The Children Act in Practice

The Children Act in Practice

Fourth Edition

Richard White
LLB, Consultant Solicitor, McMillan Williams, Thornton Heath

AP Carr
District Judge (Magistrates' Courts)

Nigel Lowe
LLB, LLD, Barrister
Professor of Law,
Cardiff Law School,
Cardiff University

Alistair MacDonald
BA (Hons), Dip Law, Barrister

Consulting Editor

V Rt Hon The Baroness Hale of Richmond
DBE, MA (Cantab)
Lord of Appeal in Ordinary

 LexisNexis®

Members of the LexisNexis Group worldwide

United Kingdom	LexisNexis, a Division of Reed Elsevier (UK) Ltd, Halsbury House, 35 Chancery Lane, London, WC2A 1EL, and London House, 20–22 East London Street, Edinburgh EH7 4BQ
Australia	LexisNexis Butterworths, Chatswood, New South Wales
Austria	LexisNexis Verlag ARD Orac GmbH & Co KG, Vienna
Benelux	LexisNexis Benelux, Amsterdam
Canada	LexisNexis Canada, Markham, Ontario
China	LexisNexis China, Beijing and Shanghai
France	LexisNexis SA, Paris
Germany	LexisNexis Deutschland GmbH, Munster
Hong Kong	LexisNexis Hong Kong, Hong Kong
India	LexisNexis India, New Delhi
Italy	Giuffrè Editore, Milan
Japan	LexisNexis Japan, Tokyo
Malaysia	Malayan Law Journal Sdn Bhd, Kuala Lumpur
New Zealand	LexisNexis NZ Ltd, Wellington
Poland	Wydawnictwo Prawnicze LexisNexis Sp, Warsaw
Singapore	LexisNexis Singapore, Singapore
South Africa	LexisNexis Butterworths, Durban
USA	LexisNexis, Dayton, Ohio

© Reed Elsevier (UK) Ltd 2008

Published by LexisNexis

A CIP Catalogue record for this book is available from the British Library.

ISBN 9781405725354

Typeset by Letterpart Ltd, Reigate, Surrey

Printed in the UK by CPI William Clowes Beccles NR34 7TL

Visit LexisNexis at www.lexisnexis.co.uk

Foreword

It is now exactly twenty years since the first publication of the Bill which eventually became the Children Act 1989 (annexed to the Law Commission's Report on Guardianship and Custody, Law Com No 172, HC 594, 25 July 1988). A great deal has changed since then but the structure and principles of the law relating to the upbringing of children laid down by the Act have not. It deals with the initial allocation of parental responsibility – who has the prior claim to bring up a child. It then deals with the principles and processes for re-allocating some or all of those responsibilities, whether between parents or other private individuals or between parents and the state, in the shape of the local authorities charged with safeguarding children's welfare. It also deals with the responsibilities of those local authorities for helping, looking after and safeguarding children and their families, whether or not there are any court proceedings.

Three fundamental principles remain clear. First, parents, often with the help of their wider families, are the people who are best suited to bringing up their own children. They have both the responsibility and the right to do so. Second, court decisions about the upbringing of children should always be governed by the paramount consideration of what is best for those children, not by what is best for their parents, their relatives, their lawyers or the local children's services. And third, decisions about the upbringing of children from the least advantaged homes and families in the country should be taken with just the same amount of care as should decisions about the upbringing of children from the most advantaged homes and families.

We must never lose sight of any of these principles but perhaps the last needs particular emphasis today. The great aim of the 1989 Act was that the same principles and procedures should apply to the children of rich and poor alike. We would take as much time and trouble deciding what should happen to the children of the poor or disadvantaged as we did deciding what should happen to the children of the rich or famous. All children, whatever their backgrounds and families, deserved the best which we could do for them. And that is what the family justice system has been trying to do ever since.

The four editions of the book have marked my own transition through the legal system: from Law Commissioner in 1990 when the first edition was published, to Family Division judge in 1995 when the second appeared, to Court of Appeal judge in 2002 when the third was published, and now to the House of Lords. Each step along the way has taken me further from the day to day experience of the Act and how it works in practice. I, along with many other readers, am grateful for this compact but full, thoughtful and practical guide to an increasingly complicated area of the law. The comments, of course, are the authors' own. The usual expert team has been further strengthened (if that were possible) by the arrival of Alistair MacDonald who we hope will have the opportunity of seeing the Act through its next twenty years.

Brenda Hale
July 2008

Preface to the fourth edition

This preface is written with a tinge of regret. In the last twenty years we have seen enormous advances, which we have been privileged to be part of. As we wrote in the second edition: 'The progress made in providing a suitable legal framework should be recognised ...'.

We have, however, throughout the life of the book drawn attention to the expectations about welfare and legal services created by the Act which have not been fulfilled. In the first edition we expressed concern about the degree of power given to the Executive to amend statute and the volume of delegated legislation.

Regrettably that power is now being exercised by the Executive to draw back from involving the Courts in welfare decisions save in the more extreme cases. The Family Justice System has in a sense been a victim of its own success. Because where it works well it has been seen to produce the most effective outcomes in working with families, it has been put to greater use. Paradoxically that has led the Executive to reduce funding, leading to delays and a lack of fulfilment of the essentials of the Act.

We have attempted to state the law as we believe it to be at 31 July 2008. We have made reference to the Children and Young Persons Bill 2008 but at that date it had not completed its passage through Parliament.

The volume of delegated legislation and departmental guidance remains substantial but it is erratic in its effect and its implementation. Such is the volume of guidance that it is not possible for it all to be published even in *Clarke Hall and Morrison*. How can practitioners be expected to keep up to date? On the other hand when there are important developments to be managed such as the planned Family Procedure Rules, which we had hoped to publish in this edition, there has been substantial delay in their production. One has to ask whether we are using technology to best effect or allowing it to inhibit progress.

The social, ethical and judicial problems for which the Act provides the fundamental framework become no less complicated. The law and lawyers have much to contribute to the solution of those problems. Their involvement is necessarily dependent on a public funding system which for all the rhetoric about its importance is substantially under threat.

We have been delighted to welcome Alistair MacDonald to the team. We express the hope that he will still be writing on the subject in another twenty years time with the enthusiasm we have sustained over the last twenty. We hope that he will continue to have a professional audience as committed to the service of child and family law and to the benefit of those who have to spend often stressful parts of their lives relying on that service.

We extend our thanks to Sarah Newton and Evelyn Reid at LexisNexis for their assistance in the production of the work; to Sharon Willicombe for again typing much of the manuscript; to our consulting editor now Baroness Hale, who has advanced to a higher judicial position during the life of each edition; and to our families for the mutual enlightenment inevitably associated with any work on family law.

Richard White, Nigel Lowe, Paul Carr, Alistair MacDonald
August 2008

Preface to the third edition

The Children Act 1989 came into force on 14 October 1991. It provided a code and structure for much of the law relating to children. It could never provide simplicity for such a complex area of human relationships. A decade on there has been substantial development of policy and philosophy of core principles, volumes of statutory instruments, guidance and case law, and many treatises on the subject. It is difficult to know where to draw the boundaries when writing on a subject with so many borders.

Much of what we wrote in the preface to the second edition remains true and bears repetition.

'The effect of social legislation like the Children Act may not be fully appreciated for some years to come. As predicted, however, the Act has brought about fundamental changes in the law relating to children.

It is easy to forget some of the problems of the old system, scattered legislation, confusing concepts of custody and care, conflicting court jurisdictions and uncertain criteria in public law cases. The progress made in providing a suitable legal framework should be recognised, although inevitably a book of this nature will pay considerable attention to problems which have arisen. Many of the difficulties highlighted by practice under the Act would have come to the surface in any event, perhaps in a worse form.

Nonetheless we have to face the fact that the Act created expectations about welfare and legal services to be provided for children and their families. These expectations have not been fulfilled. Delays in legal proceedings are all too common, in spite of the acceptance of the principle that it is likely to prejudice the welfare of the child. Professional services and resources which could bring to fruition the good intentions of the legislation have simply not been sufficient.'

We have found in practice that it is most useful to have in one relatively small bound volume the Act , court rules and commentary. We have attempted to state the law as we believe it to be at 31 August 2002.

This book is not intended to be a comprehensive analysis of all the law relating to children or even the Children Act 1989. With some exceptions we have decided to maintain the structure of the second edition, seeking to lay out the core principles and the way in which they are implemented, while at the same time drawing attention to those areas where there are problems.

Constrained as ever by space, we have maintained the emphasis in the text on Parts I to V of the Act, though in the light of developments we have necessarily to take account of the Human Rights Act 1998 and the European Convention on Human Rights, parts of the Adoption and Children Bill 2002 and activities in the international field. We have not attempted to deal with the major changes in the Care Standards Act 2000 and the work of the National Care Standards Commission, nor can we begin to tackle the major changes in the field of adoption, education and youth justice.

Once again we have to thank Butterworths for their forbearance in waiting for the manuscript. We again owe an enormous debt to our consulting editor, Lady Justice Hale, for her extensive reading of the manuscript. We should also like to thank Stephen Pizzey for his observations on Chapters 6 and 7 and Sharon Willicombe for typing much of the manuscript. Finally as ever, we thank our families, who now provide us all with somewhat different insights into working with the Children Act, than when we wrote the first edition.

Richard White, Paul Carr, Nigel Lowe
September 2002

Preface to the second edition

The Children Act 1989 came into force on 14 October 1991. With it came numerous rules and regulations and extensive government guidance. A considerable body of case law has since been developed.

We have included the Act as it is in force at 1 September 1995. Constrained by space we have chosen to concentrate in the text on Parts I to V of the Act and related provisions. This involves the general principles, private law arrangements, and public law provisions relating to local authority responsibilities for the support of children and their families and the care and protection of children who may be suffering significant harm. We have also examined how the courts are operating. There have been few developments in relation to Parts VI to X concerning children's homes, private fostering and childminding and day care but substantial statutory annotation has been included. Adoption, possibly the subject of forthcoming legislation, education, another major area of new law, and financial provision, now much affected by the Child Support Act 1991, have all been excluded. The volume of material on what remains shows how extensive and complex the provisions have become in a short period.

The effect of social legislation like the Children Act may not be fully appreciated for some years to come. As predicted, however, the Act has brought about fundamental changes in the law relating to children. It is easy to forget some of the problems of the old system, scattered legislation, confusing concepts of custody and care, conflicting court jurisdictions and uncertain criteria in public law cases. The progress made in providing a suitable legal framework should be recognised, although inevitably a book of this nature will pay considerable attention to problems which have arisen. Many of the difficulties highlighted by practice under the Act would have come to the surface in any event, perhaps in a worse form.

Nonetheless we have to face the fact that the Act created expectations about welfare and legal services to be provided for children and their families. These expectations have not been fulfilled. Delays in legal proceedings are all too common, in spite of the acceptance of the principle that it is likely to prejudice the welfare of the child. Professional services and resources which could bring to fruition the good intentions of the legislation have simply not been sufficient.

The sheer volume of legal development since the first edition required extensive consideration and analysis. Accordingly the task of writing a second edition was more time consuming than expected. Some of the policy conflicts which continue to develop have made it difficult to construct a coherent analysis at times. By the time the book is published, some of the problem areas we have identified may have been resolved and others may have emerged.

We continue to owe a debt of gratitude to Butterworths, who have shown forbearance in waiting for the manuscript. We thank Mrs Justice Hale, again our consulting editor, for her insights, now from the Bench, into the operation of the Act. Thanks also to Kathryn Bates, Patricia Burns and Hilary Carr for typing much of the manuscript. Finally, we wish to thank our ever patient families, who continue to illuminate the realities of working with the Children Act.

Richard White, Paul Carr, Nigel Lowe
September 1995

Preface to the first edition

The Children Act 1989 received the Royal Assent on 16 November 1989. It will, when implemented, bring about the most fundamental change of child law this century. Much of it has been the subject of debate for six years, yet some of the most complex provisions only found final form shortly before their enactment and were, therefore, not adequately debated in Parliament.

At the time of going to press we believe that most of the Act is likely to be implemented in October 1991. Four provisions have been brought into force already. Rules of court in relation to the evidence of children and their upbringing are expected to resolve an urgent problem as to admissibility. The position of an unmarried father as regards his child in care has been improved. In paternity cases applicants have been made responsible for choosing a blood tester from an authorised list. With effect from 16 January 1990 funds can be made available for a child to be sent for treatment outside England and Wales, for example, at the Peto Institute in Hungary.

The remainder will come soon enough. There is much work still to be done on the rules and regulations, which will be so important to practice. However, we have endeavoured to produce the book as quickly as possible, because we believe it to be vital to have an early understanding of the principles of the legislation, so that the detail can be more easily placed in context as it is published over the next eighteen months.

The law is bound to reflect the complexity of the subject. It is impossible to put into the statute all the detail that one might wish to see in establishing principles of law for children. Nevertheless, we are concerned about the degree of power given to the Executive to amend statute and the volume of delegated legislation, both of which will control how practice develops.

We have had to write within constraints of time, space and ability to interpret amendments which have been tabled late in the day. We have attempted to examine all the important parts of the Act and to relate them to each other.

We owe a considerable debt of thanks to Butterworths, for their efficiency and patience and their determination to ensure that the book was published quickly. We thank Professor Brenda Hoggett, our consulting editor, who gave extensively of her wide experience and understanding of the principles underlying the legislation.

Legislation of this length inevitably generates its own complexity. The Children Act will be no exception. It would be wrong, however, to dwell on negatives, for the Act does much to improve child law and given a fair wind by Government, judiciary and practitioners will provide a sound basis for good practice for the 1990s and beyond.

Richard White, Paul Carr, Nigel Lowe
December 1989

Authors

Richard White
Richard White is a Consultant Solicitor at McMillan Williams at their Thornton Heath office and specialises in the field of child care. He is a Tribunal Judge with the Special Educational Needs and Disability Tribunal.

AP Carr
Paul Carr is a District Judge (Magistrates' Courts) who sits in the Family Proceedings Court and was formerly a Justices' Clerk. He has variously been an editor of leading works on criminal and family law.

Nigel Lowe
Nigel Lowe is Professor of Law at Cardiff Law School, Cardiff University and author of several works on family law in general and child law in particular.

Alistair MacDonald
Alistair MacDonald is a Barrister at St Philips Chambers in Birmingham. He was called to the Bar in 1995. Alistair specialises exclusively in the law relating to children, concentrating on complex public law cases under the children and adoption legislation. He is currently Co-Chair of the Association of Lawyers for Children. In this role, Alistair was heavily involved in the 2006 DCA/DfES Care Proceedings Review and is a member of the Ministerial Group on Care Proceedings. Alistair publishes extensively on legal and policy issues concerning public children law. He provides public law training to local authorities, solicitors and family panel justices and is a member of the Family Law Bar Association and the British Association for Adoption and Fostering.

Contents

Foreword . . . . *v*
Preface to the fourth edition . . . . *vii*
Preface to the third edition . . . . *ix*
Preface to the second edition . . . . *xi*
Preface to the first edition . . . . *xiii*
Authors . . . . *xv*
Table of statutes . . . . *xxxi*
Table of statutory instruments . . . . *xliii*
Table of European legislation and other international material . . . . *li*
Table of cases . . . . *liii*

Chapter 1 Introduction
The genesis of the Act 1
The development of legislation 4
The ambit of the Children Act 1989 4
Some key changes under the Act 5
   1. New concepts 5
   2. Changes in public law 6
      (a) Services for children and families 6
      (b) A single threshold for state care and supervision 7
   3. General principles 8
   4. Procedural changes 8
      (a) Procedure and evidence 8
      (b) The creation of a comprehensive liaison network 9
      (c) Role of the courts 13
Some key changes since the Act 13
   1. Welsh devolution 14
   2. The Civil Procedure Rules 1998 14
   3. The Human Rights Act 1998 15
Chapter 2 General principles
The welfare principle 21
   1. 'Paramount' not 'first and paramount' 21
   2. Is the paramountcy principle human rights compliant? 22
   3. Comparison with UN Convention 23
   4. When the principle applies 24

5. When the principle does not apply 27
  (a) Paramountcy principle does not apply outside the context
  of litigation 27
  (b) Paramountcy principles do not apply unless child's
  upbringing etc is directly in issue 28
  (c) Paramountcy principle does not apply if excluded by other
  statutory provisions 33
6. Balancing the welfare of more than one child 35
  (a) Child-parents and babies 35
  (b) Balancing the interests of siblings 36
7. The meaning of welfare 38
8. The checklist 38
  (a) When the checklist applies 39
  (b) Applying the checklist 40
9. Delay prima facie prejudicial to the child's welfare 48
Orders to be made only where the court is satisfied that
making the order is better than making no order 50
1. Introduction and background 50
2. When the principle applies 51
3. The application of s 1(5) 52
  (a) the substantive law 52
  (b) the application of s 1(5) in practice 55
4. Form of order 56
5. The inter-relationship of the welfare principle and the
'non-intervention' principle 56
6. The inter-relationship of human rights and the
'non-intervention' principle 57
Chapter 3 Parental responsibility and guardianship
Introduction 59
Parental responsibility 60
1. Contexts in which parental responsibility is relevant 60
2. The practical effects of the changed terminology 61
3. The meaning and scope of 'parental responsibility' 61
  (a) The need to define parental responsibility 61
  (b) Lack of a comprehensive statutory definition 62
  (c) Some further observations 64
  (d) What parental responsibility comprises 65
Who has parental responsibility? 78
1. The position at the child's birth 78
  (a) Married parents 78
  (b) Unmarried parents 79
  (c) Gender change 79
  (d) Non-parents 79
Acquisition of parental responsibility after the child's birth 79
1. Acquisition of parental responsibility by unmarried fathers 79
  (a) Subsequent marriage 80

(b) Registration as the father 80
(c) Guardianship 81
(d) Parental responsibility agreements 82
(d) Parental responsibility orders 84
(e) Residence orders 90
(f) The effect of parental responsibility orders and
agreements 90
2. Checklist: the effect of the unmarried father obtaining
parental responsibility 92
3. Ending parental responsibility orders or agreements 93
4. Acquisition of parental responsibility by step-parents 94
5. Acquisition of parental responsibility by other individuals 96
(a) Guardianship 97
(b) Special guardianship 97
(c) Residence orders 97
(d) Emergency protection orders 98
6. Acquisition of parental responsibility by local authorities 98
For whom responsibility exists 98
Duration of parental responsibility 98
Sharing parental responsibility for a child and the right of
independent action 99
1. The position between married parents 100
2. The effect of a third party acquiring parental responsibility 101
Delegation of parental responsibility 102
The position of those caring for a child who do not have
parental responsibility 103
Guardianship 104
1. Introduction 104
2. The court's power to appoint guardians 105
Appointing individuals 105
3. Appointing the Official Solicitor as guardian of the estate 107
4. Private appointment of guardians 108
(a) Making an appointment 108
(b) Revoking an appointment 109
(c) When the appointment takes effect 110
(d) Disclaiming the appointment 111
(e) Effect of being appointed a guardian 111
5. Termination of guardianship 113
(a) Death, majority or marriage of the child 113
(b) Death of the guardian 113
(c) Removal by the court 113
Chapter 4 Work in the courts
Introduction 115
The overriding objective 115
The courts 116
1. Jurisdiction 117

2. The High Court 118
3. County court 118
4. Magistrates' courts 119
   The justices' clerk 120
5. Judiciary 121
6. The legal profession 122
7. Unrepresented parties and McKenzie friends 123
Allocation of proceedings 126
1. Commencement of proceedings 126
2. Transfer of proceedings 127
   Contravention of order 127
Procedure 127
1. The Private Law Programme and the Public Law Outline 127
2. Rules 128
3. Forms 129
4. Filing the application 130
5. Fees 130
6. Service 131
7. Parties 132
8. First hearing 133
9. Directions 133
10. Case management 135
11. Reviewing allocation 136
    (a) Public law 136
    (b) Private law 136
    (c) Draft President's Guidance and new Allocation Order 140
12. Ordering welfare reports 143
13. Timetable for proceedings 144
14. Service of statements 144
15. Sanctions 145
16. Reading time 145
Court hearings 146
1. Privacy and restrictions on reporting proceedings 146
2. Order of speeches and evidence 147
3. Attendance of child at hearings 148
   (a) Specified proceedings 148
   (b) Private law proceedings 148
   (c) Oral evidence 150
4. Decision 153
5. Justices' reasons 154
6. Costs 156
   Personal liability of legal representative for costs 157
Chapter 5 Private law orders
Introduction and background 159
The courts' powers under Part II: the general strategy 160
   Number of orders made bi-annually 1992–2006 161

Risk assessments 162
Section 8 orders 163
  1. Residence orders 163
    (a) Joint and shared residence orders 165
    (b) 'Interim' residence orders 169
    (c) Ex parte applications and orders 170
    (d) Effect of residence orders 171
  2. Contact orders 183
    (a) Legal considerations 183
    (b) General considerations 184
    (c) Procedural considerations 191
    (d) Human rights considerations 191
    (e) Practical considerations when making contact decisions 191
  3. Prohibited steps order 202
  4. Specific issue order 203
  5. Limits on the court's powers to make prohibited steps and
  specific issue orders 205
    (a) Orders must relate to parental responsibility 205
    (b) No power to make ouster or occupation orders 206
    (c) No power to make disguised residence or contact orders 207
    (d) No power to make orders that are denied to the High
    Court acting under its inherent jurisdiction 207
    (e) Local authorities not to regard prohibited steps or specific
    issue orders as a substitute for an order under Part IV 208
  6. Additional directions and conditions 209
    (a) Directions and limited duration orders 210
    (b) Conditions and other supplemental orders 210
  7. Restrictions on making s 8 orders 215
    (a) Children aged sixteen or over 215
    (b) Children in local authority care 216
    (c) Restrictions in the case of local authorities 216
    (d) Other restrictions 217
  8. When section 8 orders can be made 217
    (a) General jurisdictional rules 217
    (b) Family proceedings 221
    (c) Any child 223
    (d) Upon application or upon the court's own motion 223
  9. Who may apply for s 8 orders? 224
    (a) Persons entitled to apply without leave 224
    (b) Persons requiring leave 225
    (c) The leave criteria 226
    (d) Applying for orders in favour of someone else 232
  10. Enforcing s 8 orders 233
    (a) Family Law Act 1986, s 34 233
    (b) The courts' general enforcement powers 234

11. The enforcement powers under the Children and Adoption
Act 2006 reforms 240
    (a) Warning notices 240
    (b) Contact enforcement orders 241
    (c) Compensation for financial loss 243
    (d) An evaluation of the new sanctions 244
12. Family assistance orders 244
    (a) When orders may be made 245
    (b) Effect of the order 246
    (c) Duration of order 247
    (d) Family assistance orders in practice 247
13. Restricting further applications under s 91(14) 249
14. Court ordered investigation under s 37 253
15. The relationship between private law orders and public law
proceedings 254
Enhanced residence orders 255
Special guardianship 256
  1. Introduction 256
  2. The power to make special guardianship orders 257
    (a) Jurisdiction 260
    (b) Local authority involvement in making applications 261
    (c) Principles upon which orders are made 262
    (d) Powers when making a special guardianship order 263
    (e) The effects of special guardianship orders 264
    (f) Variation and discharge 266
Duration of order 267
  1. Special guardianship support services 267
  2. The use of special guardianship orders and the comparison
with adoption orders 269
  3. A comparison between special guardianship and residence
orders 271
Chapter 6 Local Authority Support for Children and Families
Introduction 279
Children in need 281
  1. Definitions 281
    (a) 'Child' 281
    (b) 'In need' 282
    (c) 'Health' and 'development' 282
    (d) 'Family' 282
  2. Assessment 282
  3. Co-operation between local authorities 284
  4. General duty to children in need 284
  5. Services for children with disabilities 286
  6. Specific powers and duties 287
    (a) Identification of children in need 287
    (b) Prevention of abuse and neglect 288

(c) Provision of accommodation to third party to protect
children 288
(d) Promoting upbringing of children by their families 288
(e) Maintenance of the family home 289
(f) Duty to consider racial groups 290
(g) Day care 290
Children under five years old 291
Services for all children 291
Accommodation of children 291
1. Duty to accommodate 291
(a) Children who must be accommodated 291
(b) Children who may be accommodated 293
(c) Homeless families 293
(d) Homeless adolescents 294
(e) Refuges for children at risk 294
2. Duties prior to providing accommodation under s 20 296
3. Limits on providing accommodation 298
4. Restricting removal from accommodation 299
5. Partnership with parents 300
Children 'looked after' 300
1. Duties to 'looked after' children 301
2. The duty to rehabilitate 303
3. The duty to promote contact 304
4. Placement of 'looked after' children 305
(a) Placement with parents and those with parental
responsibility 305
(b) Placement with relatives or friends 306
(c) Foster placements 306
(d) Residential placements 307
(e) Placement outside the jurisdiction 307
Leaving 'looked after' provision 308
1. Overall duty 309
2. Duties to the 'eligible child' 310
3. Duties to the 'relevant child' 311
4. Duties to 'former relevant children' 312
5. Persons qualifying for advice and assistance 312
6. Pathway plans 313
7. Personal adviser 313
8. Financial support 313
9. Employment, education and training support 314
Implementing Part III services 314
Chapter 7 Enquiry, Assessment and Emergency Protection
Introduction 317
Enquiry 317
1. Statutory duty to investigate 319

Contents

2. Section 47 319
   (a) Duty to investigate 319
   (b) Threshold for enquiry 320
   (c) Aims of a s 47 enquiry 322
   (d) The s 47 enquiry process 322
   (e) Strategy discussion 327
3. Section 37 327
   (a) Criteria for making the order 327
   (b) Procedure upon the granting of a s 37 order 328
   (c) Local authority duty 330
4. The assessment process 330
   (a) The assessment framework 330
   (b) Cardinal principles 331
Child-centred approach 331
Child development 332
Ecological approach 332
Equality of opportunity 332
Working with children and families 333
Strengths as well as weaknesses 334
Inter-agency approach 334
Continuing process 334
Concurrent action 335
Evidence-based knowledge 335
1. Judicial guidance 336
2. Interviewing children 336
Child assessment orders 338
1. Criteria for making the order 338
2. Procedure 340
3. Effect of a child assessment order 341
Emergency protection orders 342
1. Introduction 342
2. Grounds for an emergency protection order 343
   (a) The grounds 343
   (b) Likely to suffer harm 344
   (c) Denial of access to the child 344
   (d) Statutory guidance 345
   (e) Judicial guidance 346
3. Application for an emergency protection order 348
   (a) Applicants and respondents 348
   (b) Court 348
   (c) Applications without notice 349
   (d) The hearing 350
4. Effect of an emergency protection order 351
   (a) Automatic directions 351
   (b) Parental responsibility 352
   (c) Discretionary directions 352

5. Duration of an emergency protection order 355
6. No right of appeal 356
7. Discharge of the order 356
Police protection 356
Recovery orders 358
Ancillary protection under a care order 359
Chapter 8 Care Proceedings
Introduction 361
The 'Public Law Outline' 363
1. Endemic delay 363
2. The 2003 Case Management Protocol 364
3. The Care Proceedings Review 365
4. Revised Children Act 1989 Guidance and Regulations, Vol 1,
Court Orders (2008) 366
5. The Public Law Outline 367
The need for orders before intervention 368
Grounds for an order 368
1. The grounds 368
2. Threshold criteria 369
    (a) The 'threshold' 369
    (b) Burden and standard of proof 370
    (c) The child concerned 374
    (d) Is suffering 375
    (e) Is likely to suffer 377
    (f) Harm 378
    (g) Significant harm 379
    (h) Similar child 380
    (i) Attributable 381
    (j) Care given to the child 383
    (k) Beyond parental control 383
    (l) Agreed threshold 384
3. The welfare stage 384
    (a) Welfare 384
    (b) Proportionality 385
    (c) Kinship care 385
    (d) Care plans 386
4. Contact arrangements 388
    Duty to consider arrangements for contact 388
Application for an order 388
1. Considering whether to apply for an order 388
2. The 'pre-proceedings' stage 389
    (a) Revised Children Act 1989 Guidance and Regulations,
    Vol 1, Court Orders (2008) 389
    (b) Key principles 390
3. Proceedings 394
    (a) Key principles 394

(b) Application 399
(c) PLO Stage 1 – Issue and the first appointment 401
(d) Interim orders 407
(e) PLO Stage 2 – case management conference 415
(f) PLO Stage 3 – issues resolution hearing 418
(g) PLO Stage 4 – final hearing 419
(h) Applications for placement orders 430
Effect of Orders 431
1. Care Orders 431
(a) Designated authority 431
(b) Effect of order 432
(d) Effect on other orders 435
2. Supervision orders 435
(a) Effect 435
(b) Duration 436
(c) Requirements 436
(d) Enforcement 438
(e) Use 438
(f) Education supervision order 439
Contact with children in care 440
1. Summary 440
2. Duties of the local authority 442
(a) Duty to promote contact 442
(b) Duty to child in care 442
3. The care contact order 443
4. Powers of the court 445
5. Variation and discharge 446
6. Refusal of contact 447
Variation, discharge and appeal 449
1. Variation 449
2. Discharge of care order 449
3. Appeals 451
Withdrawing care proceedings 451
Conclusions 452
Chapter 9 Secure Accommodation
Introduction 457
Deprivation of liberty 458
Children looked after by local authorities and other
organisations 459
Restriction on the use of secure accommodation 459
(a) Definition of secure accommodation 460
(b) Who may be subject to the use of secure
accommodation 461
(c) Criteria for the use of secure accommodation 462
(d) Approved secure accommodation 464

(e) Using secure accommodation without the authorisation of
a court 464
Family proceedings for a secure accommodation order 465
1. Applicant 466
2. Transfer 466
3. Children's guardian 467
4. Legal representation 467
5. Directions 467
The hearing 467
1. Presence of the child 468
2. Evidence 468
3. Interim orders 469
4. Length of order 470
5. Effect of the order 470
6. Renewal of order 471
7. Appeal 471
Criminal proceedings 472
1. Security requirement 473
2. Application for secure accommodation order 474
(a) The court to which application is made 474
(b) Criteria 474
(c) Procedure 475
(d) Evidence 476
(e) Length of order 476
(f) Renewals 477
(g) Crown Court 477
(h) Appeal 477
Chapter 10 Welfare Reporting and the Representation of Children
Introduction 479
Context 479
1. The voice of the child 479
2. Developmental issues 483
3. Rights versus welfare 483
CAFCASS 484
1. Background 484
2. Officers of the service 485
3. The National Practice Standards 486
4. Welfare reports 487
5. Attendance of CAFCASS officers at court 491
6. Separate representation in private law proceedings 494
7. Children's guardian in specified proceedings 494
(a) 'Specified proceedings' 494
(b) Appointment of children's guardian 496
(c) Duties of the children's guardian 497
(d) Children's guardian's right to inspect records 500

Legal representation for children 501
  1. Appointment of a solicitor for the child in specified
  proceedings 501
    (a) Duties of the solicitor for the child 502
    (b) Instructions from the child in specified proceedings 502
    (c) Termination of the solicitor's instructions 503
  2. Right of child to instruct a solicitor in non-specified
  proceedings 503
  3. CAFCASS Legal and the Official Solicitor 505
    (a) CAFCASS Legal 506
    (b) The Official Solicitor 506
Attendance of the child at court 507
Chapter 11 Evidence
Introduction 511
Proving the case 512
  1. Burden of proof 512
  2. Standard of proof 512
Evidence 514
  1. General 514
  2. Evidence of harm 515
  3. Certificate of conviction 515
  4. Hearsay Evidence 516
  5. Estoppel 517
  6. Covert video surveillance 519
  7. Expert evidence 519
    (a) Leave for expert evidence 521
    (b) Instructing an expert 525
    (c) The duties of expert witnesses 528
  8. Evidence from the child 529
Disclosure 535
  1. General duty 535
  2. Exceptions to the general duty – the local authority 536
    (a) Public interest immunity 536
    (b) Real harm 541
  3. Exceptions to the general duty – the parents 541
  4. Court ordered disclosure for other proceedings 544
  5. Disclosure where there are no proceedings 548
  6. Disclosure by solicitors 550
  Duties 550
  7. Conclusions on disclosure 553
Chapter 12 Wardship and the High Court's inherent jurisdiction
Introduction 555
The impact of the 1989 Act on the wardship jurisdiction 556
  1. Public law 556
    (a) No independent power to commit wards of court into
    care or supervision of a local authority 556

(b) Wardship and care incompatible 557
(c) Circumstances in which local authorities might still look
to wardship 557
2. Private law 559
(a) Status 559
(b) Some possible remaining uses of wardship 560
(c) The use of wardship when dealing with child abduction 564
(d) Other cases involving an international element 567
The inherent jurisdiction 567
1. Procedure 567
2. Jurisdiction 568
3. Powers 569
(a) The general extent of the inherent powers 569
(b) Express restriction of powers under the CA 1989 569
(c) Other restrictions on the exercise of inherent powers 570
(d) Exclusion from the family home 571
4. Local authority use of the jurisdiction 573
(a) The need to obtain leave 573
(b) Criteria for granting leave 573
(c) Circumstances when the leave criteria have been or might
be satisfied 574
5. Individual's use of the jurisdiction 576
Chapter 13 Challenging decisions
Appeals 579
1. Generally 579
2. Routes of appeal and procedure 581
(a) Appeals from magistrates' courts 581
(b) Appeals from county courts and the High Court 583
(c) Appeals to the House of Lords/Supreme Court 587
3. The position pending appeal 589
4. The powers of appellate courts – the general position 589
5. The powers of the Court of Appeal 590
6. Reform proposals 591
Judicial review 592
1. Nature of the remedy 592
2. The requirements for judicial review 593
3. Circumstances in which judicial review has been sought 595
Summary of reported judicial review cases involving children
and local authorities 598
Reviews, complaints and other remedies 608
1. Generally 608
(a) Review of children's cases 608
(b) Complaints about after care 608
2. Complaints procedures 609
(a) Who may complain? 610
(b) What may be complained about? 611

Contents

(c) Procedure and outcome 612
Default powers of the Secretary of State 614
Applying to the Local Government Ombudsman 615
Children's Commissioners 616
Habeas corpus 616
Claims for damages for failure by local authorities to carry
out their statutory duties 617
1. Limited liability for negligence 617
2. The retreat from Bedfordshire 618
3. The East Berkshire limits 620
4. The Strasbourg rulings 622
5. Actions under ss 7 and 8 of the Human Rights Act 1998 623
Chapter 14 Conclusions
Overview 627
The family justice system 628
The courts 629
1. Openness in courts 630
2. What court? 631
3. Court rules 632
4. Legal aid/Public funding 632
5. Parental responsibility 632
6. Private law in the courts 633
7. The local authority context 634
(a) Local authority support for children and families 634
(b) Care proceedings 635
8. Privatisation of children's services 637
9. Representation of children and their interests 637
(a) Welsh devolution 639
(b) Children's Commissioners 639
11. Human rights 640
12. International developments 640
Fit for the 21st century? 640
Appendices
Appendix 1 – Children Act 1989 643
Appendix 2 – Secondary legislation
Family Proceedings Rules 1991 877
Family Proceedings Courts (Children Act 1989) Rules 1991 933
Children (Allocation of Proceedings) Order 1991 990
Appendix 3 – The Public Law Outline: Guide to Case
Management in Public Law Proceedings 1017
Appendix 4 – Practice Direction
Experts in Family Proceedings Relating to Children 1053
Appendix 5 – Timeline 1069
Index 1073

Table of Statutes

All references in the right-hand column are to paragraph numbers. Paragraph numbers printed in **bold** type indicate where an Act is set out in part or in full.

PARA

Access to Justice Act 1999 .... 1.39, 14.16
Pt I (ss 1–26) 9.20
s 54(4) 13.13
Administration of Estates Act 1925
s 46 .... 3.74
Administration of Justice Act 1960
s 12 .... 4.47
13 .... 5.170
Administration of Justice Act 1969
s 12 .... 13.22
15 .... 13.22
Administration of Justice (Appeals)
Act 1934
s 1(1) 13.23
Adoption Act 1976 .... 2.42
s 6 .... 2.26
Adoption and Children Act 2002 .... 1.10,
1.14, 1.23, 1.39, 3.2,
3.52, 3.81, 3.104,
4.15, 5.9, 5.136,
5.210, 5.212, 5.213,
5.230, 5.233, 8.17,
8.40, 8.62, 8.148,
10.38, 10.59, 13.2,
14.5, 14.21, 14.41
s 1(2) 2.7, 2.14, 2.42
(4) 5.221
(f) 5.234
(5) 3.41
(6) 2.65
21 .... 4.11, 4.49, 10.36
22 .... 8.169
26 .... 5.137
29(1) 8.171
(5) 5.216, 5.222
(6) 5.216, 5.219
(7)(a) 5.226
46(2) 3.94, 3.101, 8.171
47(2) 3.89, 3.97
(5) 2.7

PARA

Adoption and Children Act 2002—*contd*
Pt 1 Ch 4 (ss 66–76) 3.43
s 109 .... 2.60
111 .... 14.18
(7) 3.50
112 .... 14.18
114 .... 5.209
115(7) 3.109
118 .... 8.161, 8.162, 8.163
120 .... 2.55, 4.21
122 .... 10.37, 14.31
(1)(b) 4.49
144(1) 3.89
Adoption of Children Act 1926
s 3(b) 2.42
Appellate Jurisdiction Act 1876 .... 13.22

Bail Act 1976 .... 9.30
s 4 .... 9.35
Births and Deaths Registration
Act 1953
s 10(1)(a)–(c) 3.50
10A(1)(a)–(c) 3.50
14A 3.50

Care and Disabled Children Act 2000
s 6, 7 .... 6.22
Care Standards Act 2000 ... 1.39, 14.5, 14.41
s 1 .... 6.63
(2) 6.68
4(4) 6.67
23(1) 9.13
74 .... 13.70
Pt II (ss 11–42) 6.63
Child Abduction Act 1984 .... 2.71, 5.95,
11.97, 11.98, 12.20
s 1 .... 3.19, 3.77, 3.97
(5) 5.40
2 .... 3.19, 6.43

Table of Statutes

PARA

Child Abduction and Custody
    Act 1985 ...... 5.139, 11.97, 11.98, 14.5
  s 9 .... 12.23
    27 .... 12.23
Child Care Act 1980 .... 1.13, 8.17, 9.15
  s 21A 9.6
Child Support Act 1991 ..... 2.66, 3.74, 4.15,
                             11.20
  s 2 .... 2.27
    (1) 3.11
Child Support, Pensions and Social
  Security Act 2000
  s 21(3) 2.17
Children Act 1975 .... 1.13
  Pt II (ss 33–46) 5.233
Children Act 1989 ..... 1.2, 1.3, 1.4, 1.6, 1.8,
               1.10, 1.11, 1.13, 1.15,
               1.16, 1.25, 1.26, 1.28,
               1.29, 1.30, 1.31, 1.32,
               1.34, 1.35, 1.38, 1.39,
               1.41, 1.43, 1.44, 2.13,
               2.36, 2.71, 3.3, 3.17,
               3.95, 4.7, 4.17, 4.20,
               4.52, 4.59, 5.2, 5.11,
               5.44, 5.83, 5.153,
               6.55, 6.71, 6.88, 7.4,
               8.2, 8.4, 8.6, 8.8,
               8.14, 8.43, 8.50, 8.52,
               8.57, 8.65, 8.66, 8.68,
               8.70, 8.71, 8.72, 8.73,
               8.86, 8.106, 8.110,
               8.159, 8.169, 8.232,
               8.233, 8.234, 10.2,
               10.3, 10.9, 10.10,
               10.11, 10.17, 10.59,
               10.60, 10.63, 10.64,
               11.2, 11.24, 11.34,
               11.35, 11.48, 11.57,
               11.58, 11.81, 11.90,
               11.97, 11.98, 12.42,
               12.43, 13.1, 13.89,
               14.1, 14.4, 14.5, 14.9,
               14.17, 14.19, 14.21,
               14.22, 14.30, 14.32,
               14.38, 14.41
  Pt I (ss 1–7) 4.5, 4.8, 4.11, 4.15, 4.16,
               5.99, 5.136
  s 1 .... 2.1, 2.22, 4.2, 5.81, 5.142, 8.21,
               8.26, 8.54, 8.109,
               8.215, 14.3
    (1) 1.23, 2.3, 2.4, 2.5, 2.6, 2.7, 2.15,
               2.16, 2.17, 2.18, 2.20,
               2.23, 2.26, 2.27, 2.32,
               2.65, 2.66, 2.67, 2.77,
               3.14, 3.63, 3.80,
               3.112, 3.130, 4.1,
               5.43, 5.84, 5.91,
               5.151, 5.156, 5.202,
               5.203, 5.221, 7.54,
               7.64, 8.18, 8.55, 9.11,
               10.1, 12.17

PARA

Children Act 1989—contd
  s 1(1) (a), (b) 2.2
    (2) 1.23, 2.60, 2.62, 2.63, 4.1, 4.39,
               5.25, 5.221, 8.55,
               8.94, 10.26
    (3) ... 1.23, 2.38, 2.40, 2.41, 3.63, 3.85,
               3.112, 5.33, 5.34,
               5.91, 5.151, 5.221,
               5.234, 7.54, 8.18,
               8.208
      (a) 2.42, 5.196, 10.7, 10.12,
               10.26, 10.42
      (b) 2.44, 10.26, 10.42
      (c) 2.45, 10.26, 10.42
      (d) 10.26, 10.42
      (e) 2.55, 2.56, 2.57, 10.26, 10.42
      (f) 5.52, 10.26, 10.42
      (g) 2.39, 2.59
      (h) 10.42
    (4) 3.63, 3.112, 5.196, 7.54, 8.55,
               10.7
      (b) 2.40, 5.221
    (5) ... 1.24, 2.64, 2.65, 2.66, 2.67, 2.68,
               2.69, 2.70, 2.72, 2.73,
               2.74, 2.76, 2.77, 2.78,
               3.4, 3.63, 3.70, 3.80,
               3.112, 3.122, 4.56,
               5.58, 5.221, 6.1, 7.54,
               7.64, 8.18, 8.55, 8.64,
               8.208, 9.11, 14.28
    2(1) 3.43, 3.47, 3.97
    (2) 3.44
      (b) 3.46
    (3) 3.43, 3.47
    (4) 3.2, 3.105
    (5) 3.6, 3.96
    (6) 3.6, 3.96, 3.100, 3.101, 8.171
    (7) ... 3.6, 3.77, 3.96, 3.97, 3.99, 5.225,
               5.235
    (8) 3.6, 3.96, 8.171
    (9) 3.5, 3.101
    (10), (11) 3.101
    3(1) 3.9, 3.10, 6.1
    (2), (3) 3.9
    (4)(b) 3.9
    (5) 3.5, 3.26, 3.103, 6.54
    4 ...... 2.10, 2.40, 3.61, 3.62, 3.65, 3.70,
               3.71, 3.72, 3.74, 3.75,
               3.77, 3.78, 4.24, 13.2,
               14.18
    (1)(a) 3.50
      (b) 3.54, 3.55
      (c) 3.60
    (1B) 3.50
    (2) 3.54
    (2A) 3.51
    (3) 3.51, 3.79, 3.80
      (b) 3.63
    (4) 3.63, 3.79
    4A 3.81, 5.144, 14.18
    (1)(b) 3.84

PARA

Children Act 1989—*contd*

s 4a (3), (4) 3.86

5 .... 2.40, 3.53, 3.88, 3.105, 3.113,
3.129, 5.213, 5.215,
13.2

(1) 3.107, 3.109

(2) 3.107, 3.110

(3) 3.106, 3.116

(4) 3.89, 3.106, 3.116, 3.128, 5.227

(5)(a), (b) 3.118

(6) 3.106, 3.109, 3.125

(7)(b) 3.120

(8) 3.120

(9) 3.109, 3.120

(10) 3.116, 3.120

(11), (12) 1.1, 3.106, 3.115

6 ....3.105

(1) 3.116, 3.119

(2), (3) 3.119

(3A)(b) 3.119

(3B)(b) 3.119

(4) 3.119

(5), (6) 3.123

(7) 3.120, 3.121, 3.122, 3.129

7 .... 2.38, 3.113, 3.130, 4.55, 5.12,
5.195, 10.20, 10.22

(1) 10.23, 10.27, 10.38

(2) 10.27

(4) 10.27

Pt II (ss 8–16) ... 2.55, 4.6, 4.8, 4.11, 4.16,
4.19, 5.1, 5.4, 5.7,
5.9, 5.11, 5.12, 5.99,
5.105, 5.112, 5.121,
5.122, 5.125, 5.136,
5.207, 5.208, 5.221,
12.11, 12.12, 12.33

PARA

Children Act 1989—*contd*

s 8 .... 1.17, 1.18, 2.1, 2.10, 2.17, 2.27,
2.33, 2.40, 2.52, 2.55,
2.59, 2.63, 2.67, 3.40,
3.63, 3.71, 3.72, 3.74,
3.77, 3.80, 3.112,
3.113, 3.121, 3.129,
4.5, 4.6, 4.8, 4.10,
4.11, 4.16, 4.21, 4.24,
4.29, 4.40, 4.41, 4.43,
4.44, 4.49, 4.53, 5.1,
5.4, 5.5, 5.7, 5.10,
5.19, 5.24, 5.33, 5.42,
5.43, 5.55, 5.58, 5.98,
5.99, 5.105, 5.108,
5.110, 5.112, 5.120,
5.121, 5.124, 5.125,
5.127, 5.131, 5.134,
5.137, 5.138, 5.139,
5.140, 5.141, 5.143,
5.144, 5.145, 5.146,
5.150, 5.152, 5.155,
5.159, 5.160, 5.161,
5.164, 5.166, 5.169,
5.172, 5.173, 5.177,
5.207, 5.218, 5.221,
5.222, 5.224, 5.227,
6.45, 7.54, 8.107,
8.108, 8.178, 8.179,
8.186, 8.202, 8.203,
8.212, 10.7, 11.14,
12.8, 12.9, 12.10,
12.14, 12.15, 12.16,
12.35, 12.36, 12.38,
12.41, 13.2, 14.31

(1) 3.7, 5.13, 5.14, 5.54, 5.62, 5.94,
5.97

(2) 5.13

(3) 3.107, 5.135, 5.216, 7.25, 8.211,
12.1

(a) 12.5, 12.28

(4) 5.136, 5.216, 7.54, 7.64

9 .... 5.142

(1) 5.54, 5.124, 5.125, 5.137, 5.154,
8.179, 8.203, 12.35

(2) 5.54, 5.125, 8.17, 8.108, 12.35

(3) 5.126, 5.146, 5.147, 5.154,
5.216, 8.224

(5) 5.125

(a) 5.102, 5.103

(b) 5.104, 5.208

(6) 3.63, 3.112, 5.67, 5.122, 5.123,
5.209, 5.222

(7) 5.67, 5.122, 5.123

10 .... 1.18, 4.11, 5.7, 5.143, 12.41

(1) 3.113, 5.134, 5.140, 12.28

(a)(ii) 1.9, 5.146

(b) 2.39, 5.141, 5.142

(3) 5.142

(4) 2.72, 5.144

(5) 5.144, 8.224

PARA

Children Act 1989—*contd*

s 10 (6) 2.72, 5.55, 5.144, 5.145, 5.155
(7) 5.145
(7A) 5.227
(8) 1.9, 3.80, 5.148, 5.149, 5.155,
5.156, 5.216, 10.55
(9) 1.9, 2.27, 5.148, **5.150**, 5.156,
5.204, 5.216, 8.100,
8.204, 10.55
(a) 5.151, 5.152
(b) 5.149
(c) 2.67, 5.151
(d)(i) 5.151, 5.154
(10) 5.216
11(1) 1.23, 2.60, 2.63
(3) 5.24, 5.61, 5.110, 8.108
(4) 3.80, 5.17, 5.23
(5) 5.16
(6) 5.59
(7) 5.13, 5.14, 5.23, 5.39, 5.41,
5.51, 5.58, 5.99,
5.101, 5.103, 5.108,
5.113, 5.115, 5.116,
5.121, 5.167, 5.179,
5.201, 5.204, 8.108,
8.186, 8.220, 13.26
(a) 5.109
(b) 5.68, 5.73, 5.111, 5.112,
5.120, 5.181, 5.188
(c) 5.24, 5.110, 5.224
(d) 5.111, 5.112
11A 5.63
(1) 5.64
(3) 5.64
(4)–(6) 5.65
(7) 5.64
(8) 5.66
(9) 2.7, 5.66, 5.67
11B 5.63
(1)–(3) 5.64
(4) 5.64, 5.68, 5.73, 5.180, 5.187
(5)–(7) 5.64
11C 5.63
(1), (2) 5.67
(3) 5.68
(4)–(6) 5.69
11D 5.63
(1)–(3) 5.68
11E 5.63
(1)–(7) 5.66, 5.69
11F 5.63
(1)–(7) 5.70
11G(2) 5.63, 5.71
(3) 5.71
11H 5.12
(2), (3) 5.73
(6), (7) 5.73
(9), (10) 5.73
11I 5.178, 5.180, 5.187
11J(1) 5.184
(3) 5.180

PARA

Children Act 1989—*contd*

s 11J (4) 5.180, 5.187
(5)–(7) 5.181
(9) 5.179
(13) 5.184
11K 5.179
(1)–(4) 5.180
11L 5.179
(1)–(6) 5.182
(7) 2.18, 2.27, 5.182
11M 5.179
(1), (2) 5.183
11N 5.179, 5.184
11O 5.185
(2) 5.186, 5.187
(3) 5.187
(5) 5.188
(6) 5.186, 5.188
(7), (8) 5.188
(9) 5.186, 5.189
(10), (11) 5.189
(14) 2.18, 2.27, 5.189
11P 5.185
(1)–(3) 5.187
12(1) 3.71, 3.72, 3.84, 5.30, 5.52
(2) 3.90, 3.94, 5.15, 5.24, 5.30,
5.159
(3) 3.13, 3.126, 5.15, 5.30
(b), (c) 3.90
(5) 5.122, 5.123, 5.209, 5.212
(6) 5.209, 5.212, 5.235
13 .... 2.10, 5.36, 5.43, 5.98, 5.166, 13.2
(1) 2.40, 5.52
(a) 5.31, 5.32, 5.33, 5.95
(b) 5.14, 5.39, 5.95
(2) 5.24, 5.40, 5.95
(3) 5.42
14 .... 5.172
14A 2.10, 4.16, 5.213
(1) 5.215
(2)(a) 5.215, 5.223
(b) 5.215
(3)(b) 5.216
(4) 5.216
(5)(d) 5.216
(6)(b) 5.211, 5.216, 5.220
(7) 5.219
(8) 5.217, 5.219, 5.220
(9) 5.219, 5.220
(10) 5.219
(11) 5.211, 5.219
(12), (13) 5.216
14B 5.213
(1)(a), (b) 5.222
(2)(b) 5.224
14C 5.213
(1) 3.89, 5.225
(a) 3.89
(b) 3.89, 3.100, 5.235
(2)(a) 5.226
(b) 3.89, 5.226

PARA

Children Act 1989—*contd*

s 14c (3) 4.15
    (a), (b) 5.226
    (4) 5.226
    (5) 5.227
14D 5.213
    (1)(a), (b) 5.228
    (c) 5.227, 5.228
    (d), (e) 5.228
    (2) 5.228
    (3)(d) 5.228
    (4) 5.228
    (5) 5.228, 5.235
    (6) 5.228
14E 5.213, 5.221
    (4), (5) 5.224
14F 5.213
    (3), (4) 5.230
    (6) 5.230
14G 5.213, 5.230
    (3) 5.221
15 .... 3.125, 5.1
    (1) 6.8
16 .... 5.8, 5.197, 5.201
    (1) 5.191, 5.193
    (2) 5.191
    (3)(a) 5.194
    (b) 5.195
    (4), (4A) 5.198
    (5) 5.199
    (6) 5.198
    (7) 5.191, 5.195
16A 2.55, 14.20
    (2), (3) 5.11
Pt III (ss 17–30) 1.14, 2.15, 3.22, 4.16,
                5.207, 5.208, 6.2, 6.3,
                6.4, 6.5, 6.6, 6.7, 6.9,
                6.16, 6.21, 6.25, 6.41,
                6.57, 7.40, 7.46, 8.40,
                8.192, 8.228, 8.229,
                8.239, 9.11, 13.52,
                13.53, 13.55, 13.57,
                13.58
s 17 ..... 6.12, 6.14, 6.22, 6.41, 6.72, 6.87,
             6.91, 6.92, 7.6, 7.12,
             7.25, 7.31, 9.9
    (1) 2.15, 6.9, 6.17, 6.18
    (3) 6.11
    (4) 6.23
    (4A) 6.15
    (5) 6.6
    (b) 6.3
    (6) 6.19, 6.20
    (7) 6.19
    (8), (9) 6.15
    (10) 6.9, 6.11
    (11) 6.10, 6.21
17A 6.22
18(1) 6.31
    (2) 6.33
    (3)–(5) 6.31

PARA

Children Act 1989—*contd*

s (6) 6.35
19 .... 6.32
20 ..... 3.4, 5.18, 6.17, 6.24, 6.72, 8.228,
                14.27
    (1) 6.36, 6.38, 6.42, 6.63
    (c) 6.40
    (2) 6.38
    (3) 6.37, 6.42
    (4) 6.39
    (5) 6.42, 9.9
    (6) 6.39, 6.47, 6.48
    (7) 5.104, 6.39, 6.50, 6.51
    (8) 1.19, 6.54
    (9) 6.51
    (10) 6.50
    (11) 6.51
21 .... 6.37
22 .... 13.64
    (1) 8.197, 9.9, 9.30
    (2) 6.57, 9.9
    (3) 2.15, 5.146, 5.154, 6.54, 9.11,
                9.26
    (a), (b) 6.58
    (4) 6.48, 6.58, 8.210
    (5) 6.48, 6.58
    (c) 2.53
    (6) 2.15, 6.58, 9.11
23 .... 8.164, 8.170
    (1) 6.63
    (b) 6.58
    (2) 6.63
    (f)(ii) 6.66
    (3) 6.66
    (4) 6.58, 6.59, 6.64, 6.66, 8.91
    (5A) 6.48
    (6) 6.63, 8.112
    (7) 6.61
    (b) 6.48
    (8) 6.48, 6.63
23A 6.77, 6.78
23B 6.78, 9.9
23C 6.80
    (4) 6.85, 6.86
23D 6.84
23E 6.83
24(1) 6.58, 6.81
    (2), (3) 6.81
    (5) 6.81
24A 6.82
24B 9.9
24D 13.54, 13.55
    (1) 13.52
25 ...... 2.67, 8.163, 9.1, 9.8, 9.14, 9.16,
             9.19, 9.29, 9.33,
             10.36, 13.12
    (1) 6.48, 9.6, 9.7, 9.9, **9.10**, 9.25,
             9.32, 9.34
    (b) 2.27, 9.11
    (3) 9.11
    (4) 9.11, 9.26

PARA

Children Act 1989—*contd*
s 25 (5) 9.11, 9.25
  (6) 9.20
  (9) 9.26
26 ...... 6.23, 8.155, 8.161, 13.39, 13.51,
                            13.54, 13.64
  (1), (2) 6.58
  (2A) 6.58, 8.162
  (2ZB) 13.60
  (3) 6.58, 13.53, 13.55
  (3A), (3B) 13.53, 13.58
  (4) 13.53
  (7) 13.61
    (b) 13.60
  (8) 13.53
26A(1), (2) 13.54
  (4) 13.54
  (5) 13.53, 13.54
26ZB 13.60
27 .... 6.2, 6.16, 6.41
28(1) 6.48
29(1) 6.3
  (4) 3.125
Pt IV (ss 31–42) ... 2.27, 2.40, 2.63, 3.112,
                     4.6, 4.11, 4.16, 4.43,
                     4.49, 5.99, 5.105,
                     5.125, 5.136, 5.137,
                     5.207, 5.208, 6.3, 6.9,
                     6.92, 7.2, 7.11, 7.40,
                     7.46, 7.54, 8.1, 8.7,
                     8.54, 8.55, 8.56, 8.88,
                     8.91, 8.94, 8.137,
                     8.192, 8.228, 8.229,
                     8.239, 10.7, 11.76,
                     11.85, 13.53, 13.57,
                                    13.58
s 31 ..... 1.22, 2.11, 2.56, 2.74, 4.11, 4.21,
                     4.23, 4.36, 4.38, 4.43,
                     5.105, 5.106, 5.125,
                     5.192, 5.201, 5.206,
                     5.220, 6.37, 7.11,
                     7.17, 7.58, 8.13, 8.17,
                     8.19, 8.34, 8.56, 8.62,
                     8.64, 8.100, 8.138,
                     8.167, 8.181, 8.198,
                     8.227, 9.10, 9.16,
                     10.36, 12.4, 12.5,
                     12.17, 12.37, 14.33
  (1) 8.16
  (2) 8.18, 8.20, 8.21, 8.28, 8.30,
                                 8.40, 8.109
    (a) 7.67, 8.25, 8.36, 8.37, 8.39
    (b) 8.27, 8.46, 8.47
  (3) 8.28
  (4), (5) 8.87
  (8) 6.38, 8.170
  (9) 2.55, 6.10, 7.75, 8.40, 8.89
  (10) 8.44, 8.45
  (11) 8.16, 8.112
31A(1) 8.58
  (3) 8.18

PARA

Children Act 1989—*contd*
s 32(1) 1.23, 2.60, 2.63
33 .... 8.171
  (3) 3.94, 7.105, 7.107, 8.112
    (a) 3.92
    (b) 5.226, 8.172
  (5) 8.173
  (6) 8.174
    (a) 3.13, 3.41
    (b) 3.13
  (7) 2.10, 5.31, 8.175, 8.176, 9.16,
                                      10.36
  (8) 5.31, 8.177
    (a) 8.176
  (9) 8.173
34 ...... 1.7, 2.11, 2.33, 3.74, 4.11, 5.54,
                     5.122, 5.202, 5.227,
                     7.54, 7.58, 7.60,
                     8.197, 8.202, 8.203,
                     8.208, 8.218, 9.16,
                                      10.36
  (1) 3.23, 6.62, 8.201, 8.216
  (2) 5.162, 8.206
  (3) 6.62, 8.204
    (a), (b) 8.202
  (4) 2.12, 2.31, 5.161, 6.62, 8.214,
                                 8.215, 8.217
  (6) 6.62, 8.207
  (7) 8.202, 8.209
  (9) 2.12, 8.212
  (11) 8.18, 8.61, 8.205
35(1) 8.112
    (c) 8.180
36 .... 3.39, 4.11, 8.191, 9.16
  (3)–(5) 8.193
  (6) 8.195
  (8), (9) 8.192
37 ... 1.22, 3.104, 5.8, 5.207, 7.26, 7.29,
                     7.31, 7.58, 7.78, 8.88,
                     8.109, 10.38, 12.5,
                                      12.18
  (1) 7.25, 7.27, 7.28, 7.29, 8.87,
                                 8.123, 10.36
    (b) 5.206
  (2)(a)–(c) 7.30
  (3) 5.206, 7.30
  (4) 5.206, 7.30, 8.123
  (7) 7.61
38 .... 4.11, 7.91, 8.116, 8.151, 13.8
  (1) 8.109
    (b) 7.26, 7.30
  (2) 7.8, 7.26, 8.109
  (3) 8.107
  (4), (5) 8.122
  (6) 1.9, 2.18, 2.62, 8.107, 8.112,
                     8.113, 8.115, 8.117,
                     8.119, 12.32, 12.38,
                                       13.2
  (9) 8.187
  (10) 8.122
38A 12.34

PARA

Children Act 1989—*contd*

s 38a (1)(a) 8.120
   (10) 8.121
38B 8.121
39 .... 2.11, 5.207, 8.182
   (1) 8.220
   (3) 4.11
   (3A) 8.121
   (4) 8.219, 10.36
   (5) 8.219, 8.220
40 .... 13.28
   (1), (2) 8.226, 13.27
   (3) 13.27
   (4), (6) 13.27
41 .... 8.195, 9.19, 9.35, 10.36, 11.3,
              14.31
   (1) 7.29, 7.59, 11.65
   (2) 11.65
     (b) 10.42
   (3) 10.49, 11.65
   (4) 10.49
   (6) 4.49, 10.35, 10.36
     (b) 7.29
     (g) 7.59
   (6A) 10.37
   (11) 10.42
   (13) 7.58
42 .... 10.42, 10.47
   (2), (3) 10.48
Pt V (ss 43–52) 2.27, 4.16, 4.49, 5.125,
          5.139, 5.208, 6.37,
         7.12, 7.54, 7.64, 8.88,
        10.36, 11.85, 13.53,
            13.57
s 43 ..... 7.3, 7.55, 7.62, 7.74, 7.91, 8.119,
            9.9, 9.16
   (1) 7.53
   (3), (4) 7.56
   (5), (6) 7.61
   (7) 7.54
   (8) 1.9, 7.57, 12.38
   (9), (10) 7.54
   (11) 7.58
44 ...... 7.3, 7.64, 7.65, 7.71, 7.73, 7.74,
        7.100, 8.119, 9.16
   (1) 7.70, 7.75, 7.77
     (a) 7.8, 7.66
     (b), (c) 7.66, 7.68, 7.69
   (2) 7.66
     (a) 7.75
     (b)(i) 7.75
   (4) 3.91, 7.84
     (c) 3.92, 3.94, 7.63
   (5) 3.91, 7.85, 7.86
     (b) 3.13, 3.27
   (6) 7.91, 7.92
     (b) 3.27
   (7) 1.9, 7.91, 12.38
   (8) 7.91, 7.92
   (10)(a) 7.86
   (11)(a) 7.86

PARA

Children Act 1989—*contd*

s 44 (12) 7.86
   (13) 3.23, 3.74, 7.92
   (14) 7.89
   (15), (16) 7.84
44A 12.34
   (2) 7.93
   (5) 7.94
44B(2), (3) 7.94
45 .... 9.16
   (1) 7.95
   (3)–(5) 7.95
   (7) 7.82
   (8) 3.74, 7.98
   (8A) 7.98
   (8B) 7.94, 7.98
   (9) 7.98
   (10) 7.97, 7.98, 13.4
   (11) 7.98
46 .... 7.3, 7.101
   (1) 7.8, 7.100
   (3)(d) 7.103
     (f) 6.37
   (5), (6) 7.103
   (7) 7.13, 9.16
   (9) 7.103
47 .... 5.208, 7.5, 7.8, 7.9, 7.12, 7.14,
        7.15, 7.16, 7.18, 7.19,
        7.20, 7.22, 7.24, 7.25,
        7.31, 7.49, 7.55, 7.66,
            13.53
   (1), (2) 7.7, 7.13
   (3) 7.13
   (4) 7.17, 7.68
   (4A)–(5) 7.17
   (5A) 7.34
   (6) 7.17, 7.68
   (7), (8) 7.21
   (9)–(12) 7.17
48 .... 9.16
   (1) 7.88
   (3) 7.88
   (4) 7.88, 7.89
   (5), (6) 7.89
   (7) 7.88
   (9) 7.90
49 .... 6.42, 7.3
   (2) 7.104
50 .... 7.3, 7.104, 9.16
51(1), (2) 6.43, 8.98
Pt VI (ss 53–58) 1.14
Pt VII (ss 59–62) 1.14
s 59 .... 6.57
   (1) 6.66
   (4), (5) 13.53
Pt VIII (ss 63–65A) 1.14
Pt IX (ss 66–70) 1.14
s 66 .... 6.65, 6.66
Pt X (ss 71–79) 1.14
Pt XA (ss 79A–79X) 1.14
s 84 .... 13.53, 13.65

PARA

Children Act 1989—*contd*

s 84 (2), (3) 13.64
91 .... 8.178
  (1) 5.24, 8.212, 8.224
  (2) 8.203
  (4) 5.209, 12.6
  (5A) 5.227
  (7), (8) 3.79, 3.86, 3.127
  (10), (11) 5.122
  (12) 8.171
  (14) 1.53, 2.12, 5.88, 5.88, 5.108,
                5.122, 5.150, 5.201,
                5.202, 5.203, 5.204,
                5.205, 5.224, 5.227,
                8.218
  (15) 1.53, 2.12, 5.202, 7.61, 8.220,
                8.223
  (17) 1.53, 2.12, 5.202, 8.218
92(2) 5.135, 9.24, 11.20
  (4) 4.3
  (6), (7) 9.16
  (7) 3.60, 3.129, 4.3, 5.134, 5.179,
                5.216
93(1) 4.26
94 .... 13.28
94(1) 9.30, 9.40, 13.2, 13.7
  (a), (b) 8.225
  (2), (3) 13.4
  (4), (5) 13.10, 13.29
  (9) 13.10
96(2) 11.49
  (3) 10.20, 11.3
97(2) 4.47
  (4) 4.47
98 .... 11.88, 11.101
  (1) 11.85
  (2) 11.85, 11.86, 11.89, 11.89
100 ...... 7.105, 12.1, 12.3, 12.17, 12.34,
                12.41
  (1) 12.4
  (2) 12.4, 12.18, 12.35
    (b) 5.104, 12.8
    (c) 12.6
    (d) 12.8, 12.29
  (3) 12.8, 12.26, 12.35
  (4)(a) 12.8, 12.36
    (b) 12.8, 12.37, 12.39
  (5)(b) 12.36
101 .... 5.39
102 .... 7.102, 9.16
105 .... 2.16
  (1) 2.26, 2.55, 2.60, 3.55, 3.60,
                3.93, 3.111, 3.117,
                5.131, 5.140, 5.144,
                5.229, 6.65, 8.16,
                8.17, 8.40, 9.34
  (4) 9.9
  (6) 6.38, 8.170
108(12) 5.39

PARA

Children Act 1989—*contd*

Sch A1
  Pt 2 .... 5.184
    para 4 .... 5.179
Sch 1 ... 1.12, 2.26, 3.125, 4.16, 4.24, 5.1,
                5.106, 12.40, 13.4
  para 10, 11 .... 2.66
    15 .... 5.211, 6.15
Sch 2 .... 1.14, 5.142, 6.23, 7.44
  Pt 1
    para 1 .... 6.24
      2 .... 6.22, 7.6
      3 .... 6.12
      4(1), (2) 6.25
      5 .... 6.26, 7.70
      6 .... 6.22
      7 .... 6.25
        (a)(i) 6.3
      8(a)–(e) 6.28
      9 .... 6.34, 8.170
      10 .... 6.29
      11 .... 6.31
  Pt 2
    15 .... 8.199
      (1) 6.58, 6.62
      (2)(a) 6.58
      (4)–(6) 6.58
    16 .... 8.200
      (2), (3) 6.62
    17(4) 6.58
    19 .... 8.177, 9.16
      (1), (2) 6.69
      (3)(d) 6.69
      (9) 6.69
    19A 6.58, 6.72
    19B(2) 6.75
      (4), (5) 6.76
    20 .... 6.58
  Pt 3 .... 13.39
    21(3) 3.125
Sch 3 .... 8.186, 8.190
  para 1 .... 8.184
    2(2), (3) 8.183
    3 .... 8.185, 8.188
    4(4) 8.188
    6 .... 8.182
      (3) 10.36
    9 .... 8.180
  Pt III 8.196
    para 15 .... 8.204, 8.205
      (2) 4.11
    17(1) 4.11
    19(1) 10.36
Sch 5 .... 9.11
Sch 6 .... 9.11
Sch 11 .... 4.3
  Pt I 9.16
Sch 13
  para 1 .... 3.116
    45(2) 12.6

PARA

Children Act 1989—*contd*
Sch 14
  para 8(2) 3.109, 3.120
    12 .... 3.106
  Sch 15 .... 3.2, 3.105
Children Act 2004 ...... 1.10, 1.19, 1.21, 6.2,
                        6.16, 14.3, 14.4,
                        14.23, 14.37, 14.41
  Pt I (ss 1–9) 13.70
  s 10(2) 1.20
    11 .... 8.69
  Pt IV (ss 35–43) 10.13
  s 53 .... 7.17
    58(3)–(5) 3.20
    67(7)(f) 3.20
    175 .... 8.69
Children and Adoption Act 2006 ... 1.10, 5.9,
                        5.18, 5.54, 5.63, 5.67,
                        5.74, 5.81, 5.89,
                        5.175, 5.177, 5.178,
                        5.179, 5.200, 5.201
  s 6 .... 5.194
    (4) 5.199
    7 .... 2.55, 5.11, 14.20
Children and Young Persons Act 1933
  Pt I (ss 1–17) 3.21
  s 1 .... 3.26, 3.102, 3.103
    (2)(a) 3.125
    (7) 3.20
    17 .... 3.102
    49 .... 4.47
    107(1) 9.34
Children and Young Persons
    Act 1938 .... 9.34
Children and Young Persons
    Act 1956 .... 9.34
Children and Young Persons
    Act 1963 .... 9.34
Children and Young Persons
    Act 1969 .... 1.13, 9.34, 12.4
  s 23 .... 3.92, 9.13
    (1) 6.37, 9.31, 9.37
    (4)–(5A) 9.31
    32(3) 6.43
Children and Young Persons
    (Amendment) Act 1986 .... 1.13
Children (Leaving Care) Act 2000 .... 1.39
Children (Scotland) Act 1995
  s 1(1) 3.11
    (1)(d) 3.24
    2(1) 3.11
    7 .... 3.122
    82, 83 .... 6.43
Chronically Sick and Disabled Persons
    Act 1970 .... 6.12
Civil Evidence Act 1968
  s 11 .... 11.18
Civil Evidence Act 1995 .... 5.170
  s 1 .... 11.20
    4 .... 11.21
    9(1) 11.20

PARA

Civil Partnership Act 2004 ...... 3.125, 5.131
  Pt 5 Ch 3 (ss 219–238) 3.119
  s 261(1) 11.87
  Sch 5, Sch 6 .... 5.136
  Sch 27
    para 132 .... 11.87
Constitutional Reform Act 2005
  s 7 .... 4.11
    (2)(c) 4.9
    9 .... 4.11
    12, 13 .... 4.11
    23 .... 13.25
  Sch 1
    Pt 1 .... 4.11
  Sch 2
    Pt 1 .... 4.11
Contempt of Court Act 1981
  s 12 .... 9.3
    14 .... 9.3
County Courts Act 1984
  s 38 .... 12.25
    (1) 7.106
    77(1) 13.11
Courts Act 2003
  s 26(4) 4.9
    27(2) 4.10
    (5) 4.10
    28, 29 .... 4.10
    81 .... 4.11
    92 .... 4.23
Courts and Legal Services Act 1990
  s 27(2)(c) 4.13
    28 .... 4.13
  Sch 16
    para 12 .... 6.59
Crime and Disorder Act 1998 .... 1.39, 7.7
  s 8 .... 3.39, 8.191
    9 .... 3.39
    11 .... 5.136
    12 .... 5.136, 7.13, 8.18, 8.87
Criminal Justice Act 1991 .... 4.7
  s 60(3) 9.30, 9.33, 9.38, 9.39
    62 .... 9.31
    98 .... 9.31
Criminal Justice Act 2003
  s 174 .... 9.35
  Pt 11 Ch 2 (ss 114–136) 9.36
Criminal Justice and Court Services
    Act 2000 .... 1.40, 10.13
  s 12(1) 10.14
    (5)(b) 8.189, 10.38
    15 .... 10.15, 10.29, 10.42, 10.58
    16 .... 10.29, 10.44
    17 .... 10.14
Criminal Justice and Police Act 2001
  s 133 .... 9.13, 9.31

Data Protection Act 1998
  s 7 .... 11.63
Diplomatic Privileges Act 1964 .... 2.28
  Sch 1 .... 5.130

PARA

Disabled Persons (Services,
  Consultation and Representation)
  Act 1986 .... 6.12
Domestic and Appellate Proceedings
  (Restrictions of Publicity)
  Act 1968
  s 1 .... 4.47
Domestic Proceedings and Magistrates'
  Courts Act 1978 .... 1.13, 4.15, 5.136
Domicile and Matrimonial Proceedings
  Act 1973 .... 5.131
  Sch 1
    para 8 (1) 2.27
    9 .... 2.27

Education Act 1996 .... 8.173, 9.2
  s 7, 8 .... 3.39, 3.125
  9 .... 3.40
  17 .... 6.33
  Pt IV (ss 312–349) 6.12
  s 408 .... 3.40
  437 .... 8.191, 8.193
  443 .... 3.39, 8.191
  444 .... 8.191, 8.193
    (8A) 3.39
  447(1), (2) 8.191
  497 .... 13.65
  508 .... 6.35
  548 .... 3.20, 9.3
  549–550B 9.3
  576(1) 3.39, 3.125
Education and Inspections Act 2006
  s 93 .... 9.3

Family Law Act 1986 .... 2.71, 5.139
  Pt I (ss 1–43) 5.127, 5.132, 5.133,
                              5.218, 12.20
  s 1(1)(a) 4.5, 5.127, 5.129, 5.130
    (aa) 5.218
    (d) 4.5, 5.130, 12.27
  2(1) 5.127
    (a) 5.218
    (2), (2A) 5.218
    (3)(b) 12.27
      (ii) 5.130
  2A(1)(c) 5.131
    (2) 5.131
    (4) 5.130
  3(1) 4.6, 12.27
    (2) 5.218
  5 .... 5.130
  6(1) 5.133
  11(4) 5.89
  15(1) 5.133
  23(1) 5.133
  34 .... 12.20
  37 .... 12.20
  42 .... 5.129
    (1)(b) 5.99
    (2), (3) 5.131

PARA

Family Law Act 1986—*contd*
  s 42 (4)(a) 5.131
  43 .... 5.129, 10.59
  Pt II (ss 44–54) 3.119, 5.89
  Pt III (ss 55–63) 10.59
  s 55A(7) 3.50
  56(4) 3.50
  63 .... 5.99
  Pt IV (ss 64–69) 1.14, 10.59
Family Law Act 1996 ..... 5.136, 6.27, 12.34
  Pt II (ss 2–25) 1.32
  Pt IV (ss 30–63) 5.101, 8.96
  s 50 .... 5.171
Family Law Reform Act 1969 ..... 1.13, 2.17
  s 7 .... 12.4
  8 .... 3.33, 3.34
    (1) **3.31**, 3.32
    (2) 3.28, 3.31
    (3) 3.32
  21 .... 12.32
    (3) 3.28
  28(2) 7.100
Family Law Reform Act 1987 .... 1.4
  s 1 .... 8.201
    (1) 3.74
    (2) 3.43
    (3) 3.43
      (b) 3.47
    (4) 3.43
Family Law (Scotland) Act 2006
  s 23 .... 3.50

Gender Recognition Act 2004
  s 12 .... **3.45**
Guardianship of Infants Act 1925
  s 1 .... 3.41
Guardianship of Minors Act 1971 .... 1.13,
                                          2.3
  s 3 .... 3.2, 3.105
Guardianship of Minors Act 1973 .... 1.13

Housing Act 1985
  s 75 .... 3.93
Housing Act 1996 .... 5.52
  Pt VII (ss 175–218) 6.41
Human Fertilisation and Embryology
  Act 1990 .... 3.47, 4.7, 5.55
  s 28 .... 3.43
  30 .... 2.26, 3.43, 3.94, 3.101, 4.15,
                                         10.36
    (8)(a) 5.136
  Sch 3 .... 3.93
Human Fertilisation and Embryology
  Act 2008
  s 54 .... 5.135

PARA

Human Rights Act 1998 ...... 1.7, 1.41, 1.44,
1.45, 2.3, 2.20, 3.6,
5.44, 5.100, 5.130,
5.203, 6.1, 7.4, 7.40,
7.65, 8.63, 8.157,
9.29, 11.64, 13.78,
13.82, 13.87, 14.38
s 2(1)(a)–(d) 1.49
3 .... 1.50, 8.158
4 .... 1.51, 4.40
(5) 1.45
6(1) 9.27
(3) 1.52, 13.88
7 .... 1.54, 8.158, 8.162, 13.74, 13.79,
13.88, 13.92, 13.93
(1)(a), (b) 13.89
(5) 1.52, 13.90
(7) 1.52, 13.90
8 .... 1.52, 1.53, 1.54, 8.158, 13.74,
13.88, 13.90, 13.92,
13.93
(4) 13.91
9(3), (4) 1.52
10 .... 1.51
Sch 1
Art 6 .... 4.13

Interpretation Act 1978
s 6(c) 3.108, 5.17

Learning and Skills Act 2000
s 141 .... 1.21
Legitimacy Act 1976
s 1 .... 3.43
10 .... 3.43
Local Authority Social Services
Act 1970 .... 6.57, 10.47
s 7 .... 7.17, 8.13, 8.58, 11.68
Local Government Act 1974 .... 13.66
s 26(4), (5) 13.67
Local Government Act 1988
s 29 .... 13.67
Sch 3 .... 13.67
Local Government Act 2000
s 2 .... 6.19
Local Government (Miscellaneous
Provisions) Act 1976
s 19(1) 6.35

Magistrates' Courts Act 1980
s 5(1) 9.3
10(4) 9.3
17C 9.3
18(4) 9.3
63(3) 4.45, 5.162, 5.163, **5.171**,
5.172, 5.173, 5.175,
5.184, 13.10
(a) 5.174
66(1), (2) 4.9
68 .... 4.9

PARA

Magistrates' Courts Act 1980—*contd*
s 69 .... 4.47
71 .... 4.47
145A(2) 4.59
Matrimonial and Family Proceedings
Act 1984
Pt III (ss 12–27) 5.136
s 38 .... 4.17, 12.25, 12.26
39 .... 4.17
Matrimonial Causes Act 1973 ... 1.13, 3.125,
5.131, 5.136
s 11 .... 1.51
25(1) 2.26
Mental Capacity Act 2005 .... 8.102
Mental Health Act 1983 .... 9.3, 9.6, 12.19
s 1(2) 6.21
2, 3 .... 9.3
7 .... 3.104

National Assistance Act 1948 .... 6.21

Offences Against the Person Act 1861
s 18 .... 3.20
20 .... 3.20
47 .... 3.20

Police and Criminal Evidence
Act 1984 .... 7.51
s 17 .... 7.102
25(3)(e) 7.102
38(6) 6.37, 9.34
Powers of Criminal Courts
(Sentencing) Act 2000
s 63(1) 6.38
90 .... 9.6
91 .... 9.3, 9.6
100 .... 9.3
Sch 6
para 5 .... 6.37
Sch 7
para 7(5) 6.37
Protection of Children Act 1999 .... 1.39

Registration of Births, Deaths and
Marriages (Scotland) Act 1965
s 2(6) 3.50
18(1)(a)–(c) 3.50
20(1)(a) 3.50
Regulation of Investigatory Powers
Act 2000 .... 11.28

School Standards and Framework
Act 1998
s 71 .... 3.42
86 .... 3.40
92 .... 3.40
Sexual Offences Act 2003
s 104 .... 5.88

Table of Statutes

PARA

Social Security Administration
   Act 1992
  s 78(6) 3.74, 3.125
    105(3) 3.74, 3.125
Supreme Court Act 1981
  s 16 .... 13.11
    18(1) 13.3
    31(3) 13.38
    37 .... 8.173, 12.25, 12.35, 12.36
      (1) 7.105, 7.106
    41(2), (2A) 12.6
    51 .... 4.58
      (6), (7) 4.59

PARA

Supreme Court Act 1981—*contd*
  s 51 (13) 4.59
    81 .... 9.3
  Sch 1
    para 3(b)(ii) 12.26

Wills Act 1837
  s 1 .... 3.116
    9 .... 3.118
    20 .... 3.119

Youth Justice and Criminal Evidence
   Act 1999
  Pt II (ss 16–63) 10.60

Table of Statutory Instruments

All references in the right-hand column are to paragraph numbers. Paragraph numbers printed in **bold** type indicate where legislation is set out in part or in full.

PARA

Adoption Agencies Regulations 2005,
SI 2005/389
r 11–17 .... 8.169

Adoption and Children Act 2002
(Commencement No 7)
Order 2004, SI 2004/3203
art 2(2) 2.26

Adoption and Children Act 2002
(Commencement No 9)
Order 2005, SI 2005/2213 .... 5.209,
5.213

Adoption and Children Act 2002
(Commencement No 10
Transitional and Savings
Provisions) Order 2005,
SI 2005/2897
art 14 .... 2.26

Advocacy Services and Representations
Procedure (Children)
(Amendment) Regulations 2005,
SI 2005/719
reg 4 .... 13.54

Advocacy Services and Representations
Procedure (Children) (Wales)
Regulations 2004, SI 2004/1448
reg 4 .... 13.54

Arrangements for Placement of
Children (General)
Regulations 1991, SI 1991/890 .... 6.63,
6.65, 10.47
reg 3(1) 6.48
    (3) 6.48
    (5) 6.48
5 .... 6.48
7(1) 6.48
    (2) 6.58
Sch 1 .... 6.48
Sch 4 .... 6.48

PARA

Assistants to Justices' Clerks
Regulations 2006,
SI 2006/3405 .... 4.10

Births and Deaths Registration
(Northern Ireland) Order 1976,
SI 1976/1041
art 14(3)(a)–(c) 3.50

Care Homes Regulations 2001,
SI 2001/3965 .... 6.63

Children Act 1989 (Commencement
and Transitional Provisions)
Order 1991, SI 1991/828 .... 1.1

Children Act 1989 Representations
Procedure (England)
Regulations 2006,
SI 2006/1738 .... 6.49, 6.58

Children Act 2004 (Amendment of
Miscellaneous Regulations)
(Wales) Regulations 2005,
SI 2005/774 .... 6.16

Children Act 2004 (Children's Services)
Regulations 2005,
SI 2005/1972 .... 6.2, 6.16

Children (Admissibility of Hearsay
Evidence) Order 1993,
SI 1993/621 ... 5.170, 9.24, 9.36, 10.20,
10.60, 11.3, 11.20,
11.22, 11.23

Children (Allocation of Proceedings)
(Appeals) Order 1991,
SI 1991/1801 .... 4.35

Children (Allocation of Proceedings)
Order 1991, SI 1991/1677 .... 1.12, 4.2,
4.3, 4.14, 4.32, 4.33,
4.41, 8.96, 9.1, 9.18
art 3 .... 4.15, 8.88
    (1) 7.58, 7.78
    (a) 9.16

PARA

Children (Allocation of Proceedings)
Order 1991, SI 1991/1677—*contd*
art 3 (2) 7.58, 7.78
    (3) 7.58, 7.78, 9.16
    3A–3C 4.15
    4 .... 4.15
    5, 6 .... 4.17
    7 .... 4.17, 4.39
        (2) 7.78
    8 .... 4.39
    9 .... 4.17, 4.34
        (4) 4.39
    10 .... 4.17
    11 .... 4.17, 4.34
        (2) 4.39
    12 .... 4.17, 4.35, 4.40
    13 .... 4.17
    14 .... 4.16
    16 .... 4.8
        (1) 4.16
    17 .... 4.8
    18 .... 4.8
        (1) 4.16
    19 .... 4.8
    21 .... 4.18
Sch 1–Sch 4 .... 4.8
Children and Adoption Act 2006
(Commencement No 1)
Order 2007, SI 2007/2287 ... 2.55, 5.11,
                                        5.198
Children and Family Court Advisory
and Support Service (Reviewed
Case Referral) Regulations 2004,
SI 2004/2187 .... 8.162
Children (Leaving Care)
Regulations 2001,
SI 2001/2874 .... 6.58, 6.84
reg 4 .... 6.77, 6.78
    5 .... 6.75
    8, 9 .... 6.83
    11 .... 6.79
Children (Leaving Care) (Wales)
Regulations 2001,
SI 2001/2189 .... 6.77
Children (Prescribed Orders -Northern
Ireland, Guernsey and Isle of
Man) Regulations 1991,
SI 1991/2032 .... 5.39
Children (Protection from Offenders)
(Miscellaneous Amendments)
Regulations 1997,
SI 1997/2308 .... 12.16
Children (Secure Accommodation)
(No 2) Regulations 1991,
SI 1991/2034 .... 9.1
reg 2 .... 9.6, 9.17
Children (Secure Accommodation)
Regulations 1991,
SI 1991/1505 .... 9.1
reg 3, 4 .... 9.12
    5 .... 9.6

PARA

Children (Secure Accommodation)
Regulations 1991, SI 1991/1505—*contd*
reg 5 (2)(a), (b) 9.9
    6(1) 9.34
        (b) 9.32
        (2) 9.34
    7 .... 9.6
    8 .... 9.17
    9 .... 9.14
    10(1) 9.6, 9.14
        (2), (3) 9.14
    11 .... 9.26
    12 .... 9.26, 9.38
    13(1), (2) 9.37
    15 .... 9.27
    17 .... 9.27
Children's Commissioner for Wales
(Appointment) Regulations 2001,
SI 2001/3121 .... 2.6
Children's Commissioner for Wales
Regulations 2001, SI 2001/2787
reg 5, 6 .... 13.70
Children's Homes Regulations 2001,
SI 2001/3967 .... 6.63, 6.68, 9.3
reg 17(1) 9.7
    (4) 9.7
    (5) 9.7
        (a) 3.20
    24 .... 13.53
Children's Homes (Wales)
Regulations 2002, SI 2002/327
reg 17 .... 9.3
    (5)(a) 3.20
Civil Procedure Rules 1998,
SI 1998/3132 .... 1.26, 1.41
Pt 2
    r 2.1 .... 1.43, 13.11
Pt 8
    r 8.2 .... 13.41
Pt 16
    PD 16 .... 13.89
Pt 21
    r 21.12(1), (2) 3.115
Pt 25 .... 13.40
    r 25.1(1)(a), (b) 12.25
Pt 31
    r 31.6 .... 11.66
    31.19 .... 11.66
Pt 43 .... 1.43
Pt 44 .... 1.43
    r 44.3(2)(a), (b) 4.58
Pt 47 .... 1.43
Pt 48 .... 1.43
Pt 52 .... 13.11
    r 52.3 .... 1.43, 13.1
        (1) 5.170, 13.12
        (a)(iii) 9.29
        (2) 13.13
        (b) 13.15
        (3), (4) 13.13
        (6) 8.100, 13.14

PARA

Civil Procedure Rules 1998,
SI 1998/3132—*contd*
Pt 52—*contd*
  r 52.3 (7) 13.14
    52.4(1)–(3) 13.16
    52.5(1) 13.16
      (5), (6) 13.16
    52.6 .... 13.16
    52.7 .... 13.17
    52.8 .... 13.16
    52.10 .... 13.32
    52.11(1), (2) 13.33
      (3), (4) 13.34
      (5) 13.33
    52.13 .... 13.12
      (2) 13.14
    52.17 .... 13.30
  PD 52 .... 13.11
    para 4.6 .... 13.13, 13.15
      4.7, 4.8 .... 13.13
      4.9 .... 13.12
      4.11–4.15 .... 13.15
      5.2 .... 13.16
      5.5 .... 13.17
      5.6 .... 13.18
      5.9 .... 13.19
      5.10, 5.11 .... 13.20
      6.2–6.6 .... 13.21
      15.3 .... 13.18
Pt 54 .... 1.43
  r 54.1(1)(f) 13.38
    (2)(a) **13.37**
    54.2 .... 13.41
    54.3 .... 13.39
      (2) 13.40
    54.4, 54.5 .... 13.41
    54.10(2) 13.39
    54.12(3) 13.42
    54.19 .... 13.39
  PD 54
    para 5.1 .... 13.41
      5.6, 5.7 .... 13.41
      8.4 .... 13.42
  Sch 1–Rules of the Supreme Court
    Ord 40 .... 11.36
    Ord 45
      r 7(4) 5.165
    Ord 52
      r 7(1) 5.175
    Ord 59 .... 13.1
    Ord 55
      r 1(1), (2) 13.8
  Sch 2–County Court Rules
    Ord 29
      r 1(3) 5.165
    Ord 37
      r 1 .... 13.11
Community Legal Services (Financial)
  Regulations 2000, SI 2000/516
  reg 3(1)(c) 9.20

PARA

Contact with Children
  Regulations 1991, SI 1991/891
  reg 2 .... 8.207
    3 .... 8.213
    4 .... 8.207
  Schedule 8.207, 8.213
County Court Rules 1981,
  SI 1981/1687 .... 1.43
Courts Act 2003 (Consequential
  Provisions) (No 2) Order 2005,
  SI 2005/617 .... 1.27
Criminal Justice and Police Act 2001
  (Commencement No 3)
  Order 2001, SI 2001/3736 .... 9.13
Criminal Procedure Rules 2005,
  SI 2005/384
  r 3.5(6) 4.45
    6.4 .... 11.18

Data Protection (Processing of Sensitive
  Personal Data) Order 2000,
  SI 2000/417 .... 11.96
Data Protection (Subject Access
  Modification) (Education)
  Order 2000, SI 2000/414 .... 11.63
Data Protection (Subject Access
  Modification) (Health)
  Order 2000, SI 2000/413 .... 11.63
Data Protection (Subject Access
  Modification) (Social Work)
  Order 2000, SI 2000/415 .... 11.63
Day Care and Child Minding
  (National Standards) (England)
  Regulations 2003, SI 2003/1996
  reg 5 .... 3.20
Disabled Children (Direct Payments)
  (England) Regulations 2001,
  SI 2001/442 .... 6.22

European Communities (Jurisdiction
  and Judgments in Matrimonial
  and Parental Responsibility
  Matters) Regulations 2005,
  SI 2005/265 .... 5.127

Family Law Act 1986 (Dependent
  Territories) Order 1991,
  SI 1991/1723 .... 5.129
Family Procedure (Adoption)
  Rules 2005, SI 2005/2795 .... 1.34
Pt 17
  PD 17 .... 11.34
Family Proceedings (Amendment)
  Rules 1996, SI 1996/816
  r 3 .... 3.119
Family Proceedings (Amendment No 2)
  Rules 2005, SI 2005/412 .... 2.55

PARA

Family Proceedings Courts (Children
Act 1989) Rules 1991,
SI 1991/1395 ..... 1.26, 1.27, 1.43, 4.20,
9.37, 11.66, 14.15
r 1 .... 4.26
(1) 7.63
(2) 4.49, 10.15
2(2) 4.49, 9.19, 9.35, 10.36
(3) 7.60
(4) 7.92
(5) 7.63
(c) 4.42
3(1) 5.158
(2) 5.158
4 .... 8.98, 9.17
(1)(a) 4.22, 8.88
(2) 4.24, 4.27
(3) 4.26
(4) ... 4.21, 5.26, 5.96, 5.98, 7.79, 7.90,
7.104, 9.16
4A 5.178
5 .... 4.24, 4.42, 8.227, 10.23
7(2) 4.26
(5) 8.99
8(7) 4.26
(8) 4.24, 9.16
9 .... 4.24
10 .... 4.29, 10.35, 10.42
(1) 9.19, 10.39
(2), (3) 10.40
(4A) 10.39
(8) 9.28, 10.39
(9), (10) 10.41
11 .... 9.19
(1) 2.41, 10.42
11A 9.19
(1)(a) 10.42, 10.49
(b) 10.42
(2) 10.49
(b) 10.51
(3) 10.42, 10.49, 10.50
(4) 4.28
(e) 10.42
(6) 10.42
(8)–(10) 10.42
11AA 5.12, 9.19
11B 9.19, 10.26
12 .... 10.50
(1)(a) 10.42, 10.51
(3) 10.52
13(3) 4.28, 10.29
14 .... 9.21
(2) 4.27, 8.93
(h) 8.111
(5) 4.28
(11) 4.28
16 .... 4.28
(1) 9.23
(2) 4.49, 10.60, 11.48
(7) 4.47, 4.49, 10.60, 11.48
17 .... 9.22

PARA

Family Proceedings Courts (Children
Act 1989) Rules 1991,
SI 1991/1395—*contd*
r 17 (1) 4.44, 11.13
(2) 4.44
(4) 4.21, 4.44, 11.14
18 .... 7.91, 8.118
(1) 11.33
(3) 11.33
19 .... 4.44
20 .... 4.10, 4.30, 7.80, 9.22
21(1) 4.46
(2) 4.48, 8.111, 8.141
(3) 9.22
(4) 4.55
(5) 4.10, 4.55, 4.56, 7.80
(6) 2.75, 4.55, 4.56, 7.80
(8) 7.80
21AA 5.180
22(1) 4.58
22A 10.44
23 .... 11.80, 11.100
(1)–(4) 11.83
23A 4.13, 4.47, 10.27, 11.80, 11.83,
11.84, 11.100
(1)(c)(vii) 11.33
24 .... 5.173
25 .... 7.93, 8.120
27 .... 7.27
(2), (3) 7.28
28 .... 4.10, 4.29, 8.124
31A(4) 5.162
32 .... 4.10
Sch 1 .... 1.12, 8.88
Sch 2 .... 4.24, 4.25, 6.45, 8.98, 9.17
column (iii) 7.76
(iv) 7.58, 7.76
Sch 4 .... 8.98
Family Proceedings Courts (Children
Act 1989) (Amendment No 2)
Rules 2005, SI 2005/413 .... 2.55
Family Proceedings Courts
(Constitution of Committees and
Right to Preside) Rules 2007,
2007/1610
r 2 .... 4.9
3(2), (3) 4.9
5(2) 4.9
Family Proceedings Fees Order 2008,
SI 2008/1504 .... 4.23, 8.104
Family Proceedings Rules 1991,
SI 1991/1247 ...... 1.26, 1.27, 1.43, 4.2,
4.20, 4.51, 8.88,
8.124, 9.37, 11.66,
12.26, 14.15
r 2.57 .... 10.59
4.1 .... 4.26
(1) 4.49, 10.15
(2)(a) 5.33, 5.42
(c) 5.33, 5.42
4.2 .... 9.19, 10.36

PARA

Family Proceedings Rules 1991,
SI 1991/1247—*contd*

r 4.2 (2) 4.49, 9.35
  (3) 7.60
  4.3(1) 5.158
  (2) 5.158
  4.4 .... 9.16, 9.17
  (1)(a) 4.22
  (2) 4.24, 4.27
  (3) 4.26
  (4) 5.26, 5.96, 5.98, 7.79
  4.4A 5.178
  4.5 .... 4.24, 4.42, 8.227, 10.23
  4.7(2) 4.26
  (5) 8.99
  4.8 .... 9.16
  (7) 4.26
  (8) 4.24
  4.9 .... 4.24
  4.10 .... 10.35, 10.42
  (1) 9.19, 10.39
  (2), (3) 10.40
  (4A) 10.39
  (8) 9.28, 10.39
  (9), (10) 10.41
  4.11 .... 9.19, 10.33
  (1) 2.41, 10.42
  (2) 10.16, 10.49
  (4) 10.29, 10.45
  4.11A 10.16, 10.33, 10.42
  (1)(a) 10.42, 10.49
  (b) 10.42
  (2) 10.49
  (3) 10.42, 10.49
  (b) 10.51
  (4) 4.28
  (e) 10.42
  (6) 10.42
  (8)–(11) 10.42
  4.11AA 5.12
  4.11B 10.16, 10.26
  4.12 .... 10.50
  (1)(a) 10.42, 10.51
  (3) 10.52
  4.13(3) 4.28, 10.29
  (3A) 10.30
  4.14 .... 9.21
  (2) 4.27
  (3) 4.28
  (9) 4.28
  (10) 4.30
  4.16 .... 4.28, 9.23
  (2) 4.49, 10.60, 11.48
  (7) 4.47
  4.17 .... 9.22
  (1) 4.44, 11.13
  (2) 4.44
  (4) 4.21, 4.44, 11.14
  (5) 4.21, 4.44
  4.18 .... 7.91, 8.118
  (1) 11.33

PARA

Family Proceedings Rules 1991,
SI 1991/1247—*contd*

r 4.18 (3) 11.33
  4.19 .... 4.44
  4.20 .... 4.10, 4.30, 9.22
  4.21(2) 8.141, 9.22
  (3) 4.55
  (4) 2.75
  (5) 5.33, 5.42
  4.21A 5.165, 5.169
  4.21AA 5.180
  4.22 .... 9.22, 13.1
  (3)(c) 13.8
  (5), (6) 13.8
  (7) 13.7
  4.23 .... 11.80
  (1)(f) 11.33
  4.24 .... 7.93, 8.120
  4.26 .... 7.27
  (2), (3) 7.28
  5.1 .... 12.13
  6.11(4) 12.23
  6.17(4) 5.162
  9.1 .... 4.26
  (1) 10.53
  9.2 .... 4.26, 4.50
  (1) 10.53
  9.2A 4.26, 4.50, 5.156, 10.33, 10.58,
                                        12.11
  (1)(a) 10.53, 10.55
  (b) 10.53
  (10) 10.54
  (11) 10.56
  9.5 ..... 4.50, 5.206, 10.32, 10.34, 10.37,
                                        10.59
  (1), (2) 10.31
  (4) 10.31
  (6) 10.33
  10.14A 10.44
  10.20(5) 11.82
  10.20A 4.13, 4.47, 10.27, 11.80,
                  11.83, 11.84, 11.100,
                                        14.11
  (1) 11.81
  (2) 11.81
  (a) 11.82, 11.90
  (c)(vii) 11.33, 11.82
  (3) 11.81
  (5) 11.82
  App 3 .... 6.45, 9.17, 10.35
  column (iii), (iv) 7.58, 7.76
  App J 4.24

Family Proceedings (Miscellaneous
  Amendments) Rules 1999,
  SI 1999/1012 .... 4.58

Foster Placement (Children)
  Regulations 1991, SI 1991/910
  reg 4(4A) 2.10

PARA

Fostering Services Regulations 2002,
  SI 2002/57 ...... 2.10, 6.43, 6.64, 6.65,
                              6.66, 12.17
  reg 28(5)(b) 3.20
    32 .... 13.43
    40 .... 6.67
  Sch 5
    point 8 .... 3.20
Fostering Services (Wales)
  Regulations 2003, SI 2003/237 .... 6.67,
                                      12.17
  Sch 5
    point 8 .... 3.20

Homelessness (Priority Need for
  Accommodation) (England)
  Order 2002, SI 2002/2051 .... 6.42
Human Rights Act 1998
  (Commencement No 2)
  Regulations 2000,
  SI 2000/1851 .... 1.44

Justices' Clerks Rules 2005,
  SI 2005/545 .... 4.10
  Schedule
    para 38 .... 4.29
Justices of the Peace (Training and
  Development Committee)
  Rules 2007, SI 2007/1609
  r 37 .... 4.9

Magistrates' Courts (Children and
  Young Persons) Rules 1992,
  SI 1992/2071
  Pt III (rr 13–22) 9.35
Magistrates' Courts (Costs Against
  Legal Representatives in Civil
  Proceedings) Rules 1991,
  SI 1991/2096 .... 4.59
Magistrates' Courts Fees Order 2008,
  SI 2008/1052 .... 4.23, 8.104
Magistrates' Courts (Hearsay Evidence
  in Civil Proceedings) Rules 1999,
  SI 1999/681 .... 11.20
Magistrates' Courts Rules 1981,
  SI 1981/552
  r 68 .... 11.18

Parental Orders (Human Fertilisation
  and Embryology)
  Regulations 1994,
  SI 1994/2767 .... 2.26
  Sch 1 .... 3.101
Parental Responsibility Agreement
  (Amendment) Regulations 1994,
  SI 1994/3157 .... 3.56
Parental Responsibility Agreement
  (Amendment) Regulations 2001,
  SI 2001/2262 .... 3.56, 3.57

PARA

Parental Responsibility Agreement
  (Amendment) Regulations 2005,
  SI 2005/2808 .... 3.57, 3.83
Parental Responsibility Agreement
  Regulations 1991,
  SI 1991/1478 .... 3.54
  reg 3(1)–(3) 3.56
Placement of Children (Wales)
  Regulations 2007, SI 2007/310 .... 6.48,
                                      6.58
Placement of Children with Parents etc
  Regulations 1991, SI 1991/893 .... 6.59,
                                  6.64, 6.66

Refuges (Children's Homes and Foster
  Placements) Regulations 1991,
  SI 1991/1507 .... 6.43
  reg 2(1) 6.44
    3(2) 6.44
    (9) 6.44
Representations Procedure (England)
  Regulations 2006, SI 2006/1738
  reg 3, 4 .... 13.53
    6 .... 13.59
    7, 8 .... 13.59
    9(1), (2) 13.59
    11 .... 13.59
    13 .... 13.62
    14 .... 13.60
    15(1), (2) 13.60
    17(1)–(3) 13.60
    18, 19 .... 13.60
    20(2), (3) 13.60
    21 .... 13.53
Representations Procedure (Children)
  (Wales) Regulations 2005,
  SI 2005/3365
  reg 7 .... 13.53
    8 .... 13.59
    11, 12 .... 13.59
    14 .... 13.59
    15(1)–(8) 13.60
    19 .... 13.62
Review of Children's Cases
  Regulations 1991, SI 1991/895 .... 6.49,
                                      8.238
  reg 1(2) 13.51
    6 .... 6.58
    8A 6.58
  Sch 2 .... 8.221
Review of Children's Cases
  (Amendment) (England)
  Regulations 2004,
  SI 2004/1419 .... 8.162
Review of Children's Cases (Wales)
  Regulations 2007, SI 2007/307 ..... 6.58
  reg 1(2) 13.51

PARA

Rules of the Supreme Court 1965,
  SI 1965/828 .... 1.43

Social Services Complaints Procedure
  (Wales) Regulations 2005,
  SI 2005/3366
  reg 22 .... 13.60
Special Guardianship
  Regulations 2005,
  SI 2005/1109 .... 5.214, 5.233
  reg 1(3) 5.231
  2(1) 5.230
  3(1)(a)–(d) 5.231
  (2) 5.231
  6(2) 5.232
  7, 8 .... 5.232
  9 .... 5.232
  (d) 5.229
  10 .... 5.232
  11(1)–(3) 5.230
  14 .... 5.230

PARA

Special Guardianship Regulations 2005,
  SI 2005/1109—*contd*
  reg 18 .... 5.232
  Schedule 5.219
  para 10 .... 5.222
Special Guardianship (Wales)
  Regulations 2005,
  SI 2005/1513 .... 5.214, 5.233
  reg 1(3) 5.230
  2 .... 5.231
  3 .... 5.231
  4 .... 5.230
  (1), (2) 5.232
  5 .... 5.230
  12 .... 5.230
  (2) 5.232
  Schedule 5.219

Transfer of Functions (Magistrates'
  Courts and Family Law)
  Order 1992, SI 1992/709 .... 4.20

Table of European Legislation and other International Material

All references in the right-hand column are to paragraph numbers. Paragraph numbers printed in **bold** type indicate where legislation is set out in part or in full.

PARA

PRIMARY LEGISLATION
CONVENTIONS

European Convention of Human
  Rights and Fundamental
  Freedoms (Rome, 4 November
  1950) 1.45, 1.54, 2.3, 3.20, 5.100,
                6.5, 8.2, 8.6, 8.214,
                9.1, 11.40, 12.15,
                12.40, 14.38
  art 3 .... 13.85, 13.86
    (1) 1.47
    5 .... 9.3, 9.6, 9.27
    (1) **1.47, 9.2**, 9.4
    (5) 1.52
    6 .... 2.4, 2.24, 2.61, 5.152, 7.40, 8.5,
              8.98, 8.100, 8.158,
              11.64, 11.71, 11.75,
              11.89, 13.75, 13.84,
              14.13, 14.14
    (1) **1.46**, 4.43, 4.47, 5.203, 8.159,
              8.160, 8.161, 9.5
    (3) 9.5

PARA

European Convention of Human Rights and
  Fundamental Freedoms (Rome,
  4 November 1950)—*contd*
  art 8 .... 1.7, 1.48, 1.51, 1.52, 2.20, 2.21,
          2.24, 2.28, 2.50, 3.16,
          3.17, 3.19, 3.23,
          3.44 4.55, 5.44, 5.75,
          5.83, 5.93, 5.152,
          5.234, 6.1, 7.19, 7.40,
          7.101, 8.4, 8.5, 8.56,
          8.63, 8.98, 8.100,
          8.153, 8.158, 8.160,
          8.165, 9.3, 11.55,
          11.64, 13.86, 13.92,
          13.94, 14.13
    (1) 5.75
    (2) **1.46**, 2.4, 5.76, 13.79
    10 .... 2.20, 2.21, 11.64
    12 .... 1.51
    13 ... 3.23, 13.69, 13.85, 13.86, 13.88
    14 .... **1.47**, 2.50, 3.44, 5.76
    34 .... 1.52, 13.90
    41 .... 13.91
  Protocol No 1
    art 2 .... 3.38
  Protocol No 12 .... 1.47

li

PARA

European Convention on the Exercise
of Children's Rights (1996)
art 3, 4 .... 10.6
European Convention of Recognition
and Enforcement of Decisions
Concerning Custody of Children
(1980) 12.21, 2.7, 2.28
Hague Convention on the Civil
Aspects of International Child
Abduction (1980) 12.22, 12.42, 2.7,
2.28, 2.71, 14.40
art 3 .... 12.21
13 .... 4.40
Hague Convention on the Protection
of Children (1996) 14.40
UN Convention on the Rights of the
Child (1989) 1.8, 10.10
art 3(1) 2.5, 2.6, 2.14
9 .... 5.83
(3) 3.23, **5.74**
12 .... 2.77, 10.4
(1) 2.42
13 .... 10.4
Vienna Convetion on Diplomatic
Relations (1961)
art 32 .... 5.130

PARA

SECONDARY LEGISLATION
REGULATIONS

Council Regulation (EC)
No 2201/2003 ('Brussells II
Revised') 2.71, 3.55, 3.105, 5.127,
5.129, 5.130, 12.20,
12.21, 14.39
art 1(b) 3.55, 3.61
2(3) 5.128
8 .... 3.55, 3.61, 5.128, 5.218
9, 10 .... 5.128
11 .... 5.128
(6) 5.53, 12.23, 12.42
(7) 5.53, 12.42
(8) 5.53
12 .... 5.218
(1)(b) 5.128
(3) 5.128
13 .... 3.55, 3.61, 5.128, 5.218
(b) 4.5
14–16 .... 5.128
19(2) 5.218
20 .... 5.128
46 .... 3.55
Recital 5 .... 3.61
(b) 3.55

Table of Cases

A

PARA

A (minors) (residence order), Re [1992] Fam 182, [1992] 3 All ER 872,
    [1992] 3 WLR 422, 91 LGR 401, [1992] 2 FCR 174, [1992] Fam Law 439, sub
    nom A and W (minors) (residence order: leave to apply), Re [1992] 2 FLR
    154, CA 2.12, 2.17, 2.27, 2.67, 5.151, 5.154, 5.156, 12.43
A (a minor) (residence order: leave to apply), Re (1993). See A v A and Newham
    London Borough Council
A (a minor), Re (1994) 92 LGR 615, sub nom Oldham Metropolitan Borough
    Council v E 92 LGR 615, sub nom A (a minor), Re [1994] 2 FCR 125, sub
    nom Oldham Metropolitan Borough Council v E [1994] 1 FLR 568,
    [1994] Fam Law 494, CA 4.57, 8.39
A (a minor), Re [1995] 3 All ER 401, [1995] 1 WLR 482, [1995] 2 FCR 114,
    [1995] 1 FLR 335, 138 Sol Jo LB 228, CA 8.182, 8.219
A (a minor), Re [1995] 2 FCR 298, [1995] 1 FLR 767, [1995] Fam Law 413 .... 3.97
A, Re [1995] 2 FCR 686, [1995] 1 FLR 599, [1995] Fam Law 291 .... 8.220
A (section 8 order: grandparents' application), Re [1996] 1 FCR 467, [1995] 2 FLR
    153, [1995] Fam Law 540, CA 5.83, 5.152
A (a minor) (parental responsibility), Re [1996] 1 FCR 562 .... 3.74
A (child of the family), Re [1998] 1 FCR 458, [1998] 1 FLR 347, [1998] Fam Law
    14, CA 5.144
A (a minor) (disclosure of medical records to General Medical Council), Re
    [1999] 1 FCR 30, [1998] 2 FLR 641, [1998] Fam Law 586, 47 BMLR 84,
    [1998] NLJR 1088 .... 11.94
A (a minor) (contact: parent's application for leave), Re [1999] 1 FCR 127,
    [1998] 1 FLR 1, [1998] Fam Law 71, CA 5.150, 5.204
A (a minor) (holiday in non-convention country), Re [1999] 1 FCR 284,
    [1999] 2 FLR 1 .... 5.50
A (minors) (contact: domestic violence), Re [1999] 1 FCR 729, [1998] 2 FLR 171,
    [1998] Fam Law 456 .... 5.90
A (medical treatment: male sterilisation), Re [2000] 1 FCR 193, [2000] 1 FLR 549,
    [2000] 02 LS Gaz R 30, CA 2.36
A (children) (conjoined twins: surgical separation), Re [2001] Fam 147,
    [2000] 4 All ER 961, [2001] 2 WLR 480, [2000] 3 FCR 577, [2001] 1 FLR 1,
    [2001] Fam Law 18, 57 BMLR 1, 9 BHRC 261, CA 2.2, 2.7, 2.34, 2.35, 2.36, 3.26,
                                                                                                                    3.35
A (children) (specific issue order: parental dispute), Re [2001] 1 FCR 210,
    [2001] 1 FLR 121, [2001] Fam Law 22, CA 5.98
A (children) (conjoined twins) (No 2), Re [2001] 1 FCR 313, [2001] 1 FLR 267,
    [2001] Fam Law 100, [2000] All ER (D) 1700, CA 10.41
A (a child) (separate representation in contact proceedings), Re [2001] 2 FCR 55,
    [2001] 1 FLR 715, [2000] All ER (D) 1898, CA 4.50, 10.30, 10.33, 10.58
A (secure accommodation order), Re [2001] Fam Law 806 .... 9.25
A (a child) (mental health of mother), Re [2001] EWCA Civ 162, [2001] 1 FCR 577,
    [2001] All ER (D) 106 (Feb) 4.55
A (children) (shared residence), Re [2001] EWCA Civ 1795, [2002] 1 FCR 177,
    [2002] 1 FLR 495, [2001] All ER (D) 170 (Nov) 5.4, 5.22

Table of Cases

PARA

A (temporary removal from jurisdiction), Re [2004] EWCA Civ 1587, [2005] 1 FLR
   639, [2005] Fam Law 215 .... 5.47
A (contact: risk of violence), Re [2005] EWHC 851 (Fam), [2006] 1 FLR 283 ...... 5.74, 11.12
A (contact: witness protection scheme), Re [2005] EWHC 2189 (Fam), [2006] 2 FLR
   551, [2006] Fam Law 528 .... 5.55, 5.61
A (children: split hearings), Re [2006] EWCA Civ 714, [2007] 1 FLR 905,
   [2007] Fam Law 16, (2006) Times, 7 September 8.144
A (a child) (wardship: habitual residence), Re [2006] EWHC 3338 (Fam),
   [2007] 1 FCR 390, [2007] 1 FLR 1589, [2007] Fam Law 401, [2006] All ER
   (D) 367 (Dec) 12.20
A (a child) (residence order), Re [2007] EWCA Civ 899, [2008] 1 FCR 599,
   [2007] Fam Law 1061, [2007] All ER (D) 156 (Jun) 5.87
A (a child) (custody), Re [2007] EWHC 2016 (Fam), [2008] 1 FLR 289,
   [2007] Fam Law 1058, (2007) Times, 2 November, [2007] All ER (D) 156
   (Aug) 4.5, 4.40, 5.53, 12.42
A (an infant),Re, Hanif v Secretary of State for Home Affairs. See Arif (Mohamed)
   (an infant), Re
A v A (custody of children) [1988] FCR 205, [1988] Fam Law 57, sub nom (custody
   appeal: role of appellate court) [1988] 1 FLR 193, CA 13.30
A v A (minors) [1995] 1 FCR 91, [1994] 1 FLR 669, [1994] Fam Law 431, CA 5.19
A v A (children) (shared residence order) [2004] EWHC 142 (Fam), [2004] 3 FCR
   201, [2004] 1 FLR 1195, [2004] Fam Law 416, [2004] All ER (D) 54 (Feb) ... 5.20, 5.21,
                                                         5.23, 5.122, 5.206
A v A and Newham London Borough Council [1993] 1 FCR 870, sub nom A (a
   minor) (residence order: leave to apply), Re [1993] 1 FLR 425, [1993] Fam Law
   191 .... 5.151
A v A Health Authority [2002] EWHC 18 (Fam/Admin), [2002] Fam 213,
   [2002] 3 WLR 24, [2002] 1 FCR 481, [2002] 1 FLR 845, (2002) Times,
   11 March, 146 Sol Jo LB 37, [2002] All ER (D) 187 (Jan) 12.1
A v Essex County Council [2003] EWCA Civ 1848, [2004] 1 WLR 1881,
   [2004] LGR 587, [2004] 1 FCR 660, [2004] 1 FLR 749, (2004) Times,
   22 January, 148 Sol Jo LB 27, [2003] All ER (D) 321 (Dec) 13.77
A v L (contact) [1998] 2 FCR 204, [1998] 1 FLR 361, [1998] Fam Law 137 .... 5.55, 5.83,
                                                           5.85
A v Liverpool City Council [1982] AC 363, [1981] 2 All ER 385, [1981] 2 WLR
   948, 79 LGR 621, 2 FLR 222, 145 JP 318, 125 Sol Jo 396, HL 2.28, 5.154, 12.31,
                                                           12.42
A v M and Walsall Metropolitan Borough Council [1994] 1 FCR 606, [1993] 2 FLR
   244, [1993] Fam Law 619 .... 8.209, 8.214
A v N (committal: refusal of contact) [1997] 2 FCR 475, [1997] 1 FLR 533,
   [1997] Fam Law 233, CA 2.18, 5.160, 5.175
A v United Kingdom (human rights: punishment of child) (Application 25599/94)
   (1998) 27 EHRR 611, [1998] 3 FCR 597, [1998] 2 FLR 959, [1998] Fam Law
   733, [1998] Crim LR 892, 5 BHRC 137, ECtHR 1.47, 1.54, 3.20, 13.90
A v Y (child's surname) [1999] 1 FCR 577, [1999] 2 FLR 5, [1999] Fam Law 443 .... 5.36
A and B (minors) (No 2), Re [1995] 3 FCR 449, [1995] 1 FLR 351 .... 2.63, 4.1, 4.28, 4.29,
                                                   4.30, 8.106, 10.25, 11.78
A and B v United Kingdom [1998] 1 EGRLR 82 .... 1.52
A and W (minors) (residence order: leave to apply), Re. See A (minors) (residence
   order), Re (1992)
A Care Hearing, Re [2002] Fam Law 484 .... 4.46
A County Council v K, D and L [2005] EWHC 144 (Fam), [2005] 1 FLR 851,
   [2005] Fam Law 450, [2005] All ER (D) 201 (Mar) 11.31, 11.40
A Health Authority v X [2001] EWCA Civ 2014, [2002] 2 All ER 780,
   [2002] 2 FCR 357, [2002] 1 FLR 1045, (2002) Times, 1 February, [2001] All
   ER (D) 357 (Dec) 11.84
A Local Authority v D (Chief Constable of Thames Valley Police intervening). See
   Borough Council v A (Chief Constable intervening)
A Local Authority v N [2005] EWHC 2956 (Fam), [2007] 1 FLR 399,
   [2007] Fam Law 298 .... 2.78, 8.44, 12.8, 12.9

PARA

A Local Authority v Mother (care proceedings: medical evidence) [2005] EWHC 31
(Fam), [2005] 2 FLR 129, [2005] Fam Law 350, [2005] All ER (D) 146 (Feb) 7.52,
11.31
A Local Authority v S, W and T (by his guardian) [2004] EWHC 1270 (Fam),
[2004] 2 FLR 129, [2004] Fam Law 636 .... 11.7, 11.31
A Metropolitan Borough Council v DB. See B (a minor) (treatment and secure
accommodation), Re (1997)
AB (a minor), Re [1995] 1 FCR 280, [1995] 1 FLR 181, [1995] Fam Law 62 .... 11.46
AB (adoption: shared residence order), Re [1996] 1 FCR 633, [1996] 1 FLR 27,
[1995] Fam Law 663 .... 5.17
AB (care proceedings: disclosure of medical evidence to police), Re [2002] EWHC
2198 (Fam), [2003] 2 FCR 385, [2003] 1 FLR 579, [2003] Fam Law 152,
[2002] All ER (D) 132 (Nov) 11.86, 11.90, 11.91, 11.92, 11.101
AE v Staffordshire County Council [1995] 2 FCR 84, 159 JP 367 .... 9.35, 9.40
A-H (infants), Re [1963] Ch 232, [1962] 3 All ER 853, [1962] 3 WLR 1430, 106 Sol
Jo 1011 .... 12.31
AJ (a child) (adoption order or special guardianship order), Re [2007] EWCA Civ 55,
[2007] 1 FCR 308, [2007] 1 FLR 507, [2007] Fam Law 387, [2007] All ER (D)
82 (Feb) 5.214, 5.234, 5.236
A, J and J (minors), Re [1993] Fam Law 568 .... 3.109, 3.117
A-K (minors) (foreign passport: jurisdiction), Re [1997] 2 FCR 563, [1997] 2 FLR
569, [1997] Fam Law 365, CA 12.20
AMR (adoption: procedure), Re [1999] 3 FCR 734, [1999] 2 FLR 807,
[1999] Fam Law 684 .... 3.94
AS (secure accommodation order), Re [1999] 2 FCR 749, [1999] 1 FLR 103,
[1999] Fam Law 20 .... 9.16, 9.19, 9.24
AZ (a minor) (abduction: acquiescence), Re [1993] 1 FCR 733, [1993] 1 FLR
682, CA 5.27, 5.96
Abdulaziz, Cabales and Balkandali v United Kingdom (Applications 9214/80,
9473/81, 9474/81) (1985) 7 EHRR 471, ECtHR 2.28
Al Habtoor v Fotheringham [2001] EWCA Civ 186, [2001] 1 FCR 385,
[2001] 1 FLR 951, [2001] Fam Law 352, [2001] All ER (D) 172 (Feb) 12.20, 12.27
Allington v Allington [1985] FLR 586, [1985] Fam Law 157, CA 2.47
An NHS Trust v A [2007] EWHC 1696 (Fam), [2008] 1 FCR 34, [2008] 1 FLR 70,
98 BMLR 141, [2007] All ER (D) 270 (Jul) 3.35
Andrews v Salt (1873) 8 Ch App 622, 37 JP 374, 21 WR 616, 28 LT 686 .... 3.38, 3.41
Ansah v Ansah [1977] Fam 138, [1977] 2 All ER 638, [1977] 2 WLR 760, 121 Sol
Jo 118, CA 5.175
Anufrijeva v Southwark London Borough Council [2003] EWCA Civ 1406,
[2004] QB 1124, [2004] 1 All ER 833, [2004] 2 WLR 603, [2004] LGR 184,
[2003] 3 FCR 673, [2004] 1 FLR 8, [2004] Fam Law 12,
[2003] 44 LS Gaz R 30, (2003) Times, 17 October, [2003] All ER (D) 288
(Oct), 15 BHRC 526 .... 13.91
Arif (Mohamed) (an infant), Re [1968] Ch 643, [1968] 2 WLR 1290, sub nom Re A
(an infant), Hanif v Secretary of State for Home Affairs [1968] 2 All ER 145,
112 Sol Jo 295, CA 2.28, 12.31
Associated Provincial Picture Houses Ltd v Wednesbury Corpn [1948] 1 KB 223,
[1947] 2 All ER 680, 45 LGR 635, 112 JP 55, [1948] LJR 190, 92 Sol Jo 26,
177 LT 641, 63 TLR 623, CA 13.44
A-G v Harris [2001] 3 FCR 193, [2001] 2 FLR 895, [2001] All ER (D) 217 (Apr) 5.204

B

B (a minor), Re [1975] Fam 36, [1974] 3 All ER 915, [1975] 2 WLR 302, 72 LGR
691, 5 Fam Law 27, 139 JP 87, 119 Sol Jo 165 .... 12.40
B (a minor), Re (1981) 3 FLR 117, 12 Fam Law 25; revsd [1990] 3 All ER 927,
[1981] 1 WLR 1421, 80 LGR 107, 3 FLR 117, 12 Fam Law 25, 125 Sol Jo
608, CA 3.35, 12.9

PARA

B (a minor), Re [1988] AC 199, [1987] 2 All ER 206, [1987] 2 WLR 1213, 86 LGR
417, [1987] 2 FLR 314, [1987] Fam Law 419, 131 Sol Jo 625, [1987] NLJ Rep
432, HL 3.29, 3.36, 5.97
B, Re [1991] FCR 889, [1991] 2 FLR 426, [1991] Fam Law 379 .... 3.35
B, Re (1991). See R v Gwynedd County Council, ex p B
B (minors), Re [1992] Fam 162, [1992] 3 All ER 867, [1992] 3 WLR 113,
[1992] 1 FCR 555, [1992] 2 FLR 1, [1992] Fam Law 384, CA 5.27, 5.103, 5.113,
5.167
B (minors), Re [1992] 2 FCR 631, [1993] Fam Law 209, CA 4.57
B (a minor), Re [1993] Fam 142, [1993] 1 All ER 931, [1993] 2 WLR 20,
[1992] 2 FCR 617, [1993] 1 FLR 191, [1993] Fam Law 26, CA 11.71
B (minors) (termination of contract: paramount consideration), Re [1993] Fam 301,
[1993] 3 All ER 524, [1993] 3 WLR 63, 91 LGR 311, [1993] 1 FCR 363,
[1993] 1 FLR 543, [1993] Fam Law 291, [1993] 5 LS Gaz R 42, 137 Sol Jo LB
13, CA 2.11, 2.28, 8.208, 8.216, 12.43
B (a minor), Re [1993] 1 FCR 565, [1993] 1 FLR 815, [1993] Fam Law 335 .... 2.55, 2.74,
8.46
B (minors) (abduction) (No 2), Re [1993] 1 FLR 993 .... 5.96
B (minors), Re (1993). See Barking and Dagenham London Borough Council v O
B (a minor), Re (1993). See Cheshire County Council v B
B (a minor), Re [1994] 1 FCR 905, [1994] 2 FLR 269, [1994] Fam Law 614 .... 2.62, 5.109
B (minors) (contact), Re [1994] 2 FCR 812, [1994] 2 FLR 1, [1994] Fam Law
491, CA 4.52, 4.55, 5.60, 5.122, 8.141
B (child abduction: wardship: power to detain), Re [1994] 2 FCR 1142,
[1994] 2 FLR 479, [1994] Fam Law 607, CA 12.20, 12.30
B (a minor), Re [1995] 1 WLR 232, [1995] 1 FCR 142, [1994] 2 FLR 707, CA 9.11, 9.25,
9.26
B (T) (a minor), Re [1995] 2 FCR 240, CA 2.44
B (a minor) (supervision order: parental undertaking), Re [1996] 1 WLR 716,
[1996] 3 FCR 446, [1996] 1 FLR 676, [1996] Fam Law 267, CA 8.164, 8.183
B (minors) (change of surname), Re [1996] 2 FCR 304, [1996] 1 FLR 791,
[1996] Fam Law 346, 140 Sol Jo LB 28, CA 2.10, 2.40, 5.31, 5.32, 5.33, 5.36, 5.42,
5.98
B (minors) (care proceedings: issue estoppel), Re [1997] Fam 117, [1997] 3 WLR 1,
[1997] 1 FCR 477, sub nom B (minors) (care proceedings: evidence), Re
[1997] 2 All ER 29, [1996] 45 LS Gaz R 30, 140 Sol Jo LB 252, sub nom Re B
(Children Act proceedings) (issue estoppel) [1997] 1 FLR 285 .... 8.222, 11.26
B (Minors) (care proceedings: evidence), Re [1997] 2 All ER 29, [1997] 3 WLR 1,
sub nom Re B (Children Act proceedings) (issue estoppel) [1997] 1 FLR 285 .... 8.222
B (care or supervision order), Re [1997] 1 FCR 309, [1996] 2 FLR 693,
[1997] Fam Law 86 .... 8.164, 8.165
B (a minor) (treatment and secure accommodation), Re [1997] 1 FCR 618, sub nom
A Metropolitan Borough Council v DB [1997] 1 FLR 767, [1997] Fam Law
400 .... 3.37, 9.8
B (hearing open court), Re noted at [1997] Fam Law Brief 508 .... 11.89
B (Children Act proceedings) (issue estoppel), Re (1997). See B (minors) (care
proceedings: issue estoppel), Re (1997)
B (residence order), Re [1998] 1 FCR 549, [1998] 1 FLR 368, [1998] Fam Law
73, CA 2.46, 5.87, 10.29
B (contact: stepfather's opposition), Re [1998] 3 FCR 289, [1997] 2 FLR 579,
[1997] Fam Law 720, CA 5.86
B (threshold criteria: agreed facts), Re [1999] 2 FCR 328, [1998] Fam Law 583, sub
nom Re B (agreed findings of fact) [1998] 2 FLR 968, CA 8.168
B (psychiatric therapy for parents), Re [1999] 3 FCR 20, [1999] 1 FLR 701,
[1999] Fam Law 206, CA 8.116
B (care proceedings: notification of father without parental responsibility), Re (1999).
See K (care proceedings: joinder of father), Re (1999)
B (a minor) (split hearings: jurisdiction), Re [2000] 1 WLR 790, [2000] 1 FCR 297,
[1999] 48 LS Gaz R 39, 144 Sol Jo LB 23, CA 8.145
B (sexual abuse: expert's report), Re [2000] 2 FCR 8, [2000] 1 FLR 871,
[2000] Fam Law 479, CA 11.32, 11.40

PARA

B (a child) (adoption by one natural parent), Re [2001] UKHL 70, [2002] 1 All ER
641, [2002] 1 WLR 258, [2002] 1 FCR 150, [2002] 1 FLR 196, 11 BHRC 702,
(2001) Times, 19 December, [2001] All ER (D) 240 (Dec) 13.31
B (disclosure to other parties), Re [2002] 2 FCR 32, [2001] 2 FLR 1017,
[2001] Fam Law 798, [2001] All ER (D) 22 (Aug) 11.64, 11.67, 11.71, 11.100
B (a child: interim care order), Re [2002] EWCA Civ 25, [2002] 2 FCR 367,
[2002] 1 FLR 545, [2002] Fam Law 252, 146 Sol Jo LB 36, [2002] All ER (D)
29 (Jan) 8.115, 8.116
B (a child) (care proceedings: diplomatic immunity), Re [2002] EWHC 1751 (Fam),
[2003] Fam 16, [2003] 2 WLR 168, [2003] 1 FLR 241, [2003] Fam Law 8,
[2002] 41 LS Gaz R 27, (2002) Times, 14 October, [2002] All ER (D) 134
(Oct) 8.18
B (a child) (residence order), Re [2003] All ER (D) 107 (Aug) 4.57
B (care proceedings: disclosure), Re [2003] All ER (D) 196 (Oct) 4.57
B (children) (care: interference with family life), Re [2003] EWCA Civ 786,
[2004] 1 FCR 463, [2003] 2 FLR 813, (2003) Times, 1 July, [2003] All ER (D)
286 (May) 4.55, 8.4, 8.55, 8.56
B (a child) (immunisation), Re [2003] EWCA Civ 1148. See C (welfare of child:
immunisation), Re [2003] EWHC 1376 (Fam)
B, Re (children) (non accidental injury) [2003] UKHL 18, [2004] 1 AC 523,
[2003] 2 All ER 305, [2003] 2 WLR 1075, [2003] 1 FCR 673, [2003] 1 FLR
1169, [2003] 23 LS Gaz R 36, (2003) Times, 4 April, [2003] All ER (D) 64
(Apr) 2.11, 8.48
B (a child) (serious injury: standard of proof), Re [2004] EWCA Civ 567, [2005] Fam
134, [2004] 3 WLR 753, [2004] 2 FCR 257, [2004] 2 FLR 263,
[2004] Fam Law 565, [2004] NLJR 824, (2004) Times, 27 May, [2004] All ER
(D) 197 (May 11.7
B (a child: court's jurisdiction), Re [2004] EWCA Civ 681, [2004] 2 FCR 391,
[2004] 2 FLR 741, [2004] Fam Law 788, [2004] All ER (D) 433 (May) 5.131
B (children) (termination of contact), Re [2004] EWCA Civ 956, [2005] 1 FCR 480,
[2004] All ER (D) 16 (Jul), sub nom B (leave to remove: impact of refusal), Re
[2005] 2 FLR 239 .... 5.45, 5.46
B (a child) (disclosure), Re [2004] EWHC 411 (Fam), [2004] 3 FCR 1, [2004] 2 FLR
142, [2004] Fam Law 493, [2004] NLJR 498, [2004] All ER (D) 500 (Mar) 4.47
B (leave to remove: impact of refusal), Re (2005). See B (children) (termination of
contact), Re (2004)
B (a child) (separate representation), Re [2006] EWCA Civ 716, 150 Sol Jo LB 572,
[2006] All ER (D) 236 (Apr) 10.33
B (leave to remove), Re [2006] EWHC 1783 (Fam), [2007] 1 FLR 333, sub nom B (a
child) (permission to remove from the jurisdiction), Re [2006] All ER (D) 270
(Jul) 5.45
B (a child), Re [2007] EWCA Civ 556, [2007] 2 FLR 979, [2007] Fam Law 798, 151
Sol Jo LB 673, [2007] All ER (D) 241 (May) 11.39
B (a child), Re [2007] EWCA Civ 1055, [2008] 1 FLR 613, (2007) Times,
10 October, [2007] All ER (D) 371 (Jul) 5.51, 5.117
B (role of biological father), Re [2007] EWHC 1952 (Fam), [2008] 1 FLR 1015,
[2008] Fam Law 411 .... 3.63, 3.65, 3.68, 3.69
B (children) (sexual abuse: standard of proof), Re [2008] UKHL 35, [2008] 3 WLR
1, [2008] 2 FCR 339, [2008] Fam Law 619, (2008) Times, 12 June, [2008] All
ER (D) 134 (Jun) 2.56, 8.21, 8.22, 8.23, 8.24, 8.26, 8.37, 8.144, 8.236, 11.5, 11.8,
11.9, 14.24
B v A and B [2005] EWHC 1291 (Fam) 12.21
B (BPM) v B (MM) [1969] P 103, [1969] 2 WLR 862, 133 JP 245, 112 Sol Jo 985,
sub nom B (B) v B (M) [1969] 1 All ER 891, P, D and Admlty 5.171, 13.10
B v B [1992] 1 FCR 223, [1991] 2 FLR 487, [1991] Fam Law 518 .... 11.71
B v B (grandparent: residence order) [1993] 1 FCR 211, sub nom B v B (a minor)
(residence order) [1992] 2 FLR 327, [1992] Fam Law 490 .... 2.72, 3.103
B v B [1994] 1 FCR 805, [1994] 1 FLR 323n, [1994] Fam Law 377 .... 11.14
B v B [1994] 1 FCR 809, [1994] 2 FLR 713, [1994] Fam Law 377 ..... 2.63, 4.12, 4.29, 5.201
B v B (minors) [1994] 2 FCR 667, [1994] 2 FLR 489, [1994] Fam Law 613,
[1994] 21 LS Gaz R 40, CA 2.63, 4.42, 10.23, 10.64, 11.57

Table of Cases

PARA

B v B [1994] Fam Law 250, Cty Ct 2.26

B v B (Scottish contact order: jurisdiction to vary) [1996] 1 WLR 231, [1996] 1 FCR
705, [1996] 1 FLR 688, [1996] Fam Law 348 .... 5.131

B v B (residence order: restricting applications) [1997] 2 FCR 518, [1997] 1 FLR
139, [1997] Fam Law 139, CA 2.44, 5.202

B v B (Wasted Costs: Abuse of Process) [2001] 3 FCR 724, [2001] 1 FLR 843,
[2001] Fam Law 340, [2001] All ER (D) 55 (Feb) 4.59, 13.5

B v B (a child) (residence order: condition) [2004] 2 FLR 979, [2004] Fam Law 651,
(2004) Times, 7 July, [2004] All ER (D) 387 (May) 5.118

B v Derbyshire County Council [1992] 2 FCR 14, [1992] 1 FLR 538,
[1992] Fam Law 287 .... 11.25

B v Lewisham London Borough Council [2008] EWHC 738 (Admin),
[2008] Fam Law 640, [2008] All ER (D) 248 (Apr) 5.232, 13.49, 13.50

B v Reading Borough Council. See L v Reading Borough Council

B v United Kingdom (Application 9840/82) (1987) 10 EHRR 87, ECtHR 1.7

B v United Kingdom (Application 39067/97) [2000] 1 FCR 289, [2000] 1 FLR 1,
[2000] Fam Law 88, ECtHR 1.54, 3.44

B v United Kingdom (Applications 36337/97, 35974/97) [2001] 2 FCR 221,
[2001] 2 FLR 261, [2001] Fam Law 506, 11 BHRC 667, [2001] All ER (D) 241
(Apr), ECtHR 4.47

B v W [1979] 3 All ER 83, [1979] 1 WLR 1041, 143 JP 681, 123 Sol Jo 536, 143 JP
Jo 568, HL 13.30, 13.31

B and G (minors), Re [1985] FLR 493, [1985] Fam Law 127, CA 2.50

B and T (care proceedings: legal representation), Re [2001] 1 FCR 512, [2001] 1 FLR
485, [2001] Fam Law 180, CA 4.43, 8.98

BC (a minor) (care order: appropriate local authority), Re [1995] 3 FCR 598 .... 8.170

BM (a minor), Re [1993] 2 FCR 388, [1993] 1 FLR 979, [1993] Fam Law 516 .... 12.21

Barking and Dagenham London Borough Council v O [1993] Fam 295,
[1993] 4 All ER 59, [1993] 3 WLR 493, [1993] 2 FLR 651, [1993] Fam Law
670, sub nom B (minors), Re [1993] 2 FCR 241 .... 11.74

Barnet London Borough Council v Y [2006] 2 FLR 988, [2006] Fam Law 740 .... 6.5

Barrett v Enfield London Borough Council [2001] 2 AC 550, [1999] 3 All ER 193,
[1999] 3 WLR 79, [1999] LGR 473, [1999] 2 FCR 434, [1999] 2 FLR 426,
[1999] Fam Law 622, 49 BMLR 1, [1999] PIQR P 272, [1999] 4 LRC
473, HL 13.75

Bellinger v Bellinger (Lord Chancellor intervening) [2003] UKHL 21, [2003] 2 AC
467, [2003] 2 All ER 593, [2003] 2 WLR 1174, [2003] 2 FCR 1, [2003] 1 FLR
1043, 72 BMLR 147, [2003] NLJR 594, (2003) Times, 11 April, 147 Sol Jo LB
472, [2004] 1 LRC 42, [2003] All ER (D) 178 (Apr), 14 BHRC 127 .... 1.51

Berkshire County Council v B [1997] 3 FCR 88, [1997] 1 FLR 171, [1997] Fam Law
234 .... 8.198

Berkshire County Council v C [1993] Fam 205, [1993] 2 WLR 475, [1993] 1 FCR
608, [1993] 1 FLR 569 .... 8.113, 8.117

Birmingham City Council v D [1994] 2 FCR 245, [1994] 2 FLR 502,
[1994] Fam Law 610 .... 3.108, 8.29

Birmingham City Council v H (a minor) [1994] 2 AC 212, [1994] 1 All ER 12,
[1994] 2 WLR 31, 92 LGR 349, [1994] 1 FCR 896, [1994] 1 FLR 224,
[1994] 6 LS Gaz R 36, [1994] NLJR 17, 138 Sol Jo LB 13, HL ... 2.30, 2.31, 5.148, 8.55,
8.208, 8.217

Birmingham City Council v H [1993] 1 FCR 247, [1992] 2 FLR 323 .... 5.113

Birmingham City Council v M [1994] 2 FCR 245, [1994] 2 FLR 502,
[1994] Fam Law 610 .... 3.108, 8.29

Birmingham City Council v M [2008] EWHC 1085 (Fam), [2008] All ER (D) 389
(Jun) 9.25

Birmingham City Council v R [2006] EWCA Civ 1748, [2007] Fam 41,
[2007] 2 WLR 1130, [2007] Fam Law 307, (2006) Times, 29 December, sub
nom Re R (a child) (special guardianship order) [2007] 1 FCR 121, [2006] All
ER (D) 299 (Dec) 5,216, 5.217, 5.220

Borough Council v A (Chief Constable intervening) [2006] EWHC 1465 (Fam),
[2007] 1 All ER 293, [2007] 1 WLR 1932, [2007] 1 FCR 105, [2006] Fam Law
738, [2006] All ER (D) 211 (Jun), sub nom A Local Authority v D (Chief
Constable of Thames Valley Police intervening), [2006] 2 FLR 1053, 92 BMLR
1 .... 11.82, 11.90
Bradford, Re [2007] 1 FLR 530, sub nom Re B (a Child) (2006) Times,
6 October, CA 5.204
Bradford City Metropolitan Council v K [1990] Fam 140, [1990] 2 WLR 532, 88
LGR 201, [1989] FCR 738, [1989] 2 FLR 507, [1990] Fam Law 136 .... 11.3
Bramblevale Ltd, Re [1970] Ch 128, [1969] 3 All ER 1062, [1969] 3 WLR 699,
[1971] 3 WLR 821n, 113 Sol Jo 775, CA 5.165
British Airways Board v Laker Airways Ltd [1985] AC 58, [1984] 3 All ER 39,
[1984] 3 WLR 413, 128 Sol Jo 531, [1984] LS Gaz R 2849, 134 NLJ
746, HL 10.4
BBC v Rochdale Metropolitan Borough Council [2005] EWHC 2862 (Fam),
[2007] 1 FLR 101, [2006] EMLR 117 .... 2.20
Brixey v Lynas [1997] 1 FCR 220, [1996] 2 FLR 499, [1997] Fam Law 10, 1997 SC
(HL) 1, 1996 SLT 908, HL 2.47
Buchanan v Milton [1999] 2 FLR 844, [1999] Fam Law 692 .... 2.18

C

C (MA) (an infant), Re [1966] 1 All ER 838, [1966] 1 WLR 646, 64 LGR 280, 130
JP 217, 110 Sol Jo 309, CA 2.49
C (minors), Re [1978] Fam 105, [1978] 2 All ER 230, [1977] 3 WLR 561, 121 Sol
Jo 693, CA 2.50
C (a minor) (wardship proceedings), Re [1984] FLR 419, [1984] Fam Law
273, CA 13.30
C (a minor) (wardship: surrogacy), Re [1985] FLR 846, [1985] Fam Law 191, [1985]
NLJ Rep 106 .... 12.9
C (minors) (wardship: adoption), Re [1989] 1 All ER 395, [1989] 1 WLR 61, 87
LGR 73, [1989] FCR 774, [1989] 1 FLR 222, [1989] Fam Law 107, 133 Sol Jo
20, [1989] 18 LS Gaz R 35, CA 3.114
C (a minor), Re [1990] Fam 26, [1989] 2 All ER 782, [1989] 3 WLR 240,
[1990] FCR 209, [1990] 1 FLR 252, [1990] Fam Law 60, 133 Sol Jo 876,
[1989] 28 LS Gaz R 43, [1989] NLJR 612, CA 3.36, 12.39
C (a minor), Re [1991] FCR 308, [1991] 2 FLR 438, [1992] Fam Law 14, CA 11.71
C (a minor), Re [1991] FCR 969, [1992] 1 FLR 309, [1992] Fam Law 147, CA 5.83
C (a minor), Re [1991] FCR 1018, [1991] 2 FLR 168, [1991] Fam Law 525, CA 12.31
C (minors), Re [1992] 2 All ER 86, [1991] FCR 856, [1992] 1 FLR 1,
[1992] Fam Law 153, 135 Sol Jo LB 100, CA 3.64, 3.67, 3.74
C (a minor) (care proceedings), Re [1992] 2 FCR 341, sub nom C v Solihull
Metropolitan Borough Council [1993] 1 FLR 290, [1993] Fam Law 189 .... 2.62, 4.37,
5.113, 8.94, 8.151
C (minors) (hearsay evidence: contempt proceedings), Re [1993] 4 All ER 690, sub
nom C v C [1993] 1 FCR 820, [1993] 1 FLR 220, [1993] Fam Law 223, CA 5.170
C (minors), Re [1994] Fam 1, [1993] 3 All ER 313, [1993] 3 WLR 249, 91 LGR
192, sub nom M v C and Calderdale Metropolitan Borough Council
[1993] 1 FCR 431, [1993] 1 FLR 505, [1993] Fam Law 401, CA 3.74, 5.144
C (a minor) (care: childs wishes), Re (1993). See G (a minor) (appeal), Re (1993)
C (child cases: evidence and disclosure), Re (1994) 159 LG Rev 849, [1995] 2 FCR
97, [1995] 1 FLR 204 .... 11.62, 11.64, 11.65, 11.66, 11.69
C (a minor) (leave to seek section 8 orders), Re [1994] 1 FCR 837, [1994] 1 FLR
26 .... 5.156
C, Re [1994] 2 FCR 1153, [1994] 2 FLR 922, [1995] Fam Law 19 .... 9.9, 9.30, 9.37
C (a minor), Re [1994] Fam Law 468 .... 5.17
C (a minor), Re (1994). See C v Surrey County Council (1994)
C (a minor), Re [1995] 2 FCR 276, sub nom C (section 8 order: court welfare
officer), Re [1995] 1 FLR 617, CA 2.63, 4.49, 10.28, 10.64

Table of Cases

PARA

C (minors), Re [1996] Fam 79, [1995] 3 WLR 30, [1995] 2 FCR 701, [1995] 1 FLR
777, [1995] Fam Law 403, CA 5.125
C (residence: child's application for leave), Re [1996] 1 FCR 461, [1995] 1 FLR 927,
[1995] Fam Law 472 .... 5.156
C (a baby), Re [1996] 2 FCR 569, [1996] 2 FLR 43, [1996] Fam Law 533, 32
BMLR 44 .... 12.9, 12.15
C (a minor) (family assistance order), Re [1996] 3 FCR 514, [1996] 1 FLR 424,
[1996] Fam Law 202 .... 5.195
C (disclosure), Re [1996] 3 FCR 765, [1996] 1 FLR 797, [1996] Fam Law 462 ..... 4.40, 10.42
C (a minor) (interim care order: residential assessment), Re [1997] AC 489,
[1996] 4 All ER 871, [1996] 3 WLR 1098, 95 LGR 367, [1997] 1 FCR 149,
[1997] 1 FLR 1, [1997] 01 LS Gaz R 32, [1996] NLJR 1777, 141 Sol Jo LB
12, HL 8.116, 8.117
C (a minor) (care proceedings: disclosure), Re [1997] Fam 76, [1997] 2 WLR 322,
[1996] 3 FCR 521, sub nom EC (disclosure of material), Re [1996] 2 FLR 725,
[1997] Fam Law 160, CA 11.89, 11.100
C (a minor) (detention for medical treatment), Re [1997] 3 FCR 49, [1997] 2 FLR
180, [1997] Fam Law 474 .... 3.37, 7.91, 12.38
C (minors) (change of surname), Re [1997] 3 FCR 310, [1997] Fam Law 722, sub
nom Re PC (change of surname) [1997] 2 FLR 730 .... 3.77, 3.99, 5.31, 14.17
C (care order: appropriate local authority), Re (1997). See Hackney London Borough
Council v C
C (medical treatment), Re [1998] 1 FCR 1, [1998] 1 FLR 384, [1998] Fam Law 135,
40 BMLR 31, [1998] Lloyd's Rep Med 1 .... 9.8
C (minors) (change of surname), Re [1998] 2 FCR 544, [1998] 1 FLR 549,
[1998] Fam Law 250, [1997] 48 LS Gaz R 29, 142 Sol Jo LB 20, CA 5.33, 5.38
C (adoption: freeing order), Re [1999] Fam 240, [1999] 2 WLR 1079, [1999] 1 FLR
348, [1999] Fam Law 11, 142 Sol Jo LB 263, sub nom SC (a minor) (adoption:
freeing order), Re [1999] 1 FCR 145, [1998] All ER (D) 465 .... 12.32
C (a minor) (change of surname), Re [1999] 1 FCR 318, [1998] 2 FLR 656,
[1998] Fam Law 659, CA 5.35, 5.38
C (adoption: notice), Re [1999] 1 FLR 384, [1998] Fam Law 725 .... 5.146
C (care or supervision order), Re [1999] 2 FLR 621 .... 8.164
C (a child) (HIV testing), Re [2000] Fam 48, [2000] 2 WLR 270, [1999] 3 FCR 289,
[1999] 2 FLR 1004, [2000] Fam Law 16, 30 BMLR 283, [1999] All ER (D)
1004 .... 2.44, 3.35, 5.107, 12.9, 12.36
C (leave to remove from jurisdiction), Re [2000] 2 FCR 40, [2000] 2 FLR 457,
[2000] Fam Law 813, CA 13.31
C (contact: no order for contact), Re [2000] 2 FLR 723, [2000] Fam Law 699 .... 5.86
C (children) (residential assessment), Re [2001] EWCA Civ 1305, [2001] 3 FCR 164,
[2001] All ER (D) 53 (Jul) 8.117
C (secure accommodation order: representation), Re (2001). See M (a child) (secure
accommodation), Re (2001)
C (adoption: religious observance), Re [2002] 1 FLR 1119, (2002) Times, 18 April,
[2002] All ER (D) 24 (Apr) 13.43, 13.50
C (sexual abuse: disclosure to landlords), Re [2002] EWHC 234 (Fam),
[2002] 2 FCR 385, [2002] 2 FLR 375, [2002] Fam Law 590, [2002] All ER (D)
302 (May) 11.96
C (care proceedings: disclosure of local authority's decision making process), Re
[2002] EWHC 1379 (Fam), [2002] 2 FCR 673, [2002] All ER (D) 226 (Jul), sub
nom L (care: assessment: fair trial), Re [2002] 2 FLR 730 ...... 6.4, 7.19, 7.40, 8.4, 8.172,
11.64
C (permission to remove from jurisdiction), Re [2003] EWHC 596 (Fam),
[2003] 1 FLR 1066, [2003] All ER (D) 393 (Mar) 5.49
C (welfare of child: immunisation), Re [2003] EWHC 1376 (Fam), [2003] 2 FLR
1054, [2003] 31 LS Gaz R 31, (2003) Times, 26 June, [2003] All ER (D) 179
(Jun); affd sub nom B (a child) (immunisation), Re [2003] EWCA Civ 1148,
[2003] 3 FCR 156, 73 BMLR 152, 147 Sol Jo LB 934, [2003] All ER (D) 498
(Jul), sub nom C (welfare of child: immunisation), Re [2003] 2 FLR 1095 ...... 3.35, 3.99,
5.98, 5.226. 5.236

PARA

C (care: consultation with father not in child's best interests), Re [2005] EWHC 3390
(Fam), [2006] 2 FLR 787, [2006] Fam Law 625 .... 6.48, 13.64
C (a child) (contact: conduct of hearing), Re [2006] EWCA Civ 144, [2006] 1 FCR
447, [2006] 2 FLR 289, [2006] Fam Law 525, [2006] All ER (D) 214 (Jan) 4.52
C (breach of human rights: damages), Re [2007] EWCA Civ 2, [2007] 3 FCR 288,
[2007] 1 FLR 1957, sub nom P v South Gloucestershire County Council
[2007] Fam Law 393, sub nom C (a child) (care order), Re [2007] All ER (D)
05 (Jan) 13.91, 13.94
C (a child) (residence), Re [2007] EWCA Civ 866, [2008] 1 FLR 211,
[2007] Fam Law 990, [2007] All ER (D) 187 (Oct) 5.87
C (abduction: separate representation of children), Re [2008] EWHC 517 (Fam),
[2008] Fam Law 498 .... 12.41
C (residence) (2008), Re. See V v T
C (section 8 order: court welfare officer), Re . See C (a minor), Re (1995)
C v A Local Authority [2001] EWCA Civ 302, [2001] 1 FCR 614, [2001] All ER (D)
149 (Feb), sub nom C v Flintshire County Council [2001] 2 FLR 33,
[2001] Fam Law 420 .... 13.83
C v B Metropolitan Borough Council [2002] EWHC 1438 (Fam), [2002] 3 FCR 608,
[2002] 2 FLR 868, (2002) Times, 25 July, [2002] All ER (D) 280 (Jul) 13.89
C v C [1988] FCR 411, [1988] 2 FLR 291, [1988] Fam Law 338,
[1988] 10 LS Gaz R 44, CA 2.44
C v C [1988] FCR 458, [1988] 1 FLR 462, [1988] Fam Law 254 .... 2.55, 11.49
C v C (evidence: privilege) [2001] EWCA Civ 469, [2002] Fam 42, [2001] 3 WLR
446, [2001] 1 FCR 756, [2001] 2 FLR 184 .... 11.77, 11.98
C v C. See C (minors) (hearsay evidence: contempt proceedings), Re (1993)
C v Finland (Application 18249/02) [2006] 2 FCR 195, [2006] 2 FLR 597,
[2006] Fam Law 633, [2006] ECHR 18249/02, ECtHR 4.52
C (a minor) v Hackney London Borough Council [1996] 1 All ER 973,
[1996] 1 WLR 789, [1996] 1 FLR 427, [1996] Fam Law 278, CA 11.26
C v Humberside County Council [1995] 1 FCR 110, [1994] 2 FLR 759 .... 9.23, 9.26
C v K (ouster order: non parent) [1996] 3 FCR 488, [1996] 2 FLR 506, sub nom C v
K (inherent powers: exclusion order) [1997] Fam Law 16 .... 3.16, 7.106, 12.34
C (child) v Plymouth City Council [2000] 2 FCR 289, [2000] 1 FLR 875,
[2000] Fam Law 460, [2000] 15 LS Gaz R 39, 144 Sol Jo LB 180, CA 8.170
C v S [1988] QB 135, [1987] 1 All ER 1230, [1987] 2 WLR 1108, [1987] 2 FLR
505, [1987] Fam Law 269, 131 Sol Jo 624, [1987] LS Gaz R 1410, CA 3.93
C v Salford City Council. See P (a minor), Re (1994)
C v Solihull Metropolitan Borough Council. See C (a minor) (care proceedings), Re
(1992)
C v Surrey County Council [1994] 2 FCR 165, sub nom C (a minor), Re
[1994] 1 FLR 111, [1993] 22 LS Gaz R 37, 137 Sol Jo LB 135 .... 4.10
C and B (children) (care order: future harm), Re [2000] 2 FCR 614, [2001] 1 FLR
611, CA 2.78, 7.72, 8.4, 8.56, 8.110, 8.165
C and V (minors) (parental responsibility and contact), Re [1998] 1 FCR 52,
[1998] 1 FLR 392, [1998] Fam Law 10, CA 3.66, 3.67, 5.86
CB (a minor), Re [1993] 1 FCR 440, [1993] 1 FLR 920, [1993] Fam Law 462 .... 3.62
CB, Re [1995] 1 FLR 622, CA 4.49, 10.28, 10.64
CB and JB (minors) (care proceedings: case conduct), Re [1998] 2 FCR 313,
[1998] 2 FLR 211, [1998] Fam Law 454 .... 8.47, 8.143, 11.40, 11.45, 11.56
CD and MD (care proceedings: practice) [1998] 1 FLR 825, [1998] Fam Law 317 .... 8.143
CE (a minor) (appointment of Guardian ad Litem), Re [1995] 1 FCR 387,
[1995] 1 FLR 26, [1995] Fam Law 67 .... 7.29, 10.38
CF v Secretary of State for the Home Department [2004] EWHC 111 (Fam),
[2004] 1 FCR 577, [2004] 2 FLR 517, [2004] Fam Law 639, [2004] All ER (D)
322 (Jan) 2.4, 14.32
CH (a minor) (care or interim order), Re [1998] 2 FCR 347, [1998] 1 FLR 402,
[1998] Fam Law 132, CA 8.152
CH (family proceedings: court bundles), Re [2000] 2 FCR 193, [2000] All ER (D)
671 .... 4.59
CN (a minor), Re. See Kent County Council v C
CT (a minor), Re. See T (a minor) (child representation), Re (1994)

PARA

Campbell and Cosans v United Kingdom (Application 7511/76) (1982) 4 EHRR 293,
ECtHR 3.20, 3.23
Caparo Industries plc v Dickman [1990] 2 AC 605, [1990] 1 All ER 568,
[1990] 2 WLR 358, [1990] BCLC 273, [1990] BCC 164, 134 Sol Jo 494,
[1990] 12 LS Gaz R 42, [1990] NLJR 248, HL 13.73
Carp v Byron [2005] EWCA Civ 1035, [2006] 1 FCR 1, [2005] All ER (D) 373
(Jun) 5.86
Cheshire County Council v B [1992] 2 FCR 572, sub nom B (a minor), Re
[1993] 1 FLR 421 .... 8.209
Cheshire County Council v M [1992] 2 FCR 817, [1993] 1 FLR 463,
[1993] Fam Law 207 .... 4.52
Cheshire County Council v P [1993] 2 FCR 397, sub nom sub nom P (minors), Re
[1993] 2 FLR 742, CA 8.152
Cheshire County Council v S. See S (children) (care proceedings: care plan), Re
(2007)
Chief Constable of Greater Manchester v KI and KW (by their children's guardian,
CAFCASS Legal) and PN [2007] EWHC 1837 (Fam), [2008] 2 FCR 172,
[2008] 1 FLR 504, [2007] Fam Law 900 .... 2.24
Ciliz v Netherlands [2000] 2 FLR 469, [2000] Fam Law 799, ECtHR 3.23, 5.76
Clarke-Hunt v Newcombe (1982) 4 FLR 482, 13 Fam Law 20, CA 2.35
Clayton v Clayton [2006] EWCA Civ 878, [2006] Fam 83, [2007] 1 All ER 1197,
[2006] 3 WLR 599, [2006] 2 FCR 405, [2007] 1 FLR 11, [2006] Fam Law 926,
[2006] NLJR 1101, (2006) Times, 4 July, 150 Sol Jo LB 890, [2007] EMLR 65,
[2006] All ER (D) 301 (Jun) 4.47
Cleveland County Council v DPP (1994) 93 LGR 596, [1995] 06 LS Gaz R 37, 139
Sol Jo LB 13, DC 9.31
Cleveland County Council v F [1995] 2 All ER 236, [1995] 1 WLR 785,
[1995] 3 FCR 174, [1995] 1 FLR 797, [1995] Fam Law 473 .... 11.87
Cleveland County Council v W [1989] FCR 625, sub nom Re W [1989] 1 FLR 246,
[1989] Fam Law 17, [1989] Fam Law 189 .... 4.47
Clibbery v Allan [2002] EWCA Civ 45, [2002] Fam 261, [2002] 1 All ER 865,
[2002] 2 WLR 1511, [2002] 1 FCR 385, [2002] 1 FLR 565, [2002] Fam Law
260, [2002] NLJR 222, (2002) Times, 5 February, 146 Sol Jo LB 38, [2002] All
ER (D) 281 (Jan) 4.47
Costello-Roberts v United Kingdom (Application 13134/87) (1993) 19 EHRR 112,
[1994] 1 FCR 65, [1994] ELR 1, ECtHR 3.20
Council of Civil Service Unions v Minister for the Civil Service [1985] AC 374,
[1984] 3 All ER 935, [1984] 3 WLR 1174, [1985] ICR 14, 128 Sol Jo 837,
[1985] LS Gaz R 437, [1985] LRC (Const) 948, sub nom R v Secretary of State
for Foreign and Commonwealth Affairs, ex p Council of Civil Service Unions
[1985] IRLR 28, HL 13.44
Croydon London Borough v A (No 3) [1992] 2 FCR 481, [1992] 2 FLR 350,
[1993] Fam Law 70 .... 8.180, 8.185
Croydon London Borough Council v A [1992] Fam 169, [1992] 3 All ER 788,
[1992] 3 WLR 267, [1992] 1 FCR 522, [1992] 2 FLR 341, [1992] Fam Law
441, [1992] 16 LS Gaz R 28, 136 Sol Jo LB 69 .... 5.99, 5.141, 13.30, 13.31

D

D (a minor) (wardship: sterilisation), Re [1976] Fam 185, [1976] 1 All ER 326,
[1976] 2 WLR 279, 119 Sol Jo 696 .... 3.35
D (minors), Re (1982) 13 Fam Law 111 .... 12.33
D (a minor), Re [1987] AC 317, [1986] 3 WLR 1080, 85 LGR 169, [1987] 1 FLR
422, [1987] Fam Law 202, 151 JP 313, 130 Sol Jo 984, [1987] LS Gaz R 574,
[1986] NLJ Rep 1184, sub nom D (a minor) v Berkshire County Council
[1987] 1 All ER 20, HL 3.93
D (a minor), Re [1992] 1 All ER 892, [1992] 1 WLR 315, [1992] 1 FLR 637, CA 5.94,
5.96, 5.98, 5.103
D (wardship: disclosure), Re [1992] 1 FCR 297, [1994] 1 FLR 346, [1994] Fam Law
246, CA 11.90

PARA

D (a minor), Re [1993] 1 FCR 964, [1993] 2 FLR 1, [1993] Fam Law 465, CA 5.84, 5.86
D, Re [1993] 2 FCR 88, [1993] 2 FLR 423, [1993] Fam Law 518 .... 8.164
D (minors) (family appeals), Re [1995] 1 FCR 301, CA 13.5
D (a minor), Re [1995] 2 FCR 681, sub nom Stockport Metropolitan Borough
   Council v D [1995] 1 FLR 873, [1995] Fam Law 405 .... 4.54, 8.53, 8.168
D, Re [1995] 3 FCR 581 .... 11.49
D, Re (1995). See D v R
D (minors) (adoption reports: confidentiality), Re [1996] AC 593, [1995] 4 All ER
   385, [1995] 3 WLR 483, [1996] 1 FCR 205, [1995] 2 FLR 687,
   [1996] Fam Law 8, [1995] NLJR 1612, HL 2.22, 10.42, 11.70, 11.71
D (a minor) (secure accommodation order), Re [1996] 2 FCR 452, [1997] 1 FLR
   197, [1997] Fam Law 161 .... 9.10, 9.23
D (minors) (residence: conditions), Re [1996] 2 FCR 820, [1996] 2 FLR 281,
   [1996] Fam Law 605, CA 5.101, 5.114
D (prohibited steps order), Re (1996). See D v D (ouster order)
D (a minor) (contact orders: conditions), Re [1997] 3 FCR 721,
   [1997] 29 LS Gaz R 28, 141 Sol Jo LB 170, sub nom D v N (contact order:
   conditions) [1997] 2 FLR 797, CA 5.99, 5.112, 5.120
D (contact: reasons for refusal), Re [1998] 1 FCR 321, [1997] 2 FLR 48,
   [1997] Fam Law 471, CA 5.87, 5.90
D (care: threshold criteria: significant harm), Re [1998] Fam Law 656 .... 8.45
D (a minor) (natural parent: presumption of care), Re [1999] 2 FCR 118,
   [1999] 1 FLR 134, [1999] Fam Law 12, CA 2.44
D (abduction: acquiescence), Re [1999] 3 FCR 468, [1998] 2 FLR 335,
   [1998] Fam Law 512, CA 4.40
D (a child) (threshold criteria: issue estoppel), Re [2001] 1 FCR 124,
   [2000] Fam Law 875, (2000) Times, 13 October, sub nom Re D (child:
   threshold criteria) [2001] 1 FLR 274, CA 8.53, 8.168, 8.222, 11.27
D (children) (shared residence orders), Re [2001] 1 FCR 147, [2001] 1 FLR 495,
   [2001] Fam Law 183, [2000] All ER (D) 1885, CA 5.19
D (grant of care order: refusal of freeing order), Re [2001] 1 FCR 501, [2001] 1 FLR
   862, [2000] All ER (D) 1364, CA 10.42
D (a child) (wardship: evidence of abuse), Re [2001] 1 FCR 707, [2001] 1 FLR 148,
   [2001] Fam Law 11, [2000] All ER (D) 983 .... 11.38, 12.9
D (a child) (IVF treatment), Re [2001] EWCA Civ 230, [2001] 1 FCR 481,
   [2001] 1 FLR 972 .... 5.55
D (sexual abuse allegations: evidence of adult victim) [2002] 1 FLR 723,
   [2002] Fam Law 259 .... 11.51
D (intractable contact dispute: publicity), Re [2004] EWHC 727 (Fam),
   [2004] 3 FCR 234, [2004] 1 FLR 1226, [2004] Fam Law 490, [2004] All ER
   (D) 41 (Apr) 4.47, 5.77, 5.79
D (contact and parental responsibility: lesbian mothers and known father), Re
   [2006] EWHC 2 (Fam), [2006] 1 FCR 556, 150 Sol Jo LB 128, sub nom B v A
   (parental responsibility) [2006] All ER (D) 25 (Jan) 3.68, 3.70
D (paternity), Re [2006] EWHC 3545 (Fam), [2007] 2 FLR 26, [2007] Fam Law
   590 .... 2.17
D (a child) (abduction: custody rights), Re [2006] UKHL 51, [2007] 1 AC 619,
   [2007] 1 All ER 783, [2006] 3 WLR 989, [2007] 1 FCR 1, [2007] 1 FLR 961,
   [2006] NLJR 1803, 150 Sol Jo LB 1532, [2006] All ER (D) 218 (Nov) 10.3
D v D (access: contempt: committal [1991] FCR 323, [1991] 2 FLR 34,
   [1991] Fam Law 365, CA 5.165, 5.168
D v D (child abduction: non convention country) [1994] 1 FCR 654, [1994] 1 FLR
   137, [1994] Fam Law 126, CA 5.96
D v D (application for contact) [1994] 1 FCR 694 .... 2.70, 13.29
D v D (child case: powers of court) [1994] 3 FCR 28, sub nom D v D (county court
   jurisdiction: injunctions) [1993] 2 FLR 802, [1993] 37 LS Gaz R 49, 137 Sol Jo
   LB 199, CA 5.121, 5.207, 5.208, 7.106, 12.25
D v D (ouster order) [1996] 2 FCR 496, sub nom Re D (prohibited steps order)
   [1996] 2 FLR 273, [1996] Fam Law 605, CA 5.101, 5.112, 12.33
D v D (custody: jurisdiction) [1996] 3 FCR 19, [1996] 1 FLR 574, [1996] Fam Law
   272 .... 5.133

PARA

D v East Berkshire Community Health NHS Trust [2003] EWCA Civ 1151,
[2004] QB 558, [2003] 4 All ER 796, [2004] 2 WLR 58, [2003] 3 FCR 1,
[2003] 2 FLR 1166, [2003] Fam Law 816, 76 BMLR 61,
[2003] 36 LS Gaz R 37, (2003) Times, 22 August, [2003] All ER (D) 547 (Jul);
affd[2005] UKHL 23, [2005] 2 AC 373, [2005] 2 All ER 443, [2005] 2 WLR
993, [2005] 2 FCR 81, [2005] 2 FLR 284, [2005] Fam Law 615, [2005]
Lloyd"s Rep Med 263, 83 BMLR 66, [2005] NLJR 654, (2005) Times, 22 April,
149 Sol Jo LB 512, [2005] All ER (D) 292 (Apr) 13.78
D v Hereford and Worcester County Council [1991] Fam 14, [1991] 2 All ER 177,
[1991] 2 WLR 753, 89 LGR 524, [1991] FCR 56, [1991] 1 FLR 205,
[1991] Fam Law 272 .... 3.67
D v M [1983] Fam 33, [1982] 3 All ER 897, [1982] 3 WLR 891, 126 Sol Jo 562,
sub nom Dicocco v Milne 4 FLR 247, 12 Fam Law 210, CA 2.45
D v N (contact order: conditions). See D (a minor) (contact orders: conditions), Re
(1997)
D v National Society for the Prevention of Cruelty to Children [1978] AC 171,
[1976] 2 All ER 993, [1976] 3 WLR 124, 120 Sol Jo 422, CA; revsd [1978] AC
171, [1977] 1 All ER 589, [1977] 2 WLR 201, 121 Sol Jo 119, HL 11.62
D v R [1995] 1 FCR 501, sub nom D, Re [1995] 1 FLR 495, [1995] Fam Law 239 .... 4.52,
                                                                              4.57, 5.61
D v S [2008] EWHC 363 (Fam), [2008] Fam Law 499 .... 12.42
D v Southwark London Borough Council [2007] EWCA Civ 182, [2007] 1 FCR 788,
[2007] 1 FLR 2181, [2007] Fam Law 701, sub nom R (on the application of D)
v A Local Authority [2007] All ER (D) 110 (Mar) 6.63, 6.72
D and K (children) (care plan: twin track planning), Re [1999] 4 All ER 893,
[2000] 1 WLR 642, [1999] 3 FCR 109, [1999] 2 FLR 872, [1999] Fam Law
1405, [1999] NLJR 1405 .... 8.59
DB and CB (minors), Re [1993] 2 FCR 607, sub nom Southwark London Borough v
B [1993] 2 FLR 559, [1994] Fam Law 73, CA 2.11, 3.112, 8.227, 12.29, 12.40
DH (a minor), Re [1994] 2 FCR 3, [1994] 1 FLR 679, [1994] Fam Law 433, 22
BMLR 146 .... 5.112, 5.192, 5.201, 8.181, 11.28, 11.78
D, L and LA (care: change of forename) [2003] 1 FLR 339 .... 3.103, 8.175
DW (a minor), Re [1984] Fam Law 17, CA 2.37
Daniels v Walker [2000] 1 WLR 1382, [2000] All ER (D) 608, CA 1.44
Dawson v Wearmouth [1999] 2 AC 308, [1999] 2 All ER 353, [1999] 2 WLR 960,
[1999] 1 FCR 625, [1999] 1 FLR 1167, [1999] Fam Law 378, 143 Sol Jo LB
114, HL 2.69, 5.32, 5.33, 5.36, 5.98
Dean v Dean [1987] FCR 96, [1987] 1 FLR 517, [1987] Fam Law 200, CA 5.165
Dellow's Will Trusts, Re, Lloyds Bank Ltd v Institute of Cancer Research
[1964] 1 All ER 771, [1964] 1 WLR 451, 108 Sol Jo 156 .... 8.22
Devon County Council v B [1997] 3 FCR 333, [1997] 1 FLR 591, [1997] Fam Law
399, CA 7.106, 12.25, 12.35
Devon County Council v S [1992] Fam 176, [1992] 3 All ER 793, [1992] 3 WLR
273, [1992] 1 FCR 550, [1992] 2 FLR 244, [1993] Fam Law 190 ...... 4.54, 5.141, 8.167
Devon County Council v S [1994] Fam 169, [1995] 1 All ER 243, [1994] 3 WLR
183, [1994] 2 FCR 409, [1994] 1 FLR 355, [1994] Fam Law 371 .... 12.29, 12.34, 12.40
Dicocco v Milne. See D v M

E

E (SA) (a minor), Re [1984] 1 All ER 289, [1984] 1 WLR 156, 82 LGR 257,
[1984] FLR 457, [1984] Fam Law 276, 128 Sol Jo 80, HL 3.96
E (a minor), Re, E v E [1987] FCR 169, [1987] 1 FLR 269 .... 11.49
E (a minor), Re [1991] FCR 771, [1991] 2 FLR 585, [1992] Fam Law 15, 7 BMLR
117; on appeal [1993] Fam Law 15, CA 3.29
E, Re (child abduction) [1992] 1 FCR 541, sub nom F v S (wardship: jurisdiction)
[1993] 2 FLR 686, CA 12.27
E (a minor), Re [1994] 1 FCR 584, [1994] 1 FLR 146, [1993] Fam Law 671, CA 8.198
E (a minor), Re [1994] 2 FCR 709, [1995] 1 FLR 392, [1995] Fam Law 121, CA ... 2.10, 3.65

PARA

E (minors) (residence: conditions), Re [1997] 3 FCR 245, [1997] 2 FLR 638,
[1997] Fam Law 606, CA 5.51, 5.115, 5.119
E (family assistance order), Re [1999] 3 FCR 700, [1999] 2 FLR 512,
[1999] Fam Law 529 .... 5.195, 5.201
E (care proceedings: social work practice), Re [2000] 2 FCR 297, [2000] 2 FLR 254,
[2000] Fam Law 610, [2000] All ER (D) 670 .... 6.5, 7.47
E v X London Borough Council [2005] EWHC 2811 (Fam), [2006] 1 FLR 730,
[2006] Fam Law 187, [2005] All ER (D) 99 (Dec) 5.206, 12.18
EC (disclosure of material), Re. See C (a minor) (care proceedings: disclosure), Re
(1997)
EO and VP v Slovakia (Applications 56193/00 and 57581/00) [2004] 2 FCR 242,
[2004] ECHR 56193/00, ECtHR 2.61
ET (serious injuries: standard of proof), Re [2003] 2 FLR 1205n, [2003] Fam Law
871 .... 11.7
EW, Re [1992] 2 FCR 441, sub nom Re R [1992] 2 FLR 481, CA 12.27
EW (No 2), Re [1993] 1 FCR 710, sub nom Re R [1993] 1 FLR 249,
[1993] Fam Law 216 .... 12.21
Elder v Elder [1986] 1 FLR 610, [1986] Fam Law 190, CA 10.64, 11.57
Elliot v Joicey [1935] AC 209, 104 LJ Ch 111, [1935] All ER Rep 578, 79 Sol Jo
144, 152 LT 398, 51 TLR 261, 1935 SC (HL) 57, HL 3.55, 3.93
Elsholz v Germany (Application 25735/94) (2002) 34 EHRR 58, [2000] 3 FCR 385,
[2000] 2 FLR 486, [2000] Fam Law 800, ECtHR 3.17, 5.76, 11.40
Essex County Council v B [1993] 1 FCR 145, [1993] 1 FLR 866, [1993] Fam Law
457 .... 4.56, 8.195, 10.31, 10.36
Essex County Council v F [1993] 2 FCR 289, [1993] 1 FLR 847, [1993] Fam Law
337 .... 4.56, 7.97, 13.4
Essex County Council v Mirror Group Newspapers Ltd [1996] 2 FCR 831,
[1996] 1 FLR 585, [1996] Fam Law 270 .... 12.37, 12.41
Essex County Council v R [1994] Fam 167n, [1994] 2 WLR 407n, [1993] 2 FLR
826, [1993] Fam Law 670, sub nom R (a minor) (discolsure of privileged
material), Re [1993] 4 All ER 702, [1994] 1 FCR 225 .... 11.74, 11.78
Evans v Amicus Healthcare Ltd [2004] EWCA Civ 727, [2005] Fam 1,
[2004] 3 All ER 1025, [2004] 3 WLR 681, [2004] 2 FCR 530, [2004] 2 FLR
766, [2004] Fam Law 647, 78 BMLR 181, (2004) Times, 30 June, 148 Sol Jo
LB 823, [2004] All ER (D) 309 (Jun) 3.93
Evans v United Kingdom (Application 6339/05) [2007] 2 FCR 5, [2007] 1 FLR 1990,
[2007] Fam Law 588, 95 BMLR 107, [2007] NLJR 599, (2007) Times, 2 May,
22 BHRC 190, [2007] All ER (D) 109 (Apr), ECtHR 3.93
Evelyn, Re [1998] Fam CA 55, Family Court Aust 2.9

F

F (a minor), Re [1973] Fam 198, [1973] 3 All ER 493, [1973] 3 WLR 461, 117 Sol
Jo 616 .... 5.57
F, Re [1988] Fam 122, [1988] 2 All ER 193, [1988] 2 WLR 1288, [1988] FCR 529,
[1988] 2 FLR 307, [1988] Fam Law 337, 132 Sol Jo 820, [1988] NLJR
37, CA 12.27
F (wardship: police investigation), Re [1989] Fam 18, [1988] 3 WLR 818,
[1989] FCR 249, [1989] FCR 752, [1989] 1 FLR 39, [1989] Fam Law 18, 132
Sol Jo 1324, CA 11.90
F, Re [1990] 2 AC 1, [1989] 2 WLR 1025, [1989] 2 FLR 376, 133 Sol Jo 265,
[1989] 10 LS Gaz R 42, [1989] NLJR 183, CA; affd [1990] 2 AC 1,
[1989] 2 WLR 1025, [1989] 2 FLR 376, [1989] Fam Law 390, 133 Sol Jo 785,
[1989] NLJR 789, sub nom F v West Berkshire Health Authority (Mental
Health Act Commission intervening) [1989] 2 All ER 545, 4 BMLR 1, HL 3.26
F (a minor), Re [1990] Fam 125, [1989] 1 All ER 1155, [1989] 3 WLR 691,
[1989] FCR 165, [1989] 1 FLR 233, [1988] Fam Law 474, CA 12.31
F (a minor), Re [1992] 1 FCR 167, [1992] 1 FLR 561, [1992] Fam Law 330, CA 13.3
F, Re [1992] 2 FCR 433, sub nom F v Kent County Council [1993] 1 FLR 432,
[1993] Fam Law 132, [1992] 34 LS Gaz R 39, 136 Sol Jo LB 258 .... 4.48, 8.218

PARA

F (a minor), Re [1993] Fam 314, [1993] 3 All ER 596, [1993] 3 WLR 369, [1993] 1 FCR 932, [1993] 1 FLR 598, [1993] Fam Law 407, [1993] NLJR 472, CA 3.59, 3.60
F (a minor), Re [1993] 1 FCR 389, [1993] 2 FLR 9, [1993] Fam Law 517 .... 4.56, 8.227
F (minors), Re [1993] 1 FCR 945, [1993] 2 FLR 677, [1993] Fam Law 673, CA 2.43, 5.86, 5.141, 5.193, 11.57
F (child: surname), Re [1994] 1 FCR 110, [1993] 2 FLR 837n, CA 5.36
F (a minor), Re [1994] 1 FCR 729, [1994] 1 FLR 240, [1994] Fam Law 424 .... 4.52, 13.6
F (a minor) (contact: child in care), Re [1994] 2 FCR 1354, [1995] 1 FLR 510, [1995] Fam Law 231 .... 2.33, 5.124, 8.203, 8.206, 8.208
F (minors), Re [1995] 2 FCR 200, [1995] 1 FLR 819, CA 2.24, 3.25, 5.98
F (a minor), Re [1995] 3 FCR 601 .... 11.36
F (minors) (contact: appeal), Re [1997] 1 FCR 523, CA 10.28
F (contact: enforcement: representation of child), Re [1998] 3 FCR 216, [1998] 1 FLR 691, [1998] Fam Law 319, CA 5.164, 5.165, 5.175
F (Mental Health Act guardianship), Re [2000] 1 FCR 11, [2000] 1 FLR 192, [2000] Fam Law 18, 51 BMLR 128, [1999] 39 LS Gaz R 38, [1999] All ER (D) 1043, CA 12.9, 12.19
F (minors) (care proceedings: contact), Re [2000] 2 FCR 481, [2000] All ER (D) 776 .... 1.44, 8.214
F (a child) (contact order), Re [2001] 1 FCR 422, [2001] All ER (D) 16 (Jan), CA 5.90
F (children) (shared residence order), Re [2003] EWCA Civ 592, [2003] 2 FCR 164, [2003] 2 FLR 397, [2003] Fam Law 568, [2003] All ER (D) 258 (Mar) 5.22
F (children) (restriction on applications), Re [2005] EWCA Civ 499, [2005] 2 FCR 176, [2005] 2 FLR 950, [2005] All ER (D) 42 (Apr) 5.204
F (family proceedings: section 37 investigation), Re [2005] EWHC 2935 (Fam), [2006] 1 FLR 1122, sub nom C v C (children)(investigation of circumstances) [2006] Fam Law 261, [2005] All ER (D) 222 (Dec) 5.206, 7.25
F (a child) (indirect contact through third party), Re [2006] EWCA Civ 1426, [2006] 3 FCR 553, [2007] 1 FLR 1015, 150 Sol Jo LB 1465, [2006] All ER (D) 14 (Nov) 3.80, 5.55
F (children) (paternity: jurisdiction), Re [2007] EWCA Civ 873, [2008] 1 FCR 382, [2008] 1 FLR 225, [2007] Fam Law 984, sub nom F (Children), Re (2007) Times, 6 August, [2007] All ER (D) 389 (Jul), CA 5.98
F (children) (contact), Re [2007] EWHC 2543 (Fam), [2008] 1 WLR 1163, [2008] 1 FLR 1163, [2007] All ER (D) 52 (Nov), sub nom F (children) (contact: change of name), Re [2007] 3 FCR 832, [2007] Fam Law 1130 .... 5.37
F v Cambridgeshire County Council [1995] 2 FCR 804, [1995] 1 FLR 516, [1995] Fam Law 240 .... 5.106, 5.125, 7.30, 12.16
F v F (contact: committal) [1999] 2 FCR 42, [1998] 2 FLR 237, [1998] Fam Law 519, CA 5.175
F v Kent County Council. See F, Re (1992)
F v Leeds City Council [1994] 2 FCR 428, [1994] 2 FLR 60, [1994] Fam Law 610, CA 2.27, 2.32, 8.55
F v R [1995] 1 FLR 227, [1995] Fam Law 123 .... 4.56, 4.57, 5.99, 5.120
F v S (wardship: jurisdiction) [1991] FCR 631, [1991] 2 FLR 349, [1991] Fam Law 312; revsd [1992] 1 FCR 542, [1993] 2 FLR 686, CA 12.27
F v West Berkshire Health Authority (Mental Health Act Commission intervening). See F, Re (1990)
F v Wirral Metropolitan Borough Council [1991] Fam 69, [1991] 2 All ER 648, [1991] 2 WLR 1132, [1991] 2 FLR 114, [1991] Fam Law 299, CA 3.16
F and H (children), Re [2007] EWCA Civ 692, [2007] Fam Law 870 .... 5.46
F and R (Section 8 order: grandparents' application), Re. See R (minors), Re (1995)
FS (minors) (care proceedings), Re [1996] 1 FCR 666, sub nom FS (child abuse: evidence), Re [1996] 2 FLR 158, [1996] Fam Law 540, CA 11.56
Fairpo v Humberside County Council [1997] 1 All ER 183, [1997] 3 FCR 181, [1997] 1 FLR 339, [1997] ELR 12 .... 3.39
Feldbrugge v Netherlands (Application 8562/79) (1986) 8 EHRR 425, ECtHR 11.64

Fitzpatrick v Sterling Housing Association Ltd [2001] 1 AC 27, [1999] 4 All ER 705,
[1999] 3 WLR 1113, [2000] 1 FCR 21, [1999] 2 FLR 1027, [2000] 1 FLR 271,
[2000] Fam Law 14, 32 HLR 178, [1999] NPC 127, [1999] 43 LS Gaz R 34,
[1999] EGCS 125, 79 P & CR D4, [2000] 3 LRC 294, 7 BHRC 200, HL 1.49
Fleming v Pratt (1823) 1 LJOSKB 194 .... 3.19
Flintshire County Council v K [2001] 2 FLR 476, [2001] 2 FCR 724,
[2001] Fam Law 578, [2001] All ER (D) 61 (Aug) 8.177

G

G (a minor), Re [1982] 2 All ER 32, [1982] 1 WLR 438, 80 LGR 596, 3 FLR 340,
12 Fam Law 119, 126 Sol Jo 135, CA 4.58
G (a minor), Re [1987] 1 FLR 164, [1987] Fam Law 52, CA 13.5
G (minors), Re [1992] 2 FCR 720, [1993] 1 FLR 910, [1993] Fam Law 460, CA ... 5.26, 5.28,
5.29
G (minor: care order), Re (1992) Times, 19 November 4.49
G (a minor) (appeal), Re [1993] 1 FCR 810, sub nom C (a minor) (care: childs
wishes), Re [1993] 1 FLR 832 .... 4.49, 10.61, 11.48, 13.30
G (minors), Re [1993] 2 FCR 557, [1993] 2 FLR 839, [1993] Fam Law 672, CA 8.110
G (minors), Re [1994] 1 FCR 37, [1993] 2 FLR 293, [1993] Fam Law 570, CA 11.62
G (minors) (expert witnesses), Re [1994] 2 FCR 106, [1994] 2 FLR 291,
[1994] Fam Law 428, 20 BMLR 10 .... 11.34, 11.36, 11.37
G, Re [1994] 2 FCR 359, [1994] 2 FLR 301, [1994] Fam Law 568 .... 6.69, 8.177
G (a minor) (parental responsibility order), Re [1994] 2 FCR 1037, [1994] 1 FLR
504, [1994] Fam Law 372, CA 2.10, 3.65, 3.67
G (a minor), Re [1995] Fam 16, [1994] 3 WLR 1211, [1994] 2 FLR 69,
[1994] Fam Law 485, sub nom Hackney London Borough Council v G
[1994] 2 FCR 216 .... 2.74, 4.54, 8.19, 8.53, 8.168
G (a minor), Re [1995] 2 FCR 53, [1994] 2 FLR 964, [1994] Fam Law 492, CA 3.77, 3.99,
5.59, 5.226, 14.17
G (a minor), Re [1995] 2 FCR 120, [1994] 2 FLR 785, CA 4.53, 8.225, 13.30, 13.31
G (a minor) (social worker: disclosure), Re [1996] 2 All ER 65, [1996] 1 WLR 1407,
[1996] 1 FLR 276, [1996] Fam Law 143, [1995] 44 LS Gaz R 30, [1996] NLJR
85, [1995] TLR 588, 140 Sol Jo LB 10, sub nom G (a minor) (care proceedings:
disclosure), Re [1996] 3 FCR 77, CA 11.87
G (child case: parental involvement), Re [1996] 2 FCR 1, [1996] 1 FLR 857,
[1996] Fam Law 459, CA 3.80, 8.100
G (a minor) (leave to appeal: jurisdiction), Re [1999] 3 FCR 281, [1999] 1 FLR 771,
[1999] Fam Law 292, CA 5.142, 6.69, 8.177
G (children) (care proceedings: wasted costs), Re [2000] Fam 104, [1999] 4 All ER
371, [2000] 2 WLR 1007, [2000] Fam Law 24, sub nom Re G, S and H (care
proceedings: wasted costs), [1999] 3 FCR 303, sub nom Re G, S and M (care
proceedings: wasted costs), [2000] 1 FLR 52 .... 4.12, 4.29, 4.59, 11.45
G (a child) (secure accommodation order), Re [2000] 2 FCR 385, [2000] 2 FLR 259,
[2000] Fam Law 716, CA 9.9, 12.8
G (a child) (non-accidental injury: standard of proof), Re [2001] 1 FCR 97, CA 11.6
G (a child) (care order: threshold criteria), Re [2001] 1 FCR 165, [2001] 1 FLR 872,
[2000] All ER (D) 2043, CA 8.144, 11.41
G (domestic violence: direct contact), Re [2001] 2 FCR 134, [2000] 2 FLR 865 ...... 3.69, 5.93
G (a child) (secure accommodation order), Re [2001] 3 FCR 47, [2001] 1 FLR 884,
[2000] All ER (D) 2498 .... 9.10, 9.25, 9.32, 9.34
G (children) (care order: evidence), Re [2001] EWCA Civ 968, [2001] 1 WLR 2100,
[2001] 2 FCR 757, [2001] 2 FLR 1111, [2001] Fam Law 727,
[2001] 29 LS Gaz R 37, (2001) Times, 5 July, 145 Sol Jo LB 166, [2001] All ER
(D) 246 (Jun) 8.31, 8.32, 8.38, 8.39, 8.144, 8.167
G (children: contact), Re [2002] EWCA Civ 761, [2002] 3 FCR 377, [2003] 1 FLR
270, [2003] Fam Law 9, [2002] All ER (D) 428 (May) 8.201
G (adoption: ordinary residence), Re [2002] EWHC 2447 (Fam), [2003] 2 FLR
944 .... 5.132, 11.8

PARA

G (care: challenge to local authority's decision), Re [2003] EWHC 551 (Fam),
[2003] 2 FLR 42, [2003] Fam Law 389 .... 6.4, 8.5, 8.172
G (protocol for judicial case management in public law children act cases: application
to become party in family proceedings), Re [2004] EWHC 116 (Fam),
[2004] 1 FLR 1119, [2004] Fam Law 327 .... 8.85
G (removal from jurisdiction), Re [2005] EWCA Civ 170, [2005] 2 FLR 166, [2005]
All ER (D) 227 (Jan) 5.45
G (residence: same-sex partner), Re [2005] EWCA Civ 462, [2006] 1 FCR 436,
[2005] 2 FLR 957, sub nom G (children) (shared residence order: parental
responsibility), Re [2005] NLJR 744, (2005) Times, 29 April, 149 Sol Jo LB
476, [2005] All ER (D) 25 (Apr) 2.72, 5.15
G (care proceedings: placement for adoption) [2005] EWCA Civ 896, [2006] 1 FLR
47, [2005] Fam Law 770, sub nom G (a child) (care proceedings: lack of
reasons), Re (2005) Times, 1 August, [2005] All ER (D) 166 (Jul) 8.57
G (children) (residence order: no order principle), Re [2005] EWCA Civ 1283,
[2006] 1 FLR 771, [2006] Fam Law 93, (2005) Times, 14 September, [2005] All
ER (D) 399 (Jul) 2.69
G (a child) (interim care order: residential assessment), Re [2005] UKHL 68,
[2006] 1 AC 576, [2006] 1 All ER 706, [2005] 3 WLR 1166, [2005] 3 FCR
621, [2006] 1 FLR 601, [2006] Fam Law 91, (2005), Times, 25 November, 149
Sol Jo LB 1455, [2005] All ER (D) 321 (Nov) 8.115, 8.117
G (a child) (parental responsibility), Re [2006] EWCA Civ 745, [2006] 2 FLR 1092,
[2006] Fam Law 744, 150 Sol Jo LB 666, [2006] All ER (D) 247 (May) 3.70, 5.201
G (a child) (education), Re [2006] EWCA Civ 1507, [2007] 1 FLR 1663,
[2006] 40 LS Gaz R 36, 150 Sol Jo LB 1328, [2006] All ER (D) 67 (Oct) 5.98
G (children) (residence: same-sex partner), Re [2006] UKHL 43, [2006] 4 All ER
241, [2006] 1 WLR 2305, [2006] 3 FCR 1, [2006] 2 FLR 629, [2006] Fam Law
932, [2006] 32 LS Gaz R 21, [2006] NLJR 1252, (2006) Times, 27 July, 150
Sol Jo LB 1021, [2006] All ER (D) 374 (Jul) 2.3, 2.8, 2.9, 2.44, 2.47, 2.72, 5.15,
5.199, 5.201
G v A [1995] 2 FCR 223n, Cty Ct 5.36
G v C (contempt: committal) [1998] 1 FCR 592, [1998] 1 FLR 43, [1997] Fam Law
785, CA 5.175
G v F (shared residence: parental responsibility) [1998] 3 FCR 1, [1998] 2 FLR 799,
[1998] Fam Law 587 .... 5.15
G v G [1985] 2 All ER 225, [1985] 1 WLR 647, [1985] FLR 894, [1985] Fam Law
321, 129 Sol Jo 315, HL 2.23, 8.225, 10.22, 13.31
G v Kirklees Metropolitan Borough Council [1993] 1 FCR 357, [1993] 1 FLR 805,
[1993] Fam Law 278 .... 5.152, 8.100
G-A (a child) (removal from jurisdiction: human rights), Re [2001] 1 FCR 43, sub
nom Re A (permission to remove child from jurisdiction) [2000] 2 FLR
225, CA 1.54, 5.44
G, S and M (care proceedings: wasted costs), Re, See G (children) (care proceedings:
wasted costs), Re (2000)
Garlick v Oldham Metropolitan Borough Council and related appeals [1993] AC
509, [1993] 2 All ER 65, [1993] 2 WLR 609, 91 LGR 287, [1993] 2 FCR 133,
25 HLR 319, [1993] 26 LS Gaz R 38, [1993] NLJR 437, HL 6.41
Gateshead Metropolitan Borough Council v L [1996] Fam 55, [1996] 3 All ER 264,
[1996] 3 WLR 426, [1996] 3 FCR 582, [1996] 2 FLR 179, [1996] Fam Law
401 .... 8.170
Gateshead Metropolitan Borough Council v N [1993] 1 FCR 400, [1993] 1 FLR 811,
[1993] Fam Law 456 .... 8.124
Ghaidan v Godin-Mendoza [2004] UKHL 30, [2004] 2 AC 557, [2004] 3 WLR 113,
[2004] 2 FCR 481, [2004] 2 FLR 600, [2004] Fam Law 641, [2004] HLR 827,
[2004] 2 EGLR 132, [2004] 27 LS Gaz R 30, [2004] NLJR 1013, (2004) Times,
24 June, 148 Sol Jo LB 792, [2004] All ER (D) 210 (Jun), sub nom Ghaidan v
Mendoza [2004] 3 All ER 411, [2005] 1 LRC 449 .... 1.49
Gillick v West Norfolk and Wisbech Area Health Authority [1986] AC 112,
[1985] 3 All ER 402, [1985] 3 WLR 830, [1986] 1 FLR 224, [1986] Crim LR
113, 129 Sol Jo 738, 2 BMLR 11, [1985] LS Gaz R 3551, [1985] NLJ Rep
1055, HL 1.9, 3.3, 3.10, 3.30, 3.32, 3.95, 8.52, 11.98, 14.30

PARA

Glaser v United Kingdom (Application 32346/96) [2000] 3 FCR 193, [2001] 1 FLR
    153, [2000] Fam Law 880, ECtHR 5.76, 5.83
Gloucestershire County Council v P [2000] Fam 1, [1999] 3 WLR 685,
    [1999] 3 FCR 114, [1999] 2 FLR 61, [1999] Fam Law 444,
    [1999] 20 LS Gaz R 39, 143 Sol Jo LB 157, [1999] All ER (D) 427, CA 5.142, 5.147
Gogay v Hertfordshire County Council [2000] IRLR 703, [2001] 1 FCR 455,
    [2001] 1 FLR 280, [2000] Fam Law 883, [2000] All ER (D) 1057, CA 7.8, 7.14, 7.19
Gojkovic v Gojkovic (No 2) [1992] Fam 40, [1992] 1 All ER 267, [1991] 3 WLR
    621, [1991] FCR 913, [1991] 2 FLR 233, [1991] Fam Law 378, CA 4.58
Görgülü v Germany (Application 74969/01) [2004] 1 FCR 410, [2004] 1 FLR 894,
    [2004] Fam Law 411, ECtHR 8.214
Griffin v Griffin [2000] 2 FCR 302, [2000] 2 FLR 44, [2000] All ER (D) 503, CA 5.175
Guzzardi v Italy (Application 7367/76) (1980) 3 EHRR 333, ECtHR 9.4

H

H (an infant), Re [1959] 3 All ER 746, [1959] 1 WLR 1163, 124 JP 74, 103 Sol Jo
    1003 .... 3.114
H (a minor), Re (1980) 2 FLR 253, 10 Fam Law 248 .... 2.50
H (a minor), Re (1989). See H v H (minor)
H (minors), Re [1990] FCR 866, [1990] 2 FLR 172, [1990] Fam Law 338, CA 4.42, 10.23
H (minors) (local authority: parental rights) (No 3), Re [1991] Fam 151,
    [1991] 2 All ER 185, [1991] 2 WLR 763, 89 LGR 537, 135 Sol Jo 16, sub nom
    H (minors) (No 2), Re [1991] FCR 361, [1991] 1 FLR 214, [1991] Fam Law
    306, CA 3.64, 3.65
H (minors) (access), Re [1992] 1 FCR 70, [1992] 1 FLR 148, [1992] Fam Law
    152, CA 5.83, 5.84
H (a minor) (care proceedings: child's wishes), Re [1992] 2 FCR 330, [1993] 1 FLR
    440, [1993] Fam Law 200 .... 4.57, 8.119, 10.51
H (a minor), Re [1993] 1 FCR 85, [1993] 1 FLR 484, [1993] Fam Law 273, CA ... 3.67, 3.72,
                                                                                            5.86
H (a minor) (shared residence order), Re [1993] 1 FCR 671, [1994] 1 FLR 717,
    [1993] Fam Law 463, CA 3.76, 5.19
H (child's circumstances: direction to investigate), [1993] 2 FCR 277,
    [1993] Fam Law 205, subnom Re H (a minor) (Section 37 direction), Re
    [1993] 2 FLR 541 .... 5.206, 7.25, 8.26
H (a minor), Re [1994] Fam 11, [1994] 4 All ER 762, [1993] 3 WLR 1109,
    [1993] 2 FCR 437, [1993] 2 FLR 552, [1993] Fam Law 614 .... 10.53
H (a minor), Re [1994] 1 FCR 673, [1994] 2 FLR 981, [1994] Fam Law 422, CA 5.29
H (minors), Re [1994] 2 FCR 1, [1994] 2 FLR 979, [1994] Fam Law 486 .... 8.184, 8.185
H (a minor), Re [1994] 2 FCR 419, [1994] 2 FLR 776, [1995] Fam Law 13, CA 5.83
H (minors), Re [1995] 4 All ER 110, [1995] 1 WLR 667, [1995] 2 FCR 547,
    [1995] 1 FLR 638, [1995] Fam Law 293, CA 5.62, 5.96, 5.103, 5.112, 5.169
H (minors) (sexual abuse: standard of proof), Re [1996] AC 563, [1996] 1 All ER 1,
    [1996] 2 WLR 8, [1996] 1 FCR 509, [1996] 1 FLR 80, [1996] Fam Law 74,
    140 Sol Jo LB 24, HL 2.56, 7.67, 8.22, 8.25, 8.26, 8.37, 11.5, 11.6, 11.8
H (contact: enforcement), Re [1996] 2 FCR 784, [1996] 1 FLR 614, [1996] Fam Law
    348 .... 5.173
H (a minor) (parental responsibility order), Re [1996] 3 FCR 49, [1996] 1 FLR 867,
    [1996] Fam Law 402, CA 3.65, 3.67
H (shared residence: parental responsibility), Re [1996] 3 FCR 321, [1995] 2 FLR
    883, [1996] Fam Law 140, CA 5.15, 5.17, 5.19, 14.19
H (a minor) (blood tests: parental rights), Re [1997] Fam 89, [1996] 4 All ER 28,
    [1996] 3 WLR 506, [1996] 3 FCR 201, [1996] 2 FLR 65, [1996] Fam Law 461,
    [1996] NLJR 406, CA 2.17
H (minors) (care: change in care plan), Re [1998] 2 FCR 657, [1998] 1 FLR 193,
    [1998] Fam Law 70, CA 8.152
H (contact: domestic violence), Re [1998] 3 FCR 385, [1998] 2 FLR 42,
    [1998] Fam Law 392, CA 5.55, 5.90, 5.91

PARA

H (parental responsibility), Re (1998). See RH (a minor) (parental responsibility), Re (1998)

H (child abduction: whereabouts order to solicitors), Re [2000] 1 FCR 499, [2000] 1 FLR 766, [1999] All ER (D) 1519 .... 12.20

H (residence order: child's application for leave) [2000] 1 FLR 780, [2000] Fam Law 404 .... 5.155, 5.156, 5.159

H (care proceedings: intervener), Re [2000] 2 FCR 53, [2000] 1 FLR 775, [2000] Fam Law 464, CA 8.101, 10.59

H (child abduction: child of sixteen), Re [2000] 3 FCR 404, [2000] 2 FLR 51 .... 12.42

H (abduction: habitual residence: consent) [2000] 2 FLR 294 .... 4.40

H (a children), Re [2001] Fam 260, [2000] 4 All ER 609, [2001] 2 WLR 339, [2000] 2 FCR 404, [2000] 2 FLR 334, [2000] Fam Law 603, 144 Sol Jo LB 222, [2000] All ER (D) 827, CA 1.54, 2.4

H (children) (contact order), Re [2001] 1 FCR 49, [2000] All ER (D) 1724, CA 5.86

H (children) (contact order), Re (No 2) [2001] 3 FCR 385, [2002] 1 FLR 22, [2001] Fam Law 795, (2001) Times, 10 August, [2001] All ER (D) 241 (Jun) 5.86

H (children) (residence order: condition), Re [2001] EWCA Civ 1338, [2001] 3 FCR 182, [2001] 2 FLR 1277, [2001] Fam Law 870, (2001) Times, 29 August, [2001] All ER (D) 427 (Jul) 2.69, 2.70, 5.14, 5.39, 5.43, 5.44, 5.45, 5.51, 5.95, 5.118, 8.176

H (a child: residence), Re [2002] 3 FCR 277, CA 2.9

H (a child: forename), Re [2002] EWCA Civ 190, [2002] 1 FLR 973, (2002) Times, 6 February, [2002] All ER (D) 247 (Jan) 5.34, 5.37

H (a child) (interim care order), Re [2002] EWCA Civ 1932, [2003] 1 FCR 350, [2002] All ER (D) 183 (Dec) 8.109, 8.110

H (a child), Re [2003] EWCA Civ 369, [2003] All ER (D) 290 (Feb) 5.152

H (a child) (care: local authority), Re [2003] EWCA Civ 1629, [2004] Fam 89, [2004] 2 WLR 419, [2004] 1 FCR 282, [2004] 1 FLR 534, [2004] Fam Law 105, [2004] 02 LS Gaz R 27, (2003) Times, 26 November, [2003] All ER (D) 250 (Nov) 8.170

H (residence order: placement out of jurisdiction), Re [2004] EWHC 3243 (Fam), [2006] 1 FLR 1140, [2006] Fam Law 349 .... 5.112

H (children) (termination of contact), Re [2005] EWCA Civ 318, [2005] 1 FCR 658, [2005] 2 FLR 408, [2005] Fam Law 526, [2005] All ER (D) 24 (Feb) 8.201

H (a child) (contact: domestic violence), Re [2005] EWCA Civ 1404, [2006] 1 FCR 102, [2006] 1 FLR 943, [2006] Fam Law 439, 149 Sol Jo LB 1452, (2005) Times, 28 December, [2005] All ER (D) 280 (Nov) 4.55, 5.91, 5.93

H (national youth advocacy service), Re [2006] EWCA Civ 896, [2007] 1 FLR 1028, sub nom H (a child) (contact), Re [2006] All ER (D) 69 (Jun) 10.33

H (children) (care proceedings and criminal proceedings), Re [2006] EWCA Civ 1875, [2006] All ER (D) 294 (Dec) 8.106

H (abduction: Dominica: corporal punishment), Re [2006] EWHC 199 (Fam), [2006] 2 FLR 314, [2006] Fam Law 522 .... 12.22

H (a child) (removal outside jurisdiction), Re [2007] EWCA Civ 222, [2007] 2 FLR 317, [2007] Fam Law 706, [2007] All ER (D) 171 (Apr) 5.45

H (children) (residence order), Re [2007] EWCA Civ 529, [2007] 2 FCR 621, [2007] All ER (D) 26 (May) 5.24

H (a child) (contact), Re [2008] All ER (D) 255 (Jan) 5.201

H (a child) (leave to apply for residence order), Re [2008] EWCA Civ 503, [2008] Fam Law 734, [2008] All ER (D) 44 (Apr) 5.154

H v Cambridgeshire County Council [1997] 1 FCR 569, [1996] 2 FLR 566, [1996] Fam Law 721 .... 2.63, 11.34, 11.36

H v D [2007] EWHC 802 (Fam), [2007] All ER (D) 77 (Apr) 12.23

H v F (refusal of leave to remove a child from the jurisdiction) [2005] EWHC 2705 (Fam), [2006] 1 FLR 776 .... 5.49

H v H [1974] 1 All ER 1145, [1974] 1 WLR 595, 118 Sol Jo 219, CA 10.64, 11.57

H v H (1989) 87 LGR 166, [1989] FCR 257, [1989] 1 FLR 212, [1989] Fam Law 148, CA 2.55

H v H (minor) [1990] Fam 86, [1989] 3 WLR 933, [1989] FCR 356, 134 Sol Jo 21, [1989] NLJR 864, sub nom H v H and C [1989] 3 All ER 740, sub nom Re H (a minor) [1989] 2 FLR 313, [1989] Fam Law 388, CA 10.20, 11.3, 11.49

PARA

H v H (a minor) (No 2) (forum conveniens) [1997] 1 FCR 603 .... 5.20
H v L [2006] EWHC 3099 (Fam), [2007] 1 FCR 430, [2007] 2 FLR 162,
    [2007] Fam Law 306, (2007) Times, 19 February, [2006] All ER (D) 96 (Dec) 5.74
H v Norfolk County Council [1997] 2 FCR 334, [1997] 1 FLR 384, CA 13.74
H v United Kingdom (Application 9580/81) (1987) 10 EHRR 95, ECtHR 1.7
H v West Sussex County Council [1998] 3 FCR 126, [1998] 1 FLR 862,
    [1998] Fam Law 317 .... 11.12
HA v MB [2007] EWHC 2016 (Fam), [2008] 1 FLR 289, [2007] Fam Law 1058,
    (2007) Times, 2 November, [2007] All ER (D) 156 (Aug) 4.5, 4.40, 5.53, 12.42
HG, Re [1993] 1 FCR 553, [1993] 1 FLR 587, [1993] Fam Law 403 .... 3.29, 4.40, 5.97,
                                                                                                         5.157, 5.159
HIV Tests, Re. See X (a minor), Re (1994)
H-S (minors), Re [1994] 3 All ER 390, [1994] 1 WLR 1141, [1994] 3 FCR 90,
    [1994] 1 FLR 519, [1994] Fam Law 251, CA 2.21, 4.40
Haase v Germany (Application 11057/02) [2004] 2 FCR 1, [2004] 2 FLR 39,
    [2004] Fam Law 500, [2004] ECHR 11057/02, ECtHR 5.75
Hackney London Borough Council v C [1997] 1 FCR 509, sub nom C (care order:
    appropriate local authority), Re [1997] 1 FLR 544, [1997] Fam Law 319,
    [1997] 7 LS Gaz R 29, 141 Sol Jo LB 34 .... 8.170
Hackney London Borough Council v G. See G (a minor), Re (1995)
Hale v Tanner [2000] 1 WLR 2377, [2000] 3 FCR 62, [2000] 2 FLR 879,
    [2000] Fam Law 876, CA 5.175
Hampshire County Council v S [1993] Fam 158, [1993] 1 All ER 944,
    [1993] 2 WLR 216, [1993] 1 FLR 559, [1993] Fam Law 284, sub nom M v
    Hampshire County Council [1993] 1 FCR 23 .... 4.46, 4.52, 8.109, 8.111
Hansen v Turkey (Application 36141/97) [2003] 3 FCR 97, [2004] 1 FLR 142,
    [2003] Fam Law 877, ECtHR 5.75, 8.3
Haringey London Borough Council v C (E intervening) [2004] EWHC 2580 (Fam),
    [2005] 2 FLR 47, [2005] Fam Law 351, (2004) Times, 27 November, [2004] All
    ER (D) 204 (Nov) 7.4, 8.29
Harmony Shipping Co SA v Saudi Europe Line Ltd [1979] 3 All ER 177,
    [1979] 1 WLR 1380, [1980] 1 Lloyd's Rep 44, 123 Sol Jo 690, CA 11.45
Harris v Pinnington [1995] 3 FCR 35, sub nom MH v GP [1995] 2 FLR 106,
    [1995] Fam Law 542 .... 4.40, 5.42
Harris v Harris [2001] 3 FCR 193, [2001] 2 FLR 895, [2001] All ER (D) 217
    (Apr) 5.204
Harrison v Surrey County Council. See T (a minor) v Surrey County Council
Hawksworth v Hawksworth (1871) 6 Ch App 539, 25 JP 788, 40 LJ Ch 534, 19
    WR 735, [1861–73] All ER Rep 314, 25 LT 115, CA in Ch 3.41
Hendricks v Netherlands (1982) 5 EHRR 223, ECtHR 2.4
Hereford and Worcester County Council v EH [1985] FLR 975, [1985] Fam Law
    229 .... 13.26
Hereford and Worcester County Council v S [1993] 1 FCR 653, [1993] 2 FLR 360,
    [1993] Fam Law 573 .... 9.6, 9.10, 9.11
Hertfordshire County Council v W [1992] 2 FCR 885, [1992] 39 LS Gaz R 33, 136
    Sol Jo LB 259, sub nom W v Hertfordshire County Council [1993] 1 FLR 118,
    [1993] Fam Law 75 .... 4.56
Hewer v Bryant [1970] 1 QB 357, [1969] 3 All ER 578, [1969] 3 WLR 425, 113 Sol
    Jo 525, CA 3.15, 3.19, 3.95, 8.52
Hillingdon London Borough Council v H [1993] Fam 43, [1993] 1 All ER 198,
    [1992] 3 WLR 521, [1992] 2 FCR 299, [1992] 2 FLR 372, [1992] Fam Law
    536 .... 4.56, 4.58
Hinds v Liverpool County Council, Liverpool City Council [2008] EWHC 665
    (QB) 13.78, 13.88
Hodak, Newman and Hadak, Re (1993) FLR 92–421 .... 2.9
Hodges v Hodges (1796) 1 Esp 441, Peake Add Cas 79 .... 3.39
Hoffmann v Austria (Application 12875/87) (1993) 17 EHRR 293, [1994] 1 FCR
    193, [1994] Fam Law 673, ECtHR 2.50, 3.42
Hokkanen v Finland (Application 19823/92) (1994) 19 EHRR 139, [1995] 2 FCR
    320, [1996] 1 FLR 289, [1996] Fam Law 22, [1994] ECHR 19823/92,
    ECtHR 3.23, 5.75

PARA

Holmes-Moorhouse v Richmond-upon-Thames London Borough Council
[2007] EWCA Civ 970, [2008] 1 WLR 1289, [2008] LGR 1, [2007] 3 FCR
736, [2008] 1 FLR 1061, [2007] Fam Law 1134, [2007] All ER (D) 130 (Oct) 2.58,
5.19, 5.52
Hoppe v Germany (Application 28422/95) [2003] 1 FCR 176, [2003] 1 FLR 384,
[2003] Fam Law 159, [2002] ECHR 28422/95, ECtHR 5.75
Hounslow London Borough Council v A [1993] 1 WLR 291, [1993] 1 FCR 164,
[1993] 1 FLR 702, [1993] Fam Law 397 .... 8.151, 8.178
Humberside County Council v B [1993] 1 FCR 613, [1993] 1 FLR 257,
[1993] Fam Law 61 .... 2.27, 8.55

I

I v D [1989] FCR 91, [1988] 2 FLR 286, [1988] Fam Law 338 .... 5.175
I v H (contact hearing: procedure) [1998] 2 FCR 433, [1998] Fam Law 327, sub
nom I and H (contact: right to give evidence), Re [1998] 1 FLR 876, CA 5.60, 10.29
Ikarian Reefer, The. See National Justice Cia Naviera SA v Prudential
Assurance Co Ltd, The Ikarian Reefer
Ismailova v Russia (Application 37614/02) [2008] 2 FCR 72, [2008] 1 FLR 533,
[2007] ECHR 37614/02, ECtHR 3.42

J

J (minor) (abduction: ward of court), Re [1989] Fam 85, [1989] 3 All ER 590,
[1989] 3 WLR 825, [1990] FCR 341, [1990] 1 FLR 276, [1990] Fam Law 177,
133 Sol Jo 876 .... 12.21
J (a minor), Re [1990] FCR 135, [1989] 2 FLR 304, [1989] Fam Law 394, CA 2.47
J (child abuse; expert evidence), Re [1991] FCR 193, sub nom R (a minor) (expert's
evidence), Re [1991] 1 FLR 291n, [1991] Fam Law 303 .... 11.46
J (a minor) (wardship: medical treatment), Re [1993] Fam 15, [1992] 4 All ER 614,
[1992] 3 WLR 507, [1992] 2 FCR 753, [1992] 2 FLR 165, [1993] Fam Law
126, 9 BMLR 10, [1992] 30 LS Gaz R 32, [1992] NLJR 1123, 136 Sol Jo LB
207, CA 3.26, 3.36, 12.31
J (a minor), Re [1993] 1 FCR 74, [1993] 1 FLR 699, [1992] Fam Law 399 .... 8.175
J (a minor), Re [1993] 2 FCR 636, [1994] 1 FLR 369, [1994] Fam Law 375 .... 4.57, 5.109,
13.26, 13.28
J (a minor), Re [1994] 2 FCR 741, [1994] 1 FLR 729, [1994] Fam Law 316, CA 5.87
J (minors), Re (1994). See R (minors), Re (1994)
J (specific issue order: leave to apply), Re [1995] 3 FCR 799, [1995] 1 FLR 669,
[1995] Fam Law 403 .... 5.99, 5.208, 8.116
J (minors) (ex parte orders) Re, [1997] 1 FCR 325, [1997] 1 FLR 606,
[1997] Fam Law 317 .... 2.46, 5.26
J (child's religious upbringing and circumcision), Re [1999] 2 FCR 345,
[1999] Fam Law 543, [1999] All ER (D) 477, Re J (specific issue orders: muslim
upbringing and circumcision) [1999] 2 FLR 678; affd sub nom J (child's
religious upbringing and circumcision), Re [2000] 1 FCR 307, [2000] Fam Law
246, 52 BMLR 82, [1999] 47 LS Gaz R 30, sub nom Re J (specific issue orders:
child's religous upbringing) [2000] 1 FLR 571, CA 2.10, 2.44, 2.49, 3.28, 3.41, 3.42,
3.99, 5.95, 5.98, 5.226, 5.236, 14.17
J (parental responsibility), Re [1999] 1 FLR 784, [1999] Fam Law 216 .... 3.69
J (adoption: revocation of freeing order), Re [2000] 2 FCR 133, [2000] Fam Law
598, [2000] 24 LS Gaz R 39, [2000] All ER (D) 610, sub nom Re J (a child)
(freeing for adoption), Re [2000] 2 FLR 58 .... 8.177
J (children) (residence: expert evidence), Re [2001] 2 FCR 44, CA 4.55
J (a child), Re [2002] EWHC 18 (Fam/Admin), [2002] Fam 213, [2002] 3 WLR 24,
[2002] 1 FCR 481, [2002] 1 FLR 845, (2002) Times, 11 March, 146 Sol Jo LB
37, [2002] All ER (D) 187 (Jan) 12.1

J (leave to issue application for residence order), Re [2002] EWCA Civ 1346,
    [2003] 1 FLR 114, [2003] Fam Law 27 .... 5.152, 5.153, 8.100
J (a child) (care proceedings: disclosure), Re [2003] EWHC 976 (Fam), [2003] 2 FLR
    522, [2003] 31 LS Gaz R 31, (2003) Times, 16 May, [2003] All ER (D) 299
    (May) 10.48
J (a child) (custody rights: jurisdiction), Re [2005] UKHL 40, [2006] 1 AC 80,
    [2005] 3 WLR 14, [2005] NLJR 972, (2005) Times, 17 June, sub nom Re J (a
    child) (return to foreign jurisdiction: convention rights) [2005] 3 All ER 291,
    [2005] 2 FCR 381, [2005] All ER (D) 150 (Jun), sub nom Re J (child returned
    abroad: convention rights) [2005] 2 FLR 802 .... 2.7, 2.25, 12.22
J (children) (residence order: removal outside jurisdiction), Re [2006] EWCA Civ
    1897, [2007] 2 FCR 149, [2007] 1 FLR 2033, [2007] Fam Law 490, [2006] All
    ER (D) 295 (Dec) 5.47
J (a child) (adoption order or special guardianship order), Re [2007] EWCA Civ 55,
    [2007] 1 FCR 308, [2007] 1 FLR 507, [2007] Fam Law 387, [2007] All ER (D)
    82 (Feb) 5.214, 5.234, 5.236
J v C [1970] AC 668, [1969] 1 All ER 788, [1969] 2 WLR 540, sub nom C (an
    infant), Re 113 Sol Jo 164, HL 2.3, 2.4, 2.7, 2.8, 3.42
J v C [2006] EWCA Civ 551, [2007] Fam 1, [2006] 3 WLR 876, sub nom J v C
    (void marriage: status of children) [2008] 1 FCR 368, [2006] 2 FLR 1098,
    [2006] Fam Law 742, (2006) Times, 1 June, sub nom C (children) (parent:
    purported marriage between two women: artificial insemination by donor), Re
    [2006] All ER (D) 216 (May) 5.98
J v C [2006] EWHC 2837 (Fam), [2007] 1 FCR 365, [2007] 1 FLR 1064, [2006] All
    ER (D) 147 (Nov) 5.98
JC (care proceedings: procedure), Re (1995) 160 LG Rev 346, [1996] 1 FCR 434,
    [1995] 2 FLR 77, [1995] Fam Law 543 .... 4.54
JS (a minor), Re [1990] Fam 182, [1990] 2 All ER 861, [1990] 3 WLR 119,
    [1990] FCR 961, [1991] 1 FLR 7, [1991] Fam Law 95,
    [1990] 24 LS Gaz R 44 .... 12.31
J-S (a child) (contact and parental responsibility), Re [2002] EWCA Civ 1028,
    [2002] 3 FCR 433, [2003] 1 FLR 399, [2003] Fam Law 81, [2002] All ER (D)
    89 (Jul) 3.64, 3.65
JT (a minor), Re [1986] 2 FLR 107, [1986] Fam Law 213 .... 12.40
Jevremovic v Serbia (Application No 3150/05) [2007] 2 FCR 671, [2008] 1 FLR 550,
    [2007] Fam Law 985, [2007] ECHR 3150/05, ECtHR 2.61
Johansen v Norway (Application 17383/90) (1996) 23 EHRR 33, [1997] EHRLR 81,
    ECtHR 2.4, 8.3, 8.8
Jones v Jones [1993] 2 FCR 82, [1993] 2 FLR 377, [1993] Fam Law 519, CA 5.175
Jones v National Coal Board [1957] 2 QB 55, [1957] 2 All ER 155, [1957] 2 WLR
    760, 101 Sol Jo 319, CA 13.3

K

K (minors), Re [1988] Fam 1, [1988] 1 All ER 214, [1987] 3 WLR 1233,
    [1988] 1 FLR 435, [1988] Fam Law 166, 152 JP 185, 131 Sol Jo 1697,
    [1987] LS Gaz R 3501 .... 12.31
K (minors) (child abuse: evidence), Re (1989). See K v K (minors)
K (incitement to breach order), Re [1992] 2 FCR 521, [1992] Fam Law 530, sub
    nom Re K (minors) (incitement to breach contact order) [1992] 2 FLR 108 .... 5.169
K (a minor), Re (1992). See K v K
K (a minor) (contact) [1993] Fam Law 552 .... 11.57
K (minors), Re [1994] 3 All ER 230, [1994] 2 FCR 805, [1994] 1 FLR 377,
    [1994] Fam Law 247, sub nom Kent County Council v K [1994] 1 WLR 912 .... 4.47,
    11.90
K (minors), Re [1994] 1 FCR 616, [1993] Fam Law 615 .... 4.56
K (minors) (care or residence order), Re [1996] 1 FCR 365, [1995] 1 FLR 675 .... 5.141, 8.164
K (contact: psychiatric report), Re [1996] 1 FCR 474, [1995] 2 FLR 432,
    [1995] Fam Law 597, CA 5.125, 10.25, 11.36

PARA

K (adoption: foreign child), Re [1997] 2 FCR 389, [1997] 2 FLR 221, sub nom K
(adoption), Re [1997] Fam Law 316, CA 12.24
K (adoption: disclosure of information), Re [1998] 2 FCR 388, [1997] 2 FLR 74 .... 11.68
K (supervision order), Re [1999] 1 FCR 337, [1999] 2 FLR 303, [1999] Fam Law
376 .... 8.164
K (care proceedings: joinder of father), Re [1999] 2 FCR 391, sub nom B (care
proceedings: notification of father without parental responsibility), Re
[1999] 2 FLR 408, [1999] Fam Law 525 .... 2.41, 4.25, 8.98
K (contact: mother's anxiety), Re [1999] 2 FLR 703, [1999] Fam Law 527 .... 5.93
K (a minor) (removal from jurisdiction: practice), Re [1999] 3 FCR 673,
[1999] 2 FLR 1084, [1999] Fam Law 754, [1999] 33 LS Gaz R 29, CA 5.42, 5.50
K (a child) (secure accommodation order: right to liberty), Re [2001] Fam 377,
[2001] 2 All ER 719, [2001] 2 WLR 1141, [2001] 1 FCR 249, [2001] 1 FLR
526, [2001] Fam Law 99, [2000] 48 LS Gaz R 36, (2000) Times, 29 November,
144 Sol Jo LB 291, [2000] All ER (D) 1834, CA 1.47, 1.54, 3.19, 9.2, 9.6, 9.11
K (Replacement of Guardian Ad Litem), Re [2001] 1 FLR 663, [2000] All ER (D)
2482 .... 10.33
K (children) (adoption: freeing order), Re [2004] EWCA Civ 1181, [2004] 3 FCR
123, [2005] Fam Law 12, [2004] All ER (D) 150 (Aug), sub nom Re K
(non-accidental injuries: perpetrator: new evidence) [2005] 1 FLR 285 .... 8.145, 11.27
K (children: interim residence order), Re [2004] EWCA Civ 1827, [2007] 2 FCR 631,
149 Sol Jo LB 29, [2004] All ER (D) 276 (Dec), sub nom Re K (procedure:
family proceedings rules) [2005] 1 FLR 764, [2005] Fam Law 275 .... 5.24
K (children) (care proceedings), Re [2005] EWCA Civ 1226, [2006] 2 FLR 868,
[2006] Fam Law 626, [2005] All ER (D) 70 (Aug) 8.28, 8.40, 8.41
K (care: representation: public funding), Re [2005] EWHC 167 (Fam), [2005] 2 FLR
422 .... 8.99
K (non-accidental injuries: perpetrator: new evidence), Re (2005). See K (children)
(adoption: freeing order), Re (2004)
K, Re [2005] EWHC 2956 (Fam), [2007] 1 FLR 399, [2007] Fam Law 298 ... 2.78, 8.44, 12.8,
12.9
K (a child) (withdrawal of treatment), Re [2006] EWHC 1007 (Fam), [2006] 2 FLR
883, [2006] Fam Law 840, 99 BMLR 98, 150 Sol Jo LB 667, [2006] All ER (D)
120 (May) 3.37
K, Re [2007] 1 FLR 1116 .... 5.223, 5.224
K (care proceedings: care plan), Re [2007] EWHC 393 (Fam), [2008] 1 FLR 1,
[2007] Fam Law 1128 .... 8.60
K (a child) (shared residence order), Re [2008] EWCA Civ 526, [2008] All ER (D) 55
(Apr) 5.17, 5.22
K v H [1993] 1 FCR 683, [1993] 2 FLR 61, [1993] Fam Law 464 .... 2.26, 2.66
K v K (minors) [1990] Fam 86, [1989] 3 All ER 740, [1989] 3 WLR 933,
[1989] FCR 356, [1989] Fam Law 388, 134 Sol Jo 21, [1989] NLJR 864, sub
nom Re K (minors) (child abuse: evidence) [1989] 2 FLR 313, CA 10.20, 11.3
K v K [1992] 2 FCR 161, [1992] 2 FLR 98, sub nom K (a minor), Re
[1992] Fam Law 240 .... 5.169
K v P [1995] 2 FCR 457, [1995] 1 FLR 248, [1995] Fam Law 178 .... 11.24
K v W (11 March 1998, unreported) 3.69
K and A, Re [1995] 1 FLR 688, [1995] Fam Law 407 .... 5.211, 6.19
K and H (children) (interim care order), Re [2006] EWCA Civ 1898, [2007] 1 FLR
2043, [2007] Fam Law 485, [2007] All ER (D) 303 (Mar) 8.110
K and T v Finland (Application 25702/94) [2001] 2 FCR 673, [2001] 2 FLR 707,
ECtHR 6.60, 8.3, 8.165
KA v Finland (Application 27751/95) [2003] 1 FCR 201, [2003] 1 FLR 696, [2003]
ECHR 27751/95, ECtHR 4.55, 6.60, 8.3
KD (a minor) (ward: termination of access), Re [1988] AC 806, [1988] 1 All ER 577,
[1988] 2 WLR 398, [1988] FCR 657, [1988] 2 FLR 139, [1988] Fam Law 288,
132 Sol Jo 301, HL 2.3, 3.23, 3.24, 5.83, 8.42
KDT (a minor), Re [1994] 2 FCR 721, sub nom T (a minor), Re [1994] 2 FLR 423,
[1994] Fam Law 558, [1994] 21 LS Gaz R 40, CA 5.119, 12.7
KR (a child) (abduction: forcible removal by parents), Re [1999] 4 All ER 954,
[1999] 2 FCR 337, [1999] 2 FLR 542, [1999] Fam Law 545 .... 12.21

PARA

KR v Bryn Alyn Community (Holdings) Ltd (in liq) [2003] EWCA Civ 85,
[2003] QB 1441, [2004] 2 All ER 716, [2003] 3 WLR 107, [2003] 1 FCR 385,
[2003] 1 FLR 1203, (2003) Times, 17 February, [2003] All ER (D) 162 (Feb) 13.83
Karcheva v Bulgaria (Application no 60939/00) [2006] 3 FCR 434, [2006] ECHR
60939/00, ECtHR 2.61
Kelly v BBC [2001] Fam 59, [2001] 1 All ER 323, [2001] 2 WLR 253, [2000] 3 FCR
509, [2001] 1 FLR 197, [2000] Fam Law 886, [2000] 39 LS Gaz R 41, 144 Sol
Jo LB 250, [2000] All ER (D) 1312 .... 4.47, 5.100
Kent County Council v C [1993] Fam 57, [1993] 1 All ER 719, [1992] 3 WLR 808,
[1993] 1 FLR 308, [1993] Fam Law 133, sub nom Re CN (a minor)
[1992] 2 FCR 401 .... 8.209, 10.38, 12.7, 12.43
Kent County Council v K. See K (minors), Re (1994)
Kirklees Metropolitan Borough Council v S and London Borough of Brent
[2004] 2 FLR 800, [2004] Fam Law 561 .... 8.170
Kirklees Metropolitan District Council v S [2005] EWHC 3494 (Fam), [2006] 1 FLR
333, [2005] Fam Law 768, sub nom A Local Authority v S (a child) (care
proceedings: contact) [2005] All ER (D) 24 (Aug) 8.208, 8.209
Koniarska v United Kingdom (12 October 2000, unreported), ECtHR 9.2
Kosmopoulou v Greece (Application 60457/00) [2004] 1 FCR 427, [2004] 1 FLR
800, [2004] Fam Law 330, ECtHR 3.23, 5.75

L

L (a minor) (wardship: freedom of publication), Re [1988] 1 All ER 418,
[1988] 1 FLR 255, [1987] NLJ Rep 760 .... 4.47
L (a minor), Re [1995] 3 FCR 684, [1995] 2 FLR 445, [1995] Fam Law 598 .... 2.56, 2.57
L, Re (1995). See L v C
L (minors) (care proceedings: issue estoppel), Re [1996] 1 FCR 221, sub nom Re S, S
and A (care proceedings: issue estoppel) [1995] 2 FLR 244, [1995] Fam Law
601 .... 11.26
L (minors) (police investigation: privilege), Re [1996] 1 FCR 419, [1995] 1 FLR 999,
[1995] Fam Law 474, 24 BMLR 69, CA; affd [1997] AC 16, [1996] 2 All ER
78, [1996] 2 WLR 395, 95 LGR 139, 160 LG Rev 417, [1996] 2 FCR 145,
[1996] 1 FLR 731, [1996] Fam Law 400, [1996] 15 LS Gaz R 30, [1996] NLJR
441, 140 Sol Jo LB 116, HL 2.22, 2.23, 11.75, 11.88
L (care proceedings: appeal), Re [1996] 2 FCR 352, [1996] 1 FLR 116,
[1996] Fam Law 73, CA 8.152
L (a minor) (interim care order), Re [1996] 2 FCR 706, sub nom L (interim care
order: power of court), Re [1996] 2 FLR 742, [1997] Fam Law 85, CA 8.116
L (minors: sexual abuse: disclosure) [1999] 1 WLR 299, 96 LGR 807, [1999] 1 FCR
308, [1999] 1 FLR 267, [1999] Fam Law 14, 142 Sol Jo LB 270, [1998] All ER
(D) 440, CA 11.95
L (care: confidentiality), Re [1999] 1 FLR 165, [1999] Fam Law 81 .... 11.89
L (medical treatment: Gillick competency), Re [1999] 2 FCR 524, [1998] 2 FLR 810,
[1998] Fam Law 591, 51 BMLR 137 .... 3.33, 12.38
L (a minor) (section 37 direction), Re [1999] 3 FCR 642, [1999] 1 FLR 984,
[1999] Fam Law 307, CA 5.206, 7.25
L (care proceedings: disclosure to third party) [2000] 1 FLR 913, [2000] Fam Law
397 .... 11.84
L (a child) (contact: domestic violence), Re [2001] Fam 260, [2000] 4 All ER 609,
[2001] 2 WLR 339, [2000] 2 FCR 404, [2000] 2 FLR 334, [2000] Fam Law
603, 144 Sol Jo LB 222, [2000] All ER (D) 827, CA 1.54, 2.4, 3.69, 4.55, 5.82, 5.91
L (minors) (care proceedings: solicitors), Re [2001] 1 WLR 100, [2000] 3 FCR 71,
[2000] All ER (D) 1087 .... 10.51, 10.52
L (removal from jurisdiction: holiday), Re [2001] 1 FLR 241, [2001] Fam Law 9 .... 5.50
L (care: assessment: fair trial), Re (2002). See C (care proceedings: disclosure of local
authority's decision making process), Re (2002)

PARA

L (a child) (special guardianship order and ancillary orders), Re [2007] EWCA Civ
196, [2007] 1 FCR 804, [2007] 2 FLR 50, [2007] Fam Law 498, [2007] All ER
(D) 208 (Mar), sub nom E (a child) (special guardianship order), Re (2007)
Times, 11 April 5.217, 5.222, 5.223
L (care: threshold criteria), Re [2007] 1 FLR 2050, [2007] Fam Law 297, Crown
Ct 8.42
L (children) (care order: residential assessment), Re [2007] EWCA Civ 213,
[2007] 3 FCR 259, [2007] Fam Law 584, [2007] All ER (D) 246 (Mar) sub
nom Re L and H (residential assessment), [2007] 1 FLR 1370 .... 2.62, 8.115
L (interim care order: power of court), Re. See L (a minor) (interim care order), Re
(1996)
L v Bexley London Borough [1997] 1 FCR 277, [1996] 2 FLR 595, [1997] Fam Law
10 .... 8.170
L v C [1995] 3 FCR 125, sub nom L, Re [1995] 2 FLR 438, [1995] Fam Law 599 .... 3.67,
5.55
L v L [1989] FCR 697, [1989] 2 FLR 16, [1989] Fam Law 311, CA 2.55
L v L (minors) (separate representation) [1994] 1 FCR 890, [1994] 1 FLR 156,
[1994] Fam Law 432, CA 10.26
L v L (alleged contempt: procedure). See Lewis v Lewis
L v Reading Borough Council [2001] EWCA Civ 346, [2001] 1 WLR 1575,
[2001] 1 FCR 673, [2001] 2 FLR 50, [2001] Fam Law 421 .... 11.96
L v Reading Borough Council [2007] EWCA Civ 1313, [2008] 1 FCR 295, [2007]
All ER (D) 142 (Dec), sub nom B v Reading Borough Council [2008] 1 FLR
797 .... 13.81
L v Tower Hamlets London Borough Council [2001] Fam 313, [2000] 3 All ER 346,
[2001] 2 WLR 909, [2000] 2 FCR 345, [2000] 1 FLR 825, [2000] Fam Law
474, CA 13.74, 13.76
L v United Kingdom (Application 34222/96) [2000] 2 FCR 145, ECtHR 11.75
L and H (residential assessment), Re. See L (children) (care order: residential
assessment), Re
LM v Essex County Council [1999] 1 FCR 673, [1999] 1 FLR 988, [1999] Fam Law
312 .... 9.27, 9.29, 13.71
LM (by her guardian) v Medway Council. See M (a child) (care proceedings: witness
summons), Re (2007)
Ladd v Marshall [1954] 3 All ER 745, [1954] 1 WLR 1489, 98 Sol Jo 870, CA 13.30
Lambeth London Borough Council v T K [2008] EWCA Civ 103, [2008] 1 FLR
1229, (2008) Times, 2 April, sub nom K v A local authority [2008] Fam Law
382, [2008] Fam Law 408, [2008] All ER (D) 308 (Feb) 5.206, 12.18
Lancashire County Council v B [2000] 2 AC 147, [2000] 2 All ER 97,
[2000] 2 WLR 590, [2000] LGR 347, [2000] 1 FCR 509, [2000] 1 FLR 583,
[2000] Fam Law 394, 144 Sol Jo LB 151, [2000] NLJR 429,
[2000] 13 LS Gaz R 42, HL 8.46, 8.47
Langley v Liverpool City Council [2005] EWCA Civ 1173, [2006] 2 All ER 202,
[2006] 1 WLR 375, [2006] LGR 453, [2005] 3 FCR 303, [2006] 1 FLR 342,
[2006] Fam Law 94, (2005) Times, 19 October, [2005] All ER (D) 96 (Oct) 5.105,
5.208, 7.99, 7.101, 12.36
Lawrence v Pembrokeshire County Council [2007] EWCA Civ 446, [2007] 1 WLR
2991, [2007] 2 FCR 329, [2007] 2 FLR 705, [2007] Fam Law 666,
[2007] Fam Law 804, 96 BMLR 158, (2007) Times, 29 May, [2007] All ER (D)
214 (May) 13.79
Lebbink v Netherlands (Application 45582/99) [2004] 3 FCR 59, [2004] 2 FLR 463,
[2004] Fam Law 643, [2004] ECHR 45582/99, ECtHR 5.75
Leeds City Council v C [1993] 1 FCR 585, [1993] 1 FLR 269, [1993] Fam Law 73 .... 5.58,
5.112, 5.201, 5.207, 8.181
Leicestershire County Council v G [1995] 1 FCR 205, [1994] 2 FLR 329,
[1994] Fam Law 486 .... 13.29
Lewis v Lewis [1991] 3 All ER 251, [1991] 1 WLR 235, [1991] 2 FLR 43,
[1991] Fam Law 469, sub nom L v L (alleged contempt:
procedure)[1991] 1 FCR 547, [1991] Fam Law 87, 135 Sol Jo 152, CA 10.64, 11.57
Liverpool City Council v B [1995] 1 WLR 505, [1995] 2 FCR 105, [1995] 2 FLR 84,
[1995] Fam Law 476 .... 9.33, 9.38

Local Administration Comr (subpoena issued by), Re (1996) 95 LGR 338,
    [1996] 3 FCR 190, 140 Sol Jo LB 108, sub nom Subpoena (adoption: Comr for
    Local Administration), Re [1996] 2 FLR 629, [1996] Fam Law 663 .... 13.69
Local Authority v W [2005] EWHC 1564 (Fam), [2007] 3 FCR 69, [2006] 1 FLR 1,
    [2005] Fam Law 868, sub nom Re W (children) (identification: restriction on
    publication) [2006] 1 FLR 1, (2005) Times, 21 July, [2005] All ER (D) 206
    (Jul) 2.20, 2.21, 2.22, 12.40
Local Authority v Y [2006] 2 FLR 41, [2006] Fam Law 448 .... 5.211, 5.219, 5.222
Lopez v Lizazo: C-68/07 [2008] 3 WLR 338, [2008] 1 FLR 582, [2008] Fam Law
    99, [2007] All ER (D) 468 (Nov), ECJ 3.55
Lough v Ward [1945] 2 All ER 338, 89 Sol Jo 283, 173 LT 181 .... 3.95

M

M (infants), Re [1967] 3 All ER 1071, [1967] 1 WLR 1479, 111 Sol Jo 618, CA 2.50
M (a minor), Re [1988] FCR 47, [1987] 1 FLR 293n 11.51
M, Re (1989) Times, 29 December, CA 4.45, 13.35
M (a minor) (disclosure of material), Re (1990) 88 LGR 841, [1990] FCR 485,
    [1990] 2 FLR 36, [1990] Fam Law 259, CA 11.67
M, Re [1993] 1 FCR 78, [1993] 1 FLR 275, [1993] Fam Law 76 .... 4.56, 5.154, 13.2
M (minors), Re [1993] 1 FCR 253, [1993] 1 FLR 822, [1993] Fam Law 456, CA 5.153,
                                                                            8.99, 11.54
M (minors) (residence orders: jurisdiction), Re [1993] 1 FCR 718, [1993] 1 FLR 495,
    [1993] Fam Law 285, CA 3.19
M (child), Re [1993] 2 FCR 721, [1993] 2 FLR 706, [1993] Fam Law 616 .... 10.65, 11.57
M (a minor) (care order: threshold conditions), Re [1994] 2 AC 424, [1994] 3 All ER
    298, [1994] 3 WLR 558, 92 LGR 701, [1994] 2 FCR 871, [1994] 2 FLR 577,
    [1994] Fam Law 501, [1994] 37 LS Gaz R 50, 138 Sol Jo LB 168, HL 4.6, 8.25, 8.30,
                                                                            8.39
M (a minor), Re [1994] 1 FCR 1, [1994] 1 FLR 54, [1994] Fam Law 373, CA 13.28
M (a minor), Re [1994] 1 FCR 678, [1994] 1 FLR 272, [1994] Fam Law 252 .... 4.57, 5.55
M (minors) (care proceedings: child's wishes), Re [1994] 1 FCR 866, [1994] 1 FLR
    749, [1994] Fam Law 430 .... 10.50, 10.51, 10.53, 11.45, 11.46
M (a minor), Re [1994] 2 FCR 750, [1994] 1 FLR 390, [1994] Fam Law 242, CA 2.28
M (a minor), Re [1994] 2 FCR 968, [1995] 1 FLR 1029, [1995] Fam Law 476 ...... 4.51, 5.60
M (child abduction: European Convention), Re [1994] 2 FCR 1209, [1994] 1 FLR
    551, [1994] Fam Law 367 .... 5.27
M (a minor), Re [1995] Fam 108, [1995] 3 All ER 407, [1995] 2 WLR 302,
    [1995] 2 FCR 373, [1995] 1 FLR 418, 138 Sol Jo LB 241, CA 2.15, 2.27, 2.67, 9.6,
                                                                            9.11, 9.19, 9.26
M, Re [1995] 1 FCR 649, [1995] 1 FLR 533, [1995] Fam Law 291 .... 4.58
M (minors) (children's welfare: contact), Re [1995] 1 FCR 753, [1995] 1 FLR 274,
    [1995] Fam Law 174, CA 5.84
M (minors), Re [1995] 2 FCR 1, [1994] 1 FLR 760, [1994] Fam Law 312, CA 11.71
M (a minor), Re [1995] 2 FCR 90, [1995] 2 FLR 100, [1995] Fam Law 599, CA 2.43,
                                                                            10.62, 11.49
M (a minor) (contact), Re [1995] 2 FCR 435, [1995] Fam Law 236, sub nom Re M
    (section 94 appeals) [1995] 1 FLR 546, CA 2.54, 4.57, 13.31
M (minors), Re [1995] 2 FCR 643, [1995] 1 FLR 825, [1995] Fam Law 404 .... 2.24, 3.25,
                                                                            5.98, 12.29, 12.40
M (a minor), Re [1995] 2 FCR 793, [1993] 2 FLR 858 .... 4.5
M, Re [1995] 3 FCR 550, [1995] 2 FLR 86, [1995] Fam Law 540, CA 5.152, 8.204, 8.205
M (care proceedings: police videos), Re (1995). See M and K (child abuse: video
    evidence), Re
M (child's upbringing), Re [1996] 2 FCR 473, [1996] 2 FLR 441, [1996] Fam Law
    458, CA 2.54, 12.24
M (application for stay of order), Re [1996] 3 FCR 185, CA 2.11
M (care order: parental responsibility), Re (1996). See MM (care order: abandoned
    baby), Re

PARA

M (a minor) (care orders: jurisdiction), Re [1997] Fam 67, [1997] 1 All ER 263,
[1997] 2 WLR 314, [1997] 1 FCR 109, [1997] 1 FLR 456,
[1997] 05 LS Gaz R 32 .... 4.6, 8.18
M (minors), Re (interim residence order) [1997] 2 FCR 28, CA 5.24
M (a minor) (adoption or residence order), Re [1998] 1 FCR 165, [1998] 1 FLR 570,
[1998] Fam Law 188, CA 5.17
M (abduction: psychological harm), Re [1998] 2 FCR 488, [1997] 2 FLR 690, CA 12.23
M (minors) (contact: evidence), Re [1998] 2 FCR 538, [1998] 1 FLR 721,
[1998] Fam Law 252, CA 5.60
M (a minor) (Official Solicitor role), Re [1998] 3 FCR 315, [1998] 2 FLR 815,
[1998] Fam Law 594, [1998] 27 LS Gaz R 26, CA 5.206, 7.25
M (a minor) (contact: supervision), Re [1998] 1 FLR 727, [1998] Fam Law 70, CA 5.83
M (residential assessment directions), Re [1998] 2 FLR 371, [1998] Fam Law 518 .... 2.18
M (a minor) (contempt of court: committal of court's own motion), Re [1999] Fam
263, [1999] 2 All ER 56, [1999] 2 WLR 810, [1999] 1 FCR 683, [1999] 1 FLR
810, [1999] Fam Law 208, 143 Sol Jo LB 36, [1998] All ER (D) 746, CA 5.170
M (disclosure), Re [1999] 1 FCR 492, [1998] 2 FLR 1028, [1998] Fam Law
729, CA 11.64
M (contact: parental responsibility: McKenzie friend), Re [1999] 1 FCR 703,
[1999] 1 FLR 75, [1998] Fam Law 727, CA 3.67, 3.69, 5.86, 5.90, 5.201
M (minors) (contact: violent parent), Re [1999] 2 FCR 56, [1999] 2 FLR 321,
[1999] Fam Law 380 .... 5.90, 5.91
M (terminating appointment of guardian ad litem), Re [1999] 2 FCR 625,
[1999] 2 FLR 717, [1999] Fam Law 541 .... 10.41
M (leave to remove child from jurisdiction), Re [1999] 3 FCR 708, [1999] 2 FLR
334, [1999] Fam Law 377 .... 2.40, 5.33, 5.42
M (sexual abuse allegations: interviewing techniques), Re [1999] 2 FLR 92,
[1999] Fam Law 445 .... 5.55, 11.49
M (threshold criteria: parental concessions), Re [1999] 2 FLR 728, [1999] Fam Law
524, CA 4.54, 8.168
M (interim contact: domestic violence), Re [2000] 2 FLR 377, [2000] Fam Law
604, CA 5.61
M (a child), Re [2001] Fam 260, [2000] 4 All ER 609, [2001] 2 WLR 339,
[2000] 2 FCR 404, [2000] 2 FLR 334, [2000] Fam Law 603, 144 Sol Jo LB
222, [2000] All ER (D) 827, CA 1.54, 2.4
M (handicapped child: parental responsibility), Re [2001] 3 FCR 454, [2001] All ER
(D) 449 (Mar), sub nom M (contact: parental control), Re [2001] 2 FLR 342,
[2001] Fam Law 594 .... 3.65, 3.69
M (Care: Challenging Decisions by Local Authority), Re [2001] 2 FLR 1300 ...... 8.158, 8.172,
13.92
M (a child) (secure accommodation), Re [2001] EWCA Civ 458, [2001] 1 FCR 692,
[2001] All ER (D) 11 (Apr), sub nom C (secure accommodation order:
representation), Re [2001] 2 FLR 169, [2001] Fam Law 507 .... 9.5, 9.25, 9.26
M (judge's discretion), Re [2001] EWCA Civ 1428, [2002] 1 FLR 730, sub nom M (a
child: interim residence order), Re [2002] Fam Law 105, [2001] All ER (D) 16
(Sep) 5.112
M (contact: parental control), Re (2001). See M (handicapped child: parental
responsibility), Re (2001)
M (Care Proceedings: Disclosure: Human rights), Re [2002] 1 FCR 655,
[2001] 2 FLR 1316, [2001] Fam Law 799, [2001] All ER (D) 302 (Oct) 11.89, 11.91
M (children: determination of responsibility for injuries), Re [2002] EWCA Civ 499,
[2002] 2 FCR 377, [2003] 1 FLR 461, [2003] Fam Law 84, [2002] All ER (D)
171 (Mar) 8.145, 11.27
M (a child) (disclosure: children and family reporter), Re [2002] EWCA Civ 1199,
[2003] Fam 26, [2002] 4 All ER 401, [2002] 3 WLR 1669, [2002] 3 FCR 208,
[2002] 2 FLR 893, [2003] Fam Law 96, [2002] 39 LS Gaz R 37, (2002) Times,
23 August, [2002] All ER (D) 482 (Jul) 5.208, 10.27
M (sperm donor father), Re [2003] Fam Law 94 .... 3.68
M (care proceedings: judicial review), Re [2003] EWHC 850 (Admin), [2004] 1 FCR
302, [2003] 2 FLR 171, [2003] All ER (D) 265 (Apr) 13.43, 13.46, 13.50

PARA

M (intractable contact dispute: interim care order), Re [2003] EWHC 1024 (Fam),
[2003] 2 FLR 636, [2003] Fam Law 719, [2003] All ER (D) 06 (Jun) ... 5.206, 7.26, 7.28,
7.29
M (children) (residence order), Re [2004] EWCA Civ 1574, [2005] 1 FLR 656,
(2004) Times, 5 November, [2004] All ER (D) 173 (Oct), sub nom M
(residence), Re [2005] Fam Law 216 .... 10.28
M (contact: long-term best interests), Re [2005] EWCA Civ 1090, [2006] 1 FLR 627,
sub nom M (children) (contact), Re (2005) Times, 27 June, [2005] All ER (D)
230 (Jun) 5.73, 5.81, 5.85
M (children) (interim care order), Re [2005] EWCA Civ 1594, [2006] 1 FCR 303,
[2006] Fam Law 258, (2005) Times, 11 November, [2005] All ER (D) 50 (Nov),
sub nom M (interim care order: removal), Re [2006] 1 FLR 1043 .... 8.110, 8.122
M (children) (transfer of proceedings to High Court), Re [2005] EWCA Civ 1712,
149 Sol Jo LB 1454, [2005] All ER (D) 305 (Nov) 5.73
M (residence), Re (2005). See M (children) (residence order), Re (2004)
M (interim care order: removal) (2006), Re. See M (children) (interim care order), Re
(2005)
M (a child) (care proceedings: witness summons), Re [2007] EWCA Civ 9,
[2007] 1 FCR 253, [2007] Fam Law 491, [2007] NLJR 142, [2007] All ER (D)
108 (Jan), sub nom LM (by her guardian) v Medway Council [2007] 1 FLR
1698 .... 4.49, 10.61, 11.48
M (a child), Re [2007] EWCA Civ 589, [2007] 2 FCR 797, [2007] 2 FLR 1006,
[2007] Fam Law 893, [2007] All ER (D) 257 (May) 11.39
M (children) (placement order), Re [2007] EWCA Civ 1084, [2008] 1 WLR 991,
[2007] 3 FCR 681, [2007] Fam Law 1124, 151 Sol Jo LB 1435, [2007] All ER
(D) 14 (Nov), sub nom M v Warwickshire County Council [2008] 1 FLR
1093 .... 2.7, 2.18, 8.100
M v Birmingham City Council [1995] 1 FCR 50, [1994] 2 FLR 141,
[1994] Fam Law 557 .... 8.52, 9.11
M v C [1993] 1 FCR 264, [1993] 2 FLR 584, [1993] Fam Law 616 .... 4.46, 5.103
M v C and Calderdale Metropolitan Borough Council. See C (minors), Re (1994)
M v Hampshire County Council. See Hampshire County Council v S
M v M [1973] 2 All ER 81, DC 3.24
M v M [1987] 1 WLR 404, [1988] FCR 39, [1987] 2 FLR 146, [1987] Fam Law
237, 131 Sol Jo 408, [1987] LS Gaz R 981, CA 2.43, 13.30
M v M [1990] FCR 80, [1989] 2 FLR 354, [1989] Fam Law 393, CA 13.30
M v M (minors) (jurisdiction) [1993] 1 FCR 5, [1993] Fam Law 396, CA 5.49
M v M (residence order: ancillary injunction) [1994] Fam Law 440 .... 5.99, 5.101
M v M (abduction: England and Scotland) [1997] 2 FLR 263, [1997] Fam Law
540, CA 2.27, 5.131
M v M (parental responsibility) [1999] 2 FLR 737, [1999] Fam Law 538 .... 3.65, 3.69
M v M (breaches of orders: committal) [2005] EWCA Civ 1722, [2006] 1 FLR 1154,
[2006] Fam Law 259 .... 2.18, 5.160, 5.170, 5.175
M v M [2005] EWHC 2769 (Fam), [2007] 1 FLR 251, [2005] All ER (D) 14 (Dec) 3.40,
5.98
M v Warwickshire County Council [1994] 2 FCR 121, [1994] 2 FLR 593,
[1994] Fam Law 611 .... 8.182
M v Warwickshire County Council. See M (children) (placement order), Re (2007)
M and B (children) (contact: domestic violence), Re [2001] 1 FCR 116, CA 5.93
M and H (children), Re [2006] EWCA Civ 499, 150 Sol Jo LB 400, sub nom M-H
(children) (sexual abuse), Re [2006] All ER (D) 132 (Mar) 5.74
M and J (wardship: supervision and residence order), Re [2003] EWHC 1585 (Fam),
[2003] 2 FLR 541 .... 8.166, 12.8, 12.9, 12.18, 12.29
M and K (child abuse: video evidence), Re [1996] 1 FCR 261, [1996] Fam Law 13,
sub nom M (care proceedings: police videos), Re [1995] 2 FLR 571 .... 11.55
M and R (minors) (sexual abuse: expert evidence), Re [1996] 4 All ER 239, sub nom
M and R (minors) (expert opinion: evidence), Re [1996] 2 FCR 617, sub nom
M and R (child abuse: evidence), Re [1996] 2 FLR 195, [1996] Fam Law
541, CA 2.56, 2.57, 11.8, 11.9, 11.11, 11.29, 11.30, 11.38, 11.56
MD and TD (minors) (time estimates), Re [1994] 2 FCR 94, [1994] 2 FLR 336,
[1994] Fam Law 488 .... 4.28, 4.59, 8.94, 8.142

PARA

MD and TD (minors) (No 2), Re [1994] Fam Law 489 .... 8.220
MH (child) (care proceedings: children's guardian) [2002] 1 WLR 189, [2002] 1 FCR
    251, [2001] 2 FLR 1334, [2001] Fam Law 869 .... 8.189
MH v GP. See Harris v Pinnington
M-H (children) (sexual abuse), Re. See M and H (children), Re
M-J (a child) (adoption order or special guardianship order), Re [2007] EWCA Civ
    56, [2007] 1 FCR 329, [2007] 1 FLR 691, [2007] Fam Law 389, [2007] All ER
    (D) 85 (Feb) 2.78, 5.234
MM (care order: abandoned baby), Re [1996] 2 FCR 521, sub nom M (care order:
    parental responsibility), Re [1996] 2 FLR 84, [1996] Fam Law 664 .... 8.29
M, T, P, K and B (care: change of name), Re [2000] 2 FLR 645 .... 8.175
Mabon v Mabon [2005] EWCA Civ 634, [2005] Fam 366, [2005] 3 WLR 460,
    [2005] 2 FCR 354, [2005] 2 FLR 1011, (2005) Times, 2 June, [2005] All ER
    (D) 419 (May) 10.4, 10.9, 10.51, 10.53, 11.57
McGinley and Egan v United Kingdom (Application 21825/93) (1998) 27 EHRR 1, 4
    BHRC 421, ECtHR 11.64
Manchester City Council v F [1993] 1 FCR 1000, [1993] 1 FLR 419n,
    [1993] Fam Law 29 .... 8.58
Manchester City Council v R [1996] 3 FCR 118, sub nom Manchester City Council
    v B [1996] 1 FLR 324, [1996] Fam Law 202 .... 11.38
Mantovanelli v France (Application 21497/93) (1997) 24 EHRR 370, ECtHR 7.19, 7.40,
    11.64
Marckx v Belgium (Application 6833/74) (1979) 2 EHRR 330, ECtHR 1.54, 5.75, 6.1
May v May [1986] 1 FLR 325, [1986] Fam Law 105, CA 2.37, 2.44
Meadow v General Medical Council [2006] EWCA Civ 1390, [2007] QB 462,
    [2007] 1 All ER 1, [2007] 2 WLR 286, [2007] ICR 701, [2006] 3 FCR 447,
    [2007] 1 FLR 1398, 92 BMLR 51, [2006] NLJR 1686, (2006) Times,
    31 October, [2006] All ER (D) 315 (Oct) 11.58
Medcalf v Mardell [2002] UKHL 27, [2003] 1 AC 120, [2002] 3 All ER 721,
    [2002] 3 WLR 172, [2002] 31 LS Gaz R 34, [2002] NLJR 1032, (2002) Times,
    28 June, [2002] All ER (D) 228 (Jun) 4.59
Medway Council v BBC [2002] 1 FLR 104, [2001] Fam Law 883, [2001] All ER (D)
    243 (Oct) 5.100
Merton London Borough Council v K [2005] EWHC 167 (Fam), [2005] 2 FLR 422,
    [2005] All ER (D) 414 (Feb) 8.99
Mir v Mir [1992] Fam 79, [1992] 1 All ER 765, [1992] 2 WLR 225, [1992] 1 FLR
    624, [1992] Fam Law 378, [1992] 4 LS Gaz R 33, 136 Sol Jo LB 10 .... 5.164
Moser v Austria (Application No 12643/02) [2006] 3 FCR 107, [2006] ECHR
    12643/02, ECtHR 4.52

N

N (a minor), Re [1991] FCR 1000, [1992] 1 FLR 134, [1992] Fam Law 149, CA 5.165
N (a minor) (sexual abuse: video evidence), Re [1996] 4 All ER 225, [1997] 1 WLR
    153, sub nom N (a minor) (child abuse: evidence), Re [1996] 2 FCR 572,
    [1996] 2 FLR 214, [1996] Fam Law 460, [1996] NLJR 715, CA 10.45, 11.29, 11.56
N (residence: hopeless appeals), Re [1996] 1 FCR 244, [1995] 2 FLR 230,
    [1995] Fam Law 600, CA 13.5
N (a minor) (residence order: appeal), Re [1996] 2 FCR 377, sub nom N
    (Section 91(14) order), Re [1996] 1 FLR 356, [1996] Fam Law 140, CA 5.204, 8.218
N (minors), Re (1999) unreported, Lexis Nexis 5.122
N (leave to withdraw care proceedings), Re [2000] 1 FCR 258, [2000] 1 FLR 134,
    [2000] Fam Law 12 .... 4.24, 8.227
N (a child) (contact: leave to defend and remove guardian), Re [2003] 1 FLR 652,
    [2003] Fam Law 154 .... 10.55
N (Section 91(14) order), Re. See N (a minor) (residence order: appeal), Re
N v B [1993] 1 FCR 231 .... 4.56, 5.15, 14.19
N v N (consent order: variation) [1994] 2 FCR 275, [1993] 2 FLR 868,
    [1993] Fam Law 676, CA 2.26

PARA

N-B (children) (residence: expert evidence), Re [2002] EWCA Civ 1052,
  [2002] 3 FCR 259, [2002] Fam Law 807, [2002] All ER (D) 51 (Jul), sub nom
  Re M (residence) [2002] 2 FLR 1059 .... 11.31
NW (a minor), Re [1994] 1 FCR 121, [1993] 2 FLR 591, [1993] Fam Law 617 .... 4.56
National Justice Cia Naviera SA v Prudential Assurance Co Ltd, The Ikarian Reefer
  [1993] 2 Lloyd's Rep 68, [1993] FSR 563, [1993] 2 EGLR 183, [1993] 37 EG
  158n; revsd [1995] 1 Lloyd's Rep 455, CA 11.46
Newham London Borough v AG [1992] 2 FCR 119, [1993] 1 FLR 281,
  [1993] Fam Law 122, CA, CA 7.67
Nielsen v Denmark (Application 10929/84) (1988) 11 EHRR 175, ECtHR 3.19, 9.3
North Yorkshire County Council v G [1994] 1 FCR 737, [1993] 2 FLR 732,
  [1993] Fam Law 623 .... 5.156, 8.99
North Yorkshire County Council v SA [2003] EWCA Civ 839, [2003] 3 FCR 118,
  [2003] 2 FLR 849, [2003] 35 LS Gaz R 34, [2003] All ER (D) 16 (Jul), sub
  nom A (a Child) (Care proceedings: Non-accidental injury), Re (2003) Times,
  22 August 8.48
North Yorkshire County Council v Selby Youth Court Justices [1994] 1 All ER 991,
  [1995] 1 WLR 1, 93 LGR 226, [1994] 2 FCR 1184, [1994] 2 FLR 169,
  [1994] Fam Law 490, DC 3.92
Northamptonshire County Council v Islington London Borough Council [2001] Fam
  364, [2000] 2 WLR 193, [2000] LGR 125, [1999] 3 FCR 385, [1999] 2 FLR
  881, [1999] Fam Law 687, [1999] All ER (D) 832, CA 8.170
Northamptonshire County Council v S [1993] Fam 136, [1992] 3 WLR 1010,
  [1993] 1 FCR 351, [1993] 1 FLR 554, [1993] Fam Law 274 .... 8.32, 8.39
Nottinghamshire County Council v H [1995] 2 FCR 365, [1995] 1 FLR 115,
  [1995] Fam Law 63 .... 10.47, 11.68
Nottinghamshire County Council v J (26 November 1993, unreported) 6.54
Nottinghamshire County Council v P [1994] Fam 18, [1993] 3 WLR 637, 92 LGR
  72, [1994] 1 FCR 624, [1993] 2 FLR 134, [1993] 26 LS Gaz R 37, 137 Sol Jo
  LB 147, sub nom Nottinghamshire County Council v P; Re P (minors)
  [1993] 3 All ER 815, CA 3.25, 5.62, 5.103, 5.105, 5.121, 5.125, 5.206, 5.208, 7.30,
  8.17, 8.87, 12.5

O

O (infants), Re [1962] 2 All ER 10, [1962] 1 WLR 724, 106 Sol Jo 429, CA 2.37
O (a minor), Re [1992] 4 All ER 905, [1992] 1 WLR 912, [1992] 1 FCR 489,
  [1992] 2 FLR 7, [1992] Fam Law 487, [1992] 21 LS Gaz R 26 ... 4.57, 8.41, 8.45, 8.226,
  13.28
O (minors) (medical examination), Re [1992] 2 FCR 394, [1993] 1 FLR 860,
  [1993] Fam Law 473, [1993] NLJR 814 .... 8.113, 8.117, 13.2
O (a minor) (medical treatment), Re [1993] 1 FCR 925, [1993] 2 FLR 149,
  [1993] Fam Law 454, [1993] 4 Med LR 272, 19 BMLR 148, 137 Sol Jo LB
  107 .... 12.36, 12.38
O (minors) (leave to seek residence order), Re [1993] 2 FCR 482, [1994] 1 FLR 172,
  [1994] Fam Law 127 .... 4.26, 5.25, 5.158
O, Re [1995] 1 FCR 721, [1994] 2 FLR 349, [1994] Fam Law 482 .... 5.27
O (a minor) (contact: imposition of conditions), Re [1996] 1 FCR 317, [1995] 2 FLR
  124, [1995] Fam Law 541, CA 5.79, 5.84, 5.120
O (a minor) (legal aid costs), Re [1997] 1 FCR 159, sub nom O (costs: liability of
  Legal Aid Board), Re [1997] 1 FLR 465, CA 13.5
O (care or supervision order), Re [1997] 2 FCR 17, [1996] 2 FLR 755,
  [1997] Fam Law 87 .... 8.164
O (family appeals: management), Re [1998] 3 FCR 226, [1998] Fam Law 191,
  [1998] 1 FLR 431n, CA 12.24
O (care: discharge of care order), Re [1999] 2 FLR 119, [1999] Fam Law 442 .... 8.220
O (a child) (blood tests: constraint), Re [2000] Fam 139, [2000] 2 All ER 29,
  [2000] 2 WLR 1284, [2000] 1 FCR 330, [2000] 1 FLR 418, [2000] Fam Law
  324, 55 BMLR 229, [2000] 06 LS Gaz R 35, 144 Sol Jo LB 85 .... 12.32

PARA

O (a child) (supervision order: future harm), Re [2001] EWCA Civ 16, [2001] 1 FCR
    289, [2001] 1 FLR 923, [2001] Fam Law 336, [2001] All ER (D) 52 (Jan) 2.78, 8.165
O (care proceedings: evidence), Re [2003] EWHC 2011 (Fam), [2004] 1 FLR 161,
    [2004] Fam Law 16, [2003] 39 LS Gaz R 37, (2003) Times, 26 September ... 10.62, 11.48
O (a child) (contact: withdrawal of application), Re [2003] EWHC 3031 (Fam),
    [2004] 1 FCR 687, [2004] 1 FLR 1258, [2004] Fam Law 492, (2004) Times,
    13 January, [2003] All ER (D) 226 (Dec) 5.78, 5.81, 5.82
O (children) (hearing in private: assistance), Re [2005] EWCA Civ 759, [2006] Fam
    1, [2005] 3 WLR 1191, [2005] 2 FCR 563, [2005] 2 FLR 967, [2005] Fam Law
    773, (2005) Times, 27 June, [2005] All ER (D) 238 (Jun) 4.13
O (costs: liability of Legal Aid Board), Re. See O (a minor) (legal aid costs), Re
    (1997)
O v United Kingdom (Application 9276/81) (1987) 10 EHRR 82, ECtHR 1.7
O and N (children) (non-accidental injury: burden of proof), Re [2002] EWCA Civ
    1271, [2002] 3 FCR 418, [2002] Fam Law 1181, [2002] All ER (D) 401 (Jul),
    sub nom Re O and N (care: preliminary hearing) [2002] 2 FLR 1167; on appeal
    sub nom O and N (children) (non accidental injury), Re [2003] UKHL 18,
    [2004] 1 AC 523, [2003] 2 All ER 305, [2003] 2 WLR 1075, [2003] 1 FCR
    673, [2003] 1 FLR 1169, [2003] 23 LS Gaz R 36, (2003) Times, 4 April, [2003]
    All ER (D) 64 (Apr) 2.3, 2.11, 2.56, 8.48, 8.144
O'Connell, Re[2007] 1 FLR 530, sub nom Re O (Children) (2006) Times,
    6 October, CA 5.204
Official Solicitor to the Supreme Court v K [1965] AC 201, [1963] 3 All ER 191,
    [1963] 3 WLR 408, 107 Sol Jo 616, HL 2.22, 11.71
Oldham Metropolitan Borough Council v E. See A (a minor), Re (1994)
Omychund v Barker (1745) 1 Atk 21, sub nom Omichund v Barker 2 Eq Cas Abr
    397, Willes 538, sub nom Ormichund v Barker 1 Wils 84 .... 11.23
Osman v United Kingdom (1998) 29 EHRR 245, [1999] 1 FLR 193,
    [1999] Fam Law 86, [1999] Crim LR 82, 5 BHRC 293, ECtHR 13.75
Oxfordshire County Council v L [1998] 1 FLR 70, [1998] Fam Law 22 .... 8.164
Oxfordshire County Council v L and F [1997] 3 FCR 124, [1997] 1 FLR 235,
    [1997] Fam Law 249 .... 10.38, 11.89
Oxfordshire County Council v M [1994] Fam 151, [1994] 2 All ER 269,
    [1994] 2 WLR 393, [1994] 1 FCR 753, [1994] 1 FLR 175, CA 4.1, 11.74
Oxfordshire County Council v P [1995] Fam 161, [1995] 2 All ER 225,
    [1995] 2 WLR 543, [1995] 2 FCR 212, [1995] 1 FLR 552, [1995] Fam Law
    294 .... 11.78, 11.86
Oxfordshire County Council v S [2000] Fam Law 20, (1999) Times, 11 November 3.90,
    8.178
Oxfordshire County Council v S [2003] EWHC 2174 (Fam), [2004] 1 FLR 426,
    [2004] Fam Law 15, sub nom A local authority v S (children) (interim care
    order: justices' reasons) [2004] All ER (D) 270 (Mar) 8.109

P

P (infants), Re [1962] 3 All ER 789, [1962] 1 WLR 1296, 60 LGR 532, 127 JP 18,
    106 Sol Jo 630 .... 3.22
P (A J) (an infant), Re [1968] 1 WLR 1976, 112 Sol Jo 861 .... 12.31
P (minors), Re [1990] 1 WLR 613, [1990] FCR 909, [1990] 2 FLR 223,
    [1990] Fam Law 399, 134 Sol Jo 661, CA 5.33, 5.165
P, Re (1991). See, R v B County Council, ex p P
P (a minor), Re [1992] 1 FCR 145, [1992] 1 FLR 316, [1992] Fam Law 108, CA 2.42
P (minors), Re [1992] 2 FCR 681, CA 2.43, 10.12
P (a minor), Re [1993] 2 FCR 417, [1993] 1 FLR 915, [1993] Fam Law 462, CA ... 5.28, 5.29
P (minors) (contact with children in care), Re [1993] 2 FLR 156, [1993] Fam Law
    394 .... 8.201
P (minors), Re. (1993) See Cheshire County Council v P
P (a minor), Re [1994] 2 FCR 1093, sub nom sub nom C v Salford City Council
    [1994] 2 FLR 926, [1995] Fam Law 65 .... 5.138, 5.147, 12.11, 12.43

PARA

P (a minor) (parental responsibility order), Re [1994] 1 FLR 578, [1994] Fam Law
378 .... 2.70, 3.67, 3.70, 3.74
P (terminating parental responsibility), Re [1995] 3 FCR 753, [1995] 1 FLR 1048,
[1995] Fam Law 471 .... 3.69, 3.80
P (minors) (representation), Re [1996] 1 FCR 457, [1996] 1 FLR 486,
[1996] Fam Law 274, CA 10.42, 10.50
P (a minor) (abduction: declaration), Re [1996] 2 FCR 133, [1995] 1 FLR 831,
[1995] Fam Law 398, CA 5.16
P (a minor) (inadequate welfare report), Re [1996] 2 FCR 285, sub nom P (welfare
officer: duty), Re [1996] Fam Law 664 .... 10.26
P (emergency protection order), Re [1996] 3 FCR 637, [1996] 1 FLR 482,
[1996] Fam Law 273 .... 7.97, 13.4
P (sexual abuse: standard of proof), Re [1996] 3 FCR 714, [1996] 2 FLR 333,
[1996] Fam Law 531, CA 2.56
P (welfare officer: duty), Re (1996). See P (a minor) (inadequate welfare report), Re
(1996)
P (minors) (contact: parental hostility), Re [1997] 1 FCR 458, sub nom P (contact:
supervision), Re [1996] 2 FLR 314, CA 5.84, 5.87
P (a minor) (care proceedings: witness summons), Re [1997] 3 FCR 322,
[1997] 2 FLR 447, CA 2.18, 10.61, 11.48
P (parental responsibility: change of name), Re [1997] 3 FCR 739, [1997] 2 FLR
722, [1997] Fam Law 723, CA 3.69, 5.38
P (contact: supervision), Re (1997). See P (minors) (contact: parental hostility), Re
(1997)
P (a minor) (care order: designated local authority), Re [1998] 1 FCR 653,
[1998] 1 FLR 80, [1998] Fam Law 20 .... 8.170
P (minors) (diplomatic immunity), Re [1998] 2 FCR 480, [1998] 1 FLR 624,
[1998] Fam Law 12 .... 2.28, 5.130, 10.4
P (parental responsibility), Re [1998] 3 FCR 98, [1998] 2 FLR 96, [1998] Fam Law
461, CA 3.69
P (minors) (contact: discretion), Re [1999] 1 FCR 566, [1998] 2 FLR 696,
[1998] Fam Law 585, [1998] 34 LS Gaz R 32, 142 Sol Jo LB 214 .... 5.55, 5.87, 5.90
P (contact: indirect contact), Re [1999] 2 FLR 893, [1999] Fam Law 751 .... 5.55
P (a minor) (residence order: child's welfare), Re [2000] Fam 15, [1999] 3 All ER
734, [1999] 3 WLR 1164, [1999] 2 FCR 289, [1999] Fam Law 531,
[1999] 21 LS Gaz R 38, [1999] NLJR 719, 143 Sol Jo LB 141, sub nom P
(Section 91(14) guidelines) (residence and religious heritage), Re [1999] 2 FLR
573, CA 2.10, 2.12, 2.54, 3.42, 5.202, 5.203, 5.204
P (care orders: injunctive relief), Re [2000] 3 FCR 426, [2000] 2 FLR 385,
[2000] Fam Law 696 .... 7.3, 7.105, 7.106, 8.173, 12.25, 12.35, 12.36
P (a child) (Children Act 1989, ss 22 and 26: local authority compliance)
[2000] 2 FLR 910, [2000] Fam Law 792 .... 2.15, 2.18, 5.202, 13.64
P (Care Proceedings: Father's Application to be joined as Party), Re [2001] 3 FCR
279, [2001] 1 FLR 781 .... 4.25, 8.98
P (a child) (residence: grandmother's application for leave), Re [2002] EWCA Civ
846, [2002] All ER (D) 554 (May) 8.100, 8.204
P (parental dispute: judicial determination), Re [2002] EWCA Civ 1627,
[2003] 1 FLR 286, [2003] Fam Law 80, (2002) Times, 5 November, [2002] All
ER (D) 80 (Oct) 3.40, 5.98
P (children) (shared residence order), Re [2005] EWCA Civ 1639, [2006] 1 FCR 309,
[2006] 2 FLR 347, [2006] Fam Law 447, [2005] All ER (D) 116 (Nov) 5.20
P (a child) (adoption order: leave to oppose making of adoption order), Re
[2007] EWCA Civ 616, [2007] 1 WLR 2556, [2007] 2 FCR 407, [2007] 2 FLR
1069, [2007] Fam Law 889, (2007) Times, 29 June, 151 Sol Jo LB 894, [2007]
All ER (D) 334 (Jun) 2.7
P (residence: appeal), Re [2007] EWCA Civ 1053, [2008] 1 FLR 198, sub nom N (a
child) (residence order), Re [2007] All ER (D) 404 (Jul) 12.18
P (surrogacy: residence), Re [2008] 1 FLR 177 .... 12.18
P (children) (adoption: parental consent), Re [2008] EWCA Civ 535, [2008] 2 FCR
185, [2008] All ER (D) 265 (May), sub nom SB v X County Council (2008)
Times, 29 May 5.221

PARA

P (Section 91(14) guidelines) (residence and religious heritage), Re. See P (a minor) (residence order: child's welfare), Re (2000)

P v Bradford Metropolitan Borough Council [1996] 2 FCR 227, sub nom S and P (discharge of care order), Re [1995] 2 FLR 782, [1996] Fam Law 11 .... 8.222

P v P [2006] EWHC 2410 (Fam), [2007] 2 FLR 439, [2007] Fam Law 599 .... 12.21

P v W [1984] Fam 32, [1984] 1 All ER 866, [1984] 2 WLR 439, 128 Sol Jo 171, sub nom Patterson v Walcott [1984] FLR 408, [1984] Fam Law 209, 148 JP 161, DC 5.174

P-B (hearings in open court), Re [1997] 1 All ER 58, [1996] 3 FCR 705, [1996] 2 FLR 765, [1996] Fam Law 606, CA 4.47

P-B (a child) (placement order), Re [2006] EWCA Civ 1016, [2007] 3 FCR 308, [2007] 1 FLR 1106, [2006] All ER (D) 64 (Nov) 8.169

PC (change of surname), Re. See C (minors) (change of surname), Re (1997)

P, C and S v United Kingdom (Application 56547/00) (2002) 35 EHRR 1075, [2002] 3 FCR 1, [2002] 2 FLR 631, [2002] Fam Law 811, 12 BHRC 615, (2002) Times, 16 August, [2002] All ER (D) 239 (Jul), ECtHR 6.60, 7.19, 7.40, 7.72, 8.56, 8.98

Palau-Martinez v France (Application 64927/01) [2004] 2 FLR 810, [2004] Fam Law 412, ECtHR 2.50, 3.42

Paton v British Pregnancy Advisory Service Trustees [1979] QB 276, [1978] 2 All ER 987, [1978] 3 WLR 687, 142 JP 497, 122 Sol Jo 744 .... 3.93

Patterson v Walcott. See P v W

Payne v Payne [2001] EWCA Civ 166, [2001] Fam 473, [2001] 2 WLR 1826, [2001] 1 FCR 425, [2001] 1 FLR 1052, [2001] Fam Law 346, [2001] All ER (D) 142 (Feb) 1.54, 2.4, 2.10, 2.40, 5.43, 5.44, 5.48

Pearson v Franklin [1994] 2 All ER 137, [1994] 1 WLR 370, [1994] 2 FCR 545, [1994] 1 FLR 246, [1994] Fam Law 379, CA 12.33

Pelling v Bruce-Williams [2004] EWCA Civ 845, [2004] Fam 155, [2004] 3 All ER 875, [2004] 3 WLR 1178, [2004] 3 FCR 108, [2004] 2 FLR 823, [2004] Fam Law 784, [2004] All ER (D) 15 (Jul) 4.47

Phelps v London Borough of Hillingdon [2001] 2 AC 619, [2000] 4 All ER 504, [2000] 3 WLR 776, [2000] LGR 651, [2000] 3 FCR 102, [2000] ELR 499, 56 BMLR 1, [2000] NLJR 1198, 144 Sol Jo LB 241, [2000] All ER (D) 1076, HL 13.77

Pierce v Doncaster Metropolitan Borough Council [2007] EWHC 2968 (QB), [2008] 1 FCR 122, [2008] 1 FLR 922, 100 BMLR 76, [2007] All ER (D) 188 (Dec) 13.83

Poplar Housing and Regeneration Community Association Ltd v Donoghue [2001] EWCA Civ 595, [2002] QB 48, [2001] 4 All ER 604, [2001] 3 WLR 183, 33 HLR 823, 145 Sol Jo LB 122, [2001] 3 FCR 74, [2001] 2 FLR 284, [2001] Fam Law 588, [2001] 19 LS Gaz R 38, [2001] 19 EG 141 (CS), [2001] All ER (D) 210 (Apr) 1,50, 1.52

Portsmouth NHS Trust v Wyatt. See Wyatt, Re

Practice Direction (disclosure of addresses by government departments) [1989] 1 All ER 765, [1989] 1 WLR 219 .... 12.20

Practice Direction (appeals from magistrates' courts) [1992] 1 All ER 864, [1992] 1 WLR 261, [1992] 1 FLR 563 .... 13.9

Practice Direction (distribution and transfer between the High Court and County Courts of Family business and family proceedings) [1992] 2 All ER 151, [1992] 1 WLR 586, [1992] 2 FLR 87 .... 8.96

Practice Direction (applications by children: leave) [1993] 1 All ER 820, [1993] 1 WLR 313, [1993] 1 FLR 668 .... 4.40, 5.149

Practice Direction (children's cases: time estimates) [1994] 1 All ER 155, [1994] 1 WLR 16, [1994] 1 FLR 108 .... 4.59

Practice Direction (minor: change of surname: deed poll) [1995] 1 All ER 832, [1995] 1 WLR 365 .... 5.31

Practice Direction (family proceedings: allocation to judiciary 1999) [1999] 2 FLR 799 .... 4.11

Practice Direction (family proceedings: court bundles) [2000] 1 FCR 521, [2000] 1 FLR 536 .... 11.14

PARA

Practice Direction (Human Rights Act 1998: citation of authorities) [2000] 2 FCR
768, [2000] 2 FLR 429 .... 4.40
Practice Direction (judicial continuity) [2002] 3 All ER 603, [2002] 1 WLR 2183,
[2002] 2 FCR 667, [2002] 2 FLR 367 .... 8.144, 11.14
Practice Direction (criminal: consolidated) [2002] 3 All ER 904, [2002] 1 WLR
2870 .... 4.10
Practice Direction (family proceedings: allocation to judiciary (amendment) 2002)
[2002] 2 FLR 692, [2002] Fam Law 769 .... 4.11
Practice Direction (guide to case management in public law proceedings)
[2003] 1 WLR 737, [2003] 1 FLR 719 .... 4.12, 4.19, 4.24, 4.27, 4.29, 4.31, 4.33
Practice Direction (family proceedings: allocation to judiciary (amendment) 2003)
[2003] 2 FLR 373 .... 4.11
Practice Direction (protocol for judicial case management in public law Children Act
Cases) [2003] 2 FLR 719 .... 7.6, 7.28, 7.30, 8.8, 8.83
Practice Direction (care cases: judicial continuity and case management)
[2003] 1 WLR 2209, [2003] 2 FLR 798 .... 8.10
Practice Direction (family proceedings: representation of children) [2004] 2 FCR
123 .... 4.50
Practice Direction (family proceedings: court bundles) [2006] 2 FCR 833 .... 4.31, 4.59
Practice Direction (family proceedings: allocation to judiciary (amendment) 2005)
[2006] 1 FLR 1147 .... 4.11
Practice Direction (family proceedings: allocation to judiciary (amendment No 2)
2005) [2006] 1 FLR 1150 .... 4.11
Practice Direction (family proceedings: allocation to judiciary (amendment) 2007)
[2007] 1 FLR 1150 .... 4.11
Practice Direction (Children Act 1989: risk assessments under section 16A)
[2007] 2 FLR 625 .... 5.12
Practice Direction (family assistance orders: consultation) [2007] 2 FLR 626, [2007]
All ER (D) 59 (Sep) 5.195
Practice Direction (residence and contact orders) [2008] 2 FCR 273, [2008] 2 FLR
103 .... 4.22, 4.29, 4.42, 4.56
Practice Direction (residence and contact orders: domestic violence) [2008] 1 WLR
1062 .... 2.55, 5.12, 5.61, 5.62, 5.74, 5.76, 5.92, 5.120
Practice Note (child: abduction: press publicity) [1980] 2 All ER 806 .... 12.20
Practice Note (sterilisation: minors and mental health patients) [1993] 3 All ER 222,
[1993] 2 FLR 222 .... 3.29, 5.97
Practice Note (case management) [1995] 1 All ER 586, [1995] 1 WLR 332,
[1995] 2 FCR 340, [1995] 1 FLR 456 .... 4.1, 4.45, 4.46, 4.51, 4.59, 11.14, 11.36, 11.59
Practice Note (official solicitor: sterilisation) [1996] 3 FCR 94, [1996] 2 FLR 111,
[1996] Fam Law 439 .... 4.40
Practice Note (procedure) [1999] 1 All ER 186, CA 13.5
Practice Note (devolution issues: Wales) [1999] 3 All ER 466, [1999] 1 WLR 1592,
[1999] 2 Cr App Rep 486 .... 2.60
Practice Note (CAFCASS: appointment in family proceedings) [2001] 2 FCR 562,
[2001] 2 FLR 151 .... 10.54, 10.58, 12.15
Practice Note (official solicitor: appointment in family proceedings) [2001] 2 FCR
566, [2001] 2 FLR 155 .... 10.54, 10.59, 12.15
Practice Note (CAFCASS and National Assembly for Wales: appointment of
guardians in private law proceedigns [2006] 2 FLR 143 .... 10.32
President's Direction (representation of children in family proceedings pursuant to
family proceedings rules 1991, rule 9.5) [2004] 1 FLR 1188, HC 10.32
President's Guidance: McKenzie Friends [2005] Fam Law 405 .... 4.13
Procedural Directive [1992] 2 FCR 601, [1992] 2 FLR 503 .... 13.9

Q

Q (contact: natural father), Re [2001] All ER (D) 172 (Apr) 5.93
Q v Q (costs: summary assessment) [2002] 2 FLR 668, [2002] Fam Law 804,
[2002] 32 LS Gaz R 33 .... 2.18
Quinn v Quinn (1983) 4 FLR 394, 126 Sol Jo 481, 133 NLJ 615, CA 12.33

PARA

R

R (MJ) (publication of transcript), Re [1975] Fam 89, [1975] 2 All ER 749,
    [1975] 2 WLR 978, 5 Fam Law 154, 119 Sol Jo 338 .... 12.20
R (a minor), Re [1988] FCR 497, [1988] 1 FLR 206, [1988] Fam Law 129, CA 2.55
R (a minor) (expert's evidence), Re (1991). See J (child abuse; expert evidence), Re
    (1991)
R (a minor), Re [1992] Fam 11, [1991] 4 All ER 177, [1991] 3 WLR 592,
    [1992] 2 FCR 229, [1992] 1 FLR 190, [1992] Fam Law 67, [1992] 3 Med LR
    342, 7 BMLR 147, [1991] NLJR 1297, CA 3.26, 3.33, 3.95, 12.30
R, Re (1992). See EW, Re
R (a minor), Re [1993] 1 FCR 954, [1993] 2 FLR 762, [1993] Fam Law 570, CA 5.83
R (a minor), Re [1993] 2 FCR 525, [1993] 2 FLR 163, [1993] Fam Law 460, CA 2.43,
    2.50, 2.51, 5.108, 5.201, 10.64, 11.57, 13.4
R (a minor), (medical treatment) Re [1993] 2 FCR 544, 15 BMLR 72, sub nom Re R
    (a minor) (blood transfusion) [1993] 2 FLR 757, sub nom Camden London
    Borough Council v R (a minor) 91 LGR 623, 137 Sol Jo LB 151 .... 3.35, 5.98, 5.107,
    12.36, 12.38
R (a minor) (discolsure of privileged material), Re (1993). See Essex County Council
    v R
R, Re (1993). See EW (No 2), Re
R (a minor), Re [1994] Fam 254, [1994] 3 All ER 658, [1994] 3 WLR 36,
    [1994] 2 FCR 468, [1994] 2 FLR 637, [1994] Fam Law 623, CA 12.30
R (a minor), Re [1994] 2 All ER 144, [1994] 1 WLR 487, [1994] 2 FCR 629,
    [1994] 2 FLR 185, [1994] Fam Law 435, CA 12.9
R (minors), Re [1994] 2 FCR 136, sub nom J (minors), Re [1994] 1 FLR 253,
    [1994] Fam Law 248 .... 8.60, 8.152
R (a minor), Re [1995] 1 WLR 184, [1994] 2 FCR 1251, [1995] 1 FLR 123,
    [1995] Fam Law 123, CA 13.3
R (minors), Re [1995] 1 FCR 563, sub nom F and R (Section 8 order: grandparents'
    application), Re [1995] 1 FLR 524, [1995] Fam Law 235 .... 4.53
R, Re [1995] 2 FCR 573, [1995] 1 FLR 451, [1995] Fam Law 237 .... 11.36, 11.55
R (care orders: jurisdiction), Re [1995] 3 FCR 305, [1995] 1 FLR 711,
    [1995] Fam Law 292 ....4.6, 8.18
R (a minor), Re [1995] 3 FCR 334, [1995] 2 FLR 612, [1995] Fam Law 601, CA 2.38
R (a minor) (legal aid: costs), Re [1997] 1 FCR 613, sub nom R v R (costs: child
    case) [1997] 2 FLR 95, [1997] Fam Law 391, [1997] 06 LS Gaz R 27, CA 4.58
R (a minor) (leave to make applications), Re [1998] 2 FCR 129, [1998] Fam Law
    247, sub nom R (residence: contact: restricting applications), Re [1998] 1 FLR
    749, CA 2.12, 5.202, 5.203, 8.218
R (recovery order), Re [1998] 3 FCR 321, [1998] 2 FLR 401, [1998] Fam Law
    401 .... 7.104, 13.43, 13.46
R (care proceedings: adjournment), Re [1998] 3 FCR 654, [1998] 2 FLR 390,
    [1998] Fam Law 454, CA 8.60, 8.152
R (residence: contact: restricting applications), Re (1998). See R (a minor) (leave to
    make applications), Re (1998)
R (inter-country adoption), Re [1999] 1 FCR 385, [1999] 1 FLR 1014,
    [1999] Fam Law 289 .... 12.24
R (adoption: disclosure), Re [1999] 3 FCR 334, [1999] 2 FLR 1123,
    [1999] Fam Law 806 .... 8.59
R (care proceedings: disclosure) [2000] 2 FLR 751,CA 10.47, 11.65
R (Surname: Using Both Parents'), Re [2001] EWCA Civ 1344, [2002] 1 FCR 170,
    [2001] 2 FLR 1358, [2002] Fam Law 9, [2001] All ER (D) 241 (Oct) 5.31, 5.36
R (care: disclosure: nature of proceedings), Re [2002] 1 FLR 755 .... 4.1, 4.12, 11.41, 11.42,
    11.61, 11.62, 11.67, 11.100
R (residence: shared care: children's views), Re [2005] EWCA Civ 542, [2006] 1 FLR
    491, 149 Sol Jo LB 510, sub nom R (children) (shared residence order), Re
    [2005] All ER (D) 238 (Apr) 2.70, 5.20, 5.21
R (a child) (adoption: contact), Re [2005] EWCA Civ 1128, [2007] 1 FCR 149,
    [2006] 1 FLR 373, (2005) Times, 15 September, [2005] All ER (D) 78 (Aug) 5.152
R (care: plan for adoption: best interest), Re [2006] 1 FLR 483 .... 13.10

PARA

R (children) (care proceedings: maternal grandmother's applications), Re
    [2007] EWCA Civ 139, [2007] 1 FCR 439, [2007] All ER (D) 349 (Feb) 5.234
R (a child) (contact), Re [2007] EWCA Civ 943, [2007] All ER (D) 46 (Aug) 5.61
R (a child) (special guardianship order), Re (2007). See Birmingham City Council v R
R v A [2001] UKHL 25, [2002] 1 AC 45, [2001] 3 All ER 1, [2001] 2 WLR 1546,
    [2001] 2 Cr App Rep 351, 165 JP 609, [2001] Crim LR 908, (2001) Times,
    May 24, [2002] 1 LRC 347, [2001] UKHRR 825, [2001] All ER (D) 222
    (May), 11 BHRC 225 .... 1.50
R v Avon County Council, ex p Crabtree [1996] 3 FCR 773, [1996] 1 FLR 502,
    [1996] Fam Law 277, CA 13.47, 13.50
R v B County Council, ex p P [1991] 2 All ER 65, [1991] 1 WLR 221, [1991] 1 FLR
    470, [1991] Fam Law 313, sub nom Re P [1991] FCR 337, [1991] NLJR
    163, CA 10.27, 10.61, 11.22, 11.48
R v Barnet London Borough Council, ex p B [1994] 2 FCR 781, [1994] 1 FLR 592,
    [1994] ELR 357 .... 6.23, 13.39, 13.53, 13.65
R v Birmingham City Council, ex p A [1997] 2 FCR 357, [1997] 2 FLR 841 ..... 13.43, 13.46,
                                      13.50, 13.57, 13.58
R v Birmingham Juvenile Court, ex p G (minors) [1988] 3 All ER 726,
    [1988] 1 WLR 950, [1989] FCR 22, [1988] 2 FLR 423, [1988] Fam Law 469,
    132 Sol Jo 1117, [1988] NLJR 143; affd [1990] 2 QB 573, [1989] 3 All ER
    336, [1989] 3 WLR 1024, 87 LGR 798, [1989] FCR 460, [1989] 2 FLR 454,
    [1990] Fam Law 134, CA 8.227
R v Birmingham Juvenile Court, ex p R (a minor) [1988] 3 All ER 726,
    [1988] 1 WLR 950, [1989] FCR 22, [1988] 2 FLR 423, [1988] Fam Law 469,
    132 Sol Jo 1117, [1988] NLJR 143; affd [1990] 2 QB 573, [1989] 3 All ER
    336, [1989] 3 WLR 1024, 87 LGR 798, [1989] FCR 460, [1989] 2 FLR 454,
    [1990] Fam Law 134, CA 8.227
R v Brent London Borough, ex p S [1994] 2 FCR 996, [1994] 1 FLR 203,
    [1994] Fam Law 249, CA 6.25, 13.50, 13.61, 13.64, 13.65
R v Bubb (1850) 14 JP 562, 4 Cox CC 455 .... 3.21
R v Calder Justices, ex p C (4 May 1993, unreported) 9.10
R v Cannings [2004] EWCA Crim 01, [2004] 1 All ER 725, [2004] 1 WLR 2607,
    [2004] 2 Cr App Rep 63, [2004] 1 FCR 193, [2005] Crim LR 126,
    [2004] 05 LS Gaz R 27, (2004) Times, 23 January, [2004] All ER (D) 124
    (Jan) 11.58
R v Central Criminal Court, ex p S [1999] 1 FLR 480, [1999] Fam Law 93, 163 JP
    776, [1999] Crim LR 159 .... 10.4
R v Central Independent Television plc [1994] Fam 192, [1994] 3 All ER 641,
    [1994] 3 WLR 20, [1995] 1 FCR 521, [1994] 2 FLR 151, [1994] Fam Law
    500, CA 2.21, 12.30
R v Chattaway (1922) 17 Cr App Rep 7, CCA 3.21
R v Chief Constable of Cheshire, ex p K [1990] FCR 201, [1990] 1 FLR 70,
    [1990] Fam Law 17 .... 5.161
R v Chief Constable of North Wales Police, ex p Thorpe [1999] QB 396,
    [1998] 2 FLR 571, [1998] Fam Law 529, sub nom R v Chief Constable of
    North Wales Police, ex p AB [1998] 3 All ER 310, [1998] 3 WLR 57,
    [1998] 3 FCR 371, [1998] 17 LS Gaz R 29, CA 11.96, 13.41
R v Chief Constable of Nottinghamshire Constabulary, ex p Sunderland [1995] 1 AC
    274, [1994] 3 All ER 420, [1994] 3 WLR 433, 159 LG Rev 181,
    [1994] 40 LS Gaz R 35, [1994] NLJR 1008, 138 Sol Jo LB 156, HL 11.62, 11.63
R v Chief Constable of West Midlands Police, ex p Wiley [1995] 1 AC 274,
    [1994] 3 All ER 420, [1994] 3 WLR 433, 159 LG Rev 181, [1995] 1 Cr
    App Rep 342, [1994] 40 LS Gaz R 35, [1994] NLJR 1008, 138 Sol Jo LB
    156, HL 11.62, 11.63
R v Children and Family Court Advisory and Support Service [2003] EWHC 235
    (Admin), [2003] 1 FLR 953, [2003] Fam Law 392, [2003] 11 LS Gaz R 31,
    (2003) Times, 24 January, [2003] All ER (D) 102 (Jan) 2.63, 10.39
R v Cornwall County Council, ex p E [1999] 2 FCR 685, [1999] 1 FLR 1055,
    [1999] Fam Law 291, CA 13.50

Table of Cases

PARA

R v Cornwall County Council, ex p L [2000] LGR 180, [2000] 1 FCR 460,
  [2000] 1 FLR 236, [2000] Fam Law 89, [1999] 45 LS Gaz R 31, 143 Sol Jo LB
  282, [1999] All ER (D) 1216 .... 13.39, 13.48, 13.50
R v D [1984] AC 778, [1984] 2 All ER 449, [1984] 3 WLR 186, 79 Cr App Rep
  313, [1984] FLR 847, [1984] Fam Law 311, [1984] Crim LR 558, 128 Sol Jo
  469, [1984] LS Gaz R 2458, HL 3.19
R v D [2005] EWCA Crim 3660, [2006] 2 All ER 726, [2006] 2 Cr App Rep (S)
  204, [2006] Crim LR 364, (2006) Times, 3 January , [2005] All ER (D) 254
  (Dec), sub nom R v D (sexual offences: prevention order) [2006] 1 WLR 1088,
  [2006] 1 FLR 1085, [2006] Fam Law 273 .... 5.88
R v Derby Magistrates' Court, ex p B [1996] AC 487, [1995] 4 All ER 526,
  [1995] 3 WLR 681, [1996] 1 Cr App Rep 385, [1996] 1 FLR 513,
  [1996] Fam Law 210, 159 JP 785, [1996] Crim LR 190, [1995] NLJR 1575,
  139 Sol Jo LB 219, HL 2.23, 11.75
R v Derriviere (1969) 53 Cr App Rep 637, CA 3.20
R v Devon County Council, ex p L [1991] FCR 599, [1991] 2 FLR 541,
  [1991] Fam Law 369 .... 13.41
R v Devon County Council, ex p O [1997] 3 FCR 411, [1997] 2 FLR 388,
  [1997] Fam Law 390 .... 13.47, 13.50
R v East Berkshire Health Authority, ex p Walsh [1985] QB 152, [1984] 3 All ER
  425, [1984] 3 WLR 818, [1984] ICR 743, [1984] IRLR 278, CA 13.38
R v East Sussex County Council, ex p W [1999] 1 FCR 536, [1998] 2 FLR 1082,
  [1998] Fam Law 736, [1998] All ER (D) 359 ..... 8.63, 13.43, 13.46, 13.50, 13.57, 13.58
R v Exeter Juvenile Court, ex p RKH [1988] FCR 474, [1988] 2 FLR 214,
  [1988] Fam Law 334 .... 8.106
R v Gibbins and Proctor (1918) 13 Cr App Rep 134, 82 JP 287, CCA 3.21
R v Gwynedd County Council, ex p B [1992] 3 All ER 317, [1991] 2 FLR 365,
  [1991] Fam Law 377, 7 BMLR 120, sub nom Re B [1991] FCR 800, CA 3.13, 3.94,
                                                                         3.127, 5.236
R v H [2004] UKHL 03, [2004] 2 AC 134, [2004] 1 All ER 1269, [2004] 2 WLR
  335, [2004] 2 Cr App Rep 179, [2004] Crim LR 861, [2004] 08 LS Gaz R 29,
  (2004) Times, 6 February, 148 Sol Jo LB 183, [2004] 5 LRC 293, 16 BHRC
  332, [2004] All ER (D) 71 (Feb) 11.64
R v Hammersmith and Fulham London Borough Council, ex p D [1999] LGR 575,
  [1999] 2 FCR 401, [1999] 1 FLR 642, [1999] Fam Law 213, 31 HLR 786,
  [1999] 02 LS Gaz R 28 .... 13.50
R v Hampshire County Council, ex p H [1999] 3 FCR 129, [1999] 2 FLR 359,
  [1999] Fam Law 537, [1998] 29 LS Gaz R 27, 142 Sol Jo LB 188, CA 13.48, 13.50
R v Hampshire County Council, ex p K [1990] 2 QB 71, [1990] 2 All ER 129,
  [1990] 2 WLR 649, 88 LGR 618, [1990] FCR 545, [1990] 1 FLR 330,
  [1990] Fam Law 253 .... 11.60
R v Harrow London Borough Council, ex p D [1990] Fam 133, [1990] 3 All ER 12,
  [1989] 3 WLR 1239, 88 LGR 41, [1989] FCR 729, [1990] 1 FLR 79,
  [1990] Fam Law 18, 133 Sol Jo 1513, [1989] NLJR 1153, CA 13.39, 13.48
R v Hayes [1977] 2 All ER 288, [1977] 1 WLR 234, 64 Cr App Rep 194, 141 JP
  349, 120 Sol Jo 855, CA 10.63
R v Hereford and Worcester County Council, ex p D [1992] 1 FCR 497,
  [1992] 1 FLR 448, [1992] Fam Law 238 .... 13.39
R v High Peak Magistrates' Court, ex p B [1995] 3 FCR 237, [1995] 1 FLR 568,
  [1995] Fam Law 295 .... 13.43
R v Highbury Corner Magistrates' Court ex p Deering [1997] 2 FCR 569,
  [1997] 1 FLR 683, [1997] Fam Law 318, 161 JP 138, [1997] Crim LR
  59, DC 2.18
R v Hopley (1860) 2 F & F 202 .... 3.20
R v Inner London Juvenile Court, ex p G [1988] FCR 316, [1988] 2 FLR 58,
  [1988] Fam Law 292 .... 8.106
R v Kingston upon Thames Royal Borough, ex p T [1994] 1 FCR 232, [1994] 1 FLR
  798, [1994] Fam Law 375 .... 13.43, 13.46, 13.50, 13.55, 13.61
R v Kirklees Metropolitan Borough Council, ex p C (a minor) [1992] 2 FCR 321,
  [1992] 2 FLR 117, [1992] Fam Law 334, 8 BMLR 110; affd [1993] 2 FCR 381,
  [1993] 2 FLR 187, [1993] Fam Law 455, 15 BMLR 6, CA 3.26

PARA

R v L [2006] EWCA Crim 1902, [2006] 1 WLR 3092, [2007] 1 Cr App Rep 1,
[2006] 2 FCR 724, [2007] Crim LR 472, [2006] All ER (D) 408 (Jul), sub nom
R v Levey [2007] 1 FLR 462, (2006) Times, 24 August 8.106
R v Lambert [2001] UKHL 37, [2002] 2 AC 545, [2001] 3 All ER 577,
[2001] 3 WLR 206, [2001] 2 Cr App Rep 511, [2001] 31 LS Gaz R 29, (2001)
Times, 6 July, (2001) Independent, 19 July, 145 Sol Jo LB 174, [2002] 1 LRC
584, [2001] All ER (D) 69 (Jul) 1.50
R v Lambeth London Borough Council, ex p Caddell [1998] 2 FCR 6, [1998] 1 FLR
253, [1998] Fam Law 20, [1997] 30 LS Gaz R 30, 141 Sol Jo LB 147 .... 13.52
R v Lancashire County Council, ex p M [1992] 1 FCR 283, [1992] 1 FLR 109,
[1992] Fam Law 146, CA 13.43, 13.50
R v Legal Aid Board, ex p W [2000] 1 WLR 2502, [2000] 3 FCR 352, [2000] 2 FLR
821, [2000] Fam Law 802, [2000] 38 LS Gaz R 44 [2000] NLJR 1453, 144 Sol
Jo LB 252, [2000] All ER (D) 1033, CA 10.49
R v Local Authority and Police Authority in the Midlands, ex p LM [2000] 1 FCR
736, [2000] 1 FLR 612, [2000] Fam Law 83 .... 11.96
R v Local Comr for Administration for the North and East Area of England,
ex p Bradford Metropolitan City Council [1979] QB 287, [1979] 2 All ER 881,
[1979] 2 WLR 1, 77 LGR 305, 122 Sol Jo 573, [1978] JPL 767, CA 13.68
R v London Borough of Wandsworth, ex p P (1989) 87 LGR 370, [1989] 1 FLR
387, [1989] Fam Law 185 .... 13.48
R v Newham London Borough Council, ex p Dada [1996] QB 507, [1995] 2 All ER
522, [1995] 3 WLR 540, 160 LG Rev 341, [1995] 2 FCR 441, [1995] 1 FLR
842, [1995] Fam Law 410, 27 HLR 502, CA 3.93
R v Norfolk County Council Social Services Department, ex p M [1989] QB 619,
[1989] 2 All ER 359, [1989] 3 WLR 502, 87 LGR 598, [1989] FCR 667,
[1989] Fam Law 310, [1989] NLJR 293, sub nom R v Norfolk County Council,
ex p X [1989] 2 FLR 120 .... 13.47, 13.48
R v Northampton Juvenile Court, ex p London Borough of Hammersmith and
Fulham [1985] FLR 193, [1985] Fam Law 124 .... 9.8
R v Northavon District Council, ex p Smith [1994] 2 AC 402, [1994] 3 All ER 313,
[1994] 3 WLR 403, 92 LGR 643, [1994] 2 FCR 859, [1994] 2 FLR 671,
[1995] Fam Law 16, 26 HLR 659, [1994] 38 LS Gaz R 42, [1994] NLJR 1010,
138 Sol Jo LB 178, HL 6.16, 6.41
R v Oxfordshire County Council (Secure Accommodation Order) [1992] Fam 150,
[1992] 3 All ER 660, [1992] 3 WLR 88, [1992] 2 FCR 310, [1992] 1 FLR 648,
[1992] Fam Law 338 .... 4.57, 5.135, 9.11, 9.24, 9.26, 9.29, 9.36, 11.20, 13.9
R v Plymouth Juvenile Court, ex p F [1987] 1 FLR 169, [1987] Fam Law 18, 151 JP
355 .... 10.46, 10.50
R v Portsmouth Hospitals NHS Trust, ex p Glass [1999] 3 FCR 145, [1999] 2 FLR
905, [1999] Fam Law 696, 50 BMLR 269, [1999] 32 LS Gaz R 31, 143 Sol Jo
LB 220, [1999] All ER (D) 836, CA 12.15
R v R (children) (residence order: removal from jurisdiction) [2004] EWHC 2572
(Fam), [2005] 1 FLR 687, [2004] All ER (D) 169 (Nov) 5.49
R v R (costs: child case). See R (a minor) (legal aid: costs), Re (1997)
R v Rahman (1985) 81 Cr App Rep 349, [1985] Crim LR 596, 129 Sol Jo 431,
[1985] LS Gaz R 2500, CA 3.19, 3.20
R v Rotherfield Greys Inhabitants (1823) 1 B & C 345, 1 Dow & Ry MC 294, 2
Dow & Ry KB 628 .... 3.95
R v Secretary of State for Foreign and Commonwealth Affairs, ex p Council of Civil
Service Unions. See Council of Civil Service Unions v Minister for the Civil
Service
R v Secretary of State for Health, ex p Luff [1991] FCR 821, [1992] 1 FLR 59,
[1991] Fam Law 472, [1991] Imm AR 382 .... 13.50
R v Secretary of State for Social Security, ex p W [1999] 3 FCR 693, [1999] 2 FLR
604, [1999] Fam Law 526 .... 3.60, 3.74
R v Secretary of State for the Home Department, ex p Gangadeen [1998] 2 FCR 96,
[1998] 1 FLR 762, [1998] Fam Law 248, [1998] 01 LS Gaz R 24, 142 Sol Jo
LB 27, sub nom Gangadeen and Jurawan v Secretary of State for the Home
Department [1998] Imm AR 106, CA 2.28

PARA

R v Secretary of State for the Home Department, ex p Khan [1998] 2 FCR 96,
[1998] 1 FLR 762, [1998] Fam Law 248, [1998] 01 LS Gaz R 24, 142 Sol Jo
LB 27, sub nom Khan v Secretary of State for the Home Department
[1998] Imm AR 106, CA 2.28
R v Secretary of State for the Home Department, ex p Teame [1994] 3 FCR 132; on
appeal [1995] 1 FLR 293, CA 2.28
R v Somerset County Council, ex p Prospects Care Services [2000] 1 FLR 636 .... 13.50
R v South East Hampshire Family Proceedings Court, ex p D [1994] 2 All ER 445,
[1994] 1 WLR 611, [1994] 1 FCR 620, [1994] 2 FLR 190, [1994] Fam Law
560 .... 4.39
R v Tameside Metropolitan Borough Council, ex p J [2000] 1 FCR 173,
[2000] 1 FLR 942, [2000] Fam Law 9 .... 3.103, 6.39, 6.55, 6.56, 13.50
R v United Kingdom (Application 10496/83) (1987) 10 EHRR 74, [1988] 2 FLR
445, ECtHR 1.7, 3.16, 3.23, 5.75, 5.83
R v W(E) [1996] Crim LR 904, CA 11.67
R v W(G) [1996] Crim LR 904, CA 11.67
R v Waltham Forest Juvenile Court, ex p KB [1988] FCR 474, [1988] 2 FLR 214,
[1988] Fam Law 334 .... 8.106
R v West Glamorgan County Council, ex p T [1990] FCR 142, [1990] 1 FLR 339,
[1990] Fam Law 180 .... 8.218
R v Wilmington Inhabitants (1822) 5 B & Ald 525 .... 3.95
R v Woods (1921) 85 JP 272 .... 3.20
R v Z [1990] 2 QB 355, [1990] 2 All ER 971, [1990] 3 WLR 113, 91 Cr App Rep
203, [1991] Fam Law 137, CA 10.63
R (on the application of A) v Chief Constable of C [2001] 1 WLR 461,
[2001] 2 FCR 431, (2000) Times, 7 November, [2000] All ER (D) 1524 .... 11.96
R (on the application of A) v Lambeth London Borough Council [2003] UKHL 57,
[2004] 2 AC 208, [2004] 1 All ER 97, [2003] 3 WLR 1194, [2003] LGR 569,
[2003] 3 FCR 419, [2004] 1 FLR 454, [2004] Fam Law 21, [2004] HLR 117,
[2003] 45 LS Gaz R 29, (2003) Times, 24 October, 147 Sol Jo LB 1242, [2003]
All ER (D) 385 (Oct) 6.18, 6.19, 6.36, 6.41
R (on the application of AB and SB) v Nottingham City Council [2001] EWHC
Admin 235, [2001] 3 FCR 350, [2001] All ER (D) 359 (Mar) 6.18, 6.83, 13.50
R (on the application of Anton) v Secretary of State for the Home Department, Re
Anton [2005] EWHC 2730/2731 (Admin/Fam), [2005] EWHC 2731 (Fam),
[2005] 2 FLR 818, [2005] Fam Law 442 .... 12.31
R (on the application of Axon) v Secretary of State for Health (Family Planning
Association intervening) [2006] EWHC 37 (Admin), [2006] QB 539,
[2006] 2 WLR 1130, [2006] 1 FCR 175, [2006] 2 FLR 206, [2006] Fam Law
272, 88 BMLR 96, [2006] 08 LS Gaz R 25, (2006) Times, 26 January, [2006]
All ER (D) 148 (Jan) 3.30
R (on the application of B) v Islington London Borough Council [2007] EWHC 1082
(Admin), [2007] 2 FCR 378, [2007] 2 FLR 822, [2007] Fam Law 802, 10
CCLR 441, [2007] All ER (D) 08 (Jun) 6.17
R (on the application of B) v Merton London Borough Council [2003] EWHC 1689
(Admin), [2003] 4 All ER 280, [2005] 3 FCR 69, [2003] 2 FLR 888,
[2003] Fam Law 813, (2003) Times, 18 July, [2003] All ER (D) 227 (Jul) 6.8
R (on the application of B) v Stafford Combined Court [2006] EWHC 1645 (Admin),
[2007] 1 All ER 102, [2007] 1 WLR 1524, [2006] 2 Cr App Rep 505, [2006]
All ER (D) 22 (Jul) 11.64
R (on the application of B by her litigation friend MB) v Lambeth London Borough
Council [2006] EWHC 639 (Admin), [2007] 1 FLR 2091, [2006] All ER (D)
108 (Apr) 13.39, 13.50
R (on the application of Barhanu) v Hackney London Borough Council
[2007] EWHC 1082 (Admin), [2007] 2 FCR 378, [2007] 2 FLR 822,
[2007] Fam Law 802, 10 CCLR 441, [2007] All ER (D) 08 (Jun) 6.17
R (on the application of Bibi) v Camden London Borough Council [2004] EWHC
2527 (Admin), [2005] 1 FLR 413, [2005] Fam Law 108, (2004) Times,
25 October, [2004] All ER (D) 123 (Oct) 5.18

PARA

R (on the application of Burkett) v Hammersmith and Fulham London Borough
Council [2002] UKHL 23, [2002] 3 All ER 97, [2002] 1 WLR 1593, (2002)
Times, 24 May, [2002] All ER (D) 363 (May) 13.41
R (on the application of CD) v Secretary of State for the Home Department
[2003] EWHC 155 (Admin), [2003] 1 FLR 979, [2003] Fam Law 315, (2003)
Times, 27 January, [2003] All ER (D) 88 (Jan) 6.24
R (on the application of G) v Barnet London Borough Council [2003] UKHL 57,
[2004] 2 AC 208, [2004] 1 All ER 97, [2003] 3 WLR 1194, [2003] LGR 569,
[2003] 3 FCR 419, [2004] 1 FLR 454, [2004] Fam Law 21, [2004] HLR 117,
[2003] 45 LS Gaz R 29, (2003) Times, 24 October, 147 Sol Jo LB 1242, [2003]
All ER (D) 385 (Oct) 6.18, 6.19, 6.36, 6.41
R (on the application of H) v Wandsworth London Borough Council [2007] EWHC
1082 (Admin), [2007] 2 FCR 378, [2007] 2 FLR 822, [2007] Fam Law 802, 10
CCLR 441, [2007] All ER (D) 08 (Jun) 6.17, 6.72
R (on the application of Heather) v Leonard Cheshire Foundation [2002] EWCA Civ
366, [2002] 2 All ER 936, [2002] HLR 893, 69 BMLR 22, (2002) Times,
8 April, [2002] All ER (D) 326 (Mar) 1.52
R (on the application of J) v Caerphilly County Borough Council [2005] EWHC 586
(Admin), [2005] 2 FCR 153, [2005] 2 FLR 860, [2005] Fam Law 528,
[2005] Fam Law 611, (2005) Times, 21 April, [2005] All ER (D) 94 (Apr) 6.83, 6.84
R (on the application of J) v Enfield London Borough Council [2002] EWHC 432
(Admin), [2002] LGR 390, [2002] 2 FLR 1, [2002] Fam Law 662, [2002] HLR
694, [2002] 21 LS Gaz R 32, (2002) Times, 18 April, 146 Sol Jo LB 116,
[2002] All ER (D) 209 (Mar) 6.19, 13.50
R (on the application of L) v Manchester City Council [2001] EWHC Admin 707,
[2002] 1 FLR 43, [2002] Fam Law 13, (2001) Times, 10 December, [2001] All
ER (D) 111 (Sep) 13.50, 13.65
R (on the application of L) v Nottinghamshire County Council [2007] EWHC 2364
(Admin), [2007] All ER (D) 158 (Sep) 6.72
R (on the application of M) v Barking and Dagenham London Borough Council
[2002] EWHC 2663 (Admin), [2002] All ER (D) 408 (Nov) 6.16
R (on the application of M) v Bromley London Borough Council [2002] EWCA Civ
1113, [2002] 3 FCR 193, [2002] 2 FLR 802, [2003] Fam Law 20, (2002)
Times, 20 July, [2002] All ER (D) 243 (Jul) 13.43, 13.50
R (on the application of M) v Hammersmith and Fulham London Borough Council
[2006] EWCA Civ 917, [2007] LGR 127, [2006] 2 FCR 647, [2007] 1 FLR
256, [2006] All ER (D) 41 (Jul); affd [2008] UKHL 14, [2008] 1 WLR 535,
[2008] LGR 159, [2008] 1 FLR 1384, [2008] Fam Law 515, [2008] Fam Law
383, [2008] NLJR 370, (2008) Times, 3 March, 152 Sol Jo (no 9) 28, [2008]
All ER (D) 390 (Feb) 6.36, 6.42, 6.72, 13.39, 13.50
R (on the application of M) v Sheffield Magistrates' Court [2004] EWHC 1830
(Admin), [2005] LGR 126, [2004] 3 FCR 281, [2005] 1 FLR 81,
[2004] Fam Law 790, [2004] 39 LS Gaz R 34, [2004] NLJR 1410, (2004)
Times, 30 August, [2004] All ER (D) 474 (Jul) 13.50
R (on the application of P) v London Borough of Hackney [2007] EWHC 1365
(Admin), [2007] Fam Law 867, [2007] All ER (D) 127 (Jul) 13.46
R (on the application of P) v London Borough of Newham [2004] EWHC 2210
(Admin), [2005] 2 FCR 171, [2004] All ER (D) 89 (Sep) 6.83
R (on the application of P) v Secretary of State for the Home Department
[2001] EWCA Civ 1151, [2001] 1 WLR 2002, [2001] 3 FCR 416,
[2001] 2 FLR 1122, [2001] Fam Law 803, [2001] 34 LS Gaz R 41, (2001)
Times, 1 August, 145 Sol Jo LB 203, [2001] All ER (D) 278 (Jul) 2.14, 2.17, 7.19,
11.64, 13.45
R (on the application of P, W, F and G) v Essex County Council [2004] EWHC 2027
(Admin), [2004] All ER (D) 103 (Aug) 13.39
R (on the application of Q) v Secretary of State for the Home Department
[2001] EWCA Civ 1151, [2001] 1 WLR 2002, [2001] 3 FCR 416,
[2001] 2 FLR 1122, [2001] Fam Law 803, [2001] 34 LS Gaz R 41, (2001)
Times, 1 August, 145 Sol Jo LB 203, [2001] All ER (D) 278 (Jul) 2.14, 2.17. 7.19,
11.64, 13.45

PARA

R (on the application of Raines) v Orange Grove Foster Care Agency [2006] EWHC
    1887 (Admin), [2006] 2 FCR 746, [2007] 1 FLR 760, [2006] All ER (D) 328
    (Jun) 13.41, 13.47, 13.50
R (on the application of S) v Haringey London Borough Council [2003] EWHC 2734
    (Admin), [2004] 1 FLR 590, [2004] Fam Law 100, [2004] 01 LS Gaz R 21,
    (2003) Times, 27 November 13.71
R (on the application of S) v London Borough of Wandsworth, London Borough of
    Hammersmith and Fulham,London Borough of Lambeth [2001] EWHC Admin
    709, [2002] 1 FLR 469, [2002] Fam Law 180, [2001] All ER (D) 08 (Oct) ... 6.12, 13.39,
                                                          13.50
R (on the application of S) v Secretary of State for the Home Department
    [2002] EWHC 18 (Fam/Admin), [2002] Fam 213, [2002] 3 WLR 24,
    [2002] 1 FCR 481, [2002] 1 FLR 845, (2002) Times, 11 March, 146 Sol Jo LB
    37, [2002] All ER (D) 187 (Jan) 12.1
R (on the application of S) v Sutton London Borough Council [2007] EWHC 1196
    (Admin), [2007] 2 FLR 849, [2007] Fam Law 699, [2007] All ER (D) 327
    (May); revsd in part [2007] EWCA Civ 790, [2007] All ER (D) 422 (Jul) 6.36, 6.72
R (on the application of S) v Swindon Borough Council [2001] EWHC Admin 334,
    [2001] LGR 318, [2001] 3 FCR 702, [2001] Fam Law 659, (2001) Times,
    27 June, [2001] All ER (D) 78 (May), sub nom S (sexual abuse allegations: local
    authority response), Re [2001] 2 FLR 776 .... 7.8, 13.46, 13.50
R (on the application of Stevens) v Plymouth City Council [2002] EWCA Civ 388,
    [2002] 1 WLR 2583, [2002] LGR 565, [2002] 1 FLR 1177, [2002] All ER (D)
    414 (Mar) 11.67
R (on the application of T) v A Local Authority. See T (judicial review: local
    authority decisions concerning child in need), Re (2003)
R (on the application of the Howard League for Penal Reform) v Secretary of State
    for the Home Department [2002] EWHC 2497 (Admin), [2003] 1 FLR 484,
    [2003] Fam Law 149, [2003] 03 LS Gaz R 30, (2002) Times, 5 December, 147
    Sol Jo LB 61, [2002] All ER (D) 465 (Nov) 2.14, 6.24, 13.39
R (on the application of the National Association of Guardians Ad Litem) v Children
    and Family Court Advisory and Support Service [2001] EWHC Admin 693,
    [2002] 1 FLR 255, [2001] Fam Law 877, [2001] All ER (D) 32 (Sep) 13.45
R (on the application of W) v Lambeth London Borough Council [2002] EWCA Civ
    613, [2002] 2 All ER 901, [2002] LGR 351, [2002] 2 FCR 289, [2002] 2 FLR
    327, [2002] Fam Law 592, [2002] HLR 758, (2002) Times, 23 May, 146 Sol Jo
    LB 125, [2002] All ER (D) 56 (May): affd [2003] UKHL 57, [2004] 2 AC 208,
    [2004] 1 All ER 97, [2003] 3 WLR 1194, [2003] LGR 569, [2003] 3 FCR 419,
    [2004] 1 FLR 454, [2004] Fam Law 21, [2004] HLR 117,
    [2003] 45 LS Gaz R 29, (2003) Times, 24 October, 147 Sol Jo LB 1242, [2003]
    All ER (D) 385 (Oct) 6.18, 6.19, 6.36, 6.41, 13.50
R (on the application of W) v Leicestershire County Council [2003] EWHC 704
    (Admin), [2003] 2 FLR 185 .... 13.46, 13.50
R (on the application of Williamson) v Secretary of State for Education and
    Employment [2001] EWHC Admin 960, [2002] 1 FLR 493, [2002] Fam Law
    257, (2001) Times, 12 December, [2001] All ER (D) 405 (Nov); affd
    [2002] EWCA Civ 1926, [2003] QB 1300, [2003] 1 All ER 385, [2003] 3 WLR
    482, [2003] 1 FCR 1, [2003] 1 FLR 726, [2003] 09 LS Gaz R 27, (2002)
    Times, 18 December, [2002] All ER (D) 192 (Dec); affd on other grounds
    [2005] UKHL 15, [2005] 2 AC 246, [2005] 2 All ER 1, [2005] 2 WLR 590,
    [2005] 1 FCR 498, [2005] 2 FLR 374, [2005] NLJR 324, (2005) Times,
    25 February, 149 Sol Jo LB 266, 19 BHRC 99, [2005] 5 LRC 670, [2005] All
    ER (D) 380 (Feb) 3.20
R and G (minors), Re [1994] 1 FLR 793, [1994] Fam Law 314 .... 4.57, 8.180, 8.189
RH (a minor) (parental responsibility), Re [1998] 2 FCR 89, sub nom H (parental
    responsibility), Re [1998] 1 FLR 855, [1998] Fam Law 325, CA 2.10, 3.63, 3.65, 3.69
RJ (foster placement), Re [1998] 3 FCR 579, [1998] 2 FLR 110, [1998] Fam Law
    459; revsd , sub nom RJ (minors) (fostering: person disqualified), Re
    [1999] 1 WLR 581, [1998] 3 FCR 579, [1999] 1 FLR 605, [1999] Fam Law 19,
    [1998] 39 LS Gaz R 34, [1998] NLJR 1550, 142 Sol Jo LB 259, CA 2.10, 5.24, 5.25,
                                                          6.66, 12.16, 12.32

PARA

RJ (minors) (fostering: wardship), Re [1999] 3 FCR 646, [1999] 1 FLR 618,
 [1999] Fam Law 90 .... 3.90, 5.106, 6.66, 12.9, 12.16, 12.29
Ramsbotham v Senior (1869) LR 8 Eq 575, 34 JP 85, 17 WR 1057, 21 LT 293 .... 11.98
Redbridge London Borough v Newport City Council [2003] EWHC 2967 (Fam),
 [2004] 2 FLR 226, [2004] Fam Law 562 .... 8.170
Rennick v Rennick [1978] 1 All ER 817, [1977] 1 WLR 1455, 121 Sol Jo 792, CA 12.33
Rice v Miller (1993) FLC 92–415 .... 2.9
Richards v Richards [1984] AC 174, [1983] 2 All ER 807, [1983] 3 WLR 173,
 [1984] FLR 11, 13 Fam Law 256, 147 JP 481, 12 HLR 73, 127 Sol Jo 476,
 [1983] LS Gaz R 2134, 133 NLJ 725, HL 12.33
Richardson v Richardson [1989] Fam 95, [1989] 3 All ER 779, [1989] 3 WLR 865,
 [1990] FCR 232, [1990] 1 FLR 186, [1990] Fam Law 176 .... 5.164
Ridehalgh v Horsefield [1994] Ch 205, [1994] 3 All ER 848, [1994] 3 WLR 462,
 [1994] 2 FLR 194, [1994] Fam Law 560, [1994] BCC 390, CA 4.59
Riley v Riley [1986] 2 FLR 429, [1987] Fam Law 15, 150 JP 439, CA 5.18
Rochdale Borough Council v BW [1991] FCR 705, sub nom Rochdale Borough
 Council v A [1991] 2 FLR 192, [1991] Fam Law 374 .... 2.20
Roddy (a child) (identification: restriction on publication), Re [2003] EWHC 2927
 (Fam), [2004] 1 FCR 481, [2004] 2 FLR 949, [2004] Fam Law 793,
 [2004] EMLR 127, [2004] All ER (D) 150 (Feb) 10.8

S

S (an infant), Re [1958] 1 All ER 783, [1958] 1 WLR 391, 122 JP 245, 102 Sol Jo
 250 .... 5.171
S (infants), Re [1967] 1 All ER 202, [1967] 1 WLR 396, 65 LGR 158, 110 Sol Jo
 944 .... 12.14
S (minors), (wardship: police investigation), Re [1987] Fam 199, [1987] 3 All ER
 1076, [1987] 3 WLR 847, [1988] Fam Law 90, 131 Sol Jo 1390,
 [1987] LS Gaz R 3177 .... 2.18
S (a minor), Re [1992] 2 FCR 554, [1993] 1 FLR 110, [1993] Fam Law 129,
 [1992] 31 LS Gaz R 35, 136 Sol Jo LB 206, CA 10.15
S (a minor), Re (20 July 1992, unreported) 4.37
S (a minor) (independent representation), Re [1993] Fam 263, [1993] 3 All ER 36,
 [1993] 2 WLR 801, [1993] 2 FCR 1, [1993] 2 FLR 437, [1993] Fam Law 465,
 [1993] NLJR 435, CA 5.155, 10.53
S (J) (a minor), Re [1993] 2 FCR 193, [1993] 2 FLR 919, [1993] Fam Law 621 .... 8.164
S (minors), Re [1993] 2 FCR 499, [1994] 1 FLR 297, [1994] Fam Law 244, CA 5.27, 5.96
S (a minor) (medical treatment), Re [1993] 1 FLR 376, [1993] Fam Law 215 .... 12.36
S (minors) (abduction: wrongful retention), Re [1994] Fam 70, [1994] 1 All ER 237,
 [1994] 2 WLR 228, [1994] 1 FCR 83, [1994] 1 FLR 82, [1994] Fam Law 70,
 [1993] 36 LS Gaz R 37, 137 Sol Jo LB 188 .... 3.97
S (a minor), Re [1994] 1 FCR 604, [1994] 2 FLR 1065, [1995] Fam Law 20 .... 3.33
S, Re [1994] 2 FCR 414, [1994] 2 FLR 222, [1994] Fam Law 425, CA 8.209
S (minors), Re [1994] 2 FCR 986, [1994] 1 FLR 623, [1994] Fam Law 426 .... 12.34
S, Re (residence order: jurisdiction) [1995] 1 FCR 497, sub nom S v S (custody:
 jurisdiction) [1995] 1 FLR 155, [1995] Fam Law 120 .... 5.24, 5.133
S, Re [1995] 1 FCR 617, [1994] 2 FLR 1057, [1995] Fam Law 12, CA 4.51, 8.218
S (residence order: forum conveniens), Re [1995] 2 FCR 162, [1995] 1 FLR 314 .... 5.127,
 5.132
S, Re [1995] 2 FCR 697, [1995] 1 FLR 151, [1995] Fam Law 64, CA 8.106
S (a minor), Re [1995] 3 FCR 225, [1995] 2 FLR 648, [1995] Fam Law 596, CA ... 3.66, 3.75,
 3.77, 3.78
S (a minor), Re [1995] 3 FCR 564 .... 3.66, 3.74
S (minors), Re (child abduction: sequestration) [1995] 3 FCR 707, [1995] 1 FLR 858,
 [1995] Fam Law 351 .... 5.169
S (care or supervision order), Re [1996] 2 FCR 719, [1996] 1 FLR 753,
 [1996] Fam Law 268, CA 8.164, 8.183

Table of Cases

PARA

S (minors) (care orders: appeal out of time), Re [1996] 2 FCR 838, sub nom S
(minors) (discharge of care order), Re [1995] 2 FLR 639, [1995] Fam Law 667,
[1995] 31 LS Gaz R 33, CA 2.11, 11.26, 13.4

S (contact: grandparents), Re [1996] 3 FCR 30, [1996] 1 FLR 158, [1996] Fam Law
76, CA 2.72, 5.87, 7.29

S (care proceedings: split hearing), Re [1996] 3 FCR 578, [1996] 2 FLR 773,
[1997] Fam Law 11 .... 8.143

S (a minor) (abduction: European and Hague conventions), Re [1997] 1 FCR 588,
[1997] Fam Law 388, sub nom S (a minor) (custody: habitual residence), Re
[1997] 2 FLR 958, CA; affd [1998] AC 750, [1997] 4 All ER 251,
[1997] 3 WLR 597, [1997] 3 FCR 293, [1998] 1 FLR 122,
[1997] 34 LS Gaz R 28, [1997] NLJR 1310, HL 3.103, 4.5

S (appeal from Principal Registry: procedure), Re [1997] 2 FCR 119, [1997] 2 FLR
856, [1998] Fam Law 22 .... 13.11, 13.31

S (care: residence: intervener), Re [1997] 2 FCR 272, [1997] 1 FLR 497,
[1997] Fam Law 232, CA 8.101

S (a minor) (parental responsibility: jurisdiction), Re [1998] 1 WLR 1701,
[1999] 2 FCR 27, [1998] 2 FLR 921, [1998] Fam Law 528,
[1998] 21 LS Gaz R 36, 142 Sol Jo LB 157, CA 3.55, 3.61, 3.65

S (application for judicial review), Re [1998] 1 FCR 368, [1998] 1 FLR 790, CA 13.41

S (a minor) (contact: evidence), Re [1998] 3 FCR 70, [1998] 1 FLR 798,
[1998] Fam Law 316, CA 4.52, 5.60, 11.26

S (a minor) (adopted child: contact), Re [1999] Fam 283, [1999] 1 All ER 648,
[1999] 3 WLR 504, [1999] 1 FCR 169, [1998] 2 FLR 897, [1998] Fam Law
581 .... 2.33, 5.148, 5.156

S (change of surname), Re [1999] 1 FCR 304, [1999] 1 FLR 672, [1999] Fam Law
207, CA 2.10, 8.175

S (removal from jurisdiction), Re [1999] 1 FLR 850, [1999] Fam Law 219 .... 5.50

S (violent parent: indirect contact), Re [2000] 1 FLR 481, [2000] Fam Law 239 ...... 5.55, 5.90

S (foster placement (children) Regulations 1991) [2000] 1 FLR 648 .... 6.66

S (Change of names: Cultural Factors), Re [2001] 3 FCR 648, [2001] 2 FLR 1005,
[2001] Fam Law 728, [2001] All ER (D) 30 (Jul) 5.37

S (contact: appeal), Re [2001] Fam Law 505 .... 5.83

S (a child) (residence order: condition), Re [2001] EWCA Civ 847, [2001] 3 FCR
154, [2001] All ER (D) 159 (May) 5.14, 5.39, 5.43, 5.51, 5.95, 5.116

S (sexual abuse allegations: local authority response), Re (2001). See R (on the
application of S) v Swindon Borough Council

S (children) (abduction: asylum appeal), Re [2002] EWCA Civ 843, [2002] 1 WLR
2548, [2002] 2 FCR 642, [2002] 2 FLR 465, [2002] Fam Law 650,
[2003] Imm AR 52, [2002] 27 LS Gaz R 33, (2002) Times, 3 June, 146 Sol Jo
LB 159, [2002] All ER (D) 424 (May) 12.22

S (a child) (residence order: condition), Re [2002] EWCA Civ 1795, [2003] 1 FCR
138, [2002] All ER (D) 30 (Dec) 5.118

S (children: care plan), Re [2002] UKHL 10, [2002] 2 AC 291, [2002] 2 All ER 192,
[2002] 2 WLR 720, [2002] LGR 251, [2002] 1 FCR 577, [2002] 1 FLR 815,
[2002] 17 LS Gaz R 34, (2002) Times, 15 March, [2002] All ER (D) 212
(Mar) 13.88, 13.90, 13.93

S (minors) (care order: implementation of care plan), Re (2002). See W and B
(children) (careplan)

S (a child) (removal from jurisdiction), Re [2003] EWCA Civ 1149, [2003] 2 FCR
673, [2003] 2 FLR 1043, [2003] Fam Law 820, (2003) Times, 29 August,
[2003] All ER (D) 519 (Jul) 5.45

S (a child) (contact), Re [2004] EWCA Civ 18, [2004] 1 FCR 439, [2004] 1 FLR
1279, [2004] Fam Law 400, [2004] All ER (D) 257 (Jan) 5.79, 5.81, 5.83, 5.85, 5.89,
5.164, 5.176

S (unco-operative mother), Re [2004] EWCA Civ 597, [2004] 2 FLR 710,
[2004] Fam Law 637, (2004) Times, 28 May, [2004] All ER (D) 31 (May) 4.40, 5.73,
5.74, 5.85

S (a child) (care: parenting skills: personality tests), Re [2004] EWCA Civ 1029,
[2005] 2 FLR 658, [2004] All ER (D) 593 (Jul) 11.38

PARA

S (specific issue order: religion: circumcision), Re [2004] EWHC 1282 (Fam),
[2005] 1 FLR 236 .... 2.49
S (children) (termination of contact), Re [2004] EWCA Civ 1397, [2005] 1 FCR 489,
[2004] All ER (D) 129 (Sep), sub nom S (care: parental contact), Re
[2005] 1 FLR 469, [2005] Fam Law 14 .... 8.215
S (a child) (contact order: committal), Re [2004] EWCA Civ 1790, [2005] 1 FLR
812, [2005] Fam Law 206, (2004) Times, 9 December, [2004] All ER (D) 09
(Dec) 5.175
S (a child) (identification: restriction on publication), Re [2004] UKHL 47,
[2005] 1 AC 593, [2004] 4 All ER 683, [2004] 3 WLR 1129, [2004] 3 FCR
407, [2005] 1 FLR 591, [2005] Fam Law 113, [2005] Crim LR 310,
[2004] NLJR 1654, (2004) Times, 29 October, 148 Sol Jo LB 1285,
[2005] EMLR 11, [2004] All ER (D) 402 (Oct) 2.20, 2.24, 5.100, 12.15, 12.40
S (children) (care proceedings: additional expert evidence), Re [2006] EWCA Civ
981, [2007] 1 FLR 90, 150 Sol Jo LB 705, [2006] All ER (D) 347 (May),
[2006] Fam Law 831 .... 11,36. 11.39
S (children) (permission to seek relief), Re [2006] EWCA Civ 1190, [2006] 3 FCR
50, [2007] 1 FLR 482, (2006) Times, 13 September, [2006] All ER (D) 92
(Aug) 5.56, 5.108, 5.202, 5.204
S (practice: Muslim women giving evidence), Re [2007] 2 FLR 461, [2007] Fam Law
986 .... 11.15
S (a child) (adoption order or special guardianship order), Re [2007] EWCA Civ 54,
[2007] 1 FCR 271, [2007] 1 FLR 819, [2007] Fam Law 390, (2007) Times,
9 February, [2007] All ER (D) 81 (Feb) 5.213, 5.216, 5.217, 5.221, 5.222, 5.223,
5.224, 5.226, 5.227, 5.233, 5.234
S (a child) (adoption order or special guardianship order), Re [2007] EWCA Civ 90,
[2007] 1 FCR 340, [2007] 1 FLR 855, [2007] All ER (D) 175 (Feb) 5.217, 5.219
S (children) (care proceedings: care plan), Re [2007] EWCA Civ 232, [2007] 1 FCR
721, [2007] 2 FLR 275, [2007] All ER (D) 281 (Mar), sub nom Cheshire
County Council v S [2007] Fam Law 488, (2007) Times, 30 March 13.43
S (child proceedings: urgent appeals), Re [2007] EWCA Civ 958, [2007] 2 FLR 1044,
[2007] Fam Law 1126 .... 13.26
S (N) (an infant), Re, Singh v Secretary of State for Home Affairs. See Singh
(Nirbhai) (an infant), Re
S v B and Newport City Council [2007] 1 FLR 1116 .... 5.223, 5.224
S v Gloucestershire County Council [2001] Fam 313, [2000] 3 All ER 346,
[2001] 2 WLR 909, [2000] 2 FCR 345, [2000] 1 FLR 825, [2000] Fam Law
474, CA 13.74, 13.76
S v Knowsley Borough Council [2004] EWHC 491 (Fam), [2004] 2 FLR 716, sub
nom Re S, (a child) (secure accommodation order: right to liberty)
[2004] Fam Law 652, [2004] All ER (D) 76 (Jun) 9.10, 9.11, 9.26, 13.43, 13.71
S v M (access order). See Sanderson v McManus
S v Merton London Borough [1994] 1 FCR 186, [1994] Fam Law 321 .... 4.46, 4.51
S v Oxfordshire County Council [1993] 2 FCR 676, [1993] 1 FLR 452,
[1993] Fam Law 74 .... 4.57
S v P (contact application: family assistance order) [1997] 2 FCR 185, [1997] 2 FLR
277, [1997] Fam Law 533, [1997] 06 LS Gaz R 28 .... 5.195
S v R (parental responsibility) [1993] 1 FCR 331, [1993] Fam Law 339 .... 2.75, 3.65, 4.56
S v S [1972] AC 24, [1970] 3 All ER 107, [1970] 3 WLR 366, 114 Sol Jo 635, HL 2.17,
2.78
S (BD) v S (DJ) [1977] Fam 109, [1977] 1 All ER 656, [1977] 2 WLR 44, 121 Sol Jo
34, CA 2.37
S v S [2006] EWCA Civ 1617, [2006] 3 FCR 604, [2007] 1 FLR 1532, [2006] All
ER (D) 403 (Nov) 5.204
S v S (custody: jurisdiction). See S, Re (residence order: jurisdiction) (1995)
S v W (1980) 11 Fam Law 81, CA 2.46
S and B (minors), Re [1991] FCR 175, [1990] 2 FLR 489, [1991] Fam Law
99, CA 11.56
S and D (child case: powers of court), Re [1995] 1 FCR 626, [1995] 2 FLR 456,
[1995] Fam Law 602, CA 5.104, 5.208, 8.60, 8.151, 8.164, 12.25

PARA

S and P (discharge of care order), Re. See P v Bradford Metropolitan Borough
Council

S County Council v B [2000] 3 WLR 53, [2000] 1 FCR 536, [2000] 2 FLR 161,
[2000] Fam Law 462, [1999] All ER (D) 1517 .... 11.76, 11.100, 11.103

SA (vulnerable adult with capacity: marriage), Re [2005] EWHC 2942 (Fam),
[2007] 2 FCR 563, [2006] 1 FLR 867, [2006] Fam Law 268 .... 12.8, 12.40

SB (children) (care proceedings: children's guardian) [2002] 1 WLR 189,
[2002] 1 FCR 251, [2001] 2 FLR 1334, [2001] Fam Law 869 .... 8.189, 10.38

SB v X County Council. See P (children) (adoption: parental consent), Re

SC (a minor) (adoption: freeing order), Re. See C (adoption: freeing order), Re (1999)

SC (a minor) (leave to seek residence order), Re [1994] 1 FLR 96, [1993] Fam Law
618 .... 5.126, 5.156, 5.159

SH (care order: orphan), Re [1996] 1 FCR 1, [1995] 1 FLR 746, [1995] Fam Law
354 .... 3.108, 3.123, 5.215, 8.29

S-H v Kingston upon Hull City Council [2008] EWCA Civ 493, (2008) Times,
28 May, [2008] All ER (D) 176 (May) 2.18, 12.6

S, S and A (care proceedings: issue estoppel), Re. See L (minors) (care proceedings:
issue estoppel), Re (1996)

SW (a minor), Re [1986] 1 FLR 24, [1985] Fam Law 322 .... 5.122

Sahin v Germany (Application 30943/96) [2002] 3 FCR 321, [2002] 1 FLR 119,
[2002] Fam Law 94, 36 EHRR 43, ECtHR 3.17, 5.75, 5.76, 6.4, 10.5

Sahin v Germany (Application 30943/96) [2003] 2 FCR 619, [2003] 2 FLR 671,
[2003] Fam Law 727, 15 BHRC 84, ECtHR 10.5

Sanderson v McManus 1997 SC (HL) 55, 1997 SLT 629, sub nom S v M (access
order) [1997] 1 FLR 980, HL 2.69, 3.23, 5.84

Scott v Scott [1986] 2 FLR 320, [1986] Fam Law 301, 150 JP 333, CA 2.58

Secretary, Department of Health and Community Services v JWB and SMB (1992)
175 CLR 218, 106 ALR 385, 66 ALJR 300, Aus HC 3.29, 12.30

Shah v Barnet London Borough Council [1983] 2 AC 309, [1983] 1 All ER 226,
[1983] 2 WLR 16, 81 LGR 305, 127 Sol Jo 36, HL 6.38

Singh (Nirbhai) (an infant), Re [1968] Ch 643, [1968] 2 WLR 1290, sub nom S (N)
(an infant), Re, Singh v Secretary of State for Home Affairs [1968] 2 All ER
145, CA 12.31

Smith v Secretary of State for Work and Pensions [2006] UKHL 35, [2006] 3 All ER
907, [2006] 1 WLR 2024, [2006] 2 FCR 487, [2007] 1 FLR 166,
[2006] Fam Law 834, (2006) Times, 14 July, 150 Sol Jo LB 986, [2006] All ER
(D) 161 (Jul) 2.6, 10.4

Sommerfeld v Germany (Application 31871/96) [2003] 2 FCR 647, ECtHR 3.17, 5.75, 5.76

South Glamorgan County Council v W and B [1993] 1 FCR 626, [1993] 1 FLR 574,
[1993] Fam Law 398, 11 BMLR 162 .... 7.91, 8.119, 12.32, 12.38

Southwark London Borough v B. See DB and CB (minors), Re

Southwark London Borough Council v B [1999] 1 FCR 550, [1998] 2 FLR 1095,
[1998] Fam Law 657 .... 4.6, 8.32, 8.38, 8.39

Spindlow v Spindlow [1979] Fam 52, [1979] 1 All ER 169, [1978] 3 WLR 777, 1
FLR 133, 9 Fam Law 22, 122 Sol Jo 556, CA 12.33

Stephenson v Stephenson [1985] FLR 1140, [1985] Fam Law 253, CA 2.44

Stockport Metropolitan Borough Council v D. See D (a minor), Re (1995)

Subpoena (adoption: Comr for Local Administration), Re. See Local Administration
Comr (subpoena issued by), Re

Suffolk County Council v C [1999] 1 FCR 473n, [1999] 1 FLR 259n,
[1999] Fam Law 13 .... 13.29

Suss v Germany (Application No 40324/98) [2005] 3 FCR 666, [2006] 1 FLR 522,
[2006] Fam Law 261, [2005] ECHR 40324/98, ECtHR 2.61, 5.75

Suter v Suter and Jones [1987] Fam 111, [1987] 2 All ER 336, [1987] 3 WLR 9,
[1987] FCR 52, [1987] 2 FLR 232, [1987] Fam Law 239, 151 JP 593, 131 Sol
Jo 471, [1987] LS Gaz R 1142, CA 2.26

Sutton London Borough Council v Davis [1994] Fam 241, [1995] 1 All ER 53,
[1994] 2 WLR 721, 92 LGR 732, [1994] 2 FCR 1129, [1994] 1 FLR 737,
[1994] Fam Law 493, [1994] 19 LS Gaz R 33 .... 3.20

PARA

Sutton London Borough Council v Davis (No 2) [1995] 1 All ER 65, [1994] 1 WLR
1317, 92 LGR 746, [1994] 2 FCR 1199, [1994] 2 FLR 569, [1994] Fam Law
616, [1994] 31 LS Gaz R 36, 138 Sol Jo LB 140 .... 4.58

T

T (a minor), Re (1977) 1 FLR 59 .... 11.57
T (minors), Re (1981) 2 FLR 239, CA 2.50
T (a minor), Re [1993] 1 FCR 973, [1993] 2 FLR 450, [1993] Fam Law 572, CA 3.69,
5.86, 5.203
T (a minor) (child representation), Re [1994] Fam 49, [1993] 4 All ER 518,
[1993] 3 WLR 602, [1993] 2 FCR 445, sub nom Re CT (a minor)
[1993] 2 FLR 278, [1993] Fam Law 568, [1993] NLJR 776, CA 5.138, 10.54, 12.11,
12.12, 12.15
T (a minor), Re [1994] 1 FCR 663, [1994] 1 FLR 103, [1994] Fam Law 75, CA 8.164
T (a minor) (guardian ad litem: case record), Re [1994] 1 FLR 632, [1994] NLJR
123, CA 10.47
T (a minor), Re (1994). See KDT (a minor), Re
T, Re [1995] 1 FCR 517, [1995] 1 FLR 159, [1995] Fam Law 125 .... 13.39, 13.50
T (a minor) (order as to residence), Re [1996] 3 FCR 97, sub nom T (removal from
jurisdiction), Re [1996] 2 FLR 352, [1996] Fam Law 463, CA 5.48
T (minors) (termination of contact: discharge of order), Re [1997] 1 All ER 65,
[1997] 1 WLR 393, [1997] 1 FLR 517, CA 2.11, 2.12
T (a minor) (wardship: medical treatment), Re [1997] 1 All ER 906, [1997] 1 WLR
242, 96 LGR 116, [1997] 2 FCR 363, [1997] 1 FLR 502, 35 BMLR 63,
[1996] 42 LS Gaz R 28, [1996] NLJR 1577, 140 Sol Jo LB 237, CA 3.37
T (a child) (DNA tests: paternity), Re [2001] 3 FCR 577, [2001] 2 FLR 1190,
[2001] Fam Law 738, [2001] All ER (D) 82 (Jul) 2.17
T (a child: contact), Re [2002] EWCA Civ 1736, [2003] 1 FCR 303, [2003] 1 FLR
531, [2003] Fam Law 151, (2002) Times, 30 October, [2002] All ER (D) 372
(Oct) 5.82
T (judicial review: local authority decisions concerning child in need), Re
[2003] EWHC 2515 (Admin), [2004] 1 FLR 601, sub nom R (on the
application of T) v A Local Authority [2004] Fam Law 176, [2003] All ER (D)
02 (Nov) 6.18, 6.58, 13.50
T (a child) (sexual abuse: guidance), Re (2003). See Y (evidence of abuse: use of
photographs), Re (2003)
T (children) (sexual abuse: standard of proof), Re [2004] EWCA Civ 558,
[2004] 2 FLR 838, [2004] All ER (D) 277 (May) 11.7, 11.38
T (a child) (order for costs), Re [2005] EWCA Civ 311, [2005] 1 FCR 625,
[2005] 2 FLR 681, [2005] Fam Law 534, [2005] All ER (D) 335 (Mar) 4.58
T (a minor) v Surrey County Council [1994] 4 All ER 577, [1994] NLJR 319, sub
nom Harrison v Surrey County Council [1994] 2 FCR 1269 .... 13.77
T (removal from jurisdiction), Re. See T (a minor) (order as to residence), Re (1996)
T v T [1992] 1 FCR 329, [1992] 1 FLR 43, [1992] Fam Law 194 .... 5.133
T v W (contact: reasons for refusing leave) [1997] 1 FCR 118, [1996] 2 FLR 473,
[1996] Fam Law 666 .... 5.152
T and A (children) (risk of disclosure), Re [2000] 1 FCR 659,
[2000] 03 LS Gaz R 37, 144 Sol Jo LB 49, CA 10.51
T and E (proceedings: conflicting interests), Re [1995] 3 FCR 260, [1995] 1 FLR
581, [1995] Fam Law 232 .... 2.11, 2.34, 10.42, 11.45
TB (care proceedings:criminal trial), Re [1996] 1 FCR 101, [1995] 2 FLR 801,
[1996] Fam Law 13, CA 2.62
TP and KM v United Kingdom (Application 28945/95) (2001) 34 EHRR 42,
[2001] 2 FCR 289, [2001] 2 FLR 549, [2001] ECHR 28945/95, ECtHR 3.19, 8.153,
11.55, 13.84, 13.86
Taylor v Lawrence [2002] EWCA Civ 90, [2003] QB 528, [2002] 2 All ER 353,
[2002] 3 WLR 640, [2002] 12 LS Gaz R 35, [2002] NLJR 221, (2002) Times,
8 February, 146 Sol Jo LB 50, [2002] All ER (D) 28 (Feb) 13.30, 13.31
Thompson v Thompson [1986] FLR 212n, CA 10.27

PARA

Thompson v Thompson [1987] Fam Law 89, 150 JP 625, CA 2.37
Tyler v Tyler [1990] FCR 22, [1989] 2 FLR 158, [1989] Fam Law 316, CA 5.49

U

U (application to free for adoption), Re [1993] 2 FCR 64, [1993] 2 FLR 992,
     [1994] Fam Law 71, CA 5.201
U (T) (a minor), Re [1993] 2 FCR 565, [1994] Fam Law 316 .... 13.8
U (children) (contact), Re [2004] EWCA Civ 71, [2004] 1 FCR 768, [2004] All ER
     (D) 118 (Jan) 4.52
U (a child) (serious injury: standard of proof), Re [2004] EWCA Civ 567,
     [2005] Fam 134, [2004] 3 WLR 753, [2004] 2 FCR 257, [2004] 2 FLR 263,
     [2004] Fam Law 565, [2004] 22 LS Gaz R 31, [2004] NLJR 824, (2004) Times,
     27 May, [2004] All ER (D) 197 (May) 8.23, 11.7
U (re-opening of appeal), Re. See Uddin (a child) (serious injury: standard of proof),
     Re
Uddin (a child) (serious injury: standard of proof), Re [2005] EWCA Civ 52,
     [2005] 3 All ER 550, [2005] 1 WLR 2398, [2005] 1 FCR 583, [2005] NLJR
     325, (2005) Times, 31 March, 149 Sol Jo LB 266, [2005] All ER (D) 385 (Feb),
     sub nom U (re-opening of appeal), Re [2005] 2 FLR 444 .... 11.27, 13.30

V

V (a minor), Re (1979) 123 Sol Jo 201 .... 12.33
V (care or supervision order), Re [1996] 2 FCR 555, [1996] 1 FLR 776,
     [1996] Fam Law 269, CA 8.164, 8.183
V (minors) (sexual abuse: disclosure), Re [1999] 1 WLR 299, 96 LGR 807,
     [1999] 1 FCR 308, [1999] 1 FLR 267, [1999] Fam Law 14, 142 Sol Jo LB 270,
     [1998] All ER (D) 440, CA 11.95
V (a child), Re [2001] Fam 260, [2000] 4 All ER 609, [2001] 2 WLR 339,
     [2000] 2 FCR 404, [2000] 2 FLR 334, [2000] Fam Law 603, 144 Sol Jo LB
     222, [2000] All ER (D) 827, CA 1.54, 2.4, 5.91
V (a child) (care proceedings: human rights claims), Re [2004] EWCA Civ 54,
     [2004] 1 All ER 997, [2004] 1 WLR 1433, [2004] 1 FCR 338, [2004] 1 FLR
     944, [2004] Fam Law 328, [2004] 11 LS Gaz R 33, (2004) Times, 17 February,
     [2004] All ER (D) 52 (Feb) 4.40, 8.117, 13.71, 13.89
V v T [2007] EWHC 2312 (Fam), [2007] Fam Law 1134, [2007] All ER (D) 159
     (Oct), sub nom C (residence), Re [2008] 1 FLR 826 .... 5.87
V v V (children) (intractable contact dispute) [2004] EWHC 1215 (Fam),
     [2004] 2 FLR 851, (2004) Times, 28 May, [2004] All ER (D) 304 (May) 5.87, 5.160,
                                                                        5.176, 5.195, 5.200
Venema v Netherlands (Application 35731/97) [2003] 1 FCR 153, [2003] 1 FLR
     552, [2002] ECHR 35731/97, ECtHR 7.19, 7.40, 8.172
Vernon v Bosley (No 2) [1999] QB 18, [1997] 1 All ER 614, [1997] 3 WLR 683,
     [1997] RTR 275, [1998] 1 FLR 304, 35 BMLR 174, [1997] NLJR 89, 141 Sol
     Jo LB 27, CA 11.46, 11.74

W

W (minor), Re (1980). See W v Sunderland Borough Council
W (a minor) (custody), Re (1983) 4 FLR 492 .... 10.26
W (a minor), Re [1985] AC 791, [1985] 2 WLR 892, 83 LGR 669, [1985] FLR 879,
     [1985] Fam Law 326, 149 JP 593, 129 Sol Jo 347, [1985] LS Gaz R 2087,
     [1985] NLJ Rep 483, sub nom W v Hertfordshire County Council
     [1985] 2 All ER 301, HL 12.42
W, Re (1989). See Cleveland County Council v W

PARA

W (minors), Re (1990) 88 LGR 544, [1990] FCR 286, [1990] 1 FLR 203,
[1990] Fam Law 216, CA 10.27, 11.22, 11.51
W (minors) (residence order), Re [1992] 2 FCR 461, CA 2.43
W (a minor) (residence order: baby), Re [1992] 2 FCR 603, [1992] 2 FLR 332,
[1992] Fam Law 493, CA 2.47, 3.59
W (a minor) (medical treatment), Re [1993] Fam 64, [1992] 4 All ER 627,
[1992] 3 WLR 758, [1992] 2 FCR 785, [1993] 1 FLR 1, [1992] Fam Law 541,
9 BMLR 22, [1992] NLJR 1124, CA 3.26, 3.29, 3.30, 3.31, 3.33, 3.35, 3.95, 7.91,
10.8, 12.2, 12.28, 12.30, 12.38
W (a minor), Re [1993] 2 FCR 589, [1993] 2 FLR 625, CA 2.43, 5.17
W (child), Re [1993] 2 FCR 731, [1994] 1 FLR 843, [1994] Fam Law 376 ... 4.10, 4.56, 11.57
W (a minor) (secure accommodation order), Re, (1993). See W v North Yorkshire
County Council
W (minors), Re [1994] 1 FCR 842 .... 3.55
W (a minor) (contact), Re [1994] 2 FCR 1216, [1994] 2 FLR 441, [1994] Fam Law
614, CA 2.70
W (a minor) (interim care order), Re [1994] 3 FCR 102, [1994] 2 FLR 892,
[1994] Fam Law 612, CA 8.109, 8.111, 8.124
W, Re [1994] 3 FCR 242, [1994] 2 FLR 1087, [1995] Fam Law 119 .... 4.53
W, Re [1994] 3 FCR 248, [1994] 2 FLR 1092, [1995] Fam Law 19 ... 4.49, 9.23, 10.61, 11.48
W (a minor), Re [1995] 2 FCR 184 .... 2.44
W (a minor) (secure accommodation: jurisdiction), Re [1995] 2 FCR 708n 9.9, 9.37
W (welfare reports), Re [1995] 3 FCR 793, [1995] 2 FLR 142, [1995] Fam Law
544, CA 4.42, 10.22, 13.4
W (wardship: discharge: publicity), Re [1996] 1 FCR 393, [1995] 2 FLR 466,
[1995] Fam Law 612, CA 2.14, 5.100, 12.15
W (application for leave: whether necessary), Re [1996] 3 FCR 337n,
[1996] Fam Law 665 .... 5.55, 5.98, 5.145, 5.155
W (discharge of party to proceedings), Re [1997] 2 FCR 190, [1997] 1 FLR 128,
[1997] Fam Law 230 .... 2.18, 4.25, 8.98
W (contact: application by grandparent) [1997] 2 FCR 643, [1997] 1 FLR 793,
[1997] Fam Law 390 .... 5.83, 5.152
W (minors) (social worker: disclosure), Re [1998] 2 All ER 801, [1999] 1 WLR 205,
[1999] LGR 157, [1998] 2 FCR 405, [1998] 2 FLR 135, [1998] Fam Law 387,
142 Sol Jo LB 132, CA 11.89, 11.93
W (a minor) (care proceedings: assessment), Re [1998] 1 FCR 287, [1998] 2 FLR
130, [1998] Fam Law 318, CA 8.116
W (a minor) (staying contact), Re [1998] 2 FCR 453, [1998] 2 FLR 450, CA 5.61
W (residence), Re [1999] 3 FCR 274, [1999] 2 FLR 390, [1999] Fam Law
454, CA 10.28
W (a minor) (parental contact: prohibition), Re [2000] Fam 130, [2000] 2 WLR
1276, [2000] 1 FCR 752, [2000] 1 FLR 502, [2000] 03 LS Gaz R 36, sub nom
W (Section 34(2) orders), Re [2000] Fam Law 235, CA 8.209
W (contact application: procedure), Re [2000] 1 FCR 185, [2000] 1 FLR 263,
[2000] Fam Law 82 .... 5.152, 5.158
W (exclusion: statement of evidence), Re (2000). See W v A local authority (exclusion
requirement)
W (a child), (illegitimate child: change of surname) Re [2001] Fam 1, [2000] 2 WLR
258, [1999] 3 FCR 337, [1999] 2 FLR 930, [1999] Fam Law 688,
[1999] 33 LS Gaz R 29, 143 Sol Jo LB 242, CA 5.33, 5.34, 5.37, 5.98, 13.31
W (children) (threshold criteria: parental concessions), Re [2001] 1 FCR 139, [2000]
All ER (D) 2058, CA 4.54, 8.168
W (children) (care plan), Re [2001] EWCA Civ 757, [2001] 2 FCR 450,
[2001] 2 FLR 582, [2001] Fam Law 581, [2001] All ER (D) 285 (May); revsd
sub nom W (minors) (care order:adequacy of care plan), Re [2002] UKHL 10,
[2002] 2 AC 291, [2002] 2 All ER 192, [2002] 2 WLR 720, [2002] LGR 251,
[2002] 1 FCR 577, [2002] 1 FLR 815, [2002] 17 LS Gaz R 34, (2002) Times,
15 March, [2002] All ER (D) 212 (Mar) 1.50, 1.51, 8.60, 8.148, 8.156, 8.159, 8.172,
8.238, 12.6, 13.89
W (a child: non-accidental injury), Re [2002] EWCA Civ 710, [2003] 2 FCR 346,
[2002] All ER (D) 312 (Apr) 4.55

Table of Cases

PARA

W (children) (education: choice of school), Re [2002] EWCA Civ 1411,
[2002] 3 FCR 473, [2002] All ER (D) 83 (Aug) 3.40
W (a child) (abduction: jurisdiction), Re [2003] EWHC 1820 (Fam), [2003] 2 FLR
1105, [2003] Fam Law 712, [2003] All ER (D) 442 (Jul), sub nom H (a minor)
(child abduction: mother's asylum), Re (2003) Times, 8 August 12.22
W (a child) (care proceedings: leave to issue application), Re [2004] EWHC 3342
(Fam), [2005] 2 FLR 468, [2005] Fam Law 527, (2004) Times, 22 November,
[2004] All ER (D) 197 (Nov) 5.152, 5.153, 8.204
W (a child: care order), Re [2005] EWCA Civ 649, [2005] 2 FCR 277, 149 Sol Jo LB
710, [2005] All ER (D) 395 (May) 4.55
W (a child) (non-accidental injury: expert evidence), Re [2005] EWCA Civ 1247,
[2005] 3 FCR 513, [2005] All ER (D) 370 (Oct), sub nom W v Oldham
Metropolitan Borough Council [2006] 1 FLR 543, (2005) Times, 7 November 11.39,
11.40
W v A (child: surname) [1981] Fam 14, [1981] 1 All ER 100, [1981] 2 WLR 124, 11
Fam Law 22, 124 Sol Jo 726, CA 5.32
W v A Local Authority (exclusion requirement) [2000] 2 FCR 662, [2000] All ER
(D) 966, sub nom Re W (exculsion: statement of evidence) [2000] 2 FLR 666 .... 5.171,
8.120
W v Ealing London Borough Council [1994] 1 FCR 436, [1993] 2 FLR 788,
[1993] Fam Law 575, CA 4.52
W v Essex County Council [1999] Fam 90, [1998] 3 All ER 111, [1998] 3 WLR 534,
96 LGR 337, [1998] 2 FCR 269, [1998] 2 FLR 278, [1998] Fam Law 455,
[1998] 20 LS Gaz R 33, CA; revsd [2001] 2 AC 592, [2000] 2 All ER 237,
[2000] 2 WLR 601, [2000] LGR 281, [2000] 1 FCR 568, [2000] 1 FLR 657,
[2000] Fam Law 476, 53 BMLR 1, [2000] 13 LS Gaz R 44, 144 Sol Jo LB
147, HL 13.77
W v Hertfordshire County Council. See W (a minor), Re (1985)
W v Hertfordshire County Council. See Hertfordshire County Council v W
W v North Yorkshire County Council [1993] 1 FCR 693, sub nom Re W (a minor)
(secure accommodation order), [1993] 1 FLR 692, [1993] Fam Law 345 .... 4.57, 9.11,
9.23, 9.26
W v Official Solicitor (or W) [1972] AC 24, [1970] 3 All ER 107, [1970] 3 WLR
366, 114 Sol Jo 635, HL 2.17, 2.78
W v Oldham Metropolitan Borough Council . See W (a child) (non-accidental injury:
expert evidence), Re (2005)
W v Sunderland Borough Council [1980] 2 All ER 514, [1980] 1 WLR 1101, 78
LGR 487, 2 FLR 153, 145 JP 117, sub nom Re W (minor) 10 Fam Law 120,
124 Sol Jo 272 .... 10.65, 11.57
W v United Kingdom (Application 9749/82) (1987) 10 EHRR 29, ECtHR 1.7, 8.2
W v Wakefield City Council [1994] 2 FCR 564, [1995] 1 FLR 170, [1995] Fam Law
68 .... 5.150, 10.25
W and B (children) (care plan), [2001] EWCA Civ 757, [2001] 2 FCR 450,
[2001] 2 FLR 582, [2001] Fam Law 581, [2001] All ER (D) 285 (May); revsd
in part sub nom S (minors) (care order: implementation of care plan), Re
[2002] UKHL 10, [2002] 2 AC 291, [2002] 2 All ER 192, [2002] 2 WLR 720,
[2002] LGR 251, [2002] 1 FCR 577, [2002] 1 FLR 815,
[2002] 17 LS Gaz R 34, (2002) Times, 15 March, [2002] All ER (D) 212
(Mar) 1.50, 1.51, 8.60, 8.148, 8.154, 8.156, 8.157, 8.172, 8.238, 10.38, 12.6, 13.89
W and X (wardship: relatives rejected as foster carers), Re [2003] EWHC 2206
(Fam), [2004] 1 FLR 415, [2003] Fam Law 883 .... 6.66, 8.166, 12.17, 12.29, 12.32
WB (minors) (residence orders), Re [1995] 2 FLR 1023, [1993] Fam Law 395 ...... 5.15, 14.19
WSP v Hull City Council [2006] EWCA Civ 981, [2007] 1 FLR 90, [2006] Fam Law
831, 150 Sol Jo LB 705 .... 11,36, 11.39
Walker v Walker and Harrison noted at [1981] NZ Recent Law 257 .... 2.36
Watson v Nikolaisen [1955] 2 QB 286, [1955] 2 All ER 427, [1955] 2 WLR 1187,
119 JP 419, 99 Sol Jo 370 .... 6.52
Webb v Webb [1986] 1 FLR 541, [1986] NLJ Rep 843, CA 12.33
Webster, Re, Norfolk County Council v Webster [2006] EWHC 2733 (Fam),
[2008] STC 440, [2007] 1 FLR 1146, [2007] Fam Law 399, [2006] All ER (D)
32 (Nov), sub nom Webster (a child), Re [2007] EMLR 199 .... 2.20

PARA

Webster v Southwark London Borough Council [1983] QB 698, [1983] 2 WLR 217,
  81 LGR 357, 127 Sol Jo 53 .... 5.172
West Glamorgan County Council v P [1992] 2 FCR 378, [1992] 2 FLR 369,
  [1992] Fam Law 532 .... 8.214
Westminster City Council v RA [2005] EWHC 970 (Fam), [2005] 2 FLR 1309,
  [2005] fam law 687, (2005) Times, 6 June, sub nom Westminster City Council v
  B [2005] All ER (D) 461 (May)... 13.89
Westminster Social and Community Services Department v C [2008] EWCA Civ 198,
  [2008] 2 FCR 146, [2008] Fam Law 517, [2008] NLJR 479, (2008) Times,
  3 April, 152 Sol Jo (no 13) 29, [2008] All ER (D) 276 (Mar) 12.40
Wilde v Wilde [1988] FCR 551, [1988] 2 FLR 83, [1988] Fam Law 202, CA 12.33
Wilson v First County Trust Ltd [2003] UKHL 40, [2004] 1 AC 816,
  [2003] 4 All ER 97, [2003] 2 All ER (Comm) 491, [2003] 3 WLR 568,
  [2003] 35 LS Gaz R 39, (2003) Times, 11 July, 147 Sol Jo LB 872,
  [2004] 2 LRC 618, [2003] All ER (D) 187 (Jul)... 1.50
Wood v Collins [2006] EWCA Civ 743, [2006] All ER (D) 165 (May)....................... 5.170
Woolgar v Chief Constable of Sussex Police [1999] 3 All ER 604, [2000] 1 WLR 25,
  50 BMLR 296, [1999] 23 LS Gaz R 33, [1999] NLJR 857, CA 11.96
Wyatt, Re [2005] EWHC 2293 (Fam), [2005] 4 All ER 1325, 87 BMLR 183,
  [2005] NLJR 1634, [2005] All ER (D) 246 (Oct), sub nom Portsmouth NHS
  Trust v Wyatt [2006] 1 FLR 652, [2006] Fam Law 188 .... 3.26

X

X (a minor), Re [1975] Fam 47, [1975] 1 All ER 697, [1975] 2 WLR 335, 119 Sol
  Jo 12, CA 2.21, 12.30
X (a minor) (adopton details: disclosure), Re [1994] Fam 174, [1994] 3 All ER 372,
  [1994] 3 WLR 327, 92 LGR 656, [1995] 1 FCR 135, [1994] 2 FLR 450,
  [1994] Fam Law 555, CA 12.25
X (a minor), Re [1994] 2 FCR 1110, sub nom Re HIV Tests [1994] 2 FLR 116,
  [1994] Fam Law 559 .... 4.40
X (care: notice of proceedings), Re [1996] 3 FCR 91, [1996] 1 FLR 186,
  [1996] Fam Law 139 .... 2.18, 4.25, 8.98
X (minors) (care proceedings: parental responsibility), Re [2000] Fam 156,
  [2000] 2 All ER 66, [2000] 2 WLR 1031, [2000] Fam Law 244,
  [2000] 01 LS Gaz R 23, 144 Sol Jo LB 25, sub nom Re X (parental
  responsibility agreement: children in care) [2000] 1 FCR 379, [2000] 1 FLR
  517,... 3.55, 8.171
X (non-accidental injury: expert evidence), Re [2001] 2 FLR 90 .... 11.38
X (Disclosure of Information), Re [2001] 2 FLR 440 .... 2.22
X (children) (adoption: confidentiality), Re [2002] EWCA Civ 828, [2002] 3 FCR
  648, [2002] 2 FLR 476, [2002] All ER (D) 489 (May) 11.64
X, Re [2006] 2 FLR 988, [2006] Fam Law 740 .... 6.5
X (emergency protection orders), Re [2006] EWHC 510 (Fam), [2007] 1 FCR 551,
  [2006] 2 FLR 701, [2006] Fam Law 627, (2006) Times, 21 April, 150 Sol Jo LB
  435 .... 7.4, 7.61, 7.63, 7.65, 7.69, 7.73, 7.74, 7.75, 7.79, 7.80, 7.82, 7.83, 8.110
X (minors) v Bedfordshire County Council [1995] 2 AC 633, [1995] 3 All ER 353,
  [1995] 3 WLR 152, 160 LG Rev 103, [1995] 3 FCR 337, [1995] 2 FLR 276,
  [1995] Fam Law 537, [1995] ELR 404, 26 BMLR 15, [1995] NLJR 993, HL 13.63,
                                                                        13.72, 13,84
X v Dempster [1999] 3 FCR 757, [1999] 1 FLR 894, [1999] Fam Law 300 .... 4.47
X and Y (application to remove children from jurisdiction), Re [2001] 2 FCR 398,
  [2001] 2 FLR 118, [2000] All ER (D) 2543 .... 2.69, 5.44
X Council v B (emergency protection orders) [2004] EWHC 2015 (Fam),
  [2005] 1 FLR 341, [2005] Fam Law 13, [2004] All ER (D) 163 (Aug) 7.4, 7.61, 7.63,
                                           7.65, 7.73, 7.74, 7.77, 7.79, 7.80, 7.82, 7.85,
                                                                 7.86, 7,92, 7.96, 7.97

PARA

Y

Y (a minor), Re [1993] 2 FCR 422, [1994] Fam Law 127 .... 5.25, 5.28
Y, Re [1994] 2 FCR 367, [1994] 2 FLR 699, [1994] Fam Law 615 .... 8.218
Y (evidence of abuse: use of photographs), Re [2003] EWHC 3090 (Fam),
    [2004] 1 FLR 855, sub nom T (a child) (sexual abuse: guidance), Re [2003] All
    ER (D) 301 (Dec) 11.38
Y (leave to remove from jurisdiction), Re [2004] 2 FLR 330, [2004] Fam Law 650 .... 5.48
Y and K (children) (care proceedings: split hearing), Re [2003] EWCA Civ 669,
    [2003] 3 FCR 240, [2003] 2 FLR 273, [2003] Fam Law 554, (2003) Times,
    18 April, [2003] All ER (D) 98 (Apr) 8.143, 8.144, 11.16
Yousef v Netherlands (Application 33711/96) (2002) 36 EHRR 20, [2002] 3 FCR
    577, [2003] 1 FLR 210, [2003] Fam Law 89, [2002] ECHR 33711/96,
    ECtHR 2.4

Z

Z (a minor) (freedom of publication), Re [1997] Fam 1, [1995] 4 All ER 961,
    [1996] 2 WLR 88, [1996] 2 FCR 164, [1996] 1 FLR 191, [1996] Fam Law
    90, CA 2.17, 2.21, 3.38, 5.100, 12.2, 12.26, 12.30
Z v United Kingdom (Application 29392/95) (2001) 34 EHRR 97, [2001] 2 FCR
    246, [2001] 2 FLR 612, [2001] Fam Law 583, (2001) Times, 31 May, [2001]
    ECHR 29392/95, 10 BHRC 384, ECtHR 1.47, 13.69, 13.84, 13.85
Z v Z (refusal of contact: committal) [1996] 1 FCR 538n, [1996] Fam Law 255 .... 5.175
Z and A (contact: supervision order), Re [2000] 2 FLR 406, [2000] Fam Law 700 .... 8.181
Zawadka v Poland (Application 48542/99) [2006] 1 FCR 371, [2005] 2 FLR 897,
    [2005] Fam Law 774, [2005] ECHR 48542/99, ECtHR 5.76

Chapter 1

INTRODUCTION

1.1 The Children Act 1989 (CA 1989) brought about the most fundamental change in our child law and was well described by Lord Mackay LC as: 'the most comprehensive and far reaching reform of child law which has come before Parliament in living memory'.[1] Apart from two minor provisions[2] the CA 1989 was fully implemented on 14 October 1991. The Act has been widely regarded as a structural masterpiece providing an admirable framework for the promotion of the interests of children and families within a system of support services and court intervention where appropriate. The difficulties in practice have arisen from a shortage of resources in children's services and delays in the family justice system.

1   502 HL Official Report (5th series) col 488.
2   Namely s 5(11) and (12) which came into force on 1 February 1992 (SI 1991/828), discussed at para 3.115. A few provisions had been implemented before 14 October 1991.

1.2 In association with the CA 1989, Court Rules (since modified in the light of practice) brought about important changes in procedure and rules of evidence. Fundamental changes were also made to the court structure creating, in effect, a specialist division at every level. Rules have provided for the allocation and transfer of cases. Even the very function and role of the courts when dealing with children was changed by the Act and its accompanying rules. Extensive practical guidance was also provided from Government Departments. In short, the 1991 reform was not simply directed to substantive law change but radically affected all aspects of legal practice concerning children. What then prompted this wholesale change in this key area of law?

THE GENESIS OF THE ACT

1.3 The CA 1989 was the product of a long and thorough consultation process[1]. That process began with the Review of Child Care Law set up in 1984[2] by the then Department of Health and Social Security and assisted by the Family Law team at the Law Commission. That review concerned the public law relating to children, and in particular the local authority services to be provided for children and their families and the procedures to protect children where families fail. It produced twelve informal consultation papers

1

during 1984 and 1985 and a Report to Ministers in September 1985 which was published as a further consultation paper.[3] The Review's recommendations were essentially accepted by the government in their White Paper, 'The Law on Child Care and Family Services'.[4]

[1] See The Making of the Children Act: A Private History, Peter G Harris Family Law, December 2006, p 1054.
[2] In response to a recommendation of the Second Report of the House of Commons Social Services Select Committee, 1983/84 on Children in Care HC 360–361 (the Short Report).
[3] Review of Child Care Law (DHSS, 1985).
[4] 1987 Cm 62.

1.4 At the same time as the Review was investigating the public law relating to children, the Law Commission was undertaking a full-scale review of the private law on the allocation of responsibility between parents and other individuals. That review began with an examination of the law dealing with the consequences of birth outside marriage[1] and the resulting legislation, the Family Law Reform Act 1987, removed most of the remaining differences between children whose parents were married to each other at the time of their birth, and those who were not. Against this background the Commission examined most of the remaining aspects of the private law, publishing a series of Working Papers[2] and its final Report on Guardianship and Custody in 1988[3] Annexed to that Report was a Bill which eventually became the Children Act 1989.

[1] Law Com No 118, Illegitimacy (1982) and Law Com No 157, Illegitimacy (1986).
[2] Working Papers 1985, Nos 91 and 96 and 1987 Nos 100 and 101.
[3] Law Com No 172.

1.5 Important though the reviews of the public and private law were, it was the 'Cleveland crisis' that provided the final impetus for reform. As Lord Mackay LC said, it was a coincidence of the two reviews together with the Cleveland Report[1] which provided 'an historic opportunity to reform English law into a single rationalised system as it applies to the care and upbringing of children'.[2]

[1] Report of the Inquiry into Child Abuse in Cleveland 1987 (also known as the 'Butler-Sloss Report' or the Cleveland Report, 1988 Cm 412.
[2] 'The Child: A View Across the Tweed' [1988] Denning LJ 89, 93.

1.6 The Cleveland Report was concerned with the removal of scores of children from their families because of alleged sexual abuse. In those cases the concern was that the authority had acted too precipitately but in a number of other inquiries, notably those investigating the deaths of Jasmine Beckford,[1] Tyra Henry,[2] Kimberley Carlile[3] and Doreen Aston,[4] all of whom either were or had been in local authority care, the concern was that the local authority had not acted quickly enough. However, all these reports were influential in the final shaping of the CA 1989 and contributed much to a balanced view of the procedures needed to protect children, especially in the early stages where abuse is suspected.

[1] A Child in Trust: Report of the Panel of Inquiry Investigating the Circumstances Surrounding the Death of Jasmine Beckford, London Borough of Brent, 1985.

2   Whose Child? The Report of the Public Inquiry into the Death of Tyra Henry, London Borough of Lambeth, 1987.
3   A Child in Mind: Protection of Children in a Responsible Society, Report of the Inquiry into the Circumstances Surrounding the Death of Kimberley Carlile, London Borough of Greenwich, 1989.
4   Report to the Area Review Committee for Lambeth, Lewisham and Southwark London Boroughs, 1989.

1.7 Another important influence on the final shape of the CA 1989 was the European Convention on Human Rights (ECHR). Even before its direct incorporation into English domestic law by the Human Rights Act 1998,[1] there had been pressure from Europe for reform of English law to give effect to the fundamental rights of parents and children especially in relation to family life as protected by art 8. In particular there had been concern about the then inability of parents to challenge local authority decisions restricting parental access to children in care.[2] As others have pointed out,[3] many of the reforms relating to care proceedings and in particular those giving parents and others the right to challenge contact decisions made by local authorities,[4] were inspired, if not positively mandated by the United Kingdom's obligations under the ECHR.

1   For a discussion of the 1998 Act see paras 1.41 ff.
2   See eg *R v United Kingdom* [1988] 2 FLR 445, ECtHR, *O v United Kingdom* (1987) 10 EHRR 82, *H v United Kingdom* (1987) 10 EHRR 95, ECtHR and *W v United Kingdom* (1987) 10 EHRR 29, *B v United Kingdom* (1987) 10 EHRR 87, ECtHR.
3   Eg Bainham *Children: The New Law, The Children Act 1989*, p 5.
4   Under s 34, discussed at paras 8.141 ff.

1.8 Coincidentally, at the same time that the CA 1989 was being debated, the final touches to the United Nations Convention on the Rights of the Child 1989 were also being made, and no doubt the latter's provisions were borne in mind by those drafting the domestic Act.

1.9 Another influence on the CA 1989 was the House of Lords' decision in *Gillick v West Norfolk and Wisbech Area Health Authority*[1] which was concerned with an older child's capacity to consent to medical treatment in cases where he has sufficient understanding to make up his own mind. The Act recognises the importance of ascertaining and taking into account the child's own wishes to an extent commensurate with his age and understanding. The question of whether the preferences of a mature child should not only be taken into account but be determinative of the matter in question provoked considerable debate during the passage of the Bill. In general, however, save in certain specified instances,[2] the Act does not give mature children the right to act independently of those with parental responsibility. On the other hand, the effect of the Act's promotion of the child's own view, and in particular of provisions allowing the child himself to apply for leave to seek certain orders,[3] has been important.

1   [1986] AC 112, [1985] 3 All ER 402, HL.
2   Namely under ss 38(6), 43(8) and 44(7), discussed at paras 8.119, 7.57 and 7.91 respectively.
3   Namely under s 10(1)(a)(ii), (8) and (9), discussed at paras 5.155 ff.

THE DEVELOPMENT OF LEGISLATION

1.10 Since implementation, the Act has been amended on a number of occasions to take account of developing practice. Important substantive changes have been made by the Adoption and Children Act 2002[1] and the Children and Adoption Act 2006[2]. Changes to the court system have been introduced to try to meet the problems of delay[3]. Reorganisation of children's services has given a more specific focus to the welfare needs of children and families.[4]

1   In particular with the introduction of special guardianship: see paras 5.213 ff.
2   In particular with regard to the introduction of contact activities and the enforcement of contact: see paras 5.178.
3   See paras 4.2 ff.
4   See the Children Act 2004 and para 14.22.

1.11 It can readily be seen that the Act was brought to fruition following extensive and careful thought and discussion among all those experienced in the fields of working with children. This is an important factor when considering recent attempts to amend the structure put in place by the 1989 Act.

THE AMBIT OF THE CHILDREN ACT 1989

1.12 The CA 1989 has a wide ambit covering both the private and public law relating to the care and upbringing of children and the provision of services to them and their families. Under the Act there is a unified structure both of law and jurisdiction. In general all courts have the same powers when dealing with children.[1] There is now concurrent jurisdiction at all levels to hear care proceedings.[2] Similarly, proceedings can be transferred from a magistrates' court to a county court and vice versa, as well as between county courts and the High Court.

1   Save for the powers to make financial provision for children under Sch 1 to the CA 1989, the magistrates' courts having more limited powers than the two higher courts. See further *Clarke Hall and Morrison on Children*, Division 4.
2   Under the Children (Allocation of Proceedings) Order 1991, SI 1991/1677 proceedings must normally be commenced in the magistrates' court, see Family Proceedings Courts (Children Act 1989) Rules 1991, SI 1991/1395, Sch 1 and Chapter 8.

1.13 In providing a uniform set of powers the Act replaced much of the previous legislation. For example, the Guardianship of Minors Acts 1971 and 1973, the Children Act 1975, the Child Care Act 1980 and the Children and Young Persons (Amendment) Act 1986 were repealed together with those provisions of the Children and Young Persons Act 1969 dealing with care and supervision orders in civil proceedings and those of the Family Law Reform Act 1969 conferring statutory powers in wardship proceedings. The Matrimonial Causes Act 1973 and the Domestic Proceedings and Magistrates' Courts Act 1978 were amended as to ensure that the powers to make orders relating to children in those proceedings are governed by the CA 1989.

1.14 Apart from providing for new orders in both the private and public law field, the Act rewrote the law relating to the provision of services for children and families by local authorities,[1] children's homes[2] and private fostering and child minding.[3] Adoption law was amended but has now been substantially rewritten by the Adoption and Children Act 2002, which also introduced the concept of special guardianship. Amendments were made to provisions dealing with child abduction to bring them into line with the CA 1989. The Act affected domestic violence proceedings under Pt IV of the Family Law Act 1986, whereby courts can exercise their s 8 powers.

[1] Under Pt III and Sch 2, discussed in Chapter 6.
[2] Under Pts VI–VIII, (substantially revised by the Care Standards Act 2000), not discussed in this work.
[3] Under Pts IX, X and XA (substantially revised by the Care Standards Act 2000), not discussed in this work.
[4] The Adoption and Children Act 2002 is not discussed in this work in relation to the substantive law of adoption.

SOME KEY CHANGES UNDER THE ACT

1. New concepts

1.15 In producing what the Department of Health's Introduction to the Children Act 1989[1] describes as a 'practical and consistent code', the CA 1989 embodied three fundamental changes of concept, namely: parenthood replacing guardianship as the primary concept, 'parental responsibility' replacing the concept of parental rights and duties, and new powers to make residence orders rather than custody orders.

[1] (1989) HMSO, Foreword.

1.16 The introduction of the new concept of 'parental responsibility' is of particular importance under the Act. As Professor Hoggett (now Baroness Hale) said:[1]

'The [Act] assumes that bringing up children is the responsibility of their parents and that the State's principal role is to help rather than to interfere. To emphasise the practical reality that bringing up children is a serious responsibility, rather than a matter of legal rights, the conceptual building block used throughout the [Act] is "parental responsibility". This covers the whole bundle of duties towards the child, with their concomitant powers and authority over him, together with some procedural rights for protection, against interference ... It therefore represents the fundamental status of parents.'

The meaning and scope of this vital concept is discussed in Chapter 3.

[1] 'The Children Bill: The Aim' [1989] Fam Law 217.

1.17 The third change is the provision through s 8 of a fresh set of powers replacing the former powers to make custody and access orders. These powers are more flexible than the former and are intended to be less emotive. To this end they are drafted in clear and simple terms designed to settle practical questions (principally with whom the child is to live and whom the child can

5

see) and not to confer abstract rights. In this way it was hoped that the symbolism of victory that had come to be attached to custody and related orders would not be associated with these new s 8 orders.

1.18 Section 8 orders provide the 'basic menu' of the Act in that they can be made, either upon application or by the court acting on its own motion, in any 'family proceedings' including, therefore, proceedings brought by individuals or by local authorities. Another change relates to who can initiate or intervene in existing proceedings to seek a s 8 order. This is controlled by s 10[1] under which the Act adopts an 'open door' policy by allowing anyone (not otherwise entitled to seek an order) to seek the court's leave to apply for an order.

[1]   Discussed at paras 5.112 ff.

2. Changes in public law

(a) Services for children and families[1]

1.19 The CA 1989 provided a comprehensive statement of the welfare services that must be provided by local authorities[1] for families and children. For the first time services for disabled children were brought under the same umbrella as those for other children in need. An important objective of the Act is to promote these services as positive help for children in need. Emphasis is placed on the need for local authorities and families to work in partnership. Authorities are under a positive duty to consult the parents and children, and to promote contact between the child and his parents, family and friends. Even if compulsory measures are taken, the authorities remain under the positive duty to promote contact. The Act ended the local authorities' former powers to assume parental rights by administrative means. Instead, if compulsory measures are thought necessary, the authority must apply for a court order. Unless and until such an order is made, those with parental responsibility can remove the child from accommodation.[2]

[1]   Now the Children's Services Authorities: see the Children Act 2004, s 18 of which transfers what were formerly known as social services functions to that authority and requires that authority to appoint a Director of Children's Services.
[2]   See s 20(8) discussed at para 6.54.

1.20 Recent legislative policy[1] has focussed on the development of strategies for vulnerable children. Policy has provided for every child to benefit from:

(a)   physical and mental health and emotional well-being;
(b)   protection from harm and neglect;
(c)   education, training and recreation;
(d)   the contribution made by them to society;
(e)   social and economic well-being.

[1]   See the Children Act 2004, s 10(2) and Every Child Matters (2003) Cm 5860, (TOS) and the many related policy documents, especially the Children's Plan published in December 2007 from the Department of Children, Schools and Families or its predecessor the Department for Education and Skills.

1.21 The Children Act 2004 provides for the establishment of Local Safe-guarding Children's Boards by each Children's Services Authority.[1] The Board shall have as its partners:

(a)   where the authority is a county council for an area for which there is also a district council, the district council;

(b)   the chief officer of police for a police area any part of which falls within the area of the authority;

(c)   a local probation board for an area any part of which falls within the area of the authority;

(d)   a youth offending team for an area any part of which falls within the area of the authority;

(e)   a Strategic Health Authority and a Primary Care Trust for an area any part of which falls within the area of the authority;

(f)   an NHS trust and an NHS foundation trust, all or most of whose hospitals, establishments and facilities are situated in the area of the authority;

(g)   a person providing services under S 114 of the Learning and Skills Act 2000 in any part of the area of the authority;

(h)   the Children and Family Court Advisory and Support Service;

(i)   the governor of any secure training centre in the area of the authority (or, in the case of a contracted out secure training centre, its director);

(j)   the governor of any prison in the area of the authority which ordinarily detains children (or, in the case of a contracted out prison, its director).

The objective of the Board is to:

(a)   co-ordinate what is done by each person or body represented on the Board for the purposes of safeguarding and promoting the welfare of children in the area of the authority by which it is established; and

(b)   ensure the effectiveness of what is done by each such person or body for those purposes.

[1]   Section 10.

(b) A single threshold for state care and supervision[1]

1.22 Among other key changes in the public law field is the creation of a single statutory route into care: only if the statutory threshold in s 31 has been satisfied can the courts make a care or supervision order. Consistent with this philosophy, the courts' former powers in matrimonial and wardship proceedings to commit children into care of their own motion was ended.[2] The underlying philosophy of this threshold was explained by Lord Mackay LC in his Joseph Jackson Memorial Lecture:

'the integrity and independence of the family is the basic building block of a free and democratic society and the need to defend it should be clearly perceivable in the law. Accordingly, unless there is evidence that a child is being or is likely to be positively harmed because of a failure in the family, the state, whether in the guise of a local authority or a court, should not interfere.'[3]

[1]   Discussed in Chapter 6.

² Though note the powers under s 37, discussed at paras 5.158 and 7.5.
³ (1989) 139 NLJ 505 at 508.

3. General principles¹

1.23 Section 1 of the CA 1989 sets out a number of basic principles intended to be of general application both in the private law and public law context. The basic controlling principle in all cases where a court is considering what order, if any, to make is, pursuant to s 1(1), to treat the child's welfare as the paramount consideration. Additionally, the Act provided² for the first time a statutory checklist to help the courts determine what is for the child's welfare. Similarly new to English law is the enjoinder to the courts under s 1(2) to have regard to the general principle that delay in determining questions about a child's upbringing is 'likely to prejudice the welfare of the child'. To avoid delay the court was given for the first time both the power and the duty to impose timetables for proceedings.³

¹ Discussed in Chapter 2.
² Section 1(3).
³ Under ss 11(1) and 32(1), discussed in Chapter 4, paras 4.43 ff. Similar duties are imposed in adoption proceedings by the Adoption and Children Act 2002.

1.24 Another innovation of the CA 1989 is the direction to the court by s 1(5) not to make an order 'unless it considers that doing so would be better for the child than making no order at all'. This provision requires justification in every case of why it is in the child's interests that any order be made. It is no longer sufficient that each party consents to an order being made, though the court is not prevented from making an order in such circumstances. The operation of this provision is discussed in chapter 2.¹

¹ See paras 2.64 ff.

4. Procedural changes

1.25 The 1991 reforms radically affected all aspects of legal practice concerning children. These changes ranged from the introduction of entirely new rules governing procedure and evidence to changes in court structure and the creation of new Committees charged with overseeing the working of the Act.

(a) Procedure and evidence

1.26 Procedure under the CA 1989 is principally governed by two sets of rules, namely, the Family Proceedings Rules 1991¹ (FPR 1991) for the High Court and county court and the Family Proceedings Courts (Children Act 1989) Rules 1991 (FPC(CA 1989)R 1991) for the magistrates' court. They have both been considerably amended and are in the process of being rewritten, rather more belatedly than expected, for publication in 2009/10 to make them consistent with the Civil Procedure Rules 1998.

¹ SI 1991/1247.

1.27 The rules are a virtual mirror image of each other both in content and chronological order differing only where court structure dictates. For example, while the Family Proceedings Rules 1991 refer to the 'proper officer' the FPC(CA 1989)R 1991 (as amended[1]) refer to the 'designated officer for a local justice area' for procedure and 'justices' clerk' for quasi-judicial decisions. In line with the principle of unity of jurisdiction between the courts and of facilitating easy transfer from one level to another, applications and orders are made on a common set of forms, copies of which are set out at the end of each set of rules.

[1]   The Courts Act 2003 (Consequential Provisions) (No 2) Order 2005, SI 2005/617, amended by SI 2005/2804 and SI 2006/1970.

(b) The creation of a comprehensive liaison network

1.28 Another important innovation of the 1991 reforms was the creation of a comprehensive liaison network to underpin the working of the Act. This network was intended to promote co-operation not only between the courts themselves but also among court users. In this way it was hoped to promote some of the key aims of the Act, namely, to avoid delay and ensure commonality of practice throughout the country and at each court level.[1] It was also intended to provide the means by which the major issues can be quickly identified and addressed, not just locally, but also nationwide.[2] While this may have proved beneficial in some areas, it has clearly not proved successful in achieving a consistently improved standard of family justice nationally, either in the development of policy or court services or practices. The responsibilities of the Family Justice Council[3] might lead to improvements in the system but until more respect is given to their proposals, any improvement is likely to be limited[4].

[1]   See the Children Act Advisory Committee's Annual Report (CAAC Report) 1992/93, p 4.
[2]   See the CAAC Report 1993/94, p 4.
[3]   See para 1.33.
[4]   See para 14.7 for further discussion.

(I) Family Division Liaison Judge

1.29 An important part of the liaison network is the appointment of a High Court Judge of the Family Division as Liaison Judge for each of the seven circuits in England and Wales. The Liaison Judge has the following role, namely, to:

(a)   identify which circuit judges should be appointed to hear Children Act cases;
(b)   act as a channel between the Lord Chancellor and the judiciary;
(c)   assist in bringing together others, including magistrates and those responsible for support agencies to discuss matters of concern;
(d)   preside over the annual regional conference on family proceedings on their own circuit.

9

It is through this mechanism that there is a regular review at a circuit level of work at all court levels.

(II) THE CHILDREN ACT ADVISORY COMMITTEE, THE ADVISORY BOARD ON FAMILY LAW AND CHILDREN ACT SUB-COMMITTEE

1.30 The overall operation of the CA 1989 was initially monitored by the Children Act Advisory Committee (CAAC). Established in 1991 and chaired by a High Court judge with membership comprising, inter alia, representatives of various government departments, and key personnel concerned with the everyday working of the courts, the Committee continued to function until July 1997. During its six years of work the CAAC's terms of reference and consequent centre of focus changed. Originally, the terms were:[1]

> 'To advise the Lord Chancellor, the Home Secretary, the Secretary of State for Health and the President of the Family Division on whether the guiding principles of the Children Act 1989 are being achieved and whether the court procedures and the guardian ad litem system are operating satisfactorily.'

In 1993 these terms were broadened[2] to comprise both the giving of advice:

> 'On the progress of Children Act cases through the court system, with a view to identifying special difficulties and reducing avoidable delay; and to promote through local Family Court Business Committees commonality of administrative practice and procedure in the family proceedings courts and the county courts and to advise on the impact on Children Act work of other family initiatives.'

These terms were reviewed again in 1995 but although they were not formally changed, in view of the continuing problems experienced in connection with the issue of delay, the CAAC was asked to make that issue its focus of work during what turned out to be its last two years of office.[3]

[1]   CAAC Report 1991/92, p 5.
[2]   CAAC Report 1992/93, p 4.
[3]   CAAC Report 1994/95, p 7.

1.31 The CAAC did invaluable work, producing a total of five Annual Reports. Its Final Report, published in 1997, contains a useful summary of the recommendations it made in its previous reports and of the action taken.[1] In addition to its Final Report, the Committee also produced a 'Handbook of Best Practice in Children Act cases' which was intended as a 'comprehensive reference tool for use by all those involved in the preparation and conduct of public and private law Children Act proceedings'.

[1]   CAAC Final Report, 1997, at p 8.

(III) THE ADVISORY BOARD ON FAMILY LAW

1.32 As mentioned in its 1994/95 report,[1] Lord Mackay had indicated that as the CAAC was set up to monitor a new Act it should have a finite existence. The Committee was eventually wound up in 1997. Some of the CAAC's work was taken over by the Advisory Board on Family Law which was created in 1997 primarily to advise the Lord Chancellor on the implementation of the Family Law Act 1996. That Board's remit[2] included maintaining 'an overview of the working of the policy embodied in the Children Act within the family court system' and, to provide continuity with the work of the former Advisory Committee, it was decided that membership of the Board would include a Family Division judge or a Court of Appeal judge with Family Division experience.[3] The appointed member was Wall J. At the Board's first meeting it was agreed to establish a Children Act Sub-Committee, chaired by Wall J, and which would report to the Advisory Board. The Sub-Committee thus assumed some of the responsibilities of the former Advisory Committee though its remit was rather different, being 'to maintain a more strategic overview of the major policy issues and not to become involved in operational issues.'[4] Following the Government's decision not to implement Pt II of the Family Law Act 1996, it was decided to wind up the Advisory Board at the end of 2001 and with it, the Children Act Sub-Committee.

[1]   CAAC Report 1994/95, at p 8.
[2]   See the Advisory Board on Family Law's Fourth Annual Report, para 1.9.
[3]   CAAC Final Report 1997, at p 7.
[4]   Advisory Board's Fourth Annual Report, at paras 1.10–1.12.

(IV) THE FAMILY JUSTICE COUNCIL

1.33 In 2002 the Lord Chancellor's Department consulted on the desirability of creating a Family Justice Council which was ultimately established on 1 July 2004. Its terms of reference were to facilitate the delivery of better and quicker outcomes for families and children who use the family justice system. The Council's primary role is to promote an inter-disciplinary approach to family justice, and through consultation and research, to monitor how effectively the system, both as a whole and through its component parts, delivers the service the Government and the public need and to advise on reforms necessary for continuous improvement. In particular its responsibilities are to:

- promote improved interdisciplinary working across the family justice system through inclusive discussion, communication and co-ordination between all agencies, including by way of seminars and conferences as appropriate;
- identify and disseminate best practice throughout the family justice system by facilitating a mutual exchange of information between local family justice councils and the national Council, including information on local initiatives, and by identifying priorities for, and encouraging the conduct of, research;
- provide guidance and direction to achieve consistency of practice throughout the family justice system and submit proposals for new practice directions where appropriate;
- provide advice and make recommendations to Government on changes to legislation, practice and procedure, which will improve the workings of the family justice system.

(V) THE FAMILY COURT BUSINESS COMMITTEES AND THE FAMILY
COURT FORUMS[1]

1.34 In 1991, two new local committees were set up to provide local reviews
of the working of the CA 1989. The first were the Family Court Business
Committees which are concerned with the management of cases in terms of
the availability of resources, priorities in relation to other litigation and sound
practice in transferring cases between courts. The Committee is chaired by the
designated family judge and serviced by the court administrator. The Business
Committees at first reported to the CAAC and then to the Children Act
Sub-Committee and minutes of their meetings are disseminated among other
Business Committees in the surrounding areas.

[1]   See the review in the 2002 LCD Consultation Paper: 'Promoting inter-agency working in
the family justice system'.

1.35 The Second Committee, originally known as the Family Court Services
Committee, was intended to provide a forum for professional concerns about
issues arising under the CA 1989 and the conduct of the various agencies and
professions in safeguarding children's welfare. Like the Business Committee,
the Services Committee was chaired by the designated family judge, but had a
wider membership than the former.

1.36 The role of the two committees was reviewed by the Council for Family
Proceedings which concluded, inter alia, that there was a need to distinguish
more clearly between the committees' respective roles.[1] In particular it
recommended that the Services Committees should be replaced by a more
flexible style of meeting to be called the family court forums. This change was
implemented in August 1994. The amended terms of reference of the Forums
are:

(i)   to promote discussion and encourage co-operation between all the
       professions, agencies and organisations involved in or concerned with
       family proceedings and to provide occasions for this to occur at each
       care centre;
(ii)   to consider issues which arise locally in the conduct of family proceed-
       ings;
(iii) to recommend action which can be taken locally to improve the service
       provided to the parties to family proceedings; and
(iv)   in addition to routine meetings family court forums will consider
       whether special events, seminars, study days or conferences are required
       locally to disseminate good practice, new arrangements and ideas or to
       examine problems.

[1]   See the CAAC's Annual Report 1993/94, p 5 and [1994] Fam Law 662.

(IV) COURT USER COMMITTEES

1.37 The Advisory Committee regarded the role of the Business Committee as
'pivotal' to its own role. In fact both committees provide an important

opportunity for local and national problems of administration to be discussed and remedied outside the context of particular litigation. They are not, however, the only committees. Even before the 1991 reforms some areas had developed court user committees comprising practitioners and representatives from agencies concerned in family proceedings. Some courts have retained this committee which again provides a forum for identifying and resolving any problems that they may have. The key difference, however, is that the Business Committee and Family Court Forum provide the opportunity of discussing local problems facing both the county court and family proceedings court.

(c) Role of the courts

1.38 An important result of the many procedural changes is that the courts' role changed. For example, all courts have a greater managerial role consequent upon the duty to impose timetables and to give directions to adhere to that timetable. Indeed, it is under the CA 1989 that for the first time the courts themselves were placed under a duty to ensure the speedy disposal of cases. All courts are expected to take an active role in the case management of proceedings. As the Department of Health's Introduction to the Children Act 1989 puts it:[1]

> 'Under the Act the courts have an independent duty to do what is best for the child. If the courts are to discharge that duty often they will have to take an active part in the proceedings rather than simply acting as umpires between the contending parties.'

Further encouragement to take a proactive role is the general requirement of advance disclosure of evidence and the greater powers of the court to control what further evidence should be adduced. The impact of this proactive duty is discussed in Chapter 4.

[1]   (1989) HMSO, para 1.51.

SOME KEY CHANGES SINCE THE ACT

1.39 During the seventeen years since the CA 1989 first came into force there have been numerous decisions concerned with its interpretation and application. Similarly, there have been numerous amendments both to the Act and the Rules; these developments will be discussed throughout this work. There has also been a number of important new statutes, such as the Crime and Disorder Act 1998, the Access to Justice Act 1999, the Protection of Children Act 1999, the Care Standards Act 2000, the Children (Leaving Care) Act 2000 and the Adoption and Children Act 2002, which we do not have space to consider in detail in this work.

1.40 A vital part of the family justice system is the Children and Family Court Advisory and Support Service (CAFCASS) created by the Criminal Justice and Court Services Act 2000 which came into operation on 1 April 2001. This service brought together under a single umbrella, the former court welfare service, the guardian ad litem service and some of the functions of the Official Solicitor. This service is discussed further in Chapter 10.

1.41 There have been three major developments outside the CA 1989 but which nevertheless affect its operation, that should be adverted to more specifically in this introduction. They are Welsh Devolution, the Civil Procedure Rules 1998, and the implementation of the Human Rights Act 1998.

1. Welsh devolution

1.42 Consequent upon Welsh devolution is the need for separate Welsh statutory instruments and regulations to govern devolved issues such as those relating to child care. This means that care now needs to be exercised when determining the application of regulatory law. It is noticeable that the Welsh regulations tend to be published some time after their English counterparts. Furthermore they may not be identically expressed, so that divergence is beginning to develop in some areas[1], for example in relation to complaints procedures and the Commissioners for Children, who in Wales but not in England has powers to deal with individual complaints.

[1] See Rees: 'Devolution and the Development of Family Law in Wales' [2008] CFLQ 45.

2. The Civil Procedure Rules 1998

1.43 Following the so-called 'Woolf Reforms'[1] the civil litigation system was radically overhauled and the former Rules of the Supreme Court 1965 and the County Court Rules 1981 were replaced by a new set of rules known as the Civil Procedure Rules 1998 (CPR). In some ways these reforms built upon ideas pioneered in the Family Division particularly following the CA 1989.[2] The CPR themselves, however, do not generally apply to family proceedings,[3] which instead continue to be governed by the FPR 1991 (in the higher courts) and the FPC(CA 1989)R 1991 (in the magistrates' courts). However, this does not mean that the family practitioner can ignore the CPR. The CPR provisions apply to the assessment of costs in the higher court proceedings,[4] and govern both appeals to the higher courts[5] and applications for judicial review.[6] It is intended that there will be harmonisation of rules with the FPR 1991 in due course. The reforms, which have already been introduced for adoption in the Family Proceedings (Adoption) Rules 2005, are intended to: improve access to justice and reduce the cost of litigation; reduce complexity and modernise technology and improve unnecessary distinctions of practice and procedure.[7]

[1] See *Access to Justice* (HMSO 1996).
[2] See e g Burrows 'Woolf and the Family Lawyer' [1999] Fam Law 223.
[3] See CPR 2.1.
[4] Namely in accordance with Pts 43, 44, 47 and 48. See further paras 4.61 ff.
[5] CPR Pt 52. Note in this respect the important change that, even in family proceedings, leave to appeal to the Court of Appeal is generally required: CPR 52.3, discussed further at paras 13.11 ff.
[6] CPR Pt 54.
[7] See *Access to Justice* (Interim Report, HMSO, 1995), Introduction.

3. The Human Rights Act 1998

1.44 A most significant post-Children Act development has been the Human Rights Act 1998 (HRA 1998), which came into force in October 2000.[1] It is not intended here to provide a definitive discussion of the application of the 1998 Act[2] but rather to highlight some key points and to stress the underlying importance of the ECHR when applying the CA 1989 and determining lawfulness of the acts of local authorities and the courts.[3]

[1] SI 2000/1851.
[2] For a fuller discussion of the Human Rights Act 1998 see eg Swindells, Neaves, Kushner and Skilbeck *Family Law and the Human Rights Act 1998*; Horowitz, Kingscote and Nicholls *The Human Rights Act 1998 – A Special Bulletin for Family Lawyers*; Supperstone, Goudie and Coppel *Local Authorities and the Human Rights Act 1998*; *Clarke Hall and Morrison on Children*, 1[65] ff and *Butterworths Family Law Service*, Vol 5A, Ch 6.
[3] Though note the warnings against making unnecessary and unhelpful references to the ECHR, see *Daniels v Walker (Practice Note)* [2000] 1 WLR 1382 and *Re F (care proceedings: contact)* [2001] 1 FCR 481.

1.45 Although the United Kingdom was one of the original signatories to the ECHR (having ratified it in 1951) and, since 1966, has allowed individuals to take their complaints to the European Court of Human Rights in Strasbourg, the Convention remained an international obligation and did not form part of domestic law. This meant that the UK courts were not obliged to take the ECHR into account when applying domestic law.[1] What the Act does is:

- oblige all domestic courts at all levels to take ECHR case law into account when deciding a question relating to a ECHR right;
- provide that, so far as it is possible to do so, primary and subordinate legislation must be read and given effect to in a way that is compatible with ECHR rights;
- empower the higher courts[2] to make declarations of incompatibility if satisfied that a statutory provision is incompatible with a ECHR right;
- make it unlawful for public authorities to act in a way that is incompatible with a ECHR right save where the authorities are obliged to do so by primary legislation;
- permit persons to bring proceedings against a public authority acting or proposing to act in a way made unlawful by the 1998 Act; and
- empower the courts to give an appropriate remedy, including damages in respect of any act (or proposed act) of a public authority which is (or would be) found to be unlawful.

[1] Though this did not prevent courts from having regard to the ECHR particularly when construing legislative ambiguities. For a discussion of the pre-1998 Act position see eg Duffy 'English law and the European Convention on Human Rights' (1980) 29 ICLQ 585.
[2] Namely the High Court and the appellate courts, see s 4(5).

1.46 So far as child law is concerned the most relevant 'Convention rights' for the above mentioned purposes are those provided by arts 8 and 6(1) of the ECHR.[1] The former provides:

'Everyone has the right to respect for his private and family life, his home and his correspondence.'

15

However, this right is qualified by art 8(2) which states:

'There shall be no interference by a public authority with the exercise of this right except such as in accordance with the law and is necessary in a democratic society in the interests of national security, public safety or the economic well-being of the country, for the prevention of disorder or crime, for the protection of health or morals, or for the protection of the rights and freedoms of others'.

Article 6(1) provides:

'In the determination of his civil rights and obligations or of any criminal charge against him, everyone is entitled to a fair and public hearing within a reasonable time by an independent and impartial tribunal established by law. Judgment shall be pronounced publicly but the press and public may be excluded from all or part of the trial in the interest of morals, public order or national security in a democratic society, where the interests of juveniles or the protection of the private life of the parties so require, or to the extent strictly necessary in the opinion of the court in special circumstances where publicity would prejudice the interests of justice'.

1   These and all other 'incorporated' arts are contained in Sch 1 to the HRA 1998. The extent to which these basic rights are likely to continue to be protected is discussed further in Chapter 14.

1.47 These, however, are not the only ECHR rights of relevance to child law. For example, both arts 3(1) and 5(1) have already been relied upon in certain crucial cases.[1] Article 3 provides:

'No one shall be subjected to torture or to inhuman or degrading treatment or punishment'.

Article 5(1) provides:

'Everyone has the right to liberty and security of person. No one shall be deprived of his liberty save in the following cases and in accordance with a procedure prescribed by law: ... (d) the detention of a minor by lawful order for the purpose of educational supervision or his lawful detention for the purpose of bringing him before the competent legal authority; ... '

Furthermore art 14 also has to be taken into account.[2] This provides:

'The enjoyment of the rights and freedoms set forth in this Convention shall be secured without discrimination on any ground such as sex, race, colour, language, religion, political or other opinion, national or social origin, association with a national minority, property, birth or other status'.

1   Article 3 has obvious relevance to the issue of disciplining the child, see eg *A v United Kingdom (human rights: punishment of child)* [1998] 3 FCR 597, [1998] 2 FLR 959, 27 EHRR 611, ECtHR, but its significance can go beyond this, see *Z v United Kingdom* [2001] 2 FCR 246, [2001] 2 FLR 612, ECtHR, in which it was held that a local authority's failure to take adequate measures to protect children who were known to be ill-treated by their parents breached art 3. Article 5 has obvious relevance to secure accommodation, see *Re K (A Child) (Secure Accommodation Order: Rights to Liberty)* [2001] Fam 377, [2001] 2 WLR 1141, [2001] 2 All ER 719, CA, discussed at para 9.2.
2   Article 14 can only be relied upon in conjunction with another article. It does not provide an independent ECHR right. Protocol No 12 does make discrimination an independent right but the UK has not signed it.

1.48 The ECHR does not specifically confer rights on children, rather it confers rights on everyone, including children. This, however, means that art 8, for example, confers the right to respect for family life both on parents and children which therefore calls for a balancing exercise should those rights conflict.

1.49 The obligation to take ECHR case law into account when deciding a question relating to a ECHR right is provided for by s 2 of the HRA 1998. By 'case law' is meant not only the judgments of the European Court of Human Rights but also the opinions of the former Commission and includes decisions on the admissibility of claims.[1] The obligation, however, is only to take such case law into account. The jurisprudence is not binding in any strict sense of precedence and indeed it is open to the English courts to go further than the European Court.[2] Clearly however, a court that ignores ECHR case law will clearly run the risk of an appeal.

[1] See s 2(1)(a)–(d) of the HRA 1998. A useful chart of relevant ECHR case law can be found in *Clarke Hall and Morrison on Children* at 1[4001] ff.
[2] See eg *Fitzpatrick v Sterling Housing Association Ltd* [2001] 1 AC 27, [1999] 3 WLR 113, [1999] 4 All ER 705, HL and *Ghaidan v Godin-Mendoza* [2004] UKHL 30, [2004] 2 AC 557, [2004] 2 FCR 481, [2004] 2 FLR 600.

1.50 A crucial provision in the 1998 Act is s 3 which provides that so far as possible primary and subordinate legislation must be read and given effect in a manner that is compatible with the ECHR. Although this provision entitles the courts to depart from earlier domestic precedents insofar as they are thought to be incompatible with ECHR rights, as Lord Nicholls stressed in *Re S (Minors) (Care Order: Implementation Of Care Plan), Re W (Minors) (Care Order: Adequacy Of Care Plan)*,[1] it does not entitle the courts to legislate. As he put it: 'Interpretation of statutes is a matter for the courts, the enactment of statutes, and the amendment of statutes, are matters for Parliament'. As against this, however, it has also been stressed[2] that s 3 of the HRA 1998 obliges courts to find an interpretation of a statute which is compatible with the ECHR if at all possible. As Hale LJ said[3] 'the 1998 Act was carefully designed to promote the search for compatibility, rather than incompatibility'.

[1] [2002] UKHL 10, [2002] 2 AC 291, [2002] 2 WLR 720, [2002] 2 All ER 192 at para [39], applying *Poplar Housing Regeneration Community Association Ltd v Donoghue* [2001] EWCA Civ 595 at para [75], [2002] QB 48, [2001] 4 All ER 604, per Lord Woolf CJ and *R v Lambert* [2001] UK HL 37 at paras [79]–[81], [2002] 2 AC 545, [2001] 3 All ER 577, per Lord Hope.
[2] *R v A (No 2)* [2001] UKHL 25, [2002] 1 AC 45, [2001] 2 WLR 1546, [2001] 3 All ER 1, per Lord Steyn.
[3] In *Re W and B (children) (care plan), Re W (children) (care plan)* [2001] EWCA Civ 757 at para [50], [2001] 2 FCR 450, [2001] 2 FLR 582, not directly commented upon by HL on appeal, reported as *Re S*, above at n 1. In *Wilson v First Country Trust Ltd (No 2)* [2003] UKHL 40, [2004] 2 AC 816, [2003] 3 WLR 568, [2003] 4 All ER 97 the House of Lords held that the power to make a declaration of incompatibility did not arise until the court concluded that it was not possible to read and give effect to the legislation in a way that was compatible with ECHR rights.

1.51 Notwithstanding the encouragement to find compatibility, s 4 of the 1998 Act specifically empowers the High Court and the appellate courts to make a formal declaration that a provision of primary legislation is incompatible with a ECHR right. Although such declarations do not affect the validity of the legislation in question, which will continue to apply, the expectation nevertheless is that the offending provision(s) will consequently be amended.[1] Given the importance placed on finding compatibility it is not surprising that s 4 declarations are rare (but for an example see *Bellinger v Bellinger*[2]). Furthermore, declarations can only be made in respect of specific provisions. It is not therefore sufficient to allege that the whole scheme of an Act is incompatible.[3]

1 See s 10.
2 [2003] UKHL 21, [2003] 2 AC 467, [2003] 2 FCR 1, [2003] 1 FLR 1043 in which the House of Lords declared that the limitation of marriage to a male and female in the Matrimonial Causes Act 1973, s 11 was incompatible with arts 8 and 12 of the ECHR.
3 See *Re W and B (children) (care plan), Re W (children) (care plan)* [2001] EWCA Civ 757 at para [50], [2001] 2 FCR 450, [2001] 2 FLR 582, per Hale LJ, impliedly upheld on this point by HL on appeal, see *Re S (Minors) (Care Order; Implementation of Care Plan), Re W (Minors) (Care Order: Adequacy of Care Plan)* [2002] UKHL 10, [2002] 2 AC 291, [2002] 2 WLR 720, [2002] 2 All ER 192 at para [41], per Lord Nicholls.

1.52 Another significant part of the Act is that enabling individuals to enforce their ECHR rights against a public authority. A 'public authority' for these purposes is widely defined and includes local authorities and the courts.[1] The scheme of the Act in this respect was well described by Lord Nicholls in *Re S*.[2] As he put it:

> 'Sections 7 and 8 of the Human Rights Act 1998 have conferred extended powers on the courts. Section 6 makes it unlawful for a public authority to act in a way which is incompatible with a Convention right. Section 7 enables victims of conduct made unlawful by s 6 to bring court proceedings against the public authority in question. Section 8 spells out, in wide terms, the relief a court may grant in those proceedings. The court may grant such relief or remedy, or make such order, within its powers as it considers just and appropriate. Thus, if a local authority conducts itself in a manner which infringes the article 8 rights of a parent or child, the court may grant appropriate relief on the application of a victim of the unlawful act'.

Actions, which can only be brought by victims of the unlawful conduct,[3] must generally be brought within one year of the act complained of, or 'such longer period as the court or tribunal considers equitable in all the circumstances.'[4] Insofar as a complaint is sought in respect of a judicial act, it can only be by way of an appeal or judicial review.[5]

1 Section 6(3) states that ' "public authority" includes: (a) a court or tribunal, and (b) any person of whose functions are functions of a public nature ... ' on which see *Poplar Housing and Regeneration Community Association Ltd v Donoghue* [2001] EWCA Civ 595, [2002] QB 48, [2001] 4 All ER 604, CA. But note *R (on the application of Heather) v Leonard Cheshire Foundation* [2002] EWCA Civ 366, [2002] 2 All ER 936, voluntary sector home for the disabled funded by local authority held not to be exercising public functions.
2 *Re S (Minors) (Care Order: Implementation of Care Plan), Re W (Minors) (Care Order: Adequacy of Care Plan)* above at para [45].
3 Section 7(7) defines such victims by reference to art 34 of the ECHR. It is confined to a person who is directly affected by the act or omission. In *A and B v United Kingdom* [1998] 1 EHRLR 82, for example, a father of a son who was beaten by his stepfather was not considered a 'victim'.

4   Section 7(5).
5   Section 9. Damages cannot be awarded for judicial acts committed in good faith except under art 5(5) (for an arrest or detention contravening art 5), when they are payable by the Crown, s 9(3), (4).

1.53 We discuss the impact of the ECHR on specific aspects of the application of the CA throughout the book. At the time of the implementation of the HRA 1998 it was not anticipated that the 1989 Act would be vulnerable to many successful substantive law challenges, since it had been drafted with the ECHR in mind. There was speculation about the compatibility of the paramountcy principle, the status of unmarried fathers and the lawfulness of secure accommodation orders. There was concern too not so much as to the lawfulness of the power to make care orders (given the need to satisfy the threshold provisions) but rather whether a particular order is proportionate to the needs of the situation. In particular it was questioned whether it could be justified to make a care order where the child will be living at home. Concern was also expressed as to whether the lack of power of the courts to oversee care plans was compliant with the 1998 Act. There was speculation, for instance, both as to whether requiring grandparents to have court leave to apply for a s 8 order and requiring local authority foster parents to have local authority consent to apply for court leave, was human rights compliant. There was concern too as to compatibility of s 91(14), (15) and (17), which impose respectively discretionary and automatic leave requirements. Further concerns had been expressed about the rules of hearsay and the right of cross examination as they applied in children's cases. There were worries about the ability to obtain ex parte orders, particularly emergency protection orders and speculation about the legality of hearing children's cases in private.

1.54 As will be seen, many of these concerns have already been addressed either domestically, as for example, regarding the compatibility of the paramountcy principle[1] and the lawfulness of secure accommodation orders,[2] or by the European Court, as in the case of not giving unmarried fathers automatic parental responsibility.[3] Other issues remain to be addressed while still others that were not speculated upon earlier, have since been brought before the courts. In this latter regard it seems that the remedies provided for by ss 7 and 8 may well prove rather more extensive than originally envisaged.[4] One important matter that does appear to have been resolved is whether or not the HRA 1998 Act can have a so-called 'horizontal effect', that is, determining the rights as between individuals.[5] Contrary to earlier suggestions,[6] it now seems accepted that it can.[7] That is not to say that the Act directly allows individuals to sue one another under the ECHR; rather it is accepted that ECHRjurisprudence[8] establishes that there are positive obligations upon the State to ensure that individuals' rights are protected.[9] Furthermore, since courts, as public authorities, are obliged to act compatibly with ECHR rights, they must, when deciding an application between individuals, apply domestic law in accordance with those rights. Since so much of family law is concerned with private litigation, this conclusion is not without significance for the future development of child law.

1   See eg *Re L (A Child) (Contact: Domestic Violence), Re V (A Child), Re M (A Child), Re H (children)* [2001] Fam 260, [2000] 4 All ER 609, discussed at para 2.4.

2 See *Re K (A Child) (Secure Accommodation Order: Right to Liberty)* [2001] Fam 377, [2001] 2 WLR 1141, [2001] 2 All ER 719, CA, discussed at para 9.2.
3 See *B v United Kingdom* [2000] 1 FCR 289, [2000] 1 FLR 1 in which the European Court held that English law did not breach the ECHR, see further 3.44.
4 See further paras 13.88 ff.
5 For extensive discussion of this issue see Wade 'Human Rights and the Judiciary' [1998] EHRLR 520, Buxton 'The Human Rights Act and Private Law' (2000) 116 LQR 48 and Hunt 'The "Horizontal effect" of the Human Rights Act' [1998] Public Law 423.
6 See eg Buxton LJ in *Re G-A (permission to remove child from jurisdiction: human rights)* [2001] 1 FCR 43, sub nom *Re A (Permission to Remove Child From Jurisdiction)* [2000] 2 FLR 225.
7 See *Payne v Payne* [2001] EWCA, Civ 166, [2001] 1 FCR 425, [2001] 1 FLR 1052, per Thorpe LJ and Butler-Sloss P.
8 As established by *Marckx v Belgium* (1979) 2 EHRR 330, ECtHR.
9 See eg *A v United Kingdom (human rights: punishment of a child)* [1998] 3 FCR 597, [1998] 2 FLR 959, ECtHR.

Chapter 2
GENERAL PRINCIPLES

2.1 Section 1 of the CA 1989 sets out the general principles that are to be applied in court proceedings, namely:

(1) the child's welfare is paramount in deciding all questions about his upbringing and the administration of his property;
(2) regard is to be had to the general principle that delay in deciding any question with respect to the child's upbringing is likely to prejudice the child's welfare;
(3) in contested applications for s 8 orders and in all care and special guardianship proceedings, the courts should, when applying the welfare principle, pay particular regard to certain specific matters contained in the statutory welfare checklist; and
(4) the court should not make any order under the CA 1989 unless to do so is considered better for the child than making no order.

THE WELFARE PRINCIPLE

2.2 Section 1(1) lays down the cardinal principle in child law that:

'When any court determines any question with respect to:
(a) the upbringing of the child; or
(b) the administration of the child's property or the application of any income arising from it,
the child's welfare shall be the court's paramount consideration.'

As Ward LJ observed in *Re A (Children) (Conjoined Twins: Surgical Separation):*[1]

'The peremptory terms of this section should be noted. It places the court under a duty to do what is dictated by the child's welfare'.

[1] [2001] Fam 147 at 180, [2000] 4 All ER 961 at 993, CA.

1. 'Paramount' not 'first and paramount'

2.3 Unlike the 1971 Act, which directed the court to treat the child's welfare as its first and paramount consideration, s 1(1) of the CA 1989 simply directs the court to treat the child's welfare as its paramount consideration. The CA 1989's paramountcy formulation reflects the previous well established position encapsulated by Lord MacDermott when he said in the leading case, *J v C*,[1] that the principle connotes:

> 'A process whereby, when all the relevant facts, relationships, claims and wishes of parents, risks, choices and other circumstances are taken into account and weighed, the course to be followed will be that which is most in the interests of the child's welfare as that term has now to be understood. That is the first consideration because of its first importance and the paramount consideration because it rules upon or determines the course to be followed.'

In the past it was said[2] that in effect *J v C* established, and s 1(1) confirmed, that the child's welfare is the court's sole concern and other factors are relevant only to the extent that they can assist the court in ascertaining the best solution for the child. However, it is clear, following the implementation of the Human Rights Act 1998 (HRA 1998), that such an approach cannot be correct since too little attention is paid to the need to respect the rights of parents. In other words, in interpreting s 1(1), respect must be given to *each* person's rights, though where a child's interests conflict with other persons' interests, the former should prevail. Whether even this interpretation is compatible with the European Convention on Human Rights (ECHR) is discussed below.

[1]   In *J v C* [1970] AC 668 at 710–711, [1969] 1 All ER 788 at 820–821, HL. Expressly cited eg by Baroness Hale in *Re G (Children) (Residence: Same Sex Partners)* [2006] UKHL 43, [2006] 1 WLR 2305, [2006] 4 All ER 241 at [27], and by Lord Nicholls in *Re O (Minors) (Care: Preliminary Hearing)* [2003] UKHL 18, [2004] 1 AC 523, [2003] 2 All ER 305, [2003] 2 WLR 1025 at [24].See also *Re K D (a Minor) (Ward: Termination of Access)* [1988] AC 806, [1988] 1 All ER 577, HL. For a detailed discussion of the development and application of the welfare principle, see Lowe 'The House of Lords and the Welfare Principle' in Bridge (ed) *Family Law Towards the Millennium – Essays for PM Bromley* (1997) Butterworths at 125 ff.

[2]   See eg para 2.4 of the second edition of this work.

2. Is the paramountcy principle human rights compliant?

2.4 In cases governed by s 1(1) it is clear that where the parents' and the child's interests conflict, as in *J v C*[1] itself, it is the child's interests that must prevail. In *Re L (A Child) (Contact: Domestic Violence)*[2] Butler-Sloss P commented that this prevailing preference for children's interests was entirely compatible with art 8(2) of the European Convention on Human Rights. As she pointed out, in *Hendricks v Netherlands*[3] it was held that where there was a serious conflict between the interests of a child and one of his or her parents which could only be resolved to the disadvantage of one of them, it was the child's interests that had to prevail under art 8(2). Further, in *Johansen v Norway*[4] the ECHR commented that a parent was not entitled under art 8 to have such measures taken that would harm the child's health and development. Similarly, Thorpe LJ had no doubts as to the compatibility of the paramountcy principle with the ECHR, observing:[5]

> 'whilst the advent of the 1998 Act requires revision of the judicial approach to conclusion, as a safeguard to an inadequate perception and application for a father's rights under Articles 6 and 8, it requires no re-evaluation of the judge's

primary task to evaluate and uphold the welfare of the child as the paramount consideration, despite its inevitable conflict with adult rights.'

The European Court of Human Rights has itself now said in *Yousef v Netherlands*:[6]

'that in judicial decisions where the rights under Article 8 of parents and those of the child are at stake, the child's rights must be the paramount consideration. If any balancing of interests is necessary, the interests of the child must prevail ...'.

This was the first time that the European Court expressly referred to the *paramountcy* of the child's rights and the decision effectively ends the debate as to whether the paramountcy principle is human rights compliant.[7]

1   [1970] AC 668, [1969] 1 All ER 788, HL.
2   *Re L (A Child) (Contact: Domestic Violence), Re V (A Child) Re M (A Child), Re H (Children)* [2001] Fam 260 at 277, [2000] 4 All ER 609, at 620.
3   (1982) 5 EHRR 223. In fact this case was decided by the Commission and not the ECHR as suggested by Butler-Sloss P.
4   (1996) 23 EHRR 33.
5   *Payne v Payne* [2001] EWCA Civ 166 at [57], [2001] 1 FCR 425, [2001] 1 FLR 1051.
6   (2002) 36 EHRR 20, [2002] 3 FCR 577, [2003] 1 FLR 210 at [73].
7   In *CF v Secretary of State for the Home Department* [2004] EWHC 111 (Fam), [2004] 1 FCR 577, [2004] 2 FLR 517 at [103]. Munby J referred to *Yousef* as establishing that the welfare principle was a core principle of human rights law. Not everyone will agree with this analysis see eg S Harris-Short 'Family Law and the Human Rights Act 1998 – Restraint or Resolution?' [2005] CFLQ 329.

3. Comparison with UN Convention

2.5 Section 1(1) might be compared with art 3(1) of the UN Convention on the Rights of the Child 1989 (to which the UK is a party) which states:

'In all actions concerning children, whether undertaken by public or private social welfare institutions, courts of law, administrative authorities or legislative bodies, the best interests of the child shall be a primary consideration.'

2.6 This article provides an international obligation[1] to apply the best interests of the child test and as such is clearly similar to the paramountcy test under s 1(1) of the CA 1989. However, the enjoinder to regard the best interests as a *primary* consideration is not as strong (though possibly more Human Rights compliant) as to regard the child's welfare as the *paramount* consideration. On the other hand, by applying both to administrative authorities and legislative bodies, art 3(1) is wider than s 1(1) which only applies in court proceedings.

1   As a matter of strict law, since the UN Convention has not been incorporated by statute into English domestic law, courts are not bound to apply it. Nevertheless, as Baroness Hale said in *Smith v Secretary of State for Work and Pensions* [2006] UKHL 35, [2006] 1 WLR 2024, [2006] 3 All ER 907 at [78]: 'Even if an international treaty has not been incorporated into domestic law, our domestic legislation has to be construed as far as possible so as to comply with the international obligations which we have undertaken. When two interpretations ... are possible, the interpretation chosen should be that which better complies with the commitment to the welfare of children which this country has made in ratifying the United Nations Convention on the Rights of the Child'. Under the

Children's Commissioner for Wales Appointment Regulations 2001, SI 2001/3121, the Children's Commissioner for Wales has to 'have regard' to the UN Convention in the discharge of his duties, the first reference to the UN Convention in UK legislation.

4. When the principle applies

2.7 As s 1(1) states, the paramountcy principle applies whenever a court is called upon to determine any question about the child's upbringing or the administration of his property. Section 1(1) is therefore of general application and is not restricted to Children Act proceedings. It is established, for example, that the provision is applicable to wardship proceedings,[1] including non-Convention[2] child abduction cases,[3] and to the exercise of the High Court's inherent jurisdiction.[4] The paramountcy principle also applies when considering whether to make contact activity directions[5] and whether to make an adoption order but this is by reason of s 11A(9) of the CA 1989 and s 1(2) of the Adoption and Children Act 2002 respectively.[6]

1   *J v C* [1970] AC 668, [1969] 1 All ER 788, HL (discussed further at para 2.8). The wardship jurisdiction is discussed in Chapter 12.
2   Ie cases not governed by either the 1980 European Custody Convention or 1980 Hague Abduction Convention on international child abduction. For details see *Clarke Hall and Morrison on Children*, Division 2.
3   *Re J (A Child)(Custody Rights: Jurisdiction)* [2005] UKHL 40, [2006] 1 AC 80, sub nom *Re J (a child)(return to foreign jurisdiction: convention rights)* [2005] 3 All ER 291.
4   See eg *Re A (Children) (Conjoined Twins: Surgical Separation)* [2001] Fam 147, [2000] 4 All ER 961, CA. The inherent jurisdiction is discussed in Chapter 12.
5   Discussed below at paras 5.64 ff.
6   Which applies inter alia when deciding whether or not to grant a parent leave to defend adoption proceedings under s 47(5), per Wall LJ in *Re P (Adoption: Leave Provisions)* [2007] EWCA Civ 616, [2007] 2 FLR 1069. Cf *M v Warwickshire County Council* [2007] EWCA Civ 1084, [2008] 1 WLR 991, [2008] 1 FLR 1093 – welfare not paramount in determining whether to give leave to apply for the revocation of an adoption placement order.

2.8 *J v C*[1] clearly established that the paramountcy principle applies equally to disputes between parents and other individuals as well as to disputes between parents and this was again emphasised in *Re G (Children)(Residence: Same Sex Partner)*.[2] As Baroness Hale said:[3]

'The statutory position is plain: the welfare of the child is the paramount consideration. As Lord MacDermott explained [in *J v C*], this means that "it rules upon or determines the course to be followed". There is no question of a parental right. As the Law Commission explained [in Working Paper No 96 on *Custody*, 1986], "the welfare test itself is well able to encompass any special contribution which natural parents can make to the emotional needs of their child" or, as Lord MacDermott put it, the claims and wishes of parents "can be capable of ministering to the total welfare of the child in a special way" '.

1   [1970] AC 668, [1969] 1 All ER 788, HL.
2   [2006] UKHL 43, [2006] 1 WLR 2305, [2006] 4 All ER 241.
3   [2006] UKHL 43, [2006] 1 WLR 2305, [2006] 4 All ER 241 at [30]. See also Lord Nicholls who said at [2]: 'as in all cases concerning the upbringing of children, the court seeks to identify the course which is in the best interests of the children. Their welfare is the court's paramount consideration. In reaching its decision the court should always

have in mind that in the ordinary way the rearing of a child by his or her biological parent can be expected to be in the child's best interests, both in the short term and also, and importantly, in the longer term'.

2.9 Notwithstanding the above comments, as Baroness Hale said in *Re G*[1] "None of this means that the fact of parentage is irrelevant" and she quoted with approval an Australian judge's[2] following comment:

'I am of the opinion that *the fact of parenthood is to be regarded as an important and significant factor in considering which proposals better advance the welfare of the child.* Such fact does not, however, establish a presumption in favour of the natural parent, nor generate a preferential position in favour of the natural parent from which the Court commences its decision-making process ... Each case should be determined upon an examination of its own merits and of the individuals there involved'. (emphasis added)

Lord Nicholls, however, expressed the issue rather differently commenting:[3]

'I decry any tendency to diminish the significance of this factor. A child should not be removed from the primary care of his or her biological parents without compelling reason. Where such a reason exists the judge should spell this out explicitly'.

This, however, may be thought to be putting too much stress on the *biological* factor for as Baroness Hale was at pains to stress[4] 'parenthood' can comprise genetic, gestational and social and psychological parenthood. In relation to this last 'type' as Thorpe LJ had previously pointed out in *Re H (a child: residence)*[5] the biological parent may not always be the natural parent in the eyes of the child. In cases where the child has long been in the settled care of a non-parent, that non-parent will effectively have become the child's psychological parent and in those circumstances the court must, when applying the welfare principle, weigh the rival claims in the light of that finding.

[1] [2006] UKHL 43, [2006] 1 WLR 2305, [2006] 4 All ER 241 at [31].
[2] Namely Lindenmayer J in *Hodak, Newman and Hadak* (1993) FLR 92–421, approved by the Full Court of the Family Court of Australia in *Rice v Miller* (1993) FLC 92–415 and *Re Evelyn* [1998] Fam CA 55.
[3] [2006] UKHL 43, [2006] 1 WLR 2305, [2006] 4 All ER 241 at [2]. See also Lord Scott, who at [3] commented that mothers are 'special'.
[4] [2006] UKHL 43, [2006] 1 WLR 2305, [2006] 4 All ER 241 at [32]–[36].
[5] [2002] 3 FCR 277, CA (decided in 2000).

2.10 As the original Guidance to the CA 1989 stated,[1] the paramountcy principle applies whenever a court is considering whether to make a s 8 order[2] (ie regardless of who the parties are or in which proceedings the issue is raised or what the issue is).[3] It applies when considering whether to make a parental responsibility order under s 4,[4] a special guardianship order under s 14A,[5] and to applications made under s 13 both for leave to change a child's surname[6] and to remove a child from the jurisdiction.[7]

[1] Children Act 1989 Guidance and Regulations, Vol 1, Court Orders (1991) Department of Health, para 2.57. This comment is not included in the revised Guidance (2008). Sed quaere?
[2] This must surely also include the making of a contact activity condition (discussed at paras 5.67 ff) since that is part of a contact order.

3   Including for example, a child's religious upbringing and determining whether a boy should be ritually circumcised: *Re J (child's religious upbringing and circumcision)* [1999] 2 FCR 345, sub nom *Re J (specific issue orders: muslim upbringing and circumcision)* [1999] 2 FLR 678 per Wall J – decision upheld by Court of Appeal see [2000] 1 FCR 307, [2000] 1 FLR 571. See also, *Re P (A Minor) (Residence Order: Child's Welfare)* [2000] Fam 15, sub nom *Re P (a child) (residence order: restriction order)* [1999] 3 All ER 734, CA. Note also *Re J (fostering: person disqualified)* [1998] 3 FCR 579, [1999] 1 FLR 605, CA, held that, what were then the Foster Placement (Children) Regulations 1991, SI 1991/910, reg 4(4A) inserted by SI 1997/2308) and now replaced in England by the Fostering Services Regulations 2002, SI 2002/57 did not prevent the court from applying the paramountcy principle when considering whether to make a residence order or a care and control order in wardship.

4   *Re RH (a minor) (parental responsibility)* [1998] 2 FCR 89 at 94, sub nom *Re H (Parental Responsibility)* [1998] 1 FLR 855 at 899, CA, per Butler-Sloss LJ. This issue, however, may not be beyond doubt: see *Re G (a Minor) (Parental Responsibility Order)* [1994] 1 FLR 504 at 507–508, CA and *Re E (a minor) (parental responsibility)* [1994] 2 FCR 709 at 715, [1995] 1 FLR 392 at 397, CA in which Balcombe LJ pointed out that it was at least arguable that such applications do not concern questions relating to a child's upbringing. But for convincing arguments to the contrary, see Hershman at [1994] Fam Law 650.

5   Discussed at paras 5.213 ff.

6   *Re B (Change of Surname)* [1996] 1 FLR 791 at 795, CA, per Wilson J. The paramountcy principle equally applies to applications to change names under s 33(7) (discussed at para 8.175), see *Re S (change of surname)* [1999] 1 FCR 304 at 307, [1999] 1 FLR 672 at 674, CA, per Thorpe LJ.

7   *Payne v Payne* [2001] EWCA Civ 166, [2001] 1 FCR 425, [2001] 1 FLR 1052, per Thorpe LJ.

2.11 With regard to public law proceedings under the CA 1989, the paramountcy principle applies to the welfare stage of care proceedings, that is deciding what, if any, order should be made *after* deciding whether or not the statutory threshold under s 31 has been satisfied.[1] It also applies to applications to discharge care orders under s 39,[2] whether or not to make contact orders under s 34,[3] and both to the question of whether leave should be given to a local authority to withdraw their application for a care order[4] and to whether to grant a stay of order.[5]

1   See eg *Re O and N (Minors)(Care: Preliminary Hearing); Re B (A Minor)* [2003] UKHL 18, [2004] 1 AC 523, [2003] 2 All ER 305, [2003] 2 WLR 1075 at [23], per Lord Nicholls.

2   See eg *Re S (minors)(care orders: appeal out of time)* [1996] 2 FCR 838, sub nom, *Re S (Discharge of Care Order)* [2005] 2 FLR 639, CA, and *Re T and E (Proceedings: Conflicting Interests)* [1995] 1 FLR 581.

3   *Re T (minors) (termination of contact: discharge of order)* [1997] 1 All ER 65, [1997] 1 WLR 393, CA and *Re B (Minors) (Termination of Contact: Paramount Consideration)* [1993] Fam 301, [1993] 3 All ER 524, CA.

4   *Re DB and CB (Minors)* [1993] 2 FCR 607, sub nom *Southwark London Borough v B* [1993] 2 FLR 559, CA.

5   *Re M (application for stay of order)* [1996] 3 FCR 185, CA.

2.12 Although there is some authority for saying that the paramountcy principle applies to considering whether to make s 91(14) orders,[1] the matter is not free from doubt as there is also authority for saying that the paramountcy principle does not apply to s 91(15) and (17) applications,[2] which is in line with the ruling that it does not apply to deciding whether to give leave to a non-parent to make a s 8 order application.[3] Whether a sensible distinction can be made between imposing a leave requirement to make an application and granting leave may be doubted since in each case the issue is essentially the same, namely, having to weigh in the balance restricting freedom of access to the court and protecting the child. Accordingly, the better view seems to be that in none of these cases is the child's welfare paramount in the sense that it is the exclusive and automatic overriding concern[4] but rather to recognise, as Wilson J suggested,[5] that 'in the discretionary exercise under s 91(14) the best interests of the child must be weighed fully against the fundamental freedom of access to the courts without even an initial screening process.'

1   *Re P (A Minor) (Residence Order: Child's Welfare)* [2000] Fam 15 at 37, sub nom *Re P (a minor) (residence order: restriction order)* [1999] 3 All ER 734 at 752, CA, per Butler-Sloss LJ. But note the questioning of this by Wilson J in *Re R (a Minor)(Leave to Make Applications)* [1998] 2 FCR 129, sub nom *Re R (Residence: Contact: Restricting Applications)* [1998] 1 FLR 749, CA. Section 91(14) orders are discussed at paras 5.202 ff.
2   This seems to be the implication of Simon Brown LJ's comment in *Re T (minors) (termination of contact: discharge of order)* [1997] 1 All ER 65 at 74, [1997] 1 WLR 393 at 402, that the court should consider a s 34(9) application for the discharge of a s 34(4) order 'with the child's welfare in mind as the paramount consideration – *save only in the limited circumstances provided for by s 91(7) when the court's leave is required'.* [Emphasis added[.
3   See *Re A (Minors) (Residence Orders: Leave to Apply)* [1992] Fam 182, [1992] 3 All ER 872, discussed at paras 2.17 and 2.27.
4   Though note such an interpretation is not in any event 'human rights compliant', see para 2.4.
5   In *Re R (Residence: Contact: Restricting Applications)* [1998] 1 FLR 749 at 757, CA.

5. When the principle does not apply

2.13 The paramountcy principle is not of unlimited application. It does not directly apply outside the context of court litigation and even where an issue is before a court it will only apply provided the child's upbringing or the administration of his property is directly in question and even then only if the principle has not been expressly or impliedly excluded either by the CA 1989 itself or by some other statute.

(a) Paramountcy principle does not apply outside the context of litigation

2.14 The paramountcy principle only applies, if at all, in the course of litigation.[1] Unlike art 3(1) of the UN Convention[2] it has no direct application to institutions (such as prison authorities),[3] administrative authorities (such as local authorities)[4] or legislative bodies. Furthermore it does not apply to parents or other individuals with respect to their day to day or even long-term decisions affecting the child. As one commentator put it:[5]

'It can hardly be argued that parents, in taking family decisions affecting a child, are bound to ignore completely their own interests, the interests of other members of the family and, possibly, outsiders. This would be a wholly undesirable, as well as an unrealistic objective.'

Accordingly, parents are not bound to consider their children's welfare in deciding whether to make a career move, to move house or whether to separate or divorce.[6]

1 Cf the Adoption and Children Act 2002, s 1(2) which applies both to the courts and adoption agencies when coming to a decision relating to the adoption of the child.
2 Set out in para 2.5.
3 See e g *R (on the application of P) v Secretary of State for the Home Department, R (on the application of Q) v Secretary of State for the Home Department)* [2001] EWCA Civ 1151, [2001] 1 WLR 2002, [2001] 3 FCR 416, [2001] 2 FLR 112.
4 See e g *R (on the application of Howard League for Penal Reform) v Secretary of State for the Home Department)* [2002] EWHC 2497 (Admin), [2003] 1 FLR 484, at [35] per Munby J.
5 Bainham *Children: The Modern Law* (3rd edn) p 48.
6 See Dickens: 'The Modern Function and Limits of Parental Rights' 97 LQR 462, 471, who asserts, correctly it is submitted, that parental responsibility is not to do positive good, but to avoid harm. But cf *Re W (Wardship: Discharge: Publicity)* [1996] 1 FCR 393 at 405, [1995] 2 FLR 466 at 477 in which Hobhouse LJ commented that a parent's parental responsibility may restrict his freedom of action. 'He is required, where his children's upbringing is involved, to have regard also to the welfare of his children'.

2.15 The paramountcy principle does not govern the application of Pt III of the CA 1989.[1] As Butler-Sloss LJ said in *Re M (Secure Accommodation Order)*:[2]

> 'The framework of Pt III of the Act is structured to cast upon the local authority duties and responsibilities for children in its area and being looked after. The general duty of a local authority to safeguard and promote the child's welfare[3] is not the same as that imposed upon the court in s 1(1) placing welfare as the paramount consideration.'

In Butler-Sloss LJ's view[4] 's 1 was not designed to be applied to Pt III of the Act'. Accordingly, in deciding, pursuant to s 17(1), what level of services to provide for children in need in their area, local authorities are not obliged to treat the welfare of individual children as their paramount consideration,[5] nor similarly, when deciding pursuant to s 22, on how best to discharge their duties in relation to children looked after by them[6] though in this latter instance the welfare of the child will remain an important consideration.[7]

1 Part III is fully discussed in Chapter 6.
2 [1995] Fam 108 at 115, [1995] 3 All ER 407 at 412, CA, discussed further at para 9.11.
3 Ie pursuant to ss 17(1) and 22(3).
4 [1995] Fam 108 at 116, [1995] 3 All ER 407 at 413, expressly disagreeing with comments to the contrary in the Children Act 1989 Guidance and Regulations, Vol 1, Court Orders (1991) Department of Health (see para 5.7 of the original version) and Vol 4, Residential Care, para 8.8.
5 Indeed, s 17 is so phrased so as to avoid the duty being applied to individual children at all, see further para 6.18.
6 Section 22(6) expressly states that the need to protect members of the public from serious injury overrides any duty even to promote and safeguard the interests of any individual child let alone treating that child's welfare as the paramount consideration.
7 Per Charles J in *Re P (Children Act 1989, ss 22 and 26: Local Authority Compliance)* [2000] 2 FLR 910 at 923.

(b) Paramountcy principles do not apply unless child's upbringing etc is directly in issue

2.16 Even if an application relating to a child is before a court, that child's welfare will only be the paramount consideration provided the issue falls squarely within the terms of s 1(1), that is, it must *directly* concern the child's upbringing[1] or the administration of his property.

[1]   Note: s 105 excludes 'maintenance' from the definition of 'upbringing', see further para 2.26.

2.17 The paramountcy principle does not apply to applications that only indirectly concern the child's upbringing, that is, where the central issue is not one which relates to how the child is being reared.[1] It was on the basis that it was held in *R (P) v Home Secretary*[2] that the paramountcy principle had no application to the lawfulness of prison policy to separate children once they reached 18 months from their imprisoned mothers and partly on this basis, that it was held in *Re A (Minors) (Residence Orders: Leave to Apply)*[3] that s 1(1) does not apply when determining whether to grant adults[4] leave to apply for a s 8 order, since, in Balcombe LJ's words:

> 'in granting or refusing an application for leave to apply for a s 8 order, the court is not determining a question with respect to the upbringing of the child concerned. That question only arises when the court hears the substantive application.'

Similarly, it is clear that the child's welfare is not the paramount consideration when determining whether to give directions for what is now scientific testing (formerly blood testing) in paternity cases.[5]

[1]   Cf *Re Z (A Minor)(Identification: Restrictions on Publication)* [1997] Fam 1 at 29E, sub nom *Re Z (a minor)(freedom of publication)* [1995] 4 All ER 961 at 983c, per Ward LJ.

[2]   *(P) v Secretary of State for the Home Department, (Q) v Secretary of State for the Home Department and another* [2001] EWCA Civ 1151, [2001] 1 WLR 2002 [2001] 3 FCR 416, [2001] 2 FLR 1112. See in particular para [89] per Lord Phillips MR.

[3]   [1992] Fam 182 at 191G–H, [1992] 3 All ER 872 at 878a–b.

[4]   For the position of children seeking leave see paras 5.155 ff.

[5]   *Re H (A Minor)(Blood Tests: Paternal Rights)* [1997] Fam 89, [1996] 4 All ER 28, CA, applying *S v S, W v Official Solicitor* [1972] AC 24, [1970] 3 All ER 107, HL, which ruled that it was applying its protective rather than its custodial jurisdiction. Note, however, that following the amendment of the Family Law Reform Act 1969 by the Child Support, Pensions and Social Security Act 2000, s 21(3)(b) now provides that in the absence of the consent of the person having care and control of a child under the age of 16, a bodily sample may nevertheless be *taken from the child* 'if the court considers that it would be *in his best interests* for the sample to be taken' [Emphasis added] for the application of which see *Re D (Paternity)* [2006] EWHC 3545 (Fam), [2007] 2 FLR 26 and *Re T (a child) (DNA tests: paternity)* [2001] 3 FCR 577, sub nom *Re T (Paternity: Ordering Blood Tests)* [2001] 2 FLR 1190. It is submitted that the correct approach is *first* to decide upon the principles established by *S v S* whether to make a direction at all and *then* to apply s 21(3) to determine whether or not a sample should be taken from the child.

2.18 Other cases in which the paramountcy principle does not apply are:

●   determining whether an unmarried father should be served with notice of care proceedings;[1]

●   resolving a mother's application that the father cease to be a party to the discharge of care proceedings;[2]

●   considering whether a parent be committed to prison for a flagrant breach of a court order concerning a child;[3]

●   considering whether to make enforcement orders or financial compensation orders for breaches of contact orders;[4]

- determining whether to issue a witness summons against a child;[5]
- deciding whether to make directions for interim assessments under s 38(6);[6]
- in resolving a dispute between a birth mother and an adoptive mother over the disposal of their deceased child's remains, the deceased's daughter's interests were not paramount;[7]
- determining whether to grant permission to use evidence previously admitted in wardship proceedings in subsequent criminal proceedings;[8]
- in determining whether costs should be given in family proceedings;[9] and
- deciding whether to give leave to apply for a revocation of an adoption placement order.[10]

[1] *Re X (Care: Notice of Proceedings)* [1996] 1 FLR 186, per Stuart-White J.

[2] *Re W (Discharge of Party to Proceedings)* [1997] 1 FLR 128, per Hogg J.

[3] *A v N (Committal: Refusal of Contact)* [1997] 1 FLR 533, CA. In such cases, however, the child(ren)'s welfare remains a material consideration. See also *M v M (Breaches of Orders: Committal)* [2005] EWCA Civ 1722, [2006] 1 FLR 1154.

[4] CA 1989, ss 11L(7) and 11O(14) inserted by the Children and Adoption Act 2006 which merely direct a court 'to take into account the welfare of the child concerned'.

[5] *Re P (Witness Summons)* [1997] 2 FLR 447, CA on the basis, per Wilson J, 'that the question of whether to issue a witness summons against a child is not a question with respect to her or his upbringing [so] that s 1(1) does not apply ...' See also *R v Highbury Corner Magistrates' Court, ex p Deering* [1997] 1 FLR 683, DC, per Schiemann LJ and the cases there cited.

[6] Per Holman J in *Re M (Residential Assessment Directions)* [1998] 2 FLR 371 at 381–382 and per Charles J in *Re P (Children Act 1989, ss 22 and 26: Local Authority Compliance)* [2000] 2 FLR 910 at 923.

[7] Per Hale J in *Buchanan v Milton* [1999] 2 FLR 844 at 857.

[8] *Re S (Minors) (Wardship: Police Investigation)* [1987] Fam 199, [1987] 3 All ER 1076.

[9] *Q v Q (Costs: Summary Assessment)* [2002] 2 FLR 668, per Wilson J.

[10] *Re M (children)(placement order)* [2007] EWCA Civ 1084, [2008] 1 WLR 991, sub nom *M v Warwickshire County Council* [2008] 1 FLR 1093. See also *S-H v Kingston upon Hull City Council* [2008] EWCA Civ 493, (2008) Times, 28 May.

2.19 It can be a matter of fine judgment as to what matters directly concern a child's upbringing and what do not. There are two areas in particular in which the application of the paramountcy principle is problematic, namely, with regard to publicity and to procedural issues.

(i) Publicity

2.20 *In Re S (A Child) (Identification: Restrictions on Publication)*[1] the House of Lords held that since the implementation of the Human Rights Act 1998 the foundation of the jurisdiction to restrain publicity now derives from the European Convention on Human Rights and involves, since neither are unqualified rights, the balancing of the right to respect for private and family life under art 8 and the right to freedom of expression under art 10. Consequently, in the case before them and any similar case it was no longer necessary to consider the preceding case law about the existence and scope of the inherent jurisdiction of the High Court to restrict publicity to protect children. However, such case-law was thought not to be wholly irrelevant to the ultimate balancing exercise to be carried out under the ECHR. In *Re S* itself the House of Lords upheld the decision[2] not to grant an injunction prohibiting the identification of a defendant in a criminal trial charged with the murder of an elder son, to protect her younger son from harm. It was implicit in the judgment that the younger child's welfare was not paramount, ie s 1(1) of the CA 1989 did not apply.[3] Similarly, in *British Broadcasting Co v Rochdale Metropolitan Borough Council and X and Y,*[4] the BBC wishing to make a documentary, successfully sought the discharge of an injunction protecting the identities of the children and two social workers involved in previous proceedings[5] in which allegations of ritual and satanic abuse of several children were found not to have been made out. Given that the children were now adults and wished to be identified and to relate their experiences to the public, the justification for the original anonymity was held no longer to exist. In contrast, in the first post-*Re S* decision, *A Local Authority v W, L, W, T and R (By the Children's Guardian),*[6] an injunction was granted. In that case a mother of two children was awaiting sentence having pleaded guilty to a charge that she had knowingly infected the father of one of the children with HIV. Both children were in foster care and the elder (who was not HIV positive) attended a nursery away from the immediate area where the mother's identity was not known. The applicant local authority, fearing that if publicity were to be given to the mother's identity and HIV status it could give rise to a general outcry at the nursery and also make it more difficult to find alternative carers for the children, successfully sought an injunction preventing the publication of the names and addresses of the mother and father in connection with the criminal proceedings and of the details of the nursery placements.

1   [2004] UKHL 47, [2005] 1 AC 593, [2004] 3 FCR 407, [2005] 1 FLR 591.
2   Namely that of Hedley J which had been upheld by the CA (Hale LJ dissenting).
3   Note Lord Steyn's comment at [2004] UKHL 47 at [37] that Hedley J had gone too far in saying that he would have come to the same conclusion had he been persuaded that the child's welfare was the paramount consideration under s 1(1) of the CA 1989. Note also the Press Complaints Commission's Code of Practice for journalists, cl 6 of which is designed to protect the welfare of children.
4   [2005] EWHC 2862 (Fam), [2007] 1 FLR 101. See also *Re Webster; Norfolk County Council v Webster* [2006] EWHC 2733 (Fam), [2007] 1 FLR 1146.
5   *Rochdale Borough Council v A* [1991] 2 FLR 192.
6   [2005] EWHC 1564 (Fam), [2006] 1 FLR 1.

2.21 Having to balance art 8 and art 10 rights in fact reflects the line generally taken previously, namely, that since the curbing of publicity (even that directly concerning the child) only indirectly concerns the child's upbringing, the child's welfare was not paramount but instead had to be weighed in the balance with the freedom of the press.[1] *Re S*, however, does call into question the line taken in at least two earlier decisions, namely, *R v Central Independent Television plc*[2] and *Re Z (A Minor)(Identification: Restrictions on Publication).*[3] In the former it was held that if the allegedly harmful publication does not relate to the care and upbringing of children over whose welfare the court is exercising a supervisory role then not only is the child's welfare not paramount it is not relevant at all. In *Re Z*, in which the mother wanted her child to perform for the making of the film about her treatment at a unit dealing with special educational needs. It was held that because, unlike other cases, the issue concerned a parent's exercise of parental responsibility in waiving the child's rights to confidentiality with respect to her education, the child's welfare was paramount and that, therefore, the film should not be broadcast. Whether these analyses can survive *Re S* remains to be seen.[4]

1   See eg *Re H-S (Minors)* [1994] 1 WLR 1141, [1994] 3 All ER 390, CA and *Re X (A Minor)(Wardship: Jurisdiction)* [1975] Fam 47, [1975] 1 All ER 679, [1975] 2 WLR 335.
2   [1994] Fam 192, [1994] 3 All ER 641.
3   [1997] Fam 1, sub nom *Re Z (a minor)(freedom of publication)* [1995] 4 All ER 961, CA.
4   In *A Local Authority v W, L, W, T and R* [2005] EWHC 1564 (Fam), [2006] 1 FLR 1 at [24], Potter P referred specifically to *Re Z* as having limited value but this was in respect of its analysis of the *protective* powers of the High Court under its inherent jurisdiction.

(II) PROCEDURAL ISSUES

2.22 Although, on one view it may be said that the paramountcy principle can also apply to procedural issues,[1] an alternative analysis[2] is that in certain instances the courts, motivated by their concern to protect children generally, will not rigidly apply all procedural rules designed to produce overall justice to parties to litigation but will nevertheless only refrain from applying them in a particular case where they are satisfied that to do so would be harmful to the individual child concerned. Such an analysis can be justified upon the basis that issues such as disclosure[3] only indirectly concern the child's welfare and is arguably supported by the majority's reasoning in *Re L (A Minor) (Police Investigation: Privilege)*[4] in which leave was given to the police to see a medical report written by an expert engaged by the mother in the course of care proceedings.

1   It is certainly arguable that, in deciding that a parent did not have a right to see the Official Solicitor's report compiled in connection with an application to look after the child, and that the court had the power to withhold it from the parties, the House of Lords in *Official Solicitor v K* [1965] AC 201, [1963] 3 All ER 191 was applying the paramountcy principle. The headnote, for example, at [1965] AC 202, states 'that the paramount consideration of the Chancery Division in exercising its jurisdiction over wards of court was the welfare of the infants'. The headnote to the All England report is in similar terms: see [1963] 3 All ER 191.
2   See Lowe 'The House of Lords and the welfare principle' in *Family Law Towards the Millennium Essays for PM Bromley* (ed Caroline Bridge, 1997) Butterworths, ch 4, and Lowe and Douglas *Bromley's Family Law* (10th edn, 2006) OUP, 461.
3   On which see *Re X (Disclosure of Information)* [2001] 2 FLR 440 and *A Local Authority v K* [2007] EWHC 1250 (Fam), [2007] 2 FLR 914. See also *Re D (Minors) (Adoption Reports: Confidentiality)* [1996] AC 593, [1995] 4 All ER 385, HL, which establishes that non-disclosure of reports should be ordered only when the case for doing so is compelling.
4   [1997] AC 16, [1996] 2 All ER 78, HL. At first instance Bracewell J, whose judgment was upheld by the House of Lords, expressly said (see [1995] 1 FLR 999 at 1007]) 'The application before me does not relate to the upbringing of the child and, therefore, is not governed by s 1 of the Children Act 1989'.

2.23 It is implicit in *Re L*[1] that not all procedural rules can be changed even to protect children. Legal professional privilege attaching to solicitor-client communications, for example, is absolute[2]. The same is true for the rules of appeal, as was established in *G v G*,[3] in which the House of Lords rejected the argument based on the paramountcy principle that special rules of appeal apply in custody cases. Put in theoretical terms, the issue of when an appellate court should intervene does not directly concern a child's upbringing and hence the paramountcy principle does not apply. Furthermore, as the normal rules of appeal do not inhibit the courts from performing their proper role of safeguarding the child's interests, there is no need to provide special rules.

1   *Re L (A Minor) (Police Investigation: Privilege)* [1997] AC 16, [1996] 2 All ER 78, HL, discussed further in Chapter 11.
2   Following the House of Lords' ruling in *R v Derby Magistrates' Court, ex p B* [1996] AC 487, [1995] 4 All ER 526.
3   [1985] 2 All ER 225, HL.

(III) OTHER AREAS OF UNCERTAINTY

2.24 There is uncertainty as to whether the paramountcy principle applies to giving leave to interview children involved in court proceedings with a view to preparing a third party's defence in criminal proceedings,[1] but the better view is that it does not. At any rate, this was Ryder J's conclusion after careful analysis of the relevant authorities in *Chief Constable of Greater Manchester v KI and K (W) children and PN*.[2] In his view there can be few clearer examples of the interdependence of rights and interests: 'The administration of criminal justice and the rights of others are clearly engaged and may well be in conflict with a simple welfare analysis'. In his view it was both helpful and necessary to analyse the issue in terms of human rights. So done it was clear that not only were the child's art 8 rights involved but so too were the defendant's art 6 rights to a fair trial. By analogy with *Re S (A Child)(Identification: Restrictions on Publication)*[3] it was therefore incumbent upon the court to 'conduct a balancing exercise between the competing rights, considering the proportionality of the potential interference with each right independently'.

1   *Re F (Specific Issue: Child Interview)* [1995] 1 FLR 819, CA, in which Waite LJ was prepared to assume in that case that s 1(1) of the CA 1989 did apply and *Re M (Care: Leave to Interview Child)* [1995] 1 FLR 825, in which Hale J held that the child's welfare was not the overriding consideration. But in the light of the case law on the issue of witness summons, it is submitted that the child's welfare is *not* the paramount consideration.
2   [2007] EWHC 1837 (Fam), [2008] 2 FCR 172, [2008] 1 FLR 504.
3   [2004] UKHL 47, [2005] 1 AC 593, [2004] 4 All ER 683.

2.25 The former uncertainty as to the application of the paramountcy principle in non-Convention abduction cases has been authoritatively resolved in favour of its application.[1] By implication the principle also applies to the determination of forum conveniens in children cases.[2]

1   *Re J (A Child)(Custody Rights: Jurisdiction)* [2005] UKHL 40, [2006] 1 AC 80, sub nom *Re J (a child)(return to foreign jurisdiction: convention rights)* [2005] 3 All ER 291.
2   For previous conflicting case-law on this issue see the discussion in *Clarke Hall and Morrison on Children* at 1[103].

(c) Paramountcy principle does not apply if excluded by other statutory provisions

2.26 Even if the child's upbringing is directly in issue, the paramountcy principle might not always apply. It will not if statute expressly provides an alternative test or expressly excludes its operation. For example, applications for parental orders under the Human Fertilisation and Embryology Act 1990, s 30 directly concern the child's upbringing but in determining them the court is bound[1] to treat the child's welfare as its first (but not paramount) consideration. The child's welfare is similarly expressed to be the first consideration in proceedings relating to the adjustment of property and financial matters on divorce.[2] Section 105(1) of the CA 1989 expressly excludes maintenance from the definition of child's upbringing and so disapplies the paramountcy principle not just to maintenance applications but also to any other application for financial provision (ie a lump sum or property order) for a child under Sch 1 to the CA 1989. In this latter regard Sir Stephen Brown P observed in *K v H (Child Maintenance)*,[3] that the provisions of Sch 1 deal comprehensively with financial provision for children[4] and should not be confused with applications relating to upbringing or the administration of the child's own property to which s 1(1) does apply.

1   By the Adoption Act 1976, s 6 as applied to parental orders by the Parental Orders (Human Fertilisation and Embryology) Regulations 1994, SI 1994/2767 which has been expressly preserved for this purpose by the Adoption and Children Act 2002 (Commencement No 10 Transitional and Savings Provision Order) 2005, SI 2005/2897, art 14.
2   Matrimonial Causes Act 1973, s 25(1), see *N v N (consent orders: variation)* [1994] 2 FCR 275, [1994] 2 FLR 868, CA and *Suter v Suter and Jones* [1987] Fam 111, [1987] 2 All ER 336, CA.
3   [1993] 2 FLR 61 at 64. See also *B v B (Transfer of Tenancy)* [1994] Fam Law 250 (Salisbury County Court), on which see Douglas [1994] Fam Law at 251.
4   For a discussion of these powers see *Clarke Hall and Morrison on Children*, 4[31] ff.

2.27 Statute can impliedly exclude the application of s 1(1). It is established that the paramountcy principle is inconsistent with the duties of a local authority under s 25(1)(b)[1] and therefore has no application to the question of making secure accommodation orders.[2] Similarly, the criteria set out in s 10(9) for determining whether to grant adults leave to apply for s 8 orders have been held to be inconsistent with the application of the paramountcy principle.[3] Most importantly, although in general terms the paramountcy principle applies to proceedings under Pts IV and V of the CA 1989, it will only come into play provided the applicant can satisfy the court that the preconditions for a care order or for an emergency protection order have been made out.[4] It has also been said that the question of whether the future of children should be decided in one part of the UK rather than another is determined by statute and that their welfare is not the paramount consideration in reaching that decision.[5] It is implicit in the direction[6] 'to take into account the welfare of the child' that the paramountcy principle does not apply when considering whether to make enforcement orders or financial compensation orders for breaches of contact orders nor when the Secretary of State is considering the exercise of his discretionary powers under the Child Support Act 1991.[7]

1   Namely 'that if he is kept in any other description of accommodation he is likely to injure himself or other persons'. See further para 9.10.
2   *Re M (A Minor) (Secure Accommodation Order)* [1995] Fam 108, [1995] 3 All ER 407, CA, discussed at para 9.11.
3   *Re A (Minors) (Residence Orders: Leave to Apply)* [1992] Fam 182, [1992] 3 All ER 972, CA.
4   See eg *Humberside County Council v B* [1993] 1 FLR 257 and *F v Leeds City Council* [1994] 2 FLR 60, CA, discussed further at para 8.55.
5   Per Millett LJ in *M v M (Abduction: England and Wales)* [1997] 2 FLR 263 at 275 F, applying the Domicile and Matrimonial Proceedings Act 1973, Sch 1, para 8(1), which provides for mandatory stays if matrimonial proceedings have been instituted in a related

jurisdiction in which the parties were habitually resident for one year when they last lived together. Cf para 9 which gives the court a discretion to stay if the parties were not so habitually resident.

6   See CA 1989 ss 11L(7) and 11O(14) inserted by the Children and Adoption Act 2006, discussed at paras 5.182 and 5.189 respectively.
7   Child Support Act 1991, s 2.

2.28 In other cases it is the whole scheme of the legislation rather than a specific provision that impliedly excludes the paramountcy principle. The courts have refused, for example, to apply the paramountcy principle to interfere with discretionary powers clearly vested by Parliament in another body or court. Accordingly, the principle cannot be invoked to interfere with the discretionary powers vouchsafed to local authorities to look after and manage children in their care,[1] nor to interfere with the discretionary power vested in the immigration service.[2] It is clear that the child's welfare is not the paramount consideration when determining applications under the 1980 Hague Abduction Convention.[3] The paramountcy principle is ousted by a successful claim to diplomatic immunity under the terms of the Diplomatic Privileges Act 1964.[4]

1   *A v Liverpool City Council* [1982] AC 363, [1981] 2 All ER 385, HL which remains good law. See also *Re B (Minors) (Termination of Contact: Paramount Consideration)* [1993] Fam 301 at 309, [1993] 3 All ER 524 at 529–530, per Butler-Sloss LJ.
2   *Re Mohamed Arif (An Infant)* [1968] Ch 643, [1968] 2 All ER 145, CA. It was held in *R v Secretary of State for the Home Department, ex p Gangadeen, R v Secretary of State for the Home Department, ex p Khan* [1998] 1 FLR 762, [1998] 2 FCR 96, CA that treating the child's welfare as an important but not paramount consideration is not contrary to art 8 of the ECHR, having regard to such decisions as *Abdulaziz v United Kingdom* (1985) 7 EHRR 471. Note also *R v Secretary of State for the Home Department, ex p Teame* [1994] 3 FCR 132, 1 [1995] 1 FLR 293, CA – residence order does not prevent deportation.
3   See eg *Re M (A Minor) (Child Abduction)* [1994] 1 FLR 390 at 392, CA, per Butler-Sloss LJ. A similar position applies to the European or Luxembourg Convention on the Recognition and Enforcement of Custody 1980. Both these Conventions are discussed in *Clarke Hall and Morrison on Children*, Division 2.
4   See *Re P (Children Act: diplomatic immunity)* [1998] 2 FCR 480, [1998] 1 FLR 624.

6. Balancing the welfare of more than one child

2.29 One of the inherent difficulties in applying the paramountcy principle is with respect to cases involving two or more children with conflicting interests. This issue can arise either where the applicant is a child or where the application concerns siblings.

(a) Child-parents and babies

2.30 In *Birmingham City Council v H (A Minor)*[1] in which a 15-year-old mother sought contact with her baby[2] the question was raised as to whose welfare was paramount, the baby's or the mother's. At first instance Connell J held that the baby's welfare took priority over the mother's. The Court of Appeal disagreed. Taking the view that the question of contact with the baby related to the upbringing of the mother and that the question of contact with the mother related to the upbringing of the baby, they held that while the welfare of both taken together should be considered as paramount to the interests of any adults concerned in their lives, as between themselves the court should approach the question of their welfare without giving one priority over the other.

1   [1994] 2 AC 212, [1994] 1 All ER 12, HL.
2   Both mother and baby had been made the subjects of interim care orders.

2.31 The House of Lords allowed the baby's appeal. Confining their observations to the application of s 34 in general and of s 34(4) in particular,[1] their Lordships ruled that it is the child in respect of whom the application is being made (ie the baby) whose interests are paramount. In reaching this decision their Lordships expressly left open the more general question[2] 'as to whether an application by a parent who is a child for contact with its own child could be a question with respect to the 'upbringing' of the child who is a parent or whether that question related only to the child's position as a parent and not to its "upbringing".' It is submitted that that approach would have provided a simpler test and would have been in line with the jurisprudence just discussed of confining the paramountcy principle to issues *directly* concerning the child's upbringing.

1   Section 34, which deals with the specific question of contact with a child in care, is discussed at paras 8.197 ff. The narrowness of the House of Lords' approach has not escaped criticism, see Douglas: 'In Whose Best Interests?' (1994) 110 LQR 379.
2   [1994] 2 AC 212 at 223, [1994] 1 All ER 12 at 19, per Lord Slynn.

2.32 *Birmingham* was followed in *F v Leeds City Council*[1] which concerned a care order application in respect of a baby removed from a 17-year-old mother within hours of the birth. The mother appealed against the making of a care order arguing that the baby's welfare alone should not have been taken into account as the paramount consideration, since she herself was a child whose upbringing was in question. Rejecting her appeal, it was held that following the *Birmingham* decision the correct approach in determining whether the baby's welfare or that of the child-parent was paramount, was to identify which child was the subject of the application, and which child it was whose welfare was directly involved.[2] In the case before them the answer was clear since it was the baby and not the child's mother with respect to whom the application was being made and who was thus the subject of the application and the only child to be named in the order. It therefore followed that no question relating to the mother's upbringing arose and hence the court was not required by s 1(1) to treat the child-mother's welfare as the paramount consideration.

1   [1994] 2 FCR 428, [1994] 2 FLR 60, CA.
2   [1994] 2 FCR 428 at 432, [1994] 2 FLR 60 at 63, per Ward J.

(b) Balancing the interests of siblings

2.33 The position where siblings are involved is complicated. In some instances the relative weighting of their respective welfare interests may simply be determined by the form of the litigation. In *Re F (Contact: Child in Care)*[1], where a child in care wanted contact with his four siblings who were not in care, Wilson J observed that where an application was properly made under s 34 of the CA 1989 (viz where the parents or siblings were content to have contact but which was opposed by the local authority) the welfare of the child in care would be the paramount consideration, since that child would be the 'named person'. On the other hand, if that child applied for a s 8 order with his siblings, it would be the latter's welfare that would be paramount since the siblings would be the 'named persons'.

1   [1995] 1 FLR 510. See also *Re S (Contact: Application by Sibling)* [1998] 2 FLR 897 at 908, per Charles J.

2.34 Where each child is the 'subject' of the same proceedings their welfare should be equally weighted which theoretically means that *each* child's welfare should be the court's paramount consideration. In practice, however, where the siblings' interests conflict, it may be impossible to accord paramountcy to each child. In such cases the approach applied in both the *Birmingham* and *Leeds* decisions is of no help and instead one is driven to the approach applied by the Court of Appeal in the *Birmingham* case, namely, to balance the children's interests and find a preponderance in favour of one or the other.[1] A similar approach also seems inevitable in resolving applications concerning sibling children where their interests conflict. As Wall J commented in *Re T and E (proceedings: conflicting interests)*:

'... where a number of children are all the subject of an application or cross-application to the court in the same set of proceedings, and where it is impossible to achieve what was in the paramount interests of each child, the balancing exercise described in the Court of Appeal [in the *Birmingham* case] has to be undertaken and the situation of least detriment to all the children achieved.'

This approach has since been authoritatively endorsed by *Re A (Children) (Conjoined Twins: Surgical Separation)*.[2]

1   [1995] 1 FLR 581 at 587.
2   [2001] Fam 147, [2000] 4 All ER 961, CA.

2.35 *Re A* concerned the issue of whether conjoined twins should be separated when to do so would preserve the life of the one (Jodie) but inevitably kill the other (Mary). In reaching the decision to sanction the operation Ward LJ, applying the Court of Appeal approach taken in the *Birmingham* case, said:[1]

'If the duty of the court is to make a decision which puts Jodie's interests paramount and that decision would be contrary to the paramount interests of Mary, then, for my part, I do not see how the court can reconcile the impossibility of properly fulfilling each duty by simply declining to decide the very matter before it. That would be a total abdication of the duty which is imposed upon us. Given the conflict of duty, I can see no other way of dealing with it than by choosing the lesser of the two evils and so finding the least detrimental alternative. A balance has to be struck somehow and I cannot flinch from undertaking that evaluation, horrendously difficult though it is.'

A less dramatic example of the balancing approach is the pre-1989 decision in *Clarke-Hunt v Newcombe*[2] in which the Court of Appeal, having commented that there was not really a right solution but which of two 'bad solutions was the least dangerous' to the children's long-term interests, upheld a decision not to separate two brothers but to place them together with their mother even though it was against the elder boy's wishes and possibly slightly detrimental to his interests.

1   [2001] Fam 147 at 192, [2000] 4 All ER 961 at 1006.
2   (1982) 4 FLR 482, CA.

7. The meaning of welfare

2.36 The term 'welfare' as such is not defined in the CA 1989 but a good explanation is that given in a New Zealand case by Hardie Boys J who said:[1]

> ' "Welfare" is an all encompassing word. It includes material welfare, both in the sense of adequacy of resources to provide a pleasant home and a comfortable standard of living and in the sense of adequacy of care to ensure that good health and due personal pride are maintained. However, while material considerations have their place they are secondary matters. More important are the stability and the security, the loving and understanding care and guidance, the warm and compassionate relationships, that are essential for the full development of the child's own character, personality and talents.'

1   In *Walker v Walker and Harrison*, noted in [1981] NZ Recent Law 257 and cited by the Law Commission in its Working Paper No 96, Custody (1985), para 6.10. Note also Butler-Sloss P's comment in *Re A (medical treatment: male sterilisation)* [2000] 1 FCR 193 at 200, [2001] 1 FLR 549 at 555, CA that 'best interests encompasses medical, emotional and all other welfare issues', referred to by Ward LJ in *Re A (Children) (Conjoined Twins: Surgical Separation)* [2001] Fam 147 at 180, [2000] 4 All ER 961 at 994.

2.37 Ideally, the court should be concerned to promote the child's long-term future.[1] However, while there are cases where the court has clearly anticipated future contingencies such as parental acquisition of employment and remarriage,[2] or where regard has been had to furthering the child's education and general prospects,[3] inevitably the court will tend to concentrate on the immediate ties and environment of the child.

1   Unless perhaps where the short-term disadvantages are so overwhelming as to rule out the long-term option: see eg *Thompson v Thompson* (1986) 150 JP 625, [1987] Fam Law 89, CA.
2   See respectively, *Re DW (A Minor) (Custody)* [1984] Fam Law 17, CA and *S (BD) v S (DJ)* [1977] Fam 109, [1977] 1 All 656, CA.
3   See *May v May* [1986] 1 FLR 325, CA (order made in favour of father who was more academic than the mother) and cf *Re DW (A Minor) (Custody)* [1984] Fam Law 17, CA and *Re O (infants)* [1962] 2 All ER 10, CA (boy's long-term future better in Sudan, girls' in England).

8. The checklist

2.38 Although the CA 1989 does not define 'welfare', it introduced a checklist of relevant factors to which in certain circumstances the court must have regard when deciding what, if any, order to make. The checklist, which is contained in s 1(3), is as follows:

'(a)   the ascertainable wishes and feelings of the child concerned (considered in the light of his age and understanding);

(b)   his physical, emotional and educational needs;

(c)   the likely effect on him of any change in his circumstances;

(d)   his age, sex, background and any characteristics of his which the court considers relevant;

(e)   any harm which he has suffered or is at risk of suffering;

(f)   how capable each of his parents, and any other person in relation to whom the court considers the question to be relevant, is of meeting his needs; and

(g)   the range of powers available to the court under this Act in the proceedings in question'.

This checklist is not exhaustive and indeed might properly be regarded as the minimum that will be considered by the court.[1] It is always open to the court to specify other matters which it would like to see included in a welfare report.[2]

[1]   In *Re R (a minor) (residence order: finance)* [1995] 3 FCR 334, [1995] 2 FLR 612 , it was held that it was quite proper to take into account financial considerations.

[2]   Namely under s 7, see below paras 10.20 ff. See also Law Com No 172, paras 3.18 and 3.21.

2.39 The content of the checklist follows that recommended by the Law Commission, save for that under s 1(3) (g), the purpose of which is to emphasise the court's duty to consider not only whether the order being sought is the best for the child but also to consider the alternatives that the Act makes available.[1] This duty also reflects the general policy of vesting in the courts at all levels greater responsibility for the management and conduct of children cases.

[1]   Under s 10(1)(b), discussed at para 5.141, courts are empowered to make s 8 orders on their own motion.

(a) When the checklist applies

2.40 Section 1(4) directs the courts to have regard to the checklist in contested s 8 applications[1], all applications for special guardianship,[2] and all proceedings under Pt IV of the CA 1989 (ie in all care and supervision applications).[3] There is, however, nothing to prevent the courts from considering the checklist in other applications if they so choose and indeed particularly in contested applications under ss 4, 5 and 13[4] it would seem prudent to do so. In *Re B (Minors) (Change of Surname)*[5] Wilson J commented that, notwithstanding that he did not have to apply the checklist to determine an application for leave to change a child's surname, the list remained 'a most useful aide memoire of the factors that may impinge on the child's welfare.' In *Payne v Payne*,[6] in which an application for leave to remove a child from the jurisdiction was made under s 13, Thorpe LJ went further commenting 'Although technically an application brought under s 13(1) is not subject to the welfare checklist, it has been held that the trial judge should nevertheless take the precaution of regarding the checklist factors when carrying out his welfare appraisal'.

1   Restricting the application of the checklist to contested cases follows the Law Commission's recommendation (see Law Com No 172, para 3.19) which felt that if s 1(3) applied to all cases the court might have felt compelled to investigate even those cases where there was no choice as to where and with whom the child should live. In their view such an investigation would not only have been a waste of resources but also an unwarranted intrusion into family autonomy.
2   Section 1(4)(b) as amended by the Adoption and Children Act 2002, s 115(3).
3   For discussion of the practice where it is mandatory to apply the checklist, see para 4.57.
4   Discussed respectively at paras 3.60 ff, 3.107 ff and 5.31 ff.
5   [1996] 2 FCR 304 at 306, [1996] 1 FLR 791 at 793, CA. But whether he was right to consider applications for leave to change names were properly made under s 13 rather than s 8 has been questioned by Hale J in *Re M (leave to remove child from jurisdiction)* [1999] 3 FCR 708 at 715, [1999] 2 FLR 334 at 340, discussed at para 5.42.
6   [2001] EWCA Civ 166, para [30], [2001] 1 FCR 425, [2001] 1 FLR 1052, CA.

2.41 Although s 1(3) specifically directs *the court* to have regard to the checklist, it will clearly be useful to legal advisers and their clients both in preparing and in arguing their case. The Law Commission envisaged[1] that the list would enable parties to prepare relevant evidence and, by focussing clients' minds on the real issues, might help to promote settlements. In this sense the list is perhaps best regarded as being applicable in the context of litigation rather than as being confined to actual court proceedings. In any event, as Holman J pointed out,[2] the Rules[3] require the now named children's guardians[4] to have regard to the checklist when carrying out their duties.

1   Law Com No 172, para 3.18.
2   In *Re K (care proceedings: joinder of father)* [1999] 2 FCR 391 at 398, sub nom *Re B (Care Proceedings: Notification of Father Without Parental Authority)* [1999] 2 FLR 408 at 415.
3   FPR 1991, r 4.11(1); FPC(CA 1989)R 1991, r 11(1).
4   Formerly known as 'guardians ad litem'.

(b) Applying the checklist

(I) ... THE ASCERTAINABLE WISHES AND FEELINGS OF THE CHILD CONCERNED CONSIDERED IN THE LIGHT OF HIS AGE AND UNDERSTANDING

2.42 Although reflecting pre-CA 1989 practice,[1] s 1(3)(a) provides the first statutory enjoinder on the courts to consider the child's own views in the private law context other than in adoption.[2] Such an enjoinder was long overdue[3] and, in any event, is now reflective of an international obligation pursuant to art 12(1) of the UN Convention of the Rights of the Child 1989 which provides:

'States Parties shall assure to the child who is capable of forming his or her own views the right to express those views freely in all matters affecting the child, the views of the child being given full weight in accordance with the age and maturity of the child.'

By referring to the child's 'wishes and feelings', s 1(3)(a) is wider than art 12, which is confined to 'views'. Very young children can have discernible 'feelings' even if they cannot yet express their 'views'.

1   See *Re P (A Minor) (Education)* [1992] 1 FLR 316 at 321, CA, per Butler-Sloss LJ.

2   In adoption proceedings it has always been incumbent upon the court to give due consideration to the wishes of the child concerned having regard to their age and understanding, see the Adoption of Children Act 1926, s 3(b) which was re-enacted in subsequent Adoption Acts up to the 1976 Act. It is now part of the Adoption and Children Act 2002, s 1(4).

3   Though whether it should have been part of the checklist can be debated. It could be argued that such wishes are independent of their welfare. Moreover, having a separate requirement to listen to children would have given greater recognition to children being treated as individuals in their own right. For the importance of listening to children and the impact of the CA 1989 in this respect see *The Children Act Now – Messages from Research* (Department of Health 2001), ch 5.

2.43 Despite being placed first in the welfare checklist, the child's view is not expressed to be determinative.[1] As Butler-Sloss LJ put it in *Re P (minors) (wardship: care and control)*:[2]

> 'How far the wishes of children should be a determinative factor in their future placement must of course vary on the particular facts of each case. Those views must be considered and may, but not necessarily must, carry more weight as the children grow older'.

On the other hand, it has also been said that where all other factors are evenly balanced it is appropriate to recognise the extra significance of an older child's views.[3] Nevertheless the court's *obligation* is to consider the child's wishes and feelings but not necessarily to give effect to them. It must be remembered that the child may have been coached or brainwashed[4] by one parent and that sometimes even an older child's wishes can be so contrary to their long-term welfare that the court may feel justified in overriding them. In *Re M (Family Proceedings: Affidavits)*,[5] for example, a father applied for a residence order based largely on his 12-year-old daughter's wishes. Although the welfare report indicated that either parent was suitable as a carer, since the child had hitherto lived with her mother and had not had the opportunity to have any clear idea of what living with her father would really be like (the contact visits to her father had always taken place at the paternal grandparents' home), the judge upheld the welfare officer's 'instinct' that her long-term welfare would be better governed by her remaining with her mother. The Court of Appeal agreed and rejected the argument that, given either parent was suitable, the child's view should have tipped the balance. It accepted that the judge had properly taken the child's wishes into account but was not obliged to follow them, if, as here, it was not felt to be in the child's interests to do so.

1   *Re W (minors) (residence order)* [1992] 2 FCR 461, CA; *Re W (A Minor) (Residence Order)* [1993] 2 FLR 625, CA.

2   [1992] 2 FCR 681 at 687. See also *M v M (Minor:Custody Appeal)* [1987] 1 WLR 404 at 411, CA, per May LJ.

3   *Re F (Minors) (Denial of Contact)* [1993] 2 FLR 677, CA. Note also *R (on the application of CD) v Isle of Anglesey County Council* [2004] EWHC 1635 (Admin), [2004] 3 FCR 171, [2005] 1 FLR 59, in which it was accepted that the wishes and feelings of a 15 year old with grave disabilities should carry no less weight than for any other 15 year old.

4   See eg *Re R (A Minor) (Residence: Religion)* [1993] 2 FLR 163, CA, in which the wishes of a nine-year-old boy to remain with a member of the Exclusive Brethren were overridden.

5   [1995] 2 FLR 100, CA.

(II) ... THE CHILD'S PHYSICAL, EMOTIONAL AND EDUCATIONAL NEEDS

2.44 A wide variety of 'needs' can be relevant under s 1(3)(b) ranging from:

- *physical needs* in the sense of adequate accommodation;[1]
- *emotional needs* in the sense of attachment to a particular parent[2] or to a sibling or even to a family. It is also considered to be a fundamental emotional need of a child to have an enduring relationship with both parents. With regard to sibling support, as Purchas LJ said in *C v C (Minors: Custody)*:[3]

  > 'It is really beyond argument that unless there are strong features indicating a contrary arrangement ... brothers and sisters should wherever possible, be brought up together, so that they are an emotional support to each other in the stormy waters of the destruction of their family.'

Attachment to the family becomes important in disputes between parents and third parties.[4] It has also been held[5] that in resolving disputes between same-sex couples where one is the biological parent and by, parity of reasoning, between a parent and a step-parent, that it is wrong to ignore inter alia the 'biological factor'[6] though the final outcome is dependent upon the child(ren)'s welfare.

- *medical needs* so that provided it is for the child's benefit it is within the court's power to make an order for taking a bodily sample to ascertain whether the child is HIV positive,[7] and
- *educational needs* either in the sense of parental commitment to the importance of schooling and completion of homework[8] or from the point of view of religious upbringing.[9]

In practice, the child's needs together with the parent's capabilities are the major concern in most cases.

1   Cf *Stephenson v Stephenson* [1985] FLR 1140, CA.
2   See the discussion at para 2.48.
3   [1988] 2 FLR 291 at 302, CA. Cf *Re B (T) (a minor) (residence order)* [1995] 2 FCR 240, CA in which it was held that on the facts maintaining the status quo was more important to the child than being with his siblings. See also *B v B (Residence Order: Restricting Applications)* [1997] 1 FLR 139, CA, in which on the facts a decision to split the siblings was upheld on appeal, and *Re D (Care: Natural Parent Presumption)* [1999] 1 FLR 134, CA, in which it was held that too much importance had been attached in that case to the need to keep the siblings together.
4   See the discussion at para 2.9.
5   *Re G (Children)(Residence: Same Sex Partner)* [2006] UKHL 43, [2006] 1 WLR 2305, [2006] 4 All ER 241.
6   Though note Baroness Hale's analysis of 'parenthood', see the discussion at para 2.9.
7   *Re C (HIV Test)* [1999] 2 FLR 1004, FD and CA, and *Re W (a minor) (HIV test)* [1995] 2 FCR 184.
8   *May v May* [1986] 1 FLR 325, CA.
9   See *Re J (child's religious upbringing and circumcision)* [1999] 2 FCR 345, sub nom *Re J (Specific Issue Orders: Muslim Upbringing and Circumcision)* [1999] 2 FLR 678 – decision upheld by Court of Appeal, see [2000] 1 FCR 307, [2000] 1 FLR 571.

(III) ... THE LIKELY EFFECT ON THE CHILD OF ANY CHANGE IN
HIS CIRCUMSTANCES

2.45 Section 1(3)(c) is the statutory enactment of the 'status quo' or continuity factor which in practice is a particularly important factor in resolving private law disputes, the courts being well aware of the dangers of removing a child from a well-established home. As Ormrod LJ said in *D v M (Minor: Custody Appeal):*[1]

> 'it is generally accepted by those who are professionally concerned with children that particularly in the early years, continuity of care is a most important part of a child's sense of security and that disruption of established bonds are to be avoided whenever it is possible to do so.'

It is worth adding that the CA 1989 refers to a change of the child's *circumstances* not specifically their carer. Hence other factors such as school and friends are also relevant.

[1]   [1983] Fam 33 at 41, [1982] 3 All ER 897 at 902–903, CA.

2.46 Good reasons need to be adduced to justify moving a child from a well-established home[1] even on an interim basis.[2] Nevertheless the status quo is only a factor and the court may well think that the child's welfare in any particular case might be better served by being moved. As Ormrod LJ pointed out in *S v W:*[3]

> 'the status quo argument depends for its strength wholly and entirely on whether the status quo is satisfactory or not. The more satisfactory the status quo, the stronger the argument for not interfering. The less satisfactory the status quo, the less one requires before deciding to change.'

[1]   See eg *Re B (residence order)* [1998] 1 FCR 549, [1998] 1 FLR 368, CA, in which the first instance judge was held wrong to have placed speculative improvements in contact over and above the consideration of continuity of care.
[2]   See eg *Re J (Children: Ex Parte Order)*[1997] 1 FLR 606 in which Hale J observed (at 609) that ex parte orders handing over a young child to a parent with whom she has not lived for 20 months should surely be exceptional.
[3]   (1981) 11 Fam Law 81 at 82, CA.

2.47 The maintenance of the status quo becomes a stronger argument the longer the child has been with the party and is especially powerful if the other party has lost contact with the child. On the other hand, if, as in *Allington v Allington,*[1] the parties have only been separated for a few weeks and the absent parent has maintained regular contact with the child there can effectively be no status quo argument at all. In assessing what the status quo is the courts should examine the whole history of the case and not simply the position immediately before the hearing. Hence, where a parent has 'snatched' a child from the other, the court may properly regard the status quo as being the position prior to the snatch. There is, however, no *principle* where a child has been detained by the non-residential parent beyond the agreed period that the child be automatically returned to the residential parent pending the court decision as to the child's future.[2]

[1]   [1985] FLR 586, CA.
[2]   *Re J (A Minor) (Interim Custody)* [1989] 2 FLR 304, CA.

(IV) ... THE CHILD'S AGE, SEX, BACKGROUND AND ANY CHARACTERISTICS OF HIS WHICH THE COURT CONSIDERS RELEVANT

2.48 Consideration of the child's age is obviously linked to other matters such as the child's wishes and when combined with sex can be relevant to the choice of parents. In *Re W (A Minor) (Residence Order)*,[1] Lord Donaldson MR considered that 'there is a rebuttable presumption of fact that the best interests of a baby are served by being with its mother' but this is difficult to square with *Re G (Children)(Residence: Same Sex Partner)*[2] in which the House of Lords eschewed the application of *any* presumptions in this context stressing the general application of the paramountcy principle. However, within this approach the court is prepared to acknowledge that certain arrangements are more often consistent with good child raising than others. As Lord Jauncey put it in *Brixey v Lynas*:[3]

'the advantage to a very young child of being with its mother is a consideration which must be taken into account in deciding where lie its best interests in custody proceedings in which the mother is involved. It is neither a presumption nor a principle but rather recognition of a widely held belief based on practical experience and the workings of nature ... However, where a very young child has been with its mother since birth and there is no criticism of her ability to care for the child only the strongest competing advantages are likely to prevail.'

1   [1992] 2 FLR 332 at 336, CA.
2   [2006] UKHL 43, [2006] 1 WLR 2305, [2006] 4 All ER 241. See particularly Baroness Hale at [30]–[31], discussed at paras 2.8 and 2.9.
3   1996 SLT 908, [1996] 2 FLR 499, HL (Scotland).

2.49 The child's 'background' can include his religious upbringing. In the case of very young children (and probably any child of no fixed religious beliefs) the question of religious upbringing will have little bearing on the outcome of the case.[1] In *Re J (child's religious upbringing and circumcision)*[2] where the child concerned (aged 5) was being brought up as a non-practising Christian in accordance with the convictions of his mother with whom he lived and as a non-practising Muslim when staying with his father, and who could therefore be said to have no settled religious faith, Wall J declined to make a specific issue order that the child be brought up in the Muslim religion.

1   See *Re C (MA) (an infant)* [1966] 1 All ER 838 at 856 and 864–865, CA.
2   [1999] 2 FCR 345, sub nom *Re J (Specific Issue Orders: Muslim Upbringing and Circumcision)* [1999] 2 FLR 678–decision upheld by Court of Appeal, see [2000] 1 FCR 307, [2000] 1 FLR 571. See also *Re S (Specific Issue Order: Religion: Circumcision)* [2004] EWHC 1282 (Fam), [2005] 1 FLR 236.

2.50 On the other hand, where religious faith is clearly part of the child's upbringing, the court may well consider that continuation of religious observance is vital if the evidence suggests that otherwise the child could suffer emotional disturbance.[1] In this respect it is to be noted that as Scarman LJ commented:[2]

'it is not for the court to pass any judgment on the beliefs of parents where they are socially acceptable and consistent with a decent respectable life ... '

Being a Jehovah's Witness, for example, does not ipso facto mean that that parent should not be granted a residence order.[3] Indeed to deny a residence order on the ground of religion would amount to a violation of human rights.[4] In *Re H (a Minor) (Custody: Religious Upbringing),*[5] the court considered that:

> 'mere indoctrination with the beliefs and tenets of this narrow faith is not of itself indicative of harm or that harm will occur to the child so indoctrinated, provided there is an understanding and level-headed parent in charge of the child.'

A similar latitude might not, however, be given in respect of membership of what the court considers to be an extreme sect. In *Re B and G (Minors) (Custody)*[6] the decisive factor in denying a father and stepmother of what would now be a residence order in respect of children they had been looking after for five years was that they were scientologists and so held views which were found to be 'immoral and obnoxious'.

[1] This certainly influenced Willmer LJ in *Re M (infants)* [1967] 3 All ER 1071 at 1074, CA.
[2] *Re T (Minors) (Custody Upbringing)* (1975) 2 FLR 239, CA and repeated in Purchas LJ in *Re R (A Minor) (Residence Religion)* [1993] 2 FLR 163, CA.
[3] Although parties are sometimes asked to undertake not to involve their children, for example, in the house-to-house visiting conducted by Jehovah's Witnesses: see eg *Re C (Minors) (Wardship: Jurisdiction)* [1978] Fam 105, [1978] 2 All ER 230, CA.
[4] Namely art 8 taken in conjunction with art 14 of the European Convention, see eg *Palau-Martinez v France* [2004] 2 FLR 810, ECtHR and *Hoffmann v Austria* [1994] 1 FCR 193, ECtHR.
[5] (1980) 2 FLR 253.
[6] [1985] FLR 493, CA. The court felt that it could not rely on the father's undertaking to remove the children from 'the evil forces of scientology'.

2.51 Notwithstanding the foregoing there is no rule or legal principle that it can never be right to force a child to abandon his religious beliefs, since ultimately such beliefs are subservient to what is perceived as being overall in a child's best interests.[1]

[1] See *Re R (A Minor) (Residence: Religion)* [1993] 2 FLR 163, CA.

2.52 In appropriate cases, for example where the care giver has a different religion from that of the child, it is open to the court to make a residence order on condition that the child's upbringing will be continued.[1] On the other hand it could be a condition of a residence or contact order that the adult does not involve the child in his religion.[2]

[1] For the power to impose conditions on s 8 orders see paras 5.11 ff.
[2] See eg *Re R (A Minor) (Residence: Religion)* [1993] 2 FLR 163, CA.

2.53 Racial origin, cultural and linguistic background[1] are issues that should be considered under this head and on occasion are likely to prove difficult in both private and public law proceedings.

[1] Consideration to which local authorities must have specific regard under s 22(5)(c), see para 6.58.

2.54 The preservation of links with the child's culture and heritage are important issues that should not be overlooked. Such considerations were a key motivating force in *Re M (child's upbringing)*[1] in which a Zulu boy was ordered to be returned to his mother in South Africa, while in *Re M (a minor) (section 94 appeals)*[2] the failure to address the question of race when denying contact of a mixed race girl (who was confused about her racial origin) to her black father, was held to justify the Court of Appeal reversing the decision. Nevertheless, important though culture and heritage may be, the rule remains that it is the child's welfare that is the paramount consideration. Thus in *Re P (A Minor) (Residence Order: Child's Welfare)*,[3] in which Jewish Orthodox parents sought to have their child (born with Downs Syndrome) returned to them, notwithstanding that for the previous four years she was living with a non-practising Catholic couple under a residence order, it was held that on the evidence of the child's limited ability to understand and appreciate the Jewish religion, her religious and cultural heritage was *not* an overwhelming factor.

1   [1996] 2 FCR 473, [1996] 2 FLR 441, CA.
2   [1995] 2 FCR 435, [1995] 1 FLR 546.
3   [2000] Fam 15, sub nom *Re P (a child) (residence order: restriction order)* [1999] 3 All ER 734, CA.

(V) ... ANY HARM WHICH THE CHILD HAS SUFFERED OR IS AT RISK OF SUFFERING

2.55 The 'harm' referred to in s 1(3)(e) has the same meaning as it does for the purposes of establishing the threshold conditions under s 31 and accordingly means both ill-treatment and the impairment of health or development.[1] It clearly covers both physical and psychological trauma. It also covers sexual abuse which, if proved, is likely to be a significant factor,[2] but even so may not inevitably mean that the abuser should not, for example, be allowed contact.[3] Following an amendment by the Adoption and Children Act 2002[4] the definition of 'harm' has been extended to include 'impairment suffered from seeing or hearing the ill-treatment of another'. This amendment is intended to emphasise the potential harm caused to a child, for example, by witnessing violence perpetrated by one parent on another. Note may also be taken of the power, conferred by s 16A,[5] for CAFCASS and Welsh family proceedings officers to carry out a risk assessment and provide it to the court, if in the course of carrying out *any* function in family proceedings under Pt II of the CA 1989, the officer is given cause to suspect that the child concerned is at risk of harm.[6] *Practice Direction (Residence and Contact Orders: Domestic Violence)*[7] further provides that at all stages of residence or contact order proceedings, the court must consider whether domestic violence is raised as an issue and must not make a consent order for residence or contact or give permission for such an application to be withdrawn unless the parties are present in court, except where it is satisfied that there is no risk of harm to the child in so doing.

1   Section 105(1) provides that 'harm' has the same meaning as in s 31(9), discussed at para 8.40.
2   See e g *Re B (A Minor) (Care Order: Criteria)* [1993] 1 FLR 815.

3   *H v H (Child Abuse: Access)* [1989] 1 FLR 212, CA; *L v L (Child Abuse: Access)* [1989] 2 FLR 16, CA; *C v C (A Minor) (Child Abuse: Evidence)* [1988] 1 FLR 462. Cf *Re R (A Minor) (Access)* [1988] 1 FLR 206, CA.

4   Section 120, amending s 31(9) of the CA 1989, which was brought into force on 31 January 2005 by the Adoption and Children Act 2002 (Commencement No 7) Order 2004, SI 2004/3203, art 2(2). *Note* information about any harm alleged must be filed with the application for a parental responsibility order or s 8 order: see SI 2005/412 and SI 2005/413, referred to at para 4.21.

5   Introduced with effect from 1 October 2007: see the Children and Adoption Act 2006 (Commencement No 1) Order 2007, SI 2007/2287, which brought s 7 of the 2006 Act into force.

6   Risk assessments are discussed in more detail at paras 5.11–5.12.

7   [2008] 1 WLR 1062.

2.56 Apart from actual harm, s 1(3)(e) also encompasses 'risk' of harm. Such a risk could, for example, emanate from the parents' past alcoholism,[1] or sexual abuse. It is, however, established that s 1(3)(e) deals with actual harm or risk of harm and not with possibilities. As Butler-Sloss LJ said in *Re M and R (Child Abuse: Evidence)*:[2]

'The court must reach a conclusion based on facts, not on suspicion or mere doubts. If, as in the present case, the court concludes that the evidence is insufficient to prove sexual abuse in the past, and if the fact of sexual abuse in the past is the only basis for asserting a risk of sexual abuse in the future, then it follows that there is nothing (except suspicion or mere doubts) to show a risk of future sexual abuse'.

Lord Nicholls subsequently commented in *Re O (Minors)(Care: Preliminary Hearing)*[3] that, without hearing full arguments on the matter he found conclusions of *Re M and R* 'attractive' adding

'It would be odd if, on this point, the approach in proceedings for section 8 orders were different from the approach in care proceedings'.

Re M and R has since been explicitly approved by the House of Lords in *Re B (Children) (Care Proceedings: Standard of Proof) (CAFCASS intervening)*.[4]

1   See eg *Re L (residence: justices' reasons)* [1995] 2 FLR 445.

2   [1996] 2 FLR 195 at 203, applying the same test as applies to s 31 following the House of Lords' ruling in *Re H (Minors) (Sexual Abuse: Standard of Proof)* [1996] AC 563, sub nom *Re H (minors) (child abuse: threshold conditions)* [1996] 1 All ER 1 discussed at paras 8.22 ff. See also *Re P (Sexual Abuse: Standard of Proof)* [1996] 2 FLR 333, CA.

3   [2003] UKHL 18, [2004] 1 AC 523, [2003] 2 All ER 305 at [45].

4   [2008] UKHL 35, [2008] 3 WLR 1.

2.57 *Re M and R* also establishes that the appropriate standard of proof is the preponderance of probabilities.[1] However, the undoubted difficulties of proving primary allegations in some cases do not justify not investigating them at all.[2] The proper approach is to consider first whether the primary allegation on which the risk of harm is said to be based can be proved and then, assuming it can, to decide whether or not that is a risk of harm to satisfy s 1(3)(e).

1   [1996] 2 FLR 195 at 203, expressly rejecting the contention that because the child's welfare was paramount the standard of proof for establishing harm should be less than the preponderance of probabilities.

2.57 *General principles*

²   See eg *Re L (Residence: Justices' Reasons)* [1995] 2 FLR 445, in which magistrates were held wrong not to deal expressly with the father's contention that the mother's former alcohol problems had resumed.

(VI) ... HOW CAPABLE EACH OF THE CHILD'S PARENTS, AND ANY OTHER PERSON IN RELATION TO WHOM THE COURT CONSIDERS THE QUESTION TO BE RELEVANT, IS OF MEETING HIS NEEDS

2.58 A wide variety of circumstances can be brought under this factor, ranging from capability to provide housing,[1] the medical condition of the parents to their lifestyle. It is to be noted that as well as parents the capability of any other persons in relation to whom the court considers the question to be relevant must also be examined. This will clearly include any new partner (formal or informal) of a parent.[2]

¹   See *Holmes-Moorehouse v Richmond-upon-Thomas London Borough Council* [2007] EWCA Civ 970, [2008] 1 FLR 1061, discussed at para 5.52.
²   *Scott v Scott* [1986] 2 FLR 320, CA.

(VII) ... THE RANGE OF POWERS AVAILABLE TO THE COURT UNDER [THE 1989] ACT IN THE PROCEEDINGS IN QUESTION

2.59 Section 1(3)(g) directs the court to consider not only whether the order being sought is best for the child but also to consider the alternatives that the Act makes available. This is particularly important in the context of care proceedings, since it is therefore incumbent upon the court to consider not only whether or not to make the care order but whether, for example, a residence order under s 8 or a special guardianship order, would better serve the child's interests.

9. Delay prima facie prejudicial to the child's welfare[1]

2.60 Section 1(2) enjoins the court, in any proceedings in which any question with respect to a child's upbringing arises, 'to have regard to the general principle that any delay in determining the question is likely to prejudice the welfare of the child'.[2] Since this provision applies to any proceedings concerning any question concerning a child's upbringing,[3] it is not confined to proceedings under the CA 1989 but applies equally, to proceedings under the High Court's inherent jurisdiction[4] (separate provision is now made for adoption proceedings).[5] However, the timetabling provisions[6] are confined to proceedings under the CA 1989 (though in practice they are applied to proceedings under the inherent jurisdiction).

¹   A study, commissioned by the Lord Chancellor has reviewed the reasons for delay and assessed the need for reform, see *Scoping Study on Delay in Children Act Cases* (Lord Chancellor's Department, March 2002). For comments on the draft Report, see Finlay 'Delay and the Challenges of the Children Act' in *Delight and Dole* (eds Thorpe and Cowton) 5 at 10 ff. See further the discussion in Chapter 4.
²   Attention to the need to avoid delay is specifically mentioned in para 15.1 of the *Practice Note: Devolution Issues and Crown Office Applications)* [1999] 3 All ER 466.

3   Note, however, the exclusion of maintenance from the definition of 'upbringing' under s 105(1).

4   The inherent jurisdiction is discussed in Chapter 12.

5   Namely by s 1(3) of the Adoption and Children Act 2002.

6   Ie those provided by ss 11(1) and 32(1) and discussed further at paras 4.43 ff. Separate timetabling provisions apply to adoption proceedings, see s 109 of the Adoption and Children Act 2002.

2.61 The need for speed is also underscored by art 6 of the European Convention on Human Rights under which everyone is entitled to a fair and public hearing in the determination of his civil rights and obligations *within a reasonable time.*[1]

1   For examples of where undue delay has been held to be a breach of art 6 see e.g. *Süss v Germany* [2006] 1 FLR 522, ECtHR, protracted access dispute for over a decade only ending when the child became 18; *Jevremovic v Serbia* [2007] 2 FCR 671, [2008] 1 FLR 550, ECtHR, and *Karcheva v Bulgaria* [2006] 3 FCR 434, ECtHR both involving unduly protracted proceedings to establish paternity, and *EO and VP v Slovakia* [2004] 2 FCR 242, ECtHR, protracted dispute over the education of a 14-year-old child which had to be discontinued when the child became 18.

2.62 Notwithstanding s 1(2), it should not be thought that delay[1] is always detrimental to a child's welfare. As Ward J observed in *C v Solihull Metropolitan Borough Council*,[2] while delay is ordinarily inimical to the welfare of a child, planned and purposeful delay may well be beneficial. Hence, the delay of a final decision in order to ascertain the result of an assessment is obviously for rather than against the child's interests. In *Re B (a Minor) (Contact) (Interim Order)*,[3] magistrates were held to be 'plainly wrong' in refusing to make an interim contact order during which arrangements for the reintroduction of contact were to be assessed because it infringed the principle of the avoidance of delay as set out in s 1(2). As the criterion to be applied is the welfare of the *child,* detriment to the *family* is not of itself a relevant factor. It was on this basis that *Re T-B (Care Proceedings: Criminal Trial)*[4] held that the fact there was a pending criminal trial was not enough to justify delaying the hearing of care proceedings.

1   As has been observed (Butler et al: 'Children Act and the Issue of Delay' [1993] Fam Law 412): 'delay is a relative phenomenon and needs to be distinguished from 'duration'. A complex case may, quite appropriately and expeditiously, remain in the courts for several weeks while a relatively simple matter that ought to be dealt with within days may take three weeks and hence be subject to significant delay, yet still be of moderate duration'.

2   [1993] 1 FLR 290 at 304.

3   [1994] 2 FLR 269. See also *Re L and H (Residential Assessment)* [2007] EWCA Civ 213, [2007] 1 FLR 1370, on the application of s 1(2) to s 38(6) assessments.

4   [1995] 2 FLR 801, CA.

2.63 Although the principal effect of s 1(2) is to place the onus upon the courts to ensure that all proceedings concerning children are conducted as expeditiously as possible, practitioners also have a duty to ensure that a case does not drift. As Wall J has said:[1]

'Solicitors for the parties, whatever their forensic stance and irrespective of whether or not delay may be tactically advantageous to their client, have a duty in children's cases to ensure that a case does not drift and is either brought to a hearing or resolved in some other way with the minimum of delay.'

According to the same judge in another case:[2]

> 'The courts have a duty to be positive in ensuring that applications once launched are not allowed to moulder'.

To this end, courts are directed[3] in applications for s 8 orders and orders under Pt IV of the CA 1989 to draw up a timetable and to give appropriate directions for adhering to that timetable. These powers are discussed in Chapter 4. It has been held that in view of s 1(2), a court can, in appropriate cases, depart from the recommendations of a children and family reporter even though the reporter did not attend court to give oral evidence.[4]

1   In *B v B (Child Abuse: Contact)* [1994] 2 FLR 713, at 736.
2   *B v B (Minors) (Interviews and Listing Arrangements)* [1994] 2 FLR 489 at 492, CA. See also *Re A and B (Minors) (No 2)* [1995] 1 FLR 351. Nevertheless, s 1(2) does not of itself mean that CAFCASS must make an officer available for appointment as a guardian in care proceedings on receiving a request from the court: *R v Children and Family Court Advisory and Support Service* [2003] EWHC 235 (Admin), [20031] 1 FLR 953.
3   Namely under ss 11(1) and 32(1).
4   Per Hale J in *Re C (Section 8 Order: Court Welfare Officer)* [1995] 1 FLR 617, CA (welfare officers are now known as children and family reporters). Note also, *H v Cambridgeshire County Council* [1996] 2 FLR 566, leave refused for a mother to show papers to a consultant child psychiatrist given her own delay in taking steps to identify a suitable expert under the terms of an earlier order for leave.

ORDERS TO BE MADE ONLY WHERE THE COURT IS SATISFIED THAT MAKING THE ORDER IS BETTER THAN MAKING NO ORDER

1. Introduction and background

2.64   An important principle is provided by s 1(5), namely, that whenever a court is considering whether to make one or more orders under the CA 1989 with respect to a child, it 'shall not make the order or any of the orders unless it considers that doing so would be better for the child than making no order at all'. This provision[1] is intended to focus attention as to whether any court order is necessary. It was part of an underlying philosophy of the CA 1989, namely, to respect the integrity and independence of the family save where court orders have some positive contribution to make towards the child's welfare. According to the revised Children Act 1989 Guidance and Regulations,[2] s 1(5) has three aims:

> 'The first is to discourage unnecessary court orders being made, for example as part of a standard package of orders. If orders are restricted to those cases where they are necessary to resolve a specific problem this should reduce conflict and promote parental agreement and co-operation. The second aim is to ensure that the order is granted only where it will positively improve the child's welfare and not simply because the grounds for making the order are made out. For example, in care proceedings where the court may decide that it would be better for a particular child not to be made the subject of a care order, which would place that child in local authority care. The application by the court of this 'no order' should not deter local authorities from bringing proceedings in those cases where they believe that a care or supervision order is necessary in order to safeguard and promote a child's welfare. The third aim is to discourage the making of unnecessary applications'.[3]

1   Which implements the Law Commission's recommendations with regard to private law
     proceedings, see Law Com No 172, paras 3.2–3.4, and those of the Child Care Review
     (DHSS, 1985) paras 15.24–15.25 and the government's White Paper, The Law on Child
     Care and Family Services Cm 62, 1987, para 59, with respect to public law proceedings.
2   Guidance and Regulations, Vol 1, Court Orders (2008) Department for Children, Schools
     and Families, para 1.15.
3   For a comment on the new Guidance see Doughty 'The "No Order Principle" – A Myth
     Revived?' [2008] Fam Law 561.

2. When the principle applies

2.65 As s 1(5) itself states, it applies where a court is considering whether or
not to make one or more orders under the CA 1989. Accordingly, it has no
direct application in proceedings in which courts are considering whether or
not to make orders relating to children outside the Act.[1] In this respect, s 1(5)
has a narrower ambit than either s 1(1) or (2).

1   Eg orders under the wardship or inherent jurisdiction though, presumably, there is nothing
     to prevent a court from taking a similar approach, if it so chooses. A similar enjoinder now
     applies in adoption proceedings, see s 1(6) of the Adoption and Children Act 2002.

2.66 In *K v H (Child Maintenance)*[1] it was held that s 1(5) does not apply to
applications for financial provision[2] for a child under Sch 1 to the Act since,
like s 1(1), which Sir Stephen Brown P took to be the general controlling
provision for the overall application of s 1, s 1(5) 'is principally directed to
orders relating to the upbringing of a child, the administration of a child's
property or the application of any income arising from it'. Accordingly, since
an application for financial provision neither concerns the child's upbringing
nor the administration of his property, s 1(5) does not apply. The alternative
reason for holding s 1(5) inapplicable was that, given that it is clearly in a
child's interests that proper provision be made for his financial needs, a court
order is preferable to relying on the parties' oral agreement[3] since that
provides a better means of safeguarding the future both in the sense of
providing for future variations and of being able to deal with any subsequent
enforcement issues.

1   [1993] 2 FLR 61.
2   Namely periodical payments, which was what *K v H* concerned, or lump sums or property
     orders.
3   Aliter for written agreements which can, subject to the Child Support Act 1991, be varied
     by the court eg under the CA 1989, Sch 1, paras 10 and 11.

2.67 Whether Sir Stephen Brown P was right to say that s 1(1) provides
overall control of the operation of s 1 may be debated but in practice it is
likely to be the case that s 1(5) will not apply if s 1(1) does not. For example,
in *Re M (a Minor) (Secure Accommodation Order)*,[1] which established that
s 1(1) does not apply to the question of whether to make a secure accommodation order under s 25,[2] Butler-Sloss LJ expressly held that because of the
need to protect the public as well as the child, s 1(5) does not apply either.
Again, in deciding whether to grant leave to apply for a s 8 order where it is
established that the paramountcy principle does not apply[3] it seems right to
say that s 1(5) is also subsumed by the criteria set out in s 10(9).[4]

[1] [1995] Fam 108, [1995] 3 All ER 407, CA.
[2] Secure accommodation is discussed in Chapter 9.
[3] See *Re A (Minors) (Residence Orders: Leave to Apply)* [1992] Fam 182, [1992] 3 All ER 872, CA, discussed at paras 2.27 and 5.151 ff.
[4] In particular s 10(9)(c) which directs the court to consider the risk of harm to the child that the proposed application might cause. See further paras 5.150 ff.

3. The application of s 1(5)

2.68 The application of s 1(5) has proved problematic. It quickly became referred to as establishing a 'non intervention principle' or 'no order principle'[1] but insofar as these epithets suggest that orders are presumed to be unnecessary, their use has been deprecated in some quarters. As one commentator has pointed out,[2] neither the Law Commission nor statute says that court orders are presumed to be unnecessary and 'most certainly' neither suggested that in public care proceedings there is a legal presumption against the making of care or supervision orders. In his view, if epithets are required, a more accurate one would be the 'no *unnecessary* order principle'.

[1] It was memorably described as 'privatising the family' by Cretney 'Privatising the Family: The Reform of Child Law' (1989) Denning LJ 15. See also Bainham 'The Privatisation of The Public Interest in Children' (1990) 53 MLR 206. Others (eg Douglas 'Family Law under the Thatcher Government' (1990) 17 JLS 411 at 415, n 17) referred to it as establishing a policy of deregulation or non-intervention.
[2] Bainham 'Changing families and changing concepts – reframing the language of family law' (1998) 10 CFLQ 1 at 2–4.

(a) the substantive law

2.69 Although the clear import of s 1(5) is that orders should not be made under the CA 1989 unless they are considered to be for the *child's* welfare, the precise application of the sub-section remains uncertain. In *Re X and Y (leave to remove from jurisdiction: no order principle)*[1] Munby J held, relying on principles said to be distilled from the House of Lords' decision in *Dawson v Wearmouth*,[2] that the 'burden is on the party applying for an order to make out a positive case that on a balance of probabilities it is in the interests of the child that that order should be made'. However, this analysis was disapproved of by the Court of Appeal both in *Re H (children) (residence order: condition)*[3] in which Thorpe LJ commented, that he did not think that the dicta drawn from the House of Lords' cases bears 'the weight of the edifice that Munby J sought to build on them' and in *Re G (Children)*,[4] in which Ward LJ considered s 1(5) to be:

> 'perfectly clear. It does not ... create a presumption one way or another. All it demands is that before the court makes any order it must ask the question: will it be better for the child to make the order than making no order at all?'

[1] [2001] 2 FCR 398, [2001] 2 FLR 118. On which, see the comment by Douglas at [2001] Fam Law 345–346.
[2] [1999] 2 AC 308, [1999] 2 All ER 353, relying in particular on comments made by Lord Mackay (at 321A and 359(c)–(d)) and Lord Hobhouse (at 325H–326E, 363(g)–(364(d)). According to Munby J there is no difference in substance between what was said by the House of Lords in this case and what they said in the earlier Scots case, *S v M (Access Order)* [1997] 1 FLR 980, sub nom *Sanderson v McManus* 1997 SC (HL) 55.

³   [2001] EWCA Civ 1338, [2001] 3 FCR 182, [2001] 2 FLR 1277.
⁴   [2005] EWCA Civ 1283, [2006] 1 FLR 771.
⁵   At para [10].

2.70 Notwithstanding that it is wrong to place weight on the burden of proof the court must nevertheless be satisfied that an order is for the benefit of the child and that in carrying out this task the court must evaluate the evidence rather than applying any presumption.¹ Convincing the court of the benefit to the particular child of the order sought will be easier to satisfy in contested applications particularly in the private law context. Indeed, it has been said that making 'no order' is inappropriate if the court is clearly charged with the responsibility for settling a dispute. In *Re W (A Minor) (Contact)*,² upon a father's application for defined contact following the mother's refusal to comply with a previous order for reasonable contact and her declared intention not to obey any further order, the first instance decision to make a 'no order' was held to be an abdication of responsibility. The point has also been made that there is a clear distinction between dismissing an application and making a 'no order'. If the making of the latter is tantamount to dismissing a parent's application for contact, as opposed to holding that an order was not necessary, then, according to *D v D (application for contact)*,³ the court should at least take a proactive role and consider whether any further application should be made and, if so, when and in what circumstances.

¹   A good example is where a shared residence order (discussed at paras 5.17 ff) is being sought but there exists a harmonious relationship between the parents. As Thorpe LJ said in *Re R (Residence: Shared Care: Children's Views)* [2005] EWCA Civ 542, [2006] 1 FLR 491, [2005] All ER (D) 238 at [11]:

> 'the presence of that sort of harmonious relationship is a contra-indication of a shared residence order since such parents would fall within the no order principle emphasised by s 1(5) ...'.

²   [1994] 2 FLR 441, CA. Note Thorpe LJ's comment in *Re H (children) (residence order: condition)* [2001] EWCA Civ 1338, para [19], [2001] 3 FCR 182, [2001] 2 FLR 1277, referred to above at para 2.69. See also *Re P (A Minor) (Parental Responsibility Order)* [1994] 1 FLR 578.
³   [1994] 1 FCR 694, per Wall J.

2.71 While it might be easier to persuade the court to make an order in contested cases it by no means follows that no order can be granted if the parties are agreed. In this respect reference can usefully be made to the revised Guidance on the CA 1989:¹

> 'There are several situations where the court is likely to consider it better for the child to make an order than not. If the court has had to resolve a dispute between the parents, it is likely to be better for the child to make an order about it. Even if there is no dispute, the child's need for stability and security may be better served by making an order. There may also be specific legal advantages in doing so. '

In the Guidance as originally drafted² two examples were given of where an order might be justified notwithstanding the absence of a dispute. The first is where abduction of the child is thought to be a possibility since a court order is necessary for enforcement proceedings in other parts of the United Kingdom under the Family Law Act 1986 and, one might now add, an order is also useful for enforcement purposes in other EU Member States.[3] For unmarried fathers and third parties a residence order could also be essential in establishing 'rights of custody' for the purposes of the 1980 Hague Abduction Convention. The original Guidance also said:

> 'An advantage of having a residence order is that the child may be taken out of the country for periods of less than one month without the permission of other persons with parental authority or the court, whereas without an order this could amount to an offence under the Child Abduction Act 1984.[4] Also if a person has a sole residence order in his favour and appoints a ... guardian for the child, the appointment will take effect immediately on that person's death, even where there is a surviving parent. Depending on the circumstances of the case, the court might therefore be persuaded that an order would be in the child's interests.'

This Guidance still remains relevant.

[1] Children Act 1989 Guidance and Regulations, Vol 1, Court Orders (2008) Department for Children, Schools and Families, para 2.73.
[2] Children Act 1989 Guidance and Regulations, Vol 1, Court Orders (1991) Department of Health, para 2.56.
[3] Ie to meet the criteria under Council Regulation (EC) No 2201/2003 of 27 November 2003, discussed further at paras 5.127 ff.
[4] In practice, given the defences, an offence will only be committed where it can be proved that the abducting parent knew that the other parent would object.

2.72 One circumstance not mentioned in the Guidance but which could justify the making of a residence or contact order is where the applicant, for example an unmarried father, relative or cohabitant, has no parental responsibility, since it can always be argued that unless an order is made he or she will not otherwise have legal standing in relation to the child.[1] In *Re G (Residence: Same-Sex Partner)*[2] a shared residence order was made specifically to give the non-parent partner parental responsibility to prevent her being marginalised by the mother with whom she had been cohabiting. In *B v B (a Minor) (Residence Order)*[3] Johnson J accepted this argument when he granted in what he described as 'the unusual circumstances of the case' an unopposed application for a residence order by a grandparent with whom the child had been living for 10 years. The Court of Appeal has also warned of the dangers that might result from deciding to make no order simply because the parties appear to be in agreement. In *Re S (a minor) (contact: grandparents)*[4] a grandparent sought a contact order. By the time the matter came to court, the judge was persuaded that the mother would permit contact, and therefore, did not make a contact order, relying on s 1(5). On appeal it was felt that, having decided that it was in the child's welfare to have contact with the grandparent, and given the history of antagonism between the parties, the contact order should be made, even if the parties were in agreement at the time of the court hearing. The making of the order would ensure that contact did take place and avoid the need to return to court in the event of a disagreement.

[1] See s 10(4) and (6).
[2] [2005] EWCA 462, [2005] 2 FLR 957, [2005] All ER (D) 25 (Apr). Note the case eventually went to the House of Lords, which upheld the order albeit reversing the time allowed to each home in favour of the biological mother – see *Re G (Children)(Residence: Same Sex Partner)* [2006] UKHL 43,[2006] 1 WLR 2305, [2006] 4 All ER 411.

3   [1992] 2 FLR 327.
4   [1996] 3 FCR 30, [1996] 1 FLR 158.

(b) the application of s 1(5) in practice

2.73 A study conducted in the late 1990s by Bristol University found that 'no orders' were made in about 5% of cases[1]. National statistics point to a declining proportion of 'no orders'. The early indicators were that about 9% of all private law orders were of 'no orders',[2] a proportion which was still reflected for example in 1996.[3] However, in 2000 this proportion declined to about 4% of orders and to only 1½% in 2006.[4] Interestingly, among the findings by HM Inspectorate of Courts Administration in their 2007 Report, *Assisting Families by Court* Order,[5] was that the importance of the 'no order principle' was not given sufficient priority when recommending a family assistance order.[6]

1   See Bailey-Harris, Barron and Pearce: 'Settlement culture and the use of the "no order" principle under The Children Act 1989' [1999] CFLQ 53. They also found that at county court level practitioners and district judges took a variety of approaches to s 1(5).
2   See the second edition of this work at para 2.49, based upon the analysis of the CAAC Reports 1991/92 and 1992/93.
3   See the analysis of Lowe and Douglas, *Bromley's Family Law* (10th edn) p 583 based on Table 5.3 of the Judicial Statistics Annual Report 1996.
4   Based respectively on an analysis of Table 5.3 of the Judicial Statistics Annual Reports 2000, (2001, Cm 5223), and Table 5.4 of the Court and Judicial Statistics 2006 (2007, Cm 7273).
5   HMICA Report, March 2007.
6   Family assistance orders are discussed at paras 5.191 ff.

2.74 Although, s 1(5) at one time seemed to have led local authorities not to bring cases before the court, in fact relatively few 'no orders' were made in the public law context. In the first nine months after implementation 'no orders' accounted for 3% of the total number of disposals made in public law proceedings[1] and, based on the 2006 statistics, now accounts for about 2% of the disposals.[2] This should occasion little surprise since one would have expected fewer 'no orders' being made in the public law context, particularly in care proceedings under s 31 since if the statutory threshold is satisfied there is likely to be a good reason to make an order.[3] Conversely if s 31 is not satisfied a dismissal seems more likely than an order of 'no order'. In the former case there is likely to be a good reason for making an order whether or not proceedings are contested. In other words, in public law proceedings, the issue of consent is much less significant than in private law.[4]

1   See CAAC Report 1991/92 Table 2.
2   Based on Table 5.4 Judicial and Court Statistics 2006 (2007, Cm 7273).
3   In many cases not making an order would amount to a dereliction of the court's duty: see eg *Re B (A Minor) (Care Order: Criteria)* [1993] 1 FLR 815 at 821.
4   However, the fact that the parties are agreed does not absolve a court from investigating the facts for itself; see *Re G (A Minor) (Care Order: Threshold Condition)* [1995] Fam 16, sub nom *Re G (A Minor) (Care Proceedings)* [1994] 2 FLR 69.

4. Form of order

2.75 If the court decides to make no order then a formal order to that effect must be made.[1] A decision not to make an order still ranks as a 'decision' and reasons for making it should therefore be given.[2]

[1]   FPR 1991, r 4.21(4); FPC(CA 1989)R 1991, r 21(6).
[2]   *S v R (parental responsibility)* [1993] 1 FCR 331.

5. The inter-relationship of the welfare principle and the 'non-intervention' principle

2.76 Although s 1(5) can be seen as complementing the welfare principle since it cannot be in the best interests of a child to be the subject of unnecessary court orders, it has been argued[1] that in reality the welfare principle has been 'hijacked by non-interventionism' on the basis that the non-interventionist stance taken in the CA 1989 means that parental wishes, especially where both are in agreement, will determine an increasing number of issues affecting children.

[1]   Bainham 'The Privatisation of the Public Interest in Children' (1990) 53 MLR 206, 221. See also Bainham 'The Children Act 1989, Welfare and Non-Interventionism' [1990] Fam Law 143, 145.

2.77 Although there is some tension between s 1(1) and (5) it is surely going too far to say that the welfare principle has been 'hijacked' by the operation of s 1(5). As has been seen,[1] even in the private law context, the proportion of 'no orders' made under s 1(5) is relatively small (though of course it is unknown how many applications are simply not being pursued).[2] Furthermore, most agreements are likely to provide the best arrangements that can be made for the children in the circumstances. In any case it may be questioned whether the pre-1989 Act law was so very different.[3] Under the former law the courts were generally reluctant to interfere with arrangements agreed between the parents. Under the CA 1989 the difference may simply be that the court may make no order at all rather than making an order reflecting the parents' agreement. Nevertheless there is a danger that by making no order in the light of parental agreement the court could overlook the child's wishes. If they do so in the case of older children there could be a breach of art 12 of the UN Convention on the Rights of the Child.[4] Accordingly, courts should be alive to this possibility and seek some assurance that the child in question does not object to the arrangements agreed between the parents.

[1]   See para 2.73.
[2]   Although according to the Government's Working Paper *Children's Needs and Parental Responsibilities* (July 2004) only 10% of separating couples with children had their contact arrangements ordered by the courts. Nor should the number of withdrawn applications be overlooked, since a proportion of these withdrawals may have been motivated by a desire to avoid a 'no order'. The number of withdrawals greatly exceeds that of 'no orders'. For example, in 2006, 325 care order applications were withdrawn compared with 289 'no orders'; 143 contact in care applications were withdrawn compared with 27 'no orders' while in private law proceedings 1,148 applications for residence orders were withdrawn compared with 424 'no orders' and 2046 contact

applications were withdrawn compared with 991 'no orders' Judicial and Court Statistics 2006 (Cm 7273, November 2007), Table 5.4.

3   In any event, it can be questioned whether the welfare principle itself is truly child-centred. See eg Maidment *Child Custody and Divorce*, p 149 who argues that decisions in the past were 'made by adults for adults about adults'.

4   Under which there is an international obligation for courts to give due weight to a child's views. See also para 2.42.

6. The inter-relationship of human rights and the 'non-intervention' principle

2.78 In the public law context and, by analogy, when exercising the court's protective jurisdiction[1] another consideration comes into play, namely, the need from a human rights perspective for the response to any harm to be proportionate.[2] It may be, notwithstanding that harm has been found, that the child will be adequately protected without any order being made. In such a case no order would be justified both on human rights grounds and on the basis of s 1(5).[3] It is important, however, not to muddle these considerations. Section 1(5) operates to determine whether *any* order should be made, whereas human rights considerations dictate that whatever order is made must be proportionate to the harm found. In other words, even where an order is considered necessary, human rights, but not s 1(5), still operates to determine what type of order is appropriate. But neither consideration should derogate from the overarching principle of the paramountcy of the child's welfare.[4]

1   Ie the High Court's inherent jurisdiction to protect children from harm, as first espoused by the House of Lords in *S v S, W v Official Solicitor* [1972] AC 24, [1970] 3 All ER 107, see para 2.17, n 5 and for further discussion, see Lowe and White *Wards of Court* (2nd edn) 7–17 ff.

2   See in particular *Re C and B (Care Order: Future Harm)* [2001] 1 FLR 611, CA and *Re O (Supervision Order)* [2001] EWCA Civ 16, [2001] 1 FLR 923, discussed at para 8.56.

3   See, for example, *Re K; A Local Authority v N* [2005] EWHC 2956 (Fam), [2007] 1 FLR 399, particularly at [55]–[58], per Munby J.

4   See *Re M-J (Adoption Order or Special Guardianship)* [2007] EWCA Civ 56, [2007] 1 FLR 691, particularly at [19], per Wall LJ.

Chapter 3

PARENTAL RESPONSIBILITY AND GUARDIANSHIP

INTRODUCTION

3.1 The Law Commission[1] recommended that parenthood rather than guardianship should become the primary concept and that the term 'guardian' should be reserved for those formally appointed to take the place of parents upon their death. Further it pointed out that, scattered throughout the statute book were such terms as 'parental rights and duties', or 'powers and duties' or the 'rights and authority' of a parent. Not only were these terms inconsistent with one another but as the Commission had earlier commented:[2] 'it can be cogently argued that to talk of "parental rights" is not only inaccurate as a matter of juristic analysis but also a misleading use of ordinary language'. Accordingly, the Commission recommended the introduction of the concept of 'parental responsibility' to replace all the ambiguous and misleading terms referred to above, arguing that although such a change 'would make little difference in substance ... it would reflect the everyday reality of being a parent and emphasise the responsibility of all who are in that position'.[3]

[1] Report on Guardianship and Custody, Law Com 1988, No 172, Pt III.
[2] Law Com No 118, Illegitimacy, 1982, para 4.18.
[3] Law Com No 172, para 2.4.

3.2 The government accepted the Commission's recommendations and 'parental responsibility' is a pivotal concept of the CA 1989. Guardianship, on the other hand, now exclusively refers to the status of those formally appointed to take the place of parents after their death.[1] The concept of parental guardianship has been abolished.[2]

[1] Not to be confused with 'Children's Guardian' which is the term introduced by CAFCASS to replace what were formerly known as 'guardians ad litem' and who represent children either in public law proceedings (see paras 10.35 ff) or adoption proceedings, nor with 'Special Guardians' introduced by the Adoption and Children Act 2002 which provide a more permanent status for non-parents than under a residence order but unlike adoption does not extinguish the legal relationship between the child and his or her birth family (see paras 5.213 ff).
[2] CA 1989, s 2(4) expressly abolishes the rule of law that a father is the natural guardian of his legitimate children, while s 3 of the Guardianship of Minors Act 1971, which provided (in the case of legitimate children) that upon the death of one parent, the other became the guardian, has been repealed (see Sch 15).

PARENTAL RESPONSIBILITY

1. Contexts in which parental responsibility is relevant

3.3 Parental responsibility is concerned with a number of different relationships. It can embrace both the idea that parents must behave dutifully towards their children and that responsibility for child care belongs to parents and not to the state.[1] Both these important ideas are embodied in the CA 1989. The former is well summed up by the comment[2] that the concept of 'parental responsibility':

'emphasises that the days when a child should be regarded as a possession of his parent – indeed when in the past they had a right to his services and to sue on their loss are now buried forever. The overwhelming purpose of parenthood is the responsibility for caring for and raising the child to be a properly developed adult both physically and morally'.

The Department of Health's introductory guide to the Children Act[3] similarly states that parental responsibility:

'emphasises that the duty to care for the child and to raise him to moral, physical and emotional health is the fundamental task of parenthood and the only justification for the authority that it confers.'

Both these comments reflect in turn the earlier landmark decision of *Gillick v West Norfolk and Wisbech Area Health Authority*[4] in which, at any rate, Lords Fraser and Scarman emphasised that parental power to control a child exists not for the benefit of the parent but for the benefit of the child.

[1] Eekelaar, 'Parental Responsibility: State of Nature or Nature of the State?' [1991] JSWFL 37.
[2] Per Lord Mackay LC, when introducing the Bill at 502 HL Official Report (5th series), col 490.
[3] 'Introduction to the Children Act 1989', HMSO 1989, para 1.4.
[4] [1986] AC 112, [1985] 3 All ER 402, HL. See further para 3.32.

3.4 It is the enduring nature of responsibility, particularly when allied with the need to justify intervention under s 1(5),[1] that encapsulates the idea that responsibility for child care belongs to parents rather than the state. By providing that responsibility should continue despite, for example, a court order that the child should live with one of them, parents 'are to understand that the state will not relieve them of their responsibilities'.[2] This is underscored by the fact that responsibility cannot be voluntarily surrendered to a public body[3] and that even where a care order is made compulsorily placing the child in local authority care, parents still retain their responsibility.[4] In short, the CA 1989 through the concept of parental responsibility, emphasises the idea that 'once a parent, always a parent' and that prima facie responsibility for deciding what should happen to their children even upon their separation should rest with the parents themselves.

[1] Discussed at paras 2.64 ff.
[2] Cretney 'Defining the Limits of State Intervention: The Child and Courts' *in Children and the Law*' (ed Freestone, 1990) 58 at p 67.

3 Ie where the child is 'accommodated' by a local authority under s 20 (discussed in ch 6) parental responsibility is not acquired by the authority, see the discussion by Eekelaar, cited at para 3.3 above at pp 40–42.
4 The effect of care orders is discussed at paras 8.171 ff.

3.5 Apart from the parent-child and parent-state relationships, the concept of parental responsibility is also relevant to the relationship between parents and other individuals. It can be as important to parents that they can look after their children without interference by other individuals as by the state. On the other hand, de facto carers need some authority to take normal 'day-to-day' decisions whilst looking after the child. These potentially conflicting standpoints are resolved by the CA 1989 in that parents with parental responsibility, are nevertheless permitted to 'arrange for some or all [of their responsibility] will be met by one or more persons acting on his behalf.'[1] Furthermore, those without parental responsibility but who have care of the child can 'do what is reasonable in all the circumstances of the case for the purpose of safeguarding or promoting the child's welfare'.[2]

1 Section 2(9), discussed further at para 3.102.
2 Section 3(5), discussed further at para 3.103.

2. The practical effects of the changed terminology

3.6 Although the change of terminology from rights and duties to responsibility was neither intended nor expected to make a change in substance to the law, its effect upon lay persons should not be underestimated, for saying a parent has responsibilities rather than rights in itself conveys a quite different message. In any event there is more to the notion of parental responsibility than just a change in terminology. As s 2 makes clear not only can more than one person have parental responsibility at the same time but perhaps more importantly a person does not cease to have responsibility because someone else acquires it.[1] Furthermore, each holder of responsibility can in theory[2] continue to exercise it by himself or herself without having to consult any other holder subject only to the overriding condition that he or she must not act incompatibly with any existing court order.[3] These detailed provisions created a scheme which gave effect to a coherent general philosophy much more consistent with a 'responsibility' based framework than with 'rights' based notions'[4] Ironically, following the implementation of the Human Rights Act 1998, this framework now has to operate in a much more 'rights' orientated context, though even this seems to have made little practical difference.

1 Section 2(5) and (6), discussed at paras 3.96 ff.
2 But note the case law discussed at para 3.99.
3 Section 2(7) and (8), discussed at para 3.96.
4 Cretney, cited at para 3.4 above.

3. The meaning and scope of 'parental responsibility'[1]

(a) The need to define parental responsibility

3.7 Parental responsibility needs to be definable so that parents can know what they can or cannot do in relation to their child and, equally importantly, so others can know what the parents' position is. It is also important because the court's powers can sometimes be dependent on its scope. A 'prohibited steps order' can only be made to prevent any 'step which could be taken by a parent in meeting his parental responsibility for a child'.[2] A 'specific issue order' can only be made to determine 'a specific question which has arisen, or which may arise in connection with any aspect of parental responsibility for a child'.[3]

1   For a more extensive discussion of this issue see Lowe and Douglas' *Bromley's Family Law* (10th edn) 3.72 ff.
2   Section 8(1), discussed at paras 5.94 ff.
3   Section 8(1), discussed at paras 5.97 ff. Jurisdiction may also depend upon its scope since within Member States of the EU (other than Denmark) matters relating to parental responsibility are governed by Council Regulation (EC) No 2201/2003 of 27 November 2003 (Brussels II Revised), discussed at para 5.127. In this respect, however, regard must be had to its international meaning under the Regulation, the final arbiter upon which, is the European Court of Justice at Luxembourg.

3.8 The question remains whether parental responsibility should be defined by means of a general statutory provision or simply left to case law and statutory provisions dealing with specific points. While the English Law Commission favoured the latter strategy, the Scottish Law Commission considered that there are advantages in having a general statutory definition, namely:[1]

(a)   that it would make explicit what was already implicit in the law;
(b)   that it would counteract any impression that a parent has rights but no responsibilities; and
(c)   that it would enable the law to make it clear that parental rights are not absolute or unqualified, but are conferred in order to enable parents to meet their responsibilities.

1   Scot Law Com Discussion Paper No 88 Parental Responsibilities and Rights, Guardianship and the Administration of Children's Property (1990) para 2.3.

(b) Lack of a comprehensive statutory definition

3.9 The CA 1989 does not contain a comprehensive definition of what 'parental responsibility' comprises. Section 3(1) states that it means 'all the rights, duties, powers, responsibility and authority which by law a parent of a child has in relation to the child and his property'. Responsibility is also stated to include the rights, powers and duties which a guardian of the child's estate (appointed before the CA 1989 came into force) had, namely the right 'to receive or recover in his own name, for the benefit of the child, property of whatever description and wherever situated which the child is entitled to receive or recover'.[1] On the other hand, by s 3(4)(b), parental responsibility does not include rights of succession to the child's property. This implements the Law Commission's recommendation[2] and emphasises that the incidents of parenthood with which the parental responsibility concept is concerned are those which relate to the care and upbringing of a child until he grows up. While this must include some power to administer the child's property on his behalf it does not include the right of succession. The latter right is a feature of being related to the deceased in a particular way and operates irrespective of who has responsibility for his upbringing.

¹   Section 3(2) and (3).
²   Law Com No 172, para 2.7.

3.10 Section 3(1) is unhelpful particularly as it refers one back to the rights and duties model which 'responsibility' was supposed to replace. However, the Law Commission did not consider it practicable to include a list of what parental responsibility comprises, pointing out¹ that such a list would have to change from time to time to meet differing needs and circumstances and, in the light of *Gillick v West Norfolk and Wisbech Area Health Authority*,² would have to vary with the age and maturity of the child and circumstances of the case.

¹   Law Com No 172, para 2.6.
²   [1986] AC 112, [1985] 3 All ER 402, HL.

3.11 In contrast, the Children (Scotland) Act 1995, provides by s 1(1):

'a parent has in relation to his child the responsibility—
(a)   to safeguard and promote the child's health, development and welfare;
(b)   to provide, in a manner appropriate to the stage of development of the child;
        (i)   direction
        (ii)   guidance
        to the child;
(c)   if the child is not living with the parent to maintain personal relations and direct contact with the child on a regular basis; and
(d)   to act as the child's legal representative, but only in so far as compliance with this section is practicable and in the interests of the child.'

To enable a parent to fulfil those parental responsibilities, s 2(1) provides that a parent: has the right:

'(a)   to have the child living with him or otherwise to regulate the child's residence;
(b)   to control, direct or guide, in a manner appropriate to the stage of development of the child, the child's upbringing;
(c)   if the child is not living with him, to maintain personal relations and contact with the child on a regular basis; and
(d)   to act as the child's legal representative.'

3.12 Although the Scottish legislation might be thought to provide helpful *general* guidance as to the meaning of parental responsibility, the absence of such guidance in English law has not so far proved problematic. Nevertheless, there was been discussion during the passage of the Children and Young Persons Bill 2008¹ of introducing an amendment that in relation to the making of residence orders the court should consider 'whether or not the person with whom it is proposed that the child should live is likely to be able and willing to accept the responsibilities of parenthood in relation to the child' and that for these purposes the 'responsibilities of parenthood' 'means insofar as it is practicable and in the best interests of the child, safeguarding and promotion of the child's health, development and welfare, and the provision of direction and guidance to the child in a manner appropriate to his age and development'. Such an amendment would have reflected the Scottish position albeit that it would have been confined to the issue of residence orders.

[1] See the discussion of Amendment No 102 in Grand Committee debate on 17 January 2008.

(c) Some further observations

3.13 A distinction needs to be drawn between the responsibility of parents with parental responsibility, guardians or special guardians and that of other persons.[1] It is only the former, for example, whose consent is required for the child's adoption; who can appoint a guardian[2] and who (probably) have a right to bury or cremate the deceased child.[3] The responsibility of local authorities is narrower still in that they cannot cause a child in their care 'to be brought up in any religious persuasion other than that in which he would have been brought up if the order had not been made'.[4] Responsibility is narrowest for those in whose favour an emergency protection order has been made.[5]

[1] It may be that some responsibilities are properly regarded as incidents of parenthood rather than of parental responsibility. In this respect, note the Law Commission's comment (Law Com. No. 172 at para 2.7) that they were only concerned with incidents of parenthood relating to the care and upbringing of children and not specifically with incidents that attached to parents qua parents.

[2] Sections 12(3) and 33(6)(b) expressly state that those with responsibility by virtue of a residence or care order made in their favour do not have the right to agree to refuse to agree or the making of an adoption order or to appointing a guardian for a child.

[3] Cf *R v Gwynedd County Council, ex p B* [1991] 2 FLR 365, CA.

[4] Section 33(6)(a).

[5] Namely only to take 'such action in meeting his parental responsibility for the child as is reasonably required to safeguard or promote the welfare of the child, (having regard in particular to the duration of the order)': s 44(5)(b), discussed at para 7.86.

3.14 The exercise of parental responsibility may be qualified by agreement (for example, the father agreeing that the child is to live with the mother) or by order of the court. In the latter instance the extent to which responsibility can be asserted is effectively limited by the paramountcy of the child's welfare which principle the court is bound to apply in any proceedings concerning his upbringing or the administration of his property.[1]

[1] Ie under s 1(1) discussed at paras 2.2 ff.

3.15 The older the child is the less extensive and important parental responsibility may become. As Lord Denning MR so eloquently put it in respect of custody:[1]

' ... it is a dwindling right which the court will hesitate to enforce against the wishes of the child, the older he is. It starts with the right of control and ends with little more than advice.'

[1] *Hewer v Bryant* [1970] 1 QB 357 at 369, [1969] 3 All ER 578 at 582, CA. Even so parents may not lose all their responsibility even where their child is 'Gillick competent' see below, paras 3.30 ff.

3.16 There is no known tort of interference with parental rights nor therefore with parental responsibility.[1] In *F v Wirral Metropolitan Borough Council*[2] the parents argued that what was originally understood by them to be a short-term placement with foster parents and to which arrangement they had agreed but which became a long-term arrangement to which they had not agreed, constituted a wrongful interference with their rights. The parents argued that art 8 of the European Convention on Human Rights (ECHR) and the European Court's decision of *R v United Kingdom*[3] recognised a right of consortium between parent and child as one of the 'fundamental elements of family life'. After an exhaustive review the Court of Appeal unanimously concluded, in Purchas LJ's words:

> 'neither under the old common law, apart from the action per quod servitium amisit nor under modern authority is there a parental right necessary to found a cause of action against a stranger upon which the common law would grant a remedy in damages.'

[1]   Note, however, *C v K (Inherent Powers: Exclusion Order)* [1996] 2 FLR 506 in which Wall J pointed out that persons can be restrained from interfering with the exercise of parental responsibility and that the courts could use their powers to exclude a third party from the family home to protect the exercise of that responsibility.

[2]   [1991] Fam 69, [1991] 2 All ER 648, CA, on which see Bainham 'Interfering with Parental Responsibility. A New Challenge for the Law of Torts' (1990) 3 Jo of Child Law 3. See also *Re S (a Minor) (Parental Rights)* [1993] Fam Law 572.

[3]   [1988] 2 FLR 445, ECtHR.

3.17 The absence of responsibility does not necessarily mean that a person has no obligation towards the child. For example, unmarried fathers have a statutory duty to maintain their children regardless of whether they also have parental responsibility.[1] Conversely, as the Department of Health's *Introduction to the Children Act 1989* observes:[2]

> ' ... the effect of having parental responsibility is to empower a person to take most decisions in the child's life.' It does not make him a parent or relative of the child in law, for example, to give him rights of inheritance, or to place him under a statutory duty to maintain a child.'

> But, the absence of responsibility does not automatically mean that an individual has no 'rights', for if a person has a relationship with the child which amounts to 'family life' within the meaning of art 8 of the ECHR then that right must be respected by public authorities.[3]

[1]   De facto carers also have a statutory duty to protect the child and to ensure that the child is properly educated, see respectively, paras 3.26 and 3.39.

[2]   HMSO, 1989, at para 2.4.

[3]   See e g *Sahin v Germany, Sommerfeld v Germany* [2003] 2 FCR 619 and 647, [2003] 2 FLR 671, ECtHR (Grand Chamber) and *Elsholz v Germany* [2000] 3 FCR 385, [2000] 2 FLR 486, ECtHR in which failing to respect an unmarried father's position with regard to contact was held to be in breach of art 8.

(d) What parental responsibility comprises

3.18 While it may not be possible to state with certainty the precise ambit of responsibility, the following would seem to be the more important aspects:[1]

●   Providing a home for the child;

- Having contact with the child;
- Protecting and maintaining the child;
- Disciplining the child;
- Determining and providing for the child's education;
- Determining the child's religion;
- Consenting to the child's medical treatment;
- Choosing the child's name and agreeing to its subsequent change;
- Consenting to the child's marriage;
- Consenting to the child's adoption;
- Applying for or vetoing the issue of a child's passport;
- Taking the child outside the United Kingdom and consenting to the child's emigration;
- Administering the child's property;
- Representing the child in legal proceedings;
- Appointing a guardian for the child; and
- Disposing of the child's corpse.

[1] For detailed discussion see Lowe and Douglas, above at 377 ff, *Clarke Hall and Morrison on Children* at 1[197] ff and, in the context of mentally disordered children, see Fennell *Mental Health – The New Law*, ch 11.

(I) HOUSING AND LOOKING AFTER THE CHILD

3.19 The key aspect of parental responsibility is that of looking after and bringing up the child. Based upon the common law right of a person to possession of his child, it now seems better to say that those with responsibility have a prima facie[1] responsibility to provide a home for the child and the power to determine where the child should live.[2] However expressed, parental responsibility embodies the right to bring up a child free from the arbitrary interference by the State (which right is protected by art 8 of the ECHR)[3] and from interference by other individuals (which right is protected by the criminal law to the extent that persons without responsibility commit the crime of child abduction if they remove the child without lawful authority).[4] As between individuals with parental responsibility the right is qualified to the extent that removal of a child outside the United Kingdom without the consent of other individuals with parental responsibility can amount to a crime.[5] Associated with providing a home is the necessary accompanying power, inter alia, physically to control children at any rate until the years of discretion. As Lord Lane CJ commented, restraint of a child's movement is usually well within the realms of reasonable parental discipline.[6] Responsibility also includes the power to control the child's movements whilst in someone else's care.[7] On the other hand a parent and, presumably therefore, any other person with parental responsibility, can commit the common law crime of kidnapping[8] or unlawful imprisonment[9] if a child (old enough to make up his own mind) is forcibly taken or detained against his will.

[1] Ie unless a court order (namely a residence, care or emergency protection order) has been made giving someone else that prima facie right.
[2] See *Re M (Minors) (Residence Order: Jurisdiction)* [1993] 1 FLR 495 at 499 per Balcombe LJ.

3   See eg *TP and KM v United Kingdom* (2001) 34 EHRR 42, [2001] 2 FCR 289, [2001] 2 FLR 549 in which a local authority's failure properly to investigate an allegation of child abuse resulting in the mother and child being wrongfully separated for a year was held to violate art 8.

4   Child Abduction Act 1984, s 2.

5   Child Abduction Act 1984, s 1.

6   *R v Rahman* (1985) 81 Cr App Rep 349 at 353, CA. See also *Re K (A Child) (Secure Accommodation: Right to Liberty)* [2001] Fam 377, [2001] 2 WLR 1141, [2001] 2 All ER 719, CA (but cf Butler-Sloss P and Thorpe LJ applying *Nielsen v Denmark* (1989) 11 EHRR 175, ECtHR, discussed at para 9.3); *Hewer v Bryant* [1970] 1 QB 357 at 373, [1969] 3 All ER 578, at 585, CA, per Sachs LJ.

7   *Fleming v Pratt* (1823) 1 LJOS KB 194.

8   *R v D* [1984] AC 778, [1984] 2 All ER 449, HL.

9   *R v Rahman*, above.

(II) DISCIPLINE

3.20 Associated with the power of physical control is the power to discipline the child. At common law a person with parental responsibility could lawfully chastise and inflict reasonable corporal punishment upon the child.[1] However, this right has been limited by s 58(4) of the Children Act 2004,[2] which provides that in relation to charges of wounding and causing grievous bodily harm, assault causing actual bodily harm and cruelty to children under the age of 16 'battery of a child cannot be justified on the ground that it constituted reasonable punishment'.[3] Section 58(3) also provides that: 'Battery of a child causing actual bodily harm to the child cannot be justified in any civil proceedings on the ground that it constituted reasonable punishment'. However, even though the general defence of reasonable chastisement under the Children and Young Persons Act 1933, s 1(7) has also been repealed,[4] the right to smack the child has not in itself been removed. The defence of reasonable chastisement can still be pleaded in proceedings for common assault before magistrates' courts[5] while batteries *not* occasioning actual bodily harm (popularly translated as hitting without leaving a mark) are still permitted.

If chastisement goes beyond what is reasonable or because of battery cannot be pleaded as reasonable, it is unlawful and renders the individual criminally liable for assault, or, depending on the gravity, for more serious offences.[6] If it amounts to degrading punishment,[7] or is inflicted without parental consent it is in breach of the ECHR.[8] The power to discipline a child may be delegated[9] but it seems it can only be exercised by those in loco parentis to the child.[10] However, corporal punishment is forbidden in all schools,[11] children's homes,[12] and foster placements.[13]

1   See the review by Elias J in *R (on the Application of Williamson) v Secretary of State for Education and Employment* [2001] EWHC Admin 900, [2002] 1 FLR 493 at 498, paras [19] ff. *R v Hopley* (1860) 2 F & F 202; *R v Woods* (1921) 85 JP 272. The defence had statutory force by reason of Children and Young Persons Act 1933, s 1(7).

2   The section was brought into force on 15 January 2005 by s 67(7)(f) of the 2004 Act. For a review of this provision see *Review of Section 58 of the Children Act 2004* (Cm 7232, DCSF, 2007), following which the Government has decided to retain the law in its existing form in the absence of evidence that it is not working satisfactorily.

3   Respectively under ss 18, 20, 47 of the Offences Against the Person Act 1861, and s 1 of the CYPA 1933.

4   By s 58(5) of the 2004 Act.
5   See the Explanatory Notes to the 2004 Act, para 236.
6   CYPA 1933, s 1 and *R v Derriviere* (1969) 53 Cr App Rep 637, CA. Note that an unreasonable restraint of a child's movement can render a parent guilty of unlawful imprisonment: *R v Rahman* (1985) 81 Cr App Rep 349, CA.
7   Cf *Costello-Roberts v United Kingdom* [1994] ELR 1 – slippering a 7 year old held not to be 'degrading'.
8   See eg *A v United Kingdom (Human Rights: Punishment of Child)* [1998] 2 FLR 959, ECtHR, and *Campbell and Cosans v United Kingdom* (1982) 4 EHRR 293, ECtHR.
9   Either expressly as in *Sutton London Borough Council v Davis* [1994] 1 FLR 737, (though note the actual decision has now been reversed – see Day Care and Child Minding (National Standards) (England) Regulations 2003, SI 2003/1996, reg 5) or impliedly, as in the case of schools.
10 See eg *R v Woods* (1921) 85 JP 272 – unlawful for an elder brother to administer corporal punishment on his sibling where both were living with their father.
11 Education Act 1996, s 548, as substituted by s 131 of the School Standards and Framework Act 1998, which as Elias J pointed out in *R (on the Application of Williamson)*, above, at para [16], removes the defence of justification which is necessary if the intentional infliction of physical harm is not to be considered unlawful, rather than prohibits corporal punishment as such.
12 Children's Homes Regulations 2001, SI 2001/3967, reg 17(5)(a) (England) and Children's Homes (Wales) Regulations 2002, SI 2002/327, reg 17(5)(a), which simply prohibits the use of any form of corporal punishment.
13 Fostering Services Regulations 2002, SI 2002/57, reg 28(5)(b), Sch 5, point 8 (England) and Fostering Services (Wales) Regulations 2003, SI 2003/237, Sch 5, point 8, which requires foster parents to make a written agreement not to administer corporal punishment.

(III) PROTECTION

3.21 The common law duty to protect, inter alia, a child[1] has largely been replaced by the Children and Young Persons Act 1933, Pt I, which makes certain forms of behaviour criminal offences.[2] The offences are dependent on the likelihood of the child being caused unnecessary suffering or injury.

1   In fact the common law duty is owed by anyone who willingly undertakes to look after another who is incapable of looking after himself. It can therefore continue after the child's majority, see *R v Chattaway* (1922) 17 Cr App Rep 7, CCA (starvation of a helpless daughter aged 25), and can extend to a step-child or foster child, see *R v Bubb* (1850) 4 Cox CC 455; *R v Gibbons and Proctor* (1918) 13 Cr App Rep 134, CCA.
2   See *Clarke Hall and Morrison on Children*, 7[1001] ff for further details.

3.22 A parent has no duty parallel with the statutory duty placed on a local authority having the care of a child, to promote his or her welfare.[1] On the other hand it has been said that there is a 'natural and moral duty of a parent to show affection, care and interest'.[2]

1   CA 1989, Pt III, see Chapter 6.
2   *Re P (infants)* [1962] 3 All ER 789, [1962] 1 WLR 1296, an adoption case.

(IV) CONTACT WITH THE CHILD

3.23 Prima facie parental responsibility encompasses seeing or otherwise having contact with the child. While not an absolute right since in any litigation it will be contingent upon the child's welfare, nevertheless as

Lord Oliver said in *Re KD (a Minor) (Ward: Termination Of Access):*[1] 'As a general proposition a natural parent has a claim to [contact with] his or her child to which the court will pay regard and it would not I think, be inappropriate to describe such a claim as a "right" '. This 'claim' is protected to the extent that there is a statutory presumption of reasonable contact between a child in local authority care or under emergency protection and, inter alia, those with parental responsibility.[2] These latter provisions were enacted following the European Court of Human Rights ruling[3] that the absence of any right to challenge a termination of contact by a local authority amounted to a breach of arts 8 and 13 of the Convention. Article 9(3) of the UN Convention on the Rights of the Child 1989 also provides:

> 'State Parties shall respect the right of the child who is separated from one or both parties to maintain personal relations and direct contact with both parents on a regular basis, except if it is contrary to the child's best interests.'

1 [1988] AC 806 at 827, [1988] 1 All ER 577 at 590.Cf *Sanderson v McManus* 1997 SLT 629, sub nom *S v M (Access Order)* [1997] 1 FLR 980, HL (Scotland) in which Lord Hope held that the onus was on the unmarried father to establish that continued contact was for the child's welfare.
2 Sections 34(1) and 44(13).
3 See *R v United Kingdom* [1988] 2 FLR 445. Note also the subsequent decisions: *Kosmopoulou v Greece [2004] 1 FCR 427, [2004] 1 FLR 800, Hokkanen v Finland* (1994) 19 EHRR 139, [1996] 1 FLR 289, ECtHR – failure by the Sate to enforce a parent's right of access held to be in breach of art 8; *Elsholz v Germany* [2000] 3 FCR 385, [2000] 2 FLR 486, ECtHR – denial of continuing contact with his child by an unmarried father without obtaining expert psychological opinion together with a dismissal without a hearing of the father's appeal, held to be a breach of art 8; *Ciliz v Netherlands* [2000] 2 FLR 469, ECtHR – deportation of divorced father before the conclusion of a contact hearing also held to be in breach of art 8.

3.24 Given that it is a normal assumption that a child will benefit from continued contact with both parents[1] it may be that parental responsibility properly encompasses the prima facie duty to allow the child to have contact with either or both parents. Whether such responsibility extends to a parent having an obligation him or herself to maintain contact with the child can be debated.[2]

1 See e g Lord Oliver in *Re KD,* above at 827 and 590 respectively and *M v M (child: access)* [1973] 2 All ER 81, per Wrangham J at 85 and per Latey J at p 88.
2 Cf the Children (Scotland) Act 1995, s 1(1)(d) (set out at para 3.11) which clearly states that a parent has a responsibility to maintain personal relations and direct contact with the child. But even supposing that there is a theoretical duty to see the child, it would be difficult to enforce this order against an unwilling parent or even on an unwilling child. See further para 5.56.

3.25 If parental responsibility encompasses the power to control the child's movements it seems to follow that it includes the power to restrict those with whom the child may have contact. In *Nottingham County Council v P,*[1] in which it was sought to exclude the father from the matrimonial home and to restrict his contact with the children, Ward J saw 'the force of the submission' that steps taken by a parent in meeting his parental responsibility are necessarily wide steps and could extend to controlling contact with the other parent. In *Re M (Care: Leave to Interview Child)*[2] Hale J was more forthright, commenting: 'Until the child is old enough to decide for himself, a parent undoubtedly has some control over whom he may see and who may see him.'

1 [1994] Fam 18, [1993] 3 All ER 815.
2 [1995] 1 FLR 825, following *Re F (Specific Issue: Child Interview)* [1995] 1 FLR 819, CA.

(V) MEDICAL TREATMENT[1]

3.26 Any person over the age of 16 who has responsibility (in the sense of having de facto control) for a child under the age of 16 has a duty to obtain essential medical assistance for that child.[2] However, in most cases,[3] before any treatment can be given, medical practitioners need a valid consent, for without it they may be open to a prosecution for battery upon the child or for one of the graver forms of assault, or be subject to a claim in tort for trespass for which the practitioner may be liable for loss regardless of fault.[4] Prima facie anyone with parental responsibility, including a local authority,[5] can give a valid consent to the child's surgical, medical or dental treatment. But this is not an unqualified right, there being what has neatly been referred to in the context of mental health as the "parental zone of responsibility".[6] Hence, for example, the parental power of consent does not necessarily extend to all forms of treatment. Furthermore, this power is without prejudice to the ability of a 16-to-17 year old or a 'Gillick competent' child under the age of 16 to give a valid consent, nor does it preclude the court from subsequently overriding an otherwise valid consent or from sanctioning treatment otherwise opposed. In any event no practitioner can be forced to give treatment contrary to their clinical judgement.[7] Hence, as Lord Donaldson MR observed in *Re W (A Minor) (Medical Treatment: Court's Jurisdiction)*,[8] no question of consenting or refusing consent arises unless and until a medical or dental practitioner advises such treatment and is willing to undertake it and:

'Regardless of whether the minor or anyone else with authority to do so consents to the treatment, that practitioner will be liable to the minor in negligence if he fails to advise with reasonable skill and care and to have due regard to the best interests of his patient'.

1 For a valuable discussion of this issue in the context of mental health see Fennell *Mental Health – The New Law*, ch 11.
2 Children and Young Persons Act 1933, s 1. This is also facilitated by the CA 1989, s 3(5) which empowers carers without parental responsibility to do what is reasonable in all the circumstances to safeguard and promote the child's welfare. See further para 3.103.
3 Medical practitioners have long been advised that on the basis of the common law defence of necessity emergency treatment may be given if the well-being of the child could suffer by delay caused by obtaining consents. Ministry of Health Circular F/19/1/1967 and Home Office Circular 63/1968. See also *Re F (Mental Patient: Sterilisation)* [1990] 2 AC 1 at 52, sub nom *F v West Berkshire Health Authority (mental health act comr intervening)* [1989] 2 All ER 545 at 548, per Lord Bridge, and, in particular *Re A (Children) (Conjoined Twins: Surgical Separation)* [2001] Fam 147, [2000] 4 All ER 961, CA, per Brooke LJ.
4 See eg *Re R (A Minor) (Wardship: Medical Treatment)* [1992] Fam 11 at 22, [1991] 4 All ER 177 at 184, CA per Lord Donaldson MR.
5 *R v Kirklees Metropolitan Borough Council, ex p C* [1992] 2 FLR 117, CA.
6 See *Mental Health Act 1983 Draft Revised Code of Practice* (Dept of Health, 2007), which advises inter alia "Clinicians will need to determine whether it is appropriate to rely on parental consent. In order for consent to be relied upon it should be a decision which comes within the parental zone of responsibility".

⁷   *Re J (A Minor) (Child In Care: Medical Treatment)* [1993] Fam 15, [1992] 4 All ER 614, CA. See also *Portsmouth NHS Trust v Wyatt* [2005] EWHC 2293 (Fam), [2006] 1 FLR 652.

⁸   [1993] Fam 64 at 83, [1992] 4 All ER 627 at 639, CA.

3.27

The position of those with parental responsibility

The general rule that anyone with parental responsibility can give a valid consent to the child's medical treatment, is subject to a number of qualifications. First, not all those with parental responsibility are in the same position. In particular those having responsibility by virtue of an emergency protection order only have authority to take such action 'as is reasonably required to safeguard or promote the welfare of the child'.[1] Hence, while such persons can give a valid consent to day-to-day treatment they cannot agree to major elective surgery. In these cases, however, a court direction can be sought.[2]

1   Section 44(5)(b).
2   Section 44(6)(b).

3.28 Secondly, although the power of consent vested in those with parental responsibility extends to most forms of surgical, medical or dental treatment including treatment of drugs or for drug abuse and, by analogy with s 8(2) of the Family Law Reform Act 1969, diagnostic procedures such as HIV testing and, by reason of s 21(3) of that Act, (as amended), the taking of bodily samples from the child to be used in tests to determine paternity, and ritual male circumcision,[1] even parents with parental responsibility are not empowered to consent to all forms of treatment.

1   *Re J (child's religious upbringing and circumcision)* [2000] 1 FCR 307, sub nom *Re J (Specific Issue Orders: Child's Religious Upbringing)* [2000] 1 FLR 571, CA.

3.29 According to Lord Templeman in *Re B (a Minor) (Wardship: Sterilisation)*,[1] sterilisation of a girl under 18 should only be carried out with the leave of a High Court judge. In other words, even parents, with parental responsibility cannot give a valid consent. Notwithstanding that Lord Templeman was the only Law Lord to suggest this, Lord Donaldson MR subsequently commented[2] that parties might be well advised to apply to the court for guidance. Whether a similar requirement extends to other forms of treatment has yet to be decided.[3] However, High Court leave is not required to perform an operation for therapeutic reasons even though a side effect (but not the main purpose) will be to sterilise the child.[4] Furthermore it has been held that notwithstanding that a decision as to sterilisation is a matter for the judge, parents (or others with parental responsibility) nevertheless retain the responsibility for bringing the issue before the High Court.[5]

1   [1988] AC 199 at 205, [1987] 2 All ER 206 at 214.
2   In *Re W (A Minor)(Medical Treatment)* [1993] Fam 64, [1992] 4 All ER 627, CA. This is also the position in Australia: see *Department of Health and Community Services (NT) Secretary v JWB and SMB* (1982) 66 ALJR 300 (Australian High Court).
3   It might conceivably cover all irreversible treatment for non-therapeutic reasons.

4   *Re E (a minor) (medical treatment)* [1991] FCR 771 [1991] 2 FLR 585, per Sir Stephen
     Brown P. Note that in *Re B (A Minor) (Wardship: Sterilisation)* [1988] AC 199, [1987]
     2 All ER 206, the Law Lords rejected the legal relevance of the notion of a non-therapeutic
     sterilisation.
5   *Re HG (specific issue order: sterilisation)*[1993] 1 FCR 553, [1993] 1 FLR 587, discussed
     further at para 5.197. See also *Practice Note* [1993] 3 All ER 222.

3.30 A third qualification on the power of consent of those with parental
responsibility is the age of the child. Although according to, *Re W (A Minor)
(Medical Treatment: Court's Jurisdiction),*[1] those with parental responsibility
retain their power to give a valid consent throughout the child's minority, it
seems clear[2] that:

(1)   a child aged 16 or 17 or who is 'Gillick competent' if under the age of
       16 can give a valid consent which cannot be countermanded by an
       adult;[3]

(2)   although in theory a valid consent may be given by an adult with
       parental responsibility notwithstanding the opposition of the 'Gillick
       competent' or 16 or 17-year-old child, in practice no treatment should
       be given without prior court sanction;[4] and

(3)   any decision by a parent can subsequently be overridden by the High
       Court.[5]

1   [1993] Fam 64, [1992] 4 All ER 627, CA.
2   This view was most clearly expressed by Lord Donaldson MR but seemed also to be
     accepted by Balcombe LJ, both of whom expressly rejected the contention that Lord Scar-
     man should have been taken to be saying in *Gillick v West Norfolk and Wisbech Area
     Health Authority* [1986] AC 112, [1985] 3 All ER 402, HL that parents of a 'Gillick
     competent' child had no right at all to consent to medical treatment of the child.
3   See Lord Donaldson in *Re W (A Minor) (Medical Treatment: Court's Jurisdiction* [1993]
     Fam 64 at 83–84, [1992] 4 All ER 627 at 639. The child's consent can, however, be
     overridden by the court: see para 3.35. But to the contrary, note *R (on the application of
     Axon) v Secretary of State for Health* [2006] EWHC 37 (Admin), [2006] 1 FCR 175,
     [2006] 2 FLR 206, per Silber J.
4   This, at any rate, was Nolan LJ's view in *Re W (A Minor) (Medical Treatment: Court's
     Jurisdiction* 1993] Fam 64 at 94, [1992] 4 All ER 627 48–649. Lord Donaldson MR, at 84
     and 640 respectively, thought that a child's refusal was a very important consideration for
     parents deciding whether themselves to give consent.
5   See para 3.35.

3.31

The position of children

The Family Law Reform Act 1969, 8(1) provides that the consent of a minor
over the age of 16:

> 'to any surgical, medical or dental treatment which, in the absence of consent,
> would constitute a trespass to his person, shall be as effective as it would be if
> he were of full age; and where a minor has by virtue of this section given an
> effective consent to any treatment it shall not be necessary to obtain any
> consent for it from his parent or guardian.'

By s 8(2) the power to give a valid independent consent extends to 'any
procedure undertaken for the purposes of diagnosis' (which would include
HIV tests) and 'to any procedure (including, in particular, the administration

of an anaesthetic) which is ancillary to any treatment ... ' However, this statutory right of consent does not extend to the donation of blood or organs.[1] It would also seem that the power of consent does not extend to the child's own sterilisation.[2]

[1] *Re W (a Minor) (Medical Treatment: Court's Jurisdiction) [1993]* Fam 64, [1992] 4 All ER 627, per Lord Donaldson MR. Nevertheless there would seem to be a non-statutory power to consent to such treatment provided the child is 'Gillick competent'; see para 3.32.

[2] See para 3.29.

3.32 It might have been inferred from s 8(1) that a child below the age of 16 cannot give a valid consent. However, relying in part on s 8(3) which provides that 'Nothing in this section shall be construed as making ineffective any consent which would have been effective if this section had not been enacted', it was established by *Gillick v West Norfolk and Wisbech Area Health Authority*[1] that provided they are of sufficient age and understanding, children under the age of 16 can give valid consent. In *Gillick* it was specifically held that a doctor may in certain circumstances lawfully prescribe contraception for a girl under 16 years of age without the consent of her parents. In so holding the majority of the House of Lords considered that a girl could have legal capacity to give a valid consent to contraceptive advice and treatment including medical examination. Whether she gave a valid consent in any particular case would depend on circumstances, including her intellectual capacity to understand the advice. There is no absolute parental right requiring the parents' consent to be sought. Speaking of medical treatment generally, Lord Scarman said:

> 'It will be a question of fact whether a child seeking advice has sufficient understanding of what is involved to give a consent valid in law. Until the child achieves the capacity to consent, the parental right to make the decision continues save only in exceptional circumstances. Emergency, parental neglect, abandonment of the child, or inability to find the parent are examples of exceptional situations justifying the doctor proceeding to treat the child without parental knowledge and consent, but there will arise, no doubt, other exceptional situations in which it will be reasonable for the doctor to proceed without the parent's consent.'

Applying this to contraceptive advice and treatment he said:

> ' ... there is much that has to be understood by a girl under the age of 16 if she is to have legal capacity to consent to such treatment. It is not enough that she should understand the nature of the advice which is being given: she must also have a sufficient maturity to understand what is involved'.

Lord Fraser set out five preconditions before a doctor would be considered justified in prescribing contraceptive treatment:

(a) that the girl (although under 16 years of age) will understand his advice;

(b) that he cannot persuade her to inform her parents or to allow him to inform the parents that she is seeking contraceptive advice;

(c) that she is very likely to begin or to continue having sexual intercourse with or without contraceptive treatment;

(d) that unless she receives contraceptive advice or treatment her physical or mental health or both are likely to suffer; or

(e)   that her best interests require him to give her contraceptive advice, treatment or both without the parental consent.

¹   [1986] AC 112, [1985] 3 All ER 402, HL.

3.33 The test for determining what has become known as 'Gillick competence' seems particularly strict in the case of contraception and the courts seem similarly cautious when considering a child's competence to refuse life saving treatment.¹ In *Re R (a Minor) (Wardship: Medical Treatment)*² it was held that competence is not to be assessed at a particular moment in time but in conjunction with the child's whole medical history and background. 'Gillick competence' cannot therefore fluctuate on a day-to-day basis so that a child is one day regarded as competent but not on another. If the child is held competent then, unlike the statutory right conferred by s 8 of the Family Law Reform Act 1969, the power of consent extends to donating blood and organs.³

¹   See, for example, *Re L (medical treatment: Gillick competency)* [1999] 2 FCR 524, [1998] 2 FLR 810 – 14-year-old girl who had had a 'sheltered life' and who was in a life threatening condition but who could not be told of the potentially 'horrible nature' of her death if she did not have a blood transfusion, held not be 'competent'; and *Re S (a Minor) (Consent to Medical Treatment)* [1994] 2 FLR 1065 – 15½ year old girl, who appeared not to understand the inevitability of her death and of the pain and distress if her treatment was discontinued, held not to be 'competent'.
²   [1992] Fam 11 at 25–26 (per Lord Donaldson MR) and 31 (per Farquaharson LJ), [1991] 4 All ER 177 at 187 and 191 respectively.
³   *Re W (A Minor) (Medical Treatment: Court's Jurisdiction)* [1993] Fam 64 at 84, [1992] 4 All ER 627 at 639, per Lord Donaldson MR.

3.34 Although s 8 of the 1969 Act and *Gillick* establish that 16 or 17 year olds and those who are 'Gillick competent' under the age of 16 can give valid consents to medical treatment, they are not to be taken to imply that such children have a right of veto. On the contrary it is established that the court can override such children's refusal and, at any rate according to Lord Donaldson MR in *Re W*, even parents can in theory give a valid consent.¹

¹   See para 3.30 above.

3.35

The courts' powers

A court can override a parental decision to consent or refuse consent to the child's medical treatment. In *Re D (A Minor) (Wardship: Sterilisation)*,¹ Heilbron J declined to permit a sterilisation operation on a child after the mother had consented. Conversely, in *Re A (Children; Conjoined Twins: Surgical Separation)*² the court sanctioned, contrary to the parents' wishes, the separation of conjoined twins notwithstanding that the inevitable result would be to kill the weaker twin but preserve the life of the stronger twin. In *Re C (a minor) (HIV testing)*³ the court ordered, contrary to the parents' wishes, an HIV test to be carried out on a baby, and in *Re B (a child: immunisation)*⁴ the court ordered, contrary to the wishes of the one-parent carer, that the children concerned should have the MMR vaccination, while in *NHS Trust v A*⁵ the court overrode the parents' refusal to consent to their 7-month-old baby having a bone marrow transplant. Other examples include *Re B (A Minor) (Wardship: Medical Treatment)*[6] in which an operation to save the life of a Down's Syndrome baby was sanctioned notwithstanding the parents' opposition; *Re B (Wardship: Abortion)*,[7] in which the court, overruling the mother's objections, gave permission for a 12 year old to have an abortion and *Re R (a minor) (blood transfusion)*,[8] in which the court overrode the opposition to a blood transfusion for their baby by parents who were Jehovah's Witnesses. It is equally established that the court can override both a 16 year old and a 'Gillick competent' child's refusal to consent to treatment. In *Re W (A Minor) (Medical Treatment: Court's Jurisdiction)*[9] it was held that a 16-year-old anorexic child's refusal of life saving treatment should be overruled, though it was also emphasised that such a refusal should not be overridden lightly since it 'is a very important consideration in making clinical judgments and for parents and the court in deciding whether themselves to give consent'.[10]

1   [1976] Fam 185, [1976] 1 All ER 326.
2   [2001] Fam 147; [2000] 4 All ER 961, CA.
3   [1999] 3 FCR 289, [1999] 2 FLR 1004, per Wilson J. But note the judge declined to order the mother to stop breast feeding her child. After detailed consideration the Court of Appeal refused permission to appeal against Wilson J's judgment, see [1999] 2 FLR at 1017.
4   [2003] EWCA Civ 1148, [2003] 3 FCR 156, sub nom *Re C (Welfare of Child: Immunisation)* [2003] 2 FLR 1095.
5   [2007] EWHC 1696 (Fam), [2008] 1 FLR 70.
6   (1981) 3 FLR 117.
7   [1991] 2 FLR 426.
8   [1993] 2 FCR 544, [1993] 2 FLR 757, discussed further at para 12.36.
9   [1993] Fam 64, [1992] 4 All ER 627, CA. For other examples, see *Clarke Hall and Morrison on Children* at 1[233].
10 Per Lord Donaldson MR at [1993] Fam 84, [1992] 4 All ER 640.

3.36 The High Court's powers of consent are wider than those of a parent. They can extend to sanctioning a child's sterilisation,[1] and, in relation to a terminally ill child, to authorising treatment to relieve the child's suffering but not to achieve a short prolongation of life.[2] On the other hand it is established that the court has no power to order a medical practitioner to treat a child contrary to his clinical judgement.[3]

1   See *Re B (A Minor) (Wardship: Sterilisation)* [1988] AC 199 at 205, [1987] 2 All ER 206 at 214, per Lord Templeman.
2   *Re C (A Minor) (Wardship: Medical Treatment)* [1990] Fam 26, [1989] 2 All ER 782, CA. For other examples, see *Clarke Hall and Morrison on Children* at 1[234].
3   *Re J (A Minor) (Child in Care: Medical Treatment)* [1993] Fam 15, [1992] 4 All ER 614, CA.

3.37 In deciding what order to make the primary decision for the court is what is in the best interests of the child and not the reasonableness of the parents' refusal of consent.[1] But as Potter P observed[2] the court must reach its own conclusion on what is in the best interests of the child on the basis of a broad spectrum of considerations and bearing in mind that English law places a very heavy burden on those advocating a course which would inevitably lead to the cessation of human life. It has been held[3] in a case of a 16-year-old anorexic child, that the court's inherent power includes the authorisation of her detention in the clinic for the purposes of treatment as well as the power to authorise the use of reasonable force, if necessary, for the purpose.

1 Per Butler-Sloss LJ in *Re T (a minor) (wardship: medical treatment)* [1997] 1 All ER 906, [1997] 1 WLR 242, 'on the most unusual facts of the case' it was held that the child's best interests required that his future treatment should be left in the hands of his devoted parents. Accordingly, the Court of Appeal declined to override a parental refusal (contrary to medical advice) to consent to their 18-month-old child having a liver transplant.

2 *Re K (Medical Treatment: Declaration)* [2006] EWHC 1007 (Fam), [2006] 2 FLR 883 at [42] and [48].

3 Per Wall J in *Re C (Detention: Medical Treatment)* [1997] 2 FLR 180. See also *Re B (a minor)(treatment and secure accommodation)* [1997] 1 FCR 618 sub nom *A Metropolitan Borough Council v DB* [1997] 1 FLR 767.

(VI) EDUCATION

3.38 As Ward LJ has observed[1] 'arranging for education commensurate with the child's intellectual needs and abilities is [an] ... incident of the parental responsibility which arises from the duty of the parent to secure the child's education'. This responsibility derives from the common law right of a parent to determine what education the child should receive.[2] Parents' rights to determine their children's education are also protected by the European Convention on Human Rights to the extent of respecting their religious and philosophical convictions.[3]

1 *Re Z (A Minor) (Identification: Restrictions on Publication)* [1997] Fam 1 at 26, sub nom *Re Z (a minor) (freedom of publication)* [1995] 4 All ER 961 at 980, CA.

2 For a striking example, see *Tremain's Case* (1719) 1 Stra 167. See also *Andrews v Salt* (1873) 8 Ch App 622 – father's wishes to be respected after his death.

3 Protocol No 1, art 2.

3.39 At common law, because the duty was unenforceable,[1] parents could formerly choose not to have their children educated. However, under the Education Act 1996 parents of every child between the ages of five and 16 have to ensure that the child receives 'efficient full-time education suitable (a) to his age, ability, aptitude and (b) to any special education needs he may have, either by regular attendance at school other otherwise'.[2] 'Parent' for these purposes includes any person who is not a parent but who has parental responsibility for the child or who has care of the child.[3] Failure to perform this duty can result in a criminal prosecution[4] and the child may be subject to an education supervision order.[5]

1 *Hodges v Hodges* (1796) Peake Add Cas 79.

2 Education Act 1996, ss 7 and 8.

3 Education Act 1996, s 576(1). This definition can cover a local authority foster parent: *Fairpo v Humberside County Council* [1997] 1 FLR 339.

4 Education Act 1996, s 443. Formerly, parents could be fined but not imprisoned for a breach of a school attendance order for failure to secure regular attendance at school. However, under the Education Act 1996, s 444(8A), parents can now be imprisoned for up to three months where they know that their child is failing to attend regularly at the school and fail without reasonable justification to cause him to do so. See further *Clarke Hall and Morrison on Children*, 6[621]. They can also be made the subject of a parenting order under the Crime and Disorder Act 1998, ss 8 and 9, see *Clarke Hall and Morrison on Children* at 6[611]–[620].

5 CA 1989, s 36, see paras 8.191 ff.

3.40 Those with parental responsibility or who have care of children can discharge their duty by ensuring that they attend independent rather than state schools or by educating them at home, provided in this latter instance the local education authority is satisfied that the child is receiving efficient and full-time education suitable to his age etc. Disputes between individuals (usually divorcing parents) about appropriate schooling may be resolved by means of a specific issue or prohibited steps order under s 8 of the CA 1989.[1] Where State education is relied upon, except in the case of a child permanently excluded from two or more schools, education authorities are required to comply with 'parental' wishes as to choice of school save, importantly where compliance would 'prejudice the provision of efficient education or the efficient use of resources; if the preferred school is a foundation or voluntary aided school and compliance would be incompatible with any arrangements between the governing body and local education authority or if arrangements for admission to the preferred school are based on pupils with high ability or with aptitude and compliance would be incompatible with those criteria.[2] To enable a reasoned choice to be made 'parents' must be given information about the primary and secondary education available[3] and inter alia the curriculum and subject choice.[4]

[1] See eg *M v M (Specific Issue: Choice of School)* [2005] EWHC 2769 (Fam), [2007] 1 FLR 251; *Re P (Parental Dispute: Judicial Determination)* [2002] EWCA 1627, [2003] 1 FLR 286 and *Re W (children)(education: choice of school)* [2002] EWCA Civ 1411, [2002] 3 FCR 473. See further paras 5.94 ff.
[2] Education Act 1996, s 9 and the School Standards Framework Act 1998, s 86 ff. See further *Clarke Hall and Morrison on Children* at 6[522]. For the position of children with special educational needs, see *Clarke Hall and Morrison on Children*, 6[901] ff.
[3] School Standards and Framework Act 1998, s 92.
[4] Education Act 1996, s 408.

(VII) RELIGIOUS UPBRINGING

3.41 A person with parental responsibility has a right to determine the child's religious education, though there is no duty to give a child a religious upbringing. As Wall J said in *Re J (child's religious upbringing and circumcision)*:[1] 'Parental responsibility ... clearly includes the right to bring up children in a particular religious faith, or in none.' Based on the common law,[2] this right to determine the child's religious education is protected to the extent that a local authority cannot cause a child in their care 'to be brought up in any religious persuasion other than that in which he would have been brought up if the order had not been made.'[3]

[1] [1999] 2 FCR 345 at 353, sub nom *Re J (Specific Issue Orders: Muslim Upbringing and Circumcision)* [1999] 2 FLR 678 at 685 – decision upheld by Court of Appeal, see [2000] 1 FCR 307, [2000] 1 FLR 571, CA.
[2] *Andrews v Salt* (1873) 8 Ch App 622. The rule, see eg *Hawksworth v Hawksworth* (1871) 6 Ch App 539, that unless there were exceptional circumstances, children had to be brought up in the religion of their father, was abolished by the Guardianship of Infants Act 1925, s 1.
[3] CA 1989, s 33(6)(a). Note that adoption agencies should 'give due consideration' to the child's religious persuasion when placing for adoption: Adoption and Children Act 2002, s 1(5).

3.42 Parents with parental responsibility and those caring for the child can require a child's exclusion from religious studies lessons and school assembly.[1] Although the courts will seek to pay 'serious heed to the religious wishes of a parent'[2] (indeed preventing a parent bringing up his child *simply* on the basis of his religious belief is contrary to the European Convention on Human Rights),[3] in the event of a dispute the court must treat the child's welfare as the paramount consideration.[4]

1   School Standards and Framework Act 1998, s 71, discussed in *Clarke Hall and Morrison on Children* at 6[607].
2   *J v C* [1969] 1 All ER 788 at 801, per Ungoed-Thomas J.
3   Article 9 on which see *Palau-Martinez v France* [2004] 2 FLR 810, ECtHR and *Hoffmann v Austria* (1993) 17 EHRR 293, [1994] 1 FCR 913, ECtHR. Note the comment at [1994] Fam Law 673. But a parent's right to manifest his religion has to be balanced against the welfare of the child and the rights of the other parent – see Thorpe LJ in *Re J (child's religious upbringing and circumcision)* [2000] 1 FCR 307 at 311, [2000] 1 FLR 571 at 575, CA. See also *Ismailova v Russia* (Application 3761402), [2008] 1 FLR 533, ECtHR.
4   See eg *Re P (a Minor) (Residence Order: Child's Welfare)* [2000] Fam 15, [1999] 2 FCR 289, sub nom *Re P (a child) (residence order: restriction order)* [1999] 2 FCR 289, sub nom *Re P (a child) (residence order: restriction order)* [1999] 3 All ER 734, CA, discussed at para 2.54, and *Re J (child's religious upbringing and circumcision)* [1999] 2 FCR 345, sub nom *Re J (Specific Issue Orders: Muslim Upbringing and Circumcision)* [1999] 2 FLR 678 – decision upheld by Court of Appeal, see [2000] 1 FCR 307, [2000] 1 FLR 571, discussed at para 2.49.

WHO HAS PARENTAL RESPONSIBILITY?

1. The position at the child's birth

(a) Married parents

3.43 By the CA 1989, s 2(1) provides that where the father and mother of the child who were married to each other at the time of the child's birth each have parental responsibility. The reference to a child whose parents were married to each other at the time of his birth must, as s 2(3) emphasises, be interpreted in accordance with s 1 of the Family Law Reform Act 1987. Read with s 1(2)–(4) of the 1987 Act, s 2(1) refers to a child whose parents were married to each other at any time during the period beginning with insemination or (where there was no insemination) conception and ending with birth, but also includes a child who:

(a)   is treated as legitimate by virtue of the Legitimacy Act 1976, s 1;
(b)   is a legitimate person within the meaning of s 10 of the 1976 Act;
(c)   is an adopted child within the meaning of the Adoption and Children Act 2002, Ch 4, Pt 1; or
(d)   is otherwise treated in law as legitimate.

Stated simply s 2(1) means that both the father and the mother automatically each have parental responsibility in respect of their 'legitimate children'.[1]

1   Which expression should be taken to include adopted children, children in respect of whom a parental order has been obtained under s 30 of the Human Fertilisation and Embryology Act 1990 (HFEA 1990), discussed in *Clarke Hall and Morrison on Children* at 1[378] ff and children conceived by assisted reproduction to which HFEA 1990, s 28 applies applies.

(b) Unmarried parents

3.44 Where the father and mother of the child were not married to each other at the time of the child's birth,[1] s 2(2) provides that the mother but not the father has parental responsibility for the child. In *B v United Kingdom*[2] an unmarried father complained that by only according to married fathers automatic responsibility, English law discriminated against unmarried fathers in the protection given to their relationships with their children as compared with the protection given to married fathers. This was, therefore, in breach of art 14 taken in conjunction with art 8 of the ECHR. The European Court of Human Rights ruled the complaint inadmissible since, given the range of possible relationships between unmarried fathers and their children, there exists 'an objective and reasonable justification for the difference in treatment between married and unmarried fathers with regard to the automatic acquisition of parental rights.'

[1] For the meaning of which see para 3.43 above.
[2] [2000] 1 FCR 289, [2000] 1 FLR 1, ECtHR.

(c) Gender change

3.45 Section 12 of the Gender Recognition Act 2004 states:

'The fact that a person's gender has become the acquired gender under this Act does not affect the status of the person as the father or mother of the child'.

Consequently a subsequent formal change of gender will not affect the attribution of parental responsibility with regard to parents.

(d) Non-parents

3.46 Since only parents have automatic parental responsibility for a child, no other person has such responsibility at the time of the child's birth.

ACQUISITION OF PARENTAL RESPONSIBILITY AFTER THE CHILD'S BIRTH

3.47 Although parental responsibility is automatically assigned either to each of the married parents or to the unmarried mother at the time of the child's birth, the Act makes clear provision for others to acquire responsibility after the child's birth.

1. Acquisition of parental responsibility by unmarried fathers

3.48 As s 2(2)(b) states, an unmarried father does not have parental responsibility for his child unless he acquires it in accordance with the provisions of the CA 1989. He can acquire responsibility in the following ways:

(1)   by subsequently marrying the child's mother;
(2)   by being registered as the child's father on the birth certificate;
(3)   upon taking office as a formally appointed guardian of the child;
(4)   by making a parental responsibility agreement with the mother;
(5)   by obtaining a parental responsibility order;
(6)   by obtaining a residence order in which case a separate parental responsibility order must be made.

(a) Subsequent marriage

3.49 By subsequently marrying the mother, the father brings himself within s 2(1) of the CA 1989[1] and, provided the child is under the age of 18 at the time, will therefore automatically have parental responsibility. Although the Act does not expressly say so, because conferment of responsibility is an *automatic* consequence, the parents' subsequent marriage must be regarded as overriding any prior parental responsibility order or agreement, which means that responsibility cannot then be ended by a court order[2] other than adoption or a parental order under the Human Fertilisation and Embryology Act 1990.

---

[1]   Which, pursuant to s 2(3), must be interpreted in line with the Family Law Reform Act 1987, s 1(3)(b) of which, includes the parents' subsequent marriage.
[2]   Cf parental responsibility agreements and orders which can be ended by a court order, see paras 3.79–3.80.

(b) Registration as the father

3.50 Based on a suggestion canvassed in a Lord Chancellor's Consultation Paper,[1] s 4 of the CA 1989 was amended[2] to provide for the unmarried father's acquisition of parental responsibility following his registration as the child's father. For these purposes the registration must be under either ss 10(1)(a)–(c) or 10A(1)(a)–(c) of the Births and Deaths Registration Act 1953 (or their Scottish or Northern Irish equivalents).[3] Although re-registrations can confer parental responsibility they will only do so if they fall within the terms of s 10A of the 1953 Act, namely, where no father has been previously named and the re-registration is with the mother's consent. Re-registrations following a declaration of parentage[4] (which is the only means that an unmarried man of registering his fatherhood without the mother's consent) do not confer parental responsibility since they fall within s 14A of the 1953 Act. Although at first sight this might seem anomalous, men who have not been registered as fathers are thereby prevented from circumventing the requirement, when seeking parental responsibility orders (effectively against the mother's wishes) of having to show that the making of such an order is in the child's best interests.[5] Because the legislation is *not* retrospective[6] only relevant registrations made on or after 1 December 2003 confer parental responsibility.[7]

---

[1]   (1) Court Proceedings for the Determination of Paternity; (2) The Law on Parental Responsibility for Unmarried Fathers (1998) paras 39 ff.
[2]   Namely s 4(1)(a) as amended by the Adoption and Children Act 2002, s 111, with effect from 1 December 2003 (SI 2003/3079). A similar change has been made in Scotland – see the Family Law (Scotland) Act 2006, s 23.

3   Namely the Registration of Births, Deaths and Marriages (Scotland) Act 1965, ss 18(1)(a)–(c), 2(6) and 20(1)(a) and the Births and Deaths Registration (Northern Ireland) Order 1976, art 14(3)(a)–(c). As the law now stands, registrations in the Channel Islands and the Isle of Man or in any foreign jurisdiction do *not* confer parental responsibility, though under s 4(1B) of the CA 1989 the Lord Chancellor has the power to add to the list of enactments under which registration confers parental responsibility.
4   Under the Family Law Act 1986, ss 55A(7), 56(4).
5   See the discussion below at paras 3.63 ff.
6   See s 111(7) of the Adoption and Children Act 2002.
7   Query whether the reform makes it harder to refuse to make an order in favour of a man registered as the father before 1 December 2003? See further para 3.64, n 2.

3.51 Although the acquisition of parental responsibility is an automatic consequence of a relevant registration it does not put unmarried fathers in exactly the same position as married fathers since, unlike the latter, the court can, upon application by any person with parental responsibility or, with court leave, the child, order that the father shall cease to have that responsibility.[1] Another difference is that parental responsibility dates from the registration, not the child's birth. Consequently, if the mother dies before the father's registration, since he cannot register himself as the father, the unmarried father can only acquire parental responsibility by court order or upon being appointed a guardian.

1   CA 1989, s 4(2A), (3).

3.52 Presumably, in cases of registrations made subsequent to a parental responsibility agreement or even order, parental responsibility should be considered to result from the registration rather than the agreement or order though nothing seems to turn on this.[1] On the other hand, the fact that births outside marriage are commonly registered by both parents, means that since the 2002 Act's reforms the vast majority of unmarried fathers of children now being born have parental responsibility without having to take further action. This in turn, one would have thought, would have led to a significant reduction in the number of parental responsibility orders and the virtual elimination of the making of agreements. So far as the former are concerned, though they declined 6% on 2005, the number of applications, 11,059, made in 2006, was still surprisingly high.[2]

1   Cf where the parents subsequently marry, see para 3.49 above.
2   Judicial and Court Statistics 2006 (Cm 7273, November 2007), Table 5.3.

(c) *Guardianship*

3.53 To become a guardian, the father must formally have been appointed as such by the child's mother, or by the court in accordance with s 5 of the CA 1989.[1] Such an appointment can only take effect after the mother's death.

1   Discussed at paras 3.104 ff.

(d) Parental responsibility agreements

3.54 Pursuant to s 4(1)(b) the father and mother may, by a parental responsibility agreement, provide for the father to have parental responsibility for the child. Such agreements, however, only have effect if they are made in prescribed form and recorded in the prescribed manner,[1] as provided for by the Parental Responsibility Agreement Regulations 1991.[2] Once made, an agreement remains in effect notwithstanding that the couple live together or subsequently separate, though it can be ended by a court order.[3]

[1] Section 4(2).
[2] SI 1991/1478, as amended, discussed at para 3.56.
[3] See paras 3.79 and 3.80.

3.55 There are no prescribed age limits on those making agreements and there is no reason to suppose that valid agreements cannot be made by parents under the age of 18.[1] On the other hand, agreements cannot be made with respect to an unborn child.[2] A care order does not empower a local authority to prevent the mother from making a parental responsibility agreement with the father.[3] Although it is clear from the prescribed formalities (discussed at para 3.56 below) that agreements can only be completed in England and Wales there is uncertainty as to the required connection of the parties to the jurisdiction. According to *Re S (A Minor)(Parental Responsibility)*[4] jurisdiction to make parental responsibility *orders* is not dependent upon the child's habitual residence or even presence in England and Wales. So by analogy no such connection is required to make a valid agreement. However, *Re S* pre-dates the revised Brussels II Regulation[5] which clearly applies both to the making of parental responsibility agreements and orders,[6] and which requires jurisdiction to be based on the child's habitual residence or, failing that, presence.[7] This Regulation applies in matters of jurisdiction, recognition and enforcement within Member States of the European Union (except Denmark) and therefore does not directly affect the decision in *Re S* which involved a child reputedly in India, though whether that decision will now be revisited remains to be seen. In cases falling outside the Regulation[8] and, assuming *Re S* continues to apply, presumably at least one of the parents must have a real connection with England and Wales.

[1] Ie an analogy should not be drawn with capacity to make contracts since parental responsibility agreements are probably best regarded as being agreements sui generis and not strict contracts since it is difficult to see what consideration is given by the father when making the agreement.
[2] Agreements may only be made in respect of a 'child' as defined by s 105(1). There is a presumption against interpreting such definitions as including children en ventre sa mere, see *Elliot v Joicey* [1935] AC 209, HL See further para 3.93, n 3. Query whether an agreement can take effect after the mother's death?
[3] *Re X (Minors) (Care Proceedings: Parental Responsibility)* [2000] Fam 156, [2000] 2 All ER 66 in which Wilson J held that the facility under s 4(1)(b) is self-contained and does not depend upon the exercise of parental responsibility. Cf *Re W (minors) (removal from jurisdiction)* [1994] 1 FCR 842 in which the High Court accepted an undertaking not to make a parental responsibility agreement.
[4] [1998] 1 WLR 1701, [1993] 2 FLR 921, CA, discussed further at para 3.61.
[5] Namely Council Regulation (EC) No 2201/2003 of 27 November 2003, discussed at para 5.127.

6   The Regulation applies inter alia to all civil matters relating to the *attribution* of parental responsibility (see art 1(b) and recital 5(b)) and applies to agreements as well as court orders (see art 46).

7   See arts 8 and 13 respectively.

8   Meaning that *no* Member State has jurisdiction: see *Sundelind Lopez v Lopez Lizazo*, Case C-68/07, [2008] 1 FLR 582, ECJ.

3.56 As a matter of procedure, applicants must first complete the details set out in the form[1] (a separate form is required for each child) and then take it to a local family proceedings court or county court or to the Principal Registry, where a justice of the peace, a justices' clerk[2] or court officer authorised by a judge to administer oaths, will witness the parents' signature and sign the certificate of the witness. The duly completed form, together with two copies, should then be taken or posted to the Principal Registry.[3] Sealed copies will be returned to the mother and the father,[4] while the record is open to public inspection. No fee is charged to the parents for the formal recording of their agreement though a charge is payable by those wishing to inspect the record.[5]

1   Namely the child's name, gender, date of birth and date of 18th birthday and name and address of both mother and father. A new form, issued by SI 1994/3157, was re-issued by SI 2000/2262 and now contains updated accompanying notes.

2   There would appear to be no power to delegate this function to Deputy Clerks or other authorised legal officers. In any event, as acknowledged by Court Business (June 1998) item 10.18 (on which see Hershman and McFarlane *Children Law and Practice* A [215]–[217]) there may be occasions where the requirements cannot be met which mean that the person witnessing the signature must exercise some discretion as to the nature of the evidence accepted. According to Court Business, there is no requirement for both parties to the agreement to have their signatures witnessed at the same time by the same person.

3   Regulation 3(1) of the Parental Responsibility Regulations 1991, as amended.

4   Regulation 3(2).

5   Regulation 3(3).

3.57 The Notes attached to the Agreement Form[1] warn mothers that as they will need to prove their maternity they should take to court the child's full birth certificate. There is, however, no comparable advice concerning the man's paternity. Both the mother and father are, however, required to prove their own identity and signature and are advised to bring a photocard, official pass or passport. There is no investigation of whether the agreement is in the child's best interests or of why the parents are entering into it.

1   Revised in 2001 by SI 2001/2262 and again by SI 2005/2808.

3.58 The notes explain that the agreement will not take effect until the form has been received and recorded at the Principal Registry but that once it has, it can only be brought to an end by a court order or upon the child reaching 18. It also warns: 'The making of this agreement will affect the legal position of mother and father. You should both seek legal advice before you make the Agreement.'

It explains that the name and address of a solicitor can be obtained from the Children Panel, local family proceedings court or county court, Citizens Advice Bureau, a Law Centre or a local library. It also mentions that the parents could be eligible for public funding.

3.59 Whether such warnings, coupled with the need to take the agreement to court for witnessing, are sufficient to allay the fears[1] that mothers may be bullied into conferring rights upon the fathers at a time when they are particularly vulnerable to pressure,[2] is hard to say. Perhaps not surprisingly, following the introduction of the requirement of having to have agreements witnessed in court, after a steady rise between 1992 and 1994, the number of agreements fell substantially in 1995,[3] but rose again in 1996.[4] Since 1996 no national statistics have been published. However, it must be assumed, now that unmarried fathers acquire parental responsibility by reason of being registered as the child's father,[5] that there are likely to be few agreements made between mothers and fathers.

[1] See particularly Lord Banks, 502 HL Official Reports (5th series) cols 1180–1182 and 503 HL Official Report col 1319, and Doggett, 'Unmarried fathers and s 4 before and after the Children Act 1989' (1992) 4 JCL 39, 40.
[2] In *Re W (A Minor) (Residence Order)* [1992] 2 FLR 332, CA, a mother did assert that she had signed an agreement under pressure, though this was under the old procedure.
[3] According to the CAAC Report 1993–94, Appendix 1, 2,941 agreements were registered in 1992, 4411 in 1993 and 'around' 5280 in 1994. In 1995, the numbers fell 36% to an estimated 3455 (CAAC Report 1994/1995, Appendix 1).
[4] To an estimated 3590 (CAAC Final Report 1997, Appendix 2).
[5] See the discussion above at paras 3.50 ff.

(d) Parental responsibility orders

3.60 Under s 4(1)(c) the court may, upon an application by an unmarried father (ie not upon its own motion nor upon an application by the mother) order that he shall have parental responsibility for the child. Applications may be made to the High Court, county court or the family proceedings court.[1] If there is a doubt about the applicant's paternity, and a fortiori if paternity is disputed, it will have to be proved before the action may proceed.[2] It is implicit in every order made under s 4 that the man in question has been found or adjudged to be the father of the child in question.[3] An application may be made only in respect of a 'child', that is a person under the age of 18.[4]

[1] Section 92(7). In practice the majority of applications are made to the county court. In 2006, 7,531 of the 11,059 (68%) were made to the county court (Judicial and Court Statistics 2006, (Cm 7273, November, 2007) Table 5.3. This contrasts with the early experience in which the majority of applications were made to the family proceedings courts; nearly 70% of the 3,332 orders made in 1992/93 were made by magistrates – CAAC Report 1992/93, Appendix 1, p 93.
[2] See *Re F (a Minor) (Blood Tests: Parental Rights)* [1993] Fam 314, [1993] 3 All ER 596, CA.
[3] Per Johnson J in *R v Secretary of State for Social Security, ex p W* [1999] 3 FCR 693, [1999] 2 FLR 604.
[4] Section 105(1). For the reasons discussed at paras 3.55, n 2 and 3.97, n 3 it is not thought orders can be made in respect of unborn children.

3.61 According to *Re S (A Minor) (Parental Responsibility: Jurisdiction)*[1] it is not necessary for the child to be habitually resident, present or even born in England and Wales to found jurisdiction to make a s 4 order. However, as discussed at para 3.55 above, that decision predates the revised Brussels II Regulation[2] which clearly applies to such orders[3] and which requires for recognition and enforcement purposes within Member States of the European

Union (except Denmark) that jurisdiction be founded upon the child's habitual residence or, failing that, presence in the Member State.[4] Whether the existence of the Regulation will provide a reason for revisiting *Re S* remains to be seen but even were it to be applied in cases not caught by the Regulation then presumably, though this is by no means clear from *Re S*, the applicant (or mother) must have some connection (namely habitual residence or domicile) with England and Wales.

1   [1998] 1 WLR 1701, [1998] 2 FLR 921, CA per Butler-Sloss LJ who pointed out that the jurisdictional rules set out by the Family Law Act 1986 (see *Clarke Hall and Morrison on Children* at 1[577.24] ff) do not expressly apply to s 4 orders and which should therefore be interpreted as not curbing jurisdiction to make such orders.
2   Namely Council Regulation (EC) No 2201/2003 of 27 November 2003.
3   See art 1(b) and recital 5, referred to at para 3.55, n 6.
4   See arts 8 and 13 respectively.

3.62 Section 4 applications are sometimes referred to as freestanding applications to distinguish them from residence order applications by unmarried fathers in which s 4 orders are made as an ancillary but automatic consequence of making the residence order.[1] As Waite J once commented:[2]

> 'there is an unusual duality in the character of a parental responsibility order: it is on the one hand sufficiently ancillary by nature to pass automatically to a natural father without inquiry of any kind when a residence order is made in his favour; and, on the other hand, sufficiently independent, when severed from the context of a residence order, to require detailed consideration upon its merits as a freestanding remedy in its own right.'

1   Discussed at para 3.71.
2   *Re CB (a minor) (parental responsibility order)* [1993] 1 FCR 440 at 450, [1993] 1 FLR 920 at 929.

(I) DECIDING WHETHER TO MAKE A S 4 ORDER

3.63 It is generally accepted that in deciding whether to make a parental responsibility order the court should treat the child's welfare as its paramount consideration,[1] and be satisfied that making the order 'would be better for the child than making no order at all'.[2] There is no enjoinder to have regard to the welfare checklist[3] though there is nothing to prevent the court from considering it if it so wishes. In theory this means that the court is not obliged to have regard to older children's wishes yet, as has been pointed out,[4] given that, if the father applies instead for a residence order which is opposed by the mother, the court must have regard to the child's wishes, it is difficult to see why the checklist should not apply to contested s 4 applications. Furthermore, since a child with sufficient understanding may, with leave, apply to have the order ended[5] it is logical to assume that such a child's view is relevant to deciding whether to make the order in the first place.[6] The restriction under s 9(6) which prevents the court from making s 8 orders in respect of a child aged 16 or over, save where the circumstances are 'exceptional', does not apply to s 4 orders.

1   Pursuant to s 1(1), see *Re RH (a minor) (parental responsibility)* [1998] 2 FCR 89 at 94, sub nom *Re H (Parental Responsibility)* [1998] 1 FLR 855 at 859, CA, per Butler-Sloss LJ, but note the arguments discussed at para 2.10, n 4.

2   Pursuant to s 1(5), discussed at paras 2.65 ff, and on which see *Re B (Role of Biological Father)* [2007] EWHC 1952 (Fam), [2008] 1 FLR 1015. It could be argued that this provision does not apply because a parental responsibility order relates to the parent and not the child. Although this argument seems stronger than that in relation to the inapplicability of s 1(1), it is still likely to be rejected since it can reasonably be said that as parental responsibility exists for the benefit of the child, parental responsibility orders also relate to the child.

3   Set out by s 1(3), discussed at para 2.39. Under s 1(4) a court is only required to consider s 1(3) when hearing contested s 8 applications or applications under Pt IV.

4   Doggett, cited at para 3.59, n 1 above, at p 41.

5   Section 4(3)(b) and (4) discussed at para 3.79 and 3.80.

6   In practice it is not unusual to ask for a welfare report when no doubt the child's view can be brought to the court's notice.

3.64 According to, *Re H (Minors) (Local Authority: Parental Rights) (No 3)*,[1] in deciding whether to make an order the following factors will undoubtedly be material namely:

• the degree of commitment which the father has shown towards the child;

• the degree of attachment which exists between the father and the child; or

• the father's reasons for applying for the order.[2]

1   [1991] Fam 151, sub nom *Re H (minors) (adoption: putative father's rights) (No 3)* [1991] 2 All ER 185, CA. See also *Re C (minors)* [1992] 2 All ER 86 at 93, CA in which Mustill LJ stated the basic test to be: ' ... was the association between the parties sufficiently enduring; and has the father by his conduct during and since the application shown sufficient commitment to the children, to justify giving the father a legal status equivalent to that which he would have enjoyed if the parties had married?'

2   The basic application form, CI, specifically asks the applicant to state his reasons for making the application. Query whether, given that unmarried fathers now automatically acquire parental responsibility upon being registered as the father, a *pre*-December 2003 registration should be regarded as a relevant factor? For a possible hint that it might be so regarded see *Re J-S (contact: parental responsibility)* [2002] EWCA Civ 1028, [2002] 3 FCR 435, [2003] 1 FLR 399 at [54] per Ward LJ.

3.65 It became established that the so-called '*Re H*'[1] considerations should be expressly considered in all freestanding s 4 applications,[2] and furthermore, provided a concerned though absent father fulfilled the '*Re H* test' then 'prima facie it would be for the welfare of the child that such an order be made'[3]. However, in *Re RH (a minor) (parental responsibility)*.[4] Butler-Sloss LJ, in particular, disapproved of the notion that case law had created a presumption that a devoted father will ordinarily be granted an order. As she put it, the '*Re H*' requirements' are an important starting point when considering the making of a s 4 order but they are not the only factors and even if they are satisfied the court still has an overriding duty to apply the paramountcy test and to determine whether the making of an order is for the child's welfare. The point is well put in *Re M (handicapped child: parental responsibility)*:[5]

'parental responsibility is not a reward for the father for his commitment to and involvement with [the child] but an order which would only be made in [the child's] best interests.'

An example of where the child's welfare trumped the '*Re H* considerations' is *Re B (Role of Biological Father)*[6] in which the court declined to make a s 4 order in favour of the brother of one of the partners to a lesbian relationship who had provided sperm for artificial insemination.

1   *Re H (Minors) (Local Authority: Parental Rights) (No3)* [1991] Fam 151 at 158, sub nom *Re H (minors) (adoption: putative father's rights) (No 3)* [1991] 2 All ER 185 at 189.
2   Per Thorpe J in *S v R (parental responsibility)* [1993] 1 FCR 331, [1993] Fam Law 339. See also *Re JS (a child)(contact: parental responsibility)* [2002] EWCA Civ 1028, [2002] 3 FCR 433, [2003] 1 FLR 399 at [49], per Ward LJ.
3   Per Leggatt LJ in *Re H (Parental Responsibility: Maintenance)* [1996] 1 FLR 867 at 872 and per Balcombe LJ in *Re G (a minor) (parental responsibility)* [1994] 2 FCR 1037, [1994] 1 FLR 504, CA. See also Balcombe LJ's similar comments in *Re E (a minor) (parental responsibility)* [1994] 2 FCR 709 at 716g.
4   [1998] 2 FCR 89 at 94–95, [1998] 1 FLR 855 at 859–860, sub nom *Re H (parental responsibility)* CA and repeated by Butler-Sloss LJ in *Re S (Parental Responsibility: Jurisdiction)* [1998] 2 FLR 921, CA. See also *M v M (Parental Responsibility)* [1999] 2 FLR 737, CA, referred to in para 3.69.
5   [2001] 3 FCR 454.
6   [2007] EWHC 1952 (Fam), [2008] 1 FLR 1015.

3.66 Courts are generally disposed to grant orders to committed fathers. In *Re C and V (contact and parental responsibility)*,[1] Ward LJ commented that because it is desirable for the sake of a child's self esteem to grow up wherever possible having a favourable positive image of an absent parent then, applying the paramountcy test, 'wherever possible, the law should confer on a concerned father that stamp of approval because he has shown himself willing and anxious to pick up the responsibility of fatherhood and not to deny or avoid it'. This is reminiscent of his earlier comment in *Re S (Parental Responsibility)*:[2]

> 'It is wrong to place undue and therefore false emphasis on the rights and duties and the powers comprised in "parental responsibility" and not to concentrate on the fact that what is at issue is conferring upon a committed father the status of parenthood for which nature has already ordained that he must bear responsibility'.

1   [1998] 1 FCR 52, [1998] 1 FLR 392, CA in which an order was made notwithstanding that the father had been convicted of possessing obscene literature (comprising indecent photographs of children) and was not paying maintenance to the children.
2   [1995] 2 FLR 648, CA. See also *Re A (a minor) (parental responsibility)* [1996] 1 FCR 562 and *Re S (a minor)(parental responsibility)* [1995] 3 FCR 564.

3.67 Consistent with the emphasis upon the consequent status conferred by a parental responsibility order it has been held that orders can be made notwithstanding that the child is in local authority care nor is the question of enforcement necessarily decisive.[1] In *Re H (a minor) (contact and parental responsibility)*,[2] an order was made even though the father had been denied a contact order. In *Re C and V (contact and parental responsibility)*[3] it was stressed that applications for contact and parental responsibility were to be treated as wholly separate applications so that the dismissal of the former did not necessarily mean that the latter should also be dismissed. On the other hand, in *Re H (Parental Responsibility: Maintenance)*[4] it was held that the court should not use its power to make a parental responsibility order a weapon to force a father to make maintenance payments for the upkeep of his child. In all cases, however, the test remains whether it is for the child's welfare that an order be made. Lack of insight into a daughter's needs and an inability to get on with social workers is not reason in itself to refuse an order,[5] nor is it justifiable to base a refusal solely on the acrimony between the parents,[6] nor because of transsexuality.[7]

1 See respectively *D v Hereford and Worcester County Council* [1991] Fam 14, [1991] 2 All ER 177, [1991] FCR 56 and *Re C (minors) (parental rights)* [1992] 2 All ER 86, [1991] FCR 856, [1992] 1 FLR 1, CA.
2 [1993] 1 FCR 85, [1993] 1 FLR 484, CA.
3 [1998] 1 FCR 52, [1998] 1 FLR 392, CA. See also *Re M (Contact: Family Assistance: McKenzie Friend)* [1999] 1 FLR 75, CA, per Ward LJ.
4 [1996] 1 FLR 867, CA.
5 See *Re G (a minor) (parental responsibility order)* [1994] 2 FCR 1037, [1994] 1 FLR 504, CA.
6 *Re P (a Minor) (Parental Responsibility Order)* [1994] 1 FLR 578.
7 *L v C* [1995] 3 FCR 125, sub nom *Re L (Contact: Transsexual Application)* [1995] 2 FLR 438 – in which a 'father' who to outward appearances was a woman was granted a s 4 order.

3.68 Although failure to satisfy the so-called '*Re H*' criteria is likely to lead to a refusal to make a parental responsibility order it may be that where the commitment and attachment criteria cannot presently be met because, for example, the father has never seen the child, it may be appropriate to adjourn the application to see whether the criteria can be established in the future.[1]

1 See *Re M (Sperm Donor Father)* [2003] Fam Law 94. In this case a parental responsibility order was subsequently made subject to the father undertaking not to visit the child's school nor to contact any health professional connected with the child's care: *Re D (contact and parental responsibility: lesbian mothers and known fathers)* [2006] EWHC 2 (Fam), [2006] 1 FCR 556. Cf *Re B (Role of Biological Father)* [2007] EWHC 1952 (Fam), [2008] 1 FLR 1015, in which in not dissimilar circumstances Hedley J made a 'no order'.

3.69 In practice, parental responsibility orders are usually but not always granted.[1] For reported examples of where an order was refused see:

- *M v M (Parental Responsibility)*[2] in which it was held that because the father was mentally incapable of discharging the functions embraced within the concept of parental responsibility, it was not in the child's interests to make a s 4 order;
- *Re J (Parental Responsibility)*[3] the child, now aged 12 and who was born after the parents' separation, had infrequent contact with her father and between whom there was minimal attachment (the child herself not wanting to see her father). Moreover, the raison d'être for the father applying, namely his concern about the mother's involvement with drugs, no longer existed;
- *Re P (parental responsibility)*[4] in which the father was found likely to use the order inappropriately (namely he was deeply confused over sexual boundaries and had little appreciation of the difference between abusive and appropriate behaviour);
- *Re RH (a minor) (parental responsibility)*[5] in which the father had been violent towards the child;
- *Re T (a minor) (parental responsibility: contact)*[6] in which the father was violent towards the mother;
- *Re L (A Child) (Contact: Domestic Violence)*[7] – in which the father was violent and desired to control the child;

- *Re P (Parental Responsibility)*[8], in which the Court of Appeal dismissed an appeal against a refusal to make an order based in part on the father's criminal conduct, holding that a court was entitled to take into account, as relevant but not conclusive, factors that the father was in prison and the circumstances of the criminal conduct for which the sentence was imposed;
- *Re G (a child) (domestic violence: direct contact)*[9] – in which the order was refused because of the child's fear and anxiety about the father; and
- *Re M (handicapped child: parental responsibility)*[10] – in which the order was refused because the father was likely to misuse it to interfere with the mother's care thus causing her stress and potentially undermining her ability to care properly for the child.
- *Re B (Role of Biological Father)*[11] – no order made pursuant to s 1(5) in respect of a brother of one of the partners to a lesbian relationship who had provided sperm for artificial insemination on the understanding that he would have nothing to do with the child.

[1] In 2006, 148 (1.5% of all disposals) applications were refused: Judicial and Court Statistics 2006 (Cm 7273) Table 5.4. This, however, is a decline from 214 (2%) in 2004, 374 (4%) in 2001 and 686 (8%) in 1999, see Table 5.3 of the Judicial Statistics for each of those years.

[2] [1999] 2 FLR 737, per Wilson J.

[3] [1999] 1 FLR 784.

[4] [1998] 3 FCR 98, [1998] 2 FLR 96, CA – father found in possession of a number of photographs of pre-pubescent children.

[5] [1998] 2 FCR 89, sub nom *Re H (Parental Responsibility)* [1998] 1 FLR 855, CA.

[6] [1993] 1 FCR 973, [1993] 2 FLR 450, CA. See also *Re P (Terminating Parental Responsibility)* [1995] 1 FLR 1048, discussed below at para 3.80. But note that even where a mother has a genuine fear of the father, it might still nevertheless be appropriate in the child's interests to make a parental responsibility order, see *Re M (Contact: Family Assistance: McKenzie Friend)* [1999] 1 FLR 75, CA.

[7] [2001] Fam 260, [2000] 4 All ER 609, CA.

[8] [1997] 2 FLR 722, CA. See also *K v W* (11 March 1998, unreported), per Judge Anwyl QC, in which an order was refused because of the mother's vulnerability due to mental illness; this in turn made her vulnerable to stress with a resulting high risk of stress to the children.

[9] [2001] 2 FCR 134, per Butler-Sloss P.

[10] [2001] 3 FCR 454.

[11] [2007] EWHC 1952 (Fam), [2008] 1 FLR 1015.

3.70 Once it is found to be in the child's interests that both parents should have parental responsibility it should be reflected by the making of a s 4 order and not by making 'no order' pursuant to s 1(5) of the CA 1989.[1] It is within the court's power to accept, when making a s 4 order, an undertaking from the unmarried father not to exercise certain aspects of that responsibility,[2] but there is no power to suspend a parental responsibility order.[3]

[1] Per Wilson J in *Re P (A Minor) (Parental Responsibility Order)* [1994] 1 FLR 578. For discussion of the effect of s 1(5), see paras 2.68 ff. Despite this ruling there continue to be a number of 'no orders'; see the statistics cited at para 3.69, n 1.

[2] See *Re D (contact and parental responsibility: lesbian mothers and known fathers)* [2006] EWHC 2 (Fam), [2006] 1 FCR 556, see para 3.68, fn 1.

[3] *Re G (A Child)(Parental Responsibility Order)* [2006] EWCA Civ 745, [2006] 2 FLR 1093, [2006] All ER (D) 247 (May).

(e) Residence orders

3.71 An unmarried father can apply for a s 8 order without also applying for a parental responsibility order. However, in such cases if a court grants the father a residence order then by s 12(1) it is also bound to make a *separate* s 4 order. The importance of the s 4 order being made separately is that it will not automatically come to an end if the residence order is ended but will require an express order ending it, if the child is still a minor.

3.72 The obligation under s 12(1) to make a separate s 4 order only applies where the court makes a residence order. It does not apply if the court only makes a contact order in his favour. Since the father will be in a stronger legal position if he has a parental responsibility order in his favour rather than simply a contact order[1], and a fortiori than if he has no order at all, it is generally sound advice to couple applications for s 8 orders with a s 4 order application.[2] Since contact and parental responsibility do not go hand in hand, each application should be considered separately.

[1]   See para 3.76 below.
[2]   As *Re H (A Minor) (Contact and Parental Responsibility)* [1993] 1 FLR 484, CA shows, the court on occasion may grant a s 4 order even if it refuses to make a contact order.

(f) The effect of parental responsibility orders and agreements

3.73 The effect of a court order or a properly recorded agreement is the same, namely, each confers parental responsibility upon the unmarried father. In most cases he will share responsibility with the mother or, if the mother is dead, with any formally appointed guardian. He could also share responsibility with some other person in whose favour a residence order has been made.

3.74 In general terms an unmarried father with parental responsibility is in the same legal position with regard to the child as if he had married the mother.[1] However, without responsibility the father is regarded as a 'parent' for most purposes of the CA 1989.[2] He has, for example, the right to apply without leave to the court for a s 8 order[3] and a prima facie entitlement to reasonable contact with a child in local authority care.[4] He must be informed of an application for an emergency protection order[5] and has a right to apply for its discharge.[6] He also has rights of succession to his child's estate.[7] Furthermore, the lack of parental responsibility does not prevent him from being liable for child support.[8] On the other hand conferring parental responsibility upon unmarried fathers does not alter the status of the child. Hence, the child will still not take British citizenship through the father, nor be able to succeed to a title of honour through his parents. Furthermore, as the courts have stressed,[9] the granting of a s 4 order does not per se entitle the father to interfere with the day-to-day running of affairs affecting the child, at any rate whilst the child is living with another carer.

[1]   See eg the Children Act 1989 Guidance and Regulations, Vol 1, Court Orders (1991) Department of Health, para 2.5. The comment is not repeated in the revised Guidance (Children Act 1989 Guidance and Regulations, Vol 1, Court Orders (2008) Department for Children, Schools and Families).

2   The term 'parent' includes the unmarried father unless the provision indicates to the contrary: Family Law Reform Act 1987, s 1(1).

3   Ie under s 10(4). See *Re C (Minors) (Adoption: Residence Order)* [1994] Fam 1, sub nom *Re C (minors) (parent: residence order)* [1993] 3 All ER 313, CA.

4   Ie under s 34.

5   Section 44(13).

6   Section 45(8).

7   Administration of Estates Act 1925, s 46.

8   On the contrary unmarried fathers can be 'non-resident parents' for the purposes of the Child Support Act 1991 and are 'liable relatives' under the Social Security Administration Act 1992, ss 78(6) and 105(3). For this reason Waite J must be regarded as being mistaken when he commented in *Re C (Minors) (Parental Rights)* [1992] 1 FLR 1 at 9 that upon being vested with parental responsibility the father assumes 'an immediately enforceable burden' to maintain the child. Nevertheless it is implicit in the making of every s 4 order that the man in question has been found or adjudged to be the father and can be so relied upon by the Child Support Agency: *R v Secretary of State for Social Security, ex p W* [1999] 3 FCR 693, [1999] 2 FLR 604.

9   See *Re S (a minor) (parental responsibility)* [1995] 3 FCR 564; *Re A (a minor) (parental responsibility)* [1996] 1 FCR 562 and *Re P (A minor) (Parental Responsibility Order)* [1994] 1 FLR 578.

3.75 Notwithstanding the courts' entreaties not to concentrate on the rights conferred by a s 4 order,[1] it is nevertheless instructive to enquire how the legal position of an unmarried father changes once he has parental responsibility. The principal effects are set out in the following chart.

1   See e g Ward LJ's comments in *Re S (a minor) (parental responsibility)* [1995] 3 FCR 225 at 234, [1995] 2 FLR 648 at 657, CA.

2. Checklist: the effect of the unmarried father obtaining parental responsibility

3.76

Effect	Authority
1. He becomes a 'parent' for the purposes of the adoption legislation and can therefore refuse to consent to his child's adoption.	Adoption and Children Act 2002, ss 21, 47(2) and 52(6).
2. He can remove his child (under the age of 16) from local authority accommodation, and, if he is willing and able to provide accommodation or to arrange for accommodation to be provided for his child, may object to his child being accommodated in the first place.	CA 1989, s 20(7), (8).
3. He will *automatically* be a party to care proceedings.	FPR 1991, Appendix 3 FPC(CA 1989)R 1991, Sch 2.
4. He can appoint a guardian.	CA 1989, s 5(3).
5. He can give a valid consent to his child's medical treatment and require full medical details from the child's practitioner.	*Re H (A Minor)(Shared Residence)* [1994] 1 FLR 717.
6. He can consent to his child's marriage.	Marriage Act 1949, s 3(1A)(a)(i).
7. He is empowered to express a preference as to the school at which he wishes his child's education to be provided; to withdraw his child from sex education in local authority or grant maintained schools and to receive full comprehensive reports from his child's school; and to be involved in the procedure for statementing of a child with special educational needs.	School Standards and Framework Act 1998, ss 86, 71 and the Education Act 1996, Pt IV.
8. He may refuse to give consent for his child (under the age of 16) to be taken outside the United Kingdom.	Child Abduction Act 1984, s 1(3)(a)(ii).
9. He will be entitled to sign passport applications and to oppose the granting of a passport for his child.	UK Passport Agency Guidance.
10. He has 'rights of custody' for the purposes of the Hague Abduction Convention.	Hague Convention on the Civil Aspects of International Child Abduction 1980, art 3.

3.77 Although a s 4 order strengthens the unmarried father's legal position in relation to his child, the mother loses relatively little by the making of the order. She is under no general obligation (but see below) to consult with the father about the child's upbringing[1] and, so long as the child is living with her, the father has no right to interfere with the day-to-day management of the child's life and any attempt or threat to do so can be controlled by a s 8 order.[2] What the mother undoubtedly loses is the unilateral right to remove the child from the UK[3] and, more controversially, it may be that she needs to consult the father about a change of school[4] or surname.[5] She also loses the ability to appoint a guardian to take effect upon her death, unless she has a residence order in her favour.[6]

1 By reason of s 2(7), discussed further at paras 3.97 ff.
2 See eg Ward LJ's comments in *Re S (Parental Responsibility)* [1995] 2 FLR 648 at 657.
3 Under s 1 of the Child Abduction Act 1984 she will require the father's consent (unless she is unable to communicate with him or he is unreasonably refusing to give it).
4 See *Re G (a minor) (parental responsibility: education)* [1995] 2 FCR 53, [1994] 2 FLR 964, CA, discussed at para 3.99.
5 See *Re PC (Change of Surname)* [1997] 2 FLR 730, discussed at para 3.99.
6 Section 5(7), discussed at para 3.120.

3.78 The fact that a s 4 order does not entitle an unmarried father to intermeddle in his child's day-to-day upbringing prompts the question as to why applications are made. The judiciary themselves have commented that the growing number of applications is based on a fundamental misunderstanding of the nature of the order.[1] For some, however, formal recognition of what has been described[2] as the exercise of their 'social parenthood' will undoubtedly be important. Whatever the reasons, the number of such has steadily increased from 2,762 in 1992, to 7,786 in 2000 to a high of 10,522 in 2004.[3] They declined to 8,702 in 2006[4] reflecting no doubt the change in law giving unmarried fathers automatic parental responsibility by virtue of being registered as the father.

1 See eg *Re S (a minor) (parental responsibility)* [1995] 3 FCR 225, [1995] 2 FLR 648, in which Ward LJ commented that s 4 applications 'have become one of those little growth areas born of misunderstanding.
2 Eekelaar 'Parental Responsibility – A New Legal Status?' (1996) 112 LQR 233 at 235.
3 See Table of *Judicial Statistics* respectively for 1992, 2000 and 2004.
4 See Judicial and Court Statistics 2006 (Cm 7273) Table 5.4.

3. Ending parental responsibility orders or agreements

3.79 Parental responsibility orders and agreements remain effective notwithstanding that the couple live together or subsequently separate. They will, however, automatically end once the child attains his majority[1] and, as already discussed,[2] if the father subsequently marries the mother during the child's minority. Apart from these instances parental responsibility may be brought to an end only upon a court order to that effect. Such an order may be made upon the application (ie not of the court's own motion) of:

- any person who has parental responsibility for the child (this will include the father himself) or,
- with leave of the court, the child himself.[3]

In the latter case, the court may grant leave only if it is satisfied that the child has sufficient understanding to make the proposed application.[4] The court may not end a s 4 order while a residence order in favour of the unmarried father remains in force.[5]

1 Section 91(7) and (8).
2 At para 3.49.
3 Section 4(3).
4 Section 4(4). For a similar requirement when seeking leave to apply for a s 8 order, see s 10(8), discussed at para 5.155.
5 Section 11(4). Read literally, this would allow a court to end a s 4 *agreement* even though a residence order in favour of the father is still in force, but it seems inconceivable that a court would do so; see further para 3.80.

3.80 In deciding whether to end a s 4 order or agreement, the court must regard the child's welfare as its paramount consideration and be satisfied that discharging the order is better than making no order at all.[1] Nevertheless, the court should surely be slow to bring a s 4 *order*[2] to an end. It should not, for example, be thought that the ending of a residence order in the father's favour automatically means that parental responsibility should also come to an end. In any event, a separate order expressly ending the s 4 order will be required to end the father's parental responsibility. In *Re P (terminating parental responsibility)*,[3] Singer J emphasised that the ability to apply to terminate parental responsibility should not be used as a weapon by the dissatisfied mother of a non-marital child. Nevertheless, on the facts responsibility was terminated, the father having been responsible for inflicting appalling injuries on the child.

1 Section 1(1) and (5) and see *Re P (terminating parental responsibility)* [1995] 3 FCR 753, [1995] 1 FLR 1048.
2 There may be more reason to end an agreement. For example, if it could be shown that the mother had been subjected to undue pressure to sign, that might provide a good reason to make an order under s 4(3).
4 Above. For another example see *Re F (Indirect Contact)* [2006] EWCA Civ 1426, [2007] 1 FLR 1015 in which the father's anger towards the mother and propensity to violence justified the 'revocation' of the parental responsibility order. Cf *Re G (child care: parental involvement)* [1996] 2 FCR 1, [1996] 1 FLR 857, CA, in which an appeal against revocation of a parental responsibility agreement was successful.

4. Acquisition of parental responsibility by step-parents

3.81 The CA 1989 originally made no special provision for step-parents to acquire parental responsibility. However, with effect from 30 December 2005 provision is made[1] for a step-parent who is married to or the civil partner of the child's parent who has parental responsibility[2] to obtain parental responsibility either by agreement or by court order. According to the Explanatory Notes to the 2002 Act,[3] the intention of this provision is:

'to provide an alternative to adoption where a step-parent wishes to acquire parental responsibility for his or her step-child. It has the advantage of not removing parental responsibility from the other birth parent and does not legally separate the child from membership of the family of the other birth parent'.

It is not open to a *cohabiting* partner of the parent to seek parental responsibility by agreement or order.[4]

1   By s 4A (inserted by s 112 of the Adoption and Children Act (brought into force by the Adoption and Children Act 2002 (Commencement No 9) Order 2005, SI 2005/2213) and amended by s 75(2) of the Civil Partnership Act 2004.

2   Accordingly, the provisions will only apply to a step-mother if she is married to a father with parental responsibility. But presumably this provision can be triggered if the father acquires parental responsibility *after* his subsequent marriage to his step-mother.

3   Paragraph 268.

4   But such a couple could apply for a joint residence order, the effect of which is to vest, for the duration of the order, parental responsibility in the parent's partner, see paras 5.17 and 5.30.

3.82 So far as agreements are concerned, if both parents have parental responsibility (ie because they were married, the father was registered as the child's father, or because of a parental responsibility order or agreement) then the agreement must be made between the step-parent and *both* the child's mother and father.[1]

1   Aliter where only the mother has parental responsibility, in which case the agreement should only be with her. The mandatory involvement of the non-resident parent who has parental responsibility has not escaped criticism, see Lowe and Douglas' *Bromley's Family Law* (10th edn) at 423–424.

3.83 The formalities for making these agreements are basically the same as for those between unmarried parents[1] save that provision is made to accommodate it being made by each parent with parental responsibility and the step-parent.[2] Parties are required to complete a separate Step-Parent Parental Responsibility Agreement Form (FORM C (PRA 2)). As with agreements between unmarried parents, the notes attached to the form warn the parties that there are legal consequences of making the agreement and advises them to seek legal advice. Parents are advised that they will need to prove that they have parental responsibility (namely by producing the child's full birth certificate and a marriage certificate, a copy of a court order for parental responsibility, a copy of a parental responsibility agreement, or in the case of a post-1 December 2003 registered birth, the child's birth certificate showing a joint registration). The step-parent is advised that he or she must produce a marriage certificate or a certificate of civil partnership to the parent. No specific provision is made regarding age requirements for those making an agreement; on who can be made the subject of an agreement or as to any general jurisdictional requirements. However, the position must clearly be the same as for agreements with unmarried fathers.[3]

1   See para 3.56.

2   See the Parental Responsibility Agreement (Amendment) Regulations 2005, SI 2005/2808.

3   See the discussion at para 3.55.

3.84 The court's power to make a parental responsibility order is exercisable only upon the application of the step-parent[1] which is the same position as for orders for unmarried fathers. However, unlike the unmarried father, no provision is made for the automatic making of a parental responsibility order,

following the making of a residence order in a step-parent's favour.[2] Consequently, unless the step-parent has a separate parental responsibility order in
his favour (or responsibility by way of agreement) responsibility will cease
upon the ending of the residence order.[3]

1   Section 4A(1)(b).
2   Ie s 12(1) of the CA 1989 applies only to unmarried fathers.
3   For this reason, step-parents might well be advised when applying for a residence order to
     also seek a parental responsibility order.

3.85 No specific provision is made regarding jurisdiction to make orders but
the position must be the same as for making orders in favour of unmarried
fathers.[1] Similarly, by analogy with unmarried fathers,[2] and in line with the
general principles of the CA 1989 in deciding whether or not to make an
order, the court must treat the child's welfare as its paramount consideration
and be satisfied that making the order is better than making no order at all.
On the other hand, there is no obligation to apply the welfare checklist under
s 1(3) and thus no necessity to have regard even to an older child's wishes,
though whether it would be human rights compliant to ignore those wishes
can be debated. No doubt the jurisprudence on whether to make a parental
responsibility order in favour of the unmarried father[3] will be relevant to
step-parent applications but the analogy is not exact since in most cases the
application will be made with the mother's consent and the opposition will
come from the non-resident father.

1   See the discussion at para 3.61.
2   See para 3.63.
3   See paras 3.64–3.69.

3.86 Parental responsibility agreements and orders remain effective notwithstanding the couple's subsequent separation or even divorce. They will,
however, automatically end once the child attains his majority.[1] As with
agreements and orders as between parents, those with step-parents can be
brought to an end by a subsequent court order,[2] either upon application by
any person[3] with parental responsibility, *or*, with leave of the court,[4] by the
child himself.

1   Section 91(7), (8) as amended by the Adoption and Children Act 2002, Sch 3, para 68(b).
2   Section 4A(3).
3   Ie the non-resident parent can apply.
4   The court must be satisfied that the child has sufficient understanding to make the
     application: s 4A(4).

5. Acquisition of parental responsibility by other individuals

3.87 Individuals who are not parents of the child (including step-parents) can
acquire parental responsibility by becoming that child's guardian, by becoming the child's special guardian, by being granted a residence order in respect
of the child; or by being granted an emergency protection order in respect of
the child.

(a) Guardianship

3.88 To become a guardian, an individual must formally have been appointed as such either by a parent with parental responsibility or a guardian, or by the court in accordance with s 5 of the CA 1989.[1] Such an appointment can only take effect after the death of the parent or parents with parental responsibility.[2]

[1] Discussed at paras 3.107 ff.
[2] Or, if a residence order is in force, on the death of the appointing parent in whose favour the order had been made; see para 3.120.

(b) Special guardianship

3.89 Individuals who are appointed as special guardians[1] have parental responsibility for the duration of the order,[2] and which they can exercise to the exclusion of anyone else, apart from another special guardian.[3] Unlike those with residence orders in their favour, special guardians can appoint a guardian[4] and can consent or withhold consent to the child's adoption (but not to the exclusion of the parents' right to do so).[5]

[1] Special guardianship is discussed at paras 5.213 ff.
[2] Section 14C(1)(a).
[3] Section 14C(1)(b).
[4] Section 5(4), as amended by s 115(4)(b) of the Adoption and Children Act 2002.
[5] The power of consent is vested in parents and guardians, see s 47(2) of the Adoption and Children Act 2002 and for this purpose 'guardians' includes 'special guardians', see s 144(1). However, s 14C(2)(b) of the CA 1989 preserves the parents' right to consent.

(c) Residence orders

3.90 Any person, who is not a parent or guardian and, in whose favour a residence order is made, has parental responsibility while the order remains in force.[1] Such persons do not, however, thereby acquire the right to consent, or refuse consent, to the making of an adoption order nor to appoint a guardian.[2] It is only a residence order that gives parental responsibility. Consequently, other s 8 orders, for example, contact orders, do not have this effect. Furthermore, non-parents with care and control under wardship[3] do not have parental responsibility since legal control of the child will remain vested with the court.[4]

[1] Section 12(2). Because parental responsibility only lasts as long as the order it will come to an end when a care order or even an interim care order is made since that supersedes previous orders: *Oxfordshire County Council v S (a Child) (Care Order)* [2000] Fam Law 20.
[2] Section 12(3)(b) and (c).
[3] Wardship is discussed in Chapter 12.
[4] See eg *Re RJ (minors) (fostering: wardship)* [1999] 3 FCR 646, sub nom *Re RK (Wardship)* [1999] 1 FLR 618.

(d) Emergency protection orders

3.91 Any individual who has an emergency protection order in their favour has limited parental responsibility for the duration of the order.[1]

¹   Section 44(4) and (5), discussed at para 7.86.

6. Acquisition of parental responsibility by local authorities

3.92 Local authorities can acquire parental responsibility namely, by having a care order[1] or an emergency protection order[2] made in their favour. We discuss this issue in Chapters 8 and 7 respectively. Local authorities cannot acquire parental responsibility by any other means. They do not acquire responsibility, for example, when children are remanded to local authority accommodation under the Children and Young Persons Act 1969, s 23.[3]

¹   Section 33(3)(a).
²   Section 44(4)(c).
³   *North Yorkshire County Council v Selby Youth Court Justices* [1994] 1 All ER 991, [1994] 2 FLR 169. For discussion of s 23 of the 1969 Act see *Clarke Hall and Morrison on Children*, 7[156] ff.

FOR WHOM RESPONSIBILITY EXISTS

3.93 Parental responsibility exists in respect of a 'child', that is, a person under the age of 18.[1] It is a moot point whether responsibility can exist for a married child.[2] In the absence of any indications to the contrary, references to 'child' in the CA 1989 must be taken to mean a live child.[3] Accordingly, no-one can be considered to have parental responsibility until the child is born.[4]

¹   Section 105(1).
²   Cf para 3.95.
³   Following the 'rule' in *Elliot v Joicey* [1935] AC 209, HL. For a similar interpretation of 'child' under the Children and Young Persons Act 1969, see *Re D (a minor)* [1987] AC 317 sub nom *D (A Minor) v Berkshire County Council* [1987] 1 All ER 20, HL. See also *R v Newham London Borough Council, ex p Dada* [1996] QB 507, [1995] 2 All ER 522, CA, interpreting s 75 of the Housing Act 1985.
⁴   It therefore remains the case that fathers have no right to prevent the mother having an abortion, see *Paton v British Pregnancy Advisory Service Trustees* [1979] QB 276, [1978] 2 All ER 987 and *C v S* [1988] QB 135, [1987] 1 All ER 1230, CA. They do, however, have a power of veto over the use, storage or disposal of an embryo in vitro: Human Fertilisation and Embryology Act 1990, Sch 3. Either parent has an unconditional right to withdraw their consent and following that withdrawal the embryo(s) must be destroyed: *Evans and Amicus Healthcare Ltd* [2004] EWCA Civ 727, [2005] Fam 1, which position has since been ruled human rights law compliant: *Evans v United Kingdom* [2007] 2 FCR 5, [2007] 1 FLR 1990, ECtHR (Grand Chamber).

DURATION OF PARENTAL RESPONSIBILITY

3.94 An important aspect of parental responsibility is that it is not lost merely because someone else acquires it. Nevertheless responsibility does not have unlimited duration. As it can only exist in respect of a 'child', parental responsibility ends in all cases upon the child attaining his majority. It will clearly end upon the child's death.[1] Upon the making of a parental order[2] or an adoption order[3], parental responsibility is transferred to the person or persons in whose favour the order is made.[4] Non-parents who have responsibility by reason of a residence order and local authorities that have responsibility by reason of a care order only have responsibility for the duration of the order.[5] Similarly, those who have responsibility by reason of an emergency protection order only do so for the duration of the order.[6]

[1]   Though note *R v Gwynedd County Council, ex p B* [1992] 3 All ER 317, CA, which establishes that a parent retains the right to bury (or, presumably, cremate) the child notwithstanding that the child had until his death been in care.
[2]   Namely an order made under the Human Fertilisation and Embryology Act 1990, s 30.
[3]   Adoption and Children Act 2002, s 46(2).
[4]   Apart from these orders there is no other means of depriving parents of their *automatic* parental responsibility during the child's minority. However, if such power exists in a foreign jurisdiction then the courts in this jurisdiction may be forced to recognise it, see eg *Re AMR (adoption: procedure)* [1999] 3 FCR 734, [1999] 2 FLR 807 – in which an order made in Poland depriving Polish parents of their parental authority was held to deprive them of parental responsibility under English law. It was insufficient for the latter purposes that the parents retained a right to seek contact.
[5]   Sections 12(2) and 33(3).
[6]   Section 44(4)(c).

3.95   There is pre-CA 1989 authority for saying that parental guardianship ended upon the female child's marriage[1] and that it was suspended whilst the child was serving in the armed forces[2] but it remains to be seen whether a similar position will be taken with regard to parental responsibility. There is conflicting opinion as to whether responsibility ceases in respect of any aspect of a child's upbringing about which the child himself is sufficiently mature to make his own decisions.[3] Perhaps the better view in each of these situations is that parental responsibility does not end but that the scope for its exercise is limited.

[1]   *Hewer v Bryant* [1970] 1 QB 357 at 363, [1969] 3 All ER 578 at 585, CA, per Sachs LJ; *R v Wilmington Inhabitants* (1822) 5 B & Ald 525 at 526 and *Lough v Ward* [1945] 2 All ER 338 at 348.
[2]   *R v Rotherfield Greys Inhabitants* (1823) 1 B & C 345 at 349–50.
[3]   Cf Lord Scarman's comment in *Gillick v West Norfolk and Wisbech Area Health Authority* [1986] AC 112 at 186, [1985] 3 All ER 402 at 421–422, which suggests it does, but which was specifically rejected by Lord Donaldson MR in *Re R (A Minor) (Wardship: Medical Treatment)* [1992] Fam 11 at 23 [1991] 4 All ER 177 at 185 and by both Lord Donaldson MR and Balcombe LJ in *Re W (A Minor) (Medical Treatment) (Court's Jurisdiction)* [1993] Fam 64 at 75–76 and 87, [1993] 4 All ER 627 at 633 and 642–643, CA.

SHARING PARENTAL RESPONSIBILITY FOR A CHILD AND THE RIGHT OF INDEPENDENT ACTION

3.96   As s 2(5) provides, more than one person may have parental responsibility for the same child at the same time, while s 2(6) makes it clear that a person with parental responsibility does not cease to have it solely because some other person subsequently acquires it.

Where parental responsibility is shared then, by s 2(7), each person who has it 'may act alone and without the other (or others) in meeting that responsibility' except where a statute expressly requires the consent of more than one person in a matter affecting the child. This power to act independently, however, is subject to the important limitation under s 2(8), that a person with parental responsibility is not entitled to act in any way that would be incompatible with a court order.[1] Since ultimate responsibility for a ward of court vests with the court,[2] the warding of a child must operate at least to limit the freedom to exercise parental responsibility. Accordingly, notwithstanding s 2(8) the absence of a court order[3] does not necessarily mean that a parent may always exercise his responsibility without qualification.

[1] But note also certain limitations placed upon the ambit of s 2(7), discussed at para 3.99 below.
[2] See eg *Re E (SA) (a minor) (wardship)* [1984] 1 All ER 289 at 290, per Lord Scarman. Wardship is discussed in Chapter 12.
[3] A child becomes a ward of court immediately the originating summons is issued, ie, without the need for any court order.

1. The position between married parents

3.97 Under s 2(1) each married parent has parental responsibility and by s 2(7) each may act independently and without the other, subject only to express statutory provisions to the contrary. This latter qualification preserves, for example, the embargo imposed by s 1 of the Child Abduction Act 1984, against one parent taking the child (under the age of 16) outside the United Kingdom without the other's consent[1] and maintains the need to obtain each parent's consent to an adoption order as laid down by s 47(2) of the Adoption and Children Act 2002. Where parents separate or divorce, each continues to have parental responsibility even if a residence order has been made in favour of one of them. A parent whose child does not live with him should still be regarded in law as a parent and should be treated as such by, for example, schools and therefore be given information and an opportunity to take part in his child's education. Furthermore it was envisaged that where that parent has the child with him then, subject to not acting in a way that is incompatible with any court order, he would be able to exercise his responsibilities to the full.

[1] Note: neither parent can unilaterally change the child's habitual residence: *Re S (Minors) (Child Abduction: Wrongful Retention)* [1994] 1 FLR 82, per Wall J and *Re A (Wardship: Jurisdiction)* [1995] 1 FLR 767, per Hale J.

3.98 The ability to act independently was intended to mean not simply that neither parent has a right of veto but also that there is no legal duty upon parents to consult each other[1] since, such a duty was both unworkable and undesirable.[2] It was expressly contemplated that even where a residence order had been granted in one parent's favour, subject to not acting incompatibly with a court order, each parent could still exercise that responsibility without having to consult the other and with neither having a right of veto over the other's action. Referring to the example of child living with one parent and going to a school nearby the Law Commission considered that while it would be incompatible for the other parent to arrange for the child to have his hair done in a way which would exclude him from the school, it would be permissible for that parent to take the child to a sporting occasion over the weekend, no matter how much the parent with whom the child lived might disapprove.[3] The intended independence of each parent should be seen as part of the general aim of encouraging both parents to feel concerned and responsible for the welfare of the children.[4]

[1] Thus resolving the uncertainty of the former law which seemed to impose no duty to consult but did confer a power of veto. See Law Com Working Paper No 96, *Custody*, paras 2.34 ff.
[2] See Law Com No 172, para 2.7.
[3] See Law Com No 172, para 2.11.
[4] aw Com No 172, para 2.10. For a criticism of this position see Bainham [1990] Fam Law 192, 193 who argues that it is difficult to see how failing to provide for consultation could promote joint parenting following marital breakdown.

3.99 Despite the apparently clear wording of s 2(7), it was held in *Re G (a minor) (parental responsibility: education)*[1] that there remains a duty to consult at any rate over certain decisions. In that case a father who had custody, care and control under a court order, arranged for his son to attend a local education authority boarding school without informing the mother. In Glidewell LJ's view:

> ' ... the mother, having parental responsibility, was entitled to and indeed ought to have been consulted about the important step of taking her child away from day school that he had been attending and sending him to boarding school. It is an important step in any child's life and she ought to have been consulted'.

It has since been held that s 2(7) does not entitle one spouse to change the child's surname without the consent of the other,[2] while in *Re J (child's religious upbringing and circumcision)*[3] it was accepted that notwithstanding s 2(7) no one holder of parental responsibility should be able to have an incompetent child circumcised against the wishes of any of the others. Accordingly, where holders of parental responsibility disagree, circumcision should not be carried out without leave of the court. It has also been held[4] that hotly contested issues of immunisation belong to that small group of important decisions that ought not to be carried out or arranged by the one-parent carer in the absence of agreement of those with parental responsibility. Although in one sense it makes no difference whether or not there is a duty to consult, for in either case in the event of a disagreement the burden will be on the complaining parent to take the issue to court; the courts' approach to s 2(7) seems questionable.

[1] [1995] 2 FCR 53, [1994] 2 FLR 964.
[2] Per Holman J in *Re C (minors) (change of surname)* [1997] 3 FCR 310 at 316–317 sub nom *Re PC (Change of Surname)* [1997] 2 FLR 730 at 735–736.
[3] [2000] 1 FCR 307, sub nom *Re J (Specific Issue Orders) (Muslim Upbringing and Circumcision)* [2000] 1 FLR 571.
[4] Per Thorpe LJ in *Re B (a child)(immunisation)* [2003] EWCA Civ 1148, [2003] 3 FCR 156, sub nom *Re C (Welfare of Child: Immunisation)* [2003] 2 FLR 1095 at [16]–[17].

2. The effect of a third party acquiring parental responsibility

3.100 By s 2(6) neither parent loses parental responsibility solely because someone else acquires it through a court order. This means, for example, that upon divorce a father does not lose parental responsibility for the child even if a step-parent acquires it under a court order or agreement. In this situation the mother, step-father and father all share responsibility and, subject to not acting incompatibly with a court order, and subject to the case law discussed above,[1] each will be able to exercise their responsibilities independently of the others. A similar situation arises if grandparents or other relatives or foster parents have residence or even special guardianship orders made in their favour.[2] Another effect of s 2(6) is that parents do not lose parental responsibility when a local authority obtains a care order, nor when an emergency protection order is made.[3]

[1] See para 3.99.
[2] Though in the case of special guardianship, the effect is stated more forcibly by s 14C(1)(b), discussed at para 5.225.
[3] See further paras 8.171 ff and 7.86 respectively.

3.101 Although by s 2(6) parental responsibility is not lost *solely* because someone else acquires it, that does not mean that a court order can *never* end a parent's responsibility. An adoption order will clearly do so. As Lord Mackay LC said during the debates on the Bill[1] the word 'solely' is used advisedly here. An adoption order deprives a parent of parental responsibility not solely because adoptive parents acquire it but because s 46(2) of the Adoption and Children Act 2002[2] expressly extinguishes the previous parents' responsibility.

[1] 588 HL Official Report (5th Series) col 1175.
[2] A similar position obtains on making a parental order under s 30 of the Human Fertilisation and Embryology Act 1990, see Parental Orders (Human Fertilisation and Embryology) Regulations 1994, SI 1994/2767, Sch 1.

DELEGATION OF PARENTAL RESPONSIBILITY

3.102 Whilst preserving the previous position that a person with parental responsibility may not surrender or transfer that responsibility to another person save by a court order, s 2(9) permits those with parental responsibility to delegate some or all of their responsibility to one or more persons acting on their behalf. As the revised Children Act 1989 Guidance and Regulations state:[1]

> 'Informal arrangements for the delegation of parental responsibility are covered by s 2(9), which provides that a person with parental responsibility cannot surrender or transfer any part of their responsibility to another, but may arrange for some or all of it to be met by one or more persons acting on his behalf'.

Such delegation can be made to another person who already has parental responsibility[2] or to those who have not, such as schools or holiday camps. This provision is primarily intended to encourage parents (regardless of whether or not they are separated) to agree among themselves on what they believe to be the best arrangements for their children. Section 2(9) does not, however, make such arrangements legally binding. Consequently, they can be revoked or changed at will. Furthermore, as s 2(11) provides, delegations will not absolve a person with parental responsibility from any liability for failure on his part to discharge his responsibilities to the child.[3]

1. Children Act 1989 Guidance and Regulations, Vol 1, Court Orders (2008) Department for Children, Schools and Families, para 2.15.
2. Section 2(10).
3. For example, not to neglect, abandon, expose or cause or procure a child under the age of 16 to be assaulted or ill-treated etc under ss 1 and 17 of the Children and Young Persons Act 1933.

THE POSITION OF THOSE CARING FOR A CHILD WHO DO NOT HAVE PARENTAL RESPONSIBILITY

3.103 Section s 3(5) provides that those who are caring for a child but who do not have parental responsibility, 'may (subject to the provisions of this Act) do what is reasonable in all the circumstances for the purpose of safeguarding or promoting the child's welfare'. As the revised Children Act 1989 Guidance and Regulations observe,[1] what is reasonable 'will depend upon the urgency and gravity of what is required and the extent to which it is practicable to consult a person with parental responsibility'. In other words all that s 3(5) does is to clothe de facto carers with the minimum power necessary to provide for the day-to-day care of the child. So, for example, while a carer may be able to consent to the child's medical treatment in the event of an accident, he will not be able to consent to major elective surgery.[2] Whether a significantly greater latitude for action should be given to those caring for orphans remains an interesting point. It is on the basis of s 3(5) that it is thought that a foster parent of a child being accommodated by a local authority could properly refuse immediately to hand over the child to a parent who is drunk or who turns up in the middle of the night. On the other hand, s 3(5) does not empower a de facto carer to change a child's habitual residence merely by taking him out of the jurisdiction[3] nor to obtain a passport for the child[4] or to change the child's surname.[5] It has also been held[6] that because they do not have parental responsibility local authorities have no power to transfer an 'accommodated' child from residential care to foster care without the parent's permission. Anyone who cares for a child is obliged not to assault, ill-treat, neglect, abandon or expose the child in a manner likely to cause unnecessary suffering or injury to health.[7]

1. Children Act 1989 Guidance and Regulations, Vol 1, Court Orders (2008) Department for Children, Schools and Families, para 2.16.
2. It may be difficult for the carer to convince a doctor that he has sufficient authority to consent to medical treatment which may be desirable but not essential. Cf Johnson J's comments in *B v B (A Minor) (Residence Order)* [1992] 2 FLR 327 at 330 that notwithstanding s 3(5) a maternal grandmother who was the de facto carer, found in practice that the education authorities were reluctant to accept her authority to give consent, for example, to the child going on a school trip, and insisted upon having the mother's written authority.
3. Per Lord Slynn in *Re S (A Minor) (Custody: Habitual Residence)* [1998] AC 750, [1997] 3 WLR 597, [1997] 4 All ER 251, HL.
4. Per Butler-Sloss LJ in *Re S (Abduction: Hague and European Conventions)* [1997] 2 FLR 958 at 962.
5. *Re D, L and LA (Care: Change of Surname)* [2003] 1 FLR 339.
6. *R v Tameside Metropolitan Borough Council, ex p J* [2000] 1 FCR 173, [2000] 1 FLR 942.
7. Children and Young Persons Act 1933, s 1.

GUARDIANSHIP

1. Introduction

3.104 The term 'guardian' has a variety of meanings[1] but the specific concern of the following discussion is the institution of legal guardianship over children during their minority. Formerly, the concept of guardianship was a complex one. However, following its reform by the CA 1989 guardianship can now be said to be the legal status under which a person has parental responsibility for a child following the death of one or both of the child's parents. In other words a 'guardian' is someone who has been formally appointed to take the place of the child's deceased parent. Guardianship is not to be confused with 'Special Guardianship' which was introduced by the Adoption and Children Act 2002.[2] The crucial difference is that unlike the former the latter normally takes effect during the parent's lifetime.

[1] See, for example, the use of 'guardianship' under the Mental Health Act 1983, s 7 (as amended by the Mental Health Act 2007) under which a guardian may be appointed for a person who has attained the age of 16 and who is, or appears to be suffering from a mental disorder (on which, see Fennell *Mental Health – The New Law* 8.15 ff) and s 37 under which a person convicted before the Crown Court of an offence punishable with imprisonment can be placed under the guardianship of a local social services authority. The term 'guardian' is not to be confused with a 'children's guardian' who is a person appointed to represent a child in legal proceedings. See paras 10.35 ff.

[2] See paras 5.213 ff.

3.105 The law of guardianship is exclusively controlled by ss 5 and 6 of the CA 1989.[1] The concept of parental guardianship is abolished following the express abolition by s 2(4) of the rule of law that a father is the natural guardian of his legitimate children and the repeal (in Sch 15) of the Guardianship of Minors Act 1971, s 3 which provided that upon the death of one parent the other became the guardian of any legitimate child. Accordingly, save for the exceptional case where the unmarried father becomes a guardian[2] the status is now confined to non-parents formally appointed to take the place of a deceased parent or parents.

[1] This is not to say that an English court will not recognise a guardianship appointment made abroad. Indeed it is bound to recognise a guardianship order competently made in another EU Member State (other than Denmark) under the terms of Council Regulation (EC) No 2201/2003 of 27 November 2003 ('Brussels II Revised') see art 21. See more generally Lowe 'Do Foreign Appointed Guardians Qualify as "Guardians" for the purposes of the Adoption and Children Act 2002?' [2008] Fam Law 163.

[2] Eg upon the mother's death following an appointment by her or the court.

3.106 With one exception it is not possible to appoint different types of guardian.[1] The exception is the High Court's inherent power, preserved by s 5(11) and (12),[2] to appoint the Official Solicitor to be a guardian of a child's estate. Guardians of the estate apart, any person appointed a guardian under s 5 has parental responsibility.[3] This conferment of full parental responsibility was considered by the Law Commission to be central to the role of guardians. As they put it:[4]

'The power to control a child's upbringing should go hand in hand with the responsibility to look after him or at least to see that he is properly looked after.

Consultation confirmed our impression that it is now generally expected that guardians will take over any responsibility for the care and upbringing of a child if the parents die. If so, it is right that full legal responsibility should also be placed upon them.'

One consequence of having parental responsibility is that guardians can themselves appoint guardians.[5] Appointments can also be made by the court, a parent with parental responsibility or a special guardian.[6]

1   For a detailed discussion of the various types of guardian that existed before the CA 1989 see Guardianship (Law Com Working Paper No 91, 1985) pp 29–46.
2   See further para 3.115.
3   Section 5(6). However, those appointed as guardians of the child's estate, or for one specific purpose (eg to give or to withhold agreement to the child's marriage) before s 5 came into force, can only act within the terms of their appointment: Sch 14, para 12.
4   Law Com No 172, para 2.23.
5   Section 5(4). This was new under the CA 1989.
6   Section 5(3), (4) (as amended).

2. The court's power to appoint guardians

Appointing individuals

(I) WHEN THE POWER MAY BE EXERCISED

3.107 Under s 5(1) the court[1] may appoint an 'individual' to be a child's guardian if:

(a)   the child has no parent with parental responsibility for him; or
(b)   a residence order has been made with respect to the child in favour of a parent, guardian or special guardian of his who has died while the order was in force.

Under s 5(2) the above powers of appointment may be exercised in any 'family proceedings'[2] either upon application or 'if the court considers that the order should be made even though no application has been made for it'.

1   Ie the High Court, county court or magistrates' court: s 92(7).
2   Defined by s 8(3), see paras 5.135 ff.

3.108 Applying s 6(c) of the Interpretation Act 1978 (which states that, unless there is a contrary intention in the statute, the singular includes the plural), the court may appoint more than one guardian. On the other hand, by confining the power to appoint an 'individual', it is clear that the court cannot appoint a body such as a local authority to be a guardian nor can it appoint what has been described as an 'artificial individual' such as a director of children's services, who would in effect be the local authority.[1]

1   Per Hollis J in *Re SH (Care Order: Orphan)* [1995] 1 FLR 746 at 749. This restriction is contrary to the recommendations made in the Government's White Paper *The Law on Child Care and Family Services* (Cm 62 (1987)), and has already proved inconvenient, see *Birmingham City Council v D, Birmingham City Council v M* [1994] 2 FLR 502, in which the local authority unsuccessfully sought care orders in respect of orphans accommodated by them, essentially to obtain parental responsibility.

3.109 In line with the general restriction against appointing guardians during the lifetime of a parent with parental responsibility, s 5(1) provides that the court's power only arises: (1) where the child has no parent with parental responsibility; (2) upon the death of a parent, guardian or special guardian in whose favour a residence order was in force,[1] or (3) point (2) does not apply and the child's only or surviving special guardian dies.[2] Although the first embargo is strict[3] it nevertheless only applies where the child has no parent with parental responsibility. The court can therefore appoint a guardian even though the child already has a guardian (other than the child's unmarried father[4]) and it can also make an appointment notwithstanding that the child's unmarried father is still alive provided he has not obtained parental responsibility.

1   Unless a residence order or an existing custody order was also made in favour of the surviving parent: s 5(9) and Sch 14, para 8(2).
2   The references to special guardianship were added by the Adoption and Children Act 2002, s 115(4).
3   See *Re A, J and J (Minors) (Residence and Guardianship Orders)* [1993] Fam Law 568 – no power to appoint an elder sibling to be a guardian because father was still alive notwithstanding that he was living out of the jurisdiction and was believed to be suffering from mental illness.
4   Since a guardian has parental responsibility (s 5(6)) presumably an unmarried father who is a guardian will for these purposes be regarded as a parent with parental responsibility.

(II) WHO MAY APPLY?

3.110 The CA 1989 is silent as to who can apply to become a guardian but it is generally thought that any individual[1] (including, in theory, a child) may apply to be appointed. There is no requirement that leave of the court must first be obtained. On the other hand, an application can only be made under s 5 by an individual himself wishing to be a guardian. However, since under s 5(2) the court has power in any family proceedings to make an appointment of its own motion, once proceedings are in train there would seem nothing to stop any other interested person, including the child himself, from applying to seek the appointment of another individual to be a guardian.[2]

1   But not a 'body' such as the local authority, see para 3.108.
2   Such a possibility was canvassed by the Law Commission in their Working Paper No 91, para 3.49.

(III) IN RESPECT OF WHOM MAY APPLICATIONS BE MADE?

3.111 An application may be made only in respect of a 'child', that is, a person under the age of 18.[1] There is no express embargo against making an appointment in respect of a married child, although it remains to be seen whether in practice the courts would be prepared to make an appointment in such a case.[2] On normal principles of construction there is no power to appoint a guardian of a child until he or she is born.[3]

1   Section 105(1).
2   A similar problem obtained in respect of the former law, but the Law Commission Paper (see Working Paper No 91, para 3.64) was inclined to leave the question open.
3   See the authorities cited at para 3.93, n 3.

(IV) EXERCISING THE POWER

3.112 In deciding whether to make an appointment, the court must regard the child's welfare as the paramount consideration and to be satisfied that making an order is better than making no order at all.[1] It is not however, obliged to have specific regard to the factors set out in s 1(3),[2] though the court is free to do so if it so wishes.[3] There is no restriction comparable to that under s 9(6) with respect to s 8 orders that appointments relating to 16 or 17 year olds should only be made in 'exceptional circumstances'.

[1] Section 1(1) and (5).
[2] This is because the direction to do so under s 1(4) applies only to contested applicant for a s 8 order or to application for an order under Pt IV of the Act.
[3] Cf *Southwark London Borough v B* [1993] 2 FLR 559, CA. In contested cases it would seem prudent to apply the checklist.

3.113 Since s 5 proceedings rank as 'family proceedings' the court can make either upon application or upon its own motion, any s 8 order in addition to, or instead of, appointing a guardian.[1] To help the court to decide what, if any, order to make, it may order a welfare report pursuant to its powers under s 7.[2]

[1] Section 10(1) discussed at paras 5.141 ff.
[2] Discussed at paras 10.20 ff. This power implements one of the Law Commission's suggestions (Working Paper No 91, para 3.54) for improving the procedure and criteria for court appointments of guardians.

3.114 Although the court is empowered to appoint more than one guardian at one time or on different occasions, it seems unlikely that a court would appoint a subsequent guardian knowing that two or more guardians would be in conflict.[1] It has also been said[2] that it would be unusual, though not an absolute bar, to appoint persons as guardians who have never actually seen the child in question.

[1] See Hershman and McFarlane *Children, Law and Practice* J [30] relying on *Re H (an infant)* [1959] 3 All ER 746, [1959] 1 WLR 1163.
[2] Per Purchas LJ in *Re C (minors) (adoption by relatives)* [1989] 1 All ER 395, [1989] 1 WLR 61, CA.

3. Appointing the Official Solicitor as guardian of the estate

3.115 Contrary to the Law Commission's recommendation,[1] the High Court's inherent power to appoint a guardian of a child's estate is preserved.[2] However, only the Official Solicitor can be so appointed and even then only when the consent of the persons with parental responsibility has been signified to the court or when, in the court's opinion, such consent cannot be obtained or may be dispensed with.[3] Furthermore appointments may be made only in certain defined circumstances, namely, when the Criminal Injuries Compensation Board notifies the court that it has made or intends to make an award to the child; when payment to the child has been ordered by a foreign court or tribunal or when the child is absolutely entitled to the proceeds of a pension fund; or in any other case only where such an appointment seems desirable to the court.[4] In practice such appointments are likely to be confined to cases where the parents are dead or where it is unsuitable for them to be involved (for example, where they had caused the injuries to the child).

1   See Law Com No 172, para 2.24 in which the Commission recommended the abolition of the power arguing that trusteeship would adequately and more appropriately fill any gap.
2   By s 5(11) and (12).
3   CPR 21.12(2).
4   CPR 21.12(1).

4. Private appointment of guardians

(a) Making an appointment

3.116 Any parent with parental responsibility (ie not an unmarried father without such responsibility nor other individuals having parental responsibility by reason of a residence order being made in their favour), any guardian and any special guardian may appoint an individual to be the child's guardian.[1] Although reference is made to 'an individual', it is clear that more than one person may be appointed as a guardian.[2] Furthermore an additional guardian or guardians can be appointed at a later date.[3] There is nothing to prevent an appointment being made by two or more persons jointly.[4]

1   Section 5(3) and (4), as amended. The power of a guardian to make appointments was new under the CA 1989. Note the consequential amendment of s 1 of the Wills Act 1837 in Sch 13, para 1.
2   This is implicit in s 6(1) which refers to 'an additional guardian'. But 'individual' does not include a 'body', see para 3.108.
3   Section 6(1).
4   Section 5(10).

3.117 There is no restriction or control on who may be appointed (even another child, it seems, could be appointed)[1] nor are there any means of scrutinising an appointment unless a dispute or issue is subsequently brought before the court.[2] Appointments can be made only in respect of children under the age of 18.[3]

1   Although it may seem questionable for one child to have parental responsibility over another, there are occasions when such a power could be useful, see *Re A, J and J (Minors) (Residence and Guardianship Orders)* [1993] Fam Law 568, referred to at para 3.109, n 3.
2   See para 3.129 for discussion of the court's power to remove a guardian.
3   Section 105(1). Query whether: (a) an appointment can take effect once the child is married; or (b) an appointment is valid if made before the child is born but where the child is alive at the time of the appointer's death? On this last point cf para 3.111.

3.118 Whereas before the CA 1989 the appointment had to be by deed or by will, under s 5(5), it is sufficient that the appointment 'is made in writing, is dated and is signed by the person making it'. This simpler method of appointment is intended to encourage parents (particularly young parents who are notoriously reluctant to make wills) to appoint guardians.[1] Section 5(5) does not preclude appointments being made in a will or deed, since clearly such means will satisfy the minimum prescribed requirements.[2] An appointment made by will but not signed by the testator, will be valid if it is signed at the direction of the testator in accordance with the Wills Act 1837, s 9.[3] An appointment will also be valid in any other case provided it is signed at the direction of the person making the appointment, in his presence and in the presence of two witnesses who each attest the signature.[4] These latter provisions cater for the blind or physically disabled persons who cannot write, but not for those who are absent or mentally incapacitated.[5]

[1] See the Law Commission's comments at Law Com No 172, para 2.29.
[2] See Lord Mackay LC's comments at 502 HL Official Report (5th Series), col 1199.
[3] Section 5(5)(a).
[4] Section 5(5)(b).
[5] Cf the original Children Act 1989 Guidance and Regulations, Vol 1, Court Orders (1991) Department of Health, para 2.18. The revised Children Act 1989 Guidance and Regulations, Vol 1, Court Orders (2008) Department for Children, Schools and Families, para 2.22 omits this comment.

(b) Revoking an appointment

3.119 Section 6 deals with the formerly complex question of revocation of appointments. Under s 6(1), a later appointment revokes an earlier appointment (including one made in an unrevoked will or codicil) made by the same person in respect of the same child, unless it is clear that the purpose of the later appointment is to appoint an additional guardian.[1] It is also open to the person who made the appointment (including one made in an unrevoked will or codicil) expressly to revoke it in a signed written and dated instrument.[2] Under s 6(3A) a dissolution or annulment of marriage on or after 1 January 1996 revokes an appointment of the former spouse as a guardian unless a contrary intention appears from the appointment.[3] For the purposes of this provision the dissolution or annulment includes both those made by a court of civil jurisdiction in England and Wales and those recognised in England and Wales by virtue of Pt II of the Family Law Act 1986.[4] In the case of a registered partnership, the dissolution or annulment of the partnership by a court order, will revoke an appointment by the former partner unless a contrary intention appears by the appointment.[5] Section 6(4) further provides that an appointment made in a will or codicil is revoked if the will or codicil is revoked. An appointment, other than one made by will or codicil, will also be revoked if the person making it destroys the document with the intention of revoking the appointment.[6]

[1] This reverses the former position following s 20 of the Wills Act 1837 that an appointment under a will cannot be revoked by a subsequent appointment by deed and it ends the debate (on which, see Bromley and Lowe's *Family Law* (7th edn) p 531) as to whether an appointment by deed can be revoked by a later deed.
[2] Section 6(2).
[3] This provision was added by the Law Reform (Succession) Act 1995 and note the consequential changes made to Forms M5, M9 and M10 by the Family Proceedings (Amendment) Rules 1996, SI 1996/816, r 3. As Barton and Wells 'A Matter of Life and Death – The Law Reform (Succession) Act 1995' [1996] Fam Law 172, 174 point out, the appointment of a *cohabitant* would not be revoked by the couple's subsequent estrangement.
[4] Section 6(3A)(b).
[5] Section 6(3B) added by the Civil Partnership Act 2004, s 76. For these purposes the dissolution includes both those made by a court in England and Wales and those recognised in England and Wales by virtue of the Civil Partnership Act 2004, Pt 5, ch 3: s 6(3B)(b).
[6] Section 6(3B).

(c) When the appointment takes effect

3.120 Under s 5(7) the appointment only takes effect immediately upon the death of the appointing person where:

(a)   following that death the child has no parent with parental responsibility[1] (but it will take effect where a non-parent has responsibility, for example, by having a residence order in their favour); or

(b)   there was a residence order in favour of the person making the appointment immediately before his death (unless a residence or 'existing custody order' was also made in favour of the surviving parent[2]); or

(c)   he was the child's only (or last) surviving special guardian.[3]

In the case of (b), the surviving parent has no right to object but he can apply to the court for an order ending the appointment.[4] Where the child does have a parent with parental responsibility, the appointment will take effect only upon the death of that person.[5]

[1]   It will, therefore, take effect if the child's unmarried father is still alive, unless he has obtained parental responsibility in one of the ways discussed at paras 3.48 ff.

[2]   Section 5(9) and Sch 14, para 8(2). Query whether the position is the same where a joint appointment is made. Hershman and McFarlane, cited at J [27], consider that the appointment will still not take effect until the death of the surviving parent, relying on s 5(10), but the position is perhaps not beyond doubt.

[3]   Section 5(7)(b), as amended by the Adoption and Children Act 2002.

[4]   Section 6 (7). See further para 3.129 below.

[5]   Section 5(8).

3.121 The rationale of delaying the operation of a guardianship appointment is to avoid unnecessary conflict between a surviving parent and a guardian appointed by the deceased parent. As the Law Commission said,[1] there seems little reason why the surviving parent should have to share parental responsibility with a guardian who almost invariably will not be sharing the household. In effect, the law protects the surviving parent from interference by an outsider though if that parent wishes informally to seek the help of the appointee he can also do so without jeopardising his parental status. In such circumstances, however, the surviving parent can no longer object to the appointment although he can, under s 6(7), seek a court order to end it. On the other hand if the appointee wishes to challenge this position he will need to seek the court's leave to obtain a s 8 order.

[1]   Law Com No 172, para 2.27.

3.122 While this basic standpoint seems right where the child was living with both parents in a united family before the death of one of them, different considerations apply where the parents are divorced or separated. The law takes the position[1] that if there was a court order that the child should live with the parent who had died, that parent should be able to provide for the child's upbringing in the event of his death. But this standpoint has been questioned by one commentator, who said:[2]

'The survivor will, of course, have joint parental responsibility with the guardian but will have the onus of bringing the child's position before the court in the event of a disagreement between them.[3] This is not very easy to reconcile with the ethos of continuing parental responsibility following divorce. It casts the non-residential parent in the role of an outsider who is liable to interfere with the child rather than that of a concerned parent who is anxious to step in to the breach left by the deceased'.

There has also been criticism of not making provision for cases where the spouses are separated, or even divorced but where there is no residence order.[4] The father, for example, may simply have abandoned his family. As the Scottish Law Commission said: 'In many of these cases it might well be desirable for an appointment of a guardian to be capable of coming into operation, even though there is a surviving parent somewhere'.[5]

[1] Endorsing the Law Commission's view: Law Com No 172, para 2.28.
[2] Bainham: *Children: The New Law* (1990), para 2.40. See also Bainham: Children: *The Modern Law* (3rd edn, 2004) 229.
[3] Eg under s 6(7) application can be made to the court to end the appointment.
[4] Such a scenario is now more likely to arise since it will be by no means uncommon, because of the so-called non intervention principle under s 1(5), for no residence orders to have been made.
[5] Scot Law Com No 135 *Report on Family Law* (1992) reporting what was said in Discussion Paper No 88, *Parental Responsibilities and Rights, Guardianship and the Administration of Children's Property* (1990) para 3.11. Accordingly, no change was recommended, so that in Scotland (see the Children (Scotland) Act 1995, s 7) it remains the case that a guardianship appointment made by the deceased parent comes into effect notwithstanding the survival of the other parent.

(d) Disclaiming the appointment

3.123 Section 6(5) provides a formal right to disclaim an appointment. This right, which applies only to private appointments and not to those made by a court, must be exercised 'within a reasonable time of his first knowing that the appointment has taken effect'.[1] Furthermore, it must be disclaimed by an instrument in writing, signed by the appointee, and recorded in accordance with any regulations that may be made by the Lord Chancellor.[2]

[1] See by way of example, *Re SH (Care Order: Orphan)* [1995] 1 FLR 746, in which it was said that local authority foster parents intended to revoke a guardianship appointment by the mother.
[2] Section 6(6). To date, no regulations have been made.

3.124 Welcome as this power is, it does make it all the more important for parents to discuss their proposed appointment with the person concerned. It seems desirable for some official guidance to be published reminding parents of the desirability of prior consultation.

(e) Effect of being appointed a guardian

3.125 Except where the Official Solicitor is appointed guardian of a child's estate,[1] all persons appointed as guardians, whether privately or by the court, have parental responsibility for the child.[2] This places guardians in virtually the same legal position as parents with parental responsibility. The key difference is that, unlike a parent, a guardian is not a 'liable relative' under the Social Security Administration Act 1992,[3] nor a 'non-resident parent' under the Child Support Act 1991,[4] and no court may order a guardian to make financial provision for or transfer property to the child.[5] This means that although guardians are under a duty to see that the child is provided with adequate food, clothing, medical aid and lodging[6] and to educate the child properly,[7] no financial orders can be made against them[8] nor are they liable to contribute to the maintenance of a child who is being looked after by the local authority.[9] The absence of any legal liability on guardians to maintain their children might seem at odds with the general policy of awarding them full parental responsibility. The Law Commission, however, considered[10] that apart from representing a major change of policy, the imposition of financial liability upon guardians might 'act as a serious deterrent to appointments being made or accepted'. Guardians have no rights of succession upon the child's death, nor can a child take British citizenship from his guardian.

[1]   For an account of the legal position of a guardian of the estate see Law Com Working Paper No 91, para 2.23.
[2]   Section 5(6).
[3]   Sections 78(6) and 105(3).
[4]   Under s 3 of the 1991 Act (as amended by the Child Support, Pensions and Social Security Act 2000) only 'legal' parents can be 'absent or non resident parents' and hence liable for child support.
[5]   Namely under the powers conferred by the CA 1989, s 15 and Sch 1. However, in divorce, nullity and separation proceedings between a guardian and his or her spouse or the equivalent proceedings between a guardian and his or her civil partner, there is power under the Matrimonial Causes Act 1973 and the Civil Partnership Act 2004 to make financial provision for the child, provided he or she is a 'child of the family'.
[6]   Under the Children and Young Persons Act 1933, s 1(2)(a).
[7]   Under the Education Act 1996, ss 7, 8 and 576(1).
[8]   This will be so even if the guardian has obtained a residence order, see *Clarke Hall and Morrison on Children*, 4[4].
[9]   Only parents are so liable, see Sch 2, para 21(3). Similarly, guardians cannot be liable to contribute to the costs of services provided by a local authority for a child and his family: s 29(4).
[10] Law Com No 172 at para 2.25.

3.126 A guardian is in a stronger legal position than a non-parent in whose favour a residence order has been made. Unlike the latter[1] a guardian has the right to consent or withhold consent to the child's placement for adoption and to the making of an adoption order and to appoint a guardian. Furthermore, although the process of granting residence orders to third parties bears some resemblance to the court process of appointing guardians, the resulting orders are conceptually different in that the guardian replaces the deceased parent or parents, whereas in person will normally be granted a residence order whilst the child's parents are alive and will therefore share parental responsibility with them.

[1]   See s 12(3), discussed at para 3.90.

5. Termination of guardianship

(a) Death, majority or marriage of the child

3.127 The guardian's duties cease if the child dies.[1] They automatically end when the child attains the age of 18.[2] Whether the guardian's powers cease upon the child's marriage is perhaps debatable for, while s 5 imposes no such express limitation, it may well be held that there is no scope for the operation of guardianship. In any event, it seems unlikely that a guardian would be permitted to interfere with the activities of a married child even if the guardianship continues.

[1] Though query whether a guardian has a duty to bury or cremate a child? Cf *R v Gwynedd County Council, ex p B* [1992] 3 All ER 317, CA.
[2] Section 91(7), (8).

(b) Death of the guardian

3.128 Guardianship ends upon the death of a sole guardian unless, pursuant to the powers vested by s 5(4), the guardian has appointed another individual to be the child's guardian in his place. If a guardian dies leaving others in office, the survivors continue to be guardians.

(c) Removal by the court

3.129 Section 6(7) provides that a court[1] can make an order bring to an end any guardianship appointment made under s 5. Such an order can be made at any time upon the application of:

(1) any person who has parental responsibility; or
(2) the child himself, with leave of the court; or
(3) upon the court's own motion in any family proceedings, if the court considers that it should be brought to an end.[1]

In deciding whether to end the guardianship, the court must be guided by the welfare principle.[2] In reaching its decision the court is entitled to order a welfare report.[3] If it decides to end the guardianship, the court may appoint another individual to take the former guardian's place. It is also open to the court to make a s 8 order. Where the court orders a guardian's removal it may well have to consider appointing a new guardian (or alternatively making a residence order) to prevent a hiatus in parental responsibility for the child.[4]

[1] Ie The High Court, county court or a magistrates' court: s 92(7).
[2] Ie pursuant to s 1(1). If the guardian expresses his unwillingness to continue, it is unlikely that the court will hold it to be in the child's interests for the appointment to continue. For cases where the court has forcibly removed a guardian in the past, see the cases cited by Lowe and Douglas *Bromley's Family Law* (10th edn) p 448.
[3] Ie under s 7, discussed at paras 10.20 ff.
[4] See Bainham *Children – The Modern Law* (3rd edn, 2004) 232.

Chapter 4
WORK IN THE COURTS

INTRODUCTION

4.1 The principles in s 1 of the CA 1989 have affected substantive law, practice and procedure and underlie developments towards a unified family court. The requirement of s 1(1) that the welfare of the child is paramount[1] is reflected in procedures that are less confrontational and non-adversarial.[2] The avoidance of delay[3] is reflected most clearly in the obligation on courts to monitor the course of proceedings and work to a timetable, and to be proactive in the management of cases.[4] Since one means by which delay may be reduced is the more efficient use of resources, the structure of courts under the Act has more nearly aligned the jurisdiction of the courts dealing with family cases and facilitated the allocation of cases to the most suitable tribunal.

[1] See paras 2.2 ff.
[2] See *Oxfordshire County Council v M* [1994] 1 FLR 175, per Stephen Brown P and *Practice Note: Case Management* [1995] 1 All ER 586, [1995] 1 FLR 456 and see also *Re R (Care: Disclosure: Nature of Proceedings)* [2002] 1 FLR 755 at p 771D.
[3] CA 1989, s 1(2).
[4] See, for an early statement of this, *Re A and B (Minors) (No 2)* [1995] 1 FLR 351, per Wall J and now the *Practice Direction (Guide to Case Management in Public Law Proceedings)* at Appendix 3 below.

THE OVERRIDING OBJECTIVE

4.2 In addition to the general principle in s 1 of the 1989 Act, the *Practice Direction (Guide to Case Management in Public Law Proceedings)*[1] makes clear the approach which is required in cases involving children:

'The overriding objective
2.1   This Practice Direction has the overriding objective of enabling the court to deal with cases justly, having regard to the welfare issues involved.

Dealing with a case justly includes, so far as is practicable—
(1)   ensuring that it is dealt with expeditiously and fairly;
(2)   dealing with the case in ways which are proportionate to the nature, importance and complexity of the issues;
(3)   ensuring that the parties are on an equal footing;

(4) saving expense; and

(5) allotting to it an appropriate share of the court's resources, while taking into account the need to allot resources to other cases.

Application by the court of the overriding objective

2.2 The court must seek to give effect to the overriding objective when it—

(1) exercises the case management powers referred to in this Practice Direction; or

(2) interprets any provision of this Practice Direction.

Duty of the parties

2.3 The parties are required to help the court further the overriding objective.'

Although the *Practice Direction* only applies to public law proceedings, it is the same to all intents as the statement in *The Private Law Programme* and para 2 above reproduces what will clearly be the overriding objective of the revised Family Proceedings Rules when they are ultimately issued[2]. However, in the interim, there is a degree of complexity introduced by the existing general procedural rules being supplemented by Practice Directions on more specific issues. An example of this is the Children (Allocation of Proceedings) Order 1991[3] which is now to be read in the light of the *Draft Allocation Guidance*[4].

[1] See Appendix 3.
[2] See para 4.4.
[3] SI 1991/1677 as amended, see Appendix 2.
[4] See paras 4.41 ff.

THE COURTS

4.3 The High Court, county courts and magistrates' courts are given jurisdiction over proceedings under the CA 1989.[1] Although this creates a largely concurrent jurisdiction there are express restrictions on the jurisdiction of magistrates' courts which may not entertain any application or make any order involving the administration or application of any property belonging to, or held in trust for, a child or the income of any such property.[2] In addition the Children (Allocation of Proceedings) Order 1991[3] specifies that particular proceedings must be commenced in specified courts.[4]

[1] CA 1989, s 92(7).
[2] CA 1989, s 92(4).
[3] SI 1991/1677 amended by SI 1993/624, SIs 1994/2164 and 3138, SI 1995/1649, SI 1997/1897, SI 1998/2166, SI 1999/524, SI 2000/2670, SIs 2001/775 and 1656 and SI 2003/331, SIs 2005/520 and 2797, SI 2006/1541 and SI 2007/1099 made under Sch 11 to the CA 1989.
[4] See paras 4.15 ff.

4.4 In 2005 the Government issued a consultation paper *A Single Civil Court?*. This was stated to be the first phase in a scoping study to assess the case for unifying the civil jurisdictions of the High Court, county courts and family proceedings courts.[1] Then in August 2006, the Government issued a further consultation paper *'Family Procedure Rules – a new procedural code for family proceedings'*.[2] In its response[3], the Government accepted the strong support for an alignment of procedures in all levels of court. Procedures and powers would be aligned in the following areas: to order disclosure against a third party; to stay proceedings; to issue a witness summons; appointing, changing and removing a solicitor; authenticating documents; and providing for evidence by way of affidavit. There would also be consideration of other procedures suitable for alignment, in particular, whether magistrates' courts should have a general power to grant interim injunctions in family proceedings.

1   Consultation Paper CP 06/05 (03/02/2005). Responses were published on 19 October 2005. As regards proposals to unify family jurisdiction, responses were largely favourable. Ministers concluded that reform to create single Civil and Family Courts with unified jurisdictions would be feasible and beneficial and decided to adopt this as a long-term objective, although primary legislation would be required.
2   CP 19/06.
3   Published on 22 February 2008.

1. Jurisdiction

4.5 Jurisdiction to make 'Part I orders'[1] over children is governed by the Family Law Act 1986.[2] Accordingly, jurisdiction to make a s 8 order other than in circumstances where divorce, nullity or judicial separation proceedings are continuing, vests in the UK court of the jurisdiction where the child is habitually resident;[3] and failing that, in the UK court of the place where the child is physically present.[4]

Jurisdiction of the courts in England and Wales is amended by the European Communities (Matrimonial Jurisdiction and Judgments in Matrimonial and Parental Responsibility Matters) Regulations 2005[5] so as to comply with Council Regulation (EC) No 2201/2003 of 27 November 2003[6] which has direct effect on domestic law.

1   Ie a s 8 order (but not an order varying or discharging such an order) and orders (other than a variation or a revocation) made by the High Court under its inherent jurisdiction so far as it gives care of a child to any person or provides for contact with, or the education of the child: Family Law Act 1986, s 1(1)(a), (d).
2   As amended by Council Regulation (EC) No 2201/2003 of 27 November 2003 (Brussels II Revised), see para 4.5.
3   See eg *Re S (A Minor) (Custody Habitual Residence)* [1998] AC 750, [1997] 4 All ER 251, [1997] 1 FLR 122, CA.
4   See eg *Re M (a minor) (immigration: residence order)* [1995] 2 FCR 793, [1993] 2 FLR 858.
5   SI 2005/265.
6   For discussion of which see paras 5.127 ff and further see *Clarke Hall and Morrison on Children*, 1[577.1] and see *Re A; HA v MB (Brussels II Revised: Article 11(7) Application)* [2007] EWHC 2016 (Fam), [2008] 1 FLR 289 where a contact order was made in respect of a child whose return the French court had declined to order under art 13(b).

4.6 There is no specific provision establishing the jurisdiction for an application under Pt IV of the CA 1989. In relation to s 8 orders there is jurisdiction if the child was habitually resident in England or Wales or present in England and Wales at the relevant[1] time and not habitually resident in any other part of the United Kingdom.[2] In relation to public law proceedings it has been held that, as the child may be in need of care and protection, a non-restrictive interpretation of jurisdiction should be adopted. Accordingly, the jurisdiction under Pt IV is at least as extensive as that for s 8 orders under Pt II of the CA 1989.[3] Indeed it is more extensive in that it has been held that where a child was living in England at the time of the application but was habitually resident in Scotland, the child's presence at the time of the application gave the court jurisdiction throughout the duration of the proceedings, since any other interpretation would undermine the scheme of the Act to provide protection for children where appropriate.[4]

[1]   Relevant time, ie at the commencement of the proceedings or any continuous action preceding them: *Re M (a minor) (care order: significant harm)* [1994] 2 AC 424, [1994] 3 All ER 298. The relevant date is the same whether it is alleged that the child is suffering harm or is likely to suffer harm: *Southwark London Borough Council v B* [1998] 2 FLR 1095.
[2]   Family Law Act 1986, s 3(1).
[3]   *Re R (Care Orders: Jurisdiction)* [1995] 1 FLR 711.
[4]   *Re M (care orders: jurisdiction)* [1997] 1 FCR 109, [1997] 1 FLR 456. For jurisdiction in respect of parental responsibility orders or agreements, see paras 3.55, 3 61.

2. The High Court

4.7 The jurisdiction of the High Court was amended so far as was necessary to take account of the CA 1989 and was subsequently modified to accommodate proceedings under the Human Fertilisation and Embryology Act 1990 ,appeals under the Criminal Justice Act 1991 in respect of orders authorising the use of secure accommodation[1] and the provisions of Brussels II Revised[2]. The Human Embryology and Fertilisation Bill before Parliament will make substantial amendments to the 1990 Act and will further impact on the work of the Family Division.

[1]   See para 9.40.
[2]   See note to para 4.5.

3. County court

4.8 There are, for the purposes of the Children (Allocation of Proceedings) Order 1991, the following classes of county court: divorce county courts, family hearing centres[1] and care centres.[2] In addition there are non-designated county courts which retain jurisdiction over domestic violence proceedings and also adoption centres and intercountry adoption centres.[3]

Family hearing centres are competent to hear applications under Pts I and II of the CA 1989.[3] The general scheme is that these centres hear all contested s 8 applications made under Pt II.[4] Family hearing centres are not competent to hear care and related proceedings transferred from the family proceedings court. Such applications have to be heard by the care centres.[5] Care centres and the Principal Registry of the Family Division have full jurisdiction in both public and private law cases. Designated care judges, who act as the Chairman of the local Family Justice Council[6] are based at care centres together with nominated care judges and nominated district judges. Special jurisdictional arrangements have been made for London in that the Principal Registry of the

Family Division is designated for the purposes of the 1991 Order as being a divorce county court, a family hearing centre and a care centre.[7]

1   Listed in Sch 1 to the Order.
2   Listed in Sch 2 to the Order.
3   Listed in Schs 3 and 4 to the Order.
3   Children (Allocation of Proceedings) Order 1991, arts 16 and 17.
4   Children (Allocation of Proceedings) Order 1991, art 16.
5   Children (Allocation of Proceedings) Order 1991, art 18.
6   See para 1.33.
7   Children (Allocation of Proceedings) Order 1991, art 19.

4. Magistrates' courts

4.9 Jurisdiction in family proceedings in the magistrates' court is that of a District Judge (Magistrates' Court) or justices sitting in the family proceedings court. A District Judge (Magistrates' Court) must be nominated by the Lord Chief Justice to sit in family proceedings courts[1] and must sit as chairman with one or two lay justices unless it is impracticable to do so.[2] The Bench Training and Development Committee (or in Greater London or in those areas where the Lord Chief Justice has made a direction, the Family Training and Development Committee) has responsibility for granting an authorisation, on behalf of the Lord Chief Justice, for a justice to hear family proceedings[3].

A family panel comprises those justices authorised to sit as a member of a family proceedings court[4] and there is a family panel for each local justice area except where the Lord Chief Justice has given approval for combination of two or more panels[5]. In Greater London there is one family panel[6]. After appointment but before commencing to sit, panel members are required to undertake induction training and a course of basic training after they have commenced sitting. Responsibility for appraisal of family magistrates and for the list of those approved to sit as chairmen of family proceedings courts, is that of the Bench Training and Development Committee or in Greater London or in those areas where the Lord Chief Justice has made a direction, the Family Training and Development Committee[7].

A bench which includes lay justices must include so far as is practicable both a man and a woman.[8]

1   Constitutional Reform Act 2005, s 7(2)(c) and the Family Proceedings Courts (Constitution of Committees and Right to Preside) Rules 2007, SI 2007/1610, r 3(3). In practice, the President of the Family Division, as Head of Family Justice, exercises the power of nomination on behalf of the Lord Chief Justice.
2   Magistrates' Courts Act 1980, s 66(1) and see the Courts Act 2003, s 26(4).
3   Justices of the Peace (Training and Development Committee) Rules 2007, SI 2007/1609, r 37.
4   Family Proceedings Courts (Constitution of Committees and Right to Preside) Rules 2007, rr 2 and 3(2).
5   Family Proceedings Courts (Constitution of Committees and Right to Preside) Rules 2007, rr 3 and 5.
6   Family Proceedings Courts (Constitution of Committees and Right to Preside) Rules 2007, r 5(2).
7   Justices of the Peace (Training and Development Committee) Rules 2007, r 37.
8   Magistrates' Courts Act 1980, s 66(2).

The justices' clerk

4.10 The function of the justices' clerk is to provide expert legal advice to the lay justices and to conduct the ordinary business of the court[1]. The number of justices' clerks is reducing and there will (outside London) be one justices' clerk for each area of HM Courts' Service (and three in the London area, including one with exclusive responsibility for family proceedings courts). Justices' clerks are required to be barristers or solicitors of five years' standing and are appointed by the Lord Chancellor after consultation with the Lord Chief Justice[2]. One or more assistants to the justices' clerk may be appointed by the Lord Chancellor and be specifically designated as such[3]. Assistant justices' clerks must have such qualifications as may be prescribed[4]. The role of the clerk may be performed by the Clerk to the Justices himself or may be delegated to one of the assistants to justices' clerks under the FPC(CA 1989)R 1991[5], which also extend the clerk's powers in interlocutory matters.

Both justices' clerks and assistant justices' clerks exercising any function exercisable by a justice of the peace or any advisory functions on matters of law, practice and procedure, are not subject to the directions of the Lord Chancellor or any other person.[6]

The clerk is required by the rules[7] in consultation with the justices to record the reasons for their decision in writing before[8] the decision is announced. This requires a greater presence in the retiring room than in other proceedings[9] and it is acknowledged that the clerk will frequently assist with the structure of the reasons.[10]

No transcript is taken of proceedings in the family proceedings court but the clerk is required to keep a note of the oral evidence that is given at the hearing[11] and the clerk must take notes which are as complete as possible and which must be sufficient to support the findings of the justices.[12]

The clerk has some powers to make interlocutory orders in proceedings. However, these powers are limited as follows. A clerk may not make any s 8 order and may only make an interim order in public law proceedings in the limited circumstances set out in r 28 of the FPC(CA 1989)R 1991, ie not unless:

(a)   a written request for such an order has been made to which the parties and any children's guardian consent and which they or their representatives have signed;

(b)   a previous such order has been made in the same proceedings, and

(c)   the terms of the order sought are the same as those of the last such order made.

---

1   See the Courts Act 2003, s 28 and the *Practice Direction: (criminal: consolidated)* [2002] 3 All ER 90.
2   See the Courts Act 2003, s 27(2).
3   Courts Act 2003, s 27(5).
4   See the Assistants to Justices' Clerks Regulations 2006, SI 2006/3405.
5   Rule 32 and see the Justices' Clerks Rules 2005, SI 2005/545 amended by SI 2005/2796 and SI 2006/2493.
6   Courts Act 2003, s 29 (other than a justices' clerk in the case of an assistant).

7   FPC(CA 1989)R 1991, r 21(5).
8   FPC(CA 1989)R 1991, r 21(5).
9   *Practice Direction: (criminal: consolidated) [2002] 3 All ER 904 55.*
10 CAAC Report 1991/92, p 10 and see *Re W (A Minor) (Contact)* [1994] 1 FLR 843. Also, J Hunt *Professionalising Lay Justice – The Role of the Court Clerk in Family Proceedings* (Lord Chancellor's Dept 2002).
10 FPR 1991, r 4.20; FPC(CA 1989)R 1991 r 20.
11 See *C v Surrey County Council* [1994] 2 FCR 165, sub nom *Re C (A Minor) (Contribution Notice)* [1994] 1 FLR 111.

5. Judiciary

4.11 The President of the courts of England and Wales, including the High Court, county courts and magistrates' courts, is the Lord Chief Justice whose functions include training and guidance of the judiciary and the maintenance of appropriate arrangements for the deployment of the judiciary and the allocation of work within courts.[1] Statutory provision is made for rule-making and for the giving of directions.[2] The President of the Family Division of the High Court is 'Head of Family Justice'[3]. responsible for approving the various types of judge to whom family proceedings may be allocated.[4] Authorisation to sit in family proceedings is by the obtaining of a 'ticket' of which the relevant ones for proceedings under the CA 1989 are for 'public law' and 'private law' (there is also an 'adoption ticket' for proceedings under the Adoption and Children Act 2002). Circuit judges and recorders with a public law ticket, and district judges of the Principal Registry have jurisdiction to hear *any* application under the 1989 Act, as do district judges with a public law ticket who are nominated to hear all proceedings. Other district judges with a public law ticket may hear all proceedings except that in care proceedings under Pt IV they may only hear: interlocutory/unopposed/opposed hearings where the application is for an order under s 34 (a contact order) and the principle of contact is unopposed, proceedings for interim care or supervision orders under s 38 and the variation of such orders under s 39(3), proceedings for an education supervision order under s 36 and for the extension and discharge of such orders under paras 15(2), or 17(1) of Sch 3.

Even where they do not have an adoption ticket, circuit judges and those district judges nominated to hear all proceedings may hear applications under the Adoption and Children Act 2002, s 21 (placement orders) when they are heard in conjunction with care proceedings under s 31 of the CA 1989 and relate to the same child.

Designated family judges are circuit judges based at the care centres and have primary responsibility for hearing the care cases transferred from the magistrates' courts and chair the local Family Justice Councils.

District judges who do not have a private ticket have a more limited jurisdiction in that they have jurisdiction only in respect of interlocutory hearings and unopposed trials, but also have jurisdiction in applications under s 10 of the CA 1989 for a s 8 order in *opposed* trials limited to where:

'(a)   the application is for a contact order and the principle of contact with the applicant is unopposed; or

(b)   the order is (or is one of a series of orders which is):
      (i)   to be limited in time until the next hearing or order, and
      (ii)   the substantive application is returnable before a judge ... who
              has full jurisdiction in all circumstances.'[5]

A deputy district judge only has jurisdiction in interlocutory matters or unopposed hearings.

The effect of the 2002 Amendments to the Allocation Directions was to create a private law ticket for district judges enabling them to hear a wide range of cases under Pts I and II of the 1989 Act. The 2007 amendments take the process further and enable the creation of a cadre of district judges who may hear all proceedings under the Act. The policy underlying this is to establish three tiers of judiciary across the family courts: the High Court, circuit bench and the third tier across the county courts and magistrates' courts comprising district judges, district judges (magistrates' courts) and lay justices.

1   Constitutional Reform Act 2005, s 7.
2   Constitutional Reform Act 2005, s 12 and Sch 1, Pt 1 and s 13 and Sch 2, Pt 1 and the Courts Act 2003, s 81.
3   Constitutional Reform Act 2005, s 9.
4   By means of the Family Proceedings (Allocation to Judiciary) Directions [1999] 2 FLR 799 amended by the Family Proceedings (Allocation to Judiciary) (Amendment) Directions 2002 [2002] 2 FLR 692; (Amendment) Directions 2003 [2003] 2 FLR 373; (Amendment) Directions 2005 [2006] 1 FLR 1147; (Amendment No 2) Directions 2005 [2006] 1 FLR 1150; (Amendment) Directions 2007 [2007] 1 FLR 1150.
5   Family Proceedings (Allocation to Judiciary) Directions as amended.

6. The legal profession

4.12 The need for a non-adversarial approach and the avoidance of delay in the conduct of proceedings requires advocates to have the necessary expertise.[1] In public law cases representation of children is usually undertaken by solicitors from the Law Society's Children Panel who are specially trained and assessed as having the necessary skills but this does not necessarily apply to representation of parents which may cause undue delay. Solicitors may also be members of the Law Society's Family Panel and many solicitors who practise in family cases are also members of 'RESOLUTION' (formerly the Solicitors' Family Law Association) and, if they have passed the necessary written examination, members of the family panel. There is no equivalent Panel for barristers although they may become members of the Family Law Bar Association and they are subject to continuing professional development including the completion of an annual quota of training.

The Law Society has published a 'Family Law Protocol' with the support of the Solicitors' Family Law Association, the Legal Services Commission and the Lord Chancellor's Department which sets out best practice for practitioners in all aspects of private law family disputes and incorporates the Solicitors' Family Law Association Code of Practice for members.[2]

Consideration of the duties on parties in the *Practice Direction*[3] highlights that the practitioner in public law proceedings will need to have considerable skills and experience if they are to meet the requirement of helping the court to further the overriding objective. Other duties imposed on them include: assisting in preparing a timetable for the child; preparing a case summary; assisting in preparing draft case management orders (para 3.5); retaining their own record containing copies of the documents on the court's Case Management Record (para 3.8); attending advocates' meetings (para 3.11); monitoring compliance with the court's directions (para 5.5).

1   For the responsibility of solicitors and counsel to prevent delay, see *B v B (Child Abuse: Contact)* [1994] 2 FLR 713; and in pre-hearing reviews, see *Re G (children) (care proceedings: wasted costs)* [1999] 4 All ER 371, [1999] 3 FCR 303, [2000] 1 FLR 52 and to ensure proper preparation of the case, see *Re R (Care: Disclosure: Nature of Proceedings)* [2002] 1 FLR 755.
2   The Law Society 2002. See particularly, Pt III: Children (private law).
3   *Practice Direction (Guide to Case Management in Public Law Proceedings)*, see Appendix 3.

7. Unrepresented parties and McKenzie friends

4.13 Subject to the discretion of the magistrates, it had been a long-standing practice that any person may be assisted in proceedings before the family proceedings court by a 'McKenzie friend'[1] or by representation by a person who does not have a statutory right of audience. In the higher courts, the practice has generally been to restrict representation to those advocates who have a statutory right of audience although the court has discretion to grant a right of audience to any person in any proceedings[2].

Unrepresented litigants became an issue for the High Court as more parties were appearing unrepresented owing to the shrinking availability of legal aid and the shift to the provision of 'support services' for the unrepresented. However, there was a problem about the disclosure of the case papers to persons providing the assistance or a mediation service. Disclosure was initially addressed by guidance from the President[3] and this guidance was amplified by the Court of Appeal in *Re O (children) (Hearing in Private: Assistance)*[4]. In fact disclosure in these circumstances was subsequently dealt with by amendments to the procedure rules[5] and the President has complemented the rules with the following guidance:

> 'In the light of the growth of litigants in person in all levels of family court, the President issues this guidance, which supersedes that of 13th May 2005 [2005] Fam Law 405, and is to be regarded as a reminder that the attendance of a McKenzie friend will often be of advantage to the court in ensuring the litigant in person receives a fair hearing.
>
> A litigant who is not legally represented has the right to have reasonable assistance from a layperson, sometimes called a McKenzie Friend ("MF"). This is the case even where the proceedings relate to a child and are being heard in private.
> - A litigant in person wishing to have the help of a MF should be allowed such help unless the judge is satisfied that fairness and the interests of justice do not so require. The presumption in favour of permitting a MF is a strong one.

- A litigant in person intending to make a request for the assistance of a MF should be encouraged to make the application as soon as possible indicating who the MF will be.
- It will be most helpful to the litigant in person and to the court if the particular MF is in a position to advise the litigant in person throughout the proceedings.
- A favourable decision by the court, allowing the assistance of a MF, should be regarded as final and not as something which another party can ask the court to revisit later, save on the ground of misconduct by the MF or on the ground that the MF's continuing presence will impede the efficient administration of justice.
- When considering any request for the assistance of a MF, the Human Rights Act 1998 Sch 1 Part 1 Article 6 is engaged; the court should consider the matter judicially, allowing the litigant reasonable opportunity to develop the argument in favour of the request.
- The litigant in person should not be required to justify his desire to have a MF; in the event of objection, it is for the objecting party to rebut the presumption in favour of allowing the MF to attend.
- Factors which should not outweigh the presumption in favour of allowing the assistance of a MF include
  − the fact that proceedings are confidential and that the court papers contain sensitive information relating to the family's affairs
  − the fact that the litigant in person appears to be capable of conducting the case without the assistance of a MF
  − the fact that the litigant in person is unrepresented through choice
  − the fact that the objecting party is not represented
  − the fact that the hearing is a directions hearing or case management hearing
  − the fact that a proposed MF belongs to an organisation that promotes a particular cause
- The proposed MF should not be excluded from the courtroom or chambers while the application for assistance is made, and the MF should ordinarily be allowed to assist the litigant in person to make the application.
- The proposed MF should produce a short curriculum vitae or other statement setting out relevant experience and confirming that he/she has no interest in the case and understands the role of a MF and the duty of confidentiality.
- If a court decides in the exercise of its discretion to refuse to allow a MF to assist the litigant in person, the reasons for the decision should be explained carefully and fully to both the litigant in person and the would-be MF.
- The litigant may appeal that refusal, but the MF has no standing to do so.
- The court may refuse to allow a MF to act or continue to act in that capacity where the judge forms the view that the assistance the MF has given, or may give, impedes the efficient administration of justice. However, the court should also consider whether a firm and unequivocal warning to the litigant and/or MF might suffice in the first instance.
- Where permission has been given for a litigant in person to receive assistance from a MF in care proceedings, the court should consider the attendance of the MF at any Advocates' Meetings directed by the court, and, with regard to cases commenced after 1.4.08, consider directions in accordance with paragraph 13.2 of the Practice Direction. Guide to Case Management in Public Law Proceedings.

- The litigant in person is permitted to communicate any information, including filed evidence, relating to the proceedings to the MF for the purpose of obtaining advice or assistance in relation to the proceedings.
- Legal representatives should ensure that documents are served on the litigant in person in good time to seek assistance regarding their content from the MF in advance of any hearing or advocates' meeting.

What a McKenzie Friend May Do
- Provide moral support for the litigant
- Take notes
- Help with case papers
- Quietly give advice on:
  points of law or procedure;
  issues that the litigant may wish to raise in court;
  questions the litigant may wish to ask witnesses.

What a McKenzie Friend May Not Do
- A MF has no right to act on behalf of a litigant in person. It is the right of the litigant who wishes to do so to have the assistance of a MF.
- A MF is not entitled to address the court, nor examine any witnesses. A MF who does so becomes an advocate and requires the grant of a right of audience.
- A MF may not act as the agent of the litigant in relation to the proceedings nor manage the litigant's case outside court, for example, by signing court documents.

Rights of Audience
- Sections 27 & 28 of the Courts and Legal Services Act 1990 govern exhaustively rights of audience and the right to conduct litigation. They provide the court with a discretionary power to grant lay individuals such rights.
- A court may grant an unqualified person a right of audience in exceptional circumstances and after careful consideration. If the litigant in person wishes the MF to be granted a right of audience or the right to conduct the litigation, an application must be made at the start of the hearing.

Personal Support Unit & Citizens' Advice Bureau
- Litigants in person should also be aware of the services provided by local Personal Support Units and Citizens' Advice Bureaux. The PSU at the Royal Courts of Justice in London can be contacted on 020 7947 7701, by email at cbps@bello.co.uk or at the enquiry desk. The CAB at the Royal Courts of Justice in London can be contacted on 020 7947 6564 or at the enquiry desk.'[6]

---

[1] It was first confirmed that the term 'McKenzie friend' had judicial approval in *Re O (Children) (Hearing in Private: Assistance)* [2005] EWCA Civ 759, [2006] Fam 1, [2005] 2 FCR 563.

[2] Courts and Legal Services Act 1990, s 27(2)(c).

[3] Guidance issued by the Office of the President of the Family Division relating to McKenzie Friends [2005] Fam Law 405.

[4] [2005] EWCA Civ 759, [2006] Fam 1, [2005] 2 FCR 563.

[5] FPR 1991, r 10.20A and the FPC(CA 1989)R 1991, r 23A.

[6] [2008] 2 FCR 90.

ALLOCATION OF PROCEEDINGS

4.14 The CA 1989 for practical purposes created a single jurisdiction in family matters exercisable by magistrates' courts, county courts and the High Court.[1] The allocation of proceedings is principally governed by the Children (Allocation of Proceedings) Order 1991. However, for the purpose of piloting the provisions of the Public Law Outline, courts have been using the President's draft allocation guidance. It was expected that a new Allocation Order would be made to replace the 1991 Order in time for the implementation of the Public Law Outline. Unfortunately, the making of the new Order has been delayed. Proposals for a new Order are currently the subject of a consultation exercise with a view to a final version being made in the Autumn of 2008.

[1] See paras 4.2 ff. The 1991 Order is to be revoked and replaced by a new order in due course.

1. Commencement of proceedings

4.15 By art 3 of the Children (Allocation of Proceedings) Order 1991 certain proceedings, namely those concerning local authorities (including, principally, care and related proceedings, those concerning the Child Support Act 1991 and applications for parental orders under the Human Fertilisation and Embryology Act, s 30) have to be commenced in a magistrates' court. Under art 4, applications to extend, vary or discharge orders made under the CA 1989 must be made to the court that made the original order. Apart from these provisions the 1991 Order does not regulate the court level at which other proceedings under the 1989 Act must be started. However many other cases will be 'self regulating' in the sense that those concerning children in divorce cases must be made, in the first instance, to a divorce county court, while those concerning children in maintenance applications under the Domestic Proceedings and Magistrates' Court Act 1978 must be made to a magistrates' court. Where a special guardianship order is in force, an application for leave to change the child's name or remove the child from the United Kingdom under s 14C(3) of the Act is to be made to the court which made the order.[1] There is, however, no substantive restriction on the initial allocation of 'free standing' applications for s 8 orders or other Pt I orders under the CA 1989 but practice has determined the more suitable venue for certain applications.[2]

[1] Children (Allocation of Proceedings) Order 1991, art 3C as inserted by the Children (Allocation of Proceedings) (Amendment No. 2) Order 2005, SI 2005/2797. Specific provision is made for adoptions with a foreign element or where an application is made under the Adoption and Children Act 2002 when an application for an adoption is pending, see arts 3A and 3B (as inserted by SI 2005/2797).
[2] See paras 4.27 and 4.32.

4.16 Where an application under the CA 1989, Pts I, II and Sch 1 is made to a county court, it is to be commenced in a 'designated county court' i.e a divorce or civil partnership proceedings county court.[1] If, however, an application is made for a s 8 or s 14A (special guardianship) order in a divorce county court which is not also a family hearing centre then if the court is notified that the application will be contested, it must be transferred to a family hearing centre[2]. Where applications under Pts III to V of the CA 1989 are to be commenced in a county court, they must be commenced in a care centre.[3]

1 Children (Allocation of Proceedings) Order 1991, art 14.
2 Children (Allocation of Proceedings) Order 1991, art 16(1).
3 Children (Allocation of Proceedings) Order 1991, art 18(1).

2. Transfer of proceedings

4.17 The rules for transferring proceedings under the CA 1989 are solely governed by the Children (Allocation of Proceedings) Order 1991 as amended.[1] Provision is made for the transfer of proceedings under the CA 1989 from one magistrates' court to another by art 6; from one county court to another by art 10 and for the transfer of proceedings from a magistrates' court to a county court by arts 7 and 9 and vice versa by art 11. Provision is also made for the transfer of cases from a county court to the High Court and vice versa under arts 12 and 13.

1 Ie ss 38 and 39 of the Matrimonial and Family Proceedings Act 1984 do not apply: art 5.

Contravention of order

4.18 Article 21 of the Children (Allocation of Proceedings) Order 1991[1] specifically provides that proceedings commenced or transferred in contravention of the order are not invalid and no appeal lies against the determination of proceedings on the basis of such contravention alone.

1 SI 1991/1677, as amended.

PROCEDURE

1. The Private Law Programme and the Public Law Outline

4.19 The statutory Rules remain as the procedural framework for proceedings under the CA 1989 but, as has been noted above[1], these have been supplemented by Practice Directions. As regards private and public law proceedings it is essential to be aware of this additional guidance.

The Private Law Programme[2] provides that where an application is made to the court under Pt II of the CA 1989, the welfare of the child will be safeguarded by the application of the overriding objective[3] of the family justice system in three respects:

- Dispute resolution at first hearing;
- Effective court control including monitoring outcomes against aims;
- Flexible facilitation and referrals (matching resources to families).

A *First Hearing Dispute Resolution* hearing is listed in a target window of four to six weeks from issue of the application. At this stage the court would identify immediate safety issues; identify the aim of the proceedings and set the timescale. Importance is placed on early dispute resolution and arrangements in court conciliation have been put in place in county courts[4] for a CAFCASS officer to be available to facilitate early dispute resolution rather than the provision of a formal report, and, where appropriate, the family may be referred to locally available resolution services. The *Private Law Programme* emphasised the need for effective court control, judicial continuity, continuous case management and correct allocation which were taken up in public law proceedings, first in the *Judicial Protocol*[5] and then in the new *Public Law Outline.*

The latest *Practice Direction (Guide to Case Management in Public Law Proceedings)*[6] includes within it an outline of the stages applicable to proceedings in public law proceedings. These are referred to in more detail below, but in essence, there are four stages:

- *First Appointment* to confirm allocation of the case and give initial case management directions.
- *Case Management Conference* to enable the case management judge or case manager, with the co-operation of the parties, actively to manage the case and, at the earliest practicable opportunity to—
  (1) identify the relevant and key issues; and
  (2) give full case management directions including confirming the Timetable for the Child.
- *Issues Resolution Hearing* before the Final Hearing to—
  (1) identify any remaining key issues; and
  (2) as far as possible, resolve or narrow those issues.
- *Hearing*

1 See para 4.2.
2 Office of the President of the Family Division 9 November 2004.
3 Set out in more detail in the Guide to Case Management in Public Law Proceedings *para 2.*
4 Similar arrangements have been made for family proceedings courts where practicable.
5 *Protocol for Judicial Case Management in Public Law in Public Law Children Act Cases* annexed to *Practice Direction (Care Cases: Judicial Continuity and Judicial Case Management)* [2003] 1 WLR 737, [2003] 1 FLR 719.
6 Set out in full at Appendix 3. The new guidance is referred to as the *Public Law Outline* (this title is given precedence in the published version) but the PLO is actually the title of a table in Part 9 of the *Practice Direction.*

2. Rules

4.20 Proceedings under the Children Act are governed by two sets of rules: the FPR 1991[1] in the case of High Court or county court applications, and the FPC(CA 1989)R 1991[2] in the case of magistrates' courts. At the time the 1989 Act was implemented, it was not possible to formulate one set of rules for all three courts, however, the rules are, so far as practicable, to the same effect.[3] Responsibility for making rules for all three levels of courts is now that of the Family Procedure Rule Committee. Following an earlier consultation, *Family Procedure Rules – a new procedural code for family proceedings,*[4] the

Ministry of Justice has announced[5] proposals for new rules to provide a single code of practice for all family courts in modern language accessible to all court users. Examples of modernised procedures would be service of documents by e-mail and the replacement of affidavits by 'statements of truth'.[6]

1   SI 1991/1247, amended by SI 1991/2113, SIs1992/456 and 2067, 1993/295, SIs 1994/808, 2165, 2890 and 3155, SIs 1996/816 and 1674, SIs 1997/637, 1056 and 1893, SI 1998/1901, SIs 1999/1012 and 3491, SI 2000/2267, SI 2001/821, SIs 2003/184 and 2839, SI 2004/3375, SIs 2005/264, 412, 559, 617, 1976 and 2922, SIs 2006/352 and 2080 and SIs 2007/1622, 2187 and 2268.

2   SI 1991/1395, amended by SI 1991/1991, SI 1992/2068, SI 1993/627, SIs 1994/809, 2166 and 3156, SI 1997/1895, SIs 2001/615 and 818, SI 2003/2840, SI 2004/3376, SIs 2005/229, 413, 585, 617, 1977 and 2930 and SI 2007/2188.

3   The Lord Chancellor was responsible for the High Court and county courts and the Home Secretary for the magistrates' courts. Responsibility for magistrates' courts was transferred to the Lord Chancellor by the Transfer of Functions (Magistrates' Courts and Family Law) Order 1992, SI 1992/709.

4   CP 19/06 30 August 2006. The consultation was part of the implementation of the White Paper 'Justice for All' (Cm 5563) and the proposals for a unified court administration,

5   News Release 020–08 22 February 2008.

6   Post-consultation report February 2008. See further, para 4.4 above.

3. Forms

4.21 At all court levels proceedings are commenced by application either on a prescribed form or where there is no form, in writing. In certain applications such as those under s 8 where the applicant is not entitled to make an application, he must obtain the leave of the court.[1] In the magistrates' court the applicant must obtain the leave of the justices' clerk[2] when making an ex parte application or an emergency protection order.[3] The Rules prescribe a number of forms which include a 'core' application form, which for certain applications is supplemented by an additional form. Application is made in respect of a family where appropriate instead of each child as formerly[4]. In accordance with the non adversarial, inquisitorial nature of proceedings, the object of the forms is to ensure disclosure of relevant information at any early stage. In addition to full details of the child and the applicants, forms may require a description of the child's circumstances, the family structure, the reasons for making the application and proposals for the child's upbringing if an order is made; full disclosure is expected. As 'harm' to a child includes harm arising from seeing domestic violence[5], particular provision is made for identifying this as an issue at an early stage.[6] In private law proceedings for a s 8 order however, the emphasis is on avoiding the situation being inflamed by restricting the opportunity of the parties to make allegations and counter allegations so as to provide an opportunity for mediation to be explored. Accordingly, the information which may be supplied with the forms is limited and parties may not, for example, file statements until such time as the court directs.[7]

1   See paras 5.112 ff.

2   Or authorised legal adviser, see para 4.10.

3   FPC(CA 1989)R 1991, r 4(4).

4   Although for statistical purposes the number of individual children is still recorded.

5   Section 120 of the Adoption and Children Act 2002 amended the definition of 'harm' in s 31 of the Children 1989 Act to include impairment suffered from seeing or hearing the ill-treatment of another. See also Chapter 2, above.

6   Various forms were amended by SI 2005/412 (FPR 1991) and SI 2005/413 (FPC(CA 1989)R 1991) to include a question whether a child concerned has suffered or is at risk of suffering harm form domestic abuse.
7   FPC(CA 1989)R 1991, r 17(4), (5); FPR 1991, r 4.17(4), (5).

4. Filing the application

4.22 The applicant must file his application together with sufficient copies to be served on each applicant.[1] A case number will then be applied to each application and a court file created. In public law proceedings the provisions of the current rules have been overlaid by the obligations imposed by the *Practice Direction (Guide to Case Management in Public Law Proceedings)*[2] and require the local authority to file not only the application form but also the supplemental PLO 1 and the 'Checklist documents' ie those documents it is required to disclose from its files and those and the following documents it is required to prepare for the proceedings: Schedule of Proposed Findings; Initial Social Work Statement; Care Plan and Allocation Record and Timetable for the Child. In accordance with the *Practice Direction: Residence and Contact Orders (9 May 2008)*[3] where in proceedings for a contact or residence order, any question arises about residence or about contact between a child and a parent or other family member, immediately on receipt of an application for a residence order or a contact order, the court must send a copy of the application to CAFCASS for an initial screening to be undertaken in accordance with their safeguarding policies.

Files are in a standard format to facilitate transfer between the three levels of court and there are additional requirements in public law proceedings, the *Practice Direction (Guide to Case Management in Public Law Proceedings)*[4] provides:

'The Case Management Record
    3.7   The court's filing system for the case will be known as the Case Management Record and will include the following main documents—
        (1)   the Supplementary Form PLO1 which will be the index of documents on the Record;
        (2)   in care and supervision proceedings, any Letter Before Proceedings and any related subsequent correspondence confirming the Local Authority's position to parents and others with parental responsibility for the child;
        (3)   the Case Management Documentation[4];
        (4)   Standard Directions on Issue and on First Appointment;
        (5)   the Draft Case Management Orders approved by the court.
    3.8   Parties or their legal representatives will be expected to retain their own record containing copies of the documents on the court's Case Management Record.'

1   FPR 1991, r 4.4(1)(a); FPC(CA 1989)R 1991, r 4(1)(a).
2   See Appendix 3.
3   [2008] 2 FCR 273, [2008] 2 FLR 103.
4   Defined in para 3.5 of the *Practice Direction*.

5. Fees

4.23 In contrast to criminal courts, civil and family courts are mostly funded by court users through fees. A new fee structure was been implemented from

1 May 2008 by HMCS[1]. There was an alignment of fees in family proceedings in county courts and family proceedings courts but the most significant change was the increase in fees for child care proceedings and the introduction of a system of incremental fees. One aim of the new fee structure is to support the PLO as, for example, cases identified for an early final hearing are likely to attract significantly lower fees than those cases which proceed through all stages where the total fee would amount to £4,825 (not including any fee for a placement application)[2]. However, the greatly increased level of fees required a transfer of subsidy from HMCS to local authorities[3].

The fees payable in care proceedings are a first fee of £2,225 payable on an application. The second fee of £700 is payable if an issues resolution hearing or pre-hearing review is listed, the third fee of £1,900 is payable if a final hearing is listed (both the second and third fee are payable at least 14 days before the hearing). Provisions are made for refunds in certain circumstances.

[1]   Family Proceedings Fees Order 2008, SI 2008/1054; Magistrates' Courts Fees Order 2008, SI 2008/1052 made under the Courts Act 2003, s 92.
[2]   The total of approximately £5000 matches the estimate of the cost of a s 31 case to HMCS as set out in the *Review of Care Proceedings* (DCA/DfES 2006 para 3.2).
[3]   Although there was a process of consultation, the introduction of higher fees prompted the Family Justice Council, the judiciary, the Law Society and the NSPCC to express their concern that such fees would deter local authorities from seeking care orders promptly, or at all, as the money transferred to local authorities was not ring fenced ((2008) Times, 28 April). See further, paras 14.16 and 14.26.

6. Service

4.24   On receipt of the filed documents the court must fix the date, time and place for a hearing or directions appointment,[1] endorse the date so fixed on form C6 (and form C6A where appropriate – notice of hearing to parties and non-parties) and return them to the applicant.[2] The applicant must then serve the endorsed copy of the application within the number of days prescribed before the date fixed for the hearing or directions appointment on each respondent. The respondents and those on whom notice must be given are prescribed for each type of proceeding by the Schedule to the rules.[3] Detailed rules about service are contained in the FPR 1991, r 4.8 and the FPC(CA 1989)R 1991, r 8. Once an application has been made it may only be withdrawn with leave of the court.[4] In the case of applications for a parental responsibility order under s 4, an order under s 8 of or Sch 1 to the Act or special guardianship, the respondent must file and serve an acknowledgement in 14 days.[5] The court has power, inter alia, to abridge the times specified for sending documents.[6] In public law proceedings, detailed provision is made in the *Public Law Outline* as to what steps must be taken at each stage of the proceedings, including issue and the first hearing.[7]

[1]   This will be the 'First Appointment' see The Private Law Programme (private law proceedings) and the *Practice Direction (Guide to Case Management in Public Law Proceedings) Public Law Outline.*
[2]   FPR 1991, r 4.4(2); FPC(CA 1989)R 1991, r 4(2).
[3]   FPR 1991, App J; FPC(CA 1989)R 1991, Sch 2.
[4]   FPR 1991, r 4.5; FPC(CA 1989)R 1991, r 5. See *Re N (Leave to Withdraw Care Proceedings)* [2000] 1 FLR 134.

7. Parties

4.25 In public law proceedings, the child and any person with parental responsibility for the child will automatically be given party status.[1] The court may also direct that others be joined to the proceedings. The court may direct that a father not having parental responsibility should not be served with notice[2] or that he be discharged from the proceedings.[3] If a father, without parental responsibility, wishes to participate in the proceedings, he should be permitted to do so, unless there was some justifiable reason for not joining him as a party.[4] Similarly, a person against whom allegations have been made (but who is not a party) could be given leave to intervene and permitted to take part in the proceedings to the limited extent of his involvement, but has no right to be made a party.

1 FPC(CA 1989)R 1991, Sch 2.
2 *Re X (care: notice of proceedings)* [1996] 3 FCR 91, [1996] 1 FLR 186.
3 *Re W (Discharge of Party to Proceedings)* [1997] 1 FLR 128.
4 *Re B (Care Proceedings: Notification of Father Without Parental Responsibility)* [1999] 2 FLR 408. See *Re P (care proceedings: father's application)* [2001] 3 FCR 279, [2001] 1 FLR 781 where a very late application to be joined as a party was refused as to grant the application would disrupt and delay the proceedings which had already been listed for trial. The father's human rights had to be balanced against the child's need to obtain a resolution of proceedings.

4.26 In addition to the parties and others on whom notice must be served as specified in the rules, in 'relevant'[1] proceedings, any person may file a request in writing[2] that he or another be joined as a party (or cease to be a party).[3] The court may of its own motion, join a person as a party. At or before the first directions appointment in, or hearing of, relevant proceedings, the applicant shall file a statement that service of a copy of the application has been made on each respondent, and notice of the proceedings has been effected under the FPR 1991, r 4.4(3); FPC(CA 1989)R 1991, r 4(3); and the statement shall indicate:

(a)   the manner, date, time and place of service; or
(b)   where service was effected by post, the date, time and place of posting.[4]

In private law proceedings, a child is not normally a party and is not represented before the court. The child's views are made known to the court by a CAFCASS officer if one has been appointed. However, in some circumstances, these provisions are not sufficient. In such cases, the rules in county courts and the High Court[5] provide for a child to have the right to instruct a solicitor. This is discussed below[6].

Service on behalf of a child shall be effected by the solicitor acting for the child, or where there is no such solicitor, the children's guardian, or the court administration. Service on a child shall be effected by service on the solicitor acting for the child, or where there is no solicitor, the guardian, or where there is neither a solicitor nor a guardian, with leave of the justices' clerk or the court, the child.

1 Ie proceedings under the CA 1989, any statutory instrument made under the CA 1989 or any amendment made by the CA 1989 in any other enactment: FPC(CA 1989)R, r 1; the CA 1989, s 93(1) and see the FPR 1991, r 4.1.
2 Form C2. The absence of a written request does not automatically invalidate the order. The facts and circumstances, including the urgency of the situation, must be considered: *Re O (Minor) (Leave to Seek Residence Order)* [1994] 1 FLR 162, per Ewbank J.
3 FPR 1991, r 4.7(2); FPC(CA 1989)R 1991, r 7(2).
4 FPR 1991, r 4.8(7), FPC(CA 1989)R 1991, r 8(7).
5 FPR 1991, rr 9.1, 9.2, 9.2A.
6 See paras 10.49 ff.

8. First hearing

4.27 On receipt of an application in public or private law proceedings, the court administration must fix a date for a hearing or directions appointment.[1] In private law proceedings this may be a *First Hearing Dispute Resolution Appointment* in a county court or analogous hearing in a family proceedings court[2] or in public law proceedings, the *First Appointment*[3]. Directions may be given by the court or by a district judge (High Court and county court) or a single justice or justices' clerk (family proceedings court). Directions may be issued under the FPR 1991, r 4.14(2) or the FPC(CA 1989)R 1991, r 14(2). In public law proceedings, the court will issue standard directions in accordance with the Public Law Outline[3] and the expectations of the court in private law proceedings are set out in *the Private Law Programme*.

There will be further hearings in public law proceedings, such as the *Issues Resolution Hearing,* in accordance with the Public Law Outline[4].

1 FPR 1991, r 4.4(2); FPC(CA 1989)R 1991, r 4(2).
2 See *The Private Law Programme* (2005).
3 See the *Practice Direction (Guide to Case Management in Public Law Proceedings)*.
4 See Appendix 3.

9. Directions

4.28 Directions may be given of the court's own motion, in which case the parties must have been given notice and the opportunity to make representations, or on the written request of one party either on notice to the other parties or with their written consent.[1] In difficult child cases it is bad practice for directions to be sought and given in writing without the attendance of the parties.[2] In practice, the most convenient course is for the court to arrange an oral hearing at which the parties are required to attend.[3] Counsel who have conduct of the substantive hearing should attend if possible.[4] In 'specified' (ie public law) proceedings the children's guardian must attend unless excused by the court,[5] whereas in private law proceedings a children and family reporter may be ordered to attend.[6] Directions given in one court can be carried forward until amended, if the case is allocated to another court.[7]

1 FPR 1991, r 4.14(3); FPC(CA 1989)R 1991, r 14(5).

2 *Re A and B (Minors) (No 2)* [1995] 1 FLR 351, per Wall J.
3 FPR 1991, r 4.16; FPC(CA 1989)R 1991, r 16.
4 *Re MD and TD (children's cases: time estimates)* [1994] 2 FCR 94.
5 FPR 1991, r 4.11A(4); FPC(CA 1989)R 1991, r 11A(4).
6 FPR 1991, r 4.13(3); FPC(CA 1989)R 1991, r 13(3).
7 FPR 1991, r 4.14(9); FPC(CA 1989)R R 1991, r 14(11).

4.29 In a county court where a difficult case is likely to be heard by the judge, the district judge should direct that an appointment for directions should be listed before the judge who is to hear it or before the designated judge[1] who may then maintain control over the course of the case.[2] In a family proceedings court for practical reasons the majority of directions appointments are conducted by the justices' clerk. However, the justices' clerk does not have the same extensive powers to deal with interlocutory matters as that of a district judge. The justices' clerk may not grant leave for a person to become a party to proceedings and where he considers it inappropriate to make a direction on a particular matter he must refer it to a full court. The justices' clerk may not make any s 8 order and may only make an interim order in public law proceedings in the limited circumstances set out in r 28 of the FPC(CA 1989)R 1991.[3] Accordingly, directions appointments may be conducted by the justices' clerk before the normal sitting of the court.[4] If, for example, the parties agree to an interim or final order the matter can then be referred to a full court sitting later that day although with the increase in business in some courts, directions appointments may be listed separately with time slots of sufficient length to permit full exploration of the issues while reducing waiting time for the parties.

In care proceedings in the family proceedings court, the justices' clerk must, in accordance with the Public Law Outline, fix a return date for a hearing before the court which may then determine whether any interim order is required although a children's guardian may be appointed in advance by the justices' clerk.[5]

Where initial screening[6] by CAFCASS indicates that there are issues of domestic violence which may be relevant to the court's determination, the court may give directions about the conduct of the hearing,for written evidence to be filed by the parties before the hearing and, where appropriate, for special arrangements to secure the safety of any party or child attending any hearing. At the first hearing, the court must inform the parties of the content of any screening report or other information which has been provided by CAFCAS unless it considers that to do so would create a risk of harm to a party or the child and determine as soon as possible whether it is necessary to conduct a fact-finding hearing. Reasons must be recorded for a finding that such a hearing is not necessary. The court should consider the need for a s 7 report and separate representation of any child (for which upward transfer would be necessary).[7]

Otherwise an application under the CA 1989 should be listed for an early directions appointment. A directions appointment is more informal than a court hearing and in the county court will be in the district judges' chambers, in the magistrates' court in any available room or a court room whichever is most suitable. The court is expected to adopt a proactive and rigorous approach to the issues in the case with a view to ensuring that all the issues have been appropriately defined and addressed.[8]

1   *B v B (Child Abuse: Contact)* [1994] 2 FLR 713 at 736, per Wall J.
2   *Re A and B (Minors) (No 2)* [1995] 1 FLR 351. For judicial continuity, see para 4.34.
3   See para 4.10.
4   CAAC Report 1992/93, p 50.
5   Justices Clerks' Rules 2005, Sch, para 38; FPC(CA 1989)R 1991, r 10.
6   See para 4.22.
7   See the *Practice Direction: Residence and Contact Orders* (9 May 2008) [2008] 2 FCR 273, [2008] 2 FLR 103.
8   See the *Practice Direction (Guide to Case Management in Public Law Proceedings)* and the *Private Law Programme*, also *Re G (children) (care proceedings: wasted costs)* [1999] 4 All ER 371, [1999] 3 FCR 303, [2000] 1 FLR 52.

4.30 The court is required to make a note of any oral evidence that is given although proceedings are normally conducted by representations.[1] Directions must be recorded in writing and served on parties who were not present[2] but this is in reality done in all cases. Each direction should specify precise dates for compliance and should not be left open ended.[3] Good practice would suggest that the court administration should record in a diary the dates by which the various directions should be complied with. Documents received by the court should be date stamped on receipt and the listing officer can prompt the parties where necessary. At the conclusion of a directions appointment the case must never be adjourned generally; a date must be set for either a further directions appointment or a hearing before the court.[4]

1   FPR 1991, r 4.20; FPC(CA 1989)R 1991, r 20. For considerations whether the court should limit oral evidence see paras 4.51 ff.
2   FPR 1991, r 4.14(10); FPC(CA 1989)R 1991, r 14(12).
3   See *Re A and B (Minors) (No 2)* [1995] 1 FLR 351.
4   See the *Handbook of Best Practice in Children Act Cases* (CAAC 1997).

10. Case management

4.31 Guidance on case management in public law cases has been given by the President in the *Practice Direction (Guide to Case Management in Public Law Proceedings)*[1] and the detailed steps in care proceedings are discussed below. The key principles of case management are set out in the initial paragraphs of the *Practice Direction* in the form they will assume when the new Family Proceedings Rules are issued. In relation to private law proceedings, the *Private Law Programme* is to similar effect although not as detailed.

This guidance is supplemented by the *Practice Direction (Family Proceedings: Court Bundles)*:[2] which has the aim of achieving consistency in the preparation of court bundles and other related matters.

The *Practice Direction* provides that in care proceedings, case management functions may normally be performed in the High Court and a county court by a judge or district judge, and in a magistrates' court by a family proceedings court, a single justice or the 'case manager' i.e. a justices' clerk (including an assistant justices' clerk specifically authorised by a justices' clerk to exercise case management functions),

The main principles of case management in Public Law Proceedings are set out in the *Practice Direction*:

– *judicial continuity* of case management judges (in the case of magistrates' courts, case managers), who will be responsible for every case management stage in the proceedings through to the Final Hearing and, in relation to the High Court or county court, one of whom may be – and where possible should be – the judge who will conduct the Final Hearing;
– *main case management tools*: each case will be managed by the court by using the appropriate main case management tools;
– *active case management*: each case will be actively case managed by the court with a view at all times to furthering the overriding objective;
– *consistency*: each case will, so far as compatible with the overriding objective, be managed in a consistent way and using the standardised steps provided for in this Direction.

1 [2008] which is set out in full in Appendix 3.
2 [2006] 2 FCR 833.

11. Reviewing allocation

4.32 The allocation decision is currently regulated by the Children (Allocation of Proceedings) Order 1991.[1] However, there will in due course, be a new Allocation Order. In the interim period, allocation of public law proceedings is to be made in accordance with the *President's Guidance* which, although described as 'draft' and used initially for those courts piloting the Public Law Outline, is now to be followed by all courts in public law cases.[2]

1 SI 1991/1677, as amended.
2 See para 4.41.

(a) Public law

4.33 On receipt of the application, the clerk of the court will consider whether the proceedings should be transferred to a higher court or consolidated with other proceedings. The Children (Allocation of Proceedings) Order 1991[1] provides that a magistrates' court may, on application by a party or of its own motion, transfer a case to the county court, where it considers it in the interests of the child having regard to delay, whether it would be appropriate for the proceedings to be heard with other pending proceedings and whether the proceedings are exceptionally grave, important or complex in particular because of:

(a) complicated or conflicting evidence about the risks involved to the child's physical or moral well-being or about other matters relating to the welfare of the child;
(b) the number of parties;
(c) a conflict with the law of another jurisdiction;

(d)   some novel or difficult point of law; and
(e)   some question of general public interest.

In public law and private law cases, the purpose of the First Appointment is to confirm allocation of the case and give initial case management directions.[2] Previous studies had shown that the average delay between application and decision to transfer was 10 weeks[3] but there appeared to be wide variations in practice.[4]

[1]   SI 1991/1677, as amended.
[2]   *Practice Direction* (*Guide to Case Management in Public Law Proceedings*) para 3.9 and the *Private Law Programme*, p 5, para 4.
[3]   *Scoping Study on Delay in Children Act Cases* (Lord Chancellor's Dept 2002) para 103.
[4]   In a sample considered by MCSI the period varied between nil and 22 weeks: MCSI *A Review of Case Administration in Family Proceedings Courts* (May 2001) para 2.13.

4.34 Article 9 provides that, in the event of a refusal by a magistrates' court to transfer such proceedings, any party to the case may then apply to the appropriate care centre for a transfer. In that latter event the proceedings can be transferred to the care centre, the High Court or sent back to the magistrates' court. If a district judge orders the transfer of proceedings to a magistrates' court in accordance with art 11, an appeal against that decision may be made to a judge of the Family Division of the High Court or to a circuit judge (except where the order was made by a district judge or deputy district judge of the Principal Registry).[1]

[1]   Children (Allocation of Proceedings) (Appeals) Order 1991, SI 1991/1801.

4.35 The county court may transfer a case to the High Court, having regard to:[1]

(a)   delay;
(b)   whether the proceedings are appropriate for determination in the High Court; and
(c)   whether such determination would be in the interests of the child.

[1]   The Children (Allocation of Proceedings) Order 1991, SI 1991/1677, art 12.

4.36 In earlier editions of this work, we noted that transfers aimed at significantly accelerating proceedings to the county court did not appear to be common. Nor were lateral transfers as these were generally confined to the need to consolidate proceedings, or because one or more of the parties was resident within the receiving court's jurisdiction.[1] The 'complexity' provisions were the most common reason for transfer.[2] The power to transfer public law cases down from the county court to the family proceedings court was reported as being rarely used.[3] We suggested that the significance of proper use of the power to transfer cases would seem now to be greater because of the pressure on court resources created by a steady increase in the number of applications in care proceedings.[4] Furthermore, the *Review of Care Proceedings*[5] highlighted the increasing cost of care proceedings[6] and, although there were severe capacity issues in care centres, 66% of cases were being disposed of there. Even though there was capacity in FPCs, the proportions of cases being transferred (to the county court) was increasing[7]. In the context of a downturn in performance, the Chief Executive of HMCS commented:

'Significant increases in the volume of applications in 2005 and increased complexity due to legislation requiring concurrent planning of care/placement orders are felt to be key contributors this downturn.'[8]

1   See the third edition (2002) para 4.29.
2   75% of all transfers in public law cases: *Scoping Study on Delay in Children Act Cases* (Lord Chancellor's Dept 2002) para 99 (a figure remarkably consistent with the 74% in the CAAC Report 1993/94, Table 1B, p 70).
3   Seventy four cases over the three-year period 1996–1998: *Scoping Study on Delay in Children Act Cases* (Lord Chancellor's Dept 2002) para 100.
4   From 2,657 care applications in 1992 (artificially low post the implementation of the CA 1989) to 13,421 in 2006 (Judicial Statistics 2006, Table 5.3) The figures refer to the number of children subject to each application. The 2006 figure show a decrease of 7% from 2005. There is some doubt as to the accuracy of the official figures (which acknowledge known data quality issues with the figures for family proceedings courts which are likely to be an undercount. See Beckett *The Great Care Proceedings Explosion* BJSW (2001) 31, 493–501.
5   *Review of the Child Care Proceedings System in England and Wales* (DCA/DfES 2006).
6   The average cost of s 31 care and supervision proceedings was estimated at £25,000 and although the volume of legal aid bills for care proceedings had risen by 42% in the previous five years, expenditure in real terms had increased by 102%.
7   *Review of the Child Care Proceedings System in England and Wales* 2006, para 3.3.
8   HMCS Chief Executive's Report 2006/07.

COMPLEXITY

4.37 In *C v Solihull Metropolitan Borough Council*[1] Ward J said that a serious and unexplained injury to a baby was a grave and important case and should be transferred up from a magistrates' court. Where there is a conflict in the evidence of professionals of significant experience eg medical experts, the magistrates should consider whether the case should be transferred to a county court which could then consider whether to transfer the case to High Court.[2]

1   [1993] 1 FLR 290.
2   *Re S (A Minor)* (20 July 1992, unreported), FD (referred to in CAAC Report 1993/94, p 50).

4.38 Early estimates of the impact of the allocation provisions were that between 15% to 25% of all cases would make their way to the higher courts.[1] More recent data suggested that family proceedings courts dealt with about two thirds of public law cases[2] but there was some evidence that these proportions varied considerably in different areas. Variations between circa 6–7% and 50% of cases being transferred up to the county court from family proceedings courts had been identified[3] and in one case more than 50%.[4] There was considerable debate about the length of cases which could be tried in magistrates' courts but views settled on four to five days provided magistrates were available to sit on consecutive days and there were no complex issues[5].

The *Scoping Study on Delay in Children Act Cases*[6] examined perceptions of the level of service provided by family proceedings courts. Local authorities and children's guardians considered family proceedings courts provided an efficient and effective service but legal professionals considered that they could be slow and sometimes lacked case management skills. The *Scoping Study* identified the following problems:

- case management in some family proceedings courts;
- waiting for magistrates' written reasons;
- justices' clerks having insufficient sanctions to enforce directions.

1   CAAC Report 1992/93, p 46. The CAAC Report 1993/94 (Table 1A, p 70) suggested that approximately 80% of public law cases are dealt with by the magistrates' court.
2   *Scoping Study on Delay in Children Act Cases* (Lord Chancellor's Dept 2002) para 80 and see *Review of the Child Care Proceedings System in England and Wales* (2006) para 3.13.
3   (Beckett: Anglia Polytechnic University 2000).
4   The MCSI thematic review *A Review of Case Administration in Family Proceedings Courts* (May 2001) identified a Magistrates' Courts Committee where more than 50% of cases had been transferred (Table 1). The *Review of the Child Care Proceedings* para 3.13 reported that 66% of s 31 proceedings are disposed of in care centres,
5   CAAC Report 1993/94, p 50. Subsequently followed in practice, see MCSI *A Review of Case Administration in Family Proceedings Courts* (May 2001).
6   Lord Chancellor's Department 2002.

(b) Private law

4.39 The rules governing the transfer of private law proceedings are less specific than those governing public law. In contrast to art 7, art 8 merely states that where a magistrates' court 'having regard to the principle set out in s 1(2) [ie the need to avoid unnecessary delay] ... considers that in the interests of the child the proceedings can be dealt with more appropriately in [a] county court it may order the transfer accordingly'. *R v South East Hampshire Family Proceedings Court, ex p D*[1] however, establishes that when considering whether to transfer a case to a county court, a magistrates' court shall not limit consideration merely to the single issue of delay as provided for by art 8 but have regard to the overriding principle that the welfare of the child is the paramount consideration and consider other matters, such as complexity, before refusing an application. Applications can now be made under art 9(4) to the county court following a magistrates' clerk's refusal to transfer a private law case. Further, art 11(2) permits a county court to transfer a private law case back down to a magistrates' court.

1   [1994] 2 All ER 445, [1994] 1 FCR 620, [1994] 2 FLR 190.

4.40 Article 12 of the 1991 Order[1] empowers county courts to transfer proceedings to the High Court. In the private law context it is established that the following types of cases should be heard in the High Court:

- applications by children for leave to apply for s 8 orders;[2]
- applications for sterilisation of a child;[3]
- cases in which HIV tests for children are being sought;[4]
- cases in which it is sought to impose a restraint upon the freedom of the press;[5]
- contact cases where the mother has persistently opposed and withheld contact;[6]

- cases in which a party seeks leave of the court to withhold information from the parties;[7]
- claims for declarations of incompatibility under s 4 of the Human Rights Act 1998 or cases raising an issue which may lead to the court considering making such a declaration;[8] (but it is neither necessary nor desirable to transfer proceedings to a superior court level merely because a breach of convention rights is alleged).[9]
- cases, particularly those involving litigants in person, in which there are unresolved allegations of possible breaches of the Hague or European conventions on International Child Abduction.[10]
- cases in which applicants are seeking the return of a child following an art 13 Hague Abduction convention non-return order made by another EU Member State (other than Denmark).[11]

Applications for leave to remove children from the jurisdiction should be made either to the High Court or county court depending upon the complexity or difficulty.[12]

[1]   The Children (Allocation of Proceedings) Order 1991, SI 1991/1677, art 12.
[2]   *Practice Direction (applications by children: leave)* [1993] 1 All ER 820 (but only the application for leave and not necessarily the substantive application).
[3]   *Re HG (Specific Issue Order: Procedure)* [1993] 1 FLR 587; *Practice Note (Official Solicitor: Sterilisation)* [1996] 2 FLR 111.
[4]   *Re X (a minor)* [1994] 2 FCR 1110, sub nom *Re HIV Tests* [1994] 2 FLR 116n.
[5]   *Re H-S (minors) (protection of identity)* [1994] 3 All ER 390, sub nom *Re H (Minors) (Injunction: Public Interest)* [1994] 1 FLR 519, CA.
[6]   *Re S (Children: Uncooperative Mother)* [2004] EWCA Civ 597, [2004] 2 FLR 710.
[7]   *Re C (Disclosure)* [1996] 1 FLR 797.
[8]   *Practice Direction (Human Rights Act 1998: citation of authorities)* [2000] 2 FCR 768, [2000] 2 FLR 429.
[9]   *Re V (Care Proceedings: Human Rights)* [2004] EWCA Civ 54, [2004] 1 FCR 338, [2004] 1 FLR 944, per Wall LJ.
[10] *Re D (Abduction: Acquiescence)* [1998] 2 FLR 335, see also *Re H (Abduction: Habitual Residence: Consent)* [2000] 2 FLR 294. (The same principle would suggest that Brussels II issues should also be moved to the High Court).
[11] See *Re A, HA v MB (Brussels II Revised: Article 11(7) Application)* [2007] EWHC 2016 (Fam), [2008] 1 FLR 289.
[12] *Harris v Pinnington* [1995] 3 FCR 35, sub nom *MH v GP (Child Emigration)* [1995] 2 FLR 106.

(c) Draft President's Guidance and new Allocation Order

4.41 As referred to above[1], the President has issued guidance on allocation as part of the development of the *Public Law Outline* and it is intended that it will be replaced by a new Allocation Order in due course. The new guidelines lay emphasis on a more case specific and local approach and the need for close consultation and agreement between the family proceedings court and the county court on such matters as the availability/experience of magistrates and judges and present/anticipated pressures on listing.

General considerations include:

- allocation must be addressed speedily at the outset of every case and be kept under effective review to enable for example cases whose complexity has reduced to be transferred to the family proceedings court and vice versa;
- whilst the bulk of the work suitable for trial by lay magistrates may fall in the 2–3 day hearing category, there may occasionally be cases of up to 5 days which it would be appropriate for them to hear (but rarely exceeding 5 days);
- time estimates should include all aspects of procedure from the reading of the documents to the preparation and delivery of the magistrates' reasons.
- Some District Judges (Magistrates' Courts) could be expected to handle slightly longer cases and length of trial is a factor in the county court as between a circuit judge and district judge having regard to complexity and listing difficulties for district judges in accommodating cases of any length;
- volume of written evidence might indicate a case is not suitable for the family proceedings court;
- where judicial continuity is likely to be required over a period of time;
- the possibility of transferring to the county court to determine a single issue of difficulty or sensitivity rather than transferring the whole case;
- listing availability may be the deciding factor where the decision on allocation is finely balanced.

Once a case has been allocated, similar factors will decide which of the available tribunals will hear the case ie lay justices or district judge (magistrates' court) in the family proceedings court, circuit judge, district judge or recorder in the county court.

In all allocation/listing decisions, attention must be paid to the personal circumstances of the litigants which make it particularly difficult for them, eg travel or expenditure, to attend at certain courts.

In private law proceedings, the 1991 Allocation Order contains minimal guidance and the President has supplemented this with the following factors:

Against hearing in the family proceedings court

- recent proceedings in the county court (other than divorce and ancillary relief proceedings which have been concluded);
- other proceedings pending in the county court;
- disputed allegations of sexual abuse or of serious non-accidental injury or serious emotional or physical abuse or ill treatment of a child or disputed allegations of particularly serious domestic violence;
- where the instant hearing is unlikely to resolve the issues finally and significant possibility of an intractable or prolonged dispute and enforcement proceedings;
- relatively complex cases eg because of amount of evidential material; number of parties; characteristics of the parties eg age or mental incapacity etc; possible need for appointment of guardian for child in private proceedings; particularly demanding conflicts in the evidence of

141

lay witnesses; disputed expert evidence with a degree of complexity;[2] number of witnesses; sensitivity of the case; novel or difficult points of law, unusual features of eg cultural, religious or racial considerations not within the expertise of the family proceedings court, the active involvement of another jurisdiction, international considerations such as abduction or considerations as to the wider family abroad;

- where a child may be invited to give evidence or request to do so;
- where there is an issue as to whether part of the evidence should be withheld from a party;
- where there is real reason to suppose that the process or the outcome may have consequences for those involved which are unusually grave;
- contested applications to remove a child permanently or temporarily from the jurisdiction.

Factors for trial in the family proceedings court:

- straightforward applications for parental responsibility or s 8 order;
- special guardianship even where the application involves disputed facts eg as to whether there has been domestic violence etc provided the dispute does not introduce particular complexity;
- other proceedings pending in the family proceedings court.

Other relevant factors

- availability of conciliation facilities.

Cases for hearing in the Family Division of the High Court

The draft guidance makes it plain that the resources of the High Court are limited and should be reserved for exceptional cases. Except in exceptional cases, no case should be transferred to the High Court without prior consultation with the Family Division Liaison Judge for the Circuit by the Designated Family Judge for the court in which the case is proceeding. The draft guidance lists factors which will *not* normally justify transfer to the High Court. These include:

- Intractable problems with regard to contact;
- Sexual abuse;
- Injury to a child which is neither life-threatening nor permanently disabling;
- Routine neglect, even if it spans many years and there is copious documentation;
- Temporary or permanent removal to a Hague Convention country;
- Standard human rights issues;
- Uncertainty as to immigration status;
- Celebrity of the parties;
- Anticipated length of the hearing;
- Quantity of the evidence, written and oral;
- Number of experts;
- Possible availability of a speedier hearing.

The draft guidance then sets out twelve examples of where a High Court hearing is likely to be appropriate.

It is not clear, why the making of a new Allocation Order has been delayed. The thrust of the draft allocation guidance is to cascade work from the High Court to the county court. In turn this requires a new distribution of business between the county courts and family proceedings courts. Magistrates are reported as being anxious to take on more family business and this will require some tuning of any final settlement.

1 Paragraph 4.32.
2 Very few cases where there is a disagreement between two or more experts other than social work witnesses on material issues, will be suitable for hearing in the family proceedings court. However, dependant on the subject matter, it may be appropriate for the family proceedings court to hear certain cases in which the dispute is between unanimous experts and a parent or party on the other, e g that a bruise on a non-ambulant child was inflicted but such a court should never hear a case in which a parent contests unanimous medical evidence as to the cause of cerebral bleeding.

12. Ordering welfare reports

4.42 The court is not bound to order welfare reports in every case.[1] If delay would prejudice the child's welfare, the court might have to balance the advantages to be gained from a report against the disadvantage of the time it takes to obtain it.[2] It has been held that the decision whether to ask for a welfare report lies within the judge's discretion and cannot be appealed.[3] Reports can be ordered at any stage of proceedings. In the case of magistrates' courts proceedings a single justice can order a report.[4] In any case where domestic violence is raised as an issue, the court should consider directing that a report on the question of contact, or any other matters relating to the welfare of the child, be prepared under s 7 of the 1989 Act unless it is satisfied that it is not necessary to do so in order to safeguard the child's interests.[5] If a report is ordered, a date for the hearing should be fixed and not listed for hearing 'on the first open date after the court welfare officer's report is available'. The desirable practice is to ascertain when the report can be expected and to fix a specific date in the light of that information.[6] Once appointed, the proper officer or justices' clerk must notify the welfare officer of any decisions made during the course of the proceedings and of the date for hearings, for example, in connection with applications to withdraw an application.[7]

1 The appointment and duties of CAFCASS officers are considered in Chapter 10.
2 Cf *Re H (Minors) (Welfare Reports)* [1990] 2 FLR 172, CA.
3 *Re W (Welfare Reports)* [1995] 2 FLR 142, CA.
4 FPC(CA 1989)R 1991, r 2(5)(c).
5 *Practice Direction: Residence and Contact Orders (9 May 2008)* [2008] 2 FCR 273, [2008] 2 FLR 103.
6 *B v B (minors: residence and care disputes)* [1994] 2 FCR 667, sub nom *B v B (Minors) (Interviews and Listing Arrangements)* [1994] 2 FLR 489, per Wall J. New National Standards have been issued by CAFCASS see para 10.10 and see '*Putting Children and Young Persons First: Principles and National Standards Draft Policy – A Consultation Paper.*' (CAFCASS May 2002).
7 FPR 1991, r 4.5; FPC(CA 1989)R 1991, r 5.

13. Timetable for proceedings

4.43 In proceedings in which any question of making a s 8 order arises, ie generally private law proceedings, and where the court is hearing an application under Pt IV (care and supervision proceedings), a court is required to draw up a timetable with a view to disposing of the application without delay and to give such directions as it considers appropriate for the purpose of ensuring, so far as is reasonably practicable, that the timetable is adhered to.[1] The court may be robust in insisting that any timetable is met such as in *Re B and T (care proceedings: legal representation)*[2] where parents who had failed to comply with directions were effectively precluded from legal representation by the refusal of an application made by solicitors who had just been instructed for an adjournment on the first day of a five day hearing. Having regard overall to the fairness of the proceedings and the need to balance the rights of the parents against the rights of the children to an early determination of their future, the parents' rights under art 6(1) of the European Convention on Human Rights (ECHR) were not breached.

[1] At present on average, a s 31 case takes 51 weeks in Care Centres and 42 weeks in FPCs from application to disposal (*Review of the Child Care Proceedings* para 3.2). Delay in public law proceedings has been an ongoing concern since the implementation of the 1989 Act. It was initially expected that care proceedings would be concluded in three months (CAAC Report 1991/92, p 2) but this proved not to be the case and there followed a sequence of reports aimed at tackling delay, eg Dame Margaret Booth: *Avoiding Delay in Children Act Cases* (Lord Chancellor's Dept 1996); MCSI *A Review of Case Administration in Family Proceedings Courts* (May 2001); Lord Chancellor's Dept *Scoping Study on Delay in Children Act Cases* (2002). Public Service Agreement 4 between the Ministry of Justice and HMCS aims to increase the proportion of s 31 cases completed within 40 weeks.

[2] [2001] 1 FCR 512.

14. Service of statements

4.44 Parties must file and serve on the parties and any officer of CAFCASS:

(a) written statements of the substance of the oral evidence which the party intends to adduce at the hearing or directions appointment; and

(b) copies of any documents, including experts' reports upon which the party intends to rely, at or by such time as the court directs.[1]

In proceedings for a s 8 order or a special guardianship order no statement or copy may be filed until such time as the court directs,[2] and no file, document information or statement, other than those required or authorised by the Rules, should be served or made without leave of the court.[3] Subject to any direction of the court about the timing of statements, supplementary statements may be filed, as can, with leave, written amendments to the documents already served.[4]

Evidence or documents not filed in accordance with the Rules cannot be addressed or relied on at the subsequent directions appointment or hearing without leave of the court.[5] The principles of the law of evidence and their application to proceedings relating to children are discussed in detail in Chapter 11.

¹   FPR 1991, r 4.17(1); FPC(CA 1989)R 1991, r 17(1).
²   FPR 1991, r 4.17(5); FPC(CA 1989)R 1991, r 17(5).
³   FPR 1991, r 4.17(4); FPC(CA 1989)R 1991, r 17(4).
⁴   FPR 1991, rr 4.17(2) and 4.19; FPC(CA 1989)R 1991, rr 17(2) and 19.
⁵   FPR 1991, r 4.17(4); FPC(CA 1989)R 1991, r 17(4).

15. Sanctions

4.45   There are no direct sanctions for breach of directions and the nature of family proceedings makes it difficult to apply direct sanctions to a party or his representative without putting at risk the paramountcy of the child's welfare. Nevertheless, some breaches might amount to professional misconduct[1] and, as the *Practice Note (Case Management)*[2] makes plain, the court does have power in appropriate circumstances to make an award of costs against a party or personally against his representative. In addition, where in the High Court and county court the direction is properly phrased in injunctive terms,[3] it is clear that a failure to comply would be punishable as a contempt. In the magistrates' court a similarly worded direction made by the court (but not by a single justice or the clerk) might be punishable under s 63(3) of the Magistrates' Courts Act 1980.[4]

¹   Cf *Re M* (1989) Times, 29 December, CA.
²   [1995] 1 All ER 586, [1995] 1 FLR 456, (now superseded by the *Practice Direction (Guide to Case Management in Public Law Proceedings)* and the *Private Law Programme* see para 4.36. In the similarly constructed Criminal Procedure Rules 2005, SI 2005/384 as a result of amendments introduced as from 1 April 2008 by SI 2007/3662, a new r 3.5(6) provides:

'If a party fails to comply with a rule or a direction, the court may—

(a)   fix, postpone, bring forward, extend, cancel or adjourn a hearing;

(b)   exercise its powers to make a costs order; and

(c)   impose such other sanction as may be appropriate'.

³   See para 5.164.
⁴   See para 5.171.

16. Reading time

4.46   Justices who are to deal with a case must read any documents before the hearing.[1] They should be able to do this at their leisure rather than under the pressure of knowing that the parties, their advocates and witnesses are waiting.[2] Justices' clerks are encouraged where practicable to deliver the papers to the justices at their homes.[3] There is no equivalent procedural rule for the higher courts but in complex cases the same judge should have conducted the final directions appointment and should be familiar with the case. If not, it would be difficult for proper control to be exercised over the course of the evidence[4] and it is difficult to see how the *Public Law Outline* will be effective without adequate reading time. Furthermore, in all issues of any substance, the directions hearings should always consider judicial reading time and the listing offices should be contacted to ensure that the required reading time is allocated.[5]

1 FPC(CA 1989)R 1991, r 21(1). This is mandatory: *S v Merton London Borough* [1994] 1 FCR 186, even for an interim hearing: *Hampshire County Council v S* [1993] Fam 158, [1993] 1 All ER 944.
2 *M v C (Children Order: Reasons)* [1993] 2 FLR 584.
3 CAAC Report 1992/93, p 51.
4 See *Practice Note: Case Management* [1995] 1 All ER 586, [1995] 1 FLR 456.
5 *Re A Care Hearing* [2002] Fam Law 484, FD.

COURT HEARINGS

1. Privacy and restrictions on reporting proceedings

4.47 There is a restriction on the persons who may be present at hearings of 'family proceedings' before family proceedings courts[1] and where it is considered expedient in the interests of the child, representatives of the press may be excluded.[2] Hearings and direction appointments in the High Court and county court concerning proceedings under the CA 1989, are, unless the court otherwise directs, heard in chambers.[3]

Although the general rule in art 6(1) of the European Convention on Human Rights requires civil proceedings to be held in public, a state may designate a class of proceedings as an exception to the general rule. Exclusion of press and public can be justified in order to protect the privacy of a child and parties and to avoid prejudicing the interests of justice. Furthermore, the publishing of such judgments is not required to be made available to the public.[4]

Publicity in proceedings before magistrates is restricted by statute.[5] In all family courts, it is an offence to publish any material intended or likely to identify any child involved in the proceedings[6] but this protection only applies until the proceedings are concluded[7]. In the higher courts limited protection is given by s 12 of the Administration of Justice Act 1960[8] but the High Court may impose specific restrictions under its inherent jurisdiction[9] or may, conversely, give leave for confidential information to be disclosed for other purposes.[10]

In *Re D, F v M*[11], Munby J expressed the view that 'In view of the current climate and increasing complaints of "secrecy" in the family justice system, a broader approach to make judgments public may be desirable'[11]. As a response to another decision of Munby J[12] and amendments to s 12 of the Administration of Justice Act 1960, the rules have been amended to provide greater clarity to the circumstances in which information relating to proceedings concerning children being heard in private can be communicated from one person/body to another[13]. The Department of Constitutional Affairs also issued a consultation paper in 2006 entitled *'Confidence and Confidentiality: Improving Transparency and Privacy in Family Courts'*.[14] A summary of responses was published on 22 March 2007, and the Government responded by publishing proposals for change in *'Confidence and confidentiality: Openness in family courts – a new approach'*.[15] In the light of the degree of opposition from those representing children's interests, the Government focussed on improving the openness of family courts not by the numbers or types of people going *in* to the courts, but by the amount and quality of information coming *out* of the courts. The new measures were to be piloted. The proposals also invited consultation[16] on two further aspects: whether to widen disclosure rules on information and how best to protect the identity of children beyond the end of proceedings. The results of the pilot schemes and the consultation are awaited.

1 Magistrates' Court Act 1980, s 69.
2 FPC(CA 1989)R 1991, r 16(7).
3 FPR 1991 r 4.16(7). For the appellate courts, see the Domestic and Appellate Proceedings (Restrictions of Publicity) Act 1968, s 1 (appellate courts). See *Re P-B (a minor) (child cases: hearing in open court)* [1997] 1 All ER 58, [1996] 2 FLR 765, CA. See also *Re B (Hearings in Open Court)* [1997] Fam Law 508. For a review of privacy in family proceedings generally, see *Clibbery v Allen* [2002] EWCA Civ 45, [2002] 1 All ER 865, [2002] 1 FCR 385.
4 *B v United Kingdom* [2001] 2 FCR 221, [2001] 2 FLR 261, ECtHR.
5 See the Magistrates' Courts Act 1980, s 71. See also the Children and Young Persons Act 1933, s 49 (proceedings in youth courts).
6 CA 1989, s 97, and see *Pelling v Bruce-Williams* [2004] EWCA Civ 845, [2004] Fam 155, [2004] 3 All ER 871, [2004] 3 FCR 108 (the provisions of s 97(2), (4) restricting publicity of child proceedings, Convention compatible).
7 *Clayton v Clayton* [2006] EWCA Civ 878, [2006] Fam 83, [2007] 1 FLR 11.
8 Section 12 does not prevent publication of the names and addresses or photograph of the child nor of details about the order: *Re L (a minor) (wardship: freedom of publication)* [1988] 1 All ER 418, *Re W (Wards) (Publication of Information* [1989] 1 FLR 246, sub nom *Re W (Minors) (Wardship: Contempt)* [1989] Fam Law 17. What s 12 protects is the privacy and confidentiality: (i) of the documents on the court file; and (ii) of what has gone on in front of the judge in his courtroom, *Kelly v BBC* [2001] Fam 59, [2001] 1 FLR 197; See *X v Dempster* [1999] 1 FLR 894 for Wilson J's list of what may be published.
9 See *Clarke Hall and Morrison on Children*, 1[1215]ff.
10 For example in criminal proceedings, see eg *Re K (Minors) (Disclosure)* [1994] 1 FLR 377.
11 [2004] EWHC 727 (Fam), [2004] 1 FLR 1226, [2004] All ER (D) 41 (Apr).
12 *Re B (A Child: Disclosure)* [2004] EWHC 411 (Fam), [2004] 2 FLR 142.
13 New r 10.20A inserted in the FPR 1991 by SI 2005/1976 (reproduced in Appendix 2); new r 23A inserted in the FPC(CA 1989)R by SI 2005/1977. This rule prescribes who can communicate/disclose what information to whom and for what purpose. Where communication of information is not specifically permitted, it is prohibited, and the rules require that the party should make an application to the court to consider whether disclosure is appropriate.
14 (CP11/06) 11 July 2006.
15 Cm 3171 June 2007.
16 (CP 10/07) 20 June 2007.

2. Order of speeches and evidence

4.48 Subject to any directions given by the court, evidence is adduced in the following order:

- the applicant;
- any party with parental responsibility for the child;
- other respondents;
- the children's guardian; and
- the child if he is a party to the proceedings and there is no children's guardian.[1]

There is no prescribed order for speeches. This is subject to the direction of the court whose power may extend for example, to declining to hear an advocate's closing speech, although this would be extremely rare.[2]

¹ FPC(CA 1989)R 1991, r 21(2).
² *Re F* [1992] 2 FCR 433, sub nom *F v Kent County Council* [1993] 1 FLR 432.

3. Attendance of child at hearings

(a) *Specified proceedings*

4.49 The child is a party to specified proceedings,¹ but the Rules provide²
that they shall take place in the absence of the child if the court considers it in
the interests of the child, having regard to the matters to be discussed or the
evidence likely to be given, and the child is represented by a children's
guardian or solicitor. The child therefore has no absolute right to attend the
hearing. It should not be routine practice for children to be in the court
throughout care proceedings. This approach has not be affected by the more
recent availability of video link evidence³.

Children's guardians should think carefully about arrangements for children
to be present and be prepared to explain them to the court.³ If a child is likely
to be unruly the court could refuse to allow him to attend.⁴ The decision
whether or not to see the child is a matter for the discretion of the judge.⁵

¹ CA 1989, s 41(6); FPR 1991, rr 4.1(1), 4.2(2); FPC(CA 1989)R 1991, rr 1(2), 2(2),
ie applications in public law proceedings under Pts IV and V of the CA 1989, for secure
accommodation, to cause a child in care to be known by a new surname or to be removed
from the jurisdiction, to approve arrangements for a child in care to live outside England
and Wales, to extend the duration of a supervision order, for the making or revocation of a
placement order under s 21 of the Adoption and Children Act 2002. The Adoption and
Children Act 2002, s 122(1)(b) adds, in circumstances established by rules of court, s 8
private law proceedings to the list of specified proceedings. However, at the date of going
to press, no such rules have been made.
² FPR 1991, r 4.16(2); FPC(CA 1989)R 1991, r 16(2), (7).
³ *Re M (a child) (care proceedings: witness summons)* [2007] EWCA Civ 9, [2007] 1 FCR
253.
³ *Re G (a minor)(appeal)* [1993] 1 FCR 810, sub nom *Re C (A Minor) (Care: Children's
Wishes)* [1993] 1 FLR 832; *Re G (Minor: Care Order)* (1992) Times, 19 November.
⁴ *Re W (A Minor) (Secure Accommodation order: Attendance at Court)* [1994] 2 FLR 1092.
⁵ *Re C (Section 8 Order: Court Welfare Officer)* [1995] 1 FLR 617 and *Re CB (Access:
Court Welfare Report)* [1995] 1 FLR 622. See paras 11.57 ff.

(b) *Private law proceedings*

4.50 In proceedings in the High Court and the county court, the child may
begin and prosecute any family proceedings only by a next friend and may
defend such proceedings only by a guardian ad litem,¹ except where he has the
leave of the court to proceed without a next friend or guardian ad litem or has
a solicitor who is able and willing to take instructions from him². In any
family proceedings, if it appears that it is in the best interest of a child to make
him a party to the proceedings, the court may appoint a guardian ad litem to
take part in the proceedings on his behalf³. The practice formerly was for the
views of the child to be conveyed to the court by means of the report of the
court welfare officer (now children and family reporter). However, this may
not always be a sufficient mechanism by which the court could see and hear

children and give effect to their rights under the European Convention in Human Rights. For example, in *Re A (a Child) (Separate Representation in Contact Proceedings)*[4] there had been allegations that the father had sexually abused the child during supervised contact. The court was satisfied that as there was a possible conflict of interest with the mother. The child needed to be separately represented for the allegations of sexual abuse to be properly investigated as this could not be achieved by a welfare report alone. In any family proceedings where it appears to the court that the child should be made a party and be separately represented, the court will refer the matter to CAFCASS Legal.[5] The circumstances in which it may be appropriate to provide for separate representation is now regulated by the *Practice Direction (Family Proceedings: Representation of Children)* and the accompanying *Practice Note (CAFCASS)*.[6] The *Practice Direction* recognises that an appointment of a guardian ad litem is a step that will be taken only in cases which involve an issue of significant difficulty and consideration should be given to whether an alternative route might be preferable, such as asking a CAFCASS officer to carry out further work or by making a referral to social services or possibly, by obtaining expert evidence. However, circumstances which may justify the making of an order include where:

–   a CAFCASS officer is of the opinion the child should be made a party;
–   the child has a standpoint or interests which are inconsistent with or incapable of being represented by any of the adult parties;
–   there is an intractable dispute over residence or contact, implacable hostility to contact or where the child may be suffering harm associated with the contact dispute;
–   the views and wishes of the child cannot be adequately met by a report to the court;
–   an older child is opposing a proposed course of action;
–   there are complex medical or mental health issues to be determined or there are other unusually complex issues that necessitate separate representation of the child;
–   there are international complications outside child abduction;
–   there are serious allegations of physical, sexual or other abuse in relation to the child or allegations of domestic violence not capable of being resolved with the help of a CAFCASS officer;
–   proceedings concern more than one child and the welfare of the children is in conflict or one child is in a particularly disadvantaged position;
–   there is a contested issue about blood testing.

An appointment may be made by any appropriately nominated judge or district judge[7].

1   FPR 1991, r 9.2.
2   FPR 1991, r 9.2A.
3   FPR 1991, r 9.5.
4   [2001] 2 FCR 55, CA.
5   See *A (a Child) (Separate Representation in Contact Proceedings)* above.
6   *Practice Direction (Family Proceedings: Representation of Children)*, *Practice Note (CAF-CASS)* [2004] 2 FCR 123,
7   *President's Guidance: Appointment of guardians in accordance with Rule 9.5* (15 April 2008) [2008] 2 FCR 184.

(c) Oral evidence

4.51 Originally perceived by the Rules as a form of written disclosure of oral evidence to be given at the hearing,[1] the statements have been accepted as a hybrid form of evidence between submissions which do not count as evidence at all, and oral evidence given in the witness box.[2] Judicial attention has increasingly been given to the extent to which written statements may supplant the right to give oral evidence.

The evidence to be relied on at the hearing is required to have been served on the parties and the court in advance, otherwise a party may not seek to adduce such evidence without the leave of the court. At the hearing therefore it is not necessary for a witness to recite his statement but he may confirm that it is true, amplifying and updating the contents where necessary and answer the questions of the other parties and of the court: 'The practice of inviting witnesses to give evidence in chief of matters contained in their statements is to be discouraged.'[3]

In some situations the parties do not have the right to insist on oral evidence being given.[4]

[1] See para 4.44.
[2] *S v London Borough of Merton* [1994] 1 FCR 186, [1994] Fam Law 321.
[3] CAAC Report 1993/94, p 23 and see *Practice Note (Case Management)* [1995] 1 All ER 586, [1995] 1 FLR 456.
[4] Cf also where the court refuses to entertain the application at all, a power assumed to exist in *Re S (Contact: Prohibition of Applications)* [1994] 2 FLR 1057; see para 8.218 but not to be exercised unless the case is 'hopeless', see *Re M (Contact)* [1995] 1 FLR 1029.

4.52

An applicant in all applications for which leave is not required is entitled to a full trial unless the respondent can satisfy the stringent test required to justify striking out proceedings in ordinary civil litigation, since a distinction is to be drawn in proceedings concerning children.[2] In proceedings for an interim order 'the circumstances prevailing will almost certainly not permit full evidence to be heard',[3] and it is not always necessary for oral evidence to be called.[4] In *C v Finland*[5], it was held by the European Court of Human Rights that a custody application should not, inter alia, be dealt with without an oral hearing. However, that decision was made in respect of an appeal from the Appeal Court which had wrongly reversed the decision of the lower courts without affording the parties an oral hearing. The decision was therefore unfair as the parties had not had the opportunity to deal with the issues. In *Moser v Austria*[6], the European Court of Human Rights considered that a fair trial required each party to be afforded a reasonable opportunity to present his case and to have knowledge of, and comment on, the evidence produced by the other party. This would normally require an oral hearing. In *Re S (a minor) (contact: evidence)*[7] it was held that a subpoena duces tecum should be issued against the police to produce a video of an interview with a five-year-old child in which she made allegations of sexual abuse against her father so as to have the best evidence available to determine the contact application. Nevertheless, Hale J observed that it was not always wrong to consider proportionality between the benefits to the welfare of the child and the resources to be expended on the inquiry. In *Re B (Minors) (Contact)*[8] the domestic courts had previously extended the principle that a judge is not obliged to hold a full hearing, permitting the parties to call oral evidence and cross-examine any witnesses they choose:

> 'In my view a judge in family cases has a much broader discretion both under The Children Act 1989 and previously to conduct the case as is most appropriate for the issues involved and the evidence available ... There is a spectrum of procedure for family cases from the ex parte application on minimal evidence to the full and detailed investigations on oral evidence which may be prolonged. Where on that spectrum a judge decides a particular application should be placed is a matter for his discretion. Applications for residence orders or for committal to the care of the local authority or revocation of a care order are likely to be decided on full oral evidence, but not invariably. Such is not the case on contact applications which may be and are heard sometimes with and sometimes without oral evidence or with a limited amount of oral evidence.'[9]

This approach was reaffirmed in *Re C (a child) (contact: conduct of hearing)*[10] where Wilson LJ stated:

> '[33] Judges exercising jurisdiction in relation to children have, in my view, a broader discretion in the mode of their conduct of the hearing than do judges in the exercise of a conventional civil jurisdiction. Put another way, the sort of hearing which might be adjudged unfair, and therefore unlawful, in an ordinary civil context may, nevertheless, be lawful in a child context. The difference is largely attributable to the facts that, although of course the welfare of the child is not the paramount consideration in the judge's determination as to how to conduct the hearing, it is a relevant consideration; and that, unless to do so is essential to a proper determination of future arrangements for him, the child's welfare will not be served by taking a course likely to fan the flames of the animosities of the adults who surround him. Furthermore this court must consistently strive to be imaginative about the reasons, often deliberately left unexpressed at least in part, why a trial judge in a child case takes a particular decision, whether substantive or procedural; and it must also be constantly alive to the need, and even in the absence of need at any rate to the entitlement, of the judge often to act robustly in the exercise of this jurisdiction.'

The considerations which should weigh with the court are:

(1) whether there is sufficient evidence upon which to make the relevant decision;

(2) whether the proposed evidence (which should be available at least in outline) which the applicant for a full trial wishes to adduce is likely to affect the outcome of the proceedings;

(3) whether the opportunity to cross-examine the witnesses for the local authority, in particular expert witnesses, is likely to affect the outcome of the proceedings;

(4) the welfare of the child and the effect of further litigation – whether the delay in itself will be so detrimental to the child's well-being that exceptionally there should not be a full hearing. This may be because of the urgent need to place the child, or the emotional stress suffered by the child;

(5)   the prospects of success of the applicant for a full trial;
(6)   does the justice of the case require a full investigation with oral
       evidence?[11]

1   *Cheshire County Council v M* [1993] 1 FLR 463.
2   *W v Ealing London Borough Council* [1993] 2 FLR 788.
3   Per Cazalet J in *Hampshire County Council v S* [1993] Fam 158, [1993] 1 All ER 944.
4   See *Re F (A Minor) (Care Order: Procedure)* [1994] 1 FLR 240 and *Re D (Contact: Interim Order)* [1995] 1 FLR 495 (where the principle of contact is not disputed).
5   (Application 18249/02), [2006] 2 FCR 195.
6   (Application 12643/02) [2006] 3 FCR 107.
7   [1998] 3 FCR 70, CA.
8   [1994] 1 FLR 1.
9   [1994] 2 FLR 1 at 5, per Butler-Sloss LJ. See by way of contrast *Re U (children) (contempt)* [2004] EWCA Civ 71, [2004] 1 FCR 768 where an appeal was allowed against a decision to hear an application for direct contact on the papers was quashed as there should have been an oral hearing to explore all the issues.
10   [2006] EWCA Civ 144, [2006] 1 FCR 4476.
11   See *Re B (Minors) (Contact)* [1994] 2 FLR 1 at 6.

4.53 The gravity of the potential outcome of the proceedings is an important factor in determining whether any of the criteria are met. Therefore, in determining an application for the grant of leave to place a child who was the subject of a care order in an adoptive placement in Scotland which was in accordance with the parents' previously expressed wishes, the court had little difficulty in refusing a full hearing especially where the delay caused by an adjournment would have been detrimental to the child.[1]

On the other hand where the relevant evidence does not point clearly in one direction, the court will normally require oral evidence. So, for example, in an application for leave to apply for a s 8 order, where two contentious views are put before the court in writing, the court will not normally form a view without some further evidence, usually from the witness box.[2] The more relaxed and flexible procedures of the family court must be handled with the greatest care and in such a way that, unless the interests of the child make it necessary, the rules of natural justice and the rights of the parents are fully and properly observed.[3]

1   *Re W (Care: Outside Jurisdiction)* [1994] 2 FLR 1087.
2   *Re R (minors)* [1995] 1 FCR 563, sub nom *Re F and R (Section 8 Order)* [1995] 1 FLR 524.
3   *Re G (a Minor) (Care: Evidence)* [1994] 2 FLR 785.

4.54 Where the parties are agreed that a care order is appropriate and on the facts supporting the fulfilment of the threshold criteria, the court's investigative duty can be limited to reading the documents and approving an agreed order. The process of agreement is facilitated where the statements of the local authority are objective and balanced.[1] Proceedings should not be prolonged to resolve differences as to expressions in admissions made which pass the 'threshold'; the terminology of those making them should be accepted.[2] Where the need for an order is agreed but the factual basis is disputed, the court should limit its investigation to those parts of the evidence which are directly relevant to the issue of significant harm and findings which are necessary for the proper disposal of the case.[3] However, if the concessions are not sufficient to give a full understanding of allegations of sexual abuse and the care plan depends on the harm which has actually occurred, or where the credibility of the children has been impugned, further investigation may warranted.[4] Parental concessions need to be sufficient for the local authority to draw up a care plan for the court's approval.[5] CAAC advised that the court should invite parties in such cases to submit an agreed statement of facts so that the need for oral evidence will be unlikely and that where feelings are running high the court may adopt the statement without reading it aloud.[6]

1   *Re JC (Care Proceedings: Procedure)* [1995] 2 FLR 77.
2   *Re D (a minor)* [1995] 2 FCR 681, sub nom *Stockport Metropolitan Borough Council v D* [1995] 1 FLR 873.
3   *Re G (A Minor) (Care Proceedings)* [1994] 2 FLR 69 and see *Devon County Council v S* [1992] Fam 176, [1992] 3 All ER 793.
4   *Re M (Threshold Criteria: Parental Concessions)* [1999] 2 FLR 728, CA.
5   *Re W (children) (threshold criteria: parental concessions)* [2001] 1 FCR 139, CA.
6   CAAC Report 1993/94, p 32.

4. Decision

4.55 All tiers of family court must give reasons for the court's decision and state any findings of fact when making an order or refusing an application.[1] This is particularly important where the decision is contrary to expert evidence and the general weight of evidence[2] or departing from advice from a professional witness in a s 7 report.[3] There is a duty clearly to state the court's findings as to any crucial expert opinion or diagnosis[4] and to give a reasoned judgment for the step between finding the threshold criteria satisfied and endorsing the care plan.[5] In a domestic violence case, a decision may be quashed where no adequate reference has been made to *Re L*[6] and the guidelines therein.[7]

After the final hearing the court must deliver its judgment as soon as is practicable.[8] Where it is in the interests of the child, the higher courts can take the 'unusual' step of giving the court's decision at the conclusion of the argument with reasons to be given later.[9]

In the family proceedings court, however, there is an additional requirement that before the court makes an order or refuses an application, the court must state any findings of fact and complete Form 22 and state the reasons for the court's decision. The clerk must record in writing the names of the justices constituting the court and, in consultation with the justices, the reasons for the decision and any findings of fact.[10]

1   FPR 1991, r 4.21; FPC(CA 1989)R 1991, r 21(6). See also, *KA v Finland* (Application 27751/95) [2003] 1 FCR 201, for the duty under the ECHR to give detailed reasons under art 8.
2   See *Re A (a child) (mental health of mother)* [2001] EWCA Civ 162, [2001] 1 FCR 57.
3   *Re J (children) (residence: expert evidence)* [2001] 2 FCR 44, CA. See also *Re W (a child: care order)* [2005] EWCA Civ 649, [2005] 2 FCR 277 where the judge was in error for failing to give reasons for not following the opinions of two experts and the guardian.
4   *Re W (a child: non-accidental injury)* [2002] EWCA Civ 710, [2003] 2 FCR 346.
5   *Re B (children: interference with family life)* [2003] EWCA Civ 786, [2004] 1 FCR 462.
6   [2001] Fam 260, [2000] 4 All ER 609, [2000] 2 FCR 404.

7   *Re H (a child) (contact: domestic violence)* [2005] EWCA Civ 1404, [2006] 1 FCR 102, [2006] 1 FLR 943.
8   FPR 1991, r 4.21(3); FPC(CA 1989)R 1991, r 21(4).
9   See *Re B (Minors) (Contact)* [1994] 2 FLR 1, CA.
10 FPC(CA 1989)R 1991, r 21(5).

5. Justices' reasons

4.56 The giving of reasons and announcing of any decision[1] may be adjourned and deputed to one of the justices constituting the court by which the decision was made[2]. But it is not permissible, even with the consent of the parties, for the justices to announce their decision immediately after the hearing but defer giving their reasons and findings of fact to a later date.[3] The requirements of r 21(5) of the FPC(CA 1989)R 1991 are mandatory and a failure to record the reasons before announcing the decision will mean that the decision cannot stand.[4] These requirements apply on the hearing of an application for an interim order as they do for a substantive order[5] and for a decision on an interim application as to disclosure of a medical report;[6] also when hearing an application for leave[7] or to withdraw an application[8] or when refusing an application for an adjournment.[9] Reasons must also be given when considering an application for an education supervision order.[10] In its judgment or reasons the court should always make clear how its findings on the issue of domestic violence have influenced its decision on the issue of residence or contact. In particular, where the court has found domestic violence proved but nonetheless makes an order, the court should always explain, whether by way of reference to the welfare check-list or otherwise, why it takes the view that the order which it has made is in the best interests of the child.[11]

On appeal, the only findings of fact and reasons to support the justices' decision will be those announced at the time the decision is delivered and it is therefore not possible for the justices subsequently to elaborate on their original reasons.[12] The rationale of the rule is that it will be necessary for the bench of three justices to have a prior discussion before the decision is made and to have the opportunity to retire and, with the assistance of their clerk, to record their findings and reasons.[13] In this way the clerk can assist the justices where necessary to structure their reasons and distil them into written form.

Waiting around for justices to give their written reasons is cited as a procedure which makes the family proceedings court less attractive than the county court[14] and the Government has accepted that the rules should be amended to permit justices to announce a decision, give the parties the order with a summary of reasons for the decision and supply full written reasons by the end of the day wherever practicable.[15]

1   The decision to make 'no order' under s 1(5) is a 'decision' and requires the giving of reasons: *S v R (parental responsibility)* [1993] 1 FCR 331. See further paras 2.64 ff.
2   FPC(CA 1989)R 1991, r 21(6).
3   *Re K (minors) (justices' reasons)* [1994] 1 FCR 616.
4   *W v Hertfordshire County Council* [1993] 1 FLR 118, and *Re W (A Minor) (Contact)* [1994] 1 FLR 843.

5   *W v Hertfordshire County Council*, above and *F v R (Contact: Justices' Reasons)* [1995]
    1 FLR 227.
6   *Re NW (A Minor) (Medical Reports)* [1993] 2 FLR 591.
7   *Re M (Prohibited Steps Order: Application for Leave)* [1993] 1 FLR 275.
8   *Re F (a minor) (care proceedings: withdrawal)* [1993] 1 FCR 389.
9   *Essex County Council v F* [1993] 1 FLR 847.
10 *Essex County Council v B* [1993] 1 FLR 866.
11 *Practice Direction Residence and Contact Orders* (9 May 2008) [2008] 2 FCR 273, [2008]
    2 FLR 103.
12 See *Hillingdon London Borough Council v H* [1993] Fam 43, [1993] 1 All ER 198; *N v B
    (children: orders as to residence)* [1993] 1 FCR 231.
13 *Re W (A Minor) (Contact)*, n 4 above, and see *Essex County Council v B*, n 10 above.
14 Scoping Study on Delay in Children Act Cases (Lord Chancellor's Dept 2002) para 115.
15 Response to the consultation paper 'Family Procedure Rules – a new procedural code for
    family proceedings' (CP 19/06) (February 2008).

4.57 Although the High Court is mindful that lay justices are not trained
lawyers[1] nevertheless their reasons must attain a minimum standard which
will, it is submitted, explain their decision not only to the appellate court but
most importantly to the parties concerned.[2] Guidance on the structure of
justices' reasons has been given in *R v Oxfordshire County Council (Secure
Accommodation Order)*[3] and in *S v Oxfordshire County Council*[4]. In these
cases justices had used a proforma which was commended to magistrates[5] but
nevertheless justices should be careful that any proforma caters for the
situation with which they are dealing.[6]

Justices' reasons should address the welfare checklist where this is applicable
to the proceeding:[7]

> 'It is unacceptable for any court to make a bland statement that it has
> "considered all aspects of the welfare checklist" without further particularisa-
> tion unless, elsewhere in the course of its judgment or reasons, it has, in
> considering the evidence or in making findings, dealt in detail with the relevant
> aspects on the checklist, thereby demonstrating that it has applied its mind to
> the relevant factors'.[8]

The court should therefore address important issues in the case such as race[9]
and record facts significant in the making of the decision and the court's
assessment of the credibility and reliability of at least the more important
witnesses.[10] Important issues of disputed fact must be resolved[11] or if, on the
making of an interim order, the justices have deliberately refrained from
making findings, the fact that they have so refrained, and the reasons why
should be explained.[12] Reasons must also be given for departing from the
recommendation of a children's guardian[13] or children and family reporter.[14]
A decision may be quashed where the reasons show the justices had addressed
irrelevant considerations.[15]

1   *Re J (A Minor) (Residence)* [1994] 1 FLR 369 per Singer J, also *Re B (Procedure: Family
    Proceedings Court)* [1993] Fam Law 209 and *Re M (a Minor) (Contact: Conditions)*
    [1994] 1 FLR 272.
2   See *Re J (A Minor) (Residence)* above.
3   [1992] Fam 150, sub nom *R (J) v Oxfordshire County Council* [1992] 3 All ER 660.
4   [1993] 1 FLR 452. See now *Justices' Reasons in the Family Proceedings Court in Children
    Act Cases* Joint Guidance from the Justices' Clerks' Society and the Magistrates' Associa-
    tion (November 2007).
5   See also *Re B (Procedure: Family Proceedings Court)* [1993] Fam Law 209, CA.

6   See *Re R and G (Minors) (Interim Care or Supervision Orders)* [1994] 1 FLR 793.

7   *Re O (a minor)* [1992] 4 All ER 905, [1992] 1 WLR 912.

8   *Re D (Contact: Interim Order)* [1995] 1 FLR 495, per Wall J and see *D v R* [1995] 1 FCR 501. However, on appeal the court has been prepared to assume that judges approved to sit in family cases have had the welfare checklist in mind; *Re A (a minor)* [1994] 2 FCR 125, sub nom *Oldham Metropolitan Borough Council v E* [1994] 1 FLR 568, and see further for the checklist, para 2.38.

9   *Re M (Section 94 Appeals)* [1995] 1 FLR 546.

10   *H (a minor) (care proceedings)* [1992] 2 FCR 330 and see *Re M (A Minor) (Contact: Conditions)* [1994] 1 FLR 272.

11   See *F v R (Contact: Justices' Reasons)* [1995] 1 FLR 227.

12   *F v R (Contact: Justices' Reasons)* [1995] 1 FLR 227.

13   Formerly 'guardian ad litem'. *Re W (A Minor) (Secure Accommodation)* [1993] 1 FLR 692.

14   Formerly 'welfare officer'. *Re M (Section 94 Appeals)* [1995] 1 FLR 546 and *F v R (Contact: Justices' Reasons)* [1995] 1 FLR 227 and *Re B (a child) (residence order)* [2003] All ER (D) 107 (Aug).

15   *Re B (care proceedings: disclosure)* [2003] All ER (D) 196 (Oct).

6. Costs

4.58   Costs are generally at the discretion of the court.[1] In children cases it is unusual to order costs[2] but this is not a presumption.[3]

The principles relating to costs in family proceedings relating to children are to be found in *Re T (a child) (order for costs)* where the Court of Appeal approved the exposition of the judge at first instance:

> '2.1   The Civil Procedure Rules apply. Under normal circumstances, according to r 44.3(2)(a), the general rule is that costs should follow the event, although the court can make a different order (r 44.3(2)(b)[5].
>
> 2.2   However, this general rule does not apply to family proceedings. (Family Proceedings (Miscellaneous Amendments) Rules 1999, SI 1999/1012.)
>
> 2.3   It is suggested that even in family proceedings, the general rule is probably the starting point but can more easily be displaced. (*Gojkovic v Gojkovic (No 2)* [1991] FCR 913, [1992] 1 All ER 267.)
>
> 2.4   In cases involving children in particular, costs awarded against one parent or another are exceptional since the court is anxious to avoid the situation where a parent may feel "punished" by the other parent which will reduce co-operation between them. This will only impinge ultimately on the welfare of the child or the children concerned. (*Sutton London BC v Davis (No 2)* [1994] 2 FCR 1199, [1995] 1 All ER 65; *Re M (child case: costs)* [1995] 1 FCR 649.)
>
> 2.5   The conduct of the parties is in reality the major consideration when deciding whether or not an exceptional order for costs should be made. It should only be made if the penalised party has been unreasonable in his or her conduct. Moreover the 'unreasonableness' must relate to the conduct of the litigation rather than the welfare of the child. (*R v R (costs: child case)* [1997] 1 FCR 613.)
>
> 2.6   One has to be very careful in this distinction when, as in the case of (the mother), the apparent unreasonableness is as a result of the personality of the relevant party. In such circumstances, there is often an overlap of that party's conduct of the litigation and the conduct relating to the welfare of the child.
>
> 2.7   At the beginning of my involvement (the father) was applying for contact in relation to A as well as J. His welfare has also been a concern

from time to time throughout. However, the costs in dispute have been incurred in relation to J's welfare alone.'

¹ Supreme Court Act 1981, s 51; FPC(CA 1989)R 1991, r 22(1). For assessment of the amount of costs, see *Clarke Hall and Morrison on Children*, 1[1431]ff. For consideration of the exercise of the power to order costs against a local authority, see *Hillingdon London Borough Council v H* [1993] Fam 43, [1992] 2 FCR 299.
² *Re G (a minor) (wardship: costs)* [1982] 2 All ER 32; *Gojkovic v Gojkovic (No2)* [1992] Fam 40; *Sutton London Borough Council v Davis (Costs) (No 2)* [1994] 2 FLR 569.
³ *Re M (Local Authority's Costs)* [1995] 1 FLR 533.
⁴ [2005] EWCA Civ 311, [2005] 1 FCR 625, [2005] 2 FLR 681.
⁵ For the magistrates' courts the FPC(CA 1989)R 1991, r 22(1) applies.

Personal liability of legal representative for costs

4.59 The court may disallow wasted costs or order a legal representative to meet such costs. 'Wasted costs' means any costs incurred by a party as a result of any improper, unreasonable or negligent act or omission on the part of any legal or other representative or any employee of such a representative; or which, in the light of any such act or omission occurring after they were incurred, the court considers it is unreasonable to expect the party to pay.[1] Failure to comply with the *Public Law Outline*, and delays caused by practitioners could be dealt with under these provisions.[2] Practitioners have been warned that liability for wasted costs might arise if adequate time estimates are not provided[3]; where important information was not communicated to expert witnesses thereby incurring delay[4]; and where documents were bundled incompletely[5]. In *B v B (wasted costs order)*[6] a wasted costs order was made in respect of an 'unsustainable' appeal against a direction of a deputy district judge setting a trial date. The appeal was without merit and incapable of succeeding so as to amount to an abuse of the appellate process. As the matter was discrete from the main issues in the case, the court felt able to make a wasted costs order before the final substantive hearing. A solicitor who has instructed counsel does not abdicate his professional responsibility although the more specialist the advice sought from counsel, the more reasonable it is likely to be for the solicitor to rely on it.[7] For general guidance on the making of wasted costs orders see *Ridehalgh v Horsefield*[8]. In *Re G, S and M (Wasted Costs)*[9] Wall J set the decision in *Ridehalgh* in the context of non-adversarial care proceedings:

'Unlike most civil proceedings, care proceedings under the Children Act 1989 are non-adversarial. Furthermore, public law care proceedings, in particular, are almost invariably conducted between parties all of whom, on one basis or another, are publicly funded. The local authority has to pay for care proceedings out of its annual budget: the parents and the child or children concerned (through their guardian ad litem) are usually both funded by the tax payer through legal aid. In cases where the Official Solicitor is involved, he too, derives his budget from public funds.

Contested care proceedings are extremely expensive. However, inter partes orders for costs are rare. I cannot recall ever making an order for costs in care proceedings against parents or a guardian ad litem in favour of a local authority. Cases in which the court orders a local authority to pay the costs of the other parties are, in my experience, also very rare and the order in such circumstances is usually a mark of disapprobation for the way the local authority has behaved in relation to the children or their parents.

Parents facing care proceedings often contest them in circumstances where the likelihood of care orders being made is very high, and where the parents' case is effectively hopeless. As *Ridehalgh v Horsefield* [1994] Ch 205 at 233, [1994] 3 All ER 848 at 863 makes clear, however, lawyers for parents in these circumstances are not to be penalised for pursuing a hopeless case. Parents in such cases are at risk of losing their children; no decision could be more important for both the children and their parents, and all parents at such risk are entitled to proper representation and to have their cases put ...

It follows that a local authority which obtains a care order in a "hopeless" case will be unlikely either to obtain or even seek an order for costs against impecunious parents, or the Legal Aid Board or the lawyers conducting the parents' case.

In these circumstances, in my judgment, and in clear contrast to commercial or other adversarial civil litigation, it is the court which has to be the watchdog over the proper expenditure of public funds. The 1989 Act specifically gives the court a pro-active, case management responsibility in both public and private law cases: see ss 11 and 32, and the numerous cases dealing with case management. In my judgment, therefore, in care proceedings it is frequently likely to be the court which will need to initiate proceedings relating to wasted costs orders ...'

1   Supreme Court Act 1981 s 51(6), (7) and (13). See *Medcalf v Mardell* [2002] UKHL 27, [2003] 1 AC 120, [2002] 3 All ER 721 for jurisdiction to make costs against the legal representative of any other party to the same proceedings including a barrister in respect of conduct other than when exercising a right of audience in court. For magistrates' courts, see the Magistrates' Courts Act 1980, s 145A(2). The relevant rules are the Magistrates' Court (Costs Against Legal Representatives in Civil Proceedings) Rules 1991, SI 1991/2096.
2   See para 4.45.
3   *Practice Direction* [1994] 1 All ER 155, [1994] 1 FLR 108, see *Clarke Hall and Morrison on Children*, para [13106] and *Re MD and TD (Minors) (Time Estimates)* [1994] 2 FCR 94, [1994] 2 FLR 336.
4   *Re G, S and M (Wasted Costs)* [1999] 3 FCR 303, [2000] 1 FLR 52, FD.
5   *Practice Note* [1995] 1 All ER 586, [1995] 1 FLR 456. See also *Practice Direction* [2006] 2 FCR 833 and *Re CH (family proceedings: court bundles)* [2000] 2 FCR 193.
6   [2001] 3 FCR 724, FD.
7   In *B v B (wasted costs order)* above, responsibility was apportioned as 75% to counsel and 25% to the solicitor.
8   [1994] 2 FLR 194, CA.
9   [1999] 3 FCR 303, [2000] 1 FLR 52, FD.

Chapter 5

PRIVATE LAW ORDERS

INTRODUCTION AND BACKGROUND

5.1 In this chapter consideration is given to the court's powers under Pt II of the CA 1989 to make orders, other than financial orders,[1] in what are termed 'family proceedings'.

[1] The powers to make financial orders are governed by s 15 and Sch 1. For a discussion of these powers see *Clarke Hall and Morrison on Children*, Division 4.

5.2 In its report on Guardianship and Custody the Law Commission commented[1] that while the main principles of the pre-1989 Act were reasonably clear and well accepted, the details, particularly concerning custody, were complicated and confusing.[1] The Commission was also concerned that the law made the stakes too high pointing out that all the research evidence[2] shows that children who fare best after their parents' separation are those who are able to maintain a good relationship with both parents. While recognising the obvious limitation that law cannot make people co-operate, the Commission argued that at least it should not stand in their way. Hence, if the parties can co-operate with one another, the law should intervene as little as possible, but if they cannot, the law should at least try to 'lower the stakes' and avoid the impression that the 'loser loses all'.

[1] Law Com No 172, 1988, para 1.1.
[2] Notably, that of J S Wallerstein and J B Kelly *Surviving the Breakup* (1980, Grant McIntyre). See also Wallerstein and Blakeslee *Second Chances: Men, Women and Children A Decade After Divorce* (1989, Bantam). See now eg Harold and Murch 'Inter-parental conflict and children's adaptation to separation and divorce: theory, research and implications for family law, practice and policy' [2005] CFLQ 185 and Rodgers and Pryor *The Development of Children from Separated Families: A Review of Research from the United Kingdom* (1998).

5.3 With the above considerations in mind, and with the general aim of making the law 'clear, simple and, we hope, fairer for families and children alike' the Law Commission recommended, inter alia, that the differing powers of the various courts under the different jurisdictions to make custody and access orders should be replaced by a new set of powers designed to be less emotive and more flexible and which are common to all courts.

THE COURTS' POWERS UNDER PART II: THE GENERAL STRATEGY

5.4 Replacing the previous diverse statutory powers to make custody, care and control, custodianship and access orders, the courts are empowered to make a range of orders, collectively known as 'section 8 orders', namely, 'residence orders', 'contact orders', 'prohibited steps orders' and 'specific issue orders'. Overall, the s 8 powers are intended to concentrate both the court's and the parties' minds on the practical issues which generally arise with respect to children, rather than on the allocation of theoretical rights and duties.[1]

[1] See Hoggett 'The Children Bill: The Aim' [1989] Fam Law 217 at 219. But for a classic example of not applying the CA 1989, see the first instance decision in *Re A (children) (shared residence)* [2001] EWCA Civ 1795, [2002] 1 FCR 177, CA.

5.5 Although s 8 orders are closely associated with private law disputes they can be made in *any* family proceedings[1] including, therefore, in public law proceedings. In other words the s 8 powers provide a basic menu of orders available under the Act.

[1] For the full meaning of which see paras 5.135 ff.

5.6 To put these powers into perspective it is of interest to note the number of orders made annually respectively in private and public proceedings in alternate years 1992–2006.

Number of orders made bi-annually 1992–2006[1]

Order	1992		1994		1996		1998		2000		2002		2004		2006	
	Private Law	Public Law	Private Law	Public Law	Private Law	Public Law	Private Law	Public Law	Private Law	Public Law	Private Law	Public Law	Private Law	Public Law	Private Law	Public Law
Residence	16515	1234	23919	1502	27660	1075	24204	761	25809	1365	30006	2453	31848	2976	30035	2941
Contact	17589	n/a	31486	n/a	40330	n/a	39500	n/a	46070	1177	61356	2725	70169	2045	62672	1848
Prohibited Steps	6103	773	5971	299	5783	194	4307	141	5345	227	8889	243	9556	235	9081	304
Specific Issues	1379	127	1807	41	2277	74	1834	60	2457	79	2940	173	3893	162	3893	115

1 The 1992, 1994, 1996 and 1998 statistics are taken from the Children Act Report 1995–1999 (2000, Cm 4579) Tables 10.1 and 10.2, the 2000, 2002 and 2004 statistics are taken from the Judicial Statistics Annual Reports for those years, Tables 5.2 and 5.3, and the 2006 statistics are taken from the Judicial and Court Statistics 2006, Table 5.4. For a collection of other relevant statistics, see *Clarke Hall and Morrison on Children*, 1[631.1]–[631.7].

5.7 Part II provides a clear plan governing who can apply for an order. The basic scheme (under s 10) is that some people, for example, parents (with or without parental responsibility), guardians or special guardians, are entitled to apply for any s 8 order, while others, for example, relatives, are able to seek the court's leave either to intervene in existing 'family proceedings' or to initiate their own proceedings to seek a s 8 order.

5.8 Another important change made by the CA 1989 was the removal of the court's power in matrimonial and other private law proceedings concerning children to make committal to care or supervision orders. Instead, under s 37[1] the courts can direct the local authority to investigate the circumstances but it is for the authority and not the court to decide whether an application for a care or supervision order should be made. However, courts are empowered under s 16, to make 'family assistance' orders, the object of which is to provide short-term help to the family.[2]

1   Discussed at paras 5.206 and 7.25 ff.
2   See paras 5.191 ff.

5.9 After operating for many years virtually unamended there has been a number of changes to Pt II, first under the Adoption and Children Act 2002 and then by the confusingly named Children and Adoption Act 2006. Under the former Act new powers to make special guardianship and enhanced residence orders were introduced. These powers are discussed at the end of the chapter. The 2006 Act contains a raft of new powers both to promote contact (ie by making contact activity directions and conditions) and to enforce contact orders (ie the power to impose a community work sanction and to order financial compensation for the loss occasioned by the breach). These powers are respectively discussed in the context of contact orders (at paras 5.63 ff) and enforcement powers (at paras 5.179 ff). Further changes principally to improve the position of relatives, are being proposed under the Children and Young Persons Bill 2008.

5.10 The fact that it was felt necessary to introduce new powers with respect to contact is indicative that these orders are the most problematic of the s 8 powers. They are also a response in part to an influential report *Making Contact Work*[1] and in part to a high profile campaign by pressure groups such as Families Need Fathers and Fathers 4 Justice.[2]

1   A Report to the Lord Chancellor by the Advisory Board on Family Law; Children Act Sub-Committee (2002).
2   See eg Collier 'Fathers 4 Justice, the law and the new politics of Fatherhood' [2005] CFLQ 511.

RISK ASSESSMENTS

5.11 One innovation of the Children and Adoption Act 2006 is the introduction of risk assessments. Section 7 of the 2006 Act adds a new s 16A to the CA 1989. This provision, which was brought into force in October 2007,[1] requires CAFCASS and Welsh family proceedings officers to carry out a risk assessment and provide it to the court, if in the course of carrying out *any* function in family proceedings under Pt II of the CA 1989,[2] the officer is given cause to suspect that the child concerned is at risk of harm.[3]

[1] By the Children and Adoption Act 2006 (Commencement No 1) Order 2007, SI 2007/2287.
[2] According to the Explanatory Notes to the 2006 Act (at para 48) the power arises in 'private law family proceedings under the Act' but this is not strictly accurate since it does not arise in proceedings under Pt I of the CA 1989, namely, parental responsibility order applications and guardianship proceedings.
[3] Section 16A(2). Note that by s 16A(3) 'A risk assessment, in relation to a child who is at risk of suffering harm of a particular sort, is an assessment of the risk of that harm being suffered by the child'. But quite what this means is hard to say.

5.12 As the Explanatory Notes to the 2006 Act explain,[1] 'the duty applies whenever an officer is involved in any function connected with [Part II] proceedings including, for instance, preparing a report for the court under section 7 of the 1989 Act, monitoring of contact orders as provided for by the new section 11H of the 1989 Act or working on alternative dispute resolution. It also applies where an officer is carrying out functions under a family assistance order'. Furthermore, under *Practice Direction: Children Act 1989: Risk Assessments under Section 16A*,[2] the duty to report arises irrespective of outcome so that a report must still be made even if the officer concludes there is no risk of harm. As the *Direction* points out, the fact that a risk assessment has been carried out is a material fact that should be placed before the court, whatever the outcome of the assessment. In reporting the outcome to the court, the officer should make clear the factor(s) that triggered the decision to carry out the assessment.

[1] Paragraph 48.
[2] [2007] 2 FLR 625. See also the FPR 1991, r 4.11AA, as amended; FPC(CA 1989)R 1991, r 11AA, as amended. Note also *Practice Direction (Residence and Contact Orders: Domestic Violence)* [2008] 1 WLR 1062 which provides inter alia that consent residence and contact orders should not be made, nor permission given to withdraw such applications unless the parties are present in court, except where the court is satisfied that there is no risk of harm to the child.

SECTION 8 ORDERS

5.13 The expression 'a section 8 order' means any of the orders mentioned in s 8(1), that is, a contact order, a prohibited steps order, a residence order and a specific issue order. It also includes any order varying or discharging such an order.[1] In making any of these orders the court has further supplemental powers under s 11(7)[2] which are designed to ensure maximum flexibility.

[1] Section 8(2).
[2] Discussed at paras 5.108 ff.

1. Residence orders

5.14 By s 8(1) a residence order 'means an order settling the arrangements to be made as to the person with whom the child is to live'.

5.14 *Private law orders*

Residence orders determine with whom the child is to live, and indeed, in their simplest form the order need do no more than name the person *with whom* the child is to live. Although determining with whom the child will live effectively determines *where* the child will live, in the absence of a prohibited steps order[1] or, unless the court adds a direction or a condition,[2] the person in whose favour the residence order has been made is free to live in, or subsequently move to, any location *within* the UK.[3]

---

[1]   See *Re H (children) (residence order: condition)* [2001] EWCA Civ 1338, [2001] 3 FCR 182, [2001] 2 FLR 1277, CA.
[2]   Namely under s 11(7) (discussed at paras 5.109 ff). See in particular *Re S (a child) (residence order: condition)* [2001] EWCA Civ 847, [2001] 3 FCR 154.
[3]   But not *outside* the UK without either court leave or the consent of everyone with parental responsibility: s 13(1)(b), discussed at paras 5.39 ff.

5.15 Residence orders should be seen for what they are, namely, orders determining with whom the child is to live and nothing more. They should not normally be regarded as a means of reallocating parental responsibility. This is more obviously so as between married parents since, based on the fundamental principle that 'changes in the child's residence should interfere as little as possible in his relationship with both his parents',[1] each parent retains full parental responsibility and with it the power to act independently unless this is incompatible with a court order, regardless of who has a residence order.[2] But even where the making of a residence order does have the effect of conferring parental responsibility, as it does when made in favour of those who do not already have it,[3] it is inappropriate to make the order *solely* for that purpose. That, at any rate, was Thorpe J's view in *N v B (children: order as to residence)*[4] in which a cohabitant, having discovered just before the hearing that he was not the father, failed in his attempt to obtain a shared residence order.[5] However, in a later decision, *Re G (Children)(Residence: Same Sex Partner)*,[6] the Court of Appeal made a shared residence order in respect of two children conceived by AID, to both partners to a same-sex relationship, specifically to give the non-parent partner parental responsibility to prevent her being marginalised by the mother. Furthermore *N v B* had earlier been distinguished *Re H (shared residence: parental responsibility)*,[7] in which the making of a shared residence order so that the stepfather had parental responsibility for his stepson was upheld, since on the facts the child would otherwise be confused if he did not have the comfort and security of knowing not only that his stepfather (whom he had only just discovered was not his natural father) wished to treat him as his child but that the law would not give some stamp of approval to that de facto position. Perhaps the best summary of the current law is by Bracewell J who, in *G v F (shared residence: parental responsibility)*,[8] considered that a shared residence order may be appropriate for the purposes of conferring parental responsibility on a non-parent provided it is not simply a device or the sole reason for the application.

---

[1]   See Law Com No 172, para 4.16.
[2]   See paras 3.96 ff. But note the exceptions discussed at para 3.99.
[3]   Ie under s 12(2), (3); see para 5.30.
[4]   [1993] 1 FCR 231, sub nom *Re WB (Residence Orders)* [1995] 2 FLR 1023.
[5]   Shared residence orders are discussed at paras 5.17 ff.

6   See *Re G (Residence: Same-sex Partner)* [2005] EWCA Civ 462, [2005] 2 FLR 957, [2005] All ER (D) 25 (Apr). The House of Lords subsequently upheld this order, albeit reversing the times allocated to each home in favour of the biological mother, see *Re G (Children) (Residence: Same-Sex Partner)* [2006] UKHL 43, [2006] 1 WLR 2305, [2006] 4 All ER 241.

7   [1996] 3 FCR 321, [1995] 2 FLR 883, CA.

8   [1998] 3 FCR 1, sub nom *G v F (Contact and Shared Residence: Applications for Leave)* [1998] 2 FLR 799.

5.16 Under s 11(5) where as a result of a residence order 'the child lives, or is to live with one of two parents who each have parental responsibility for him', that order will cease to have effect if the parents live together for a continuous period of more than six months.[1]

1   For an example of where such an order did come to such an end see *Re P (Abduction: Declaration)* [1995] 1 FLR 831 at 834, CA.

(a) Joint and shared residence orders

5.17 Although residence orders are said to settle the arrangements to be made as to *the person* with whom the child is to live,[1] they can, both because of the general presumption under the Interpretation Act 1978, s 6(c) that words appearing in a statute in the singular include the plural and the implication of s 11(4) (see below), also be made in favour of more than one person.[2] A court can therefore make an order in favour of a parent and step-parent,[3] a cohabiting couple,[4] grandparents,[5] or foster parents[6]. In these cases, what may be conveniently described[7] as 'joint residence orders' are made in favour of couples living together, but the power is not so restricted, for residence orders may also be made in favour of two or more persons who do not live together. These latter type of orders have become known as 'shared residence' orders. In theory it is within the court's powers to make both a joint and shared residence order in favour of both parents and their respective new partners, though as yet there is no reported example of such an order.

1   A residence order cannot, therefore, be made in favour of the child himself, see further para 5.159, n 2.

2   In theory there is nothing to stop the court making an order in favour of more than two people, although in practice it is rarely likely to do so.

3   See eg *Re H (shared residence: parental responsibility)* [1996] 3 FCR 321, [1995] 2 FLR 883, CA.

4   See eg *Re AB (a minor) (adoption: parental consent)* [1996] 1 FCR 633, sub nom *Re AB (Adoption: Joint Residence)* [1996] 1 FLR 27 (see above para 5.15, n 9), and *Re C (A Minor) (Residence Order: Lesbian Co-Parents)* [1994] Fam Law 468 (joint residence order made to the mother and her female cohabitant).

5   See eg *Re W (A Minor) (Residence Order)* [1993] 2 FLR 625, CA.

6   See eg *Re M (a minor) (adoption or residence order)* [1998] 1 FCR 165, [1998] 1 FLR 570, CA.

7   Ie it is not a legal term of art, though it is the accepted terminology, see Wilson LJ in *Re K (Shared Residence Order)* [2008] EWCA Civ 526, [2008] All ER (D) 55 (Apr) at [15].

5.18 Shared care arrangements vary: at one end of the spectrum is the case of the child spending half his time with each parent,[1] at the other end is the more common situation of the child spending weekdays with one and weekends with the other parent or living during term-time with one parent and school holidays with the other. Rather than having to reflect these arrangements by making a residence order in favour of one parent and contact in favour of the other, the Law Commission believed[2] that it would be 'a far more realistic description of the responsibilities involved ... to make a residence order covering both parents'. In so recommending the Commission were not suggesting that children *should* share their time more or less equally between their parents, which arrangement they thought would rarely be practicable or for the child's benefit. Rather, they were recommending the reversal of a pre-CA decision[3] in which it had been held that courts could not as a matter of principle make what would be now a shared residence order. As the Department of Health's Children Act 1989 Guidance and Regulations put it at the time of Act's implementation:[4]

> ' ... it is not expected that it will become a common form of order because most children will still need the stability of a single home, and partly because in the cases where shared care is appropriate there is less likely to be a need for the court to make any order at all. However, a shared care order has the advantage of being more realistic in those cases where the child is to spend considerable amounts of time with both parents, [and] brings with it certain other benefits (including the right to remove the child from accommodation provided by a local authority under s 20), and removes any impression that one parent is good and responsible whereas the other parent is not.'

1   So-called '50/50 shared residence orders' are relatively rare, see *R (on the application of Bibi) v Camden London Borough Council* [2004] EWHC 2527 (Admin), [2005] 1 FLR 413 at [42(3)], per Davis J. Calls for a presumption of shared residence following divorce or separation were rejected by the government in the discussion leading to the Children and Adoption Act 2006, see [2006] Fam Law 30 at 34.
2   Law Com No 172, para 4.12.
3   *Riley v Riley* [1986] 2 FLR 429, CA.
4   Children Act 1989 Guidance and Regulations, Vol 1, Court Orders (1991) Department of Health, para 2.28. This comment is not repeated in the revised Guidance (2008) Department for Children, Schools and Families, see para 2.34, which simply states that a 'shared residence order may be appropriate in those cases where the child is to spend considerable amounts of time with both parents'.

5.19 The courts' approach to the making of such orders has been an evolving one. Early post-CA 1989 authority[1] suggested that shared residence orders should only be made in exceptional circumstances but this was resiled from in *A v A (minors) (shared residence order)*[2]. In upholding an order dividing equally the time the children were to live with each parent outside school term time, Butler-Sloss LJ commented[3] that whilst it was a matter for individual discretion, in general terms it had to be demonstrated that there was a positive benefit in making what she termed the unusual order of shared residence as opposed to making the more conventional one of residence to other and contact to other. But in *Re D (Children) (Shared Residence Orders)*[4] the Court of Appeal distanced itself both from the requirement of exceptional circumstances and of the need to show positive benefit. Hale LJ said that she:[5]

> 'would not add any gloss on the legislative provisions, which are always subject to the paramount consideration of what is best for the children concerned.'

Butler-Sloss P agreed and, having pointed to the Court of Appeal's developing application of the new concept, said:[6]

'Now nine years later with far greater experience of the workings of the Act it is necessary to underline the importance of the flexibility of the Children Act 1989 in s 8 orders and, consequentially, that the Court of Appeal should not impose restrictions upon the working of the statute not actually found within the words of the section.'

1   *Re H (a minor) (residence order)* [1993] 1 FCR 671 at 682–683, [1994] 1 FLR 717 at 728, per Purchas LJ.
2   [1995] 1 FCR 91 at 101, [1994] 1 FLR 669 at 678, CA.
3   [1995] 1 FCR 91 at 100, [1994] 1 FLR 669 at 677. See also *Re H (shared residence: parental responsibility)* [1996] 3 FCR 321, [1995] 2 FLR 883, CA, in which Ward LJ referred to shared residence orders as being 'unusual'.
4   [2001] 1 FLR 147, sub nom *D v D (Shared Residence Order)* [2001] 1 FLR 495.
5   [2001] 1 FLR 147 at para (32) at 154, [2001] 1 FLR 495 at 501. See also *Holmes C Moorhouse v Richmond-upon Thames London Borough Council* [2007] EWCA Civ 970, [2008] 1 WLR 1289, [2008] 1 FLR 1061.
6   [2001] 1 FLR 147 at para (39) at 155, [2001] 1 FLR 495 at 502 respectively.

5.20 In *Re D* a shared residence order was upheld on appeal where the children were in effect living with both parents, had homes with each of them and appeared to be coping well with the arrangements, but where the parents themselves were at loggerheads over the arrangements and had frequently resorted to court proceedings. The hope was that the order would reduce the conflict between the parties.[1] Similarly, a shared residence order was made in *A v A (Shared Residence)*[2] in which the children were happily spending 50% of their time with each parent while the adults themselves were incapable of working in harmony. In Wall J's view this was a prime case for a shared residence order since it not only reflected the reality that the children were dividing their time equally between their parents but it also reflected the fact that the parents were equal in the eyes of the law having equal duties and responsibilities towards their children. Moreover, it avoided the risk that a sole residence order could have been misinterpreted as enabling control by one parent when what the family needed was co-operation as recognised by the shared residence order. As Wall LJ later put it,[3] while it does not automatically follow that because children divide their time between their parents in proportion approaching equality, a shared residence order should be made, good reasons were required for not making one in such circumstances. Another factor that may be influential in making a shared residence order is the child's views.[4] Conversely, as we discuss below, it is not the case that shared residence orders are only apt where children alternate between the homes equally.

1   Cf *H v H (a minor) (No 2) (forum conveniens)* [1997] 1 FCR 603, in which Bracewell J refused to make a shared residence order because she thought that in that case it would be 'a recipe for conflict.'
2   [2004] EWHC 142 (Fam), [2004] 1 FLR 1195.
3   *Re P (children)(shared residence order)* [2005] EWCA Civ 1639, [2006] 1 FCR 309, [2006] 2 FLR 347.
4   As emphasised in *Re R (Residence: Shared Care: Children's Views)* [2005] EWCA Civ 542, [2006] 1 FLR 491, [2005] All ER (D) 238 (Apr), though on the facts a shared residence order was not made.

5.21 In *Re R (Residence: Shared Care: Children's Views)*[1] it was held that a harmonious relationship between the parents is not a prerequisite for making such an order. In *A v A* Wall J commented:[2]

'*D v D* makes it clear that a shared residence order is an order that the children live with both parents. It must therefore reflect the reality of the children's lives. Where children are living with one parent and are either not seeing the other parent or the amount of time to be spent with the other parent is limited or undecided, there cannot be a shared residence order. However, where the children are spending a substantial amount of time with both their parents, a shared residence order reflects the reality of the children's lives. It is not necessarily to be considered an exceptional order and should be made if it is in the best interest of the children concerned'.

1   [2005] EWCA Civ 542, [2006] 1 FLR 491, [2005] All ER (D) 238 (Apr).
2   [2004] EWHC 142 (Fam), [2004] 1 FLR 1195 at [119].

5.22 Illustrative of these two themes are *Re A (Children)(Shared Residence)*[1] and *Re F (Shared Residence Order)*.[2] The former concerned two girls who lived with their mother and a boy who lived with his father. The boy was unwilling to see his mother and was not doing so and there was some uncertainty about one of the girls' contact with her father. In setting aside the shared residence orders[3] Hale LJ emphasised that since a residence order was about where a child is to live it was difficult to make a shared residence order 'about a child who is not only living with one of the parents but is for the foreseeable future, unlikely even to visit with that parent'. In *Re F*, on the other hand, a shared residence order (with the children spending school terms with the mother and holidays with the father) was made in respect of two young children notwithstanding the fact that the mother lived in Edinburgh which was a considerable distance and in another jurisdiction from the father's home in Hampshire and with whom the children were to spend 38% of each year. Repeating the view that a shared residence order had to reflect the underlying reality of where the children lived and not deal with parental status, Thorpe LJ specifically rejected the notion that a shared residence order was only apt where the children alternated their two homes evenly. As Wall J later commented in *A v A*[4] in relation to *Re F* 'If the home offered by each parent was of equal status and importance to the children an order for shared residence would be valuable'. Building on this notion, Wilson LJ emphasised in *Re K (Shared Residence Order)*[5] that the two issues, the division of the child's time and whether the favoured division should be expressed in terms of a shared residence order or a contact order, were separate questions which needed to be adjudicated upon sequentially.

1   [2001] EWCA Civ 1795, [2002] 1 FCR 177.
2   [2003] EWCA Civ 592, [2003] 2 FLR 397.
3   These orders were originally coupled with others for care and control respectively to the mother in respect of the girls and the father in respect of the boy, which was clearly outside the CA 1989 powers.
4   Above at para [121].
5   [2008] EWCA Civ 526, [2008] All ER (D) 55 (Apr) at [14]. In that case the court upheld a shared residence order in which there was a 40%–60% division between the parents.

5.23 Where a residence order is made in favour of two persons who do not live together, then, under s 11(4), the order may specify the periods during which the child is to live in the different households concerned. Such directions may be general rather than specific and in some cases may not be needed at all. Since a residence order only settles the arrangements as to the person with whom the child is to live, any other conditions that are needed must be specified separately by the court acting under the powers vested by s 11(7),[1] or possibly at large.[2] Given that under a shared residence order neither carer is obliged to consult the other unless this is specified in the order, it is important that the order is clear on points which are fundamental to the success of the arrangement.[3]

[1] Section 11(7) is discussed at paras 5.108 ff.
[2] See *A v A (Shared Residence)* [2004] EWHC 142 (Fam), [2004] 1 FLR 1195 in which a Schedule was attached.
[3] For an attempt to do this see the Schedule attached to the residence order made in *A v A*, above.

(b) 'Interim' residence orders

5.24 The combination of s 11(3), which permits a court to make a s 8 order 'even though it is not in a position to dispose finally of [the] proceedings', and s 11(7)(c), under which orders can be made for a specified period, enables courts to make interim provision by way of a residence order for a limited period.[1] The Act, however, makes no distinction between a final residence order and one made as an interim measure.[2] Hence *all* such orders, even those expressed to last for a matter of days, have the same effect, and will, for example, discharge any existing care order,[3] confer, for the duration of the order, parental responsibility on those who do not already have it,[4] and empower the residence holder to remove the child from the UK for a period of less than one month.[5] It is established[6] that interim changes of residence are only justified if they are in the interests of children or there is otherwise an emergency.

[1] It is apparently possible to make an interim residence order to run alongside the main order; see *Re M (minors) (interim residence order)* [1997] 2 FCR 28, CA.
[2] As Bracewell J observed in *S v S (Custody: Jurisdiction)* [1995] 1 FLR 155 at 157; 'it has become common parlance to speak of "interim residence orders", but in fact there is no such creature within the Children Act 1989'.
[3] Section 91(1) and note *Re R-J (fostering: disqualified person)* [1998] 3 FCR 579, [1999] 1 FLR 605, CA.
[4] Section 12(2).
[5] Section 13(2). Presumably this power of removal is subject to the length of the order – an order expressed to last only a few days cannot be taken to vest a power of removal in excess of that.
[6] *Re H (children)(residence order)* [2007] EWCA Civ 529, [2007] 2 FCR 631 and *Re K (Interim Residence Order)* [2004] EWCA Civ 1827, [2005] 1 FLR 764, sub nom *Re K (procedure: family proceedings rules)* [2007] 2 FLR 631.

5.25 Where an 'interim' order is thought justified, careful thought needs to be given to its length, and mindful of the general enjoinder under s 1(2) to treat 'delay' as prima facie detrimental to the child's interest, courts should ensure that they are no longer than absolutely necessary.[1] It has been held[2] in relation to children in the interim care of a local authority that even a so-called 'interim residence order' should not be made as a temporary expedient.

[1] See eg *Re O (Minors) (Leave to Seek Residence Order)* [1994] 1 FLR 172, where, on the facts, five weeks' duration was thought too long. See also *Re Y (a minor) (ex parte interim orders)* [1993] 2 FCR 422, discussed below, para 5.28.
[2] *Re R-J (fostering: disqualified person)* [1998] 3 FCR 579, [1999] 1 FLR 605, CA.

(c) Ex parte applications and orders

5.26 Although applications for residence orders can be made ex parte,[1] they should only be granted exceptionally. In *Re G (minors) (ex parte interim residence order),*[2] Butler-Sloss LJ commented:

> 'In my judgment, it is very rare indeed that it is necessary to have an ex parte interim residence order. The only situation that I can think of is where there is a "snatch" situation – child abduction. There obviously will from time to time be other exceptional circumstances in which it is necessary for the protection of children that there should be an ex parte order'.

Furthermore, as Hale J observed in *Re J (minors) (ex parte orders):*[3]

> 'courts obviously have a special responsibility to ensure that ex parte orders which could cause harm to the interests of an adult or a child are not made without good reason. Orders requiring the handing over of a very young child to a parent with whom she has not lived for 20 months should surely be made only in exceptional circumstances.'

1   FPR 1991, r 4.4(4), as amended by SI 1992/2067 and FPC(CA 1989)R 1991, r 4(4), as amended by SI 1992/2068. Originally no such provision had been made.
2   [1992] 2 FCR 720 at 722, [1993] 1 FLR 910 at 912D.
3   [1997] 1 FCR 325 at 329, [1997] 1 FLR 606 at 609.

5.27 Ex parte orders are most likely to be justified in the context of abduction. In *Re B (Minors) (Residence Orders),*[1] for example, in which a mother 'snatched' one of four children of the family from the father (from whom she had separated a few days earlier) it was held justifiable to make ex parte residence orders to secure the return of the child and to prevent further snatches of the remaining children. Ex parte orders are commonly sought and sometimes granted in the context of international child abduction, ironically not infrequently at the behest of the parent who has wrongfully brought the child to the UK.[2]

1   [1992] Fam 162, [1992] 3 All ER 867, CA.
2   See eg *Re O (child abduction: undertakings)* [1995] 1 FCR 721 [1994] 2 FLR 349, *Re M (Child Abduction) (European Convention)* [1994] 1 FLR 551, and *Re AZ (A Minor) (Abduction: Acquiescence)* [1993] 1 FLR 682, in which ex parte orders were granted and *Re S (minors) (abduction)* [1993] 2 FCR 499, [1994] 1 FLR 297 where the application was refused.

5.28 Although ex parte residence orders can justifiably be made to protect a child from immediate physical or moral danger, the circumstances need to be compelling. In *Re G (minors) (ex parte interim residence order),*[1] an allegation that the mother had been taking cannabis was not thought to justify making an ex parte order in favour of the father. Even where an ex parte order is justified, as in *Re Y (a minor) (ex parte residence orders)*[2] where a grandmother successfully applied after the mother, who had a history of mental instability, had phoned her, threatening to commit suicide, it was held wrong to make the order stand for 12 weeks. In Johnson J's view it was unacceptable to make an order ex parte with no prospect for an inter partes hearing within seven days save in exceptional circumstances.

¹ [1992] 2 FCR 720, [1993] 1 FLR 910, CA. See also *Re P (a minor) (ex parte interim residence order)* [1993] 2 FCR 417, [1993] 1 FLR 915, CA, in which it was held wrong to have made an ex parte order because the child was in no immediate danger since she was already under the scrutiny of the local authority.

² [1993] 2 FCR 422.

5.29 In most cases¹ those wishing to challenge an ex parte order should await the full hearing rather than appeal it,² though an absent party wishing to challenge an ex parte order can apply to the court that made it for a discharge or variation.³ Such applications should be on notice but normally on short notice.⁴

¹ An appeal might, however, be justified if the return hearing is fixed too far ahead as in *Re Y (a minor) (ex parte residence orders)* [1993] 2 FCR 422.

² See *Re G (minors)* [1992] 2 FCR 720, [1993] 1 FLR 910, CA.

³ Per Purchas LJ in *Re P (a minor) (ex parte interim residence order)* [1993] 2 FCR 417 at 420, [1993] 1 FLR 915 at 917–918. See also to similar effect, *Re H (a minor) (wardship: challenging ex parte order)* [1994] 1 FCR 673, [1994] 2 FLR 981, CA.

⁴ Per Purchas LJ in *Re P (a minor) (ex parte interim residence order)* [1993] 2 FCR 417 at 420, [1993] 1 FLR 915 at 918.

(d) *Effect of residence orders*

(I) PARENTAL RESPONSIBILITY

5.30 Whilst in force residence orders confer parental responsibility on those in whose favour they are made such as relatives or foster parents who would not otherwise have that responsibility.¹ In the case of unmarried fathers who do not already have parental responsibility, the court is *bound*, upon making a residence order in his favour, to make a *separate* parental responsibility order under s 4.² This obligation is presumably also triggered by the making of a shared or joint residence order.

¹ Section 12(2), but note the restriction of that responsibility under s 12(3), discussed at para 3.90.

² Section 12(1), discussed at paras 3.71–3.72.

(II) CHANGE OF CHILD'S SURNAME

5.31 Under s 13(1)(a), it is an automatic condition of *all* residence orders¹ that no person may cause the child to be known by a new surname without either the written consent of every person who has parental responsibility or leave of the court.² Although it is not a *statutory* requirement to have the child's consent,³ Holman J left open⁴ whether the consent of an older child, particularly those aged 16 or over, was both necessary and sufficient. In any event if the child objects to the change of name he can seek leave to apply for a prohibited steps order to prevent the change.⁵ Applications for formal changes of surname should be made to the Central Office (Filing Department), and must be supported by the production of the consent in writing of every person having parental responsibility. In the absence of such consent the application will be adjourned until court leave is given.⁶

5.31 *Private law orders*

1   For a similar rule where the child is subject to a care order, see s 33(7) and (8) discussed at para 8.177.
2   Note in *Re R (a child)* [2001] EWCA Civ 1344, [2002] 1 FCR 170, sub nom *Re R (Surname: Using Both Parents)* [2001] 2 FLR 1358, in which the parents were urged to use both their names, there was no suggestion that in absence of the parties' agreement, court leave was not required to sanction the change. For the difficulties of enforcing an embargo against a name change see paras 5.166 ff.
3   Though attempts had been made to amend s 13 so as to require the child's consent, see 502 HL Official Report (5th Series) col 1262 by Lord Meston and 503 HL Official Report (5th Series), col 1347 per Lord Elwyn Jones.
4   In *Re C (minors)(change of surname)* [1997] 3 FCR 310 at 320, sub nom *Re PC (Change of Surname)* [1997] 2 FLR 730 at 739. Nonetheless the support of a 16 year old for a name change did not inhibit the court from refusing the change in *Re B (a minor) (change of surname)* [1996] 2 FCR 304, [1996] 1 FLR 791.
5   See Lord Mackay LC 502 HL Official Report (5th Series) col 1264.
6   *Practice Direction (minor: change of surname: deed poll)* [1995] 1 All ER 832, [1995] 1 WLR 365.

5.32 Section 13(1)(a) implements the Law Commission's recommendation[1] which, like the court in *W v A (Child: Surname)*,[2] considered a child's surname to be an important symbol of his identity and relationship with his parents and that while it may be in his interests for it to be changed, it was not a matter on which a parent with whom the child lives should be able to take unilateral action. Case law since the Act reflects this attitude. In *Dawson v Wearmouth*[3] the House of Lords held that a court should not sanction a change of a child's surname unless there is some evidence that it would lead to an improvement in his or her welfare. In any event s 13(1)(a) can only operate as an inhibition on the adult residence holder. As Wilson J observed in *Re B (minors) (change of surname):*[4]

> 'It does not, because in effect it cannot, prescribe the surname which the children ask teachers, friends and relatives to attribute to them'.

1   Law Com No 172, para 4.14.
2   [1981] Fam 14, [1981] 1 All ER 100, CA.
3   [1999] 2 AC 308, [1999] 2 All ER 353.
4   [1996] 2 FCR 304 at 308, [1996] 1 FLR 791 at 795, CA.

5.33 It has been held[1] that wherever there is a pre-existing residence order,[2] applications to change names are properly made under s 13(1)(a) rather than for a specific issue order under s 8[3] (conversely, where there is no pre-existing order application must be made for a s 8 order).[4] Although technically this means that there is no *obligation* to apply the welfare checklist,[5] it remains a useful aide mémoire.[6] A more serious consequence of requiring applications to be made under s 13 is that the consequential directions are probably not enforceable.[7] As with all applications directly concerning children's upbringing, in resolving disputes over children's names, whether under s 13 or s 8, the child's welfare is the court's paramount consideration.

1   By *Re B (minors) (change of surname)* [1996] 2 FCR 304, [1996] 1 FLR 791, CA. But note the query raised by Hale J in *Re M (leave to remove child from jurisdiction)* [1999] 3 FCR 708, [1999] 2 FLR 334, discussed at para 5.42.
2   Similarly if there is a pre-existing custody or care and control order made before the CA 1989, as in *Re B*, above.
3   This in any event is implicit in r 4.1(2)(a) and (c) of the FPR 1991 and by the different form for the order under s 13, namely Form C44 as opposed to C43, which is required by r 4.21(5).

⁴   *Re C (minors) (change of surname)* [1998] 2 FCR 544 at 545, [1998] 1 FLR 549 at 550, CA, per Wilson J *Dawson v Wearmouth* [1999] 2 AC 308 at 325 [1999] 2 All ER 353 at 363, per Lord Hobhouse and *Re W (A Child) (Illegitimate Child: Change of Surname)* [2001] Fam 1, [2000] 2 WLR 258, CA, per Butler-Sloss LJ at para (9).
⁵   Namely that provided by s 1(3), discussed at paras 2.38 ff.
⁶   Per Wilson J in *Re B*, above. In *Re C*, above, Ward LJ suggested the checklist would apply regardless of whether the application was under s 8 or s 13.
⁷   See *Re P (Minors) (Custody Order: Penal Notice)* [1990] 1 WLR 613, discussed at para 5.166.

5.34 In *Re W (a Child) (Illegitimate Child: Change of Surname)*[1] Butler-Sloss LJ summarised the position with regard to names as follows:

'(a)   If parents are married they both have the power and the duty to register their child's names.[2]

(b)   If they are not married the mother has the sole duty and power to do so.

(c)   After registration of the child's names, the grant of a residence order obliges any person wishing to change the surname to obtain the leave of the court for the written consent of all those who have parental responsibility.

(d)   In the absence of a residence order, the person wishing to change the surname from the registered name ought to obtain the relevant written consent or the leave of the court by making an application for a specific issue order.

(e)   On any application the welfare of the child is paramount, and the judge must have regard to the s 1(3) criteria.

(f)   Among the factors to which the court should have regard is the registered surname of the child and the reasons for the registration, for instance recognition of the biological link with the child's father. Registration is always a relevant and an important consideration but it is not in itself decisive. The weight to be given to it by the court will depend upon the other relevant factors or valid countervailing reasons which may tip the balance the other way.

(g)   The relevant considerations should include factors which may arise in the future as well as the present situation.

(h)   Reasons given for changing or seeking to change a child's name based on the fact that the child's name is or is not the same as the parent making the application do not generally carry much weight.

(i)   The reasons for an earlier unilateral decision to change a child's name may be relevant.

(j)   Any changes of circumstances of the child since the original registration may be relevant.

(k)   In the case of a child whose parents were married to each other, the fact of the marriage is important and I would suggest that there would have to be strong reasons to change the name of the father's surname if the child was so registered.

(l)   Where the child's parents were not married to each other, the mother has control over registration. Consequently on an application to change the surname of the child, the degree of commitment of the father to the child, the quality of contact, if it occurs, between father and child, the existence or absence of parental responsibility are all relevant factors to take into account.'

¹   [2001] Fam 1 at 7–8, [2000] 2 WLR 258 at 263–264, (para 9).
²   Where both register independently of one another, the first registration prevails, see *Re H (Child's Name: First Name)* [2002] EWCA Civ 190, [2002] 1 FLR 973, CA.

5.35   This summary is intended only as guidance with each case having to be decided upon its own facts and upon the basis of the paramountcy principle. Nevertheless it is clear that the burden of having to show that a change of name is for the child's benefit is a hard one to discharge. Ward LJ put it well in *Re C (a minor) (change of surname)*[1] when he said:

'... there is a heavy responsibility on those who seek to change a child's surname ... good and cogent reasons should be shown to allow a change.'

1   [1999] 1 FCR 318, [1998] 2 FLR 656, CA.

5.36   For examples of judicial refusals to sanction name changes see:

- *Re F (minors) (change of name)*:[1] leave was refused since there was no reason to suppose that a young girl was going to be embarrassed or particularly unusual in being registered at a school under a different name from the current surname of her mother.
- *Re B (a minor) (change of surname)*,[2] in which the Court of Appeal upheld a refusal despite the children's wish for change. Whilst agreeing that 'orders which ran flatly contrary to the wishes of normal adolescent children were virtually unknown to family law', that principle did not extend to the formal change of surname from that of the father to the stepfather since[3] that would only serve to injure the link between the father and the children, which was not in the latter's best interests. In so ruling Wilson J said 'there was no opprobrium nowadays for a child to have a different surname from that of adults in the household'.
- *A v Y (child's surname)*:[4] a specific issue order that a child be known by his father's name or a double surname was refused on the basis that he would be confused by a change of a name he had known for four years.
- *Dawson v Wearmouth*:[5] a father's application for a specific issue order to change his one-month-old child's name to his, (registered by the mother in her ex-husband's name) was refused because he could not demonstrate that such a change would be for the benefit of the child.
- *Re R (Change of Surname: Spanish Practice)*:[6] a mother was not permitted to change a child's surname on taking up residence in Spain since no benefit to the child could be shown. The parents, were, however, encouraged to consider the use of both surnames in line with Spanish practice.

1   [1994] 1 FCR 110, [1993] 2 FLR 837 n.
2   [1996] 2 FCR 304, [1996] 1 FLR, CA. See also *G v A (children: surname)* [1995] 2 FCR 223n.
3   This was because the prohibition against a change of name lay against the mother rather than against the child. As Wilson J pointed out, the child himself is free to ask others to address him in whatever name he chooses regardless of any s 13 directions.
4   [1999] 1 FCR 577, [1999] 2 FLR 5.
5   [1999] 2 AC 308, [1999] 2 All ER 353, HL.
6   [2001] EWCA Civ 1344, [2001] 2 FLR 1358, CA.

5.37   For examples of permitted name changes see:

- *Re S (Change of Names: Cultural Factors)*:[1] A Muslim mother, divorced from the Sikh father and now living in a Muslim community, was permitted to use Muslim names, including her current Muslim nick-name for the child in daily life and at school but not formally to change the child's name since that would contribute to an undesirable elimination of his Sikh identity.

- *Re W (Child) (Illegitimate Child: Change of Surname)*[2] in which one mother[3] was permitted to change her son's name to avoid him having the same name as his father who was a notorious criminal and thus to protect him from what she genuinely feared was a real risk of harm if his identity was revealed in the new locality where they were living, and another mother[4] was similarly allowed to do so following the father's convictions for indecent assaults both upon a 17-year-old girl and his 11-year-old niece.

- *Re H (Child's Name: First Name)*[5], in which a mother, whose own registration of name was cancelled because it was made after the father's registration, was permitted to use her given name for the child, though no order to that effect was thought necessary.

- *Re F (children)(Contact: change of name)*[6] – change of name permitted because of threat of abduction by father.

[1]   [2001] 2 FLR 1005, per Wilson J.
[2]   [2001] Fam 1, [2000] 2 WLR 258, CA. This case comprised three separate appeals.
[3]   Namely in the *Re A* case.
[4]   Namely in the *Re B* case.
[5]   [2002] EWCA Civ 190, [2002] 1 FLR 973.
[6]   [2007] EWHC 2543 (Fam), [2007] 3 FCR 832, [2008] 1 WLR 1163.

5.38 Case law suggests that it might be easier to persuade the court to sanction a change of name that has already occurred than to permit a prospective change. In *Re P (minors) (parental responsibility: change of name)*[1] the court rejected an unmarried father's application that his name be restored to his two children. The names had been changed some time ago, following the father's long-term imprisonment, when the mother decided to make a fresh start both for herself and her children and it was not in their interests for the name to be changed back. In *Re C (a minor) (change of surname)*,[2] notwithstanding that the unmarried mother's original decision to change her child's surname following the breakdown of her relationship with the father was not initially justified, the Court of Appeal resolved nevertheless that a further change now was not in the child's interests.

[1]   [1997] 3 FCR 739, [1997] 2 FLR 722, CA.
[2]   [1999] 1 FCR 318, [1998] 2 FLR 656, CA. See also *Re C (minors) (change of surname)* [1998] 2 FCR 544, [1998] 1 FLR 549, CA.

(III) REMOVAL OF CHILD FROM THE UNITED KINGDOM

5.39 Under s 13(1)(b), where a residence order is in force, no person may remove the child from the United Kingdom (ie England and Wales, Scotland and Northern Ireland) without either the written consent of every person who has parental responsibility or leave of the court. In *Re H (children) (residence order: condition)*[1] the Court of Appeal rejected the argument[2] that s 13(1)(b) requires court leave to remove the child from the jurisdiction rather than from the UK. Accordingly, there is no obligation upon the person with a residence order to seek permission to relocate anywhere *within* the UK though it is open to someone else (normally the other parent) to seek to prevent that relocation either by means of a prohibited steps order[3] or, possibly, by the imposition of a s 11(7) condition.[4] However, to succeed in such an application the circumstances will need to be exceptional.[5]

1   [2001] EWCA Civ 1338, [2001] 3 FCR 182, [2001] 2 FLR 1277, CA.
2   Relying on inter alia the side note to s 13 which refers to 'removal from jurisdiction', s 108(12) which applies particular provisions of the CA 1989, but not s 13, to Northern Ireland and to the exercise of power under s 101 to make delegated legislation in making the Children (Prescribed Orders – Northern Ireland, Guernsey and Isle of Man) Regulations 1991, SI 1991/2032.
3   Prohibited steps orders are discussed at paras 5.94 ff.
4   Section 11(7) conditions are discussed at paras 5.111 ff.
5   See *Re S (a child) (residence order: condition)* [2001] EWCA Civ 847, [2001] 3 FCR 154 and *Re H*, above, in which a prohibited steps order was made preventing the father, in whose favour a residence order had been granted, from taking the children to Northern Ireland on a permanent basis.

5.40

Temporary removals for less than one month

Under s 13(2), a person in whose favour a residence order has been made can remove the child for a period of less than one month without anyone's permission. This latter provision places those with a residence order in a special position since under the Child Abduction Act 1984[1] it is an offence to remove a child under the age of 16 outside the UK without the consent[2] of those having parental responsibility or leave of the court. Presumably, a shared residence order gives each parent the right to remove the child for less than one month.

1   For a discussion of this Act, see *Clarke Hall and Morrison on Children*, 2[11].
2   Though, unlike the requirement under the CA 1989, the consent does not have to be in writing. Note the qualifications to the consent requirement under s 1(5) of the 1984 Act.

5.41   Permitting unrestricted temporary removals, is intended[1] to allow persons in whose favour a residence order has been made to make arrangements for holidays without having to seek the permission of the 'non-residential' parent(s) and without even having to give notice. There is no limit on the number of temporary removals permitted. In cases of dispute a prohibited steps order can be made to curtail the right or a restriction of the right can be added to the residence order under s 11(7).[2]

1   See the Law Commission's recommendations (Law Com No 172), para 4.15.
2   See e g revised Children Act 1989 Guidance and Regulations, Vol 1, Court Orders (2008) Department for Children, Schools and Families, para 2.33 and Lord Mackay LC 503 HL Official Report (5th Series), col 1354. Section 11(7) is discussed at paras 5.108 ff.

5.42

Removals for more than one month

Where permission is sought to take the child out of the UK for more than one month, specific application for leave must be made to the court.[1] Where leave is sought under s 13 then under s 13(3) the court may grant leave either generally or for a specified purpose. However, it is not entirely settled whether leave should be sought under s 13 rather than by way of a specific issue order. Applying *Re B (minors) (change of surname)*[2] in relation to names, it seems that they should. However, this was queried by Hale J in *Re M (leave to remove child from jurisdiction)*.[3] As she pointed out, in the absence of a residence order an application must be made for a s 8 order, but 'if a person can apply [for a s 8 order] when there is no residence order in force, it is odd that they should have to use a different route when there is a residence order. The Family Proceedings Rules[4] may provide for a different route but it does not follow that it is the exclusive or only route'.

[1] According to Thorpe J in *Harris v Pinnington* [1995] 3 FCR 35, sub nom, *MH v GP (Child Emigration)* [1995] 2 FLR 106 such applications should be heard either in the High Court or county court depending upon the complexity of the case. But in *Re K (removal from jurisdiction: practice)* [1999] 3 FCR 673, 676, [1999] 2 FLR 1084, 1086–1087, Thorpe LJ said that where applications involve considerations of foreign legal systems and which may require the putting in place of mirror orders, they should normally be dealt with by a Family Division judge.
[2] [1996] 2 FCR 304, [1996] 1 FLR 791, CA, discussed at para 5.33.
[3] [1999] 3 FCR 708 at 715, [1999] 2 FLR 334 at 340.
[4] Namely the FPR 1991, rr 4.1(2)(a) and (c) and 4.21(5).

5.43 No matter by what route or by whom (it is equally open to the non-residential parent, for example, to seek leave to remove a child) the matter is raised, the court's general approach should be the same, namely, that in deciding whether to grant leave the court must apply the paramountcy of the child's welfare under s 1(1).[1] However, in applying that principle a distinction is to be drawn between seeking leave to remove children outside the UK (the so-called 'external relocation cases') and applications to take children to another part of the UK (the so-called 'internal relocation cases').[2]

[1] See *Re S (a child) (residence order: condition)* [2001] EWCA Civ 847, [2001] 3 FCR 154, CA. Technically, whereas it is mandatory to apply the welfare checklist in contested s 8 applications, it is only discretionary to do so under s 13, though even then Thorpe LJ has said in *Payne v Payne* [2001] EWCA Civ 166, [2001] Fam 473, [2001] 1 FCR 425, [2001] 1 FLR 1052 at [33] that courts should nevertheless take the precaution of having regard to it.
[2] See Thorpe LJ's summary in *Re H (children) (residence order: condition)* [2001] EWCA Civ 1338, [2001] 3 FCR 182, [2001] 2 FLR 1277 at [16]–[17].

5.44

External relocation applications

In Payne v Payne,[1] the Court of Appeal held that the CA 1989 had not altered the underlying factors that should be taken into account in determining whether to give leave and that the 'internal application' of the European Convention on Human Rights (ECHR) following the implementation of the Human Rights Act 1998 did not 'necessitate a revision of the fundamental approach to relocation applications formulated by this court and consistently applied over so many years.'[2] Nevertheless to guard against a risk of 'too perfunctory an investigation resulting from too ready an assumption that the [primary carer]'s proposals are necessarily compatible with the child's welfare', Thorpe LJ suggested that courts should adopt the following discipline, namely:

> '[40](a)Pose the question: is the mother's application genuine in the sense that it is not motivated by some selfish desire to exclude the father from the child's life? Then ask is the mother's application realistic, by which I mean founded on practical proposals both well researched and investigated? If the application fails either of these tests refusal will inevitably follow.
>
> (b)   If however the application passes these tests then there must be a careful appraisal of the father's opposition: is it motivated by genuine concern for the future of the child's welfare or is it driven by some ulterior motive? What would be the extent of the detriment to him and his future relationship with the child were the application granted? To what extent would that be offset by extension of the child's relationships with the maternal family and homeland?
>
> (c)   What would be the impact on the mother, either as the single parent or as a new wife, or a refusal of her realistic proposal?
>
> (d)   The outcome of the second and third appraisals must then be brought into an overriding review of the child's welfare as the paramount consideration directed by the statutory checklist insofar as appropriate.
>
> [41]   In suggesting such a discipline I would not wish to be thought to have diminished the importance that this court has consistently attached to the emotional and psychological well-being of the primary carer. In any evaluation of the welfare of the child as the paramount consideration great weight must be given to this factor'.

¹   [2001] EWCA Civ 166, [2001] Fam 473, [2001] 1 FCR 425, [2001] 1 FLR 1052, CA. Note that Munby J's application of a different test in *Re X and Y (leave to remove from jurisdiction: no order principle)* [2001] 2 FCR 398, [2001] 2 FLR 118, was expressly disapproved by the Court of Appeal in *Re H (children) (residence order: condition)* [2001] EWCA Civ 1338, [2001] 3 FCR 182, [2001] 2 FLR 1277. For comments of the *Payne* test see e g Pressdee 'Relocation, Relocation: Rigorous Scrutiny Revisited' [2008] Fam Law 220 and Geekie 'Relocation and Shared Residence: One Route or Two?' [2008] Fam Law 446.

²   Above at para 35, per Thorpe LJ agreeing with Ward LJ's earlier conclusions in *Re G-A (a child) (removal from jurisdiction: human rights)* [2001] 1 FCR 43, sub nom *Re (A Permission to Remove Child from Jurisdiction: Human Rights)* [2000] 2 FLR 225, CA, in which it was held that permission to remove a child permanently from the jurisdiction does not, per se, breach the other parent's 'right to family life' under art 8 of the European Convention on Human Rights.

5.45 Although Thorpe LJ has since said¹ that trial judges should direct themselves only by reference to *Payne* he has also acknowledged² that his guidance is unhelpful in its layout inasmuch as it is easy to assume that para [40] contains the totality of the discipline whereas it is important to understand that para [41] (stressing the importance of the primary carer's well-being) is as much part of the discipline as if it had been expressed in para [40] (c). A number of post-*Payne* refusals of leave at first instance have either been overturned or remitted for retrial because too little regard was paid to the primary carer's well being. In *Re B (Leave to Remove)*,³ for example, a lesbian mother (who conceived through her partner's brother agreeing to act as a sperm donor) wanted to return to the USA where she had been offered a good position in the film world (her former career) and to look after her own mother who lived in Florida by herself and who was in poor health. Leave was granted inter alia because the impact upon the mother if leave were to be refused would have been 'dramatic' and would have affected her care of the child (changing primary carer was not even an option). *Re B* may be compared with *Re H (A Child)*[4] in which leave was refused inter alia because the mother conceded that if her disabled husband (whom the mother had married following her divorce from the father) were to be denied permission permanently to enter the USA she should 'make the best of it'.

1   In *Re H (Children)(Residence Order: Condition)* [2001] EWCA Civ 1338, [2001] 2 FLR 1277 at [17].
2   *Re B (Leave to Remove: Impact of Refusal)* [2004] EWCA Civ 956, [2005] 2 FLR 239.
3   [2006] EWHC 1783 (Fam), [2007] 1 FLR 333. See also eg *Re B (Leave to Remove: Impact of Refusal)* above; *Re G (Removal From Jurisdiction)* [2005] EWCA Civ 170, [2005] 2 FLR 166 and *Re B (Removal From Jurisdiction); Re S (Removal From Jurisdiction)* [2003] EWCA Civ 1149, [2003] 1 FLR 1043.
4   [2007] EWCA Civ 222, [2007] 2 FLR 317.

5.46 Whether there is a difference in principle between so-called 'lifestyle cases', that is, where the desire to relocate is inspired by a desire to improve general living conditions and those more familiar cases of the carer wishing to return to her native country or where a specific employment opportunity has arisen for a member of the family, is a matter of debate. In *Re B (Leave To Remove: Impact of Refusal)*[1] the court rejected the argument that there was a difference. According to Thorpe LJ[2] there is but one standard to be applied to all cases. The applicant's explanation for relocating is the core of the case and the judge must assess that application and weigh it in the balance with the other considerations outlined in *Payne*. In contrast, in *Re F and H (children)*,[3] in upholding a decision to permit an American mother and her child to relocate to the USA, the Court of Appeal commented that in the case of a cross-border family where the primary carer was returning to a completely familiar environment, the bar was set far lower than in a case where the applicant was pursuing a dream in an unknown and untried environment. It was even lower where the proposal was to return to a completely familiar home life after a brief absence.

1   [2004] EWCA Civ 956, [2005] 2 FLR 239.
2   At [17].
3   [2007] EWCA Civ 692, [2007] Fam Law 870.

5.47 There are other examples in which the '*Payne* discipline' may have less relevance. In *Re A (Temporary Removal From Jurisdiction)* it was accepted that a distinction should be made between applications for permanent removal and those for a temporary removal. As Thorpe LJ put it[2] 'The more temporary the removal, the less regard should be paid to the principles stated in *Payne v Payne*'. In that case the trial judge was held to have underestimated the impact on the mother's career plans of his refusal to grant her leave to go to South Africa for two years to carry out her research and complete her PhD. Leave was accordingly granted. Compelling urgency is another example. In *Re J (Leave to Remove: Urgent Case)*[3] the two children in question were living with the father and had no contact with, nor wished to see, their mother. The father, however, was in dire straits. The family home had burnt down; he was bankrupt and unemployed and his parents, who had been financially support-ing him, were planning to move to Bulgaria. The father had been offered a job in Bulgaria. In upholding the granting of leave, it was observed that the discipline espoused by *Payne* was hardly applicable to these facts but insofar as it was, it pointed in the direction of granting the request.

¹   [2004] EWCA Civ 1587, [2005] 1 FLR 639.
²   At [13].
³   [2006] EWCA Civ 1897, [2007] 2 FCR 149, [2007] 1 FLR 2033.

5.48 *Payne* is predicated upon the premise that the application for leave is being made by the sole primary carer but that will not always be the case. In *Re Y (Leave To Remove From Jurisdiction)*¹ a five-year-old child was effectively sharing his home equally with each parent and on the facts he was found to be well settled, bilingual and bicultural. In these circumstances it was held that the cost to the child of a move from Wales to Texas was too high and leave to remove him by the mother, was refused. In *Payne* itself, Butler-Sloss P said² that the observations were made upon the premise that residence is not a live issue. If there is a finely balanced dispute as to which parent the child should live with, then the future plans of each parent are clearly relevant, but if that issue is clear then the plans for removal from the jurisdiction are not likely to be significant in the decision about residence. The corollary of this is that it by no means automatically follows that because an application for leave to remove has been refused, the applicant should lose residence of the child.³

¹   [2004] 2 FLR 330.
²   [2001] EWCA Civ 166, [2001] Fam 473, [2001] 1 FCR 425, [2001] 1 FLR 1052 at [86].
³   *Re T (Removal From Jurisdiction)* [1996] 2 FLR 352, CA.

5.49 Although a reasonable application (in the sense that it is genuine, not motivated by an inappropriate selfish desire, and practical) does not create a presumption in favour of leave being given, nevertheless in practice such an application will only be refused if it is incompatible with the child's welfare. In this latter regard the detrimental impact that a refusal of leave might have upon the care that the primary carer would give usually outweighs the likelihood of harm following from a reduction of contact with the non-residential parent.¹ In short, the best chance of opposing a leave application is to show that it should fail at the first hurdle, namely, that the applicant was inappropriately motivated or that the plans were ill thought out. An example of the former is *Tyler v Tyler*² in which a father, who had enjoyed frequent contact with his two sons, successfully opposed the mother's request for leave to emigrate to Australia to join her family, it being found that the mother's dominant motive was bitterness towards her husband and that furthermore she would be able to cope with the disappointment if permission was refused. An example of the latter is *H v F (Refusal of Leave to Remove a Child from the Jurisdiction)*,³ in which a mother of Jamaican origin wanted to return to Jamaica together with her nearly 10 year old son and her father. She planned to establish a bed and breakfast business in a property owned by her father but these plans were found not to be well thought-out and did not seem viable. This finding together with the value of continued contact with the father and the ambivalence of the child himself towards the move led to leave being refused.[4]

1 See *Re C (Permission To Remove From Jurisdiction)* [2003] EWHC 1596 (Fam), [2003] 1 FLR 1066, per Charles J.
2 [1989] 2 FLR 158, CA.
3 [2005] EWHC 2705 (Fam), [2006] 1 FLR 776. See also *R v R (Leave to Remove)* [2004] EWHC 2572 (Fam), [2005] 1 FLR 687 – mother refused leave to take her children to France because she did not have the emotional stability to establish a new life in another country and her plans to do so were insufficiently thought out.
4 See also *M v M (Minors)(Jurisdiction)* [1993] 1 FCR 5, CA – leave refused because of the children's (aged 12 and 10) opposing views.

5.50 When granting leave, the court should assess all risks (for example, enforcement of a contact order) and build in all practical safeguards (for example, notarised agreements and mirror orders),[1] not simply trusting the parent or accepting undertakings.[2] The court may, in granting leave, impose conditions, for example requiring the deposit of a sum of money until the parent with leave obtains 'authentication' of the contact order in the foreign court and complies with an order relating to the child's education; upon evidence of compliance, the deposit would be released,[3] or requiring the swearing of a solemn oath on the Quran.[4]

1 Ie an order made in the jurisdiction to which the child is being taken.
2 *Re K (removal from jurisdiction: practice)* [1999] 3 FCR 673, [1999] 2 FLR 1984, CA.
3 *Re S (Removal From Jurisdiction)* [1999] 1 FLR 850, CA. In *Re L (Removal From Jurisdiction: Holiday)* [2001] 1 FLR 241 the mother was required to deposit a bond which was to be released upon the child's return.
4 *Re A (security for return to jurisdiction) (note)* [1999] 1 FCR 284, [1999] 2 FLR 1n, *Re L (Removal From Jurisdiction: Holiday)* above.

5.51

Internal relocation applications[1]

There is no statutory restriction in respect of moving a child *within* the UK.[2] Consequently the person with residence does not require leave to so relocate. Nevertheless such a proposed move can be challenged by the non resident parent seeking a prohibited steps order[3] or the imposition of a condition on the residence order under s 11(7). The '*Payne* test' has no application[4] but rather the approach is, as established in *Re S (a child) (residence order: condition)*,[5] only to restrict the principal carer's right to reside anywhere within the UK in exceptional circumstances. The rationale for this less stringent approach compared with giving leave to relocate externally is that, in Thorpe LJ's words in *Re H (children) (residence order; condition)*,[6] within 'the same sovereignty there will be the same system of laws, with the same rights of the citizen, rights for instance to education, health care and statutory benefits'. He added 'Equally it can be said that within Europe, while perhaps the burden upon the applicant may be greater it is equally mitigated by the fact that within the community there is the same fundamental approach to social issues and a real endeavour to achieve harmonisation, obviously in social policy but also in family justice'.

1   See also the discussion at paras 5.114 ff.
2   Aliter outside the UK, including therefore to the Isle of Man or the Channel Isles.
3   Discussed at paras 5.94 ff.
4   See eg *Re B (Prohibited Steps Order)* [2007] EWCA Civ 1055, [2008] 1 FLR 613 at [13],
    per Lloyd LJ relying on *Re E (Residence: Imposition of Conditions)* [1997] 2 FLR 638 at
    643, per Butler-Sloss LJ.
5   [2001] EWCA Civ 847, [2001] 3 FCR 154.
6   [2001] EWCA Civ 1338 at para 20, [2001] 3 FCR 182 at 188, [2000] 2 FLR 1277 at
    1283.

(IV) THE EFFECTS OF SHARED RESIDENCE ORDERS

5.52 The CA 1989 does not distinguish between different types of residence orders. On the face of it, therefore, shared residence orders must have the same effect as sole residence orders.[1] But it has become apparent than on occasion the consequences of making a shared residence order requires careful thought. For example, in *Holmes-Moorhouse v Richmond-up-Thames London Borough Council*[2] the question arose as to what impact a shared residence order had on the local housing authority's obligation under the Housing Act 1996, ie whether the order (under which the children were to spend alternative weekends and half the school holidays with the father) obliged the authority to treat the father as having a priority housing need as a person with whom dependent children might reasonably be expected to reside. It was held that notwithstanding the order the authority still had to satisfy itself as to the reasonableness of the expectation that the dependent children could live with the father.[3]

1   Eg upon granting an unmarried father without parental responsibility a shared residence
    order the court must, pursuant to s 12(1), make a separate parental responsibility order in
    his favour and, pursuant to s 13(1), each person with a shared residence order has the right
    to remove the child outside the UK for a period of less than one month without anyone's
    permission. See paras 5.30 and 5.40 respectively.
2   [2007] EWCA Civ 970, [2008] 1 WLR 1289, [2008] 1 FLR 1061.
3   But in judging what weight to place on the shared residence order a distinction had to be
    drawn to an order made despite opposition, in which case the court would have had to
    consider, pursuant to s 1(3)(f) of the CA 1989, the parent's capability to provide
    accommodation, and one made by consent, where such an enquiry might not have been
    made. In the former case there would be no room for the authority to make a fresh
    assessment of the reasonableness of the parent's expectations, whereas there would be
    room in the latter case. Though in that case if the authority considered that the
    expectations were not reasonable the parties could return to the court to review the
    consent order, see Moses LJ, [2007] EWCA Civ 970, [2008] 1 FLR 1061 at [52].

5.53 The making of a shared residence order rather than a contact order can also be significant for the purposes of the revised Brussels II Regulation. In particular where, following a refusal to return an abducted child by another Member State, an application is brought before the domestic court[1] and that court then makes a shared residence order the question arises whether that order constitutes 'a judgment which requires the return of the child' within the meaning of art 11(8) and which has to be recognised and immediately enforced by the 'non-returning jurisdiction'.[2]

1   Ie under the scheme provided for by art 11(6), (7) of the Regulation, for details of which,
    see *Clarke Hall and Morrison on Children*, 2[35–21] ff and Lowe, Everall and Nicholls
    The New Brussels II Regulation 31 ff.

2   In Singer J's view in *Re A; HA v MB (Brussels II Revised: Article 11(7) Application)* [2007]
EWHC 2016 (Fam), [2008] 1 FLR 289, [2007] All ER (D) 156 (Aug), discussed by Lowe
'The Current Experience and Difficulties of Applying Brussels II Revised', [2007] IFL 183,
it did not matter whether it was a contact or a shared residence order, as neither would
trigger the obligation but the matter is not free from doubt.

2. Contact orders[1]

5.54 Section 8(1) defines a contact order as an order requiring the person
with whom the child lives, or is to live, to allow the child to visit or stay with
the person named in the order, or for that person and the child otherwise to
have contact with each other'.

Section 8 contact orders should not be confused with 'care contact orders'
under s 34. The former exclusively control contact between individuals and
cannot be made in favour of a local authority nor while the child is in care.[2]
The latter exclusively control contact with a child in local authority care.[3]

1   For studies into how contact is working see eg Trinder 'The Longer Term Outcomes in
Court Consideration' (Dept for Children, Schools and Families, November 2007) summarised at [2008] Fam Law 81, a follow-up study to her research 'Making Contact Happen
or Making Contact Work: The Process and Outcomes of In-Court Conciliation' (DCA,
2006) summarised at [2006] Fam Law 416; the many studies referred to in Adam's
challenging article 'Parents' Rights v Children's Needs in Private Cases' [2007] Fam Law
257 (though note a reply by Pugsley at [2007] Fam Law 454; and the seminal report
Making Contact Work (A Report to the Lord Chancellor by the Advisory Board on Family
Law; Children Act Sub-Committee, 2002) which was instrumental in the reforms introduced by the Children and Adoption Act 2006.
2   Section 9(1) and (2), discussed at paras 5.124 and 5.125.
3   Discussed at paras 8.204 ff.

(a) Legal considerations

5.55 In general terms contact orders provide for the child to visit or stay with
the person named in the order, the emphasis thus being on the child rather
than parent. Contact orders embrace both physical and non-physical contact
and may therefore range from long or short visits to contact by letter or
telephone.[1] Indirect contact can also be by email, texting or by other means.[2]
For the purposes of protection, indirect contact can be facilitated by third
parties.[3] For the purposes of s 10(6), under which applications may be made
without leave to vary certain s 8 orders,[4] there is no rigid compartmentalisa-
tion between direct and indirect contact.[5]

1   For examples of contact by post see *Re P (minors) (contact: discretion)* [1999] 1 FCR 566,
[1998] 2 FLR 696, *A v L (contact)* [1998] 2 FCR 204, [1998] 1 FLR 361 and *Re M (a
minor) (contact: conditions)* [1994] 1 FCR 678, [1994] 1 FLR 272, each involving letter
contact with a father in prison; *Re P (Contact: Indirect Contact)* [1999] 2 FLR 893 indirect
contact with a father who had just been released from prison; *L v C* [1995] 3 FCR 125,
sub nom *Re L (Contact: Transsexual Applicant)* [1995] 2 FLR 438 – indirect contact with
transsexual father; and *Re D (a child) (IVF treatment)* [2001] EWCA Civ 230, [2001]
1 FCR 289, sub nom *Re D (Parental Responsibility: IVF Baby)* [2001] 1 FLR 972, indirect
contact with a man deemed to be the father under the Human Fertilisation and
Embryology Act 1990. For examples of indirect contact being ordered with violent or
abusive parents, see *Re S (Violent Parent: Indirect Contact)* [2000] 1 FLR 481; *Re H*

(Contact: Domestic Violence) [1998] 3 FCR 385, [1998] 2 FLR 42, CA and *Re M (Sexual Abuse Allegations: Interviewing Techniques)* [1999] 2 FLR 92.

2 Including video recordings, see eg *Re A (Contact: Witness Protection Scheme)* [2005] EWHC 2189 (Fam), [2006] 2 FLR 551 and see 'Indirect Contact via Video-tape' [1997] Fam Law 310, which might be a particularly useful way of re-establishing contact.

3 Eg via CAFCASS, see eg *Re F (Indirect Contact)* [2006] EWCA Civ 1426, [2007] 1 FLR 1015.

4 See para 5.145.

5 *Re W (application for leave: whether necessary)* [1996] 3 FCR 337n.

(b) General considerations

5.56 Orders may provide for the child to have contact with any person (including, where appropriate, a sibling) and more than one contact order may be made in respect of a child. In theory, it is within the court's powers to provide for the child to have contact with an unwilling parent[1] but it seems an impracticable option and therefore questionable in terms of the child's welfare. In fact the Joint Committee on the Draft Children (Contact) and Adoption Bill were in favour of such a power[2] but the Government, dismissed the suggestion saying:[3]

> 'We would be concerned about the implications that would arise if contact orders were to be used to force someone, against their wishes, to have contact with a child. The child's welfare must be the paramount consideration in making decisions about their upbringing and there are serious issues raised about the potential distress, or even harm, such contact could cause to the child or children involved'.

1 But note Wall LJ's comment in *Re S (children)(restriction on applications), Re E (a child) (restriction on applications)* [2006] EWCA Civ 1190, [2006] 3 FCR 50, sub nom *Re S (Permission to Seek Relief)* [2007] 1 FLR 482 at [88] 'There is currently no power to compel absent parents to have contact with their children.'

2 See their First Report HL Paper 100–1/HC 400–1.

3 See the Government Reply to the Report from the Joint Committee Cm 6583 (June 2005).

5.57 A contact order can be the sole order even between parents and may be appropriate where there is no dispute as to the person with whom the child is to live. Orders can provide for contact to take place at Contact Centres. The role of these Centres has been said[1] to be 'one of the most important developments of the last ten years'. They are useful as a means of providing a temporary venue for supported contacted in cases where the child's parents are unable to provide an alternative. They are not, however, intended to be places for contact over the long term, nor are they ipso facto the equivalent of professionally supervised contact. Orders can provide for contact to take place abroad.[2]

1 See *Making Contact Work*, above at ch 8.

2 *Re F (a Minor) (Access out of Jurisdiction)* [1973] Fam 198, [1973] 3 All ER 493.

5.58 Although courts can make orders for 'reasonable contact',[1] if that is the sole order between the parents then, having regard to s 1(5),[2] one may question the need to make the order at all. Such an order might, however, be justifiable where the applicant is not a parent, for example a grandparent, since without an order that person has no locus standi in relation to the child[3] and it might be valuable if the person with whom the child lives is hostile to the absent parent having contact and who might therefore seek to prevent it. Where restricted or supervised contact is thought appropriate the court may attach directions or conditions under s 11(7).[4]

1   Before the CA 1989 orders for 'reasonable' access were common and the original Children Act 1989 Guidance and Regulations, Vol 1, Court Orders (1991) Department of Health at para 2.29 anticipated that orders for reasonable contact would be the 'usual order'. The revised Guidance (2008) Department for Children, Schools and Families, para 2.35 merely refers to 'reasonable contact' as one of the options.
2   Discussed at paras 2.64 ff.
3   Cf the similar arguments, discussed at para 2.72, as to making s 8 orders generally.
4   Section 11(7) is discussed at paras 5.108 ff. Note also *Leeds County Council v C* [1993] 1 FCR 585, [1993] 1 FLR 269 which establishes that there is no power under s 11(7) to order a local authority to supervise contact.

5.59 Contact orders requiring one parent to allow the child to visit the other parent[1] will automatically lapse if the parents subsequently live together for a continuous period of more than six months.[2] While the child is with a parent on a contact visit that parent may exercise parental responsibility, at any rate with respect to short-term matters,[3] without consulting the other provided he does nothing which is incompatible with any existing court order.[4]

1   Note: if the order is directed against someone other than a parent or if the child is permitted contact with a third party it will not lapse because of the parents' cohabitation.
2   Section 11(6).
3   But not to take important steps that have long-term consequences for the child, see eg *Re G (a minor) (parental responsibility: education)* [1995] 2 FCR 53, [1994] 2 FLR 964, CA and the other cases discussed at para 3.99.
4   See paras 3.96 ff.

5.60 In *Re S (a minor) (contact: evidence)*[1] it was held that a *subpoena duces tecum* should be issued against the police to produce a video of an interview with a five-year-old child in which she made allegations of sexual abuse against her father so as to have the best evidence available to determine the contact application. Nevertheless, Hale J observed that it was not always wrong to consider proportionality between the benefits to the welfare of the child and the resources to be expended on the inquiry. In *Re B (minors) (contact)*[2] it was held that a full hearing permitting the parties to call oral evidence and cross-examine any witnesses they may choose is not always necessary. A judge has a broad discretion to decide a contact application on the basis of written evidence provided there is sufficient evidence upon which to make the decision and having duly taken into account such factors as whether the evidence sought to be addressed at the full hearing was likely to effect the outcome; whether the delay that could be caused by the full hearing would be exceptionally detrimental to the child's welfare; the prospects of success of the applicant at the full trial and whether the justice of the case required a full investigation with oral evidence. *Re B*, however, represents the exceptional case and where oral evidence is heard, including evidence from a Children and Family Reporter, the parties, no matter how weak their case may be, ought to be allowed to cross-examine and be given the opportunity to give their own oral evidence.[3] Where expert evidence is adduced it is wrong for a judge to ignore it.[4]

1   [1998] 3 FCR 70, CA.
2   [1994] 2 FCR 812, [1994] 2 FLR 1, CA. See also *Re M (Contact)* [1995] 1 FLR 1029.
3   *Re I and H (Contact: Right to Give Evidence)* [1998] 1 FLR 876, CA.
4   *Re M (minors) (contact: evidence)* [1998] 2 FCR 538, CA, judge erred in following welfare officer's opinion rather than the expert opinion of a doctor.

(I) INTERIM CONTACT ORDERS

5.61 Section 11(3) permits a court to make an interim contact order where it is not in a position finally to dispose of the proceedings. But, courts should be cautious about making interim orders if the principle of contact is in dispute and substantial factual issues are unresolved.[1] Where sexual abuse is alleged against a parent and the child is showing behavioural problems then, even if on the available evidence abuse is not likely to be established but further investigation is necessary, while it might be appropriate to allow contact to continue, it is not appropriate to make an order for staying contact.[2] In cases of domestic violence where directions are given for a fact-finding hearing the court should consider whether an interim order is in the child's interests bearing in mind whether the safety of the child and the residential parent can be secured before, during and after any contact.[3]

1   Per Wall J in *D v R* [1995] 1 FCR 501, sub nom *Re D (Contact: Interim Order)* [1995] 1 FLR 495. See also *Re R (a child)(contact)* [2007] EWCA Civ 943, [2007] All ER (D) 46 (Aug).
2   *Re W (a minor) (staying contact)* [1998] 2 FCR 453, [1998] 2 FLR 450, CA. It may not, however, be possible, particularly in domestic violence cases, to make an interim order without hearing oral evidence or the advice of a Children and Family Reporter: see *Re M (Interim Contact: Domestic Violence)* [2000] 2 FLR 377, CA; *D v R* above and *Re A (Contact: Witness Protection Scheme)* [2005] EWHC 2189 (Fam), [2006] 2 FLR 551.
3   *Practice Direction (Residence and Contact Orders: Domestic Violence)* [2008] 1 WLR 1062, paras 18 ff.

(II) PROHIBITING CONTACT

5.62 When the CA 1989 was first implemented it was thought that orders denying contact required a prohibited steps order. As the Department of Health's original Children Act 1989 Guidance and Regulations stated:[1]

> 'a s 8 order is a positive order in the sense that it requires contact to be allowed between an individual and a child and cannot be used to deny contact'.

However, this reasoning was rejected in *Nottingham County Council v P*,[2] Sir Stephen Brown P commenting:

> 'We agree with the judge that the sensible and appropriate construction of the term "contact order" includes a situation where a court is required to consider whether any contact should be provided for. An order that there shall be "no contact" falls within the general concept and common sense requires that it should be considered to fall within the definition of "contact order" in s 8(1).'

On this analysis prohibiting contact has to be considered as part of a s 8 contact order. However, in *Re H (minors) (prohibited steps order)*,[3] the Court of Appeal subsequently made a prohibited steps order against a mother's former cohabitant preventing him from having or seeking contact with the children to whom it was considered he posed a risk. It was held that it was only by this means that an order could be directed (and thus enforced) against the man. Butler-Sloss LJ commented that had a 'no contact' order been made it would have been directed against the mother who would thus have been obliged to prevent contact. That would have been inappropriate in this case since she neither wanted the children to have such contact nor, more importantly, had she the power to control it.[4] This ruling seems preferable to *Nottingham* and it is suggested that all prohibitions of contact are best achieved by a prohibited steps order.

1   Children Act 1989 Guidance and Regulations, Vol 1, Court Orders (1991) Department of Health, para 2.30. The revised Guidance (2008) para 2.35 merely states that an order 'may provide for no contact'.
2   [1994] Fam 18 at 38–39, [1993] 3 All ER 815 at 824, CA, discussed further at para 5.105.
3   [1995] 4 All ER 110, [1995] 1 WLR 667. *Nottingham* was not cited by the court.
4   The children were of school age and, as Butler-Sloss LJ said, 'With the best will in the world the mother could not protect her children going to or from school or at school or at play ... '

(III) CONTACT ACTIVITY DIRECTIONS AND CONDITIONS

5.63 As part of the strategy to facilitate contact, powers to make contact activity directions and conditions have been introduced by the Children and Adoption Act 2006 via the insertions of ss 11A–11G into the CA 1989.[1] Directions can be made at any stage in proceedings prior to a final order being made as to contact. Conversely, conditions can only be made upon the making (or variation) of a final contact order. The latter are part of a formal order and are therefore enforceable on pain of contempt, by an enforcement order or by a financial compensation order.[2] Although there are no formal sanctions for non-compliance with directions, due account can be taken of any breaches[3] in the final disposal of the contact issue.

1   For the background to these measures, see paras 5.9–5.10 above.
2   Discussed respectively at paras 5.164 ff, 5.179 ff and 5.185 ff.
3   A CAFCASS or a Welsh family proceedings officer can be asked to monitor compliance with a direction and to report to the court any failure to comply: s 11G(2).

(IV) CONTACT ACTIVITY DIRECTIONS

5.64 A contact activity direction requires 'an individual who is a party to the proceedings to take part in an activity that promotes contact with the child concerned'.[1] A direction can only be made when a court is *considering* whether to make, vary or discharge a contact order but not when it is making a final contact order.[2] Even then the power is limited to disputed cases.[3] Furthermore individuals must be habitually resident in England and Wales[4] and no direction can be made if the contact order 'is, or would be if made, an excepted order' (effectively contact orders made in the context of adoption proceedings (other than step-parent adoptions)).[5] Children can only be made to take part in an activity if they are the parent of the child in relation to whom the court is considering provision about contact.[6] In other words there is no coercive power over children qua children.

1   Section 11A(3).
2   Section 11A(1), (7). In such cases the court must make a contact activity *condition*.
3   Section 11B(1). This restriction has been criticised as unnecessarily limiting the court's powers. Furthermore, there is no requirement that contact must be disputed when imposing conditions, see para 5.68.
4   Section 11B(7). A direction ceases to have effect if the individual subject to the direction ceases to be habitually resident in England and Wales.
5   Section 11B(3). An 'excepted order' is fully defined by s 11B(4)–(6).
6   Section 11B(2).

5.65 A direction must specify both the activity and the person providing the activity.[1] The activities that may be so required include (a) programmes, classes and counselling or guidance sessions of a kind that may assist a person as regards establishing, maintaining or improving contact with a child and, may, by addressing a person's violent behaviour, enable to facilitate contact; (b) sessions in which information or advice is given as regards making or operating arrangements by means of mediation.[2] A direction cannot be used to require medical or psychiatric examinations or mediation.[3]

1   Section 11A(4).
2   Section 11A(5).
3   Section 11A(6).

5.66 In deciding whether to make a direction, 'the welfare of the child concerned is to be the court's paramount consideration'.[1] The court must also be satisfied that the activity is appropriate in the circumstances of the case; that the provider of the activity concerned is suitable to provide it and the activity is available in a place to which it is reasonable to expect the person in question to travel.[2] Before making a direction the court must obtain and consider information about the individual who would be subject to the direction and its likely effect upon him in particular with regard to any conflict with his religious beliefs or any interference with the times that he is at work or attending an educational establishment.[3] Courts can seek information on any of these points from a CAFCASS or Welsh family proceedings officer.[4]

1   Section 11A(9).
2   Section 11A(8) applying s 11E(1)–(4).
3   Section 11E(5), (6).
4   Section 11E(7). The appropriate officer is bound to comply with such a request.

(V) CONTACT ACTIVITY CONDITIONS

5.67 Like a direction, a contact activity condition 'requires an individual ... to take part in an activity that promotes contact with the child concerned.[1] But unlike directions, they are made when making or varying (but not discharging) a final contact order.[2] Conceptually the 2006 Act reforms are predicated upon the view that conditions are part of the final contact order and are therefore subject to the same principles and restrictions.[3] It was for this reason, for example, that it was not felt necessary to provide that the making of conditions are subject to the paramountcy principle.[4] It is precisely because they are part of the final order that unlike directions, conditions are enforceable.[5]

1   Section 11C(2).
2   Section 11C(1).
3   Presumably, therefore, conditions can only be made in exceptional circumstances where the child concerned has reached the age of 16, ie the restrictions contained in s 9(6) and (7) (discussed at para 5.122) apply.
4   Cf s 11A(9) which expressly applies the paramountcy principle to the making of directions.
5   Ie either through enforcement and/or financial compensation orders (discussed at paras 5.179 ff) or through the more traditional enforcement methods of imprisonment and/or fine (see paras 5.163 ff).

5.68 Although conditions are made at a later stage in proceedings than directions, there is no requirement that conditions can only be made following the making of directions. Moreover, in the absence of any specific provision, unlike directions a dispute over contact is not a prerequisite for the imposition of a condition. On the other hand, conditions may only be imposed on the person with whom the child lives, or is to live, the person in whose favour the contact order is made and any person on whom a s 11(7)(b) condition[1] is imposed.[2] Like directions, conditions may only be imposed on individuals who are habitually resident in England and Wales[3] and cannot be made with respect to an 'excepted order'.[4] Children cannot be made subject to a condition unless they are a parent of the child concerned.[5]

1   These conditions are discussed at paras 5.111 ff.
2   Section 11C(3).
3   Section 11D(3). Any condition ceases to have effect if the individual subject to the condition ceases to be habitually resident in England and Wales.
4   Section 11D(2). 'Excepted orders' are defined by s 11B(4), see above at para 5.64.
5   Section 11D(1).

5.69 The condition must specify the activity and the person providing the activity.[1] The activities that can be so specified are the same as those that can be specified in a direction and are subject to the same prohibitions.[2] For the reasons already discussed,[3] although there is no express requirement to do so, in deciding whether to impose a condition, the court must treat the child's welfare as its paramount consideration. It must also be satisfied that the activity is appropriate in the circumstances of the case; that the provider of the activity concerned is suitable to provide it and the activity is available in a place to which it is reasonable to expect the person in question to travel.[4] Before imposing a condition the court must obtain and consider information about the individual who would be liable to the condition and its likely effect upon him in particular with regard to any conflict with his religious beliefs or any interference with the times that he is at work or attending an educational establishment.[5] Courts can seek information on any of these powers from a CAFCASS or Welsh family proceedings officer.[6]

1   Section 11C(4).
2   Section 11C(5). Note in particular that conditions cannot require medical or psychiatric examinations or mediation.
3   See para 5.67 above.
4   Section 11C(6) applying s 11E(1)–(4).
5   Section 11E(5), (6).
6   Section 11E(7). The appropriate officer is bound to comply with such a request.

(VI) FINANCIAL SUPPORT AND MONITORING OF DIRECTIONS AND CONDITIONS

5.70 Section 11F enables the Secretary of State and the National Assembly for Wales to make regulations authorising payments to assist individuals ordinarily resident respectively in England and Wales paying the charge and fees of those providing the activities.[1] Regulations may provide that the activity provider must have been approved either by the Secretary of State or the National Assembly for Wales in order for financial assistance to be provided in respect of their activities.[2] Regulations may also set a maximum amount of financial assistance that will be paid for a contact activity; set a sliding scale to determine how much assistance individuals may receive depending upon their financial circumstances and provide for payments to be made directly to the activity provider rather than to individuals.[3]

[1]   Section 11F(1–5).
[2]   Section 11F(6).
[3]   Section 11F(7).

5.71 Section 11G(2) empowers a court, when making a contact activity direction or condition, to request[1] that a CAFCASS or Welsh family proceedings officer monitor or arrange for the monitoring of the individual's compliance with the direction or condition and to report any failure to the court.

[1]   Officers have a duty to comply with such a request: s 11G(3).

(VII) MONITORING CONTACT

5.72 In addition to CAFCASS or Welsh family proceedings officers being asked to monitor compliance with contact activity directions and conditions, they can be requested more generally to monitor compliance with a contact order (other than those made in adoption proceedings)[1] and to report to the court on such matters relating to compliance as the court may specify.[2] Such monitoring roles can last up to one year.[3] Those who can be subject to monitoring are a person (a) who is required to allow contact with the child; (b) whose contact with the child is provided for; and (c) who is subject to a s 11(7)(b) condition.[4]

[1]   Ie an 'excepted order' as defined by s 11B(4) (on which see para 5.64): s 11H(10).
[2]   Section 11H(2). Officers have a duty to comply with the request: s 11H(7).
[3]   Section 11H(6).
[4]   Section 11H(3). Section 11(7)(b) conditions are discussed at paras 5.111 ff. Individuals who are children cannot be monitored unless they are the parent of the child concerned: s 11H(9).

(c) Procedural considerations

5.73 Contact cases should not be transferred from the county court to the High Court 'too readily', for example, because they are difficult or the judge had a growing frustration at the absence of apparent achievement.[1]

1   *Re M (children)(transfer of proceedings to High Court)* [2005] EWCA Civ, [2005] All ER (D) 305 (Nov). But in an appropriate case a transfer will be made, see e.g. *Re M (Contact: Long-Term Best Interests)* [2005] EWCA Civ 1090, [2006] 1 FLR 627, sub nom *Re M (Children)(contact)* [2005] All ER (D) 230 (Jun), and *Re S (Unco-operative Mother)* [2004] EWCA Civ 597, [2004] 2 FLR 710.

5.74 Allegations of sexual abuse in contact applications may be determined as a preliminary issue for the purpose of making findings of fact.[1] In one such case concerning allegations of sexual abuse by a father of his daughter, the Attorney-General exceptionally agreed to provide an advocate to the court for the purpose of cross-examining the daughter since the father was disqualified from receiving public funding because of his earnings but was unable otherwise to fund the continuing litigation.[2] A fact-finding hearing may similarly be held with regard to allegations of domestic violence.[3] One advantage of a split hearing is that it offers the opportunity both of making directions for therapeutic interventions[4] and of making contact activity directions,[5] before making a final order.

1   See eg *Re A (Contact: Risk of Violence)* [2005] EWHC 851 (Fam), [2006] 1 FLR 283 which inter alia provides important guidance on how such fact-finding hearings should be conducted, namely, that it is the legal representatives' responsibility to provide the best possible evidence to the court including providing full statements identifying facts in issue between the parties (preferably in tabular form) and giving realistic time estimates and informing the listing office if the estimate is inadequate.
2   *H v L* [2006] EWHC 3099 (Fam), [2007] 1 FCR 430, [2006] All ER (D) 96 (Dec). But there is no power to order a parent to undergo therapy (though adverse inferences can be drawn from a refusal to so participate): *Re S (Unco-operative Mother)* [2004] EWCA Civ 597, [2004] 2 FLR 710. The recommendation that the power be included in the Children and Adoption Act 2006 fell on deaf ears but note contact activity directions and conditions can include counselling sessions, see above at para 5.65.
3   See *Practice Direction (Residence and Contact Orders: Domestic Violence)* [2008] 1 WLR 1062 paras 13–15, 21–23.
4   See eg *Re M and H (children)(sexual abuse)* [2006] EWCA Civ 499, 150 Sol Jo LB 400, discussed in *Clarke Hall and Morrison on Children* at 1[648.3].
5   Discussed above at paras 5.64 ff.

(d) Human rights considerations

5.75 Article 9(3) of the UN Convention on the Rights of the Child states:

> 'States Parties shall respect the right of the child who is separated from one or both parents to maintain personal relations and direct contact with both parents on a regular basis, except if it is contrary to the child's best interests'.

It is equally well established that contact between a parent and child falls within art 8(1) of the European Convention on Human Rights as a right to respect for private and family life both within marriage-based relationships[1] and to children and parent relationships outside marriage.[2]

5.75 Private law orders

1   See eg *R v United Kingdom* [1988] 2 FLR 445, ECtHR; *Hokkanen v Finland* [1995] 2 FCR 320, [1996] 1 FLR 289, ECtHR and *Sahin v Germany, Sommerfeld v Germany* [2003] 2 FCR 619 and 647, [2003] 2 FLR 671, ECtHR (Grand Chamber).
2   See *Lebbink v Netherlands* [2004] 3 FCR 59, [2004] 2 FLR 463, ECtHR, and *Sahin v Germany, Sommerfeld v Germany*, above.

5.76 The consequences of contact being an art 8 right are twofold: first States are under an obligation not to interfere with it arbitrarily – in other words a denial of contact is a breach of art 8 unless it is justified in the child's interests within the meaning of art 8(2);[1] and secondly States are under a positive obligation[2] to facilitate contact so far as can be reasonably expected in the circumstances of each case and hence failure of a State's authority to take adequate and effective measures to enforce contact may constitute a violation of art 8.[3] The application of art 8 can also have procedural implications particularly with whether or not to hear the child,[4] though as the Grand Chamber held in *Sahin v Germany, Sommerfeld v Germany*[5] it was going too far to say that domestic courts should always hear evidence from a child in court. In *Sahin*, for example, the child was only aged 5 at the relevant time and the domestic court was held to have been entitled to rely upon the findings of the expert.

1   Compare eg *Haase v Germany* [2004] 2 FCR 1, [2004] 2 FLR 39, ECtHR, where a breach was found, with *Hoppe v Germany* [2003] 1 FCR 176, [2003] 1 FLR 384, ECtHR and *Süss v Germany* [2005] 3 FCR 666, [2006] 1 FLR 522, ECtHR where art 8 was not found to be violated notwithstanding that the margin of appreciation was narrower in relation to access disputes than in relation to custody.
2   See *Marckx v Belgium* (1979) 2 EHRR 330, ECtHR.
3   See eg *Zawadka v Poland* [2006] 1 FCR 371, [2005] 2 FLR 897, ECtHR; *Kosmopolou v Greece* [2004] 1 FCR 427, [2004] 1 FLR 800, ECtHR and *Hansen v Turkey* [2003] 3 FCR 97, [2004] 1 FLR 142, ECtHR, where a violation was found and *Glaser v United Kingdom* [2000] 3 FCR 193, [2001] 1 FLR 153, ECtHR, where no violation was found.
4   See eg *Elsholz v Germany* [2000] 3 FCR 385, [2000] 2 FLR 486, ECtHR, in which a refusal to order an independent psychological report and to give the father an oral hearing was held to violate art 8. Note also *Ciliz v Netherlands* [2000] 2 FLR 469, ECtHR, in which deporting the father before the conclusion of a contact hearing was held to violate art 8.
5   [2003] 2 FCR 619 and 647, [2003] 2 FLR 671, ECtHR. Note, however, Germany was found to be in breach of art 14 inter alia for placing a heavier burden on unmarried fathers than on divorced fathers in respect of access claims.

5.77 In *Re D (a child)(intractable contact dispute: publicity)*[1] Munby J helpfully considered the impact of the Convention on the English law concerning contact and extracted the following most important points:

- 'the mutual enjoyment by parent and child of each other's company constitutes a fundamental element of family life';
- the courts have 'a duty to exercise exceptional diligence in view of the risk that the passage of time may result in a de facto determination of the matter';
- in private law cases, just as much as in public law cases, there is an obligation on national authorities to take action for the reuniting of a parent with his child;
- there is a positive obligation on the domestic legal system that final binding judicial decisions do not remain inoperative to the detriment of one party;

- this positive obligation extends in principle to the taking of coercive measures not merely against the recalcitrant parent but even against children;
- national authorities cannot shelter behind the applicant's lack of action.

[1] [2004] EWHC 727 (Fam), [2004] 3 FCR 234, [2004] 1 FLR 1226 at [26] ff.

(e) Practical considerations when making contact decisions

(I) OVERVIEW OF DIFFICULTIES

5.78 There are more disposals of contact applications (59% in 2006)[1] than of any other s 8 order application. They also pose some of the greatest problems. As Wall J has said:[2]

'Disputes between separated parents over contact to their children are amongst the most difficult and sensitive cases which judges and magistrates have to hear. Nobody should pretend they are easy, or that there is any one-size-fits-all solution'.

[1] Judicial and Courts Statistics 2006 (2007 Cm 7273) Table 5.4.
[2] *Re O (Contact: Withdrawal of Application)* [2003] EWHC 3031 (Fam), [2004] 1 FLR 1258 at [6] (1).

5.79 One of the scourges of the system is the protracted contact dispute. Although, as Butler-Sloss P said in *Re S (Contact: Promoting Relationship With Absent Parent)*[1] it is important that parents 'should not be encouraged or permitted to think that the more intransigent ... and the more unco-operative they are, the more likely they are to get their own way', there are, sadly, cases where the person seeking contact has, in the face of such obduracy and the apparent impotence of the legal system, simply given up. A depressing example is *Re D (a child)(intractable contact dispute: publicity)*[2] in which the mother continually sabotaged contact arrangements over a five-year period, resulting in court orders, penal notices, suspended prison sentences and finally a period of imprisonment. There were 43 hearings conducted by 16 different judges after numerous adjournments. Eventually the father gave up. He had, in the words of Munby J, been let down by the system. There had been appalling delays in the legal system, the courts had failed to get to grips with the mother's groundless allegations and her defiance of its orders and had failed to enforce them.

[1] [2004 EWCA Civ 18 [2004] 1 FLR 1279, in turn citing Sir Thomas Bingham in *Re O (Contact: Imposition of Conditions)* [1995] 2 FLR 124 at 129.
[2] [2004] EWHC 727 (Fam), [2004] 3 FCR 234, [2004] 1 FLR 1226.

5.80 It was to meet cases like *Re D* that new measures designed both to facilitate contact in the first place (ie the power to make contact activity directions or conditions and more easily to make family assistance orders) and to enforce orders that are made (through enforcement and financial compensation orders) are contained in the Children and Adoption Act 2006.[1] But it would be idle to assume that the obdurate parent will suddenly disappear and protracted contact disputes will become a past phenomenon.

1   Discussed at paras 5.63, 5.179 and 5.185 respectively.

5.81 Although many of the obdurate parents frustrating contact in the reported cases are mothers, they are by no means exclusively so.[1] But, as Butler-Sloss P observed in *Re S (Contact: Promoting Relationship with Absent Parent)*,[2] in practice after separation the majority of children remain with the mother so that it is the father who is the more likely parent to seek a contact order. This means that it is all too easy to make the accusation of gender bias if contact is denied. However, the courts are adamant about their gender neutrality. As Wall J put it:[3]

'The courts are not anti-father and pro-mother or vice versa. The court's task, imposed by Parliament in s 1 of the Children Act 1989, in every case is to treat the welfare of the child or children concerned as paramount, and to safeguard and promote the welfare of every child to the best of its ability'.

1   See e.g. *Re M (Contact: Long-Term Best Interests)* [2005] EWCA Civ 1090, [2006] 1 FLR 627, sub nom *Re M (Children)(Contact)* [2005] All ER (D) 230 (Jun).
2   [2004] EWCA Civ 18, [2004] 1 FLR 1279 at [19].
3   *Re O (Contact: Withdrawal of Application)* [2003] EWHC 3031 (Fam), [2004] 1 FLR 1258 at [6] (3).

5.82 Another issue that is sometimes raised before the courts is that of parental alienation, that is, an allegation that the children's hostility towards one parent (normally the non-resident parent) has been deliberately fostered by the other (normally the resident parent). There is little doubt about the existence of this phenomenon but one debate (particularly prevalent in the USA) is whether there is such a thing as 'Parental Alienation Syndrome'.[1] The English court's attitude is that it is inappropriate to call it a syndrome[2] but at the same time it should not be assumed that a child's hostility to contact has been deliberately fostered by the residential parent.[3] As with all issues, the allegation of hostility requires careful investigation and evaluation.[4]

1   See the discussion by C Bruch 'Parental Alienation Syndrome and Alienated Children – getting it wrong in child custody cases' [2002] CFLQ 381.
2   See in particular the paper prepared by Drs Sturge and Glaser for the Court of Appeal in *Re L; V, M and H (Contact: Domestic Violence)* [2001] Fam 260 published under the title 'Contact and Domestic Violence – The Experts' Court Report' [2000] Fam Law 615 at 622–3 and Lord Justice Wall 'Enforcement of Contact Orders' [2005] Fam Law at 29.
3   See eg *Re O (Contact: Withdrawal of Application)* [2003] EWHC 3031 (Fam), [2004] 1 FLR 1258, in which the father's assertion of alienation by the mother was rejected, the children's hostility being found to be due to the father's own behaviour.
4   See *T (Contact: Parental Alienation: Permission to Appeal)* [2002] EWCA Civ 1736, [2003] 1 FLR 531, where the alienation was held not to have been adequately investigated.

(II) PREDISPOSITION TO MAINTAIN CONTACT WITH BOTH PARENTS

5.83 As with all issues directly concerning the child's upbringing, the controlling principle in deciding whether or not to make a contact order is the paramountcy of the child's welfare.[1] This principle applies regardless of whether the child's parents are married to each other,[2] and whether it is sought to end or reintroduce contact.[3] Bearing this principle in mind, it would be wrong to say that *as a matter of law* there is a presumption that a parent (but not a step-parent or grandparents)[5] should be permitted contact. Nevertheless, the de facto position is that the courts are predisposed to maintaining contact with both parents[6] it being repeatedly said that the court should be slow to deny contact between a child and his or her parents. As Butler-Sloss P said in *Re S (Contact: Promoting Relationship With Absent Parent):*[7]

> 'No parent is perfect but "good enough parents" should have a relationship with their children for their own benefit and even more in the best interests of the children. It is, therefore, most important that the attempt to promote contact between a child and the non-residential parent should not be abandoned until it is clear that the child will not benefit from continuing the attempt'.

As Butler-Sloss LJ pointed out in *Re R (a minor) (contact),*[8] the principle of continued contact is underlined by art 9 of the United Nations Convention on the Rights of the Child 1989 and endorsed in the CA 1989. Furthermore, as the European Court of Human Rights held in *Glaser v United Kingdom,*[9] art 8 of the ECHR 'includes a right for a parent to have measures taken with a view to his or her being reunited with the child and an obligation of national authorities to take measures' both in public and private law proceedings. However, the court also acknowledged that the obligation of national authorities to take measures to facilitate contact by a non-custodial parent after divorce was not absolute and that where it might appear to threaten the child's interests or interfere with his or her art 8 rights, it was for those authorities 'to strike a fair balance between them'.

1   See generally *Re KD (A Minor)(Ward: Termination of Access)* [1988] AC 806, [1988] 1 All ER 577, HL, which rejected the argument based on art 8 of the European Convention for the Protection of Human Rights following the decision in *R v United Kingdom* (1987) 10 EHRR 74, [1988] 2 FLR 445, that what is now contact was a parental right which should only be displaced where the court was satisfied that the exercise of the right would be positively inimical to the child's interests.

2   See eg *Re M (Contact: Supervision)* [1998] 1 FLR 727, CA in which an unmarried father was granted supervised contact notwithstanding his problems concerning drug and alcohol abuse, occasional lack of control over his temper and the lack of a permanent home. Step-parents and grandparents are not in such a strong position: see respectively *Re H (A Minor)(Contact)* [1994] 2 FLR 776, *Re W (Contact: Application by Grandparent)* [1997] 1 FLR 793 and *Re A (Section 8 Order: Grandparent Application)* [1995] 2 FLR 153, CA.

3   See eg *Re R (A Minor)(Contact)* [1993] 2 FLR 762, CA, in which the court stressed the need for a five year old to be told who her father was and to be reintroduced to him despite not having seen him for three years. See also *A v L (Contact)* [1998] 1 FLR 361 (discussed further at para 5.85) and *Re H (Minors)(Access)* [1992] 1 FLR 148, CA.

4   *Re H (A Minor) (Contact)* [1994] 2 FLR 776. Cf *Re C (a minor) (access)* [1991] FCR 969, [1992] 1 FLR 309, CA.

5   *Re A (section 8 order: grandparent application)* [1996] 1 FCR 467, [1995] 2 FLR 153, CA. See also *Re W (contact: application by grandparent)* [1997] 2 FCR 643, [1997] 1 FLR 793; *Re S (Contact: Appeal)* [2001] Fam Law 505.

6   Indeed, according to Adams *'Parents' Rights v Children's Needs in Private Cases'* [2007] Fam Law 257, contact orders follow 98% of applications.

7   [2004] EWCA Civ 18, [2004] 1 FLR 1279 at [32].

8   [1993] 1 FCR 954 at 961, [1993] 2 FLR 762 at 767.

9   [2000] 3 FCR 193 at 209, paras (65)–(66), [2001] 1 FLR 153 at 168.

5.84 The general approach, established by *Re H (minors) (access),*[1] is for the judge to ask himself whether there are cogent reasons why the child should be denied contact with a parent. It has since been said to be helpful to cast the relevant principles into the framework of the welfare checklist, namely, to consider whether the fundamental need of every child to have an enduring relationship with both parents is outweighed by the depth of harm that, might thereby be caused.[2] In *Re P (minors) (contact: parental hostility)*,[3] Wall J summarised the principles as follows:

'(1)   Overriding all else, as provided by s 1(1) of the CA 1989, the welfare of the child is the paramount consideration, and the court is concerned with the interests of the mother and the father only insofar as they bear on the welfare of the child.

(2)   It is almost always in the interests of the child whose parents are separated that he or she should have contact with the parent with whom the child is not living.

(3)   The court has powers to enforce orders for contact, which it should not hesitate to exercise where it judges that it will overall promote the welfare of the child to do so.

(4)   Cases do, unhappily and infrequently but occasionally, arise, in which a court is compelled to conclude that in existing circumstances an order for immediate direct contact should not be ordered, because so to order would injure the welfare of the child: see *Re D (a Minor) (Contact: Mother's Hostility)* [1993] 2 FLR 1 at 7G, per Waite LJ.

(5)   In cases, in which, for whatever reason, direct contact cannot for the time being be ordered, it is ordinarily highly desirable that there should be indirect contact so that the child grows up knowing of the love and interest of the absent parent with whom, in due course, direct contact should be established.'

---

1   [1992] 1 FCR 70 at 74F,[1992] 1 FLR 148 at 152C, per Balcombe LJ, CA.
2   *Re M (minors) (contact)* [1995] 1 FCR 753, [1995] 1 FLR 274, CA.
3   [1997] 1 FCR 458 at 473, sub nom *Re P (Contact: Supervision)* [1996] 2 FLR 314 at 328, CA, relying on *Re O (a minor) (contact: indirect contact)* [1996] 1 FCR 317 at 323–325, sub nom *Re O (Contact: Imposition of Conditions)* [1995] 2 FLR 124 at 128–130, CA. Cf *S v M (Access Order)* [1997] 1 FLR 980, sub nom *Sanderson v McManus* 1997 SLT 629 in which the House of Lords held, on an appeal from Scotland, that technically the onus of proof is on a parent (in this case an unmarried father) to show that continued contact is for the child's welfare, though as Lord Clyde observed 'true questions of the burden of proof will almost invariably fade into insignificance after any inquiry.'

5.85   Even where direct contact might be inappropriate, the court should still consider indirect contact as a means of preserving some kind of relationship with the absent parent. In *A v L (Contact)*,[1] the father was serving a long-term prison sentence and, notwithstanding the unwillingness of any relative to facilitate any form of contact, the court thought it right to make an order for indirect contact (using the good offices of the mother's solicitors), Holman J stressing the child's fundamental right to have some knowledge of and some contact with his natural father. In many other cases the court has been concerned that every effort is made to preserve contact or the possibility of contact to the extent of referring the parents to therapy or other professional help[2] and, it is for these cases that contact activity directions or conditions[3] will be particularly appropriate.

---

1   [1998] 1 FLR 361. Holman J, anxious that (a three-year-old boy) should know who his father was, held that it was wrong for the justices to have accepted the mother's view (even though this was also accepted by the father) that the child should not be told about his parentage until he grew older.

² See eg *Re M (Contact: Long-Term Best Interests)* [2005] EWCA Civ 1090, [2006] 1 FLR
627; *Re S (Unco-operative Mother)* [2004] EWCA Civ 597, [2004] 2 FLR 710 and *Re S
(Contact: Promoting Relationship With Absent Parent)* [2004] EWCA Civ 18, [2004]
1 FLR 1279.

³ Discussed above at paras 5.63 ff.

(III) DENYING CONTACT WITH A PARENT

5.86 Notwithstanding the predisposition to preserve contact with both parents, there are occasions when it is not in the child's interests to do so.
Examples include:

- *Re C (Contact: No Order for Contact)*¹ in which indirect contact was
  refused with a father who had been absent over a three year period and
  against whom the child had an extreme adverse reaction;
- *Re F (minors) (denial of contact)*,² in which contact with a transsexual
  father was refused primarily because of the children's (boys aged 12 and
  9) own wishes;
- *Re H (children) (contact order) (No 2)*³ where, contrary to the
  children's wishes, no contact order was made with a father who was
  suffering from Huntingdon's disease and who had in the past threatened to kill himself and (unknown to them) the children, it being found
  that the mother was at risk of suffering a nervous breakdown if a
  contact order was made;
- *Re T (a minor) (parental responsibility: contact)*,⁴ in which an unmarried father was denied contact because of his violence towards the
  mother and his blatant disregard for the child's welfare;
- *Carp v Bryon*,⁵ a father who had two convictions for common assault
  against the mother, and who, contrary to his belief, was proved by
  DNA testing not to be the child's biological father;
- *Re C and V (minors) (parental responsibility and contact)*,⁶ in which
  the child had severe medical problems requiring constant and informed
  medical attention which the mother, but not the father, was able to give;
  and
- *Re D (a minor) (contact: mother's hostility)*⁷ and *Re H (a minor)
  (parental responsibility)*⁸ in which respectively the mother's and the
  stepfather's implacable hostility towards contact with an unmarried
  father was held to justify prohibiting contact.

¹ [2000] 2 FLR 723.
² [1993] 1 FCR 945, [1993] 2 FLR 677, CA.
³ [2001] 3 FCR 385. This was the rehearing of the case remitted by the Court of Appeal
reported as *Re H (children) (contact order)* [2001] 1 FCR 49. Cf *Re M (contact: parental
responsibility: McKenzie friend)* [1999] 1 FCR 703, [1999] 1 FLR 75, CA, in which
previously successful contact was overshadowed by the mother's fear of the father, though
in this case, indirect contact was still granted.
⁴ [1993] 1 FCR 973, [1993] 2 FLR 450, CA.
⁵ [2005] EWCA Civ 1035, [2006] 1 FCR 1.
⁶ [1998] 1 FCR 52, [1998] 1 FLR 392, CA.
⁷ [1993] 1 FCR 964, [1993] 2 FLR 1, CA.
⁸ [1993] 1 FCR 85, [1993] 1 FLR 484. See also *Re B (a minor) (contact: stepfather's
opposition)* [1998] 3 FCR 289, [1997] 2 FLR 579, CA, in which the dismissal of the
father's contact application was justified because of the child's stepfather's threat to reject
the child and the mother.

5.87 Despite the foregoing cases concerning parental hostility, it has been said[1] that judges should be reluctant to allow one parent's implacable hostility to deter them from making a contact order where they believe the child's welfare requires it. In *Re P (minors) (contact: discretion)*[2] Wilson J considered that hostility towards contact can arise in three different situations. The first is where there are no rational grounds for the parent's hostility, in which case the court should only refuse an order for contact if satisfied that it would create a serious risk of emotional harm to the child. The second is where the parent advances grounds for the hostility which the court regards as sufficiently potent as to displace the presumption that contact is in the child's best interests. In this case the hostility as such becomes largely irrelevant. The third is where the parent advances sound arguments for the displacement of the presumption of contact but where there are also sound arguments the other way (ie the arguments are rational but not decisive). In such a case the hostility 'can itself be of importance, occasionally of determinative importance, provided, as always, that what is measured is its effect upon the child'. Where one parent makes contact difficult or impossible for the other the court could transfer residence. However, this is a remedy of last resort and should not be adopted to solve a relatively straightforward contact problem.[3] As Bracewell J observed in *V v V (Children: Contact: Implacable Hostility)*[4] such a transfer should only be made if it is 'fully justified by affording paramount consideration to the child's welfare. It must not be used to punish a parent'.

---

[1] Per Balcombe LJ in *Re J (a minor)(contact)* [1994] 2 FCR 741 at 749, [1994] 1 FLR 729 at 736. See also *Re S (Contact: Grandparents)* [1996] 3 FCR 30, [1996] 1 FLR 158 and *Re P (minors) (contact: parental hostility)* [1997] 1 FCR 458, sub nom *Re P (Contact: Supervision)* [1996] 2 FLR 314, CA. But note *Re D (contact: reasons for refusal)* [1998] 1 FCR 321, [1997] 2 FLR 48, CA, in which Hale J observed that the term 'implacable hostility' usually refers to the type of case where no good reason could be discerned for a parent's opposition to contact.
[2] [1999] 1 FCR 566 at 574–575, [1998] 2 FLR 696 at 703–704.
[3] Per Thorpe LJ in *Re B (residence order: status quo)* [1998] 1 FCR 549, [1998] 1 FLR 368, CA. See also *V v T* [2007] EWHC 2312 (Fam), [2007] All ER (D) 159 (Oct).
[4] [2004] EWHC 1215 (Fam), [2004] 2 FLR 851, [2004] All ER (D) 304 (May) at [48]. In fact the court did order a transfer. See also *Re C (Residence Order)* [2007] EWCA Civ 866, [2008] 1 FLR 211, [2007] All ER (D) 187 (Oct); *Re A (a child)(residence order)* [2008] 1 FCR 599, [2007] All ER (D) 156 (Jun), in which transfers were also made.

5.88 As between parents it is rarely necessary to make formal orders prohibiting contact. It is normally sufficient simply to refuse an application thereby leaving the primary carer in sole control. In addition to refusing to make a contact order, the court can also make a s 91(14) order restraining future applications without leave,[1] though as discussed below,[2] this is a draconian measure requiring special justification. It is also possible to prevent contact by a Sexual Offences Prevention Order issued under the Sexual Offences Act 2003, s 104, but as *R v D (Sexual Offences Prevention Order)*[3] establishes, such an order is similarly draconian and should not be imposed as a matter of routine.

---

[1] Section 91(14) orders are discussed below at paras 5.202 ff.
[2] See paras 5.203 ff.
[3] [2005] EWCA Crim 3660, [2006] 1 FLR 1085.

(IV) SHOULD THE PREDISPOSITION TO PRESERVE CONTACT BE PUT IN
STATUTORY FORM?

5.89 Although there has been debate as to whether there ought to be a
statutory presumption of contact with both parents, or an amendment to the
welfare checklist to ensure that courts have regard to the importance of
sustaining a relationship between the child and the non-resident parent, the
government declined to insert it into the Children and Adoption Act 2006.[1]
Ironically, had the plans to implement Pt II of the Family Law Act 1996 not
been abandoned there would effectively have been a statutory presumption of
contact at any rate in the context of divorce or separation cases since by
s 11(4) of that Act the courts were to have been directed 'to have particular
regard to:

> '... the general principle that, in the absence of evidence to the contrary, the
> welfare of the child will be best served by
> (i)   his having regular contact with those who have parental responsibility
>   for him and with other members of his family ...'.'

But since the courts have made it crystal clear that they recognise the
importance of maintaining the child's relationship with both parents there is
no need for such reform and indeed there are dangers of so-called satellite
litigation were some poorly drafted statutory provision to be introduced. A
fortiori it would be wrong to legislate, as some have argued, for a presumption of equality of time spent by a child with each parent. As Butler-Sloss P has
convincingly said:[2]

> 'This approach to contact would not be in the best interests of many children
> whose welfare is the issue before the courts. The court is not and should not be
> tied to a certain number of days which would be automatically ordered to be
> spent by the absent parent with the child. Children of all ages and circum-
> stances may be the subject of contact orders and one blanket type of order may
> inhibit the court arriving at the decision which reflects the best interests of each
> individual child'.

[1]   See the Government Reply to The Report from the Joint Committee on the Draft Children
       (Contact) and Adoption Bill Cm 6583 (June 2005) para 121.
[2]   In *Re S (Contact: Promoting Relationship With Absent Parent)* [2004] EWCA Civ 18,
       [2004] 1 FLR 1279 at [26].

(V) CONTACT AND DOMESTIC VIOLENCE[1]

5.90 Violence does not per se justify a refusal of contact;[2] it is a matter of
discretion, not principle. But in *Re M (minors) (contact: violent parent)*[3] Wall
J commented that too little weight was sometimes given to the need of a
violent parent to change behaviour so as to demonstrate fitness to have
contact. In *Re H (minors) (contact: domestic violence)*[4] the court refused to
interfere with a decision that despite the judge's misgivings about the father,
including his violence, there was not enough to outweigh the normal principle
that contact was in the children's interests.[5] In *Re A (minors) (domestic
violence)*[6] resumption of contact with a previously violent father was denied.

5.90 *Private law orders*

Interim contact orders in cases of domestic violence raise particularly difficult issues. The court may allow indirect contact in cases where direct contact is not considered appropriate.[7]

1 For a general discussion see [2000] Fam Law 630. See also Butler-Sloss P at [2001] Fam Law 355.
2 *Re F (a child) (contact order)* [2001] 1 FCR 422 and *Re H (minors) (contact: domestic violence)* [1998] 3 FCR 385, [1998] 2 FLR 42, CA.
3 [1999] 2 FCR 56, [1999] 2 FLR 321 – contact was refused.
4 [1998] 3 FCR 385, [1998] 2 FLR 42, CA.
5 Note also that under the FLA 1996, s 42(2)(b) non-molestation orders may be made in any family proceedings of the court's own motion.
6 [1999] 1 FCR 729; and see also *Re D (Contact: Reasons for Refusal)* [1997] 2 FLR 48; *Re P (Contact: Discretion)* [1998] 2 FLR 696; *Re M (contact: parental responsibility McKenzie friend)* [1999] 1 FCR 703, [1999] 1 FLR 75.
7 *Re S (violent parent: Indirect Contact)* [2000] 1 FLR 481.

5.91 In *Re L (a Child), Re V (a child), Re H (a Child) (Contact: Domestic Violence)*,[1] the Court of Appeal dismissed four appeals by fathers against orders allowing them indirect contact, but refusing them direct contact in cases of a background of domestic violence between the spouses and partners. Approving the approach previously taken[2] it was held that there were no presumptions for or against contact with a violent parent, and the only principle applicable was the paramountcy of the child's welfare as set out in the CA 1989, s 1(1) and the checklist in s 1(3).[3] Drawing both on *A Report to the Lord Chancellor on the Question of Parental Contact in Cases Where There is Domestic Violence*[4] which was presented to the Lord Chancellor on 29 February 2000, and on an expert report (now published)[5] prepared by Drs Sturge and Glaser on contact from a child and adolescent psychiatry perspective, Butler-Sloss LJ commented:[6]

'The family judges and magistrates need to have a heightened awareness of the existence of and consequences (some long-term) on children of exposure to domestic violence between their parents or other partners. There has, perhaps, been a tendency in the past for courts not to tackle allegations of violence and to leave them in the background on the premise that they were matters affecting the adults and not relevant to issues regarding the children. The general principle that contact with the non-residence parent is in the interests of the child may sometimes have discouraged sufficient attention being paid to the adverse effects on children living in the household where violence has occurred. It may not necessarily be widely appreciated that violence to a partner involves a significant failure in parenting – failure to protect the child's carer and failure to protect the child emotionally. In a contact or other s 8 application, where allegations of domestic violence are made which might have an effect on the outcome, those allegations must be adjudicated upon and found proved or not proved. It will be necessary to scrutinise such allegations which may not always be true or may be grossly exaggerated. If however there is a firm basis for finding that violence has occurred, the psychiatric advice becomes very important. There is not, however, nor should there be, any presumption that, on proof of domestic violence, the offending parent has to surmount a prima facie barrier of no contact. As a matter of principle, domestic violence of itself cannot constitute a bar to contact. It is one factor in the difficult and delicate balancing exercise of discretion. The court deals with the facts of a specific case in which the degree of violence and the seriousness of the impact on the child and on the resident parent have to be taken into account. In cases of proved domestic violence, as in cases of other proved harm or risk of harm to the child, the court has the task of weighing in the balance the seriousness of the domestic violence, the risks involved and the impact on the child against the positive factors, if any, of contact between the parent found to have been violent and the child. In this context, the ability of the offending parent to recognise his past conduct, be aware of the need to change and make genuine efforts to do so, will be likely to be an important consideration.'

1   [2001] Fam 260, [2000] 4 All ER 609, CA.
2   Eg in *Re H (minors)(contact: domestic violence)* [1998] 3 FCR 385, [1998] 2 FLR 42, CA, and *Re M (minors)(contact: violence parent)* [1999] 2 FCR 56, [1999] 2 FLR 321.
3   But note that the definition of 'harm' has been extended by the Adoption and Children Act 2002 to include 'impairment suffered from seeing or hearing the ill-treatment of another' discussed at para 2.55.
4   The Advisory Board on Family Law: Children Act Sub-Committee, Chairman Wall J. See http://www.open.gov.uk/lcd/family/abfla/dvconreport.pdf. See its full report, *Making Contact Work*, above.
5   [2000] Fam Law 615.
6   At 272–273 and 616 respectively.

5.92   In *Re L* Waller LJ set out the following propositions:[1]

'(1)   That the effect of children being exposed to domestic violence of one parent as against the other might up until now have been underestimated by judges and adverse alike.

(2)   That alleged domestic violence was a matter which should be investigated and findings of fact should be made because if it was established, its effect on the children exposed to it and the risk to the residential carer were highly relevant factors in considering orders for contact and their form.

(3)   That in assessing the relevance of past domestic violence it was likely to be highly material whether the perpetrator had shown an ability to recognise the wrong, or less commonly she, had done and the steps taken to correct the deficiency in that perpetrator's character.

(4)   That there should, however, be no presumption against contact simply because domestic violence was alleged or proved. It was one highly material factor among many which might offset the assumption in favour of contact when the difficult balancing exercise was carried out.'

Important procedural guidance is provided by *Practice Direction (Residence and Contact Orders: Domestic Violence)*,[2] which directs courts to determine as soon as possible whether a fact-finding hearing in relation to any disputed allegation of domestic violence is necessary. Where such hearings are considered necessary directions to ensure that matters are heard expeditiously and fairly must be given and at the same time as fixing a fact-finding hearing a further hearing for the determination of the application must also be fixed. Where violence has been found, information about any available local facilities to assist the party or the child must be obtained and if, having regard to the welfare checklist, the court considers that direct contact is in the best interests of the child the court should consider what, if any, direction or conditions are required to enable the order to be carried into effect.

1   Above at 301 and 643–644 respectively.
2   [2008] 1 WLR 1062.

5.93 *Re L* is an important decision to which judges should have regard.[1] Subsequent to *Re L*, Butler-Sloss P refused direct contact to a violent father who had killed his wife.[2] All contact was also refused in a case,[3] where there had been 'unusually high levels of domestic violence', because of the harm to the living child with the mother suffering from psychological and emotional conditions induced by that contact. Refusal of contact in cases of domestic violence where there is a risk of emotional destabilisation to the child promotes the child's right to family life with its primary carer pursuant to art 8 of the ECHR.[4]

1 In *Re H (Contact: Domestic Violence)* [2005] EWCA Civ 1404, [2006] 1 FLR 943, the trial judge was severely criticised for having no regard to *Re L*, The Sturges/Glaser report and the guidelines set out in *Making Contact Work* and approved in *Re L*.
2 *Re G (Direct Contact: Domestic Violence)* [2000] 2 FLR 865, FD.
3 *Re M and B (children) (contact: domestic violence)* [2001] 1 FCR 116, CA; and see also *Re K (Contact: Mother's Anxiety)* [1999] 2 FLR 703, CA.
4 *Re Q (Contact: Natural Father)* [2001] All ER (D) 172 (Apr).

3. Prohibited steps order

5.94 By s 8(1) a prohibited steps order:

> 'means an order that no step which could be taken by a parent in meeting his parental responsibility for a child, and which is of a kind specified in the order, shall be taken by any person without the consent of the court.'

This is one of the two orders under the CA 1989 (the other being a specific issue order, discussed below) modelled on the wardship jurisdiction and intended to broaden all courts' powers when dealing with children. The two orders are not mutually exclusive and on occasion both might be necessary.[1]

1 See eg *Re D (a minor)(child: removed from jurisdiction)* [1992] 1 All ER 892, [1992] 1 WLR 667, CA – specific issue order for the child's return and a prohibited steps order prohibiting a further removal from the jurisdiction.

5.95 A prohibited steps order empowers a court to place a *specific* embargo upon the exercise of parental responsibility. This is in contrast to the vague requirement in wardship that no important step in the child's life be taken without the court's prior consent.[1] This order can be put to a variety of uses, for example, to prohibit contact with a parent or someone else (discussed further below), restrain a particular operation, including the circumcision of a boy without the consent of the other parent or the court,[2] prevent the child's schooling or religion from being changed or to stop a parent from changing the child's name.[3] Another example, instanced by the Law Commission,[4] is to impose an embargo that the child should not be removed from the UK which they said might be useful in cases where no residence order had been made so that the automatic restrictions against removal under s 13 do not apply.[5] Even where the s 13 restrictions do apply it might still be possible to obtain a prohibited steps order to prevent repeated removal of children outside the UK for periods of less than one month by the residential parent. Furthermore, since s 13 only prevents removing a child outside the UK, if it is sought to prevent relocations *within* the country then a prohibited steps order must be sought, though as emphasised in *Re S (a child) (residence order: condition)*[6] and *Re H (children) (residence order: condition)*[7] such orders will only be justified in exceptional circumstances.

1   Wardship is discussed in Chapter 12. It is assumed that an order as vague as prohibiting any important step could not be made as a prohibited steps order.
2   *Re J (child's religious upbringing and circumcision)* [1999] 2 FCR 345, sub nom *Re J (Specific Issue Orders: Muslim Upbringing and Circumcision)* [1999] 2 FLR 678, per Wall J, upheld an appeal at [2000] 1 FCR 307, [2000] 1 FLR 571, CA.
3   Note that under s 13(1)(a) a person with residence is not allowed to change the child's name without the consent of all those having parental responsibility or with leave of the court, see the discussion at paras 5.31 ff.
4   Law Com No 172, para 4.20. See also the revised Children Act 1989 Guidance and Regulations, Vol 1, Court Orders (2008) Department for Children, Schools and Families, at para 2.37.
5   The embargo under s 13(1)(b) and (2) is discussed at paras 5.39 ff. In the absence of a residence order the unilateral removal by a joint holder of parental responsibility can be an offence under the Child Abduction Act 1984.
6   [2001] EWCA Civ 847, [2001] 3 FCR 154, discussed at paras 5.51 and 5.116.
7   [2001] EWCA Civ 1338, [2001] 3 FCR 182, [2001] 2 FLR 1277, discussed at paras 5.51 and 5.118.

5.96 Although the order itself must relate to parental responsibility[1] it can be made against anyone regardless of whether they have parental responsibility. A prohibited steps order can, for example, be made against an unmarried father whether or not he has parental responsibility or against a third party, for example to restrain a former cohabitant from contacting or seeking to have contact.[2] An order can be made against non-parties.[3] Provided the order is of some value to the applicant it can be made even though the child is abroad.[4] Applications for prohibited steps orders can be made ex parte[5] and an order may be made either in conjunction with another s 8 order or on its own.

1   See paras 5.100 ff.
2   *Re H (minors) (prohibited steps order)* [1995] 4 All ER 110, [1995] 1 WLR 667, CA.
3   *Re H*, above. Nevertheless such an order could not be enforced until it has been specifically served.
4   See *Re D (a minor) (child: removal from jurisdiction)* [1992] 1 All ER 892, [1992] 1 WLR 315, CA.
5   FPR 1991, r 4.4(4); FPC(CA 1989)R 1991, r 4(4). Such orders are sometimes made in the context of international child abduction, often at the request of the abducting parent, to prevent removal by the other. See eg *Re AZ (a minor) (abduction: acquiescence)* [1993] 1 FCR 733, [1993] 1 FLR 682; *Re B (Minors) (Abduction) (No 2)* [1993] 1 FLR 993; *D v D (child abduction: non-convention country)* [1994] 1 FCR 654, [1994] 1 FLR 137 and *Re S (minors) (abduction)* [1993] 2 FCR 499, [1994] 1 FLR 297.

4. Specific issue order

5.97 By s 8(1) a specific issue order:

'means an order giving directions for the purpose of determining a specific question which has arisen, or which may arise, in connection with any aspect of parental responsibility for a child.'

These orders enable a specific question relating to the child to be brought before the court, the aim of which is not to give one parent or the other a general 'right' to make decisions in a particular respect but to enable a particular issue to be settled.[1] It was held in *Re HG (a minor) (application for sterilisation)*[2] that there is no necessity for there to be a dispute between the parties before the power arises to make a specific issue order; it is sufficient that there is a question to be answered. In that case an unopposed application[3] for a specific issue order was granted giving High Court sanction for the sterilisation of a 17-year-old mentally disabled child.

[1] Children Act 1989 Guidance and Regulations, Vol 1, Court Orders (1991) Department of Health, para 2.32. The latter part of the comment is not repeated in the revised Guidance (2008) see para 2.38.
[2] [1993] 1 FCR 533, sub nom *Re HG (Specific Issue Order: Sterilisation)* [1993] 1 FLR 587.
[3] The application was thought necessary in view of Lord Templeman's lone dictum in *Re B (a Minor) (Wardship: Sterilisation)* [1988] AC 199 at 205, [1987] 2 All ER 206 at 214 that High Court sanction is always required for a child's sterilisation. See also *Practice Note* [1993] 3 All ER 222.

5.98 Applications for specific issue orders may be made ex parte[1] and orders may be made either in conjunction with another s 8 order or on their own. Examples include

- *Re C (Welfare of Child: Immunisation)*,[2] in which the court ordered, contrary to the mother's wishes, the child's immunisation;
- *Re R (a minor) (medical treatment)*,[3] in which the court ordered inter alia that in an imminently life-threatening situation, the child in question be given a blood transfusion without the consent of her parents who were Jehovah's Witnesses;
- *Re F (minors) (solicitors' interviews)*,[4] in which an order was made permitting a defence solicitor to interview children for the purpose of providing evidence in criminal proceedings against their father;
- *Re D (a minor) (child removal from jurisdiction)*,[5] in which a mother was ordered to return the child to the jurisdiction;
- *Re A (children) (specific issue order: parental dispute)*,[6] in which an order was made at the French father's request that notwithstanding that they were now living with their English mother in England, the two children should attend the Lycée Français in London;
- *Re P (Parental Dispute: Judicial Determination)*,[7] in which a dispute over which private school the children should attend was resolved.

Specific issue orders can also be brought to resolve disputes over a child's religious upbringing;[8] and, provided no residence order is in force,[9] to obtain court leave to change a child's name[10] or to take the child out of the United Kingdom.[11] After some doubts[12] it is now established that a specific issue order can be made requiring a parent to disclose to the child the truth of his or her parentage.[13] Such orders can be made on the court's own motion.[14]

[1] FPR 1991, r 4.4(4); FPC(CA 1989)R 1991, r 4(4). See eg *Re D (a minor) (child removal from jurisdiction)* [1992] 1 All ER 892, [1992] 1 WLR 315, CA.
[2] [2003] EWHC 1376 (Fam), [2003] 2 FLR 1054, upheld on appeal: [2003] EWCA Civ 1148, [2003] 2 FLR 1095.
[3] [1993] 2 FCR 544, sub nom *Re R (A Minor) (Blood Transfusion)* [1993] 2 FLR 757. See also *Re C (HIV Test)* [1999] 2 FLR 1004, CA – in which a specific issue order was granted that a baby be tested for HIV.

4 [1995] 2 FCR 200, sub nom *Re F (Specific Issue: Child Interview)* [1995] 1 FLR 819, CA. See also *Re M (minors) (solicitors' interviews)* [1995] 2 FCR 643, sub nom *Re M (Care: Leave to Interview Child)* [1995] 1 FLR 825, discussed at para 3.25.

5 Above.

6 [2001] 1 FCR 210, [2001] 1 FLR 121, CA.

7 [202] EWCA Civ 1627, [2003] 1 FLR 286. In that case the court overturned a first instance order that the dispute should be finally determined by the mother in consultation with the father, since that amounted to the 'plainest failure to adjudicate' the dispute. See also *M v M (Specific Issue: Choice of School* [2005] EWHC 2769 (Fam), [2007] 1 FLR 251 in which the court made a direction giving permission for a father to take his child to have a voice test to see if he could qualify for a choral scholarship at a particular school; and *Re G (Contact)* [2006] EWCA Civ 1507, [2007] 1 FLR 1663 in which an order re schooling (made originally in Australia) had become impractical.

8 See eg *Re J (child's religious upbringing and circumcision)* [1999] 2 FCR 345, sub nom *Re J (Specific Issue Orders: Muslim Upbringing and Circumcision)* [1999] 2 FLR 678 in which a father unsuccessfully sought a specific issue order requiring the non-Muslim mother to raise the child as a Muslim – not appealed on this point see [2000] 1 FCR 307, [2000] 1 FLR 571, CA.

9 Where there is a residence order in force, leave applications should be made under s 13, see *Re B (minors) (change of surname)* [1996] 2 FCR 304, [1996] 1 FLR 791, CA, discussed at para 5.33.

10 See eg *Dawson v Wearmouth* [1999] 2 AC 308, [1999] 2 All ER 353, HL and *Re W (A Child) (Illegitimate Child: Change of Surname)* [2001] Fam 1, [2000] 2 WLR 258, CA, discussed at paras 5.33 ff.

11 *Re D (a minor) (child: removal from jurisdiction)* [1992] 1 All ER 892, [1992] 1 WLR 667 and see paras 5.39 ff.

12 See in particular *J v C* [2006] EWCA Civ 551, [2007] Fam 1, [2006] 3 WLR 376 'clarifying' earlier comments to the contrary made in sub nom *J v C (Void Marriage: Status of Children)* [2008] 1 FCR 368, [2006] 2 FLR 1098.

13 *Re F (Paternity: Jurisdiction)* [2007] EWCA Civ 873, [2008] 1 FLR 225.

14 *Re J (Paternity: Welfare of Child)* [2006] EWHC 2837 (Fam), [2007] 1 FLR 1064.

5. Limits on the court's powers to make prohibited steps and specific issue orders

(a) Orders must relate to parental responsibility

5.99 An important limitation both on prohibited steps and specific issue orders is that they must concern an aspect of parental responsibility. Courts cannot, therefore, make a prohibited steps order forbidding contact between parents,[1] or protecting one parent from being assaulted by the other[2] nor can a specific issue order be made to compel a local authority to provide support services.[3]

1 *Croydon London Borough Council v A* [1992] Fam 169, [1992] 3 All ER 788, but see *F v R (Contact)* [1995] 1 FLR 227 in which Wall J accepted that such an embargo could nevertheless be incorporated as a condition to a residence or contact order under s 11(7), though this decision is now difficult to square with *Re D (a minor) (contact: conditions)* [1997] 3 FCR 721, sub nom *D v N (Contact Order: Conditions)* [1997] 2 FLR 797, CA, discussed at para 5.121.

2 *M v M (Residence Order: Ancillary Jurisdiction)* [1994] Fam Law 440 but Johnson J also held that an injunction could nevertheless be sought under the appropriate family protection legislation, as an ancillary action to the Children Act application. Note: by s 42(1)(b) of the Family Law Act 1996, the court can make a non-molestation order of its own notion in any 'family proceedings', which by s 63 includes proceedings under Pts I, II and IV of the CA 1989.

3 *Re J (specific issue order: leave to apply)* [1995] 3 FCR 799, [1995] 1 FLR 669.

5.100 The initial assumption[1] that neither a prohibited steps order restricting, nor a specific issue order sanctioning publicity about a child could be made, since that could not be considered to be an aspect of parental responsibility, was reflected in the majority view in *Re W (minors) (continuation of wardship)*.[2] However, note may be taken of Hobhouse LJ's well-reasoned dissenting judgment in *Re W*[3] that determining whether an immature child should become involved with the media 'falls within the scope of the proper discharge of parental duties', and of *Re Z (A Minor) (Identification: Restriction on Publication)*,[4] in which the Court of Appeal made a prohibited steps order restraining publicity upon the basis that the mother's waiver of the child's right of confidentiality to the particular information (namely the attendance at a specialist unit dealing with children's educational needs) was an aspect of parental responsibility. Although, account must now be made of *Re S (A Child)(Identification: Restrictions on Publication)*,[5] in which the House of Lords ruled that in the light of the Human Rights Act 1998 the foundation of the jurisdiction now derives from the European Convention on Human Rights rather than the inherent jurisdiction, it remains an open question of whether a s 8 order can be used to restrain publicity.

1 See original Children Act 1989 Guidance and Regulations, Vol 1, Court Orders (1991) Department of Health at para 2.31. This comment has not been repeated in the revised Guidance (2008), see para 2.37.
2 [1996] 1 FCR 393, sub nom *Re W (Wardship: Discharge: Publicity)* [1995] 2 FLR 466.
3 Above at 404 and 476 respectively.
4 [1997] Fam 1, sub nom *Re Z (a minor) (freedom of publication)* [1995] 4 All ER 961, CA. For analysis of this decision, see inter alia, *Kelly v BBC* [2001] Fam 59, [2001] 1 All ER 323 [2001] 2 WLR 253, per Munby J and *Medway Council v BBC* [2001] 1 FLR 104, per Wilson J.
5 [2004] UKHL 47, [2005] 1 AC 593, [2004] 4 All ER 683.

(b) No power to make ouster or occupation orders

5.101 It is settled that there is no jurisdiction under the CA 1989 to exclude a parent from the home for the protection of the child. In *D v D (ouster order)*[1] Ward LJ clearly stated that there is no jurisdiction to make an ouster order under the CA 1989.[2] Aside from justifying this position as a matter of policy (ie that because of their draconian effect Parliament should be taken to confer the power to make ouster orders only where a statute clearly so provides) a possible theoretical justification for this lack of power is that ouster orders relate to matters of occupation rather than parental responsibility.[3]

1 [1996] 2 FCR 496, sub nom *Re D (Prohibited Steps Order)* [1996] 2 FLR 273, CA. See also *Re D (Minors) (Residence: Conditions)* [1996] 2 FCR 820 [1996] 2 FLR 281. Both these cases also establish that the inability to make an ouster order cannot be overcome by using s 11(7), see below at paras 5.113 ff.
2 Though probably an application for an occupation order under Pt IV of the Family Law Act 1996 can be brought as an ancillary action to the CA 1989 application – cf *M v M (Residence Order: Ancillary Injunction)* [1994] Fam Law 440, discussed above at paras 5.99, n 2. For the power to make an ouster order under the High Court's inherent jurisdiction see para 12.33, and upon making an emergency protection or interim care order, see paras 7.93–7.94 and 8.120–8.121 respectively.
3 This line of argument was hinted at by Nourse LJ in *Pearson v Franklin* [1994] 2 All ER 137, [1994]1 WLR 370, CA but it is not beyond question since ouster orders are viewed as being primarily about protection and only incidentally about occupation. See also the discussion at paras 12.33–12.34.

(c) No power to make disguised residence or contact orders

5.102 Section 9(5)(a) prevents the court from making a specific issue or a prohibited steps order 'with a view to achieving a result which could be achieved by a residence or contact order.' This provision was made to guard against the slight risk, particularly in uncontested cases, that the orders might be used to achieve the same practical results as residence or contact orders but without the same legal effects.[1]

[1]   Law Com No 172, para 4.19. The revised Guidance (2008), para 2.40.

5.103 A clear example of the type of order forbidden by s 9(5)(a) is *M v C (children orders: reasons)*[1] in which justices purported to make a specific issue order returning the children to their mother which could and should have been achieved by a residence order. However, other examples are less obvious. For instance, in *Re B (Minors) (Residence Order)*[2] it was held that s 9(5)(a) operates to prevent the making of a specific issue order to return a child to a parent in the case of a snatch since such an order could be made by means of a residence order with appropriate conditions attached under s 11(7).[3] There has also been debate about whether s 9(5)(a) prevents the making of a prohibited steps order to prevent contact.[4]

[1]   [1993] 1 FCR 264, [1993] 2 FLR 584.
[2]   [1992] Fam 162, [1992] 3 All ER 867, CA. Cf *Re D (a Minor) (Child: Removal From Jurisdiction)* [1992] 1 All ER 892, [1992] 1 WLR 315 in which a specific issue order was made ordering a parent abroad to return the child to the jurisdiction.
[3]   The power to add conditions etc under s 11(7) is discussed at paras 5.108 ff.
[4]   See *Nottingham County Council v P* [1994] Fam 18, [1993] 3 All ER 815, CA, and *Re H (minors)(prohibited steps orders)* [1995] 4 All ER 110, [1995] 1 WLR 667, CA, discussed at para 5.62.

(d) No power to make orders that are denied to the High Court acting under its inherent jurisdiction

5.104 Section 9(5)(b) prevents the court from exercising its power to make a specific issue or prohibited steps order 'in any way which is denied to the High Court (by s 100(2)) in the exercise of its inherent jurisdiction.'[1] According to the Department of Health's original Children Act 1989 Guidance and Regulations,[2] s 9(5)(b) prevents local authorities applying for a prohibited steps or specific issue order as a way of obtaining (a) the care or supervision of a child; (b) that the child be accommodated by them or (c) any aspect of parental responsibility. In *Re S and D (Child Care: Powers of Court)*[3] it was held that by reason of s 9(5)(b) and s 100(2)(b) there was no power to restrain a parent from removing the child from local authority accommodation[4] pursuant to the rights conferred by s 20(7). It must also follow that there is similarly no power to restrain a parent from objecting to his child being accommodated in the first place pursuant to the right conferred by s 20(7).[5]

[1]   The inherent jurisdiction is discussed in Chapter 12.
[2]   Children Act 1989 Guidance and Regulations, Vol 1, Court Orders (1991) para 2.33. The revised Guidance (2008) Department for Children, Schools and Families at para 2.41 omits to mention the bar on local authorities obtaining parental responsibility.

3 [1995] 1 FCR 626, sub nom *Re S and D (Children: Powers of Court)* [1995] 2 FLR 456, CA.
4 Accommodation is discussed in Chapter 6. For the position where one parent seeks to prevent the other from objecting, see para 5.208.
5 Discussed at paras 6.50–6.51. Query whether it is possible for a prohibited steps order to be made upon the parent's application to prevent the other parent from objecting to the child's accommodation?

(e) Local authorities not to regard prohibited steps or specific issue orders as a substitute for an order under Part IV

5.105 Notwithstanding their entitlement to seek leave to apply for a prohibited steps or specific issue order in respect of a child *not* in their care,[1] *Nottingham County Council v P*[2] establishes that where intervention is thought necessary to protect children from significant harm authorities must take direct action under Pt IV of the CA 1989[3] rather than seeking to invoke the court's powers under Pt II. In that case, following allegations of sexual abuse made against her father by the eldest daughter, the local authority obtained emergency protection orders in respect of two younger children. The father voluntarily left the family home leaving the two girls residing with their mother. The local authority, resisting judicial encouragement to bring care proceedings,[4] persisted in their application for a prohibited steps order[5] requiring the father neither to reside in the same household as the girls nor to have any contact with them unless they wished it. In rejecting their application, Sir Stephen Brown P commented:[6]

> 'We consider that this court should make it clear that the route chosen by the local authority in this case was wholly inappropriate. In cases where children are found to be at risk of suffering significant harm within the meaning of s 31 of the Children Act 1989 a clear duty arises on the part of local authorities to take steps to protect them. In such circumstances a local authority is required to assume responsibility and to intervene in the family arrangements in order to protect the child. A prohibited steps order would not afford the local authority any authority as to how it might deal with the children. There may be situations for example, where a child is accommodated by a local authority, where it would be appropriate to seek a prohibited steps order for some particular purpose. However, it could not in any circumstances be regarded as providing a substitute for an order under Pt IV of the CA 1989.'

This comment was endorsed in *Langley v Liverpool City Council*.[7] Indeed, having observed[8] that a prohibited steps order was 'a private law remedy required to prevent threatened or repeated misconduct, generally in a warring family', Thorpe LJ went as far as to say that he had 'yet to encounter a case in which a local authority has decided that it can achieve the end that its child protection duties require by applying for a [prohibited steps order]'.[9]

1 See post, para 5.125.
2 [1994] Fam 18, [1993] 3 All ER 815, CA.
3 Ie by initiating care proceedings, for which see Chapter 8.
4 Both Judge Heald, at first instance, and Ward J had made s 37 directions.
5 For which they had been granted leave to apply.
6 [1994] Fam at 39, [1993] 3 All ER at 824. In any event it was doubted whether there was any power to make an ouster order under s 8. For a critique of this decision see inter alia Cobley and Lowe: 'Ousting Abusers 'Public or Private Law Solution?' (1994) 110 LQR 38.

⁷   [2005] EWCA Civ 1173, [2006] 1 FLR 342 at [78].
⁸   [2005] EWCA Civ 1173, [2006] 1 FLR 342 at [77].
⁹   But note the examples to the contrary discussed at para 5.107 below.

5.106 In *F v Cambridgeshire County Council*[1] a father, a Sch 1 offender, sought limited contact with his children who were living with their mother. The local authority were opposed to the father having contact but did not themselves seek a care order since they accepted that the mother was able to look after the children properly. Stuart-White J held, following *Nottingham*, that unless and until the s 31 threshold had been met, the local authority could not intervene in family life and hence leave to join as a party to private law proceedings should be refused.

¹   [1995] 2 FCR 804, [1995] 1 FLR 516. Query whether this embargo could be overcome by invoking wardship proceedings? Cf *Re RJ (Minors) (Fostering: Wardship)* [1999] 3 FCR 646, [1999] 1 FLR 618, discussed at para 12.16.

5.107 Although *Nottingham* clearly restricts local authorities seeking prohibited steps or specific issue orders even in respect of children they are 'looking after' but who are not in care, neither it nor *Langley v Liverpool City Council* should be read as establishing that such orders should never be sought. They might be appropriate, for example, where there is concern about a specific aspect of a parent's care of a child and the authority, while not wanting to seek a care order, nevertheless wishes to protect the child.[1] The classic example is where the authority is concerned about the child's medical treatment. In *Re C (HIV Test)*,[2] the local authority successfully applied for a specific issue order that a baby born to an HIV positive mother be tested for HIV. Similarly, in *Re R (a Minor) (Medical Treatment)*[3] a local authority successfully applied for a specific issue order to sanction a blood transfusion for a child contrary to his parent's (who were Jehovah's Witnesses) wishes.

¹   See the revised Guidance (2008) at para 2.41.
²   [2000] Fam 48, [1999] 2 FLR 1004, CA.
³   [1993] 2 FCR 544, sub nom *Re R (a Minor) (Blood Transfusion)* [1993] 2 FLR 757, discussed also at para 12.36.

6. Additional directions and conditions

5.108 The power to make interim orders, to delay implementation or to attach other special conditions is contained in s 11(7),[1] which provides that a s 8 order[2] may:

(a)   contain directions as to how the order is to be carried out;

(b)   impose conditions to be complied with by any person in whose favour the order has been made or any parent or any non-parent who has parental responsibility, or any person with whom the child is living;

(c)   specify the period for which the order or any provision in it is to have effect; and

(d)   make such incidental, supplemental or consequential provision as the court thinks fit.

These powers are exercisable by *any* court making a s 8 order.

¹ Occasionally, however, courts accept undertakings rather than imposing conditions. See eg *Re R (a Minor) (Religious Sect)* [1993] 2 FCR 525, sub nom *Re R (a Minor) (Residence: Religion)*, [1993] 2 FLR 163, CA, aunt granted contact on the undertaking that she would not speak or communicate with the child in relation to religious or spiritual matters.

² But not any other order, for example, a s 91(14) order, see *Re S (Permission to Seek Relief)* [2006] EWCA Civ 1190, [2007] 1 FLR 482 at [73].

(a) Directions and limited duration orders

5.109 The power under s 11(7)(a) to give directions as to how an order is to be put into effect enables the court to smooth the transition in cases, for example, where the child's residence is changed or to define more precisely what contact is to take place under a contact order. It also provides a means by which a first instance court can stay an order, for example by directing that any transfer of residence be delayed pending an appeal.[1]

¹ See *Re J (a Minor) (Residence)* [1993] 2 FCR 636 at 642, [1994] 1 FLR 369 at 375, per Singer J.

5.110 The power under s 11(7)(c) to specify the period for which a s 8 order, or any provision in it, empowers the court inter alia to make what are effectively interim orders (although the Act itself does not make a rigid distinction between 'interim' and 'final' orders under s 8).[1] Accordingly, the court can make an order for a limited duration coupled with a direction that the matter be brought back to court at a later specific date. This type of order could be useful in cases where more information is required[2] or to allow time to monitor the effectiveness of, for example, contact arrangements.[3] Another use of a limited duration order might be to make a holding order pending an appeal.

¹ See, for example, para 5.24 for discussion of 'interim' residence orders.

² Under s 11(3) courts can make a s 8 order even though they are not in a position finally to dispose of proceedings.

³ As in *Re B (a Minor) (Interim Order for Contact)* [1994] 1 FCR 905, [1994] 2 FLR 269.

(b) Conditions and other supplemental orders

5.111 While not expecting the frequent use of power under s 11(7)(b) and (d) to add conditions and to make such incidental, supplemental or consequential provision as is thought, the Law Commission instanced[1] three examples of when they could be useful, namely:

(1)   in the case of a dispute about which school the child should attend, making it a condition of a residence order that the child attend a particular school;

(2)   where there is a real fear that on a contact visit the parent will remove the child from the country and not return him, making it a condition of the contact order that any such removal is prohibited;[2] and

(3)   where there is real concern that the person with whom the child will live will not agree to a blood transfusion, making it a condition of the residence order to require the parent to inform the other parent so that the latter can agree to it.

¹ Law Com No 172, paras 4.23. All that the original Children Act 1989 Guidance and Regulations, Vol 1, Court Orders (1991) Department of Health at para 2.22 stated was that the supplemental etc powers 'enable the new orders [ie s 8 orders] to be as flexible as possible and so reduce or remove the need to resort to wardship.' Even this minimal guidance is omitted from the revised Guidance (2008), see para 2.27.

² Lord Mackay LC at 505 HL Official Report (5th Series) col 345 envisaged conditions being imposed forbidding a parent from moving the child to another town. See further paras 5.115 ff.

5.112 In *Re D (a Minor) (Contact: Conditions)*¹ Sir Stephen Brown P commented 'that it may be necessary for a court in the future to give further consideration to the true nature, meaning and effect of conditions imposed under s 11(7)'. Nevertheless, certain things are clear. First, s 11(7) only vests ancillary or supportive powers to those under s 8. It does not therefore give completely novel and independent powers to make, for example, conditions about the parties' finances or property ownership. It is on this basis, for instance, that it is established² that s 11(7) cannot be used to interfere with rights of occupation. Given their supportive role, Hedley J was surely right to doubt³ whether the s 11(7) powers can be used to deal with matters as profound as a change of residence and contact. Secondly, as with all Pt II powers, s 11(7) is governed by the paramountcy principle and should only be invoked where the child's welfare requires.⁴ Thirdly, as s 11(7)(b) itself expressly states, conditions may only be imposed on the persons there listed and, according to Booth J in *Leeds County Council v C*⁵ the power to make incidental etc orders under s 11(7)(d) is similarly confined.⁶ Consequently as they are not listed, there is no power under s 11(7) to order contact to be supervised by a local authority.⁷ Nevertheless, the list is wide and enables the courts to impose obligations not only upon the person in whose favour the s 8 order is made, but also upon any parent,⁸ any other person who has parental responsibility, or any other person with whom the child is living. Furthermore, provided the person is included in the list it is no objection that he is not a party.⁹

¹ [1997] 3 FCR 721 at 726–727, sub nom *D v N (Contact Order: Conditions)* [1997] 2 FLR 797 at 802, CA.

² See *D v D (Ouster Order)* [1996] 2 FCR 496, at 502–503, sub nom *Re D (Prohibited Steps Order)* [1996] 2 FLR 273 at 279, CA.

³ *Re H (Residence Order: Placement Out Of Jurisdiction)* [2004] EWHC 3243 (Fam), [2006] 1 FLR 1140 at [23].

⁴ See Law Com No. 172 at para 4.21.

⁵ [1993] 1 FCR 585, [1993] 1 FLR 269. See also *Re M (Judge's Discretion)* [2001] EWCA Civ 1428, [2002] 1 FLR 730, CA.

⁶ As Booth J pointed out, above at 590 and 273 respectively, if it were not, then s 11(7)(b) would be unnecessary. See also *Re DH (a Minor) (Care Proceedings: Evidence and Orders)* [1994] 2 FCR 3 at 41, sub nom *Re DH (a Minor) (Child Abuse)* [1994] 1 FLR 679 at 700–1, per Wall J.

⁷ In Booth J's view the appropriate remedy is a family assistance order, discussed below, paras 5.191 ff.

⁸ Including, therefore, the unmarried father who does not have parental responsibility for the child.

⁹ See *Re H (Minors) (Prohibited Steps Order)* [1995] 4 All ER 110, [1995] 1 WLR 667, discussed at paras 5.62 and 5.96, in which it was held that when making a prohibited steps order against a non-party there was power under s 11(7)(d) to give that person liberty to apply on notice to vary or discharge the order.

5.113 *In Re B (a Minor) (Residence Order)*,¹ Butler-Sloss LJ commented:

'Speaking for myself, I read [s 11(7)] very broadly as giving the judge who makes a residence order the jurisdiction to attach conditions or directions which I think are very much the same thing, as to how the children should be cared for and where they should be once the residence order has been made.'

She accordingly held that s 11(7) empowered a court, when making a residence order, to require a child to be returned; to direct the return of the child to the former matrimonial home and to the interim care of one parent, and to direct that the child remain with that parent pending the full inter partes hearing. It has become apparent, however, that a significant restriction on the application of s 11(7) is that the condition must not be incompatible with the residence order itself. In *Birmingham City Council v H*[2], Ward J refused to make a residence order with the conditions that the mother was to live at a particular unit and comply with all reasonable instructions from the unit's staff, perhaps even to hand over the child to the care of the staff. As he pointed out, this latter condition was tantamount to saying that some other person could assume parental responsibility, which was clearly inconsistent with the residence order to which the condition would have been attached.

[1]   [1992] Fam 162 at 165; [1992] 3 All ER 867 at 869, CA.
[2]   [1993] 1 FCR 247, [1992] 2 FLR 323; cf *Re C (a Minor) (Care Proceedings)* [1992] 2 FCR 341, sub nom *C v Solihull Metropolitan Borough Council* [1993] 1 FLR 290 in which Ward J made a residence order conditional upon the parents undertaking a programme of assessment, and co-operating with all reasonable requests by the local authority to participate in that programme.

5.114 In *Re D (Minors) (Residence: Conditions)*,[1] a consent order was made under which two children were returned to live with their mother on condition inter alia that she did not in the interim bring the children into contact with a former partner. Subsequently, the mother applied to the court to allow her former partner to reside at her home. At first instance, the application was refused, but on appeal the judge was held to have failed to look at the matter as a contested residence application and remitted the case for a full consideration of the competing claims of the mother and the father and grandmother. Ward LJ commented:[2]

' ... The court was not in a position so to override her right to live her life as she chose. What was before the court was whether, if she chose to have him back, the proper person with whom the children should reside was herself or whether it would be better for the children that they lived with their father or with the grandmother'.

[1]   [1996] 2 FCR 820, [1996] 2 FLR 281.
[2]   Above at 823 and 284 respectively.

5.115 This restrictive view was followed in *Re E (Minors) (Residence: Condition)*,[1] in which the court had to consider the principles governing the imposition of conditions on a residence order preventing the primary carer from moving from the Blackpool to the London area on the grounds that the mixed race child would more readily integrate in the former community. It was held that s 11(7) did not empower a court to impose upon the carer of a child the condition that he or she should reside at a particular address, since such a restriction 'sits uneasily with the general understanding of what is meant by a residence order'. It was accepted, however, that there may be exceptional cases in which the imposition of a condition in a residence order may be justified.

1   [1997] 3 FCR 245, [1997] 2 FLR 638.

5.116 In *Re S (a Child) (Residence Order: Condition)*[1] Thorpe LJ considered that:

> 'in defining the possibility of exception [in *Re E*] Butler-Sloss LJ was guarding against the danger of never saying never in family litigation. The whole tenor of her judgment is plain to me, in that she was giving the clearest guide to courts of trial that, whereas it was not safe to say never in cases in which the imposition of such a condition would be justified, it would be highly exceptional and probably restricted to a case, as yet unforeseen and may be difficult to foresee, in which the ability of the primary carer to perform to a satisfactory level required the buttress of a s 11(7) order'.

In Thorpe LJ's view[3] *Re E* was not to be interpreted as giving trial judges a 'general latitude to strive for some sort of ideal over and above the rival proposals of the available primary carers'. It was accordingly held that the judge had been wrong to grant the mother a residence order in respect of a Down's Syndrome child coupled with a condition that she should reside in Croydon (she wanted to live in Cornwall) although the matter was remitted to the first instance court for further investigation (for the outcome of which see para 5.118 below).

1   [2001] EWCA Civ 847, [2001] 3 FCR 154 at [24].
2   Above at [25].

5.117 These decisions make it clear that, in the private law context particularly, it will be difficult to justify imposing on any residence order conditions restricting the primary carer's movements and choice of where and with whom to live because to do so would, save in exceptional circumstances, be an unsustainable restriction on adult liberties and would be likely to have an adverse effect on the welfare of the child. The proper approach is, as one commentary put it:[1]

> 'to look at the issue of where the children will live as one of the relevant factors in the context of the cross-applications for residence and not as a separate issue divorced from the question of residence. If the case is finely balanced between the respective advantages and disadvantages of the parents, the proposals put forward by each parent will assume considerable importance. If one parent's plan is to remove the children against their wishes to a part of the country less suitable for them, it is an important factor to be taken into account by the court and might persuade the court in some cases to make a residence order in favour of the other parent'.

1   Lowe, Everall and Nicholls *International Family Law, Law Practice and Procedure* at 6.4 cited with approval by Thorpe LJ in *Re B (Prohibited Steps Order)* [2007] EWCA Civ 1055, [2008] 1 FLR 613, at [9].

5.118 As *Re E* and *Re S* recognised, there will be exceptional circumstances justifying the imposition of restrictive conditions on a residence order. At the remitted hearing in *Re S* the trial judge, bearing in mind the evidence that the loss of contact with her father consequent upon the mother and child's move from Croydon to Cornwall would be harmful to the Downs Syndrome child, considered the case to be 'highly exceptional' and imposed the same conditions as those originally imposed. On further appeal,[1] the Court of Appeal held that it could not interfere with the trial judge's findings. In *Re H (Children) (Residence Order: Condition)*[2] it was considered justifiable to couple a residence order with a prohibited steps order to prevent the father taking the children to Northern Ireland, inter alia, because their sense of loss of their mother as a close and regular contact would be akin to a bereavement. In *B v B (Residence: Condition Limiting Geographic Area)*[3] a condition that the mother should reside within an area 'bounded by the A4 to the north, the M25 to the west and the A3 to the south and east', was temporarily imposed inter alia in the context of the mother making two applications to go to Australia with the prime motive of getting away from the father.

1   *Re S (a child)(residence order: condition)(No 2)* [2002] EWCA Civ 1795, [2003] 1 FCR 138.
2   [2001] EWCA Civ 1338, [2001] 3 FCR 182, [2001] 2 FLR 1277.
3   [2004] 2 FLR 979.

5.119   While in the private law context such conditions will rarely be justified. However, as Butler-Sloss LJ indicated in *Re E*,[1] tighter restrictions may be justified in the public law context in which, given the choice between local authority care and a residence order, it might be right to opt for the latter, provided the court is given some degree of control. In *Re KDT (a Minor)*,[2] for example, rather than make a care order the court made both a supervision order and a residence order, coupling the latter with a condition that the father was not to share a bed with the child in any circumstances. In adding the latter condition the court was aware of the practicalities of enforcing any such order, but given the rigorous scrutiny which the court was confident that the local authority would exercise, it felt that any breach was likely to come to the authority's attention and as such the condition was 'a useful addition to the child protection measures already in force.'

1   [1997] 3 FCR 245 at 250, [1997] 2 FLR 638 at 642.
2   [1994] 2 FCR 721, sub nom *Re T (a Minor) (Care Order: Conditions)* [1994] 2 FLR 423, CA.

5.120   There seems greater latitude to attach conditions to contact orders. In *Re O (a Minor) (Contact: Indirect Contact)*[1] Sir Thomas Bingham MR considered that ss 8 and 11(7) give the court a wide and comprehensive power to make orders and set conditions which effectively ensure and facilitate contact between the child and the non-residential parent. Accepting that judges should not impose duties which parents could not realistically be expected to perform, his Lordship considered they could compel the person with a residence order and who is hostile to contact to read the other parent's communications with the child without censorship. It was also held to be wrong to place unnecessary limits on the number of letters the absent parent could send.[2] It might also be possible to make an order for supervised contact provided the supervisor is one of the persons listed in s 11(7)(b).[3] There are, however, limits about what can be imposed. In *Re D (a Minor) (Contact:*

Conditions)[4] it was held that when making an order for defined contact it was wholly inappropriate to use s 11(7) to make orders (inter alia forbidding the father to molest the mother or her relatives, from entering or damaging certain premises belonging to those relatives, or from corresponding with the mother's employers) which related more to the protection of the mother from perceived harassment than to the management of contact.

1   [1996] 1 FCR 317, sub nom *Re O (Contact: Imposition of Conditions)* [1995] 2 FLR 124, CA. For position where domestic violence has been proved, see *Practice Direction (Residence and Contact Orders: Domestic Violence)* [2008] 1 WLR 1062, para 28.
2   See also *F v R (Contact: Justices' Reasoning)* [1995] 1 FLR 227 in which Wall J approved an agreed condition to an indirect contact order that the father was not to contact or enter a day centre or school at which the child was a pupil without either the mother's or the court's prior permission.
3   See para 5.112.
4   [1997] 3 FCR 721, sub nom *D v N (Contact Order: Conditions)* [1997] 2 FLR 797, CA.

5.121 The restraints on making s 8 orders in the public law context apply equally to the exercise of the supplemental powers under s 11(7). As Balcombe LJ observed in *D v D (Child Case: Powers of Court)*:[1]

' ... s 11, just as much as s 8, falls within Pt II (the private law part) of the CA 1989 and those words cannot be construed as giving the court a power to interfere with the exercise by other bodies[2] of their statutory or common law powers, whether derived from other parts of the CA 1989 or elsewhere.'

Similarly, as *Nottingham County Council v P*[3] shows, courts should not use their s 11(7) powers, even when acting on their own motion, effectively allowing local authorities to intervene in family life under the Act's private law provisions.

1   [1994] 3 FCR 28 at 41, sub nom *D v D (County Court: Jurisdiction: Powers of Court)* [1993] 2 FLR 802 at 813, CA.
2   Ie, in this case, the local authority and the police.
3   [1994] Fam 18, [1993] 3 All ER 815, CA, discussed at paras 5.105 ff.

7. Restrictions on making s 8 orders

(a) Children aged sixteen or over

5.122 Reflecting the reality that 'as young people mature through their teenage years it becomes inappropriate to make orders concerning them against their wishes,'[1] s 9(7) and (6) respectively currently[2] provide that, subject to s 12(5),[3] a s 8 order (other than a variation or discharge) should not be made in respect of a child who has attained the age of sixteen, nor should any order be expressed to have effect beyond a child's sixteenth birthday, unless the court is satisfied that the 'circumstances' of the case are exceptional'.[4] The Act gives no guidance on what ranks as 'exceptional' but the revised Guidance instances the case where the child concerned has impaired cognitive development.[5] The requirement was held to be satisfied in *A v A (children)(shared residence)*[6] in which a shared residence order was made until each child reached their majority and coupled with a s 91(14) order as a package designed to put an end to the parents' litigation over the children and to encourage them to exercise their responsibility in a responsible manner. In the context of contact orders it has been held[7] that there was nothing unusual about a child being unable to come to a happy arrangement as to their future relationship and consequently s 9(6) was not satisfied. Orders not expressed to extend beyond the child's sixteenth birthday automatically end when he reaches sixteen.[8] Where a direction is made, the order will cease to have effect when the child reaches eighteen.[9]

1 See the Revised Guidance (2008) at para 2.58.
2 Note the proposed reform under the Children and Young Persons Bill 2008, discussed at para 5.123 below.
3 See para 5.123.
4 As Butler-Sloss LJ pointed out in *Re B (Minors) (Application for Contact)* [1994] 2 FCR 812 at 818, [1994] 2 FLR 1 at 6, CA, although there is no equivalent restriction 'for contact in the public law area under s 34' in practice, a similar regime operates. Cf the power to make enhanced residence orders (but no other s 8 order) under s 12(5) (discussed at paras 5.209–5.212) in favour of non-parents which last until the child's 18th birthday without the need to prove 'exceptional circumstances'.
5 Revised Guidance (2008), para 2.58. The Law Commission (Law Com No 172), para 3.25, instanced the case in which it is necessary to protect an older child from the consequences of immaturity, citing *Re SW (a Minor) (Wardship: Jurisdiction)* [1986] 1 FLR 24 where a 17-year-old girl was made a ward for the few remaining months of her minority in an attempt to control her behaviour.
6 [2004] EWHC 142 (Fam), [2004] 3 FCR 201, [2004] 1 FCR 1195.
7 *Re N (Minors)* (1999, unreported, LexisNexis).
8 Section 91(10).
9 Section 91(11).

5.123 The restrictions on making residence orders imposed by s 9(6) and (7) are subject to the court's power, when making such an order in favour of a person who is *not* a parent or guardian of the child, to direct, upon request of that person, that the order continue until the child reaches the age of 18 *without* the need to prove exceptional circumstances.[1] Furthermore under the Children and Young Persons Bill 2008, the restriction on the duration of residence orders will be removed altogether.[2]

1 See s 12(5) inserted by the Adoption and Children Act 2002, s 114. See further para 209.
2 Ie s 9(6) will be amended so as not to apply to residence orders and s 12(5) will be repealed.

(b) Children in local authority care

5.124 Section 9(1) prevents the court from making a s 8 order, other than a residence order, with respect to a child who is already the subject of a local authority care order.[1]

1 But note there is no embargo against a s 8 contact order being made at the behest of a child in care for contact with siblings who are not in care: *Re F (a Minor) (Contact: Child in Care)* [1994] 2 FCR 1354, [1995] 1 FLR 510.

(c) Restrictions in the case of local authorities

5.125 Section 9(2) prevents local authorities from applying for, and the courts from granting them, a residence or contact order.[1] The embargo is intended to prevent local authorities from obtaining parental responsibility other than by a care order under s 31. If local authorities wish to restrict contact with a child accommodated by them, they must seek a care order and have the matter dealt with in those proceedings. The combined effect of s 9(1) and (2) is that where a child is in care, a local authority cannot apply for any s 8 order. On the other hand, authorities may seek leave to obtain a prohibited steps or specific issue order in respect of a child accommodated by them, though this provision may not be used as a disguised route to seeking a residence or contact order[2] nor should local authorities seek to use Pt II powers in substitution for the public law powers under Pts IV or V of the Act.[3] Similarly, it has been held inappropriate to grant a local authority leave to intervene in private law proceedings so as to challenge contact being made with one of the parents.[4]

[1]   This embargo also extends to variations of residence and contact orders, see *Re C (Contact: Jurisdiction)* [1995] Fam 79, [1995] 1 FLR 777, CA.
[2]   Section 9(5), discussed at para 5.102.
[3]   *Nottingham County Council v P* [1994] Fam 18, [1993] 3 All ER 815, CA discussed on this point at para 5.105.
[4]   See *F v Cambridge County Council* [1995] 2 FCR 804, [1995] 1 FLR 516, discussed at para 5.106. Note also *Re K (Contact: Psychiatric Report)* [1996] 1 FCR 474, [1995] 2 FLR 432, CA in which it was again emphasised that local authority's powers to become involved in private law proceedings are limited. See also the comments of Wall 'The courts and child protection – the challenge of hybrid cases' [1997] CFLQ at 355–356.

(d) Other restrictions

5.126 According to Booth J residence orders cannot be made in favour of the child applicant, at any rate, where the child is seeking to live with someone else.[1] However, it must surely be open to the court to make a residence order in favour of a mother who herself is a child in respect of her own child and there seems no objection in principle[2] to granting in appropriate cases such an order in favour of a child applicant in respect of a sibling.[3]

[1]   *Re SC (a Minor) (Leave to Seek Residence Order)* [1994] 1 FLR 96 at 100.
[2]   Ie it cannot be objected that because the making of a residence order confers parental responsibility on those who do not already have it, an order cannot be made in favour of a child since of course mothers (and married fathers) have parental responsibility even if they are minors.
[3]   For discussion of whether courts can make residence orders on their own motion in favour of local authority foster parents when the parties themselves are barred from doing so under s 9(3), see para 5.142.

8. When section 8 orders can be made

(a) General jurisdictional rules

5.127 Jurisdiction to make, but not to vary or discharge,[1] s 8 orders is governed by Pt 1 of the Family Law Act 1986 which has been amended[2] to take account of the revised Brussels II Regulation (hereinafter 'BIIR').[3] For the purposes of this Act s 8 orders are known generally as 'Part I orders' but more specifically as 's 1(1)(a) orders'. According to s 2(1) of the FLA 1986 a court shall not make a s 1(1)(a) order unless:

'(a)   it has jurisdiction under the Council Regulation [ie BIIR], or
(b)   the Council Regulation does not apply but
    (i)   the question of making the order arises in or in connection with matrimonial proceedings and the condition in section 2A ... is satisfied, or
    (ii)   the condition in section 3 ... is satisfied.'

[1] Family Law Act 1986, s 1(1)(a). See *Re S (Residence Order: Forum Conveniens)* [1995] 1 FLR 314 in which jurisdiction to vary a contact order was exercised notwithstanding that the child was living in Holland with his mother. But note that this case would now be governed by BIIR. Although it makes sense to exclude variations and discharges of orders within a purely intra-United Kingdom context since courts keep jurisdiction over continuing orders (see below) it is a mistake to exclude them, as s 1(1)(a) apparently does, from the operation of the BIIR.

[2] By the European Communities (Jurisdiction and Judgments in Matrimonial and Parental Responsibility Matters) Regulations 2005, SI 2005/265.

[3] Namely Council Regulation (EC) No 2001/2003 of 27 November 2003 concerning jurisdiction and the recognition and enforcement of judgments in matrimonial matters and the matters of parental responsibility, repealing Regulation (EC) No 1347/2000.

(I) THE APPLICATION OF BIIR

5.128 BIIR provides rules for the determination of jurisdiction over matters of parental responsibility as between *all* Member States of the European Union[1] except Denmark.[2] In outline[3] the rules are as follows:

(a)   Primary jurisdiction is given to the State in which the child is habitually resident at the time the court is seised[4] (art 8);
(b)   If habitual residence cannot be established and art 12 (see below) does not apply, jurisdiction is based on the child's presence (art 13);
(c)   Where no Member State has jurisdiction under arts 8–13 then a Member State can assume jurisdiction according to its own domestic rules (art 14).

This scheme is subject to the following exceptions:

(i)   in the case of a child's *lawful* movement to another Member State, the court that made an access order retains jurisdiction to modify it for three months (art 9),[5]
(ii)   special rules apply in cases of a child's *wrongful* removal or retention (art 10);
(iii)   courts having jurisdiction to deal with divorce, legal separation or annulment have jurisdiction 'in any matter relating to parental responsibility connected with that application' provided at least one of the spouses has parental responsibility for the child and *any* other holder of responsibility accepts the jurisdiction *and* that is in the child's best interests[6] to exercise it (art 12(I));
(iv)   jurisdiction is also conferred on a Member State if the child has a 'substantial connection' with that State in particular by virtue of one of the holders of parental responsibility being habitually resident there or that the child is a national of that State *and* jurisdiction of the court has been accepted by all the parties to the proceedings at the time the court is seised *and* that it is in the child's best interests (art 12(3)).

None of the foregoing rules prevents courts of a Member State 'from taking such provisional, including protective measures in respect of persons or assets in that State' according to domestic law (art 20). Provision is also made by art 15 to allow a transfer of a case in whole or in part from a court with jurisdiction to a court of another Member State.

1 Ie including the ten States acceding to the Union in May 2004 and Bulgaria and Romania which acceded in January 2007.
2 See art 2(3).
3 For more detail, see *Clarke Hall and Morrison on Children*, 1[577.7] ff and Lowe: 'The Current Experiences and Difficulties of Applying Brussels II Revised' [2007] IFL 183.
4 'Seised' is defined in art 16 as lodging the document that institutes the proceedings 'provided that the applicant has not subsequently failed to take the steps he was required to take to have service effected on the respondent'.
5 Jurisdiction is lost if the holder of access rights accepts jurisdiction of the new court by participating in proceedings there.
6 Article 12(1)(b) actually refers to the 'superior' interests of the child but this is a mistake which is not made in other language versions nor elsewhere in BIIR.

(II) The application of the Family Law Act 1986[1]

5.129 Apart from incorporating BIIR the general aim of the Family Law Act 1986 is to avoid conflicts of jurisdiction arising within the United Kingdom[2] and specified dependent territories (that is, at the moment, the Isle of Man). To this end the Act provides for uniform jurisdictional rules when making 's 1(1)(a) orders', the scheme of which is:

(a) jurisdiction is prima facie vested in the UK court in which divorce, nullity or separation proceedings are continuing; but

(b) if there are no such proceedings, jurisdiction is vested in the UK court of the jurisdiction in which the child is habitually resident; and

(c) where neither (a) or (b) applies, jurisdiction is vested in the UK court of the place where the child is physically present.

1 This Part implements the recommendations of the English and Scottish Law Commissions in their Report, *Custody of Children – Jurisdiction and Enforcement within the United Kingdom* (Law Com No 138, Scot Law Com No 91, 1985). For a full discussion and critique of the Act, see Lowe 'The Family Law Act 1986 – A Critique' [2002] Fam Law 39 and Lowe, Everall and Nicholls *International Movement of Children, Law Practice and Procedure* ch 3.
2 Meaning England and Wales, Scotland and Northern Ireland: s 42.
3 Section 43 and the Family Law Act 1986 (Dependent Territories) Order 1991, SI 1991/1723. References to the UK court also include the Isle of Man court.

5.130 As under BIIR, notwithstanding that a court properly has jurisdiction on one of the above bases there is a discretion to refuse or stay applications.[1] Unlike BIIR, however, there is *no* emergency jurisdiction to make a s 1(1)(a) order.[2] There is no jurisdiction to make orders under the CA 1989 in relation to children who are members of the household of a parent claiming diplomatic immunity.[3] Save where the person enjoying immunity initiates proceedings, that immunity can only be waived by the sending State and not the individual concerned.[4]

1 Section 2A(4), which is confined to matrimonial proceedings and s 5, which is of general application.

2   The emergency jurisdiction, based on the child's presence, is confined to the High Court's inherent power (discussed in Chapter 12) to make s 1(1)(d) orders: s 2(3)(b)(ii).
3   *Re P (Children Act: Diplomatic Immunity)* [1998] 1 FLR 624, per Stuart-White J (on which see Barker 'Re P (*Minors*) Child abduction and international immunities – balancing competing policies' [1998] CFLQ 211) applying the Vienna Convention on Diplomatic Relations 1961 as incorporated into English law by the Diplomatic Privileges Act 1964 Sch1. Query whether this is human rights compliant? At the time of the decision the Human Rights Act 1998 was not in force.
4   *Re P (Children Act: Diplomatic Immunity)*, above, applying art 32 of the Vienna Convention.

5.131 While divorce or nullity proceedings under the Matrimonial Causes Act 1973 or dissolution or nullity proceedings under the Civil Partnership Act 2004, (where jurisdiction is based on a spouse's or civil partner's domicile or habitual residence for one year)[1] are continuing, the court can make a s 8 order in relation to children of the family.[2] Proceedings are 'continuing' for this purpose from the time the petition is filed until the child reaches 18 in Northern Ireland or the Isle of Man or 16 in Scotland, unless those proceedings have been dismissed.[3] Even if the proceedings have been dismissed, there is still jurisdiction to make a s 8 order if it is made forthwith or where an application had been made on or before the dismissal.[4] A similar position obtains in respect of judicial separation (and separation order) proceedings save that there is no jurisdiction to make a s 8 order if divorce or nullity proceedings are 'continuing' in Scotland, Northern Ireland or the Isle of Man.[5]

1   See the Domicile and Matrimonial Proceedings Act 1973, which also provides a not dissimilar scheme of priority within the UK, for the application of which see *M v M (Abduction: England and Scotland)* [1997] 2 FLR 263, CA.
2   Defined by ss 42(4)(a) and 4A in line with the definition in s 105(1) of the CA 1989.
3   Section 42(2)–(3). See eg *B v B (Scottish Contact Order: Jurisdiction to Vary)* [1996] 1 WLR 231, and note *Re B (Court's Jurisdiction)* [2004] EWCA Civ 681, [2004] 2 FLR 741 – stayed proceedings cease to be 'continuing'. English orders also 'continue' until the child reaches 18.
4   Section 2A(1)(c).
5   Section 2A(2).

5.132 Although on its face the 1986 Act provides a simple overall scheme the legislation is bedevilled by complexity and inadequate drafting which have been commented upon on more than one occasion by the judiciary. Thorpe J, for example, commented that 'Part I of the Family Law Act 1986 is not easy to understand either in its layout or its language', and Wall J referred[2] to it as 'a complex, much amended and thoroughly unsatisfactory statute'. More damning still, the 1986 Act has failed to prevent conflicts of jurisdiction arising between the UK courts, the very raison d'être of its original enactment.

1   *Re S (Residence Order: Forum Conveniens)* [1995] 1 FLR 314 at 320.
2   *Re G (Adoption: Ordinary Residence)* [2002] EWHC 2447 (Fam), [2003] 2 FLR 944 at 951.

5.133 Two main defects defeat the simplicity of the scheme. The first is that matrimonial proceedings take precedence *whenever* they are instituted. This means that while in the absence of matrimonial proceedings jurisdiction can properly be taken on the basis of the child's habitual residence, such proceedings are liable to be overtaken or 'trumped' by subsequent matrimonial proceedings.[1] Similarly, proceedings based on the child's presence can be trumped by those subsequently based on the child's habitual residence. The second complication concerns so-called superseding orders, that is, Pt I orders made during the subsistence of another Pt I order.[2] Provided the second order is competently made,[3] it will supersede the earlier order. Even interim or holding orders have that effect however unintentional.[4]

[1] See, for example, *A v A (Forum Conveniens)* [1999] 1 FLR 1.
[2] See the FLA 1986, ss 6(1) (England and Wales), 15(1) (Scotland) and 23(1) (Northern Ireland).
[3] This is made expressly clear in s 15(1) and has been held to be implicit in ss 6(1) and 23(1): *D v D (Custody: Jurisdiction)* [1996] 1 FLR 574 at 582, per Hale J.
[4] *S v S (Custody: Jurisdiction)* [1995] 1 FLR 155. See also *T v T (Custody: Jurisdiction)* [1992] 1 FLR 43.

(*b*) *Family proceedings*

5.134 Under the CA 1989, s 10(1) the court (ie the High Court, county court or magistrates' court)[1] is empowered to make a s 8 order in 'any family proceedings in which a question arises with respect to the welfare of the child'.

[1] Section 92(7).

5.135 The term 'family proceedings' is defined by s 8(3)[1] as meaning any proceedings 'under the inherent jurisdiction of the High Court in relation to children' or under the enactments listed in s 8(4). With regard to the former, which refers both to wardship and to proceedings under the general inherent jurisdiction of the High Court,[2] s 8(3) states that local authority applications for leave to invoke the High Court's inherent jurisdiction fall outside the definition.

[1] Note: s 8(3) only provides the exclusive definition of 'family proceedings' for the purpose of making s 8 orders and special guardianship orders. For other purposes, eg the admission of hearsay evidence, recourse might also be had to the definition in s 92(2): *R v Oxfordshire County Council (Secure Accommodation Order)* [1992] Fam 150, sub nom *R (J) v Oxfordshire County Council* [1992] 3 All ER 660, discussed further at para 9.24.
[2] Wardship and the High Court's general inherent jurisdiction are discussed in Chapter 12.

5.136 The enactments listed in s 8(4), as amended, are as follows:

• Pts I, II and IV of the CA 1989;
• the Matrimonial Causes Act 1973;
• the Domestic Proceedings and Magistrates' Courts Act 1978;
• the Matrimonial and Family Proceedings Act 1984, Pt III;
• the Family Law Act 1996;
• Adoption and Children Act 2002;
• Crime and Disorder Act 1998, ss 11 and 12,[1] and
• Civil Partnership Act 2004, Schs 5 and 6.

Applications for parental orders under s 30 of the Human Fertilisation and Embryology Act 1990 also rank as 'family proceedings'.[2]

¹ Under which a child safety order, placing a child under the age of 10 who has committed an act which would have been an offence had the child been aged 10 or over, under the supervision of a social worker or a member of a youth offending team, can be made. See further *Clarke Hall and Morrison on Children* at 7[10.2].

² Human Fertilisation and Embryology Act 1990, s 30(8)(a). For a discussion of parental orders see *Clarke Hall and Morrison on Children*, 1[378] ff. Note: the 1990 Act will prospectively be replaced by a new Act but at the time of going to press the relevant Bill had not completed its passage through Parliament.

5.137 The inclusion of Pt IV of the CA 1989 means that in care proceedings the court can make s 8 orders.¹ Section 8 orders can also be made in adoption, family protection proceedings and financial relief proceedings. The reason for including all these proceedings is that by extending the range of options the court will be able best to meet the child's needs.² However, the position in adoption is not straightforward since s 26 of the Adoption and Children Act 2002 makes express provision for the making of contact orders upon a placement for adoption order which presumably excludes the s 8 power to do so.³

¹ But note s 9(1) prevents the court from making a s 8 order *and* a care order, though there is nothing to prevent a court making both a supervision order and a s 8 order.

² As the Law Commission had observed (Law Com No 172, para 4.37) it seemed 'highly artificial' for the court to be able to exclude one person from the matrimonial home at least in part for the children's sake, yet not to be able to order that the child should live with the parent remaining in the home. It might be noted that in family protection proceedings the court is not obliged to consider the children and in many cases the matter will be too urgent for it to do so.

³ A consequence of this is none of the other provisions of the CA 1989 apply.

5.138 The inclusion of wardship proceedings under 'family proceedings' furthers the policy of reducing the need to resort to the jurisdiction, the strategy being¹ that if the outcome is likely to be the same as in other proceedings there will be less incentive to use it. Furthermore, even where an application is made the expectation is that, where appropriate, the court will make a s 8 order and discharge the wardship.²

¹ See Law Com No 172, para 4.35.

² As was done in *Re T (Minor) (Care: Representation)* [1994] Fam 49, [1993] 4 All ER 518, CA, discussed further at para 12.11 and *Re P (a Minor) (Leave to Apply: Foster Parents)* [1994] 2 FCR 1093, sub nom *C v Salford City Council* [1994] 2 FLR 926, discussed further at para 5.147.

5.139 Wide though the definition is it does not include all proceedings concerning children. In particular it does not include proceedings under Pt V of the CA 1989,¹ which means that in applications for emergency protection or child assessment orders the court has no power to make a s 8 order. There is similarly no power to make s 8 orders in international child abduction proceedings under the Child Abduction and Custody Act 1985, nor in proceedings under the Family Law Act 1986.²

¹ Part V is discussed in Chapter 7.

² The 1986 Act deals, inter alia, with abductions within the UK and with declarations of status.

(c) Any child

5.140 Section 10(1) empowers a court in family proceedings to make a s 8 order in respect of any child (ie a person under the age of eighteen).[1] In other words, the court's powers are not limited to 'children of the family' nor to the biological children of the parties. On the other hand, as has been discussed,[2] the power is restricted in the case of children who have reached the age of sixteen. Upon normal rules of interpretation[3] 'child' only refers to live persons. There is therefore no power to make s 8 orders in respect of unborn or deceased children.

1 Section 105(1).
2 See paras 5.122–5.123.
3 See the cases cited at para 3.93, n 3.

(d) Upon application or upon the court's own motion

5.141 Section 10(1) provides that s 8 orders can be made either upon application or, once proceedings have begun, by the court itself whenever it 'considers that the order should be made even though no such application has been made'.[1] Although the Law Commission expected[2] that orders would normally be made upon application the significance of the court's ability to make s 8 orders on their own motion should not be overlooked. However, if a court is minded to make an order that has not been argued for, it should inform the parties of that intention and give them the opportunity to make submissions on the desirability of the proposed option.[3] It has also been said[4] that it should only be in wholly exceptional circumstances that a residence order should be imposed on unwilling recipients.

1 Section 10(1)(b).
2 Law Com No 172, para 4.38.
3 See eg *Croydon London Borough Council v A* [1992] Fam 169, [1992] 3 All ER 788 and *Devon County Council v S* [1992] Fam 176 [1992] 3 All ER 793. In both these cases the observations were made in respect of magistrates' court decisions but the principle ought to be of general application. Query the position on appeal, see eg *Re F (Minors) (Denial of Contact)* [1993] 1 FCR 945, [1993] 2 FLR 677 in which the Court of Appeal refused to make a family assistance order inter alia because the point had not been argued at first instance.
4 Per Stuart-Smith J in *Re K (Minors) (Care or Residence Orders)* [1996] 1 FCR 365 at 374, [1995] 1 FLR 675 at 683, in which devoted grandparents did not wish to have legal responsibility in respect of two grandsons (who were suffering from a muscle-wasting disease) they were looking after.

5.142 In *Gloucestershire County Council v P*[1] it was held that the flexibility given to a judge by s 10(1)(b) to make a residence order upon his own initiative is not limited by the restrictions imposed by ss 9 and 10(3).[2] It was thus held to be no bar on the court granting a residence order in favour of foster parents that the parties themselves were prohibited from seeking court leave to apply for such an order though it would only be in 'a most exceptional' case that it would be right to make an order in favour of foster parents who could not themselves apply. A similarly purposive interpretation was applied in *Re G (a Minor) (Leave to Appeal: Jurisdiction)*[3] when upholding a decision to make an 'interim' residence order upon an application for leave to allow a child in care to go to Scotland, even though this evaded the difficulties of Sch 2 to the CA 1989. Butler-Sloss LJ said:[4]

> 'Judges cannot dispense with the Children Act. What they can dispense with are unnecessary procedural difficulties within the general powers of the Children Act to arrive at what the judge thinks under s 1 of the Children Act to be the best interests of the child, with the child's welfare being the paramount consideration'.

1   [2000] Fam 1, [1999] 3 FCR 114, [1999] 2 FLR 61, CA (Thorpe LJ dissenting).
2   Discussed at para 5.125.
3   [1999] 3 FCR 281, [1999] 1 FLR 771.
4   Above at 284 and 773 respectively.

9. Who may apply for s 8 orders?

5.143 The Act adopts a so-called 'open door' policy whereby some are entitled to apply, while others can, with leave of the court, apply for s 8 orders either by intervening in existing 'family proceedings'[1] or by initiating their own proceedings. The detailed scheme provided for by s 10 (which governs both initiating and intervening in family proceedings), is described below.

1   For the meaning of which, see paras 5.135 ff.

(a) Persons entitled to apply without leave

5.144 Parents, guardians, special guardians, step-parents who have parental responsibility by virtue of a s 4A order or agreement and those with a residence order in their favour are entitled to apply for any s 8 order.[1] For these purposes 'parents' includes the unmarried father[2] but not 'former parents' whose child has been adopted.[3] In addition certain other persons are entitled to apply for a residence order or a contact order without leave,[4] namely:[5]

(a)   any party to a marriage (whether or not subsisting) or any civil partner in a civil partnership (whether or not subsisting) in relation to whom the child is a 'child of the family';
(b)   any person[6] with whom the child has lived for a period of at least three years (this period need not be continuous but must not have begun more than five years before, or ended more than three months before the making of the application);[7]
(c)   any person having the consent of:
       (i)   each of the persons in whose favour a residence order is in force;
       (ii)   the local authority, if the child is subject to a care order; or
       (iii) in any other case, each of the persons who have parental responsibility for the child.

Group (a) primarily refers to step-parents but can include any married person or persons[8] or civil partner(s) who has treated the child as a 'child of the family'.[9] Under the Children and Young Persons Bill 2008 it is proposed that relatives will be entitled to apply for a residence order (but not a contact order) if the child has lived with them for one year.

1   Section 10(4), as amended.
2   *Re C (Minors) (Adoption: Residence Order)* [1994] Fam 1, sub nom *Re C (Minors) (Parent: Residence Order)* [1993] 3 All ER 313, CA (sometimes referred to as 'the Calderdale case') reversing Johnson J's ruling that for the purposes of s 10(4) 'parents' referred only to those who have parental responsibility.
3   *Re C (Minors) (Adoption: Residence Order)*, above.
4   Ie leave is still required to apply for a specific issue or prohibited steps order.
5   Section 10(5).
6   But note the prospective change (see below) in respect of relatives.
7   Section 10(6).
8   Including grandparents: see *Re A (Child of the Family)* [1998] 1 FCR 458, [1998] 1 FLR 347, CA.
9   'Child of the family' is defined by s 105(1) as a child of both the married parents and 'any other child, not being a child who is placed with those parties as foster parents by a local authority or voluntary organisation, who has been treated by both of those parties as a child of their family'.

5.145 Those not otherwise included in the above-mentioned categories will nevertheless be entitled, pursuant to s 10(6), to apply for a variation or discharge of a s 8 order if either the order in question was made on his application or, in the case of a contact order, he is named in that order. This means, for instance, that a child named in a contact order will not need leave to apply to vary it.[1] Section 10(7) reserves the power of rules of court to prescribe additional categories of people who may make applications without prior leave. These powers have not yet been exercised.

1   *Re W (Application For Leave: Whether Necessary)* [1996] 3 FCR 337n, per Wilson J.

(b) Persons requiring leave

5.146 In general anyone, including the child himself and any body, local authority or organisation professionally concerned with children, who is not entitled to apply, can seek leave of the court to apply for any s 8 order.[1] However, local authorities cannot in any event apply for residence or contact orders,[2] while any person 'who is, or was at any time during the last six months, a local authority foster parent' (the term 'local authority foster parent' refers to any person with whom any child is 'looked after' by a local authority within the meaning of s 22(3),[3] and therefore includes those with whom the child has been placed as prospective adopters)[4] must have the consent of the local authority to apply for the court's leave unless he is a relative of the child or the child has been living with him for at least one year preceding the application.[5] According to Lord Mackay LC[6] the reason for imposing the additional restrictions on applications by local authority foster parents is to prevent premature applications unduly interfering with local authority plans for the child and so undermining their efforts to bring stability to the child's life. It is also intended to guard against the risk of deterring parents from voluntarily using the fostering services provided by local authorities which, it is argued, could easily happen if the restrictions were relaxed.

1   Section 10(1)(a)(ii).
2   Discussed at para 5.125.
3   Discussed at para 6.58.
4   Per Judge Foster QC, in *Re C (Adoption: Notice)* [1999] 1 FLR 384.

5   Section 9(3), as amended by s 113 of the Adoption and Children Act 2002, which reduced the period from an anomalous three years.
6   In 502 HL Official Report (5th series), cols 1221–1222. This provision had not been recommended by the Law Commission.

5.147 Ironically, in the first case to consider s 9(3), *Re P (A Minor) (Leave to Apply: Foster Parents)*,[1] parents sought to challenge the propriety of the consent given by the local authority. In that case a child suffering from Down's Syndrome had been accommodated by the local authority and placed with foster parents. Subsequently, the foster parents expressed their wish to adopt but as Roman Catholics they were unacceptable as prospective adopters to the parents who were Jewish. They accordingly, and with the consent of the local authority, sought leave to apply for a residence order. The parents argued that because of their dual function as an adoption agency and as an accommodating local social services authority the local authority should not or could not have consented to the foster parents' application. Rejecting this argument, it was held that for the purposes of s 9(3) it was the consent of the social services authority accommodating the child that was required, and that therefore the authority's role as adoption agency was not part of that consent. It was further held that because the balance of the welfare factors made the case a difficult one, that was justification in itself in having the issues resolved by the court. Leave was accordingly granted.

1   [1994] 2 FCR 1093, sub nom *C v Salford City Council*, [1994] 2 FLR 926, per Hale J. But note this restriction does not bar the court from making an order on its own motion, see *Gloucestershire County Council v P* [2000] Fam 1, [1999] 3 FCR 114, [1999] 2 FLR 61, CA (Thorpe LJ dissenting), discussed at para 5.142.

(c) The leave criteria

5.148 So far as the leave criteria are concerned two provisions of the CA 1989 are relevant, namely, s 10(8) and (9). At one time it was thought that the former applied to children seeking leave, while the latter applied to adults seeking leave. However, in *Re S (A Minor) (Adopted Child: Contact)*[1] Charles J considered it is too simplistic to say that s 10(8) applies to child applicants and s 10(9) to adult applicants. As he pointed out, the application of these provisions is not dependent upon whether or not the applicant is a child but upon whether or not the applicant is 'the child concerned'. He considered that for these purposes the phrase 'the child concerned' means the child who is the subject of the application.[2] If he is not then s 10(9) applies rather than s 10(8). In *Re S* itself the child (who was adopted) was seeking contact with another sibling and could not therefore be considered the subject-matter of the action and hence not the 'child concerned'. Accordingly, s 10(9) was held to apply.

1   [1999] Fam 283, [1999] 1 All ER 648, sub nom *Re S (Adopted Child: Contact by Sibling)* [1999] 1 FCR 169, [1998] 2 FLR 897.
2   Which interpretation reflects the case law on the application of the paramountcy test as established by *Birmingham City Council v H (a Minor)* [1994] 2 AC 212, [1994] 1 All ER 12, HL, discussed at paras 2.30 ff.

5.149 On Charles J's analysis s 10(9) can apply both to adults and children seeking leave while s 10(8), though confined to child applicants, will only apply where the child is regarded as the subject of the action, as for example, where a residence order or contact order with another adult is being sought. It remains to be seen whether it will become the accepted approach. One problem of applying s 10(9) to child applicants is that it might appear that the child's age and understanding (referred to in s 10(8)) are not relevant. However, according to Charles J that factor can be taken into account since the criteria listed in 10(9) are not meant to be exclusive. But even if this solution is accepted there remains the difficulty that s 10(9)(b) directs the court to consider 'the applicant's connection with the child' which does not sit easily with the interpretation that s 10(9) can apply to child applicants. It should be added that regardless of whether leave is sought by the child under s 10(8) or (9), applications should be made to the High Court.[1]

[1]   *Practice Direction (Application by Children: Leave)* [1993] 1 All ER 820, [1993] 1 WLR 313.

(I) THE APPLICATION OF S 10(9)

5.150 Section 10(9) states:

'Where the person applying for leave to make an application for a s 8 order is not the child concerned, the court shall, in deciding whether or not to grant leave, have particular regard to:
(a)   the nature of the proposed application for the s 8 order;
(b)   the applicant's connection with the child;
(c)   any risk there might be of that proposed application disrupting the child's life to such an extent that he would be harmed by it; and
(d)   where the child is being looked after by a local authority'
        (i)   the authority's plans for the child's future; and
        (ii)   the wishes and feelings of the child's parents'.[1]

[1]   Although s 10(9) only applies where leave is sought to apply for a s 8 order, it has been held that the underlying thinking behind the provision is also applicable to an application by a non-parent for proceedings to be consolidated: *W v Wakefield City Council* [1994] 2 FCR 564, at 576, [1995] 1 FLR 170 at 179, per Wall J. But note s 10(9) does *not* apply to the question of granting leave following the making of a s 91(14) order, per Thorpe LJ in *Re A (a Minor) (Contact: Parent's Application for Leave)* [1999] 1 FCR 127, [1998] 1 FLR 1, CA. See further para 5.204.

5.151 It was held in *Re A (Minors) (Residence Orders: Leave to Apply)*[1] that in deciding whether to grant adult applicants leave, the paramountcy of the child's welfare principle under s 1(1) has no application for three reasons:

(1)   in granting or refusing a leave application the court is not determining a question with respect to the child's upbringing. That question only arises when the court hears the substantive application.
(2)   furthermore some of the guidelines, for example, s 10(9)(a), (c) and (d)(i) would be otiose if the child's welfare was paramount, while
(3)   in any event there 'would have been little point in Parliament providing that the court was to have particular regard to the wishes and feelings of the child's parents, if the whole decision were to be subject to the overriding (paramount) consideration of the child's welfare'.

5.151 *Private law orders*

Notwithstanding *Re A*, s 10(9) should not be regarded as providing the exclusive guidelines and in particular as preventing the court from considering the checklist under s 1(3). It is therefore proper to consider the child's own views,[2] and, when applying s 10(9) to child applicants, to consider the child's age and understanding.[3]

1   [1992] Fam 182, [1992] 3 All ER 872, CA.
2   *Re A (a Minor) (Residence Order: Leave to Apply)* [1993] 1 FLR 425, per Hollings J.
3   Per Charles J in *Re S (A Minor) (Adopted Child: Contact)*, above, at para 5.148.

5.152 A leave application should not be treated as a substantive application (in other words judges should avoid considering the merits of the prospective action). Consequently even where leave has been given it by no means follows that the eventual application will succeed.[1] At one time it was held[2] that in deciding whether or not to grant leave, the court should assess whether the substantive application would have a reasonable prospect of success, but in *Re M (Care: Contact: Grandmother's Application for Leave)*[3] it was held that this test was too rigid. According to *Re M* the applicant had to satisfy the court that there 'is a serious issue to try and must present a good arguable case'. But in turn *Re M* was called into question in *Re J (Leave to Issue Application for Residence Order)*[4] in which Thorpe LJ expressed concern that the courts had been substituting the 'good-arguable case' test for that laid down by Parliament which anxiety was heightened 'where applicants manifestly enjoy art 6 rights to a fair trial and, in the nature of things, are also likely to enjoy art 8 rights'. In *Re R (Adoption: Contact)*[5] the issue was again considered with Wall LJ concluding that notwithstanding '*Re J* it is permitted to make a broad assessment of the merits of the particular application but what a court cannot do is to determine the application on the 'no reasonable prospects of success' criterion'. As he pointed out, s 10(9)(a) expressly enjoins the court to consider 'the nature of the proposed application for the s 8 order' which, in his view, entitles the court to take into account the relevant jurisprudence. Hence, in *Re R* the trial judge had been right when refusing leave to have regard to the fact that courts are reluctant to make a contact order in the face of reasonable opposition from the prospective adopters.[6] The refusal to give leave is a serious issue and failure to give reasons for the decision constitutes a fundamental defect.[7]

1   See e g *Re A (Section 8 Order: Grandparent Application)* [1996] 1 FCR 467, [1995] 2 FLR 153, CA and *Re W (Contact: Application by Grandparent)* [1997] 2 FCR 643, [1997] 1 FLR 793.
2   *G v Kirklees Metropolitan Borough Council* [1993] 1 FCR 357, [1993] 1 FLR 805.
3   [1995] 3 FCR 550 at 562–563, sub nom *Re M (Care: Contact: Grandmothers Application for Leave)* [1995] 2 FLR 86 at 98.
4   [2003] 1 FLR 114. Note also *Re H* [2003] EWCA Civ 369, [2003] All ER (D) 290 (Feb), referred to in *Re R (Adoption: Contact)* [2005] EWCA Civ 1128, [2006] 1 FLR 373 at [38], and *Re W (Care Proceedings: Leave to Apply)* [2004] EWHC 3342 (Fam), [2005] 2 FLR 468.
5   [2005] EWCA Civ 1128, [2006] 1 FLR 373.
6   But while it can be right to look at the likely outcome of the prospective application from a legal point of view, it must be surely wrong to do so from a factual point of view since that would seem to venture into investigating the substantive merits of the case.
7   Per Connell J in *T v W (Contact Reasons for Refusing Leave)* [1997] 1 FCR 118, [1996] 2 FLR 473; and *Re W (a Child) (Contact: Leave to Apply)* [2000] 1 FCR 185, sub nom *Re W (Contact Application: Procedure)* [2000] 1 FLR 263.

5.153 The leave requirement is intended to act as a filter to protect the child and his family against unwarranted interference with their comfort and security, whilst ensuring that the child's interests are properly respected.[1] The more tenuous the applicant's connection with the child the harder it will be to obtain leave. Conversely, the closer the connection the more readily leave should be given. As the Law Commission put it,[2] the requirement of leave will 'scarcely be a hurdle at all to close relatives such as grandparents … who wish to care for or visit the child'. On the other hand, as Lord Mackay LC commented in response to attempts during the passage of the Bill to give grandparents an entitlement to apply for a residence or contact order:[3]

> '[t]here is often a close bond … between a grandparent and a grandchild … and in such cases leave, if needed, will no doubt be granted. Indeed, in many cases it will be a formality; but we would be naive if we did not accept that all interest shown by a grandparent in a child's life is not necessarily benign, even if well intentioned. Arguably, at least until we have some experience of wider rights of application, the law should provide some protection to children and their parents against unwarranted applications by grandparents when they occur'.

Since implementation another concern voiced by the court is the consequential delay in having too many parties and Butler-Sloss LJ has specifically said that it is undesirable that grandparents whose interests are identical with those of the mother should be separately represented.[4] In contrast in *Re J (Leave to Issue Application for Residence Order)*[5] Thorpe LJ commented:

> 'it is important that trial judges should recognise the greater appreciation that has developed of the value of what grandparents have to offer, particularly to children of disabled parents. Judges should be careful not to dismiss such opportunities without full enquiry'.

Nevertheless, it is in the nature of the requirement that even grandparents are not always given leave.[6]

1 As Lord Mackay LC eloquently put it (502 HL Official Report (5th Series), col 1227): 'There is clearly a danger both in limiting and expanding the categories of persons who may apply for orders in respect of children. On the one hand, a too wide and uncontrolled gateway can expose children and families to the stress and harm of unwarranted interference and the harassment of actual or threatened proceedings. If too narrow or over-controlled the gateway may prevent applications which would benefit or safeguard a child from harm'.

2 Law Com No 172, para 4.41.

3 503 HL Official Report (5th series), col 1342.

4 *Re M (Minors) (Sexual Abuse: Evidence)* [1993] 1 FCR 253 at 257, [1993] 1 FLR 822 at 825. The difficulty in practice is that the parties themselves will not always consider their interests identical. See also *Re W (Care Proceedings: Leave to Apply)* [2004] EWHC 3342 (Fam), [2005] 2 FLR 468.

5 [2002] EWCA Civ 1346, [2003] 1 FLR 114 at [19].

6 For a defence of the leave requirement for grandparents see Douglas '*Re J (Leave to Issue Application for Residence Order)* Recognising grandparents' concern or controlling their interference?' [2003] CFLQ 103. For a general discussion of the legal position of grandparents under the CA 1989, see *The Children Act: What's in it for Grandparents?* (4th edn, 2007) published by The Grandparents' Association. But for a moving account of a grandparent's experience, see 'The Judicial Inconsistency and the Family Court System' [2007] Fam Law 721.

5.154 Careful consideration needs to be given to applications for leave by individuals in respect of children in care. In *Re A (Minors) (Residence Orders:*

Leave to Apply)[1] the court refused leave to apply for a residence order in respect of children originally placed with the applicant for long-term fostering but who had been removed from her by the local authority nearly six months earlier.[2] The court accepted that the power under s 9(1) to make a residence order notwithstanding that the child is in care represented a fundamental change in that the so-called '*Liverpool* principle'[3] no longer had direct application but that did not mean that no weight should be given to the local authority's views. On the contrary s 10(9)(d)(i) provides that the court is to have particular regard to the authority's plans for the child. Furthermore, in view of the duty under s 22(3) to safeguard and promote the welfare of any child in its care, it was held that the court should approach the application for leave on the basis that 'the authority's plans for the child's future are designed to safeguard and promote the child's welfare and that any departure from those plans might well disrupt the child's life to such an extent that he would be harmed by it'.[4] In other words, courts should not allow such applications to become a back-door means of reviewing local authority decisions.[5]

1   [1992] Fam 182, [1992] 3 All ER 872.
2   In fact the application was made one week before the expiry of six months from the removal but it was agreed between the parties that the local authority would not object to the application as they could have done under s 9(3), and that the mother would not pursue her action for judicial review. For an unusual case where leave was given notwithstanding that the child had been freed for adoption, see *Re H (A Child)* [2008] EWCA Civ 503, [2008] Fam Law 734.
3   Named after *A v Liverpool City Council* [1982] AC 363, [1981] 2 All ER 385, HL which established that the appropriate means of challenging local authority decisions was via judicial review rather than wardship. See further paras 12.42 and 12.43.
4   Per Balcombe LJ [1992] Fam at 189 [1992] 3 All ER at 879.
5   See also *Re M (Prohibited Steps Order: Application for Leave)* [1993] 1 FCR 78, [1993] 1 FLR 275 in which a former guardian sought leave to challenge a local authority's decision not to take care proceedings' application remitted to justices for a re-hearing.

(II) THE APPLICATION OF S 10(8)

5.155 Where the applicant for leave to make a s 8 application[1] is the 'child concerned', s 10(8) provides that leave can only be granted provided the court is satisfied that the child has sufficient understanding to make the proposed application. There is no hard and fast rule for determining whether the child is of sufficient age and understanding. As Sir Thomas Bingham MR said in *Re S (a Minor) (Independent Representation):*[2]

'the rules eschew any arbitrary line of demarcation based on age and wisely so. Different children have differing levels of understanding at the same age. And understanding is not absolute. It has to be assessed relatively to the issues in the proceedings. Where any sound judgment on these issues calls for insight and imagination which only maturity and experience can bring, both the court and the solicitor will be slow to conclude that the child's understanding is sufficient'.

Even if the child is found to be competent, leave might not necessarily be granted. For example in *Re H (Residence Order: Child's Application For Leave)*[3] a child, of sufficient understanding to make the application, was refused leave to make it because his father could adequately represent his views to the court.

1   Note: a child who has previously been given leave and who has been named in a contact order does not need fresh leave to apply to vary that order; per Wilson J in *Re W (Application for Leave: Whether Necessary)* [1996] 3 FCR 337n, applying s 10(6), see para 5.145.
2   [1993] Fam 263 at 276, [1993] 3 All ER 36 at 43–44, CA. See also Chapter 10.
3   [2000] 1 FLR 780.

5.156 Apart from requiring the court to be satisfied about the child's understanding, the Act gives little further guidance, particularly as it seems to be accepted that the guidelines under s 10(9) do not apply where a child is seeking leave under s 10(8).[1] According to Charles J in *Re S (A Minor) (Adopted Child: Contact)*[2] this lack of guidance is indicative that the court is to have regard to the interests of the child. It is, however, generally accepted that in determining whether to grant leave the child's welfare is *not* the paramount consideration. As Booth J held in *Re SC (a Minor) (Leave to Seek Residence Order)*,[3] applying *Re A (Minors) (Residence Orders: Leave to Apply)*,[4] when determining an application for leave under s 10 (whether it be under s 10(8) or (9)) the court is *not* determining a question in respect of the upbringing of the child concerned (that question only arises if leave is granted and the court determines the substantive application) and that therefore s 1(1) *does* not apply.[5] To this might be added, that not regarding the child's welfare as paramount has the merit of according a child of sufficient understanding to make the application some degree of independence which seems more in keeping with the spirit of the Act.[6]

1   See *Re C (Minor: Leave to Apply for Order)* [1994] 1 FCR 387, sub nom *Re C (A Minor) (Leave to Seek Section 8 Orders)* [1994] 1 FLR 26 and *Re SC (A Minor) (Leave to Seek Residence Order)* [1994] 1 FLR 96 both of which were predicated upon the view that s 10(8) applied to children seeking leave, while s 10(9) applied to adults seeking leave. But it was also implicitly accepted by Charles J in *Re S (A Minor) (Adopted Child: Contact)* [1999] Fam 283, [1999] 1 All ER 648, who, as discussed at paras 5.148–5.149, considered the application of s10(8) and (9) to be dependent upon whether or not the applicant was the child concerned.
2   Above.
3   [1994] 1 FLR 96 at 99. See also in *Re C (Residence: Child's Application for Leave)* [1995] 1 FLR 927; *North Yorkshire County Council v G* [1994] 1 FCR 737, [1993] 2 FLR 732, and *Re S (a Minor) (Adopted Child: Contact)*, above, per Charles J. See also *Re H (Residence Order: Child's Application For Leave)* [2000] 1 FLR 780 in which Johnson J resiled from his earlier position to the contrary.
4   [1992] Fam 182, [1992] 3 All ER 872, discussed at para 5.151.
5   See the discussion at para 2.17.
6   And with FPR 1991, r 9.2A which allows children of sufficient age and understanding to initiate proceedings without a next friend or guardian ad litem. See further paras 10.53–10.55

5.157 According to *Re HG (Specific Issue Order: Sterilisation)*[1] parents, at any rate when applying for leave that their child be sterilised, can apply for leave on that child's behalf in cases where the child lacks the necessary understanding to apply on his own behalf. The advantage of this ruling is that in these cases public funding can be sought on behalf of the child rather than the parents.[2]

1   [1993] 1 FCR 553, [1993] 1 FLR 587, per Peter Singer QC (as he then was).
2   In *Re HG* the parents did not qualify for legal aid.

(III) PROCEDURE FOR SEEKING LEAVE

5.158 Any person seeking leave must file a written request setting out the reasons for the application and a draft of the application for making of which leave is sought.[1] Leave can be granted by the court or a single justice, with or without a hearing.[2] However, according to Wilson J in *Re W (a Child) (Contact Leave to Apply)*[3] it should be exceptional to grant leave ex parte.[4] Notice of an application for leave to apply should generally be given to all parties likely to be affected if leave is granted. Moreover, in almost all cases, it is appropriate for the respondent, together with the applicant, to be invited to attend the hearing for the grant of leave. Where magistrates proceed in the absence of notice to the respondent and grant leave, they should record reasons for both decisions.

1 FPR 1991, r 4.3(1); FPC(CA 1989)R 1991, r 3(1). Nevertheless the fact that an order has been made without a written request does not automatically invalidate the order: per Ewbank J in *Re O (Minors) (Leave to Seek Residence Order)* [1993] 2 FCR 482, [1994] 1 FLR 172.
2 Rules 4.3(2) and 3(2) respectively.
3 [2000] 1 FCR 185, sub nom *Re W (Contact Application: Procedure)* [2000] 1 FLR 263, per Wilson J.
4 Wilson J said (at 189 and 266 respectively) while he could imagine a case where an ex parte application could be justified, for example, a mature teenage child leaving home and seeking leave to apply for a residence order to secure his position in the home of another family, he could not readily think of an example of a proposed application for contact where an ex parte application would be justified.

(d) Applying for orders in favour of someone else

5.159 The Act is silent on whether applications may be made for a s 8 order in favour of someone else. However, as has been seen, an adult can apply for leave on behalf of a child,[1] and, implicit in the ability of a child being able to obtain leave to apply for such orders, is that they can seek a residence order in favour of another person.[2] As Booth J said in *Re SC (a Minor) (Leave to Seek Residence Order)*[3] who commented:

> 'In my judgment the court should not fetter the statutory ability of the child to seek any s 8 order, including a residence order, if it is appropriate for such an application to be made. Although the court will undoubtedly consider why it is that the person in whose favour a proposed residence order would be made is not applying, it would in my opinion be wrong to import into the Act any requirement that only he or she should make the application.'

Whether the courts would be disposed to permit applications other than by children for residence or contact orders in favour of someone else remains to be seen.[4]

1 See *Re HG (Specific Issue Order: Sterilisation)* [1993] 1 FCR 553, [1993] 1 FLR 587, discussed at para 5.97.
2 Cf *Re H (Residence Order: Child's Application For Leave)* [2000] 1 FLR 780 in which a child unsuccessfully sought leave to apply for a residence order to his father failed on the facts rather than the legal impossibility of such an action. As Booth J pointed out in *Re SC (a Minor) (Leave to Seek Residence Order)* [1994] 1 FLR 96 at 100, residence orders cannot be made in favour of the child applicant himself since that would confer parental responsibility on him by reason of s 12(2).

³ Above, at 100E–F.
⁴ See further, Lowe and Douglas *Bromley's Family Law* (10th edn) 550.

10. Enforcing s 8 orders

5.160 Enforcing s 8 orders, particularly contact orders, can be difficult and protracted.[1] The imposition of penal sanctions for breaking court orders should not be thought of as being the norm in children cases. On the contrary, they should be sought only where all other alternatives are seen to be ineffective or inappropriate.[2] Even then careful thought needs to be given to the provocative and emotional effect that applications for penal notices and committals can have in themselves. It is important not to lose sight of the child's welfare in these disputes though, as will be seen, in deciding whether to impose a penal sanction the child's welfare has been held *not* to be the paramount consideration.[3]

1 See generally Lowe 'Enforcing orders relating to children' (1992) 4 Jo of Child Law 26, and especially in relation to enforcing contact orders, see *Making Contact Work* (A Report to the Lord Chancellor by the Advisory Board on Family Law: Children Act Sub-Committee, 2002), ch 14 and, inter alia, the Government's Green Papers *Parental Separation: Children's Needs and Parents' Responsibilities* CM 6273 (July 2004) and *Children's Needs and Parents' Responsibilities: Next Steps* CM 6452 (January 2005).
2 For example, transferring residence from one parent to another, in the face of repeated breaches of contact orders, should only be made where it is in the child's interests and not as punishment of the recalcitrant parent, see *V v V (Children: Contact: Implacable Hostility)* [2004] EWHC 1215 (Fam), [2004] 2 FLR 851, [2004] All ER (D) 304 (May), discussed at para 5.87.
3 *A v N (Committal: Refusal of Contact)* [1997] 2 FCR 475, [1997] 1 FLR 533, CA and *M v M (Breaches of Orders: Committal)* [2005] EWCA Civ 1722, [2006] 1 FLR 1154, discussed below at para 5.175.

(a) Family Law Act 1986, s 34

5.161 Under the Family Law Act 1986, s 34,[1] where a person is required by a s 8 order[2] to give up a child to another person (this will most commonly apply in the enforcement of a residence order) and the court that made the order is satisfied that the child has not been given up, it may make a 'search and recovery' order authorising an officer of the court or a constable to take charge of the child and deliver him to that other person.[3] Since this power enables such orders to be implemented without recourse to penal procedures, it should normally be preferred to those latter powers. However, because an order under s 34 cannot be granted unless or until the order to give up the child has been disobeyed, it might be preferable in emergencies to obtain an ex parte order under the High Court's inherent jurisdiction[4] authorising the tipstaff to find and recover the child.[5] The court may also pre-empt an unlawful removal of a child from the care of the person with a residence order or from the jurisdiction by making an order preventing such removal and attaching a penal notice thereto.

1 See generally Fricker and Bean: *Enforcement of Injunctions and Undertakings*, p 80 ff and by Fricker, Adams, Pearce, Salter, Stevens and Wybrow: *Emergency Remedies and Procedures* (2nd edn) p 158 ff and Lowe, Everall and Nicholls *International Movement of Children – Law Practice and Procedure* 10.36–10.38.

2   Or any existing statutory custody or care and control order.
3   Note that the police generally have a duty to assist in the handing over of a child where there is a threat of danger or a breach of the peace: *R v Chief Constable of Cheshire, ex p K* [1990] FCR 201, [1990] 1 FLR 70. Note also the power under s 33 of the 1986 Act for a court to order any person who it has reason to believe may have relevant information as to the child's whereabouts to disclose it to the court.
4   This jurisdiction is discussed in Chapter 12. Although as s 34(4) makes clear, the power under s 34 is without prejudice to any power conferred in the court by or under any other enactment or rule of law.
5   See Fricker et al, above, at p 248 and Fricker, 'Injunctive Orders Relating to Children' [1993] Fam Law 226, 229–230.

5.162   A s 34 order confers the power to enter and search any premises where the person acting in pursuance of the order has reason to believe the child may be found and to use such force as may be necessary to give effect to 'the purpose of the order'.[1] However, the order only gives authority to officers of the court and police officers in England and Wales. If the child is in another part of the UK or the Isle of Man recovery orders will be required from a court of the relevant jurisdiction.[2] Applications for a s 34 order may be made ex parte.[3] The procedure and prescribed forms are set out in the FPR 1991, r 6.17 (for the two higher courts) and in the FPC(CA 1989)R 1991, r 31A (magistrates).[4]

1   Section 34(2).
2   See Lowe, Everall and Nicholls, cited at para 5.161, at 10.37.
3   FPR 1991, r 6.17(4), FPC (CA) R 1991, r 31A(4).
4   Breach of an order is enforceable under the higher courts' contempt powers (discussed below) or under the Magistrates' Courts Act 1980, s 63(3) – discussed below at paras 5.168 ff.

(b)   The courts' general enforcement powers

5.163   General powers of enforcement are provided by the law of contempt, in the case of the High Court and county court, and by the Magistrates' Courts Act 1980, s 63(3) in the case of magistrates' courts.

(I)   THE HIGH COURT AND COUNTY COURT POWERS

5.164   As far as the two higher courts are concerned (in this respect the powers of the High Court are no greater than those of the county court)[1] the breaking of an order or an undertaking incorporated in an order constitutes a contempt of court for which the contemnor may be fined, imprisoned or have his property sequestered.[2] The first remedy is unusual.[3] The latter remedy (under which the contemnor's assets are frozen)[4] is useful in cases where the offender is abroad but has assets in this country.[5] The major sanction for breaking a s 8 order is by committal by which means the offender can be imprisoned.

1   See *Re F (Contact: Enforcement: Representation of Child)* [1998] 3 FCR 216, [1998] 1 FLR 691, CA.

2   These powers are briefly referred to in the CAAC Report 1992/93, ch 5 but for detailed discussion reference should be made to Arlidge and Eady and Smith on *Contempt* (2nd edn), ch 12; Borrie and Lowe's *The Law of Contempt* (3rd edn) ch 14; and Miller: *Contempt of Court* (3rd edn) ch 14.

3   See Butler-Sloss P in *Re S (Contact: Promoting Relationship With Absent Parent)* [2004] EWCA Civ 18, [2004] 1 FLR 1279 at 28 in the context of enforcing contact orders. See more generally Borrie and Lowe, cited at n 2 above at 635–9 and Miller, cited at n 2 above, at p 2.16.

4   There is, however, power both to order the sale of sequestered assets and to direct that money raised by the sequestrators be used to pay for the costs of tracing the child and instituting proceedings abroad, see respectively *Mir v Mir* [1992] Fam 79, [1992] 1 All ER 765 and *Richardson v Richardson* [1989] Fam 95, [1989] 3 All ER 779.

5   It is therefore particularly useful in cases of international child abduction, see *Clarke Hall and Morrison on Children*, Division 2.

5.165 Before any committal order may be made the court must be satisfied beyond reasonable doubt[1] that the defendant knowingly broke the order. It is also a fundamental requirement[2] that a penal notice (that is, a notice in writing formally warning the person against whom the order is made that failure to obey it constitutes a contempt of court for which the offender may be sent to prison) has been attached to the order in question.[3] Penal notices, however, can only be attached to injunctions or to orders that are injunctive in form.[4] In other words to be enforceable the order must, as the CAAC states:[5] 'set out in explicit terms precisely what it is that the person in question must do, or must refrain from doing' and in the former case it must also specify the time within which the act is to be done.

1   See *Dean v Dean* [1987] 1 FLR 517, CA and *Re Bramblevale Ltd* [1970] Ch 128, [1968] 3 All ER 1062, CA.

2   CPR Sch 1 RSC Ord 45 r 7(4) (High Court) and CCR 1981 Ord 29 r 1(3) and FPR 1991, r 4.21A (county court).

3   Even so, courts are not *bound* to attach penal notices even where disobedience to an order is a real issue, see *Re F (Contact: Enforcement: Representation of Child)* [1998] 3 FCR 216, [1998] 1 FLR 691, CA where it was held justified not to attach a penal notice on a contact order with the father in respect of a disabled child whose mother and grandmother were against such contact. See also *Re N (a Minor) (Access: Penal Notice)* [1991] FCR 1000, [1992] 1 FLR 134, in which the Court of Appeal upheld a refusal to make a specific issue order incorporating a penal notice, where the judge had found the child no longer wished to see the father and would suffer serious emotional upset if he was forced against his will to do so.

4   See *Re P (Minors) (Custody Order: Penal Notice)* [1990] 1 WLR 613, CA and *D v D (Access: Contempt: Committal)* [1991] 2 FLR 34, CA, discussed by Lowe, 'Enforcing orders relating to children' (1992) 4 Jo of Child Law 271.

5   CAAC Report 1992/93, at p 44. For the procedure of adding a penal notice see the FPR 1991, r 4.21A.

5.166 The requirement that the order be in injunctive form means that not all s 8 orders and associated directions can be enforced by committal. For example, the embargoes against changing the child's surname and removing him from the UK as provided for by s 13[1] and clearly stated on the face of a residence order[2] are not per se enforceable by committal orders.[3] If sanctions for contempt[4] are being sought it will be necessary to obtain a prohibited steps order clearly setting out what action must be refrained from and backed by a penal notice.

1   Discussed at paras 5.31 ff.
2   Namely Form C43.

3 Cf *Re P (Minors) (Custody Order: Penal Notice)*, above.
4 However, because of the direction against removal, residence orders per se remain useful (though not absolutely essential) for persuading the police to issue an 'all ports warning' to prevent the child's removal from the UK by the non-residential parent. See further *Clarke Hall and Morrison on Children*, 2[12] ff.

5.167 Since residence orders only settle 'the arrangements to be made as to the person with whom a child is to live' they are clearly not injunctive in form and are not therefore enforceable in themselves in the two higher courts.[1] To make such orders prima facie enforceable courts must attach precise directions or conditions,[2] for example that the child be returned to a specific place at a specific time.[3]

1 This at any rate is the conclusion of Fricker et al, at 483, and Lowe: Enforcing orders relating to children (1992) 4 Journal of Child Law 26, 27. The position is different with regard to orders made by magistrates' courts, see paras 5.171 ff.
2 Ie under s 11(7), discussed at paras 5.108 ff.
3 For an example of this type of order see *Re B (Minors) (Residence Order)* [1992] Fam 162, [1992] 3 All ER 867, CA.

5.168 Although in their statutory form contact orders are injunctive in terms and are therefore prima facie enforceable, as *D v D (Access: Contempt: Committal)*[1] shows, an order which is declaratory in terms providing, for example for reasonable contact, cannot have a penal notice attached to it and cannot therefore be enforced by committal. As the CAAC has said:[2] 'To be enforceable by committal, an order for contact … [has] … to specify when and probably where, the child [is] to be allowed contact as well as with whom.' It is similarly necessary to spell out in a prohibited steps or specific issue order precisely what is prohibited or required and in the latter case by when the act in question is required to be completed.

1 [1991] 2 FLR 34.
2 CAAC Report 1992/93, p 44.

5.169 Provided the s 8 order is enforceable by committal order, FPR 1991, r 4.21A provides that:

> 'the judge may, on the application of the person entitled to enforce the order, direct that the proper officer shall issue a copy of the order, indorsed with or incorporating a penal notice as to the consequences of disobedience, for service … and no copy of the order shall be issued with any such notice indorsed or incorporated save in accordance with such a direction.'

Orders are normally only enforceable against parties to the proceedings, but it can also be a contempt for someone else knowingly to frustrate a court order.[1]

1 See *Re K (incitement to breach order)* [1992] 2 FCR 521, sub nom *Re K (minors)(incitement to breach contact order)* [1992] 2 FLR – solicitor held guilty of contempt for advising a client mother to break an access order; *Re S (Abduction: Sequestration)* [1995] 1 FLR 858 contempt for a friend to assist mother in abducting child. Cf *Re H (Minors) (Prohibited Steps Order)* [1995] 4 All ER 110, [1995] 1 WLR 667, CA in which it was held that an order can be made against a non-party, see above, para 5.96.

5.170 Committal proceedings can be initiated on the court's own motion but only when it is urgent and imperative to act immediately to prevent justice being obstructed.[1] Contempt of court must be proved upon the criminal standard of proof, ie beyond all reasonable doubt. The Children (Admissibility of Hearsay Evidence) Order 1993[2] can apply to these proceedings provided the evidence 'shows a substantial connection with the upbringing, maintenance or welfare of the child.'[3] Both parties have a right of appeal to the Court of Appeal by virtue of s 13 of the Administration of Justice Act 1960 and insofar as it is against a committal, but not otherwise[4], then, pursuant to CPR 52.3(1), no permission is required.[5]

1 *Re M (Minors) (Breach of Contact Order: Committal)* [1999] Fam 263, [1999] 2 All ER 56, CA.
2 SI 1993/621. Note also the Civil Evidence Act 1995. See further paras 11.20 ff
3 *Re C (Minors) (Hearsay Evidence: Contempt Proceedings)* [1993] 4 All ER 690, sub nom *C v C (Contempt: Evidence)* [1993] 1 FCR 820, [1993] 1 FLR 220.
4 See *M v M (Breaches of Orders: Committal)* [2005] EWCA Civ 1722, [2006] 1 FLR 1154, in which, notwithstanding repeated breaches, in the interests of the children, no committal order was made.
5 According to *Wood v Collins* [2006] EWCA Civ 743, [2006] All ER (D) 165 (May) (noted in *Butterworths Family and Child Law Bulletin* No 96 – September 2006) the exoneration against the need for permission should be interpreted as applying to both the claimant *and* the contemnor.

(II) MAGISTRATES' COURTS' GENERAL ENFORCEMENT POWERS

5.171 Magistrates' enforcement powers are governed by the Magistrates' Courts Act 1980, s 63(3) which provides:

'Where any person disobeys an order of a magistrates' court ... to do anything other than the payment of money or to abstain from doing anything the court may:
(a)   order him to pay a sum not exceeding £50 for every day during which he is in default or a sum not exceeding £5000; or
(b)   commit him to custody until he has remedied his default for a period not exceeding 2 months; but a person who is ordered to pay a sum for every day during which he is in default or who is committed to custody until he has remedied his default shall not by virtue of this section be ordered to pay more than [£5000[1]] or be committed for more than 2 months in all for doing or abstaining from doing the same thing contrary to the order (without prejudice to the operation of this section in relation to any subsequent default).'

There is no power under s 63(3) both to fine *and* commit an offender nor is there a statutory power to suspend a committal order.[2]

1 The provision in fact still specifies £1000 but it clearly should be changed in line with the maximum fine provided by para (a).
2 See *B (BPM) v B(MM)* [1969] P 103. Notwithstanding this apparent absence of power, a committal order was suspended in *Re W (Exclusion: Statement of Evidence)* [2000] 2 FLR 666. There is power under the Family Law Act 1996, s 50 to suspend committal orders in relation to orders made under that legislation. There is a power to grant a stay of execution pending an appeal, see *B (BPM) v B (MM)*, above, following *Re S (an infant)* [1958] 1 All ER 783, [1958] 1 WLR 391.

5.172 Section 14 of the CA 1989 provides that where a residence order is in force and 'any other person (including one in whose favour the order is also in force) is in breach of the arrangements settled by that order', the person named in the order, may, as soon as a copy of the residence order has been served on the other person, enforce the order under the Magistrates' Courts Act 1980, s 63(3), 'as if it were an order requiring the other person to produce the child to him'. The reason for making specific provision in respect of residence orders is because, as already discussed, without such provision such orders are likely to be regarded as declaratory only and therefore not enforceable.[1] No such difficulty attaches to the other s 8 orders (at any rate in their statutory form) and accordingly all such orders are prima facie enforceable under s 63(3).

1   Following *Webster v Southwark London Borough Council* [1983] QB 698, [1983] 2 WLR 217. Query why the opportunity was not taken to make s 14 applicable to residence orders made in the High Court and county court?

5.173 Unlike the higher courts there is no provision for adding a penal notice to a magistrates' court's order. According to the FPC(CA 1989)R 1991, r 24 a person (in whose favour a residence order has been made) wishing to enforce it must:

'file a written statement describing the alleged breach of the arrangements settled by the order, whereupon the justices' clerk shall fix a date, time and place for a hearing of the proceedings and give notice as soon as practicable, to the person whom it is alleged is in breach of the arrangements settled by that order, of the date fixed.'

No specific rule is laid down for the enforcement of s 8 orders other than residence orders but it seems sensible to assume that a similar procedure is applicable. To be enforceable under s 63(3) an order must specify exactly what is to be done. In *Re H (Contact: Enforcement)*[1] it was held that the failure to specify in a contact order where the handover was to take place was fatal to the complaint.

1   [1996] 2 FCR 784, [1996] 1 FLR 614.

5.174 Section 63(3) of the 1980 Act is not happily worded and seems more apt for dealing with continuing breaches. However, as Wood J said in *P v W (Access Order: Breach)*[1] the word 'or' in both s 63(3)(a) and (b) makes it 'possible to argue that the first part of each phrase makes provision for continuing disobedience and the second half provides for punishment of a past contempt.' This latter point, however, was left open in *P v W* and has yet to be authoritatively resolved. For this reason where a party is thought likely to disobey a court order it might be better to seek orders in the higher courts.

1   [1984] Fam 32 at 40.

(III) Determining whether to impose a penalty

5.175 Even if the court is satisfied that an order has been knowingly broken by the defendant, it should regard the enforcement powers both under contempt and under the 1980 Act to imprison or fine the offender as a remedy of the last resort.[1] As Hale LJ observed in *Hale v Turner:*[2]

'Family cases, it has long been recognised, raise quite different considerations from those elsewhere in the civil law. The two most obvious are the heightened emotional tensions that arise between family members and often the need for those family members to continue to be in contact with one another because they have children together or the like ... '

Nevertheless, in appropriate cases it will be right to imprison an offender.[3] In *A v N (Committal: Refusal of Contact)*,[4] it was held that in considering whether to commit a mother for her persistent and flagrant breach of a contact order with the father, the child's welfare was a material but not the paramount consideration, making it potentially easier to impose such a sanction,[5] (though with respect to breach of contact orders regard will now have to be had to the power to make an enforcement order under the provision introduced by the Children and Adoption Act 2006[6] which one would anticipate being used in preference to committal orders). Although in principle similar caution should be exercised when considering the imposition of penal sanctions upon the non-residential parent, there may nevertheless be less concern for the child's welfare in so doing.[7]

1   See *Ansah v Ansah* [1977] Fam 138 at 143, [1977] 2 All ER 638 at 643, CA. Note also Bennett J's comment in *Re H*, above, that magistrates should 'take the greatest caution before proceeding with a hearing under s 63 ... they should proceed with the greatest possible caution to use a weapon of last resort'. See also *I v D (Access Order: Enforcement)* [1989] FCR 91, [1988] 2 FLR 286.

2   [2000] 1 WLR 2377, [2000] 3 FCR 62, [2000] 2 FLR 879, at para (25), CA. See the comments thereon by Kay (2001) 64 MLR 595, particularly at 598–601.

3   See *Jones v Jones* [1993] 2 FCR 82, [1993] 2 FLR 377, CA. See also *Hale v Tanner*, above, in which helpful general guidance is given with regard to imposing sentences for contempt.

4   [1997] 2 FCR 475, [1997] 1 FLR 533, CA in which a mother was committed to prison for 42 days for her persistent and repeated breaches and note the discussion of this decision in *Making Contact Work*. The importance but not paramountcy of the child's welfare when considering committal orders was repeated by Ward LJ in *M v M (Breaches of Orders: Committal)* [2005] EWCA Civ 1722, [2006] 1 FLR 1154 – but a refusal to make a committal order having regard to the welfare of the children was nevertheless upheld. See also *Re S (Contact Dispute Committal)* [2004] EWCA Civ 1790, [2005] 1 FLR 812 – mother's committal for seven days (with an interim residence order to father) for repeated breaches – upheld on appeal; *F v F (Contact: Committal)* [1999] 2 FCR 42, [1998] 2 FLR 237, CA, committal order for seven days suspended for six months, upheld by Court of Appeal, and *Z v Z (Refusal of Contact: Committal)* [1996] 1 FCR 538 n.

5   Though this is not to say that the penal remedy should be readily resorted to, cf *Re F (Contact: Enforcement: Representation of Child)* [1998] 3 FCR 216, [1998] 1 FLR 691, CA and, note also the power to suspend committals, see CPR 1998, Sch 1, RSC Ord 52, r 7(1) on which note *Griffin v Griffin* [2000] 2 FCR 302, [2000] 2 FLR 44, CA.

6   See paras 5.179 ff.

7   Cf *G v C (Contempt: Committal)* [1998] 1 FCR 592, sub nom *G v C (Residence Order: Committal)* [1998] 1 FLR 43, CA in which eight months' imprisonment of a father for breaking contact conditions was held justifiable.

(IV) LIMITATIONS OF THE CONTEMPT POWERS

5.176 As Bracewell J observed in *V v V (Contact: Implacable Hostility)*[1] the option of committing the contemnor to prison or to suspend the prison term, always at best a blunt remedy,

'may well not achieve the object of reinstating contact; the child may blame the parent who applied to commit the carer to prison; the child's life may be disrupted if there is no-one capable of or willing to care for the child when the parent is in prison; it cannot be anything other than emotionally damaging for a child to be suddenly removed into foster care by social services from a parent, usually a mother, who in all respects except contact is a good parent'.

Nor is a fine any better, for as Bracewell J said: 'This option is rarely possible because it is not consistent with the welfare of the child to deprive a parent on a limited budget'. Research[2] has also identified another issue, namely, children's concern that their own reluctance to have contact with their non-residential parent might be misinterpreted by the court that their parental carer was being intractable or, more broadly, that they are responsible for any sanctions being imposed on their parents.

²   [2004] EWHC 1215 (Fam), [2004] 2 FLR 851 at [10]. See also *Re S (Contact: Promoting Relationship With Absent Parent)* [2004] EWCA Civ 18, [2004] 1 FLR 1279 at [28], per Butler Sloss P and Lord Justice Wall 'Enforcement of Contact Orders' [2005] Fam Law 26 at 30–31.

³   *Douglas, Murch, Miles and Scanlon* Research into the Operation of Rule 9.5 of the Family Proceedings Rules 1991 *(DCA, March 2006)* 7.61 ff.

5.177 It was a response to criticisms such as those outlined above that new measures have been introduced by the Children and Adoption Act 2006 to increase the options of the court when dealing with breaches of contact orders.[1]

¹   But not for breaches of any other s 8 order. For the background to these measures see the Government Green papers Parental Separation: Children's Needs and Parents' Responsibilities Cm 6273 (July 2004); Parental Separation: Children's Needs and Parents' Responsibilities: Next Steps Cm 6452 (January 2005); the Draft Children (Contact) and Adoption Bill Cm 6462 (February 2005); the Joint Committee on the Draft Children (Contact and Adoption Bill; First Report HL Paper 100–1/HC 400–1 (the so-called 'Scrutiny Committee') and The Government Reply to the Report from the Joint Committee Cm 6583 (June 2005). For comments on the proposals see J Masson and C Humphreys 'Facilitating and Enforcing Contact: The Bill and the Ten Per Cent' [2005] Fam Law 548 and J Edwards 'Enforcement of Contact Orders – a New Era?' [2007] Fam Law 125.

11. The enforcement powers under the Children and Adoption Act 2006 reforms

(a) Warning notices

5.178 As part of the package of measures introduced by the Children and Adoption Act 2006 to improve the enforcement of contact orders, it is provided by s 11I of the CA 1989 (as inserted by the 2006 Act) that whenever a court makes or varies a contact order,[1] it must attach a notice warning of the consequences for failing to comply. Applications should be made ex parte and the court may deal with the application without a hearing.[2]

¹   Including, it is submitted, when adding a contact activity condition.
²   FPR 1991, r 4.4A, FPC(CA 1989) 1991, r 4A.

(b) Contact enforcement orders

5.179 A new sanction for failing to comply with contact orders, the enforcement order, has been introduced by the Children and Adoption Act 2006, via the insertion of ss 11J–11N into the CA 1989. Under s 11J where the court[1] is satisfied beyond all reasonable doubt that a person has failed to comply with a contact order it may make an enforcement order which is an order imposing an unpaid work requirement up to a maximum of 200 hours[2] on the person who has broken the order. According to the Explanatory Notes to the Act,[3] a breach of a contact activity condition,[4] or of a condition attached to a contact order under s 11(7), constitutes a breach of a contact order for these purposes though the Act does not expressly say so. A fortiori the sanction can be imposed for a breach of the contact order. Any enforcement order that is imposed can be suspended for such a period as the court thinks fit.[5]

[1] Ie High Court, county court or magistrates' court: CA 1989, s 92(7).
[2] CA 1989, Sch A1, para 4 as added by Sch 1 to the 2006 Act. Note that the more draconian of the suggested sanctions, namely, curfews and tagging were not included in the 2006 Act.
[3] At para 30.
[4] But note, not an activity direction. Contact activity directions and conditions are discussed above at paras 5.63 ff.
[5] Section 11J(9).

5.180 No enforcement order may be made if the court is satisfied that the person in breach had a reasonable excuse for failing to comply though the burden is on the person in breach to prove on the balance of probabilities that he had a reasonable excuse;[1] nor can an order be made against someone who was under 18 at the time of the breach,[2] nor if the contact order was an 'excepted order'.[3] Furthermore, a court may not make an enforcement order unless it is satisfied that the person had been given a copy of or otherwise informed of the terms of a s 11I warning notice.[4] No enforcement order can be made against a person unless he or she is habitually resident in England and Wales and any such order ceases to have effect if the person concerned ceases to be so habitually resident.[5]

[1] Section 11J(3),(4). Note the difference in the standard of proof necessary to establish non compliance and the lack of a reasonable excuse.
[2] Section 11K(2).
[3] Section 11K(3). An excepted order issue where an adoption order is being considered or where, post-adoption, a court is considering making, varying or discharging a contact order in relation to someone who, but for the adoption, would have been a relative of the child, see s 11B(4).
[4] Section 11K(1).
[5] Section 11K(4). Rules dealing with service are governed by FPR 1991, r 4.21AA, FPC (CA) 1991, r 21AA.

5.181 Orders can only be made on the application of:

'(a) the person who is, for the purposes of the contact order; the person with whom the child concerned lives or is to live;

(b) the person whose contact with the child concerned is provided for in the contact order;

(c) any individual subject to a condition under section 11(7)(b) or a contact activity condition imposed by the contact order; or

(d) the child concerned'.[1]

In the latter case the child must obtain the leave of the court and leave may only be given if the court is satisfied that the child has sufficient understanding to make the proposed application.[2] The inclusion of (a) above means that in theory a resident parent can seek an enforcement order against a non-resident parent. However, it is by no means clear that a contact order can be made against such a person under s 8[3] and still less against an unwilling parent[4] though it is true that the non-resident parent could be in breach of conditions attached to an order under s 11(7), for example, for failing to return the child at a certain time and place or for breach of a contact activity condition.

[1] Section 11J(5).
[2] Section 11J(6),(7).
[3] Note the similar criticism made by Masson and Humphreys, cited at para 5.177 above, at 552.
[4] Ironically, the Government itself rejected the proposal that the court should have the power to compel an unwilling parent to have contact with the child, see above para 5.56.

5.182 Before making an enforcement order the court must be satisfied that it is necessary to secure compliance and that 'the likely effect on the person of the enforcement order proposed to be made is proportionate to the seriousness of the breach ...'.[1] The court is also required, before making the order, to obtain and consider information about the person upon whom the order would be imposed and the likely effect of the order on him including, in particular, any conflict with his religious beliefs or any interference with times he is at work or attending an educational establishment.[2] The unpaid work must be local and the court must be satisfied that the enforcement measures are available within the local justice area in which the person resides.[3] Any information required under this section can be sought from a CAFCASS or Welsh family proceedings officer.[4] In making an enforcement order the court 'must take into account the welfare of the child'[5] but implicit in that is that the child's welfare is not the paramount consideration. Whether this is adequate protection for the child can be debated. Some advocate that, at the very least, provision should be made for the child's separate representation in enforcement proceedings.[6]

[1] Section 11L(1).
[2] Section 11L(3), (4).
[3] Section 11L(2).
[4] Section 11L(5). It is the officer's duty to comply with any such request: s 11L(6).
[5] Section 11L(7).
[6] Douglas et al, cited at para 5.176 above at paras 7.61 ff.

5.183 On making an enforcement order 'the court is to ask' a CAFCASS officer or a Welsh family proceedings officer to monitor compliance and to report to the court,[1] and it is the officer's duty to comply with the request.[2]

[1] Section 11M(1).
[2] Section 11M(2).

5.184 More than one enforcement order may be made in relation to the same person on the same occasion and such an order is said to be 'without prejudice' to s 63(3) of the Magistrates' Courts Act 1980 as it applies in relation to contact orders.[1] An enforcement order can subsequently be revoked or amended, and, if it is itself broken, the court may amend it or make it more onerous, or impose another enforcement order.[2] When making the enforcement order the court must attach to that order a notice warning of the consequences of non-compliance.[3]

[1] Section 11J(1) and (13) respectively. Query why the higher courts' contempt powers are also not expressly preserved.
[2] Schedule A1, Part 2.
[3] Section 11N. This is the equivalent of a penal notice having to be attached to an order before contempt sanctions may be imposed, but in this instance, all courts are under the same obligation.

(c) Compensation for financial loss

5.185 A second type of order may be imposed upon breach of a contact order, introduced by the Children and Adoption Act 2006 (by inserting ss 11O and 11P into the CA 1989), namely a financial compensation order for financial loss occasioned by the breach. The example commonly cited is the cost of a holiday that has been lost because of the breach but it can also include wasted travel costs though presumably these will have to be substantial enough to justify court time being spent on the issue.

5.186 Where a court is satisfied[1] that an individual has failed to comply with a contact order (including breaching a condition attached to a contact order)[2] and that a relevant party[3] has suffered loss because of the breach, it can order the person in breach to pay compensation up to the amount of the loss.[4]

[1] Query on what standard of proof? Unless the court takes the view that a compensation order is a similar sanction to a fine for contempt, the standard of proof must be the balance of probabilities. The fact that the Act makes no special provision as distinct from enforcement orders suggests that Parliament must have intended the civil standard of proof to apply.
[2] See the Explanatory Notes to the Act at para 42.
[3] Ie a person entitled to apply for an order under s 11O(6), see para 5.188 below.
[4] Section 11O(2). Note that the amount of compensation cannot exceed the amount of the applicant's loss: s 11O(9), discussed below at para 5.189.

5.187 No compensation order may be made if the court is satisfied that the person in breach had a reasonable excuse for failing to comply though the burden is on the person in breach to prove (presumably, on the balance of probabilities)[1] that he had a reasonable excuse;[2] nor can an order be made against someone who was under 18 at the time of the breach[3] nor if the contact order was an 'excepted order'.[4] Furthermore a court may not make a compensation order unless it is satisfied that the person in question had been given a copy of or otherwise informed of the terms of a s 11I warning notice.[5]

[1] The Act is silent on this but the burden cannot be greater than proving a reasonable excuse in relation to enforcement orders which s 11J(4) states to be on the balance of probabilities.
[2] Section 11O(2), (3).
[3] Section 11P(2).
[4] Section 11P(3). For the meaning of 'excepted order' see s 11B(4), discussed at para 5.64.

5   Section 11P(1). Note: unlike enforcement orders there is no requirement when making compensation orders that the individual concerned is habitually resident in England and Wales.

5.188 Only the person suffering loss can apply and in any event claimants are limited to the resident parent; the person with whom contact was ordered; an individual subject to a condition under s11(7)(b) or a contact activity condition; or, with court leave, the child.[1] In deciding whether to give a child leave, the court must be satisfied that he or she has sufficient understanding to make the application.[2]

1   Section 11O(5), (6), (7).
2   Section 11O(8).

5.189 The amount of compensation is determined by the court but cannot exceed the amount of the applicant's loss.[1] In deciding what compensation to order, the court must take into account the financial circumstances of the individual in breach and the child's welfare (which, as for enforcement orders, is not the paramount consideration).[2] An amount ordered to be paid as compensation may be recovered as a 'civil debt'.[3]

1   Section 11O(9).
2   Section 11O(10), (14).
3   Section 11O(11).

(d) An evaluation of the new sanctions

5.190 How effective the new sanctions of enforcement and compensation orders prove to be, remains to be seen. Although the new powers will undoubtedly have their uses it has to be said that many of the limitations and difficulties attendant on the contempt sanctions[1] apply equally to enforcement orders, while compensation orders are only likely to be appropriate in a minority of cases where the carer has sufficient resources to pay without adversely impacting upon the child(ren) they are looking after.

1   See the discussion at para 5.176.

12. Family assistance orders

5.191 Section 16 empowers the court to make a 'family assistance order'. Such an order requires either a CAFCASS officer (England) or a Welsh family proceedings officer to be made available or the local authority to make an officer of the authority available[1] to 'advise, assist and (where appropriate) befriend any person named in the order'.[2] Those who may be named in the order are: any parent (which includes the unmarried father) or guardian, any person with whom the child is living or in whose favour a contact order is in force with respect to the child, and the child himself.[3]

1   Subject to s 16(7); see para 5.195 below.
2   Section 16(1).
3   Section 16(2).

5.192 This power replaced the former power to make supervision orders in private law proceedings and must in turn be distinguished from supervision orders made under s 31 of the CA 1989.[1] As the original Children Act 1989 Guidance and Regulations put it:[2]

> 'A supervision order is designed for the more serious cases, in which there is an element of child protection involved. By contrast, a family assistance order aims simply to provide short-term help to a family, to overcome the problems and conflicts associated with their separation or divorce. Help may well be focused more on the adult rather than the child.'

[1]   Discussed at paras 8.180 ff.
[2]   Children Act 1989 Guidance and Regulations, Vol 1, Court Orders (1991) Department of Health, para 2.50 and cited by Wall J *Re DH (a Minor) (Care Proceedings: Evidence and Orders)* [1994] 2 FCR 3 at 43, sub nom in *Re D H (a Minor) (Child Abuse)* [1994] 1 FLR 679 at 702. The revised 2008 Guidance at para 2.67 omits the reference to supervision orders and to adult focused help, commenting: 'The nature of the help to be provided will normally be in assessment or case analysis provided by CAFCASS to the court'.

(a) When orders may be made

5.193 Family assistance orders may be made in any 'family proceedings'[1] whether or not any other order has been made.[2] The power may be exercised only by the court acting upon its own motion though there is nothing to stop parties requesting the court to make such an order during the course of family proceedings.[3] However, the lack of the right to apply for such an order means that parties cannot apply to court *solely* for a family assistance order.

[1]   For the definition of which see paras 5.135 ff.
[2]   Section 16(1).
[3]   Though note *Re F (Minors) (Contact)* [1993] 1 FCR 945, [1993] 2 FLR 677 in which the Court of Appeal refused to consider making a family assistance order since the point had not been argued at first instance and in the absence of being able to show that the original order was wrong had no power to make such an order or remit the case back.

5.194 As originally enacted, before any order could be made, the court had to be satisfied that the circumstances of the case were 'exceptional'.[1] The Act did not define what was meant by 'exceptional circumstances' but in general it was clear that the order could not be made as a matter of routine. With effect from October 2007, however, the need to prove exceptional circumstances was removed[2] as part of a policy to enable such orders to be used more often particularly to facilitate contact.[3] Whether this change will result in more orders remains to be seen but, at all events, the revised Children Act 1989 Guidance and Regulations comment[4] that 'it will be particularly important in all orders for the court to make plain at the outset why family assistance is needed and what it is hoped to achieve by it.'

[1]   Section 16(3)(a) as originally enacted.
[2]   Namely by s 6 of the Children and Adoption Act 2006, brought into force by SI 2007/2287.
[3]   See e g the Explanatory Notes to the 2006 Act, para 45.
[4]   Children Act 1989 Guidance and Regulations, Vol 1, Court Orders (2008) Department for Children, Schools and Families, para 2.69. For examples of reported cases of which such orders have been made see para 5.200 below.

5.195 *Private law orders*

5.195 According to *Practice Direction: Family Assistance Orders: Consultation*[1] before making an assistance order the court must have obtained the opinion (either orally or in writing, for example, as part of a s 7 report) of the appropriate officer[2] about whether it would be in the best interests of the child in question for such an order to be made and, if so, how the order could operate and for what period. It must also give any person whom it proposes to name in the order an opportunity to comment upon any opinion given by the appropriate officer. Another requirement before making an order is that the court must be satisfied that the consent of every person named in the order, *other than the child,* has been obtained.[3] Furthermore, an order may not be made requiring a local authority to make one of its officers available unless either the authority agrees or the child concerned lives or will live in its area.[4] It is not a proper use of a family assistance order to require a local authority to provide someone for escort duty where no family member is prepared to take the children to visit their father in prison.[5]

[1] [2007] 2 FLR 626, [2007] All ER (D) 59 (Sep).
[2] Namely a CAFCASS officer (England) or a Welsh family proceedings officer or an officer of a local authority, depending upon the category of officer the court proposes to require to be made available under the order.
[3] Section 16(3)(b). The Government rejected the recommendation both of Bracewell J in *V v V (Contact: Implacable Hostility)* [2004] EWHC 1215 (Fam), [2004] 2 FLR 851 at [11] and of the Joint Committee on the Draft Children (Contact) and Adoption Bill, HL Paper 100–1/HL 400–1 that the requirement of consent be removed, on the basis that it would not be constructive to 'advise, assist and befriend' an unwilling or even hostile party. But note the findings of the HMICA Report, Assisting Families by Court Order (March, 2007) discussed at 5.200.
[4] Section 16(7). But see *Re C (a Minor) (Family Assistance Order)* [1996] 3 FCR 514, [1996] 1 FLR 424 where, having made an assistance order directing the local authority to make an officer available, the local authority subsequently returned to the court to say that it did not have the resources to carry the order out. Johnson J declined to take further action.
[5] *S v P (Contact Application: Family Assistance Order)* [1997] 2 FCR 185, [1997] 2 FLR 277. Cf *Re E (Family Assistance order)* [1999] 3 FCR 700, [1999] 2 FLR 512, discussed at para 5.201.

5.196 There is no formal requirement that the child himself consents, nor is there a statutory requirement to ascertain the child's own wishes and feelings about such an order.[1] Nevertheless, there is nothing to prevent the court from discovering the child's view (nor from applying the whole checklist under s 1(3)) if it so chooses and in cases where the child is mature enough to make his own decisions, it would seem prudent to do so.

[1] The enjoinder to do so by s 1(3)(a) does not apply, (see s 1(4), discussed at para 2.40).

(b) *Effect of the order*

5.197 Section 16 gives no guidance as to which officer should be appointed neither is it clear whether the court is empowered to appoint a particular CAFCASS officer or Welsh family proceedings officer or a particular type of local authority officer. In the latter case, for example, in certain circumstances it might be preferable to appoint a housing officer rather than an officer from social services.[1] In the private law context the most appropriate appointee is likely to be the officer who has compiled the welfare report for the court, while in care proceedings the obvious candidate is the social worker attached to the particular case.

¹   See the discussion by Coubrough at [1993] Fam Law 598–599.

5.198 Under s 16(4), a family assistance order may direct the person named in the order or, such of the persons so named as may be specified, to take such steps as may be so specified with a view to enabling the officer to be kept informed of the address of any person named in the order and to be allowed to visit each person. If a contact order is also in force the order may also 'direct the officer concerned to give advice, and assistance as regards establishing, improving and maintaining contact to such of the persons named in the order as may be specified in the order.¹ Furthermore the original power conferred upon officers that where a s 8 order was also in force, the officer concerned could refer to the court the question of whether the s 8 order should be varied or discharged,² has now been strengthened inasmuch as the officer concerned can be *directed* to report to the court 'on such matters relating to the section 8 order as the court may require (including the question of whether the section 8 order ought to be varied or discharged)'.³

¹   Section 16(6) (as originally enacted).
²   Section 16(4A), added with effect from 1 October 2007 (see SI 2007/2287), by s 6(3) of the Children and Adoption Act 2006.
³   Section 16(6) as inserted, with effect from 1 October 2007 (see SI 2007/2287) by s 6(5) of the 2006 Act.

(c) Duration of order

5.199 A family assistance order is intended to be a short-term remedy. Hence, s 16(5) originally provided that unless a shorter period is specified the order will have effect only for six months from the day on which it is made. However, as part of the policy to encourage more extensive use of such orders this period has, with effect from October 2007, been extended to 12 months.¹ There is, in any event, no restriction on making any further order.²

¹   By the Children and Adoption Act 2006, s 6(4) brought into force by SI 2007/2287.
²   See the revised Children Act 1989 Guidance and Regulations, Vol 1, Court Orders (2008) Department for Children, Schools and Families, para 2.69. For an example of where a 'fresh' order was made by the House of Lords, see *Re G (Children)(Residence: Same Sex Partner)* [2006] UKHL 43, [2006] 1 WLR 2305, [2006] 1 All ER 241 at [45].

(d) Family assistance orders in practice¹

5.200 Before the changes introduced by the Children and Adoption Act 2006 were brought into force, the number of family assistance orders was relatively constant. According to the *Children Act Report 1995–1999*,² the 'level of Family Assistance Orders made throughout the 1990s ranged from about 600 to around 1,000 annually'. While according to the CAFCASS Annual Report 2005–2006 the service responded to 645 family assistance orders during 2005–2006 compared with 530 in the previous year.⁴ In the latter case the figures referred to are for England only, Wales having its own CAFCASS service. The clear intention of the 2006 Act is to increase the use of such orders[4] but it remains to be seen whether this will be achieved. One important factor will be the availability of resources.[5] An insight as to how family assistance orders were working before the implementation of the 2006 Act reforms is provided by the HM Inspectorate of Courts Administration's 2007 report, *Assisting Families by Court Order*.[6] Although it was found that service users valued the importance of the independent view and advice by CAFCASS, the lack of information provided about family assistance orders meant that users were not always clear as to what they had consented to when agreeing to State support through a court order. Furthermore, there was found to be no explicit set of agreed criteria used by CAFCASS systematically to inform when an assistance order might be appropriate. Indeed there was wide variation in recommending such orders both between CAFCASS regions and between practitioners in the same teams. The Report therefore recommended (1) that to help users to give informed consent, CAFCASS should provide information, before an assistance order was recommended, explaining what might be required if the order were made; and (2) to help improve service delivery, CAFCASS should further develop its draft guidance and procedures.

[1]   See *Making Contact Work* (A Report to the Lord Chancellor by the Advisory Board on Family Law: Children Act Sub Committee, 2002) ch 11; Trinder and Stone 'Family assistance orders – professional aspiration and partly frustration' (1998) 10 CFLQ 291 and Seden 'Family Assistance Orders and the Children Act: Ambivalence About Intervention or a Means of Safeguarding and Promoting Children's Welfare?' (2001) 15 Int Jo of Law, Policy and the Family 226.

[2]   Cm 4579, January 2000.

[3]   HC 1310 (July 2006) p 10.

[4]   See para 45 of the Explanatory Notes to 2006 Act.

[5]   Lack of funding was one of the problems of having effective family assistance orders identified by Bracewell J in *V v V (Contact: Implacable Hostility)* [2004] EWHC 1215 (Fam), [2004] 2 FLR 851 at [11]. But another factor that might weigh against expanded use is the continuing nature of such orders and the consequential problems that that poses for the courts and support services alike in meeting performance indicators.

[6]   HMICA Report, March 2007.

5.201 The few reported cases show that a major role of family assistance orders is in facilitating contact and this will clearly be expanded by the 2006 Act's reforms. Among the more recent examples is *Re G (Children)(Residence: Same Sex Partner)*[1] in which a family assistance order was initially made together with a shared residence order in the context of a residence and a contact dispute between same-sex partners and which was renewed by the House of Lords essentially to help the parties make the contact arrangements work in the light of the decision that the primary residence of the children should be with their biological mother. Earlier examples include *Re M (Contact: Parental Responsibility: McKenzie Friend)*,[2] in which the Court of Appeal proposed (subject to obtaining the mother's consent)[3] making a family assistance order to facilitate indirect contact between the children and their father in respect of whom the mother had a genuine fear. In *Leeds County Council v C*[4] Booth J held that the only appropriate way in which a court could make provision for the supervision of contact by a local authority was by an order under s 16 and not by attaching a condition under s 11(7). However in the *Re D H (a Minor) (Care Proceedings: Evidence and Orders)*[5] Wall J observed that while:

' ... in the conventional case a supervision order under s 31 will not be appropriate where the object is simply to achieve contact supervised by a local authority ... where the threshold criteria under s 31 are met in relation to the necessity for contact to be supervised, it may be appropriate to make a supervision order rather than an order under s 16.'

Despite this comment it is evident that a family assistance order can have a useful role to play in providing local authority assistance to supervise contact.[6] In *Re E (Family Assistance Order)*[7] a family assistance order was made against the wishes of a local authority (into whose area the family had moved) in order to supervise contact between a child and her mother in a psychiatric unit. A family assistance order was also made in *Re U (Application to Free for Adoption)*,[8] where, having rejected a local authority's application to free a child for adoption and granting instead a residence order to the grandparents, it was held that the order was a useful way of monitoring the child's placement.

1   [2006] UKHL 43, [2006] 1 WLR 2305, [2006] 4 All ER 241. See also *Re G (Parental Responsibility Order)* [2006] EWCA Civ 745, [2006] 2 FLR 1092, [2006] All ER (D) 247 in which a family assistance order was made in the context of a mother's hostility to the father having contact.
2   [1999] 1 FCR 703, sub nom *Re M (Contact: Family Assistance Order)* [1999] 1 FLR 75, CA. Note also the use of the s 91(14) powers (discussed at paras 5.202 ff) in that case to prevent the father making an application to court without leave before the expiration of the family assistance order.
3   This part of the order was directed to lie on the file for 14 days to give the mother (who was not at the appellate hearing) through her solicitors the opportunity to consent to the order being made.
4   [1993] 1 FCR 585, [1993] 1 FLR 269. But cf *Re H (a child)(contact)* [2008] All ER (D) 255 (Jan) – in which an order was refused – the real issue being contact.
5   [1994] 2 FCR 3 at 42, sub nom *Re DH (a Minor) (Child Abuse)*, [1994] 1 FLR 679 at 702.
6   See *B v B (Procedure: Alleged Sexual Abuse)* [1994] 1 FCR 809 at 836, sub nom *B v B (Child Abuse: Contact)* [1994] 2 FLR 713 at 737–738, ironically also per Wall J. See also *Re R (a Minor) (Religious Sect)* [1993] 2 FCR 525, sub nom *Re R (a Minor) (Residence: Religion)* [1993] 2 FLR 163, CA – a case involving a father who was a member of the Exclusive Bretheren. Note also the conclusions of *Making Contact Work*, above, at paras 11.9 ff, including the recommendation that CAFCASS prepare proposals, inter alia, for educational programmes for parenting and support packages to be operated under a family assistance order.
7   [1999] 3 FCR 700, [1999] 2 FLR 512.
8   [1993] 2 FCR 64, [1993] 2 FLR 992, CA.

13. Restricting further applications under s 91(14)

5.202 Section 91(14) allows the court on 'disposing of any application for an order' under the CA 1989 to restrain future applications without permission[1] of the court. Although perhaps more associated with private law orders, this power can be exercised both in respect of private *and* public law proceedings.[2] In deciding whether to make a s 91(14) order it is established[3] that the court should apply the paramountcy principle under s 1(1). Accordingly, restrictions on applications by a parent who wishes to raise issues concerning the child's welfare should only be imposed where the welfare of the child so requires.[4]

1   Section 91(14) itself refers to 'leave of the court' but in Wall LJ's view in *Re S (children)(restriction on applications), Re E (a child)(restriction on applications)* [2006] EWCA Civ 1190, [2006] 3 FCR 50, sub nom *Re S (Permission to Seek Relief)* [2007]

1   FLR 482 at [50] in the light of the CPR 1998, 'leave' has been superseded by 'permission' though there is no difference between the two words.

2   See *Re P (Children Act 1989, ss 22 and 26: Local Authority Compliance)* [2000] 2 FLR 910. But note s 91(15) imposes an automatic leave requirement to make further applications within six months of a previous application to discharge a care, supervision or education supervision order or for the substitution of a supervision order for a care order or a child assessment order and similarly s 91(17) does so following the refusal of a contact application under s 34.

3   See *Re P (A Minor) (Residence Order: Child's Welfare)* [2000] Fam 15 at 17, sub nom *Re P (a Minor) (Residence Order: Restriction Order)* [1999] 3 All ER 734 at 752, but note the discussion at para 2.12.

4   *B v B (Residence Order: Restricting Applications* [1997] 2 FCR 518, [1997] 1 FLR 139, CA. Compare the more cautionary approach of Wilson J in *Re R (a Minor) (Leave to Make Applications)* [1998] 2 FCR 129, sub nom *Re R (Residence: Contact: Restricting Applications)* [1998] 1 FLR 749, CA, who said, in the context of making a restricting order together with a contact order after a renewed residence application had been made with no fresh evidence, that the court had to weigh the best interests of the child against the fundamental freedom of access to the courts.

5.203 Section 91(14) orders represent a substantial interference with a citizen's right of unrestricted access to the courts and how this should be balanced against the child's welfare was carefully considered in *Re P (A Minor) (Residence Order: Child's Welfare)*.[1] Butler-Sloss LJ commented:

'A number of guidelines might be drawn from the cases ... It is, however, important to remember that these are only guidelines intended to assist and not to replace the wording of the section ...

(1)   Section 91(14) should be read in conjunction with section 1(1) of the CA 1989 which made the welfare of the child the paramount consideration.

(2)   The power to restrict applications to the court was discretionary and in the exercise of its discretion the court had to weigh in the balance all the relevant circumstances.

(3)   An important consideration was that to impose a restriction was a statutory intrusion into the right of a party to bring proceedings before the court and to be heard in matters affecting his/her child.

(4)   The power was therefore to be used with great care and sparingly: the exception and not the rule.

(5)   It was generally to be seen as a useful weapon of last resort in cases of repeated and unreasonable applications.

(6)   In suitable circumstances, and on clear evidence, a court might impose the leave restriction in cases where the welfare of the child required it, although there was no past history of making unreasonable applications.

(7)   In cases under paragraph 6 above, the court would need to be satisfied: first, that the facts went beyond the commonly encountered need for a time to settle to a regime ordered by the court and the all too common situation where there was animosity between the adults in dispute or between the local authority and the family and; second, that there was a serious risk that, without the imposition of the restriction, the child or the primary carers would be subject to unacceptable strain.

(8)   A court might impose the restriction on making applications in the absence of a request from any of the parties, subject, of course , to the rules of natural justice such as an opportunity for the parties to be heard.

(9)   A restriction might be imposed with or without limitation of time.

(10)   The degree of restriction should be proportionate to the harm it was intended to avoid. Therefore the court imposing the restriction should carefully consider the extent of the restriction to be imposed and specify, where appropriate, the type of application to be restrained and the duration of the order.

(11)   It would be undesirable in other than the most exceptional cases to make the order ex parte.'

Her Ladyship continued:

'It was suggested to us that s 91(14) may infringe the Human Rights Act 1998 and European Convention for the Protection of Human Rights and Fundamental Freedoms 1950, Article 6(1), by depriving a litigant of the right to a fair trial. I do not consider that submission to be correct. The applicant is not denied access to the court. It is a partial restriction[2] in that it does not allow him the right to an immediate inter partes hearing. It thereby protects the other parties and the child from being drawn into the proposed proceedings unless or until a court had ruled that the application should be allowed to proceed.'

1   [2000] Fam 15 at 37–38, sub nom *Re P (a Minor) (Residence Order: Restriction Order)* [1999] 3 All ER 734 at 752–753, CA and the cases there cited.
2   Although *Re T (A Minor)(Parental Responsibility: Contact)* [1993] 2 FLR 450, CA, stands as authority for saying it is possible to impose an absolute prohibition under the inherent jurisdiction, such an order was described as 'particularly controversial' by Wilson J in *Re R (a Minor) (Leave to Make Application)* [1998] 2 FCR 129, sub nom *Re R (Residence: Contact: Restricting Applications)* [1998] 1 FLR 749. Query whether the inherent power survives s 91(4) and, if it does, is it human rights compatible?

5.204   *Re P* must now be read with *Re S (children)(restriction on applications), Re E (a child)(restriction on applications)*[1] which, after a comprehensive review of the authorities, established the following:

●   It is not permissible to attach conditions to a s 91(14) order beyond stating how long it is to last and identifying the type of relief to which it applies.

As Wall LJ put it,

'Had Parliament intended s 91(14) to create a power to impose conditions under it, Parliament we think [especially in view of the express power under s 11(7)] would have said so'.[2]

●   It is permissible to tell the litigant that unless he addresses a particular issue and can show that he has addressed it any application for permission to apply is unlikely to succeed.

As Wall LJ put it:[3]

'The need to address the court's findings and reasons for the imposition of the s 91(14) order are matters of evidence which go to the success or failure of the application for permission to apply: the imposition of conditions on a s 91(14) order is an impermissible bar to an application for permission to apply being made at all'.

●   There is no inconsistency between requiring the applicant to demonstrate a need for renewed judicial investigation[4] and having to persuade the judge that he has an arguable case with some chance of success'.[5]

As Wall LJ said the two tests complement each other for a judge will not 'see a need for a renewed judicial investigation into an application which he does not think sets out an arguable case'.[6]

• Although s 91(14) orders can be made without time limit or expressed to last until the child attains the age of 16 such orders should be the exception rather than the rule. Where they are made the reasons for doing so should be fully and carefully expressed.

As Wall LJ said:

'It behoves the court to consider carefully what mischief the [order] is designed to address, and in particular whether or not it is going to be possible, at the end of the defined period, to re-investigate the question, and to attempt the restoration of the relationship between the absent parent and the child ... An order which is indeterminate, or which is expressed to last until the sixteenth birthday ... is, in effect, an acknowledgement by the court that nothing more can be done ... If the court has indeed reached that stage, it needs to spell out its reasons, clearly, so that the parents – and in particular the parent who is the subject of the s 91(14) order knows precisely where he or she stands, and precisely what issues he or she had to address if an application for permission to apply is going to be possible'.[7]

• Before a s 91(14) order is made the person affected by it should have a proper opportunity if necessary, by means of a short adjournment, to consider it and be heard on it.[8]

• On the other hand, flexibility is permissible in deciding whether the resident parent should be served in the first instance with a permission to apply applications. In certain sensitive circumstances, for example, where the stress of previous litigation has destabilised the family, it may be proper for the application to be considered by the judge on paper who can then decide whether or not an inter partes hearing is required.[9]

---

[1]   [2006] EWCA Civ 1190, [2006] 3 FCR 50, sub nom *Re S (Permission to Seek Relief)* [2007] 1 FLR 482.

[2]   Above at [74]. Section 11(7) is discussed above at paras 5.108 ff.

[3]   Above at [80] and reemphasised by Wall LJ in *Stringer v Stringer* [2006] EWCA Civ 1617, [2007] 1 FLR 1532.

[4]   Namely, the test set out by Thorpe LJ in *Re A (a minor)(contact: parent's application for leave)* [1999] 1 FCR 127, sub nom *Re A (Application for Leave)* [1998] 1 FLR 1.

[5]   Namely, the test set out by Butler-Sloss LJ in *Re P (A Minor)(Residence Order: Child's Welfare)* [2000] Fam 15, [1999] 3 All ER 734.

[6]   Above at [78]. It will be noted that permission to apply is not governed by the criteria set out in s 10(9), discussed above at para 5.105.

[7]   Above at paras [89]–[90]. But for a post-*Re S* example of a s 91(14) order expressed to last until the elder of two children reach 18 and younger, 16, see *Re Bradford; Re O'Connell* [2006] EWCA Civ 1199, [2007] 1 FLR 530.

[8]   Above at [91]. On occasion informal notice might be sufficient, see *Re F (children)(restriction on applications)* [2005] EWCA Civ 499, [2005] 2 FCR 176, [2005] 2 FLR 950.

[9]   Above at [91]–[92]. Accordingly, caution should be exercised about following dicta in *Re N (a minor)(residence order: appeal)* [1996] 2 FCR 377, sub nom *Re N (Section 91(14) Order)* [1996] 1 FLR 356, per Hale J and in *Re A (a minor)(contact: parent's application for leave)*, above, at n 4, per Thorpe LJ on the need for an inter partes hearing.

[10] Above at [95], which therefore limits the earlier ruling of Munby J in *Harris v Harris, A-G v Harris* [2001] 3 FCR 193, [2001] 2 FLR 895. An oral hearing is provided for by FPR 1991.

5.205 The appropriate procedure for applying to discharge the order or for applying for leave, notwithstanding a s 91(14) order, is to issue the application on Form C2. If the application is successful, then Form C1 should be issued.

14. Court ordered investigation under s 37

5.206 Under s 37 where, in any family proceedings[1] it appears to the court that it may be appropriate to make a care or supervision order under s 31, the court may direct a local authority to investigate the child's circumstances. Section 37 empowers a court to direct that an investigation is undertaken but it has no power to direct a local authority to bring care proceedings.[2] All that an authority is bound to do under the direction is undertake the investigation but if after doing so they decide not to apply for a care or supervision order they must inform the court of their reasons for so deciding.[3] Although it is implicit in a s 37 direction that there must be: (a) a 'child'; (b) family proceedings; and (c) a question arises with respect to the child's welfare, these are issues to be determined by the court, not the local authority.[5] Although courts are not empowered to commit a child into care they can, when making a direction, make an interim care order (provided the relevant criteria are satisfied).[4] As the section itself says and the courts have subsequently emphasised, s 37 directions should only be made where it appears that it might be appropriate to make a public law order. It is therefore generally inappropriate in a purely private law dispute, but while not a panacea it can on occasion be useful in intractable contact disputes provided there is a coherent care plan of which temporary or permanent removal of the children from the parents is an integral part.[6] Even so it is a drastic order and should not be resorted even in intractable contact disputes unless there is no alternative.[7]

---

[1] For the meaning of which see paras 5.135 ff.

[2] The absence of any such power was criticised in *Nottingham County Council v p* [1994] Fam 18, by Sir Stephen Brown P. See also Mr Justice Wall 'The courts and child protection – the challenge of hybrid cases' [1997] 9 CFLQ 345 at 348–50. Note also *E v London Borough of X* [2005] EWHC 2811 (Fam), [2006] 1 FLR 730 – local authority took no further action having found the 'child' in question to be at least 20; *Re M (a minor) (official solicitor's role)* [1998] 3 FCR 315, [1998] 2 FLR 815, CA – inappropriate to use s 37 if the Official Solicitor is invited to investigate; and *Re H (Child's Circumstances: Direction to Investigate)* [1993] 2 FCR 277, sub nom *Re H (a Minor) (Section 37 Direction)* [1993] 2 FLR 541 – where direction is given 'child's circumstances' should be widely construed. There is some evidence that FPR 1991 r 9.5 is being used to appoint a guardian ad litem (Douglas et al *Research into the Operation of Rule 9.5 of the Family Proceedings Rules 1991* (DCA, 2006) 5.22) instead of giving a s 37 direction because of local authorities' lack of resources.

[3] Section 37(3). Unless the court directs otherwise, the local authority must inform the court within eight weeks of the directions: s 37(4).

[4] See *Lambeth London Borough Council v TK and KK* [2008] EWCA Civ 103, [2008] 1 FLR 1229.

[5] Section 38(1)(b). Interim care orders are discussed below at paras 8.109 ff.

[6] See e.g. *Re M (Intractable Contact Dispute: Interim Care Order)* [2003] EWHC 1024 (Fam), [2003] 2 FLR 636 and *Re F (Family Proceedings: Section 37 Investigation)* [2005] EWHC 2935 (Fam), [2006] 1 FLR 1122 – in which a father supported and was complicit in the children's hostility and refusal to have contact with their mother. But cf *A v A (Shared Residence)* [2004] EWHC 142 (Fam), [2004] 1 FLR 1195 where a direction was held inappropriate because of the substantial delay that it would engender when the

children were in urgent need of respite and crucially because foster care was inappropriate; and *Re L (Section 37 Direction)* [1999] 1 FLR 984 CA where the case was nowhere near the public law threshold.

6   See *Re F (Family Proceedings: Section 37 Investigation)* [2005] EWHC 2935 (Fam), [2006] 1 FLR 1122, a s 37 report not ordered provided the father agreed to a child psychiatrist seeing children (whose negative views of the mother had been encouraged by the father) and assessing their views.

15. The relationship between private law orders and public law proceedings

5.207 Notwithstanding that the Act itself provides for some interplay between Pt II and Pts III and IV[1] (for example, the duty of the courts in care proceedings to consider whether to make a s 8 order instead of a care order or in addition to a supervision order; the ability of individuals to seek a discharge of a care order by means of an application for a residence order rather than an application under s 39;[2] the power of the courts to order a local authority to supervise a s 8 contact order by means of a family assistance order;[3] and the power in any family proceedings to direct a local authority to investigate the child's circumstances),[4] it is evident that the courts consider that a clear distinction should be drawn between the so-called 'private law' and 'public law' provisions of the CA 1989. As Balcombe LJ said in *D v D (Child Care: Powers of Court)*,[5] 'There is no statutory link between the private and public law parts of the Children Act 1989'.

1   See paras 2.76–2.77 of the revised Guidance (2008).
2   See further paras 8.220 ff.
3   See *Leeds County Council v C* [1993] 1 FCR 585, [1993] 1 FLR 269.
4   Namely under s 37, discussed at para 5.206.
5   [1994] 3 FCR 28 at 158, sub nom *D v D (County Court Jurisdiction: Injunctions)* [1993] 2 FLR 802 at 812, CA.

5.208 The rulings in *Nottingham County Council v P*[1] and *D v D (Child Care: Powers of Court)*[2] taken together with other limitations on the power to make prohibited steps or specific issue orders, namely, that the orders themselves must relate to an aspect of parental responsibility[3] and cannot be used so as to confer any aspect of parental responsibility upon a local authority that it does not already have,[4] effectively means that Pt II cannot be looked to either as a means of forcing local authorities to act under Pts III to V[5] nor as a means of preventing to them from so doing. What remains unclear, however, is the extent to which orders can be made against individuals which have a direct impact on public law powers. Hence, while it seems clear that the court cannot under a Pt II order require a local authority to provide accommodation against the wishes of a parent,[6] it remains a moot point whether one parent could obtain a prohibited steps order preventing the other from objecting to the child being accommodated. However, in view of *Re S and D (Child Case: Powers of Court)*[7] which held that the court had no power to restrain a mother from removing her children from accommodation, it seems unlikely that such an order could be made. On the other hand, Balcombe LJ commented in *D v D*[8] that while there was no direct power under Pt II to prevent local authorities from investigating the child's circumstances under s 47, nevertheless if satisfied:

'that a person with parental responsibility for a child was exercising the rights attaching to that responsibility in a way which would be detrimental to the child's welfare, eg. by permitting the child to be exposed to unnecessary interviews or examinations, *the court in the exercise of its private law jurisdiction could make a prohibited steps order under s 8 restraining that person from exercising those rights.* Once such an order had been made neither the Council nor the police (except in the exercise of their emergency powers under s 46 so far as those extend) could have taken any step invasive of the lives of these children without first applying to the court'. [Emphasis added.]

In other words Pt II orders can apparently be made against individuals which directly impact upon local authority powers under other Parts of the CA 1989.

1   [1994] Fam 18, [1993] 3 All ER 815, CA, and endorsed by Thorpe LJ in *Langley v Liverpool City Council* [2005] EWCA Civ 1173, [2006] 1 FLR 342, discussed at para 5.107.
2   [1994] 3 FCR 28, sub nom *D v D (County Court Jurisdiction: Injunctions)* [1993] 2 FLR 802, CA, and referred to by Wall J (as he then was) in *Re M (Disclosure: Children and Family Reporter)* [2002] EWCA Civ 1199, [2002] 2 FLR 893 at [99] discussed at para 5.105.
3   See paras 5.99–5.100.
4   See s 9(5)(b), discussed at para 5.104.
5   Eg to force local authorities to accommodate children or to bring care proceedings: see *Re J (a Minor) (Specific Issue Order: Leave To Apply)* [1995] 3 FCR 799, [1995] 1 FLR 669.
6   This would seem to be the result of s 9(5)(b).
7   [1995] 1 FCR 626, sub nom *Re S and D (Children: Powers of Court)* [1995] 2 FLR 456, CA.
8   [1994] 3 FCR 28 at 40, sub nom *D v D (County Court Jurisdiction: Injunctions)* [1993] 2 FLR 802 at 812– 813.

ENHANCED RESIDENCE ORDERS

5.209 As part of the strategy to offer alternatives to adoption, the Adoption and Children Act 20021 amended s 12 of the CA 1989 so as to provide for 'enhanced residence orders'. By s 12(5) the court is empowered when making a residence order in favour of any person who is not a parent or guardian of the child 'to direct, at the request of that person, that the order continue in force until the child reaches the age of eighteen …'. Furthermore and, importantly, by s 12(6) where a residence order includes such a direction, an application to vary or discharge the order may only be made with the leave of the court.2 Although even without these provisions it is possible to make a similar order, namely, to extend a residence order until the child is 18 under s 9(6) and to couple that order with a s 91(4) direction, the circumstances need to be exceptional.3 Under s 12(5) the circumstances do not have to be 'exceptional'. Indeed to the contrary, provided an application is made one would expect an enhanced order to be granted as a matter of routine.

1   Section 114, brought into force on 30 December 2005 by the Adoption and Children Act 2002 (Commencement No 9) Order 2005, SI 2005/2213.
2   But note the prospective repeal of these provisions by the Children and Young Persons Bill 2008, discussed at para 5.212.
3   See para 5.122.

5.210 As the Explanatory Notes to the 2002 Act state, the intention behind this reform is 'to provide a further means of delivering enhanced security where the holder of the residence order who is not the child's parent is caring for the child on a long term basis'[1]. The hope is that these changes will provide greater legal security for such persons as grandparents or other relatives, step-parents or foster parents while retaining the legal relationship between the birth family and the child which would be lost on adoption.

1   According to the Review of Adoption Law (HMSO, 1992) para 6.4 residence orders per se were 'not perceived as being likely to offer a sufficient sense of permanence for a child and his carers'.

5.211 Enhanced residence orders offer would-be applicants less protection than special guardianship (discussed below), In particular, while it may be possible to obtain a residence order allowance[1] it might well be easier to obtain financial support with a special guardianship order.[2] On the other hand, unlike special guardianship, enhanced residence orders offer non-parents a remedy without the necessity of having to involve local authorities. But even in this respect the absence of local authority involvement cannot be guaranteed since it lies within the court's power in any 'family proceedings' to consider making a special guardianship order,[2] in which case it must call for a local authority report.[3]

1   Under Sch 1, para 15 to the Children Act 1989 as amended by s 78(3) of the Civil Partnership Act 2004, local authorities have a non-enforceable discretion (compare *Re K and A (Local Authority: Child Maintenance)* [1995] 1 FLR 688) to pay to persons other than parents or their spouses or civil partners with a residence order in their favour, a contribution towards the cost of the accommodation and maintenance of the child.
2   Section 14A(6)(b).
3   Section 14A(11) and see *A Local Authority v Y, Z* [2006] 2 FLR 41.

5.212 It seems that enhanced residence orders will be short-lived, for under the Children and Young Persons Bill 2008 general provision is made for residence orders to last until the child reaches the age of 18 unless the court directs otherwise.[1] At the same time s 12(5) and (6) are to be repealed. Ironically, according to the Explanatory Notes to the Bill the general intention is 'to provide enhanced security for the child where the holder of a residence order who is not the child's parent is caring for the child on a long-term basis'. Yet, with the repeal of s 12(6), that protection will be less than under the 2002 Act's reforms since parents will no longer require court leave to seek a discharge.[2]

1   See the discussion at para 5.144 above.
2   No explanation for this change is given, nor at the time of writing, is it clear whether there will be any transitional provision to preserve s 12(6) in relation to existing orders.

SPECIAL GUARDIANSHIP

1. Introduction

5.213 A key part of the strategy to offer alternative legal options to adoption introduced by the Adoption and Children Act 2002 is the creation of the status, special guardianship. The proposal to have a new form of guardianship was first made in the Consultative Document on Adoption Law in 1992.[1] At that stage it was proposed that there should be power to appoint what was to be called the child's 'inter vivos guardian'. Such guardians were to have all the rights, duties and powers of a guardian under s 5 of the CA 1989 save for the power to agree to the child's adoption. This proposal was not, however, included in the draft Adoption Bill 1996[2] but eventually re-emerged in its current form, namely, as ss 14A–14G of the CA 1989, as inserted by s 115 of the 2002 Act. These provisions came into force on 30 December 2005.[3]

[1] Department of Health, para 6.5. For a detailed account of the history see eg *Re S (Adoption Order or Special Guardianship Order)* [2007] EWCA Civ 54, [2007] 1 FCR 271, [2007] 1 FLR 819 at [5]–[13] per Wall LJ.
[2] Published as part of a government White Paper: 'Adoption – A Service for Children' (Department of Health and Welsh Office).
[3] Adoption and Children Act 2002 (Commencement No 9) Order 2005, SI 2005/2213.

5.214 Special guardianship orders are intended to provide a more permanent status for non-parents than that provided by a residence order (even an enhanced one)[1] but unlike adoption they do not extinguish the legal relationship between the child and his or her birth family. In other words these orders are intended to meet the needs of children for whom adoption is not appropriate (eg older children who do not wish to be adopted) but who cannot return to their birth parents and who 'would benefit from the permanence provided by a legally secure family placement'.[2] Special guardians are distinguishable from guardians since unlike the latter, who, as we have seen, replace the deceased parents, they take office during the parents' life-time. Furthermore unlike guardians, special guardians have to be appointed by court, ie there is no power to make private appointments.

[1] For further discussion of the differences between special guardianship and residence orders, see para 5.235 below.
[2] See the Explanatory Notes to the Act, para 18 and the Explanatory Memorandum to the Special Guardianship Regulations 2005, SI 2005/1109 (England) para 7.2. For a more detailed account of the differences between special guardianship and adoption see the chart annexed to *Re AJ (Adoption Order or Special Guardianship Order)* [2007] EWCA Civ 55, [2007] 1 FCR 308, [2007] 1 FLR 507 reproduced at para 5.236 below.

2. The power to make special guardianship orders

5.215 A special guardianship order is an order appointing one or more individuals to be a child's special guardian, or special guardians.[1] By confining the power to appoint 'individuals' the court cannot appoint a body such as a local authority nor what has been described as an 'artificial individual' such as a director of children's services.[2] On the other hand, orders can be granted to a single individual or a couple, whether married or not. Parents cannot be appointed.[3] Individuals must be aged 18 or over.[4]

[1] Section 14A(1).
[2] See the similar restriction in appointing guardians under s 5 of the CA 1989 and applied in *Re SH (Care Order: Orphan)* [1995] 1 FLR 746, discussed at para 3.108.
[3] Section 14A(2)(b).
[4] Section 14A(2)(a).

5.216   The court (ie the High Court, county court or magistrates' court)[1] may make a special guardianship order either upon application or upon its own motion in any 'family proceedings'.[2] Guardians, those with a residence order in their favour, those with whom the child has lived for a period of at least three years[3] (under the proposed amendment by the Children and Young Persons Bill 2008 relatives with whom the child has lived for at least one year will be entitled to apply) and any person having the consent of: (i) each of the persons in whose favour a residence order is in force; (ii) the local authority if the child is subject to a care order; or (iii) in any other case, each of the persons who have parental responsibility for the child, are *entitled* to apply for a special guardianship order.[4] Anyone else, for example, grandparents who have not provided a home for the child, and the child himself must obtain court leave.[5] In deciding whether to grant leave the court must have regard to the same criteria as for deciding whether to grant leave to apply for a s 8 order.[6] Local authority foster parents (unless relatives) will additionally need the consent of the local authority, if the child has not lived with them for one year.[7] These provisions are summarised in the following chart annexed to *Birmingham City Council v R*.[8]

	Individuals entitled to apply for Special Guardianship: (involves reading together ss 14A(5) and 10(5)(b)(c) and 10(10))
14A(2)(a) 14A(2)(b)	A special guardian – must be aged 18 or over; and must not be a parent of the child
14A(5)(a)	Any guardian of the child
14A(5)(b)	Any individual in whose favour a residence order is in force with respect to the child
14A(5)(c) 10(5)(b) 10(10)	Any individual listed in s 10(5)(b), read with s 10(10): i.e. Any person with whom the child has lived for a period of at least 3 years;* which need not be continuous but must have begun not more than 5 years before, or ended more than 3 months before, the making of the application
14A(5)(c)	Any individual listed in s 10(5)(c): ie. any person who: (i) has the consent of each person in whose favour a residence order is in force; (ii) has the consent of the local authority where the child is in care; or (iii) has the consent of those who have parental responsibility for the child.
14A(5)(d)	A local authority foster parent with whom the child has lived for at least one year immediately preceding the application.

Section 14A(4) brings in s 9(3) as it applies to s 8 orders: local authority foster parents 'within the last six months' may not apply for leave to apply unless: (a) has the consent of the authority; (b) is a relative of the child; or (c) the child has lived with him for at least one year preceding the application.

Section 14A(13): when an adoption placement order is in force, leave to apply for a special guardianship order is required under s 29(5) and (6) of the Adoption and Children Act 2002.

* Note the prospective change for relatives under the Children and Young Persons Bill 2008.

---

1   Section 92(7).
2   Section 14A(6)(b). 'Family proceedings' are defined by s 8(3), (4) of the CA 1989, see paras 5.135 ff. Inter alia this means the court has power to make special guardianship orders in adoption proceedings. But on this issue note *Re S (Adoption Order or Special Guardianship Order)* [2007] EWCA Civ 54, [2007] 1 FCR 271, [2007] 1 FLR 819, discussed at para 5.217.

3   The period of three years need not be continuous but must not have begun more than five years before nor ended three months before the making of the application: s 14A(5)(c) applying s 10(10) of the CA 1989.

4   Section 14A(5).

5   Section 14A(3)(b). Note: without leave an individual cannot give the required notice to the local authority of the intention to apply for a special guardianship order see *Birmingham City Council v R* [2006] EWCA Civ 1748, [2007] Fam 41, [2007] 2 WLR 1130, [2006] All ER (D) 299 (Dec) discussed further at para 5.220.

6   Section 14A(12), applying s 10(8) and (9), discussed at paras 5.150 ff.

7   Section 14A(4), applying s 9(3) (as amended), and s 14A(5)(d).

8   [2006] EWCA Civ 1748, [2007] Fam 41, [2007] 2 WLR 1130, [2006] All ER (D) 299 (Dec), Appendix 1.

5.217 It was pointed out in *Re S (Adoption Order or Special Guardianship Order)*[1], that implicit in the power to make a special guardianship order upon its own motion is that the court can impose such an order on unwilling parties. This is most likely to arise in cases where, as in *Re S* itself, the applicant(s) are seeking to adopt the child but the court thinks that a special guardianship would better serve the child's interests.[2] As Wall LJ said:[3]

> 'The jurisdictional position is very clear: the court has the power to impose a special guardianship order on an unwilling party to the proceedings. Whether or not it should do so will depend upon the facts of the individual case, including the nature of the refuser's case and its interrelationship with the welfare of the particular child. What seems to us clear is that if the court comes to the view on all the facts and applying the welfare checklist under the 1989 Act (including the potential consequences to the child of the refuser implementing the threat to refuse to be appointed a special guardian) that a special guardianship order will best serve the welfare interests of the child in question, that is the order which the court should make'.

However, when making special guardianship orders in such circumstances regard must still be had to requirement under s 14A(8) for there to be a local authority report on the suitability of such an order.[4]

1   [2007] EWCA Civ 54, [2007] 1 FCR 271, [2007] 1 FLR 819.

2   For another example, see *Re L (a child)(special guardianship order and ancillary orders)* [2007] EWCA Civ 196, [2007] 1 FCR 804, [2007] All ER (D) 208 (Mar), sub nom *Re L (Special Guardianship: Surname)* [2007] 2 FLR 50.

3   [2007] EWCA Civ 54 at [77].

4   See *Re S (Adoption Order or Special Guardianship Order)(No 2)* [2007] EWCA Civ 90, [2007] 1 FCR 340, [2007] 1 FLR 855, discussed further at para 5.219.

(a) Jurisdiction

5.218 Special guardianship orders rank as Part 1 orders for the purposes of the Family Law Act 1986[1] under which freestanding applications[2] can only be made if the child is habitually resident in England and Wales or present there and not habitually resident in any part of the United Kingdom or specified dependent territory.[3] Although the 1986 Act implies otherwise,[4] special guardianship is surely also governed by Council Regulation (EC) No 2201/2003 ('BIIR')[5] which provides for the child's habitual residence as the primary basis of jurisdiction[6] (but allowing for jurisdiction to be based on presence inter alia if habitual residence cannot be established)[7] but which also prevents jurisdiction being taken if a court of another Member State of the EU (except Denmark) is seised first.[8] A key difference between the two sets of rules is that whereas under the 1986 Act primary jurisdiction is given to that part of the UK or specified dependent territory in which matrimonial proceedings are also continuing[9] under the Regulation courts hearing matrimonial proceedings can only have jurisdiction to hear matters concerning parental responsibility if the parties agree and that it is in the child's interests to do so.[10] To reconcile this position the 1986 Act should be understood as only applying to resolve conflicts of jurisdiction within the United Kingdom with the Regulation applying as *between* Member States.

[1]   Family Law Act 1986, s 1(1)(aa), inserted by the Adoption and Children Act 2002, Sch 3, para 47.
[2]   Aliter if matrimonial or civil partnership proceedings are continuing in another part of the United Kingdom or specified dependent territory: s 3(2).
[3]   Family Law Act, ss 2(2A) and 3. The only specified dependent territory is the Isle of Man.
[4]   Inasmuch as jurisdiction to make s 8 orders under the CA 1989 are expressly made subject to BIIR by s 2(1)(a) but special guardianship is not under s 2(2A).
[5]   Ie it falls within the concept of 'parental responsibility' under the Regulation as defined by art 1(1)(a) and (2). Article 2(2) expressly includes custody, guardianship and placements in foster care and must surely therefore encompass 'special guardianship'.
[6]   See art 8.
[7]   See art 13.
[8]   See art 19(2).
[9]   Family Law Act 1986, s 3(2). For the meaning of 'continuing' see para 5.131.
[10] Article 12.

(b) Local authority involvement in making applications

5.219 Applicants must give three months' written notice to the local authority of their intention to apply for such an order.[1] Individuals requiring leave to make an application cannot give notice until leave is granted.[2] Upon receiving notice the local authority[3] must then investigate the matter and prepare a report for the court about the suitability of the applicant and any other relevant matters.[4] The court, too, has power to direct a local authority to make such an investigation and report[5] and must do so if it wishes to make such an order.[6] *In other words, in no circumstances may a special guardianship order be made without a local authority report.*[7] According to *Re S (Adoption Order or Special Guardianship Order)(No 2)*,[8] however, where a court is minded to make a special guardianship order rather than an adoption order for which application has been made and for which a local authority report has been filed, although a s 14A(8) report has still to be filed before a special guardianship order can be made, it need not be entirely new. It will be sufficient for the court to ask the local authority to provide the missing information required under s 14A(8) and to get out the remaining information by way of cross references. There is no power for the court to restrict the nature and scope of a s 14A(8) report.[9]

[1]   Section 14A(7). But note this three-month period does not apply where a person has leave to make a competing application for a special guardianship order at a final hearing: Adoption and Children Act 2002, s 29(6). As Bridge and Swindells *Adoption The Modern Law* point out (at 7.118), this prevents the competing application delaying the adoption hearing.
[3]   But they can arrange for someone else to carry out the investigation: s 14A(10).

5.219 *Private law orders*

4   Section 14A(8). The matters to be dealt with in the report are specified in the Schedule to the Special Guardianship Regulations 2005, SI 2005/1109 (England) and to the Special Guardianship (Wales) Regulations 2005, SI 2005/1513 (Wales). They include a detailed assessment of the child and the child's family (including in each case their wishes and feelings), of the prospective special guardian or guardians and details of the local authority including details of any past involvement with the applicant; a summary of support services available and, where the local authority has decided not to provide any, their reason why; and their overall recommendations on whether or not a special guardianship order should be made and what arrangements there should be for contact between the child and his relatives.
5   Section 14A(9).
6   Section 14A(11).
7   See *A Local Authority v Y, Z* [2006] 2 FLR 41.
8   [2007] EWCA Civ 90, [2007] 1 FCR 340, [2007] 1 FLR 853.
9   *Birmingham City Council v R* [2006] EWCA Civ 1748, [2007] Fam 41, [2007] 2 WLR 1130, [2006] All ER (D) 299 (Dec).

5.220 The interaction of these provisions can be complicated. In *Birmingham City Council v R*[1] the local authority sought a care order (it was common ground that the threshold criteria under s 31 were satisfied and that neither of the child's parents was capable of caring for the child) but the mother and maternal grandparents (who had party status in the care proceedings) wanted the child to live with the grandparents under a special guardianship order. Notwithstanding that the grandparents had not sought leave to apply for such an order[2] the judge, pursuant to s 14A(9), directed the local authority to prepare a s 14A(8) report. It was held that he had been wrong to do so since he had no power to order a report at the behest of a person who requires, but has not obtained, leave to apply for a special guardianship order, which meant that he could only do so provided, pursuant to s 14A(6)(b), he was satisfied that such an order should be made. However, when he ordered the report he could not be satisfied and hence he had no power under s 14A(9) to make the direction.

1   [2006] EWCA Civ 1748, [2007] Fam 41, [2007] 2 WLR 1130, [2006] All ER (D) 299 (Dec).
2   The judge was held to have erred in recording the grandparents' undertaking to make an application for a special guardianship order within 7 days.

(c) Principles upon which orders are made

5.221 In deciding whether or not to make a special guardianship order the court must regard the child's welfare as the paramount consideration and be satisfied that making an order is better than making no order at all.[1] It *must* also apply the welfare checklist under s 1(3).[2] It is also obliged to be mindful of the general principle[3] that delay is likely to prejudice the child's welfare and to that end courts are empowered to set timescales for proceedings involving special guardianship applications.[4] As Wall LJ observed in *Re S (Adoption Order or Special Guardianship Order)*[5] where the court is considering whether to make a special guardianship or an adoption order it will be incumbent upon the court to apply both the welfare checklist under s 1(3) of the CA 1989 in relation to special guardianship and s 1(4) of the Adoption and Children Act 2002 in relation to adoption. Given that in most cases the issue will not be the actual placement but what form of order should be made, the 'no order' principle will have little relevance and the risk of prejudice caused by delay 'may be of less pivotal importance'.

¹ Section 1(1) and (5) of the CA 1989 (discussed above at paras 2.2 ff and 2.64 ff respectively). These provisions apply by reason of the fact that the special guardianship provisions are inserted into Pt II of the CA 1989.
² See the specific amendment by s 14G(3) to s 1(4)(b) of the CA 1989. Note: unlike s 8 order applications, it is mandatory to apply the checklist to all special guardianship applications regardless of whether or not they are opposed.
³ Under s 1(2) of the CA 1989, discussed at paras 2.60 ff.
⁴ See s 14E.
⁵ [2007] EWCA Civ 54, [2007] 1 FCR 271, [2007] 1 FLR 819 at [48]. Note also that the welfare test is different under the two Acts, see *SB v X County Council* [2008] EWCA Civ 535, (2008) Times, 29 May.

(d) Powers when making a special guardianship order

5.222 Before making an order the court must consider whether a contact order (for example, to enable continued contact with the both parents or other members of the family) should be made at the same time.¹ Although this latter power seems to signal that unlike adoption orders, special guardianship with contact is not to be regarded as 'unusual' it is clear that should not be a priori position but instead be regarded as an issue which is dependent upon what is thought to be for the child's welfare.² More generally, the court must consider whether *any* s 8 order in force which respect to the child should be varied or discharged.³ This obligation seems surprising particularly with regard to residence orders the continuation of which do seem incompatible with a special guardianship order. This was certainly Wall LJ's view when he commented⁴ that 'it is plain that a special guardianship order ... has the effect of discharging any residence order in relation to the same child'. However, given that a special guardianship order does *not automatically* discharge a residence order,⁵ the courts need to be aware that an express discharge order should be made. There is no restriction comparable to that under s 9(6) with respect to s 8 orders, that orders relating to 16 or 17 year olds should only be made in exceptional circumstances. However, no special guardianship order may be made where an adoption placement order is in force unless an application for a final adoption order has been made *and* the applicant has obtained leave to make the application or is the guardian of the child.⁶

¹ Section 14B(1)(a). The local authority report should contain a recommendation on suitable contact arrangements, see the English Special Guardianship Regulations 2005, Sch, para 10.
² See particularly *Re S (Adoption Order or Special Guardianship Order)* [2007] EWCA Civ 54, [2007] 1 FCR 271, [2007] 1 FLR 819 and *Re L (a child)(special guardianship order and ancillary orders)* [2007] EWCA Civ 196, [2007] 1 FCR 804, [2007] All ER (D) 208 (Mar), sub nom *Re L (Special Guardianship: Surname)* [2007] 2 FLR 50 in which the CA upheld an order granting supervised contact with the mother and indirect contact to the father (with details of the number of cards and letters and presence). See also *A Local Authority v Y, Z* [2006] 2 FLR 41 in which contact was left to the special guardians to determine.
³ Section 14B(1)(b).
⁴ In *Re S (Adoption Order or Special Guardianship Order)* [2007] EWCA Civ 54, [2007] 1 FCR 271, [2007] 1 FLR 819 at [30].
⁵ Nor vice versa, see para 5.227 below.
⁶ Adoption and Children Act 2002, s 29(5).

5.223   On making a special guardianship order the court may also give leave for the child to be known by a new surname.[1] This express power will no doubt encourage such applications and signals a difference both between these orders and adoption, where a new surname is automatic, and a residence order where a change of name is not encouraged.[2] This is not to say that such orders should always be made. Indeed, as *Re L (a child)(special guardianship order and ancillary orders)*[3] shows, such an order should not be made where it would interfere with the child's identity needs. In that case a decision to grant special guardianship[4] to 'devoted excellent grandparents' (with whom the three year old child had lived from the age of three months) but refusing their application for the child's surname to be changed, on the basis that it would interfere with her emotional identity needs, was upheld on appeal. In so ruling, the court rejected the grandparents' contention that there was a fatal inconsistency between the granting of a special guardianship order on the one hand and on the other the restrictive effect the orders under attack had upon the free exercise of the overriding parental responsibility conferred on them by the order. As Ward LJ put it 'Links with the natural family are not severed as in adoption but the purpose undoubtedly is to give freedom to the special guardians to exercise parental responsibility in the best interests of the child. That, however, does not mean that the special guardians are free from the exercise of judicial oversight'.

1   Section 14A(2)(a). Such leave was given by Hedley J in *S v B and Newport City Council*; *Re K* [2007] 1 FLR 1116.
2   See paras 5.31 ff.
3   [2007] EWCA Civ 196, [2007] 1 FCR 804, [2007] All ER (D) 208 (Mar),sub nom *Re L (Special Guardianship: Surname)* [2007] 2 FLR 50.
4   In fact the grandparents had originally applied for an adoption order.

5.224

The court can give permission for the child to be taken outside the UK for more than three months.[1] As with s 8 orders the court is empowered to add directions and conditions to any special guardianship order,[2] and to make provisions which have effect for a specified period.[3] The court can also make other supporting orders such as a prohibited steps or a specific issue order or a s 91(14) order.[4]

1   Section 14B(2)(b). See further para 5.225 below.
2   Section 14E(4).
3   Section 14E(5), applying s 11(7) of the CA 1989 except for s 11(7)(c) under which there is a general power to make an order for a specified time.
4   See *S v B and Newport City Council*; *Re K* [2007] 1 FLR 116, referred to in *Re S (Adoption Order or Special Guardianship Order)* [2007] EWCA Civ 54, [2007] 1 FCR 271, [2007] 1 FLR 819 at [59]. For further discussion of the use of s 91(14), see paras 5.202 ff.

(e)   The effects of special guardianship orders

5.225   Special guardians have, for the duration of the order, parental responsibility for the child which, for the most part, they will be able to exercise to the exclusion of anyone else, apart from another special guardian.[1] The power to act to the *exclusion* of anyone else is put in stronger terms than under s 2(7) which permits co-holders of parental responsibility to 'act alone and without the other (or others) in meeting that responsibility'.[2] As another commentary puts it,[3] whereas a residence order is based upon the concurrent exercise of parental responsibility, special guardianship is based upon its exclusive exercise. However, notwithstanding this conceptual difference, it is doubtful whether there is any practical difference since even a residence holder is in a stronger position than others with parental responsibility. Moreover, like a residence holder special guardians are not empowered to exercise responsibility independently in circumstances where the law requires the consent of *all* parties with parental responsibility (see para 5.226). According to the Explanatory Notes to the Act:[4]

'The intention is that the special guardian has a clear responsibility for all the day to day decisions about caring for the child or young person and for taking decisions about his upbringing. But the order retains the basic link with the birth parents, unlike adoption. They remain legally the child's parents, though their ability to exercise their parental responsibility is limited. They retain the right to consent or not to the child's adoption or placement for adoption'.

1   Section 14C(1)(b).
2   Discussed at paras 3.96 ff.
3   *Butterworths Family Law Service*, 3A[4485].
4   See para 236.

5.226 The exceptions to the special guardians' power to exercise responsibility independently are: (1) circumstances where the law requires the consent of *all* parties with parental responsibility,[1] for example, sterilisation,[2] ritual circumcision,[3] immunisation,[4] changes in the child's education;[5] (2) consenting to the child's adoption or placement for adoption;[6] (3) causing the child to be known by a new surname[7] or removing him from the UK for a period of more than three months.[8] Furthermore, if an adoption placement order is in force the special guardian's exercise of parental responsibility may be restricted by the adoption agency.[9] A third restriction is that if a care order is subsequently made, the local authority has the power to determine the extent to which a special guardian may meet his parental responsibility for the child.[10]

1   Section 14C(2)(a). But note that in *Re S (Adoption Order or Special Guardianship Order)* [2007] EWCA Civ 54, [2007] 1 FCR 271, [2007] 1 FLR 819, at [46] Wall LJ reserved his position on this.
2   This example is given in the Explanatory Notes to the Act, at para 277.
3   Cf *Re J (Child's Religious Upbringing and Circumcision)* [2000] 1 FCR 307, sub nom *Re J (Specific Issue Orders) (Muslim Upbringing and Circumcision)* [2000] 1 FLR 571, CA, discussed at para 3.92.
4   *Re B (a child)(immunisation)* [2003] EWCA Civ 1148, [2003] 3 FCR 156 sub nom, *Re C (Welfare of Child: Immunisation)* [2003] 2 FLR 1095 discussed at para 3.99.
5   Cf *Re G (a Minor) (Parental Responsibility: Education)* [1995] 2 FCR 53, [1994] 2 FLR 964, CA, discussed at para 3.99.
6   Section 14C(2)(b).
7   Section 14C(3)(a).
8   Section 14C(3)(b) and (4). It will be noted that unlike residence orders which entitle a residence holder to remove a child from the UK for a period of less than one month, special guardians are entitled to remove the child from the UK for a period of less than *three* months.
9   Adoption and Children Act 2002, s 29(7)(a).
10   CA 1989, s 33(3)(b), as amended by the 2002 Act, Sch 3, para 63(a)(i).

5.227 Special guardians can appoint a guardian to take their place upon their death.[1] Conversely, they have an obligation to take reasonable steps to inform parents with parental responsibility and guardians that the child has died.[2] A special guardianship order automatically discharges any existing care order and related s 34 contact order[3] but, as we have seen (see para 5.222), does not automatically discharge any existing s 8 order (even a residence order). Nor does an order prevent a subsequent application being made for a residence order though leave of the court will be required.[4] A subsequent residence order does not automatically discharge a special guardianship order but the residence holder can apply for its discharge.[5] An apparent anomaly in this scheme was identified in *Re S (Adoption Order or Special Guardianship Order)*[6] inasmuch as there appears to be no leave requirements for parents to apply for a s 8 order other than a residence order. The only apparent way to restrict this right is to make a s 91(14) order with indefinite duration.[7]

1. CA 1989, s 5(4) as amended by the Adoption and Children Act 2002, s 115(4)(b).
2. Section 14C(5).
3. Section 91(5A), added by Sch 3 to the 2002 Act. Section 34 orders are discussed at paras 8.197 ff.
4. Section 10(7A) added by Sch 3, para 56(d) to the 2002 Act.
5. Section 14D(1)(c).
6. [2007] EWCA Civ 54, [2007] 1 FCR 271, [2007] 1 FLR 819 at [64]ff, per Wall LJ.
7. Even then, as Wall LJ pointed out, the test for overcoming the leave restriction has historically been seen as relatively low.

(f) Variation and discharge

5.228 Unlike adoption orders, special guardianship orders may be varied or discharged, either upon application[1] or upon the court's own motion.[2] Those entitled to apply[3] are: (a) the special guardian; (b) any parent or guardian of the child (but only one year after the order has been made and with leave of the court, which may only be given if it is satisfied that there has been a significant change of circumstances since the making of the order);[4] (c) the child, subject to leave of the court, which may only be granted if it is satisfied that the child has sufficient understanding to make the application;[5] (d) if a residence order is subsequently made, the person in whose favour it is made; (e) any other individual not falling into the above categories who has, or immediately before the making of the special guardianship order had, parental responsibility for the child;[6] and (f) if a care order is subsequently made, the designated local authority. Presumably when considering whether to grant a variation or discharge the court must apply the paramountcy of the child's welfare principle.

1. Section 14D(1).
2. Section 14D(2).
3. Section 14D(1)(a)–(e).
4. Section 14D(3), (5) and (6). These safeguards are intended to provide additional security for special guardians.
5. Section 14D(3), (4).
6. Leave is required if at the time of application, the applicant no longer has parental responsibility: s 14D(3)(d).

DURATION OF ORDER

5.229 No specific provision is made for the duration of a special guardian-ship order but in accordance with general principles it is submitted that it comes to an end upon the child attaining 18[1] or upon the death of the child or special guardian (or surviving special guardian in the case of a joint appoint-ment).[2] It is a moot point whether it ends upon the child's marriage.

[1] References to a 'child' in the CA 1989 generally refer to a child under 18, see s 105(1). It is also the underlying assumption in the provision of financial support, see reg 9(d) of the Special Guardianship Regulations 2005 (England).

[2] This would be in line with the position in guardianship, see paras 3.127–3.128. But note the query on this in the Chart reproduced at para 5.236.

1. Special guardianship support services

5.230 Section 14F makes important provision requiring local authorities to make arrangements within their area for special guardianship support services to provide counselling, advice and information and any other services as prescribed in regulations.[1] The intention[2] is to ensure that local authorities put in place a range of support services, including financial support, to be available where appropriate for special guardians and their children. To this end the local authority is obliged upon the request of a relevant child[3] looked after by them (or previously looked after before the making of a special guardianship order or a parent of such a child) to carry an assessment of that person's needs (including the need for financial support) for special guardian-ship support services.[4] In other cases the local authority may carry out such an assessment upon the written request, inter alia, of a child with respect to whom a special guardianship order is in force, of a special guardian or any person whom the local authority considers to have a significant and ongoing relationship with a relevant child[5] but if they are minded not to, they must give the person 'notice of the proposed decision (including the reasons for it) and must allow him a reasonable opportunity to make representations in relation to that decision.[6] Where the local authority decides to provide support services (other than advice or information) on more than one occasion they must provide a plan[7] and keep that plan under review.[8] These provisions are given additional teeth by the obligation under s 14G for local authorities to establish a procedure for considering representations (including complaints) made to them in respect of these support services by either special guardians or their children.

[1] Namely the Special Guardianship Regulations 2005 (England); Special Guardianship (Wales) Regulations 2005. For an interesting discussion of the policy behind the introduc-tion of these Regulations, see the Explanatory Memorandum to each of the Regulations.

[2] See the Explanatory Notes to the Adoption and Children Act 2002.

[3] Namely a child subject to a special guardianship order, or to an application for such an order or in respect of whom the court is considering such an order and has asked the local authority to investigate and report: Special Guardianship Regulations 2005 (England), reg 2(1), (reg 1(3) of the Welsh Regulations).

[4] Section 14F(4) and reg 11(1) of the 2005 Regulations (England). Cf reg 5 of the Welsh Regulations.

[5] Section 14F(3) and reg 11(2) of the 2005 Regulations (England). Cf reg 4 of the Welsh Regulations.

[6] Regulation 11(3) of the 2005 Regulations (England).

7   Section 14F(6) and reg 14 of the 2005 Regulations (England).
8   Chapter 4 of the 2005 Regulations (England); reg 12 of the Welsh Regulations..

5.231 Under the Special Guardianship Regulations both for England and Wales the prescribed services (in addition to counselling advice and information) comprise financial support; assistance to enable relevant children,[1] the special guardians or prospective special guardians and the parents of relevant children, to discuss matters relating to special guardianship; assistance, including mediation services in relation to contact arrangements; services in relation to a relevant child's therapeutic needs and assistance to ensure the continuance of the relationship between a relevant child and a special guardian, or prospective special guardian.[2] In each of these cases the services may include giving assistance in cash.[3]

1   Defined by reg 2 of the 2005 Regulations (England); (reg 1(3) of the Welsh Regulations).
2   Regulation 3(1)(a)–(d) of the 2005 Regulations (England); (reg 3 of the Welsh Regulations).
3   Regulation 3(2) of the 2005 Regulations (England); the Welsh Regulations are silent on this.

5.232 A key part of the special guardianship support services is financial support. Such support is only payable in the circumstances provided for under reg 6 of the 2005 Special Guardianship Regulations (England) (reg 4 of the Welsh Regulations) and is only payable to the special guardian or prospective special guardian where the local authority considers:[1]

● it is necessary to ensure that the special guardian or prospective special guardian can look after the child;

● that the child needs special care which requires a greater expenditure of resources than would otherwise be the case because of his illness, disability, emotional or behavioural difficulties or the consequences of his past abuse or neglect;

● it is appropriate to contribute to any legal costs;

● it is appropriate to contribute to the expenditure necessary for the purposes of accommodating and maintaining the child, including the provision of furniture and domestic equipment, alternations to and adaptations of the home, provision of meals, of transport and of clothing and toys and other items necessary for the purpose of looking after the child.

Support may also include a remuneration element in cases where it was paid to the former local authority foster parent of a child who has now become the special guardian or prospective special guardian.[2] Payments may be paid periodically or as a single sum.[3] Support ceases to be payable if the child:

● ceases to have a home with the special guardian or prospective special guardian;

● ceases full-time education or training and commences employment;

● qualifies for income support or jobseekers' allowance in his own right; or

● attains the age of 18 unless he continues in full-time education or training, when it may continue until the end of the course of training he is then undertaking.[4]

Financial support is reviewable upon any relevant change of circumstances and, in any event, annually.[5] In *B v London Borough of Lewisham*[6] it was held wrong for a local authority when fixing the appropriate rate for special guardianship allowances to ignore fostering allowances and ally them instead to adoption allowances.

1   Regulation 6(2) of the 2005 Regulations (England). Compare reg 4(1) of the Welsh Regulations.
2   Regulation 7 of the 2005 Regulations (England); the Welsh Regulations are silent on this.
3   Regulation 8 of the 2005 Regulations (England). Note also no support is payable until the conditions set in reg 10 (England) have been complied with. There are no comparable provisions in the Welsh Regulations.
4   Regulation 9 of the 2005 Regulations (England); (reg 4(2) of the Welsh Regulations).
5   Regulation 18 of the 2005 Regulations(England); (reg 12(2) of the Welsh Regulations).
6   [2008] EWHC 738 (Admin), [2008] Fam Law 640, [2008] All ER (D) 248 (Apr).

2. The use of special guardianship orders and the comparison with adoption orders[1]

5.233 Although these provisions are reminiscent of the former custodianship provisions,[2] which did not prove successful, there is every reason to believe that they will prove to be more useful. Certainly the name is better, while the provisions themselves are much more straightforward. Moreover, special guardianship clearly offers more security than residence orders while the provisions governing support are likely to be a further inducement to potential applicants. Illustrations of circumstances where special guardianship may be appropriate include:[3]

- older children who do not wish to be *legally* separated from their birth families;.
- children being cared for on a permanent basis by members of their wider family (commonly grandparents);
- children in some minority ethnic communities, who have religious and cultural difficulties with adoption as it is set out in law;
- unaccompanied asylum-seeking children who need secure, permanent homes, but have strong attachments to their families abroad;
- sibling groups where the older child is the carer and the sibling relationship is more important to a younger child than the need for adoption;
- long-term foster parents, particularly of older children, who feel they can take over parental responsibility from the local authority.

But as Wall LJ said in *Re S (Adoption Order or Special Guardianship Order)*,[4] the above are only illustrations: 'There can be no routine solutions. Each case needs to be decided on the application of the statutory provisions to the best interests of the particular child or children concerned'. This means that there are no paradigm situations and no a priori assumptions can be made as, for example, grandparents looking after grandchildren.[5] According to the Judicial and Court Statistics it is estimated that just over 900 orders were made in 2006, the vast majority of which (726, 80%) were made in public law proceedings.[6]

1   See generally Hall 'Special Guardianship: A Missed Opportunity – Findings from Research' [2008] Fam Law 148, and by the same author 'Special Guardianship – Themes Emerging from Case-Law' [2008] Fam Law 244.
2   Namely those provided under the Children Act 1975, Pt II (brought into force in December 1985) which were repealed by the CA 1989.
3   This list is taken from a variety of sources including the White Paper *Adoption: a new approach* (CM 5017), referred by Wall LJ in *Re S (Adoption Order or Special Guardianship Order)* [2007] EWCA Civ 54, [2007] 1 FCR 271, [2007] 1 FLR 819 at [42] and the Explanatory Notes to the 2002 Act and to the Special Guardianship Regulations 2005 (both the English and Welsh versions).
4   See the Explanatory Memorandum to the Special Guardianship Regulations 2005 (England), p 11.
5   Above, at n 2, at [43] and [61].
6   Cm 7273 (November, 2007) Table 5.4.

5.234 Litigation has so far concentrated on the decision of whether to grant a special guardianship order or an adoption order.[1] According to *Re S (Adoption Order or Special Guardianship Order)*:[2]

'[48] … There is nothing in the statutory provisions themselves which limits the making of a special guardianship order or an adoption order to any given set of circumstances. The statute itself is silent on the circumstances in which a special guardianship order is likely to be appropriate, and there is no presumption contained within the statute that a special guardianship order is preferable to an adoption order in any particular category of case. Each case must be decided on its particular facts; and each case will involve the careful application of a judicial discretion to those facts. (iii) 'The key question which the court will be obliged to ask itself in every case in which the question of adoption as opposed to special guardianship arises will be: which order will better serve the welfare of this particular child?'

'[49] … The court will need to bear Article 8 of the European Convention for the Protection of Human Rights and Fundamental Freedoms 1950 in mind, and to be satisfied that its order is a proportionate response to the problem, having regard to the interference with family life which is involved. In choosing between adoption and special guardianship, in most cases Article 8 is unlikely to add anything to the considerations contained in the respective welfare checklists. Under both statutes the welfare of the child is the court's paramount consideration, and the balancing exercise required by the statutes will be no different to that required by Article 8. However, in some cases, the fact that the welfare objective can be achieved with less disruption of existing family relationships can properly be regarded as helping to tip the balance'.

'[51] A particular concern is that an adoption order has, as a matter of law, the effect of making the adopted child the child of the adopters for all purposes. Accordingly, where a child is adopted by a member of his wider family, the familial relationships are inevitably changed. This is frequently referred to as the "skewing" or "distorting" effect of adoption, and is a factor which the court must take into account when considering whether or not to make an adoption order in such a case. This is not least because the checklist under section 1 of the 2002 Act requires it to do so: – see section 1(4)(f) ("the relationship which the child has with relatives"). However, the weight to be given to this factor will inevitably depend on the facts of the particular case, and it will be only one factor in the overall welfare question'.

On the other hand:

'[68] ... it must be accepted that special guardianship does not always provide the same permanency of protection as adoption. In our judgment this is a factor, which, in a finely balanced case could well tip the scales in favour of adoption'.

Wall LJ also observed that:

'[48] ... Provided the judge has carefully examined the facts, made appropriate findings in relation to them and applied the welfare checklists contained in section 1(3) of the 1989 Act and section 1 of the 2002 Act, it is unlikely that this court will be able properly to interfere with the exercise of judicial discretion, particularly in a finely balanced case. (We think it is no co-incidence that all three of the appeals with which these judgements are concerned fall to be dismissed, although each reaches a different result)'.

In *Re S* itself the Court of Appeal upheld a decision to grant a foster mother special guardianship rather than the adoption she applied for. In contrast in both *Re AJ (Adoption Order or Special Guardianship Order)*[3] and *Re M-J (Adoption Order or Special Guardianship Order)*[4] the Court of Appeal upheld decisions granting adoption orders rather than special guardianship to respectively a paternal aunt and uncle and an aunt.

[1] Which judging from the 2006 statistics, referred to in para 5.233, is the common context in which special guardianship arises. But see *Re R (children)(care proceedings: maternal grandmother's application)* [2007] EWCA Civ 139, [2007] 1 FCR 439 in which a grandmother's application for a residence order or alternatively a special guardianship order was refused.
[2] [2007] EWCA Civ 54, [2007] 1 FCR 271, [2007] 1 FLR 819.
[3] [2007] EWCA Civ 55, [2007] 1 FCR 308, [2007] 1 FLR 507.
[4] [2007] EWCA Civ 56, [2007] 1 FCR 329, [2007] 1 FLR 691.

3. A comparison between special guardianship and residence orders

5.235 Although special guardians are in a similar position to non-parent residence holders inasmuch as they have parental responsibility for the child for the duration of the order which they share with the parents, there are some important differences. For example, the power to act independently of the parents is expressed in stronger terms: under s 14C(1)(b) special guardians are 'entitled to exercise parental responsibility to the exclusion of any other person with parental responsibility for the child (apart from another special guardian)'. Whereas s 2(7) permits, in the case of multi-holders of parental responsibility that each 'may act alone without the other (or others) in meeting that responsibility'. More significantly, and importantly from the point of view of security, it is more difficult for parents to apply to vary or discharge a special guardianship order than to apply to vary or discharge a residence order. In the former case not only do they require court leave but that leave cannot be given 'unless there has been a significant change in circumstances since the making of the order ...'[1] whereas in the latter case there is a simple leave requirement.[2] Other differences are that unlike non-parent residence holders, special guardians are entitled to appoint a guardian and can remove a child from the UK for any period of less than three months as opposed to one month in the case of residence holders. Finally, provision is made for local authority support of special guardians.

5.235 *Private law orders*

1   Section 14D(5).
2   Section 12(6).

SCHEDULE OF MAIN DIFFERENCES BETWEEN SPECIAL GUARDIANSHIP ORDERS AND ADOPTION[1]		
	SPECIAL GUARDIANSHIP	*ADOPTION*
1. STATUS OF CARER	Special Guardian: *If related to child retains existing relative status*	Parent for all purposes: *If related to child existing relative status changes.*
2. STATUS OF CHILD	A child living with relatives/carers who remains the child of birth parent	The child of the adoptive parent as if born as a child of the marriage and not the child of any other person, therefore adoption includes a vesting of 'parenthood' *Section 39(1), (2) of the Adoption Act 1976 Act/s 67 of the Adoption and Children Act 2002 (the 2002 Act)*
3. DURATION OF ORDER	Ceases automatically on reaching 18 if not revoked by court earlier *The legal relationship created is therefore time limited and not lifelong Section 91(3) of the Children Act 1989 (the 1989 Act).*	Permanent *The legal relationship is lifelong. Section 39(2) of the 1976 Act/s 46 of the 2002 Act.*
4. EFFECT ON BIRTH PARENT PR	PR retained by birth parents *SG can impose limitations in use (see 6 below). Section 14C(1), (2) of the 1989 Act.*	Birth Parent PR extinguished. *Section 39(2) of the 1976 Act/s 46 of the 2002 Act.*
5. CARER'S PR	PR vests in special guardian/s *Section 14C(1),(2) of the 1989 Act Subject to limitations (see 6 below).*	PR vested in adopter/s *Section 39(1) of the 1976 Act/s 49 of the 2002 Act/s 2 of the 1989 Act No limitations (but see joint operation* below)*
6. LIMITATION /RESTRICTION OF PR		

SCHEDULE OF MAIN DIFFERENCES BETWEEN SPECIAL GUARDIANSHIP ORDERS AND ADOPTION[1]		
	SPECIAL GUARDIANSHIP	*ADOPTION*
(*a*) *removal from jurisdiction*	(a) up to 3 months without leave, thereafter only with written consent of all PR holders or leave of court unless court gave general leave on making SG order. *Section 14C(3)(b) and 14C(4)/14B(2)(b) of the 1989 Act.*	(a) No restriction
(*b*) *change of name*	(b) cannot change surname without written consent of all PR holders or order of the court *Section 14C(3)(a)/14B(2)(a) of the 1989 Act.*	(b) No restriction *name change may take place at time of making adoption order or thereafter*
(*c*) *consent to adoption*	(c) consent required from birth parents *and* special guardians or court must dispense with consent of birth parents *and* special guardians. *Sections 19, 20, 52 and 144 of the 2002 Act/s 14C(2)(b) of the 1989 Act.*	(c) consent required from adopters only or court must dispense with consent of adopters only.
(*d*) *medical treatment*	(d) may be difficulties where each special guardian agrees but birth parents do not in the following circumstances: **Sterilisation of a child** *This is the example given in the government guidance to SGO in 'Every Child Matters; in Relation to effect of s 14C(2)(a) – no authority is cited.* **Ritual Circumcision** See *Re J (Specific Issue Orders: Child's Religious Upbringing and Circumcision) [2000] 1 FLR 571 Suggests that like sterilisation the consent of all PR holders would be required for this procedure*	(d) no restrictions where each adoptive parent agrees (subject to age/Gillick competence of child) on giving consent for medical treatment. **However, where adoptive parents themselves disagree in these scenarios a court order may be required (see below).*

SCHEDULE OF MAIN DIFFERENCES BETWEEN SPECIAL GUARDIANSHIP ORDERS AND ADOPTION[1]	
SPECIAL GUARDIANSHIP	*ADOPTION*
Immunisation *See Re C (Welfare of Child: Immunisation) [2003] EWCA Civ 1148, [2003] 2 FLR 1095. This added contested immunisations to the small group of important decisions where the consent of both parents was required* **Life prolonged/Life shortening** *If the above scenarios require consent of all with PR surely it must then extend to issues of whether treatment should be given or withheld in terminal cases.* **Section 14C(1)(b) with (2)(a)** Section 14C(1)(b) does not effect the operation of any enactment or rule of law which requires the consent of more than one person with PR in a matter effecting the child. If consent of all PR holders is required for these type of decisions does this then impose a duty upon SG to consult with birth parents in advance and to bring the matter back to court for determination if birth parents indicate an objection.	**Section 2(7) of the 1989 Act.* Where more than one person has PR for a child each may act alone and without the other but nothing in this part shall be taken to affect the operation of any enactment which requires the consent of more than one person in a matter affecting the child.

275

SCHEDULE OF MAIN DIFFERENCES BETWEEN SPECIAL GUARDIANSHIP ORDERS AND ADOPTION[1]

	SPECIAL GUARDIANSHIP	*ADOPTION*
(e) *voluntary accommodation*	(e) If SG objects LA cannot accommodate child unless court order. If all SGs consent but birth parents object would appear that LA cannot accommodate child unless court order if birth parent willing and able to provide accommodation or arrange for accommodation to be provided, *This is not the case if there is in force a residence order and the residence order holder consents nor if there is a care and control order pursuant to wardship or inherent jurisdiction and the person in whose favour the order is made consents.*	(e) where adoptive parents agree they can accommodate voluntarily.
(f) *removal from voluntary accommodation*	(f) Any person may remove from voluntary accommodation at any time. *This is not the case if residence order holder or carer under wardship/inherent jurisdiction agrees to the voluntary accommodation.* *How is the 'exclusive' nature of the SG's PR intended to operate in these circumstances? It appears that the statute requires the consent of all PR holders therefore if SGs consent to accommodation but parents do not the parents can simply remove the child.* *Section 20 (7), (8) and (9) of the 1989 Act.*	(f) adoptive parents can remove from voluntary accommodation.
(g) *consent to marriage under 18*	(g) if all SGS agree no restriction. the Marriage Act 1949 has been amended to enable SGs to give valid consent where SGO in force (unless also care order in force) s 3(1), (1A)(a) and (b).	(g) if all agree no restriction.

SCHEDULE OF MAIN DIFFERENCES BETWEEN SPECIAL GUARDIANSHIP ORDERS AND ADOPTION[1]		
	SPECIAL GUARDIANSHIP	*ADOPTION*
<u>7. DEATH OF A CHILD</u>	Special guardian must notify parents with PR. *Section 14C(5) of the 1989 Act. Special guardians may not be able to arrange for burial/cremation in circumstances where parents wish to undertake such a task if the SGO ends on death. See by way of analogy Re v Gwynedd County Council, ex p B [1991] 2 FLR 365.*	No requirements for notification. *The rights and duties of legal parents do not end on death therefore would be no such conflict.*
<u>8. REVOCATION OF ORDER</u>	Specific statutory provision for birth parents to apply for discharge of SGO with leave of the court, leave not to be granted unless there has been a significant change of circumstances. Specific statutory provision for court to discharge of its own motion even where no application in any 'family proceedings'. *Section 14D of the 1989 Act.*	No statutory provision for revocation. *In wholly exceptional circumstances court may set aside adoption order, normally limited to where has been a fundamental breach of natural justice. See for example, Re K (Adoption and Wardship) [1997] 2 FLR 221.*
<u>9. FUTURE APPLICATIONS BY PARENTS</u> *(a) Residence* *(b) Contact* *(c) Prohibited Steps* *(d) Specific Issue*	(a) Leave required (b) no automatic restriction (c) no automatic restriction (d) no automatic restriction *Section 10(4)(7A) and (9) of the 1989 Act A parent is entitled to apply for any section 8 order except residence where is SGO.*	(a) Leave required. (b) Leave required. (c) Leave required. (d) Leave required. *Section 10(2)(b), (4) and (9) of the 1989 Act.*
<u>10. RESPONDENTS TO FUTURE LEGAL PROCEEDINGS RE CHILD</u>	Birth parents would be respondents in addition to the SGs to any applications in relation to the child for s 8 orders. EPOs, Care/Supervision Orders, Secure accommodation..	Only adopters would be automatic respondents.

SCHEDULE OF MAIN DIFFERENCES BETWEEN SPECIAL GUARDIANSHIP ORDERS AND ADOPTION[1]		
	SPECIAL GUARDIANSHIP	*ADOPTION*
11. <u>MAINTENANCE</u>	Does not operate to extinguish any duty on birth parents to maintain the child	Operates to extinguish any duty on birth parents to maintain the child. *Section 12(3)(b) of the 1976 Act/s 46(2)(d) of the 2002 Act.*
1. INTESTACY	Child placed under SGO will not benefit from the rules relating to intestacy if the SGs die intestate.	Adopted Child will have rights of intestate succession.

[1] See the Chart annexed to *Re AJ (Adoption Order or Special Guardianship Order)* [2007] EWCA Civ 55, [2007] 1 FCR 308, [2007] 1 FLR 507.

Chapter 6

LOCAL AUTHORITY SUPPORT FOR CHILDREN AND FAMILIES

INTRODUCTION

6.1 Integral to the ethos of the CA 1989 is that family life should be independent and free from unjustified interference by the State. This ethos is crystallised within the Act by the central concept of parental responsibility, whereby 'all the rights, duties, powers, responsibilities and authority which by law a parent has in relation to a child and his property'[1] are ordinarily discharged by the parent(s) of a child as part of 'the every day reality of being a parent'.[2] This central concept is further reinforced by the presumption that no court order modifying or restricting the exercise of parental responsibility should be made unless it will promote the child's welfare (the so called 'no order' principle').[3] This statutory foundation for an independent and free family life is further underpinned by the Human Rights Act 1998, which incorporates into domestic law the provisions of the European Convention on Human Rights and Fundamental Freedoms 1950. Article 8 of the Convention operates not only to impose on the State a duty to refrain from interfering in family life (and to ensure that any such interference is necessary and proportionate) but also a positive duty to act to protect family life.[4]

---

[1] CA 1989, s 3(1).
[2] Guardianship and Custody (Law Com 1988 No 172), para 2.4. See Chapter 2.
[3] CA 1989, s 1(5).
[4] *Marckx v Belgium* (1979) 2 EHRR 330, ECtHR.

6.2 Part III of the CA 1989 sets out the general and specific duties imposed on local authorities in respect of the services which they must or may provide for children and their families. In providing these services, the local authority has a duty to consider whether any local education authority, local housing authority, health authority or other local authority can help in the provision of services and, if they can, to seek that help.[1] The scheme set out under Pt III imposes:

(a)   A general duty in respect of the welfare of children in need (including children with a disability) coupled with specific duties and powers aimed at facilitating the general duty of the local authority to provide a range and level of services to children in need.

279

(b)   Duties and powers in respect of children under five (whether they are in need or not).

(c)   Duties and powers in respect of other children (whether or not they are under five and whether or not they are in need).

(d)   Duties and powers in relation to the accommodation of children including children who are 'looked after' by the local authority.

(e)   Duties and powers in respect of children leaving care and formerly looked after by the Local Authority.

---

¹   CA 1989, s 27; It should be noted that the Children Act 2004 and the Children Act 2004 (Children's Services) Regulations 2005, SI 2005/1972, now creates a framework whereby the provision by local government, national government and non-governmental organisations of 'children's services' is carried out co-operatively having regard to the need to safeguard and promote the welfare of children.

6.3 Local authorities may in certain circumstances charge a reasonable sum[1] for the services and can delegate the discharge of their duties.[2] Each of the duties prescribed under Pt III is intended to enable local authorities to work with a family in a manner which seeks to promote the independent exercise of parental responsibility. Specifically, the work of local authorities under Pt III should be directed at avoiding the need for proceedings under Pt IV of the Act.[3] One of five key recommendations of the *Review of the Child Care Proceedings System in England and Wales*[4] stipulated that greater efforts should be made to ensure that applications under Part IV are only issued after all safe and appropriate alternatives have been explored. The recommendations of this review, coupled with the pre-proceedings requirements of the Public Law Outline[5] governing case management of proceedings under Pt IV, is likely to see an increased focus on the extent to which the local authority has fulfilled its duty to work under Pt III in a manner designed to promote the upbringing of the child by his family and avoid proceedings.

---

¹   CA 1989, s 29(1).
²   CA 1989, s 17(5)(b).
³   CA 1989, Sch 2, para 7(a)(i).
⁴   DCA/DfES 2006.
⁵   See para 8.7.

6.4 Working in partnership with those holding parental responsibility and members of the wider family is the guiding principle in the effective discharge of the local authority's duties under Pt III.[1] This requires local authorities to maximise the involvement of families at all stages of the planning and decision-making process such that the decision-making process in respect of those families is characterised by transparency and fairness[2]. This means that issues affecting a family's ability to participate in the decision-making process, for example a learning disability, should not be allowed to frustrate the principle of working in partnership[3] and that families should be provided with correct and complete information to facilitate that partnership.[4] It should be remembered however, that partnership cannot be permitted to compromise the duty to safeguard and promote the child's welfare.[5]

---

¹   The concept of partnership was introduced in the Guidance to the Act. See the Children Act 1989 Guidance and Regulations, Vol 2, Family Support, Day Care and Educational Provision for Young Children (1991) Department of Health, para 2.1 and Care of Children: Principles and Practice in Regulations and Guidance (1989) HMSO.

2   *Re L (Care: Assessment: Fair Trial)* [2002] EWHC 1379 (Fam), [2002] 2 FLR 730.
3   *Re G (Care: Challenge to Local Authority's Decision)* [2003] EWHC 551 (Fam), [2003] 2 FLR 42.
4   *Sahin v Germany* [2002] 1 FLR 119, [2002] Fam Law 94, ECtHR.
5   Report of the CAAC (1992).

6.5 For an effective balance to be struck between working in partnership with families under Pt III and ensuring that the child's welfare is safeguarded and promoted, the decision-making process deployed by local authorities when discharging their duties must itself be a rigorous one. Those with the power of decision making should never make a judgment without having a full knowledge of the files and consulting those professionals who know the family.[1] Local authorities must carefully consider all available information relevant to the decision, to ensure that adequate regard is paid to the Convention rights of the family and the child, including allowing them adequate participation in the decision-making process.[2]

1   *Re E (Care Proceedings: Social Work Practice)* [2000] 2 FLR 254.
2   *Re X; Barnett London Borough Council v Y and X* [2006] 2 FLR 998.

6.6 Authorities are required to facilitate the provision of Pt III services by others, in particular voluntary organisations, and may make such arrangements as they see fit for others to provide such services (for example, day care or fostering services).[1]

1   Section 17(5). See also the Children Act 1989 Guidance and Regulations, Vol 2, Family Support, Day Care and Educational Provision for Young Children (1991) Department of Health, at para 2.11.

6.7 Wide-ranging advice on the whole of Pt III is given in the Department of Health's publications, the Children Act 1989 Guidance and Regulations, in Volume 2 on Family Support, Day Care and Educational Provision for Young Children, Volume 3 on Family Placements, Volume 4 on Residential Care, the Framework Document on the Assessment of Children in Need and their Families[1] and the National Minimum Standards for Fostering Services.[2] The most comprehensive discussion of the implementation of these provisions is contained in Children Act Now: Messages from Research.[3]

1   Department of Health (2000) TSO.
2   Department of Health (2002) TSO.
3   (2001) TSO.

CHILDREN IN NEED

1. Definitions

(a) 'Child'

6.8 A child is defined by the CA 1989 as a person under the age of 18 years old.[1] Where there is a dispute as to whether the child in question is a child for the purposes of the Act, it is for the local authority to decide that issue.[2] In deciding that issue, the local authority must adopt a procedure which adheres to the minimum standards of enquiry and fairness and one which provides for adequate reasons to be given for the decision reached.[3]

1   CA 1989, s 15(1).
2   R (*on the application of B*) *v Merton London Borough Council* [2003] EWHC 1689 (Admin), [2003] 2 FLR 888.
3   R (*on the application of B*) *v Merton London Borough Council* [2003] EWHC 1689 (Admin), [2003] 2 FLR 888.

(b) 'In need'

6.9 A child is 'in need' for the purposes of Pt III if he is unlikely to achieve or maintain, or to have the opportunity of achieving and maintaining, a reasonable standard of health or development without the provision for him of services by the local authority under Pt III, or his health or development is likely to be significantly impaired, or further impaired, without the provision of such services, or he is disabled.[1] It is implicit in the definition provided by the Act that children who *may* suffer if assistance is not given by the local authority are also children 'in need' for the purposes of s 17(1). The Guidance states that the definition of 'in need' provided by the Act is deliberately wide to ensure emphasis is maintained on the need for proactive preventative services.[2] The longer a child in need is without the services anticipated by Pt III the greater the likelihood of proceedings under Pt IV being required.

1   CA 1989, s 17(10).
2   Children Act 1989 Guidance and Regulations, Vol 2, Family Support, Day Care and Educational Provision for Young Children (1991) Department of Health), para 2.4.

(c) 'Health' and 'development'

6.10 'Health' means physical or mental health and 'development' means physical, intellectual, emotional, social or behavioural development.[1]

1   Section 17(11). The same definitions are provided in s 31(9).

(d) 'Family'

6.11 'Family' is defined in wide terms by the Act and includes any person who has parental responsibility for the child and any other person with whom he has been living and thus is not limited to relatives.[1] A local authority service may be provided for a family if that service is being provided with a view to safeguarding or promoting the child's welfare.[2]

1   CA 1989, s 17(10).
2   CA 1989, s 17(3).

2. Assessment

6.12 Where a local authority believes that a child in its area (ie physically present in its area[1]) is in need for the purposes of the CA 1989, that local authority *may* assess the child's needs for the purposes of s 17 at the same time as the local authority assesses the child's needs under any other Act and in particular under the Chronically Sick and Disabled Persons Act 1970, the Education Act 1996, Pt IV and the Disabled Persons (Services, Consultation and Representation) Act 1986.[2]

[1] *R (on the Application of S) v London Borough of Wandsworth, London Borough of Hammersmith and Fulham, London Borough of Lambeth* [2001] EWHC Admin 709, [2002] 1 FLR 469).

[2] CA 1989, Sch 2, para 3 and see *Clarke Hall and Morrison on Children*, Part 6.

6.13 Guidance as to the effective assessment of need is contained in the original Guidance.[1] Assessments should not be process based but rather sufficiently analytical to assist in planning the appropriate intervention.

[1] Children Act 1989 Guidance and Regulations, Vol 2, Family Support, Day Care and Educational Provision for Young People (1991) Department of Health, paras 2.7–2.9.

6.14 Co-ordinated assessments should be carried out in accordance with the Assessment Framework considered in Chapter 7. Assessments should be carefully planned and should encompass the context in which concerns have arisen as well as the specific concerns themselves. Assessment should always include consideration of the existing strengths and skills of a family as well as any vulnerabilities. The assessment should involve all those caring for the child and be undertaken in an open way. Interventions may be short term but should be geared to the long-term interests of the child. They should also take account of the capacity of the whole community to support a family and not just the social services department. Services provided under s 17 should work alongside other services, notably health and education, to promote the well-being of children and young people. This community approach is particularly important given the prevalence of mental disorders in children aged 5 to 15.[1]

[1] Survey of Mental Health of Children and Young People in Great Britain (Office of National Statistics 2004). This report showed a prevalence of mental disorder of 1 in 10 for this age group.

6.15 Pursuant to s 17(4A), before determining what (if any) services to provide for a particular child in need, a local authority shall, so far as is reasonably practicable and consistent with the child's welfare ascertain the child's wishes and feelings regarding the provision of those services and give due consideration (having regard to his age and understanding) to such wishes and feelings of the child as they have been able to ascertain.[1] Authorities are required to have regard to the means of the child and each of his parents, although no person is liable for repayment at any time when he is in receipt of income support, family credit or disability working allowance.[2] This would suggest that an authority must consider the means of the child concerned and each of his parents before giving assistance or cash and must not have a blanket policy in relation to any group, and that authorities could impose a condition as to repayment when a person became able to pay. An authority may also contribute to the cost of looking after a child who is living with a person under a residence order, such as a relative or foster parent, except where that person is a parent or step-parent.[3]

1   CA 1989, s 17(4A) as amended by s 53 of the Children Act 2004.
2   CA 1989, s 17(8) and (9).
3   CA 1989, Sch 1, para 15.

3. Co-operation between local authorities

6.16 A local authority may request the help of another authority, including an education authority, a housing authority, or a health authority or special health authority, Primary Care Trust or National Health Service Trust, to carry out duties under Pt III. An authority so requested shall comply with the request if it is compatible with its own statutory or other duties and obligations and does not unduly prejudice the discharge of any of their functions.[1] A housing authority is not obliged to provide accommodation, but it does have a duty to ascertain whether it could provide a solution to the problems of homeless families so as to prevent children suffering from lack of accommodation.[2] In addition to the conditional duty to co-operate prescribed by s 27, the Children Act 2004 and the Children Act 2004 (Children's Services) Regulations 2005[3] now create a framework whereby the provision by local government, national government and non-governmental organisations of 'children's services' is carried out co-operatively having regard to safeguarding and promoting the welfare of children. Where more than one local authority is involved (for example because there is an issue as to which area the child is within) arguments between local authorities as to who considers and meets the needs of the child should not hold up the provision of services.[4] Part 1 of the Children and Young Persons Bill currently being considered by Parliament makes provision for local authorities to be able to enter into arrangements with a body corporate for the discharge by that body of social services functions in relation to looked after children using registered social workers. Such functions will be treated as carried out by the local authority.[5]

1   CA 1989, s 27.
2   *R v Northavon District Council, ex p Smith* [1994] 2 AC 402, HL.
3   SI 2005/1972. See also the Children Act 2004 (Amendment of Miscellaneous Regulations) (Wales) Regulations 2005.
4   *R (on the application of M) v of Barking and Dagenham London Borough Council* [2002] EWHC 2663 (Admin), [2002] All ER (D) 408 (Nov).
5   Children and Young Persons Bill 2008. Note that the functions of Independent Reviewing Officers and Adoption Agencies where the other party is not a registered adoption agency are excluded from this provision by s 2 of the Bill.

4. General duty to children in need

6.17 Section 17 imposes on every authority a general duty to safeguard and promote the welfare of children in their area who are 'in need' and, so far as is consistent with that duty, to promote the upbringing of such children by their families by providing a range and level of services appropriate to those children's needs.[1] This provision is intended to underpin a central philosophy of the legislation that children should, wherever possible, be brought up by their families. Services should be available so as to alleviate the suffering of children and to avoid, if possible, the removal of children from their families. It is important to note that a local authority cannot avoid a specific or particular duty by claiming merely to act under the general duty imposed by s 17. For example, if a local authority provides accommodation for a child in need, and if on the facts a duty to do so arose under s 20, the local authority must be regarded as providing that accommodation under s 20 and not under s 17.[2]

1 CA 1989, s 17(1).
2 R (*on the application of H, Barhanu and B*) *v London Borough of Wandsworth, London Borough of Hackney, London Borough of Islington* [2007] EWHC 1082 (Admin), [2007] 2 FLR 822 and see para 6.72.

6.18 The duty under s 17 is a general duty; it is not enforceable by an individual and does not require a local authority to meet every assessed need of each child in need in its area. The House of Lords has held that the correct analysis of s 17(1) is that it sets out duties of a general character which are intended to be for the benefit of all the children in need in the local social services authority's area in general. The other duties and the specific duties which then follow, including the duty to assess the needs of a child, are to be performed in each individual case by reference to the general duties set out in s 17(1). The House of Lords made clear that the assessment of a child's needs did not crystallise the general duty under s 17(1) so that it became a specific duty owed to the child as an individual.[1] However, a local authority may not discriminate against an individual for no good reason and on that basis the authority must at least carry out an adequate assessment of the need in each case, so that they can establish whether the degree of need requires a service.[2] Further, where it is alleged that a local authority has failed to comply with its duties under s 17, for example by deciding not to provide services where an assessment has indicated that they are required, the individual concerned may challenge the local authority by means of the complaints procedure under the Act and thereafter by way of judicial review.[3]

1 R (*on the application of G*) *v Barnet London Borough Council; R* (*on the application of W*) *v Lambeth London Borough Council; R* (*on the application of A*) *v Lambeth London Borough Council* [2003] UKHL 57, [2004] 2 AC 208, [2004] 1 FLR 454. It should be noted that Lord Nicholls and Lord Steyn gave a dissenting judgment in which they held that s.17 does impose a duty in respect of the individual child, requiring the local authority to take reasonable steps to assess the needs of an individual child in need and to provide a range and level of services 'appropriate' to those needs.
2 R (*on the application of AB & SD*) *v Nottinghamshire County Council* [2001] EWHC Admin 235, [2001] 3 FCR 530.
3 Re T (*Judicial Review: Local Authority Decisions Concerning Children in Need*) [2003] EWHC 2515 (Admin), [2004] 1 FLR 601.

6.19 The general duty to provide services provided under s 17 may include giving assistance in kind or, in exceptional circumstances,[1] in cash unconditionally or conditionally as to repayment.[2] Regard must be had to the means of the child and his parents before such assistance is given. The authority may provide cash to assist with accommodation under s 17[3] and has a general discretion to make provision for the economic or social well-being of its area under s 2 of the Local Government Act 2000.[4] It is doubtful that the court has the power to *order* the local authority to make financial provision pursuant to s 17.[5]

1 The Children and Young Persons Bill 2008 removes the reference to 'exceptional circumstances' in s 17(6).
2 Section 17(6) and (7).
3 *R (on the Application of W) v Lambeth London Borough Council* [2002] EWCA Civ 613, [2002] 2 FLR 327.
4 *R (on the application of J) v London Borough of Enfield* [2002] EWHC 432 (Admin), [2002] 2 FLR 1.
5 *Re K and A (Local Authority: Child Maintenance)* [1995] 1 FLR 688.

6.20 Under the general duty pursuant to s 17 a local authority may provide accommodation for a child in need and his family.[1] Whilst the local authority may provide accommodation for a child in need and his family under s 17(6) the local authority is not obliged to make such provision.[2]

1 *CA 1989, s 17(6) as amended by the Adoption and Children Act 2002, s 116.*
2 *R (G) v Barnet London Borough Council; R (W) v Lambeth London Borough Council; R (A) v Lambeth London Borough Council* [2003] UKHL 57, [2004] 2 AC 208, [2004] 1 FLR 454.

5. Services for children with disabilities

6.21 A child is disabled for the purposes of Pt III if 'he is blind, deaf, dumb, suffering from a mental disorder of any kind or is substantially and permanently handicapped by illness, or congenital deformity, or suffering some other disability as may be prescribed.[1] This definition is the same as that provided by the National Assistance Act 1948 allowing a person who is disabled to obtain assistance both before and after they attain their majority. Pursuant to the Mental Health Act 1983 s 1(2)[2] 'mental disorder' means 'any disorder or disability of the mind.'

1 CA 1989, s 17(11).
2 As amended by the Mental Health Act 2007, s 1.

6.22 As children in need, disabled children will be able to benefit from the same services as other children. Additionally, the Act imposes on local authorities a duty to provide services for children with disabilities so as to minimise the effect of their disabilities and give such children the opportunity to lead lives which are as normal as possible.[1] The local authority is required to keep a register of disabled children in its area.[2] Where a carer provides or intends to provide a substantial amount of care on a regular basis for a disabled child and requests an assessment of his ability to provide that care the local authority must carry out an assessment, which assessment will indicate the services the local authority should provide under s 17 or, pursuant to s 17A, pay the carer to secure.[3] Further guidance as to the local authority's duty to in respect of disabled children can be found in the Children Act 1989 Guidance and Regulations, Vol 6, Children with Disabilities.[4]

1 CA 1989, Sch 2, para 6.

² CA 1989, Sch 2, para 2 and Children Act 1989 Guidance and Regulations, Vol 6, Children with Disabilities (1991) Department of Health, Chapter 4.

³ Care and Disabled Children Act 2000, ss 6 and 7; Disabled Children (Direct Payments)(England) Regulations 2001, SI 2001/442.

⁴ The Children and Young Persons Bill 2008 makes provision for breaks for carers of disabled children.

6. Specific powers and duties

6.23 In pursuance of the general duty under s 17, local authorities have specific duties and powers.¹ These may be amended or added to by the Secretary of State,² which should enable the government to ensure the development of good local authority practice without recourse to Parliament. As the provisions exist at present, they leave wide discretion to the local authority, since duties are expressed in terms of 'taking reasonable steps' or providing services 'as they consider appropriate'. The duty of the local authority to provide specific services for children in need is one which is subject to the local authority's budgetary constraints.³ There are only three absolute duties: to publish information about services provided, to open and maintain a register of disabled children and to establish a complaints procedure.⁴ In addition to the specific duties as to the assessment of children's needs, the maintenance of a register of disabled children and to reduce the need for care proceedings,⁵ the Act stipulates the following specific powers and duties in relation to children in need.

¹ See CA 1989, Sch 2 generally.
² CA 1989, s 17(4).
³ *R (on the application of B) v Barnet London Borough Council, ex p B* [1994] 1 FLR 592.
⁴ See CA 1989, s 26.
⁵ See paras 6.17– 6.20.

(a) Identification of children in need

6.24 Every local authority must take reasonable steps to identify the extent to which there are children in need in their area. This includes children who are placed in a young offenders institution subject to the necessary requirement of imprisonment.¹ The local authority is required to publish information² about the services they provide under the general duty, day care services under s 18, accommodation for children under s 20, and their duties to children leaving or who have left care. Where it considers it appropriate, the local authority must publish information about similar services provided by others. The local authority must also take such steps as are reasonably practicable to ensure that those who might benefit from the services receive the information relevant to them.

¹ *R (on the application of Howard League for Penal Reform) v Secretary of State for the Home Department* [2002] EWHC 2497 (Admin), [2003] 1 FLR 484; *R (on the application of CD) v Secretary of State for the Home Department* [2003] EWHC 155 (Admin), [2003] 1 FLR 979.
² CA 1989, Sch 2, para 1.

(b) Prevention of abuse and neglect

6.25 Every authority shall take reasonable steps through the provision of Pt III services to prevent children in their area suffering ill-treatment or neglect.[1] There is a duty to inform another authority if a child who the authority believes is likely to suffer harm, lives or proposes to live in the area of that authority together with particulars of the harm the child is likely to suffer and (if possible) where the child lives or proposes to live.[2] Schedule 2, para 7 provides a connected duty to take reasonable steps, through the provision of services under Pt III, to reduce the need to bring proceedings for care or supervision orders, family or other proceedings which might lead to placement in care, High Court proceedings under the inherent jurisdiction or criminal proceedings in respect of children. Authorities should also encourage children not to commit criminal offences and avoid the need for placing them in secure accommodation. In respect of both Sch 2, paras 4 and 7 the phrase 'reasonable steps' is likely to be interpreted as requiring the local authority to do its best within the bounds of what is reasonably practicable.[3] Further guidance is provided in Working Together to Safeguard Children (2006).

[1]   CA 1989, Sch 2, para 4(1).
[2]   CA 1989, Sch 2, para 4(2).
[3]   *R v London Borough of Brent, ex p S* [1994] 1 FLR 203.

(c) Provision of accommodation to third party to protect children

6.26 Where it appears to an authority that a child is suffering or is likely to suffer ill-treatment at the hands of another person living at the same premises and that other person proposes to move from those premises, rather than removing the child (with disruption attendant thereon) the authority may assist that other person to obtain alternative accommodation, including assistance in kind,[1] on conditions as to repayment if applicable.

[1]   CA 1989, Sch 2, para 5.

6.27 This provision is a response to concern expressed in the Report of the Enquiry into Child Abuse in Cleveland 1987[1] that children, who were allegedly sexually abused, were removed from the family home, when it might have been in their interests for the alleged abuser to have left, if he could have been provided with alternative accommodation. It is intended to allow local authorities to assist those who are willing to leave voluntarily.[2]

[1]   CM 412, 1988. See also provisions on exclusion of individuals under emergency protection orders and interim care orders in Chapters 7and 8.
[2]   The limited powers under the Family Law Act 1996 may be utilised to order an abuser to leave the property by means of an 'exclusion order.'

(d) Promoting upbringing of children by their families

6.28 In order to discharge the general duty to promote the upbringing of children by their families, local authorities are given a number of duties in relation to what might broadly be described as family support mechanisms, designed to support the care of children within their families and to prevent family breakdown where difficulties within the family environment arise. These provisions stipulate the following support local authority's are under a general duty to provide:[1]

Advice, guidance and counselling

Where a child is in need, the local authority must make such provision as it considers appropriate for advice, guidance and counselling, which may be provided at a family centre.[2] The local authority is not able to charge for advice, guidance and counselling.

Occupational, social, cultural and recreational activities

Where a child is in need, the local authority must make such provision as it considers appropriate for occupational, social, cultural and recreational activities, which again may be provided at a family centre.[3]

Home help

Where a child is in need, the local authority must make such provision as it considers appropriate for the services of a home help, which assistance may include laundry facilities.[4]

Travel assistance

So that a child in need and its family may access effectively the services provided by the local authority pursuant to its duties under the Act, without which access such services would be useless, the local authority must provide such facilities as it considers appropriate for, or assistance with, travelling to and from home for the purpose of taking advantage of any service provided under the Act or any similar service.[5]

Holiday

Where a child in need is living at home, the local authority must make such provision as it considers appropriate for assistance to be provided to enable the child concerned and his family to have a holiday.[6]

1   CA 1989, Sch 2, para 8.
2   CA 1989, Sch 2, para 8(a).
3   CA 1989, Sch 2, para 8(b).
4   CA 1989, Sch 2, para 8(c).
5   CA 1989, Sch 2, para 8(d).
6   CA 1989, Sch 2, para 8(e).

(e) Maintenance of the family home

6.29 Where a child is in need, not looked after by the local authority and living apart from his family, the local authority must take such steps as are reasonably practicable if it thinks it necessary in order to safeguard or promote his welfare to enable him to live with his family or to promote contact between him and his family.[1]

¹   CA 1989, Sch 2, para 10.

(f) Duty to consider racial groups

6.30 In making any arrangements either for the provision of day care or designed to encourage persons to act as local authority foster parents, the authority shall have regard to the different racial groups to which children in need in their area belong.[1]

¹   CA 1989, Sch 2, para 11.

(g) Day care

6.31 Every local authority is required to provide such day care as is appropriate for children in need within their area who are five and under and not yet attending school.[1] Day care is defined as any form of care or supervised activity provided for children during the day, whether or not on a regular basis.[2] The authority may provide day care for such children even though they are not in need. They may also provide facilities including training, advice, guidance and counselling for those caring for children in day care or who accompany children in day care.[3] An authority is required to provide for children in need who are attending school, such care or activities supervised by a responsible person, as is appropriate outside school hours or during school holidays and may make such provision for children who are not in need.[4]

¹   CA 1989, s 18(1).
²   CA 1989, s 18(4).
³   CA 1989, s 18(3).
⁴   CA 1989, s 18(5).

6.32 Authorities are required to review their day care provision.[1] Department of Health Guidance makes detailed observations on the development of services and states that local authorities should have an agreed policy for discharging their general duty to provide day care for children in need.[2] Past research suggests that, while there was enthusiasm for the provisions of the Act which gave some prominence to day care services, there has been little progress in coordinated action, identification of levels of need or increase in provision. Lack of resources had made it difficult to develop or expand day care for children in need or other children.[3]

¹   CA 1989, s 19.
²   Children Act 1989 Guidance and Regulations, Vol 2, Family Support, Day Care and Educational Provision for Young Children (1991) Department of Health.
³   Implementing the Children Act for Children under 8: Thomas Coram Research Unit (1994) HMSO. See also Petrie P, Poland G and Wayne S 'Play and Care out of School' (1994) HMSO and Petrie P, Egharevba I, Oliver C and Poland G 'Out-of-school Services, Out-of-school Lives' (2000) TSO.

CHILDREN UNDER FIVE YEARS OLD

6.33 The local authority may provide day care for any child under five and not attending school whether that child is in need or not. Where a child under five is attending school, and accordingly does not come within the provisions in respect of day care, the local authority may provide care or supervised activities for that child outside school hours or during school holidays.[1] A local education is empowered, but is not under a duty, to make educational provision for children under five (save where a child has special educational needs, in which case the local authority is under a duty to ensure adequate educational provision for that child between the ages of two and five).[2]

[1] CA 1989, s 18(2).
[2] Education Act 1996, s 17.

SERVICES FOR ALL CHILDREN

6.34 Every local authority must provide such family centres as they consider appropriate in relation to children within their area whether those children are in need or not.[1] A 'family centre' is a centre at which a child, his parents, a person with parental responsibility for him or any other person looking after him may attend for: (a) occupational, cultural, social or recreational activities; or (b) advice, guidance or counselling; and in which, when receiving advice, guidance or counselling (b), he may be accommodated at the same time. The Children Act 1989 Guidance and Regulations, Vol 2, Family Support, Day Care and Educational Provision for Young Children provides for three types of family centre, namely therapeutic, community and self-help.[2]

[1] CA 1989, Sch 2, para 9.
[2] (1991) Department of Health, para 3.20.

6.35 A local authority may provide care or supervised activities for any child attending school, outside school hours or during holidays whether that child is in need or not and may assist those caring for children in day care.[1] A local authority may provide, either inside or outside its area, such recreational facilities as it sees fit for all children with or without charge.[2] A local authority may also establish, maintain and manage for all children camps, holiday classes, playing fields and play centres.[3]

[1] CA 1989, s 18(6).
[2] Local Government (Miscellaneous Provisions) Act 1976, s 19(1).
[3] Education Act 1996, s 508.

ACCOMMODATION OF CHILDREN

1. Duty to accommodate

(a) Children who must be accommodated

6.36 Subject as set out below local authorities must provide accommodation for a child in need who requires it as a result of there being no person with parental responsibility for him, or because he is lost or abandoned, or because the person who has been caring for him is prevented[1] (whether or not permanently and for whatever reason) from providing suitable accommodation or care.[2] The words 'for whatever reason' mean that accommodation may be provided because of the disability of the child as well as that of the parent.[3] On the face of it, s 20 imposes a mandatory duty to provide accommodation once any of the conditions for the imposition of the duty are satisfied. However, Department of Health guidance[4] indicates that the findings of the authority's assessment should be used to determine whether any such accommodation should be provided. Section 20 thus applies only if the child requires accommodation.[5]

[1] See *R (on the application of S) v Sutton London Borough Council* [2007] EWHC 1196 (Admin), [2007] 2 FLR 849 where the court held that the question of whether the person caring for the child is prevented from providing accommodation involves an objective test.
[2] CA 1989, s 20(1).
[3] *R(G) v Barnett London Borough Council; R(W) v Lambeth London Borough Council, R(A) v Lambeth London Borough Council* [2003] UKHL 57, [2004] 2 AC 208, [2003] 1 All ER 97, [2004] 1 FLR 454.
[4] Guidance on Accommodating Children in Need and their Families (LAC(2003)13) DOH.
[5] *R (on the application of S) v Sutton London Borough Council* [2007] EWHC 1196 (Admin), [2007] 2 FLR 849 and see *R (on the application of M) v Hammersmith and Fulham London Borough Council* [2006] EWCA Civ 917, [2006] 2 FCR 647.

6.37 Local authorities must also provide accommodation for any child in its area who has reached the age of 16, is in need and whose welfare the local authority consider is likely to be seriously prejudiced if it does not provide accommodation.[1] Further, local authorities must provide[2] for the reception and accommodation of children removed or kept away from home under Pt V of the Act under an emergency protection order or police protection order. The duty to provide accommodation for a child arises where he:

(a) has been removed into police protection and the authority is requested to provide accommodation under s 46(3)(f);

(b) has been kept in police detention and arrangements are made for him to be accommodated under the Police and Criminal Evidence Act 1984, s 38(6);

(c) is on remand under para 7(5) of Sch 7 to the Powers of Criminal Courts (Sentencing) Act 2000 or s 23(1) of the Children and Young Persons Act 1969;

(d) is the subject of a supervision order imposing a residence requirement under para 5 of Sch 6 to the Act of 2000; or

(e) is in the care of a local authority under s 31.

[1] CA 1989, s 20(3).
[2] CA 1989, s 21.

6.38 If the child is ordinarily resident[1] in another authority, that authority may take over the provision of accommodation provided pursuant to s 20(1) within three months of being notified in writing that the child is being provided with accommodation or such other longer period as may be prescribed.[2] In determining the 'ordinary residence' of a child for any purpose of the Act there shall be disregarded any period in which he lives in any place:

(a)   which is a school or other institution;
(b)   in accordance with the requirements of a supervision order under this Act or an order under s 63(1) of the Powers of Criminal Courts (Sentencing) Act 2000; or
(c)   while he is being provided with accommodation by or on behalf of a local authority.[3]

The Court of Appeal has provided detailed guidance on the proper interpretation of s 105(6) of the Act within the context of determining which local authority is the designated authority for the purposes of s 31(8).[4]

[1]   'Ordinarily resident' refers to a man's abode in a particular place or country which he has adopted voluntarily and for settled purposes as part of the regular order of his life for the time being, whether of short or long duration': *Shah v Barnet London Borough Council* [1983] 1 All ER 226 at 235, HL.
[2]   CA 1989, s 20(2).
[3]   CA 1989, s 105(6).
[4]   See para 8.170.

(b) Children who may be accommodated

6.39 Authorities have a discretion but not a duty to provide accommodation for any child (ie not simply a child in need) if they consider that to do so would safeguard or promote his welfare. This discretion to provide accommodation is exercisable even though a person with parental responsibility for the child is able to provide that child with accommodation[1] although it would appear that the exercise of this discretion is still subject to the prohibition provided by s 20(7) on providing accommodation against objection of those with parental responsibility who are 'willing and able' to provide accommodation for the child.[2] A local authority may also provide accommodation for any person who has reached the age of sixteen but is under twenty-one in any community home which takes children who have reached the age of sixteen if the local authority considers that to do so would safeguard and promote his welfare.[3]

[1]   CA 1989, s 20(4).
[2]   *R v Tameside Metropolitan Borough Council, ex p J* [2000] 1 FLR 942.
[3]   CA 1989, s 20(6).

(c) Homeless families

6.40 In spite of the duty placed on a local authority to provide accommodation for a child where the person caring for him is prevented from providing him with suitable accommodation for whatever reason,[1] the provisions of the Act are not intended to be used to look after children where their parents are homeless. However, where the local authority is dealing with homeless children the statutory guidance given to both housing and social services departments stresses the need for joint protocols for assessing the needs of homeless 16 and 17 year olds.[2]

[1]   CA 1989, s 20(1)(c).
[2]   See para 6.42.

6.41 Whilst the local authority has the power, but is not obliged, to provide accommodation for a family under the provisions of s 17,[1] and there may be circumstances where that would be necessary in an emergency, the principal responsibility for accommodating homeless families lies with the housing authority under the Housing Act 1996, Pt VII. Whilst the local authority may request the help of the housing authority to enable it to carry out its functions under Pt III and the housing authority is obliged to assist with the request if it is compatible with their own statutory or other duties and obligations, and if it does not prejudice the discharge of any of their functions,[2] the House of Lords has held that the nature and scope of the functions of housing and social services departments were not intended to change as a result of the duty to co-operate.[3] If the parents have made themselves intentionally homeless within the terms of the Housing Act 1996, Pt VII, the housing authority could decline to help the family even though the children of that family are in need, on the grounds that giving priority to such a family would unduly prejudice the discharge of its functions. The courts have sought to avoid undermining this housing policy.[4] This leaves open the possibility that an authority will accommodate a child apart from his family, where the child's need for accommodation can be met as an individual but not as part of his family because of the limits of the housing stock.

[1]   R (G) v Barnett London Borough Council; R(W) v Lambeth Borough Council; R(A) v Lambeth London Borough Council [2003] UKHL 57, [2004] 2 AC 208, [2004] 1 FLR 454.
[2]   CA 1989, s 27.
[3]   R v Northavon District Council, ex p Smith [1994] 2 AC 402.
[4]   See Garlick v Oldham Metropolitan Borough Council [1993] AC 509, [1993] 2 All ER 65, HL.

(d) Homeless adolescents

6.42 A local authority has duties and powers relating to accommodation in respect of young persons found in their area who are between 16 and 21 years old. They are required to provide accommodation for 16 and 17 year olds in need, if they consider their welfare is likely to be seriously prejudiced if they are not provided with accommodation.[1] The authority may provide accommodation in a community home for any person between 16 and 21 years old, if they consider that it would safeguard or promote that person's welfare.[2] The duty to provide accommodation under s 20(1) also applies to homeless adolescents.[3] If the criteria in s 20 are met, social services rather than the housing authority should take the long-term responsibility for them.[4]

[1]   CA 1989, s 20(3).
[2]   CA 1989, s 20(5).
[3]   R (on the application of M) v London Borough of Hammersmith and Fulham [2008] UKHL 14, [2008] 1 WLR 535 and see the Homelessness Code of Guidance for Local Authorities (Department for Communities and Local Government, 2006, para 10.39).
[4]   Homelessness Code of Guidance for Local Authorities (Department for Communities and Local Government, 2006, para 10.39) and see the Homelessness (Priority Need for Accommodation) (England) Order 2002, SI 2002/2051.

(e) Refuges for children at risk

6.43 Section 51 enables organisations, which provide refuges for runaway youngsters, to be exempted by certificate of the Secretary of State from prosecution for assisting or inducing youngsters to run away or stay away or for harbouring them or for child abduction. Regulations relating to certificates and the requirements to be complied with while a certificate is in force are contained in the Refuges (Children's Homes and Foster Placements) Regulations 1991.[1] The Secretary of State may issue a certificate with respect to a home or approved foster parents.[2] The certificate has the effect that the home or foster parent is exempt from prosecution for:

(a)   abduction of children in care;[3]
(b)   abduction of child by persons other than parent;[4]
(c)   compelling, persuading, inciting or assisting any person to be absent from detention;[5]
(d)   harbouring children who have absconded from residential establishments.[6]

Any applicant for a certificate will normally be expected first to have registered the home as a children's home or have made an application in respect of a foster parent approved under the Fostering Services Regulations 2002.[7] The objectives of the project will be expected to include the rehabilitation of the young person with his or her parent(s) or whoever else is responsible for the young person, provided this is consistent with the welfare of the child.[8] Protection from prosecution extends to the organisation itself and to those persons providing the home in which the refuge is situated, or the foster parent providing the refuge, but not those involved in outreach work, whether or not they are employed by the refuge.[9] Such a person would have, at the least, to 'assist or incite' in the absence of the refugee from detention to be vulnerable to prosecution, so that responsible counselling should not be criminal behaviour.

[1]   SI 1991/1507.
[2]   CA 1989, s 51(1) and (2).
[3]   CA 1989, s 49.
[4]   Child Abduction Act 1984, s 2.
[5]   Children and Young Persons Act 1969, s 32(3).
[6]   Children (Scotland) Act 1995, ss 82 and 83.
[7]   SI 2000/57.
[8]   Children Act 1989 Guidance and Regulations, Vol 4, Residential Care (1991) Department of Health, paras 9.5 and 9.7.
[9]   Children Act 1989 Guidance and Regulations, Vol 4, Residential Care (1991) Department of Health, paras 9 and 10.

6.44 Regulation 3 of the Refuges (Children's Homes and Foster Placements) Regulations 1991 provides the criteria for the provision of placement in a refuge. A child may not be provided with a refuge unless it appears to the person providing the refuge that the child is at risk of harm unless the child is, or continues to be, provided with a refuge.[1] As soon as is reasonably practicable after admitting a child to a home for the purpose of providing a refuge or after a foster parent provides a refuge for a child, and in any event within 24 hours of such provision, the person providing the refuge for the child shall notify the 'designated officer'[2] that a child has been admitted to the home, or provided with refuge by a foster parent, together with the telephone number by which the person providing the refuge for the child may be contacted. The child's name and address must be given if known. He must also give the name and address of the 'responsible person'. A child may be accommodated in a refuge for no more than 14 days or no more than 14 days in any three-month period.[3]

1   Refuges (Children's Homes and Foster Placements) Regulations 1991, r 3(2).
2   'Designated officer' means a police officer designated for the purposes of those see r 2(1).
3   Refuges (Children's Homes and Foster Placements) Regulations 1991, r 3(9).

6.45 Notice must be given to the person who is providing the refuge of any proceedings under the Act taken in respect of a child who is alleged to be placed in that refuge. The person providing the refuge can seek leave to be joined as a party to those proceedings should he wish to challenge the application, apply for an emergency protection order, or ask the police to take the child into police protection, if they believe the child would suffer significant harm by being removed from the refuge.[1]

1   Family Proceedings Rules 1991, Appendix 3 and the Family Proceedings Court Rules 1991, Sch 2.

6.46 Where a child ceases to be provided with a refuge, the person who provided him with the refuge shall notify the designated officer. Where a child remains in the refuge for more than 14 consecutive days, or more than 21 days in any period of three months, the protection from prosecution which a certificate provides will apply but the certificate can be withdrawn from the refuge. This emphasises the short-term aims of the refuge provisions.

2. Duties prior to providing accommodation under s 20

6.47 Before providing accommodation under s 20, the authority must, as far as is reasonably practicable and consistent with the child's welfare, ascertain the child's wishes regarding the provision of accommodation and give due consideration to them having regard to his age and understanding.[1]

1   CA 1989, s 20(6).

6.48 In addition to the duty under s 20(6) the local authority must fulfil the following additional duties before providing accommodation for the child:

(a)   So far as is reasonably practicable, agree the arrangements with a person with parental responsibility for the child or, if there is no such person, the person who is caring for the child.[1]

(b)   So far as is reasonably practicable, make immediate and long-term arrangements for the placement and for promoting the welfare of the child who is placed[2] recorded in writing.[3] Planning is required from the earliest possible time after recognition of need or referral where the provision of accommodation is likely to be necessary and the plan should be reviewed on an ongoing basis. Even where it is not possible (for example, by reason of emergency) to draw up a long-term plan, a provisional outline plan should always exist and a firm plan drawn up as soon as possible thereafter.[4] In making the placement arrangements the local authority must have regard to those matters set out in Schs 1 and 4 to the Arrangements for Placement of Children (General) Regulations 1991.

(c) Ascertain the wishes and feelings of the child, his parents, those persons with parental responsibility and others whose wishes and feelings the local authority considers to be relevant.[5] This duty to ascertain the wishes and feelings of the parents may be removed or limited by application for a declaration under the inherent jurisdiction of the High Court.[6]

(d) Give due consideration to those wishes and feelings and to the religious persuasion, racial origin and cultural and linguistic background of the child.[7] The correct approach to making placement decisions where there are issues of race and culture is set out in a DOH circular entitled 'Issues of Race and Culture in the Family Placement of Children.'[8]

(e) So far as is reasonably practicable and reasonably consistent with the welfare of the child, provide accommodation which is near to the child's home.[9]

(f) So far as is reasonably practicable and reasonably consistent with the welfare of the children provide accommodation for siblings together.[10]

(g) Provide accommodation for a child who is disabled which is not unsuitable for that child's particular needs.[11]

(h) Make arrangements to enable the child to live with his parents, a person with parental responsibility, the holder of a residence order in respect of the child or the holder of an existing order for care and control or other person connected with the child, unless to do so would not be reasonably practicable or consistent with his welfare. 'Living with' is defined as staying with for a period of more than 24 hours.[12]

(i) Not to place the child in accommodation restricting his liberty unless the conditions for placing the child in such accommodation are satisfied.[13]

(j) To consult with the local education authority if it is proposed to provide the child with accommodation or to accommodate him where education is to be provided.[14]

(k) So far as is reasonably practicable, arrange for the child to be examined by a registered medical practitioner, and require that practitioner to make a written assessment of the state of health of the child and his need for health care (save where the an examination of a similar nature has taken place in the previous 3 months or where the child is of sufficient age and understanding and refuses to submit to a medical examination).[15]

(l) Give notice of the placement arrangements to the child, his parents, any other person with parental responsibility, any other person whose wishes and feelings the local authority considers to be relevant, the district health authority, the local education authority, the child's registered medical practitioner, the area authority, any former carer before the arrangements were made any holder of a contact order.[16] As a matter of good practice, the social worker should explain personally to the parents and the child what the placements arrangements entail.[17]

---

[1] Arangement for Placement of Children (General) Regulations 1991, reg 3(3).

2   Arrangements for Placement of Children (General) Regulations 1991, reg 3(1). Note that since July 2007 these Regulations have applied only in England. From that date the position in Wales has been governed by the Placement of Children (Wales) Regulations 2007, SI 2007/310.

3   Arrangement for Placement of Children (General) Regulations 1991, reg 3(5).

4   The Children Act 1989 Guidance and Regulations, Vol, 3 Family Placements (1991) Department of Health, paras 2.9 and 2.17.

5   CA 1989, s 22(4) as amended by s 53 of the Children Act 2004.

6   *Re C (Care; Consultation with Parents Not in Child's Best Interests)* [2005] EWHC 3390 (Fam) [2006] 2 FLR 787.

7   CA 1989, s 22(5).

8   (C1 90(2)).

9   CA 1989, s 23(7)(b).

10   CA 1989, s 23(7)(b).

11   CA 1989, s 23(8).

12   CA 1989, s 23(5A).

13   CA 1989, s 25(1).

14   CA 1989, s 28(1).

15   Arrangement for Placement of Children (General) Regulations 1991, reg 7(1).

16   Arrangement for Placement of Children (General) Regulations 1991, reg 5.

17   The Children Act 1989 Guidance and Regulations Volume 3 Family Placement, para 2.70.

6.49 The foregoing duties must also be satisfied before a local authority accommodates a child in care. In addition, the following duties must also be satisfied by the local authority prior to the accommodation of a child in care:

(a)   To ensure that the required statutory records and registers are kept in relation to the child, including the written case record to include the placement arrangements, any written reports, any record or document considered or created in connection wit the review of the child's case, details of contact arrangements, details of others acting on behalf of the local authority.

(b)   To consider representations or complaints made by any person coming within the Children Act 1989 Representations Procedure (England) Regulations 2006.

(c)   To carry out reviews in accordance with the Review of Children's Cases Regulations 1991.

1   SI 2006/1738.

2   SI 1991/895.

3. Limits on providing accommodation

6.50 In the absence of a care order or an emergency protection order the local authority does not have parental responsibility for the child and may not provide accommodation for that child where those with parental responsibility are willing and able to provide accommodation for the child, or arrange for accommodation to be provided, for the child, and object to the local authority providing accommodation.[1]

1   CA 1989, s 20(7) and (10).

6.51 Section s 20(7) regarding the objection of those with parental responsibility does not apply where the holder of a residence order or special guardianship order in respect of the child or an order made by the High Court under the inherent jurisdiction as to who has care of the child consents to accommodation under s 20.[1] Thus, if a person with a residence order, a special guardian or a person who has care of the child pursuant to an order under the High Court's inherent jurisdiction, or all of them if there are more than one, agrees to the child being accommodated, another person with parental responsibility may not object or remove the child. Likewise, s 20(7) regarding the objection of those with parental responsibility do not apply where the child has reached the age of sixteen and consents to accommodation by the local authority.[2]

[1]   CA 1989, s 20(9).
[2]   CA 1989, s 20(11).

6.52 If there is no person with parental responsibility, accommodation should normally be a short-term solution. The authority cannot obtain parental responsibility without a care order but, for a young child, someone should be exercising parental responsibility.[1] The authority could seek a guardian or person who would be willing to obtain a residence order for the child (but cannot itself be made a guardian). If the child is temporarily lost, he needs to be looked after, and his parent will resume care as soon as he is found. 'Abandoned' was not defined in previous child-care legislation, but it has been held that in adoption legislation it means 'leaving the child to its fate'.[2] Again, such a child should not be accommodated for more than the shortest period. Either the parent will come forward and the child returned or an agreement for looking after the child will be reached in partnership with the parent, or more secure plans will be made for the child's future.

[1]   See para 8.29 for discussion as to taking proceedings in respect of orphans.
[2]   *Watson v Nikolaisen* [1955] 2 QB 286, [1955] 2 All ER 427.

6.53 Where a person is prevented from providing a child with suitable accommodation or care, whether an agreement for the child to be accommodated or care proceedings is the more appropriate must depend on the circumstances. If the child is suffering significant harm, the authority will have to consider carefully, in consultation with those having parental responsibility, whether the welfare of the child requires a care order rather than an agreement for accommodation.

4. Restricting removal from accommodation

6.54 Subject to the same exceptions set out in para 6.51 above, any person with parental responsibility for the child may remove the child from accommodation provided by the local authority at any time.[1] There is no requirement that the parent has to give notice of intention to remove the child from accommodation after a specified period. A person who does not have parental responsibility but has care of a child may (subject to other provisions of the Act) do what is reasonable in all the circumstances of the case for the purpose of safeguarding or promoting the child's welfare.[2] The primary purpose of s 3(5), however, is to enable a de facto carer to make routine or urgent decisions, such as consenting to medical treatment, in the interests of the child, provided they are not controversial. The provision would not allow a foster parent or local authority to refuse to hand over the child to a parent seeking to remove a child accommodated under the provisions of s 20 even where that parent may not be capable of caring for the child nor would the general duty of the local authority to safeguard and promote the child's welfare under s 22(3).[3] The proper course of action in these circumstances is for the local authority to apply for an emergency protection order or an interim care order or invite an appropriate person (if any) to apply for a residence order.

[1]   CA 1989, s 20(8).
[2]   CA 1989, s 3(5).
[3]   *Nottinghamshire County Council v J* (26 November 1993, unreported).

5. Partnership with parents

6.55   Parental responsibility includes the right to decide where the child lives.[1] It is central to the philosophy of the Act that an authority should seek to reach agreement with the parent or other person with parental responsibility on such matters as the purpose of accommodating the child and the period for which it might be provided, schooling and contact with the child. The Children Act 1989 Guidance and Regulations Volume 2, Family Support, Day Care and Educational Provision for Young Children states that 'The Act assumes a high degree of co-operation between parents and the local authority in negotiating and agreeing what form of accommodation can be offered and the use to make of it.[2] Care must be taken by local authorities when seeking to accommodate children that the principles governing the giving and taking of informed consent are strictly adhered to. Local authorities should ensure that they involve all those with parental responsibility in the initial negotiations and written agreements on the provision of accommodation, and consider carefully whether accommodation is in the child's interests, given the nature of the agreement which may be reached.

[1]   *R v Tameside Metropolitan Borough Council, ex p J* [2000] 1 FLR 942.
[2]   (1991) Department of Health, para 2.25.

6.56   The authority cannot move an accommodated child without the consent of the persons having parental responsibility. If a parent refused to agree to a necessary move, the authority would have to consider whether to seek a care order.[1]

[1]   *R v Tameside Metropolitan Borough Council, ex p J* [2000] 1 FCR 173: see also para 3.103.

CHILDREN 'LOOKED AFTER'

6.57   Children who are in the care of the local authority pursuant to a care order or who are provided with accommodation (for a continuous period of more than 24 hours) pursuant to any of the functions of a social services authority,[1] are 'looked after' by the authority.[2] Children may also be looked after by or on behalf of a voluntary organisation.[3] When considering the duties of local authorities to looked after children there is a high degree of commonality between the duties of the local authority to children who are 'looked after' by virtue of being in the care of the local authority and those who are 'looked after' by reason of their being provided with accommodation.[4]

1   As provided by the Local Authority Social Services Act 1970.
2   CA 1989, s 22(2).
3   CA 1989, s 59.
4   The Children and Young Persons Bill 2008 significantly amends Pt III of the Children Act 1989 in relation to the duties of the local authority to accommodate and maintain looked after children.

1. Duties to 'looked after' children

6.58 Subject to s 22(6) of the Act conferring upon local authorities a power to act in a manner inconsistent with their duties under s 22 where it is necessary to do so to protect members of the public from serious injury, the local authority has the following duties towards children 'looked after' by reason of their being accommodated by the Local Authority. The following duties are also owed to children 'looked after' by reason of their being in the care of the local authority:

(a)   To safeguard and promote the child's welfare.[1] In satisfying this duty there is no obligation upon a local authority to follow a particular course of action.[2]

(b)   To rehabilitate a child whom it is looking after to the care of its parents or the person(s) holding parental responsibility for the child unless to do so would not be reasonably practicable or consistent with the child's welfare.[3]

(c)   To make use of services available to children who are cared for by their parents as appears to the local authority reasonable in each case.[4]

(d)   To ascertain the wishes and feelings of the child, the child's parents, those persons with parental responsibility and any other person whose wishes and feelings the local authority considers to be relevant.[5]

(e)   Before making any decision with respect to a child they are looking after to give due consideration to such wishes and feelings of the child the local authority has been able to ascertain, having regard to his age and understanding, to such wishes and feelings of the child's parents, those persons with parental responsibility and any other person whose wishes and feelings the local authority has been able to ascertain and to the child's religious persuasion, racial origin, and cultural and linguistic heritage.[6]

(f)   To maintain children accommodated in other respects aside from the provision of accommodation.[7]

(g)   To advise, assist and befriend the child accommodated with a view to promoting that child's welfare when the child ceases to be provided with accommodation by the Local Authority.[8] A local authority has a duty to carry out an assessment of the needs of an 'eligible child'[9] with a view to determining what advice, assistance and support it would be appropriate to provide while they are still looking after him, and after they cease to look after him. They must prepare a pathway plan and keep it under regular review and arrange for the child to have a personal adviser.[10]

(h)   To promote contact between the looked after child and his parents, any person who has parental responsibility, any relative (including relatives by marriage or civil partnership), friends and any other person connected with the child unless it is not reasonably practicable or consistent with the welfare of the child.[11]

(i)   To appoint a visitor[12] where it appears to the local authority that communication between the child and the child's parent or any person with parental responsibility has been infrequent or the child has not visited or been visited (or lived with) any such person during the preceding 12 months and it would be in that child's best interests for an independent person to be appointed to be his visitor.[13] A child of sufficient understanding may object to the appointment of a visitor, which objection the local authority must honour.[14]

(j)   To ensure that the child is examined medically once every six months prior to the child's second birthday and thereafter once every year unless the child is of sufficient age and understanding and objects to the medical examination.[15] The local authority must also ensure that every looked after child is provided with health care services.[16]

(k)   To ensure that the required statutory records and registers are kept in relation to the child, including the written case record to include the placement arrangements, any written reports, any record or document considered or created in connection with the review of the child's case, details of contact arrangements, details of others acting on behalf of the local authority.[17]

(l)   To provide a procedure for considering representations or complaints.[18]

(m)   To draw up an individual plan for the child being looked after and carry out regular reviews with the regulations and amended if necessary pursuant to s 26(1) of the Act.[19] The planning in respect of the child should take place with the aim of safeguarding and promoting that child's welfare, preventing drift and focussing work with the family and child. The planning process should comprise the stages set out in the Children Act 1989 Guidance and Regulations, Vol 4, Residential Care (1991) paras 2.43–2.72. The process of review should ensure that the child's welfare is being promoted and safeguarded in the most effective manner and should result in amendments to the individual plan if necessary. Any failure to implement a recommendation of the review process must be notified by the local authority to the Independent Reviewing Officer.[20]

(n)   To notify the parents, those with parental responsibility (as far as is reasonably practicable) and the Secretary of State where the child dies whilst being looked after.[21]

(o)   In so far as is reasonably practicable, provide information as to where the child is accommodated to the child's parents and any person with parental responsibility.[22] Where the child is 'looked after' by reason of the child being in care the local authority is not required to inform a person of the child's whereabouts if it considers that giving out that information would prejudice the child's welfare.[23]

(p)   Where the child is 'looked after' by reason of the child being in the care of the local authority to consider whether to apply to discharge the care order under s 26(2) of the Act.

1   CA 1989, s 22(3)(a).
2   *Re T (Judicial review: Local Authority Decisions Concerning Child in Need)* [2003] EWHC 2515, [2004] 1 FLR 601.
3   CA 1989, s 23(4).
4   CA 1989, s 22(3)(b).
5   CA 1989, s 22(4) .
6   CA 1989, s 22(5).
7   CA 1989, s 23 (1)(b).
8   CA 1989, s 24(1).
9   An 'eligible child' is one aged 16 or 17, who has been looked after by a local authority for a period (prescribed under the regulations as thirteen weeks), or periods amounting in all to that period, which began after he reached fourteen years of age and ended after he reached the age of sixteen: Sch 2, para 19A and the Children (Leaving Care) Regulations 2001, SI 2001/2874. In Wales the position is governed by Children (Leaving Care)(Wales) Regulations 2001, SI 2001/2189.
10   See paras 6.70 ff.
11   CA 1989, Sch 2, para 15(1).
12   See the Children Act 1989 Guidance and Regulations, Vol 3, Family Placements (1991) Department of Health, paras 7.12–7.17. The Children and Young Persons Bill 2008 amends the provisions as to the appointment and duties of visitors.
13   CA 1989, Sch 2, para 17.
14   CA 1989, Sch 2, para 17(4).
15   Review of Children Cases Regulations 1991, SI 1991/895, r 6.
16   Arrangements for Placement of Children (General) Regulations 1991, r 7(2).
17   See also rhe Children Act 1989 Guidance and Regulations, Vol 3, Family Placements(1991) Department of Health, para 2.83.
18   CA 1989, s 26(3) and see the Children Act 1989 Representations Procedure (England) Regulations 2006, SI 2006/1738.
19   The Arrangements for Placement of Children (General) Regulations 1991 and the Review of Children's Cases Regulations 1991. Note that from July 2007 the regulations apply to England only. Cases in Wales are governed by the Placement of Children (Wales) Regulations 2007 and the Review of Children's Cases (Wales) Regulations 2007.
20   Review of Children's Cases Regulations 1991, r 8A. See also the CAFCASS *Practice Note, Cases Referred by Independent Reviewing Officers* (November 2004) which explains the functions and duties of the CAFCASS Officer where a case is referred by an IRO.
21   CA 1989, Sch 2, para 20.
22   CA 1989, Sch 2, para 15(2)(a). The child's parents and any person with parental responsibility must secure that the local authority are kept informed of their address. Failure to discharge this duty is an offence carrying a sentence of a fine not exceeding level 2 on the standard scale: CA 1989, Sch 2, para 15(5). Note that there is a statutory defence to this offence set out in Sch 2, para 15(6).
23   CA 1989, Sch 2, para 15(4).

2. The duty to rehabilitate

6.59 There is a clear duty upon the local authority to rehabilitate a child whom it is looking after to the care of its parents, person(s) holding parental responsibility for the child or the holder of a residence order immediately before the making of a care order. Unless to do so would not be reasonably practicable or consistent with the child's welfare, the authority must make arrangements to enable him to live with his parents or other person with parental responsibility or a relative, friend or other person connected with him.[1] Where a child is in the care of the local authority the local authority may only permit the child to live with his parents, person(s) holding parental responsibility for the child or the holder of a residence order immediately before the making of a care order in accordance with the Placement of Parents etc Regulations 1991.[2] For the purposes of s 23 of the Act, 'live with' means 'staying with for a continuous period of more than 24 hours.'[3]

[1]   CA 1989, s 23(4).
[2]   SI 1991/893.
[3]   Courts and Legal Services Act 1990, Sch 16, para 12.

6.60   This statutory duty is reinforced by statutory guidance to local authority's which describes the duty under the Act as a duty on local authorities to make all reasonable efforts to rehabilitate the child with his or her family wherever possible unless it is clear that the child can no longer live with his family or that the authority has sufficient evidence to suggest that further attempts at rehabilitation are unlikely to succeed.[1] The statutory duty is further underscored by Convention case law, the European Court in *KA v Finland*[2] observing:

'As the court has reiterated time and again, the taking of a child into public care should normally be regarded as a temporary measure, to be discontinued as soon as circumstances permit, and any measures implementing such care should be consistent with the ultimate aim of reuniting the natural parent and the child. The positive duty to take measures to facilitate family reunification as soon as reasonably feasible will begin to weigh on the responsible authorities with progressively increasing force as from the commencement of the period of care, subject always to its being balanced against the duty to consider the best interests of the child.'[3]

[1]   Local Authority Guidance (98) 20, Appendix 4.
[2]   [2003] 1 FLR 696.
[3]   See also *P, C and S v United Kingdom* (2002) 35 EHRR 1075, [2002] 2 FLR 631 and *K and T v Finland* [2001] 2 FLR 707.

6.61   As far as is reasonably practicable and consistent with the welfare of the child, the authority must secure that the accommodation is near to his home and that siblings are accommodated together.[1]

[1]   CA 1989, s 23(7).

3. The duty to promote contact

6.62   There is also a clear duty on the local authority to promote contact between the looked after child and his parents, any person who has parental responsibility, any relative (including relatives by marriage or civil partnership), friends and any other person connected with the child unless it is not reasonably practicable or consistent with the welfare of the child.[1] In addition, the local authority has a general duty to allow contact between a child in care and his parents and others.[2] This duty is subject to an order of the court prescribing the level of contact or authorising the local authority to refuse contact.[3] In cases where it is necessary to safeguard and promote the welfare of the child, the local authority may deny contact to a child 'looked after' by reason of his being in care without order of the court for a maximum period of 7 days.[4] The local authority has a discretion to make payments in respect of travelling, subsistence or other expenses to facilitate contact pursuant to this duty where circumstances justify the payment and it appears that contact could not otherwise take place without causing undue financial hardship.[5]

1   CA 1989, Sch 2, para 15(1).
2   CA 1989, s 34(1). For a detailed discussion of the provisions of s 34 see paras 8.197 ff.
3   CA 1989, s 34(3) and (4).
4   CA 1989, s 34(6).
5   CA 1989, Sch 2, paras 16(2) and 16(3).

4. Placement of 'looked after' children

6.63 When a local authority is looking after a child, they must[1] provide him with accommodation while he is in their care and must maintain him. In carrying out this duty the local authority may place the child with a family, a relative of his or any other suitable person, on such terms as to payment or otherwise as the authority determines. Placement may also be made in an appropriate children's home or by making such other arrangements as seem appropriate to the authority and comply with regulations.[2] The Arrangements for Placement of Children (General) Regulations 1991[3] apply to all these placements, including those by a local authority or a voluntary organisation or in an appropriate children's home. They require the local authority to plan by making immediate and long-term arrangements for the placement and provide for the content of those arrangements and who should be consulted about them. In relation to a disabled child, accommodation should not be unsuitable to his particular needs.[4] It is a question of fact whether in the circumstances a private fostering arrangement has become available in such a way as to permit a local authority, which had been on the verge of having to provide accommodation for a child, to 'side-step' that duty by helping to make a private fostering arrangement. In considering whether a duty falls on a local authority, a child is 'looked after' at the point the duty under s 20(1) arose and a child does not have to be looked after for 24 hours before either a placement under s 23(2) or an arrangement under s 23(6) can be made.[5]

1   CA 1989, s 23(1).
2   Children's Homes Regulations 2001, SI 2001/3967. These Regulations apply only to England but there are comparable regulations for Wales. 'Appropriate children's home' means a children's home in respect of which a person is registered under Pt II of the Care Standards Act 2000; and an establishment is a children's home (subject to reservations) if it provides care and accommodation wholly or mainly for children': Care Standards Act 2000, s 1. Where a child is accommodated in a care home the position will be regulated by the Care Homes Regulations 2001.
3   SI 1991/890.
4   CA 1989, s 23(8).
5   *D v Southwark London Borough Council* [2007] EWCA Civ 182, [2007] 1 FCR 788.

(a) Placement with parents and those with parental responsibility

6.64 In respect of a child who is 'looked after' by reason of being in the care of the local authority pursuant to a care order, the local authority may only allow him to live with a parent or other person with parental responsibility for him, or with a person in whose favour there was a residence order immediately before the care order was made,[1] after the local authority has carried out the requirements contained in the Placement of Children with Parents etc Regulations 1991.[2] Guidance in respect of such placements is given in the Children Act 1989 Guidance and Regulations, Vol 3, Family Placements. The Fostering Services Regulations 2002 do not apply to such placements.

1   CA 1989, s 23(4).
2   SI 1991/893. These regulations have only a limited application to children who have reached the age of 16.

(b) Placement with relatives or friends

6.65 If the child is placed by the local authority with a relative[1] or friend that placement will be governed by the Arrangements for Placement of Children (General) Regulations 1991 and the Fostering Services Regulations 2002. Where the child is placed with a relative or friend privately, such a placement will be unregulated as it does not come within the definition of 'private fostering.'[2]

1   As defined by CA 1989, s 105(1) as a grandparent, brother, sister, uncle or aunt (whether of the full blood or the half blood or by marriage or civil partnership) or step-parent. Cohabitants are not relatives for the purposes of the Act.
2   CA 1989, s 66.

(c) Foster placements

6.66 Unless with the child's parent(s), a person with parental responsibility for the child or a person who held a residence order in respect of the child immediately prior to the child becoming looked after,[1] the placement of a child looked after by a local authority with a family is a foster placement with a 'local authority foster parent'[2] and will be subject to the Fostering Services Regulations 2002.[3] In addition to the placement of a child by the local authority with local authority foster parents, fostering arrangements may also comprise a private fostering arrangement governed by statute[4] a fostering arrangement organised by a voluntary organisation[5] or a placement within wardship proceedings under the inherent jurisdiction of the High Court.[6]

1   In which case the placement will be governed by the Placement with Parents etc Regulations 1991.
2   CA 1989, s 23(3) – a local authority foster parent means a person with whom a child is placed who is not a person falling within s 23(4).
3   Section 23(2)(f)(ii).
4   CA 1989, s 66.
5   CA 1989, s 59(1).
6   For example where the court wishes to maintain a placement under a care order with carers who for some reason cannot be approved as foster carers, see *Re RJ (Minors) (Fostering: Person Disqualified)* [1999] 1 FLR 605; *Re RJ (Minors) (Fostering: Wardship)* [1999] 1 FLR 618; *Re S (Foster Placement (Children) (Regulations 1991)* [2000] 1 FLR 648 and *Re W and X (Wardship: Relative Rejected as Foster Carers)* [2003] EWHC 2206 (Fam), [2004] 1 FLR 415. This is discussed further in Chapter 12.

6.67 As each of these different fostering arrangements results in a different legal position as between the child, the child's parents and the organisation arranging the foster placement, care must be taken to establish the precise nature of the foster placement when considering the legal status of the child and his carers. Regulations[1] provide for the registration and duties of fostering agencies, approval of foster parents and the requirements to be satisfied on and after placement of a child with a local authority foster parent. A fostering agency may be either a local authority or an independent fostering agency, which can include a voluntary organisation.[2] A local authority may make arrangements for its fostering functions to be delegated to an independent fostering agency, save that it must be satisfied that a placement with a foster parent is the most suitable way of performing its duties of placement for a child.[3]

[1] Fostering Services Regulations 2002, SI 2002/57 and see generally Fostering Services, National Minimum Standards, Department of Health (The Stationery Office, 2002). In Wales the Fostering Services (Wales) Regulations 2003 apply.
[2] Care Standards Act 2000, s 4(4).
[3] Fostering Services Regulations 2002, reg 40.

(d) Residential placements

6.68 The Care Standards Act 2000[1] and the Children's Homes Regulations 2001[2] provide for the welfare of children placed in children's homes.[3] These provisions are outside the scope of this work.[4]

[1] Care Standards Act 2000, s 1(2).
[2] SI 2001/3967.
[3] An establishment is a children's home (subject to exceptions) if it provides care and accommodation wholly or mainly for children: Care Standards Act 2000, s 1. Reference should be made to Children's Homes Guidance and Regulations.
[4] See the Care Standards Legislation Handbook (4th edn) Jordans by His Honour Judge David Pearl.

(e) Placement outside the jurisdiction

6.69 Where a child is looked after (whether or not in care) the local authority may arrange or assist in arranging for that child to live outside England and Wales provided every person with parental responsibility consents.[1] Where the child is in care, the permission of the court must also be obtained.[2] Where a parent withholds their consent to the placement abroad of a child in the care of the local authority the court may dispense with the parents' consent on the grounds it is being withheld unreasonably.[3] Where the procedural requirements for the placing abroad of a child who is in care have not been complied with, but the placement is nonetheless appropriate, the court may make a residence order, thereby discharging the care order.[4] These provisions do not apply where the local authority seeks to place the child with prospective adopters outside the jurisdiction.[5] Detailed guidance on the placement of 'looked after' children outside the jurisdiction is contained in the Children Act 1989 Guidance and Regulations, Vol 8, Private Fostering and Miscellaneous.[6]

¹   CA 1989, Sch 2, paras 19(2) and (3)(d).
²   CA 1989, Sch 2, para 19(1).
³   See *Re G (Minors)(Care: Leave to Place Outside Jurisdiction)* [1994] 2 FLR and *Re W (An Infant)* [1971] AC 682, [1971] 2 All ER 49.
⁴   *Re G (Leave to Appeal: Jurisdiction)* [1999] 1 FLR 771.
⁵   CA 1989, Sch 2, para 19(9).
⁶   (1991) Department of Health, para 4.7.

LEAVING 'LOOKED AFTER' PROVISION

6.70 In 2006, 9.6% of looked after children aged 10 or over, were cautioned or convicted for an offence during the year, almost three times the rate for all children of this age. This rate was similar over the previous three years.¹ A study by McCann et al in 1996 demonstrated that, in relation to children being looked after by one local authority in England the total weighted prevalence rate of psychiatric disorder for this group was 67%, with 96% of adolescents in residential units and 57% in foster care having psychiatric disorders. The prevalence of psychiatric disorder in the comparison group was 15%.² Whilst recent figures suggest improvement, with 37% gaining at least one GCSE or GNVQ, school performance for looked after children still compares poorly with that of the general population, 94% of whom attain at least one GCSE or GNVQ. Between 12 and 19% of care leavers go on to further education, compared with 68% of the general population.³ Fifty per cent of young people will be unemployed on leaving care and 20% will experience some kind of homelessness within two years.⁴

¹   Outcome Indicators for Looked After Children: Twelve Months to September 2006, England, DfES, 2007.
²   McCann et al 1996.
³   Department of Health, 2001*b*; Biehal et al, 1995; Richardson and Lelliot, Mental health of looked after children, Advances in Psychiatric Treatment (2003) 9: 249–256,
⁴   Biehal et al, 1995; Broad, 1998.

6.71 Concerns for the welfare of children formerly looked after by a local authority¹ have led to much enhanced duties being imposed on local authorities in respect of children who are leaving or have left 'looked after' provision.² It should of course be noted that the difficulties identified in respect of children leaving the looked after system stem not just from previous deficiencies in the manner in which such children are prepared for leaving that system but also from deficiencies in the looked after system itself that urgently require remedy.³

¹   See for example *Moving On: Young People and Leaving Care Schemes*, Biehal et al (HMSO 1995) and *Leaving Care in Partnership: Family Involvement with Care Leavers*, Marsh and Peel (The Stationery Office 1999).
²   By way of amendment to the CA 1989 according to the provisions of the Children (Leaving Care) Act 2000. Further amendments may arise by virtue of the Children and Young Persons Bill 2008.
³   The Government has namely issued a Green Paper provision for children and young people looked after entitled 'Care Matters: Transforming the Lives of Children and Young People in Care' (2006) DCSF.

1. Overall duty

6.72 It is the duty of the local authority looking after a young person to advise, assist and befriend him with a view to promoting his welfare when they have ceased looking after him.[1] The duty of the local authority is rooted in the fact that the child has been looked after. These provisions thus make the choice between assisting a young person under s 17 and assisting a young person under s 20 much more important as only the latter assistance will result in the young person becoming 'eligible' for continuing assistance under the leaving care provisions.[2] Whilst there is concern that this difference will lead to local authority's choosing to assist children under s 17 in order to avoid those children becoming eligible under the leaving care provisions (and in any event from benefiting from being a looked after child), Baroness Hale stated in *R(on the application of M) v London Borough of Hammersmith and Fulham*:[3]

'For my part, I am entirely sympathetic to the proposition that where a local children's services authority provide or arrange accommodation for a child, and the circumstances are such that they should have taken action under section 20 of the 1989 Act, they cannot side-step the further obligations which result from that duty by recording or arguing that they were in fact acting under section 17 or some other legislation. The label which they choose to put upon what they have done cannot be the end of the matter.'[4]

[1] CA 1989, Sch 2, para 19A as inserted by the Children Leaving Care Act 2000, s.1.
[2] See paras 6.75–6.80.
[3] [2008] UKHL 14, [2008] 1 WLR 535.
[4] See also *Southwark London Borough Council v D* [2007] EWCA Civ 182, [2007] 1 FLR 2181; *H v Wandsworth London Borough Council* [2007] EWHC 1082 (Admin), (2007) 10 CCLR 441; *R (on the application of S) v Sutton London Borough Council* [2007] EWCA Civ 790, [2007] All ER (D) 422 (Jul); and *R (on the application of L) v Nottinghamshire County Council* [2007] EWHC 2364 (Admin), [2007] All ER (D) 158 (Apr).

6.73 In discharging its duty under the leaving care provisions, the local authority must have regard to the principles set out in the Children Act 1989 Guidance and Regulations, Vol 3, Family Placements,[1] Vol 4, Residential Placements[2] and Vol 6, Children with Disabilities.[3] The Guidance sets out three areas that must be considered when preparing a young person for leaving 'looked after' provision,[4] namely:

(a) Enabling the young person to build and maintain relationships with others.

(b) Enabling the young person to develop their self esteem.

(c) Teaching the young person practical and financial skills and knowledge.

[1] (1991) Department of Health, para 9.18.
[2] (1991) Department of Health, para 9.19.
[3] Chapter 6.
[4] Children Act 1989 Guidance and Regulations, Vol 3, Family Placements (1991) Department of Health, para 9.43 and Vol 4, Residential Placements, para 7.43.

6.74 In ensuring that a young person is properly prepared for leaving 'looked after' provision in these three broad areas, the Guidance makes clear that the preparation work should accord with the following seminal principles of effective child care practice generally:[1]

(a)   Preparation for leaving 'looked after' provision must fully involve the young persons in discussions and plans for their future and a continuing plan formulated with the young person well before they leave care.

(b)   The plan should be formulated in consultation with the young person's parents and/or foster carers where possible.

(c)   Preparations for leaving 'looked after' provision should always take account of the young person's religious persuasion, racial origin, cultural and linguistic background and other needs.

(d)   Carers should be prepared to take some risks and to take responsibility for taking those risks when helping the young person to develop culturally and socially, including allowing the young person to take some risks to this end.

(e)   The services provided to the young person in preparation for them leaving 'looked after' provision must take account of the fact that the process of transition from childhood to adulthood is a lengthy one and requires services to reflect a gradual transition from dependence to independence.

(f)   The preparation for the young person leaving 'looked after' provision should be planned in conjunction and co-operation with other interested agencies.

[1]   Children Act 1989 Guidance and Regulations, Vol 3, Family Placements (1991) Department of Health, para 9.18; Vol 4, Residential Placements, para 7.18 and Vol 6, Children with Disabilities, Chapter 6.

2. Duties to the 'eligible child'

6.75 An 'eligible child' is one aged 16 or 17, who has been looked after by a local authority for 13 weeks, or periods amounting to that, which began after he reached the age of 14 and ended after he reached the age of 16.[1] A child does not come within the definition if the local authority has arranged to place him in a pre-planned series of short-term placements, none of which individually exceeds four weeks (even though they may amount in all to the prescribed period) and at the end of each such placement the child returns to the care of his parent, or a person who is not a parent but who has parental responsibility for him.[2] Where there is a dispute as to whether a child is an 'eligible child' for the purposes of the Act the court is likely to take a 'common sense' approach to determining whether previous arrangements mean that the child is an 'eligible child.'[3]

[1]   CA 1989, Sch 2, para 19B(2) as inserted by the Children Leaving Care Act 2000, s 1.
[2]   Children (Leaving Care) Regulations 2001, reg 5.
[3]   *R (on the application of Berhe) v Hillingdon London Borough Council* [2003] EWHC 2075 (Admin), [2004] 1 FLR 439. See para 6.72.

6.76 In respect of an eligible child the authority must, in addition to its other duties to looked after children:

(a)   Carry out an assessment of his needs with a view to determining what advice, assistance and support it would be appropriate for them to provide him under the Act while they are still looking after him and after they cease to look after him.[1]
(b)   Prepare a pathway plan for him and review it regularly.[2]
(c)   Where the child is still being looked after, arrange a personal adviser.[3]

[1]   CA 1989, Sch 2, para 19B(4).
[2]   CA 1989, Sch 2, para 19B(4). See para 6.83.
[3]   CA 1989, Sch 2, para 19B(5). See para 6.84.

3. Duties to the 'relevant child'

6.77 A 'relevant child' is one, aged 16 or 17, who is not being looked after by a local authority, but was, before last ceasing to be looked after, an eligible child.[1] A child will also be a relevant child if at the time that child attained the age of 16 he was detained in hospital but otherwise would have been a relevant child.[2]

[1]   CA 1989, s 23A.
[2]   Children (Leaving Care) Regulations 2001, reg 4. In Wales the Children (Leaving Care) (Wales) Regulations 2001 apply.

6.78 A child is not to be treated as a relevant child where:

(a)   he has lived with a family for a period of six months (unless that placement breaks down);[1] Given the likely vulnerability of children returning to their families, this provision does appear to fly in the face of the overall positive effect of the Regulations.
(b)   the period of looking after the child would only be 13 weeks if time during pre-planned short-term placements at the end of which the child returned to a parent or person with parental responsibility were included.[2]

[1]   Children (Leaving Care) Regulations 2001, reg 4.
[2]   Children (Leaving Care) Regulations 2001, reg 4.

6.79 In respect of a relevant child the local authority has a duty to take the following steps:[1]

(a)   To take reasonable steps to keep in touch whether or not the child remains in the area of the local authority. Where the local authority has lost touch it must, without delay, consider how to re-establish contact, take reasonable steps to re-establish contact and continue to take those steps until it succeeds.
(b)   To appoint a personal adviser.
(c)   To carry out an assessment of his needs with a view to determining what advice, assistance and support it would be appropriate to provide under the Act.
(d)   To prepare a pathway Plan and review that Pathway Plan regularly.
(e)   To safeguard and promote the child's welfare unless satisfied that his welfare does not require it, support him by maintaining him, by

311

providing or maintaining him in suitable accommodation and by providing him with assistance to meet his needs in relation to education, training or employment as provided for in the Pathway Plan.[2]

1   CA 1989, ss 23A and 23B.
2   Children (Leaving Care) Regulations 2001, reg 11.

4. Duties to 'former relevant children'

6.80 A former relevant child is a person who has been a relevant child (and would be one if he were under 18) and a person who was being looked after by an authority when he attained the age of 18, and immediately before ceasing to be looked after was an eligible child.[1] In relation to such a child the authority must take reasonable steps to keep in touch, and if they lose touch with him, seek to re-establish contact. They must continue the appointment of a personal adviser and continue to keep the pathway plan under regular review. They must give a former relevant child assistance to the extent that his welfare and his educational or training needs require it by contributing to expenses or making a grant. These duties subsist until the child reaches the age of 21, or until the end of a programme for education and training.

1   CA 1989, s 23C.

5. Persons qualifying for advice and assistance

6.81 A young person who is under 21 qualifies for advice and assistance[1] if at any time after reaching the age of 16 but while still a child, he was but is no longer, looked after, accommodated or fostered (whether privately or otherwise) by a local authority or a voluntary organisation, in a private children's home or in any accommodation provided (for three months) by an education authority, Health Authority, Special Health Authority, Primary Care or National Health Service Trust or in a care home or independent hospital. The responsible local authority is that which last looked after him, wherever he is living in England or Wales. If he was not looked after by an authority, the authority where he resides is responsible.[2]

1   CA 1989, s 24(1)–(3).
2   CA 1989, s 24(5).

6.82 In relation to a young person who qualifies for assistance, the authority must[1] take such steps as they think appropriate to contact him at such times as they think appropriate to discharge their duties. They must consider whether the young person needs help by way of advice or assistance. If he does they must advise and befriend him if he was being looked after by a local authority or was accommodated by or on behalf of a voluntary organisation. If he was otherwise accommodated they may advise and befriend him, and in either case may give assistance in kind or, exceptionally, in cash. They may give assistance by contributing to expenses incurred in living near the place where employed or seeking employment and may make a grant to meet expenses connected with his education or training. The duties apply to a person under twenty-four. If the person proposes to live, or is living, in the area of another local authority they must inform that other authority.

1   CA 1989, s 24A.

6. Pathway plans

6.83 All eligible and relevant and former relevant children must have a pathway plan.[1] This is required to set out the advice, assistance and support which the authority intend to provide while looking after and when ceasing to look after the child. It must be maintained and reviewed until the young person is at least 21, and longer if it is to cover education, training, career plans and support. The pathway plan, which must be in writing and provided to the young person, must set out the manner in which the responsible authority proposes to meet the needs of the child, and the date by which, and by whom, any action required to implement any aspect of the plan, will be carried out.[2] The plan should contain sufficient detail of the assessment, the care plan and service provision.[3] Overall, the pathway plan should state clearly 'who does what, where and when.'[4] The pathway plan must be reviewed either when the young person requests a review or in any event, at least once every six months.[5]

1   CA 1989, s 23E.
2   Children (Leaving Care) Regulations 2001, r 8; see also *R (on the application of P) v London Borough of Newham* [2004] EWHC 2210, [2005] 2 FCR 171.
3   *R (on the application of AB and SB) Nottingham City Council* [2001] EWHC 235 (Admin), [2001] 3 FCR 350.
4   *R (J) v Caerphilly County Borough Council* [2005] EWHC 586 (Admin), [2005] 2 FLR 860, per *on the application of* Munby J.
5   Children (Leaving Care) Regulations 2001, reg 9.

7. Personal adviser

6.84

All eligible, relevant and former relevant children must have a personal adviser,[1] whose responsibility it is to help draw up the pathway plan. He must ensure that the plan is implemented and developed with the young person's changing needs. He must keep in touch until the young person is 21 and ensure the provision of advice and support. The detailed duties of the personal adviser are set out in the Children (Leaving Care) Regulations 2001.

1   CA 1989, s 23D. Note that an employee of the local authority can be appointed as a personal advisor to the child provided care is taken to ensure that the employee is not given other responsibilities that may place him in a conflicted or ambiguous position, see: *R (J) v Caerphilly County Borough Council* [2005] EWHC 586 (Admin), [2005] 2 FLR 860.

8. Financial support

6.85 Relevant children and former relevant children are removed from entitlement to means-tested benefits. They remain the responsibility of the local authority, who have to ensure that the vulnerable young people they have looked after receive the care and help they need to grow into independence. They must continue to ensure that young people in and leaving care are suitably accommodated, supported and advised according to their needs.[1]

[1] CA 1989, s 23C(4).

9. Employment, education and training support

6.86 The local authority has a duty[1] to give a former relevant child assistance (and may assist other care leavers), to the extent that his welfare requires it, by contributing to expenses incurred in living near the place where he is or will be employed or where he is seeking employment. Similarly to the extent that his welfare and his educational or training needs require it, the authority has a duty to assist in kind or, in exceptional circumstances, in cash until he reaches the age of 21, or longer if his pathway plan sets out a programme of education or training which extends beyond his 21st birthday.

[1] CA 1989, s 23C(4).

IMPLEMENTING PART III SERVICES

6.87 The history of the implementation of Part III services under the Act does not make for encouraging reading. The Children Act Report 1992 stated: 'most authorities are providing a range of services commensurate with the purposes of the Children Act'.[1] Closer analysis of the information threw doubt on that statement even at that time. Only 55% of authorities responded; they were likely to be those providing better services. The 1993 Report stated:[2] 'most authorities are providing most relevant services and were planning to develop missing services or improve existing ones'. The response rate had increased to 76% but it was still a matter for concern that the Report appeared to express satisfaction that in addition to advice, child protection, accommodation and fostering, only two thirds of authorities 'also provided a range of other services'.[3]

[1] Cm 2144, para 3.15.
[2] Cm 2584, para 2.15.
[3] Cm 2584, para 2.15.

6.88 Studies in the mid to late 1990s[1] showed a different picture. Information about children in need was limited. Definitions of need were limited. Although practitioners would have liked to give a higher priority to proactive, preventive work, in practice resources were shown to be focused on 'high risk' cases. This was at the expense of promoting the welfare of a broader group of children through the provision of family support services. There was a considerable level of unmet need and many families struggled for a long time before any assistance was available from social services. A particular problem was the lack of services for children with emotional and behavioural difficulties in the 7 to 12 age group, a group likely to create more serious problems in subsequent years.

[1] See Aldgate and Tunstill 'Making Sense of Section 17: Implementing Services for Children in Need within the Children Act 1989' (1995) HMSO; Colton et al 'Children in Need: Family Support under the Children Act 1989' (1995) Gower; Tunstill and Aldgate 'Services for Children in Need: from Policy to Practice' ((2000) TSO and most recently the Children Act Report 2000 (2001) Department of Health.

6.89 Until 2000 there was little information about children in need apart from those looked after by authorities or whose names appeared on child protection registers. The Children Act Report 2000[1] noted the advent of a statistical collection called the Children in Need census. Information was to be collected by means of a census of activity and expenditure over seven consecutive working days. The first set of data was gathered in February 2000.[2] Similar surveys have been completed in September 2001,[3] February 2003[4] and February 2005.[5]

[1] Department of Health (2001).
[2] Department of Health (2001).
[3] Deprtment of Health (2002).
[4] Department for Education and Skills (2003).
[5] Department for Education and Skills (2005).

6.90 The 2005 survey[1] available suggests that during the survey week in February 2005 there were approximately 385,900 Children in Need known to local authorities as requiring some form of Social Services provision. Of these, 72,600 (19%) were Children Looked After, and the remaining 313,300 (81%) were other Children in Need supported in families or living independently. During the census week, social services departments undertook active work on behalf of around 234,700 (61%) children. Of these children, 65,900 (28%) were Children Looked After and 168,700 (72%) were other Children in Need. Once again, the proportion of children receiving a service in the week was much higher for Children Looked After (91%) than for other Children in Need (54%).

[1] Information for 2006 is not available. In July 2006, the decision was taken by the DfES not to run the census in February 2007 because of 'changes to Local Authority funding streams which have made the current approach unworkable and the feedback we have received from authorities that they do not find the current census helpful': letter from Richard Bartholomew (Divisional Manager – Children, Young People and Families Analysis and Research DfES) to Local Authorities, 6 July 2006.

6.91 This data only provides information about the needs of those children who are in receipt of social services, how they are responded to and what costs are involved. There is as yet no means of capturing the outcomes for children of social care intervention which must be the best measure of how effective work done under Pt III is for the children concerned. It is planned that this will be possible following the full implementation of the Integrated Children's System[1] although it is still unclear exactly when and how effectively this aim will be achieved. More importantly there is at present no means of capturing the unmet need. The latest figure of 385,000 Children in Need is subject to a number of caveats centring on the local authority practice on the recording of open cases, the coverage of the Children in Need databases in a few authorities and differences in reporting of numbers of cases between 2000, 2001, 2003 and 2005. A lack of comprehensive and reliable data continues to be a significant stumbling block when seeking to remedy deficiencies in the provision of services under Pt III as very basic questions on outcomes and the use of resources cannot be answered.[2]

1 The Every Child Matters website describes the Integrated Children's System as 'a conceptual framework, a method of practice and a business process to support practitioners and managers in undertaking the key tasks of assessment, planning, intervention and review' (www. everychildmatters.gov.uk).
2 Review of the Child Care Proceedings System in England and Wales, DCA and DfES (2006).

6.92 What is clear is that the major weaknesses of the CA 1989 still lie, 16 years after it came into force, in the failure to resource Pt III provision or to co-ordinate services for children throughout social services, education, including special needs, physical and mental health and the criminal and civil justice system. In particular, the research that is available has shown that social services departments are unable to deliver the basic level of service by reason of a woeful lack of experienced social workers.[1] Lack of resources at present critically limits the ability of the available social workers to provide an effective service to Children in Need.[2] Without a level of human, structural and financial resourcing that permits an effective level of service provision under Pt III of the Act it is inevitable that more children will enter the care system long term, be involved in the criminal justice system, be unemployed and suffer mental health problems. A Social Services Inspectorate's report in 1997 found that 23% of adult prisoners and 38% of young prisoners had been in care.[3] According to a study in 2004, the children identified in the study as 'persistent' offenders had higher rates of contact with social services and were more likely to have come to the attention of a social services department through supervision orders or to have been accommodated compulsorily.[4] The deficiencies in the services provided by local authorities under Pt III of the Act, and the chronic resource deficits that underpin those difficulties, are likely to become more acute in light of the reforms signalled by the 2006 Review of the Care Proceedings System in England and Wales, under which there will be an ever increasing emphasis on the need for effective 'pre-proceedings' work aimed at avoiding where possible and preparing effectively for proceedings under Pt IV where needed.

1 Finch, DfES, (2004); Final Report on the Judicial Case Management Protocol (2003) Lord Chancellor's Advisory Committee.
2 Final Report on the Judicial Case Management Protocol (2003).
3 SSI, 1997.
4 Hagell & Newburn (2004).

Chapter 7

ENQUIRY, ASSESSMENT AND EMERGENCY PROTECTION

INTRODUCTION

7.1 Four key processes are identified in the statutory guidance[1] as underpinning work that is effective in achieving improvements in children's lives. In order of application, those four processes are assessment, planning, intervention and reviewing. Proper assessment is thus the foundation stone of effective and sustainable outcomes for children in need and for those children suffering or at risk of suffering significant harm. State intervention in family life should always be based on a sound and thorough prior assessment of the situation leading to the intervention, in order that that situation can be effectively and efficiently addressed in a manner which safeguards and promotes the child's welfare. Even where the intervention takes place on an emergency basis it should proceed from the starting point of careful planning based on as thorough an assessment of the situation giving rise to the emergency as is possible in the circumstances.

[1] Working Together to Safeguard Children (2006) para 5.5.

7.2 Problems with the timing and the quality of enquiries and assessments both in emergency and non-emergency situations are still encountered. Enquiries and assessments are still often process based and insufficiently analytical to form the proper basis for effective decision making and care planning. Too often it is the incident giving rise to the referral rather than the circumstances giving rise to the incident which are investigated. It is in these circumstances that a reactive approach to intervention can become embedded to the detriment of the child and his family. It remains the case that some 34% of cases under Pt IV commence without a core assessment having been completed.[1] A failure to consult and involve the child and the family sufficiently in the process of enquiry, assessment and decision making is a still perennial deficiency. Each of these deficiencies militates against sustainable outcomes being achieved for the children and young people intended to benefit from the intervention of the local authority.

[1] Brophy (2006).

317

7.3 Where, following enquiry into and assessment of the child's circumstances, emergency measures are required to safeguard that child's welfare, emergency protection provisions are provided for by the Act in the form of the emergency protection order[1] and police protection.[2] Where a local authority is being frustrated in its enquiry into and assessment of the child's circumstances, the Act provides a remedy in the form of a child assessment order where there is reasonable cause to suspect that he is or is likely to be suffering significant harm and an assessment of him is needed but cannot be carried out because his parents will not co-operate.[3] The Act also protects against the abduction of a child from the care of a local authority, from emergency protection and from police protection[4], as well as making provision for the court ordered recovery of the child.[5] Where a child who is the subject of a care order requires additional protection, the court may grant injunctive relief ancillary to that care order.[6]

[1]   CA 1989, s 44.
[2]   CA 1989, s 46.
[3]   CA 1989, s 43.
[4]   CA 1989, s 49.
[5]   CA 1989, s 50.
[6]   *Re P (Care Orders: Injunctive Relief)* [2000] 2 FLR 385 and in the High Court and county court only.

7.4 Within the context of the Human Rights Act 1998 and the growing appreciation of the detrimental impact caused to a child by the sudden removal from its family, attention on the use of the emergency protection provisions of the Act has focused increasingly on the need to utilise such measures sparingly. In particular the courts have concentrated on emphasising the need for awareness of the extreme gravity of emergency relief and the need for scrupulous regard to be paid to the human rights of both child and parents when considering the use of such remedies; with emergency intervention under the Act ordered only in circumstances where there is 'exceptional justification' and 'extraordinarily compelling reasons' for such intervention.[1] This approach once again emphasises the need for careful planning based on thorough enquiry and assessment when considering intervention.

[1]   *X Council v B (Emergency Protection Orders)* [2004] EWHC 2015 (Fam); [2005] 1 FLR 341; *Harringey London Borough Council v C (E intervening)* [2004] EWHC 2580 (Fam), [2005] 2 FLR 47; *Re X (Emergency Protection Orders)* [2006] EWHC 510 (Fam), [2006] 2 FLR 701.

7.5 The words 'enquiry', 'investigate' and 'assessment' are often used interchangeably within the context of the duties and obligations under the Act. For example, the suggested[1] tool by which the local authority fulfils its duty to enquire into a child's circumstances under s 47 is the 'Framework for the Assessment of Children in Need and their Families' dealt with below.[2] Whether 'enquiring', 'investigating' or 'assessing', the key to safeguarding and promoting the welfare of the subject child is the rigorous application of the principles of good practice contained in the guidance which underpins the application of the Act and which is covered in more detail below.[3]

[1]   Working Together to Safeguard Children (2006) paras 5.37 and 5.46.
[2]   DOH, (HMSO 2000).

3   See in particular 'Working Together to Safeguard Children (2006) Chapter 5; Framework for the Assessment of Children in Need and their Families (2000) DOH; Communicating with Children (2002) TSO: Department of Health; and Achieving Best Evidence in Criminal Proceedings: Guidance for Vulnerable or Intimidated Witnesses, including Children (2002) TSO. See also communicating with Vulnerable Children: A Guide for Practitioners (2003) Department of Health.

ENQUIRY

1. Statutory duty to investigate

7.6 As seen in Chapter 6, local authorities are under a wide-ranging general duty to safeguard and promote the welfare of children in their area who are 'in need' and, so far as is consistent with that duty, to promote the upbringing of children by their families by providing a range and level of services appropriate to those children's needs. Where a local authority believes that a child in its area is in need for the purposes of the CA 1989, that local authority *may* assess the child's needs for the purposes of s 17.[1] In most cases that duty can be carried out in conjunction with the family who may require the service. In some cases it may appear that a child is in need of protection from harm. It may then be necessary to carry out an enquiry to establish the facts before a proper assessment can be made. It may also be necessary to take legal proceedings to protect the child and enable appropriate plans to be made in the interests of the child. In certain circumstances there is, in addition to the general duty imposed by s 17 of the Act, a statutory duty on a local authority to investigate the child's circumstances with a view to determining what action, if any, should be taken. An 'Aide-Memoir' providing an overview of the statutory enquiry and assessment process is contained in the Protocol for the Judicial Case Management of Public Law Children Act Cases Appendix F.[2]

1   CA 1989, Sch 2, para 3.
2   [2003] 2 FLR 719. The 'Aide-Memoir' has not been incorporated into the Public Law Outline that replaces the Protocol for Judicial Case Management (see Chapter 8) and it is likely that, moving forward, Working Together (2006) will remain the definitive guide to the enquiry and assessment process.

2. Section 47

(a) Duty to investigate

7.7 Pursuant to s 47 of the Act, where a local authority is informed that a child who lives or is found in its area is:

(a)   the subject of an emergency protection order;
(b)   is in police protection;
(c)   has contravened a ban imposed by a curfew notice under the Crime and Disorder Act 1998;
(d)   is the subject of an emergency protection order in favour of the local authority;
(e)   a child in respect of whom the local authority have reasonable cause to suspect is suffering or is likely to suffer significant harm;

the local authority shall make, or cause to be made, such enquiries as it considers necessary to enable it to decide whether to take action to safeguard and promote the child's welfare.[1] Where the child comes within the terms of s 47 by virtue of being in breach of a curfew notice, the enquiry by the local authority must commence within 48 hours of the local authority receiving the information concerning the child.[2]

[1] CA 1989, s 47(1) and (2).
[2] CA 1989, s 47(1).

(b) Threshold for enquiry

7.8 The test for whether the duty to investigate under s 47 is triggered in relation to a child who may be suffering or at risk of suffering significant harm is whether there is 'reasonable cause to suspect' that this is the case. There are distinctions between the standard of 'reasonable cause to suspect' in this provision, by contrast with the power of police protection where the constable must have 'reasonable cause to believe that a child would be likely to suffer significant harm',[1] the court's power to make an emergency protection order where there must be 'reasonable cause to believe that the child is likely to suffer significant harm'[2] and the court's power to make an interim care order where it must be satisfied that 'there are reasonable grounds for believing that' the necessary criteria are made out.[3] Suspicion is a standard that is 'quite low' and it is not necessary to establish facts on a balance of probabilities[4] but there must still be objectively reasonable grounds and not simply what the decision-maker thinks reasonable.[5]

[1] CA 1989, s 46(1).
[2] CA 1989, s 44(1)(a).
[3] CA 1989, s 38(2).
[4] *Re S (Sexual Abuse Allegations: Local Authority Response)* [2001] EWHC Admin 334, [2001] 2 FLR 776.
[5] *Gogay v Hertfordshire County Council* [2001] 1 FLR 280.

7.9 In determining whether the threshold for initiating an enquiry under s 47 is met in cases where a child may be suffering or at risk of suffering significant harm it is important that the initial assessment of the child's circumstances following a referral is conducted in accordance with the statutory guidance.[1]

[1] Working Together (2006) Chapter 5.

7.10 Where a referral is received a decision should be taken about what response is required within one working day of receiving a referral or new information being provided about an open case[1]. Parents' permission should be sought before discussing a referral about them with other agencies[2], unless permission-seeking may itself place a child at risk of significant harm. Initially the local authority should normally expect to seek the co-operation of those persons having parental responsibility, but applications may be made to the court for a child assessment order, or an emergency protection order if the child requires immediate protection. Within 7 working days of receiving a referral the local authority should carry out a carefully planned initial assessment by a qualified social worker to establish[3]:

(a)   What are the developmental needs of the child?
(b)   Whether the parents are able to respond appropriately to the child's identified needs? Is the child being adequately safeguarded from significant harm, and are the parents able to promote the child's health and development?
(c)   What impact are family functioning and history, the wider family and environmental factors having on the parents' capacity to respond to their child's needs and the child's developmental progress?
(d)   Whether action is required to safeguard and promote the welfare of the child?

[1]   Working Together (2006) para 5.31.
[2]   Working Together (2006) para 5.34.
[3]   Working Together (2006) para 5.38.

7.11 Initial assessment of the child's circumstances subsequent to the receipt by the local authority of a referral should adhere to the following process[1]:

(a)   Seeing and speaking to the child (according to age and understanding) and family members as appropriate.
(b)   Drawing together and analysing available information from a range of sources (including existing records).
(c)   Involving and obtaining relevant information from professionals and others in contact with the child and family.

The child should be seen within a timescale commensurate with the nature of the concerns expressed at the time of the referral and care should be taken to communicate with the child in a way which facilitates the provision of accurate and complete information.[2] Following assessment the authority may decide to initiate court proceedings under Pt IV. With that in mind it is important to ensure that the enquiries are conducted in such a way as to provide evidence acceptable in proceedings under s 31 of the Act.

[1]   Working Together (2006) para 5.39.
[2]   Working Together (2006) para 5.41.

7.12 The aim of the initial assessment is to establish in respect of the child who is the subject of the referral whether:

(a)   The child is 'in need' for the purposes of s 17.
(b)   There is reasonable cause to suspect that the child is suffering, or is at risk of suffering, significant harm for the purposes of s 47.

The statutory guidance recognises that an initial referral may, following initial assessment, require responses under different sections of the CA 1989 depending on the findings of that assessment. Where there are no substantiated concerns the family may still benefit from support and practical help to promote a child's health and development[1]. Accordingly, the local authority should still consider whether or not to proceed with a 'core assessment', so as to undertake an in-depth assessment of the developmental needs of the child and what services may be required. Likewise, where the outcome of the initial assessment points to the child being at risk of immediate significant harm the local authority should consider whether any action is necessary for the child's immediate protection under Pt V of the Act.[2]

1   Working Together (2006) para 5.44.
2   Working Together (2006) para 5.49.

(c) Aims of a s 47 enquiry

7.13 Where a s 47 enquiry is triggered by satisfaction of the criteria laid down by s 47(1) or s 47(2) that enquiry must be directed towards the following aims:[1]

(a)   Establishing whether the local authority should make any application to the court, or exercise any of its powers under the Act or s 11 of the Crime and Disorder Act 1998 (child safety orders) with respect to the child.[2]
(b)   Whether, in the case of a child in respect of whom an emergency protection order has been made and who is not in accommodation provided by or on behalf of the local authority, it would be in the child's best interests (whilst an emergency protection order remains in force) for him to be in such accommodation.
(c)   Whether, in the case of a child who has been taken into police protection, it would be in the child's best interests for the local authority to ask for an application to be made under s 46(7) of the Act for an emergency protection order.

1   CA 1989, s 47(3).
2   Section 11 provides for local authorities to apply for a child safety order, which is aimed at children under ten years old and is designed to prevent them becoming involved in criminal or anti-social behaviour. See the Crime and Disorder Act Guidance Document: Child Safety Orders (June 2000) Home Office.

7.14 The fact that a child is 'looked after' by the local authority does not prevent a s 47 enquiry being carried out where the criteria for such an enquiry is met. Three investigative areas that should be pursued where there is concern that a member of staff may be involved in the harm suffered or likely to be suffered by the child are as follows:[1]

(a)   The inter-departmental and inter-agency child protection investigation to an initial child protection case conference. This should not be confused with any disciplinary action taken in relation to staff.
(b)   The police investigation into whether criminal conduct is involved.
(c)   The employer's disciplinary procedure to determine whether the member of staff is guilty of misconduct.

1   *Gogay v Hertfordshire County Council* [2001] 1 FLR 280 per Hale LJ.

(d) The s 47 enquiry process

7.15 The local authority's s 47 enquiry should be carried out by means of undertaking a 'core assessment' utilising the Framework for the Assessment of Children in Need and their Families[1] in order to provide sound evidence on which to base the often difficult professional judgments about whether to intervene to safeguard a child and promote his welfare and, if so, how best to do so and with what intended outcomes.[2] The Guidance recommends that a Social Services Department has a maximum of 35 working days to complete this assessment.[3]

1   DOH (2000) and covered in detail below. See also Working Together (2006) para 5.48.
2   Working Together (2006) para 5.48.
3   The Assessment Framework, para 3.11.

7.16 Throughout the s 47 enquiry, a Social Services Department should consider whether statutory intervention is required. Where there is considered to be a risk to the life of a child or a likelihood of serious immediate harm, emergency action can take place following an immediate strategy discussion between police, social services and other agencies as appropriate. Where a single agency has to act immediately to protect a child, a strategy discussion should take place as soon as possible after such action has been taken.

7.17 Section 47 of the Act stipulates a number of obligations which the local authority must meet during the course of its enquiries.

Access to the child

In making enquiries the local authority must take such steps as are reasonably practicable to obtain access to the child or to ensure that access to him is obtained on their behalf by a person authorised by them for the purpose unless they are satisfied that they already have enough information to decide what action to take.[1] If the authority are refused access to the child or are denied information as to his whereabouts, the authority should apply for an emergency protection order, a child assessment order, a care order or a supervision order, unless satisfied that his welfare can be safeguarded without such an order.[2]

Consultation with education authority

Where, as a result of its enquiries, the local authority considers that there are matters in connection with the child's education that should be investigated the local authority is obliged to consult with the relevant local education authority.[3]

Child's wishes and feelings

Pursuant to the Children Act 2004, ss 53, 47 of the Act has been amended to make it a statutory obligation upon the local authority to ascertain the wishes and feelings of the child in relation to the action to be taken in respect of him and to give due consideration, having regard to his age and understanding, to such wishes and feelings.[4] As noted above, when ascertaining the wishes and feelings of the child concerned care should be taken to communicate with the child in a way which facilitates the provision of accurate and complete information which is capable of constituting acceptable evidence should proceedings under s 31 be required.[5] Accordingly, whilst the process of ascertaining the wishes and feelings of the child in respect of the course of action the local authority intends to pursue may not constitute a formal interview of the child concerning its circumstances, regard should be had nonetheless to the applicable guidance regulating the interview of children.[6] If the child is unable to take part in an interview because of age or understanding, alternative means of understanding the child's wishes or feelings should be used, including observation where children are very young or where they have communication impairments.[7]

Third party co-operation

Where enquiries under s 47 are being conducted it is the duty of any local authority, any local education authority, any local housing authority, any health authority, special health authority, primary care trust, NHS trust or NHS foundation trust, and any person authorised by the Secretary of State to assist the local authority with its enquiries (in particular by the provision of information and advice) if called upon by the local authority to do so save where it would be unreasonable in all the circumstances of the case.[8]

Consultation with other local authorities

Where a local authority is conducting enquiries under s 47 in respect of a child who it appears to the local authority is ordinarily resident in the area of another local authority, the local authority making the enquiries is under a duty to consult the other local authority, which authority may undertake the enquiries in its place.[9]

[1]   CA 1989, s 47(4).
[2]   CA 1989, s 47(6).
[3]   CA 1989, s 47(5).
[4]   CA 1989, s 47(5A) as amended by the Children Act 2004, s 53.
[5]   Working Together (2006) para 5.41.
[6]   Communicating with Children (2002) TSO: Department of Health (this provides guidance for interviewing children about adverse experiences and can be used as a basis for treatment) and Achieving Best Evidence in Criminal Proceedings: Guidance for Vulnerable or Intimidated Witnesses, including Children (2002) TSO (guidance published by the Department of Health, the Home Office and the Department for Education and Employment under s 7 of the Local Authority Social Services Act 1970). See also Dr David Jones Communicating with Vulnerable Children: A Guide for Practitioners (2003) Department of Health.
[7]   Working Together (2006) para 5.63.
[8]   CA 1989, s 47(9), (10) and (11).
[9]   CA 1989, s 47(12).

7.18 In addition to the statutory obligations governing the conduct of the s 47 enquiry, the statutory guidance provides further advice on the manner in which such an enquiry is to be appropriately conducted.[1] The enquiry should be led by a qualified and experienced social worker. It should cover all relevant dimensions in the Assessment Framework before its completion. Those making enquiries about a child should always be alert to the potential needs and safety of any siblings or other children in the household of the child in question. In addition, enquiries may also need to cover children in other households with whom an alleged offender may have had contact.[2]

1   Working Together (2006) paras 5.60 ff.
2   Working Together (2006) para 5.60.

7.19 In contrast to compulsory intervention by way of an emergency protection order or an interim care order, s 47 enquiries generally do not constitute an infringement of rights under art 8 of the European Convention.[1] However, the parents' rights under art 8 afford procedural safeguards against inappropriate interference with the substantive rights protected by that article.[2] In the circumstances, in accordance with their art 8 rights it is essential that parents are placed in a position in respect of the investigation and assessment process that allows them access to the information relied on by the local authority when taking decisions relevant to the care of their child and to permit their full participation in that process.[3] Enquiries (and in all other circumstances) should be undertaken in partnership with all family members who are being investigated or assessed where possible. Where a child is alleged to have been harmed or be likely to be harmed the same approach should be adopted wherever possible, although the safety of the child should not be compromised.[4] Where a parent is disabled, it may be necessary to provide help with communication to enable the parent to express him/herself to the best of his or her.[5]

1   *Gogay v Hertfordshire County Council* [2001] 1 FLR 280.
2   *R (on the application of P) v Secretary of State for the Home Department; R (on the application of Q) v Secretary of State for the Home Department* [2001] EWCA Civ 1151, [2001] 2 FLR 1122.
3   *Venema v Netherlands* [2003] 1 FLR 552, ECtHR applying *P, C and S v United Kingdom* [2002] 2 FLR 631, ECtHR. See also *Re L (Care Assessment)* [2002] EWHC 1379 (Fam), [2002] 2 FLR 730 and *Mantovenellli v France (Application 21497/93)*(1993) 24 EHRR 370, ECtHR.
4   Working Together (2006) paras 5.45 and 5.63.
5   Working Together (2006) para 5.63.

7.20 Section 47 enquiries should always be carried out in such a way as to minimise distress to the child, and to ensure that families are treated sensitively and with respect. Social workers should explain the purpose and outcome of s 47 enquiries to the parents and child (having regard to age and understanding) and be prepared to answer questions openly, unless to do so would affect the safety and welfare of the child. It is particularly helpful for families if social workers provide written information about the purpose, process and potential outcomes of s 47 enquiries. The information should be both general and specific to the particular circumstances under enquiry. It should include information about how advice, advocacy and support may be obtained from independent sources.[1] In short, families need to know the nature and extent of the local authority's concerns, the actions the family need to take to address those concerns, the assistance that will provided to help the family do so, the timescale within which the concerns must be addressed, the criteria for successfully addressing the concerns and the consequences of failing to do so.

1   Working Together (2006) para 5.69.

7.21 Under s 47(8), where the local authority concludes that, as a result of its enquiries, it should take action to safeguard and promote the child's welfare it is obligated to take that action in so far as it within its power to do so and is reasonably practicable. The outcome of the enquiries may be that the original concerns are not substantiated and no further action is necessary. As noted above, it may nonetheless be appropriate to continue the 'core assessment' to assist the process of deciding what services the child and family require. However, where at the conclusion of its enquiries the local authority decides not to apply for an emergency protection order, a care order a child assessment order or a supervision order, it must consider whether it would be appropriate to review the case at a later date and, if so, set a date for that review.[1]

1   CA 1989, s 47(7).

7.22 Where concerns have been substantiated and the child is judged to be at continuing risk of significant harm, an initial child protection conference must be held. The timing of the conference will depend on the urgency of the case but should always take place within 15 days of the strategy discussion at which s 47 enquiries were instigated. The Social Services Department and other agencies are required to prepare reports for the initial child protection conference[1]. The information gathering for the purposes of the core assessment informs the report to the conference. The parents (including absent parents) should be invited to attend the conference and helped to participate fully. The social worker should give parents information about local advice and advocacy agencies, and explain that they may bring an advocate, friend or supporter. The child, subject to consideration about age and understanding, should be invited to attend and to bring an advocate, friend or supporter if he wishes. Where the child does not want to attend or his attendance is not appropriate, the social worker should ascertain his wishes and feelings and make these known to the conference.[2] The involvement of family members should be planned carefully. Exceptionally, it may be necessary to exclude one or more family members from a conference, in whole or in part. If the parents are excluded, or are unable or unwilling to attend a child protection conference, they should be enabled to communicate their views to the conference by another means.[3]

1   Working Together (2006) para 5.89.
2   Working Together (2006) para 5.84.
3   Working Together (2006) paras 5.85–5.86.

7.23 The conference is required to take a decision whether the child is at continuing risk of significant harm and if so formulate an outline child protection plan and determine the category of abuse under which the child's name should be registered on the child protection register.[1] The child protection plan should include the name of a key worker from the Social Services Department and clarify whether, in addition to the core assessment, any specialist assessments of the child and family are required. The child protection plan should identify the professionals and agencies who should work together with the family, the core group, who must meet within ten days of the child protection conference to flesh out the child protection plan and decide what steps need to be taken and by whom and within what timescales to complete the core assessment and provide planned services.[2]

[1]   Working Together (2006) para 5.80 and paras 5.93–5.100.
[2]   Working Together (2006) paras 5.107 ff.

(e) *Strategy discussion*

7.24 Whenever the local authority concludes that there is reasonable cause to suspect that a child is suffering, or is likely to suffer, significant harm, it should convene a strategy discussion involving children's services and the police, and other agencies as appropriate, in particular any referring agency.[1] The primary tasks of the strategy meeting are to:

(a)   Share available information.
(b)   Agree the conduct and timing of any criminal enquiry.
(c)   Agree what action is required immediately to safeguard and promote the welfare of the child, and/or provide interim services and support. If the child is in hospital, decisions should also be made about how to secure the safe discharge of the child.
(d)   Determine what information from the strategy discussion will be shared with the family, unless such information sharing may place a child at increased risk of significant harm or jeopardise police enquiries into any alleged offence(s).[2]
(e)   Determine if legal action is required.[3]

Where a strategy discussion is held prior to the commencement of a s 47 investigation, that discussion should also decide whether enquiries under s 47 of the CA 1989 should be initiated and plan how the s 47 enquiry should be undertaken (if one is to be initiated), including the need for medical treatment, and who will carry out what actions, by when and for what purpose.

[1]   Working Together (2006) para 5.54.
[2]   See also The Challenge of Partnership in Child Protection: Practice Guide (HMSO, 1995) and Information Sharing: Practitioner Guide (DfES).
[3]   Working Together (2006) para 5.5.

3. Section 37

(a) *Criteria for making the order*

7.25 In addition to the duties imposed upon the local authority by ss 17 and 47, the need for an enquiry into the child's circumstances[1] may arise as a result of an initiative by the court which is considering the welfare of the child in other family proceedings. Where:

(a)   the proceedings are 'family proceedings' for the purposes of s 8(3) of the Act; and
(b)   a question has arisen in respect of the welfare of the child whose circumstances are to be investigated; and

(c)   it appears to the court that it might be appropriate for a care or supervision order to be made with respect to a child;

the court may direct a local authority to investigate the child's circumstances.[2] It is plain on the face of the Act that the court should not make a s 37 direction unless it appears to the court that it might be appropriate to make a public law order[3] and the court should look to pursue alternative options before deciding that an order under s 37 is the appropriate order to make.[4] The court should not fetter the discretion of the authority conducting the investigation.[5]

[1]   The phrase 'child's circumstances' is to be construed widely to include any situation which might have a bearing on the question of whether the child who is the subject of the investigation is likely to suffer significant harm at a point in the future: *Re H (A Minor)(Section 37 Direction)* [1993] 2 FLR 541.
[2]   CA 1989, s 37(1).
[3]   *Re L (Section 37 Direction)* [1999] 1 FLR 984, CA.
[4]   *Re F (Family Proceedings: Section 37 Investigation)* [2005] EWHC 2935 (Fam), [2006] 1 FLR 1122.
[5]   *Re M (A Minor) (Official Solicitor: Role)* [1998] 3 FCR 315.

7.26 The court may make an interim care or supervision order pending the completion of the s 37 investigation.[1] This is the only circumstance in which the court may make such an order without an application by the local authority. The court must still be satisfied as to the criteria in s 38.[2] Where the circumstances truly justify it s 37 of the Act can be utilised by the court in cases of intractable dispute over contact to remove children under an interim care order from a primary carer who is denying contact to the absent parent. However, Wall J was careful to point out in *Re M* that the use of s 37 in such cases came with a strong 'health warning' and was not to be considered as a panacea.[3]

[1]   CA 1989, s 38(1)(b).
[2]   CA 1989, s 38(2) and see below Chapter 8.
[3]   *Re M (Intractable Contact Dispute: Interim Care Order)* [2003] EWHC 1024 (Fam), [2003] 2 FLR 636.

(b) Procedure upon the granting of a s 37 order

7.27 The procedure to be followed on the making of a direction pursuant to s 37(1) is set out in the FPR 1991, r 4.26 (and where the direction is made in the family proceedings court, in the FPC(CA 1989)R 1991, r 27). Further guidance is to be found in the CAAC's Best Practice Guidance on Section 37(1) Directions.[1]

[1]   CAAC Annual Report 1992/93, Annex 1, p 40. The guidance is also set out in the CAAC Handbook of Best Practice in Children Act Cases (1997) CAAC.

7.28 Upon the court making a direction pursuant to s 37(1) the direction must be recorded in writing and the case adjourned to a fixed date.[1] The court must fix a date for the filing of the s 37 report by the local authority, which date should allow the local authority 36 days to complete the report[2]. The direction must then be served on the local authority together with the documentary evidence in the proceedings within 24 hours of the order being made.[3] It is important that the local authority is given a clear idea of why the court has made the s 37 direction. A transcript or very full note of the court's reasons should be provided to the local authority.[4]

[1] FPR 1991, r 4.26(2); FPC(CA 1989)R, r 27(2), Appendix G Protocol for the Judicial Case Management of Public Law Children Act Cases [2003] 2 FLR 719, para 2.
[2] Appendix G Protocol for the Judicial Case Management of Public Law Children Act Cases [2003] 2 FLR 719, para 6.
[3] FPR 1991, r 4.26(3); FPC(CA 1989)R 1991, r 27(3), Appendix G Protocol for the Judicial Case Management of Public Law Children Act Cases [2003] 2 FLR 719, para 4.
[4] *Re M (Intractable Contact Dispute: Interim Care Order)* [2003] EWHC 1024 (Fam), [2003] 2 FLR 636.

7.29 When the court has directed the local authority pursuant to s 37(1) to investigate, on the basis that it is considering making an interim care or supervision order, the proceedings become 'specified' for the purposes of s 41.[1] In specified proceedings the court will appoint a children's guardian unless it is satisfied that it is not necessary to do so in order to safeguard the child's interests.[2] The appointment of a children's guardian will not be automatic. The questions that should be considered by the court in deciding whether to appoint a children's guardian upon making a s 37 direction:

(i)   Is the court actually making an interim care order, or merely considering whether to do so?
(ii)   If only an interim order was being considered, what factors required the appointment to be made?
(iii) Would there be sufficient time for the guardian to be informed of the issues and play a useful role?
(iv)   Is there any specific role to be played by the guardian in the s 37 investigation itself?
(v)   If there was no appointment, would the child's interests be properly safeguarded in the interim and during the course of the investigation?
(vi)   Does the child have his or her own solicitor?[3]

If the case required an urgent child protection investigation, the guardian might not be able to play any useful role at that stage, unless the court had actually made an interim care order which involved a change of carer. If the case involved a longer assessment, the court should consider precisely what the role of a guardian would be and whether the work would be better done by a court welfare officer. If there was no public law element the latter would provide continuity.[4] Where the local authority produces a report setting out a decision not to apply for a care or supervision order there is no longer any basis for the appointment of the children's guardian.[5]

[1] CA 1989, s 41(6)(b).
[2] CA 1989, s 41(1).
[3] Children should have their own representation in private law proceedings where all contact has ceased and the issue of contact has become an intractable one: *Re M (Intractable Contact Dispute: Interim Care Order)* [2003] EWHC 1024 (Fam), [2003] 2 FLR 636.
[4] *Re CE (A Minor)(Section 37 Direction)* [1995] 1 FLR 26.
[5] *Re S (Contact: Grandparents)* [1996] 1 FLR 158.

(c) Local authority duty

7.30 In responding to a direction pursuant to s 37, the local authority directed to carry out the assessment must:

(a)   Consult with the family, the child and all relevant agencies.[1]
(b)   Consider whether to apply for a care or supervision order.[2]
(c)   Consider whether to provide services or assistance for the child or his family.[3]
(d)   Consider whether to take any other action with respect to the child.[4]

Where the local authority decides not to apply for an care order or a supervision order it must, within 8 weeks of the date of the s 37 direction, inform the court in writing of its reasons, any services or assistance which it is providing or intends to provide and any other action it is taking or intends to take in respect of the child.[5] Where the local authority decides not to apply for a care order or a supervision it is wrong to join the local authority to the proceedings in which the s 37 direction was made.[6] The court has no power to order the authority to take proceedings[7] but can make an interim care order when making a direction under s 37.[8]

---

[1]   Appendix G Protocol for the Judicial Case Management of Public Law Children Act Cases [2003] 2 FLR 719 at para 7. The Protocol has now been replaced by the Public Law Outline, which does not reproduce the contents of Appendix G. Full consultation with the family, the child and the relevant agencies remains however a central tenet of good practice in responding to a direction pursuant to s 37.
[2]   CA 1989, s 37(2)(a).
[3]   CA 1989, s 37(2)(b).
[4]   CA 1989, s 37(2)(c).
[5]   CA 1989, s 37(3) and (4).
[6]   *F v Cambridgeshire County Council* [1995] 1 FLR 516.
[7]   CA 1989, s 37(2).
[8]   CA 1989, s 38(1)(b) and see *Nottinghamshire Councy Council v P* [1994] Fam 18, [1993] 2 FLR 134, [1993] 1 WLR 637, [1993] 3 All ER 815, CA and the critique of Wall J in 'The Courts and Child Protection – the challenge of hybrid cases' [1997] CFLQ 345 at 348–350.

4. The assessment process

(a) The assessment framework

7.31 As noted above, the suggested[1] tool by which the local authority fulfils its duty to enquire into a child circumstances is the 'Framework for the Assessment of Children in Need and their Families.'[2] The Government issued the Framework for the Assessment of Children in Need and their Families for the purpose of assessments carried out under ss 17, 37 and 47. The three areas to be covered in an assessment are the child's developmental needs, parenting capacity, and family and environmental factors. These are represented diagrammatically by the 'Assessment Framework' triangle shown in the Diagram.

---

[1]   Working Together to Safeguard Children (2006) paras 5.37 and 5.46.
[2]   DOH 2000.

Health   Basic Care

Education

Emotional &
Behavioural
Development

CHILD'S DEVELOPMENTAL NEEDS   PARENTING CAPACITY

Ensuring
Safety

Identity

Emotional
Warmth

CHILD
Safeguarding
and promoting
welfare

Family
& Social
Relationships

Stimulation

Social
Presentation

Guidance
& Boundaries

Selfcare Skills   **FAMILY & ENVIRONMENTAL FACTORS**   Stability

Community Resources   Family's Social Integration   Income   Employment   Housing   Wider Family   Family History & Functioning

7.32 The purpose of the Framework for Assessment is to provide a systematic way of recording, analysing and understanding what is happening to a child within its family and wider community with a view to professional judgments being made as to what action, if any, the local authority needs to take to safeguard and promote that child's welfare. The Framework should ensure that planning for the child takes place on the basis of evidence-based knowledge.[1]

[1]   DOH 2000.

(b) Cardinal principles

7.33 The approach to assessment contained in the Framework is underpinned by a series of cardinal principles which should be observed during the assessment process and evident in the final assessment produced by the local authority.

CHILD-CENTRED APPROACH

7.34 All effective practice is child centred.[1] However, an alarming number of assessments continue to concentrate almost exclusively on adult issues within the pre-proceedings phase, setting a pattern for subsequent proceedings if needed and resulting in the interests of children being sidelined or otherwise obscured. The child should be seen and kept in focus throughout the assessment. This requirement is now enhanced by the addition of s 47(5A) requiring the child's wishes and feelings to be ascertained and given due consideration having regard to the child's age and understanding.[2]

[1]   Goldthorpe and Munro, Child Law Handbook, Law Society, 2005.
[2]   Framework for Assessment, para 1.34.

CHILD DEVELOPMENT

7.35 Beyond the bald use of the phrase 'commensurate with the needs of the child', it is often difficult to identify explicitly the manner in which plans and decisions have considered and taken account of the developmental stage and needs of the child concerned. In particular, it is common for there to be no readily ascertainable distinction in the decision-making process or planning for siblings of widely differing ages and developmental needs. The Framework notes that a thorough understanding of child development is critical to work with children and their families.[1] Understanding of children's development, and in particular the timescales for the progress of such development is essential to achieving comprehensive assessment, identification of issues, service provision and the avoidance of delay. Those working with children should be informed by a developmental perspective which recognises that, as children grow, they continue to develop their skills and abilities. Plans and interventions to safeguard and promote the child's welfare should be based on a clear assessment of the child's developmental progress and the difficulties a child may be experiencing. Planned action should also be timely and appropriate for the child's age and stage of development."[2]

[1]   Framework for Assessment, para 1.36.
[2]   Working Together (2006) para 5.4.

ECOLOGICAL APPROACH

7.36 The Framework makes clear that an understanding of the child and his circumstances must be located within the context of the child's family, his community and the culture in which he is growing up. This understanding is vital if the influence of environmental factors on the care given to the child is to be properly understood.[1] In particular, the interaction between the three domains of the Framework for Assessment and their effect on each other must be carefully analysed.[2]

[1]   Framework for Assessment, para 1.39.
[2]   Framework for Assessment, para 1.41.

EQUALITY OF OPPORTUNITY

7.37 Many cases of poor outcomes are rooted in a failure to address sufficiently or at all issues of diversity, or in addressing such issues with entirely inappropriate resources. Particular examples are a failure to identify and take into account learning disabilities in parents and children and a failure to consider at an early stage and, on a proactive basis, the placement needs of minority ethnic children. The Framework highlights the need to consider all children and parents as individuals and to work sensitively and knowledgably with issues of diversity.[1] Issues of diversity should be identified and dealt with on the basis of practicality and understanding[2] with descriptive information being supported by substantive detail.[3]

[1]   Framework for Assessment, paras 1.42–1.43.
[2]   Goldthorpe and Munro, Child Law Handbook, Law Society, 2005.

[3] Brophy J, Jhutti Johal and Owen (2003) *Significant Harm: Child Protection Litigation in a Uni-Cultural Context*, DCA Research Series 1/03.

WORKING WITH CHILDREN AND FAMILIES

7.38 The Framework for Assessment highlights that, in the process of determining what is happening to the child, it is critical to develop a co-operative working relationship with families so that parents and caregivers feel respected and informed, that staff are being open and honest with them and that they in turn can be confident in providing vital information about the child, themselves and their circumstances.[1]

[1] Framework for Assessment, para 1.44.

7.39 It is particularly important that families know the nature and extent of the local authority's concerns, the actions the family need to take to address those concerns, the assistance that will be provided to help the family do so, the timescale within which the concerns must be addressed, the criteria for successfully addressing the concerns and the consequences of failing to do so. It is important to note that the desirability of working in partnership with families should not override the importance of ensuring the child's safety.[1] In addition, the following elements are crucial to developing a positive and cooperative working relationship:

(a) The practical and consistent application of inclusive practice to give effect to the principle of partnership with families.

(b) Facilitating maximum involvement by families and children at all stages of the planning and decision making process.

(c) Working on the basis of openness, honesty, realism and reliability.

(d) When carrying out assessments, making clear to families and to children the nature and purpose of the assessment, the criteria for success and for failure, what will be expected from the family during the assessment, what the timetable for the assessment is, where will it take place, how will the family get to the assessment and who will pay for this. Who will let the family know what they are doing wrong and when will they be told.[2]

(e) Obtaining the consent of children, young people and their parents when sharing information unless to do so would place the child at risk of significant harm.

(f) Making documents upon which decisions are based available to parents in a timely manner to allow full consideration of the same.

(g) Holding open meetings with parents that have a written agenda in advance and full, balanced, clear and accurate notes or minutes.

(h) Making decisions by agreement, whenever possible, unless to do so would place the child at risk of significant harm.

(i) Where the exclusion of a parent is required that exclusion is based on sound reasons and alternative methods for securing their involvement is explored.

[1] Framework for Assessment, para 3.35.
[2] The Victoria Climbié Report (Cm 5730) (2003) Recommendation 25, para 4.152.

7.40 The need to work in partnership with families during the assessment process is now leant extra weight by the developing jurisprudence following the coming into force of the Human Rights Act 1998. In particular, the courts have made clear that the protection provided by the ECHR, and in particular arts 6 and 8 of the Convention, apply not only to the judicial element of proceedings under Pt IV of the Act but also to the process of assessment and intervention under Pt III.[1] In the circumstances, there is now a rights based imperative for adopting the principles of good practice for working in partnership with families listed in para 7.39.

[1]   *Venema v Netherlands* [2003] 1 FLR 552, ECtHR applying *P, C and S v United Kingdom* [2002] 2 FLR 631, ECtHR. See also *Re L (Care Assessment)* [2002] EWHC 1379 (Fam), [2002] 2 FLR 730 and *Mantovenelli v France (Application No. 21497/93)*(1993) 24 EHRR 370, ECtHR.

STRENGTHS AS WELL AS WEAKNESSES

7.41 Whilst social workers should not suspend their critical professional judgement and adopt a 'rule of optimism'[1] it important that a realistic and informed appraisal is made of the strengths and resources of the family as well as identifying the deficits which may require remedial action to be taken.[2]

[1]   Dingwall et al (1983).
[2]   Framework for Assessment, para 1.49.

INTER-AGENCY APPROACH

7.42 The local authority is not the only agency which is the assessor of the child's circumstances and the provider of services consequent upon the outcome of that assessment. The Framework highlights the fact that from birth, all children will become involved with a variety of different agencies, particularly concerning health care, day care and educational development. Accordingly, complete and comprehensive assessment should be based on an inter-agency, now usually termed multi-agency, approach.[1] Ideally, such an approach should permit of access to, and early instruction of, experts offering more specialist advice in areas such as chronic substance abuse, acute mental health issues in children, issues arising from learning disability and to advise on evidential requirements in cases of sudden unexpected death in infancy, unusual head injuries or cases of suspected fabricated illness.[2]

[1]   Framework for Assessment, para 1.50.
[2]   HHJ Newton & HHJ 'Hamilton Early Involvement of Experts' [2006] Family Law 678.

CONTINUING PROCESS

7.43 One of the key difficulties identified in the use of the 'Orange Book' assessment model[1] which preceded the 2000 Framework for Assessment was that the assessment was regarded as an event rather than a process.[2] A key problem that is still noted with assessments is a tendency to assess the incident giving rise to the referral rather than the situation giving rise to the incident, leading to a reactive events-based approach to intervention and resulting in events-based planning as opposed to situation-based planning. Relevant support for the family is thus often delayed until the 'completion' of the assessment process. The Framework for Assessment stipulates that assessment should be an iterative process which should continue throughout the period of intervention[3] in order to ensure that the needs of the child continue to be identified and met appropriately.

[1]   Protecting Children; A Guide for Social Workers Undertaking a Comprehensive Assessment (1988).
[2]   Framework for Assessment, p xii.
[3]   Framework for Assessment, paras 1.53–1.54.

CONCURRENT ACTION

7.44 The duty to both safeguard and promote the child's welfare continues throughout the assessment process and services may be provided whilst the assessment is being carried out.[1] The longer a family is without the support anticipated by Sch 2 with a view to preventing the need for proceedings, the greater the likelihood of protective intervention being required and of increasing pressure from the perspective of the child's developmental timescale[2]. The process of assessment should accordingly be therapeutic in itself. This does not preclude taking timely action either to provide immediate services or to take steps to protect a child who is suffering or is likely to suffer significant harm. Action and services should be provided according to the needs of the child and family, in parallel with assessment where necessary, and not await completion of the assessment.[3]

[1]   Framework for Assessment, para 1.27.
[2]   Goldthorpe with Munro, Child Law Handbook (2005) Law Society.
[3]   Framework for Assessment, para 1.56.

EVIDENCE-BASED KNOWLEDGE

7.45 A combination of evidence based practice grounded in knowledge with finely balanced professional judgement is the foundation for effective practice with children and families. The Framework for Assessment requires that practice in relation to the assessment of the child's situation be evidence based. To this end, the person carrying out the assessment can be expected to:

(a)   Use knowledge critically from research and practice about the needs of children and families and the outcomes of services and interventions to inform assessment and planning.
(b)   Record and update information systematically, distinguishing sources of information.
(c)   Learn from the views of children and families.
(d)   Evaluate continuously whether the intervention is effective in responding to the needs of an individual child and family and modifying their intervention accordingly.

(e)   Evaluate rigorously the information, processes and outcomes from practitioner's own intentions to develop 'practice wisdom.'[1]

¹   Framework for Assessment, para 1.58.

7.46 Proper and rigorous evidential practice during the assessment process is key to ensuring effective practice both under Pt III (by ensuring a proper and accurate foundation on which evidence-based decisions can be effectively and fairly made) and Pt IV (by ensuring the court has a proper foundation on which to base decisions as to threshold and outcome). From the outset of the assessment, the Local Authority, and in particular frontline social workers should have regard to the need to secure cogent, primary evidence upon which to make evidence-based decisions and to support findings if necessary.

1. Judicial guidance

7.47 Where there are long-running concerns about the care of children, judicial guidance has suggested the following in respect of the manner in which the local authority should conduct its enquiries, assessment and intervention:[1]

(a)   Every social work file should have as the top document a running chronology of significant events which was kept up-to-date as events unfolded; it would then be relatively straightforward to identify serious and deep rooted problems rather than the circumstances triggering the instant referral.

(b)   Lack of parental co-operation was never a reason to close a file or remove a child from a protection register; on the contrary it was a reason to investigate in greater depth.

(c)   Referrals by professionals such as health visitors and teachers should be given great weight and investigated thoroughly; they were a potential source of valuable information.

(d)   Line managers and those with power of decision making should never make a judgement to take no action without having full knowledge of the file and consulting those professionals who knew the family.

(e)   Children who were part of a sibling group should not be considered in isolation but in the context of family history; where previous children had been brought to the attention of social services the details of their cases should be considered in assessing what had gone wrong historically and whether appropriate change had been effected.

(f)   In order to avoid drift, work with families had to be time limited so that an effective timetable could be laid down within which changes needed to be achieved.

¹   *Re E (Care Proceedings: Social Work Practice)* [2000] 2 FCR 297, [2000] 2 FLR 254.

2. Interviewing children

7.48 In many cases where there is an allegation of significant harm to a child, there will be a joint investigation conducted by the police and social services department, since there may be questions involving both the civil and criminal law. If he is old enough, it is probable that the child will be interviewed jointly by a police officer and social worker in accordance with the guidance in 'Achieving Best Evidence in Criminal Proceedings: Guidance for Vulnerable or Intimidated Witnesses, including Children'.[1] This provides guidance for interviewing children about harm they may have suffered, where their evidence may be required for the purpose of criminal proceedings. The standards of procedure and interviewing set out are considered to provide the most reliable evidence. If there is a reasonable prospect that criminal proceedings will follow, it is likely that a video recording of the interview with the child witness will be made.

[1]   (2002) TSO (Issued under Circular HOC 06/2002 the Guidance it replaces the 'Memorandum of Good Practice on Interviewing Children' (1992) Home Office). See also Dr PH Jones, communicating with Vulnerable Children: A Guide for Practitioners (2003) Department of Health.

7.49 A video-recorded interview serves two purposes for criminal proceedings: the gathering of evidence and the examination in chief of a child witness. Most importantly for child protection purposes any relevant information gained during the interview can be used to inform s 47 enquiries. The Guidance sets out a number of considerations which should be taken into account in deciding whether or not to record an interview:

(a)   The needs and circumstances of the child.
(b)   Whether it is likely to maximise the quality of the child's evidence.
(c)   The type and seriousness of the offence.
(d)   The circumstances of the offence.
(e)   The child's state of mind.
(f)   Perceived fears about intimidation and recrimination.
(g)   The purpose and likely value of a video recorded interview.
(h)   The competency, compellability and availability of the child for cross-examination.
(i)   The child's ability and willingness to talk in a formal setting.

7.50 Even if the child's evidence will not be used for the purposes of criminal proceedings, the interviewing methods adopted should be followed where possible, as they provide the best source of information for civil proceedings. *Working Together* provides extensive guidance on discussions with children concerning their circumstances. In particular, the guidance highlights the fact that when children are first approached, the nature and extent of any harm suffered by them may not be clear, nor may it be clear whether a criminal offence has been committed and that, accordingly, it is important that even initial discussions with children are conducted in a way that minimises any distress caused to them and maximises the likelihood that they will provide accurate and complete information. The guidance further makes clear that It is important, wherever possible, to have separate communication with a child, that leading or suggestive communication should always be avoided and that children may need time, and more than one opportunity, to develop sufficient trust to communicate any concerns they may have, especially if they have a communication impairment, learning disabilities, are very young or are experiencing mental health problems.[1]

[1] Working Together (2006) para 5.60.

7.51 Joint interviewing has come to dominate investigation practice in child protection, where the child is old enough to communicate, not least because it provides the most effective evidence. The focus in 'Achieving Best Evidence' is on the criminal procedure and care must be taken that this does not limit the wider investigation of significant harm to children generally. Although *Working Together* gives extensive guidance on protection of the child and emphasises the importance of both the civil and criminal aspects of the investigation, there is a risk that the criminal aspects of child protection will predominate and an investigation should be carried out solely with the criminal standard of proof in mind. This may be heightened by other factors. *Working Together* procedures require the attendance of the police at child protection conferences. When the police are informed of an alleged offence, they may undertake an interview of anyone suspected of a crime in accordance with the Police and Criminal Evidence Act 1984 (a PACE interview), without a social worker being present. Indeed many areas now have guidance on when cases should be referred to the police for them to consider whether to carry out an investigation. In this context, the latest version of *Working Together* contemplates joint enquiry/investigation as the exception not the rule, such an approach being utilised only in circumstances where, for example, the possibility that a child would be threatened or otherwise coerced into silence; a strong likelihood that important evidence would be destroyed; or that the child in question did not wish the parent to be involved at that stage and is competent to take that decision.[1]

[1] Working Together (2006) para 5.65.

7.52 In spite of the importance of proper interviewing techniques it is essential to remember that proof of the tests for taking steps to protect children are not dependent on criminal standards. Local authorities have to be alert to ensure that their enquiries are conducted with the civil standard of proof in mind. In those cases which raise complex questions about whether or how the child has been harmed, an early forensic analysis with the civil tests in mind, undertaken by suitable experts from all necessary disciplines, may be crucial not only to the short-term investigation, but also to the longer term protection of the child through court proceedings.[1] It should be remembered that investigations of fact should have regard also to the wide context of social, emotional, ethical and moral factors.[2]

[1] HHJ Newton & HHJ Hamilton 'Early Involvement of Experts' [2006] Family Law 678.
[2] *A County Council v A Mother* [2005] EWHC 31 (Fam), [2005] 2 FLR 129.

CHILD ASSESSMENT ORDERS

1. Criteria for making the order

7.53 Provided the criteria are satisfied[1], where a local authority considers that it is being prevented from conducting its enquiries in respect of the child in a manner that will establish fully whether further action should be taken by the local authority to safeguard and promote the child's welfare, the local authority may apply for a child assessment order under s 43. The criteria which must be satisfied for the making of a child assessment order are:

(a)   the applicant has reasonable cause to suspect that a child is suffering, or is likely to suffer, significant harm;

(b)   an assessment of the state of the child's health or development, or of the way in which he has been treated, is required to enable the applicant to determine whether or not the child is suffering, or is likely to suffer, significant harm; and

(c)   it is unlikely that such an assessment will be made, or be satisfactory, in the absence of a child assessment order.

[1]   CA 1989, s 43(1).

7.54 Applications for a child assessment order falls under Pt V and are not therefore 'family proceedings' for the purposes of s 8(4). The power of the court is limited to making or not making the order sought (save where the Court considers an emergency protection order is justified[1]). The court is not able to make orders under Pt II or Pt IV. In considering an application for a child assessment order, the child's welfare is paramount[2] and 'no order' principle applies.[3] The 'welfare checklist' set out at s 1(3) is not considered as its application is excluded in relation to child assessment orders.[4] When making the order, the court may specify the terms of the assessment, including the nature and manner of the assessment to be carried out.[5] The child may be kept away from his or her home in accordance with the directions specified in the order, if it is necessary for the purposes of the assessment and for such a period as may be specified in the order.[6] The court may also when making the child assessment order specify the contact arrangements for a child who will be kept away from home[7] during the course of the assessment.[8] In establishing the proper level of contact, the court should be guided by the presumption of reasonable contact between a child in care and his parents established by s 34.[9]

[1]   See para 7.33.
[2]   CA 1989, s 1(1).
[3]   CA 1989, s 1(5).
[4]   CA 1989, s 1(4).
[5]   CA 1989, s 43(7).
[6]   CA 1989, s 43(9).
[7]   Under the grounds set out in s 43(9).
[8]   CA 1989, s 43(10).
[9]   The revised Children Act 1989 Guidance and Regulations, Vol 1, Court Orders (2008) Department for Children, Schools and Families, Chapter 4.

7.55 Child assessment orders should be used sparingly and should be contemplated only where there is serious concern for the child[1]. Before applying for a child assessment order there should have been substantial effort on the part of the local authority to persuade those caring for the child for the need for assessment. An application under s 43 should always be preceded by an investigation under s 47. A proposal to apply for a child assessment order should be considered at a child protection case conference on a multi-disciplinary basis. An order is not appropriate in circumstances where parents are simply reluctant to use the normal child health services.[2]

1   There were 45 applications for child assessment orders in 2006 (Judicial and Court Statistics 2006 (Cm 7273)(2007)).
2   The revised Children Act 1989 Guidance and Regulations, Vol 1, Court Orders (2008) Department for Children, Schools and Families, Chapter 4.

7.56 A child assessment order is designed to be less interventionist than an emergency protection order, an interim care order or an interim supervision order. However, a child assessment order should not be used where the circumstances of the case suggest that a more interventionist order is required.[1] The court may treat an application for a child assessment order as an application for an emergency protection order and should not make a child assessment order it is satisfied that there are grounds for making an emergency protection order and that such an order should be made rather than a child assessment order.[2]

1   The revised Children Act 1989 Guidance and Regulations, Vol 1, Court Orders (2008) Department for Children, Schools and Families, Chapter 4. Child assessments orders are not commonly used (see para 7.62, n 1 below).
2   CA 1989, s 43(3) and (4).

7.57 Where a child is of sufficient understanding to make an informed decision, that child may refuse to submit to a medical or psychiatric or other assessment notwithstanding the making of a child assessment order.[1] A child of sufficient maturity and understanding should be invited to consent to an assessment even though his parents do not agree to an assessment being carried out.[2] Care should be taken not to pressure a child into agreeing to an assessment, even where the child's reluctance to be assessed may be itself the product of coercion from those caring for him.[3]

1   CA 1989, s 43(8) .
2   Hershman & McFarlane, Children Law and Practice, para C[256].
3   Children Act 1989 Guidance and Regulations, Vol 1, Court Orders (1991) Department of Health, para 4.13.

2. Procedure

7.58 The only applicants for a child assessment order are the local authority or a person authorised for the purposes of s 41(13).[1] The applicant must take such steps as are reasonably practicable to ensure that notice of the application is given to the parents of the child, any person who has parental responsibility, any person caring for the child, any person in whose favour a contact order is in force in respect of the child, any person permitted contact with the child pursuant to s 34 and the child himself.[2] Those with parental responsibility, the child and, where there is a care order in force, all those believed to have parental responsibility prior to the making of the care order will be automatic respondents to the application.[3] The rules specify other persons who must be given notice of the application.[4] The application must be made in the family proceedings court unless the application is made as a result of an investigation directed by the court under s 37, in which circumstances the application should be made to the court which directed the investigation, or the application is made where other proceedings are pending, in which case the application should be made to the court where those proceedings are pending.[5]

[1] Namely, persons who are authorised persons under s 31 of the Act. This currently extends only to an officer of the NSPCC.
[2] CA 1989, s 43(11).
[3] FPR 1991, Appendix 3, Column (iii); FPC(CA 1989)R 1991, Sch 2, Column (iv).
[4] FPR 1991, Appendix 3, Column (iv); FPC(CA 1989)R 1991, Sch 2, Column (iv).
[5] Children (Allocation of Proceedings) Order 1991, arts 3(1), (2) and (3).

7.59 Pursuant to s 41(6)(g), an application for a child assessment order is 'specified proceedings' and accordingly, upon an application being made the court must appoint a children's guardian unless the court is satisfied that such an appointment is not necessary to safeguard the child's interests.[1]

[1] CA 1989, s 41(1).

7.60 A child assessment order may be varied or discharged on the application of the local authority or the authorised person upon whose application the child assessment order was made or the child's parents, any person who has parental responsibility, any person caring for the child, any person in whose favour a contact order is in force in respect of the child, any person permitted contact with the child pursuant to s 34 and the child himself.[1] There is a right of appeal against the granting of a child assessment order.

[1] FPR 1991, r 4.2(3); FPC(CA 1989)R 1991, r 2(3).

3. Effect of a child assessment order

7.61 Where a child assessment order has been made under s 43 the person authorised by the order to carry out the assessment may do so according to the terms of the order. The order does not vest parental responsibility in the local authority.[1] Any person who is in a position to produce the child is under a duty to produce him to the person named in the order and to comply with such directions relating to the assessment of the child as may be specified in the order.[2] Where there is a failure to produce the child, immediate enquiries should be made to determine whether there is a satisfactory explanation for the failure. Deliberate failure to comply may constitute grounds for an application for an emergency protection order.[3] The assessment must begin by the date specified in the order, which order shall have effect for a period not exceeding 7 days beginning with the date specified in the order.[4] The duration of the child assessment order is not capable of extension and no further order can be applied for within 6 months of the disposal of the previous application for an order save where the court gives leave.[5]

[1] CA 1989, s 37(7).
[2] CA 1989, s 43(6).

3   The revised Children Act 1989 Guidance and Regulations, Vol 1, Court Orders (2008)
    Department for Children, Schools and Families, Chapter 4 but see *X Council v B*
    (*Emergency Protection Orders*) [2004] EWHC 2015 (Fam), [2005] 1 FLR 341 and *Re X*
    (*Emergency Protection Orders*) [2006] EWHC 510 (Fam), [2006] 2 FLR 701.
4   CA 1989, s 43(5).
5   CA 1989, s 91(15).

7.62 Whether or not to apply for a child assessment order must largely
depend on the evidence available to the applicant and the attitude of the
parents or other person with parental responsibility or caring for the child[1]. If
there is evidence of harm but the local authority is doubtful that it will be able
to assess properly whether further action on its part is required application for
a child assessment order may be appropriate if the criteria for such an order
can be met. Experience to date has shown, however, that given the limited
scope of the order local authorities have been reluctant to use of provisions of
s 43. Even though the period of seven days need not commence on the making
of the order, that time may not be sufficient for an assessment. It is likely to
require the participation of the parents, although court directions can only be
given in relation to the child. The technical requirements of the section make it
difficult to operate and there has been little use of it in practice[2], local
authorities preferring instead to persist with efforts to obtain the co-operation
of those caring for the child.

1   Only 17 child assessment orders were made in 2006 (Judicial and Court Statistics 2006
    (Cm 7273)(2007)).
2   See 'Assessment and the Control of Social Work: an Analysis of Reasons for the Non-Use
    of the Child Assessment Order, Dickens [1993] JSWFL 88.

EMERGENCY PROTECTION ORDERS

1. Introduction

7.63 Under the CA 1989, s 44 the court may make an emergency protection
order which is an order vesting in the applicant parental responsibility for the
child who is the subject of the application additional to that of the parents and
any other person holding parental responsibility[1] and which:

(a)   Allows the applicant to remove the child to accommodation provided
      by the applicant.
(b)   Prevents to the removal of the child from hospital or other place where
      he was accommodated before the order was granted.
(c)   Compels any person who is in a position to do so to comply with a
      request to produce the child to the local applicant.

Section 44 is designed to provide for the immediate removal or retention of a
child in a genuine emergency.[2] The court[3] is empowered to make an
emergency protection order, initially limited to eight days, to ensure the safety
of a child where he is otherwise likely to suffer significant harm. The
provisions are based on the recommendations of the Review of Child Care
Law[4] following widespread criticism of place of safety orders which they
replaced. Guidance on the use of these powers is contained in '*Working
Together to Safeguard Children*'.[5]

1 CA 1989, s 44(4)(c) .
2 For what constitutes a genuine emergency see *X Council v B* (*Emergency Protection Orders*) [2004] EWHC 2015 (Fam), [2005] 1 FLR 341 and *Re X* (*Emergency Protection Orders*) [2006] EWHC 510 (Fam), [2006] 2 FLR 701 and below under Grounds for an emergency protection order.
3 'Court' includes a single justice on a without notice application for an emergency protection order: FPC(CA 1989)R 1991, rr 1(1) and 2(5).
4 (1985) DHSS, Ch 13.
5 Working Together (2006) paras 5.49–5.53.

7.64 When considering an application for an emergency protection order the child's welfare must be the court's paramount consideration and the court should not make an emergency protection order unless to do so would be better than making no order at all.[1] An application for an emergency protection is made under Pt V and therefore falls outside the definition of family proceedings under the Act.[2] There is no requirement to consider the statutory checklist when considering an application for such an order. It follows that it is not open to the court to make other orders under the Act on an application for an emergency protection order. Even if one of the conditions in s 44 applies, the court will not automatically make an emergency protection order.

1 CA 1989, s 1(1) and (5).
2 CA 1989, s 8(4).

7.65 The courts have been increasingly cautious when considering applications for emergency protection orders.[1] This caution has been grounded in the developing jurisprudence arising from the coming into force of the Human Rights Act 1998, and the consequent incorporation into domestic law of the ECHR, and a growing understanding of the detrimental impact caused to a child by the sudden removal from its family. Any consideration of the ambit and use of s 44 must now take place within this context.

1 See *X Council v B* (*Emergency Protection Orders*) [2004] EWHC 2015 (Fam), [2005] 1 FLR 341 and *Re X* (*Emergency Protection Orders*) [2006] EWHC 510 (Fam), [2006] 2 FLR 701.

2. Grounds for an emergency protection order

(a) The grounds

7.66 The court may only make an emergency protection order if the following grounds are satisfied. The grounds for making an order differ depending on the identity of the applicant.[1]

(a) The court may make an emergency protection order upon the application of any applicant if it is satisfied that there is reasonable cause to believe that the child is likely to suffer significant harm if:
  (i) he is not removed to accommodation provided by or on behalf of the applicant; or
  (ii) he does not remain in the place in which he is then being accommodated.[2]

(b) The court may make an emergency protection order on the application of a local authority if it is satisfied that:
- (i) enquiries are being made in respect of the child under s 47 of the Act; and
- (ii) those enquiries are being frustrated by access to the child being unreasonably refused to a person authorised to seek access and the applicant has reasonable cause to believe that access to the child is required as a matter of urgency.[3]

(c) The court may make an emergency protection order on the application of an authorised person[4] if it is satisfied that:
- (i) there is reasonable cause to believe that the child is likely to suffer significant harm;
- (i) enquiries are being made in respect of the child's welfare; and
- (ii) those enquiries are being frustrated by access to the child being unreasonably refused to a person authorised to seek access and the applicant has reasonable cause to believe that access to the child is required as a matter of urgency.[5]

[1] CA 1989, s 44(1).
[2] CA 1989, s 44(1)(a).
[3] CA 1989, s 44(1)(b).
[4] See para 7.75 and the CA 1989, s 44(2).
[5] CA 1989, s 44(1)(c).

(b) Likely to suffer harm

7.67 In cases where the ground relied upon is that the child is likely to suffer significant harm[1], the court has to be satisfied that there is reasonable cause to believe that significant harm is likely to occur. This is a forward-looking test. Evidence of harm which was occurring at the time of the application or has occurred in the past is not sufficient unless it gives cause to believe that harm is likely to occur in the future. Nonetheless, harm need not actually have occurred. 'Likely to suffer' should not be equated with 'on the balance of probabilities' as when looking to the future the court is only able to evaluate an element of chance.[2] In the context of s 31(2)(a) of the Act, the House of Lords has held that the phrase 'likely to suffer harm' is used in the sense of a real possibility, a possibility that cannot sensibly be ignored having regard to the nature and gravity of the feared harm in the particular case.[3]

[1] For a discussion on the definition of 'significant harm' see Chapter 8.
[2] *Newham London Borough Council v AG* [1993] 1 FLR 281.
[3] *Re H (Child Sexual Abuse: Standard of Proof)* [1996] 1 All ER 1, [1996] 1 FLR 80, HL.

(c) Denial of access to the child

7.68 A local authority may apply for an order where they are making statutory enquiries and those statutory enquiries are being frustrated by access to the child being unreasonably refused to a person authorised to seek access and they have reasonable cause to believe that access to the child is required as a matter of urgency.[1] In this respect, it should be remembered that a local authority has a duty to obtain access to a child during its statutory enquiries[2] and is required where such access is frustrated to apply for an emergency protection order or child assessment order, a care order or a supervision order in such circumstances unless satisfied that the child's welfare can be safeguarded without doing so.[3] An authorised person may apply for an order in circumstances where enquires are being made and access is being frustrated where the authorised person also has reasonable cause to suspect that the child is suffering or is likely to suffer significant harm.[4]

1   CA 1989, s 44(1)(b).
2   CA 1989, s 47(4).
3   CA 1989, s 47(6).
4   CA 1989, s 44(1)(c).

7.69 As to whether a refusal to allow the child to be seen is unreasonable, the statutory guidance states:

> 'The hypothesis of the grounds at S 44(1)(b) and (c) is that this combination of factors is evidence of an emergency or the likelihood of an emergency. The court will have to decide whether the refusal of access to the child was unreasonable in the circumstances. It might consider a refusal unreasonable if the person refusing had had explained to him the reason for the enquiries and the request for access, the request itself was reasonable, and he had failed to respond positively in some other suitable way, by arranging for the child to be seen immediately by his GP, for example. Refusal of a request to see a sleeping child in the middle of the night may not be unreasonable, but refusal to allow access at a reasonable time without good reason could well be. The parent who refuses immediate access but offers to take the child to a local clinic the following morning may not be making a reasonable refusal where the risk to the child is believed to be imminent or where previous voluntary arrangements have broken down.'[1]

1   Revised Children Act 1989 Guidance and Regulations, Vol 1, Court Orders (2008) Department for Children, Schools and Families, Chapter 4 but see *Re X (Emergency Protection Orders)* [2006] EWHC 510 (Fam), [2006] 2 FLR 701.

(d) Statutory guidance

7.70 Statutory guidance as to the application of s 44 of the Act is contained in the revised Children Act 1989 Guidance and Regulations, Vol 1, Court Orders[1] and in the revised version of Working Together to Safeguard Children.[2] In relation to the circumstances justifying an application for an emergency protection order, the statutory guidance provides as follows:

(a)   Where there is a risk to the life of a child or a likelihood of serious immediate harm, an agency with statutory child protection powers should act quickly to secure the immediate safety of the child.[3] Decisive action is essential once it appears that circumstances fall within one of the grounds in s 44(1).[4]

(b)   An emergency protection order should not be regarded as a routine response to allegations of child abuse or a routine step in the instigation of care proceedings.[5]

(b)   Where possible, emergency measures should only be taken where a comprehensive inter-agency discussion demonstrates that such measures are justified and planning has been undertaken to minimise their impact.[6]

(c)   In some cases, it may be sufficient to secure a child's safety by a parent taking action to remove an alleged perpetrator, or by the alleged perpetrator agreeing to leave the home.[7]

---

[1]   (2008) Department for Children, Schools and Families, paras 4.28–4.70.
[2]   Paragraphs 5.49–5.53.
[3]   Working Together (2006) para 5.49.
[4]   Revised Children Act 1989 Guidance and Regulations, Vol 1, Court Orders (2008) Department for Children, Schools and Families, Chapter 4.
[5]   Revised Children Act 1989 Guidance and Regulations, Vol 1, Court Orders (2008) Department for Children, Schools and Families, Chapter 4.
[6]   Working Together (2006) para 5.50.
[7]   Working Together (2006) para 5.51 and the Children Act 1989 Guidance and Regulations, Vol 1, Court Orders (1991) Department of Health, para 4.31 and see the provisions of the CA 1989, Sch 2, para 5.

(e) *Judicial guidance*

7.71 The courts have provided extensive guidance on the application of s 44 of the Act, which must be carefully considered when determining whether an application for an emergency protection order is justified and appropriate in the circumstances of the case.

7.72 In *Re C and B (Care Order: Future Harm)*[1] Hale LJ observed that emergency protection orders are intended to be made when there is an emergency and it can be shown that unless emergency action is taken the child will be a risk of significant harm during the period of the emergency protection order. Within the context of the removal of a child from the care of his parents, the European Court of Human Rights held in *P, C and S v United Kingdom*[2] that the removal of baby into public care at birth under an emergency protection order is an extremely harsh measure and one requiring extraordinarily compelling reasons.

---

[1]   [2001] 1 FLR 611, CA.
[2]   [2002] 2 FLR 631.

7.73 The foregoing case law provides the foundation for two seminal High Court decisions which now constitute the definitive guidance on the application of the jurisdiction provided by s 44, namely *X County Council v B (Emergency Protection Orders)*[1] and *Re X (Emergency Protection Orders)*.[2] McFarlane J observed in *Re X (Emergency Protection Orders)* that Munby J's list of essential factors set out in *X Council v B (Emergency Protection Orders)* should be copied and placed before the court during every hearing of an application for an emergency protection order and that applicants and their legal advisers should consider themselves under a duty to the court to ensure that the list was expressly drawn to the attention of the bench.

---

[1]   [2004] EWHC 2015 (Fam), [2005] 1 FLR 341.
[2]   [2006] EWHC 510 (Fam), [2006] 2 FLR 701.

7.74 In relation to the considerations applicable when determining whether an application for an emergency protection order is justified, *X Council v B and Re X (Emergency Protection Orders)* provide the following guidance:

(a)   Emergency protection orders should only be made in a genuine emergency, and contain only what is necessary to provide immediate short-term protection. An EPO will rarely (if ever) be warranted by: allegations of emotional harm; inchoate and non-specific allegations of sexual abuse where there is no evidence of immediate risk of harm to the child; or allegations of induced or fabricated illness, where there is no medical evidence of an immediate risk of direct physical harm to the child. Justices faced with an EPO application in a case of emotional abuse, non-specific allegations of sexual abuse and/or fabricated or induced illness, should actively consider refusing the application on the basis that the local authority should instead issue an application for an interim care order. Any such ICO application was likely to be transferred by the justices immediately to a higher court.[1]

(a)   An EPO, summarily removing a child from his parents, is a 'draconian' and 'extremely harsh' measure, requiring 'exceptional justification' and 'extraordinarily compelling reasons'. Such an order should not be made unless the FPC is satisfied that it is both necessary and proportionate and that no other less radical form of order will achieve the essential end of promoting the welfare of the child. Separation is only to be contemplated if immediate separation is essential to secure the child's safety: 'imminent danger' must be 'actually established'.

(b)   Both the local authority which seeks and the FPC which makes an EPO assume a heavy burden of responsibility. It is important that both the local authority and the FPC approach every application for an EPO with an anxious awareness of the extreme gravity of the relief being sought and a scrupulous regard for the European Convention rights of both the child and the parents.

(c)   Any order must provide for the least interventionist solution consistent with the preservation of the child's immediate safety.

(d)   If the real purpose of the local authority's application is to enable it to have the child assessed then consideration should be given to whether that objective cannot equally effectively, and more proportionately, be achieved by an application for, or by the making of, a CAO under s 43 of the CA 1989.[2] Lack of information or a need for assessment could never, of themselves, establish the existence of a genuine emergency sufficient to justify an EPO; positive evidence establishing the threshold under s 44 of the CA 1989 was necessary. Using an EPO, particularly one obtained without notice to the parents, solely for the purpose of achieving some sort of assessment or investigation would very rarely, if ever, be justified.[3]

---

[1]   *Re X (Emergency Protection Orders)* [2006] EWHC 510 (Fam), [2006] 2 FLR 701.
[2]   *X Council v B (Emergency Protection Orders)* [2004] EWHC 2015 (Fam), [2005] 1 FLR 341.
[3]   *Re X (Emergency Protection Orders)* [2006] EWHC 510 (Fam), [2006] 2 FLR 701.

3. Application for an emergency protection order

(a) Applicants and respondents

7.75 An application[1] for an emergency protection order can be made by any person authorised by the Secretary of State or any other person.[2] Where the applicant is the local authority the application can only be made by an 'authorised officer of the local authority on behalf of the local authority.[3] At present persons authorised by the Secretary of State[4] are limited to officers of the NSPCC.

1   There were 1,676 applications for emergency protection orders in 2006 (Judicial and Court Statistics 2006 (Cm 7273)(2007)).
2   CA 1989, s 44(1).
3   CA 1989, s 44(2)(b)(i). Note that the practice of permitting social workers to override the legal adviser's advice upon whether or not the grounds for an EPO had been established was deprecated by McFarlane J in *Re X (Emergency Protection Orders)* [2006] EWHC 510 (Fam), [2006] 2 FLR 701.
4   CA 1989, ss 44(2)(a) and 31(9).

7.76 Those with parental responsibility, the child and, where there is a care order in force, all those believed to have parental responsibility prior to the making of the care order will be automatic respondents to the application.[1] The rules specify other persons who must be given notice of the application.[2]

1   FPR 1991, Appendix 3, Column (iii); FPC(CA 1989)R 1991, Sch 2, Column (iii).
2   FPR 1991, Appendix 3, Column (iv); FPC(CA 1989)R 1991, Sch 2, Column (iv).

7.77 Upon an application for an emergency protection order being made the court must appoint a children's guardian unless it is satisfied that it is not necessary to safeguard his interests.[1] It is difficult to contemplate a situation in which the appointment of a children's guardian would not be necessary upon an application for an emergency protection order. In the context of an application for an emergency protection order where removal is contemplated a guardian must be appointed immediately upon issue of the proceedings.[2]

1   CA 1989, s 44(1).
2   *X Council v B (Emergency Protection Orders)* [2004] EWHC 2015 (Fam), [2005] 1 FLR 341.

(b) Court

7.78 An application for an emergency protection order must be made in the family proceedings court and may be made to a single justice[1] unless the application is made as a result of an investigation directed by the court under s 37 of the Act, in which circumstances the application should be made to the court which directed the investigation, or the application is made where other proceedings are pending, in which case the application should be made to the court where those proceedings are pending.[2] The application may not be transferred to a higher court.[3]

1   Children (Allocation of Proceedings) Order 1991, art 3(1).

2   Children (Allocation of Proceedings) Order 1991, art 3(2) and (3).
3   Children (Allocation of Proceedings) Order 1991, art 7(2).

(c) Applications without notice

7.79 The application may be made without notice with the consent of the justices' clerk.[1] When considering whether to hear an application for an emergency protection order without notice to the parents, it is important that the court has regard to the following principles:[2]

(a)   Save in wholly exceptional cases, parents must be given adequate prior notice of the date, time and place of any application by a local authority for an emergency protection order. Only if the court was fully satisfied that there was a pressing need for a without notice hearing should the court proceed on that basis.

(b)   Where the application for an EPO is made ex parte the local authority must make out a compelling case for applying without first giving the parents notice.

(c)   An ex parte application will normally be appropriate only if the case is genuinely one of emergency or other great urgency (and even then it should normally be possible to give some kind of notice, albeit informal, to the parents) or if there are compelling reasons to believe that the child's welfare will be compromised if the parents are alerted in advance to what is going on.

1   FPR 1991, r 4.4(4) and the FPC(CA 1989)R 1991, r 4(4).
2   *X Council v B (Emergency Protection Orders)* [2004] EWHC 2015 (Fam), [2005] 1 FLR 341; *Re X (Emergency Protection Orders)* [2006] EWHC 510 (Fam), [2006] 2 FLR 701.

7.80 Where it is considered appropriate to proceed on a without notice basis, the court and the applicant should nonetheless adhere strictly to the following principles during and after the hearing:

(a)   The evidential burden on the local authority is even heavier if the application is made without notice.

(b)   Those who seek relief without notice. are under a duty to make the fullest and most candid and frank disclosure of all the relevant circumstances known to them. This duty is not confined to the material facts: it extends to all relevant matters, whether of fact or of law.[1] If possible, an applicant for a without notice emergency protection order should have legal representation, and the lawyer concerned must consider him or herself under a duty not only to present the case for the authority, but also to ensure that it was presented fairly, and that the bench was fully aware of the legal context within which the application was made.[2]

(c)   It is important that those who are not present should nonetheless be able to know what oral evidence and other materials have been put before the court. The court should comply meticulously with the mandatory requirements of rr 20, 21(5) and (6) of the FPC(CA 1989)R 1991. The court must 'keep a note of the substance of the oral evidence' and must also record in writing not merely its reasons but also any findings of fact.

(d)   The fact that the court is under the obligations imposed by rr 21(5), (6) and (8) of the FPC(CA 1989)R 1991, forms no reason why the local authority should not immediately inform the parents of exactly what has gone on in their absence.[3] The local authority legal department should ensure that a clear note of proceedings is prepared and made available to parents, together with copies of any material submitted to the court, at the earliest opportunity unless there were countervailing considerations requiring confidentiality.[4]

(e)   Unless it is impossible to do so, a without notice hearing ought to be taped; otherwise, a dedicated note-taker, in addition to the clerk, should attend the hearing with the task of compiling a verbatim note.[5]

(f)   Part of the legal advice given to justices in an EPO application made without notice must be that two separate matters were to be considered:

      (i)   Should the application proceed without notice to the parents?

      (ii)   Are the grounds for the EPO made out?[6]

[1]   *X Council v B (Emergency Protection Orders)* [2004] EWHC 2015 (Fam), [2005] 1 FLR 341.
[2]   *Re X (Emergency Protection Orders)* [2006] EWHC 510 (Fam), [2006] 2 FLR 701.
[3]   *X Council v B (Emergency Protection Orders)* [2004] EWHC 2015 (Fam), [2005] 1 FLR 341.
[4]   *Re X (Emergency Protection Orders)* [2006] EWHC 510 (Fam), [2006] 2 FLR 701.
[5]   *Re X (Emergency Protection Orders)* [2006] EWHC 510 (Fam), [2006] 2 FLR 701.
[6]   *Re X (Emergency Protection Orders)* [2006] EWHC 510 (Fam), [2006] 2 FLR 701.

(d) The hearing

7.81 An application for an emergency protection order should not be fitted round a busy court list but given enough time for the justices to receive detailed evidence, to receive advice upon the legal context, and to give adequate reasons. Priority should be given to the emergency protection order hearings.[1]

[1]   *Re X (Emergency Protection Orders)* [2006] EWHC 510 (Fam), [2006] 2 FLR 701.

7.82 The strict rules of evidence do not apply to an application for an emergency protection order. The court may take account of any statement contained in any report made to the court in the course of, or in connection with, the hearing or any evidence given during the hearing, which is in the opinion of the court relevant to the application.[1] This enables the court to give proper weight to hearsay, opinions, health visiting or social work records and medical reports. However, the evidence in support of the application for an emergency protection order must be full, detailed, precise and compelling. Unparticularised generalities will not suffice. The sources of hearsay evidence must be identified. Expressions of opinion must be supported by detailed evidence and properly articulated reasoning.[2] Evidence given to the justices should come from the best available source, usually that would be the social worker with direct knowledge of the case.[3] When considering whether or not to grant an order the court will wish to know what necessitates urgent action, whether, if removal is necessary, it can be achieved with the cooperation of the parents, and whether the decision can wait for the parents to be given an opportunity to prepare for an interim hearing.[4]

1   CA 1989, s 45(7).
2   *X Council v B (Emergency Protection Orders)* [2004] EWHC 2015 (Fam), [2005] 1 FLR 341.
3   *Re X (Emergency Protection Orders)* [2006] EWHC 510 (Fam), [2006] 2 FLR 701.
4   Revised Children Act 1989 Guidance and Regulations, Vol 1, Court Orders (2008) Department for Children, Schools and Families, Chapter 4.

7.83 The emergency nature of the application did not absolve the court of its duty to give a reasoned explanation for its decision; in urgent cases, the decision could be announced and the order made with detailed reasons prepared thereafter.[1]

1   *Re X (Emergency Protection Orders)* [2006] EWHC 510 (Fam), [2006] 2 FLR 701.

4. Effect of an emergency protection order

(a) Automatic directions

7.84 An emergency protection order operates as a direction to any person who is in a position to do so to comply with any request to produce the child to the applicant, authorises removal to or prevention of removal from accommodation provided by or on behalf of the applicant. This would include, for example, a hospital.[1] A person who obstructs the applicant intentionally in exercising the applicant's power to remove or prevent the removal of the child under an emergency protection order is guilty of an offence and liable upon summary conviction to a fine not exceeding level 3 on the standard scale.[2]

1   CA 1989, s 44(4).
2   CA 1989, s 44(15) and (16).

7.85 In *X Council v B (Emergency Protection Orders)* Munby J observed in relation to the applicant's power to remove under an emergency protection order:

> 'The local authority must apply its mind very carefully to whether removal is essential in order to secure the child's immediate safety. The mere fact that the local authority has obtained an EPO is not of itself enough. The FPC decides whether to make an EPO. But the local authority decides whether to remove. The local authority, even after it has obtained an EPO, is under an obligation to consider less drastic alternatives to emergency removal. Section 44(5) requires a process within the local authority whereby there is a further consideration of the action to be taken after the EPO has been obtained. Though no procedure is specified, it will obviously be prudent for local authorities to have in place procedures to ensure both that the required decision-making actually takes place and that it is appropriately documented.'

(b) Parental responsibility

7.86 An emergency protection order gives the applicant parental responsibility for the child, but this is limited insofar as the applicant shall exercise the power to remove or prevent removal only in order to safeguard and promote the welfare of the child. If an applicant gains access and finds that the child is not harmed or likely to be harmed, he may not remove the child. [1] If during the period of the order, a return home to a parent or other connected person appears to be safe, then the applicant is required to carry that out.[2] This imposes on the local authority a continuing duty to keep the case under review day by day so as to ensure that parent and child are separated for no longer than is necessary to secure the child's safety. In this the local authority is under a duty to exercise exceptional diligence.[3] The power of removal may be exercised again while the order remains in force if a change in circumstances makes it necessary.[4] Overall, parental responsibility is to be exercised only as far as is reasonably required to safeguard or promote the welfare of the child, having regard in particular to the duration of the order.[5] It would not be appropriate to make any changes in the child's life, which would have a long-lasting effect.

[1] CA 1989, s 44(5).
[2] CA 1989, s 44(10)(a) and (11)(a).
[3] *X Council v B (Emergency Protection Orders)* [2004] EWHC 2015 (Fam), [2005] 1 FLR 341.
[4] CA 1989, s 44(12).
[5] CA 1989, s 44(5).

(c) Discretionary directions

7.87 In addition to the automatic directions contained in an emergency protection order, the order may also include discretionary directions designed to facilitate the execution of the order.

(I) TRACING AND SEARCH

7.88 The whereabouts of a child who may be in need of emergency protection are not always known. The court has power to include provision in an emergency protection order, if it appears to the court that information as to the child's whereabouts is available to a person, requiring that person to disclose, if asked to do so by the applicant, any information he may have.[1] The order may also authorise an applicant to enter premises specified by an order and search for the child with respect to whom the order was made. The court may authorise an applicant to enter specified premises and search for a child and may include another child in the order, if it believed there might be another child on the premises.[2] The statutory guidance suggests that authority for entry and search should be asked for as a matter of course.[3] It is an offence to obstruct the exercise of this power.[4] Although, where it is necessary in the execution of the order, this provision authorises entry to premises, it does not permit forced entry and may be used only where there is co-operation.

[1] CA 1989, s 48(1).

² CA 1989, s 48(3) and (4).
³ Children Act 1989 Guidance and Regulations, Vol 1, Court Orders (1991) Department of Health, para 4.52.
⁴ CA 1989, s 48(7).

(II) DISCOVERY OF OTHER CHILDREN

7.89 If the applicant believes there may be another child on the premises to be searched who ought also to be the subject of an emergency protection order, he may seek an order authorising a search for him.[1] If such an order is made and the child is found on the premises, and the applicant is satisfied that the grounds for making an emergency protection order exist, the order authorising the search has effect as if it were an emergency protection order.[2] The applicant must inform the court of the effect of an order authorising a search.[3] This provision is intended to cover circumstances where an applicant believes there may be more than one child in the family or on premises, who is likely to suffer significant harm. Although in many cases the applicant will be aware of the existence of other children, and should, if there are grounds, seek an individual emergency protection order for each child, this provision is of importance in two situations. First, the applicant may not be able to identify the specific child or children,[4] but may want to check on the well-being of children in the same circumstances as the child in respect of whom the order is made. Secondly, if the police were, for example, to discover a sexual abuse ring, they might not know the number or identity of children involved.

¹ CA 1989, s 48(4).
² CA 1989, s 48(5).
³ CA 1989, s 48(6).
⁴ As required by CA 1989, s 44(14).

(III) WARRANTS

7.90 If a person has been prevented from exercising powers under an emergency protection order, by being refused entry to premises or access to the child, or it appears to the court that he is likely to be prevented from doing so, a warrant may be issued authorising a constable to assist the entry and search, using reasonable force if necessary.[1] It would seem to be wise to obtain a warrant if difficulties in gaining entry are foreseen or there is a likelihood of threatening or intimidatory behaviour. The court may direct that the constable be accompanied by a registered medical practitioner, nurse or health visitor.

¹ CA 1989, s 48(9). The procedure for this is set out in the FPC(CA 1989)R 1991, r 4(4).

(IV) MEDICAL EXAMINATION

7.91 The court may give directions as to a medical or psychiatric examination or other assessment of the child[1] and may direct that there is to be no such examination or assessment.[2] The court should, given the combination of this provision and the requirement that no child shall have such an assessment for use in proceedings without the leave of the court,[3] be able to exert some control over excessive examinations of the child. Where a child is '*Gillick* competent'[4] and accordingly is of sufficient understanding to make an informed decision, he may refuse to submit to an examination or assessment.[5] On the face of it the court may not overrule a child who is capable of making an informed decision. However, where the objections of the child are themselves something which give rise to concern or the need for medical examination (for example where a child suffering from anorexia nervosa refuses to submit to a directed medical examination), on current authority it is arguable that the child's objection to assessment may be overridden if assessment is considered to be in the child's interests.[6]

1   CA 1989, s 44(6).
2   CA 1989, s 44(8).
3   FPR 1991, r 4.18; FPC(CA 1989)R 1991, r 18.
4   In accordance with the 'Gillick' principles discussed in Chapter 3.
5   CA 1989, s 44(7). The provision is the same as that in relation to interim care or supervision orders under s 38 and a child assessment order under s 43.
6   *Re W (A Minor)(Medical Treatment: Court's Jurisdiction)* [1993] Fam 64, sub nom *Re W (A Minor)(Consent to Medical Treatment)* [1993] 1 FLR 1, CA and *Re C (Detention: Medical Treatment)* [1997] 2 FLR 180. For a decision where the child's interests were arguably wrongly overridden see *South Glamorgan County Council v W and B* [1993] 1 FLR 574.

(V) CONTACT

7.92 The applicant who has the benefit of an emergency protection order must allow the child reasonable contact, during the period of an order, subject to the directions of the court, with his parents, any other person with parental responsibility, any person with whom he was living immediately before the court, any person in whose favour there is a contact order in relation to him and any person acting on behalf of those persons.[1] The court may (not must), on making the order, and at any time while it is force, give such directions, and impose conditions, as it considers appropriate in relation to contact between the child and any named person.[2] The direction can be varied at any time on the application of the parties to the application, the children's guardian, the local authority and any person named in the directions.[3] Arrangements for contact must be driven by the needs of the family, not stunted by lack of resources.[4] The statutory guidance states that:

> 'It is anticipated that where the applicant is the local authority the court will leave contact to the discretion of the authority or order that reasonable contact be negotiated between the parties, unless the issue is disputed'.[5]

1   CA 1989, s 44(13).
2   CA 1989, s 44(6) and (8).
3   FPC(CA 1989)R 1991, r 2(4).
4   *X Council v B (Emergency Protection Orders)* [2004] EWHC 2015 (Fam), [2005] 1 FLR 341.
5   Children Act 1989 Guidance and Regulations, Vol 1, Court Orders (1991) Department of Health, para 4.62.

(VI) EXCLUSION

7.93 To include an exclusion requirement in an emergency protection order the court has to be satisfied that:[1]

(a)   there is reasonable cause to believe that if the person is excluded from the home in which the child lives, the child will cease to suffer, or cease to be likely to suffer, significant harm; and

(b)   another person living in the home is able and willing to give the child the care which it would be reasonable to expect a parent to give, and consents to the exclusion requirement in writing or given orally to the court.[2]

1   CA 1989, s 44A(2).
2   FPR 1991, r 4.24; FP(CA 1989)R 1991, r 25.

7.94 The exclusion requirement is a provision requiring the relevant person to leave a dwelling house in which he is living with the child, prohibiting him from entering a dwelling house in which the child is living or excluding the relevant person from a defined area around the dwelling house. A power of arrest may be attached to the exclusion requirement.[1] The exclusion requirement and the power of arrest may be ordered for periods shorter than the substantive order. A person who is not entitled to apply for discharge of an emergency protection order, but to whom the exclusion requirement applies, may apply for variation of the requirement.[2] If the child is removed from the dwelling house, the requirement shall cease to have effect. The court may accept an undertaking, which is enforceable as if it were an order of the court, but no power of arrest can be attached.[3] The undertaking ceases to have effect if the applicant for the order removes the child from the house from which the person is excluded to other accommodation for a continuous period of more than 24 hours.[4]

1   CA 1989, s 44A(5).
2   CA 1989, s 45(8B).
3   CA 1989, s 44B(2).
4   CA 1989, s 44B(3).

5. Duration of an emergency protection order

7.95 The order may be granted for up to eight days,[1] though the court may order one extension for up to seven days, on the application of a person entitled to apply for a care order,[2] if it has reasonable cause to believe that the child is likely to suffer significant harm if the order is not extended.[3] If the eighth day of the order is a public holiday or Sunday the court may specify a period for the order which has the effect of extending it to noon on the first later day which is not such a holiday or a Sunday.[4] Where the child is in police protection and the designated officer applies for an emergency protection order the period of eight days of any emergency protection order granted starts from the date that the child was taken into police protection and not from the date of the emergency protection order application.[5]

1   CA 1989, s 45(1).
2   CA 1989, s 45(4).
3   CA 1989, s 45(5).
4   CA 1989, s 45.
5   CA 1989, s 45(3).

7.96 No emergency protection order should be made for any longer than is absolutely necessary to protect the child. Where the emergency protection order is made without notice very careful consideration should be given to the need to ensure that the initial order is made for the shortest possible period commensurate with the preservation of the child's immediate safety.[1] If there has been a genuine emergency and the authority believes care proceedings should follow, it should normally be possible to deal with the application for an interim care order within the initial eight-day period.

[1]   *X Council v B (Emergency Protection Orders)* [2004] EWHC 2015 (Fam), [2005] 1 FLR 341.

6. No right of appeal

7.97 There is no appeal against the making of or refusal to make an emergency protection order.[1] Local authorities which are dissatisfied with a decision will have to consider whether police protection is justified or whether to start care proceedings and seek an interim order.[2] Parents or carers who are dissatisfied that an order has been made do have available the option of judicially reviewing the decision of the local authority to apply for an order. Such an approach may be appropriate to correct an error or injustice but should not be seen as a routine procedure.[3]

[1]   Section 45(10) and *Essex County Council v F* [1993] 1 FLR 847.
[2]   *Re P (Emergency Protection Order)* [1996] 1 FLR 482.
[3]   *X Council v B (Emergency Protection Orders)* [2004] EWHC 2015 (Fam), [2005] 1 FLR 341.

7. Discharge of the order

7.98 Although there is no provision for an appeal against an emergency protection order, an application to discharge the order may be made. It may only be heard between 72 hours and eight days after the making of the order[1]. The application may be made by the child, a parent, any other person with parental responsibility or any person with whom he was living immediately before the making of the order, except where that person was present at and given notice of the hearing.[2]

[1]   The Children and Young Persons Bill 2008 removes this restriction.
[2]   CA 1989, s 45(8)–(11).

POLICE PROTECTION

7.99 Paragraph 5.1 of the revised edition of *Working Together to Safeguard Children* states in respect of police protection that 'Police powers should only be used in exceptional circumstances where there is insufficient time to seek an Emergency Protection Order, or for reasons relating to the immediate safety of the child'. The Home Office circular 44/2003 (which does not have statutory force) provides that 'Police protection powers should only be used when necessary, the principle being that wherever possible the decision to remove a child from a parent or carer should be made by a court.' Overall, within the statutory scheme the provisions for the granting of an emergency protection order take primacy over those governing the taking of a child into police protection.[1]

> [1]   *Langley v Liverpool City Council* [2005] EWCA Civ 1173, [2006] 1 FLR 342.

7.100   A constable has powers to take a child 'into police protection' for up to 72 hours, if he has reasonable cause to believe that a child would be likely to suffer significant harm if he did not remove the child to suitable accommodation, or take steps to prevent removal from a hospital or other place where the child is being accommodated.[1] The provision can only be used where the police officer has found the child, since the section has no powers of search attached. The section is the successor to s 28(2) of the Children and Young Persons Act 1969 Act, which was most frequently used by the police to hold children who had run away from home or whose parents had abandoned them. It may also be used by a police officer who attends a domestic dispute and finds the parents drunk, or for a child living in unhygienic conditions or the newborn in hospital. In accordance with the foregoing discussion as to the relationship between s 46 and s 44 of the Act, consideration should always be given to whether the child's interests will be protected by an application to the court for an emergency protection order.

> [1]   CA 1989, s 46(1) For analysis of recent research on the provision, see Masson 'Police Protection-Protecting Whom' JSWFL 24(2) 2002: 157–173. See also Borkowski 'Police Protection and s 46' [1995] Fam Law 204.

7.101   The power to remove a child under police protection pursuant to s 46 may be exercised even where an emergency protection order is in place. However, when considering whether to effect removal under s 46 the following matters must be considered:[1]

(a)   Removal should usually be effected pursuant to the emergency protection order and s 46 invoked only where it is not practicable to do so (for example, because the police officer does not know that an emergency protection order is in force).

(b)   Where a police officer knows an emergency protection order is in force he should not exercise the s 46 power of removal absent compelling reasons to do so.

(c)   In the absence of compelling reasons, a police officer who removes a child under s 46 when he knows an emergency protection order is in force acts unlawfully and in breach of the family's art 8 rights.

(d)   In deciding whether it is practicable to execute the emergency protection order the police should always have regard to the paramount need to protect the child from significant harm.

> [1]   *Langley v Liverpool City Council* [2005] EWCA Civ 1173, [2006] 1 FLR 342.

7.102   The police have powers to enter and search premises without a warrant for the purpose of saving life or limb,[1] but this provision appears to be rarely used and is limited to emergencies. The police may enter premises in order to arrest a person for an arrestable offence and to deal with or prevent a breach of the peace. They may arrest without a warrant any person who has committed any offence where the arrest is necessary to protect the child from that person.[2] They can obtain a warrant to enter premises and search for children.[3]

1   Police and Criminal Evidence Act 1984, s 17.
2   Police and Criminal Evidence Act 1984, s 25(3)(e).
3   CA 1989, s 102.

7.103 The police do not acquire parental responsibility but must do what is reasonable in all the circumstances of the case for the purpose of safeguarding or promoting the child's welfare, having regard in particular to the length of the period during which the child will be in police protection.[1] The extent of this duty is unclear but taken in conjunction with the duty to discover the wishes and feelings of the child[2], it clearly gives authority to take preliminary steps to establish what has happened to the child. It should not be taken as authority to conduct a detailed interview or assessment, nor a medical examination, unless the circumstances require it. The child must be returned to the care of the parents as soon as the police officer has determined that there is no longer reasonable cause to believe that the child would be likely to suffer significant harm[3] or at the end of the 72-hour period if no other order has been made in respect of the child.[4]

1   CA 1989, s 46(9).
2   CA 1989, s 46(3)(d).
3   CA 1989, s 46(5)
4   CA 1989, s 46(6).

RECOVERY ORDERS

7.104 A court may make a recovery order[1] in respect of a child who is in care, or is the subject of an emergency protection order or in police protection, if there is reason to believe that he has been unlawfully taken away from the 'responsible person', has run away or is staying away from the responsible person or is missing. A responsible person is anyone who has care of the child by virtue of a care order, emergency protection order or police protection.[2] The local authority may designate the responsible person and can specify who that person should be at any given time. A recovery order operates as a direction to produce the child or disclose his whereabouts and authorises a constable to enter named premises and search for the child using reasonable force if necessary. Reasonable force extends not only to entry and search, but also to the removal of the child.[3] The application may be made without notice.[4]

1   CA 1989, s 50.
2   CA 1989, s 49(2).
3   *Re R (Recovery Orders)* [1998] 2 FLR 401.
4   FPC (CA 1989) R 1991, r 4(4).

ANCILLARY PROTECTION UNDER A CARE ORDER

7.105 Section 37(1) of the Supreme Court Act 1981 provides that 'the High Court may by order (whether interlocutory or final) grant an injunction or appoint a receiver in all cases in which it appears to the court to be just and convenient to do so.' This injunctive relief may be granted either unconditionally or on such terms and conditions as the court considers to be just. Under this statutory provision, the High Court has jurisdiction to grant injunctive relief to a local authority to support the rights conferred upon the authority by a care order and in particular the power pursuant to s 33(3) to determine the extent to which a parent may exercise parental responsibility for a child who is subject to a care order in favour of the local authority. The jurisdiction of the High Court under s 37(1) of the Supreme Court Act 1981 is separate from the inherent jurisdiction. Accordingly, a local authority does not require leave under s 100 of the CA 1989 to issue an application for injunctive relief under this statutory provision.[1] Section 37 has been used to prohibit parents from obstructing a child's attendance at school by an injunction made ancillary to a care order under the CA 1989.[2]

[1] *Re P (Care Order: Injunctive Relief)* [2000] 2 FLR 385.
[2] *Re P (Care Order: Injunctive Relief)* [2000] 2 FLR 385.

7.106 The jurisdiction of the county court is derived from statute and accordingly the county court has no inherent jurisdiction to grant injunctive relief in care proceedings.[1] Whether the county court is able to grant similar injunctive relief in support of the rights conferred by a care order pursuant to s 38(1) of the County Courts Act 1984 has yet to be definitively determined. In *C v K (Inherent Powers: Exclusion Order)*[2] Wall J held that there exists: (a) an inherent jurisdiction in both the High Court and the county court to protect children from harm exercisable irrespective of the proceedings in which the need for that protection arises and (b) a co-existing jurisdiction in the High Court under s 37(1) of the Supreme Court Act 1981 and in the county court under the County Courts Act 1984, s 38(1) to grant injunctive relief in support of legal and equitable rights and, specifically, in support of the rights conferred by parental responsibility. Whilst the conclusion of Wall J that there exists in the county court an inherent jurisdiction to protect children from harm irrespective of the proceedings in which the need to protect the child arose appears to conflict with Court of Appeal authority to contrary and must be doubted[3], there is plainly a co-existing jurisdiction in the High Court under s 37(1) of the Supreme Court Act 1981 and in the county court under the County Courts Act 1984, s 38(1) to grant injunctive relief in support of legal and equitable rights, including rights conferred by parental responsibility. In the circumstances, it is suggested that the county court has the same statutory jurisdiction as the High Court to grant injunctive relief to a local authority in support of its rights under a care order (and arguably to a parent with parental responsibility in support of his or her co-existing and co-terminus rights as a parent with parental responsibility).[4]

[1] *D v D (County Court Jurisdiction: Injunctions)* [1993] 2 FLR 802; *Devon County Council v B* [1997] 1 FLR 591.
[2] [1996] 2 FLR 506.

³ *D v D (County Court Jurisdiction: Injunctions)* [1993] 2 FLR 802; *Devon County Council
   v B* [1997] 1 FLR 591.
⁴ *Re P (Care Order: Injunctive Relief)* [2000] 2 FLR 385.

7.107 Injunctive relief ancillary to an interim or final care order is likely to be
of use where the protection normally provided by a care order is insufficient
to meet the demands of the situation, for example where parents refuse to
comply with the limitations placed on the exercise of their parental responsibility under a care order pursuant to s 33(3) of the Act and seek to obstruct
the placement, schooling or health care of the child who is subject to the care
order.

Chapter 8

CARE PROCEEDINGS

INTRODUCTION

8.1 Where a child is suffering or is at risk of suffering significant harm the CA 1989 provides a mechanism by which the State can initiate care proceedings to protect the child and make arrangements to safeguard and promote his future welfare. The compulsory intervention by the State in family life by way of care proceedings constitutes one of the most draconian steps the State is able to take in respect of the family. As such, the judicial process established by Pt IV of the Children Act to regulate such intervention is one that requires the most careful application in accordance with the principles laid down by the Act and associated jurisprudence.

8.2 The incorporation into domestic law of the ECHR has thrown into further relief the obligation to act with due care when exercising a jurisdiction that may lead to the permanent separation of a child from its family of birth. In *W v United Kingdom*[1] (a decision which pre-dates the CA 1989) the European Court observed:

'... predominant in any consideration of this aspect of the present case must be the fact that the decisions may well prove irreversible: Thus where a child has been taken away from his parents and placed with alternative carers, he may in the course of time establish with them new bonds which it might not be in his interests to disturb or interrupt by reversing a previous decision to restrict or terminate parental access to him. This is accordingly a domain in which there is an even greater call than usual for protection against arbitrary interferences.'

[1] (1987) 10 EHRR 29.

8.3 The European jurisprudence on the use of care proceedings has in particular emphasised the temporary nature of public care and the principle that care proceedings should be utilised with a view to reuniting the family provided always that reunification would not prejudice the welfare of the child. The classic formulation of this principle is contained in *Johansen v Norway*[1] in which the European Court held:

'... taking a child into care should normally be regarded as a temporary measure to be discontinued as soon as circumstances permit and any measures of implementation of temporary care should be consistent with the ultimate aim of reuniting the natural parent and child. In this regard a fair balance has to be struck between the interests of the child in remaining in public care and those of the parents in being reunited with the child. In carrying out this balancing exercise, the Court will attach particular importance to the best interests of the child, which depending on their nature and seriousness may override those of the parent. In particular ... the parent cannot be entitled under Article 8 of the Convention to have such measures taken as would harm the child's health and development.'[2]

[1]   (1996) 23 EHRR 33.
[2]   The principle that public care is a temporary measure runs clearly through the line of European authority promulgated since *Johansen v Norway*. See in particular *K and T v Finland* [2001] 2 FLR 707; *KA v Finland* [2003] 1 FLR 696 and *Hansen v Turkey* [2004] 1 FLR 142 in which case the court indicated that the adequacy of the action taken to reunite the family should be judged by the speed of its implementation given the detrimental consequences of delay to the relationship between parent and child.

8.4 This principle that care proceedings should be used to safeguard the welfare of the child whilst the State works to ensure that the child can be returned safely to his family if possible has been clearly incorporated into domestic law, with emphasis being placed on the principle of 'proportionality' enshrined in art 8 of the Convention. In *Re C and B (Children) (Care Order: Future Harm)*[1] Hale LJ said:

'Nevertheless one comes back to the principle of proportionality. The principle has to be that the local authority works to support, and eventually to reunite, the family, unless the risks are so high that the child's welfare requires alternative family care.'

The domestic statutory guidance also emphasises the need for local authorities to utilise the care system as a tool to protect children whilst work is undertaken to ensure their welfare at home rather than a system of peremptory and permanent removal.[2] Further, the principle of proportionality demands that proceedings for a care order should only be pursued where no less radical form of intervention would succeed in safeguarding and promoting the welfare of the child.[3]

[1]   [2001] 1 FLR 611.
[2]   Local Authority Circular LAC (98) 20 Appendix 4 which states: Where a child is in the care of the Local Authority, the CA 1989 places a duty on them to make all reasonable efforts to rehabilitate the child with his or her family wherever possible unless it is clear that the child can no longer live with his family or that the authority has sufficient evidence to suggest that further attempts at rehabilitation are unlikely to succeed.'
[3]   *Re B (Care: Interference with Family Life)* [2003] EWCA Civ 786, [2003] 2 FLR 813.

8.5 Both the European and domestic courts have also emphasised the importance of procedural fairness in both care proceedings and the administrative procedures that lead to the decision to take care proceedings. In *Re L (Care: Assessments: Fair Trial)*[1] Munby J observed that the fair trial guaranteed by art 6 of the ECHR is not confined to the 'purely judicial' part of the proceedings and that unfairness at any stage of the litigation process may involve breaches not merely of art 8 but also of art 6 of the ECHR. In *Re G (Care: Challenge to Local Authority's Decision)*[2] Munby J stated:

'The fact that a care order is in existence does not entitle the local authority to make decisions about the child without reference to the parents, to make significant changes to the care plan or remove the child from their care without properly involving the parents in the decision-making process and without giving the parents a proper opportunity to make their case before a decision is made.'

1   [2002] EWHC 1379 (Fam), [2002] 2 FLR 730.
2   [2003] EWHC 551 (Fam), [2003] 2 FLR 42.

8.6 This chapter considers the system established by the Act by which local authorities are empowered to take care proceedings in respect of children. There have been marked differences of opinion and practice about the care of children who may be being harmed, both in different parts of the country and at different times during the currency of the Act. This has resulted in fluctuations in the number of proceedings, the outcomes of proceedings and how they are managed. Given the imperatives of the ECHR however, it is difficult to envisage how any procedure of compulsory intervention in the family could ever satisfy the State's treaty obligations other than by way of judicial procedure.

THE 'PUBLIC LAW OUTLINE'

1. Endemic delay

8.7 The original aim under the CA 1989 was for care proceedings to be completed within 12 weeks from the date of issue. This initial aim was never achieved. Whilst there is nothing fundamentally wrong with Pt IV of the Act, the implementation of its provisions has resulted in significant operational difficulties. In particular, delay in the determination of care proceedings has become an endemic problem in the care system and a problem to which considerable effort has been devoted in attempts to solve it. In his 2004 study for the Department of Education and Skills[1] Finch concluded that since 1996 there had been numerous reviews and studies on the operation of the Act to the extent that was 'no shortage of good quality analysis of the challenges that the system faces.' Each of the reviews to which Finch referred, including the 1996 Booth Report[2], the 2002 Lord Chancellor's Department Scoping Study on Delay[3] and the final report on Judicial Case Management Protocol in 2003,[4] identified delay as a major difficulty in the operation of the Act, in many cases driven by a lack of sufficient human, structural and financial resources.

1   Delays in Public Law Children Act Cases, Finch (2004) DfES.
2   Delay in Public Law Children Act Proceedings, Dame Margaret Booth DBE (1996), LCD (see also A Thematic Review of Case Administration in Family Proceedings Courts, HMSO (March 2001) Lord Chancellor's Department.
3   March 2002, LCD.
4   June 2003, LCD.

2. The 2003 Case Management Protocol

8.8 Decisions of the European Court have emphasised the need for 'exceptional diligence' in avoiding delay.[1] Whilst the concept of judicial control over case management in proceedings under the Act has long been recognised[2] it was not until 2003 that the first major attempt to tackle the issue of delay by means of a national statement of common case management practice[3] was launched in the form of the Protocol for Judicial Case Management of Public Law Children Act Cases.[4] In the Foreword to the 2003 Protocol, the then President of the Family Division, Dame Elizabeth Butler-Sloss, with the Lord Chancellor and the Secretary of State of State for Education and Skills, stated:

> 'After over a decade of otherwise successful implementation of the Children Act 1989 there remains a large cloud in the sky in the form of delay. Delay in care cases has persisted for too long. The average care case lasts for almost a year. This is a year in which the child is left uncertain as to his or her future, is often moved between several temporary care arrangements, and the family and public agencies are left engaged in protracted and complex legal wranglings. Though a fair and effective process must intervene before a child is taken from its parents, we believe it is essential that unnecessary delay is eliminated and that better outcomes for children and families are thereby achieved. This Protocol sets a guideline of 40 weeks for the conclusion of care cases. Some cases will need to take longer than this, but many more cases should take less.

1   *Johansen v Norway* (1996) 23 EHRR 33 para 88.
2   Cretney, 'Defining the Limits of State Intervention' in: The Child and the Law, Freestone (1990) Hull University Press.
3   Final Report of the Lord Chancellor's Committee on Judicial Case Management in Public Law Children Act Cases, May 2003, LCD.
4   [2003] 2 FLR 719.

8.9 The 2003 Protocol was implemented in November 2003 and set about tackling delay by placing the case management of care proceedings within a six-stage case process encompassing the issue of the application, the first hearing at the family proceedings court, an allocation hearing, a case management conference, a pre-hearing review and the final hearing. The 2003 Protocol set out in detail in relation to each of these six stages the actions to be undertaken and the timescales within which those actions should be completed. It also provided a series of 'case management tools' to facilitate its implementation, including standard directions, a case management questionnaire and checklist, a code of guidance for experts and a Practice Direction in respect of bundles. Additional guidance was provided for local authorities in the form of an 'Assessment and Care Planning Aide-Memoir' and a guide to requests under s 37 of the Act. The 2003 Protocol required that cases be completed within 40 weeks of the initial application.

8.10 The implementation of the 2003 Protocol was governed by a Practice Direction[1] which set out the overriding objective of the Protocol, namely to enable the court to deal with every care case:

a)   justly, expeditiously, fairly and with the minimum of delay;
b)   in ways which ensure, so far as is practicable, that:

    (i)   the parties are on an equal footing;
    (ii)   the welfare of the children involved is safeguarded; and
    (iii) distress to all parties is minimised;
c)   so far as is practicable, in ways which are proportionate:
    (i)   to the gravity and complexity of the issues;
    (ii)   to the nature and extent of the intervention proposed in the private; and
family life of the children and adults involved.

The Practice Direction placed the parties under a duty to assist the court to further the overriding objective and prescribed the central principles by which the court would do so, namely judicial continuity, active case management, consistency by standardisation of steps and the use of the case management conference. Overall, the 2003 Protocol sought to ensure that, in relation to each set of care proceedings issued there were no unacceptable delays in the hearing and determination of those proceedings and that, save in exceptional circumstances, every care case was finally determined within 40 weeks of the application being issued.[2]

[1] *Practice Direction (Care Cases: Judicial Continuity and Judicial Case Management)* [2003] 2 FLR 719.
[2] *Practice Direction (Care Cases: Judicial Continuity and Judicial Case Management)* [2003] 2 FLR 798.

8.11 The success of the 2003 in combating delay was limited. A consultation exercise commenced in January 2005 by the Judicial Review Team indicated an increase in delay and an inability to meet the 40 week target set by the 2003 Protocol, although 80% of all respondents felt that overall performance had been improved when measured against the paramount objective of the 2003 Protocol.[1] Once again, resource difficulties were identified as a key issue in the Protocol failing to tackle delay. The Judicial Review Team proposed additional case management measures including a Pre-Proceedings Protocol[2], a Children's Dispute Resolution Appointment[3] and the use of a Case Plan[4].

[1] Thematic Review of the Protocol for Judicial Case Management in Public Law Children Act Cases (2005) HMCS; DCA Annual Report 2003–04, Cm 6210.
[2] Thematic Review, para 46 with the intention of avoiding proceedings in appropriate circumstances and whilst concurrently preparing for proceedings by identifying key issues and goals to minimise delay and cost.
[3] Thematic Review, para 47 to permit 'early neutral evaluation' of the case by the Judge, early inter-disciplinary professional advice and case planning.
[4] Thematic Review, para 48 identifying issues, goals to be achieved, a child centred timetable, accountability for the delivery of the plan and a mechanism for review.

3. The Care Proceedings Review

8.12 In July 2005 the Department of Constitutional Affairs and the Department for Education and Skills commenced a review of care proceedings.[1] The terms of reference for the review were broad and designed to focus on keeping cases out of court and to encourage early settlement of those cases that did reach the courtroom.[2] It has been pointed out that those setting up the review seemed unaware that care proceedings have long been regarded as a 'last resort'.[3] Overall, the review was characterised by a failure by the review team to understand properly the care proceedings system.[4] Fortunately, although belatedly, the review team was able to draw heavily on both the experience of practitioners and the results of the Judicial Review Team's Thematic Review of the 2003 Protocol.

[1]   This review was announced in 'A Fairer Deal for Legal Aid' in response to the rising proportion of legal aid expenditure on care proceedings. The review therefore took place within the context of the Government's desire to reduce the cost of care proceedings.
[2]   A Fairer Deal for Legal Aid, Cm 6591 (TSO 2005) paras 7.15, 8.18 and Appendix B.
[3]   Masson, Reforming Care Proceedings – Time for Review, CFLQ [2007] 420. This article provides an interesting and detailed account of the competing agendas and pressures to which the Care Proceedings Review was subject and which shaped its final recommendations.
[4]   Masson, Reforming Care Proceedings – Time for Review, CFLQ [2007] 421.

8.13 The recommendations of the final report of the Care Proceedings Review, entitled *Review of the Child Care Proceedings System in England and Wales*[1] fell into five key categories, namely:

(a)   Ensuring that families and children understand proceedings and are as far   as possible enabled positively to engage with the system.
(b)   Ensuring that applications are only made after all safe and appropriate alternatives have been explored.
(c)   Improving the quality and consistency of applications under s 31 of the CA 1989.
(d)   Improving case management during proceedings.
(e)   Encouraging closer working relationships between agencies in the system.

The vehicle by which the pre-proceeding element of these recommendations have been implemented is the revised Children Act 1989 Guidance and Regulations, Vol 1, Court Orders (2008) issued under s 7 of the Local Authority Social Services Act 1970 by the Department of Children, Schools and Families and the Welsh Assembly Government in January 2008.[2] The recommendations for improved case management have been implemented by the new Public Law Outline[3] (replacing the 2003 Protocol) implemented via a Practice Direction from the President of the Family Division in April 2008. Improving the quality and consistency of applications under s 31 of the CA 1989 is the function of both instruments. The twin aims of these measures are to encourage early effective intervention where children's welfare is threatened, with a view to achieving partial or full resolution before cases reach court and, where proceedings are necessary, to ensure the proper preparation of applications and their effective case management.

[1]   (DCA/DfES 2006).
[2]   Department of Children, Schools and Families, January 2008.
[3]   Ministry of Justice, January 2008.

4. Revised Children Act 1989 Guidance and Regulations, Vol 1, Court Orders (2008)

8.14 The revised Children Act 1989 Guidance and Regulations, Vol 1 aims, in so far as they relate to care proceedings, to place increased emphasis on pre-proceedings preparation of cases by local authorities to ensure that all the necessary steps have been completed prior to issuing proceedings and to avoid unnecessary delay during the start of the court process. In particular, the Guidance stipulates that all kinship care options should have been fully explored, core assessments should have been carried out wherever possible before proceedings commence and care plans should have been prepared and shared with families. It is not intended that all of the work done in proceedings is to be shifted pre-proceedings. In particular, if a child's welfare is at risk, the local authority must make an immediate court application. The absence of certain pre-proceedings steps or documents is irrelevant in these circumstances.[1] Before issuing proceedings, the local authority should send out a 'Pre-Proceedings Letter' setting out its concerns about a child. This letter triggers the parents' entitlement to non-means tested publicly-funded legal advice to allow liaison and negotiations with local authorities, with the aim of avoiding proceedings or if this is not possible, identifying the key issues in dispute at an early stage.[2] The revised Guidance also encourages greater use of Family Group Conferences. Reference to the detailed provisions of the revised Guidance is made below where appropriate.

[1] A New Public Law Outline and Statutory Guidance for Local Authorities – Frequently Asked Questions, 12 December 2007, Ministry of Justice.
[2] A Pro-forma letter is appended to the revised Guidance. There are significant difficulties with the timing of these provisions and their failure to extend to legal representation of children pre-proceedings, which are discussed in more detail below.

5. The Public Law Outline

8.15 The Public Law Outline (PLO) compresses the six stages of the 2003 Protocol to four and places far greater emphasis on pre-proceedings preparation by use of a Pre-Proceedings Checklist, which aims to ensure that applications are only made where circumstances justify it and that they reach court properly prepared.[1] Once an application is issued, it will follow the following steps:

(a) First Appointment to allocate and give initial case management directions.
(b) Advocate's Meeting and Case Management Conference to identify issues and give full case management directions.
(c) Advocate's Meeting and Issues Resolution Hearing to resolve and narrow issues and identify any remaining issues.
(d) Hearing to determine remaining issues.

It is intended that enhanced case management and advocacy preparation will ensure that the key issues in the case are identified early on. A new case management template order appended to the PLO supports this process. It is also intended that a 'final hearing' will only be listed when the issues have been narrowed down, so the final hearing can focus on the main issues in dispute.[2] The timetable for progressing a case will be fixed around the needs of the child involved and all cases will be listed in accordance with these individual child-centered timetables. There will be no changes to finding of fact hearings. Where finding of fact hearings are required they will be timetabled around the case management conference so that a finding of fact hearing is directed and an adjourned case management conference can consider the outcome for further directions. The PLO will not apply retrospectively. However judges may apply some of the underlying principles of the PLO to any pre-PLO cases that are still in the system.[3] Again, reference to the detailed provisions of the PLO is made below where appropriate.

[1] See also para 8.105 for the Experts Practice Direction that accompanies the PLO.
[2] A New Public Law Outline and Statutory Guidance for Local Authorities – Frequently Asked Questions, 12 December 2007, Ministry of Justice.
[3] A New Public Law Outline and Statutory Guidance for Local Authorities – Frequently Asked Questions, 12 December 2007, Ministry of Justice.

THE NEED FOR ORDERS BEFORE INTERVENTION

8.16 A care order is an order placing a child in respect of whom an application for a care or supervision order has been made in the care of designated local authority.[1] A supervision order is an order which places a child under the supervision of a designated local authority.[2]

[1] CA 1989, ss 31(1), (11), 105(1).
[2] CA 1989, s 31(1), (11).

8.17 A local authority only has the power to intervene in the care and upbringing of a child, against the wishes of a person having parental responsibility, where an authorised court has made a care or supervision order in proceedings under s 31 of the Act.[1] A child can only be in care if the court makes a care order.[2] A local authority cannot apply for a residence order[3] nor use section 8 proceedings for the purpose of retaining control of a child.[4] The court may not require a local authority to take proceedings and cannot make an order under s 31 of the Act unless the authority has made an application.[5] Voluntary arrangements should always be fully explored ahead of any application for a care or supervision order, provided this does not jeopardise the safety of the child.[6]

[1] Revised Children Act 1989 Guidance and Regulations, Vol 1, Court Orders (2008) Department for Children, Schools and Families, para 3.6. Save in proceedings for a child assessment order or emergency protection order, described in Chapter 7, and where there is an adoption placement order under the Adoption and Children Act 2002.
[2] CA 1989, s 105(1). Under the repealed Child Care Act 1980 a child could have been in care without a court order.
[3] Section 9(2), discussed at para 5.125.
[4] *Nottingham County Council v P* [1994] Fam 18, [1993] 3 All ER 815, CA.
[5] *Nottingham County Council v P* [1994] Fam 18, [1993] 3 All ER 815, CA.
[6] Children Act 1989 Guidance and Regulations, Vol 1, Court Orders (1991) Department of Health, para 3.7.

GROUNDS FOR AN ORDER

1. The grounds

8.18 The court may only make a care order or supervision order under the Act if the following grounds are satisfied.[1]

(a)   The child in respect of whom the application is made is habitually (or ordinarily) resident in England and Wales or physically present at the time the application is made.[2]

(b)   The statutory 'threshold' criteria set out under s 31[3] of the Act are satisfied.[4]

(c)   An order is in the child's best interests having regard to the principle that the child's welfare is the court's paramount consideration,[5] having regard in particular to the matters set out in the welfare checklist[6] and having regard to the principle that the court must not make any order unless it considers that doing so would be better for the child than making no order at all.[7]

(d)   The court has considered the arrangements which the local authority has made, or proposes to make in respect of contact and has invited the parties to comment on those arrangements.[8]

(e)   In respect of a care order, the court has considered a s 31A care plan with respect to the child.[9]

[1]   The only exception to this is where a child safety order is in force and the child has failed to comply with a requirement of the order. In these circumstances, the court can discharge the child safety order and make a care order whether or not the court considers the threshold criteria pursuant to s 31(2) has been satisfied. See the Crime and Disorder Act 1998, s 12.

[2]   *Re R (Care Orders: Jurisdiction)* [1995] 1 FLR 711; *Re M (A Minor)(Care Orders: Jurisdiction)* [1997] 1 All ER 263, [1997] 1 FLR 456; *Re B (Care Proceedings: Diplomatic Immunity)* [2002] EWHC 1751 (Fam), [2003] Fam 16, [2003] 1 FLR 241 where diplomatic immunity did not prevent the court having jurisdiction to make a care order in respect of a child present in England and Wales.

[3]   CA 1989, s 31(2).

[4]   In respect of an interim order, the court must be satisfied that there are reasonable grounds for believing that the criteria under the CA 1989, s 31(2) are made out. See below para 8.109.

[5]   CA 1989, s 1(1).

[6]   CA 1989, s 1(3).

[7]   CA 1989, s 1(5).

[8]   CA 1989, s 34(11).

[9]   CA 1989, s 31A(3).

2. Threshold criteria

(a) The 'threshold'

8.19 Section 31 of the Act empowers the court to make a care order or a supervision order, in respect of a child under 17 (or 16 if married), only if it is satisfied[1] that:

(a)   the child concerned is suffering significant harm, or is likely to suffer significant harm; and

(b)   the harm or likelihood of harm is attributable to:

    (i)   the care given to the child, or likely to be given to him if the order were not made, not being what it would be reasonable to expect a parent to give to him; or

    (ii)   the child's being beyond parental control.

¹   The court must satisfy itself, and is not relieved of the duty because the parties agree: *Re G (A Minor) (Care Order: Threshold Conditions)* [1995] Fam 16, sub nom *Re G (A Minor) (Care Proceedings)* [1994] 2 FLR 69. See below para 8.167.

8.20 The conditions set out in s 31(2) of the Act are known as the 'threshold criteria' because they are not in themselves grounds or reasons for making a care or supervision order but rather only open the door to the jurisdiction to do so. As the then Lord Chancellor, Lord Mackay, said of the provisions:[1]

> 'Those conditions are the minimum circumstances which the Government considers should always be found to exist before it can ever be justified for a court even to begin to contemplate whether the State should be enabled to intervene compulsorily in family life ... Wherever rules of law apply there will always be borderline cases where it may be difficult both as a matter of law and on the merits to say whether a case falls or indeed should fall within or without a rule. The only means of avoiding borderline cases is to avoid rules and to operate a discretion ... once the court becomes involved in intervention from outside the family, and especially where State intervention is proposed, I do not believe that a broad discretion without defined minimum criteria, whatever its guiding principle, can be justified ... Unless there is evidence that a child is being, or is likely to be, positively harmed because of a failure in the family, the State, whether in the guise of a local authority or a court, should not interfere.'

¹   Joseph Jackson Memorial Lecture (1989) 139 NLJ 505.

(b) Burden and standard of proof

8.21 The burden of proving the threshold criteria rests on the local authority. The standard of proof which the local authority must meet is the civil standard of the balance of probabilities. Giving the leading judgment in *Re B (Children)(sexual abuse: standard of proof)*[1] Baroness Hale stated in the clearest terms:

> 'I would ... announce loud and clear that the standard of proof in finding the facts necessary to establish the threshold under section 31(2) or the welfare considerations in section 1 of the 1989 Act is the simple balance of probabilities, neither more nor less.'

¹   [2008] UKHL 35, [2008[2 FCR 338.

8.22 In *Re H (Minors)(Sexual Abuse: Standard of Proof)*[1] Lord Nicholls of Birkenhead held that when considering whether, on the balance of probabilities, a past event relevant to the threshold had occurred, the inherent probability or improbability of that past event is a factor to be taken into account in deciding whether it is more likely than not that the event itself occurred. This factor does *not*, however, change the standard of proof, which remains at all times the balance of probabilities. Explaining this, Lord Nicholls stated:

> 'The balance of probability standard means that a court is satisfied an event occurred if the court considers that, on the evidence, the occurrence of the event was more likely than not. When assessing the probabilities the court will have in mind as a factor, to whatever extent is appropriate in the particular case, that the more serious the allegation the less likely it is that the event occurred and,

hence, the stronger should be the evidence before the court concludes that the allegation is established on the balance of probability. Fraud is usually less likely than negligence. Deliberate physical injury is usually less likely than accidental physical injury. A stepfather is usually less likely to have repeatedly raped and had non-consensual oral sex with his under-age stepdaughter than on some occasion to have lost his temper and slapped her. Built into the preponderance of probability standard is a serious degree of flexibility in respect of the seriousness of the allegation.

Although the result is much the same, this does not mean that where a serious allegation is in issue the standard of proof required is higher. It means only that the inherent probability or improbability of an event is itself a matter to be taken into account when weighing the probabilities and deciding whether, on balance, the event occurred. The more improbable the event, the stronger must be the evidence that it did occur before, on the balance of probability, its occurrence will be established. Ungoed-Thomas J expressed this neatly in *Re Dellow's Will Trusts, Lloyd's Bank v Institute of Cancer Research* [1964] 1 WLR 451 at p 455:

> "The more serious the allegation the more cogent is the evidence required to overcome the unlikelihood of what is alleged and thus to prove it."

Thus the inherent probability or improbability of the past event in question is one of the many varied factors to be weighed in the balance when deciding if that past event is more likely than not to have occurred. It does not make any difference to the standard of proof to be applied.'

1   [1996] AC 563, [1996] 1 All ER 1, HL.

8.23 Baroness Hale identified in *Re B (Children)(sexual abuse: standard of proof)* that the effect of this passage, in which Lord Nicholls appears to treat the concepts of seriousness and improbability as interchangeable, was to ground the development of an unfortunate practice, namely:

> '... Lord Nicholls' nuanced explanation left room for the nostrum, "the more serious the allegation, the more cogent the evidence needed to prove it", to take hold and be repeated time and time again in fact-finding hearings in care proceedings (see, for example, the argument of counsel for the local authority in *Re U (A Child) (Department for Education and Skills intervening)* [2004] EWCA Civ 567, [2005] Fam 134, at p 137). It is time for us to loosen its grip and give it its quietus.'[1]

Re B makes plain that the use of the 'nostrum' that the more serious the allegation the more cogent the evidence needed to prove it is no longer appropriate in proceedings under the Act.

1   At para [64].

8.24 Whilst loosening the grip of the 'nostrum' which developed out of Lord Nicholls' proposition that the more improbable the event the stronger must be the evidence that it occurred, it is suggested that this 'nuanced' proposition itself survives *Re B*. Baroness Hale concluded later in her judgment that:

> 'Neither the seriousness of the allegation nor the seriousness of the conse-quences should make any difference to the standard of proof to be applied in

determining the facts. The inherent probabilities are simply something to be taken into account, where relevant, in deciding where the truth lies.'[1]

In examining this issue in *Re B (Children)(sexual abuse: standard of proof)* Lord Hoffman stated:

'There is only one rule of law, namely that the occurrence of the fact in issue must be proved to have been more probable than not. Common sense, not law, requires that in deciding this question, regard should be had, to whatever extent appropriate, to inherent probabilities. If a child alleges sexual abuse by a parent, it is common sense to start with the assumption that most parents do not abuse their children. But this assumption may be swiftly dispelled by other compelling evidence of the relationship between parent and child or parent and other children. It would be absurd to suggest that the tribunal must in all cases assume that serious conduct is unlikely to have occurred. In many cases, the other evidence will show that it was all too likely. If, for example, it is clear that a child was assaulted by one or other of two people, it would make no sense to start one's reasoning by saying that assaulting children is a serious matter and therefore neither of them is likely to have done so. The fact is that one of them did and the question for the tribunal is simply whether it is more probable that one rather than the other was the perpetrator.'[2]

[1] At para [70].
[2] At para [15].

8.25 In relation to the likelihood of future harm, having held that the word 'likelihood' in s 31(2)(a) means 'a real possibility, a possibility that cannot be sensibly ignored', Lord Nicholls continued in *Re H (Minors)(Sexual Abuse: Standard of Proof)*:[1]

'There is no difficulty, in applying this standard to the threshold conditions. The first limb of s 31(2)(a) predicates an existing state of affairs: that the child is suffering significant harm. The relevant time for this purpose is the date of the care order application or, if temporary protective arrangements have been continuously in place from an earlier date, the date when those arrangements were initiated. This was decided by your Lordships' House in *Re M (A Minor) (Care Order: Threshold Conditions)* [1994] 2 AC 424, [1994] 2 FLR 577. Whether at that time the child was suffering significant harm is an issue to be decided by the court on the basis of the facts admitted or proved before it. The balance of probability standard applies to proof of the facts.

The same approach applies to the second limb of s 31(2)(a). This is concerned with evaluating the risk of something happening in the future: aye or no, is there a real possibility that the child will suffer significant harm? Having heard and considered the evidence and decided any disputed questions of relevant fact upon the balance of probability, the court must reach a decision on how highly it evaluates the risk of significant harm befalling the child, always remembering upon whom the burden of proof rests.'

Thus, in determining whether there is a likelihood of future harm, the court must consider whether, on the basis of facts and circumstances proved on the balance of probabilities to have existed or to exist the risk of future harm is a real possibility?

[1] [1996] AC 563 at 587, [1996] 1 All ER 1 at 18, HL.

8.26 Thus the foundation for both the proof of past harm and the proof of future harm is facts proven on the balance of probabilities. Nothing less will suffice as a sufficient foundation for a finding of past or future harm. Lord Nicholls concluded in *Re H (Minors)(Sexual Abuse: Standard of Proof)*:

'As I read the Act, Parliament decided that the threshold for a care order should be that the child is suffering significant harm, or there is a real possibility that he will do so. In the latter regard the threshold is comparatively low. Therein lies the protection for children. But, as I read the Act, Parliament also decided that proof of the relevant facts is needed if this threshold is to be surmounted. Before the s 1 welfare test and the welfare "checklist" can be applied, the threshold has to be crossed. Therein lies the protection for parents. They are not to be at risk of having their child taken from them and removed into the care of the local authority on the basis only of suspicions, whether of the judge or of the local authority or anyone else. A conclusion that the child is suffering or is likely to suffer harm must be based on facts, not just suspicion.'

In the case of In *Re B (Children)(sexual abuse: standard of proof)* Lord Hoffmann, in considering the issue of whether a finding that future harm was a real possibility could be based on anything less than facts proved on the balance of probabilities stated:

'If a legal rule requires a fact to be proved (a "fact in issue"), a judge or jury must decide whether or not it happened. There is no room for a finding that it might have happened. The law operates a binary system in which the only values are 0 and 1. The fact either happened or it did not. If the tribunal is left in doubt, the doubt is resolved by a rule that one party or the other carries the burden of proof. If the party who bears the burden of proof fails to discharge it, a value of 0 is returned and the fact is treated as not having happened. If he does discharge it, a value of 1 is returned and the fact is treated as having happened.'

It should be noted in this context that although not satisfied the child is yet suffering significant harm, on the basis of proven facts the court may find that there is a likelihood of future harm. Lord Nicholls noted in *Re H (Minors)(Sexual Abuse: Standard of Proof)* that the range of factors which might be taken into account was infinite, including the history of members of a family, the state of relationships within a family, proposed changes within the membership of a family, parental attitudes, and omissions which might not reasonably have been expected, just as much as actual physical assault. They included threats and abnormal behaviour by a child and unsatisfactory parental responses to complaints or allegations and facts which might be minor in isolation but when taken together might suffice to satisfy the court of the likelihood of future harm.[1]

[1] *Re H (Minors)(Sexual Abuse: Standard of Proof)* [1996] AC 563, [1996] 1 All ER 1, HL. It has been held that the likelihood test would be satisfied if the parent or carer would be unlikely to satisfy the emotional needs of the child, even some years in the future: *Re H (A Minor) (Section 37 Direction)* [1993] 2 FLR 541.

8.27 In deciding whether a child is 'beyond parental control' pursuant to s 31(2)(b) the same standard of proof applies.

(c) The child concerned

8.28 It is the child[1] who is the subject of the application who the court must consider when determining whether the threshold criteria are met. In a case concerning more than one child, the wording of s 31(2) requires that the court satisfy itself in respect of the threshold criteria in relation to each individual child. The treatment of another child may be sufficient to satisfy the threshold criteria in respect of the child concerned.[2]

1. A care order cannot be made in respect of an unborn child or a child who has attained the age of 17, or 16 if married. See the CA 1989, s 31(3).
2. *Re K (Care: Threshold Criteria)* [2005] EWCA Civ 1226, [2006] 2 FLR 868 in which the Court of Appeal held that where life-threatening injuries had been caused by parents to one child, where the judge was unable to decide which of those parents had caused the injuries, and where the parents had both been found to have lied about those injuries, there must be either highly unusual circumstances or a full and reasoned explanation from the judge if the threshold criteria were to be found not to be met in relation to the parents' uninjured child.

8.29 Where orphan children who were being accommodated were leading well settled lives, it was held that it would be a distortion of the threshold criteria, to find a theoretical risk of significant harm.[1] Thorpe J considered that the local authority had adequate powers to safeguard and promote the children's interests without the making of a care order. On the other hand the court did find the criteria satisfied when the 'rescue operation' began before the parents died.[2] The child was accommodated at the time of the parents' death, but Hollis J held that at the date of the initial intervention he was suffering harm. In contrast to the *Birmingham* case he held that it was in the interests for a care order to be made, because without it the authority might have difficulties in carrying out what they thought was in his interests. In a third case Cazalet J held that an abandoned baby was suffering significant harm immediately before he was found, since the complete dereliction of parental responsibility constituted ill-treatment[3] and that he was likely to suffer significant harm as a result of the abandonment. Like Hollis J he held that it was essential that the authority had full powers to make decisions and accordingly made a care order. The consequence of these cases is that the threshold criteria can be satisfied even though the parents are dead, and it may be that if parents have failed to make arrangements for the care of their child in the event of their death, the child could be considered as likely to suffer harm. Satisfaction of the criteria does not mean that a care order necessarily has to be made. If a suitable carer emerges, the court can decline to make a care order and consider whether to make a residence order. In *Haringey London Borough Council v C (E intervening)*[4] the threshold were found satisfied in the case of a child whose place in the family was founded on a lie that the child had been born to the female carer. The harm that would be caused by allowing the lie to continue was sufficient to satisfy the threshold.

1. *Birmingham City Council v D and Birmingham City Council v M* [1994] 2 FCR 245, [1994] 2 FLR 502.
2. *Re SH (Care Order: Orphan)* [1995] 1 FLR 746.
3. *Re MM (Care Order: Abandoned baby)* [1996] 2 FCR 521, sub nom *Re M (Care Order: Parental Responsibility)* [1996] 2 FLR 84.
4. [2004] EWHC 2580 (Fam), [2005] 2 FLR 47.

(d) Is suffering

8.30 The original draft of the Bill used the words 'has suffered', but this was amended so that the test would be one of present, not past, harm. While the present tense implies an existing condition, that does not mean that the state must exist at the date of the final hearing for the criteria to be satisfied. In *Re M (A Minor) (Care Order: Threshold Conditions)*[1] the father murdered the mother of a 4-month-old baby and his half-siblings. The local authority accommodated the children and they went to live with a cousin of the mother. She felt unable to look after the baby and he was fostered. Seven months later, shortly before the father was to stand trial, the local authority started care proceedings. The cousin then felt that she could care for the child and sought a residence order. The proceedings were heard 16 months after the murder, at which time there was nothing to indicate that the child was suffering significant harm nor that he was likely to as there was a suitable home with the cousin. The trial judge held that at the time when the protection process started, the child was suffering harm by being permanently deprived of the love and care of his mother. The House of Lords held that although the child had been removed from harm by the time of the hearing, the question was whether the court could be satisfied that the child 'is suffering', because there was harm at the time that the local authority put in place protective arrangements. In the House of Lords Lord Mackay LC said:

> 'There is much to be said for the view that the hearing which Parliament contemplated was one which extended from the time the jurisdiction of the court is first invoked until the case is disposed of and that was required to be done in the light of the general principle that any delay in determining the question is likely to prejudice the welfare of the child. There is nothing in s 31(2) which in my opinion requires that the conditions to be satisfied are to be dissociated from the time of the making of the application by the local authority. I would conclude that the natural construction of the conditions in s 31(2) is that where, at the time the application is to be disposed of, there are in place arrangements for the protection of the child by the local authority on an interim basis which protection has been continuously in place for some time, the relevant date with respect to which the court must be satisfied is the date at which the local authority initiated the procedure for protection under the Act from which these arrangements follow. If after a local authority had initiated protective arrangements the need for these had terminated, because the child's welfare had been satisfactorily provided for otherwise, in any subsequent proceedings it would not be possible to found jurisdiction on the situation at the time of initiation of these arrangements.'

1 [1994] 2 AC 424, [1994] 2 FLR 577, HL.

8.31 Thus, the date relevant to whether the child in question is suffering significant harm is either:

(a) the date of hearing of the application; or
(b) where protective arrangements have been placed continuously until the date of the hearing of the application, the date those protective arrangements were initiated.

It is possible to use information acquired after the relevant date for the purposes of proving the threshold provide that information is capable of demonstrating the state of affairs at the relevant date.[1]

¹ *Re G (Care Proceedings: Threshold Conditions)* [2001] EWCA Civ 968, [2001] 2 FLR 1111.

8.32 This raises the question of what constitute 'protective arrangements' for the purposes of establishing the relevant date? Lord Mackay affirmed the judgment of Ewbank J in *Northamptonshire County Council v S*,¹ when he said that the court had 'to consider the position immediately before an emergency protection order, if there was one, or an interim care order, if that was the initiation of protection, or as in this case, when the child went into voluntary care'. The position is not without doubt. In *Re G (children) (Care Order: Evidence)*² the Court of Appeal stated that it was common ground that the threshold had to be crossed when the authority first intervened to protect the child: 'that is, either the date of the application or, if child protection measures (police protection or emergency protection order) have been *continuously* (emphasis added) in place since before then, the date when those began'. The *Northamptonshire* case was not referred to. If the authority accommodated the child as a protection measure, even though it should perhaps have sought an order, there seems to be no good reason why the period of intervention should not be deemed to have started at that time, provided it is continuous. How far the court is prepared to go into the past must be a matter for evidence and the exercise of judicial discretion.

¹ [1993] Fam 136 at 140. See also *Southwark London Borough Council v B* [1999] 1 FCR 550, [1998] 2 FLR 1095.
² [2001] EWCA Civ 968, [2001] 2 FCR 757 at [761].

8.33 By their decision in *Re M* the House of Lords maintained a flexible approach to the threshold criteria. It has, however, been argued that their decision 'realigns the balance between the family and the state in a way which substantially weakens the family's power to withstand state intervention'.¹ It can equally be argued that if the House of Lords had interpreted the phrase 'is suffering' in any other way, the protective intention of the provision would have been nullified and planning for the child's future would have been more difficult. Whenever a child had been removed from harm, the authority would have had to satisfy the court in respect of the more uncertain provision that the child would be likely to suffer harm. That was not the intention behind the introduction of the 'likely to suffer' clause.

¹ Masson J 'Social engineering in the House of Lords': *Re M* [1994] 6 JCL 170.

8.34 It is submitted that in *Re M* the House of Lords correctly decided that it was necessary to apply the s 31 criteria at an earlier stage than the final hearing. Any other interpretation would have rendered the first limb of the provision meaningless. As a matter of law the court can trace events back to any point of intervention by the local authority provided there is continuity of intervention. While this limits the application of the test that the child is likely to suffer harm, it does mean that applications are more commonly based on established facts. In any event limitation of the application of the first limb is not necessary. As Lord Mackay emphasised, being satisfied as to the criteria did not preclude the court from taking into account all the circumstances at the date of the hearing. It is an entry to the use of powers and does not necessitate intervention. If another family member was available the court could make orders other than those under s 31 or no order at all.

8.35 Neither the Court of Appeal nor the House of Lords considered in *Re M* whether the murder of the child's mother was ill treatment of the child. It has been suggested that the statutory definition requires the harm to result from an act directed at the child and not at someone else.[1] It is submitted that this view is wrong. Surely it is ill-treatment of the child to deprive him permanently of his mother. A parent who acts in such a way must be taken to understand the consequences for the child, even if the act was not aimed at him. It necessarily entails a failure of care of the child. This argument is strengthened by recognition that children can be harmed by seeing or hearing ill-treatment of another.[2]

[1] Whybrow J, '*Re M* – past, present and future harm' (1994) 6 JCL 88.
[2] See below under 'Harm' at para 8.40.

(e) Is likely to suffer

8.36 The second limb of s 31(2)(a) was introduced in the CA 1989 to deal with those cases, previously the cause of many applications in wardship, where there were grave risks to a child, but no evidence of actual harm.

8.37 In *Re H (Minors) (Sexual Abuse: Threshold Conditions)*[1] the House of Lords unanimously held that the word 'likely' was being used in s 31(2)(a) in the sense of 'a real possibility, a possibility that could not sensibly be ignored' having regard to the nature and gravity of the feared harm in the particular case, rather than in the sense of more likely than not. Thus, where the likelihood is based on facts which were alleged to have occurred previously, those facts have to be proved on the balance of probabilities. Based on those findings the court must then assess whether a risk of future harm is a real possibility. This approach was robustly endorsed by the House of Lords in *Re B (Children)(sexual abuse: standard of proof)*[2] Baroness Hale observing:

> 'To allow the courts to make decisions about the allocation of parental responsibility for children on the basis of unproven allegations and unsubstantiated suspicions would be to deny them their essential role in protecting both children and their families from the intervention of the state, however well intentioned that intervention may be. It is to confuse the role of the local authority, in assessing and managing risk, in planning for the child, and deciding what action to initiate, with the role of the court in deciding where the truth lies and what the legal consequences should be. I do not under-estimate the difficulty of deciding where the truth lies but that is what the courts are for.'

[1] [1996] AC 563, [1996] 1 All ER 1, HL.
[2] [2008] UKHL 35, [2008] 2 FCR 339.

8.38 The date relevant for determining whether the child in question is likely to suffer significant harm is either:

(a)   the date of hearing of the application; or

(b)   where protective arrangements have been placed continuously until the
        date of the hearing of the application, the date those protective
        arrangements were initiated.[1]

Again, it is possible to use information acquired after the relevant date for the
purposes of proving the threshold criteria have been satisfied provided that
information is capable of demonstrating the state of affairs at the relevant
date.[2]

[1]   *Southwark London Borough Council v B* [1999] 1 FCR 550, [1998] 2 FLR 1095 in which
        it was held that 'likelihood' was to be assessed at the date of the intervention.
[2]   *Re G (Care Proceedings: Threshold Conditions)* [2001] EWCA Civ 968, [2001] 2 FLR
        1111.

8.39 In *Oldham Metropolitan Borough Council v E*[1] the Court of Appeal
held that, where proceedings are commenced on the basis that the child is
likely to suffer significant harm when with the carer who has the care at that
time, but that carer then proposes that a suitable relative should look after the
child, the criteria were not satisfied. Although the House of Lords overruled
the Oldham case in *Re M*,[2] it is not clear that they were doing so in relation to
the test for future harm as well as the test for actual harm. The Court of
Appeal has since addressed this problem. Hale LJ noted in *Re G*:[3]

> 'It would be odd indeed if actual and likely harm had to be judged at different
> dates. Further the policy considerations [of giving the court a wide discretion to
> protect children] are equally strong in each case.'

The better view must be that in this situation the court should consider the
position as at the time of intervention, and leave questions of outcome to the
welfare stage of the proceedings. The correct approach is surely well expressed
by Ewbank J in *Northamptonshire County Council v S:*[4]

> 'The threshold test relates to the parent or other carer whose lack of care has
> caused the harm referred to in s 31(2)(a). The care which other carers might
> give to the child [in the future] only becomes relevant if the threshold test is
> met.'

[1]   [1994] 1 FLR 568, CA.
[2]   [1994] 2 AC 424, [1994] 2 FLR 577, HL.
[3]   *Re G (children) (Care Order: Evidence)* [2001] 2 FCR 757 at 762. Note also *Southwark
        London Borough Council v B* [1999] 1 FCR 550, [1998] 2 FLR 1095 in which it was held
        that 'likelihood' was to be assessed at the date of the intervention.
[4]   [1993] Fam 136, [1993] 1 FCR 351.

(f) Harm

8.40 Harm for the purposes of s 31(2) is defined by the Act[1] as ill-treatment
or the impairment of health or development including, for example, impairment suffered from seeing or hearing the ill-treatment of another. The Act[2]
further defines elements of the definition of harm as follows:

(a)   'Ill-treatment' includes sexual abuse and forms of ill-treatment which
        are not physical (although the definition must be implication include
        forms of physical abuse).

(b) 'Health' means physical or mental health.
(c) 'Development' means physical, intellectual, emotional, social or behavioural development.

The inclusion in the definition of harm of the words 'including, for example, impairment suffered from seeing or hearing the ill-treatment of another' results from an amendment effected by the Adoption and Children Act 2002 designed to reflect the increased understanding of the impact of domestic violence on children. The Court of Appeal has subsequently observed that courts should not underplay the possibility of a child suffering significant harm as a result of his exposure to domestic violence within the home.[3] It is important to recognise that the categories of abuse are not closed.[4]

[1] CA 1989, s 31(9) as amended by the Adoption and Children Act 2002, s 120. By virtue of s 105(1) these definitions apply throughout the Act. They also interlink with the definition of a child 'in need' in Pt III.
[2] CA 1989, s 31(9) as amended by the Adoption and Children Act 2002, s 120.
[3] *Re K (Care: Threshold Criteria)* [2005] EWCA Civ 1226, [2006] 2 FLR 868.
[4] Report of the Enquiry into Child Abuse in Cleveland, Cmnd 412 (1987) p.4.

8.41 When considering the issue of harm, there is a danger in compartmentalising different aspects of harm in a particular case. The correct approach is to see each aspect of harm within the overall context of the case.[1] It has been held that a child who persistently refuses to attend school and thereby misses education is suffering harm, in relation to her intellectual and social development.[2]

[1] *Re K (Care: Threshold Criteria)* [2005] EWCA Civ 1226, [2006] 2 FLR 868.
[2] *Re O (A Minor)(Care Order: Education: Procedure)* [1992] 4 All ER 905, [1992] 2 FLR 7.

(g) Significant harm

8.42 The central concept of the criteria is whether the child is or is likely to suffer harm which is *significant*. In *Re L (Care: Threshold Criteria)*[1] Hedley J observed (in a judgment delivered in public) that:

> 'What about the court's approach, in the light of all that, to the issue of significant harm? In order to understand this concept and the range of harm that it's intended to encompass, it is right to begin with issues of policy. Basically it is the tradition of the UK, recognised in law, that children are best brought up within natural families. Lord Templeman, in *Re KD (A Minor Ward) (Termination of Access)* [1988] 1 AC 806, [1988] 2 FLR 139, at 812 and 141 respectively, said this:
>
> > "The best person to bring up a child is the natural parent. It matters not whether the parent is wise or foolish, rich or poor, educated or illiterate, provided the child's moral and physical health are not in danger. Public authorities cannot improve on nature."
>
> There are those who may regard that last sentence as controversial but undoubtedly it represents the present state of the law in determining the starting point. It follows inexorably from that, that society must be willing to tolerate very diverse standards of parenting, including the eccentric, the barely adequate and the inconsistent. It follows too that children will inevitably have both very

different experiences of parenting and very unequal consequences flowing from it. It means that some children will experience disadvantage and harm, while others flourish in atmospheres of loving security and emotional stability. These are the consequences of our fallible humanity and it is not the provenance of the state to spare children all the consequences of defective parenting. In any event, it simply could not be done.'

1   [2007] 1 FLR 2050.

8.43 The court must consider whether, on the balance of probabilities, the harm caused is significant. The word 'significant' is not defined in the Act. Significant is defined by the Oxford English Dictionary as 'considerable, noteworthy or important'.[1] Factors such as the child's parents having learning difficulties or misusing substances are not grounds in themselves unless they contribute to the harm suffered or likely to be suffered.[2] 'Minor shortcomings in health care or minor deficits in physical, psychological or social development should not require compulsory intervention, unless cumulatively they are having, or are likely to have, serious and lasting effects upon the child.'[3]

1   This definition used to be contained in the statutory guidance (Children Act 1989 Guidance and Regulations, Vol 1, Court Orders (1991) Department of Health, para 3.19. The definition has not however been incorporated into the revised version of the Guidance issued in January 2008.
2   Children Act 1989 Guidance and Regulations, Vol 1, Court Orders (1991) Department of Health, para 3.9.
3   Children Act 1989 Guidance and Regulations, Vol 1, Court Orders (1991) Department of Health, para 3.12.

8.44 These are clearly matters of fact for the court, but it would appear that the significance could relate to the seriousness of the harm or the implications of it. For example, a broken leg would be a serious injury, but, depending on causation or attribution, the implications of a small cigarette burn might be more significant. Where a child has been injured but the local authority cannot prove the requisite standard that such injuries were non-accidental in nature the significant harm criteria will not be made out. Depending on the facts of the case, it may, however, be appropriate to find that the child had suffered significant harm by reason of the parents' failure to seek medical attention promptly. The court should be slow to conclude that a child has suffered harm by reason of a particular standard of parenting when the parents have done nothing wrong by the standards of their own community.[1] Where the question of whether harm suffered by a child is significant turns on the child's health or development (but not ill-treatment), his health or development is to be compared with that which could be reasonably be expected of a similar child.[2]

1   *Re K; A Local Authority v N* [2005] EWHC 2956 (Fam), [2007] 1 FLR 399.
2   CA 1989, s 31(10).

(h) Similar child

8.45 Where the facts relate to impairment of health or development, it is necessary to compare the health or development with what could reasonably be expected of a similar child.[1] How should the test of 'similar child' be applied? It has been held,[2] in relation to a truanting child, that the comparison should be made with a child who is attending school rather than one who is not, but other comparisons remain to be considered. It would seem that in relation to children with learning difficulties or similar medical problems, the court should compare the child with another child who has similar difficulties. Comparisons should not be made in respect of cultural and ethnic backgrounds.[3]

[1] Section 31(10). Note that the provision does not apply where the facts relate to alleged ill-treatment.
[2] *Re O (a minor) (care order: education procedure)* [1992] 4 All ER 905, [1992] 2 FLR 7.
[3] *Re D (Care: Threshold Criteria: Significant Harm)* [1998] Fam Law 656.

(i) Attributable

8.46 Having satisfied itself that the harm is significant, the court has also to be satisfied that it is attributable to the care given, or that the likelihood of harm is attributable to the care likely to be given to the child, not being what it would be reasonable to expect a parent to give to the child.[1] The statutory guidance defines 'care' as including the responsibility for making the proper provision for the child's health and welfare (including promoting his physical, intellectual, emotional, social and behavioural development) and not just meeting his basic survival needs.[2] In the case of a sexually abused child it includes listening to the child and monitoring its words and actions so that a professional assessment can be carried out.[3] If the child is being accommodated at the time of the proceedings, the test to be applied would be in relation to the care likely to be given to the child without the making of an order. Harm caused by a third party is not relevant unless the parent could have been expected to intervene and prevent it but did not do so.[4] The absence of a reasonable standard of care by a parent need not imply fault.[5]

[1] CA 1989, s 31(2)(b). The alternative ground is that the significant harm of the risk of significant harm attributable to the child being 'beyond parental control' and is dealt with below.
[2] Revised Children Act 1989 Guidance and Regulations, Vol 1, Court Orders (2008) Department for Children, Schools and Families, para 3.40.
[3] *Re B (A Minor) (Care Order: Criteria)* [1993] 1 FLR 815.
[4] Revised Children Act 1989 Guidance and Regulations, Vol 1, Court Orders (2008) Department for Children, Schools and Families, para 3.40.
[5] *Lancashire County Council v B* [2000] 2 AC 147, [2000] 1 FLR 583, HL.

8.47 Whilst s 31(2)(b) is expressed by reference to the care given by 'a parent', it is not necessary to prove that the significant harm suffered by the child is attributable to an identified parent. Where the court considers on the evidence that the significant harm is attributable to one or other of the child's parents but is unable on the evidence to tell which, the court may still find that the threshold criteria is met.[1] Likewise, where the care of the child is shared between his parents and others, the words 'care given to the child' encompasses any person who has had care of the child. In *Lancashire County Council v B*, a baby of six months was looked after by a child-minder, whilst her parents were at work. She sustained serious, non-accidental head injuries.

It was not possible for the court to be satisfied which of several people had been responsible for the injuries suffered by the child. The local authority commenced care proceedings, relying exclusively on the injuries sustained by the baby in a two month period during which the child-minder cared for the baby. The House of Lords held that the criteria were met where the court was satisfied that a child, whose care was shared between the parents and a child-minder whilst the parents were at work, had suffered significant harm, even though the court was unable to identify which of the carers had inflicted the injuries, and there was no more than a possibility that the parents were responsible for inflicting those injuries. In summary, although 'attributable' denotes a causal connection, it need not be the sole, dominant or direct cause and effect; a contributory causal connection will suffice provided there is harm.[2]

1   *Re CB and JB (Care Proceedings: Guidelines)* [1998] 2 FLR 211.
2   *Lancashire County Council v B* [2000] 2 AC 147, [2000] 1 FLR 583, HL.

8.48 *Lancashire County Council v B* raises the possibility of the court establishing the threshold criteria on the basis of it being satisfied that a child has suffered significant harm whilst in the care of his parents or other carers but without being able to identify which of those parents or carers caused the harm. For obvious reasons, this has significant consequences when the Court comes to consider the proper outcome for the child at the welfare stage of the proceedings. For example, in a case where the 'pool' of potential perpetrators of the significant harm encompasses all those family members who may otherwise be in a position to care for the child, the options for the future care of the child are significantly narrowed as it must proceed on the basis that all those in 'pool' are possible perpetrators of the harm.[1] Accordingly, the court should go on to consider whether it is possible to exclude one or more of the potential perpetrators of the harm from the 'pool' by asking itself 'is there a likelihood or real possibility' that one or more of a number of people with access to the child was the perpetrator or a perpetrator of the inflicted injuries?'[2] Even if this test does not narrow the pool of potential perpetrators, where possible, when considering threshold, the judge should be astute to express such views as he can to assist social workers and psychiatrists in making their assessments and preparing a care plan.[3]

1   *Re O and N; Re B* [2003] UKHL 18, [2004] 1 AC 523, [2003] 1 FLR 1169.
2   *North Yorkshire County Council v SA* [2003] EWCA Civ 839, [2003] 2 FLR 849.
3   *Re O and N; Re B* [2003] UKHL 18, [2004] 1 AC 523, [2003] 1 FLR 1169.

8.49 Where there is actual harm, the *Lancashire* case appears to provide the court with adequate power to make findings sufficient to justify the threshold criteria where necessary even if the evidence is not sufficient to identify the perpetrator of the harm. It is a difficult balance to find. As Hayes has said:

'The dilemma to be resolved is how far the legal framework, and the legal process, can best reconcile safeguarding children from suffering harm with the obligation to respect parental autonomy and family privacy.'[1]

Whilst the interpretation of the attributable condition means that parents, who might be wholly innocent and whose care might not have fallen below that of a reasonable parent, could face the possibility of losing their child with all the pain and distress that caused, so far as the threshold criteria are concerned, the factor which outweighs all others is the prospect that any unidentified, and unidentifiable, carer might inflict further injury on a child he or she had already severely damaged. It is a necessary interpretation of the provisions since an authority would otherwise have to prove who was responsible for the injury, rather than simply that the child was receiving inadequate care. As described above the finding does not necessitate an order.

[1]   'Reconciling protection of children with justice for parents in cases of alleged child abuse ' (1997) 17 Legal Studies 1.

(j) Care given to the child

CARE OF THE REASONABLE PARENT

8.50 The care given or likely to be given must be 'not what it would be reasonable to expect a parent to give the child'. This requires a test to be applied as to whether a hypothetical reasonable parent would provide adequate care, so that parents cannot argue that they have particular problems, that they are feckless, unintelligent, irresponsible, alcoholic, drug abusers, poor or otherwise disadvantaged, which justify them in providing a lower standard of care. Those matters might be relevant to the question of whether an order should be made, if their problems could be ameliorated by the provision of other services by the local authority, but they will not enable them to avoid fulfilling the threshold criteria. Previous guidance suggests that the court will wish to see professional evidence on the standard of care which reasonable parents could be expected to provide with support from community-wide services as appropriate, where the child's needs are complex or demanding, or the lack of reasonable care is not immediately obvious.[1]

[1]   Original Children Act 1989 Guidance and Regulations, Vol 1, Court Orders (1991) Department of Health, para 3.23. The revised edition of this Guidance does not contain the same stipulation.

CARE OF THE CHILD IN QUESTION

8.51 The court has to consider the care which should be given to the child in question rather than an average child. If the child has particular difficulties, say in relation to his behaviour or handicap, the court should consider what a reasonable parent would provide for him. This could require a higher or different standard of care than for an average child.

(k) Beyond parental control

8.52 The criteria can also be satisfied if the child is suffering or likely to suffer significant harm which is attributable to the child being beyond parental control.[1] The guidance provides that 'beyond parental control' means that whatever the standard of care provided by the parents, the child is suffering or is likely to suffer significant harm because of lack of parental control.[2] It is suggested that whether a child is beyond parental control must be considered in light of the age of the child concerned, as the nature and degree of parental control over a child changes with age.[3]

1 For an example of the circumstances see *M v Birmingham City Council* [1994] 2 FLR 141.
2 Revised Children Act 1989 Guidance and Regulations, Vol 1, Court Orders (2008) Department for Children, Schools and Families, para 3.41. It would seem implicit that there is no requirement to demonstrate fault on the part of the parents in order to satisfy the threshold criteria under this ground.
3 *Hewer v Bryant* [1970] 1 QB 357 at 369 per Lord Denning: 'It [*the parental right*] starts with the right of control and ends with little more than advice.' See also *Gillick v West Norfolk and Wisbech Area Health Authority* [1986] 1 AC 112.

(*l*) *Agreed threshold*

8.53 Where parties are agreed that the threshold criteria is satisfied the court remains under a duty to satisfy itself that the threshold criteria are made out and on what basis.[1] In so satisfying itself, the court must balance the time spent on its investigation and the likely evidential result.[2] It is contrary to public policy for proceedings to be prolonged to resolve differences of expression between the parties where the overall basis on which the threshold criteria is satisfied is agreed.[3] Investigation of the threshold criteria by the court may be justified notwithstanding that the facts have been conceded on a limited basis without trial in respect of a previous child.[4]

1 *Re G (A Minor)(Care Order: Threshold Conditions)* [1995] Fam 16, sub nom *Re G (A Minor)(Care Proceedings)* [1994] 2 FLR 69.
2 *Re G (A Minor)(Care Order: Threshold Conditions)* [1995] Fam 16, sub nom *Re G (A Minor)(Care Proceedings)* [1994] 2 FLR 69.
3 *Stockport Metropolitan Borough Council v D* [1995] 1 FLR 873.
4 *Re D (Child: Threshold Criteria)* [2001] 1 FLR 274.

3. The welfare stage

8.54 The satisfaction of the threshold criteria does no more than provide the court with the jurisdiction to make orders under Pt IV of the Act. The bare fact that the threshold criteria are satisfied is not a reason in itself for making an order.[1] The court must, at the 'welfare stage' go on to consider whether it is in the child's best interests for an order to be made having regard to the matters set out in s 1 of the CA 1989.

1 Revised Children Act 1989 Guidance and Regulations, Vol 1, Court Orders (2008) Department for Children, Schools and Families, para 1.14.

(*a*) *Welfare*

8.55 When deciding whether to make an order under Pt IV of the Act the welfare of the child must be the court's paramount consideration.[1] The welfare principle applies to the child who is the subject of the proceedings, and not the mother where she is also a child.[2] The statutory 'welfare checklist' applies and the court must have regard to its contents.[3] The court must also have regard to the principle that delay is ordinarily inimical to the child's welfare and must not make an order unless to do so would be better for the child than making no order at all.[4] The local authority's intentions for the child are of the utmost importance, since it justifies the making of an order.

1   CA 1989, s 1(1). See *Humberside County Council v B* [1993] 1 FLR 257 and *Re B* (*Care: Interference with Family Life*) [2003] EWCA Civ 786, [2003] 2 FLR 813.
2   *F v Leeds City Council* [1994] 2 FLR 60, CA and see *Birmingham City Council v H* (*A Child*) [1994] 2 AC 212, [1994] 1 All ER 12, HL discussed at para 2.232.
3   CA 1989, s 1(4).
4   CA 1989, s 1(2), (5).

(b) Proportionality

8.56 The principle of proportionality enshrined in art 8 of the ECHR is of crucial importance at the welfare stage in proceedings under Pt IV of the Act. In *Re B* (*Care: Interference with Family Life*)[1] Thorpe LJ considered the role of the court between being satisfied that the threshold criteria are met and granting an order and held that:

> 'Once the judge has determined to make a care order, the management of the care plan thereafter is for the local authority to determine. But there is still a vital judicial task between finding the s 31 threshold crossed and endorsing the care order. The judge must first consider all the options that are open. He must weigh the relevant factors balancing one factor against an other. He must deliver a reasoned judgment explaining his ultimate choice. Furthermore, where the application is for a care order empowering the local authority to remove a child or children from the family, the judge in modern times may not make such an order without considering the European Convention for the Protection of Human Rights and Fundamental Freedoms 1950 Article 8 rights of the adult members of the family and of the children of the family. Accordingly he must not sanction such an interference with family life unless he is satisfied that that is both necessary and proportionate and that no other less radical form of order would achieve the essential end of promoting the welfare of the children.'

The consideration of whether an order is a proportionate response to the concerns grounding the proceedings is thus central to the court's determination of the proper course of action in those cases where the threshold criteria are satisfied. In *Re C and B* (*Care Order: Future Harm*),[2] Hale LJ observed:

> 'Intervention in the family must be proportionate, but the aim should be to reunite the family when circumstances enable that, and the effort should be devoted towards that end. Cutting off all contact and the relationship between the child and their family is only justified by the overriding necessity of the interests of the child.'

1   [2003] EWCA Civ 786, [2003] 2 FLR 813.
2   [2001] 1 FLR 611. See also *P, C and S v United Kingdom* [2002] 2 FLR 631.

(c) Kinship care

8.57 When local authorities assess the needs of a child for alternative family placement, they must consider the possibility of placement with the extended family.[1] Kinship care, as it has come to be known, can make for successful placements,[2] provided they are carefully managed. It is likely to ensure better continuity of care and speedier placement, but these factors need to be balanced with an adequate assessment of whether the relatives will protect the child, where necessary, and facilitate contact appropriately. When the court is considering the best outcome for the child, it must give weight to the right of the child to grow up within his own family unless to do so would not be in his best interests. When the local authority seeks an alternative outcome for the child it is for the local authority to demonstrate why a family placement is not in the child's best interests. If the court accedes to the case put forward by the local authority it must clearly articulate the risks presented by such a placement.[3]

[1]   Children Act 1989 Guidance and Regulations, Vol 1, Court Orders (2008) Department of Health, para 3.7.
[2]   See Harwin and Owen 'A Study of Care Plans and their Implementation', in *Delight and Dole* (eds Thorpe and Cowton) (200) Jordans.
[3]   *Re G (Care Proceedings: Placement for Adoption)* [2005] EWCA Civ 896, [2006] 1 FLR 47.

(d) Care plans

8.58   In practice the application of the welfare principle means that the court must be satisfied that the outcome of the proceedings provides the best available arrangements, having applied the statutory checklist and considered what would happen if no order were to be made. In order to satisfy the court that it is better for the child to make an order, the authority should be able to indicate what plans will be put into effect as a result of the order. Thus, the local authority which it is proposed will be the 'designated authority'[1] must within such time as the court may direct, prepare a care plan for the future care of the child.[2] The statutory care plan should:

(a)   Be based on the findings of the initial and core assessments and any other assessments that have taken place and should set out the aims of the plan and the intended outcomes for the child.
(b)   Follow in structure the Assessment Framework domains and dimensions in accordance with the Integrated Children's System care plan exemplar.[3]
(c)   Be explicit about the services which will be provided by which agency and at what frequency in relation to the dimension headings.
(d)   Set out the outcomes which are being sought in relation to the needs and services identified.

Further guidance on the preparation of care plans is provided by Circular LAC (99) 29 which local authorities should follow unless there is good reason for not doing so.[4]

[1]   See below para 8.170.
[2]   CA 1989, s 31A(1). Prior to this amendment to the Act there was no statutory duty on a local authority to file a care plan although there was ample authority requiring them to do so.

3   It had previously been held in *Manchester City Council v F* [1993] 1 FLR 419n that care
     plans should follow the headings set out in the Guidance on Family Placements Depart-
     ment of Health, Vol 3, para 2.62. See also Handbook of Best Practice in Children Act
     Cases (June 1997) CAAC in *Clarke Hall and Morrison on Children*, 1[2004].
4   See Circular LAC 99(29) issued under s 7 of the Local Authority Social Services Act 1970.

8.59 Where the local authority has ruled out rehabilitation or placement with
relatives and has confirmed adoption as the preferred option, the following
should be addressed in the care plan:[1]

(a)   appropriate steps should be taken within the local authority to
       co-ordinate information between the teams responsible for the care
       proceedings application and those responsible for family finding and to
       allocate responsibilities for carrying out the necessary work;

(b)   BAAF Form E (details about the child) should be completed as far as
       possible, including obtaining from the parent(s) relevant medical and
       other details, although there may be difficulty in obtaining the neces-
       sary medical and other information from the parents;

(c)   the adoption panel should consider the case, with a view to making a
       recommendation on whether adoption is in the child's best interests;

(d)   the local authority should have identified the key steps and timetable,
       including family finding any necessary therapy, and issues of contact
       (for inclusion in the care plan) which would lead to an adoptive
       placement, if the court made a care order;

(e)   the care plan should include a contingency plan for use in specified
       circumstances if the preferred option for adoption cannot be achieved;

(f)   consideration should be given as to whether a freeing application is
       appropriate.

1   See Circular LAC(99)29. See also *Re D and K (Care Plan: Twin Track Planning)*[1999]
     3 FCR 109, [1999] 2 FLR 872. When the local authority makes its report to the adoption
     panel, it should make the views of the children's guardian known: *Re R (Minors)
     (Adoption) (Disclosure)* [1999] 2 FLR 1123.

8.60 Before making an order the court must scrutinise the care plan prepared
by the local authority and satisfy itself that the plan is in the child's best
interests.[1] Difficulties arise where the local authority seeks a final order on the
basis of a care plan which the court is not satisfied meets the child's best
interests. Where the court is faced with the dilemma of making a final order
on the basis of a care plan which does not meet the child's interests and
refusing the order plainly required for the protection of that child, the court
should adopt the least worst course of action.[2] In *Re W and B; Re W (Care
Plan)*[3] Hale LJ observed that:

> 'Only in the rare case where the court and the local authority remain at odds
> over the overall objective of the plan should it be necessary for the court to
> decline to make the care order and to retain control of the case by means of a
> series of interim care orders.'

In *Re K (Care Proceedings: Care Plan)*[4] Munby J made clear that the court is
not obliged to retreat at the first rebuff and that in an appropriate case the
court can properly require the local authority to reconsider its care plan more
than once. Where there is no realistic alternative to the care plan advanced by

the local authority, the court should make the final care order. In *Re R (Care Proceedings: Adjournment)*[5] Butler-Sloss P stated:

> 'If there had been a realistic alternative to the care plan, the judge was of course entitled to urge the local authority to look carefully at it ... the judge is not a rubber stamp. But if the threshold criteria have been met and there is no realistic alternative to a care order and to the specific plans proposed by the local authority, the court is likely to find itself in the position of being obliged to hand the responsibility for the future decisions about the child to the local authority. In this case ... [t]he child would have to stay in care and in my view there was no alternative to the care plan as the lesser of two evils.'

1 *Re R (Minors)(Care proceedings: Care Plan)* [1994] 2 FCR 136.
2 *Re S and D (Children Powers of Court)* [1995] 2 FLR 456.
3 [2001] EWCA Civ 757, [2001] 2 FLR 582.
4 [2007] EWHC 393 (Fam), [2008] 1 FLR 1.
5 [1998] 2 FLR 390. See *Clarke Hall and Morrison on Children*, 1[14454].

4. Contact arrangements

Duty to consider arrangements for contact

8.61 Before making an order the court must consider the arrangements which the local authority has made, or proposes to make, for affording any person contact with the child and invite the parties to comment on those arrangements.[1] Whilst it is the parties who must have the opportunity to comment on the local authority's contact arrangements, the local authority must make the court aware of contact arrangements with any person encompassed by the plan for contact.

1 CA 1989, s 34(11). See below para 8.202.

APPLICATION FOR AN ORDER

1. Considering whether to apply for an order

8.62 There are a range of considerations which the applicant must have in mind when deciding whether to institute proceedings under s 31 of the Act for a care or supervision order, all of which must be carefully considered by the local authority.

(a)   Can satisfactory arrangements for the welfare of the child be achieved without recourse to proceedings?
(b)   Are the threshold criteria satisfied?
(c)   What would be achieved by an order under s 31 that could not be achieved without an order?
(d)   What is in the interests of the child?
(e)   What are the plans for the child?
(f)   Should an application for a placement order be made simultaneously?[1]

1 Under the Adoption and Children Act 2002. See below para 8.169.

8.63 Before taking proceedings, the local authority must consider the position carefully.[1] Applications should be part of a carefully planned process, with liaison during the stages of investigation and assessment, and following the commencement of proceedings. Where possible, services should be provided to the child and his family on a voluntary basis, but such an approach can only be satisfactory, if it provides the child, who is suffering or likely to suffer significant harm, with adequate protection. A care or supervision order should be sought when there appears to be no better way of safeguarding and promoting the welfare of such a child. Some cases require the early initiation of care proceedings. The implementation of the Human Rights Act 1998 and in particular art 8 of the European Convention on Human Rights, has led to emphasis of the principle that throughout the proceedings intervention must be a proportionate response to the nature and gravity of the feared harm and proportionate to the legitimate aim of protecting the child.[2] The authority cannot be compelled by judicial review to institute care proceedings.[3]

[1]   See Handbook of Best Practice in Children Act Cases (June 1997) CAAC in *Clarke Hall and Morrison on Children*, 1[2001].
[2]   See para 8.56 above.
[3]   *R v East Sussex County Council, ex p W* [1998] 2 FLR 1082.

8.64 In the initial period after implementation of the CA 1989 there was a substantial drop in the number of applications for orders under s 31. The requirement that the court should make no order unless it is better for the child to make an order[1] became interpreted as a 'no order' principle. Proceedings were not taken until all alternatives had been exhausted and even though a child had suffered serious harm, simply on the basis that the parent accepted that the local authority would look after the child. The decrease was so marked that in the Children Act Report 1992 the Department of Health advised:

> 'Where a local authority determines that control of the child's circumstances is necessary to promote his welfare then compulsory intervention, as part of a carefully planned process, will always be the appropriate remedy. Local authorities should not feel inhibited by the working in partnership provisions of the Children Act from seeking appropriate court orders ... Equally, the existence of a court order should not of itself impede a local authority from continuing its efforts at working in partnership with the families of children in need. The two processes are not mutually exclusive. Each has a role to play, often simultaneously, in the case management of a child at risk.'

[1]   Section 1(5).

2. The 'pre-proceedings' stage

(a) *Revised Children Act 1989 Guidance and Regulations, Vol 1, Court Orders (2008)*

8.65 As discussed above[1] the twin aims of the reforms signalled by the Care Proceedings Review are to encourage early effective intervention where children's welfare is threatened, with a view to achieving partial or full resolution before cases reach court and, where proceedings are necessary, to

ensure the proper preparation of applications and their effective case management. To meet the first of these aims, the revised edition of the Children
Act 1989 Guidance and Regulations, Vol 1 seeks to set out a more rigorous
pre-proceedings process by which proceedings can be avoided if possible.[2]

1   See paras 8.13–8.15.
2   Some have argued that the provisions contained in the revised Guidance remain a pale
reflection of what is required to ensure that work carried out pre-proceedings operates to
divert cases away from proceedings in a manner which ensures sustainable outcomes for
children. See for example MacDonald 'Whatever Happened to the Pre-Proceedings
Protocol?' [2007] Fam Law 991.

(b) Key principles

8.66 The revised Children Act 1989 Guidance and Regulations emphasises
the following process during the pre-proceedings stage (save in circumstances
where emergency action is required to safeguard the child's welfare).[1] The
completion of this process should not be allowed to hold up the issue of
proceedings in appropriate cases[2]:

(a)   The completion where possible of a core assessment prior to the issue of
proceedings.
(b)   The early identification and, if appropriate, the assessment of potential
carers for the child within the wider family or with friends of the family.
(c)   Full inter-agency co-operation including the sharing of information for
the purpose of safeguarding children is essential.
(d)   Communication with the parents (and child, if of sufficient age and
understanding) to convey the nature and extent of the concerns held by
the local authority and the steps required to resolve them.
(e)   The expectation that the local authority will seek legal advice prior to
the decision to take proceedings.
(f)   The provision of a 'Letter Before Proceedings' to parents at the point
the local authority determines that proceedings should be issued to
enable the parents to take legal advice on the local authority's concerns.
(g)   A meeting between the local authority and the parents at which a
further plan to avoid proceedings will be formulated.
(h)   Where proceedings are required, the preparation of an application in
accordance with the 'Pre-Proceedings Checklist' to ensure the required
materials are placed before the Court.

These expectations are set out in detail in the revised Guidance[3] and are
summarised in the form of a flow chart.[4]

1   Revised Children Act 1989 Guidance and Regulations, Vol 1, Court Orders (2008)
Department for Children, Schools and Families, para 3.31.
2   *PLO Practice Direction*, para 5.1.
3   Revised Children Act 1989 Guidance and Regulations, Vol 1, Court Orders (2008)
Department for Children, Schools and Families, paras 3.1–3.34.
4   Revised Children Act 1989 Guidance and Regulations, Vol 1, Court Orders (2008)
Department for Children, Schools and Families, Annex 1.

(I) ASSESSMENT

8.67 The revised Guidance states that compliance with the requirement to complete a core assessment will be scrutinised by the responsible court as part of the court's first consideration of any application for a care or supervision order it receives.[1] Further, the Guidance makes clear that the Core Assessment constitutes the central part of the evidence supporting any application that the local authority may make.[2] The detailed requirements of the core assessment are covered in Chapter 7.[3]

[1]   Revised Children Act 1989 Guidance and Regulations, Vol 1, Court Orders (2008) Department for Children, Schools and Families, para 3.15.
[2]   Revised Children Act 1989 Guidance and Regulations, Vol 1, Court Orders (2008) Department for Children, Schools and Families, para 3.17.
[3]   See paras 7.31 ff.

(II) KINSHIP CARE

8.68 One of the drivers of delay in care proceedings that can be reliably evidenced is the late identification and assessment of potential carers for the child in the wider family. The revised Children Act 1989 Guidance and Regulations, Vol 1 provides that when assessing the wider family and environmental factors within its core assessment, the local authority should ensure it considers the capacity and willingness of the wider family to provide care for the child on a short or a longer term basis, within the context of the duty of the court to make no order unless to do so would be better for the child than making no order.[1] Before reaching a decision to take care proceedings, the local authority should have taken such steps as possible (including the use where appropriate of a family group conference) to explore whether care for the child can be safely provided by a relative or friend, have assessed the suitability of possible arrangements and considered the most appropriate legal status of such arrangements.[2]

[1]   Revised Children Act 1989 Guidance and Regulations, Vol 1, Court Orders (2008) Department for Children, Schools and Families, para 3.7.
[2]   Revised Children Act 1989 Guidance and Regulations, Vol 1, Court Orders (2008) Department for Children, Schools and Families, para 3.24.

(III) INTER-AGENCY CO-OPERATION

8.69 Within the context of the safeguarding duties now imposed upon local authorities and their relevant partners under the Children Act 2004 (including education (s 175) and health, probation and youth justice (s 11)), if families are to be successfully diverted from proceedings during the pre-proceedings stage all agencies involved with the family must take all appropriate actions to address the concerns identified, working to agreed local policies and procedures in full partnership with other agencies.[1]

[1]   Revised Children Act 1989 Guidance and Regulations, Vol 1, Court Orders (2008) Department for Children, Schools and Families, para 3.23; Safeguarding Review, 2002; Every Child Matters Green Paper, 2003.

(IV) COMMUNICATION WITH THE PARENTS AND CHILDREN

8.70 Parents and others with a legitimate interest in the child's future should, as far as possible, be involved in the pre-application assessment process and should, to the extent that it is possible to do so, be consulted on the local authority's plans for the child. Even before the local authority reaches a decision that it should apply for a care or supervision order the parents will have already been made aware of the local authority's concerns in respect of the child.[1] Ideally, the local authority should communicate to the parents at the earliest stage:

(a)   The nature and extent of the local authority's concerns.
(b)   The actions the family will need to take to address the concerns of the local authority.
(c)   The assistance, guidance and services that will be provided to the family to help them addressthe concerns of the local authority.
(d)   The timescale within which the concerns of the local authority need to be addressed.
(e)   The criteria for successfully addressing the concerns of the local authority.
(f)   The consequences of failing to address the concerns of the local authority.

Where a child is of sufficient age and understanding, it is vital that the local authority also speak to the child about its concerns and involves the child in the assessment process and its plans for the child.[2]

---

[1]   Revised Children Act 1989 Guidance and Regulations, Vol 1, Court Orders (2008) Department for Children, Schools and Families, paras 3.3 and 3.24. See also para 7.39.
[2]   Children Act 1989 Guidance and Regulations, Vol 1, Court Orders (1991) Department of Health, para 3.24. See also Chapter 10, paras 10.3–10.12.

(V) 'LETTER BEFORE PROCEEDINGS'

8.71 Where work with the family does not yield the desired improvements in the situation for the child, the local authority may take the decision to apply for a care or supervision order. Upon the local authority taking this decision, it must now send to the parents a 'Letter Before Proceedings' in the form of the standard letter annexed to the revised Guidance. The letter, the contents of which should also be explained carefully and directly to the parents, taking into account in the way the information is presented to the parents their cognitive and linguistic abilities, should include:[1]

(a)   A summary of concerns about the actual or likely harm to the child and the evidence on which these concerns are based.
(b)   Information about what the local authority has done to safeguard and promote the child's welfare, what needs to be addressed to address the local authority's continuing concerns, what support will be provided to assist the parents and what the outcome will be if the problems are not addressed.

(c)   Information about how to obtain legal help and advice (including a list of solicitors who provide a legal service in public law Children Act cases) together with encouragement to seek such advice.

In addition, the local authority should also explain to any child of sufficient age and understanding its intention to issue proceedings unless to do so would exacerbate any significant harm that they might already be suffering. Where it intends to issue proceedings, the local authority should notify CAFCASS of this intention to aid planning, though it should not identify the child to CAFCASS without the parents' consent.[2]

---

[1]   Revised Children Act 1989 Guidance and Regulations, Vol 1, Court Orders (2008) Department for Children, Schools and Families, para 3.39.

[2]   Revised Children Act 1989 Guidance and Regulations, Vol 1, Court Orders (2008) Department for Children, Schools and Families, para 3.28. The Guidance contends that absent an order, the local authority will need parental consent to discuss with the child its intention to issue proceedings although this proposition is questionable.

(VI) MEETING WITH PARENTS

8.72 Following the issue of the 'letter before proceedings', the local authority should hold a meeting with the parents to consider what steps can be taken to avoid proceedings, including parental engagement with the local authority, by further explaining the local authority's position and concerns. Where proceedings cannot be avoided, this meeting should be used to narrow the issues prior to issue.[1] Upon receipt of a 'letter before proceedings', the parents become entitled to non-means tested publicly-funded legal advice at level 2, which covers liaison and negotiation with the local authority at this stage of the pre-proceedings process.[2]

---

[1]   Revised Children Act 1989 Guidance and Regulations, Vol 1, Court Orders (2008) Department for Children, Schools and Families, para 3.27. It remains to be seen the extent to which parents who have received a letter from the local authority announcing its intention to issue proceedings in respect of their children continue to be willing to place trust in the local authority to the extent necessary to address concerns co-operatively.

[2]   Revised Children Act 1989 Guidance and Regulations, Vol 1, Court Orders (2008) Department for Children, Schools and Families, para 3.26. Both the timing and level of this funding has been the subject of criticism, the former based on concern that representation is required much earlier in the process to be effective in avoiding proceedings and the latter based on the concern that the levels of remuneration are uneconomic.

8.73 Following this meeting, the local authority should provide in writing a revised plan for the child setting out what the parents and local authority are going to do to safeguard the child (including what consideration has been given to the possibility of the child living with a relative or a friend) and what steps will be taken if these actions are not effective. The outcome of the meeting should also be explained carefully and directly to the parents, taking into account in the way the information is presented to the parents their cognitive and linguistic abilities.[1]

---

[1]   Revised Children Act 1989 Guidance and Regulations, Vol 1, Court Orders (2008) Department for Children, Schools and Families, paras 3.31 and 3.32.

8.74 Where, despite this meeting and revised plan, the local authority continues to be concerned (or again becomes concerned) that the child is suffering or is likely to suffer significant harm, the local authority remains responsible for making an application for a care or supervision order and must comply with the pre-proceedings checklist before doing so.[1] The pre-proceedings checklist is dealt with below and represents the boundary between the pre-proceedings and the proceedings stages.

[1] Revised Children Act 1989 Guidance and Regulations, Vol 1, Court Orders (2008) Department for Children, Schools and Families, para 3.33.

3. Proceedings

(a) Key principles

8.75 From 1 April 2008 the Public Law Outline and accompanying Practice Direction[1] provide the procedural framework for care proceedings.[2] The PLO sets out cardinal principles by which it seeks to achieve the second key aim of the reforms signalled by the Care Proceedings Review, namely to ensure the proper preparation of applications under Pt IV of the Act and their effective case management.[3]

[1] This Practice Direction replaces *Practice Direction: Care Cases: Judicial Continuity and Judicial Case Management* appended to the Protocol for Judicial Case Management in Public Law Children Act Cases [2003] 2 FLR 719.
[2] The PLO does not apply to applications issued before 13 April 2008 but the court may direct in any individual case that the Case Management Tools and Case management Documentation referred to in the PLO shall apply wholly or in part to that application: *Practice Direction – Guide to Case Management in Public Law Proceedings*, para 1.2.
[3] The PLO must be read together with the *Practice Direction (Family Proceedings: Court Bundles)*(*Universal Practice to be applied to all Courts except the FPC*) [2006] 2 FLR 199 with the following adjustments: (a) add 'except the First Appointment, Case Management Conference, and Issues Resolution Hearing referred to in the *Practice Direction: Guide to Case Management in Public Law Proceedings* where there are no contested applications being heard at those hearings' to para 2.2; and (b) the references to the 2003 Protocol shall be read as references to the PLO.

(I) THE OVERRIDING OBJECTIVE

8.76 The PLO Practice Direction has the overriding objective of enabling the court to deal with cases justly, having regard to welfare issues involved.[1] Dealing with the case "justly" includes, so far as is practicable:

(a)   ensuring that it is dealt with expeditiously and fairly;
(b)   dealing with the case in ways which are proportionate to the nature, importance and complexity of the issues;
(c)   ensuring that the parties are on an equal footing;
(d)   saving expense;
(e)   allotting to it an appropriate share of the court's resources, whilst taking into account the need to allot resources to other cases.[2]

[1] PLO Practice Direction, para 2.1.
[2] PLO Practice Direction, para 2.1.

8.77 The court must seek to give effect to the overriding objective when it exercises the case management powers referred to in the PLO Practice Direction or interprets any provision of the Practice Direction.[1] The parties are required to help the court to further the overriding objective.[2] In addition, the PLO Practice Direction[3] requires that throughout the proceedings the parties and their representatives should co-operate wherever reasonably practicable to help towards securing the welfare of the child as the paramount consideration. The Practice Direction further stipulates[4] that at each court appearance the court will ask the parties and their legal representatives:

(a)   What steps they have taken to achieve co-operation and the extent to which they havebeen successful?

(b)   If appropriate the reason why co-operation could not be achieved?

(c)   The steps needed to resolve any issues necessary to achieve co-operation.[5]

[1]   PLO Practice Direction, para 2.2.
[2]   PLO Practice Direction, para 2.3.
[3]   PLO Practice Direction, para 19.1.
[4]   PLO Practice Direction, para 19.2.
[5]   Given the workload of judges and the congested nature of the court lists it must be questionable whether in practice the court will undertake this exercise explicitly at each and every hearing. It is suggested that it will be incumbent on practitioners to raise issues of non-cooperation where those issues present a risk to the child's welfare and/or an impediment to proper case management.

(II) Judicial continuity

8.78 The concept of judicial continuity is central to the case management objectives of the PLO[1]. Each case will be allocated one or not more than two case management judges (or in the case of the family proceedings court, case managers) who will be responsible for every case management stage in the proceedings through to final hearing. In the High Court and the county court, one of the case management judges (where there are two) should, where possible, be the judge who will have conduct of the final hearing.[2]

[1]   See also para 8.83 below.
[2]   PLO Practice Direction, para 3.1(1).

(III) Active case management

8.79 Each case completed under the auspices of the PLO will be actively case managed by the court with a view to at all times furthering the overriding objective.[1] The PLO provides that 'active case management' includes:[2]

(a)   Identifying the Timetable for the Child (see below).

(b)   Identifying the appropriate court to conduct the proceedings and transferring theproceedings as early as possible to that court.

(c)   Encouraging the parties to co-operate with each other in the conduct of theproceedings.

(d)   Retaining the Case Management Record.

(e)   Identifying all facts and matters that are in issue at the earliest stage in theproceedings and at each hearing.

(f)   Deciding promptly which issues need full investigation and hearing and which do not.

(g)   Deciding the order in which issues are to be resolved.

(h)   Identifying at an early stage who should be a party to the proceedings.

(i)   Considering whether the likely benefits of taking a particular step justify any delay which will result and the cost of taking it.

(j)   Directing discussion between advocates and litigants in person before the CaseManagement Conference and Issues Resolution Hearing.

(k)   Requiring the use of the Draft Case Management Order and directing advocates andlitigants in person to prepare or adjust the draft order where appropriate.

(l)   Standardising, simplifying and regulating—
    (i)   the use of Case Management Documentation and forms;
    (ii)   the court's orders and directions.

(m)   Controlling—
    (i)   the use and cost of experts;
    (ii)   the nature and extent of the documents which are to be disclosed to the partiesand presented to the court;
    (iii) whether and, if so, in what manner the documents disclosed are to bepresented to the court;
    (iv)   the progress of the case.

(n)   Where it is demonstrated to be in the interests of the child, encouraging the parties touse an alternative dispute resolution procedure if the court considers such a procedureto be appropriate and facilitating the use of such procedure.

(m)   Helping the parties to reach agreement in relation to the whole or part of the case.

(o)   Fixing the dates for all appointments and hearings.

(p)   Dealing with as many aspects of the case as it can on the same occasion.

(q)   Where possible dealing with additional issues which may arise from time to time inthe case without requiring the parties to attend at court.

(r)   Making use of technology.

(s)   Giving directions to ensure that the case proceeds quickly and efficiently.

---

1   PLO Practice Direction, para 3.1(3). The ability of the court to actively case manage is dependent on the case management judge having sufficient time to consider the case and its case management requirements within the context of the court list. This is one of the many areas in which the availability or otherwise of resources will impact heavily on the operation of the PLO.

2   PLO Practice Direction, para 3.14.

8.80 The parties and their representatives must co-operate with the court in case management, including the fixing of timetables to avoid unacceptable delay, and in the crystallisation and resolution on which the case turns.[1] This assistance with case management must include using the Case Management Documentation[2], monitoring compliance with the court's directions and telling the court or court officer about any failure to comply with a direction of the court or other delay in the proceedings.[3]

1   PLO Practice Direction, para 5.4. It is difficult to see within the context of care proceedings what sanctions the court will apply if the parties do not cooperate with the case management of the case given the emotive issues involved and the needs of many families involved in the process.
2   PLO Practice Direction, para 5.3.
3   PLO Practice Direction, para 5.5.

8.81 At each case management stage of the proceedings, and particularly at the First Appointment and the Case Management Conference, the court will consider obtaining evidence about the ethnicity, language, religion and culture of the child and other significant persons involved in the proceedings and will consider the implications of this evidence for the child in the context of the issues in the case.[1]

1   PLO Practice Direction, para 6.

8.82 The court will have a filing system for the case called the 'case management record' from which it will be possible to chart the case management history of the case.[1] The case management record will include the following documents:

(a)   The Supplementary Form PLO1 which will be the index of documents on the record.

(b)   In care and supervision proceedings, any letter before proceedings and any related subsequent correspondence confirming the Local Authority's position to parents and others with parental responsibility for the child.

(c)   The case management documentation.

(d)   Standard directions on Issue and on First Appointment.

(e)   The draft case management orders approved by the court.

The parties are themselves required by the PLO Practice Direction to retain copies of the documents in the case management record.[2]

1   PLO Practice Direction, para 3.7.
2   PLO Practice Direction, para 3.8.

(IV)   CONSISTENCY

8.83 The standardisation of steps was a key element of the 2003 Protocol for the Judicial Case Management of Public Law Children Act Cases.[1] As the replacement for the 2003 Protocol, the PLO again incorporates the concept of improved case management through the adoption nationally of standardised case management steps. The PLO Practice Direction provides that each case will, so far as compatible with the overriding objective, be managed in a consistent way and using the standardised steps provided for in the Practice Direction.[2]

1   [2003] 2 FLR 719.
2   PLO Practice Direction, para 3.1(4).

(V) EXPECTATIONS

8.84 The PLO states its expectations of the court and of practitioners within the context of the foregoing key principles:[1] The expectations are that proceedings should be—

(a) Conducted using the Case Management Tools and Case Management Documentation referred to in the Practice Direction in accordance with the PLO.

(b) Finally determined within the timetable fixed by the court in accordance with the Timetable for the Child, the target times in the PLO being adhered to and being taken as the maximum permissible time for the taking of the step referred to in the Outline.[2]

[1] PLO Practice Direction, para 4.1.
[2] The requirement contained in the 2003 Protocol that cases be completed within 40 weeks of the application issued does not appear in the PLO which instead substitutes the 40-week requirement with 'The Timetable for the Child.' This change reflects the widely held view that the absolute 40-week deadline operated in some cases to the detriment of the child.

8.85 The PLO acknowledges that there may be cases where the court considers that the child's welfare requires a different approach from the one contained in the Public Law Outline.[1] In those cases, the court will:[2]

(a) Determine the appropriate case management directions and timetable; and

(b) Record on the face of the order the reasons for departing from the approach in the Public Law Outline.

[1] Following the implementation of the 2003 Case Management Protocol, the appellate courts moved quickly to prevent the injustice that could arise out of slavishly following case management procedures – see *Re G* (*Protocol for Judicial Case Management in Public Law Children Act Cases: Application to Become Party in Family Proceedings*) [2004] EWHC 116 (Fam), [2004] 1 FLR 1119.
[2] PLO Practice Direction, para 4.2.

(VI) ALTERNATIVE DISPUTE RESOLUTION

8.86 The PLO Practice direction stipulates[1] that courts will encourage the parties to use an alternative dispute resolution procedure and facilitate the use of such a procedure where it is:

(a) readily available;
(b) demonstrated to be in the interests of the child; and
(c) reasonably practicable and safe.

At any stage in the proceedings, the parties can ask the court for advice about alternative dispute resolution.[2] At any stage in the proceedings the court itself will consider whether alternative dispute resolution is appropriate[3]. If so, the court may direct that a hearing or proceedings be adjourned for such specified period as it considers appropriate:

(a) to enable the parties to obtain information and advice about alternative dispute resolution; and

(b)   where the parties agree, to enable alternative dispute resolution to take place.

The PLO expressly recognises that no party can or should be obliged to enter into any form of alternative dispute resolution if they are unwilling to do so.[4]

1   PLO Practice Direction, para 18.1.
2   PLO Practice Direction, para 18.2.
3   PLO Practice Direction, para 18.3.
4   In any event there are significant difficulties with the use of ADR in the context of public law Children Act proceedings, see in particular Research Review: Child Care Proceedings under the Children Act 1989, Brophy, DCA Research Series 5/06 May 2006 at pp 80–81.

(b) Application

(I) APPLICATION

8.87 Even where the grounds for a care or supervision order are made out, the court cannot make such an order without an application having been made[1] save where:

(a)   An application for a supervision order has been made and the court wishes to make a care order or an application has been made for a care order and the court wishes to make a supervision order.[2]

(b)   A direction for an investigation by the local authority pursuant to s 37(1) of the Act has been made (in which case the court can make an interim care order or an interim supervision order).[3]

(c)   The court has made a finding of non-compliance with a child safety order.[4]

1   *Nottingham County Council v P* [1994] Fam 18, [1993] 3 All ER 815, CA.
2   CA 1989, s 31(4) and (5).
3   CA 1989, s 37.
4   Crime and Disorder Act 1998, s 12.

8.88 Application must be made on the prescribed form.[1] Proceedings under Pts IV and V of the Act must be commenced in the family proceedings court,[2] unless they arise out of a direction for an investigation under s 37 or there are proceedings pending in another court. The application must be made on notice.[3]

1   FPC(CA 1989)R 1991, Sch 1. In the rare case when an application is made in a higher court the form is the same under the FPR 1991.
2   Children (Allocation of Proceedings) Order 1991, SI 1991/1677, art 3.
3   FPC(CA 1989)R 1991, r 4(1)(a).

(II) APPLICANTS

8.89 Application to the court for an order under s 31 may be made only by a local authority or an 'authorised person' or a person authorised[1] by the Secretary of State.

1   The NSPCC is authorised by s 31(9). There is no other authorised person.

(III) THE PRE-PROCEEDINGS CHECKLIST

8.90 The PLO Practice Direction provides that the applicant should prepare the case before the proceedings are issued and that the local authority should use the pre-proceedings checklist.[1] This means that the local authority should, where possible, have available to submit with the application the documents specified in the pre-proceedings checklist,[2] namely:

(a)   Previous orders and judgments/reasons.
(b)   Assessments, including initial and core assessment, any s 37 report and any relatives and friends materials (for, example, a genogram).
(c)   Other relevant reports and records including single, joint or inter-agency, materials (for example health, and education or Home Office and immigration documents).
(d)   Records of any discussion with the family.
(e)   Key local authority minutes and records for the child (including the Strategy Discussion Record).
(f)   Pre-existing care plans (for example, the child in need plan, looked after child plan and child protection plan).
(e)   Social work chronology.
(f)   Letters before proceedings.
(g)   Schedule of proposed findings.
(h)   Initial social work statement.
(i)   Care plan.
(j)   Allocation Record and Timetable for the Child.

[1]   PLO Practice Direction, para 5.1.
[2]   PLO Practice Direction, para 10.2.

8.91 As noted above, the PLO recognises that in some cases the circumstances are such that the safety and welfare of the child may be jeopardised if the start of proceedings is delayed until all of the documents appropriate to the case and referred to in the pre-proceedings checklist are available. Where the case has had to be commenced without full compliance with the pre-proceedings checklist, the court is likely to make directions relating to the preparation of any missing documentation upon issue of the proceedings or at the first appointment.[1] It is suggested by the authors that in cases where proceedings have had to be commenced without all pre-proceedings steps having been completed the local authority must continue within proceedings to work with the parents pursuant to its duty to facilitate rehabilitation where appropriate.[2] Further, in all cases, just because proceedings have been issued under Pt IV of the Act does not mean that the concerns that have resulted in those proceedings are necessarily irredeemable nor should they be considered to be so by the local authority at the point of issue. Pt IV of the Act cannot be allowed to become an administrative graveyard.

[1]   PLO Practice Direction, para 10.3.
[2]   CA 1989, s 23(4) and see para 6.59.

(c) PLO Stage 1 – Issue and the first appointment

(I) ISSUE

8.92 Upon the local authority filing its application with the documents set out in the pre-proceedings checklists (and supplementary Form PLO1) the court officer will issue the application and the court will nominate the case manager(s) and give standard directions including;[1]

(a)   Directions concerning compliance with the pre-proceedings checklist if necessary.

(b)   Directions pertaining to allocation and/or transfer.

(c)   Directions for the appointment of a children's guardian (in relation to care and supervision proceedings the court will expect that CAFCASS will have received notice from the local authority that proceedings are going to be started)[2].

(d)   Directions for the provision of the Case Analysis of the Children's Guardian for the First Appointment.[3]

(e)   Directions for the appointment of a solicitor for the child.

(f)   Directions where appropriate for inviting the Official Solicitor to act for protected persons (for example, non-subject children and incapacitated adults).

(g)   Directions for the listing of the case for First Appointment by Day 6 following the issue of the application.

(i)   Directions for a contested hearing (if necessary).

By Day 3 following the application, the court will expect a children's guardian to have been appointed[4] and that the local authority will have served the application form, the pre-proceedings checklist documents and the Supplementary Form PLO1 on the other parties. Whilst not explicitly stated in the PLO, given the short timescale between issue and first appointment it would appear to be incumbent on the local authority to notify the court on issue whether a contested hearing will be required at the first appointment so that the necessary arrangements can be made.

---

1   PLO Stage 1.
2   PLO Practice Direction, para 10.4(2).
3   See Chapter 10. The children's guardian will now be required to prepare a short report (verbal or written) at each case management stage of the proceedings detailing his or her analysis of the case and recommendations for the appropriate way forward – see CAFCASS Briefing on the PLO 25 January 2008, CAFCASS.
4   Following the implementation of CAFCASS organisational issues and staffing shortages contributed to significant delays in the appointment of children's guardians upon the commencement of proceedings. It remains to be seen whether the three days target for allocation under the PLO can be consistently met.

(II) THE FIRST APPOINTMENT

8.93 Within six days of the issue of the application for a care or supervision order, the court must list the case for first appointment, at which the allocation of the case will be confirmed and initial case management directions will be given. If the parties have notified the court of the need for a contested hearing, this will be dealt with at the first appointment.[1] The court will also conduct the initial case management in respect of the case and give standard directions, including:

(a)   Confirmation of the timetable for the child.
(b)   Confirmation of allocation or transfer.
(c)   Identification of additional parties and representation (including further consideration of the allocation of the children's guardian if not yet achieved).
(d)   Identification of cases appropriate for 'early final hearing'.
(e)   Scrutinisation of the care plan.
(f)   Directions for the provision of case analysis and recommendations from the children's guardian for the case management conference and the issues resolution hearing.
(g)   Directions for the local authority case summary and case summaries from the other parties.
(h)   Directions for initial witness statements.
(i)   Directions for the advocate's meeting preceding the case management conference.
(j)   Listing of the case management conference or (if appropriate) an Early Final Hearing.

In addition, the court will give consideration to making directions in relation to the following further matters:[2]

(a)   Those matters in the PLO which remain to be considered.
(b)   The joining of a person who would not otherwise be a respondent under the Rules as a party to the proceedings.
(c)   Where any person to be joined as a party may be a protected party, an investigation of that person's capacity to conduct the proceedings and the representation of that person and if appropriate invite the Official Solicitor to act for that person.
(d)   The identification of family and friends as proposed carers and any overseas, immigration, jurisdiction and paternity issues.
(e)   In public law proceedings other than care and supervision proceedings, the documents to be filed with the court.
(f)   Evidence to be obtained as to whether a parent who is a protected party is competent to make his or her own statement.

[1]   PLO Stage 1. Note that the FPC(CA 1989)R 1991, r 14(2) is still in force in respect of initial directions hearings in care proceedings although in practice it is the detailed provisions of the PLO that will be followed.
[2]   PLO Practice Direction, para 12.3(6).

(III) TIMETABLE FOR PROCEEDINGS

8.94 Section 32 requires a court hearing an application under Pt IV to draw up a timetable with a view to disposing of the application without delay and to give such directions as it considers appropriate for the purpose of ensuring, so far as is reasonably practicable, that the timetable is adhered to. The court should control the progress of care proceedings and for those directions appointments are an integral part of that process, they should not be formalities.[1] This is an extension of the duty of the court to have regard to the general principle that any delay in determining the question is likely to prejudice the welfare of the child.[2] Courts and practitioners should ensure that a timetable acts as an encouragement to bring the matter before the court expeditiously, while not discouraging sensible negotiation. Equally important the court must ensure the proper conduct of the proceedings in a way that is fair to all parties.

1   *Re MD and TD (Minors) (Time Estimates)* [1994] 2 FLR 336.
2   Section 1(2). Delay is ordinarily inimical to the welfare of the child but planned and purposeful delay may be beneficial: *C v Solihull Metropolitan Borough Council* [1993] 1 FLR 290.

8.95 One of the key developments signalled by the PLO is the 'timetable for the child' which requires that the timetable for the proceedings will be set by the court to take account of all the significant steps in the life of the child subject to the proceedings that are likely to take place during the proceedings, including not only legal steps but also social, care, health and educational steps.[1] Accordingly, the case timetable may be different for different siblings in the same case and a case can be longer or shorter depending on the circumstances. The following examples of significant steps in the child's life are provided by the Practice Direction:[2]

(a)   Any formal review by the local authority of the case of a looked after child.
(b)   The child taking up a place at a new school.
(c)   Any review by the local authority of any statement of the child's special educational needs.
(d)   An assessment by a paediatrician or other specialist.
(e)   The outcome of any review of the local authority plans for the child, for example, any plans for permanence through adoption, special guardianship or placement with parents or relatives.
(f)   A change or proposed change in the child's placement.

1   PLO Practice Direction, para 3.3.
2   PLO Practice Direction, para 3.4.

(IV) ALLOCATION AND TRANSFER

8.96 Within the context of the care proceedings review, emphasis was placed on the need to utilise more efficiently the court resources available to deal with applications for care and supervision orders. In particular, the concept of 'cascading' work down to the family proceedings court gained prominence.[1] To this end, the President of the Family Division has issued draft guidance on the allocation of proceedings between the family proceedings court, the county court and the High Court.[2] The following guidance is designed to assist in deciding whether a case should be heard in the family proceedings court, the county court or the High Court. It complements the Children (Allocation of Proceedings) Order 1991, the Family Law Act 1996 (Pt IV) (Allocation of Proceedings) Order 1997 and the Practice Direction of 5 June 1992 entitled

Family Division: Distribution of Business;[3] it does not override them. It does, however, replace the guidance formerly contained in decided authorities which pre-date it.[4]

1   House of Commons Constitutional Affairs Committee Minutes of Evidence for 22 May 2006, Sir Mark Potter P.
2   See para 8.92.
3   [1992] 2 FLR 87.
4   President's Guidance on the Distribution between Family Proceedings Courts, County Courts and High Courts of Cases Concerning Children and Proceedings under Part IV of the Family Law Act 1996.

8.97   At the first appointment the court will consider allocation of the case with a view to identifying the appropriate court to conduct the proceedings and transferring the proceedings as early as possible to that court and will transfer those cases to the county court which are obviously suitable for immediate transfer. For example, a case where there is evidence that a parent may be a protected party and require representation which currently cannot be obtained in the magistrates' court.[1]

1   PLO Practice Direction, para 11.3.

(V) PARTIES

8.98   The child and any person with parental responsibility for the child will automatically be given party status.[1] The applicant for a care or supervision order must serve a copy of the application on all the parties to the proceedings[2] and on every person who the applicant believes to be a parent without parental responsibility.[3] The court may direct that a father not having parental responsibility should not be served with notice[4] or that he be discharged from the proceedings.[5] If a father without parental responsibility wishes to participate in the proceedings, he should be permitted to do so, unless there is some justifiable reason for not joining him as a party.[6] Where a mother contends that a certain man is the father of the child, that person should be served by the local authority or an application made for a decision as to whether he should be served.[7] A father without parental responsibility who has been given notice of the proceedings but who delays an application to be joined until the final directions hearing may be refused if that would delay the resolution of the care hearing. In such cases, the father's right to access to the court has to be balanced with the right of the child to an early determination of his future, so that neither arts 6 nor 8 of the ECHR are breached by refusing the father's application.[8]

1   FPC(CA 1989)R 1991, Sch 2.
2   FPC(CA 1989)R 1991, r 4.
3   FPC(CA 1989)R 1991, Sch 4. In addition, the application must be served on any local authority providing accommodation for the child, any person with whom the child is living at the time proceedings are commenced, any person providing the child with refuge pursuant to s 51(1) or (2) of the Act and every person the local authority believes to be a party to any pending proceedings in respect of the child.
4   *Re X (Care: Notice of Proceedings)* [1996] 3 FCR 91, [1996] 1 FLR 186.
5   *Re W (Discharge of Party to Proceedings)* [1997] 1 FLR 128.

6   *Re B (Care Proceedings: Notification of Father Without Parental Responsibility)* [1999] 2 FLR 408; *Re P (Care Proceedings: Father's Application to be Joined as a Party)* [2001] 1 FLR 781.

7   *Re B (Care Proceedings: Notification of Father Without Parental Responsibility)* [1999] 2 FLR 408.

8   *Re P (Care Proceedings: Father's Application to be Joined as a Party)* [2001] 1 FLR 781 (where the father had been served with notice of the proceedings at the outset, had been advised early on to seek legal advice, and had chosen not to participate in the proceedings having been given ample opportunity to be involved); see also *Re B and T (Care Proceedings: Legal Representation)* [2001] 1 FLR 485, CA, in which it was held that it was not a breach of human rights for a parent not to have legal representation. In *P, C and S v United Kingdom* [2002] 2 FLR 631 the European court, considering an application in respect of this case, concluded that the assistance of a lawyer during the hearings of applications with such crucial consequences, was an indispensable requirement without which there was a breach of art 6. Sed quaere when lawyers had withdrawn because they were required to conduct the case in an unreasonable manner? For a wider discussion of representation in care proceedings see Lindley, Richards and Freeman 'Advice and advocacy for parents in child protection cases' [2001] CFLQ 167 and 311.

8.99   The court may direct that others be joined to the proceedings.[1] There is concern about the number of parties who become involved in care proceedings, which can cause unnecessary delay and waste of costs. The court should however be particularly cautious about giving leave to relatives whose interests are the same as the parents, and are simply standing behind them[2] nor should public funds be expended to enable a person to be a party unless they have a positive case to advance.[3]

1   FPC(CA 1989)R 1991 r.7(5); FPR 1991 r.4.7(5).
2   *Re M (Minors) (Sexual Abuse: Evidence)* [1993] 1 FCR 253, [1993] 1 FLR 822, discussed at para 5.153. See also *North Yorkshire County Council v G* [1994] 1 FCR 737, in which a brother was refused leave to become a party to care proceedings on the basis that his case was the same as that of his mother.
3   *Merton London Borough Council v K; Re K (Care: Representation: Public Funding)* [2005] EWHC 167 (Fam), [2005] 2 FLR 422.

8.100   The guidelines for leave applications set out in s 10(9) are applicable to applications for joinder in care proceedings.[1] In *G v Kirklees Metropolitan Borough Council* the court held that the applicant to be joined as a party to proceedings needed to demonstrate that their case was reasonably likely to succeed. However, in *Re G (Child Case: Parental Involvement)*[2] the Court of Appeal determined that the reasonable likelihood of success test set out in the *Kirklees* case was too high and the test should be 'is their an arguable case?' Finally, in *M v Warwickshire County Council*[3] Wilson LJ, preferred the 'real prospects of success' test used in the Civil Procedure Rules 1998[4] as being likely to be apt to the vast majority of applications. It should be noted that in *Re J (Leave to Issue an Application for a Residence Order)* Thorpe LJ stated:[5]

'I am particularly anxious at the development of a practice that seems to substitute the test "has the applicant satisfied the court that he or she has a good arguable case" for the test Parliament applied in s 10(9). That anxiety is heightened in modern times when applicants under s 10(9) enjoy Article 6 rights to a fair trial and, in the nature of things, are also likely to enjoy Articel 8 rights.'

8.100 *Care Proceedings*

It remains to be seen whether the simple statutory approach preferred by Thorpe J in *Re J* will be extended to applications for party status in cases under s 31 of the Act.

1   *G v Kirklees Metropolitan Borough Council* [1993] 1 FLR 805. See also *Re P (A Child)(residence: grandmother's application for leave)* [2002] EWCA Civ 846, [2002] All ER (D) 554 (May).
2   [1996] 1 FLR 857.
3   [2007] EWCA Civ 1084, [2008] 1 FLR 1093.
4   CPR 52.3(6).
5   [2002] WCA Civ 1346, [2003] 1 FLR 114.

8.101 A person against whom allegations are made (but who is not a party) can be given leave to intervene and permitted to take part in the proceedings to the limited extent of his involvement in the allegations which are the subject of the proceedings,[1] but has no right to be made a party.[2]

1   *Re S (Care: Residence: Intervener)* [1997] 1 FLR 497, CA.
2   *Re H (Care Proceedings: Intervener)* [2000] 1 FLR 775.

8.102 The court must consider as soon as possible whether any of the adult parties or intended adult to the proceedings lacks capacity[1] to conduct proceedings such that they require a litigation friend or guardian ad litem to conduct proceedings on their behalf. The issue of capacity must be determined before the court gives directions in respect to that adult's role in the proceedings.[2] An adult who lacks capacity is a 'protected party' within proceedings. That adult's representative must be involved in any instruction of an expert, including the instruction of an expert to assess whether the adult, although a protected party, is competent to give evidence. The representative should consider (and ask the expert to consider), if the protected party is competent to give evidence, what will serve their best interests in this regard. In particular, the representative may wish to seek advice about 'special measures' for giving evidence. The representative can put forward an argument on behalf of the protected party that the protected party should not give evidence.[3]

1   Within the meaning of the Mental Capacity Act 2005.
2   PLO Practice Direction, paras 7.1 and 7.2.
3   PLO Practice Direction, para 7.3.

8.103 Where a child is a party to the proceedings rather than the subject of them and that child is nearing his or her 18th birthday and considered likely to lack capacity to conduct the proceedings when he reaches 18 ,the court will consider giving directions relating to the investigation of a child's capacity in this respect.[1]

1   PLO Practice Direction, para 8.

(VI) EARLY FINAL HEARING

8.104 The PLO introduces the concept of the 'early final hearing'. The PLO stipulates that the cases which are suitable for an early final hearing are likely to be those cases where the child has no parents, guardians, relatives who want to care for the child, or other carers. Examples are those cases where the child is an abandoned baby or where a child has been brought into this country and abandoned. The court will identify at the first appointment whether the case is one which is suitable for an early final hearing; and set a date for that final hearing where it is appropriate to do so.[1]

1   PLO Practice Direction, para 12.4. In May 2008 the Government issued the Magistrates' Court Fees Order 2008, SI 2008/1052 and the Family Proceedings Fees Order 2008, SI 2008/1054 which have resulted in a substantial increase in the fee for issuing care proceedings (with a discount in that fee in those cases suitable for early final hearing). This step has lead to concerns that perverse incentives to delay the issue of proceedings or to rush a case to early final hearing may result.

(VII) EXPERTS

8.105 Where the parties are agreed on any matter relating to experts or expert evidence, the draft agreement must be submitted for the court's approval as early as possible in the proceedings. The issue of expert evidence should accordingly be considered at the first appointment where possible in order to mitigate delay. A party who wishes to instruct an expert should comply with the Experts Practice Direction.[1]

1   PLO Practice Direction, para 12.7; PLO Experts Practice Direction.

(VIII) CONCURRENT CARE AND CRIMINAL PROCEEDINGS

8.106 The decision whether to adjourn care proceedings, and have repeated interim care orders, may cause difficulty when there are concurrent criminal proceedings pending. Prior to the CA 1989, there was reluctance to adjourn care proceedings for the outcome of criminal proceedings.[1] The general rule is that the care proceedings will precede the criminal trial.[2] In a case where parents faced a murder charge, the Court of Appeal has held that it was preferable for the criminal trial to be heard before care proceedings, unless there were exceptional circumstances requiring the child's long-term future to be arranged without delay.[3] The family court should ensure that there is co-ordination between the different courts.[4] In cases where there are both care proceedings and criminal proceedings, consideration should be given to a joint directions hearing.

1   See *R v Inner London Juvenile Court, ex p G* [1988] FCR 316, [1988] 2 FLR 58; *R v Exeter Juvenile Court, ex p RKH, R v Waltham Forest Juvenile Court, ex p KB* [1988] FCR 474, [1988] 2 FLR 214.
2   *R v L* [2006] EWCA Crim 1902, [2006] 1 WLR 3092, *Re H (Children)* [2006] EWCA Civ 1875, [2006] All ER (D) 294 (Dec).
3   *Re S (Care Order: Criminal Proceedings)* [1995] 1 FLR 151.
4   *Re A and B (Minors) (No 2)* [1995] 1 FLR 351.

(*d*) *Interim orders*

8.107 Once care proceedings have been started, the court has the option of making:

(a)   no order;
(b)   a residence order and other s 8 orders for a limited period;
(c)   with or without an interim supervision order; or
(d)   an interim care order.[1]

If the court makes a residence order on an application for a care or supervision order, it must make an interim supervision order unless satisfied that the child's welfare will be satisfactorily safeguarded without it.[2]

[1]   Together with directions pursuant to s 38(6) if appropriate. See below at 8.113.
[2]   Section 38(3).

8.108 An order under s 8 may be made for a specified period and may impose conditions.[1] Orders may be made even though the court is not in a position to dispose of the proceedings.[2] Thus the court has power to make interim orders similar to those it could make as a final disposal in care proceedings. It could make a residence order until the next hearing in favour of a relative, and control the child's contact with a parent for the time being, through a contact order or a prohibited steps order.[3] The court cannot, however, make a contact order in favour of a local authority because of the restriction contained in s 9(2).[4]

[1]   Section 11(7), see paras 5.108 ff.
[2]   Section 11(3), see para 5.62.
[3]   See paras 5.54 ff.
[4]   See para 5.125.

(I) GROUNDS FOR AN INTERIM CARE OR SUPERVISION ORDER

8.109 Where, on an application for a care or supervision order, the proceedings are adjourned or where the court in any proceedings gives a direction for an authority to investigate the child's circumstances,[1] the court may make an interim care or supervision order[2] if it satisfied that there are reasonable grounds for believing that the threshold criteria pursuant to s 31(2) are satisfied.[3] The court must still apply the overriding principles in s 1 that the welfare of the child is paramount[4] and that no order should be made unless it is better for the child than making no order.[5] The court must hear some evidence if the interim order is opposed[6] and must be satisfied that the grounds for an interim order are made out even where all the parties agree that an order should be made.[7] The task of the court at the interim stage is simply to determine whether the threshold for an interim order are met and not to make final findings of fact with a view to deciding whether the s 31(2) threshold criteria are satisfied.[8]

[1]   Under s 37: see para 7.25.
[2]   CA 1989, s 38(1).
[3]   Section 38(2). For the threshold criteria see above.
[4]   *Re H (A Child)(Interim Care Order)* [2002] EWCA Civ 1932, [2003] 1 FCR 350.
[5]   *Hampshire County Council v S* [1993] Fam 158, [1993] 1 FLR 559.
[6]   *Re W (A Minor)(Interim Care Order)* [1994] 2 FLR 892.
[7]   Revised Children Act 1989 Guidance and Regulations, Vol 1, Court Orders (2008) Department for Children, Schools and Families, para 3.45.
[8]   *Oxfordshire County Council v S* [2003] EWHC 2174 (fam), [2004] 1 FLR 426.

8.110 At an interim stage the removal of a child from her parents is not to be sanctioned unless the child's safety requires interim protection to the extent that the child's safety demands immediate separation.[1] Where the court is considering making an interim care order in respect of a young child and it is not possible to bring the matter back to court for final hearing for a significant period, the court must balance the risk of harm to the child of long-term removal with the risk of harm to the child of being left with the parents.[2] An interim order should not be regarded as a 'automatic' step but rather a 'time-limited intervention'.[3] It is a neutral step in the proceedings favouring neither one party nor the other and enabling the court to maintain strict controls over any steps taken with respect to the child.[4]

[1] *Re K and H* [2006] EWCA Civ 1898, [2007] 1 FLR 2043 and *Re H (A Child)(Interim Care Order)* [2002] EWCA Civ 1932, [2003] 1 FCR 350. This test must be distinguished from the 'exceptional justification/extraordinarily compelling reasons' test applicable in applications for an emergency protection order, the nature of which test is formulated having regard to the nature of the emergency protection process (see *Re X (Emergency Protection Orders)* [2006] EWHC 510 (Fam), [2006] 2 FLR 701).

[2] *Re M (Interim Care Order: Removal)* [2005] 1 FCR 303, [2006] 1 FLR 1043. The action taken must be a proportionate response to the nature and gravity of the feared harm: *Re C and B (Care Order: Future Harm)* [2001] 1 FLR 611. See paras 8.56 and 8.164.

[3] Revised Children Act 1989 Guidance and Regulations, Vol 1, Court Orders (2008) Department for Children, Schools and Families, para 3.44.

[4] *Re G (Minors)(Interim Care Order)* [1993] 2 FLR 839. It is suggested however that the oft expressed idea that an interim care order represents a holding position pending the outcome of the final hearing is unhelpful when seeking to ensure delay does not adversely affect the proceedings.

(II) GUIDANCE ON INTERIM APPLICATIONS

8.111 Within the foregoing context, the following guidance to the family proceedings court remains important when courts are dealing with interim applications.[1] This guidance applies equally to the county court:[2]

(1) Justices should bear in mind that they are not, at an interim hearing, required to make a final conclusion; indeed it is because they are unable to reach a final conclusion that they are empowered to make an interim order. An interim order or decision will usually be required so as to establish a holding position, after weighing all the relevant risks, pending the final hearing.

(2) If justices find that they are unable to provide the appropriate hearing time, be it through pressures of work or for some other reason, they must, when an urgent interim order may have to be made, consider taking steps pursuant to r 14(2)(h) by transferring the proceedings laterally to an adjacent family proceedings court.

(3) At the start of a hearing which is concerned with interim relief, justices will usually be called upon to exercise their discretion under r 21(2) as to the order of speeches and evidence. Circumstances prevailing will almost certainly not permit full evidence to be heard. Accordingly, in such proceedings, justices should rarely make findings as to disputed facts.[2] These will have to be left over for the final hearing.

(4) Justices must bear in mind that the greater the extent to which an interim order deviates from a previous order or the status quo, the more

acute the need is likely to be for an early final hearing date. Any disruption in a child's life almost invariably requires early resolution. Justices should be cautious about changing a child's residence under an interim order. The preferred course should be to leave the child where it is, with a direction for safeguards and the earliest possible hearing date.

(5) When an interim order may be made which will lead to a substantial change in a child's position, justices should consider permitting limited oral evidence to be led and challenged by way of cross-examination. However, it will necessarily follow that, in cross-examination, the evidence will have to be restricted to the issues which are essential at the interim stage. To this end the court may well have to intervene to ensure that this course is followed and that there is not a 'dress rehearsal' of the full hearing.

(6) Justices should, if possible, ensure that they have before them the written advice from the children's guardian. When there are substantial issues between the parties the guardian should, if possible, be at court to give oral advice. A party who is opposed to a recommendation made by the guardian should normally be given an opportunity to put questions to him or her in regard to advice given to the court.

1   *Hampshire County Council v S* [1993] Fam 158, [1993] 1 FLR 559.
2   *Re W (A Minor)(Interim Care Order)* [1994] 2 FLR 892.

(III) EFFECT OF AN INTERIM ORDER

8.112 An interim care or supervision order has the same effect as a full care or supervision order. Under an interim care order the local authority shares parental responsibility with the parents and remains under a duty to rehabilitate the child to the care of the parents unless to do so would not be reasonably practicable or consistent with his welfare.[1] Under an interim supervision order, the local authority must advise, assist and befriend the child.[2] In addition, under an interim order the court has the jurisdiction to direct an assessment of the child under s 38(6) of the Act.

1   CA 1989, ss 31(11), 33(3) and 23(6).
2   CA 1989, s 35(1).

(IV) DIRECTIONS FOR ASSESSMENT

8.113 Section 38 provides that where a court makes an interim care or supervision order it may give such directions as it considers appropriate with regard to medical or psychiatric examination or other assessment of the child and may direct that no examination or assessment is to take place at all or unless the court directs.[1] A direction may be given or varied at any time during the period of an interim order. In deciding what directions should be given, the welfare of the child is not the court's paramount consideration.[2] A direction to carry out an assessment is a requirement and not permission to do so.[3]

1   Section 38(6).
2   See para 2.16.

³ CA 1989, s 38(6). See *Re O (Minors)(Medical Examination)* [1993] 1 FLR 860 and *Berkshire County Council v C* [1993] Fam 205, [1993] 1 FLR 569.

8.114 A parent who opposes the making of a care order is likely to make an application for an assessment, because without it the court may have no professional or expert evidence other than that of the local authority on which to base its decision. Thus that application can be determinative of the outcome of the care proceedings.

8.115 A direction pursuant to s 38(6) is a direction aimed at providing the court with the material that, in the view of the court, is required to enable it to reach a proper decision at the final hearing of the application for a care order.¹ In *Re G (Interim Care Order: Residential Assessment)*² the House of Lords stipulated in relation to applications for assessment under s 38(6) that:

'What is directed under s 38(6) must clearly be an examination or assessment of the child, including where appropriate, his relationship with his parents, the risk that his parents may present to him and the ways in which those risks may be avoided or managed, all with a view to enabling the court to make the decisions which it has to make under the Act with the minimum of delay. Any services which are provided to the child and his family must be ancillary to that end. They must not be an end in themselves.'

In *Re G* an assessment whose main purpose was to provide a continuing course of psychotherapy to the mother was held to fall outside the ambit of s 38(6). Where the assessment sought does fall within the ambit of s 38(6) and there is some evidence that such an assessment may be justified, when determining the application the court should have regard to the underlying philosophy of the CA 1989 that wherever possible children should be brought up by their parents or within their natural families and the requirement that the parents receive a fair trial at final hearing.³

¹ *Re B (Interim Care Order: Directions)* [2002] EWCA Civ 25, [2002] 1 FLR 545.
² [2005] UKHL 68, [2006] 1 AC 576, [2006] 1 FLR 601.
³ *Re L and H (Residential Assessment)* [2007] EWCA Civ 213, [2007] 1 FLR 1370.

8.116 In *Re C (A Minor) (Interim Care Order: Residential Assessment)* the House of Lords held that a court could dictate the placement of the child during an interim care order for the purpose of an assessment.¹ There may be a direction to reside in a mother and baby unit, if that management was the better course for the case.² The court may not order that a child live at home with its parent during the course of an interim care order, which is a discretion vested in the local authority.³ Although s 38 is wide enough to give the court jurisdiction to name the person to carry out an assessment, the court should not direct an individual who is unwilling to do so.⁴

¹ [1997] AC 489, [1997] 1 FCR 149, HL.
² *Re B (Interim Care Order: Directions)* [2002] EWCA Civ 25, [2002] 1 FLR 545.
³ *Re L (A Minor)(interim care order)* [1996] 2 FCR 706, CA.

⁴   *Re W (A Minor) (Care Proceedings: Assessment)* [1998] 1 FCR 287, CA and *Re B (Psychiatric Therapy for Parents)* [1999] 1 FLR 701, CA. Note also that the court cannot direct the provision of services: *Re J (a Minor) (Specific Issue Order: Leave to Apply)* [1995] 1 FLR 669.

8.117   A court can give a direction for an assessment under s 38(6) even if the application for that direction is opposed by the local authority, which must then comply with it.¹ In *Re C (A Minor) (Interim Care Order: Residential Assessment)* the House of Lords also held that the court can direct the authority to fund any necessary placement, although it would take into account the cost and the fact that local authority resources were limited. It might be necessary to consider the impact of the cost compared to the ability of the authority to provide other services for children.² For that purpose an authority should consider whether to provide budgetary evidence³ although the court should not request detailed evidence from the local authority in this regard.⁴ It is important to ensure that proper weight is given to the benefit to the child compared to the wider responsibility of the local authority generally.⁵

¹   *Re V (A Child)(Care Proceedings: Human Rights Claims)* [2004] EWCA Civ 54, [2004] 1 FLR 944.
²   [1997] AC 489, [1997] 1 FCR 149, [1997] 1 FLR 1, HL and see *Re C (children) (residential assessment)* [2001] EWCA Civ 1305, [2001] 3 FCR 164. A direction can be appealed but it must otherwise be obeyed. Lack of resources is no excuse: *Re O (Minors) (Medical Examination)* [1993] 1 FLR 860 and *Berkshire County Council v C* [1993] Fam 205, [1993] 1 FLR 569.
³   The Funding Code has now been amended so that the Legal Services Commission will no longer contribute to the funding of residential assessments, the LSC arguing that the cost of such assessment is not a proper cost for a body funding legal costs to meet. This will place an additional funding burden on local authorities and is likely to lead to more contested applications for assessments of this nature on the basis of cost.
⁴   *Re G (Interim Care Order: Residential Assessment)* [2005] UKHL 68, [2006] 1 AC 576, [2006] 1 FLR 601.
⁵   *Re C (Children)(Residential Assessment)* [2001] EWCA Civ 1305, [2001] 3 FCR 164.

8.118   Where there is no interim order in force, a party may still obtain leave to file a report, but the court has jurisdiction to order or prohibit any assessment that involves the participation of the child.¹ If a direction is given for a medical report on a parent or the child, no party will then be able to withhold the report because it is not favourable to their case.²

¹   FPR 1991, r 4.18 and the FPC(CA 1989)R 1991, r 18.
²   See paras 11.33.

8.119   If the child is of sufficient understanding to make an informed decision, he may refuse to submit to an examination or assessment.¹ The level of understanding that enables a child to make an informed decision whether to refuse to submit to a psychiatric examination is a much higher level of understanding than is required to enable him to give instructions to a solicitor on his behalf, which must be a questionable distinction.² It has been held, questionably, that the High Court can, in the exercise of its inherent jurisdiction³, override the refusal of a child to submit to an examination or assessment.⁴

¹   Section 38(6). Similar provisions apply in relation to applications for a child assessment order under s 43 or an emergency protection order under s 44.

2   *Re H (A Minor) (Care Proceedings)* [1993] 1 FLR 440.
3   See Chapter 12.
4   *South Glamorgan County Council v W and B* [1993] 1 FLR 574, for discussion of which see para 12.132, n1.

(V) Attaching an exclusion requirement to an interim order

8.120 A court may include an exclusion requirement in an interim care order.[1] (This does not include a case which is based on the child being beyond parental control).[2] The court must be satisfied of three conditions:

(a)   that there is reasonable cause to believe that if a person (the relevant person) is excluded from a dwelling house in which the child lives, the child will cease to suffer or cease to be likely to suffer significant harm; and

(b)   that a person living in the dwelling house, whether a parent or some other person, is able and willing to give the child the care which it would be reasonable to expect a parent to give; and

(c)   that that person consents to the inclusion of the exclusion requirement. Consent must be in writing or given orally to the court.[3]

1   CA 1989, s 38A. There are no available statistics in respect of such orders, but practical experience suggests they remain rare.
2   That part of the threshold criteria is specifically excluded: s 38A(1)(a).
3   FPR 1991, r 4.24 and FP(CA 1989)R 1991, r 25. See also *President's Direction* [1998] 1 FLR 495. For the procedure to be followed and evidence required see *W v A Local Authority (Exclusion Requirement)* [2000] 2 FCR 662, [2001] 2 FLR 666.

8.121 An exclusion requirement may be one or more of the following provisions:

(a)   requiring the relevant person to leave a dwelling house in which he is living with the child;

(b)   prohibiting him from entering a dwelling house in which the child is living; or

(c)   excluding the relevant person from a defined area around the dwelling house.

A power of arrest may be attached to the exclusion requirement. The exclusion requirement and the power of arrest may be ordered for periods shorter than the substantive order. If the child is removed from the dwelling house, the requirement shall cease to have effect. The court may accept an undertaking in similar terms but a power of arrest cannot be attached.[1] A person who is not entitled to apply for variation or discharge of an interim care order, but to whom the exclusion requirement applies, may apply for variation of the requirement.[2] The exclusion requirement ceases to have effect if the child is removed from the house from which the person in question was excluded for a continuous period of 24 hours.[3]

1   CA 1989, s 38B.
2   CA 1989, s 39(3A).
3   CA 1989, s 38A(10).

(VI) DURATION OF INTERIM ORDERS

8.122 An interim care or supervision order may be made for such period as the court orders but may not last longer than eight weeks in the case of an initial order or 'the relevant period' in the case of a second or subsequent order.[1] The relevant period is four weeks, or eight weeks from the date of the first order if that is longer.[2] Thus, if the first order was made for two weeks, the second order could be made for six weeks. If the first two orders were made respectively for one week and two weeks, the third order could be made for five weeks. When deciding the period, the court must consider whether a party who was or might have been opposing the order was in a position to argue the case in full.[3] Where the parents are not present at court when the first interim care order is made a 28 day order is preferable.[4]

1   CA 1989, s 38(4).
2   CA 1989, s 38(5).
3   CA 1989, s 38(10).
4   *Re M (Interim Care Order: Removal)* [2005] EWCA Civ 1594, [2006] 1 FLR 1043.

8.123 If the court orders an investigation by a local authority under s 37(1), a care or supervision order may be made for no longer than the period within which the authority must report to the court. The maximum period is eight weeks.[1] The authority may decide within that period to commence and obtain an order.

1   CA 1989, s 37(4).

(VII) RENEWING INTERIM ORDERS

8.124 There is no limit in principle to the number of repeated interim orders which the court can make, provided they are made before the expiry of the relevant period.[1] Where an initial interim care order has been made and a date fixed for a full hearing, there will probably be no further contested interim applications unless circumstances change.[2] Agreed interim care orders may be made in the family proceedings court under the following conditions:[3]

(a)   a written request for such an order has been made to which the other parties and any children's guardian consent, and which they or their representative have signed;
(b)   a previous such order has been made in the same proceedings; and
(c)   the terms of the order sought are the same as those of the last such order made.

Although family proceedings courts are encouraged to make interim care orders in accordance with these provisions, there is no similar provision in the Family Proceedings Rules 1991 but in general care centres appear to adopt a similar approach. Courts sometimes require the local authority to attend on the renewal application. In London some local authorities have developed the practice of seeking the agreement of other parties to ongoing approval to renewal of orders.[4]

1   *Gateshead Metropolitan Borough Council v N* [1993] 1 FLR 811.

² See the judgment of Glidewell LJ in *Re W (A Minor)(Interim Care Order)* [1994] 2 FLR
892 for the principles governing whether a further contested hearing is required.
³ FPC(CA 1989)R 1991, r 28.
⁴ Such local protocols are not to be discouraged: see Handbook of Best Practice in Children
Act Cases (1997) CAAC.

(e) PLO Stage 2 – case management conference

8.125 The PLO provides that there will be a case management conference
(CMC) in each case to enable the case management judge or case manager,
with the co-operation of the parties, actively to manage the case and, at the
earliest practicable opportunity to identify the relevant and key issues and give
full case management directions including confirming the timetable for the
child.[1]

¹ PLO Practice Direction, para 14.1 The early identification of issues is a key feature of the
Outline and central to its successful operation.

(I) ADVOCATES' MEETING

8.126 Before the CMC (and before the issues resolution hearing) the court
will consider directing advocates to have discussions. Such discussion is
intended to facilitate agreement and to narrow the issues for the court to
consider. It is intended that litigants in person may take part in the advocates'
meeting or discussions.[1] Where there is a litigant in person the court will
consider the most effective way in which that person can be involved in the
advocates' discussions and give directions as appropriate including directions
relating to the part to be played by any McKenzie friend.[2] An advocate who
has conduct of the final hearing should ordinarily attend the CMC (and the
issues resolution hearing). Where the attendance of this advocate is not
possible, then an advocate who is familiar with the issues in the proceedings
should attend.[3] Discussions are to take place no later than two days before the
CMC and the need for discussions outside the 'court room door' of matters,
which could have been discussed at an earlier time, is to be avoided.[4]

¹ PLO Practice Direction, para 3.11.
² PLO Practice Direction, para 13.2.
³ PLO Practice Direction, para 16.
⁴ PLO Practice Direction, para 13.3.

8.127 The main objective of the advocates' meeting or discussion (whether
before the CMC or theiIssues resolution hearing) is to prepare the draft case
management order (CMO).[1] Following discussion the advocates should prepare the draft CMO. In practice the intention is that the advocate for the
applicant, which in care and supervision proceedings will ordinarily be the
local authority, should take the lead in preparing and adjusting the draft CMO
following discussion with the other advocates.[2] Where it is not possible for the
advocates to agree the terms of the draft CMO, the advocates should specify
on the draft CMO, or on a separate document if more practicable those
provisions on which they agree and those provisions on which they disagree.[3]

¹ PLO Practice Direction, para 13.1.

2 PLO Practice Direction, para 13.4.
3 PLO Practice Direction, para 13.5.

8.128 At the advocates' meeting or discussion before the CMC, the advocates should also endeavour to agree between themselves the questions to be put to any proposed expert (whether jointly instructed or not) if not previously agreed. Under the Experts Practice Direction the questions on which the proposed expert is to give an opinion are a crucial component of the expert directions which the court is required to consider at the CMC.[1]

1 PLO Practice Direction, para 13.7.

(II) CASE MANAGEMENT ORDER

8.129 The draft form of a CMO contains directions of general application to be used as appropriate for each case. The form of order is not only to be used for drawing up orders in the form prescribed by the Rules at the end of a hearing but also as a case management checklist. It is designed to assist the parties identify the relevant issues and the procedural directions which may be required, monitor changes to the relevant issues and compliance with the court's directions and to focus on what the proceedings are intended to achieve.[1]

1 PLO Practice Direction, para 13.10.

8.130 Parties should start to consider the content of the draft CMO at the earliest opportunity either before or in the course of completing applications to the court or the response to the application. They should in any event consider the draft CMO after the first appointment. There should be ongoing consideration of the draft CMO throughout the proceedings. Thedraft CMO should serve as an aide memoire to everyone involved in the proceedings of the timetable for the child, the case management decisions and the identified issues.[1]

1 PLO Practice Direction, paras 5.7 and 5.8.

8.131 Only one draft CMO should be filed with the court for each of the CMC and the issues resolution hearing. It is the responsibility of the advocate for the applicant, which in care and supervision proceedings will ordinarily be the local authority, to prepare those drafts and be responsible for obtaining comments from the advocates and the parties.[1]

1 PLO Practice Direction, para 5.9.

8.132 Unless the court directs otherwise, the draft CMO must be filed with the court no later than 11am on the day before the CMC or the issues resolution hearing whichever may be appropriate.[1]

1 PLO Practice Direction, para 13.6.

(III) CASE MANAGEMENT CONFERENCE

8.133 The court will set a date for the CMC normally no later than 45 days from the date of issue of the proceedings and in any event in line with the timetable for the child.[1] At the CMC, the court will:[2]

(a) Review and confirm the timetable for the child.

(b) Confirm the allocation or the transfer of the case.

(c) Scrutinise the care plan.

(d) Identify the key issues.

(e) Identify the remaining case management issues.

(f) Resolve remaining case management issues by reference to the draft CMO.

(g) Identify any special measures such as the need for access for the disabled or provision for vulnerable witnesses.

(h) Scrutinise the case management record to check whether directions have been complied with and if not, consider making further directions as appropriate.

(i) Where expert evidence is required, check whether the parties have complied with the Experts Practice Direction, in particular section 4 (Preparation for the relevant hearing) and consider giving directions as appropriate.

(j) Set a date for the issues resolution hearing normally at any time between 16 and 25 weeks from the date of issue of the proceedings and in any event in line with the timetable for the child.

(k) If necessary, specify a period within which the final hearing of the application is to take place unless a date has already been set.

The parties, their advisers and the children's guardian, are encouraged to try to agree directions for the management of the proceedings.[3] To obtain the court's approval the agreed directions must[4] set out a timetable for the child by reference to calendar dates for the taking of steps for the preparation of the case and include a date when it is proposed that the next hearing will take place.

[1] PLO Practice Direction, para 12.5.
[2] PLO Practice Direction, paras 14.3 and 14.5.
[3] PLO Practice Direction, para 20.1.
[4] PLO Practice Direction, para 20.2.

8.134 The PLO emphasises[1] that a party or the children's guardian must apply to the court at the earliest opportunity if they wish to vary by extending the dates set by the court for:

(a) A directions appointment.

(b) A first appointment.

(c) A CMC.

(d) An issues resolution hearing.

(e) The final hearing.

(f) The period within which the final hearing of the application is to take place.

(g)   Any discussion between advocates or for the filing of the draft CMO.

¹   PLO Practice Direction, para21.

(f) PLO Stage 3 – issues resolution hearing

(I) ADVOCATES' MEETING

8.135 As with the CMC, prior to the Issues Resolution Hearing (IRH) the court will consider directing advocates to have discussions. Such discussion is once again intended to facilitate agreement and to narrow the issues for the court to consider. It is intended that litigants in person may take part in the advocates' meeting or discussions.[1]

¹   PLO Practice Direction, para 3.11 and see para 8.126 above.

(II) DRAFT CASE MANAGEMENT ORDER

8.136 As with the CMC the main objective of the advocates' meeting or discussion is to prepare the draft CMO.[1]

¹   PLO Practice Direction, para 13.1 and see para 8.127 above.

(III) ISSUES RESOLUTION HEARING

8.137 The PLO introduces an entirely new species of hearing to the proce-dure in applications under Pt IV of the Act. The IRH is designed to resolve and narrow issues in the case and identify key remaining issues requiring resolution, either by way of agreement or by way of determination at final hearing.[1] In addition, the IRH[2] is likely to be the last hearing before any final hearing and will thus also fulfill the role of a pre-hearing review at which final case management directions and other preparations for the final hearing will be made.[3]

¹   PLO Practice Direction, para 15.1.
²   Some consideration was given to calling this hearing an Issues Resolution Appointment. However, as an element of the PLO, there were obvious disadvantages with the acronym IRA.
³   PLO Practice Direction, para 15.2.

8.138 During the IRH the court will carry out the following tasks:

(a)   Identify the key issues (if any) to be determined.
(b)   Review and confirm the timetable for the child.
(c)   Consider giving case management directions relating to—
     (i)   any outstanding matter contained in the draft CMO;
     (ii) the preparation and filing of final evidence including the filing of witness templates;
     (iii) skeleton arguments;
     (iv) preparation and filing of bundles in accordance with the Bundles Practice Direction;

(v)   any agreement relating to the satisfaction of the threshold criteria under s 31 of the 1989 Act or facts and issues remaining to be determined in relation to it or to any welfare question which arises;

(vi)   time estimates;

(vii)   the judicial reading list and likely reading time and judgment writing time;

(viii)   issue the CMO.

8.139   In the family proceedings court the intention is that most IRH's will be conducted by legal advisers. At the IHR, the legal adviser who should have been allocated adequate time to prepare, and is a qualified or otherwise specialist family lawyer, should be able to take the parties through the evidence with them. This exercise will not just be checking that all is in order for the final hearing , but will be an analysis of what in reality remains to be determined by the court and what is no longer in dispute.[1]

[1]   A New Public Law Outline and Statutory Guidance for Local Authorities – Frequently Asked Questions, 12 December 2007, Ministry of Justice.

8.140   During the formulation of the PLO and the consultative process which accompanied its introduction in the initiative areas in which it was first piloted, concern was expressed[1] that the IRH risked becoming a hearing at which parents who were perceived to have 'weak' cases were pressured by the court to concede orders without proper opportunity to challenge the evidence against them, as distinct from a proactive but collaborative mechanism to identify and, wherever possible, narrow issues within proceedings[2]. As a result of these concerns, the PLO makes clear the function of the IRH by stating at paras 15.4 and 15.5 as follows:

'15.4   For the avoidance of doubt the purpose of an Issues Resolution Hearing is to—

(1)   identify key issues which are not agreed;

(2)   examine if those key issues can be agreed; and

(3)   where those issues cannot be agreed, examine the most proportionate method of resolving those issues.

15.5   The expectation is that the method of resolving the key issues which cannot be agreed will be at a hearing (ordinarily the Final Hearing) where there is an opportunity for the relevant oral evidence to be heard and challenged.'

[1]   See for example the responses of the Family Law Bar Association, the Association of Lawyers for Children to the draft Public Law Outline, Resolution and NAGALRO.

[2]   This concern arose largely out of the original proposal in the Judicial Review Team's Thematic Review of the Public Law Case Management Protocol (see above) that the court would subject cases to 'early neutral evaluation' at a 'Children's Dispute Resolution Hearing'.

(g)   PLO Stage 4 – final hearing

8.141   At the final hearing, the court will determine the outstanding issues between the parties. The court is in control of its own procedure and may give directions for the order or evidence and closing submissions.[1] In *Re B (Minors)(Contact)*[2] Butler-Sloss LJ said, in the context of a dispute over contact to children in care:

> 'There is a spectrum of procedure for family cases from the ex parte application on minimal evidence to the full and detailed investigations on oral evidence which may be prolonged. Where on that spectrum a judge decides a particular application should be placed is a matter for his discretion. Applications for residence orders or for committal to the care of a local authority or revocation of a care order are likely to be decided on full oral evidence, but not invariably. Such is not the case on contact applications which may be and are heard sometimes with and sometimes without oral evidence or with a limited amount of oral evidence ... The considerations which should weigh with the court include:
>
> (1) Whether there is sufficient evidence upon which to make the relevant decision?
>
> (2) Whether the proposed evidence (which should be available at least in outline) which the applicant for a full trial wishes to adduce is likely to affect the outcome of the proceedings?
>
> (3) Whether the opportunity of cross-examine [sic] the witnesses for the local authority, in particular in this case the expert witnesses, is likely to affect the outcome of the proceedings?
>
> (4) The welfare of the child and the effect of further litigation – whether the delay in itself will be so detrimental to the child's well-being that exceptionally there should not be a full hearing. This may be because of the urgent need to place the child, or as is alleged in this case, the emotional stress suffered by both children, and particularly D?
>
> (5) The prospects of success of the applicant or a full trial?
>
> (6) Does the justice of the case require a full investigation with oral evidence?'

[1] FPC(CA 1989)R 1991, r 21(2) and the FPR 1991, r 4.21(2).
[2] [1994] 2 FLR 1.

8.142 It is vital that advocates who are conducting the final hearing have provided the court with an accurate time estimate of the final hearing, including accurate times for the examination and cross examination of witnesses. The court has the power to penalise advocates in costs if the case seriously overruns due to negligent or incompetent estimation of time.[1]

[1] *Re MD and TD (Minors) (Time Estimates)* [1994] 2 FLR 336. This case contains detailed guidance as to the proper calculation of appropriate time estimates.

(I) SPLIT HEARINGS

8.143 In some cases where there is a clear issue as to whether sexual or physical abuse has taken place, the court should consider whether to have a preliminary hearing to obtain findings of fact on those issues. The substantive hearing focussing on the child's welfare can then proceed more speedily[1] and upon a firm foundation of fact.[2] Wall J has said[3] in relation to the conduct of split hearings:

> 'The essence of a split hearing is the clear identification of the issue to be tried first ... Evidence which is relevant to the assessment of the parents or other

family members if and when the threshold criteria are established should not be permitted unless for some reason it is of direct relevance to the factual issue being tried. It is the essence of a split hearing that assessments of the parties and their capacity to parent their children need to be carried out on the basis of the facts found by the court. Ex hypothesi that can only be done after the court has decided both that the threshold criteria have been satisfied and the factual basis upon which they have been satisfied ... Evidence of propensity or a psychiatric or psychological assessment of one of the parties is unlikely to be of any assistance in resolving a purely factual issue. There will in any event be before the court evidence from the local authority and the parents relating to the history of the case and the backgrounds of each of the parents.'

[1]   *Re S (Care Proceedings: Split Hearing)* [1996] 2 FLR 773, although a split hearing may of course extend materially the time it takes to get to that 'speedy' substantive hearing.
[2]   *Re Y and K (Split Hearing: Evidence)* [2003] EWCA Civ 669, [2003] 2 FLR 273.
[3]   *Re CB and JB (Minors) (Care proceedings: Case Conduct)* [1998] 2 FCR 313, [1998] 2 FLR 211. See also *Re CD and MD (Care Proceedings: Practice)* [1998] 1 FLR 825 and Handbook of Best Practice in Children Act Cases (June 1997) CAAC.

8.144 When directing a split hearing, the court should state clearly whether the first part of the split hearing is to determine whether the threshold criteria are satisfied or simply to determine the factual issues in the case as there is a clear distinction between these two purposes.[1] The pre-proceedings checklist[2] requires that a local authority files with its application a schedule of proposed findings[3]. It is essential that the factual questions to be resolved by the court are formulated as soon as possible and in such a way as to enable the court dealing with the first part of the split hearing to answer 'yes' or 'no' to the factual questions posed with the minimum of narrative.[4] A submission of 'no case to answer' is not an appropriate submission in a Children Act case.[5] The courts have previously observed that where possible the same judge *should* hear both parts of the hearing.[6] The House of Lords has now held that at the conclusion of the finding of fact hearing the case must be considered 'part heard', Baroness Hale holding in the case of *Re B (Children)(sexual abuse: standard of proof)*[7]:

'But the finding of those facts is merely part of the whole process of trying the case. It is not a separate exercise. And once it is done the case is part heard. The trial should not resume before a different judge, any more than any other part heard case should do so. In the particular context of care proceedings, where the character and personalities of the parties are important components in any decision, it makes no sense at all for one judge to spend days listening to them give evidence on one issue and for another judge to send more days listening to them give evidence on another. This is not only a wasteful duplication of effort. Much useful information is likely to fall between the gaps. How can a judge who has not heard the parents give their evidence about how the child's injuries occurred begin to assess the risk of letting them care for the child again? The experts may make their assessments, but in the end it is for the judge to make the decision on all the evidence before him. How can he properly do that when he has heard only half of it?'

Accordingly, the 'welfare' hearing following a finding of fact hearing *must* now proceed before the same judge who heard the finding of fact hearing.[8]

[1]   *Re A (Split Hearings: Practice)* [2006] EWCA Civ 714, [2007] 1 FLR 905, [2007] Fam Law 16.

2   PLO Practice Direction, para 10.2.
3   See also *Re G (Care Proceedings: Threshold Conditions)* [2001] EWCA Civ 968, [2001] 2 FLR 1111 per Hale LJ.
4   *Re O and N (Care: Preliminary Hearing)* [2002] EWCA Civ 1271, [2002] 2 FLR 1167 (reversed by the House of Lords in *Re O and N* [2003] UKHL 18, [2003] 1 FLR 1169 but not on this point).
5   *Re Y and K (Split Hearing: Evidence)* [2003] EWCA Civ 669, [2003] 2 FLR 273.
6   *Re G* [2001] 1 FCR 165, [2001] 1 FLR 822. See also *Practice Direction – Judicial Continuity* [2002] 3 All ER 603, [2002] 2 FCR 667, [2002] 2 FLR 367, FD.
7   [2008] UKHL 35, [2008] 2 FCR 339.
8   As a matter of principal, Baroness Hale's judgment that following a fact-finding hearing the case is part heard must be correct. In practice, the pressure on court lists has historically militated against the application of this principle in many cases. It remains to be seen whether and to what extent listing practices change in light of the House of Lords' clear statement of principle on this issue.

8.145 There is jurisdiction to hear an appeal against findings of fact on preliminary issues made at a split hearing.[1] The effect of this is that there does not have to be a decision before a party can appeal against findings which would be detrimental to their case. Where fresh evidence comes to light following findings being made, the court may either re-open the fact-finding decision[2] or conduct the final hearing in such a way as to allow the examination of the new evidence and the amendment of the previous findings if justified.[3] Whilst the court will be slow to grant an application to re-open findings[4] the public interest in the child's right to know the truth about who injured them and why is a powerful reason in favour of re-opening the findings previously made.[5]

1   *Re B (Split Hearings: Jurisdiction)* [2000] 1 FCR 297, [2000] 1 FLR 334.
2   *Re K (Non-Accidental Injuries: Perpatrator: New Evidence)* [2004] EWCA Civ 1181, [2005] 1 FLR 285.
3   *Re M and MC (Care: Issues of Fact: Drawing of Orders)* [2002] EWCA Civ 499, [2003] 1 FLR 461.
4   *Re M and MC (Care: Issues of Fact: Drawing of Orders)* [2002] EWCA Civ 499, [2003] 1 FLR 461.
5   *Re K (Non-Accidental Injuries: Perpatrator: New Evidence)* [2004] EWCA Civ 1181, [2005] 1 FLR 285.

(II) FINAL ORDER OR FURTHER INTERIM ORDER

8.146 It has always been a principle of the CA 1989 that there is a clear demarcation between the role of the courts and the role of local authorities in care cases ' … the court should be able to determine major issues such as the transfer of parental rights and duties where there is or may be a dispute between parents and local authorities, while the management of the case should be the responsibility of the local authority.'[1]

1   Review of Child Care Law (1985), para 2.20.

8.147 There are problems with a rigid application of this principle. In two particular cases, this may lead to an unsatisfactory outcome. First, a care plan may be unacceptable to all involved in court proceedings, save an authority which is determined not to be influenced by others, whether CAFCASS or the court. Secondly, a care order may be made on the basis of a care plan approved by the court but it is not implemented either because of a change of mind by the local authority or a lack of resources. The courts have had such concern, especially in relation to some authorities, that they have sought to find remedies.

8.148 Two issues have arisen concerning the making of a care order and its relationship with the care plan. First can the court decline to make a final order and continue to make interim orders, so as to keep control of the case, where it does not agree with the proposed care plan or it is not confident about the willingness or ability of the authority to carry out the plan? Secondly if a care order is made, is there any way in which the court can control the case thereafter? These questions have been considered in some detail by the House of Lords[1] in two cases heard together at the end of 2001 and, in respect of the latter issue, have now been the subject of statutory reform.[2]

[1] *Re S (Minors) (Care Order: Implementation of Care Plan)*; *Re W (Minors) (Care Order: Adequacy of Care Plan)* [2002] UKHL 10, [2002] 2 AC 291, [2002] 1 FLR 815.
[2] By virtue of the Adoption and Children Act 2002.

(III) INTERIM CARE ORDER IN PLACE OF FINAL CARE ORDER

8.149 In *Re W*, the local authority took care proceedings in respect of J and A, aged 12 and 10 years old. The final care plan was that the children should be placed with the maternal grandparents, with continuing direct contact with both parents. The grandparents lived in the United States. They agreed to move to England to care for the children. The judge concluded that the children were unable to return safely to the joint care of their parents: 'possibly, or even probably, it may be appropriate in twelve to eighteen months, but not now'. All the parties agreed that the maternal grandparents would be suitable carers, although the evidence that they would be able to come here was 'exiguous in the extreme'. The judge described the care plan as inchoate, because of all the uncertainties involved, but nonetheless made care orders for both children.

8.150 The Court of Appeal held it was clear that the care plan was insufficiently mature but the judge had been constrained by the case law to make the full care order. They held that the judge should have insisted on more information before making the order, or on a report back if things did not turn out as expected. The court allowed the appeal in this case, replacing the care order with an interim care order and remitting the case for further consideration.

8.151 It is difficult to improve on the analysis of Lord Nicholls in the House of Lords, when he said:

'[90] From a reading of s 38 as a whole it is abundantly clear that the purpose of an interim care order, so far as presently material, is to enable the court to safeguard the welfare of a child until such time as the court is in a position to decide whether or not it is in the best interests of the child to make a care order. When that time arrives depends on the circumstances of the case and is a matter for the judgment of the trial judge. That is the general, guiding principle. The corollary to this principle is that an interim care order is not intended to be used as a means by which the court may continue to exercise a supervisory role over the local authority in cases where it is in the best interests of a child that a care order should be made.'

'[91]   An interim care order, thus, is a temporary 'holding' measure. Inevitably, time is needed before an application for a care order is ready for decision. Several parties are usually involved: parents, the child's guardian, the local authority, perhaps others. Evidence has to be prepared, parents and other people interviewed, investigations may be required, assessments made, and the local authority must produce its care plan for the child in accordance with the guidance contained in local authority circular LAC(99)29. Although the Children Act itself makes no mention of a care plan, in practice this is a document of key importance. It enables the court and everyone else to know, and consider, the local authority's plans for the future of the child if a care order is made.'

'[92]   When a local authority formulates a care plan in connection with an application for a care order, there are bound to be uncertainties. Even the basic shape of the future life of the child may be far from clear. Over the last ten years problems have arisen about how far courts should go in attempting to resolve these uncertainties before making a care order and passing responsibility to the local authority. Once a final care order is made, the resolution of the uncertainties will be a matter for the authority, not the court.'

'[93]   In terms of legal principle one type of uncertainty is straightforward. This is the case where the uncertainty needs to be resolved before the court can decide whether it is in the best interests of the child to make a care order at all. In *C v Solihull Metropolitan Borough Council* [1993] 1 FLR 290 the court could not decide whether a care order was in the best interests of a child, there a 'battered baby', without knowing the result of a parental assessment. Ward J made an appropriate interim order. In such a case the court should finally dispose of the matter only when the material facts are as clearly known as can be hoped. Booth J adopted a similar approach, for a similar reason, in *Hounslow London Borough Council v A* [1993] 1 FLR 702.'

'[94]   More difficult, as a matter of legal principle, are cases where it is obvious that a care order is in the best interests of the child but the immediate way ahead thereafter is unsatisfactorily obscure. These cases exemplify a problem, or a 'tension', inherent in the scheme of the Children Act. What should the judge do when a care order is clearly in the best interests of the child but the judge does not approve of the care plan? This judicial dilemma was described by Balcombe LJ *in Re S and D (Children: Powers of Court)* [1995] 2 FLR 456, 464, perhaps rather too bleakly, as the judge having to choose between "the lesser of two evils".'

'[95]   In this context there are sometimes uncertainties whose nature is such that they are suitable for immediate resolution, in whole or in part, by the court in the course of disposing of the care order application. The uncertainty may be of such a character that it can, and should, be resolved so far as possible before the court proceeds to make the care order. Then, a limited period of 'planned and purposeful' delay can readily be justified as the sensible and practical way to deal with an existing problem.'

8.152 Lord Nicholls noted *Re CH (Care or Interim Care Order)*,[1] where the Court of Appeal held that the fact that a care order was the inevitable outcome should not have deflected the judge from hearing expert evidence on this issue. Even if the issue could not be finally resolved before a care order was made, it was obviously sensible and desirable that, in the circumstances of the case, the local authority should have the benefit of the judge's observations on the point. He also approved of *Re J (Minors) (Care: Care Plan)*[2] in which Wall J said:

> 'there are cases (of which this is one) in which the action which requires to be taken in the interests of children necessarily involves steps into the unknown ... provided the court is satisfied that the local authority is alert to the difficulties which may arise in the execution of the care plan, the function of the court is not to seek to oversee the plan but to entrust its execution to the local authority.'[3]

[1]   [1998] 1 FLR 402. See also *Re H (Care: Change in Care Plan)* [1998] 1 FLR 193, CA, in which it was said that if the care order was based on a flawed care plan the parent was entitled to have it reconsidered, even if the order remained in force. On the other hand, it has been held that if all the facts are known, it can seldom, if ever, be right for the court to continue adjourning a case: *Re P (Minors) (Interim Order)* [1993] 2 FLR 742, CA, *Re R (Care Proceedings: Adjournment)* [1998] 2 FLR 390, CA.

[2]   [1994] 1 FLR 253.

[3]   [1994] 1 FLR 253 at 265. See also *Re L (Sexual Abuse: Standard of Proof)* [1996] 1 FLR 116 and *Re R (Care Proceedings: Adjournment)* [1998] 2 FLR 390.

8.153 Lord Nicholls continued (at para 99):

> 'Despite all the inevitable uncertainties, when deciding whether to make a care order the court should normally have before it a care plan which is sufficiently firm and particularised for all concerned to have a reasonably clear picture of the likely way ahead for the child for the foreseeable future. The degree of firmness to be expected, as well as the amount of detail in the plan, will vary from case to case depending on how far the local authority can foresee what will be best for the child at that time. This is necessarily so. But making a care order is always a serious interference in the lives of the child and his parents. Although Article 8 contains no explicit procedural requirements, the decision making process leading to a care order must be fair and such as to afford due respect to the interests safeguarded by Article 8: see *TP and KM v United Kingdom* [2001] 2 FLR 549, 569, paragraph 72. If the parents and the child's guardian are to have a fair and adequate opportunity to make representations to the court on whether a care order should be made, the care plan must be appropriately specific.'

8.154 He noted that in the Court of Appeal Thorpe LJ[1] had expressed the view that in certain circumstances the judge at the trial should have a 'wider discretion' to make an interim care order: 'where the care plan seems inchoate or where the passage of a relatively brief period seems bound to see the fulfilment of some event or process vital to planning and deciding the future'. In an appropriate case, a judge must be free to defer making a care order until he is satisfied that the way ahead 'is no longer obscured by an uncertainty that is neither inevitable nor chronic.'

[1]   *Re W and B (children: care plan)* [2001] EWCA 757 at para 29, [2001] 2 FCR 450, [2001] 2 FLR 582.

(IV) SUPERVISING CARE PLANS

8.155 The problem presented by the separation of court and state upon the making of a care order when the care order it is not implemented has now been addressed by statutory reform.[1] However, before looking at those provisions, it is instructive to examine the decision of the House of Lords which triggered them.

[1] Adoption and Children Act 2002, s 118 amending the CA 1989, s 26.

8.156 The House of Lords considered the question of supervising or reviewing care plans after the making of a care order in *Re S*.[1] A mother had three children, P aged 14, M aged 11 and J aged 10 years. Torbay, the local authority, sought care orders in respect of all three children. Its care plan for P was that he should remain in foster care, which was agreed. The care plan for M and J was that an attempt should be made to rehabilitate them with their mother. Counsel for the mother submitted that a care order should not be made because the mother was sceptical about whether Torbay would carry out the care plan. The mother contended that interim care orders should be made. The judge made final care orders in respect of all three children, expressing confidence that Torbay would implement the care plan. This confidence proved to be misplaced. There were serious failings principally because of a financial crisis within Torbay local authority leading to substantial cuts in the social services budget.

[1] *Re S (Minors) (Care Order: Implementation of Care Plan)*; *Re W (Minors) (Care Order: Adequacy of Care Plan)* [2002] UKHL 10, [2002] 2 WLR 720, [2002] 1 FLR 815.

8.157 The Court of Appeal had held[1] that courts should not be prevented from reviewing the implementation of care plans on which the decision to make a care orders was based. It proposed a scheme of making starred care plans. It was held that only by such a mechanism could the provisions relating to care orders be considered consistent with the Human Rights Act 1998, in those cases where rights under the ECHR were being abused.

[1] *Re W and B (children: care plan)* [2001] EWCA Civ 757, [2001] 2 FCR 450, [2001] 2 FLR 582.

8.158 In his comprehensive judgment Lord Nicholls addressed the proposal of the Court of Appeal for starred care plans and the compatibility of the CA 1989 provisions in respect of a care order with arts 6 and 8 of the ECHR. He disagreed with the Court of Appeal on the basis that the court's introduction of a 'starring system' could not be justified as a legitimate exercise in interpretation of the CA 1989 in accordance with s 3 of the Human Rights Act 1998.[1] The starring system would create a new supervisory function, an amendment of statute, which was a matter for Parliament. Lord Nicholls instead said that ss 7 and 8 of the 1998 Act provided the remedy:[2]

> '[62] ... if a local authority fails to discharge its parental responsibilities properly, and in consequence the rights of the parents under Article 8 are violated, the parents may, as a longstop, bring proceedings against the authority under s 7 ... I say "as a longstop", because other remedies,

both of an administrative nature and by way of court proceedings, may also be available in the particular case ... Sometimes court proceedings by way of judicial review of a decision of a local authority may be the appropriate way to proceed. In a suitable case an application for discharge of the care order is available. One would not expect proceedings to be launched under s 7 until any other appropriate remedial routes have first been explored.'

1   For further discussion see para 1.144.
2   See paras 13.89 where the possibility of a free-standing application under s 7 is considered, as in *Re M (Care: Challenging Decisions by Local Authority)* [2001] 2 FLR 1300.

8.159 Lord Nicholls noted that the jurisprudence of the European Court of Human Rights did not hold that art 6(1) required that all administrative decisions should be susceptible of substantive appeal to a court, with the court substituting its views for the decision made by the administrator. 'The extent of judicial control required depends on the subject matter of the decision and the extent to which this lends itself to judicial decision.'[1] 'This principle that, the required degree of judicial control varies according to the subject matter of the impugned decision, is important in the context of the Children Act ...' [2] Hence the extent to which decisions by an authority affect the private law rights of parents and children also varies widely. Some affect the continuing parental responsibility of a parent, others do not.[3]

1   *Re W and B (children: care plan)* [2001] EWCA Civ 757, [2001] 2 FCR 450, [2001] 2 FLR 582. See para 8.157.
2   See para 8.157.
3   See para 8.157.

8.160 Lord Nicholls concluded that there may be circumstances when English law would not satisfy the requirements of art 6(1) regarding some child care decisions made by local authorities. 'The guarantee provided by art 6(1) can hardly be said to be satisfied in the case of a young child who, in practice, has no way of initiating judicial review proceedings to challenge a local authority's decision affecting his civil rights.'[1] It was equally true that 'where there is no parent able and willing to become involved, the art 8 rights of a young child may be violated by a local authority without anyone outside the local authority becoming aware of the violation, which might leave a child without an effective remedy'.[2] He did not consider that this meant that the CA 1989 was incompatible with the ECHR but it might signify the existence of a lacuna in the statute.

1   See para 8.157.
2   See para 8.157.

8.161 As noted above, the House of Lords determined that the starring system devised by the Court of Appeal created a new supervisory function, an amendment of statute, which was a matter for Parliament. In light of their Lordships' conclusion that there may nonetheless be circumstances when English law would not satisfy the requirements of art 6(1) regarding some child care decisions made by local authorities following the making of a care order, and their Lordships trenchant criticism of that position, Parliament acted. The result was s 118 of the Adoption and Children Act 2002 amending s 26 of the CA 1989.

8.162 The Adoption and Children Act 2002, s 118 created the role of the Independent[1] Reviewing Officer (IRO). The local authority is required to appoint an IRO who must participate in the review process following the making of a final care order, monitor the local authority's implementation of the care plan and refer the case to CAFCASS if the IRO considers it appropriate to do so having regard to the actions of the local authority.[2] Thereafter, CAFCASS may commence proceedings[3] to address any failings on the part of the local authority having referred the matter back to the children's guardian from the care proceedings.[4]

[1]   The title 'Independent' is entirely misleading as the majority of IROs are employees of the local authority.
[2]   CA 1989, s 26(2A). Detailed guidance on the role of the IRO is set out in the Review of Children's Cases (Amendment)(England) Regulations 2004, SI 2004/1419 and the Independent Reviewing Officers Guidance (DfES) 2004.
[3]   Under the Human Rights Act 1998, s 7, by way of judicial review or by way of an action for compensation.
[4]   Children and Family Court Advisory and Support Service (Reviewed Case Referral) Regulations 2004, SI 2004/2187.

8.163 In the last edition, we doubted whether the then amendments proposed to the then Adoption and Children Bill would resolve the problems identified in *Re S*, since the provisions arising from those amendments relied primarily not on a requirement to bring the matter back before the court, but on the willingness of a person working within the local authority to refer the matter to CAFCASS and on expeditious work on the part of CAFCASS. This pessimism appears to have been born out, with limited numbers of cases being referred to CAFCASS since the coming into force of s 118 in September 2004.[1]

[1]   The Children and Young Persons Bill 2008 contains provisions for strengthening the role of the IRO. Clause 11 of the Bill amends s 25 of CA 1989 to make provision for the appointment and specified functions of the IRO. Clause 12 amends s 25 of CA 1989 to make provision for a body corporate to administer the training, accreditation, appointment and management of IRO's. Clause 13 of the Bill makes provision for these reforms to apply in Wales.

(V)   CARE ORDER OR SUPERVISION ORDER?

8.164 The court may make a care order or a supervision order where the local authority intends to place the child with a parent[1] or with members of the extended family,[2] but there are important differences between the orders. The purpose of a supervision order is to help and assist a child, leaving full responsibility with the parents. Any conditions attached cannot be enforced by the court[3]. The limitations of the order do not address the problems of parents who continue to exercise their responsibilities inadequately. A care order, on the other hand, places a positive duty on the local authority, through the acquisition of parental responsibility, to ensure the welfare of the child and protect it from inadequate parenting. This is not inconsistent with seeking to work in partnership with parents, since s 23 of the CA 1989 envisages that the local authority could place a child with his parents under a care order. Where a care order is not sought by the local authority, the court should not impose a care order which is not in the interests of the child simply to encourage a local authority to perform its statutory duties towards children in need.[4] There could well be circumstances where the making of a care order was the only way to protect children placed with relatives from significant harm, even though the local authority did not want an order. The court cannot, if it disapproves a local authority care plan, make an injunction to prevent a course of action[5] nor can it accept undertakings from a parent to strengthen a supervision order.[6]

[1] *Re T (a minor) (care or supervision order)* [1994] 1 FCR 663,[1994] 1 FLR 103, CA. See also *Re D (care proceedings: appropriate order)* [1993] 2 FCR 88,[1993] 2 FLR 423; *Re S (J) (A Minor) (Care or Supervision Order)* [1993] 2 FLR 919. *Re B (Care or Supervision Order)* [1996] 2 FLR 693, *Re O (Care or Supervision Order)* [1996] 2 FLR 755; *Re K* [1999] 1 FCR 337 and *Re C (Care or Supervision Order)* [1999] 2 FLR 621.
[2] *Re K (minors)* [1996] 1 FCR 365, [1995] 1 FLR 675.
[3] *Re V (care or supervision order)* [1996] 2 FCR 555,[1996] 1 FLR 776, CA, followed in *Re S (care or supervision order)* [1996] 2 FCR 719,[1996] 1 FLR 753, CA. But see para 8.819.
[4] *Oxfordshire County Council v L (Care or Supervision Order)* [1998] 1 FLR 70.
[5] *Re S and D* [1995] 2 FLR 456.
[6] *Re B (a minor) (supervision order: parental undertaking)* [1996] 3 FCR 446, CA.

8.165 The doctrine of proportionality under art 8 of the ECHR in this context was emphasised by Hale LJ in *Re O (Supervision Order)*[1] in relation to whether to make a care or supervision order. As Hale LJ pointed out, a supervision order is quite different from a care order – not least in who has control of the child. In *Re O* a mentally ill mother and her new partner were co-operating with the local authority. The threshold criteria were satisfied, but it was held that a care order was not justified. The authority was not seeking to remove the child and the situation was unlikely to deteriorate so quickly that the child would need to be removed without a court order. On the other hand, some order needed to be made both because of the possibility that the parents might cease to co-operate and of deterioration in the mother's health. A care order as opposed to a supervision order should only be made if the stronger order is necessary to protect the child.[2] If the evidence is restricted to future rather than immediate risk a supervision order is more likely to be appropriate having regard to the principle that the intervention of the State has to be proportionate to the legitimate aim of protecting family life.[3]

[1] [2001] EWCA Civ 16, [2001] 1 FCR 289, [2001] 1 FLR 923.
[2] *Re B (Care or Supervision Order)* [1996] 2 FLR 693.
[3] *Re C and B (children) (care order: future harm)* [2000] 2 FCR 614, CA; and *Re O (Supervision Order)* [2001] EWCA Civ 16, [2001] 1 FLR 923. See also *K and T v Finland* [2001] 2 FCR 673, [2001] 2 FLR 707, Grand Chamber.

8.166 In cases of an exceptional nature the court may be justified in making a supervision order in support of a residence order and additionally making the child a ward of court where there has been a substantial amount of harm to the children but a family placement is nonetheless justified[1] or where the local authority fostering panel is unable to approve a placement with relatives under a care order but that placement is nonetheless in the child's best interests.[2]

1   *Re M and J (Wardship Supervision and Residence Orders)* [2003] EWHC 1585 (Fam), [2003] 2 FLR 541.
2   *Re W and X (Wardship: Relatives Rejected as Foster Carers)* [2003] EWHC 2206 (Fam), [2004] 1 FLR 415.

(VI) CONSENT ORDERS

8.167 Care proceedings frequently lead to a negotiated solution in which the threshold criteria may be agreed and the order itself may be agreed. Notwithstanding the agreement of the parties, the court still has a duty to investigate, where it is being asked to make an order under s 31, and to satisfy itself that findings of fact are appropriate.[1] A judgment may be important to the future management of the case. Although the court has a duty to consider whether any order should be made, the extent of an investigation by the court should reflect the fact that there is consensus among the parties especially if they include a public authority and a children's guardian.[2] If the parties are agreed that a care order should be made, the investigation could properly be limited to a perusal of documentation and approval of an agreed order.[3]

1   Note that the local authority should file a statement of the findings it wishes the court to make and where possible this should be agreed with the other parties: *Re G (children) (care order: evidence)* [2001] EWCA Civ 968, [2001] 2 FCR 757.
2   *Devon County Council v S* [1992] Fam 176, [1992] 3 All ER 793.
3   The fact that the court is required to exercise its discretion even where the parties are agreed implies that the court should give a short judgment.

8.168 If the factual basis is not agreed, the court should limit its investigation to those parts of the evidence which are relevant to the issue of significant harm and necessary for the proper disposal of the case.[1] Where a parent concedes sufficiently to satisfy the threshold criteria and the order sought, it may not be necessary to proceed with a long trial.[2] If the concessions were not sufficient to give a proper understanding of allegations of sexual abuse and the care plan depended on the harm which had actually occurred, or where the credibility of the children was impugned, the circumstances might warrant further investigation.[3] The court is not subsequently barred from reinvestigating a concession (ie issue estoppel is inapplicable).[4] Where concessions are found to be inadequate, for example because no responsibility was accepted for the children's sexualised behaviour, the case can be remitted for rehearing.[5]

1   *Re G (A Minor) (Care Order: Threshold Conditions)* [1995] Fam 16, sub nom *Re G (A Minor) (Care Proceedings)* [1994] 2 FLR 69 and *Stockport Metropolitan Borough Council v D* [1995] 1 FLR 873.
2   *Re B (Agreed Findings of Fact)* [1998] 2 FLR 968. In this case there were pending criminal proceedings on the same issues.
3   *Re M (Threshold Criteria: Parental Concessions)* [1999] 2 FLR 728, CA.
4   *Re D (a child) (threshold criteria: issue estoppel)* [2001] 1 FCR 124, [2001] 1 FLR 274, CA.
5   *Re W (a child) (threshold criteria: parental concessions)* [2001] 1 FCR 139, CA.

(h) Applications for placement orders

8.169 Where the care plan of the local authority is one of permanency by way of adoption, an application for a placement order will have to be considered.

The local authority is under a duty to make such an application where it is satisfied that the child in question ought to be placed for adoption.[1] The decision that a child ought to be placed for adoption is a complex[2] and has the potential to impact adversely on the timetable for the care proceedings.[3] It is good practice to ensure that any assessments needed to inform the decision as to adoption and to allow the court to determine whether a placement order should be granted are obtained within a time frame that allows the decision and any application for a placement order to be issued prior to the final hearing in the care proceedings.[4] The tight timescales caused by the requirements of the adoption legislation have resulted in applications for placement orders being issued only very shortly before the final hearing listed for the care proceedings. Such short notice will not necessarily justify the adjournment of the care proceedings or the application for a placement order.[5]

[1]   Adoption and Children Act 2002, s 22.
[2]   See the Adoption Agencies Regulations 2005, rr 11 to 17.
[3]   It would not appear that much thought was given to ensuring that the procedure under the Adoption and Children Act 2002 and associated regulations was aligned with the procedure for obtaining a care order under the CA 1989.
[4]   Local authorities should follow the guidance contained in LAC(98)20 'Adoption – Achieving the Right Balance' and in particular the steps set out in para 31.
[5]   *Re P-B (A Child)* [2006] EWCA Civ 1016, [2007] 3 FCR 308, [2007] 1 FLR 1106.

EFFECT OF ORDERS

1. Care Orders

(a) Designated authority

8.170 A care order can only be made in favour of one local authority (the 'designated authority') and is not transferable once made. The local authority designated in a care order must be:[1]

(a)   the authority in whose area the child is ordinarily resident;[2] or
(b)   where the child does not reside[3] in a local authority area, the authority in whose area any circumstances arose in consequence of which the order is being made.

There has been conflict about how the designated authority should be chosen, but the Court of Appeal has now held that the provisions should be given the construction which achieves a simple mechanism to determine which authority should be responsible for implementing the care order and the care plan.[4] Where the mother had moved after the commencement of care proceedings, it was held that for the purposes of deciding which should be the designated care authority, the child's ordinary residence should be judged as at the time when the authority first intervened.[5] Where a child had no recent connection with the authority which would have been designated on a strict interpretation of the CA 1989, s 105, it was held that the court had a discretion to designate an authority, because the child was not ordinarily resident in any authority.[6] If it is intended that a care order will designate an authority other than that which applied for the order, there should be early liaison between the authorities. A care plan should be prepared in co-operation between them. An authorised representative should attend court to give assurances about the authority's commitment to the plan.[7] A local authority cannot refuse designation on the making of a care order.[8]

[1]   CA 1989, s 31(8). The designation of an authority in respect of a supervision order is to the authority where the child lives or will live, unless another authority agrees to accept the order: Sch 3, para 9.

[2]   In determining ordinary residence, there shall be disregarded any period during which the child lives at school or in any institution or while he is being accommodated by or on behalf of a local authority: s 105(6). If the child has been placed at home under an interim care order, he is not regarded as being accommodated under s 23, under s 105(6) does not apply: *Re P (Care Proceedings: Designated Authority)* [1998] 1 FLR 80; *Re H (Care Order: Appropriate Local Authority)* [2003] EWCA Civ 1629, [2004] 1 FLR 534; *Kirklees Metropolitan Borough Council v S and London Borough of Brent* [2004] 2 FLR 800.

[3]   This should be read as including the word 'ordinary' before reside: *Gateshead Metropolitan Borough Council v L* [1996] Fam 55, [1996] 2 FLR 179.

[4]   *Northamptonshire County Council v Islington London Borough Council* [2001] Fam 364, [1999] 3 FCR 385, CA; and see *C (A Child) v Plymouth City Council* [2000] 1 FLR 875, CA and *London Borough of Redbridge v Newport City Council* [2003] EWHC 2967 (Fam), [2004] 2 FLR 226.

[5]   *Re BC (a minor) (care order: appropriate local authority)* [1995] 3 FCR 598.

[6]   *Gateshead Metropolitan Borough Council v L* [1996] Fam 55, [1996] 2 FLR 179. See also *Re C (Care Order: Appropriate Local Authority)* [1997] 1 FLR 544.

[7]   *L v London Borough of Bexley* [1996] 2 FLR 595.

[8]   *Re C (Care Order: Appropriate Local Authority)* [1997] 1 FLR 544.

(b) *Effect of order*

(I) PARENTAL RESPONSIBILITY

8.171 Section 33 sets out the powers and duties acquired by a local authority under a care order, but this must be read in conjunction with s 2.[1] The local authority is required to receive the child and keep him in their care while the order is in force. The authority acquires parental responsibility, but the parent does not cease to have parental responsibility solely because some other person acquires it.[2] The local authority has no power to prevent a mother from entering into a parental responsibility agreement in relation to a child subject to a care order.[3] A person with parental responsibility is not entitled to act in a way which would be incompatible with any order made under the Act,[4] so that a parent is not entitled to exercise parental responsibility inconsistently with the care order. A care order lasts until the child is eighteen,[5] unless it is brought to an end earlier by a residence order or by its discharge.[6] The making of a placement order suspends the operation of the care order (which will be resurrected if the placement order is discharged)[7] and an adoption order extinguishes any order under the CA 1989.[8]

[1]   See Chapter 3.

[2]   Section 2(6) see para 3.96.

[3]   *Re X (Minors) (Care Proceedings: Parental Responsibility)* [2000] 2 All ER 66, sub nom *Re X (Parental Responsibility Agreement: Children in care)* [2000] 1 FCR 379, [2000] 1 FLR 517.

[4]   CA 1989, s 2(8).

[5]   CA 1989, s 91(12).

[6]   See below paras 8.178–8.179.

[7]   Adoption and Children Act 2002, s 29(1).

[8]   Adoption and Children Act 2002, s 46(2).

8.172 The authority has the power to determine the extent to which a parent or guardian may meet his parental responsibility insofar as it is necessary to do so to safeguard or promote the child's welfare,[1] but this is subject to a number of reservations. Issues about contact may be referred to the court.[2] Other decisions taken by a local authority may range from the trivial to those of fundamental importance to parents and children. In *Re S*[3] Lord Nicholls drew a distinction between 'rights in respect of the control of the day to day care of the child [which] were decided by the making of the care order and the grant of parental responsibility to the local authority' and a responsibility which may be 'of fundamental importance, for example, whether rehabilitation is still a realistic possibility'. The House of Lords approved the decision in *Re M (Care: Challenging Decisions By Local Authority)*[4] in which a local authority ruled out rehabilitation but was held to have acted unfairly by not involving the parents to a degree sufficient to provide their interests with the requisite protection.

1   CA 1989, s 33(3)(b).
2   See below para 8.197–8.218.
3   *Re S (Minors) (Care Order: Implementation of Care Plan)*; *Re W (Minors) (Care Order: Adequacy of Care Plan)* [2002] UKHL 10, [2002] 2 AC 291, [2002] 1 FLR 815.
4   [2001] 2 FLR 1300. See also *Re C (Care Proceedings: Disclosure of Local Authority's Decision Making Process)* [2002] EWHC 1379 (Fam), [2002] 2 FCR 673; *Re G (Care: Challenge to Local Authority's Decision)* [2003] 2 FLR 42 and *Venema v Netherlands* [2003] 1 FLR 552 for a similar issue raised in the cause of care proceedings.

8.173 A parent or guardian is still entitled to do what is reasonable in all the circumstances of the case for the purpose of safeguarding or promoting the child's welfare[1] and retains any right, duty, power, responsibility or authority in relation to the child and his property under any other enactment.[2] These would include the right to consent to the child's marriage, rights under the Education Act 1996 in relation to the child's special educational needs, financial responsibility for the child and some responsibility for his acts if he is in the parent's charge and control. It has been held that the court could grant an order under s 37 of the Supreme Court Act 1981 in support of the rights conferred upon the local authority by s 33 of the Act, in the particular case to require a parent to allow a child to attend a college for education.[3]

1   CA 1989, s 33(5).
2   CA 1989, s 33(9).
3   *Re P (Care Orders: Injunctive Relief)* [2000] 2 FLR 385.

8.174 The local authority is not allowed to cause the child to be brought up in any religious persuasion other than that in which he would have been brought up if no order had been made. They do not have the right to consent, or refuse to consent, to the making of a placement order or to consent, or refuse to consent, to an adoption order or a proposed foreign adoption order. An authority may not appoint a guardian.[1]

1   CA 1989, s 33(6).

(II) CHANGE OF NAME

8.175 While a care order is in force no person may cause the child to be known by a new surname without the written consent of every person with parental responsibility.[1] For most children in care this would be the normal expectation, but the provision can cause difficulty for that small group of children being placed for adoption without parental consent. At some point after placement, but often before the formal adoption order, it may be in the child's interests to assume the name of the substitute family, especially, for example, if the child is about to start school. It might be thought that assumption of a new name should not occur until it is clear by adoption that the placement is permanent, but that does not necessarily recognise the importance for some children of being identified with the new family at an earlier stage or the risks of losing anonymity if the original name is used. In some cases it may be necessary for the child to be known by the new name, even though formal records retain the original name. In such circumstances, the court can give leave under s 33(7) for a change of name and application may need to be made to the court, in which the application the child's welfare is paramount and, in addition to the welfare checklist, the court must give very careful consideration to the wishes, feelings, needs and objectives of the applicant, the motives and objections of the respondents and the opinion of the children's guardian.[2] Where a foster carer wishes to change a child's name he should consult the local authority and the parent's views should be sought, with an application made to court if necessary.[3] The Court of Appeal has held that on an application by a *Gillick* competent child to determine his or her surname the child's welfare was the paramount consideration and the judge should give very careful consideration to the wishes, feelings, needs and objectives of the child.[4] In an appropriate case the order may be granted without notice.[5]

[1]   CA 1989, s 33(7).
[2]   *Re M,T,P,K and B (Care: Change of Name)* [2000] 2 FLR 645 where a local authority successfully applied for a change of name for five children in care to allay their fears of their parents or other members of an itinerant community of removing them from their foster-carers and spiriting them away to the anonymity of their community.
[3]   *Re D, L and LA (Care: Change of Forename)* [2003] 1 FLR 339.
[4]   *Re S (a minor) (change of name)* [1999] 1 FCR 304,[1999] 1 FLR 672, CA.
[5]   *Re J (A Minor) (Child: Change of Name)* [1993] 1 FLR 699.

(III) TEMPORARY REMOVAL FROM THE JURISDICTION

8.176 A child in care may not be removed from the United Kingdom[1] without the written consent of every person having parental responsibility or the leave of the court.[2] This does not prevent the local authority having the care of the child arranging for a temporary removal for no more than a month.[3] This could cover a holiday or a trip to relatives to see if a longer term residence abroad would be suitable.

[1]   That is England, Wales, Scotland and Northern Ireland: see *Re H (children) (residence order: condition)* [2001] EWCA Civ 1338, [2001] 3 FCR 182, [2001] 2 FLR 1277, discussed at para 5.39.
[2]   CA 1989, s 33(7).
[3]   CA 1989, s 33(8)(a).

(IV) ARRANGING FOR LIVING OUTSIDE ENGLAND AND WALES

8.177 If the authority wishes to arrange for a child to live outside England and Wales, it must have the written consent of every person with parental responsibility or the leave of the court.[1] The approval of the court is required under the system set out in the CA 1989, Sch 2, para 19. If consent is withheld the court has power to dispense with it. The court may dispense with unnecessary procedural difficulties in order to achieve what is in the best interests of the child.[2] The proper approach is to look at the broad band within which a reasonable person might exercise a responsible choice, taking into account the sacrifice contemplated. The band for objection is narrow because, unlike in adoption, the parent would not lose parental responsibility. The child's interests are not paramount but merely one of the factors to be taken into account.[3]

[1] CA 1989, s 33(8).
[2] *Flintshire County Council v K* [2001] 2 FLR 476.
[3] *Re G (Minors) (Care: Leave to Place Outside Jurisdiction)* [1994] 2 FLR 301. See also *Re G (Leave to Appeal: Jurisdiction)* [1999] 1 FLR 771, CA and *Re J (Freeing for Adoption)* [2000] 2 FLR 58 at 67.

(c) Effect on other orders

8.178 The making of a care order discharges any s 8 order, so that no parent can continue to have a residence order. It also operates to dismiss an application for a residence order, so the court should consider any such application carefully before making a care order.[1] A care order discharges a supervision order and a school attendance order and brings wardship to an end.[2] It also has the effect of discharging a custody order made in a foreign jurisdiction.[3]

[1] *Hounslow London Borough Council v A* [1993] 1 WLR 291, [1993] 1 FLR 702.
[2] CA 1989, s 91.
[3] *Oxfordshire County Council v S* [2000] Fam Law 20.

8.179 The court cannot make a s 8 order, other than a residence order, with respect to a child who is in care.[1] If the court does make a residence order, the care order is discharged. There is no embargo on the court combining a supervision order with a s 8 order, with supplementary directions or conditions, provided the threshold criteria apply. Nor is the court prevented from making a s 8 order in respect of a child who is accommodated.

[1] Section 9(1) and see paras 5.124–5.125.

2. Supervision orders

(a) Effect

8.180 The order puts the child under the supervision of a designated local authority, but does not give them parental responsibility.[1] The duties of the supervisor are:

(a)   to advise, assist and befriend the supervised child;
(b)   to take such steps as are reasonably necessary to give effect to the order; and

(c)   where (i) the order is not wholly complied with; or (ii) the supervisor considers that the order may no longer be necessary, to consider whether or not to apply to the court for its variation or discharge.

These basic duties are substantially expanded by Sch 3 by the importing of a scheme which had previously been used primarily for the intermediate treatment of adolescents into the general scheme under which supervision orders can be made. A parent can be required to reside at a particular place under the terms of a supervision order.[2] The provisions are enforceable in the same way as any other order made by the court.[3]

[1]   See Sch 3, para 9.
[2]   *Croydon London Borough v A (No 3)* [1992] 2 FCR 481, [1992] 2 FLR 350.
[3]   But see s 35(1)(c) and *Re R and G (Minors) (Interim Care or Supervision Orders)* [1994] 1 FLR 793.

8.181 A supervision order should not be used for the purpose of supervising contact. A family assistance order could be used for that purpose.[1] If there is a child protection element during contact sufficient to justify the court being satisfied as to the threshold criteria a supervision order might be appropriate.[2] This might arise where a parent was making false allegations about the other parent in order to influence the children against contact.[3] It would usually be preferable to make a family assistance order[4] to achieve supervised contact, but in cases involving an element of child protection, where the local authority made a s 31 application and the criteria were satisfied, a supervision order could be made.[5]

[1]   *Leeds City Council v C* [1993] 1 FCR 585, [1993] 1 FLR 269.
[2]   *Re DH (a minor) (child abuse)* [1994] 2 FCR 3, [1994] 1 FLR 679.
[3]   *Re Z and A (Contact: Supervision Order)* [2000] 2 FLR 406.
[4]   *Leeds City Council v C* [1993] 1 FLR 269.
[5]   *Re DH (A Minor) (Child Abuse)* [1994] 1 FLR 679.

(b) Duration

8.182 A supervision order lasts for up to one year, though it may be made for a shorter period.[1] It is subject to discharge[2] and extension by the court for up to a total of three years.[3] Application to extend is not like an original application for an order, so the court's decision is governed by the welfare principle. The court does not have power to vary the order to a care order without further proof of the threshold criteria on an application by the local authority.[4]

[1]   *M v Warwickshire County Council* [1994] 2 FLR 593.
[2]   Under s 39. The provisions are the same as for discharge of a care order: see below.
[3]   CA 1989, Sch 3, para 6.
[4]   *Re A (Supervision Order: Extension)* [1995] 1 WLR 482, [1995] 1 FLR 335, CA.

(c) Requirements

(I) THE SUPERVISED CHILD

8.183 A supervision order may require the supervised child to comply with any directions given from time to time by the supervisor which require him to:

(a)   live at a place or places specified in the directions for a specified period or periods;

(b)   present himself to a specified person at a place and on a day specified;

(c)   participate in specified activities, such as education or training.

The precise directions are a matter for the supervisor and not the court. He shall decide whether and to what extent and in what form he shall exercise this power. The provision does not confer on him the power to give directions in respect of any medical or psychiatric examination or treatment.[1] The court may not accept an undertaking in conjunction with a supervision order[2] nor can conditions be imposed on a supervision order.[3]

1   CA 1989, Sch 3, paras 2(2) and (3).
2   *Re B (A Minor)(Supervision Orders: Parental Undertakings)* [1996] 1 WLR 716, [1996] 1 FLR 676, CA.
3   *Re V (Care or Supervision Order)* [1996] 2 FCR 555, [1996] 1 FLR 776, CA. See also *Re S* [1996] 2 FCR 719, [1996] 1 FLR 753, CA.

(II) The responsible person

8.184   A supervision order may include requirements, with the consent of and in relation to a 'responsible person' (that is a person with parental responsibility or with whom the child is living).[1] The requirements may be that the responsible person take all reasonable steps to ensure that the child complies with any direction given by the supervisor,[2] that he takes all reasonable steps to ensure that the child complies with any requirement in relation to psychiatric and medical examination or treatment and that he complies with the supervisor's directions on attending at a specified place.

1   CA 1989, Sch 3, para 1.
2   The directions given being a matter for the responsible person and not for the court: see *Re H (Supervision Order)* [1994] 2 FLR 979. But see below para 8.189.

8.185   Paragraph 3 of Sch 3 contains provisions whereby a responsible person can be required to comply with directions to attend at a specified place for the purpose of taking part in specified activities. Such directions have to be given by the supervisor. Under this provision a responsible person could be required to comply with directions as to treatment, but these provisions are a matter for the supervisor and not for the court.[1] It has been held that a parent can be required to reside at a particular place under the terms of a supervision order.[2] The wording of para 3 makes it clear that the directions are a matter for the supervisor and not the court, though it might be possible, where appropriate, for the court to make a residence order, conditional on the person living with the child at a specific place.

1   *Re H (Supervision Order)* [1994] 2 FLR 979.
2   *Croydon London Borough v A (No 3)* [1992] 2 FCR 481, [1992] 2 FLR 350.

8.186   A supervision order can exist at the same time as a s 8 order. Thus in appropriate cases the court can consider making a residence order in combination with a contact order or prohibited steps order, and a supervision order.

Where directions are within the ambit of Sch 3, they should be made under that Schedule, rather than under s 11(7), since that provision is for the purpose of implementing s 8 orders.

(III) MEDICAL OR PSYCHIATRIC EXAMINATION OR TREATMENT

8.187 A supervision order (but not an interim supervision order)[1] may require the supervised child to:

(a)　submit to a medical or psychiatric examination;

(b)　submit to such an examination from time to time as directed by the supervisor;

(c)　submit to specified treatment in relation to his mental or physical condition.

1　CA 1989, s 38(9).

8.188 Paragraphs 3 and 4 of Sch 3 contain detailed provisions which have to be satisfied before a requirement can be imposed as to examination and treatment. Both are subject to the conditions that the child, of sufficient understanding to make an informed decision, must consent to the inclusion of the requirement in the supervision order.[1]

1　CA 1989, Sch 3, para 4(4).

(d) Enforcement

8.189 The terms of a supervision order are enforceable in the same way as any other order made by the court.[1] The supervisor may bring the matter back before the court.[2] The Criminal Justice and Court Services Act 2000, s 12(5)(b) has now been repealed by the Adoption and Children Act 2002 and accordingly the court is no longer able to provide for a continuing role for the children's guardian following the making of a final supervision order.[3]

1　But see para 8.164, n 3.
2　*Re R and G (Minors) (Interim Care or Supervision Orders)* [1994] 1 FLR 793.
3　Thus *Re MH (A Child), Re SB and MB (Children)* [2001] 2 FLR 1334 is no longer to be regarded as correct as it was based on s 12(5)(b) of the Criminal Justice and Courts Services Act 2000.

(e) Use

8.190 Supervision orders are sought and made less frequently than care orders. Applications are rarely made for a supervision order but may be made by the courts as an alternative to what may be seen as a draconian care order. However, a finding that the threshold criteria are satisfied may be a powerful statement in a suitable case. Combined with the authority to direct a treatment programme for the child and the responsible person, this can make the order a powerful tool. In the light of observations about the need to ensure that an order is proportionate to the circumstances of the case, local authorities are likely to have to consider how to use supervision orders more constructively.[1]

[1] A more imaginative use of Sch 3 might assist, but these provisions (see above) provide for directions given by the supervisor to the child, and not by the court, nor to the parent. This was what was envisaged by the Review of Child Care Law (1985) HMSO, and should perhaps be revisited in the light of current experience.

(f) Education supervision order

8.191 If it appears to an education authority that a child is not receiving suitable education, they may serve a notice on the parent requiring him to satisfy the authority that the child is receiving such education. If a parent on whom a notice has been served fails to satisfy the authority that the child is receiving suitable education or in the opinion of the authority it is expedient for the child to attend school, they shall serve on the parent a school attendance order.[1] If the parent fails to comply with the order, the parent commits an offence, unless he can show that the child is receiving suitable education.[2] There is a separate offence, if a child of compulsory school age who is a registered pupil, fails to attend school regularly.[3] In either case, before the authority institutes proceedings, it must consider whether it would be appropriate to apply instead, or in addition, for an education supervision order under s 36.[4] A court by which a person is convicted of failing to comply with a school attendance order, or before which a person is charged with failing to secure a child's regular attendance at school, may direct the education authority to apply for an education supervision order[5] and may make a parenting order.[6]

[1] Education Act 1996, s 437.
[2] Education Act 1996,s 443.
[3] Education Act 1996,s 444.
[4] Education Act 1996,s 447(1).
[5] Education Act 1996,1996, s 447(2).
[6] See the Crime and Disorder Act 1998, s 8 (*Clarke Hall and Morrison on Children*, 7 [2203]).

8.192 Before instituting proceedings for an education supervision order, the education authority must consult the appropriate social services authority.[1] That authority may decide to provide support for the child and his family under Pt III[2] or to apply for a compulsory order under Pt IV of the CA 1989.

[1] CA 1989, s 36(8) and (9).
[2] See Chapter 6.

8.193 An education authority may apply for an education supervision order on the ground that the child concerned is of compulsory school age and is not being properly educated, that is, he is not receiving efficient full-time education suitable to his age, ability and aptitude and any special education needs he may have.[1] This ground is deemed to be satisfied, unless it is proved to the contrary, where a school attendance order in force under s 437 of the

Education Act 1996 is not complied with, or he is a registered pupil at a school and is not attending regularly within the meaning of s 444 of that Act.[2]

1   CA 1989, s 36(3) and (4).
2   CA 1989, s 36(5).

8.194 The scheme encourages education authorities to consider whether an education supervision order or prosecution or both is likely to provide the more effective approach. Supervision might be more effective for parents who find it difficult to exercise proper influence over a child who has developed a pattern of poor attendance, whereas parental hostility to intervention or a structured programme of work might suggest that prosecution would be necessary.[1]

1   Children Act 1989 Guidance and Regulations, Vol 7, Guardians ad litem and other court related issues (2008) Department of Health paras 3.07 and 3.08.

8.195 The proceedings are not specified for the purposes of s 41,[1] so that a children's guardian is not appointed. The court must state any findings of fact and give reasons, when determining an application for an education supervision order.[2] The order cannot be made in respect of a child in care.[3]

1   See para 10.26.
2   See *Essex County Council v B* [1993] 1 FLR 866.
3   CA 1989, s 36(6).

8.196 An education supervision order may last for up to one year but may be extended for up to a further three years at a time.[1] It shall cease to have effect when the child reaches compulsory school leaving age or when he becomes the subject of a care order. The order may be discharged on the application of the child, parent or the education authority. The supervisor has a duty to advise, assist and befriend and give directions to the child and the parents so as to secure that the child is properly educated. If directions are not complied with, the supervisor must consider what further steps to take. He may seek new directions or apply for discharge of the order. A parent who persistently fails to comply with a direction shall be guilty of an offence. If a child persistently fails to comply with a direction, the education authority must notify the social services authority, which is obliged to investigate the circumstances of the child.

1   CA 1989, Sch 3, Pt III.

CONTACT WITH CHILDREN IN CARE

1. Summary

8.197 The CA 1989 established a structure in relation to contact with children looked after[1] by a local authority, distinct from the provisions regulating visiting or staying in the private law. There are duties to all children looked after, and further provisions in respect of children who are subject to a care order. The court has power to make what may conveniently be described as a care contact order. Unlike the position prior to the CA 1989, when the local authority had a discretion to make decisions about contact with children in care, those decisions are now ultimately a matter for the court. As the Contact Orders Study[2] points out, 'proposals from the local authority now have to face the rigours of legal challenge'.

1 Defined to include children accommodated and children subject to a care order: s 22(1). See Chapter 6.
2 Department of Health Social Services Inspectorate *A Study of Local Authority Decision Making Around Contact Applications Under Section 34* (1994).

8.198 The courts have recognised both the importance of ongoing contact following the granting of a care order and the potential difficulties of establishing whether such advantages pertain in a particular case. In *Re E (A Minor)(Care Order: Contact)*[1] Simon-Brown LJ noted:

> 'In short, even when the s 31 criteria are satisfied, contact may well be of singular importance to the long-term welfare of the child: first, in giving the child the security of knowing that his parents love him and are interested in his welfare; secondly, by avoiding any damaging sense of loss to the child in seeing himself abandoned by his parents; thirdly, by enabling the child to commit himself to the substitute family with the seal of approval of the natural parents; and, fourthly, by giving the child the necessary sense of family and personal identity. Contact, if maintained, is capable of reinforcing and increasing the chances of success of a permanent placement, whether on a long-term fostering basis or by adoption.'

In *Berkshire County Council v B*[2] Hale J stated:

> 'The question, therefore, becomes one of balancing the respective factors in the welfare of the child. At one end of the spectrum there must be cases where the child clearly needs a new family for life and contact with his family of birth will bring little or no benefit and is likely to impede this. At the other end of the spectrum are cases where the child is likely to return home in the short to medium term and contact is essential to enable this to take place.

> There are also many cases in the middle where the child is unlikely to be able to return home in the short to medium term and so needs a long-term stable placement but where the relationships with his family of origin are so important to him that they must be maintained. One reason for this may well be that adoption is unlikely to succeed so that a child must not be deprived of his existing relationships which matter to him for the sake of putative ones which may never be found.

> In these very difficult cases the court has to balance these various advantages against the difficulties that contact is likely to cause in finding and sustaining an appropriate placement for the child. Obviously contact, however important, cannot be pursued to a level which makes a successful placement impossible to find because the child needs a home and to be properly looked after, and that must be the first priority.

> The local authority are not entitled to approach the case in a "take it or leave it" manner, for two reasons: first, because, as I have already explained, the court retains control over the relationship between the child and his parents through the issues of contact and adoption. The court therefore has to balance the various factors and so must the local authority. Secondly, while I accept that local authorities are entitled to have a general approach based on their

appreciation of what is in general best for children – and we are all aware of the many reasons why adoption may well provide the best solution for most young children who have to be looked after for a long time away from their family of birth – they have a statutory duty to make decisions in the interests of the individual child in their care. They cannot approach decision-making in any particular case as if it were governed by general principles alone. It is trite law that those exercising a statutory discretion are not entitled to fetter their discretion by a reference to a general policy of which they will not admit departures in appropriate cases.'

1   [1994] 1 FLR 146.
2   [1997] 1 FLR 171.

2. Duties of the local authority

(a) Duty to promote contact

8.199 Where a child is being looked after by a local authority, whether subject to a care order or not, the authority shall, unless it is not reasonably practicable or consistent with his welfare, endeavour to promote contact between the child and his parents, others who have parental responsibility and relatives, friends and others.[1] They must take reasonable steps to keep parents and others with parental responsibility informed of his whereabouts, unless the authority has reasonable cause for believing that giving that information would be prejudicial to the child's welfare. Information must also be given where another authority takes over the provision of accommodation. Information about the child may only be withheld where it is essential for the welfare of the child, and where the child is in the care of the local authority.

1   CA 1989, Sch 2, para 15.

8.200 The local authority may promote contact by helping with costs incurred in making visits.[1] This help may be given to the parent (or other person who is entitled to contact with the child) or to the child. The local authority should ensure that the parents and child are aware that such assistance is available when plans for contact are being discussed. The original version of the Children Act 1989 Guidance and Regulations states:[2]

> 'Children with special needs, or who have difficulty in communicating, may need extra local authority support to help them to maintain contact when placed at a distance from their home area. Contact includes communication by letter and telephone, and some children may need special provisions to facilitate this type of contact. Particular consideration must also be given to the needs of children for whom their first language (or that of their parent) is not English'.

1   CA 1989, Sch 2, para 16.
2   See Section 3.

(b) Duty to child in care

8.201 Section 34(1) requires the local authority to allow a child, who is subject to a care order, reasonable contact with his parents[1] or guardian, a person in whose favour there was a residence order immediately before the making of the care order, or a person who had the care of the child by virtue of an order under the inherent jurisdiction of the High Court. Reasonable contact is not the same as contact at the discretion of the local authority. 'Reasonable' implies contact which is agreed between the local authority and the parents or in the absence of an agreement, contact which is objectively reasonable.[2] The advantages of maintaining a link via contact where to do so is in the best interests of the child operate in respect of fathers just as much as it does for mothers.[3] The local authority cannot subordinate the welfare of the child by reducing or ending contact in order to make finding a permanent placement for that child easier.[4]

[1] Parent includes the unmarried father even if he does not have parental responsibility: Family Law Reform Act 1987, s 1.
[2] *Re P (Minors) (Contact With Children In Care)* [1993] 2 FLR 156.
[3] *Re G (Adoption: Contact)* [2002] EWCA Civ 761, [2003] 1 FLR 270.
[4] *Re H (Children)(Termination of Contact)* [2005] EWCA Civ 318, [2005] 2 FLR 408.

3. The care contact order

8.202 Those persons referred to in the preceding paragraph may apply to the court as of right for a care contact order with regard to the contact they are to be allowed with a child in care.[1] Applications may also be made by any person, such as a relative, who has obtained the leave of the court.[2] The care contact order differs from a contact order under s 8, which is an order requiring the person with whom the child lives to allow contact. Under s 34 the order is described in terms of the contact which is to be allowed between the child and the applicant. The same interpretation as in s 8 may, however, be placed on the concept of contact, which includes visiting, staying or other contact, for example, by letter or telephone. The court may impose such conditions as it considers appropriate.[3] This may include restriction of contact to specific periods or places.

[1] CA 1989, s 34(3)(a).
[2] CA 1989, s 34(3)(b).
[3] CA 1989, s 34(7).

8.203 A care contact order can only exist if there is a care order in force. If the child is in care, no court can make a s 8 contact order,[1] save on an application of a child in care for contact with siblings who were not in care.[2] If there is a contact order under s 8 in existence, it is discharged on the making of a care order.[3] If the court considers that contact with a named person should continue, it must make a new order under s 34.

[1] CA 1989, s 9(1). The court can make a s 8 order in respect of a child who is accommodated but not subject to a care order.
[2] *Re F (Contact: Child in Care)* [1995] 1 FLR 510. See para 5.124.
[3] CA 1989, s 91(2).

8.204 In respect of persons not entitled to apply for a contact order as of right, in deciding whether to grant leave to a third party to make an application for contact under s 34(3), the court should take account of the criteria set out in s 10(9).[1] In *Re M (Minors in Care) (Contact: Grandmother's Application)*[2] it was held that it would be anomalous not to do so, since they were apposite to leave applications under s 34(3). The court should at least have regard to:

(a)   the nature of the contact being sought;

(b)   the connection of the applicant to the child: the more meaningful the connection, the greater the weight to be given. Although contact between grandparents and children was assumed by para 15 of Sch 3 to be beneficial, they still required leave to apply;

(c)   whether the child's need for security and stability would be disrupted; and

(d)   the wishes of the parents and the local authority were material.

In deciding whether or not to grant leave the court should adopt the following approach:

(1)   If the application was vexatious or frivolous or an abuse of process, it would fail.

(2)   If the application failed to disclose any eventual real prospect of success, it should be dismissed.

(3)   The applicant had to satisfy the court that there was a serious issue to try, and present a good arguable case.

The court should also ask itself whether the person applying for leave has a separate point to advance on contact or is advancing a position identical to that of another party. If the latter, it is unlikely the court will give leave for the applicant to become a party.[3]

¹   See para 5.150.
²   [1995] 3 FCR 550, [1995] 2 FLR 86, CA. But see also *Re P (a child)* [2002] EWCA Civ 846, [2002] All ER (D) 554 (May).
³   *Re W(Care Proceedings: leave to Apply)* [2004] EWHC 3342 (Fam), [2005] 2 FLR 468).

8.205 Since a wide range of interested persons may seek the leave of the court to apply for a contact order, the authority must give careful consideration to its duty to allow the child to have contact with any relevant person. The outline arrangements will have been submitted to the court at the care proceedings.[1] In view of the continuing responsibility vested in a parent after a care order, where possible the local authority should, in a spirit of partnership, seek to reach a written agreement on the terms for the contact and other arrangements while the child is in care.[2] Given that contact between a child and its family will be assumed to be beneficial[3] a local authority that contends contact is not in the child's best interests and/or reasonably practicable must lead evidence to establish that position.[4]

¹   CA 1989, s 34(11).
²   See the Children Act 1989 Guidance and Regulations, Vol 3, Family Placements (1991) Department of Health, para 6.33.
³   Pursuant to the CA 1989, Sch 2, para 15.
⁴   *Re M (Minors in Care) (Contact: Grandmother's Application)* [1995] 3 FCR 550, [1995] 2 FLR 86, CA.

8.206 A child in care has a right to make an application for defined contact which is to be allowed with any named person.[1] This provision has created some complex dilemmas in relationships between siblings, whose interests may differ. In most cases it would be desirable for the authority to take the proceedings if so requested by the child, but the authority may consider an application undesirable. The child may wish to take the initiative. If an applicant child in care is seeking contact with other children who are willing to see him, the interests of the applicant child are paramount, but if those children were in care, the applicant child would be the person named, and the other children would be the subject of the application, whose interests were paramount.[2]

1   CA 1989, s 34(2).
2   *Re F (Contact: Child in Care)* [1995] 1 FLR 510. See also para 2.13.

8.207 There are emergency arrangements which permit an authority to refuse to allow contact, where they would otherwise be obliged to do so, for no more than seven days, if they are satisfied that it is necessary to do so in order to safeguard or promote the child's welfare.[1] Where an authority decides as a matter of urgency to refuse contact that they would otherwise be required to promote or allow in accordance with an order under s 34, it must give certain persons specified information. These include the child if he is of sufficient understanding, other persons with parental responsibility, and others whose wishes and feelings the authority consider to be relevant.[2] The Schedule to the Contact with Children Regulations 1991 includes information as follows: the decision, its date and the reasons for it, the duration and the remedies available in case of dissatisfaction. Where arrangements have been made and are then varied or suspended, the person concerned must also be given written notice.[3]

1   CA 1989, s 34(6).
2   SI 1991/891, reg 2.
3   SI 1991/891, reg 4.

4. Powers of the court

8.208 In determining contact applications under s 34 the welfare of the child is the paramount consideration.[1] The court must also consider the checklist under s 1(3) and whether making no order is better than making any order at all under s 1(5). Where an application for contact to a child in care is made by a parent who is also a minor, the person whose upbringing is in question is the son or daughter of the parent and it is that child's welfare which is the paramount consideration.[2] In exceptional circumstances the court may order daily supervised contact between a mother and a young baby.[3]

1   *Re B (Minors) (Termination of Contact: Paramount Consideration)* [1993] Fam 301, [1993] 3 All ER 524.
2   *Birmingham City Council v H (A Minor)* [1994] 2 AC 212, [1994] 1 All ER 12, HL, discussed at para 2.13. See also *Re F (Contact: Child in Care)* [1995] 1 FLR 510.
3   *Kirklees Metropolitan District Council v S (Contact to Newborn Babies)* [2005] EWCA Civ 213, [2006] 1 FLR 333.

8.209 The court may make such order and impose such conditions as it thinks appropriate.[1] It has power to make an interim contact order at the same time as a care order with a provision for a further hearing on contact.[2] The court cannot, however, make a contact order with a direction to the children's guardian 'to keep an eye on the case',[3] nor that a guardian should have contact with a child after a care order.[4] The court does not have power to make an order prohibiting a local authority from allowing contact between child and parent, only an order authorizing the local authority to refuse contact.[5] The court should be careful on an interim application not to prejudice the main application.[6] Where the local authority contends that resource issues militate against a certain level of contact, it should submit evidence to the court of the cost to the local authority of facilitating the contact sought.[7]

[1] CA 1989, s 34(7).
[2] *Re B (A Minor) (Care Order: Review)* [1993] 1 FLR 421.
[3] *Re S (A Minor) (Care: Contact Order)* [1994] 2 FLR 222, CA.
[4] *Kent County Council v C* [1993] Fam 57, [1993] 1 FLR 308.
[5] *Re W (Parental Contact: Prohibition)* [2000] Fam 130, [2000] 1 FLR 502, CA.
[6] *A v M and Walsall Metropolitan Borough Council* [1994] 1 FCR 606, [1993] 2 FLR 244.
[7] *Kirklees Metropolitan District Council v S (Contact to Newborn Babies)* [2005] EWCA Civ 213, [2006] 1 FLR 333.

8.210 These provisions give the court power to influence the future direction of a case, although the arrangements for contact which an authority may in practice make will have to be taken into account. An authority seeking a care order or opposing discharge of an order will be obliged to consider carefully the arrangements, arguments and evidence in relation to contact with the child in respect of any connected person. Those arrangements must be discussed with the child if old enough[1] and with those connected with the child.

[1] CA 1989, s 22(4).

8.211 The court has power where a child is in care, to make an order about contact under s 34 in any family proceedings,[1] which concern the same child. This includes domestic violence, divorce and adoption cases. Authorities will have to be on the alert constantly for questions about contact with the whole range of people who might be interested in the child.

[1] As defined by s 8(3) provided of course that the judge or court is authorised to deal with care cases.

5. Variation and discharge

8.212 The court may vary or discharge an order on the application of the authority, the child or the person named in the order.[1] Although the Act is not specific on the point, the making of a residence order under s 8 must discharge a s 34 order since it is dependent upon the existence of the care order which is itself discharged by virtue of s 91(1). The court should make an appropriate contact order under s 8.

[1] CA 1989, s 34(9).

8.213 The Contact with Children Regulations 1991 provide that an authority can depart from the terms of a court order by agreement with the person to whom the order relates, subject to agreement with the child if he is of sufficient understanding, and subject to the sending of a written notice within seven days of the agreement to depart from the terms of the order.[1] The notice must be sent to the child, his parents or guardian, a person who had a residence order before a care order was made, a person who had the care of the child under an order in the exercise of the High Court's inherent jurisdiction, and any other person whose wishes and feelings the authority consider to be relevant.[2] The notice must contain information as to the decision, the date of and reasons for it, its duration and the remedies available in case of dissatisfaction.[3] The idea behind the provisions is to allow for flexibility and obviate the need to return to court where all are agreed with the revised arrangement. That would suggest that although the scope of the power is wide, it should in practice probably be limited to minor variations. If there was a major change in contact arrangements, on which plans for the child relied, and subsequently the parent objected, there would be a risk of them being reversed on application to the court.

[1] Regulation 3.
[2] Regulation 3.
[3] Schedule to the Regulations.

6. Refusal of contact

8.214 The authority or the child may also apply for an order authorising the authority to refuse to allow contact with any person with whom the authority would otherwise be required to allow the child to have contact.[1] This includes making an order on an interim basis.[2] The court should be careful on an interim application not to prejudice the main application.[3] Provided the section is used as part of a care plan approved by the court, and as a means of avoiding drift or delay in the interests of the child concerned, it has been held that the section is compliant with the ECHR.[4] However, an order giving authority to refuse contact should only be made where matters are so exceptional and the risk so severe that contact must be stopped.[5]

[1] Section 34(4). But note this is not an order terminating contact, rather an order *authorising* the refusal of contact at the discretion of the local authority.
[2] *West Glamorgan County Council v P* [1992] 2 FLR 369.
[3] *A v M and Walsall Metropolitan Borough Council* [1994] 1 FCR 606, [1993] 2 FLR 244.
[4] *Re F (Care: Termination of Contact)* [2000] 2 FCR 481. See also *Gorgulu v Germany (Application 749699/01)* [2004] 1 FLR 894.
[5] *A v M and Walsall Metropolitan Borough Council* [1994] 1 FCR 606, [1993] 2 FLR 244.

8.215 As in all contact applications, when the court is considering whether to authorise the local authority to refuse to allow contact, the child's welfare is the paramount consideration pursuant to s 1. Although a court should not readily make an order contrary to the plans of the local authority, it must still apply the welfare principle. An order under s 34(4) should not be made in a case where the option of rehabilitation remains open and the s 34(4) order will not be implemented immediately.[1]

¹   *Re S (Care: Parental Contact)* [2004] EWCA Civ 1397, [2005] 1 FLR 469, although where
an adoption is already in prospect and the order made refers specifically to the period
following the placement being made it is arguable that *Re S* should not apply.

8.216 In *Re B (Minors) (Termination of Contact: Paramount Consideration)*,¹ Butler-Sloss LJ said:

> 'Contact applications fall into two categories, those which ask for contact as
> such, and those which are attempts to set aside the care order itself. In the first
> category there is no suggestion that the applicant wishes to take over the care of
> the child and the issue of contact often depends on whether contact would
> frustrate long-term plans for the child in a substitute home, such as adoption
> where continuing contact may not be for the long term welfare of the child. The
> presumption of contact which has to be for the benefit of the child, has always
> to be balanced against the long-term welfare of the child and particularly where
> he will live in the future. Contact must not be allowed to destabilise or
> endanger the arrangements for the child and in many cases the plans for the
> child will be decisive of the contact application ...
>
> The proposals of the local authority, based on their appreciation of the best
> interests of the child, must command the greatest respect and consideration
> from the court, but Parliament has given to the court, and not to the local
> authority, the duty to decide on contact between the child and those named in
> s 34(1). Consequently the court may have the task of requiring the local
> authority to justify their long-term plans to the extent only that those plans
> exclude contact between parent and child.
>
> In the second category contact applications may be made by parents by way of
> another attempt to obtain the return of the children. In such a case the court is
> obviously entitled to take into account the failure to apply to discharge the care
> order, and in the majority of cases the court will have little difficulty in coming
> to the conclusion that the application cannot demonstrate that contact with a
> view to rehabilitation with the parent is a viable proposition at that stage,
> particularly if it had already been rejected at the earlier hearing when the child
> was placed in care.'

¹   [1993] Fam 301, [1993] 3 All ER 524, CA.

8.217 Where the mother is a child makes an application for contact with a
child in care, the welfare test should be applied to the child whose upbringing
is in question. Since s 34(4) relates to that child, no question falls to be
determined as to the upbringing of the parent, even though she is a child.¹

¹   *Birmingham City Council v H (A Minor)* [1994] 2 AC 212, [1994] 1 All ER 12, HL.

8.218 Where an applicant has been refused an order under s 34, he may not
make another such application within six months without the leave of the
court.¹ There is, however, a further provision which empowers the court to
order that no application for an order under the Act may be made by a named
person without the leave of the court.² It has been said that the order should
be used sparingly.³ It should not be made without giving the party affected due
notice.⁴ It would be appropriate where a party or child were suffering from
too frequent applications or where there had been a full hearing and a
subsequent application would have no prospect of success.⁵

1 CA 1989, s 91(17).
2 CA 1989, s 91(14). See para 5.122.
3 *R v West Glamorgan County Council, ex p T* [1990] 1 FLR 339.
4 *Re S (Contact) (Prohibition of Applications)* [1994] 2 FLR 1057, CA.
5 *Re F* [1992] 2 FCR 433 [1993] 1 FLR 432; *Re Y (Child Orders: Restricting Applications)* [1994] 2 FLR 699. See also *Re N (Section 91(14) Order)* [1996] 1 FLR 356; and *Re R (Residence: Contact: Restricting applications)* [1998] 1 FLR 749.

VARIATION, DISCHARGE AND APPEAL

1. Variation

8.219 The court may substitute a supervision order for a care order on the application of any person who has parental responsibility, the child himself or the designated local authority.[1] On such an application the court may disregard the requirements to satisfy the threshold criteria.[2] There is no similar provision relating to substitution of a care order for a supervision order, so that a fresh application by the local authority is required and the court must be satisfied as to the threshold criteria.[3] The court cannot of its own volition substitute a care order on an application to extend a supervision order.

1 CA 1989, s 39(4).
2 CA 1989, s 39(5).
3 *Re A (Supervision Order: Extension)* [1995] 1 WLR 482, [1995] 1 FLR 335, CA.

2. Discharge of care order

8.220 Application for discharge of a care order may be made by any person who has parental responsibility for the child, the child himself[1] or the local authority.[2] No application may be made without the leave of the court within six months of the determination of a previous application.[3] The court may substitute a supervision order on such an application. It needs to consider only the welfare principle and need not satisfy itself again as to the threshold criteria.[4] If the authority is seeking a care order in substitution for a supervision order, the authority must satisfy afresh the threshold criteria.[5] The court does not have power to postpone discharge of a care order to allow for a gradual return of a child to his family over a period of time, but it can vary the contact provisions consistent with a plan for return. It can also make a residence order with appropriate directions and conditions under s 11(7) of the CA 1989 coupled with a supervision order. The burden of proving that the child's welfare requires the discharge of the care order is on the person applying for discharge.[6]

1 The child does not require leave: *Re A (care: discharge application by child)* [1995] 2 FCR 686, [1995] 1 FLR 599.
2 CA 1989, s 39(1).
3 CA 1989, s 91(15).
4 CA 1989, s 39(5).
5 *Re O (Care: Discharge of Care Order)* [1999] 2 FLR 119.
6 *Re MD and TD (Minors)(No 2)* [1994] Fam Law 489.

8.221 Local authorities are required by the Review of Children's Cases Regulations 1991[1] to consider on at least every statutory review of a case of a child in care whether to apply for discharge of the care order. As part of each review the child has to be informed of steps he may take himself, which include applying for discharge of the order, applying for a contact order or variation of an existing contact order or for leave to apply for a residence order.

1 SI 1991/895, Sch 2 as amended by the Children's Cases (Amendment)(England) Regulations 2004, SI 2004/1419.

8.222 There is no strict rule of issue estoppel binding any of the parties in cases concerning children.[1] A judge has a discretion to re-open a conceded issue where necessary in the interests of a child and such a course is better characterised as case management than estoppel.[2] Having heard a parent's oral evidence and submissions from the parties, it is not a denial of justice for a court to decide at that stage that there was no realistic prospect of the care order being discharged.[3]

1 *Re B (Children Act Proceedings)(Issue Estoppel)* [1997] 1 FLR 285 per Hale J which sets out the factors to be taken into account when considering whether an issue of fact should be reopened at a subsequent hearing.
2 *Re D (a child) (threshold criteria: issue estoppel)* [2001] 1 FCR 124, CA.
3 *P v Bradford Metropolitan Borough Council* [1996] 2 FCR 227, sub nom *Re S and P (Discharge of Care Order)* [1995] 2 FLR 782.

8.223 Where an application has been made for discharge of a care order (or supervision order), no further application may be made without the leave of the court unless the period between disposal of the application and the making of the further application exceeds six months.[1]

1 CA 1989, s 91(15).

8.224 A third party such as a relative or foster parent who wishes a care order to be discharged, can seek a residence order. The making of such an order discharges the care order.[1] A person is entitled to apply for a residence order if they have the consent:[2]

(a)   of the local authority if the child is in care; or
(b)   of each of those people with parental responsibility; or
(c)   the child has lived with them for at least three years.

If they are or have been a local authority foster parent within the last six months, they require the consent of the local authority they are a relative or the child has been with them for at least one year.[1]

1 CA 1989, s 91(1).
2 CA 1989, s 10(5).
3 CA 1989, s 9(3) as amended by the Adoption and Children Act 2002.

3. Appeals[1]

8.225 All parties can appeal against the making of a care order.[2] The local authority can appeal against the refusal to make a care order.[3] In each case the principle of *G v G (Minors: Custody Appeal)*[4] applies, but there might be slightly more flexibility in care cases.[5]

1   See Chapter 13.
2   CA 1989, s 94(1)(a).
3   CA 1989, s 94(1)(b).
4   [1985] FLR 894, HL.
5   See for example *Re G (A Minor) (Care: Evidence)* [1994] 2 FLR 785, CA and Chapter 13 generally.

8.226 If the court dismisses an application for a care or supervision order, and an interim care or supervision order is in force at the time of the dismissal, it may make a care or supervision order for a specific appeal period.[1] If the court grants an application to discharge a care or supervision order, it may order that the decision shall have no effect for the appeal period.[2] There are limitations to these provisions. They do not apply if there is no previous order in force, so they cannot assist in respect of a first application. There is no corresponding provision to enable a stay of execution on the application of a parent. The proper course is said to be to apply to the High Court, where the judge has power to order a stay under the inherent jurisdiction.[3] It has been argued that justices do have a common law power to grant a stay.[4] In an appropriate case it would seem to be sensible to consider maintaining the status quo pending an appeal.

1   CA 1989, s 40(1).
2   CA 1989, s 40(2).
3   *Re O (a minor) (care order: education: procedure)* [1992] 4 All ER 905, [1992] 2 FLR 7.
4   See 'In context: Stay of Execution pending appeal' [1992] 2 FCR 896.

WITHDRAWING CARE PROCEEDINGS

8.227 The leave of the court is required before an application under s 31 can be withdrawn.[1] A person seeking leave to withdraw shall file and serve on the parties a written request setting out the reasons for the request. Application may be made orally if the parties and the children's guardian are present.[2] If all these consent in writing and the court thinks fit, it shall grant the request or it may fix a date for hearing the application. The welfare of the child is paramount.[3] Prior to the Children Act it was held that the action of a local authority in offering no evidence when refused leave to withdraw was highly questionable.[4]

1   FPR 1991, r 4.5; FPC(CA 1989)R 1991, r 5; and see *Re N (Leave to Withdraw Care Proceedings)* [2000] 1 FLR 134.
2   *Re F (a minor) (care order: withdrawal of application)* [1993] 1 FCR 389, [1993] 2 FLR 9.
3   *Southwark London Borough v B* [1993] 2 FLR 559, CA.
4   *R v Birmingham Juvenile Court, ex p G and R* [1988] 3 All ER 726, [1989] 1 WLR 950; affd in the Court of Appeal [1990] 2 QB 573, [1989] 3 All ER 336, [1989] FCR 460.

CONCLUSIONS

8.228 There remains a tension over whether and when to take care proceedings. Local authorities have to take into account a wide range of welfare, social, political, resource and jurisprudential factors. There are some real dilemmas in achieving the right balance in making decisions about when and whether to move from working under Part III of the Act to proceedings under Part IV of the Act. The sometimes uneasy relationship between local authorities and the courts and the sighting of the boundary between them can lead to impairment of the service provided in both arenas. This difficulty is exacerbated by the fact that the two systems often speak different languages. This conflict can be seen in decisions about whether support services could be mandated, when proceedings should be initiated, the evidence required to satisfy a case, when there should be an assessment, who should be responsible for it, whether there should be court control of the care plan, whether to make an interim or final care order and whether the court should have review powers. In a world of increasing pressure on limited resources there is a risk that local authorities will seek to save money by relying on unsuitable kinship placements or keeping children accommodated too long pursuant to s 20 of the Act when proceedings are in fact justified.

8.229 If the local authority is able to provide resources which are truly supportive of the family, this will often be preferable to taking proceedings. However, since local authorities cannot be required to provide services, a child may suffer significant harm with the effect that the threshold criteria come to be satisfied as a result of their failures or lack of resources. Unfortunately the evidence suggests that so far the balance between family support and compulsory intervention has been difficult to find, not least because successive governments have not made available the resources to fund the proper implementation of Pt III of the Act. In those circumstances many local authorities will continue to provide primarily a fire-fighting service to protect children, with or without an effective use of Part III of the Act, thereafter relying on Part IV to do the work with the family mandated by Part III. The shortage of staff, especially in the metropolitan areas, compounds these problems. Whilst the 'Quality Protects' project introduced in 1998 represented a step in the right direction with regard to the delivery of more family support services, the conclusions of the recent Care Proceedings Review tend to suggest that the provision of such support services remains inadequate to ensure that those cases in which proceedings could be avoided do not end up in court. Within this context, and in any event, local authorities will need to appreciate that notwithstanding the imperatives of the PLO the issue of proceedings under Part IV of the Act does not mean that the concerns that have resulted in those proceedings are necessarily irredeemable. Part IV of the Act cannot be allowed to become an administrative graveyard where families who cannot be worked with under Part III of the Act go to be buried.

8.230 Care proceedings can be expensive, time consuming and threatening (to parents and professionals) and the possible trauma involved can have an adverse impact on the family, especially if proceedings are not well managed by the court and by the professionals involved. Proceedings may nonetheless be essential to protect the child; the irony is that those most seriously damaged children will suffer further harm as a result of the delays currently being experienced in bringing about a satisfactory conclusion to the proceedings. As a society we still seem to have failed to grasp the concept that the removal of a child from harm in his own family can itself cause harm, which is a factor to be considered when deciding whether to take proceedings (especially on emotional grounds). Sadly, this latter observation remains as true for this edition as it did for the last.

8.231 Used constructively proceedings can achieve a structure and a benchmark from which to work for the future. They can provide a framework for informed discussion in which the parents will feel heard, care plans will be carefully examined and a good guardian can act as an independent mediator. In spite of these potential advantages local authorities cannot be required to take care proceedings, since, even assuming the court becomes aware of a problem, its powers are restricted to requiring the authority to carry out an investigation. This can lead to children continuing to suffer abuse and neglect at home, or to them having unplanned carers in local authority accommodation where a local authority does not act.

8.232 It remains a sad fact that the resources required for many children suffering harm and the expertise needed to achieve satisfactory planning will only be made available if they become the subject of care proceedings. This remains equally true for obtaining advice from a well-informed third party such as a guardian, the input of an expert such as a child and family psychiatrist and the commitment of the family to take seriously social services' concerns. Perhaps the greatest sadness is that these deficiencies have been recognised and reported upon for the entire currency of the Act.[1]

[1] There has been a range of work done on the operational difficulties experienced under the Children Act 1989 by reason of resource difficulties, including the Booth Report in 1995, the Lord Chancellor's Department's Scoping Study on Delay in 2002, the Final Report on the Judicial Case Management Protocol in 2003 and the Finch Report on Delay for the Department for Education and Skills in 2004, to name but a few.

8.233 Delay is the primary product of these difficulties. The new PLO is a means of managing the process to bring proceedings to a conclusion with the avoidance of delay. But the setting of a timetable for the progress of proceedings does not by itself reduce delay.[1] The Children Act Scoping Study[2] suggests that *causes* of delay are lack of experts, inflexibility of jurisdiction leading to problems with judicial availability, and lack of judicial case management.[3] Regrettably these problems remain largely unmitigated since they were first identified in the Booth Report in 1995.[4] Contributory factors within the social services field are the poor status of social work and residential care over a long period of time, now heightened by the equally poor status given to CAFCASS employees, consequential reluctance to engage in painful work with impoverished parents, all leading to staff shortages, inadequate training in areas such as child attachment and the law, a shortage of carers with the necessary skills to parent troubled children, and not least and in spite of all the rhetoric to the contrary, an overall lack of investment in child welfare and related areas of work.

1 See Plotnikoff The Timetabling of Care Proceedings before the Implementation of the Children Act 1989 (1991) Department of Health.
2 (March 2002) Lord Chancellor's Department.
3 See A Review of Case Administration in Family Proceedings Courts (May 2001) Magistrates' Courts Service Inspectorate,.
4 See the Final Report on the Judicial Case Management Protocol (2003).

8.234 The success or otherwise of the PLO in addressing issues of delay through case management will, in addition to the question of resources, depend on the extent to which its provisions are embraced by local authorities and others in the care system. Initially care proceedings were perceived as an 'event', the purpose of which was to obtain a court order enabling a pre-conceived plan to be carried out. The local authority would have formed a clear view that the only means of securing the welfare of the child was to bring care proceedings. Although local authorities do seem to explore options for supporting children within their families more thoroughly before applying for a court order, in the majority of cases in which proceedings are brought, the local authorities' goals are not fully formed in the manner now required by the PLO nor the product of a co-ordinated attempt to divert that case away from proceedings. The application of the principle of 'front-loading' underpinning the PLO risks simply transferring delay from proceedings to the pre-proceedings stage as local authorities seek to fully assess families and formulate their plans prior to issue, risking children remaining in a dangerous limbo. There is, however, clear potential for a better position to be reached. Care proceedings appear to have become a more dynamic process, in what has been described as a 'legally protected space within which to assess, and if possible work towards, a resolution of family difficulties or to demonstrate that that was not possible'.[1] The outcome of this emphasis on resolution rather than adjudication is that only 40% of care proceedings result in a contested hearing.

1 See Hunt and Macleod Statutory Intervention in Child Protection; the Impact of the Children Act 1989, (1998); Hunt, Macleod and Thomas the Last Resort: Child Protection, the Courts and the Children Act 1989 (1999) TSO; Hunt 'A moving target: care proceedings as a dynamic process' [1998] CFLQ 281.

8.235 The original model of proceedings which assumed a defined period for the conduct of the hearing[1] may not be a sound basis for this more fluid and dynamic process, a fact tentatively recognised by the PLO and its structure.[2] The challenge for the court is to apply the PLO so as to provide an effective vehicle for this process, with directions hearings needing an emphasis different from management of the 'case' in the familiar sense. The court has to assist in facilitating the process of 'problem resolution' as the case evolves. The extent to which the PLO is able to achieve this aim remains to be seen but will require sufficient human, structural and financial resources and the support of all agencies involved in the system if it is to do so. In particular, the role of the children's guardian in moderating this process has become a key feature of care proceedings and is further emphasised by the PLO[3]. This process will require CAFCASS to play an effective role, but whether the organisation will be equipped to respond to the demands remains to be seen.

1   And later reiterated and emphasised by the 2003 Case Management Protocol.
2   In particular the use of a 'timetable for the child'.
3   See Chapter 10.

8.236 There remain potential problems where the case is based on possible future harm. While it must be right that a likelihood of harm cannot be substantiated on the basis of mere suspicion, should a court exclude its powers where the evidence suggests a future risk to the child but one which then must be discounted because the local authority is unable to prove to the requisite standard the factual basis on which that risk of future harm is grounded? The House of Lords has answered this question in the affirmative in *Re B (Children)(sexual abuse: standard of proof)*.[1] Given the draconian nature of the orders that can follow a finding of likelihood of future harm, it is very difficult to see how we could now move from the current position whereby the likelihood of future harm can be grounded on anything less than facts proved to the requisite standard.

1   [2008] UKHL 35, [2008] 2 FCR 339.

8.237 There is in fact little concrete evidence that children are being left at home in danger for want of protective measures. The number of care orders has increased[1]. There is no evidence that children who are injured have been sent home by the courts because they have not been satisfied of the threshold criteria. On the other hand there is still a feeling that local authorities leave cases too late, whether it is because they dislike the court arena, because they lack confidence in their ability to prove cases or from concern as to whether they can provide anything better. Ultimately it is a matter of politics and professional judgement whether you err on the side of running the risks of leaving a child in an uncertain situation or the risks inherent in local authority care.

1   In 2006, 7,222: Judicial and Court Statistics 2006, p 88.

8.238 As we commented in the second edition the provisions for ensuring the implementation of care plans remain unsatisfactory. There had been no progress in this respect since 1995 and little attention given by Government until the problem was considered in the House of Lords in *Re S* and *Re W*.[1] There had been great frustration because the courts have been unable to impose specific action on a local authority or be confident that the care plan on which the making of a care order was based would be implemented. Although day-to-day decisions about the welfare of the child must ultimately be for the local authority, when they are more fundamental to the future of the child, it has proved to be unsatisfactory to leave decisions entirely in the hands of some local authorities. The statutory provisions brought by the Government to 'remedy' these difficulties are unsatisfactory, or at least have been implemented in a manner which means they are largely ineffective. Questioning the actions of a local authority in relation to the implementation of the care plan for a looked after child will generally require an individual (the child or a member of the child's family) to challenge the actions of the State (as embodied by the local authority). For reasons too obvious to recount, it is vital that the person charged with determining the proper course of such a challenge be independent both of the individual and of the State. Regrettably, the amendments made to the Review of Children Cases Regulations 1991 have failed to ensure that IRO's are truly independent of the local authorities in respect of which they may be asked to consider referral. Finally, in order for the role of the IRO to be effective, there must be sufficient resources available to CAFCASS to deal efficiently and expeditiously with any referrals made by the IRO.

1   *Re S (Minors) (Care Order: Implementation of Care Plan); Re W (Minors) (Care Order: Adequacy of Care Plan)* [2002] UKHL 10, [2002] 2 WLR 720. See paras 8.155–8.163.

8.239 Sustainable outcomes for children can only be consistently achieved if Pt III and Pt IV of the Act work in the complementary way in which they were designed to. Part III must involve effective and properly resourced support work with a view to avoiding proceedings where possible or narrowing significantly the issues should proceedings become necessary under Pt IV. In turn, Pt IV cannot be allowed to become what amounts to an administrative graveyard where families who cannot be worked with effectively under Pt III go to be buried and, accordingly, requires the rigorous case management of proceedings subject always to the needs of the child and the requirements of fairness. Achieving these aims remains a work in progress.

Chapter 9

SECURE ACCOMMODATION

INTRODUCTION

9.1 Any infringement of personal liberty is a tort (and in some circumstances a crime) unless authorised by law. Domestic law has recognised some circumstances where the liberty of a child may be restrained as part of the exercise of parental responsibility in the child's upbringing and for his welfare. These have been extended to a limited extent to teachers and public authorities exercising statutory responsibilities for a child eg local authorities having parental authority under a care order. Public authorities must act in accordance with the European Convention for the Protection of Human Rights and Fundamental Freedoms[1] (the 'Convention') and the use of accommodation by local authorities for the purpose of restricting a child's liberty is specifically restricted by s 25 of the CA 1989 supplemented by the Children (Secure Accommodation) Regulations 1991[2] and the Children (Secure Accommodation) (No 2) Regulations 1991.[3]

Except in relation to certain remands to local authority accommodation in criminal proceedings,[4] a child may only be kept by a local authority in secure accommodation for the purpose of restricting liberty in accordance with a secure accommodation order made by a court, except for a short period where prescribed criteria are fulfilled.[5] An attempt was made in the CA 1989, which was only partially successful, to distinguish between secure accommodation orders made in respect of children accommodated under civil provisions and those remanded in criminal proceedings. Jurisdiction in civil cases is in the family proceedings courts, and, in circumstances prescribed in the Children (Allocation of Proceedings) Order 1991,[6] county courts and the High Court. In criminal proceedings jurisdiction it is the youth court and adult magistrates' court which have jurisdiction, not the Crown Court.[7]

[1]   Rome 4 November 1950; TS 71 (1953); Cmd 8969.
[2]   SI 1191/1505, amended by SI 1992/2117, SI 1995/1398, SI 1996/692, SI 2000/694, SI 2001/2237, SI 2002/546, SI 2004/696 and SI 2006/2986 (Wales).
[3]   SI 1991/2034 amended by SI 2000/694, SI 2002/546 and SI 2004/696.
[4]   See para 9.30.
[5]   See paras 9.10 and 9.14.

⁶ SI 1991/1677 amended by SI 1993/624, SIs 1994/2164 and 3138, SI 1996/1649, SI 1997/1897, SI 1998/2166, SI 1999/524, SI 2000/2670, SIs 2001/775 and 1656, SI 2003/331, SIs 2005/520 and 2797, SI 2006/1541 and SI 2007/1099.
⁷ See para 9.39.

Deprivation of liberty

9.2 Article 5.1 of the European Convention for the Protection of Human Rights and Fundamental Freedoms (the 'Convention') provides inter alia that:

> 'Everyone has the right to liberty and security of person. No-one shall be deprived of his liberty save in the following cases and in accordance with a procedure prescribed by law:
> ... (d) the detention of a minor by lawful order for the purpose of educational supervision or his lawful detention for the purpose of bringing him before the competent legal authority.'

In *K (A Child) (Secure Accommodation Order: Right to Liberty)*[1], relying on *Koniarska v United Kingdom (Application 33670/96)* ECtHR, it was held that secure accommodation is a deprivation of liberty within the meaning of art 5 but comes within the exception in art 5(1)(d) as it is an order prescribed by law and, in the light of the compulsory education requirements of the Education Act 1996 which is embraced in the exercise by a local authority of parental rights for the benefit and protection of the child concerned, is for the purpose of educational supervision.

[1] [2001] Fam 377, [2001] 2 All ER 719, [2001] 1 FCR 249, CA. See also A Pack 'Sweet and Tender Hooligans – Secure Accommodation and Human Rights' [2001] Family Law 140 and J Masson '*Re K (A Child) (Secure Accommodation Order: Right to Liberty)* and *Re C (Secure Accommodation Order: Representation)* securing human rights for children and young people in secure accommodation' [2002] CFLQ 77.

9.3 It is not every restriction on the freedom of movement of a child which will amount to a 'deprivation of liberty' within the meaning of art 5 of the Convention as this right of the child must be balanced against the rights of parents under art 8 which guarantees respect for private and family life. A fundamental element of family life, which is protected by the Convention, is the right of parents to exercise parental authority over their children having regard to their corresponding parental responsibilities:[1]

> 'The care and upbringing of children normally and necessarily require that the parents or only parent decide where the child must reside and also impose, or authorise others to impose, various restrictions on a child's liberty. Thus the children in a school or other educational or recreational institution must abide by certain rules which limit their freedom of movement and their liberty in other respects'[2]

The position of educational establishments has been clarified by statute.[3] As regards residential accommodation, the position is clarified by guidance.[4] Deprivation of liberty in criminal proceedings is provided for by statute.[5] Patients may, in circumstances prescribed under the Mental Health Act 1983, be detained for assessment or treatment.[6]

[1] *Nielsen v Denmark* (1988) 11 EHHR 175, ECtHR.

2   *Nielsen v Denmark* (1989) 11 EHHR 175 at 191–192.
3   Education Act 1996, ss 548–550B. See also DfEE Circulars 10/98 Section 550A of the Education Act 1996: The Use of Force to Control or Restrain Pupils; 10/99 Social Inclusion: Pupil Support in *Clarke Hall and Morrison on Children* at paras 6[10151]ff and 6[10181]ff. Education and Inspections Act 2006, s 93.
4   Local Authority Circular (93)13 Guidance of Permissible Forms of Control in Children's Residential Care in *Clarke Hall and Morrison on Children* at paras 1[14291]ff and see the Children's Homes Regulations 2001, SI 2001/3937 amended by SIs 2002/865 and 2469, SI 2005/1541 and SI 2006/1738, reg 17 and the Children's Homes (Wales) Regulations 2002, SI 2002/327 amended by SI 2002/2622, SIs 2004/1756 and 2414, SIs 2005/774, 1541 and 2929, SI 2006/3251 and SI 2007/311, reg 17.
5   Magistrates' Courts Act 1980, ss 5(1), 10(4), 17C and 18(4) (remand); Powers of Criminal Courts (Sentencing) Act 2000, ss 91 and 100 (long-term detention and detention and training orders); Supreme Court Act 1981, s 81 (grant of bail by Crown Court); Contempt of Court Act 1981, ss 12 and 14.
6   Mental Health Act 1983, ss 2 and 3 as amended by the Mental Health Act 2007.

9.4 There is a point where restraint on a child's liberty exceeds ordinary acceptable parental restrictions and amounts to 'deprivation of liberty' within the meaning of art 5 of the Convention. Deprivation of liberty is only lawful in accordance with art 5 if it falls within an exception in art 5.1. In determining whether there is a deprivation of liberty, the approach of the European Court of Human Rights is to have regard to the actual situation in which the child is and account is taken of a whole range of criteria, such as the type, duration, effects and manner of implementation of the measure in question, ie the distinction between deprivation and restriction is one of fact and degree, and not one of nature or substance.[1]

1   *Guzzardi v Italy* (1980) 3 EHHR 333, ECtHR.

9.5 A child who is subject to proceedings for a secure accommodation order has the protection of the fair trial provisions in art 6(1) of the Convention and while it has not been decided whether such proceedings should be categorised as civil or criminal in nature for the purpose of the Convention, such a child should be afforded the five specific minimum rights guaranteed under art 6(3) to everyone charged with a criminal offence[1].

1   *Re M (a child) (secure accommodation)* [2001] EWCA Civ 458, [2001] 1 FCR 692, sub nom *Re C (Secure Accommodation Order: Representation)* [2001] 2 FLR 169.

CHILDREN LOOKED AFTER BY LOCAL AUTHORITIES AND OTHER ORGANISATIONS

Restriction on the use of secure accommodation

9.6 Apart from courts ordering detention in criminal proceedings, the need to impose any restriction on a child's movements to the extent that it would amount to a deprivation of liberty is likely to arise in a situation where a local authority or body providing residential accommodation is accommodating them. The deprivation of a child's liberty is an extreme step and a parent would have difficulty in justifying any detention for more than a period of a few days.[1] A local authority or other body requiring to use accommodation which deprives a child of his liberty for more than the few days justified in the case of a parent[2] would need to establish that their action was authorised by domestic law and was for a purpose which was permissible within the terms of art 5 of the Convention.

In the case of bodies providing residential accommodation, secure accommodation may not be used unless it is authorised by the Act.[3] Those bodies accommodating children which are specified in s 25 of the Act (namely a local authority) or the regulations (namely health authorities, Primary Care Trusts, National Health Service Trusts, NHS foundation trusts or local education authorities, and those providing accommodation in care homes or independent hospitals)[4] may not use secure accommodation unless the criteria in s 25 are met. The criteria applicable to a local authority are set out in s 25(1)[5] and are suitably modified for other agencies by the Children (Secure Accommodation) Regulations 1991.[6]

The restriction on the use of secure accommodation in s 25 of the Act does not apply to children detained under the provisions of the Mental Health Act 1983 or the Powers of Criminal Courts (Sentencing) Act 2000, ss 90, 91 – long-term detention as punishment for certain grave crimes[7] – since their detention is regulated by those statutory provisions.[8]

[1]   See *Re K (a child) (secure accommodation order: right to liberty)* [2001] 2 All ER 719, [2001] 2 WLR 1141, [2001] 1 FCR 249, CA at para [29], per Butler-Sloss P.

[2]   In any event, a local authority or other body providing residential accommodation may only use secure accommodation where the criteria in s 25 are met but may do so without the authority of a court where the period is less than 72 hours in any consecutive period of 28 days: Children (Secure Accommodation) Regulations 1991, SI 1991/1505, reg 10(1).

[3]   In reality, the legislation is framed in such a way as to impose a restriction on a power which is assumed already to exist since s 25 reproduces, in essence, the terms of s 21A of the Child Care Act 1980. That Act made express provision that a local authority had the same duties and powers in respect of a child in their care as a parent and might restrict the child's liberty as appropriate. Such a power is now assumed to be an ordinary incident of parental responsibility, see the comments of Hoffmann LJ in *Re M (A Minor)* [1995] 1 FLR 418 at 425 and Butler-Sloss P in *Re K (a child) (secure accommodation order: right to liberty)* [2001] 2 All ER 719, [2001] 2 WLR 1141, [2001] 1 FCR 249, CA and see the discussion at para 3.20.

[4]   Children (Secure Accommodation) Regulations 1991, reg 7. Application to court may be made by such authorities or persons by virtue of the Children (Secure Accommodation) (No 2) Regulations 1991, reg 2.

[5]   See para 9.10.

[6]   As amended by SI 1992/2117, SI 1995/1398, SI 1996/692, SI 2000/694, SI 2001/2237, SI 2002/546, SI 2004/696 and SI 2006/2986 (Wales).

[7]   Children (Secure Accommodation) Regulations 1991, reg 5.

[8]   But this does not preclude the local authority making an application in respect of such a child who has been released on leave as 'detained' (which is to be given its literal meaning). See, for an example, *Hereford and Worcester County Council v S* [1993] 2 FLR 360, where on release, the local authority would accommodate the child and considered it necessary to use secure accommodation.

(a) Definition of secure accommodation

9.7 Secure accommodation is defined by the Act as 'accommodation provided for the purpose of restricting liberty'.[1]

The current regulations provide that measures of control, restraint or discipline may be used in children's homes provided they are not excessive or unreasonable and do not comprise any form of prohibited measure such as corporal punishment.[2]

1   CA 1989, s 25(1).
2   See the Children's Homes Regulations 2001, SI 2001/3967 as amended, reg 17(1), (5) and for the duty to record details of any measures taken, see reg 17(4). Restraint means 'Use of reasonable physical intervention or force to prevent injury or serious damage to property.' 'Measure of Control' means 'A means used to maintain acceptable behaviour by children, including supervision, guidance, reward, physical restraint and disciplinary measures or punishments.' Children's Homes – National Minimum Standards, Appendix 3.

9.8 Secure accommodation is not limited to accommodation provided with the approval of the Secretary of State; it is the restriction of liberty which is the essential factor. A unit for the treatment of mentally disturbed children was secure accommodation, as its purpose was to restrict the liberty of children there with a view to modifying their behaviour.[1] However, it is not so much the *purpose* for which the accommodation is used as whether, on the facts, it is actually secure accommodation. Accordingly, in *A Metropolitan Borough Council v DB*[2] the patient was in a maternity ward at a hospital to which entry and exit could only be effected by the use of a key or pass. As the nursing staff were instructed to prevent the patient leaving so that her health and life were not seriously endangered, the court held that the ward should be regarded as secure accommodation within the meaning of s 25. In contrast, in *Re C (Medical treatment)*[3] the patient was in a ward which was not equipped with any devices which restricted entry or exit. In deciding that the patient was not held in secure accommodation, the court referred to the primary purpose of the clinic which was to provide treatment for eating disorders but also to the fact that in exercising its parens patriae jurisdiction, the court has the power to direct that the clinic should detain the patient as an in-patient, using reasonable force if necessary. If the ward was secure accommodation, the common law jurisdiction of the court would be ousted and the requirements of s 25 would apply.

1   *R v Northampton Juvenile Court, ex p London Borough of Hammersmith and Fulham* [1985] FLR 193.
2   [1997] 1 FLR 767, sub nom *Re B (a minor) (treatment and secure accommodation)* [1997] 1 FCR 618.
3   [1998] 1 FLR 384, [1998] Fam Law 135, FD.

(b) Who may be subject to the use of secure accommodation

9.9 Section 25(1) applies to children 'looked after' by a local authority. This is defined as children in their care[1] or who are provided with accommodation in the exercise of any functions which are social services functions[2] and which is accommodation provided for a continuous period of more than 24 hours.[3] The provisions do not apply to (and secure accommodation may not be used in respect of):

- children accommodated for 24 hours or less;[4]
- children over 16 years[5] accommodated under s 20(5) of the Act;[6]

- a child kept away from home under a child assessment order made under s 43 of the Act.[7]

1 CA 1989, s 105(4).
2 Apart from functions under ss 17, 23B, 24B of the CA 1989.
3 Above, s 22(1), (2). These provisions include a child who is being looked after by a local authority as a condition of bail: *Re C (secure accommodation: bail)* [1994] 2 FCR 1153, [1994]2 FLR 992. In these circumstances application for a secure accommodation order may be made to a family proceedings court: *Re W (a minor) (secure accommodation: jurisdiction)* [1995] 2 FCR 708.
4 Above, s 22(2).
5 Where the criteria have been met, the court is not inhibited from making a secure accommodation order in respect of a child aged 15 which will extend beyond the child's sixteenth birthday: *Re G (a child) (secure accommodation order)* [2000] 2 FCR 385, [2000] 2 FLR 259, CA.
6 Children (Secure Accommodation) Regulations 1991, reg 5(2)(a).
7 Children (Secure Accommodation) Regulations 1991, reg 5(2)(b).

(c) Criteria for the use of secure accommodation

9.10 Under s 25(1):

' ... a child who is being looked after by a local authority may not be placed ... in (secure accommodation) unless it appears:
(a) that
 (i) he has a history[1] of absconding and is likely to abscond from any other description of accommodation;[2] and
 (ii) if he absconds, he is likely to suffer significant harm; or[3]
(b) that if he is kept in any other description of accommodation he is likely to injure himself or other persons.'

These criteria are modified in certain criminal proceedings and are considered separately below.[4] In *S v Knowsley Borough Council*[5] Charles J considered that the standard of the test for '*likely* to abscond' and '*likely* to suffer significant harm' was the same namely it should be construed as meaning 'a real possibility' as it has in the context of s 31 where the same statutory words 'likely to suffer significant harm' are used.[6]

1 One previous absconding is sufficient to amount to a 'history' of absconding: *R v Calder Justices, ex p C* (4 May 1993, unreported).
2 For the purpose of deciding this issue, a children's guardian is entitled to enquire into alternative local authority placements and the court is required to do so as the position is distinct from that in care proceedings: *Hereford and Worcester County Council v S* [1993] 1 FCR 653, [1993] 2 FLR 360.
3 The grounds in paras (a) and (b) are disjunctive rather than conjunctive: *Re D (Secure Accommodation Order)* [1997] 1 FLR 197.
4 See para 9.32.
5 [2004] EWHC 491 (Fam), [2004] 2 FLR 716.
6 See paras 8.36 and 8.41 and *Re G (Secure Accommodation Order)* [2001] 1 FLR 884.

9.11 It is the function of the court hearing an application to determine whether the criteria have been satisfied.[1] If they are, the court 'shall make' a secure accommodation order.[2] However this has to be read subject to the power to make an interim order under s 25(5).[3] There was some initial uncertainty whether the court must have regard to the 'welfare principle' in s 1(1) and the 'no order' principle in s 1(5),[4] but it is clear that neither principle applies.[5] However, the welfare of the child is a relevant but not the paramount consideration.

Under Pt III of the Act the general duty of a local authority is to safeguard and promote the child's welfare. In coming to a decision to hold a child in secure accommodation without a court order, the local authority has to satisfy the terms of s 25(1) and must also have regard to its duty under s 22(3) to safeguard and promote the welfare of the child who is being looked after by them. In *Re M (Secure Accommodation Order)*[5] the Court of Appeal was of the view that the court has the same duty when considering an application under s 25:

> 'In coming to the decision to restrict the liberty of a child the local authority will also have regard to their duty to safeguard and promote the welfare of a child who is looked after by them (s 22(3)). The welfare principle is rightly to be considered by the local authority in coming to so serious and Draconian a decision as the restriction upon the liberty of the child. They have the power, however, to place him in secure accommodation if he is likely to injure others rather than himself (s 25(1)(b)). This power may be inconsistent with the concept of the child's welfare being paramount. The jurisdiction of the court is to be found in the same section and the court applies the same criteria in s 25(1) as the local authority ... '[6]

In *S v Knowsley Borough Council*[7] Charles J considered that the apparently mandatory language of s 25(4) does not entail that the decision-making involves the simple giving of a yes or no answer to a question of fact, as the court has a discretion as to the length of any order. The duty of the court is to put itself in the position of a reasonable local authority and to ask, first, whether the conditions in s 25 (1) are satisfied and secondly, whether it would be in accordance with the authority's duty to safeguard and promote the welfare of the child (but subject to the qualification in s 22(6)) for the child to be kept in secure accommodation and if so, for how long. The court could refuse to make an order if it was not satisfied that to do so would be in accordance with the duties of the local authority to safeguard and promote the welfare of the child. Although the court decides whether the s 25(1) criteria are met, it should assess welfare issues on the basis that the local authority is the decision maker and thus on the basis whether a placement of the child in secure accommodation is within the permissible range of options open to a local authority exercising its duties and functions to promote and safeguard the welfare of the child who is being looked after by it. A court cannot dictate how a local authority should exercise those duties and this part of the decision-making process is not analogous to the second or welfare stage involved in the making of a care order.

1   CA 1989, s 25(3).
2   CA 1989, s 25(4).
3   *Hereford and Worcester County Council v S* [1993] 1 FCR 653, [1993] 2 FLR 360.
4   See *R v Oxfordshire County Council (Secure Accommodation Order)* [1992] Fam 150, [1992] 3 All ER 660 and *Re W (A Minor) (Secure Accommodation Order)* [1993] 1 FLR 692 and *M v Birmingham City Council* [1994] 2 FLR 141.
5   *Re M (Secure Accommodation Order)* [1995] Fam 108, [1995] 1 FLR 418, CA and see *Re B (A Minor) (Secure Accommodation)* [1994] 2 FLR 707, CA and see the discussion at paras 2.15 ff. See also *Re K (a child) (secure accommodation order: right to liberty)* [2001]

9.11 Secure Accommodation

2 All ER 719, [2001] 1 FCR 249, [2001] 1 FLR 526, CA where it was made clear that the purpose of the order had to be for the educational supervision of children.

6   Per Butler-Sloss LJ at 423–442.
7   [2004] EWHC 491 (Fam), [2004] 2 FLR 716.

(d) Approved secure accommodation

9.12 Secure accommodation in a community home in England must be approved by the Secretary of State[1] and the placing of a child under the age of 13 years in secure accommodation in a community home must have the prior approval of the Secretary of State and is subject to any terms and conditions that he sees fit.[2]

The Secretary of State may approve the use of secure accommodation in voluntary homes and registered children's homes subject to any requirements in regulations to be made which may include obtaining the prior permission of the local authority.[3]

1   Children (Secure Accommodation) Regulations 1991, reg 3 (revoked in relation to Wales by SI 2006/2986).
2   Children (Secure Accommodation) Regulations 1991, reg 4.
3   CA 1989, Schs 5 and 6 as inserted by the Criminal Justice and Public Order Act 1994. At the date of going to press, no such regulations had been made.

9.13 National minimum standards for children's homes provide that apart from the measures necessary to the home's status as a secure unit, children resident in secure units should receive the same care services as they should in other children's homes and should be cared for consistently with these national minimum standards, with only those adaptations essential in the home concerned for the maintenance of security.[1] However, such is the pressure on secure places that as from 1 December 2001, s 133 of the Criminal Justice and Police Act 2001 has enabled local authorities to arrange for 12–16 year olds who are remanded by the courts to local authority secure accommodation under s 23 of the 1969 Act to be placed in secure training centres at the request of the local authority with the consent of the Secretary of State.[2]

1   Children's Homes – National Minimum Standards (Dept of Health 2002) published by the Secretary of State under s 23(1) of the Care Standards Act 2000.
2   Criminal Justice and Police Act 2001 (Commencement No 3) Order 2001, SI 2001/3736.

(e) Using secure accommodation without the authorisation of a court

9.14 The criteria in s 25[1] must be satisfied before a child may be kept in secure accommodation. The order of a court is not needed where the use is for not more than 72 hours in aggregate in any period of 28 days[2] and it will be for the authority itself to determine whether any of the criteria are met. If a child is in secure accommodation between 12.00 midday on the day before and 12.00 midday on the day after a public holiday or a Sunday and the child had in the 27 days before the day on which he was placed in secure accommodation, been placed and kept in secure accommodation for an aggregate of more than 48 hours, where the maximum period would otherwise have expired in this period, it will extend until 12.00 midday on the first day which is not itself a public holiday or a Sunday, after the public holiday or Sunday.[3] Time limits will run afresh after the making of any intervening court order.[4]

Where a child is placed in secure accommodation in a children's home managed by a person or organisation other than the local authority which is looking after him, that authority must be notified with a view to obtaining their authority to continue to keep him there if necessary.[5]

[1] See para 9.10.
[2] Children (Secure Accommodation) Regulations 1991, reg 10(1).
[3] Children (Secure Accommodation) Regulations 1991, reg 10(3).
[4] Children (Secure Accommodation) Regulations 1991, reg 10(2).
[5] Children (Secure Accommodation) Regulations 1991, reg 9.

9.15 There was some criticism that under the previous legislation namely the Child Care Act 1980, there was a tendency to see secure accommodation as a convenient method of treatment or as a means of making use of facilities available in a secure establishment after a secure environment was no longer needed. Guidance from the Department of Health makes the current position plain:

> 'Restricting the liberty of children is a serious step which must be taken only when there is no appropriate alternative. It must be a "last resort" in the sense that all else must first have been comprehensively considered and rejected, never because no other placement was available at the relevant time, because of inadequacies in staffing, because the child is simply being a nuisance or runs away from his accommodation and is not likely to suffer significant harm in doing so, and never as a form of punishment ... Secure placements, once made, should be only for so long as is necessary and unavoidable. Care should be taken to ensure that children are not retained in security simply to complete a pre-determined assessment or "treatment" programme.'[1]

[1] Children Act 1989 Guidance and Regulations, Vol 4, Residential Care (1991) Department of Health, para 8.5 (part).

FAMILY PROCEEDINGS FOR A SECURE ACCOMMODATION ORDER

9.16 As it is not usually possible to predict accurately the need for secure accommodation, the short term provisions outlined above will enable the authority to deal with the situation when it arises. In this period consideration should be given to whether secure accommodation needs to be available as a longer term option. If so, an application to the court will be required. Applications are generally made to a family proceedings court[1] except that an application may be made to a county court (care centre) or the High Court where other proceedings specified in the Children (Allocation of Proceedings) Order 1991[2] are pending in respect of the same child. An application may not be made without notice and in view of the view of the 'three day' provision, it would, we suggest, require considerable justification to abridge notice.[4] The local authority must inform the child of the making of the application so that the child has the opportunity to be legally represented and to give instructions to the legal representative[5].

1   CA 1989, s 92(6), (7), Sch 11, Pt I and the Children (Allocation of Proceedings) Order 1991, SI 1991/1677, art 3(1)(a).

2   Article 3(3), ie under the following provisions: s 25 (secure accommodation), s 31 (care and supervision orders), s 33(7) (leave to change name of or remove from United Kingdom child in care), s 34 (parental contact), s 36 (education supervision orders), s 43 (child assessment orders), s 44 (emergency protection orders), s 45 (duration of emergency protection orders etc), s 46(7) (application for emergency protection order by police officer), s 48 (powers to assist discovery of children etc), s 50 (recovery orders), s 102 (powers of constable to assist etc) and para 19 of Sch 2 (approval of arrangements to assist child to live abroad).

3   See the FPR 1991, r 4.4; FPC(CA 1989)R 1991, r 4(4).

4   Ie under the FPR 1991, r 4.8; FPC(CA 1989)R, r 8(8).

5   *Re AS (secure accommodation order)* [1999] 2 FCR 749, [1999] 1 FLR 103, FD.

1. Applicant

9.17 The applicant is the local authority looking after the child,[1] or where the child is not being looked after by a local authority, the health authority, Primary Care Trust, National Health Service Trust, NHS Foundation Trust, local education authority, or the person carrying on the independent care home or hospital as the case may be.[2] Application Form C1 and supplement C20 must be filed in respect of the child together with a copy for the respondents ie each person believed to have parental responsibility, and the child himself.[3] Copies of the application must be served not less than one day before the hearing or directions appointment.[4] Notice of the application must also be given to the persons caring for the child at the time when the proceedings are commenced.[5]

1   Children (Secure Accommodation) Regulations 1991, reg 8.

2   Children (Secure Accommodation) (No 2) Regulations 1991, reg 2.

3   FPR 1991, r 4.4 and Appendix 3; FPC(CA 1989)R 1991, r 4 and Sch 2.

4   FPR 1991, r 4.4 and Appendix 3; FPC(CA 1989)R 1991, r 4 and Sch 2.

5   FPR 1991, r 4.4 and Appendix 3; FPC(CA 1989)R 1991, r 4 and Sch 2.

2. Transfer

9.18 The transfer provisions of the Children (Allocation of Proceedings) Order 1991 apply to transfers to another magistrates' court, or to a county court (care centre), or to the High Court.[1] Proceedings are generally commenced in the family proceedings court for the area in which the child normally has his home, otherwise there would be a potential burden on that court which had a secure unit in its area and a problem in providing the services of children's guardians if they were all drawn from the area containing the secure unit.

1   See paras 4.15 ff.

3. Children's guardian

9.19 Proceedings under s 25 are 'specified proceedings' for the purpose of s 41 of the CA 1989[1] and after the commencement of the proceedings, the court (or, in a family proceedings court, the justices' clerk) must appoint a children's guardian for the child unless it is considered unnecessary.[2] A guardian should be appointed in all save the most exceptional circumstances, [3] The guardian will appoint and instruct a solicitor for the child in accordance with the normal powers and duties prescribed by rules of court[4] and the solicitor will represent the child in accordance with rule 12 as in other specified proceedings.[5] The guardian's general duties will be adapted to the specific requirements of an application having regard to the nature of the welfare considerations in secure accommodation cases.[6]

[1] FPR 1991, r 4.2; FPC(CA 1989)R 1991, r 2(2).
[2] FPR 1991, r 4.10(1); FPC(CA 1989)R 1991, r 10(1).
[3] *Re AS (secure accommodation order)* [1999] 2 FCR 749, [1999] 1 FLR 103, FD.
[4] FPR 1991, r 4.11; FPC(CA 1989)R 1991, rr 11–11B. See generally, paras 10.21 ff.
[5] See paras 10.40 ff.
[6] See *Re M (Secure Accommodation Order)* [1995] Fam 108, [1995] 1 FLR 418, and see paras 9.11 ff.

4. Legal representation

9.20 Although the court has a discretion not to appoint a guardian, it cannot make a secure accommodation order in respect of a child who is not legally represented unless the child has been informed of his right to apply for representation funded by the Legal Services Commission as part of the Community Legal Service and, having had the opportunity to do so, has refused or failed to apply.[1] A right to representation is granted under Pt I of the Access to Justice Act 1999 and is not subject to any financial contribution from the client.[2]

[1] CA 1989, s 25(6).
[2] Community Legal Service (Financial) Regulations 2000, SI 2000/516 as amended, reg 3(1)(c).

5. Directions

9.21 On filing the application the court may fix a directions appointment.[1] Although on an initial application, the time scale will generally restrict the work undertaken by the guardian before the hearing itself,[2] the court may adjourn the proceedings and make an interim order.[3]

[1] For directions appointments, see paras 4.27 ff.
[2] FPR 1991, r 4.14; FPC(CA 1989)R 1991, r 14.
[3] See para 9.25.

THE HEARING

9.22 These are family proceedings to which the Family Proceedings Rules 1991 and the Family Proceedings Courts (Children Act 1989)

Rules 1991 apply and therefore the rules regulating the provision of written statements, recording of evidence and giving of reasons apply.[1]

The court (or, in a family proceedings court, the justices' clerk) may give directions as to the order of speeches but subject to this, evidence is normally given first by the applicant, any party with parental responsibility and then the guardian or the child if there is no guardian.[2]

[1] FPR 1991, rr 4.17, 4.20 and 4.22; FPC(CA 1989)R 1991, rr 17, 20 and 21, and see generally Chapter 4.
[2] FPR 1991, r 4.21(2); FPC(CA 1989)R 1991, r 21(3).

1. Presence of the child

9.23 Rules provide that 'relevant proceedings' (which include secure accommodation proceedings) should take place in the absence of a party, including the child, if the court considers it in the interests of the child, having regard to the matters to be discussed or the evidence likely to be given and the party is represented by a children's guardian or solicitor. In considering the interests of the child, the court must give the child's guardian and solicitor and, if he is of sufficient understanding, the child, an opportunity to make representations.[1]

It has been stated that the court must be scrupulous to ensure that the statutory criteria are met before it may make an order since the liberty of the subject is at stake,[2] The court can allow the child to be in court but should bear in mind that attendance at court is likely to be harmful to the child. Indeed, the court should only allow attendance where it is satisfied it is in the interests of the child. Even then, where the court is of the view that the child could be unruly, it can refuse to allow the child into court.[3] In *Re D (Secure Accommodation Order)*[4] Singer J considered that it was unusual for a 14-year-old child to give evidence on a secure accommodation application and that if it could be avoided it should be. As yet, these decisions have not yet been tested against the 'fair trial' provisions in art 6 of the Convention, particularly in the case of older children; we would suggest that it is necessary to consider the context of the particular case before the court and the safeguards present to ensure a fair trial such as representation balanced against the potential harm to the child which would be caused by his attending the hearing.

[1] FPR 1991, r 4.16, FP (CA 1989) R 1991, r 16(1).
[2] *W v North Yorkshire County Council* [1993] 1 FCR 693, sub nom *Re W (A Minor) (Secure Accommodation Order)* [1993] 1 FLR 692, FD and see *C v Humberside County Council* [1994] 2 FLR 759, per Bracewell J.
[3] *Re W (a minor) (secure accommodation: attendance at court)* [1994] 3 FCR 248, [1994] 2 FLR 1092, FD per Ewbank J.
[4] [1996] 2 FCR 452, [1997] 1 FLR 197, FD.

2. Evidence

9.24 The Children (Admissibility of Hearsay Evidence) Order 1993[1] provides for the admission of hearsay evidence in civil proceedings in the High Court and county courts and in family proceedings in magistrates' courts in connexion with the upbringing, maintenance and welfare of a child. In *R v Oxfordshire County Council (Secure Accommodation Order)*[2] it was confirmed that 'family proceedings' means family proceedings under the CA 1989[3] and include any proceedings for a secure accommodation order.[4] In such proceedings psychiatric evidence will often be required.[5] In considering the likelihood of self-harm or threats when at large, Douglas Brown J doubted whether evidence simpliciter of an attempt at self injury and threats to others whilst in secure accommodation could be evidence on which the likelihood of self-harm or threats when at large could be assessed; psychiatric evidence would be helpful in determining this.[6] Except where matters proceed by agreement between the parties, sworn evidence must be heard so that the court may make clear recordings of facts as found by the court.[7]

[1]   SI 1993/621.
[2]   [1992] Fam 150, [1992] 3 All ER 660.
[3]   Section 92(2).
[4]   *R v Oxfordshire County Council (Secure Accommodation Order)* [1992] Fam 150, [1992] 3 All ER 660.
[5]   *R v Oxfordshire County Council (Secure Accommodation Order)* [1992] Fam 150, [1992] 3 All ER 660.
[6]   *R v Oxfordshire County Council (Secure Accommodation Order)* [1992] Fam 150, [1992] 3 All ER 660.
[7]   *Re AS (secure accommodation order)* [1999] 2 FCR 749, [1999] 1 FLR 103, FD.

3. Interim orders

9.25 Where the court is not in a position to decide whether the criteria in s 25(1) are met and adjourns consideration of the application, it may make an interim order authorising the child to be kept in secure accommodation.[1] The preliminary question for the court is whether to proceed to determine the application or to adjourn ie whether it has sufficient material to decide whether the criteria for making an order are made out and the appropriate duration of the order. If it has, there will be no grounds for adjourning the application and the court must proceed to determine the application for the secure accommodation order. If the court decides to adjourn the application, the period of adjournment should be the minimum necessary to ensure the factors justifying an adjournment are addressed and the court has either the necessary information and or procedural fairness is ensured.[2] The making of an interim order is not justified by a desire to continue the involvement of a children's guardian.[3] The function and role of the children's guardian within secure accommodation proceedings is to provide assistance to the court with the issues raised by the application. It is not to oversee the exercise by the local authority of its statutory duties, nor to perform some free-standing welfare role for the benefit of the child. It is not accordingly a proper use of the court's power to prolong secure accommodation proceedings simply in order to keep a children's guardian involved for the purposes of assisting the child, or overseeing the performance of the local authority's statutory duties.

[1]   Section 25(5) and *Re M (a child) (secure accommodation)* [2001] EWCA Civ 458, [2001] 1 FCR 692, sub nom *Re C (Secure Accommodation Order: Representation)* [2001] 2 FLR 169, CA. See also *Re A (Secure Accommodation Order)* [2001] Fam Law 806, FD and *Re G (Secure Accommodation Order)* [2001] 1 FLR 884, FD.

2   *Birmingham City Council v M* [2008] EWHC 1085 (Fam), [2008] All ER (D) 189.
3   *Re B (A Minor) (Secure Accommodation)* [1994] 2 FLR 707, CA. See *Re M (a child) (secure accommodation)* [2001] EWCA Civ 458, [2001] 1 FCR 692, sub nom *Re C (Secure Accommodation Order: Representation)* [2001] 2 FLR 169, CA where an interim order was made to enable a solicitor appointed by the child to take instructions.

4. Length of order

9.26 The court must specify the length of an order[1] and in determining its length the court will have regard to the duty imposed on the local authority by s 22(3) of the CA 1989 to safeguard and promote the welfare of the child.[2] 'Secure placements once made, should only be for so long as is necessary and unavoidable.'[3] Furthermore, any interference with the Convention rights of the child under art 8 must be 'proportionate.'[4] In any event, the court must consider carefully the purpose to be achieved by the order and must assess as best it can the time this is likely to take. It has a duty to explain carefully why it does so and make findings of fact and give reasons for specifying whatever is held to be the maximum period of time for which the order may take effect. Although the order is permissive, the court may not delegate to the local authority its decision as to the appropriate length[5] and may be assisted in its determination by the recommendation of the guardian. If the court departs from his recommendation, it must explain carefully why it does so.[6] Unless the child is placed under a care order, a person with parental responsibility may remove him at any time.[7]

The maximum length of the order initially is three months.[8] This will include the period of any prior interim order[9] and the time limit runs from the making of the order not from the date when a child is subsequently placed in secure accommodation.[10] Orders may be renewed on further application for periods of up to six months at a time.[11]

1   CA 1989, s 25(4).
2   *Re M (A Minor)* [1995] Fam 108, [1995] 1 FLR 418, CA.
3   Children Act 1989 Guidance and Regulations, Vol 1, Court Orders (1991) Department of Health, para 5(1) approved in *R v Oxfordshire County Council (Secure Accommodation Order)* [1992] Fam 150, [1992] 3 All ER 660.
4   See, for the need to safeguard the child's Convention rights: *Re M (a child) (secure accommodation)* [2001] EWCA Civ 458, [2001] 1 FCR 692, sub nom *Re C (Secure Accommodation Order: Representation)* [2001] 2 FLR 169, CA.
5   *Re W (A Minor) (Secure Accommodation Order)* [1993] 1 FLR 692.
6   Above.
7   CA 1989, s 25(9).
8   Children (Secure Accommodation) Regulations 1991, reg 11.
9   *C v Humberside County Council* [1994] 2 FLR 759.
10   *Re B (A Minor) (Secure Accommodation)* [1994] 2 FLR 707.
11   Children (Secure Accommodation) Regulations 1991, reg 12.

5. Effect of the order

9.27 The order is permissive, ie the authority are not required to use secure accommodation; they are authorised to use it when necessary and may only do so for as long as the statutory criteria are satisfied. A local authority looking after a child in secure accommodation in a children's home must appoint a minimum of three persons, at least one of whom is independent of the authority, to review the keeping of the child in such accommodation within the first month and thereafter at intervals not exceeding three months.[1] Their duty is to satisfy themselves whether the criteria still apply and whether another placement would be practicable having regard to the wishes and feelings of the child, his parents and others responsible for his case.[2] If it ceases to appear to the local authority that the criteria are satisfied, they must cease to keep the child in secure accommodation. In *LM v Essex County Council*[3] a 15-year-old girl had been subject to a series of secure accommodation orders. A review panel had been appointed[4] to review her placement which subsequently concluded that the criteria for keeping her in secure accommodation had ceased to apply and that the authority should make immediate arrangements to remove her. However, the authority was unable to make alternative arrangements for her care and intended to keep her in a secure unit until the secure accommodation order expired. In granting a writ of habeas corpus, Holman J left open whether it was incumbent on the authority to release the child at once, as this issue no longer fell to be decided on the facts although, as has been argued,[5] art 5 of the Convention would suggest that this is the case.[6]

[1]   Children (Secure Accommodation) Regulations 1991, reg 15 as amended by SI 1992/2117 and SI 1995/1398.
[2]   Children (Secure Accommodation) Regulations 1991, reg 17 as amended by SI 1992/2117 and SI 1995/1398.
[3]   *LM v Essex County Council* [1999] 1 FCR 673, [1999] 1 FLR 988, FD.
[4]   In accordance with the Children (Secure Accommodation) Regulations 1991.
[5]   G Douglas [1999] Family Law 312.
[6]   Human Rights Act 1998, s 6(1).

6. Renewal of order

9.28 Where it appears that application will be required for renewal of the order, such application, it is suggested, should be made in good time to allow for the appointment of the children's guardian and solicitor and for them to make adequate inquiries and take instructions. When appointing the children's guardian, the court (or in a family proceedings court, the justices' clerk) is required to consider the appointment of the same children's guardian who has previously acted for the child.[1]

[1]   FPR 1991, r 4.10(8); FPC(CA 1989)R 1991, r 10(8).

7. Appeal

9.29 Any appeal against the making of or refusal to make, an order by the family proceedings court lies to the Family Division of the High Court.[1] Detailed provision for appeals is made by Pt 52 of the Civil Procedure Rules 1998.[2] Since the liberty of the subject is in issue, any appeal should be listed as a matter of urgency and it is the duty of the appellant's solicitor to make the district registry aware of the need for urgency and to invite the district registry or the district judge to list the matter at the nearest court where an early hearing can take place before a High Court judge.[3] Where a secure accommodation order has been validly made by a court but subsequently it is alleged that the criteria no longer apply, there is no provision for an application to be made to the court to discharge the order and the court which made the order is functus officio. If the local authority declines to remove the child from the secure placement, the child must apply to the High Court for a writ of habeas corpus (where the local authority agrees the criteria are not met) or judicial review (where the local authority disputes whether the criteria are satisfied).[4] In *S v Knowsley Borough Council*[5] it seemed to Charles J that judicial review was likely, in most cases, to be the most appropriate remedy and it could be combined with points made under the Human Rights Act 1998. Furthermore, the existence of the requirement to obtain permission in proceedings for judicial review is a safeguard to local authorities because it protects them against having to spend time in dealing with points that are not arguable.

Further appeal lies to the Court of Appeal. Contrary to the normal rule, no leave is required where the appeal is in relation to a secure accommodation order made under s 25 of the CA 1989.[6]

1   CA 1989, s 94(1).
2   SI 1998/3132. Part 52 was added by the Civil Procedure (Amendment No 4) Rules 2000, SI 2000/2092.
3   *R v Oxfordshire County Council (Secure Accommodation Order)* [1992] Fam 150, [1992] 3 All ER 660.
4   *LM v Essex County Council* [1999] 1 FCR 673, [1999] 1 FLR 988, FD.
5   [2004] EWHC 491 (Fam), [2004] 2 FLR 716.
6   CPR 52.3(1)(a)(iii).

CRIMINAL PROCEEDINGS

9.30 The complex[1] provisions for remands in criminal proceedings may be summarised as follows.[2] When remanding[3] a child or young person under the age of 17 years, the court may grant him bail with or without conditions, or refuse bail. The decision to grant or refuse bail is made in accordance with the criteria in the Bail Act 1976.

Where a defendant is granted bail with a condition of residence where directed by the local authority, he is being 'looked after' by a local authority for the purposes of s 22(1) of the CA 1989.[4] Any application for a secure accommodation order will be made to a family proceedings court in accordance with the procedure for civil proceedings. Similarly, an application for a secure accommodation order in proceedings on an *adjourned*[5] hearing before the Crown Court is also made to the family proceedings court.

1   See further, Dawson and Stevens 'Applications for Secure Accommodation: The Legal Labyrinth' (1991) 155 JPN 777.
2   For the power to remand a juvenile, see generally *Clarke Hall and Morrison on Children*, paras 7[136]ff.
3   'Remand' includes a committal.
4   *Re C (A Minor) (Secure Accommodation Order: Bail)* [1994] 2 FLR 922.
5   An application must be made to the youth court in respect of a juvenile initially remanded or committed to the Crown Court: Criminal Justice Act 1991, s 60(3). See para 9.39.

1. Security requirement

9.31 If bail is refused, the remand is generally to local authority accommodation.[1] Such local authority accommodation is not secure and the defendant may be returned home to his parents although he is still being accommodated by the local authority. Where, however, the criteria in s 23(4)–(5) of the Children and Young Persons Act 1969 are satisfied, there is provision for the court, ie a youth or magistrates' court or the Crown Court to require the authority to comply with a 'security requirement', ie a requirement that the person in question be placed and kept in secure accommodation.

The criteria set out in s 23(4)–(5) of the Children and Young Persons Act 1969 are that the local authority has been consulted and the defendant is:

'(a) charged with or has been convicted of a violent or sexual offence, or an offence punishable in the case of an adult with imprisonment for a term of fourteen years or more;'

(b) ... charged with or has been convicted of one or more imprisonable offences which, together with any other imprisonable offences of which he has been convicted in any proceedings

(i) amount, or

(ii) would, if he were convicted of the offences with which he is charged, amount, to a recent history of repeatedly committing imprisonable offences while remanded on bail or to local authority accommodation,

and (in either case) the court is of the opinion, after considering all the options for the remand of the person, that only remanding him to local authority accommodation with a security requirement would be adequate to protect the public from serious harm from him; or to prevent the commission by him of imprisonable offences'.

These provisions apply to females aged 12–16 years and males aged 12–14 years. In respect of males aged 15–16 a modified[2] s 23 of the Children and Young Persons Act 1969 Act applies and the court may make a security requirement in the case of a male aged 15–16 whom the court has declared meets the criteria in s 23(5) as modified[3] and in particular the 'vulnerability' criterion in s 23(5A).[4] At present, the criminal court must remand a male offender aged 15–16 years who has met the criteria in s 23(5) as modified but who has not been declared to be a 'vulnerable person', to prison accommodation.[5] Nevertheless, the demand for secure places in the criminal justice system has put a severe strain on the availability of resources so that it has been necessary to provide that local authorities may place 12–16-year olds who are remanded by the courts to local authority secure accommodation under s 23 of the 1969 Act in secure training centres at the request of the local authority with the consent of the Secretary of State.[6]

---

[1] Children and Young Persons Act 1969, s 23(1). The court has no power to specify the particular accommodation to be used by the local authority: *Cleveland County Council v DPP* [1995] 06 LS Gaz R 37.

[2] By the Criminal Justice Act 1991, s 98.

[3] Ie in addition to the criteria at (a) and (b), there is secure accommodation available for him and the court is of the opinion that only remanding him to a remand centre or prison, or to local authority accommodation with a requirement that he be placed and kept in secure accommodation, would be adequate to protect the public from serious harm from him.

473

4   'If the court is of opinion that, by reason of his physical or emotional immaturity or a propensity of his to harm himself, it would be undesirable for him to be remanded to a ... prison.'
5   This power will be abolished when the transitory provisions of s 62 of the Criminal Justice Act 1991 cease to have effect and there is sufficient secure accommodation for all remanded juveniles.
6   Criminal Justice and Police Act 2001, s 133.

2. Application for secure accommodation order

9.32 Most offenders are remanded into secure accommodation under the 'security requirement' provisions outlined above. However, there is a residual number of cases where a freestanding application for a secure accommodation order must be made to a youth or magistrates' court. In the case of offenders aged 10 and 11 the court may not make a security requirement. Accordingly, if it is necessary for secure accommodation to be used, the local authority itself must make an application for a secure accommodation order. A local authority may similarly make such an application to a youth court where an offender has initially been remanded into non-secure local authority accommodation, but it subsequently appears to the authority that secure accommodation is required. This was the situation in *Re G (Secure Accommodation Order)*[1] where a 13-year-old girl had, with her mother's consent, been placed in a residential unit. She made appearances before a youth court in criminal proceedings and was remanded in those proceedings. She continued to abscond from the residential unit where she was being accommodated but had not committed an offence during the period of her absconding. Although the criteria in reg 6(1)(b) (the criteria as modified for defendants in criminal proceedings)[2] had not been met, the youth court was not precluded from considering whether the criteria in s 25(1) of the CA 1989 had been satisfied.

1   [2001] 1 FLR 884, FD.
2   See para 9.34.

(a) The court to which application is made

9.33 In the case of a child or young person remanded to local authority accommodation by a youth or magistrates' court, any application under s 25 of the 1989 Act is to 'that' court[1] ie a youth (or magistrates') court as distinct from a family proceedings court. A local youth court therefore has jurisdiction to make an order in respect of a youth remanded into local authority accommodation by a youth court outside the authority's boundary.[2]

1   Criminal Justice Act 1991, s 60(3).
2   *Liverpool City Council v B* [1995] 1 WLR 505, [1995] 2 FCR 105.

(b) Criteria

9.34 The criteria in s 25(1) of the CA 1989 are modified in respect of more serious offences by the Children (Secure Accommodation) Regulations 1991[1] in relation to children[2] of the following descriptions:

474

(a)   children detained under s 38(6) of the Police and Criminal Evidence Act 1984 (detained children), and

(b)   children remanded to local authority accommodation under s 23 of the Children and Young Persons Act 1969 (remand to local authority accommodation) but only if:

(i)   the child is charged with or has been convicted of a violent or sexual offence, or of an offence punishable in the case of an adult with imprisonment for a term of 14 years or more, or

(ii)   the child has a recent history of absconding while remanded to local authority accommodation, and is charged with or has been convicted of an imprisonable offence alleged or found to have been committed while he was so remanded, may be placed in secure accommodation if they are likely to abscond from non-secure accommodation, or are likely to injure themselves or other people if kept in any other accommodation.[3]

The modification makes it sufficient in the case of a serious offence (or a less serious offence where there is a recent history of absconding), for the court to be satisfied that the child is likely to abscond from non-secure accommodation. The court is not required to assess whether he is likely to suffer significant harm. There appears to be greater emphasis on the protection of the public, a factor not present in civil proceedings or for criminal offences where the criteria are not modified.[4] Moreover, the jurisdiction of the youth court is not dependent on the case falling within reg 6(1), (2) of the 1991 Regulations. If a child is in local authority accommodation because he has been remanded by a youth court, the youth court has exclusive jurisdiction to make a secure accommodation order where either the conditions in reg 6 are met or if they are not so satisfied, as for example where the offence does not carry more than 14 years' imprisonment in the case of an adult nor is a violent offence, where the criteria in s 25 are satisfied.[5]

[1]   See reg 6.
[2]   Ie persons under 18 years: CA 1989, s 105(1). For the purpose of the Children and Young Persons Acts 1933 to 1969 a child is defined as a person under the age of 14 years: CYPA 1933, s 107(1).
[3]   Children (Secure Accommodation) Regulations 1991, reg 6.
[4]   See *Re G (Secure Accommodation Order)* [2001] 1 FLR 884, FD.
[5]   *Re G (Secure Accommodation Order)* [2001] 1 FLR 884, FD.

(c) Procedure

9.35 The procedure in the youth and the adult magistrates' court is pre-scribed by the Magistrates' Courts (Children and Young Persons) Rules 1992, Pt III.[1] Since the FPC(CA 1989)R 1991, are inapplicable to the criminal courts, these are not 'specified proceedings' for the purpose of s 41 of the CA 1989 and a children's guardian may not be appointed.[2] Nor are statements to be filed. A criminal court is obliged to give reasons for refusing bail[3] or to give reasons for, and explain the effect of any sentence[4] and while there is no general statutory obligation on criminal courts corresponding to that on family proceedings courts to give reasons for their decisions,[5] art 6 of the

Convention requires any court to explain its decision. It is therefore incumbent on the court to give some reasons for its decision and to indicate that it has considered whether there is any alternative to making to order.

1 SI 1992/2071 and see *AE v Staffordshire County Council* [1995] 2 FCR 84.
2 Secure accommodation applications are specified proceedings by virtue of the FPR 1991, r 4.2(2); FPC(CA 1989)R 1991, r 2(2).
3 Bail Act 1976, s 4.
4 Criminal Justice Act 2003, s 174.
5 See para 9.22.

(d) Evidence

9.36 Remand hearings in criminal courts are usually conducted by representations although evidence may be called if required. In secure accommodation proceedings evidence or statements will be required to establish the criteria but as they are, for these purposes, classified as 'family proceedings'[1] hearsay will be admissible.[2]

1 See para 5.101.
2 Children (Admissibility of Hearsay Evidence) Order 1993, SI 1993/621, and see *R v Oxfordshire County Council (Secure Accommodation Order)* [1992] Fam 150, [1992] 3 All ER 660. In any event, there are now more flexible provisions for the admission of hearsay evidence, see the Criminal Justice Act 2003, Pt 11, Chapter 2 (ss 114–136).

(e) Length of order

9.37 In the case of a child before the court in criminal proceedings who is not accommodated by a local authority other than by virtue of the remand, the maximum period of authorisation is the period of the remand[1] which includes a committal.[2] In any event the period of the order shall not exceed 28 days on any one occasion without further court authorisation.[3] The terms of reg 13 would appear to bind a family court exercising jurisdiction over a child remanded to local authority accommodation where it and not a youth court has jurisdiction, ie where application is made in respect of a child who has been refused bail by the Crown Court.[4] In the case of a child remanded on bail to live where directed by the local authority, in the circumstances in *Re C (A Minor) (Secure Accommodation: Bail)*[5] reg 13 may be felt not to apply following the reasoning in *Re W (a minor) (secure accommodation: jurisdiction)*,[6] in which case the time limits applicable to civil cases would apply. Whichever court is considering the matter will be bound to include the welfare of the child in its considerations and the length of any order must be for no longer than is necessary.[7]

1 Children (Secure Accommodation) Order 1991, reg 13(1).
2 Children and Young Persons Act 1969, s 23(1).
3 Children (Secure Accommodation) Order 1991, reg 13(2).
4 Where a family court exercises jurisdiction the FPR 1991 and the FPC(CA 1989)R 1991 apply and a children's guardian may be appointed, see para 9.19.
5 [1994] 2 FLR 922. See n 3 to para 9.9.
6 [1995] 2 FCR 708n.
7 See paras 9.11 and 9.26.

(f) Renewals

9.38 An order may be renewed by further application to the court.[1] The reference to 'that court' in s 60(3) of the Criminal Justice Act 1991 refers generically to the type of court, ie youth or adult magistrates' court.[2]

[1]   Children (Secure Accommodation) Order 1991, reg 12.
[3]   See *Liverpool City Council v B* [1995] 1 WLR 505, [1995] 2 FCR 105.

(g) Crown Court

9.39 The Crown Court has no jurisdiction to make a secure accommodation order as it is not included within the terms of s 60(3). On transfer for trial or committal for sentence the youth or adult magistrates' court which remanded or committed him may have made an order for a period of up to 28 days. A renewal of such an order will be to the respective youth or magistrates' court.

Where the Crown Court has further remanded the child or young person, the position is unclear. It has been cogently argued[1] that an application in these circumstances must be made to a family proceedings court in which case the procedural provisions in civil proceedings apply including the appointment of a guardian, the filing of statements and the giving of reasons but a more attractive proposal would be for the Crown Court to have the power to make such an order.

[1]   Dawson and Stevens cited at para 9.30 above.

(h) Appeal

9.40 Appeal against the making of, or refusal to make, an order by an adult magistrates' court or a youth court is to the Family Division of the High Court as for orders made in civil proceedings.[1]

[1]   CA 1989, s 94(1) and see *AE v Staffordshire County Council* [1995] 2 FCR 84. For procedure, see para 9.29.

Chapter 10

WELFARE REPORTING AND THE REPRESENTATION OF CHILDREN

INTRODUCTION

10.1 Section 1(1) of the CA 1989 requires the court to have as its paramount consideration the welfare of the child when determining any questions with respect to that child's upbringing. For the court to be in a position to apply effectively this principle it must have before it cogent evidence in respect of the child's overall welfare and, in particular, the elements of the child's welfare upon which s 1(3) concentrates. The manner in which this evidence is brought before the court is the subject of this chapter.

CONTEXT

10.2 Whilst the two primary methods by which evidence in respect of the child's welfare is presented to the court, namely the provision of a 'welfare report' and/or in some cases the representation of the child before the court, are well established, the manner in which they are used has evolved significantly as the courts and practitioners have developed a greater understanding of children's welfare and rights and the interaction between the two. Consequently, a proper understanding of the CA 1989 provisions governing welfare reporting and the representation of the children must be grounded in an understanding of the ever developing context in which such reporting and representation takes place.

1. The voice of the child

10.3 A key influence on the manner in which the legal provisions for welfare reporting and the representation of children are presently deployed under the Act has been an increasing understanding of the rights of, and need for, children to have an effective voice in proceedings in which they are the subject and which concern their current and future welfare. The need to ensure that the child is listened to within proceedings through the proper use of the

479

reporting and representation provisions of the Act has been expressly endorsed by the House of Lords, Baroness Hale observing in *Re D (A Child)*[1] that:

> 'There is a growing understanding of the importance of listening to the children involved in children's cases. It is the child, more than anyone else, who will have to live with what the Court decides. Those who do listen to children understand that they often have a point of view which is quite distinct from that of the person looking after them. They are quite capable of being moral actors in their own right. Just as the adults may have to do what the court decides whether they like it or not, so may the child. But that is no more reason for failing to hear what the child has to say than it is for refusing to hear the parents' views.'

This understanding has been driven forward by a combination of international conventions, developing international and domestic jurisprudence and research.

[1]   [2006] UKHL 51, [2007] 1 AC 619, [2007] 1 FLR 961.

10.4 Article 12 of the United Nations Convention on the Rights of the Child[1] provides that 'States Parties shall assure to the child who is capable of forming his or her own views the right to express those views freely in all matters affecting the child, the views of the child being given due weight in accordance with the age and maturity of the child' and that 'For this purpose, the child shall in particular be provided the opportunity to be heard in any judicial and administrative proceedings affecting the child either directly, or through a representative or appropriate body, in a manner consistent with the procedural rules of   national law.' Article 13 provides that every child has the right to freedom of expression. In *Mabon v Mabon*[2] the Court of appeal acknowledged the increasing recognition of the autonomy and consequential rights of children having regard in particular to art 12, Thorpe LJ observing:

> 'Unless we in this jurisdiction are to fall out of step with similar societies as they safeguard Article 12 rights, we must, in the case of articulate teenagers, accept that the right to freedom of expression and participation outweighs the paternalistic judgment of welfare ...'

[1]   As a matter of strict law, since the UN Convention has not been incorporated by statute into English domestic law, courts are not bound to apply it (see *British Airways v Laker Airways* [1985] AC 58, [1984] 3 All ER 39, HL and more specifically *Re P (Children Act: Diplomatic Immunity)* [1998] 1 FLR 624 at 628 and *R v Central Criminal Court ex p S* [1999] 1 FLR 480 at 487). However, Baroness Hale said in *Smith v Secretary of State for Work and Pensions* [2006] UKHL 35, [2006] 1 WLR 2024, [2006] 3 All ER 907 at [78]:

> 'Even if an international treaty has not been incorporated into domestic law, our domestic legislation has to be construed as far as possible so as to comply with the international obligations which we have undertaken. When two interpretations ... are possible, the interpretation chosen should be that which better complies with the commitment to the welfare of children which this country has made in ratifying the United Nations Convention on the Rights of the Child'.

[2]   [2005] EWCA Civ 634, [2005] Fam 366, [2005] 2 FLR 1011.

10.5 The European Court of Human Rights has recognised the need to involve hear the child within the context of disputes between adults, the Court holding in *Shahin v Germany*[1] that:

'... the German courts' failure to hear the child reveals an insufficient involvement of the applicant in the access proceedings. It is essential that the competent courts give careful consideration to what lies in the best interests of the child after having direct contact with the child.'

It should be noted that the Grand Chamber later held that 'It would be going too far to say that domestic courts are always required to gear a child in court on the issue of access to a parent not having custody, but this issue depends on the specific circumstances of each case having due regard to the age and maturity of the child concerned.'[2]

1   [2002] 1 FLR 119.
2   [2003] 2 FLR 671, at para [73].

10.6 The European Convention on the Exercise of Children's Rights 1996, though not ratified by the United Kingdom, makes further provision. Article 3 states, in respect of a child considered to have sufficient understanding, that he is entitled:

(a)   to receive all relevant information;
(b)   to be consulted and express his views; and
(c)   to be informed of the possible consequences of compliance with these views and the possible consequences of any decision.'

Article 4 states that a child has the right 'to apply, in person or through other persons or bodies, for a special representative in proceedings before a judicial authority affecting the child where internal law precludes the holders of parental responsibilities from representing the child as a result of a conflict of interest with the latter.'

10.7 Section 1(3)(a) requires the court to have regard to the ascertainable wishes and feelings of the child when the court is considering in a contested case whether to make, vary or discharge an order under s 8, a special guardianship order or an order under Pt IV.[1]

1   CA 1989, s 1(3)(a) and (4) as amended.

10.8 Beyond these clear international and statutory principles, it is a matter of simple fairness that a person must have a right to participate fully in a process that is designed to determine the course of that person's future and further, that this right must apply whether that person is an adult or a child. In *Re Roddy* (*A Child*)(*Identification: Restriction on Publication*)[1] Munby J referred to *Re W* (*A Minor*)(*Medical Treatment: Court's Jurisdiction*)[2] and observed:

'In my judgment (and I wish to emphasise this) it is the responsibility – it is the duty – of the Court not merely to recognise but, as Nolan LJ said, to defend what, if I may respectfully say so, he correctly described as the right of the child who has sufficient age and understanding to make an informed decision, to make his or her own choice. This is not mere pragmatism, though as Nolan LJ pointed out, any other approach is likely to be both futile and counter productive. It is also, as he said, a matter of principle. For, as Balcombe J recognised, the Court must recognise the child's integrity as a human being.'

1   [2003] EWHC 2927 (Fam), [2004] 2 FLR 949.
2   [1993] Fam 64, [1993] 1 FLR 1, CA.

10.9 The need to listen to the voice of the child within proceedings, however, goes beyond the child's right to participate within the decision-making process pursuant to international conventions. Increasing the accuracy of the court's understanding of the views of the child, through that child's thoughts, wishes and feelings, increases the accuracy of the court's assessment of the likely outcomes of the competing options presented to the court, in turn resulting in a more sustainable outcome for the child in question[1]. Beyond this, there are wider and compelling child centred reasons for hearing the voice of the child in court. First, children want to be heard within the process that determines the future course of their lives[2]. Secondly, children have a right not only to participate in proceedings but to have a dialogue about, and an understanding of, those matters which have resulted in the case coming to court. Thirdly, a child may need to express views, wishes and feelings in order to prevent future harm, distress or disadvantage.[3] In *Mabon v Mabon*,[4] Thorpe LJ observed:

> 'In testing the sufficiency of a child's understanding, I would not say that welfare has no place. If direct participation would pose an obvious risk of harm to the child, arising out of the nature of the continuing proceedings and, if the child is incapable of comprehending that risk, then the judge is entitled to find that sufficient understanding has not been demonstrated. But judges have to be equally alive to the risk of emotional harm that might arise from denying the child knowledge of and participation in the continuing proceedings.'

1   Schofield, The Voice of the Child in Public Law Proceedings: A Developmental Model, Hearing the Children, Family Law 2004, p 33.
2   Timms JE, and Thorburn J, Your Shout! Looked After Children's Perspectives on the Children Act 1989, NSPCC, London; Timms, JE, Bailey, S and Thoburn, J (2007) Your shout too!: a survey of the views of children and young people involved in court proceedings when their parents' divorce or separate. London: NSPCC.
3   Communicating with Children, Dr David Jones, Hearing the Children, Family Law 2004, p 354.
4   [2005] EWCA Civ 634, [2005] Fam 366, [2005] 2 FLR 1011.

10.10 The need to listen to the voice of the child within proceedings under the Act is recognised in the new CAFCASS National Standards which, from September 2007, provide the following minimum standards to which CAFCASS must adhere:[1]

(a)   Children will always be seen, including in extended dispute resolution programmes (private law) and case planning (public law). The only exceptions to this are where a CAFCASS practitioner acts in the role of Reporting Officer in adoption proceedings; in short court-based dispute resolution appointments where no further assessment or continuing work is required; and in unavoidable circumstances, such as where the child is out of the jurisdiction or too ill to be seen. The reason for not seeing a child will be recorded on the case file.

(b)   Direct work with children and young people will be consistent with the United Nations Convention on the Rights of the Child as reflected in the Qualities for Children's Services standards developed by the CAFCASS Children's Rights Service.

(c)   Through evidence giving or a written CAFCASS analysis, CAFCASS aims to be the voice of the child in court when the child cannot speak directly.

(d)   CAFCASS will be alert to and sensitive to the pressures on children who may have been coached to give a false or rehearsed story for a specific purpose.

(e)   As far as possible, children will be protected from any involvement or exposure in a case in which they are likely to become more vulnerable as a result.

(f)   Where a child requires support from services outside of CAFCASS then, with parental and, if appropriate, the child's agreement, a referral will be made.

(g)   CAFCASS will ensure that the outcome of each case is fed back to the child sensitively.[2]

[1]   CAFCASS National Minimum Standards 2007, Standard 5. See para 10.17.
[2]   The Children Act Advisory Committee Handbook of Best Practice in Children Act Cases (1997) CAAC at para 59 notes that in some cases, and particularly where the court has not followed the CAFCASS Officer's recommendation, it is appropriate for the CAFCASS Officer to see the child to explain the position in person.

2. Developmental issues

10.11 The legal framework within which the voice of the child is heard within proceedings itself exists within the context of a number of key developmental theories around attachment,[2] cognitive development[1] and resilience.[3] When considering the legal position in respect of the voice of the child in court sight should not be lost of the fact that the CA 1989 provisions designed to facilitate welfare reporting and representation of children exist against, and therefore must take account of, the developmental needs of the particular child subject of the proceedings.

[1]   Bowlby, Attachment and Loss, Volume 1 Attachment (Hogarth Press 1969), Howe, Brandon, Hinings and Schofield, Attachment Theory: Child Maltreatment ant and Family Support (Macmiillan 1999).
[2]   Piaget and Inhelder, The Psychology of the Child (Routledge, Keegan and Paul, 1969).
[3]   Fonagy, Steele, Steele, Higgit and Target, Theory and Practice of Resilience, (1994) Journal of Child Psychology and Psychiatry.

3. Rights versus welfare

10.12 Within the context of the foregoing principles, it must be remembered that whilst children should feel that they have participated as partners in the decision-making process, they should not be made to feel that the burden of decision making has fallen totally upon them.[1] Further, whilst the court is duty bound by the Act to ascertain the wishes and feelings of the child[2] and is compelled by international convention and domestic authority to listen to the voice of the child, the Court is *not* restricted by the child's wishes and feelings and should disregard them if the child's welfare diverges from those wishes. In the end, the decision is that of the court and not that of the child. As Butler-Sloss LJ observed in *Re P (Minors)(Wardship: Care and Control)*:[3]

'How far the wishes of children should be a determinative factor in their future placement must of course vary on the particular facts of each case …those views must be considered and may, but not necessarily must, carry more weight as the children grow older.'

1   Schofield, The Voice of the Child in Public Law Proceedings: A Developmental Model, Hearing the Children, Family Law 2004, p 34.
2   CA 1989, s 1(3)(a).
3   [1992] 2 FCR 681.

CAFCASS

1. Background

10.13 A review conducted jointly by the Home Office in 1997, the then Lord Chancellor's Department, the Department of Health and the Welsh Office of the provision of court welfare services at that point provided by Family Court Welfare (FCW), the Guardian ad Litem and Reporting Officer Service (GALRO) and the Children's Division of the Official Solicitor's (OS) Department, concluded that an integrated service subsuming the work of each of the above services could provide an improved service to the courts, better safeguard the interests of children, reduce wasteful overlaps and increase efficiency. The Lord Chancellor announced the decision to set up the Children and Family Court Advisory and Support Service (CAFCASS) in April 2000. It is a non-departmental public body answerable through its board to the Lord Chancellor.[1] Since 1 April 2005 CAFCASS functions in Wales are the responsibility of the Welsh Assembly and are carried out by CAFCASS (Cymru).[2] CAFCASS and CAFCASS Cymru may make arrangements with organisations or individuals to perform the functions of the Service.[3]

1   Criminal Justice and Courts Services Act 2000.
2   Children Act 2004, Pt IV.
3   See 'Devolution and the development of family law' [2008] CFLQ 45 at 54–56.

10.14 Pursuant to the Criminal Justice and Court Services Act 2000[1] the functions of CAFCASS are as follows:

(a)   To safeguard and promote the welfare of children.
(b)   To give advice to any court about any application made to it in any such [family] proceedings.
(c)   To make provision for the children to be represented in such proceedings.
(d)   To provide information, advice and other support for the children and their families.

These functions are limited to 'family proceedings',[2] but in the light of (d) and the support element of the title may extend to associated activities outside the court.

1   Section 12(1).
2   Criminal Justice and Court Services Act 2000, s 17.

2. Officers of the service[1]

10.15 The name given to an officer of CAFCASS will depend on the function they are fulfilling before the court:

(a)   An officer of the service appointed to prepare a welfare report is a 'child and family reporter';

(b)   An officer of the service appointed to represent a child in public law proceedings or adoption proceedings is a 'children's guardian';

(c)   An officer appointed to receive the consent of the parent(s) who hold parental responsibility in adoption proceedings is a 'reporting officer';

(d)   An officer of the service appointed in Human Fertilisation and Embryology proceedings (parental orders) is a 'parental order reporter'; and

(e)   The court may ask a local authority to prepare a welfare report. An officer appointed by a local authority to prepare a welfare report is a 'welfare officer'.

A children and family reporter reports to the court about the child's background; a children's guardian represents the child, who may also have legal representation and prepares a report for the court. Because their functions are different, the appointment of one does not ipso facto preclude the appointment of the other, although given the scarcity of resources, the court should consider carefully what would be gained by appointing both. The distinction between a welfare officer and a guardian ad litem (as they then were) has been judicially considered:[2]

> 'The functions of the court welfare officer and those of the Guardian are not identical although they do have many features in common: each has a duty to report to the court; each has a duty to consider the welfare or the interests of the child; each may be cross-examined on any report which they give. However, a court welfare officer is not a party in the proceedings, whereas the guardian ad litem, through his representation on behalf of the child, is. Nonetheless, each has a similar duty to the court, which is to advise the court as to what is best for the child independently of the other parties to the proceedings and each of them is independent of all other parties in the proceedings. Therefore the reports of both the court welfare officer and the guardian should be given the same consideration by the court receiving such reports.'

It was therefore held that it was only in exceptional circumstances that it would be justified in appointing both a welfare officer and a guardian ad litem to report in the same proceedings. The Service may authorise an officer of the Service of a prescribed description to conduct litigation in relation to any proceedings in any court and to exercise a right of audience in any proceedings before any court in the exercise of the functions of the Service.[3]

---

[1]   FPR 1991, r 4.1(1) and the FPC(CA 1989)R 1991, r 1(2). In Wales the term 'Welsh Family Proceedings Officer' is used in place of the term 'Officer of the Service.

[2]   *Re S (A Minor)(Guardian ad Litem/Welfare Officer)* [1993] 1 FLR 110.

[3]   Criminal Justice and Court Services Act 2000, s 15.

10.16 All officers are required to make such investigations as may be necessary to carry out their duties and in particular, contact or seek to interview such persons as he thinks appropriate or as the court directs, and obtain such professional assistance as is available to him or the court directs.[1]

---

1   FPR 1991, r 4.11(2). Rule 4.11A provides additional powers for a Chidlren's Guardian in light of the additional duty of the children's guardian to represent the child in court and r 4.11B provides for additional powers and duties for the children and family reporter (see below).

3. The National Practice Standards

10.17 National standards for work previously undertaken by probation officers were issued by the Home Office in a document entitled National Standards for Probation Service Family Court Welfare Work.[1] Advice for guardians ad litem under the former panel system was available under the title Manual of Practice Guidance for Guardians ad litem and Reporting Officers,[2] A Guide for Guardians ad Litem in Public Law Proceedings under the Children Act 1989[3] and the National Standards for the Guardian ad Litem and Reporting Officer Service.[4] Many of the principles contained in these publications were incorporated into the 2003 CAFCASS Service Standards and Principles.

---

1   (1994) HMSO.
2   (1992) HMSO.
3   (1995) HMSO.
4   Copies can be obtained from DOH, Publications Unit, PO Box 410, Wetherby LS23 7LN.

10.18 CAFCASS now operates to a set of National Standards which set out what can be expected from the service.[1] They are described as safe national minimum standards and they update the 2003 CAFCASS Service Standards and Principles. It is intended that the revised National Standards will be phased in between 1 June 2007 and 1 June 2010. In summary, the CAFCASS National Standards are grouped under the following overarching principles:

(a)   CAFCASS will safeguard against harm, safeguard a child's right to maintain important attachments, safeguard a child's right to fully participate in its work with them, and safeguard a stable and secure life for the children and young people we work with as far as it can.

(b)   CAFCASS will adopt an early intervention approach, becoming involved with a case as soon as it is made aware of that case.

(c)   Case plans will be drawn up as early as possible, following a case analysis. The case plan will address how CAFCASS intervention will be applied to each case and will set out how the case will be reviewed regularly in line with CAFCASS guidance on case planning.

(d)   CAFCASS's work will comprise an evidence-based intervention for each child, whatever the case nature or type. Each intervention will have a clear goal of effecting beneficial change for children. The case analysis will identify the key issues for the child and the case plan will set out the appropriate level and type of intervention needed. The level of service provision on each case will never fall below the minimum necessary, and will be the maximum affordable, taking all the cases needing CAFCASS help into account.

(e)   CAFCASS will ensure that all children are seen, heard and understood and their active involvement in all aspects of their case is promoted, in a way that is consistent with and responds to each child's wishes, competence and understanding.

(f)   CAFCASS will aspire to excellence in every aspect of its work and commits itself to being a learning organisation, to applying the learning from research to service delivery, and to continuously improving the quality of its service to children and families.

(g)   CAFCASS will aim to be a high-performing, effective organisation, making the best possible use of modern technology.

(h)   CAFCASS will aim to operate the highest standards of customer care, internally and externally, at all levels, and in all aspects of its work.

(i)   CAFCASS will recognise the inter-dependence of partner agencies in the family justice system and that to be successful, collaborative working is essential.

(j)   CAFCASS regards strong leadership, and good governance as important principles underpinning its vision and in how these standards will be taken forward.

[1]   CAFCASS National Standards (June 2007).

10.19 In addition to its National Standards, CAFCASS has produced the CAFCASS Safeguarding Framework to ensure accountability throughout the service for the safeguarding and promoting of the welfare of children by ensuring the Service works to make certain that outcomes for children in the family court system both keep them safe and promote their welfare and ensuring that the individual child's voice is heard and is taken into account in making decisions about them.[1] Recognising the impact of domestic violence on the welfare of children, CAFCASS has also produced a Domestic Violence Toolkit.[2]

[1]   CAFCASS Safeguarding Framework (2007) para 1.6.
[2]   Available on www.cafcass.gov.uk.

4. Welfare reports

10.20 Subject to exceptions in relation to hearsay,[1] rules of evidence apply in the High Court (with the exception of wardship), the county court and the magistrates' court.[2] The wishes and feelings of the child must be communicated to the court by means of admissible evidence, including hearsay evidence.[3] A court may, when considering *any* question with respect to a child under the Act, ask either CAFCASS or a local authority to report to the court 'on such matters relating to the welfare of that child as are required to be dealt with in the report'.[4] The power to ask for a report arises in relation to *any* issue under the CA 1989, but since a children's guardian will almost invariably be appointed in public law proceedings, these provisions relate primarily to private law proceedings. Guidance given in the 'Best practice note for the judiciary and family proceedings courts when ordering a court welfare officer's report'[5] should now be routinely followed by all courts, though there are bound to be local variations in practice. The High Court may also order a report relating to the welfare of the child pursuant to its inherent jurisdiction.

1   Children (Admissibility of Hearsay Order) 1993, SI 1993/621.
2   Unless they are relaxed by agreement between the parties (see *Re H (A Minor), Re K (Minors) (Child Abuse: Evidence)* [1989] 2 FLR 313) or by order of the Lord Chancellor (See the CA 1989, s 96(3)).
3   Children (Admissibility of Hearsay) Order 1993.
4   CA 1989, s 7.
5   First published in the Children Act Advisory Committee's Annual report for 1993/1994 and then re-published in the Handbook of Best Practice in Children Act Cases (1997) CAAC.

10.21 Before a welfare report is ordered consideration should be given to referring the parties to mediation (with their consent). In some areas parties will not be granted a public funding certificate to issue proceedings, unless they have attended mediation or there are good reasons for mediation not to take place. Referral may be to a mediation service or to the children and family reporter, depending on local arrangements. This is not a welfare report and a Children and Family Reporter involved in mediation should not be the officer who undertakes the preparation of a welfare report.[1] CAFCASS, in co-operation with the courts, has introduced mediation schemes (known as dispute resolution schemes) in family courts in many parts of the country in an effort to reduce conflict when parents divorce and separate. According to figures provided by CAFCASS around 60% of dispute resolution work achieves full or partial agreements. In 2006–07 CAFCASS participated in 26,344 dispute resolution meetings.[2]

1   First published in CAAC's Annual Report for 1993/94 and then re-published in the Handbook of Best Practice in Children Act Cases (1997) CAAC.
2   Source CAFCASS (2007).

10.22 The ordering of a welfare officer's report is a judicial act entirely within the court's discretion requiring inquiry into the circumstances of the child.[1] Whilst it has been held that such an order should never be the subject of an appeal[2] this decision must be questionable. It is suggested that where a decision to order a welfare report is 'plainly wrong'[3] an appeal will be justified. A report should never be ordered when there is no live issue under the CA 1989 before the court. Although the exact procedures in different courts vary, there will always be some kind of preliminary appointment or hearing before the district judge, justices' clerk or family proceedings court in children's cases, perhaps in conjunction with a CAFCASS officer. The attendance of the parties and their solicitors is required at this time to enable the court properly to consider whether the matter can be dealt with without a report and if necessary to inquire into the issues to be covered in the report.

1   CA 1989, s 7.
2   *Re W (Welfare Reports)* [1995] 2 FLR 142.
3   See *G v G (Minors: Custody Appeal)* [1985] 1 WLR 647, [1985] 2 All ER 225, [1985] FLR 894, HL and Chapter 13 generally.

10.23 The court is not bound to order welfare reports in every case.[1] If delay would prejudice the child's welfare, the court might have to balance the advantages to be gained from a report against the disadvantage of the time it takes to obtain it.[2] On the other hand it is the general practice for a welfare report to be ordered where the matter remains contested. Whenever possible there should be one report made by one officer recording his own observations especially where the parties lived or the proposed homes are near each other, although it is recognised that it is sometimes impossible if it would cause unacceptable delay or expense. If a report is ordered, the court should ascertain when the report can be expected and fix a specific date in the light of that information[3] and must notify the reporter of any decisions made during the course of the proceedings and of the date for hearings.[4]

1   CA 1989, s 7(1).
2   *Re H (Minors) (Welfare Reports)* [1990] 2 FLR 172, CA.
3   *B v B (minors: residence and care disputes)* [1994] 2 FCR 667, sub nom *B v B (Minors) (Interviews and Listing Arrangements)* [1994] 2 FLR 489.
4   FPR 1991, r 4.5; FPC (CA 1989) R 1991, r 5.

10.24 When a welfare report is ordered the court should explain to the parties what will be involved and should emphasise the need to co-operate with the children and family court reporter and specifically to keep any appointments made. In particular, when the principle of contact is in dispute the parties should be told that the children and family court reporter will probably wish to see the applicant parent alone with the child. It should also be emphasised that the report, when received, is a confidential document and must not be shown to anyone who is not a named party to the application.[1]

1   See the Handbook of Best Practice in Children Act Cases (1997) CAAC.

10.25 The court may, in private law proceedings, ask a local authority to report rather than a children and family reporter. This can provide a useful bridge between private and public law proceedings. If a local authority has already been involved applications can properly be made to the court hearing the private law proceedings for a report, which a local authority is duty bound to provide.[1] Where there are both private law proceedings and investigations being carried out by the police and social services, the local authority should report to the court on the nature, progress and outcome of the investigations. In this way the court can ensure the co-ordination of the private law proceedings with the statutory local authority child abuse investigations.[2] Where the court decides to ask the local authority to report, it can ask them to arrange for it to be done either by one of their officers or such other person (other than a probation officer) as the authority consider appropriate, but there is no power to order a local authority to instruct a child psychiatrist to prepare a report for the court.[3]

1   *W v Wakefield City Council* [1994] 2 FCR 564, [1995] 1 FLR 170.
2   *Re A and B (Minors) (No 2)* [1995] 1 FLR 351 at 368–369.
3   *Re K (Contact: Psychiatric Report)* [1995] 2 FLR 432, CA.

10.26 In preparing a welfare report, an officer is required to have regard to the principle that delay is ordinarily inimical to a child[1] and the statutory welfare checklist.[2] The officer is further required to make such investigations as may be necessary to carry out their duties and in particular, contact or seek to interview such persons as he thinks appropriate or as the court directs, and obtain such professional assistance as is available to him or the court directs. The children and family court reporter[3] should get to know the child in his or her home and observe the relationship between the child and any adults[4]; an independent and objective assessment of the family relationships involved cannot be made in an office and must be made in a natural environment.[5] In addition, the officer is required:[6]

(a)   To notify the child of such of the contents of the report as appropriate having regard to the child's age and understanding or explain them to the child in a manner appropriate to his age and understanding,

(b)   Attend any hearing at which his report is considered,

(c)   Advise the court if he considers that the joinder of a person as a party to the proceedings would be likely to safeguard the interests of the child,

(d)   Consider whether it is in the child's best interests to be made a party to the proceedings and, if so, to notify the court of his opinion and the reasons for it.

Where the children and family court reporter, having met the child, comes to the conclusion that he is not able to represent the views of the child to the court adequately, he or she should report the matter to the court at an early stage so that consideration can be given to the separate representation of the child.[7]

1   CA 1989, s 1(2) and see para 2.60.
2   CA 1989, s 1(3)(a)–(f) and see para 2.38.
3   In Wales the Welsh Family Proceedings Officer.
4   *Re W (A Minor)(Custody)* (1983) 4 FLR 492 at 501B. Whilst it can be argued that the expectations set out in *Re W* are a counsel of perfection and are now not often achieved, if the relationship between child and non-residential parent is at the core of the proceedings it is doubtful the court can reach a satisfactory decision without sufficiently cogent evidence as to the quality of that relationship.
5   *Re P (A Minor)(Inadequate Welfare Report)* [1996] 2 FCR 285, sub nom *Re P (Welfare Officer: Duties)* [1996] Fam Law 664.
6   FPR 1991, r 4.11B and the FPC(CA 1989)R 1991, r 11B.
7   *L v L (Minors)(Separate Representation)* [1994] 1 FLR 156.

10.27   The report must contain in it such matters as are required to be dealt with by the report.[1] As a matter of good practice, the direction for the report should specify the issues that the report should cover, the court having the power to direct the officer to deal with particular matters.[2] The report may contain material that would be otherwise inadmissible as evidence and the court is entitled to take account of such information[3] subject to applying the usual caution in respect of hearsay evidence.[4] Where the officer includes hearsay evidence he should explicitly identify its source and provide his reasons for agreeing with it if he does so.[5] The report is covered by the rules governing the disclosure of documents filed with the court.[6] The Court of Appeal has given extensive guidance as to the proper course of action for an officer who becomes aware of possible child abuse during the course of preparing his report in *Re M (Disclosure: Children and Family Reporter)*.[7]

1   CA 1989, s 7(1).
2   CA 1989, s 7(2).

3   CA 1989, s 7(4).
4   *Re W (Minors)(Wardship: Evidence)* [1990] 1 FLR 203 and *R v B County Council, ex p P* [1991] 2 All ER 65, [1991] 1 FLR 470, CA.
5   *Thompson v Thompson* [1986] 1 FLR 212.
6   FPR 1991, r 10.20A and the FPC(CA 1989)R 1991, r 23A.
7   [2002] EWCA Civ 1199, [2003] Fam 26, [2002] 2 FLR 893.

10.28 The court is not bound by any recommendation in welfare reports, but if it departs from it the court should give its reasons for doing so following an adequately balanced consideration of the report.[1] On the other hand, provided the reasons given by a judge constitute a sound basis for the exercise of his discretion and for dissenting from the court welfare officer's recommendation, the failure to state expressly his reasons for not following the latter's recommendation does not vitiate the decision. Normally, clear-cut recommendations should only be rejected after hearing the welfare officer's oral evidence.[2] However, bearing in mind the principle of delay, it is within the court's power to depart from a recommendation even where the officer does not attend the hearing.[3]

1   *Re W (Residence)* [1999] 3 FCR 274, [1999] 2 FLR 390, CA and *Re M (Residence)* [2004] EWCA Civ 1574, [2005] 1 FLR 656.
2   *Re CB (Access: Court Welfare Report)* [1995] 1 FLR 622, CA. See also *Re F (minors) (contact: appeal)* [1997] 1 FCR 523, CA and *Re W (residence)* [1999] 3 FCR 274, [1999] 2 FLR 390, CA.
3   *Re C (Section 8 Order: Court Welfare Officer)* [1995] 1 FLR 617, CA.

5. Attendance of CAFCASS officers at court

10.29 Where a CAFCASS officer has filed a report the court may direct that he should attend any hearing at which the report is to be considered. Where such a direction is not made, the officer is not expected to attend.[1] A party may question an officer of CAFCASS about oral or written evidence tendered by him to the court but the court does have the power to limit such cross-examination.[2] Although it has been suggested that welfare officers are not witnesses on oath since they are officers of the court,[3] this argument is now difficult to sustain in the light of this rule. The same considerations apply to a guardian as to a children and family reporter. The Service may authorise an officer of the Service of a prescribed description to conduct litigation in relation to any proceedings in any court and to exercise a right of audience in any proceedings before any court in the exercise of the functions of the Service.[4] An officer of the Service may be cross-examined in any proceedings to the same extent as any witness but may not be cross-examined merely because he is exercising a right to conduct litigation or a right of audience.[5]

1   FPC(CA 1989)R 1991, r 13(3) and FPR 1991, r 4.13(3) (as substituted by Family Proceedings Court (Miscellaneous Amendments) Rules 1992, SI 1992/2068 and Family Proceedings (Amendment No 2) Rules 1992, SI 1992/2067).
2   FPR 1991, r 4.11(4).
3   *Re I and H (Contact: Right to Give Evidence)* [1998] 1 FLR 876, CA and see *Re B (Residence Order: Status Quo)* [1998] 1 FLR 368.
4   Criminal Justice and Court Services Act 2000, s 15.
5   Criminal Justice and Court Services Act 2000, s 16.

6. Separate representation in private law proceedings[1]

10.30 In private law disputes between parents there has been concern at the ability of child and family court reporters to 'sufficiently see and hear' the child,[2] especially where there is a conflict of interest between parents and child. There is no automatic right for the child to be represented in private family law proceedings, but increasingly the courts have recognised the need for representation. The reporter is under a duty to consider whether it is in the best interests of the child to be made a party to proceedings and notify the court of that opinion and the reasons for it.[3]

1   See also Chapter 5 generally.
2   *Re A (A Child) (Contact: Separate Representation)* [2001] 1 FLR 715, CA.
3   FPR 1991, r 4.13(3A).

10.31 Rule 9.5 of the FPR 1991 provides for a child to be made party to non-specified proceedings and for a guardian ad litem to be appointed for a child with authority to take part in proceedings on the child's behalf.[1] An appointment of a guardian ad litem on behalf of the child in private law proceedings can only be made where it appears to the court that it is in the best interests of the child to be made a party to those proceedings.[2] Once the appointment is made, the child is treated procedurally as any other party. Such an appointment may be made on the application of any party to the proceedings (who must file a written consent from the proposed guardian ad Litem to act and a certificate from a solicitor that the proposed guardian has no interest in the proceedings and is a proper person to be a guardian ad litem[3] or on the application of the guardian ad litem[4]) or by the court of its own motion.[5] The guidance issued by the President on 25 February 2005 stipulating that, save in exceptional circumstances, the jurisdiction to appoint a guardian ad litem under r 9.5 must be exercised by a circuit judge, High Court judge or district judge in the Principal Registry has now been revoked and replaced with Guidance provide for the appointment to be made by a circuit judge or a district judge.[6]

1   It should be noted that this power does not exist in the Family Proceedings Court there being no similar provision in the FPC(CA 1989)R 1991, see *Essex County Council v B* [1993] 1 FLR 866 at 882.
2   FPR 1991, r 9.5(1).
3   FPR 1991, r 9.5(4).
4   FPR 1991, r 9.5(2).
5   FPR 1991, r 9.5(2).
6   Appointment of Guardians in Accordance with Rule 9.5: President's Guidance dated 25th February 2005: Revocation – 15 April 2008.

10.32 The detailed practice provisions by which r 9.5 is applied are contained in the President's Direction (Representation of Child in Family Proceedings Pursuant to FPR 1991, r 9.5[1] and the Practice Note The Appointment of Guardians in Accordance with r 9.5 and the President's Practice Direction of 5 April 2004.[2] CAFCASS have also issued a Practice Note dated June 2006 dealing with the practical aspects of involving CAFCASS Officers in private law proceedings by means of r 9.5.[3]

1   [2004] 1 FLR 1188.

2   Family Court Practice, p 2762.
3   [2006] 2 FLR 143.

10.33 Where the court makes an appointment under r 9.5 consideration should first be given to appointing an officer of CAFCASS or Welsh Family Proceedings Officer as Guardian ad Litem. Where a CAFCASS officer is appointed as a guardian ad litem under r 9.5 the duties under FPR 1991, rr.4.11 and 4.11A apply.[1] The CAFCASS National Standards provide that early intervention in a private law case means supporting parents and carers in dispute to make a safe and 'built to last' agreement for the future care of their child/children. Where this is not possible, a plan identifying future work needed and a recommended legal framework for this will be submitted to court.[2] Whilst a child of sufficient understanding may participate in proceedings without a guardian ad litem,[3] there may be advantages to the child having a guardian ad litem in a case where there is severe acrimony between his parents within the proceedings. Where a 'proper person' is appointed in place of an officer of CAFCASS, that proper person may be a solicitor who is already a solicitor for the child (although this is undesirable)[4] or a charitable organisation, for example the National Youth Advocacy Service (NYAS).[5] The use of the NYAS has been endorsed by the Court of Appeal.[6] A protocol has been agreed between CAFCASS and the NYAS with respect to children made parties in private law proceedings.[7]

1   FPR 1991, r 9.5(6).
2   CAFCASS National Standards, Standard 2.6.
3   FPR 1991, r 9.2A.
4   Re K (Replacement of Guardian ad Litem) [2001] 1 FLR 663.
5   Re A (Contact: Separate Representation) [2001] 1 FLR 715.
6   H (National Youth Advocacy Service) [2006] EWCA Civ 896, [2007] 1 FLR 1028 and Re B (A Child) [2006] EWCA Civ 716, [2006] All ER (D) 236 (Apr).
7   Protocol of December 2005 between the National Youth Advocacy Service and the Children and Family Court Advisory and Support Service [2006] Fam Law 243.

10.34 In December 2006 the Government consulted on its proposals for reforming the use of r 9.5 in private law proceedings. Those proposals, which centred on the suggestion that separate representation under r 9.5 be limited to those cases where the child had a separate *legal* point to advance, were so roundly criticised that the Government has yet to publish its response to the consultation. In terms of the facility r 9.5 provides for children in projecting their voice within private law proceedings between their parents, research by Cardiff University research 'Research into the Operation of r 9.5 of the FPR 1991'[1] found that most of the children liked the idea of someone appointed by the court to help them have their say in the proceedings. In addition, the research found that children generally had clear ideas of what constitutes a 'good' guardian ad litem:

(a)   they wanted the person appointed to give them enough time to get to know them;

(b)   they wanted someone they could trust who could communicate with them at their level and who was not patronising;

(c)   hasty interrogations were disliked while a friendly conversational style of interviewing was preferred;

(d)   they wanted clear explanations not only about the guardian's role but about the whole court process. This was particularly important if parents had failed to explain things or had done so in a biased or inaccurate way.

[1]   G Douglas, M Murch, C Miles and L Scanlan (March, 2006)DCA.

7. Children's guardian in specified proceedings

(a) 'Specified proceedings'

10.35 Section 41(6) specifies certain proceedings in which the child is made a respondent and the court is required to appoint an officer of CAFCASS or a Welsh Family Proceedings Officer – known as a children's guardian – to represent the child, unless satisfied that it is not necessary to do so in order to safeguard the child's interests.[1] The presumption in respect of the appointment of a children's guardian applies only to a child who is the subject of the proceedings. Where a child is a respondent to the proceedings by reason of being the parent of the child who is subject to the proceedings, the representation of that child will be governed by the rules covering the legal representation of children.[2]

[1]   FPR 1991, r 4.10; FPC(CA 1989)R 1991, r 10.
[2]   See paras 10.49 ff.

10.36 The specified proceedings in which a children's guardian will be appointed under s 41 are as follows:

'(a)   on an application for a care order or supervision order;
(b)   in which the court has given a direction under section 37(1) and has made, or is considering whether to make, an interim care order;[1]
(c)   on an application for the discharge of a care order or the variation or discharge of a supervision order;
(d)   on an application under section 39(4) to substitute a care order for a supervision order;
(e)   in which the court is considering whether to make a residence order with respect to a child who is the subject of a care order;
(f)   with respect to contact between a child who is the subject of a care order and any other person;
(g)   under Part V;
(h)   on an appeal against—
    (i)   the making of, or refusal to make, a care order, supervision order or any order under section 34 (contact to a child in care);
    (ii)   the making of, or refusal to make, a residence order with respect to a child who is the subject of a care order; or
    (iii)   the variation or discharge, or refusal of an application to vary or discharge, an order of a kind mentioned in sub-paragraph (i) or (ii);
    (iv)   the refusal of an application under section 39(4); or
    (v)   the making of, or refusal to make, an order under Part V;
(hh)   on an application for the making or revocation of a placement order (within the meaning of s 21 of the Adoption and Children Act 2002); or

(i)   which are specified for the time being, for the purposes of this section, by rules of court.'

Education supervision orders do not come within the ambit of s 41(6)[2] and orders under Pt II are not provided for. The rules[3] add the following proceedings to the specified proceedings category:

(a)   family proceedings under s 25 for a child to be kept in secure accommodation;

(b)   application under s 33(7) enabling a child to be known by a new surname or removed from the United Kingdom;

(c)   proceedings under Sch 3, para 19(1) to approve a child in care living abroad;

(d)   applications under Sch 3, para 6(3) for extension of a supervision order; and

(e)   proceedings under the Human Fertilisation and Embryology Act 1990 s 30 for a parental order.

[1]   The proceedings are no longer specified when the local authority decides not to make an application under the CA 1989, s 31.
[2]   *Essex County Council v B* [1993] 1 FLR 866.
[3]   FPR 1991, r 4.2; FPC(CA 1989)R 1991, r 2(2).

10.37 Following an amendment by s 122 of the Adoption and Children Act 2002, s 41(6A) provides that proceedings which may be specified by rules of court include (for example) proceedings for the making, varying or discharging of a s 8 order. This provision was added in light of the growing number of private law cases in which applications are being made for the appointment of a guardian ad litem[1] where the dispute between the parents has become intractable. Whilst this amendment raises the prospect that private law proceedings will become specified proceedings, the rules that will give effect to s 41(6A) are still awaited and no timescale has been given for their implementation.

[1]   Pursuant to the FPR 1991, r 9.5.

10.38 Proceedings may cease to be specified proceedings, such as where a local authority, having conducted an investigation under s 37, decides not to make an application for a care or supervision order.[1] Where proceedings are no longer specified, the role of the children's guardian will cease, although it is possible to identify cases where the court has allowed the guardian's appointment for the child to continue despite the fact that proceedings were no longer specified under the Act where, subject to consent and the availability of funding, it would be appropriate for the guardian to continue.[2] Section 12(5)(b) of the Criminal Justice and Court Services Act 2000 was repealed by the Adoption and Children Act 2002 and, accordingly, it is no longer possible for the court to extend the appointment of the children's guardian following the making of a final supervision order.[3] The court has no jurisdiction to direct a children's guardian to continue his involvement following the making of a final care order.[4] A desire on the part of the court to monitor a rehabilitation process under a care order is not a matter for the children's guardian.[5]

1   If the s 37 direction has been made in private law proceedings, the court may direct a s 7
     report within those proceedings notwithstanding a s 37 report has been completed. See the
     CA 1989, s 7(1).
2   *Re CE (A Minor) (Section 37 Direction)* [1995] 1 FLR 26. See also *Oxfordshire County
     Council v L and F* [1997] 1 FLR 235 where it was held desirable for the child to be
     represented after the termination of care proceedings on an application for disclosure of
     documents. An alternative approach would be for a direction under FPR 1991, r 9.5 to be
     sought and a public funding application made.
3   Thus *Re SB and MB (Children)* [2001] 2 FLR 1334 is not longer correct.
4   *Kent County Council v C* [1993] Fam 57, [1993] 1 FLR 308.
5   See *Re S (Care Order: Implementation of Care Plan)* [2002] UKHL 10, [2002] 2 AC 291.
     For a full discussion of this case see Chapter 8. The Adoption and Children Act 2002
     amends the CA 1989 to provide for the power of referral of cases to a CAFCASS officer
     where a care plan has not been carried out: see Chapter 8.

(b) Appointment of children's guardian

10.39 A children's guardian is appointed in accordance with rules of court
which provide that the appointment shall be made as soon as practicable after
the commencement of proceedings, unless an appointment has already been
made or the court considers such an appointment is not necessary to safeguard
the interests of the child.[1] The Public Law Outline[2] provides that a children's
guardian shall be appointed by no later than the third day following issue of
proceedings and that CAFCASS should allocate the children's guardian within
the same timescale[3] although there is no statutory duty on CAFCASS to
comply with this timescale, the duty on CAFCASS being to comply 'as soon as
reasonably practicable.'[4] Where it is not possible to appoint a children's
guardian in time for the first appointment, the appointment by the court of a
solicitor for the child pending the appointment of a children's guardian is
governed by best practice guidance issued in 2003.[5] When appointing a
children's guardian the court is required to consider appointing the person
who has previously acted as the children's guardian to the same child.[6] Where
the circumstances require it, a second children's guardian may be appointed in
specified proceedings, for example where additional enquiries need to be
carried out and it is impracticable for one children's guardian to complete
them.[7]

1   FPR 1991, r 4.10(1); FPC(CA 1989)R 1991, r 10(1).
2   See para 8.7.
3   It is at this point that the 'Duty Scheme' provided for in the CAFCASS National Standards
     could present a risk to the continuity of the children's guardian in specified proceedings.
4   *R v Children and Family Court Advisory and Support Service* [2003] EWHC 235 (Admin),
     [2003] 1 FLR 953.
5   Best Practice Guidance – Appointment of Solicitors for Children where it falls to the Court
     to do so in Specified Proceedings, November 2003.
6   FPR 1991, r 4.10(8); FPC(CA 1989)R 1991, r 10(8).
7   FPR 1991, r 4.10(4A); FPC(CA 1989)R 1991, r 10(4A).

10.40 Where a children's guardian is not appointed at the commencement of
proceedings (because the court is satisfied that such an appointment is not
necessary to safeguard the interests of the child) at any stage thereafter a party
to the specified proceedings may apply without notice for such an appointment.[1] The court must grant such an application unless the court considers
such an appointment is not necessary to safeguard the interests of the child.[2]

¹   FPR 1991, r 4.10(2); FPC(CA 1989)R 1991, r 10(2).
²   FPR 1991, r 4.10(3); FPC(CA 1989)R 1991, r 10(3).

10.41 Any appointment of the guardian should be terminated by a judicial rather than an administrative act¹ and the court should give reasons for doing so.² It is possible for the court to terminate the appointment of a children's guardian who has acted manifestly contrary to the best interests of the children even if that guardian has acted in good faith and with due diligence.³

¹   See the FPR 1991, r 4.10(9); FPC(CA 1989)R 1991, r 10(9) and *Re M (Terminating Appointment of Guardian Ad Litem)* [1999] 2 FLR 717.
²   FPR 1991, r 4.10(10); FPC(CA 1989)R 1991, r 10(10).
³   *Re A (Conjoined Twins: Medical Treatment)(No 2)* [2001] 1 FLR 267.

(c) Duties of the children's guardian

10.42 The children's guardian is under a duty to safeguard the interests of the child in accordance with the rules.¹ Where there is a conflict of interest between the children involved in the case, this will not necessarily prevent the children's guardian from safeguarding the interests of each of the children concerned.² The relevant rules are the FPC(CA 1989)R 1991, rr 10, 11 and 11A and the FPR 1991, rr 4.10, 4.11 and 4.11A. Within the context of the general duty to safeguard the interests of the child, the children's guardian is under a duty to:³

(a)   Have regard to the principle that delay is likely to prejudice the welfare of the child and the matters set out at s 1(3)(a) to 1(3)(f) of the Act (the 'welfare checklist').

(b)   Make such investigations as are necessary for him to carry out his duties and, in particular, to contact or seek to interview such persons as he thinks appropriate and to obtain such professional assistance as is available to him which he thinks it appropriate or which the court directs.

(c)   Provide the court with such other assistance as it may require.

(d)   Appoint a solicitor to represent the child if one has not already been appointed⁴ or the Children's guardian is authorised for the purposes of the Criminal Justice and Court Services Act 2000, s 15.⁵

(e)   Give such advice to the child as is appropriate having regard to his understanding.⁶

(f)   Subject to the child meeting the criteria for instructing the solicitor direct⁷ to instruct the solicitor representing the child on all matter relevant to the interests of the child, including the possibilities for appeal, arising in the course of proceedings.⁸

(g)   Inform the court where it appears that the child wishes to instruct a solicitor direct and the children's guardian or the court considers the child is capable of conducting proceedings on his own behalf and thereafter to continue his duties and such other duties as the court may direct and take such part in the proceedings as the court directs (with the benefit of legal representation if given leave by the court).⁹

(h)   Attend, unless excused, all directions appointments and hearings of proceedings and shall advise on the following matters:

>   (i)   whether the child is of sufficient understanding for any purpose including the child's refusal to submit to a medical or psychiatric examination or other assessment that the court has power to require, direct or order;
>
>   (ii)   the wishes of the child in respect of any matter relevant to the proceedings, including his attendance at court;
>
> (iii)   the appropriate forum for the proceedings;
>
> (iv)   the appropriate timing of the proceedings or any part of them;
>
>   (v)   the options available to it in respect of the child and the suitability of each such option including what order should be made in determining the application;
>
> (vi)   any other matter on which the court seeks his advice or about which he considers that the court should be informed.[10]

(i)   Where practicable, notify any person whose joinder as a party to the proceedings would be likely, in the opinion of the children's guardian, to safeguard the interests of the child, of that person's right to apply to be joined and to notify the court accordingly.[11]

(j)   File a written report not less than 14 days prior to the final hearing and serve a copy of the report on the other parties.[12] This report may contain hearsay or other technically inadmissible evidence which the court may take account of subject to the usual caveats in respect of such evidence.[13] The court should not take a course of action contrary to the recommendations of the children's guardian without giving reasons for doing so.[14]

(k)   Inspect appropriate records[15] and bring to the attention of the court, such records and documents which may, in his opinion, assist in the proper determination of the proceedings.

(l)   Ensure that, if he considers it appropriate, that the child is notified of the decision of the court in a manner appropriate to the child's age and understanding.[16] A children's guardian should not promise a child to withhold information from the court,[17] but may apply to the court for directions that information should not be revealed to another party.[18]

---

1   CA 1989, s 41(2)(b).

2   *Re T and E (Proceedings: Conflicting Interests)* [1995] 1 FLR 581 but see *Re P (Representation)* [1996] 1 FLR 486.

3   FPR 1991, r 4.11(1); FPC(CA 1989)R 1991, r 11(1). Interestingly, the children's guardian is not required by the rules to have regard to s 1(3)(h), the range of orders available to the court but is required to advise the court respect of the options open to it (see FPR 1991, r 4.11A(4)(e); FPC(CA 1989)R 1991, r 11A(4)(e).

4   FPR 1991, r 4.11A(1)(a), FPC(CA 1989)R 1991, r 11A(1)(a) and see below.

5   To conduct litigation and exercise rights of audience in any proceedings before any court.

6   FPR 1991 r 4.11A(1)(b), FPC(CA 1989)R 1991, r 11A(1)(b).

7   FPR 1991 r 4.12(1)(a), FPC(CA 1989)R 1991, r 12(1)(a).

8   FPR 1991 r 4.11A(1)(b), FPC(CA 1989)R 1991, r 11A(1)(b).

9   FPR 1991, r 4.11A(3); FPC(CA 1989)R 1991, r 11A(3).

10   FPR 1991, r 4.11A(4); FPC(CA 1989)R 1991, r 11A(4).

11   FPR 1991, r 4.11A(6); FPC(CA 1989)R 1991, r 11A(6).

12   FPR 1991, r 4.11A(8); FPC(CA 1989)R 1991, r 11A(8). The requirements of this provision are now supplemented by the provisions of the Public Law Outline, which requires the Children's guardian to prepare an 'Analysis and Recommendations' before the First Appointment, the Case Management Conference, the Issues Resolution Hearing and the Final Hearing.

13   CA 1989, s 41(11).

14 *Re D (Grant of Care Order: Refusal of Freeing Order)* [2001] 1 FLR 862, see also para 10.32.
15 CA 1989, s 42; FPR 1991, r 4.11A(9); FPC(CA 1989)R 1991, r 11A(9).
16 FPR 1991, r 4.11A(10); FPC(CA 1989)R 1991, r 11A(10).
17 *Re D (minors)* [1995] 4 All ER 385, [1995] 2 FLR 687, HL.
18 *Re C (Disclosure)* [1996] 1 FLR 797.

10.43 The CAFCASS National Standards encourage early intervention in cases. According to the National Standards, early intervention in a public law case involves reviewing and quality assuring the assessments undertaken and commissioned and the care plan proposed by a local authority, highlighting the additional steps or actions needed and highlighting gaps in service provision where children's welfare is impeded and seeking to close those gaps by persuading the relevant parties, such as local authorities in public law cases, to take appropriate action. Where such persuasion fails to remedy identified difficulties, the children's guardian should return the matter to court for directions.[1] Under the Public Law Outline, upon appointment, the children's guardian will be required to prepare 'Analysis and Recommendations' in respect of the case in readiness for the first directions appointment and thereafter to provide 'Analysis and Recommendation' reports to the court prior to the Case Management Conference, the Issues Resolution Hearing and the Final Hearing.[2]

1 CAFCASS National Standards Standard 2.5, 4.8 and 4.9.
2 Public Law Outline, (MOJ 2007). See para 8.7.

10.44 The Manual of Practice for Guardians ad litem and Reporting Officers[1] previously advised guardians ad litem that:

'The guardian should not attempt to appear in court as an expert witness in matters on which he is not competent and credible in the court's eyes, as this can only undermine the child's case.'

The guardians cannot, and should not attempt to be, experts in all matters about which they have to report. Nonetheless, as experienced social workers they may well have considerable expertise in a particular area. Any party to the proceedings may cross examine the children's guardian to the same extent as any other witness (save where he is exercising a right to conduct litigation or a right of audience[2]) within the proceedings subject to the court limiting the issues on which such cross examination is permitted.[3]

1 HMSO, 1992.
2 CJCSA 2000 s 16.
3 Criminal Justice and Court Services Act 2000 s 16; FPR 1991, r 10.14A; FPC(CA 1989)R 1991, r 22A.

10.45 In relation to issues of fact, it must be acknowledged that the role of the children's guardian is, to a degree, necessarily circumscribed. However, in *Re N (Child Abuse: Evidence)*[1] the Court of Appeal, approving the Manual of Practice for Guardians ad Litem and Reporting Officers, held:

'By the Family Proceedings Rules 1991 [the Guardian's] duty is to 'advise the court' on a number of matters including what orders should be made in determining the applications: r 4.11(4). It is impossible for him to advise without having come to his own conclusion about the harm the child is alleged to have suffered. He has to decide in the exercise of his own duty to safeguard the child's interests whether or not he believes the child. Judges cannot complain if he states that belief as the reason for coming to the conclusion and giving the advice he advances. It may be better if his report and his evidence expressly acknowledge that he realises and accepts that this is the court's decision, and even if it is not expressly acknowledged, the judge must make it clear to the guardian and particularly to the parties that the ultimate decision would be his and his alone.'

It is suggested that, in addition to formulating his or her own view of the harm suffered by the child, the duty of the children's guardian to safeguard the interests of the child must mean that his or her role in relation to any fact finding exercise may extend to advancing questions designed:

(a)   To clarify the true factual position upon which the court will be invited to determine the proper outcome for the child.

(b)   To challenge expert evidence that may be controversial or otherwise impeachable.

(c)   To correct errors arising from the manner in which the case is put by other parties.

(d)   To allow the children's guardian to come to his or her own conclusion about the harm the child is alleged to have suffered.

¹   [1996] 2 FLR 214.

10.46   The foregoing list is not exhaustive. Overall, it is suggested that it is a function of the children's guardian (justified and facilitated by the nature of the guardian's role of safeguarding the child's interests) to take an investigative approach within the forensic process of court proceedings, echoing the approach under previous legislation of the appointment of a guardian ad litem who could make a close and independent investigation of the facts and circumstances of the child.[1]

¹   *R v Plymouth Juvenile Court, ex p F* [1987] 1 FLR 169.

(d) Children's guardian's right to inspect records

10.47   A children's guardian appointed for the purpose of specified proceedings has a right at all reasonable times to examine and take copies of any records of, or held by, a local authority or other authorised persons compiled in connection with the making or proposed making by any person of any application under the Act with respect to the child he represents and any other records of, or held by, an authority in relation to the child and compiled in connection with any function of the social services committee under the Local Authority Social Services Act 1970.[2] The provision is wide enough to include case conference minutes. It includes files compiled with a view to adoption[1] and a report prepared under Pt 8 of Working Together for an Area Child Protection Committee.[3] The provision is limited to the local authority or any authorised person. The Arrangements for Placement of Children (General) Regulations 1991 make additional provision so that each voluntary organisation,[4] where it is not acting as an authorised person, and every person carrying on a registered children's home, shall provide a guardian with access to the case records and registers and information from, and copies of, such records or registers held in whatever form (such as by means of computer). The guardian has no right to inspect records of the Crown Prosecution Service, but disclosure can be ordered if documents are of real importance to a care case.[5]

1 CA 1989, s 42.
2 *Re T (A Minor) (Guardian Ad Litem: Case Record)* [1994] 1 FLR 632, CA.
3 *Re R (Care Proceedings: Disclosure)* [2000] 2 FLR 751.
4 Arrangements of Placement of Children (General) Regulations 1991, r 11.
5 *Nottinghamshire County Council v H* [1995] 1 FLR 115.

10.48 Where copies of records are taken by the children's guardian they are admissible as evidence in proceedings, regardless of any enactment or rule of law which would otherwise prevent the record in question being admissible in evidence.[1] There is no issue of public interest immunity to be taken by the local authority when considering the right of the children's guardian to inspect and copy documents that fall within the ambit of s 42 of the Act although the children's guardian should be cautious about what is then disclosed to other parties.[2]

1 CA 1989, s 42(2), (3).
2 *Re J (Care Proceedings: Disclosure)* [2003] EWHC 976 (Fam), [2003] 2 FLR 522.

LEGAL REPRESENTATION FOR CHILDREN

1. Appointment of a solicitor for the child in specified proceedings

10.49 In specified proceedings, a children's guardian must appoint a solicitor to represent the child if one has not already been appointed[1] and shall instruct the solicitor on all matters relevant to the interests of the child, including appeal, in the course of proceedings.[2] Where the children's guardian is an officer of CAFCASS authorised to conduct litigation, he is not required to instruct a solicitor if he intends to have conduct of the proceedings on behalf of the child, unless the child wishes to instruct a solicitor direct and the children's guardian or the court considers that he is of sufficient understanding to do so.[3] Notwithstanding the duty to instruct a solicitor, the Legal Services Commission may decide that the merits of a case do not warrant legal representation and refuse public funding.[4] The court may appoint a solicitor if there is no guardian or if the child has sufficient understanding to instruct a solicitor and wishes to do so or if it appears to the court that it is in the child's interests for him to be represented by a solicitor.[5] Where it appears to the guardian that the child is instructing his solicitor direct, or intends to, and is capable of, conducting the proceedings on his own behalf, the guardian must inform the court. He then carries on with his duties, save for instructing the solicitor, but may, with leave, have legal representation.[6]

1 FPR 1991, r.4.11A(1)(a); FPC (CA 1989) R 1991, r 11A(1)(a) and see below.
2 FPR 1991, r 4.11(2); FPC(CA 1989)R 1991, r 11(2). See the Guidance on the Working Relationship between Children Panel solicitors and Guardians (Law Society / CAFCASS February 2004).
3 FPR 1991, r 4.11A(2).

⁴ While the LSC may seek to avoid public funding, they should take account of the mandatory requirement placed on the guardian to appoint a solicitor: *R v Legal Aid Board, ex p W* [2000] 3 FCR 352, [2000] 2 FLR 821 and Focus 32, September 2000.

⁵ CA 1989, s 41(3), (4). As a result of the shortage of guardians and the delay in their allocation, some courts are appointing solicitors who will conduct the case for the child on their own initiative pending instructions from a guardian – guidance is available from the Best Practice Guidance Note – Appointment of Solicitors for Children where it falls to the Court to do so in Specified Proceedings, November 2003. See also Winter D 'The Dilemmas of a Panel Solicitor who has no Children's guardian' [2001] Fam Law 904.

⁶ FPR 1991, r 4.11A(3); FPC(CA 1989)R 1991, r 11A(3).

(a) Duties of the solicitor for the child

10.50 As for the children's guardian, the duties of a solicitor appointed to represent the child in specified proceedings are specific and they must:[1]

(a) act in accordance with instructions received from the children's guardian;

(b) conduct the proceedings in accordance with instructions received from the child, if the solicitor considers, having taken into account the views of the children's guardian and any direction of the court under the FPC(CA 1989)R 1991, r 11A(3), that the child wishes to give instructions which conflict with those of the children's guardian and that he is able, having regard to his understanding, to give such instructions on his own behalf;

(c) act in accordance with instructions received from the child, if no children's guardian has been appointed for the child and the child has sufficient understanding to instruct a solicitor and wishes to do so;

(d) in default of any instructions, act in furtherance of the best interests of the child;[2]

(e) inform the court and other parties how the child was to be represented and what views he was expressing;[3] and

(f) not advance a local authority care plan when representing one child and at the same time represent a child, capable of giving instructions, who is opposed to the care plan.[4]

¹ FPR 1991, r 4.12; FPC(CA 1989)R 1991 , r 12 and see The Law Society's Guide to Good Practice for Solicitors Acting for Children (6th edn, 2002) Law Society and the Law Society Guidance on Representation of Children in Public Law Proceedings (October 2006) Law Society.

² The solicitor for the child is not functus officio at the conclusion of proceedings and has a duty to consider the question of appeal and to serve notice of appeal if appropriate: *R v Plymouth Juvenile Court, ex p F* [1987] 1 FLR 169.

³ *Re M (minors) (care proceedings: child's wishes)* [1994] 1 FCR 866, [1994] 1 FLR 749.

⁴ *Re P (Minors) (Representation)* [1996] 1 FCR 457, [1996] 1 FLR 486.

(b) Instructions from the child in specified proceedings

10.51 Where a children's guardian is appointed within specified proceedings and instructs a solicitor to represent the child, the solicitor is required to take instructions from the children's guardian. However, if:

(a)   The solicitor considers, having regard to the views of the children's guardian and any direction from the court[1] that the child wishes to give instructions which conflict with those of the children's guardian; and

(b)   The child is able, having regard to his understanding, to give instructions on his own behalf;

the solicitor must conduct the proceedings in accordance with the instructions given by the child to the solicitor.[2] In line with the comments of Thorpe LJ in *Mabon v Mabon*,[3] solicitors should acknowledge the growing appreciation of the autonomy and consequential rights of children when evaluating the sufficiency of a child's understanding. The solicitor should be careful to take full instructions from an intelligent and articulate, even though, disturbed child.[4] If a child is suffering emotional disturbance, his ability to instruct a solicitor depends on whether the level of disturbance is such as to remove the level of understanding required for giving rational instructions. If such a question arises it is a matter for expert opinion.[5] The children's guardian should be alert to the possibility of conflicts arising between what he considers to be in the best interests of the child and the child's wishes. Guidance as to the proper course of action in circumstances where there is a divergence between the views of the children's guardian and the views of the child is provided in *Re M (Minors)(Care Proceedings: Child's Wishes)*.[6]

1   FPR 1991, r 4.11A(3)(b); FPC(CA 1989)R 1991, r 11A(2)(b).
2   FPR 1991, r 4.12(1)(a); FPC(CA 1989)R 1991, r 12(1)(a).
3   [2005[EWCA Civ 634, [2005] Fam 366, [2005] 2 FLR 1011 per Thorpe LJ.
4   *Re T and A* [2000] 1 FLR 659.
5   *Re L (Children) (Care Proceedings: Cohabiting Solicitors)* [2000] 3 FCR 71 and *Re H (A Minor)(Care Proceedings: Child's Wishes)* [1993] 1 FLR 440.
6   [1994] 1 FLR 749.

(c) Termination of the solicitor's instructions

10.52 Where the child or the children's guardian wishes an appointment of a solicitor to be terminated, he may apply to the court for an order for its termination. The solicitor and the child or children's guardian shall be given an opportunity to make representations.[1] There is no requirement that the child be of 'sufficient understanding' before he may apply for the termination of the solicitor's appointment.[2] A solicitor whose firm had acted previously in unrelated matters for a party in family proceedings was not required to stand down unless there was a real risk of disclosure of confidential information.[3] Where solicitors representing different parties in the same proceedings have a close personal relationship, one of them should stand down.[4]

1   FPR 1991, r 4.12(3); FPC(CA 1989)R 1991, r 12(3).
2   FPR 1991, r 4.12(3); FPC(CA 1989)R 1991, r 12(3).
3   *Re T and A* [2000] 1 FLR 859.
4   *Re L (Children) (Care Proceedings: Cohabiting Solicitors)* [2000] 3 FCR 71.

2. Right of child to instruct a solicitor in non-specified proceedings

10.53 A child is a 'person under a disability'[1] for the purposes of legal proceedings. Accordingly (save in relation to children who are subject to

specified proceedings, for which see above) the rules governing the commencement, prosecution or defence of proceedings under the Act or the inherent
jurisdiction only with a litigation friend or a guardian ad litem apply to
children. In summary, the position is as follows:

(a) Every child who brings non-specified proceedings or specified proceedings of which he is not the subject child must act by a litigation friend[2]
unless:
   (i) he obtains the leave of the court (which must be satisfied that the
   child had sufficient understanding to participate as a party in the
   context of the particular proceedings without a litigation friend)[3]
   or;
   (ii) he has instructed a solicitor who considers that he is able, having
   regard to his understanding, to given instructions in relation to
   the proceedings and the solicitor has accepted instructions from
   the child to act for him and where the proceedings have begun is
   so acting.[4]
(b) Every child who responds to non-specified proceedings must act by a
Guardian ad litem[5] unless:
   (i) he obtains the leave of the court (which must be satisfied that the
   child had sufficient understanding to participate as a party in the
   context of the particular proceedings without a Guardian ad
   litem)[6] or;
   (ii) he has instructed a solicitor who considers that he is able, having
   regard to his understanding, to given instructions in relation to
   the proceedings and the solicitor has accepted instructions from
   the child to act for him and where the proceedings have begun is
   so acting..[7]

The welfare of the child must play a part in determining whether a child
should be entitled to act without a litigation friend or guardian ad litem. If
direct participation would pose an obvious risk of harm to the child, arising
out of the nature of the continuing proceedings and, if the child is incapable of
comprehending that risk, then the judge is entitled to find that sufficient
understanding has not been demonstrated. But judges have to be equally alive
to the risk of emotional harm that might arise from denying the child
knowledge of and participation in the continuing proceedings. On a wider
basis, courts should acknowledge the growing appreciation of the autonomy
and consequential rights of children when evaluating the sufficiency of a
child's understanding.[8]

1 FPR 1991, r 9.1(1).
2 FPR 1991, r 9.2(1). In the context of the representation of children in private law
   proceedings, officers of CAFCASS and Welsh Family Proceedings Officers are still called
   guardians ad litem.
3 FPR 1991, r 9.2A(1)(a); *Re S (A Minor) (Representation)* [1993] 2 FLR 437, CA; *Re H (A
   Minor) (Role of Official Solicitor)* [1993] 2 FLR 552; and *Re M (Minors)* [1994] 1 FLR
   749.
4 FPR 1991, r 9.2A(1)(b).
5 FPR 1991, r 9.2(1).
6 FPR 1991, r 9.2A(1)(a); *Re S (A Minor) (Representation)* [1993] 2 FLR 437, CA; *Re H (A
   Minor) (Role of Official Solicitor)* [1993] 2 FLR 552; and *Re M (Minors)* [1994] 1 FLR
   749.
7 FPR 1991, r 9.2A(1)(b).

8 *Mabon v Mabon* [2005] EWCA Civ 634, [2005] Fam 366, [2005] 2 FLR 1011 per Thorpe LJ.

10.54 These provisions are only available in the county court and High Court. Applications by a child in respect of himself should be commenced in the High Court.[1] Whether or not a child is able to give instructions to a solicitor is ultimately a matter for the court.[2] Where the court considers that the child does not have the capacity to give instructions, including where a solicitor's assessment of a child's capacity to instruct him is unsustainable, the court could appoint a litigation friend or guardian ad litem.[3] This will be achieved by reference to CAFCASS Legal where the child's welfare is the subject of the application. Where the child's welfare is not the subject of the application (for example, an application by a child for contact to a sibling) the appointment will be facilitated through the Official Solicitor.[4]

1 *Practice Direction – Children Act 1989 – Applications by Children* [1993] 1 FLR 668.
2 *Re T (A Minor: Child Representation)* [1994] Fam 49, [1993] 2 FLR 445, sub nom *Re CT (A Minor)(Wardship: Representation)* [1993] 2 FLR 278, CA.
3 FPR 1991, r 9.2A(10) and see *Re T* [1994] Fam 49, [1993] 2 FCR 445, sub nom *Re CT (A Minor) (Wardship Representation)* [1993] 2 FLR 278, CA.
4 *CAFCASS Practice Note* [2001] 2 FCR 562 and *Practice Note: Official Solicitor: Appointment in Family Proceedings* [2001] 2 FLR 155 and see below.

10.55 It is important to note that the issue of whether or not a child should have leave to bring non-specified proceedings without a litigation friend is separate from the issue of whether a child should have leave to bring the proceedings. For example, where a child seeks leave to apply for a s 8 order and seeks to act without a litigation friend, that child will need to satisfy the court both that he meets the requirements for acting without a litigation friend[1] *and* the requirements for the granting of leave to make the application.[2] The tests for each stage are different.

1 FPR 1991, r 9.2A(1)(a).
2 CA 1989, s 10(8), (9); *Re N (Contact: Minor Seeking Leave to Defend and Removal of Guardian)* [2003] 1 FLR 652.

3. CAFCASS Legal and the Official Solicitor

10.56 Not all children will succeed in their desire to act without a litigation friend or guardian ad litem. Moreover, a child may still act by a litigation friend or guardian ad litem even if he meets the criteria for acting without them.[1] In determining by whom such children will be represented, a distinction must be drawn between children whose welfare is the subject of family proceedings and children whose welfare is not the subject of those proceedings. Regard must also be had to the nature of the non-specified proceedings in which the question of representation arises.

1 FPR 1991, r 9.2A(11).

(a) CAFCASS Legal

10.57 CAFCASS Legal Services and Special Casework (known as CAFCASS Legal) has largely taken over the responsibilities of the Official Solicitor for representing children whose welfare is the subject of non-specified family proceedings.

10.58 The CAFCASS Practice Note[1] sets out guidance for the work of this body. The involvement of CAFCASS Legal will generally only arise where it appears to the court that the child ought to have party status and be legally represented. The cases which may require representation from CAFCASS Legal will generally arise where the child needs someone to orchestrate an investigation of the case on their behalf.[2] Further particular examples of CAFCASS Legal representing subject children are where:

(a) there is a significant foreign element such as a challenge to the English court's jurisdiction or a need for enquiries to be conducted abroad;

(b) there is a need for expert medical or other evidence to be adduced on behalf of the child in circumstances where a joint instruction by the parties is impossible;

(c) a child wants to instruct a solicitor direct but has been refused leave to instruct a solicitor in accordance with the FPR 1991, r 9.2A;

(d) an application is made for leave to seek contact with an adopted child; and

(e) there are exceptionally difficult, unusual or sensitive issues (usually dealt with in the High Court) making it necessary for the child to be granted party status within the proceedings.

CAFCASS Legal may be invited to act or instruct counsel to appear as *amicus curiae* in proceedings under the Act in which, in the opinion of the court, an issue of general public importance has arisen or is likely to arise. An officer of the Service may be authorised to conduct litigation in relation to any proceedings in any court and to exercise a right of audience in any proceedings before any court in the exercise of the functions of the Service.[3] CAFCASS Legal may not represent a child in the family proceedings court. CAFCASS Legal will liaise with the Office of the Official Solicitor to avoid duplication of representation.

[1] *CAFCASS Practice Note* [2001] 2 FCR 562.
[2] *Re A (Contact: Separate Representation)* [2001] 1 FLR 715.
[3] Criminal Justice and Courts Services Act 2000, s 15. The Government has undertaken that this power will only be used in limited circumstances, so that most children will continue to be represented by an independent Children Panel solicitor, but the rule is clearly capable of wider application. See also 'Comment', Hinchcliffe M, September [2001] Fam Law.

(b) The Official Solicitor

10.59 The Official Solicitor will continue in appropriate cases to represent the interests of children whose welfare is not the subject of the proceedings where those children do not meet the criteria for acting without a litigation friend of guardian ad litem although the Official Solicitor will generally liaise with CAFCASS to determine which body is best placed to represent the particular child. The Official Solicitor's Practice Note sets out the ambit of the cases involving children in which the Official Solicitor may become involved.[1] These include cases where:

(a) a child who is also the parent of a child, and who is a respondent to a Children Act or Adoption and Children Act application. If a child respondent is already represented by a CAFCASS officer in pending proceedings of which he or she is the subject, then the Official Solicitor will liaise with CAFCASS to agree the most appropriate arrangements;

(b) a child who wishes to make an application for a Children Act order naming another child (typically a contact order naming a sibling). The Official Solicitor will need to satisfy himself that the proposed proceedings would benefit the child applicant before proceeding;

(c) a child witness to some disputed factual issue in a children case and who may require intervener status. In such circumstances the need for party status and legal representation should be weighed in the light of *Re H (Care Proceedings: Intervener)*;[2]

(d) a child party to a petition for a declaration of status under Pt III of the Family Law Act 1986;

(e) a child intervener in divorce or ancillary relief proceedings (FPR 1991, r 2.57 or 9.5);

(f) a child applicant for, or respondent to, an application for an order under Part IV of the Family Law Act 1996. In the case of a child applicant, the Official Solicitor will need to satisfy himself that the proposed proceedings would benefit the child before pursuing them, with leave under the Family Law Act 1996, s 43 if required.

[1] *Practice Note: Official Solicitor: Appointment in Family Proceedings* [2001] 2 FLR 155.
[2] [2000] 1 FLR 775.

ATTENDANCE OF THE CHILD AT COURT

10.60 The child is a party to specified proceedings, but has no absolute right to attend the hearing. The Rules provide[1] that it shall take place in the absence of the child if the court considers it in the interests of the child, having regard to the matters to be discussed or the evidence likely to be given, and the child is represented by a children's guardian or solicitor. Except by direction of the Court children should not attend any CA 1989 hearings.[2] By reason of the admissibility of hearsay evidence in Children Act proceedings[3] and the use of video interviewing techniques it will usually be unnecessary to call children as witnesses of fact. However, it is suggested that there is no reason why special measures should not be put in place to protect children who are required to give evidence in the same way that such measures are deployed in criminal proceedings.[4]

[1] FPR 1991, r 4.16(2); FPC(CA 1989)R 1991, r 16(2), (7).
[2] See The Children Act Advisory Committee, Handbook of Best Practice in Children Act Cases (1997) CAAC, para 58.
[3] Children (Admissibility of Hearsay Evidence) Order 1993, SI 1993/621.
[4] Youth Justice and Criminal Evidence Act 1999, Pt II.

10.61 Where a child does attend specified proceedings, it should not be routine practice for children to be in the court throughout care proceedings. The court must be very cautious before it compels the attendance of a child complainant to give oral evidences in cases of abuse and the risk of harm to the child arising from the process must be carefully considered.[1] The following principles are applicable:[2]

(a)   The starting point must be that it is undesirable for a child to have to give evidence in care proceedings.

(b)   Particular justification will be required before this course will be taken.

(c)   There will be some cases in which it will be right to require oral evidence from the child but these will be rare.[3]

(d)   The forensic need for the evidence to be given orally has to be balanced against the risk of harm to the child.[4]

(e)   Where a child is called to give evidence, the court must determine whether the child is competent to give evidence (either sworn or unsworn).

(f)   If the court determines that the child is competent to give evidence, the child will be a compellable witness.[5]

(g)   Any court has an inherent jurisdiction not to require the attendance of witnesses where it would be oppressive to do so.[6] A specific issue order may be used to prevent a parent calling his or her child to give evidence.[7]

(h)   In deciding whether to issue a witness summons the child's welfare is of great relevance although not paramount.[8]

(i)   In principle, the older the child, the more arguable is the application for a witness summons.[9]

(j)   In most cases involving a child aged 12 years or younger, whether or not he or she is a family member, the court would favour the absence of oral evidence, even where that might mean the weakening of the evidence against the adult concerned.[10]

(k)   Children's guardians should think carefully about arrangements for children to be present and be prepared to explain them to the court.[11]

(l)   If a child is likely to be unruly the court could refuse to allow him to attend.[12]

---

[1]   *R v B County Council, ex p P* [1991] 1 FLR 470; *Re P (Witness Summons)* [1997] 2 FLR 447.

[2]   It should be noted that some of the authorities from which these principles are derived are now of some age. They should now all be read in light of the principles set out in *Mabon v Mabon Mabon v Mabon* [2005] EWCA Civ 634, [2005] 2 FLR 1011 and in the context of the decisions being an exercise of discretion.

[3]   *LM v Medway Council* [2007] EWCA Civ 9, [2007] 1 FLR 1698.

[4]   *LM v Medway Council* [2007] EWCA Civ 9, [2007] 1 FLR 1698.

[5]   *R v B County Council, ex p P* [1991] 2 All ER 654, [1991] 1 FLR 470.

[6]   *R v B County Council, ex p P* [1991] 2 All ER 654, [1991] 1 FLR 470.

[7]   [1992] Fam Law 278.

[8]   *Re P (Witness Summons)* [1997] 2 FLR 447.

[9]   *Re P (Witness Summons)* [1997] 2 FLR 447.

[10]   *Re P (Witness Summons)* [1997] 2 FLR 447.

[11]   *Re C (A Minor) (Care: Child's Wishes)* [1993] 1 FLR 832.

[12]   *Re W (A Minor) (Secure Accommodation Order: Attendance at Court)* [1994] 2 FLR 1092.

10.62 To date it has not been the general practice in family proceedings for children to give direct oral evidence as to their wishes and feelings in private law proceedings. In a dispute between parents, it is unfair for the child to be dragged into the arena and quite wrong for a child who is the subject of the dispute to be asked to file a statement.[1] The court may properly refuse to receive oral evidence from a child notwithstanding that he is sufficiently competent to be an independent party to the proceedings.[2]

1 *Re M (Family Proceedings: Affidavits)* [1995] 2 FLR 100.
2 *Re O (Care Proceedings: Evidence)* [2003] EWHC 2011 (Fam), [2004] 1 FLR 161.

10.63 Where a child does give evidence, at common law a child may give sworn evidence provided the court is satisfied after enquiry that the child is competent to give sworn evidence applying the test: 'the child has a sufficient appreciation of the solemnity of the occasion, and the added: responsibility to tell the truth which is involved in taking the oath, over and above the duty to tell the truth which is an ordinary duty of social conduct.[1] If in the court's opinion the child does not understand the nature of an oath, the child's evidence may still be heard by the court if, in its opinion:

(a)   The child understands that it is his or her duty to speak the truth.
(b)   The child has sufficient understanding to justify his or her evidence being heard.[2]

1 *R v Hayes* [1977] 1 WLR 234, [1977] 2 All ER 288.
2 CA 1989; *R v Z* [1990] 2 QB 355, [1990] 2 All ER 971, CA.

10.64 The decision whether or not to see the child in private is a matter for the discretion of the judge.[1] A judge should only take the decision to see a child in chambers having regard to the following principles:[1]

(a)   A judge should only decide to see a child in his chambers after hearing submissions from the parties.[3]
(b)   The discretion must be exercised cautiously; there must be good reason for him to see the child and it must be perceived to be in the child's interests to see the judge.[4]
(c)   The interview should normally take place after the close of evidence and before closing submissions.[5]
(d)   If the judge decides to see the child the judicial interview should take place at court.[6]
(e)   It is for the judge to decide who will be present when he sees the child.
(f)   The judge should not, except perhaps in the most exceptional circumstances, say anything to the child which could be understood as a promise that what the child says will remain confidential.[7]
(g)   When a judge has seen the child privately he must tell the parties what the child has said so that they may deal with it.[8]
(h)   A judge should never go to visit a child alone, for example at his school.[9]

Whilst these criteria present a hurdle apparently replete with potential pitfalls, research suggests that it is increasingly common for judges to see children in at court within public law proceedings.[10] The 'Your Shout' research by the NSPCC found that:

'The young people also gave strong support to the Act's emphasis on consultation with themselves and those who were important to them. Overall, it was encouraging to see that roughly a quarter of the sample had been to court and that a quarter of these said they had spoken to the judge. Traditionally there has been resistance to the idea of involving children directly in care proceedings. This finding indicates that practice may be slowly changing and that judges are more prepared to give children who want to be involved the chance to attend the court hearing and to speak to them.'[11]

1   *Re C (Section 8 order: Court Welfare Officer)* [1995] 1 FLR 617 and *Re CB (Access: Court Welfare Report)* [1995] 1 FLR 622.
2   Although the President of the Family Division has recently mooted the question of whether we should in fact review our reluctance to allow children to speak to judges in private (see [2006] Fam Law 150 and 170). A Family Justice Council Sub-Committee, the Voice of the Child, is currently considering the participation of children and the extent to which they should see the judge.
3   *B v B (Minors)(Interviews and Listing Arrangements)* [1994] 2 FLR 489.
4   *B v B (Minors)(Interviews and Listing Arrangements)* [1994] 2 FLR 489.
5   *B v B (Minors)(Interviews and Listing Arrangements)* [1994] 2 FLR 489.
6   *Re R (A Minor)(Residence: Religion)* [1993] 2 FLR 163.
7   *H v H (Child: Judicial Interview)* [1974] 1 WLR 595; *Elder v Elder* [1986] 1 FLR 610.
8   *H v H (Child: Judicial Interview)* [1974] 1 WLR 595; *Elder v Elder* [1986] 1 FLR 610.
9   *L v L (Access: Contempt)* [1991] 1 FCR 547.
10 For a powerful personal account of this practice see Crichton, N 'Listening to Children', [2006] Fam Law 849.
11 Timms JE, and Thorburn J, *Your Shout! Looked After Children's Perspectives on the Children Act 1989*, NSPCC, London; The current President of the Family Division, Sir Mark Potter, has encouraged judges to see children in appropriate cases: inaugural Resolution Annual Lecture 'Does the Family Justice System serve the needs of Children?' (2008).

10.65 In proceedings taking place in the family proceedings court, historically it was held that the magistrates have no right to see the child privately.[1] Under the current legislation the circumstances in which magistrates should see a child in private are 'rare and exceptional' where a children's guardian or CAFCASS Officer is involved in the case.[2]

1   *Re W (A Minor)* (1980) 10 Fam Law 120.
2   *Re M (Minor)(Justices Discretion)* [1993] 2 FLR 706.

Chapter 11
EVIDENCE

INTRODUCTION

11.1 Evidence in proceedings relating to children raises complex issues. It is necessary to consider how the court is to be satisfied of the basis for making an order, the nature of evidence required by the courts, rules of evidence peculiar to children's proceedings, the sources of evidence, the way in which that evidence is obtained, in particular from experts, disclosure of information and documents for the purpose of proceedings, withholding of information or documents on the basis of confidentiality and privilege or self-incrimination.

11.2 Evidential practice under the CA 1989 can labour under the disadvantage of certain myths, for example that there are no rules of evidence in children proceedings. This myth encompasses the idea that, in contrast to proceedings in the criminal and commercial jurisdictions, anything is admissible at any point and in any format in children proceedings regardless of the quality, source or timing of the evidence it is sought to have admitted. The second popular fiction is that all proceedings relating to children are procedurally informal in nature. This myth propagates and perpetuates the notion that the court will permit almost any procedural or evidential irregularity within the context of proceedings concerning children, provided that the same is in the children's best interests. Whilst the court will, of course, not let procedure stand in the way of a child's welfare, this myth of informality can militate against the timely prosecution of cases and runs the risk of reducing the welfare test to an excuse for procedural sloth. These two myths, which are without foundation, tend to operate against the proper presentation of cases, and in particular the proper gathering and presentation of evidence to prove cases.

11.3 In reality, the law of evidence applies, without any relaxation, to all cases under the CA 1989[1] save where specific exceptions are made under the Act.[2]

[1] *Re H (A Minor), Re K (Minors)(Child Abuse: Evidence)* [1989] 2 FLR 313 and *Bradford City Metropolitan Council v K and K* [1990] Fam 140, [1989] 2 FLR 507.

11.3 *Evidence*

2 For example, under the Children (Admissibility of Hearsay Evidence) Order 1993 (made under s 96(3) of the CA 1989) and s 41 of the CA 1989 relating to evidence given by the children's guardian in public law proceedings.

11.4 Although the applicable evidential principles have been considered primarily in the public law field, and indeed frequently in sex abuse cases, they are fundamentally the same and applicable to other types of harm,[1] such as head injuries, and to private law cases[2] where appropriate.

1 Indeed, many of the difficulties encountered with evidence in public law proceedings arise in relation to cases of long-term neglect where the primary evidence is often social work recording. Such recording is often not undertaken with rules of evidence in mind.
2 In practice, private law cases tend to be less evidentially complex than public law ones. This may account for the disparity in the number of authorities dealing with evidence in public law cases when compared to the number of authorities dealing with this issue in relation to private law.

PROVING THE CASE

1. Burden of proof

11.5 The legal burden of establishing the existence of the threshold criteria rests on the applicant. The general principle is that he who asserts must prove. The applicant must establish the existence of the pre-conditions and the facts entitling him to the order he seeks.[1]

1 *Re H (Minors) (Sexual Abuse: Standard of Proof)* [1996] AC 563, [1996] 1 All ER 1, [1996] 1 FCR 509, HL.

2. Standard of proof

11.6 It is established by the House of Lords decision in *Re B*[1] that the standard of proof required is the simple balance of probabilities, which means that a court is satisfied an event occurred if it considers that, on the evidence, the occurrence of the event was more likely than not. In *Re B* Baroness Hale stated in the clearest terms:

> 'I would ... announce loud and clear that the standard of proof in finding the facts necessary to establish the threshold under section 31(2) or the welfare considerations in section 1 of the 1989 Act is the simple balance of probabilities, neither more nor less.'

1 *Re B* [2008] UKHL 35, [2008] 3 WLR 1. See paras 8.21–8.27 and *Re H (Minors) (Sexual Abuse: Standard of Proof)* [1996] AC 563, [1996] 1 All ER 1, [1996] [1996] 1 FCR 509, HL. The same test should be applied to findings relevant to the threshold criteria and the question of whether a particular person is the perpetrator of harm: *Re G (a Child) (Non-Accidental Injury: Standard of Proof)* [2001] 1 FCR 97.

11.7 The standard of proof thus remains the balance of probabilities, as distinct from the criminal standard of beyond reasonable doubt.[1] Indeed, it is entirely appropriate for a judge in family proceedings to arrive at a different conclusion from a jury in a criminal trial given the wider range of evidence upon which the family court is concerned in respect of the child.[2]

512

1   See *Re U and Re B* [2004] EWCA Civ 567, [2004] 2 FLR 263 and *Re T (Abuse: Standard of Proof)* [2004] EWCA Civ 558, [2004] 2 FLR 838. In *Re ET (Serious Injuries: Standard of Proof)* [2003] 2 FLR 1205n the Court of Appeal expressly rejected a statement by Bodey J that the difference between the civil standard of proof and the criminal standard of proof is 'largely illusory.'

2   *A Local Authority v S, W and T (by his Guardian)* [2004] EWHC 1270 (Fam), [2004] 2 FLR 129.

11.8 The position in respect of the applicable standard of proof is complicated by the issue of establishing risk of future harm. In determining that issue, the court is examining the possibility that an event will occur in the future on the basis of the facts proved in respect of the past. When considering whether the likelihood of such future harm is proved, the court must determine whether there is a real possibility of such harm on the basis of the proven facts.[1] This assessment cannot be based on the mere suspicion of past harm but only on facts that have been established to the requisite standard.[2]

1   *Re B* [2008] UKHL 35. See paras 8.21–8.27 and *Re H (Minors) (Sexual Abuse: Standard of Proof)* [1996] AC 563, [1996] 1 All ER 1, [1996] [1996] 1 FCR 509, HL. *Re H* applies to consideration of harm under s 1(3)(e): see *Re M and R (Child Abuse: Evidence)* [1996] 2 FLR 195, CA.

2   *Re B* [2008] UKHL 35, [2008] 3 WLR 1. See paras 8.21–8.27 and *Re H (Minors) (Sexual Abuse: Standard of Proof)* [1996] AC 563, [1996] 1 All ER 1, [1996] [1996] 1 FCR 509, HL. See also *Re G (Adoption: Ordinary Residence)* [2002] EWHC 2447 (Fam), [2003] 2 FLR 944.

11.9 When the court, having made findings of fact, comes to consider the appropriate order to make (if any) the exercise of the court's discretion at this welfare stage must be based upon facts which have been established to the requisite standard of proof.[1]

1   *Re B* [2008] UKHL 35, [2008] 3 WLR 1. See paras 8.21–8.27 and *M and R (Sexual Abuse: Expert Evidence)* [1996] 4 All ER 239, CA.

11.10 The recent increase in the number of care proceedings does not suggest that the standard has created major difficulties, although there may be a few isolated, single issue, cases where problems arise because there is no supporting evidence.[1] It is a matter for concern that practice experience suggests that sexual abuse is identified in fewer cases, at least until the behaviour of children becomes more seriously disturbed. Whether this comes about as a result of the reluctance of the courts to accept the evidence or the failure of professionals to evaluate the evidence adequately is not clear. The court must take a realistic view of the evidence, but if it is more likely than not that there has been no abuse, it is difficult to justify intervention.

1   See paras 8.46 and 8.49. For further review of the problems see: Hayes 'Reconciling protection of children with justice for parents in cases of alleged child abuse' [1997] 1 Legal Studies 1, Keating 'Shifting standards in the House of Lords – *Re H and others (Minors) (Sexual Abuse: Standard of Proof)* (1996) 8 CFLQ 157, Victor Smith, 'Sexual Abuse: Standard of Proof' [1994] Family Law 626 and John Spencer 'Evidence in child abuse cases – too high a price for too high a standard?' (1994) 6 JCL 160.

11.11 The test may present a greater problem in contact proceedings between parents where allegations of abuse cannot be proved to the satisfaction of the court, although the child appears to be convinced he has been abused. The court will deal with contact on the basis of its findings, which may be contrary to the beliefs of the child.[1]

[1] See, for example, *M and R (Sexual Abuse: Expert Evidence)* [1996] 4 All ER 239, CA.

EVIDENCE

1. General

11.12 In private law and public law proceedings the court expects the best possible evidence on which to make its decision.[1] Full statements by the parties should identify which facts are in issue between them, and therefore need proof, and which were accepted. Where first-hand evidence was available, either from a witness or in documentary form, it should be presented. Attention should always be given to the issue of evidence that might be corroborative or, alternatively, give rise to doubt about the central issues.[2] Evidence should be regulated 'by way of weight rather than admissibility'.[3]

[1] *Re A (Contact: Risk of Violence)* [2005] EWHC 851 (Fam), [2006] 1 FLR 283.
[2] *Re A (Contact: Risk of Violence)* [2005] EWHC 851 (Fam), [2006] 1 FLR 283.
[3] *H v West Sussex County Council* [1998] 1 FLR 862 and see para 11.4.

11.13 Subject to the following paragraph parties must file and serve on the parties and any officer of the service or Welsh family proceedings officer:

(a) written statements of the substance of the oral evidence which the party intends to adduce at the hearing or directions appointment; and
(b) copies of any documents, including experts' reports upon which the party intends to rely, at or by such time as the court directs.[1]

[1] FPR 1991, r 4.17(1); FPC(CA 1989)R 1991, r 17(1).

11.14 In proceedings for a s 8 order no statement or copy may be filed until such time as the court directs,[1] and no file, document, information or statement, other than those required or authorised by the Rules, should be served or made without leave of the court. Subject to any direction of the court about the timing of statements, supplementary statements may be filed, as can, with leave, written amendments to the documents already served. Evidence or documents not filed in accordance with the Rules cannot be adduced or relied upon at the subsequent directions appointment or hearing without leave of the court: FPR 1991, rr 4.17(4) and 17(4). For hearings, preparation of court bundles is essential and regard should be had to *Practice Note (Case Management)*,[2] *B v B (Court Bundles: Video Evidence)*,[3] *Practice Direction (Family Proceedings: Court Bundles)*[4] *and Practice Direction: Judicial Continuity.*[5]

[1] See the FPR 1991, rr 4.17 and 17.
[2] [1995] 1 All ER 586, [1995] 2 FCR 340, [1995] 1 FLR 456, see para 4.44–4.45.
[3] [1994] 1 FCR 805, [1994] 1 FLR 323n.

⁴ [2000] 1 FCR 521, [2000] 1 FLR 536. This Practice Note does not apply in the family proceedings court.
⁵ [2002] 2 FLR 367.

11.15 The ability to observe a witness' demeanour and deportment during the giving of evidence is important and essential to assess accuracy and credibility. But in sensitive cases it is also important that a witness be permitted to present their case to the satisfaction of the court but also observing their religious observance of dress. In the case of a Muslim witness who wears the veil, there may be arrangements such as screens which may facilitate the hearing. Each case must obviously be looked at in its own circumstances, and the court must be alert to any opportunistic attempt to derail proceedings.[1]

1   *Re S (Practice: Muslim Women Giving Evidence)* [2007] 2 FLR 461.

11.16 Parents can be compelled to give evidence in any proceedings. They have no right to refuse to do so, nor to refuse to answer questions which may incriminate them.[1]

1   *Re Y and K (Split Hearing: Evidence)* [2003] EWCA Civ 669, [2003] 2 FLR 273.

2. Evidence of harm

11.17 The following matters are typical of relevant evidence:

(a)   perpetrators' admission;
(b)   third party witness to ill-treatment;
(c)   physical indicators, through height or weight charts, X-rays;
(d)   behavioural indicators;
(e)   educational problems in school age children;
(f)   behaviour in older children;
(g)   expert opinion as to the nature and cause of harm;
(h)   opportunity and circumstances;
(i)   social assessment of family;
(j)   child's complaint eg to teacher, especially if spontaneous;
(k)   exposure to pornographic material especially involving children;
(l)   interview of the child; and
(m)   family history.

3. Certificate of conviction

11.18 A conviction is prima facie evidence of the offence to which it relates.[1] A father's conviction for violence against his child, for example, is admissible to prove the commission of that offence. A conviction may be proved by a certified extract from a court register.[2]

1   Civil Evidence Act 1968, s 11.
2   Magistrates' Courts Rules 1981, SI 1981/552, r 68; Criminal Procedure Rules 2005, SI 2005/384, r 6.4.

4. Hearsay Evidence

11.19 Evidence in private and public law proceedings is likely to be a mixture of factual information, professional observation[1] and expert opinion. It can be produced by way of written statement or oral evidence. It is likely to be accumulated over a period of time through assessment and questioning of the parties and the child outside of the hearing. As a result there is likely to be a substantial amount of hearsay evidence, especially in care proceedings.

[1] Care must be taken with the evidential status of professional observation as it is likely to be a mixture of fact and opinion and thus to invoke the rules of evidence in relation to both.

11.20 The Children (Admissibility of Hearsay Evidence) Order 1993 provides that in civil proceedings before the High Court, county court and in 'family proceedings',[1] and civil proceedings under the Child Support Act 1991 before a magistrates' court, evidence given in connection with the upbringing, maintenance or welfare of a child is admissible notwithstanding any rule of law relating to hearsay.[2] Hearsay evidence is also admissible under the Civil Evidence Act 1995 but there are procedural safeguards.[3] As a result the provisions of the Civil Evidence Act 1995 appear to be little used in proceedings relating to children.

[1] Defined for this purpose by the CA 1989, s 92(2). See *R v Oxfordshire County Council (Secure Accommodation Order)* [1992] Fam 150.
[2] SI 1993/621. Evidence admissible under the 1993 Order is not confined to what the child has said but includes any evidence.
[3] Section 1. For the implementation of these provisions in magistrates' courts see the Magistrates' Courts (Hearsay Evidence in Civil Proceedings) Rules 1999, SI 1999/681. Note also that a document which is shown to form part of the records of a public authority may be received in evidence in civil proceedings without further proof: s 9(1).

11.21 The weight to be given to hearsay evidence is a matter for the court, but under the Civil Evidence Act 1995 it must have regard to any circumstances from which any inference can reasonably be drawn as to the reliability or otherwise of the evidence,[1] and in particular to:

(a) whether it would have been reasonable and practicable for the party by whom the evidence was adduced to have produced the maker of the original statement as a witness;
(b) whether the original statement was made contemporaneously with the occurrence or existence of the matters stated;
(c) whether the evidence involves multiple hearsay;
(d) whether any person involved had any motive to conceal or misrepresent matters;
(e) whether the original statement was an edited account, or was made in collaboration with another or for a particular purpose; and
(f) whether the circumstances in which the evidence is adduced as hearsay are such as to suggest an attempt to prevent proper evaluation of its weight.

[1] Civil Evidence Act 1995, s 4.

11.22 It is important that practitioners do not stop at the 1993 Order when considering hearsay evidence. There is a series of limiting principles enshrined, which are vital to consider when seeking to deploy hearsay evidence to prove a case. Prior to 1993, in *Re W (Minors) (Wardship: Evidence)*[1] the court observed that '... hearsay evidence is admissible as a matter of law, but ... this evidence and the use to which it is put has to be handled with the greatest care and in such a way that, unless the interests of the child make it necessary, the rules of natural justice and the rights of the parents are fully and properly observed'. Later, in *R v B County Council, ex p P*[2] the court concluded that 'A court presented with hearsay evidence has to look at it anxiously and consider carefully the extent to which it can properly be relied on'.

[1]   [1990] 1 FLR 203 at 227.
[2]   [1991] 2 All ER 65 at 72J.

11.23 The admissibility of hearsay pursuant to the 1993 Order can have the effect in some cases of circumscribing the search for the best evidence available on a particular issue. This can result in hearsay evidence being used where, with further investigation and effort, direct evidence could be obtained to prove the point in issue. In 1754 Lord Hardwicke in *Omychund v Barker*[1] said that 'the judges and sages of the law have laid it down that there is but one general rule of evidence, the best that the nature of the case will allow'. Whilst this is no longer a formal rule of evidence, it must remain the guiding principle for practitioners when deciding which evidence is required to prove the facts in issue in a particular case.

[1]   (1745) 1 Atk 21.

5. Estoppel

11.24 It is in the public interest that there must be an end to litigation[1]. The question arises as to the application of the doctrine of *estoppel per rem judicatam* in Children Act proceedings. In order to create an estoppel the judgment in the earlier action relied on as creating an estoppel must be:

(a)   of a court of competent jurisdiction;
(b)   final and conclusive;
(c)   on the merits;
(d)   the parties in the earlier action and those in the later action in which that estoppel is raised must be the same; and
(e)   the issue in the later action in which the estoppel is raised must be the same issue as that decided by the judgment in the earlier action.[2]

[1]   Beyond this general principle, within the context of family proceedings it is vital in the interests of the child that there is an end to litigation.
[2]   *K v P (Children Act Proceedings: Estoppel)* [1995] 1 FLR 248.

11.25 Because cases involving children are fluid, with a continuing and developing situation existing in the life of the child, the operation of res judicata in proceedings relating to children is heavily circumscribed.[1]

[1]   *B v Derbyshire County Council* [1992] 1 FLR 538.

11.26 Where a finding of abuse has been made against a party in previous proceedings, that party will rarely be allowed to challenge the finding in subsequent proceedings.[1] The court is not, however, bound by the doctrine of estoppel and has a discretion to decide whether issues should be reconsidered.[2] The court must balance the need for certainty of decision and the protection of the litigant from being vexed twice by the same complaint with the counter-vailing public interest in the protection of children, whose interests are paramount.[3] The court should bear in mind considerations of public policy such as:

(a) finality of litigation;
(b) the prejudicial effect of delay on the welfare of the child balanced against the likely effect of reliance on findings of fact that might turn out to have been erroneous;
(c) what form the previous hearings had taken;
(d) the importance of previous findings in the context of the present proceedings; and
(e) whether a rehearing of the issue would result in any substantially different finding.

[1] *Re S, S and A (Care Proceedings: Issue Estoppel)* [1995] 2 FLR 244; *Re S (Minors) (Discharge of Care Order)* [1995] 2 FLR 639,CA; *C v Hackney London Borough Council* [1996] 1 FLR 427, CA; and *Re S (a minor) (contact: evidence)* [1998] 3 FCR 70.
[2] *Re B (Children Act proceedings) (issue estoppel)* [1997] 1 FCR 477, [1997] 1 FLR 285.
[3] *Re S, S and A (Care Proceedings: Issue Estoppel)* [1995] 2 FLR 244.

11.27 In *Re D (a child) (threshold criteria: issue estoppel)*[1] the parties had entered into an agreement on a finding that a mother had failed to exercise proper supervision of her child. Subsequently in proceedings relating to a younger child, it was seen that the key question was whether she had been careless or a deliberate abuser. The Court of Appeal held that the court must retain a discretion to have the matter reopened and held that, the welfare of the child being the paramount consideration, the doctrine of estoppel had no application. Where new evidence has arisen between a fact finding hearing and a disposal hearing, the court can conduct the disposal hearing to take account of the new evidence rather than reopen the entirety of the findings.[2] In *Re K (Non-Accidental Injuries: Perpetrator: New Evidence)*[3] the Court of Appeal set out the following guidelines:

(a) It is in the public interest for those who caused serious non-accidental injuries to children to be identified, wherever such identification is possible.
(b) It is also in the public interest that children know the truth about who has injured them as children, and why.
(c) It is not in the public interest to leave the perpetrator issue open solely because orders facilitating adoption have been granted.
(d) In determining whether to re-open findings on the basis of fresh evidence it is sufficient that the fresh evidence might reasonably lead, on a rehearing, to a finding that the carer could be excluded as a possible perpetrator.

(e)   Against the argument that delay will prejudice the welfare of the children there is not only the powerful consideration of public interest, but also the possibility that the children might be reunited with the parent(s).

¹   [2001] 1 FCR 124, CA. None of the earlier authorities appear to have been considered.
²   *Re M and MC (Care: Issues of Fact: Drawing of Orders)* [2002] EWCA Civ 499, [2003] 1 FLR 461.
³   [2004] EWCA Civ 1181, [2005] 1 FLR 285. See also *Re U (Re-Opening of Appeal)* [2005] EWCA Civ 52, [2005] 2 FLR 444.

6. Covert video surveillance

11.28 Evidence may be obtained by covert video surveillance, for example if a parent is suspected of injuring a child.¹ Although it might be desirable to obtain the consent of the parent not suspected or the court, if there was a risk of more than transient harm, there should be no delay in operating the surveillance.² The Regulation of Investigatory Powers Act 2000, which seeks to ensure that investigatory powers are used in accordance with human rights, applies to covert video surveillance. There are designated authorities empowered to carry out such investigations, including the police, local authorities and health authorities. The guidance suggests that where there is any potential for use of covert video surveillance the police should be informed and, within the multi-agency team, take the lead in co-ordinating such action. Local Safeguarding Board procedures should include guidance on fabricated or induced illness in children and on the use of covert video surveillance. ³

¹   See Safeguarding Children in whom Illness is Induced or Fabricated by Carers with Parenting Responsibilities: Supplementary Guidance to Working Together to Safeguard Children, Department of Health, Home Office and Department for Education and Skills, August 2002, paras 6.46–6.51. For earlier guidance, see Guidelines for the multi-agency management of patients suspected or at risk of suffering from life threatening abuse resulting in cyanotic apnoeic episodes, Staffordshire Area Child Protection Committee January 1994.
²   *Re DH (a minor) (child abuse)* [1994] 2 FCR 3, [1994] 1 FLR 679.
³   At paras 1.20 and 1.21.

7. Expert evidence

11.29 Evidence from experts may be required in relation to the welfare of the child, the existence of specific harm, or as to its likelihood or its effect. If an allegation relates to ill-treatment, unless there is physical evidence, it is likely to depend on statements of the child. If the harm relates to health or development, expert opinion will be required as to existence of the harm, and how the child compares with a similar child. Whether the evidence comes from a social worker, health visitor, psychologist or child and family psychiatrist or other experienced person will depend on the expertise of the individual and the facts of the case. Evidence of a diagnosis of sexual abuse calls for a very high level of expertise. For the court to rely on opinion evidence, even to admit it, the qualifications of the witness must extend beyond experience gained as a social worker and require clinical experience as or akin to a child psychologist or child psychiatrist.[1] The opinion of an expert, however eminent, is not determinative, since ultimately findings are a matter for the court.[2]

[1]   *Re N (a minor) (child abuse: evidence)* [1996] 2 FCR 572, [1996] 2 FLR 214, CA.
[2]   *Re M and R (minors)* [1996] 2 FCR 617, [1996] 2 FLR 195, CA.

11.30 The foundation of the effective instruction of experts in proceedings relating to children is a proper understanding of the function of experts within such proceedings. To this end the observation of Butler-Sloss LJ in *Re M and R (Child Abuse: Evidence)*[1] is pertinent:

> '... when the judge is of the opinion that the witness' expertise is still required to assist him to answer the ultimate questions (including, where appropriate, credibility) then the judge can safely and gratefully rely upon such evidence, while never losing sight of the fact that the final decision is for him.'

[1]   [1996] 2 FLR 195.

11.31 The function of the expert must always be seen in the wider evidential context of the case and not in isolation from it. In *A Local Authority v S, W and T (By His Guardian)*[1] the High Court determined that a disagreement between experts does not absolve the judge from making a decision. Hedley J, having reminded himself that some forms of medical evidence were genuinely controversial and that understanding by experts was likely to develop over the years, nevertheless held that disagreement between experts did not absolve the judge of his responsibility for making a decision on the civil standard of proof. The court has to make findings on the totality of the evidence. It is the role of the court to take into account and weigh the expertise and speciality of the expert witnesses. It is open to the Judge to reach a conclusion on the totality of the evidence that was different or did not accord with the medical expert.[2] In *A County Council v A Mother*[3] Ryder J stated:

> '[44]   Further, I remind myself that a factual decision must be based on all available materials, i.e. be judged in context and not just upon medical or scientific materials, no matter how cogent they may in isolation seem to be. Just as best interests are not defined only by medical or scientific best interests (see, for example, *Re A (Male Sterilisation)* [2000] 1 FLR 549 at 555) likewise, investigations of fact should have regard to the wide context of social, emotional, ethical and moral factors.
>
> ...
>
> [182]   It has often been said, and I repeat it again for the record, that the welfare of the child cannot be deduced from any one sole professional perspective: welfare is not just medical best interests nor is it restricted to education or social care. It is a multi-faceted concept.'

[1]   [2004] EWHC 1270 (Fam); [2004] 2 FLR 129.
[2]   *A County Council v K D and L* [2005] EWHC 144 (Fam), [2005] 1 FLR 851 (per Charles J). See also *Re M (Residence) Re N-B* [2002] 3 FCR 259 (sub nom [2002] 2 FLR 1059 where it was held a judge was not entitled to reject the experts' assessment on matters upon which the experts, by reason of their training and professional expertise and experience were well equipped to guide the court.
[3]   [2005] EWHC 31 (Fam), [2005] 2 FLR 129.

11.32 The need for there to be an impartial opinion will often arise and this cannot be provided by an expert who is treating the child or family. The role of the expert to treat must not be confused with the role of the expert to report. Instructions for a forensic report should be impartial and, wherever possible, should be joint and agreed with the other side although in *Re B*[1] Thorpe LJ stated that the treating clinician could make *no* forensic contribution; it must be doubted whether that can be taken literally. It may be essential for there to be evidence on the medical history initially provided and as to the initial diagnosis made. An independent forensic expert, instructed jointly or by the guardian, can then comment on the diagnosis and such issues as reliability and suggestibility.

[1]   *Re B (sexual abuse: expert's report)* [2000] 2 FCR 8, [2000] 1 FLR 871, CA.

(*a*) *Leave for expert evidence*

11.33 Information relating to such proceedings (whether or not contained in a document filed with the court or recorded in any form) may be communicated only to an expert whose instruction by a party has been permitted by the court.[1] If the evidence to be given requires the child to be medically or psychiatrically examined or otherwise assessed, the leave of the court or the justices' clerk must be obtained.[2] Without leave no evidence arising out of the examination or assessment may be adduced.[3] Documents relating to the proceedings may be disclosed to an expert whose instruction by a party has been authorised by the court.[4]

[1]   FPR 1991, r 10.20A(2)(vii); FPC(CA 1989)R 1991, r 23A(1)(c)(vii).
[2]   FPR 1991, r 4.18(1); FPC(CA 1989)R 1991, r 18(1).
[3]   FPR 1991, r 4.18(3); FPC(CA 1989)R 1991, r 18(3).
[4]   FPR 1991, r 4.23(1)(f).

11.34 The courts have long endorsed the need for practitioners to make any applications for leave to instruct experts at as early a stage in the proceedings commensurate with the state of the evidence.[1] The expert's role is to assist the court in determining the issues in the case. It follows that before any steps are taken to identify and instruct an expert, the parties to the proceedings must identify as clearly as is reasonably practicable what issues the Judge will be required to determine.[2] The principle of the early identification of issues and the early instruction of experts to assist with those issues is, in respect of care proceedings, enshrined in the Public Law Outline and its associated Experts Practice Direction.[3] The Practice Direction aims to provide the court in family proceedings relating to children with early information to determine whether an expert or expert evidence will assist the court to:

(a)   identify, narrow and where possible agree the issues between the parties;
(b)   provide an opinion about a question that is not within the skill and experience of the court;
(c)   encourage the early identification of questions that need to be answered by an expert; and

(d)   encourage disclosure of full and frank information between the parties, the court and any expert instructed.[4]

1   *Re G (Minors)(Expert Witnesses)* [1994] 2 FLR 291.
2   *Re G (Minors)(Expert Witnesses)* above; see also *H v Cambridgeshire County Council* [1996] 2 FLR 566.
3   Public Law Outline para 12.7. The PLO also requires the parties to control the use and cost of expert evidence (see para 3.14(13)(a). The Expert Witness Practice Direction supersedes, for such proceedings, that contained in Appendix C (the Code of Guidance for Expert Witnesses in Family Proceedings) to the Protocol of June 2003 (Judicial Case Management in Public Law Children Act Cases) and in the Practice Direction to Part 17 (Experts) of the Family Procedure (Adoption) Rules 2005 (FP(A)R 2005, SI 2005/2795) with effect on and from 1 April 2008.
4   Experts Practice Direction, para 1.3. The Experts Practice Direction does not appear to be limited to public law cases. It is suggested that it should be considered good practice in any case under the CA 1989 where an expert is to be instructed.

11.35 The Practice Direction provides[1] that expert issues should be raised with the court and, where appropriate, with the other parties as early as possible. This means:

(a)   in public law proceedings under the Children Act 1989, by or at the Case Management Conference;[2]
(b)   in private law proceedings under the Children Act 1989, by or at the First Hearing Dispute Resolution Appointment.[3]

When experts' reports are commissioned before the commencement of proceedings, it should be made clear to the expert that he or she may in due course be reporting to the court and should therefore consider himself or herself bound by the Practice Direction. A prospective party to family proceedings relating to children (for example, a local authority) should always write a letter of instruction when asking a potential witness for a report or an opinion, whether that request is within proceedings or pre-proceedings (for example, when commissioning specialist assessment materials, reports from a treating expert or other evidential materials); and the letter of instruction should conform to the principles set out in this guidance.[4] The Practice Direction further provides that in emergency or urgent cases, where, before formal issue of proceedings, a without notice application is made to the court during or out of business hours; or where, after proceedings have been issued, a previously unforeseen need for expert evidence arises at short notice and a party wishes to call expert evidence without having complied with the Practice Direction, the party wishing to call the expert evidence must apply forthwith to the court (where possible or appropriate, on notice to the other parties) for directions as to the future steps to be taken in respect of the expert evidence in question.

1   At para 1.9.
2   See the *Practice Direction: Guide to Case Management in Public Law Proceedings* (the 'PLO') and Chapter 8.
3   See the Private Law Programme (9 November 2004), section 4 (Process).
4   Experts Practice Direction, para 2.3.

11.36 Section 4 of the Expert's Practice Direction sets out the procedure for seeking leave to instruct an expert. The court has a proactive role in the grant of leave. The court has the duty to analyse the evidence and decide the areas in which expert evidence is necessary and both the power and the duty to limit expert evidence to given categories of expertise and to specify the numbers of experts to be called. The court should be proactive:

(a)   in enquiring into:
   (i)   the category of the expert evidence sought;
   (ii)   the name of the expert;
   (iii)   the relevance of the evidence to the issues in the case;
   (iv)   whether or not the expert evidence can properly be obtained by the joint instruction of one expert by two or more parties;
   (v)   whether or not the expert evidence may properly be adduced by only one party or whether it is necessary for experts of the same discipline to be instructed by more than one party;
(b)   in laying down a timetable for the filing of evidence;
(c)   in making arrangements for the dissemination of reports; and
(d)   in giving directions for the experts to confer.[1]

The court should not give leave for an assessment, where there was no issue before the court on which the assessment was likely to assist.[2] Where no application is made by the parties for leave to instruct an expert, but the court nonetheless feels it would be assisted by expert evidence, the court is able to appoint an expert of its own volition within family proceedings[3]. This power is to be used sparingly. Whilst an adult party may not be compelled to obtain a report on their own mental health the court has jurisdiction to compel disclosure of that party's medical records for the purpose of enabling another party to obtain an opinion on any matters within those records.[4]

[1]   *Re G (Minors)(Expert Witnesses)* [1994] 2 FLR 291; see also *H v Cambridgeshire County Council* [1996] 2 FLR 566. See also *Practice Note (Case Management)* [1995] 1 FLR 456 and *Re R (child abuse: video evidence)* [1995] 2 FCR 573, [1995] 1 FLR 451.
[2]   *Re F (a minor) (care proceedings: directions)* [1995] 3 FCR 601 and *H v Cambridgeshire County Council* [1996] 2 FLR 566.
[3]   RSC Ord 40; *Re K (Contact: Psychiatric Reports)* [1995] 2 FLR 432.
[4]   *Re S; WSP v Hull City Council* [2006] EWCA Civ 981, [2007] 1 FLR 90.

11.37 In light of the court's duty to take a proactive role when considering whether leave should be give to instruct an expert witness, the Practice Direction provides that it will be necessary for the party wishing to instruct an expert to make enquiries designed so as to provide the court with information about that expert which will enable the court to decide whether or not to give permission. In practice, enquiries may need to be made of more than one expert for this purpose. This will in turn require each expert to be given sufficient information about the case to enable that expert to decide whether or not he or she is in a position to accept instructions. Such preliminary enquiries, and the disclosure of anonymised information about the case which is a necessary part of such enquiries, will not require the court's permission and will not amount to a contempt of court.[1] To this end, advocates have a positive duty to place all relevant information before the court when asking for leave and must be fully prepared to justify to the court the need for expert evidence of the specified type sought.[2]

11.37 *Evidence*

1   See Preliminary Enquiries of the Expert and Expert's Response to Preliminary Enquiries, paras 4.1 and 4.2. Section of the Practice Direction (*Preparation for the relevant hearing*) gives guidance on applying for the court's permission to instruct an expert, and on instructing the expert, in family proceedings relating to children.
2   *Re G (Minors)(Expert Witnesses)* [1994] 2 FLR 291.

11.38 In considering the identity of the expert to be instructed and the nature of the instructions the parties should have regard to the following principles:

(a)   Experts reports based solely on a 'paper review' of the documents filed in the proceedings will rarely be as persuasive as reports based on interviews and assessments, which supplement the documentation.

(b)   Following on from this, whilst there is an understandable need to avoid the need for additional intimate examinations of a child, there are potential dangers in experts being asked to give a second opinion on the issue of sexual abuse by relying on photographs of a previous examination.[1]

(c)   It is not helpful for experts to express opinions when they have a limited knowledge of the type of case in issue.[2] Accordingly, care should be taken that the expert is not only experienced in the relevant field but also that he/she has experience of the particular type of case in issue.

(e)   Reliance on diagnoses or methodology's already significantly discredited by the courts is unlikely to convince a later tribunal and may simply lead to unnecessary delay and cost.[3]

(d)   Where the medical evidence shows signs of abuse, which are compatible with sexual abuse (as opposed to probative of it), other non-medical evidence will be needed to confirm the diagnosis. The need to instruct an expert must not blind the parties to the need also to obtain the fullest possible spectrum of evidence relevant to the issues at hand.

(e)   Whilst the court is entitled to rely on expert evidence on the issue of credibility[4] the Court of Appeal has deprecated the use of personality tests to determine issues of credibility, these being for the judge to decide.[5]

1   *Re Y (Evidence of Abuse: Use of Photographs)* [2003] EWHC 3090 (Fam), [2004] 1 FLR 855 but see also *Re T (Abuse: Standard of Proof)* [2004] EWCA Civ 558, [2004] 2 FLR 838.
2   *Manchester City Council v B* [1996] 1 FLR 324.
3   See *Re X (Non-Accidental Injury: Expert Evidence)* [2001] 2 FLR 90 (deprecation of diagnosis of 'temporary brittle bone disease') and *Re D* [2001] 1 FCR 707 (deprecation of the use of 'facilitated communication').
4   *Re M and R (Child Abuse: Evidence)* [1996] 2 FLR 195.
5   *Re S (Care: Parenting Skills: Personality Tests)* [2004] EWCA Civ 1029, [2005] 2 FLR 658.

11.39 Fairness is an important factor for the court to consider when deciding whether to permit the instruction of an expert on a particular issue.[1] In certain cases where the medical evidence of alleged non-accidental injury or unascertained infant death becomes pivotal, the court should be slow to decline an application for a second expert, since such evidence was not easily challenged in the absence of another expert opinion.[2] However, such a second opinion should only be permitted where the question to be addressed goes to an issue of critical importance.[3] The court should not routinely favour the instruction of two or more experts in the same discipline additional to such experts already destined to give evidence because of their clinical involvement in the child's case.[4]

1   *Re B (Care Proceedings: Expert Witness)* [2007] EWCA Civ 556, [2007] 2 FLR 979.
2   See *Re W (a child)(non-accidental injury: expert evidence)* [2005] EWCA Civ 1247, [2005] 3 FCR 513. See also *Re M (Care Proceedings: Best Evidence)* [2007] EWCA Civ 589, [2007] 2 FLR 1006.
3   *Re W (a child)(non-accidental injury: expert evidence)* [2005] EWCA Civ 1247, [2005] 3 FCR 513.
4   *Re S; WSP v Hull City Council* [2006] EWCA Civ 981, [2007] 1 FLR 90.

(b) Instructing an expert

11.40 Detailed guidance on the instruction of experts is given in the Experts Practice Direction issued in concert with the PLO.[1] Parties should consider whether evidence can properly be obtained by joint instruction to an expert. This may put parents at a disadvantage if they are then constrained by the evidence of that expert. An alternative is to consider whether an expert should initially be instructed by the children's guardian. Parents will have to consider whether they would be permitted to obtain another report, if that report proved unacceptable[2]. A refusal to allow a party to adduce expert evidence may be a breach of that party's rights under the ECHR.[3] In any event a party instructing an expert should try to agree the terms of the letter of instruction and the letter should be in the court bundle.[4] All instructions to experts should be impartial.[5] In *A County Council v K, D and L*[6] Charles J held that rather than ask experts to express a view on the cause of injuries or death on the balance of probability they instead be asked:

(a)   To identify the possible causes of the symptoms (including if applicable an 'unknown cause'), to set out in respect of each possible cause why it might be a cause and accordingly why it should be considered.

(b)   In relation to each possible cause to state their view on the *likelihood* of each possibility being the cause, together with the reasons why they include or reject each possibility as a reasonable (as opposed to a fanciful or merely theoretical) possible cause.

(c)   To compare the likelihood of the causes identified as reasonable possibilities being the actual cause of injury or death.

(d)   To state whether they consider that a cause is the most likely cause or causes of the injury or death and the reasons for that view.

(e)   To state whether they consider that a cause is or is more likely than not to be the cause or causes of the injury or death and their reasons for that view.

1   Section 5 of the Experts Practice Direction provides detailed guidance on the compilation of the letter of instruction. Appendices to the Practice Direction provide pro forma questions for paediatricians, psychiatrists and applied psychologists.
2   See *Re W (a child)(non-accidental injury: expert evidence)* [2005] EWCA Civ 1247, [2005] 3 FCR 513.
3   *Elsholz v Germany* (2002) 34 EHRR 58, [2000] 2 FLR 486.
4   *Re CB and JB (minors) (care proceedings: case conduct)* [1998] 2 FCR 313.
5   *Re B (a minor) (sexual abuse: expert's report)* [2000] 2 FCR 8, [2000] 1 FLR 871, CA.
6   [2005] EWHC 144 (Fam), [2005] 1 FLR 871.

11.41 The letter of instruction to an expert should be prepared carefully on an individual basis. Precedents should only be used as a framework and as a check and should not be simply reproduced.[1] It is inappropriate for an expert to be given only a summary of any judgment in previous proceedings. However well meaning the summary, it is not a substitute for the full text.[2] As often as may be necessary, the expert should be provided promptly with a copy of any new document filed at court, together with an updated document list or bundle index.[3]

[1]   *Re R (Care: Disclosure: Nature of Proceedings)* [2002] 1 FLR 755.
[2]   *Re G (A Child)(Care Order: Threshold Criteria)* [2001] 1 FCR 165 CA.
[3]   Experts Practice Direction para 5.3.

11.42 There is no standard format for an experts report.[1] Where a report would benefit from clarification or restructuring to highlight or make clearer the salient points the solicitor or counsel are permitted to *re-structure* it by means of drafting a witness statement for approval by the expert.[2] When the parties receive the report of the expert, all parties and legal advisors should always check whether the expert has reported in accordance with his/her instructions, whether the parties wish to put further points to the expert and the role the expert should play at the hearing.[3]

[1]   Whilst now somewhat dated, Cottrell and Tufnell [1996] Fam Law 159 sets out good practice as to the form and content of experts' reports identified from a survey carried out in association with the Official Solicitors Office and the Lord Chancellors Department.
[2]   Bar Code of Conduct, para 606, Annexe H, para 5.8.
[3]   *Re R (Care: Disclosure: Nature of Proceedings)* [2002] 1 FLR 755.

11.43 Where the court has directed that the instructions to the expert are to be contained in a jointly agreed letter and the terms of the letter cannot be agreed, any instructing party may submit to the court a written request, which must be copied to the other instructing parties, that the court settle the letter of instruction. Where possible, the written request should be set out in an e-mail to the court, preferably sent directly to the judge dealing with the proceedings (or, in the Family Proceedings Court, to the legal adviser who will forward it to the appropriate judge or justices), and be copied by e-mail to the other instructing parties. The court will settle the letter of instruction, usually without a hearing to avoid delay; and will send (where practicable, by e-mail) the settled letter to the lead solicitor for transmission forthwith to the expert, and copy it to the other instructing parties for information.[1]

[1]   Experts Practice Direction, para 5.2.

11.44 Any party wishing to put written questions to an expert for the purpose of clarifying the expert's report must put the questions to the expert not later than 10 business days after receipt of the report. [1] The court will specify the timetable according to which the expert is to answer the written questions. [2] By the specified date, the court may – if it has not already given such a direction – direct that the experts are to meet or communicate:

(a)   To identify and narrow the issues in the case.
(b)   Where possible, to reach agreement on the expert issues.

(c)   To identify the reasons for disagreement on any expert question and what, if any, action needs to be taken to resolve any outstanding disagreement or question.

(d)   To explain or add to the evidence in order to assist the court to determine the issues.

(e)   To limit, wherever possible, the need for the experts to attend court to give oral evidence.

The Expert's Practice Direction gives detailed guidance as to the arrangement and management of experts' meetings.[3] Importantly, a global discussion between experts of different disciplines may only take place with the leave of the court.[4] Jointly instructed experts should not attend any meeting or conference which is not a joint one, unless all the parties have agreed in writing or the court has directed that such a meeting may be held, and it is agreed or directed who is to pay the expert's fees for the meeting or conference. Any meeting or conference attended by a jointly instructed expert should be proportionate to the case.[5] In public law Children Act proceedings, where the court gives a direction that a meeting shall take place between the local authority and any relevant named experts for the purpose of providing assistance to the local authority in the formulation of plans and proposals for the child, the meeting shall be arranged, chaired and minuted in accordance with the directions given by the court.[6]

[1]   Paragraph 6.1.
[2]   Paragraph 6.1.
[3]   Paragraph 6.3.
[4]   Paragraph 6.3(1).
[5]   Paragraph 6.4.
[6]   Paragraph 6.5.

11.45 The Experts Practice Direction contains detailed guidance on the management of expert evidence during the hearing.[1] There is no property in an expert witness and he or she can be called to give evidence by any party to the proceedings even if they have not instructed that expert.[2] Where the expert evidence is unanimous as to causation and timing, none of the relevant experts should be required to attend to give oral evidence, unless a party has not instructed their own expert (in which case one representative expert witness may be called for cross-examination).[3] Practitioners should ensure that experts are called in a logical sequence if possible with related experts giving evidence on the same day of the trial.[4] It is the duty of the advocate calling the expert witness to ensure that he has seen any fresh material or is aware of any fresh developments which post-date the expert's report and that the expert's opinion remains the same, or as has changed, as a consequence of the fresh material.[5] Failure to carry out this task may result in wasted costs orders being made against those responsible.[6] The solicitor instructing the expert shall inform the expert in writing of the outcome of the case, and of the use made by the court of the expert's opinion.[7]

[1]   Paragraph 8.
[2]   *Harmony Shipping Co SA v Saudi Europe Line* [1979] 1 WLR 1380 at 1386.
[3]   *Re CB and JB (Care Proceedings: Guidelines)* [1998] 2 FLR 211.
[4]   *Re M (Minors)(Care Proceedings: Child's Wishes)* [1994] 1 FLR 749.
[5]   *Re T and E (Proceedings: Conflicting Interests)* [1995] 1 FLR 581.

6   *Re G, S and M* [2000] 1 FLR 52.
7   Experts Practice Direction, para 9.1.

(c) *The duties of expert witnesses*

11.46 The following principles in respect of the duties and responsibilities of experts can be divined from the authorities and in particular *Re AB (Child Abuse: Expert Witnesses)*[1]:

(a)   Expert evidence presented to the court should be and should be seen to be the independent product of the expert uninfluenced as to form or content by the exigencies of litigation.[2]

(b)   An expert witness should provide independent assistance to the court by way of objective unbiased opinion in relation to matters within his expertise. An expert witness in the High Court should never assume the role of advocate.[3]

(c)   The expert should state the facts and assumptions on which his opinion is based.[4]

(d)   An expert should not mislead by way of omission. The expert should consider all the material facts in reaching his conclusions and must not omit to consider the material facts which could detract form his concluded opinion.[5]

(e)   Doctors who have clinical experience of the child outside the ambit of the court proceedings should review their notes before writing a court report, and ensure that all their clinical material is available for inspection by the court and other experts.[6]

(f)   In any event, the expert must make all his material available to other experts in the case.[7]

(e)   If the expert considers that insufficient data is available, he/she must say so and indicate that his/her opinion is no more than a provisional one.[8]

(g)   Where an expert advances a hypothesis to explain a given set of facts, he owes a very heavy duty to explain to the court that what he is advancing is a hypothesis, that it is controversial (if it is), and to place before the court all the material which contradicts the hypothesis.[9]

(h)   Where medical evidence points overwhelmingly to non-accidental injury, any expert who advises the parents and the court that the injury has an innocent explanation has a heavy duty to ensure that he/she has considered carefully the available material and is expressing an opinion that can be objectively justified.[10]

(i)   An expert witness should make it clear when a particular question falls outside his expertise.[11]

(i)   If after exchange of reports, an expert witness changes his view on a material matter, such change of view should be communicated ... to the other side without delay and when appropriate to the court.[12]

(i)   Where expert evidence refers to photographs, plans, calculations ... survey reports or other similar documents these must be provided to the opposite party at the same time as the exchange of reports.[13]

1   [1995] 1 FLR 181 Wall LJ having considered *National Justice Compania Naviera SA v Prudential Assurance Co Ltd, the Ikarian Reefer* [1993] 2 Lloyd's Rep 68.
2   *Re AB (Child Abuse: Expert Witnesses)* [1995] 1 FLR 181.

3   *Re R (A Minor)(Expert's Evidence)* [1991] 1 FLR 291n; *Vernon v Bosley (No 2)* [1997] 1 All ER 614, [1998] 1 FLR 304; *Re AB (Child Abuse: Expert Witnesses)* [1995] 1 FLR 181.

4   *Re AB (Child Abuse: Expert Witnesses)* [1995] 1 FLR 181.

5   See *Re R (A Minor)(Expert's Evidence)* [1991] 1 FLR 291n; *Vernon v Bosley (No 2)* [1997] 1 All ER 614, [1998] 1 FLR 304.

6   *Re M (Minors)(Care Proceedings: Child's Wishes)* [1994] 1 FLR 749.

7   *Re AB (Child Abuse: Expert Witnesses)* [1995] 1 FLR 181.

8   *Re R (A Minor)(Expert's Evidence)* [1991] 1 FLR 291n; *Vernon v Bosley (No 2)* [1997] 1 All ER 614, [1998] 1 FLR 304.

9   *Re AB (Child Abuse: Expert Witnesses)* [1995] 1 FLR 181.

10   *Re AB (Child Abuse: Expert Witnesses)* [1995] 1 FLR 181.

11   *Re AB (Child Abuse: Expert Witnesses)* [1995] 1 FLR 181.

12   *Re AB (Child Abuse: Expert Witnesses)* [1995] 1 FLR 181.

13   *Re AB (Child Abuse: Expert Witnesses)* [1995] 1 FLR 181.

11.47 In *Re AB* it was emphasised that experts have a privileged position as only they can give opinion evidence, and because they bring to court an expertise on which the court is dependent. They must only express opinions which they genuinely hold and which are not biased in favour of one party. If an expert does seek to promote a particular case, the report must make that clear, but that approach should be avoided. A misleading opinion may well inhibit a proper assessment of the case by non-medical professional advisers, increase costs and lead parties, and in particular parents, to false views and hopes.

8. Evidence from the child

11.48 Except by direction of the court children should not attend any CA 1989 hearings.[1] Even where a child is competent to be a party to the proceedings, the court is entitled to refuse to hear oral evidence from them.[2] Whilst the child is a party to specified proceedings, he has no absolute right to attend the hearing. The Rules provide[3] that a hearing shall take place in the absence of the child if the court considers it in the interests of the child, having regard to the matters to be discussed or the evidence likely to be given, and the child is represented by a children's guardian or solicitor. The court must be very cautious before it compels the attendance of a child complainant to give oral evidence and the risk of harm to the child arising from the process must be carefully considered.[4] The following principles have been endorsed by the Court of Appeal:[5]

(a)   The starting point must be that it is undesirable for a child to have to give evidence in proceedings.

(b)   Particular justification will be required before this course will be taken.

(c)   There will be some cases in which it will be right to require oral evidence from the child but these will be rare.

(d)   The forensic need for the evidence to be given orally has to be balanced against the risk of harm to the child.

The following further principles can be derived from the authorities dealing with this issue:

(e)   Where a child is called to give evidence, the court must determine whether the child is competent to give evidence (either sworn or unsworn).[6]

(f)   If the court determines that the child is competent to give evidence, the child will be a compellable witness.[7]

(g)   Any court has an inherent jurisdiction not to require the attendance of witnesses where it would be oppressive to do so.[8] A specific issue order may be used to prevent a parent calling his or her child to give evidence.[9]

(h)   In deciding whether to issue a witness summons the child's welfare is of great relevance although not paramount[10].

(i)   In principle, the older the child, the more arguable is the application for a witness summons[11].

(j)   In most cases involving a child aged 12 years or younger, whether or not he or she is a family member, the court would favour the absence of oral evidence, even where that might mean the weakening of the evidence against the adult concerned[12].

(k)   Children's guardians or guardian's ad litem should think carefully about arrangements for children to be present and be prepared to explain them to the court.[13]

(l)   If a child is likely to be unruly the court could refuse to allow him to attend.[14]

[1]   See the Handbook of Best Practice in Children Act Cases (1997) CAAC, para 58. See para 10.64 above.
[2]   *Re O (Care Proceedings: Evidence)* [2003] EWHC 2011 (Fam), [2004] 1 FLR 161.
[3]   FPR 1991, r 4.16(2); FPC(CA 1989)R 1991, r 16(2), (7).
[4]   *R v B County Council, ex p P* [1991] 1 FLR 470; *Re P (Witness Summons)* [1997] 2 FLR 447.
[5]   *LM (By Her Guardian) v Medway County Council, RM and YM* [2007] EWCA Civ 9 [2007] 1 FLR 1698.
[6]   *R v B County Council, ex p P* [1991] 2 All ER 65, [1991] 1 FLR 470.
[7]   *R v B County Council, ex p P* [1991] 2 All ER 65, [1991] 1 FLR 470.
[8]   *R v B County Council, ex p P* [1991] 2 All ER 65, [1991] 1 FLR 470.
[9]   [1992] Fam Law 278.
[10]   *Re P (Witness Summons)* [1997] 2 FLR 447.
[11]   *Re P (Witness Summons)* [1997] 2 FLR 447.
[12]   *Re P (Witness Summons)* [1997] 2 FLR 447.
[13]   *Re C (A Minor) (Care: Child's Wishes)* [1993] 1 FLR 832.
[14]   *Re W (A Minor) (Secure Accommodation Order: Attendance at Court)* [1994] 2 FLR 1092.

11.49 If it is alleged that a child has been the victim of abuse, a child who is old enough may be the best source of information, especially in sexual abuse cases, where there is no physical evidence. The child's evidence may be heard directly by the court if, in its opinion, he understands that it his duty to speak the truth and he has sufficient understanding to justify his evidence being heard.[1] It is rare for a child to give evidence directly. If the child is too young or too frightened to give evidence, or where there has been a criminal investigation, hearsay evidence will be given by an interviewer, possibly in accordance with Achieving Best Evidence.[2] The following issues should be considered where evidence is being given by a witness of an interview with a child:[3]

(a)   Should the child be called to give evidence personally?

(b)   Has the child and/or a parent given informed consent to the interview?

(c)   Has the interview been video or audiotaped and is a transcript available, and if not why not?

(d)   Where appropriate has the leave of the court been given?

(e)   What was the purpose of the interview: forensic, diagnostic, therapeutic?

(f)   Was/were appropriate person(s) conducting the interview: police, child psychiatrist, social worker and what was their experience?

(g)   Were the venue and time suitable? and

(h)   How many and how long were the interviews[4] (it must be recognised that there is a danger of pressurising the child by lengthy or repeated interviews, and yet the child may not reveal the whole story on one occasion, and may only do so when she feels safe)?

(i)   Has there been a spontaneous statement by child?

(j)   Is the child's sexual knowledge appropriate to age and development?

(k)   Is there information suggestive of sexual knowledge or experience, eg smell, touch, pain?

(l)   Have there been leading or hypothetical questions, and if so were they inappropriate?[5]

(m)   Has the child been given an opportunity to deny that abuse has taken place or provide an alternative explanation of established facts?

(n)   Has the interviewer avoided presuming that abuse has taken place?[6]

(o)   Has the interviewer taken the child seriously, and not made promises about believing or not revealing what the child has said? and

(p)   If dolls, puppets, drawings or other aids to communication have been used, has this been appropriate?

[1]   CA 1989, s 96(2). The child should not be asked to swear an affidavit to boost the chances of a parent on an appeal: *Re M (a minor)* [1995] 2 FCR 90, CA.

[2]   Home Office, 2002, see para 7.16.

[3]   See generally *Re M (Sexual Abuse Allegations: Interviewing Techniques)* [1999] 2 FLR 92.

[4]   *H v H (Minor) (Child Abuse: Evidence)* [1990] Fam 86, [1989] 3 All ER 740, CA.

[5]   *C v C (Child Abuse: Access)* [1988] 1 FLR 462 at 465.

[6]   *Re E (a minor)* [1987] FCR 169, [1987] 1 FLR 269 and *Re D (Child Abuse: Investigation Procedure)* [1995] 3 FCR 581.

11.50 In the light of the standard of proof and the importance of not focussing exclusively on specific allegations, it is important for the court to be presented with a comprehensive picture about the child. Reliance solely on children's evidence can present problems of credibility, suggestibility, retraction and confusion of events and detail, especially where there have been delays. Nonetheless children are now not necessarily regarded as less reliable than adults, although the courts will exercise caution.

11.51 Although it is likely that evidence will be sought from a formal interview of the child, especially in view of the standard of proof in relation to allegations of abuse, other sources may still be relevant, in particular where they would contribute to a range of concerns about the care of the child. Although there was a sexual abuse context to the case, there is no reason why the observations of Butler-Sloss LJ should not remain relevant, when she said in *Re W (Minors) (Wardship: Evidence):[1]*

'In wardship, therefore, the rules as to the reception of statements made by children to others, whether doctors, police officers, social workers, welfare officers, foster-mothers, teachers or others, may be relaxed and the information may be received by the judge. He has a duty to look at it and consider what weight, if any, he should give to it. The weight which he places upon the information is a matter for the exercise of his discretion. He may totally disregard it. He may wish to rely upon some or all of it. Unless uncontroversial it must be regarded with great caution. In considering the extent to which, if at all, a judge would rely on the statements of a child made to others, the age of the child, the context in which the statement was made, the surrounding circumstances, previous behaviour of the child, opportunities for the child to have knowledge from other sources, any knowledge, as in this case, of a child's predisposition to tell untruths or to fantasise, are among the relevant considerations.'

1   [1990] 1 FLR 203 at 214, CA. She referred to a number of decisions about the court's view of interviews with children for the purpose of 'disclosures'. See the [1987] Family Law Reports, principally, Latey J in *Re M (A Minor) (Child Abuse: Evidence)* [1987] 1 FLR 293n. Where an allegation was made by an adult in respect of incidents alleged to have occurred when the person was a child, oral evidence should normally be given by that person: *Re D (Sexual Abuse Allegations: Evidence of Adult Victim)* [2002] 1 FLR 723.

11.52 In relation specifically to sexual abuse great care will be exercised as the judge emphasised:

'Allegations of sexual abuse made in a statement by a child naming a perpetrator presented considerable problems and would, unsupported, rarely be sufficiently cogent and reliable for a court to be satisfied on the balance of probabilities, that the person named was the perpetrator. The evidence may, however, reveal a clear indication that the child has been exposed to inappropriate sexual activities and may be sufficiently compelling to satisfy the judge that the child has been subjected to serious sexual abuse.'[1]

1   *Re W (Minors) (Wardship: Evidence)* [1990] 1 FLR 203, CA.

11.53 The difficulties inherent in the investigation and proof of allegations of child sexual abuse have been highlighted in many cases which have considered the forensic implications of the therapeutic interviewing techniques sometimes used where children are alleged to have been sexually abused. The courts have frequently drawn attention to 'The Cleveland Report',[1] for the guidance it contains on investigating allegations of sexual abuse.

1   Report of the Inquiry into Child Abuse in Cleveland 1987, HMSO 1988, CM 412.

11.54 In *Re M (minors)*[1] Butler-Sloss LJ said:

'It is important to draw distinctions between interviews with young children for the purposes of investigation, assessment and therapy. It would be rare, I would assume, that interviews for a specifically therapeutic purpose would be provided for use in court. Generally it is desirable that interviews with young children should be conducted as soon as possible after the allegations are first raised, should be few in number and should have investigation as their primary purpose. However, an expert interview of a child at a later stage, if conducted in such a way as to satisfy the court that the child has given information after acceptable questioning, may be a valuable part of the evidence for consideration as to whether abuse has occurred. No rigid rules can be laid down and it is for the court to decide whether such evidence is or is not of assistance.'

¹ [1993] 1 FCR 253, [1993] 1 FLR 822, CA.

11.55 The practice of video recording interviews of children now seems well established, especially if there is an allegation of a criminal offence. Provided they are conducted in accordance with guidance[1] they will be useful in civil proceedings, though there may be argument about how the interview is conducted, the value of what the video shows and its relevance to other evidence. Although the video is usually the property of the police, they can be required to produce it by sub poena duces tecum. It should be disclosed subject to proper controls about who has access to it.[2] The solicitor representing the child may be asked to co-ordinate the use of the video.[3]

¹ Achieving Best Evidence (2002) Home Office, see para 7.18.
² *Re M (Child Abuse: Video Evidence)* [1995] 2 FLR 571. If the question of disclosure of the video and its transcript is not submitted promptly to the court for a decision, there may be a breach of art 8: *TP and KM v United Kingdom* [2001] 2 FCR 289, ECtHR.
³ *Re R (Child Abuse: Video Evidence)* [1995] 1 FLR 451.

11.56 An expert may give evidence of opinion as to the truthfulness of a witness or reporter of events which are in dispute but it is the judge's duty to decide whether or not a child should be believed.[1] It should be rare to extend this to a parent.[2] Earlier observations of the Court of Appeal made in relation to video recorded evidence[3] appear to remain relevant:

> '(1) The recording was admitted as a form of hearsay evidence. It was for the judge to decide its weight and credibility. He would judge the internal consistency and inconsistency of the story. He would look for any inherent improbabilities in the truth of what the child related and would decide what part, if any, he could believe.
>
> (2) The judge would receive expert evidence to explain and interpret the video. This would cover such things as the nuances of emotion and behaviour, the gestures and the body movements, the use or non-use of language and its imagery, the vocal inflections and intonations, the pace and pressure of the interview, the child's intellectual and verbal abilities, or lack of them, and any signs or the absence of signs of fantasising.
>
> (3) It was for the judge to separate admissible from inadmissible expert evidence. Proper evidence from an expert would be couched in terms that a particular fact was consistent or inconsistent with sexual abuse, and that it rendered the child's evidence capable or incapable of being accepted by the judge as true.'

¹ *Re M and R (minors)* [1996] 2 FCR 617, [1996] 2 FLR 195, CA. See also *Re S and B (minors) (child abuse: evidence)* [1991] FCR 175, [1990] 2 FLR 489, CA and *Re FS (minors) (child abuse: evidence)* [1996] 1 FCR 666, [1996] 2 FLR 158, CA.
² *Re CB and JB (minors) (care proceedings: case conduct)* [1998] 2 FCR 313.
³ *Re N (a minor) (child abuse: evidence)* [1996] 2 FCR 572, [1996] 2 FLR 214, CA.

11.57 Although it is well established that High Court and county court judges have the power to interview children in private, there are no specific rules governing when they should do so. In *Re R (A Minor) (Residence: Religion),*[1] Balcombe LJ commented that 'a judge's decision whether or not personally to interview a child must above all be a question for the exercise of judicial discretion'. The following principles apply where a judge or magistrates are considering interviewing a child.[2] They are of more relevance to private law proceedings than public law proceedings[3]:

(a) A judge should only decide to see a child in his chambers after hearing submissions from the parties[4].

(b) The discretion must be exercised cautiously; there must be good reason for him to see the child and it must be perceived to be in the child's interests to see the judge[5].

(c) The interview should normally take place after the close of evidence and before closing submissions[6].

(d) If the judge decides to see the child the judicial interview should take place at court[7].

(e) It is for the judge to decide who will be present when he sees the child.

(f) The judge should not, except perhaps in the most exceptional circumstances, say anything to the child which could be understood as a promise that what the child says will remain confidential[8].

(g) When a judge has seen the child privately he must tell the parties what the child has said so that they may deal with it[9].

(h) A judge should never go to visit a child alone, for example at his school[10].

Before the CA 1989 it was established that magistrates had no powers to interview children in private,[11] but in *Re M (a minor) (justices' discretion)*[12] Booth J held that in exceptional circumstances magistrates could see a child in private.

1   [1993] 2 FLR 163, CA. For a case where it was held appropriate to see a child in private, see *Re F (Minors) (Denial of Contact)* [1993] 2 FLR 677, CA.
2   It should be noted that some of the authorities from which these principles are derived are now of some age. They should now all be read in light of the principles set out in *Mabon v Mabon* [2005] EWCA Civ 634, [2005] Fam 366, [2005] 2 FLR 1011 and in the context of the decisions being an exercise of discretion.
3   As in public law proceedings the child will have the benefit of representation.
4   *B v B (Minors)(Interviews and Listing Arrangements)* [1994] 2 FLR 489.
5   *B v B (Minors)(Interviews and Listing Arrangements)* [1994] 2 FLR 489.
6   *B v B (Minors)(Interviews and Listing Arrangements)* [1994] 2 FLR 489.
7   *Re R (A Minor)(Residence: Religion)* [1993] 2 FLR 163.
8   *H v H (Child: Judicial Interview)* [1974] 1 WLR 595; *Elder v Elder* [1986] 1 FLR 610.
9   *H v H (Child: Judicial Interview)* [1974] 1 WLR 595; *Elder v Elder* [1986] 1 FLR 610.
10   *L v L (Access: Contempt)* [1991] 1 FCR 547.
11   *Re W (Minors)* (1980) 10 Fam Law 120; *Re T (A Minor) (Welfare Report Recommendations)* (1977) 1 FLR 59.
12   [1993] 2 FCR 721, [1993] 2 FLR 706. See also *Re W (child: contact)* [1993] 2 FCR 731, [1994] 1 FLR 843 and *Re K (A Minor) (Contact)* [1993] Fam Law 552.

11.58 All reports on the progress of the CA 1989 have concluded that delays in proceedings are compounded by the lack of availability of expert witnesses. This is in turn compounded by reluctance to accept the evidence of social workers, which in its turn has deteriorated with the decrease in their skills and numbers. It is a vicious circle. Following a number of high profile cases in which the expert evidence of Professor Sir Roy Meadows, a consultant paediatrician, was called into question[1] and the associated media backlash against him, the shortage of experts willing to undertake expert reports in relation to cases concerning children has become even more acute. This, coupled with concerns over the expense of expert witnesses, has lead to the production of a report from Chief Medical Officer entitled 'Bearing Good Witness: Proposals for reforming the delivery of medical expert evidence in family law cases'.[2] The key proposal is that the NHS should establish teams of specialist doctors and other professionals within local NHS organisations to improve the quality of the medical expert witness service by introducing mentoring, supervision and peer review. A National Knowledge Service to support the medical expert witness programme is also proposed.[3]

[1] See *R v Cannings* [2004] EWCA Crim 1, [2004] 1 WLR 2607 and *Meadows v General Medical Council (Her Majesty's A-G Intervening)* [2006] EWCA Civ 1390, [2007] 1 FLR 1398.
[2] DOH, (2006).
[3] See *Bearing Good Witness: the Reluctant Experts* [2008] Fam Law 153.

DISCLOSURE

1. General duty

11.59 'It is a duty owed to the court both by the parties and by their legal representatives to give full and frank disclosure ... in all matters in respect of children.'[1] This duty of disclosure has to be considered in conjunction with the practical need to present the case in a way which is comprehensible to the court and fair to the parties.

[1] *Practice Note (Case Management)* [1995] 1 FLR 456. It is probable that the duty of the parties under the PLO to help the court further the overriding objective encompasses a duty of full and frank disclosure.

11.60 A local authority which brings care proceedings has a duty to disclose all relevant information in its possession or power which might assist parents to rebut allegations made against them. In *R v Hampshire County Council, ex p K*[1] a child who had allegedly been sexually abused was examined by a police surgeon who found no physical evidence of abuse but because of what the child had said, sexual abuse was suspected. After a further examination two months later, another paediatrician concluded there had been sexual abuse. The court held that local authorities:

> 'had a high duty in law, not only on grounds of general fairness but also in the direct interests of a child whose welfare they served, to be open in the disclosure of all relevant material affecting that child in their possession or power (excluding documents protected on established grounds of public immunity) which might be of assistance to the natural parent or parents in rebutting charges against one or both of them of in any way ill-treating the child'.

[1] [1990] 2 QB 71, [1990] 2 All ER 129, [1990] 1 FLR 330.

11.61 Charles J subsequently observed in *Re R (Care: Disclosure: Nature of Proceedings)*[1] that 'there seems to be a general reluctance of many involved in family proceedings to disclose documents'. He noted that this was often 'incorrectly based on views relating to confidentiality and an assertion that records of the local authority are subject to public interest immunity'. He suggested that 'local authorities and guardians should be more willing than they seem to be to exhibit their notes of relevant conversations and incidents that are relied on for findings'. As he noted this is the practice which was formerly adopted by the Official Solicitor.

¹   [2002] 1 FLR 755 per Charles J.

2. Exceptions to the general duty – the local authority

(a) Public interest immunity

11.62 Evidence can be excluded from proceedings if the public interest requires it to be excluded. This is known as 'public interest immunity'. ¹ The categories of public interest immunity are not closed² and public interest immunity is unlikely to attach to material simply because it belongs to a class of documents. ³ Each claim for public interest immunity must therefore be considered by reference to the individual documents themselves.⁴ If records appear to be protected by public interest immunity, the local authority should draw the existence of the document to the attention of the other parties, so that they can apply for it to be disclosed.⁵ This is so even where the document in question is detrimental to the local authority's case.⁶ The difficulty is that the authorities do not state explicitly which records attract immunity. It would appear that the public interest immunity is based on the duty owed to children that what they say in confidence will not be disclosed without good reason. Ultimately the question of disclosure is a matter for the court. A child should not be given an undertaking that what they say will remain confidential.⁷

¹   See *D v NSPCC* [1978] AC 171, HL a case which applied to immunity from disclosure of the identity of informants.
²   *D v NSPCC* [1978] AC 178, HL.
³   *R v Chief Constable of West Midlands Police, ex p Wiley; R v Chief Constable of Nottinghamshire Police, ex p Sunderland* [1995] 1 AC 274, [1994] 3 All ER 420, HL. In *Re R (Care: Disclosure: Nature of Proceedings)* [2002] 1 FLR 755 Charles J commented that any case on public interest immunity prior to *Wiley* in 1995 should be regarded with caution and carefully reconsidered.
⁴   *R v Chief Constable of West Midlands Police, ex p Wiley; R v Chief Constable of Nottinghamshire Police, ex p Sunderland* above.
⁵   *Re C (Expert Evidence: Disclosure: Practice)* [1995] 1 FLR 204.
⁶   *Re R (Care: Disclosure: Nature of Proceedings)* [2002] 1 FLR 755.
⁷   *Re G (Minors) (Welfare Report: Disclosure)* [1993] 2 FLR 293, CA.

11.63 As a matter of practice non-disclosure of information by a professional to a parent and/or his legal advisors should only occur in exceptional cases and on the basis of the need not to disclose specific documents because of their contents rather than because of the type or class of document.¹ This is consistent with the Data Protection Act 1998, under which a parent is entitled to disclosure of records relating to their child unless disclosure would be likely to cause serious harm.²

¹   *R v Chief Constable of West Midlands Police, ex p Wiley; R v Chief Constable of Nottinghamshire Police, ex p Sunderland* [1995] 1 AC 274.
²   An individual is entitled to have communicated to him in an intelligible form personal data of which that individual is the data subject: Data Protection Act 1998, s 7. The Information Commissioner takes the view that an individual can exercise parental

responsibility in relation to his child in this regard. Data is exempt from disclosure if the supply of the information to the data subject would be likely to cause serious harm to his or any other person's physical or mental health or condition: Data Protection (Subject Access Modification) (Social Work) Order 2000, SI 2000/415. See also the Data Protection (Subject Access Modification) (Health) Order 2000, SI 2000/413 and the Data Protection (Subject Access Modification) (Education) Order 2000, SI 2000/414 for similar provisions.

11.64 The child's interests must be balanced against the principle of justice that parties are entitled to know the evidence in the case.[1] Article 6 of the European Convention on Human Rights requires that each party must be afforded an equal opportunity to present his case, including his evidence, under conditions that do not place him at a substantial disadvantage. This includes the right to the disclosure of relevant documents.[2] The fair trial guaranteed by art 6 is not confined to the 'purely judicial' part of the proceedings but extends prior to and subsequent to the proceedings themselves.[3] Article 8 affords procedural safeguards against inappropriate interference with the substantive rights protected by that Article which safeguards also arguably compel proper disclosure of documents relevant to the issue and/or proceedings in question.[4] Although the right to a fair trial under art 6 is absolute, that does not mean that there is an absolute and unqualified right to see all the documents. This is because:

(a)   The right to a fair hearing pursuant to art 6 is an unqualified right but the several ancillary rights under that Article are not themselves unqualified, including the right to disclosure of relevant evidence. In *R v H*[5] the House of Lords noted:

> 'In such circumstances some derogation from the golden rule of full disclosure may be justified but such derogation must always be the minimum derogation necessary to protect the public interest in question and must never imperil the overall fairness of the trial.'

(b)   In relation to their confidential records, a person has a right to privacy within art 8, the interference in which is subject to the application by the court of the usual principles of legality, necessity and proportionality.[6]

(c)   Subsequent to the implementation of the Human Rights Act 1998, the interests of anyone whose art 6, 8 and 10 rights are engaged in the issue of disclosure, whether as a witness, party or victim, must be considered when determining whether disclosure of confidential documents should be withheld or made.[7] The interests of anyone who could demonstrate a right to family life under art 8 were capable of denying a litigant access to documents.[8]

Accordingly, whilst relevant to the balancing exercise the court must carry out when determining whether to order or withhold disclosure, the rights guaranteed by the European Convention are not definitive in themselves on the issue of whether confidential documents should be disclosed.

[1]   *Re M (Disclosure)* [1998] 2 FLR 1028, CA in which a guardian ad litem sought leave to withhold information from a mother and her legal advisers. The appropriate procedure in these cases is set out in *Re C (child cases: evidence and disclosure)* [1995] 2 FCR 97, [1997] 1 FLR 204.

11.64 *Evidence*

2   See *Feldbrugge v Netherlands* (1986) 8 EHRR 425; *McGinley and Egan v United Kingdom* (1998) 27 EHRR 1, ECtHR.
3   *Re L (Care: Assessment Fair Trial)* [2002] EWHC 1379 (Fam), [2002] 2 FLR 730; *Mantovanelli v France (Application 21497/93)* (1997) 24 EHRR 370, ECtHR.
4   *R (on the application of P) v Secretary of State for the Home Department; R (on the application of Q) v Secretary of State for the Home Department* [2001] EWCA Civ 1151, [2001] 2 FLR 1122.
5   [2004] UKHL 30, [2004] 2 AC 134 at [18].
6   See *R (on the application of B) v Stafford Combined Court* [2006] EWHC 1645 (Admin), [2007] 1 All ER 102.
7   *Re B (Disclosure to other Parties)* [2001] 2 FLR 1017.
8   *Re B (Disclosure to Other Parties)* [2001] 2 FLR 1017. This analysis was approved by the Court of Appeal in *Re X (Children) (Adoption Reports: Confidentiality)* [2002] EWCA Civ 828, [2002] 3 FCR 648, [2002] All ER (D) 489 (May).

11.65 A children's guardian has the right to examine and take copies of any records held by a local authority or authorised person which were compiled in connection with the making or proposed making of an application under the Act with respect to the child concerned.[1] Any copy shall be admissible as evidence of the matter referred to,[2] and that rule applies regardless of any enactment or rule of law which would prevent the record being admissible.[3] The local authority should draw to the attention of the guardian any concerns within its records. If in the course of inspecting records, the guardian found relevant records which had not been disclosed, he should invite disclosure by the local authority. The guardian cannot disclose documents covered by public interest immunity and should seek an order of the court if necessary.[4]

1   Section 41(1).
2   Section 41(2).
3   Section 41(3).
4   *Re C (Expert Evidence: Disclosure: Practice)* [1995] 1 FLR 204. In *Re R (Care Proceedings: Disclosure)* [2000] 2 FLR 751, CA, it was held that a children's guardian had the right to an area child protection committee report on the child's half-sibling. The court observed that where the contents of the report were sensitive the children's guardian should be very careful as to how they are disseminated.

11.66 Under the Civil Procedure Rules 1998 standard disclosure requires a party to disclose only: (a) the documents on which he relies; (b) the documents which adversely affect his own or another party's case or support his own case; and (c) documents which he is required to disclose by a relevant practice direction.[1] A person may apply, without notice, for an order permitting him to withhold disclosure of a document on the ground that disclosure would damage the public interest.[2] These rules do not apply to children's proceedings and the FPR 1991and FPC(CA 1989)R 1991 have no similar provision but the principles are helpful. A local authority taking care proceedings has a duty to disclose all relevant information which might assist parents to rebut allegations made against them, except that which is protected by public interest immunity. If records appear to be covered by public interest immunity, the local authority should draw the existence of the document to the other parties' attention, so that they can apply for it to be disclosed.[3]

1   CPR 31.6.
2   CPR 31.19.
3   *Re C (Expert Evidence: Disclosure: Practice)* [1995] 1 FLR 204.

11.67 Where an application for disclosure is made the court must exercise its discretion by carrying out a balancing exercise between the public interest in protecting the confidentiality of social work records and the public interest in the fair administration of justice, so that a party may have access to information he requires to obtain legal redress.[1] The party seeking disclosure must establish that production of the documents, otherwise covered by public interest immunity, is necessary (ie that they are relevant, material and admissible) as containing material of real importance to him.[2] The court may inspect the documents in order to decide whether to order disclosure.[3] In cases relating to children, the following principles will apply:[4]

(a) General discovery of documents is an inappropriate procedure for children's cases, however the court retains the power to order specific discovery.

(b) Social work records (including child protection case conference minutes) are subject to the principle of public interest immunity, which is justified by the particular circumstances of the welfare of children.

(c) There is no absolute rule against disclosure.

(d) It may be necessary in some cases, for the benefit of the child concerned, for the local authority to volunteer disclosure of certain records. In such cases the leave of the court is not required to sanction such disclosure.

(e) The previous blanket immunity from production in wardship cases is no longer appropriate. The court must balance each request for disclosure, in order to decide whether the public interest in protecting social work records overrides the public interest that a party to proceedings should obtain the information in order to obtain legal redress.

(f) Unless the documents are likely to be of real importance to the party seeking disclosure, they should not be disclosed.[5]

(g) It is for the person seeking disclosure to demonstrate the need for the documents to be produced.

[1] *Re B (disclosure to Other Parties)* [2001] 2 FLR 1017; *R (on the application of Stevens) v Plymouth City Council* [2002] EWCA Civ 388, [2002] 1 FLR 1177.

[2] *Re M (A Minor) (Disclosure of Material)* [1990] 2 FLR 36. In *Re R (Care Disclosure: Nature of Proceedings)* [2002] 1 FLR 755, Charles J commented that this decision should now be treated with caution and held that the previous view that social services records are a class of document covered by public interest immunity is no longer good law. Subject to this need for caution, *Re M* remains the leading Court of Appeal authority on disclosure in cases relating to children.

[3] Rather than reading the files, the court can accept the assurances of 'an independent competent member of the Bar that the documents requested are irrelevant' (*R v W(G); R v W(E)* [1996] Crim LR 904, CA).

[4] *Re M (A Minor) (Disclosure of Material)* [1990] 2 FLR 36. Subject to the need for caution expressed in *Re R* above, *Re M* is still the leading Court of Appeal authority on disclosure in cases relating to children.

[5] The appropriate test in this regard is to ask whether the documents are necessary for the fair disposal of the proceedings. This question should be asked as a preliminary question in respect of each document in respect of which disclosure is sought (*Re R (Care: Disclosure: Nature of Proceedings)* [2002] 1 FLR 755).

11.68 While issues of public interest immunity in children's cases will usually relate to local authority records,[1] the issue may also apply to documents in the

11.68 *Evidence*

possession of the police or Crown Prosecution Service,[2] for example as a result of sharing of information under child protection procedures. Disclosure of confidential adoption records raises separate considerations.[3]

[1] Detailed guidance as to the principles of confidentiality applicable to social services records is available. These principles are set out in Local Authority Circular (88)17 (as continued by LASSL (92)9)). This guidance is issued under the Local Authority Social Services Act 1970, s 7 and therefore has statutory force.
[2] *Nottinghamshire County Council v H* [1995] 1 FLR 115.
[3] *Re K (Adoption: Disclosure of Information)* [1997] 2 FLR 74.

11.69 Guidance as to the procedure where documents may be subject to public interest immunity is set out in *Re C (Expert Evidence: Disclosure: Practice):*[1]

'It is the responsibility of the local authority actively to consider what documents they have in their possession which are or may be relevant to the issues as they affect the child, its family and any other person who is relevant in regard to an allegation of significant harm, and to the care and upbringing of the child in the context of the welfare check-list issues. The local authority should not content themselves with disclosing the documents which support their case, but must consider themselves under a duty to disclose in the interests of the child and of justice documents which may modify or cast doubt on their case. The particular concern should relate to those documents which actually help the case of an opposing party. If there is any doubt about whether the information is relevant, consideration should be given to notifying the affected parties of the existence of the material. Whilst the temptation to invite costly, intrusive and pointless fishing expeditions should be avoided, there should be a presumption in favour of disclosure of potentially helpful information. If documents are obviously relevant and not protected from disclosure by public interest immunity, then the local authority should initiate disclosure. The parties should endeavour to agree some sensible arrangement for the costs incurred in photocopying of documents.

If documents are apparently relevant but appear to be protected by public interest immunity from disclosure, a letter should be written by the local authority to the parties' legal advisers and to the guardian drawing general attention to the existence of the documents and inviting an application to the court if disclosure of the relevant documents is required.

In all cases it is particularly important that the local authority should draw the guardian ad litem's attention to any matters of concern within the documents. Whilst it is the court's task to decide any contested disclosure matter, the guardian ad litem's full knowledge of the material may enable him to assist the court as to its relevance.'

[1] [1995] 1 FLR 204.

11.70 In *Re D (Minors)(Adoption Reports: Confidentiality)* the court noted that:

'It is a fundamental principle of fairness that a party is entitled to the disclosure of all materials which may be taken into account by the court when reaching a decision adverse to that party.'[1]

[1] *Re D (Minors) (Adoption Reports: Confidentiality)* [1996] AC 593, [1996] 1 FCR 205.

(b) Real harm

11.71 Although evidence filed in proceedings relating to children should normally be disclosed to the parties, the court has a long-established power to withhold evidence from a party in exceptional cases.[1] In *Re M (A Minor) (Disclosure of Evidence)*[2] the Court of Appeal held that the test is whether real harm to the child would ensue. In *Re D (Minors)(Adoption Reports: Confidentiality)*[3] Lord Mustill said there must be a strong presumption in favour of disclosure on the grounds of natural justice before describing the process the court should follow:

> '... the Court should first consider whether disclosure of the material would involve a real possibility of significant harm to the child. If it would, the court should next consider whether the overall interests of the child would benefit from non-disclosure, weighing on the one hand the interest of the child in having material properly tested, and on the other both the magnitude of the risk that harm will occur and the gravity of the harm if it does occur. If the Court is satisfied that the interests of the child point towards non-disclosure, the next and final step is for the Court to weigh that consideration, and its strength in the circumstances of the case, against the interest of the parent or other party in having an opportunity to see and respond to the material. In the latter regard the court should take into account the importance of the material to the issues in the case. Non-disclosure should be the exception not the rule. The Court should be rigorous in the examination of the risk and gravity of the feared harm to the child and should order non-disclosure only when the case for doing so is compelling.'

The court may, if in the interests of the child, prevent the disclosure to the parents and others, reports of the child's statements.[4] In *Re B (Disclosure to Other Parties)*[5] it was held that although under art 6 a litigant was prima facie entitled to disclosure of all materials which might be taken into account by the court, the rights of other parties to the proceedings, including children, had to be afforded due respect. Non-disclosure had to be limited to what the situation demanded. The court had to be rigorous in its examination of the feared harm.

[1] *Official Solicitor v K* [1965] AC 201, applied in *Re B (A Minor) (Disclosure of Evidence)* [1993] Fam 142, [1993] 1 All ER 931, CA and *Re C (A Minor) (Irregularity of Practice)* [1991] 2 FLR 438.
[2] [1994] 1 FLR 760.
[3] [1996] AC 593.
[4] *B v B (Child Abuse: Evidence)* [1991] 2 FLR 487.
[5] [2001] 2 FLR 1017.

3. Exceptions to the general duty – the parents

11.72 Material held by or on behalf of parents may come within a number of categories:

(a) reports prepared on their behalf with or without the permission of the court and whether specifically for the purpose of children's or other proceedings;

(b) communications between client and solicitor;

(c)   statements or admissions made by parents in the course of investigations for the purposes of the proceedings in respect of themselves or others; and

(d)   material acquired by the solicitor in the course of representation of the client.

11.73 The duty of full and frank disclosure applies to all parties and their legal adviser, but consideration has to be given as to the extent this applies to parents in relation to whether:

(a)   disclosure can and should be ordered by the court for the purposes of children's proceedings; and

(b)   disclosure can and should be ordered to a third party for other purposes, such as criminal proceedings.

11.74 The extent of the duty of the parents or their advisers to disclose material in their possession has been the subject of much litigation. It was held in *Barking and Dagenham London Borough Council v O*[1] that parties could only be required to disclose reports on which they were intending to rely. Subsequently it was held in *Essex County Council v R (Legal Professional Privilege)*[2] that legal representatives having reports relevant to the determination of a matter concerning children, but contrary to the interests of their client, had a positive duty to disclose the reports to all the parties and to the courts. In *Oxfordshire County Council v M*[3] the Court of Appeal approved the *Essex* decision, but the case concerned the disclosure of experts' reports obtained in care proceedings. That left open the question of reports in the parties' possession not obtained with the leave of the court or for the purpose of other proceedings. In *Vernon v Bosley (No 2)*[4] Thorpe LJ confirmed his approach when he stated: 'The court's inquiry cannot be deflected, inhibited or disadvantaged by litigation privilege.'

[1] *Barking and Dagenham London Borough Council v O* [1993] Fam 295, [1993] 4 All ER 59, [1993] 2 FLR 651.

[2] *Essex County Council v R* [1994] Fam 167n, [1993] 2 FLR 826, sub nom *Re R (a minor) (disclosure of privileged material)* [1993] 4 All ER 702.

[3] [1994] Fam 151, [1994] 2 All ER 269, [1994] 1 FLR 175.

[4] [1999] QB 18, CA.

11.75 In *R v Derby Magistrates' Court, ex p B*[1] the House of Lords, considering the privilege attaching to communications between solicitor and client, held that 'no exception should be allowed to the absolute nature of legal professional privilege once established'. In *Re L (a Minor) (Police investigation: Privilege)*[2] the House of Lords held by a majority that there was a distinction between legal professional privilege attaching to communications between solicitor and client and that attaching to reports by third parties prepared on the instructions of a client for the purposes of litigation and upheld their disclosure. The European Court of Human Rights upheld[3] the House of Lords decision in *Re L* by ruling inadmissible a claim that the requirement to disclose an adverse medical report in Children Act proceedings was a breach of art 6 of the Convention (right to a fair trial).

[1] [1996] AC 487, [1995] 4 All ER 526, HL.

2   [1997] AC 16, [1996] 2 All ER 78, HL.
3   *L v United Kingdom (disclosure of expert evidence)* [2000] 2 FCR 145, ECtHR.

11.76 In *S County Council v B*[1] Charles J, in a detailed analysis, considered the potential conflict between the principles in *Re L* and the *Derby Magistrates' Court* case. He considered that the *Derby* case applied both to privilege between solicitor and client, and to communications with third parties for the purposes of litigation, the latter known as 'litigation privilege'. He interpreted *Re L* as a case in which litigation privilege never arose. He defined the ratio of the case as follows:

> 'In proceedings under Pt IV of the CA 1989 where the welfare of children is paramount and thus the proceedings are essentially non-adversarial, legal professional privilege does not arise in respect of the reports of an expert based on the papers disclosed in the proceedings and which the court has given leave to a party to disclose to that expert.'

Accordingly he held that the absolute right to legal professional privilege meant that a father, who had instructed different medical experts in criminal proceedings from those in the care proceedings, could refuse and should not be ordered to disclose any communications with, and the reports of, those medical experts, nor even to disclose the names of the experts he instructed for the purpose of the criminal proceedings.

1   [2000] 1 FCR 536, [2000] 2 FLR 161, FD. Charles J regarded the observations of Thorpe LJ in *Vernon v Bosley*, cited in para 11.57, as obiter. For consideration of this problem see Power E 'Legal Professional Privilege in Children Act Cases' [2002] Fam Law 465.

11.77 Threats of criminal acts do not come within the scope of legal professional privilege.[1] An affidavit sworn by a husband's former solicitors in support of their application to be removed from the record could be used by the wife in proceedings relating to the welfare of the child, even though the affidavit had been sent to the solicitors inadvertently, because it showed the husband had made grossly indecent, obscene and menacing statements in telephone calls to his solicitors.

1   *C v C (evidence: privilege)* [2001] EWCA Civ 469, [2001] 1 FCR 756, [2001] 2 FLR 184.

11.78 In practice it may be academic whether the court can order disclosure. An expert who had provided a report could be subpoenaed, provided his identity was known, and would be in difficulty declining to answer questions. If a party knows of the existence of reports, it is unlikely that the other will decline to produce them, if parenting competence is in question. If reports are withheld, the court may draw its own conclusions. The difficulty arises where documents are in the possession of solicitors, unknown to other parties. Thorpe J gave a clear view in the Essex case[1] that the duty to the child overrode professional confidence.[2] In *S County Council v B* Charles J expressed the view that this was limited to those reports which had been prepared for proceedings relating to the child. For practitioners there remains uncertainty. It is suggested that this can only be resolved by recourse to the principles set out below.[3]

1   *Essex County Council v R* [1994] Fam 167n, [1993] 2 FLR 826, sub nom *Re R (a minor) (disclosure of privileged material)* [1993] 4 All ER 702.
2   See also *Re DH (A Minor)* [1994] 1 FLR 679; *Re A and B (Minors) (No 2)* [1995] 1 FLR 351 and *Oxfordshire County Council v P* ['995] Fam 161, [1995] 1 FLR 552.
3   See para 11.82.

4. Court ordered disclosure for other proceedings

11.79 There have been similar difficulties in settling the issue of whether material which might be useful for purposes other than the care proceedings should be disclosed. This can arise in two ways, either through material which has been filed in the children proceedings, or through statements which might be made if the parents could be confident that they would not be disclosed, for example to the police for the purposes of investigation of an alleged crime. There is now one relevant statutory provision.

11.80 Rule 4.23 of the FPR 1991 and replaced by r 10.20A.[1] Rule 23 of the FPC(CA 1989)R 1991 remains in force but has been supplemented by r 23A. The purpose of these rules is now to balance the need to ensure confidentiality so that no improper disclosure of documents is made to a third party and to make easier the proper disclosure of documents to third parties where such disclosure is beneficial.

1   See para 4.47.

11.81 FPR1991, r 10.20A applies to proceedings brought under the 1989 Act, proceedings under the inherent jurisdiction of the High Court in respect of minors and proceedings which relate wholly or mainly to the maintenance or upbringing of a minor.[1] The rule provides that, for the purposes of the law relating to contempt of court, information relating to proceedings (whether or not contained within a document filed with the court) may be communicated where the court gives leave, where the court directs in accordance with the provisions of the rule or to certain specified persons including parties, legal representatives, CAFCASS and experts whose instruction by a party has been authorised by the court.[2] In addition, rule 10.20A contains a table which provides for the disclosure by specified persons of specified information to specified persons for a specified purpose.[3] For example, a party may disclose without leave any information relating to the proceedings to a spouse, civil partner, co-habitant or close family member for the purpose of confidential discussions enabling the party to receive support. To take a further example, a party may disclose without leave to a police officer the text or summary of judgment for the purpose of a criminal investigation.

1   FPR 1991, r 10.20A(1).
2   FPR 1991, r 10.20A(2).
3   FPR 1991, r 10.20A(3).

11.82 It is important when considering whether disclosure without leave is permitted under the FPR 1991, r 10.20A to have regard to the definitions provided by the rule as these act to extend further the provisions for disclosure without leave.[1] For example, whilst a party may disclose to a police officer without leave the text or summary of judgment for the purpose of a criminal investigation, if that police officer is serving in a child protection or paedophile unit he is a professional acting in furtherance of the protection of children[2] and entitled to much wider disclosure encompassing any information relating to the proceedings.[3]

1   FPR 1991, r 10.20(5).
2   FPR 1991, r 10.20A(5).
3   FPR 1991, r 10.20A(2)(c)(viii). See also *A Local Authority v D (Chief Constable of Thames Valley Police Intervening)*; *Re D* [2006] 2 FLR 1053 although care must be taken with this authority as Sumner J's conclusion in *Re D* that it is only in 'exceptional circumstances' that disclosure should not be ordered under r 10.20A(2)(a) is per incuriam and probably not correct. See below para 11.81.

11.83 In the family proceedings court, FPC(CA 1989)R 1991, r 23 continues to impose confidentiality on the parties so that no disclosure of documents is made to a third party without the leave of the court.[1] This the extent to which confidentiality is imposed is circumscribed by the specific provisions of r 23[2] and the provisions of r 23A, which mirror those of r 10.20A in the FPR 1991.

1   FPC(CA 1989)R 1991, r 23(1).
2   FPC(CA 1989)R 1991, r 23(2), (3) and (4).

11.84 FPR 1991, r 10.20A and the FPC(CA 1989)R 1991, r 23A[1] do not permit disclosure of information to the media.[2] Any disclosure issues that are not covered by these rules still require the determination of the court.[3]

1   See para 4.47.
2   For guidance on the provisions governing disclosure to the media in respect of proceedings relating to children see *Clarke Hall and Morrison on Children*, paras 1[1373] ff.
3   See for example *Re L (Care Proceedings: Disclosure to Third Party)* [2000] 1 FLR 913: disclosure of the court's judgment, expert medical reports and minutes of the experts' meetings, was allowed to the UK Central Council for Nursing, Midwifery and Health Visiting where the mother was a nurse who had been deprived of caring for her own child. The court may attach conditions to an order for disclosure: *A Health Authority v X* [2001] EWCA Civ 2014, [2002] 1 FLR 1045.

11.85 In any proceedings under Pts IV or V of the CA 1989, no person shall be excused from giving evidence on any matter or answering any question put to him in the course of his giving evidence, on the ground that doing so might incriminate him or his spouse of an offence.[1] A statement or admission made in such proceedings shall not be admissible in evidence against the person making it or his spouse in proceedings for an offence other than perjury.[2] This section was intended to protect parents against incriminating themselves or their spouses when giving evidence in civil proceedings, so as to encourage them to be truthful, without exposing themselves to prosecution.

1   Section 98(1).
2   Section 98(2).

11.86 In *Oxfordshire County Council v P*[1] Ward J held that statements made to a guardian ad litem in the course of her enquiries come within the term 'statement or admission' in s 98 and should not be disclosed to the police without the leave of the court. He suggested that:

'a practice could quickly be developed permitting the free exchange of information between the social services and police on a basis that the information was treated by the police as confidential and might be used for investigation but not as evidence in any criminal proceedings which might follow, and if the police wished to use as evidence information arising in care proceedings they must seek the court's leave'.

The provisions of s 98(2) also extend to any statement or admission given by parents to an expert witness.[2]

¹ [1995] 1 FLR 552.
² *Re AB (Care Proceedings: Disclosure of Medical Evidence to Police)* [2002] EWHC 2198 (Fam), [2003] 1 FLR 579 in which Wall J held that statements made to experts were analogous to statements made to the children's guardian and accordingly came within the protection of s 98(2).

11.87 In *Cleveland County Council v F*[1] Hale J held that this approach should extend to statements made to social workers in the course of their investigations. She expressed the hope that this afforded parents protection and an incentive to co-operate with the investigation and assessment in the interests of the children. If the parents were married, the protection extended to the spouse (or civil partner by virtue of the Civil Partnership Act 2004, s 261(1), Sch 27, para 132). In the Cleveland case they were not and the mother sought an order of the court that any statement she might make should be protected from disclosure.

¹ [1995] 2 All ER 236. See also *Re G (minor) (social worker: disclosure)* [1996] 2 All ER 65, [1996] 1 FLR 276, CA.

11.88 In *Re L (A Minor) (Police investigation: Privilege)*[1] the House of Lords considered s 98. It was said that the court should not make an order for disclosure, compliance with which was likely to involve the danger of self-incrimination. On the other hand it was also said that it would be most unsatisfactory if the court had information that a mother might have a committed a serious offence against a child but was disabled from disclosing such information to an investigating authority.

¹ [1997] AC 16, [1996] 2 All ER 78, HL.

11.89 The Court of Appeal has since held[1] that s 98(2) only gave protection against statements being admissible evidence in criminal proceedings (unless for perjury). This did not cover a police enquiry into the commission of an offence. Nothing in the subsection detracted from the power of the judge to order disclosure of any part of the proceedings in appropriate circumstances, including material covered by s 98(2). The judge should consider:

(a)   the welfare and interest of the child concerned and of other children generally;
(b)   the maintenance of confidentiality in children's cases and the importance of encouraging frankness;
(c)   the public interest in the administration of justice and the prosecution of serious crime;
(d)   the gravity of the alleged offence and the relevance of the evidence to it;

(e)   the desirability of co-operation between the various agencies concerned with the welfare of children;

(f)   fairness to the person who had incriminated himself and any others affected by the incriminating statement; and

(g)   any other material disclosure which had taken place.

¹   *Re C (A Minor) (Care Proceedings: Disclosure)* [1997] Fam 76, sub nom *Re EC (disclosure of material)* [1996] 2 FLR 725. *See also Oxfordshire County Council v L and F* [1997] 1 FLR 235; *Re B (Hearing in Open Court)* noted at [1997] Fam Law Brief 508 where Hale J refused the application of the Crown Prosecution Service that a case should be heard in open court, so that the police could hear the evidence to enable the prosecution to consider more fully the criminal case against the father; and *Re L (Care: Confidentiality)* [1999] 1 FLR 165 where Johnson J commented that the protection provided by s 98(2) could not be absolute and might offend against the requirements of a fair trial under art 6 of the European Convention on Human Rights. See *Re W (Minors) (Social Workers: Disclosure)* 1999] 1 WLR 205, [1998] 2 FCR 405, CA, where leave was given for the police to have a copy of an assessment report from child protection investigations which had been filed with the court and *Re M (disclosure: police investigation)* [2002] 1 FCR 655, [2001] 2 FLR 1316 for a case in which the court decided that the balance was tipped against disclosure of incriminating statements made by the mother in the course of care proceedings.

11.90 If the police want disclosure of potentially incriminating statements, they have to apply to the court hearing the care proceedings. The court will then have to carry out the exercise of balancing competing public interests to ensure that justice is served in the circumstances of the particular case. In *Re D (Minors)(Wardship: Disclosure)*¹ held that:

> 'The principle is quite clear, and that is that the judge hearing an application for leave to disclose such documents must in the exercise of his discretion conduct a balancing exercise – that is to say, he has to balance the importance of confidentiality in wardship proceedings and the frankness which it engenders in those who give evidence to the wardship court against the public interest in seeing that the ends of justice are properly served.'

This discretion is an unfettered discretion² and is of equal application to CA 1989 proceedings.³ There is accordingly no presumption for or against disclosure and each application for such disclosure must be decided on its own merits by conducting the required balancing exercise.⁴

¹   [1994] 1 FLR 346.
²   See *Re F (Wards)* [1989] 1 FLR 39 at 44H per Sir Stephen Brown P.
³   *Kent County Council v K* [1994] 1 WLR 912.
⁴   *Re AB (Care Proceedings: Disclosure of Medical Evidence to the Police)* [2002] EWHC 2198 (Fam), [2003] 1 FLR 579. It is suggested that the later case of *A Local Authority v D (Chief Constable of Thames Valley Police Intervening); Re D* [2006] 2 FLR 1053 in which Sumner J cam to the conclusion that it is only in 'exceptional circumstances' that disclosure should not be ordered under r 10.20A(2)(a) cannot be correct as this would operate to place the burden of proof onto the person resisting disclosure and severely, and improperly, restrict the exercise of the Court's unfettered discretion.

11.91 In *Re AB (Care Proceedings: Disclosure of Medical Evidence to the Police)*¹ Wall J observed:

> 'Depending on the seriousness of the abuse, and the practicability of rehabilitation, the court is more likely to refuse an application for disclosure to the police in a case involving child abuse where there is a frank acknowledgement of responsibility by the abusing parent. This is often perceived as a vitally

important first step towards rehabilitation between parent and child, particularly when coupled with a recognition of the harm caused and a genuine desire
for help to avoid repetition.'

Wall J continued:

'... a frank acknowledgement of the way in which they have treated their
children is a vitally important first step towards rehabilitation. Secondly, if
parents acknowledge the harm they have done and genuinely want help in
ensuring that there is no repetition in the future, rehabilitation is likely to be in
the children's interests, and the courts will do their best to facilitate it. In such
cases, and dependent upon the gravity of the injuries, the court may well
conclude, as Miss Elizabeth Lawson QC did in *Re M*[2], that the public interest
in encouraging frankness has greater weight than the public interest in the
prosecution of serious crime, and any application for permission to disclose the
papers to the police may be refused.'

[1]   [2002] EWHC 2198 (Fam), [2003] 1 FLR 579.
[2]   *Re M (Care Proceedings: Disclosure: Human Rights)* [2001] 2 FLR 1316.

11.92 Within the context of cases in which parents are contemplating
acknowledging an accidental injury, an order for disclosure can act as
significant additional deterrent to frankness. It places the parents in the
invidious position of choosing between (a) an admission that may allow the
children to return to their care but place them at risk of prosecution and (b)
maintaining a silence which will protect them from prosecution but prevent
the rehabilitation of the children. It is generally not in the public interests for
barriers to be erected between one branch of the judicature and another
because this may be inimical to the overall interests of justice. However, such
barriers may be justified where not to erect them would cause the function of
family jurisdiction to ensure children are cared for by their parents where it is
in their best interests to be effectively defeated by the function of the criminal
jurisdiction. It must be recognised that the aims and functions of agencies
involved in child protection may on occasion conflict to the potential
detriment of the children concerned. Where parents frankly acknowledge their
culpability and demonstrate a willingness to address outstanding risks, the aim
of the local authority to promote the rehabilitation of the children to the care
of their parents may be in direct conflict with the aim of the Police and Crown
Prosecution Service to prosecute those parents. In these circumstances, an
order for disclosure has the potential to achieve the opposite outcome to that
which the local authority is seeking to promote. In such circumstances, the
refusal of an order which in ordinary circumstances protects the public
interest in the prosecution of crime may be acceptable having regard to the
welfare of the children. [1]

[1]   See *Re AB (Care Proceedings: Disclosure of Medical Evidence to the Police)* [2002] EWHC
2198 (Fam), [2003] 1 FLR 579.

5. Disclosure where there are no proceedings

11.93 *Working Together* comments:

'For those children who are suffering, or at risk of suffering, significant harm, joint working is essential, to safeguard and promote welfare of the child(ren) and, where necessary, to help bring to justice the perpetrators of crimes against children. All agencies and professionals should ... share and help to analyse information so that an assessment can be made of the child's needs and circumstances.'[2]

The previous edition of *Working Together*[1] stipulated that disclosure should be appropriate for the purpose and only to the extent necessary to achieve that purpose.[3] In child protection work the degree of confidentiality will be governed by the need to protect the child.[4] Social workers and others working with a child and family must make clear to those providing information that confidentiality may not be maintained if the withholding of the information will prejudice the welfare of a child. *Working Together* recommends information sharing protocols,[5] while requiring regard for the law.[6]

[1] Working Together (2006) para 1.16.
[2] The Stationary Office, 1999.
[3] See para 7.36.
[4] See paras 7.22 and 7.23.
[5] See para 7.31 and Appendix 4 of Working Together.
[6] In *Re W (Minors) (Social Workers: Disclosure)* [1999] 1 WLR 205, [1999] 2 FCR 405, CA, it was pointed out that notes and preparatory documents in child protection investigations, while covered by confidentiality, could be shared with the police as part of the co-operation required by Working Together but the court's leave was required for an assessment report filed with the court.

11.94 All the professional bodies have published guidance on the disclosure of confidential information, which in general terms provide for disclosure only where the person to whom the confidence is owed has given consent to disclosure or there is an order of the court or there is an overriding need for disclosure in the public interest, which includes the prevention of child abuse.[1]

[1] See for example Confidentiality (1995) General Medical Council, and Guidelines for Professional Practice (United Kingdom Central Council for Nursing, Midwifery and Health Visiting, 1996). See also Child Protection: Medical Responsibilities (1994) HMSO; and see *Re A (a minor) (disclosure of medical records to the General Medical Council)* [1999] 1 FCR 30.

11.95 In spite of the general principle that information should be shared to protect children, the Court of Appeal has held that a local authority has no duty to disclose to another local authority the name of a person found in care proceedings to have abused a child, and accordingly his address would not be disclosed by the court.[1]

[1] *Re V (Sexual Abuse: Disclosure)*; *Re L (Sexual Abuse: Disclosure)* [1999] 1 FLR 267.

11.96 Records of allegations of abuse held by the police and/or a local authority may be subsequently disclosed where it was genuinely and reasonably believed that this was necessary to protect children.[1] Such disclosure should only take place if there was 'a pressing need' for it, having taken into account relevant considerations of the authority's belief as to the truth of the allegations, the interest of the third party in obtaining the information, and the degree of risk posed if the information is not disclosed.[2] Principles on disclosure of such sensitive information are established by the Data Protection (Processing of Sensitive Personal Data) Order 2000.[3]

[1]   *R v Local Authority in the Midlands, ex p LM* [2000] 1 FCR 736,[2000] 1 FLR 612, QBD; following *R v Chief Constable of North Wales Police, ex p AB* [1998] 3 FCR 371 and *Woolgar v Chief Constable of the Sussex Police* [1999] 3 All ER 604. See also *Re C (sexual abuse: disclosure)* [2002] EWCH 234 (Fam), [2002] 2 FCR 385.
[2]   *R (n the application of A) v Chief Constables of C and D, ex p A* [2001] 2 FCR 431, where it was held that the police were justified in passing information to another police force about their investigation of alleged sexual offences by a schoolteacher, even though he was not prosecuted. A duty of care is still owed to the suspected abuser as well as the child: *L v Reading Borough Council* [2001] EWCA Civ 346, [2001] 1 FCR 673.
[3]   SI 2000/417.

6. Disclosure by solicitors

Duties

11.97 Guidance has been given by the Law Society on cases where a solicitor receives information from a client which is or might be privileged, but which if revealed might protect a child from harm. The following guidance is also applicable to child abduction cases.

'General principles:
(1)   The Law Society committees take the view that child abduction is merely one example of child abuse and, therefore, any guidance given applies equally to cases of abuse and abduction.
(2)   A solicitor has two basic duties to a client, whether parent or child:

The duty to act in the client's best interests

Clearly, the nature of this duty depends on who the client is. In considering the duty to act in the client's best interests, the solicitor will need to draw a distinction between those children who are competent to give instructions and those who are not. A child who is competent to give instructions should be represented in accordance with those instructions. If a child is not competent to give instructions the solicitor should act in the child's best interests.

The duty of confidentiality

A number of preliminary points can be made before considering how the situation is affected by the question of who the client is:
(1)   Is the information confidential? It has been held at common law that when communications are made by a client to his or her solicitor before the commission of a crime, for the purpose of being guided or helped in the commission of it, this constitutes a move outside the solicitor/client relationship and any communications made are not confidential and the solicitor is free to pass them on to a third party. The solicitor will, therefore, need to consider whether or not the proposed action is in fact a crime and reference should be made to the appropriate provisions, for example the common law offence of kidnapping or the provisions of the CAA 1984 and the CACA 1985 and provisions relating to child abuse.[1]
(2)   Assuming that the information received is confidential, which will usually be the case, a solicitor also has a duty to the court (as opposed to the client). As a result, the solicitor may still be ordered by the court to disclose the information – for instance in a wardship case.[2] In all cases it is the solicitor's duty not to mislead the court.[3]

(3)   In circumstances other than those outlined above the committees are in favour of the principle of absolute confidentiality being maintained save in truly exceptional circumstances. Any solicitor considering the disclosure of confidential information, should bear in mind that he or she is bound by a duty of confidentiality and may only be entitled to depart from this duty in exceptional circumstances.

In considering what might constitute exceptional circumstances a solicitor must consider what would be in the public interest. There is a public interest in maintaining the duty of confidentiality. Without this, the public interest in being able to confide in professional advisers would be harmed and the duty of confidentiality would be brought into disrepute. There is also a public interest in protecting children at risk from serious harm. Only in cases where the solicitor believes that the public interest in protecting children at risk outweighs the public interest in maintaining the duty of confidentiality does the solicitor have a discretion to disclose confidential information.

(4)   If a solicitor, having considered the arguments set out above, feels that he or she may be entitled to disclose confidential information he or she should, in addition, consider the following points:

   (*a*)   is there any way of remedying the situation other than revealing the information? If so, thought should be given as to whether this course would have the desired effect of protecting the child and, if so, whether it should be taken;

   (*b*)   if the information is or is not disclosed, will the solicitor involved be able to justify his or her actions if called upon to do so by the court or Solicitors Complaints Bureau? Before revealing any information a junior solicitor or member of the solicitor's staff should always consult with his or her principal on the appropriate course of action to take.'

11.98

'Who is the client?

Five different situations have been considered:

An adult

(1)   An adult (parent or otherwise) who is not an abuser but is asserting that a third party is abusing a child. In this situation a solicitor's duty to act in the best interests of his client might entail suggesting that the client alerts a relevant agency, for example the police or a social services department, him or herself or accepting instructions to do so. If the client does not wish to alert a relevant agency or does not give the solicitor instructions to do so, the solicitor must accept the client's decision and may remain bound by the duty of confidentiality. A solicitor in this position should explain the legal position and can seek to persuade the client to disclose the abuse or allow the solicitor to do so. If the client refuses to follow either of these courses of action, the solicitor may still exercise his or her discretion and reveal the information. This will only be the case if the public interest in revealing the information outweighs that of keeping it confidential.

(2)   An adult who is abusing or whom the solicitor believes will abuse a child. Where the client is an abuser or potential abuser it becomes necessary to consider not only the duty to act in the client's best interests and the duty of confidentiality, but also whether or not any distinction

should be made between continuing and future abuse and how and when a solicitor should explain his duty of confidentiality and any possible limitations to it.

Where a client is continuing to commit an offence or is proposing to commit an offence, the duty to act in the client's best interests means that a solicitor should explain the legal implications of what a client has done, is doing or is proposing to do. For example, a client who tells a solicitor that he has or is proposing to abduct a child should be told about the common law offence of kidnapping, the provisions of the CAA 1984, the CACA 1985 and the client's duty to obey orders of the court, if there are any which are relevant. Similar steps should be taken in relation to cases of child abuse.

In the case of future abuse if, after receiving the solicitor's advice on the legal position, the client is dissuaded from his criminal course of action the solicitor's duty of confidentiality is absolute. In the case of a continuing offence, which as a result of the advice then ceases, this is equally the case.

In the case of a continuing crime which does not cease as a result of the advice given, or a future crime which the solicitor understands from the client may or will take place, the solicitor must then go on to consider whether or not it is justifiable to breach his or her duty of confidentiality bearing in mind the guidance set out above. In addition, it may be appropriate for the solicitor to point out that he or she has a discretion to inform a third party of the offence that is, will or may be committed.

(3)   An adult who has been abused or is being abused. As above, where the client is an adult who has been or is being abused, the duty to act in the client's best interests would entail outlining the legal position and suggesting where the client, or the solicitor on the client's behalf, could go for help. A solicitor in these circumstances is absolutely bound by the duty of confidentiality to the client but it is always permissible to try to persuade the client to reveal the abuse.

A child

The extent of a solicitor's potential entitlement to breach the duty of confidentiality will depend on whether the child is mature or immature. It will often be difficult for a solicitor to judge the maturity of a child and he or she will need to make a judgment on the basis of the child's understanding. Reference should be made to the principles in *Gillick v West Norfolk and Wisbech Area Health Authority and Department of Health and Social Security*[4] and the CA 1989. In difficult cases it may be appropriate for a solicitor to approach a third party with knowledge of the child and expertise in this area, for instance the guardian ad litem involved in the case (if any). A solicitor should never breach the duty of confidentiality unless he or she strongly suspects or knows that abuse has taken, is taking, or will take place.

(4)   A mature child who is being abused. Where a mature child is the client the guidance in (3) above applies except that a solicitor may have a discretion to breach the duty of confidentiality where he or she knows or strongly suspects that younger siblings are being abused or where the child is in fear of his or her life or of serious injury.

(5)   An immature child who is being abused. Where an immature child is the client, the solicitor's duty is as in (3) above in relation to doing the best for the client. A solicitor can try to persuade the client to reveal the abuse. If the client refuses, the solicitor is not absolutely bound by the duty of confidentiality and may feel, bearing the above arguments in mind, that he or she is entitled to disclose what the child has told him or her to a third party. This should only be done if it is in the public interest

and there is no other less oppressive method of dealing with the situation (such as a guardian ad litem disclosing the abuse).

Where the client is an immature child, the solicitor may need to consider whether or not he or she should reveal any disclosures to the child's parents. It may be that a disclosure of information to another third party, such as the police or a social services department, would best serve the interests of the client.'

1   This may be better described as a move outside the relationship of privilege: see, for example, *C v C (Evidence: Privilege)* [2001] EWCA Civ 469, [2001] 1 FCR 756, [2001] 2 FLR 184, at para 11.60.

2   *Ramsbottom v Senior* (1869) LR 8 Esq 575 (Rayden and Jackson on Divorce and Family Matters (17th edn) LexisNexis, para 42.22.

3   Chapter 14 of the Guide to the Professional Conduct of Solicitors.

4   [1986] AC 112, [1986] 1 FLR 224, HL.

11.99

'The decision to disclose and possible consequences

Any client, whether child or adult, has a right to be made aware of when and in what circumstances the solicitor's duty of confidentiality may be breached. The decision of when and how to tell the client of the solicitor's decision will clearly be a difficult one, although it is thought to be preferable to make the position clear during the first interview. This will present the solicitor with a dilemma – if he or she fails to disclose the abuse, he or she will not be in a position to help protect the child from further abuse. On the other hand, if the solicitor tells the child he or she may breach the duty of confidentiality, there is a risk that further disclosures will not be forthcoming from the child. Despite this, if a solicitor is about to breach his or her duty of confidentiality there is a high expectation that the solicitor will tell the client of his or her decision and explore with the client how this should be done. However, in the end it is for the solicitor to exercise his or her professional judgment about when and how to explain the duty of confidentiality to any client; it is impossible to formulate a rule that can be applied in all circumstances.

Any solicitor who tells the client that the solicitor will breach the duty of confidentiality should inform the client that he or she is entitled to terminate the solicitor's retainer if such disclosure is contrary to the client's wishes. However, it is almost inevitable that the breaching of the duty of confidentiality by the solicitor will cause the client to terminate the solicitor's retainer whether or not the client is informed by the solicitor of his or her intentions. Upon the termination of the retainer the duty of confidentiality still remains, subject to the solicitor being able to justify a breach of the duty in the exceptional circumstances referred to in *The duty of confidentiality* above.'

7. Conclusions on disclosure

11.100 The law on disclosure of information which could influence the future welfare of the child and for the purpose of proceedings is complex and intricate, especially in relation to disclosure by parents. The detailed analysis by Charles J in *S County Council v B,*[1] and his rationale of the leading House of Lords cases, the uncertainty of the application of the principles in *Re C (A Minor) (Care Proceedings: Disclosure)*[2] and the observations of Munby J in *Re B (Disclosure to Other Parties)*[3] and of Charles J in *Re R (Care:*

11.100 *Evidence*

Disclosure: Nature of Proceedings)[4] illustrate the difficulties. This disparate law and guidance leads directly to acute uncertainties both in agencies and individuals as to what is permissible and what is not. This in turn can compromise safeguarding and assessment by inhibiting data sharing to a child's detriment, can result in unwarranted intrusion into matters rightly confidential to children and parents and often results in delay. Whilst recent attempts have been made to simplify information sharing within the context of proceedings,[5] there remains a great deal of confusion amongst practitioners as to what information can be shared, what documents must be disclosed and the interface between confidentiality and child protection at the pre-proceedings stage.

1 [2000] 1 FCR 536, [2000] 2 FLR 161: see para 11.59.
2 [1997] Fam 76, [1996] 2 FLR 725: see para 11.68.
3 [2001] 2 FLR 1017. See para 11.53.
4 [2002] 1 FLR 755: see para 11.43.
5 FPR 1991, r 10.20A; FPC(CA 1989)R 1991, rr 23 and 23A.

11.101 It is debatable whether the original purpose of s 98 can be achieved and whether the protection now afforded by s 98 will encourage candour on the part of parents. Casual or unguarded statements made to the guardian or social worker, or indeed doctor, may be protected from use as evidence in a prosecution but still be used for investigation. Parents who fear a criminal prosecution are unlikely to make statements on the subtle basis that they could be used for investigation but not for evidence in criminal proceedings. A solicitor advising a parent would be failing in his duty not to advise of the risks in speaking to anyone, no matter what the purpose of the interview.[1]

1 The practice of legal advisers advising parents not to agree to be interviewed by experts or the children's guardian was expressly and strongly deprecated by Wall J in *Re AB (Care Proceedings: Disclosure of Medical Evidence to the Police)* [2002] EWHC 2198 (Fam), [2003] 1 FLR 579 although the learned judge did not consider it as professionally improper.

11.102 These uncertainties act to the detriment of the conduct of proceedings. The battleground lies between those who believe that, in order to ensure that the welfare of the child can be made paramount, the court should have access to all information which might be relevant to the future welfare of the child, and those who believe that the administration of justice and fairness to other parties requires that there are circumstances where they should be entitled to withhold information.

11.103 Charles J may well be correct when he says in *S County Council v B*[1] that the principles relating to privilege can only be changed by statute. Overall, this area of the law would benefit from a thorough and authoritative analysis, so that courts can concentrate on taking decisions about the welfare of the child rather than the way in which proceedings have to be conducted.

1 [2000] 1 FCR 536, [2000] 2 FLR 161.

Chapter 12

WARDSHIP AND THE HIGH COURT'S INHERENT JURISDICTION

INTRODUCTION

12.1 The principal provision under the CA 1989 governing the use of the High Court's inherent jurisdiction is s 100. That section is based on the premise that the High Court's inherent jurisdiction comprises both wardship in particular and the general or residual inherent jurisdiction.[1] Lord Mackay explained the thinking behind the provision when he commented in his Joseph Jackson Memorial Lecture:[2]

> 'In the Government's view, wardship is only one use of the High Court's inherent parens patriae jurisdiction. We believe therefore, it is open to the High Court to make orders under its inherent jurisdiction in respect of children other than through wardship'.

[1] As Parry: The Children Act 1989: Local Authorities, Wardship and the Revival of the Inherent Jurisdiction' [1992] JSWFL 212, 213 observes: 's 100 has the marginal heading for guidance, 'Restrictions on use of wardship jurisdiction,' whereas the substance of the section relates to the inherent jurisdiction as much as to wardship'. Note also the inclusion of the 'inherent jurisdiction' in the definition of 'family proceedings' in s 8(3) is intended to cover wardship as well.

[2] (1989) 139 NLJ 505 at 507. However, while the independent existence of the inherent jurisdiction was acknowledged under the pre-CA 1989 law, as Lowe and White *Wards of Court* (2nd edn, 1986) had put it (at 1–5), 'the general view seems to be taken that the inherent jurisdiction to protect children is not exclusively vested in the wardship jurisdiction but that that jurisdiction is a convenient machinery for administering it'. Note also Munby J's analysis in *A (A Patient) v A Health Authority; Re J; R (on the Application of S) v Secretary of the State for the Home Department* [2002] EWHC 18 (Fam/Admin), para 31, [2002] 1 FLR 845.

12.2 Although it has been said that the High Court's inherent jurisdiction is equally exercisable whether the child is or is not a ward of court[1] and that 'for all practicable purposes the jurisdiction in wardship and the inherent jurisdiction over children is one and the same',[2] wardship and the inherent jurisdiction are not synonymous. Unlike wardship, the exercise of the inherent jurisdiction does *not* place the child under the ultimate responsibility of the court. The inherent jurisdiction empowers the High Court to make orders dealing with particular aspects of the child's welfare whereas wardship additionally vests in the court both an immediate and a continuing supervisory function over the child.[3]

555

12.2 Wardship and the High Court's inherent jurisdiction

1   Per Lord Donaldson MR in *Re W (a Minor) (Medical Treatment: Court's Jurisdiction)* [1993] Fam 64 at 73F–G, [1992] 4 All ER 627 at 631d.
2   Per Ward LJ in *Re Z (A Minor) (Identification: Restrictions on Publication)* [1997] Fam 1 at 14, sub nom *Re Z (a minor) (Freedom of Publication)* [1995] 4 All ER 961 at 968.
3   Per Lord Donaldson MR in *Re W*, above. For detailed discussion of the wardship and inherent jurisdiction see Lowe and Douglas *Bromley's Family Law* (10th edn) ch 16.

12.3 The overall scheme under s 100 is that local authorities cannot use wardship as a means of obtaining a care order nor can they use the jurisdiction in respect of any child already in care. On the other hand, in appropriate cases, local authorities can invoke the High Court's general inherent jurisdiction to resolve specific issues concerning children provided there is no alternative statutory procedure and there is a likelihood of substantial harm to the child. There remain, however, some occasions when local authorities can still invoke wardship.

THE IMPACT OF THE 1989 ACT ON THE WARDSHIP JURISDICTION[1]

1. Public law

(a) No independent power to commit wards of court into care or supervision of a local authority

12.4 Before the 1989 Act, local authorities frequently looked to the wardship jurisdiction rather than to the then existing statutory scheme[2] as a means of having children committed into their care. The continued existence of such an alternative, however, ran counter to the philosophy of having a single route into care based on the s 31 threshold which had been carefully designed to provide the minimum circumstances justifying state intervention. Accordingly, s 100(1) repealed the former statutory power[3] to commit a ward of court into the care or supervision of a local authority. Similarly, s 100(2) expressly prevents the High Court from exercising its inherent jurisdiction to require a child to be placed in the care, or to be put under the supervision of, a local authority, or to require a child to be accommodated by or on behalf of a local authority.

1   See the excellent articles by District Judge John Mitchell: 'Whatever happened to Wardship? Part I and Part II' [2001] Fam Law 130 and 212.
2   Namely the Children and Young Persons Act 1969.
3   Namely the Family Law Reform Act 1969, s 7.

12.5 If, in wardship proceedings it appears to the court that a care or supervision order might be appropriate then, like any other court in 'family proceedings',[1] it can, pursuant to the powers under s 37,[2] direct a local authority to investigate the child's circumstances with a view to the authority making an application. In the event of such an application being made[3] a care or supervision order can only be made provided the threshold criteria under s 31 are satisfied.

1   Wardship proceedings are 'family proceedings' by reason of s 8(3)(a), see para 5.135.
2   Discussed at paras 5.206 and 7.25.

³ But there is no power to force the local authority to apply: see e g *Nottingham County Council v P* [1994] Fam 18, [1993] 3 All ER 815.

(b) Wardship and care incompatible

12.6 The Act makes wardship and local authority care incompatible. Section 91(4) provides that the making of a care order with respect to a child who is already a ward of court brings that wardship to an end, while s 100(2)(c) states that the High Court cannot exercise its inherent jurisdiction 'so as to make a child who is the subject of a care order a ward of court'.¹ Section 41(2A) of the Supreme Court Act 1981² also provides that a child in care does not become a ward of court upon the making of a wardship application.³

¹ A point emphasised by Hale LJ in *Re W and B, Re W (care plan)* [2001] EWCA Civ 757, [2001] 2 FCR 450, [2001] 2 FLR 582, at para [76] not commented upon by the House of Lords. Note also *S-H v Kingston upon Hull City Council* [2008] EWCA Civ 493, (2008) Times, 28 May in which it was held that the embargo applied equally to a child who is subject to an adoption placement order.
² Added by the CA 1989, Sch 13, para 45(2).
³ This is contrary to the normal rule that immediately upon the issue of the originating summons the child becomes a ward of court; see the Supreme Court Act 1981, s 41(2) and *Clarke Hall and Morrison on Children*, at 1[776].

12.7 These restrictions mean that the High Court cannot use wardship to keep control of a child committed to the care of a local authority.¹ Similarly, a local authority cannot look to wardship to obtain a High Court order in respect of a child already in their care. In this latter case, however, they can seek to invoke the High Court's inherent jurisdiction.²

¹ This means, for example, that wardship cannot be used to get round the embargo (see *Re KDT (a minor) (care order: conditions)* [1994] 2 FCR 721, sub nom *Re T (A Minor) (Care Order: Conditions)* [1994] 2 FLR 423 and *Kent County Council v C* [1993] Fam 57, [1993] 1 All ER 719) against making conditional care orders.
² See paras 12.25 ff. For the position of individuals seeking to challenge a local authority's decision in respect of a child in care, see paras 12.42 and 12.43.

(c) Circumstances in which local authorities might still look to wardship

12.8 Section 100 does not place an absolute embargo against local authority use of wardship.¹ Recourse to the prerogative jurisdiction remains a possible option in respect of children not in local authority care including those being accommodated by them. Although wardship cannot be used initially to bring about such an arrangement,² unlike care, accommodation is not incompatible with wardship. Similarly, it is established that a supervision order and wardship are not incompatible.³ However, to invoke wardship local authorities must first obtain court leave to invoke the jurisdiction,⁴ which may only be given upon the court being satisfied that: (a) the result sought to be achieved cannot be achieved by the making of a s 8 order⁵ (in this regard it must be remembered that it is also open to an authority to apply with court leave for a prohibited steps or specific issue order);⁶ and (b) that 'if the court's inherent jurisdiction⁷ is not exercised with respect to the child he is likely to suffer significant harm.'[8] Even if leave is given the court may choose not to exercise its jurisdiction. Furthermore, s 100(2)(d)[9] prevents the courts from making orders 'for the purpose of conferring on any local authority power to determine any question which has arisen, or which may arise, in connection with any aspect of parental responsibility for a child'.

1   As emphasised by Munby J in *Re SA (Vulnerable Adult With Capacity: Marriage)* [2005] EWHC 2942 (Fam), [2006] 1 FLR 867 at [109].
2   See s 100(2)(b). See also *Re G (a child) (secure accommodation order)* [2000] 2 FCR 385, [2000] 2 FLR 259, in which the first instance judge was held to be in 'plain breach' of s 100(2) in requiring a local authority to accommodate a child.
3   See *Re K; A Local Authority v N and Others* [2005] EWHC 2956 (Fam) [2007] 1 FLR 399 and *Re M and J (Wardship: Supervision and Residence Orders)* [2003] EWHC 1585 (Fam), [2003] 2 FLR 541.
4   Pursuant to s 100(3).
5   Section 100(4)(a), discussed further at para 12.36.
6   See paras 5.105 and 5.125.
7   Which, for these purposes, applies to wardship proceedings as well.
8   Section 100(4)(b), discussed in more detail at para 12.37.
9   Discussed in detail at para 12.29.

12.9   Since s 8 orders do not cover every situation, in cases where the local authority is not itself seeking care but is nevertheless concerned about a child's well-being, wardship might be the right solution, at any rate, where there is thought to be a need for the court's continuing control to protect the child.[1] In *Re R (a minor) (contempt)*,[2] for example, a local authority warded a 14-year-old child accommodated by them to protect her from a relationship with a 33-year-old man. Wardship might also offer the best and sometimes the only means open to a local authority seeking to protect 17 year olds when most of the public law options are unavailable.[3] Other possible examples are safeguarding the interests of orphans,[4] protecting a child from a possible forced marriage[5] and cases where a local authority is concerned about the child's welfare but is not itself seeking care as, for example, supporting foster parents' applications for care and control,[6] agreeing to a residence order being made in favour of a mother and stepfather coupled with a supervision order,[7] and upon learning of a surrogacy arrangement[8] or of a parental refusal to consent to a child's medical treatment.[9] In this latter context one advantage of wardship is the immediacy of its effect, that is, the moment the child becomes a ward, no important step may be taken without the court's consent, and hence leave to carry out the proposed operation will be required. Nevertheless, unless the continuing control of the court is desirable or useful[10] then it is unlikely that the wardship would be continued by the court. In any event it is usually equally effective simply to seek a prohibited steps or specific issue order.[11]

1   In this respect, note Munby J's comments in *Re K; A Local Authority v N)* [2005] EWHC 2956 (Fam), [2007] 1 FLR 399 at [90] that continued protection is the only justification for invoking wardship.
2   [1994] 2 All ER 144, [1994] 1 WLR 487, CA. Query whether a prohibited steps order could have been made in this case? Cf *Re C (HIV Test)* [1997] 2 FLR 1004 in which, following local authority intervention, a specific issue order was granted, ordering a baby to be tested for HIV.
3   See eg *Re F (mental health act guardianship)* [2000] 1 FCR 11, [2000] 1 FLR 192, CA, discussed further at para 12.19 and *Re D (a child) (wardship: evidence of abuse)* [2001] 1 FCR 707, sub nom *Re D (Evidence: Facilitated Communication)* [2001] 1 FLR 148. CA,

which concerned allegations made by a 17 year old with a mental age of 2 and who lived in a special care unit that he had been sexually abused by his father. In the event these allegations were not proved and the wardship was discharged.

4   See eg *Re C (a baby)* [1996] 2 FCR 569, [1996] 2 FLR 43 discussed below at para 12.15.
5   See eg *Re K; A Local Authority v N*, above at n 1, though note, the protection of wardship was not held to be justified upon the particular facts.
6   As in *Re RJ (minors) (fostering: wardship)* [1999] 3 FCR 646, [1999] 1 FLR 618, discussed at para 12.16.
7   As in *Re M and J (Wardship: Supervision and Residence Orders)* [2003] EWHC 1585 (Fam), [2003] 2 FLR 541, discussed at 12.18.
8   Cf *Re C (A Minor) (Wardship: Surrogacy)* [1985] FLR 846, and Local Authority Circular (85) 12.
9   Cf *Re B (A Minor) (Wardship: Medical Treatment)* [1981] 1 WLR 1421, (1981) 3 FLR 117, CA.
10 As in *Re C (a baby)*, *above*, discussed below at para 12.17.
11 See eg *Re C (HIV Test)* above.

2. Private law

12.10 Although the CA 1989 places no express restraint on the use of wardship by individuals, the expectation and indeed the object was that there would be a substantial decline in the private law use of the jurisdiction. As the Department of Health's original Children Act 1989 Guidance and Regulations[1] put it:

'By incorporating many of the beneficial aspects of wardship such as the "open door" policy, and a flexible range of orders, the Act will substantially reduce the need to have recourse to the High Court.'

As a result of these changes, relatives are now generally better advised to seek, albeit with leave, s 8 orders or special guardianship in the lower courts. Similarly, in most cases,[2] it is difficult to see what parents can now gain from wardship as against pursuing remedies under the CA 1989.

1   Children Act 1989 Guidance and Regulations, Vol 1, Court Orders (1991) Department of Health, para 3.98.
2   But see paras 12.13 ff below.

(a) Status

12.11 In the leading decision, *Re T (A Minor) (Child: Representation)*,[1] it was held that since the FPR 1991, r 9.2A applied to all 'family proceedings', then in wardship, as in any other family proceedings, provided the child has sufficient understanding to bring or defend proceedings on his or her own behalf, the court has no power to impose a guardian ad litem on such a child against his or her wishes. It was further held that given that there were no advantages either to the child or to the adoptive parents that were not also available in ordinary family proceedings under Pt II of the CA 1989, there was nothing which, in the words of Waite LJ, would justify giving the child 'the status, an exceptional status under the modern law as it must now be applied, of a ward of court'.[2]

1   [1994] Fam 49, [1993] 4 All ER 518, [1993] 2 FCR 445, sub nom *Re CT (A Minor) (Wardship: Representation)* [1993] 2 FLR 278, CA.

2   Ie pursuant to FPR 1991, r 9.2A, discussed above at para 10.53.
3   [1994] Fam at 65D, [1993] 4 All ER at 528. See also *Re P (a minor) (leave to apply: foster parents)* [1994] 2 FCR 1093, sub nom *C v Salford City Council* [1994] 2 FLR 926, in which Hale J could see no advantage in continuing the wardship.

12.12 In concluding that the continuation of wardship was inappropriate, Waite LJ commented that while it survives as an independent jurisdiction, the:

> 'courts' undoubted discretion to allow wardship to go forward in a suitable case is subject to their clear duty, in loyalty to the scheme and purpose of the Children Act legislation, to permit recourse to wardship only when it becomes apparent to the judge in any particular case that the question which the court is determining in regard to the minor's upbringing or property cannot be resolved under the statutory procedures in Pt II of the Act in a way that secures the best interests of the child; or where the minor's person is in a state of jeopardy from which he can only be protected by giving him the status of a ward of court; or where the court's functions need to be secured from the effects potentially injurious to the child, of external influences (intrusive publicity for example) and it is decided that conferring on the child the status of a ward will prove a more efficient deterrent than the ordinary sanctions of a contempt of court which already protect all family proceedings'.[1]

1   [1994] Fam 49 at 60, [1993] 4 All ER 518 at 524.

(b) Some possible remaining uses of wardship

12.13 Given that no material changes have been made to the rules governing the issue of an originating summons,[1] Waite LJ's comments in *Re T* ought not to be taken as restricting individuals' ability to make a child a ward of court in the first instance, though clearly, the courts will require special justification to continue the wardship once the case comes before them. It remains now to consider what advantages there may be in issuing an originating summons and when the court might consider continuing the wardship.

1   The procedure is governed by FPR 1991, r 5.1.

12.14 One important feature of the wardship jurisdiction is its immediacy: as soon as the originating summons is issued the child becomes a ward and no important step may then be taken without prior court sanction.[1] In effect the issuing of the originating summons provides a unique quasi-administrative mechanism by which the child's legal position can be immediately frozen, which is useful when dealing with emergencies, such as threatened child abduction, particularly when an international element is involved.[2] Invoking wardship can also be an effective way of halting a proposed medical operation on the child and can provide a usefully speedy means by which non-parents, who would otherwise have to seek leave to apply for a s 8 order can safeguard their position, for example, by preventing parents from removing the child from their care pending a court hearing.

1   *Re S (infants)* [1967] 1 All ER 202, [1967] 1 WLR 396, per Cross J.
2   See further paras 12.20 ff below.

12.15

The court's wardship powers are wider than those under s 8 and where advantage needs to be taken of this it would be proper both to invoke and to continue the wardship. For example, the court's overall control of its wards might be thought advantageous in the case of an abandoned child, where no-one looking after him has parental responsibility. Alternatively, it can be appropriate for a court to assist with taking responsibility in cases of grave anxiety. In *Re C (a baby)*,[1] a child developed meningitis which left her brain-damaged and unable to survive without artificial ventilation and likely to suffer increasing pain and distress with no hope of recovery. Sir Stephen Brown P commented:

> 'It appeared appropriate that the courts should take responsibility for this child and relieve the parents in some measure of the grave responsibility which they have borne since her birth.'

The jurisdiction could also provide an effective means of protecting and managing a child's property interests in the event of the parents' death. Whether wardship has any role in protecting a child from publicity can possibly be debated.[2]

1   [1996] 2 FCR 569, [1996] 2 FLR 43. See also *R v Portsmouth Hospitals NH Trust, ex p Glass* [1999] 3 FCR 145, [1999] 2 FLR 905, CA, which concerned a 12-year-old severely disabled boy with only a limited lifespan. Trust between the mother and the hospital had completely broken down and following her unsuccessful appeal against the dismissal of her action for judicial review, the mother was urged to ward her son so as to allow the Official Solicitor to be continuously involved in the case. Note the Official Solicitor's role in wardship has now largely been taken over by CAFCASS see *Practice Notes* [2001] 2 FCR 562 and [2001] 2 FCR 566, [2001] 2 FLR 155.

2   Although Waite LJ himself instanced the example of protecting the child from publicity in *Re T*, above at [1994] Fam 60, [1993] 4 All ER 524, the House of Lords has since ruled in *Re S (A Child)(Identification: Restrictions on Publicity)* [2004] UKHL 47, [2005] 1 AC 593 that the foundation of jurisdiction to restrain publicity now derives from the European Convention on Human Rights rather than the inherent jurisdiction. The continuation of wardship was found useful in *Re W (minors)(continuation of wardship)* [1996] 1 FCR 393, sub nom *Re W (Wardship: Discharge: Publicity)* [1995] 2 FLR 466, in which a father had acquiesced in his four sons talking to the press about their 'fight to stay with their Dad'.

12.16 Wardship was found to be advantageous both in the short and the long term in *Re RJ (Minors) (Fostering: Person Disqualified)*[1] and *Re RJ (minors) (fostering: wardship)*.[2] These decisions concerned three children who though happily placed with foster carers could not remain there following the implementation of the Children (Protection From Offenders)(Miscellaneous Amendments) Regulations 1997,[3] since the foster-father had previously been formally cautioned for actual bodily harm to another foster child who was now adopted by him and his wife. Following the foster parents' intervention in care proceedings at which the mother was still seeking her children's return, the Court of Appeal in the first mentioned decision, held that although the 1997 Regulations did not prevent the court from making a residence order, the preferable course was to discharge the interim care orders, make the children wards of court and grant interim care and control to the foster parents. The status quo could thereby be preserved pending the full hearing and, by not granting even interim residence orders which would have vested parental responsibility in the foster parent, any perception of prejudice by the mother could be avoided. At the subsequent full hearing (the second mentioned decision) it was held that, given the exceptional circumstances, the appropriate long-term solution was to continue the wardship and to grant care and control to the foster carers. The advantages of this solution were:

(1)   giving ultimate control to the court would be reassuring to the foster carer (who would otherwise have shared parental responsibility with the mother had they been granted residence orders);

(2)   it placed the children in a neutral setting, removing them to some extent from the pressure of the more adversarial nature of Children Act proceedings;[4]

(3)   it was only by this means that the local authority could remain involved in what had become a private law case and would therefore enable the authority to apply for certain orders which might not have otherwise been available to them given the prohibition against local authorities applying for s 8 orders;[5] and

(4)   it would similarly allow the children's guardian to continue to be involved.

As Cazalet J put it 'the use of wardship will enable this case to be managed appropriately for the future'.

1   [1999] 1 WLR 581, [1998] 3 FCR 579, [1999] 1 FLR 605, CA.
2   [1999] 3 FCR 646, [1999] 1 FLR 618.
3   SI 1997/2308. This Regulation was intended to prevent paedophiles from becoming foster parents.
4   Query if this reason would generally be thought to be justifiable?
5   Cf *F v Cambridgeshire County Council* [1995] 2 FCR 804, [1995] 1 FLR 516, discussed at para 5.106.

12.17   Wardship was also held to be the appropriate solution in *Re W and X (Wardship: Relatives Rejected As Foster Carers)*,[1] which concerned proceedings brought in respect of four children, the three eldest of whom had lived with their maternal grandparents after the death of a sibling. It was common ground that the threshold criteria (under s 31) had been satisfied. In relation to the three older children[2] the local authority's preferred option was to leave them with the grandparents but subject to a care order. However, because the local authority had previously rejected the grandparents as foster parents, Regulations[3] meant that this option could not be adopted since the authority would be obliged to remove the children from the grandparents as soon as the care order was made. In Hedley J's opinion this inability to pursue what was perceived to be the best option was a lacuna in the legislation[4] which wardship could properly remedy since it neither infringed the letter nor the spirit of s 100 given that the court were not seeking to control the local authority. Moreover, the children's placement warranted long-term external control which could not be achieved by a care order. Hedley J accordingly warded the children as well as making supervision and residence orders in favour of grandparents.

1   [2003] EWHC 2206 (Fam), [2004] 1 FLR 415.
2   No argument was raised over the youngest child in respect of whom a care order was made.

3   Namely the Fostering Services Regulations 2002, SI 2002/57 (which only apply in England
      – for the Welsh equivalent see the Fostering Services (Wales) Regulations 2003,
      SI 2003/237). Inter alia these Regulations prevent placement of children with unapproved
      foster parents.
4   Hedley J went as far as to suggest that it was worth considering whether the Regulations
      were ultra vires inasmuch as they thwarted the court's duty under s 1(1) of the CA 1989 to
      treat the child's welfare as its paramount consideration.

12.18 The above trilogy of cases demonstrate the court's willingness to use
wardship to overcome restrictions imposed by regulation on local authorities'
freedom to put children in foster placements which would otherwise operate
to the unwarranted detriment of the particular children concerned. But three
further cases are illustrative of a potentially wider use. In *Re M and J
(Wardship: Supervision and Residence Orders),*[1] a mother and stepfather
conceded the threshold criteria in care proceedings and agreed to the psychologist's recommendation that one boy should live with his father and the
other with his maternal grandmother. The local authority did not entirely
agree with these recommendations but nevertheless did not seek alternative
orders. Although he recognised it as being an 'exceptional course' Charles J
made a residence order and a supervision order coupled with wardship orders
in respect of each child, and an order for contact. The justification for the
wardship orders was to manage the inevitable future tensions that would arise
within the family which he felt that by themselves local authority may not
have been able to handle. In *E v X London Borough,*[2] on the other hand, E
who had come to England from Ghana was being temporarily accommodated
by the local authority following the breakdown of E's relationship with a
woman she believed to be her mother. E made herself a ward of court but after
a s 37 investigation, the other woman denied she was the mother and alleged
that E was 20. The local authority was asked to make an age assessment
which found E to be 'at least 20'. E then sought an order in wardship that she
was 17. The court acceded to her request, ruling it was not prevented from
doing so by s 100(2); found her to be 17 and continued the wardship until E's
majority 'in the light of the uncertainty as to her present circumstances should
she be obliged to leave her present lodging', it appearing to the court to be
'desirable' for it to'retain oversight of her welfare for the 10 months or so of
her minority'. In *Re P (Surrogacy: Residence)*[3] in the context of a dispute in
respect of a surrogacy agreement (the mother concealing the birth) it was held
appropriate, when making a residence order in favour of the biological and
commissioning father and his wife with contact to the surrogate mother and
her husband, that the child and his surrogate sibling be made wards of court
to enable there to be a level of court supervision of the situation in the absence
of any input by the local authority. Such an arrangement also enabled the
children's guardian who had played a vital role in the contact arrangements to
remain involved in the case.

1   [2003] EWHC 1585 (Fam), [2003] 2 FLR 541.
2   [2005] EWHC 2811 (Fam), [2006] 1 FLR 730. Cf *Lambeth London Borough Council v
      TK and KK* [2008] EWCA Civ 103, [2008] 1 FLR 1229, in which a dispute over the child's
      age was resolved in the context of s 37 fact-finding proceedings.
3   [2008] 1 FLR 177 – decision upheld on appeal see *Re P (Residence: Appeal)* [2007] EWCA
      Civ 1053, [2008] 1 FLR 198.

12.19 Wardship was thought to provide a preferable means of protecting a
mentally impaired 17-year-old child rather than guardianship under the

12.19 *Wardship and the High Court's inherent jurisdiction*

Mental Health Act 1983. In *Re F (mental health act: guardianship)*[1] a 17-year-old, who had a mental age of between 5 and 8 had been accommodated by a local authority because of chronic neglect. (Her seven siblings were taken into interim care for the same reason).[2] Her parents sought her return. Care proceedings were not possible because of the child's age and the local authority instead obtained a guardianship order under the Mental Health Act 1983. The Court of Appeal held that wardship was the more appropriate remedy not least because the 1983 Act was not a child centred jurisdiction and the child lacked the benefit of independent representation. Furthermore, on the particular facts wardship would enable a single judge to consider the interests both of the child in question and her seven siblings.

1   [2000] 1 FCR 11, [2000] 1 FLR 192, CA.
2   This option could not be exercised over the child in question since she was already aged 17.

(c) The use of wardship when dealing with child abduction

12.20 Although there are no published statistics on the current use of wardship it seems likely that a substantial proportion of applications are made in connection with child abduction.[1] This has long been a key role of the jurisdiction and although there are no longer any jurisdictional advantages in invoking wardship[2] and while many of the powers that were formerly unique to it are now more generally available, wardship remains a useful option because of the immediate and all round protection that it offers, in particular the embargo against the child's removal from England and Wales without court leave which automatically arises immediately that the child is warded. Applications are commonly of three types, namely, those aimed at preventing children from being wrongfully removed from England and Wales, those made by left-behind parents in respect of children abducted abroad and those, usually made by the abducting parent, in connection with children brought to this country from overseas. With regard to the first use, since under the Child Abduction Act 1984 it is a crime wrongfully to take a child outside the United Kingdom,[3] it is not necessary to have a court order to obtain police help to obtain an all ports warning.[4] Nevertheless wardship remains a useful device for convincing the police to intervene. Furthermore, a court order is advantageous if the child is missing since it enables the applicant to enlist the aid of government agencies to trace the child.[5] The court can make location and collection orders[6] and although the inherent powers are little different to those granted under s 34 of the Family Law Act 1986 there is some evidence that (at any rate, in the past) wardship cases are given higher priority by the police.[7] A court can order individuals, including solicitors, to disclose the whereabouts both of the child and proposed defendant. Moreover, in appropriate cases, it can also order solicitors not to reveal the making, content or service of the whereabouts order.[8] Alternatively, the court can order publicity to help trace a ward.[9] Wardship can also help to prevent abduction, inter alia, because a court can order the surrender of a British[10] or even a foreign passport.[11]

1   CAAC Report 1993/94, p 33. According to Mitchell [2001] Fam Law 212 at 214, a third of all wardship cases reported in *Family Law* since the implementation of the CA 1989, have concerned child abduction. See also Lowe, Everall and Nicholls *International*

Movement of Children – Law, Practice and Procedure (2004) Jordans, 9.30–9.31, who point that out that one drawback of wardship is that few foreign jurisdictions will be familiar with the concept.

2   Jurisdiction in children cases is generally governed by the Family Law Act 1986 Pt I (as amended to take account of the revised Brussels II Regulation, see *Clarke Hall and Morrison on Children*, 1[577] ff), and the Court of Appeal has ruled in *Al Habtoor v Fotheringham* [2001] EWCA Civ 186, [2001] 1 FCR 385, [2001] 1 FLR 951 that English courts should not seek to take jurisdiction on any wider basis. For an example of a refusal to exercise wardship because of the child's lack of habitual residence in England and Wales, see *Re A (Wardship: Habitual Residence)* [2006] EWHC 3338 (Fam), [2007] 1 FLR 1589. Note also Potter P's comment (at [50]) that it is not the function of the court, inter alia, in wardship proceedings to make declarations of unlawful detention abroad based upon the nationality or domicile of the child concerned.

3   For a discussion of the operation of the 1984 Act see *Clarke Hall and Morrison on Children* 2[11].

4   See *Clarke Hall and Morrison on Children*, 2[12].

5   *Practice Direction (disclosure of addresses)* [1989] 1 All ER 765, [1989] 1 WLR 219.

6   Discussed in *Clarke Hall and Morrison on Children* at 2[16]–[20].

7   *Re B (minors) (wardship: power to detain)* [1994] 2 FCR 1142 at 1146, [1994] 2 FLR 479 at 482, per Butler-Sloss LJ.

8   See *Re H (child abduction: whereabouts order to solicitors)* [2000] 1 FCR 499, [2000] 1 FLR 766.

9   *Re R (MJ) (A Minor) (Publication of Transcript)* [1975] Fam 89 and *Practice Note* [1980] 2 All ER 806, discussed in *Clarke Hall and Morrison on Children*, 2[22].

10   This power, formerly exclusively an inherent power, is now conferred on all courts by s 37 of the Family Law Act 1986.

11   See *Re A-K (minors) (contact)* [1997] 2 FCR 563, sub nom *Re AK (Foreign Passport: Jurisdiction)* [1997] 2 FLR 569, CA.

12.21 Apart from being useful both to prevent abductions and trace children within the United Kingdom, wardship can be advantageous in cases where children are subsequently taken abroad particularly to so-called non-Convention countries, that is, states that have implemented neither the 1980 Hague Convention on the Civil Aspects of International Child Abduction nor the 1980 European (or Luxembourg) Convention on Recognition and Enforcement of Decisions Concerning Custody of Children.[1] Although in non-Convention cases it is ultimately better in most instances to institute proceedings in the State to which the child has been taken, the respect that wardship commands abroad is not to be underestimated. A good example is *Re KR (a child) (abduction: forcible removal by parents)*[2] in which a 16-year-old Sikh girl living in England was taken to the Punjab by her parents for an arranged marriage. Her elder sister issued wardship proceedings and, following what has been described[3] as 'an imaginative order, replete with recitals' by Singer J which secured the co-operation of the Indian authorities, the ward was returned. Wardship can even be useful in cases where children are subsequently removed to Convention countries since it can enable those who do not otherwise have 'rights of custody'[4] to be able to apply under the 1980 Hague Convention[5] while an order giving residence or contact is enforceable under either the revised Brussels II Regulation[6] or the 1980 European Convention.[7]

1   For a list of Contracting States see *Clarke Hall and Morrison on Children*, 2[2104].

2   [1999] 4 All ER 954, [1999] 2 FCR 337, [1999] 2 FLR 542. See also *P v P* [2006] EWHC 2410 (Fam), [2007] 2 FLR 439, wards returned from Nepal in compliance with order, and *B v A and B* [2005] EWHC 1291 (Fam) – child warded in a dispute between mother and

paternal grandmother that the latter had removed the child from her to Pakistan at a time where the mother had no visa to return to England. CAFCASS was ordered to investigate the circumstances.

3 Mitchell [2001] Fam Law 212 at 215.
4 See art 3 of the Hague Convention, discussed in *Clarke Hall and Morrison on Children*, 2[51].
5 See *Re J (Minor: Abduction: Ward of Court)* [1989] Fam 85, [1989] 3 All ER 590; *Re B M (Wardship: Jurisdiction)* [1993] 1 FLR 979 and *Re R (Wardship: Child Abduction) (No.2)* [1993] 1 FLR 249, discussed by Lowe, Everall and Nicholls *International Movement of Children: Law, Practice and Procedure* (2004) Jordans, 4.43 and 9.23 and by Lowe and Nicholls, 'Child Abduction, The Wardship Jurisdiction and the Hague Convention' [1994] Fam Law 191.
6 See *Clarke Hall and Morrison on Children* at 2[35.7] ff.
7 See *Clarke Hall and Morrison on Children* at 2[74] ff.

12.22 With regard to children wrongfully brought into this country a distinction needs to be made between non-Convention applications and those made under the Hague or European Conventions. In the former case, as is authoritatively established by the House of Lords in *Re J (A Child)(Custody Rights: Jurisdiction)*,[1] the court is bound to apply the paramountcy principle and not to have regard to the special rules and concepts contained in the 1980 Hague Abduction Convention. The application of the paramountcy principle involves deciding whether the child's welfare is best served by ordering the child's immediate return to the foreign jurisdiction where he was taken without conducting a full investigation of the merits or delaying a possible return and fully investigating the case. As Baroness Hale put it:

'there is always a choice to be made. Summary return should not be the automatic reaction to any and every unauthorised taking or keeping a child from his home country. On the other hand, summary return may well be in the best interests of the individual child.'[2]

Baroness Hale identified[3] a number of factors that are important to determining the appropriate decision, namely:

- the degree of the child's connection with each country;
- the length of time the child has spent in each country;
- the difference of approach of the other foreign legal system;
- the effect of the decision upon the child's primary carer.

1 [2005] UKHL 40, [2006] 1 AC 80, sub nom *Re J (a child)(return to foreign jurisdiction: convention rights)* [2005] 3 All ER 291, [2005] 2 FCR 381.
2 Note when exercising its jurisdiction the court is not precluded from ordering the child's return (if that is in the child's best interests) merely because the child is involved in asylum proceedings, see *Re S (child abduction: asylum appeal)* [2002] EWCA Civ 843, [2002] 2 FCR 642, [2002] 2 FLR 465 and *Re W (a child)(abduction: jurisdiction)* [2003] EWHC 1820 (Fam), [2003] 2 FLR 1105.
3 [2005] UKHL 40 at [33]–[40], discussed in detail in *Clarke Hall and Morrison on Children* at 2[33.4]. For a subsequent application of *Re J* in which the court refused in wardship proceedings to return the child, see *Re H (Abduction: Non Convention Application)* [2006] EWHC 199 (Fam), [2006] 2 FLR 314.

12.23 A Convention application takes precedence over the wardship,[1] but the latter jurisdiction can come into play if the Convention application fails[2] provided art 11(6) of the revised Brussels II Regulation (which governs the position following a refusal to return)[3] is either inapplicable because the case is a non Revised Brussels II case or because art 11(6) has not been activated.

1 Child Abduction and Custody Act 1985, ss 9 (Hague) and 27 (European) and the FPR 1991, r 6.11(4).
2 See eg *H v D* [2007] EWHC 802 (Fam), [2007] All ER (D) 77 (Apr) and *Re M (abduction: psychological harm)* [1998] 2 FCR 488, [1997] 2 FLR 690, CA.
3 See the discussion in *Clarke Hall and Morrison on Children* at 2[35.21]–[35.23].

(d) Other cases involving an international element

12.24 Wardship has been found useful in cases involving an international element following a refusal to make an adoption order. One such case, *Re M (child's upbringing)*,[1] concerned a boy born in South Africa to Zulu parents, who, with his parents' consent, was brought to England by a white woman who later applied to adopt him. The parents objected to the adoption and the child was warded. The adoption application was refused and the child was ordered to be returned to his parents but the wardship was continued. The boy's return proved unsuccessful and he is now back in England living with the applicant under a wardship order.[2] In a second case, *Re K (adoption: foreign child)*[3] a Bosnian Muslim orphan baby was brought to England by an English couple initially to receive medical treatment. The couple were later granted an adoption order. However, because they had failed to reveal to the court that the child had relatives in Switzerland who wished to look after her, the adoption was set aside, but the court felt that she should nevertheless remain with the couple because of her psychological bond with them. Accordingly the couple were granted care and control, with substantial access being granted to the relatives. The wardship was continued.

1 [1996] 2 FCR 473, [1996] 2 FLR 441, CA.
2 See *Re O (family appeals: management)* [1998] 3 FCR 226, [1998] 1 FLR 431n.
3 [1997] 2 FCR 389, sub nom *Re K (Adoption and Wardship)* [1997] 2 FLR 221. See also *Re R (Inter-Country Adoption)* [1999] 1 FCR 385, [1999] 1 FLR 1014.

THE INHERENT JURISDICTION[1]

1. Procedure

12.25 The inherent jurisdiction can be invoked either upon specific application or by the court itself in cases where it is already seized of proceedings.[2] In that latter case the power is confined to the High Court[3] since it is established that county courts (and a fortiori magistrates' courts) have no inherent powers to protect children.[4] Applications for declarations, including interim directions, may also be made under the inherent jurisdiction.[5]

1 See generally *Clarke Hall and Morrison on Children*, 1[881] ff.
2 See Charles J's analysis in *Re P (care orders: injunctive relief)* [2000] 3 FCR 426, [2000] 2 FLR 385. For an example of its exercise upon the court's initiative see *Re X (A Minor) (Adoption Details: Disclosure)* [1994] Fam 174, [1994] 3 All ER 372, CA, in which it was held to be an appropriate use of the inherent jurisdiction by the High Court hearing an adoption application to order that during the minority of the child in question the Registrar General should not disclose to any person without leave of the court the details of the adoption entered in the Adopted Children Register. Note following *Re P*, above, a

distinction may have to be made between exercising the powers to support an order under s 37 of the Supreme Court Act 1981 and those under the inherent jurisdiction.

3   Unless proceedings have been transferred from the High Court to the county court under the Matrimonial and Family Proceedings Act 1984, s 38.

4   *D v D (child case: powers of court)* [1994] 3 FCR 28, sub nom *D v D (County Court Jurisdiction: Injunctions)* [1993] 2 FLR 802, CA, *Devon County Council v B* [1997] 3 FCR 333, [1997] 1 FLR 591, CA and *Re S and D (children: powers of the court)* [1995] 1 FCR 626, [1995] 2 FLR 456, CA. Note, however, where a county court has jurisdiction over the subject matter then under the County Courts Act 1984, s 38 the courts can exercise the same powers as the High Court to grant an injunction. See Fricker, 'Injunctive Orders relating to the Children' [1993] Fam Law 141, 142, para 1.4.

5   CPR 25.1(1)(a) and (b).

12.26 Applications to invoke the inherent jurisdiction must be made to the High Court (such proceedings are assigned to the Family Division)[1] but proceedings can subsequently be transferred to the county court.[2] Although no specific procedure is prescribed by the FPR 1991, in practice, application is made by originating summons and is headed 'In the Matter of the Supreme Court Act 1981'.[3] Like wardship, the claimant should, unless directed otherwise, file an affidavit in support of the application when the summons is issued. Local authorities wishing to invoke the inherent jurisdiction must first obtain leave of the court.[4]

1   Supreme Court Act 1981, Sch 1, para 3(b)(ii), as amended by the CA 1989, Sch 13, para 45(3).

2   Ie in accordance with the Matrimonial and Family Proceedings Act 1984, s 38.

3   See *Re Z (A Minor) (Identification: Restrictions on Publication)* [1997] Fam 1 at 14 sub nom *Re Z (a minor) (freedom of Publication)* [1995] 4 All ER 961 at 968, per Ward LJ.

4   CA 1989, s 100(3), discussed at paras 12.35 ff.

2. Jurisdiction

12.27 Jurisdiction to make orders giving care of a child to any person or providing for contact with, or the education of a child within the meaning of the Family Law Act 1986, s 1(1)(d), as amended to take account of the revised Brussels II Regulation, is governed by the 1986 Act and is generally confined to where the child is either habitually resident in England and Wales or physically present here and not habitually resident in another part of the United Kingdom or Isle of Man nor where under the Regulation another Member State is seised of the case.[1] Exceptionally, where the court considers that the immediate exercise of its powers are necessary for the child's protection, the child's physical presence in England and Wales will suffice to give jurisdiction.[2] Even if there is a residual jurisdiction based on the child's allegiance to the Crown to make orders not caught by s 1(1)(d),as amended,[3] it is unlikely that jurisdiction will be taken on that basis.[4]

1   FLA 1986, s 3(1). For discussion of the application of the Regulation see paras 5.127 ff. Before the implementation of the Regulation it was established that the initial burden of proof lies on the applicant to satisfy the court that it has jurisdiction but once this has been discharged the burden shifts to the defendant to show that jurisdiction has subsequently been lost by establishing, for example, that the child is no longer habitually resident in the country: *Re E (child abduction)* [1992] 1 FCR 541, sub nom *F v S (Wardship: Jurisdiction)* [1993] 2 FLR 686, CA (decided in 1991) and *Re EW* [1992] 2 FCR 441, sub nom *Re R (Wardship: Child Abduction)* [1992] 2 FLR 481, CA. Query whether this ruling applies to applications governed by the Regulation?

2   Article 20 of the revised Brussels II Regulation and the FLA 1986, s 2(3)(b).
3   As accepted by Ward J in *F v S (wardship: jurisdiction)* [1991] FCR 631, [1991] 2 FLR
    349, not commented upon on the point by the Court of Appeal. Following *Re F (In Utero)*
    [1988] Fam 122, [1988] 2 All ER 193, CA, there would appear to be no jurisdiction to
    protect an unborn child.
4   See *Al Habtoor v Fotheringham* [2001] EWCA Civ 186, [2001] 1 FCR 385, [2001] 1 FLR
    951, CA, discussed at 12.20, n 2.

3. Powers

(a) The general extent of the inherent powers

12.28 Proceedings under the inherent jurisdiction rank as 'family proceedings'[1] so that the court is empowered either upon application or its own
motion to make any s 8 order.[2] The powers under the general inherent
jurisdiction are co-extensive with those under wardship. As Lord Donaldson MR put it in *Re W (A Minor) (Medical Treatment: Court's Jurisdiction):*[3]

   'Since there seems to be some doubt about the matter, it should be made clear
   that the High Court's inherent jurisdiction in relation to children the parens
   patriae jurisdiction is equally exercisable whether the child is or is not a ward of
   court … '

1   CA 1989, s 8(3)(a).
2   Section 10(1).
3   [1993] Fam 64 at 73F, [1992] 4 All ER 627 at 641c. See also Balcombe LJ at 85 and 640
    respectively.

(b) Express restriction of powers under the CA 1989

12.29 Section 100(2)(d) of the CA 1989 prevents the High Court from
exercising its inherent jurisdiction[1] 'for the purposes of conferring on any local
authority power to determine any question which has arisen, or which may
arise, in connection with any aspect of parental responsibility for a child'. In
other words, while the High Court may make orders under its inherent
jurisdiction in respect of a child, in doing so, it must not confer any aspect of
parental responsibility upon a local authority that the authority does not
already have.[2] This is less likely to cause problems where the child is in care,
since the local authority will already have parental responsibility. Hence, the
determination of a particular question by the court, for example, obtaining a
return order against abducting parents, will not be contrary to s 100(2)(d).[3]
Similarly, the court is free to determine the scope and extent of parental
responsibility and can, for instance, make orders giving leave for a child in
care to be interviewed by the father's solicitor to prepare a defence to criminal
charges.[4] If the local authority do not have parental responsibility for the
child, the High Court may not under its inherent jurisdiction make orders
which in any way confer parental responsibility upon the authority. Hence, for
example, while the court could sanction a named couple to look after the
child[5] it could not authorise a local authority to place the child, nor a fortiori,
to place the child 'with a view to adoption'. It has, however, been held wrong
that s 100 be restrictively interpreted and that it is perfectly proper for a local
authority to invite the court to exercise its inherent jurisdiction to protect

children even if the exercise of that power would be an invasion of a person's parental responsibility, for example, by restricting a non-family member from contacting or communicating with the children in question.[6]

1   Which, for these purposes, also includes the wardship jurisdiction.
2   See eg the revised Children Act 1989 Guidance and Regulations, Vol 1, Court Orders (2008) Department for Children, Schools and Families, para 3.88.
3   See *Re DB and CB (minors)* [1993] 2 FCR 607, sub nom *Southwark London Borough v B* [1993] 2 FLR 559 at 571 per Waite LJ.
4   Per Hale J in *Re M (minors) (care: leave to interview child)* [1995] 2 FCR 643, [1995] 1 FLR 825.
5   As in *Re RJ (minors) (fostering: wardship)* [1999] 3 FCR 646, [1999] 1 FLR 618, *Re M and J (Wardship, Supervision and Residence Orders)* [2003] EWHC 1585 (Fam), [2003] 2 FLR 541, and *Re W and X (Wardship: Relations Rejected As Foster Parents)* [2003] EWHC 2206 (Fam), [2004] 1 FLR 415, discussed at paras 12.16–12.18.
6   Per Thorpe J in *Devon County Council v S* [1994] Fam 169, accepting the argument that the local authority were not seeking leave to apply to the court to confer any power upon themselves but were asking the court to exercise its own powers.

(c)   Other restrictions on the exercise of inherent powers[1]

12.30   Courts have traditionally declined to define the limits of their inherent powers to protect children which have been frequently described as theoretically unlimited.[2] Although it is accepted that the High Court's inherent power to protect children is wider than that of a parent,[3] it is equally well established that whatever may be the theoretical position, there are 'far-reaching limitations in principle' on the exercise of that jurisdiction.[4] As Ward LJ put it in *Re Z (A Minor) (Identification: Restrictions on Publication)*:[5]

> 'The wardship or inherent jurisdiction of the court to cast its cloak of protection over minors whose interests are at risk of harm is unlimited in theory though in practice the judges who exercise the jurisdiction have created classes of cases in which the court will not exercise its powers'.

However, because of the court's tendency to approach the issue on a case-by-case basis rather than by laying down general guidance the precise ambit of these limits is still far from clear. Nevertheless the courts seem to be moving to a position of saying that the inherent jurisdiction should not be exercised so as to exempt the child from the general law or to obtain rights and privileges for a specific child that are not generally available to all children.[6]

1   For a detailed discussion see Lowe and Douglas *Bromley's Family Law* (10th edn) 905 ff.
2   See eg *Re W (A Minor) (Medical Treatment: Court's Jurisdiction)* [1993] Fam 64, [1992] 4 All ER 627 per Lord Donaldson MR and Balcombe LJ; *Re R (A Minor) (Wardship: Restrictions on Publication)* [1994] Fam 254 at 271, [1994] 3 All ER 658 at 672, per Millett LJ; and *Re B (child abduction: wardship: power to detain)* [1994] 2 FCR 1142, [1994] 2 FLR 479 at 483 (per Butler-Sloss LJ) and 487 (per Hobhouse LJ).
3   See *Re R (A Minor) (Wardship: Consent to Medical Treatment)* [1992] Fam 11 at 25B and 28G and *Re W (A Minor) (Medical Treatment: Court's Jurisdiction)*, above. Note also that a similar standpoint has been taken by the Australian High Court in *Secretary, Department of Health and Community Services v JWB and SMB* (1992) 66 ALJR 300.
4   Per Balcombe LJ in *Re W*, above, at 85 and 640 respectively, citing Sir John Pennycuick in *Re X (A Minor) (Wardship: Jurisdiction)* [1975] Fam 47 at 61, CA.
5   [1997] Fam 1 at 23, sub nom *Re Z (a minor) (freedom of publication)* [1995] 4 All ER 961 at 977.

6   See eg *Re R (A Minor) (Wardship: Restrictions on Publication)* [1994] Fam 254 at 271, [1994] 3 All ER 658 at 672–673 per Millett LJ and *R v Central Independent Television plc* [1994] Fam 192, [1994] 3 All ER 641, CA.

12.31 Among the more important specific limitations established in wardship and therefore by implication under the inherent jurisdiction are that the court will not interfere with the exercise of powers clearly vested in other bodies such as local authorities,[1] the immigration service[2] or the lower courts.[3] The inherent powers cannot be used to interfere with the normal criminal process[4] nor with the normal operation of military law.[5] It has also been held that there is no inherent power to order a doctor directly or indirectly to treat a child in a manner contrary to his or her clinical judgment.[6] The court has also refused to grant a mandatory injunction against a school to educate a child against its wishes.[7]

1   *A v Liverpool City Council* [1982] AC 363, [1981] 2 All ER 385, HL, discussed at para 12.42.
2   *R (on the application of Anton) v Secretary of the State for the Home Department; Re Anton* [2004] EWHC 2730/2731 (Admin/Fam), [2005] 2 FLR 818, *Re Mohamed Arif An Infant), Re Nirbhai Singh (An Infant)* [1968] Ch 643, [1968] 2 All ER 145, CA, *Re F (A Minor) (Immigration: Wardship)* [1990] Fam 125, [1989] 1 All ER 1155, CA.
3   See eg *Re A-H (Infants)* [1963] Ch 232 and *Re P(AJ) (An Infant)* [1968] 1 WLR 1976.
4   See eg *Re K (a minor) (wardship: criminal proceedings)* [1988] 1 All ER 214.
5   *Re JS (A Minor) (Wardship: Boy Soldier)* [1990] Fam 182, [1990] 2 All ER 861.
6   *Re J (A Minor) (Child in Care: Medical Treatment)* [1993] Fam 15, [1992] 4 All ER 614, CA.
7   *Re C (a minor) (wardship: jurisdiction)* [1991] FCR 1018, [1991] 2 FLR 168, CA.

12.32 The inherent jurisdiction cannot, as a matter of principle, be exercised to override a statutory provision,[1] though it can be a matter of fine judgement to determine what the legislative intention is.[2] It is accepted that the jurisdiction can be used to fill unintended lacunas in legislative schemes.[3]

1   See *Re O (A Minor) (Blood Tests: Constraint)* [2000] Fam 139, [2000] 2 All ER 29 in which Wall J refused to exercise the inherent jurisdiction to override the refusal of a parent with care and control to consent to a blood sample being taken from her child as she was then entitled to do under the Family Law Reform Act 1969, s 21 (since amended by the Child Support, Pensions and Social Security Act 2000, s 82). It is on this ground that Douglas Brown J's decision in *South Glamorgan County Council v W and B* [1993] 1 FCR 626, [1993] 1 FLR 574 that the High Court has an inherent power to override a child's refusal to submit an examination when placed inter alia in interim care can be criticised, since there is a clear statutory power (see eg s 38(6)) to do so.
2   Compare, for example, *Re RJ (foster placement)* [1998] 3 FCR 579, [1998] 2 FLR 110 in which Brown P considered granting care and control to disqualified foster parents would subvert the policy behind the Children (Protection From Offenders) Miscellaneous Amendments Regulations 1997, with that of the Court of Appeal at [1999] 1 WLR 581, [1998] 3 FCR 579, [1999] 1 FLR 605, which was content to say that the Regulations were not directed at the courts.
3   See eg *Re W and X (Wardship: Relatives Rejected As Foster Parents)* [2003] EWHC 2206 (Fam), [2004] 1 FLR 415 (discussed at para 12.17) and *Re C (A Minor) (Adoption: Freeing Orders)* [1999] Fam 240, 1999] 2 WLR 1079, [1999] 1 FCR 145, [1999] 1 FLR 348.

(d) Exclusion from the family home

12.33 There is uncertainty about whether there is an inherent power to exclude persons from the family home, which is important given that local authorities cannot look to Pt II of the CA 1989 to obtain such a remedy.[1] Prior to *Richards v Richards*[2] there was authority for saying that what were then known as ouster orders could be made broadly on the basis of what was best for the child and it was not unknown for such orders to be made in wardship proceedings.[3] *Richards*, however, seemed to put an end to such a line of reasoning, and in particular seemed to doubt the existence of an independent jurisdiction (ie outside that provided by the family protection legislation) to protect children by means of ouster orders.[4] However, in attempting to reconcile certain post-*Richards* decisions, the Court of Appeal in *Pearson v Franklin*[5] concluded that distinctions have to be drawn according to whether the adult parties were spouses, former spouses, cohabitants or former cohabitants. Only if the adult parties were former spouses whose marriage has been dissolved by the decree absolute is there an inherent power to make ouster orders.[6]

[1] See *D v D (ouster order)* [1996] 2 FCR 496, sub nom *Re D (Prohibited Steps Order)* [1996] 2 FLR 273 CA, discussed at para 5.101.
[2] [1984] AC 174, [1983] 2 All ER 807, HL.
[3] See *Re V (A Minor) (Wardship)* (1979) 123 Sol Jo 201 and *Rennick v Rennick* [1978] 1 All ER 817 at 819 and *Spindlow v Spindlow* [1979] Fam 52 at 58 in which Ormrod LJ assumed there was such a power. The matter was not beyond doubt, however: see to the contrary *Re D (Minors)* (1983) 13 Fam Law 111.
[4] See eg Lowe and White, *Wards of Court* (2nd edn) pp 6–51.
[5] [1994] 2 All ER 137, [1994] 1 WLR 370. In doing so Nourse LJ acknowledged that the distinctions between couples who are or have been married and unmarried couples who are or have been living together 'may not, on a long view, be satisfactorily explicable'. See also the critical commentary at [1994] Fam Law 379–380.
[6] Following *Webb v Webb* [1986] 1 FLR 541, and *Wilde v Wilde* [1988] FCR 551, [1988] 2 FLR 83, CA, each in turn applying *Quinn v Quinn* (1983) 4 FLR 394, CA.

12.34 Since *Pearson*, however, there have been two first instance decisions suggesting that the inherent powers may be wider. In the first, *Re S (minors) (inherent jurisdiction: ouster)*[1] Connell J, granted a local authority's request under s 100 for leave to pursue an application to exclude a father from the matrimonial home, while in the second, *C v K (ouster order: non parent)*,[2] Wall J also concluded there remained an inherent power to protect children by means of an ouster order. Whether the appellate courts will be disposed to uphold either decision remains to be seen but so far as the former is concerned the need to do has been undermined by the power to include exclusion requirements in interim care orders and emergency protection orders introduced by the Family Law Act 1996.[3]

[1] [1994] 2 FCR 986, [1994] 1 FLR 623.
[2] [1996] 3 FCR 488, [1996] 2 FLR 506. See also *Devon County Council v S* [1994] Fam 169, [1995] 1 All ER 243 in which Thorpe J acted under the inherent jurisdiction to exclude a family friend (see further para 12.40). See the analysis by Judge Fricker QC at [1994] Fam Law 629.
[3] Namely under ss 38A (discussed at paras 8.120–8.121) and 44A (discussed at paras 7.93–7.94) of the CA 1989. Query whether it is implicit in these reforms that Parliament was anticipating courts to apply the Family Law Act 1996 when making exclusion orders?

4. Local authority use of the jurisdiction

(a) The need to obtain leave

12.35 Although local authorities cannot look to the inherent jurisdiction as a means of putting them in charge of the child's living arrangements[1] they can nevertheless seek to use it to resolve specific questions about the child's future. Indeed, because of the unavailability of wardship[2] and of s 8 orders (by reason of the embargoes in s 9(1) and (2))[3] they must do so if the child is in their care. Nevertheless, this avenue is fettered because under s 100(3) of the CA 1989 local authorities must first obtain the court's leave to apply for any exercise of the High Court's inherent jurisdiction.[4]

1   See CA 1989, s 100(2).
2   See paras 12.6–12.7.
3   Discussed at para 5.125.
4   See eg *Devon County Council v B* [1997] 3 FCR 333, [1997] 1 FLR 591, CA. But note that according to *Re P (care orders: injunctive relief)* [2000] 3 FCR 426, [2000] 2 FLR 385 insofar as powers are sought under s 37 of the Supreme Court Act 1981 (namely injunctive relief to support rights conferred by the CA 1989) leave is not required.

(b) Criteria for granting leave

12.36 Under s 100(4)(a), the court must be satisfied that the result sought to be achieved cannot be achieved under any statutory jurisdiction. This bar applies even where the statutory remedy is contingent upon the local authority having first to obtain leave before being able to seek an order.[1] This restriction makes it difficult for an authority to obtain leave for the exercise of the inherent jurisdiction in respect of a child not in their care, since in those circumstances they could seek to obtain a prohibited steps or specific issue order under s 8,[2] or possibly injunctive relief under s 37 of the Supreme Court Act 1981.[3] In *Re R (a minor) (blood transfusion)*[4] a local authority wishing to obtain sanction for a blood transfusion for a child contrary to his parents' (who were Jehovah's Witnesses) wishes, were refused leave because, as the child was not in care, an appropriate remedy could be obtained under s 8.[5]

1   Section 100(5)(b).
2   *Re C (a child) (HIV test)* [1999] 3 FCR 289, [1999] 2 FLR 1004 where a local authority successfully applied for a specific issue order to have a baby tested for HIV. But note the difficulties of doing so, see *Langley v Liverpool City Council* [2005] EWCA Civ 1173, [2005] 3 FCR 303, [2006] 1 FLR 342 at [73]–[78], per Thorpe LJ.
3   See *Re P (care orders: injunctive relief)* [2000] 3 FCR 426, [2000] 1 FLR 385 – injunction granted under the CA 1989 to require parents to allow the child (who was being fostered) to attend school without interference.
4   [1993] 2 FCR 544, [1993] 2 FLR 757, per Booth J. This point was apparently overlooked by Thorpe J in *Re S (a minor) (Medical Treatment)* [1993] 1 FLR 376. Cf *Re O (a minor) (medical treatment)* [1993] 1 FCR 925, [1993] 2 FLR 149.
5   Though Booth J was doubtful about whether a specific issue order should be granted ex parte. Sed quaere?

12.37 Even if there is no alternative remedy, before granting leave, the court must be satisfied that 'there is reasonable cause to believe that if the court's inherent jurisdiction is not exercised with respect to the child he is likely to suffer significant harm'.[1] It has been accepted[2] that cases determining the meaning of 'likely to suffer significant harm' for the purposes of s 31[3] are also relevant to its meaning under s 100(4)(b). This potentially stringent requirement has been criticised as being too restrictive. Since a local authority must of necessity not be seeking to acquire full parental responsibility but to have some specific matter of upbringing determined, the less onerous welfare test would surely have been appropriate.[4]

1   CA 1989, s 100(4)(b).
2   Per Connell J in *Essex County Council v Mirror Group Newspapers Ltd* [1996] 2 FCR 831, [1996] 1 FLR 585. Leave was refused in that case. But as Bainham, *Children – The Modern Law* (3rd edn) 537, points out, unlike s 31, s 100(4)(b) only requires the court to be 'reasonably satisfied' that significant harm might result if the jurisdiction is not exercised.
3   Discussed at paras 8.36 ff.
4   See Eekelaar and Dingwall (1989) 139 NLJ 217, 218; Lowe (1989) 139 NLJ 87, 88 407. Cf Bainham, above at 537.

(c) Circumstances when the leave criteria have been or might be satisfied

12.38 Local authorities are not expected to make frequent use of the inherent jurisdiction.[1] Where a child is in care the local authority will have parental responsibility and should normally make decisions themselves and in cases where the child is not in care, specific issue or prohibited steps orders under s 8 will normally provide an appropriate remedy. Nevertheless, there will be occasions when recourse to the High Court will be appropriate. Lord Mackay instanced[2] the exercise of the inherent power to sanction or forbid an abortion being carried out on a child in care, where there are no other statutory means of seeking a court order and the decision, if wrong, is clearly likely to cause significant harm. In *Re W (A Minor) (Medical Treatment: Court's Jurisdiction),*[3] for example, it was thought right to invoke the inherent jurisdiction to overcome the refusal of a 16-year-old anorexic child in care to consent to medical treatment. Other examples of medical treatment where leave is likely to be given include sterilisation[4] and contested cases involving emergency medical treatment of a child in care.[5]

1   See the revised Children Act 1989 Guidance and Regulations, Vol 1, Court Orders (2008) Department for Children, Schools and Families, paras 3.86 and 88.
2   (1989) 139 NLJ at 507.
3   [1993] Fam 64, [1992] 4 All ER 627, CA. See also *Re C (a minor) (detention for medical treatment)* [1997] 3 FCR 49, [1997] 2 FLR 180 and *Re L (medical treatment: Gillick competence)* [1999] 2 FCR 524, [1998] 2 FLR 810. Note also *South Glamorgan County Council v W and B* [1993] 1 FLR 574, Douglas Brown J held (dubiously it is submitted, see para 12.32, n 1) that the High Court could under its inherent power override the statutory right under the CA 1989, ss 38(6), 43(8) and 44(7) of a child of sufficient understanding to make an informed decision to refuse to submit to an examination or other assessment.
4   This is one of the examples given by the revised Guidance, above, at para 3.87. It also instances restraining harmful publicity about a child.
5   See *Re O (a minor) (medical treatment)* [1993] 1 FCR 925, [1993] 2 FLR 149, per Johnson J, as explained by Booth J in *Re R (a minor) (blood transfusion)* [1993] 2 FCR 544, [1993] 2 FLR 757.

12.39 Another issue where High Court help might be justified is whether a mentally or physically handicapped child should have a life-saving or life-prolonging operation. While such an issue is obviously crucial to the child concerned, it must not be assumed that leave will always be given. For example, if as in *Re C (A Minor) (Wardship: Medical Treatment)*,[1] a baby is terminally ill and the medical team considers that the goal should be to ease the baby's suffering rather than to achieve a short prolongation of life, then even if the local authority disagree, it is not at all certain that they would satisfy the criterion set out in s 100(4)(b). In practice, the argument of substance may well take place on the application for leave.

1   [1990] Fam 26, [1989] 2 All ER 782, CA.

12.40 The above medical problems are extreme examples of situations when High Court intervention might be justified, but circumstances do not always have to be so extraordinary. In *Re DB and CB (minors)*[1] leave was granted to a local authority first to seek an order for the return of a child in their care and then to seek to enforce that order. In other cases, for example, where a local authority seeks an injunction to prevent a violent father from discovering his child's whereabouts,[2] or from molesting his child[3] or, to restrain harmful publicity about the child[4] then, as the inherent jurisdiction is the only means of obtaining a remedy, it should not be too difficult to satisfy the leave criteria. In *Devon County Council v S*[5] it was held appropriate to exercise the inherent jurisdiction to prevent a family friend (a Sch 1 offender and a paedophile) from having contact with the children and to prevent the mother from allowing the children to have contact with him since there was no other means of obtaining such a remedy. In *Re M (Care: Leave to Interview Child)*[6] the jurisdiction was successfully invoked to permit a child in care to be interviewed by the father's solicitor with a view to preparing evidence in the father's defence in furthering criminal proceedings against him.

1   [1993] 2 FCR 607, sub nom *Southwark London Borough v B* [1993] 2 FLR 559, CA.
2   *Re JT (A Minor)* [1986] 2 FLR 107.
3   Cf *Re B (A Minor) (Wardship: Child in Care)* [1975] Fam 36, [1974] 3 All ER 915.
4   See eg *A Local Authority v W, L, W, T and R (By the Children's Guardian)* [2005] EWHC 1564 (Fam), [2006] 1 FLR 1. But note that following *Re S (A Child)(Identification: Restrictions on Publication)* [2004] UKHL 47, [2005] 1 AC 593, [2004] 4 All ER 683, the foundation of the jurisdiction is the ECHR rather the inherent jurisdiction. See further para 2.20.
5   [1994] Fam 169, [1995] 1 All ER 243, per Thorpe J.
6   [1995] 2 FCR 643, [1995] 1 FLR 825, per Hale J. Note also *Re SA (Vulnerable Adult With Capacity: Marriage)* [2005] EWHC 2942 (Fam), [2007] 2 FCR 563, [2006] 1 FLR 867, inherent jurisdiction exercised at a local authority's request to ensure that a vulnerable adult was appropriately informed about any marriage proposal; and *Westminster City Council v C* [2008] EWCA Civ 198, [2008] 2 FCR 146, [2008] 2 FLR 267, [2008] Fam Law 517, in which a local authority invoked in the inherent jurisdiction to determine the validity of a vulnerable adult's marriage.

12.41 Although in theory the granting of leave does not automatically mean that the court must exercise its jurisdiction, given that it must be satisfied that the child is likely to suffer significant harm if the jurisdiction is not exercised[1] it would be an unusual case where leave was given and the jurisdiction not subsequently exercised.[2]

1   This requirement distinguishes s 100 from leave under s 10 to apply for a s 8 order, where it by no means follows that an order be made following the granting of leave. See para 5.152.

5. Individual's use of the jurisdiction

12.42 Although individuals can invoke the inherent jurisdiction there is normally little advantage in doing so, not least because of the continued availability of wardship. Nevertheless it is invoked in abduction proceedings as, for example, where the child is 16 or over so that the 1980 Hague Abduction Convention cannot apply[1] and it can be invoked by the court itself following its refusal to order the child's return in a Hague application in cases not covered by the revised Brussels II Regulation[2] The inherent jurisdiction can also be invoked in cases brought before an English court under the procedure set out by art 11(6) and (7) of the Regulation following a refusal by a foreign court of a Member State to return a child under the Hague Convention.[3] The advantage of invoking the inherent jurisdiction is that it will guarantee that the proceedings will be heard in the High Court.[4] Where the child is in local authority care then, since wardship cannot be used, the High Court's inherent powers can only be invoked, if at all, under the wider inherent jurisdiction. However, before the CA 1989 it was well settled that the High Court would not allow the prerogative jurisdiction to be used as a means of challenging authorities' decisions over children in care. The basic rationale for what became known as the '*Liverpool* principle' was that as Parliament had vouchsafed a wide discretion in local authorities over the management of children in care, it was not for the courts to subvert that intention by allowing parents and others a right of challenge through wardship and therefore outside the statutory system. As Lord Wilberforce said in *A v Liverpool City Council:*[5]

> 'In my opinion the court has no such reviewing power. Parliament has by statute entrusted a local authority the power and duty to make decisions as to the welfare of children without any reservation of reviewing power to the court.'

1   See, for example, *Re C (Abduction: Separate Representation of Children)* [2008] EWHC 517 (Fam), [2008] Fam Law 498, in which there were several siblings, the eldest being 16; and *Re H (Abduction: Child of sixteen)* [2000] 2 FLR 51 in which the child became 16 during Hague proceedings.
2   See eg *D v S (Abduction: Acquiescence)* [2008] EWHC 363 (Fam), [2008] 2 FLR 293, [2008] Fam Law 499.
3   For a discussion of this procedure, see *Clarke Hall and Morrison on Children* at 2[35.31].
4   According to *Re A, HA v MB (Brussels II Revised: Article 11(7) Application)* [2007] EWHC 2016 (Fam), [2008] 1 FLR 289, all art 11(7) applications should be heard in the High Court but there is some debate as to what the position might be under revised Rules currently (ie at the time of writing) being discussed.
5   [1982] AC 363, [1981] 2 All ER 385, HL. See also *Re W (A Minor) (Wardship: Jurisdiction)* [1985] AC 791, [1985] 2 All ER 301, HL.

12.43 Nothing in the CA 1989 can be taken to have altered the pre-Act standpoint. This was made clear by Butler-Sloss LJ in *Re B (Minors) (Termination of Contact: Paramount Consideration)*[1] who commented:

'*A v Liverpool City Council* is still, in my opinion, of the greatest relevance beyond the confines of child care law and the principle set out by Lord Wilberforce is equally applicable today, that the court has no reviewing power over the exercise of the local authority's discretionary decisions in carrying out its statutory role.'

She further observed that the principal judicial remedy for an abuse of power is judicial review.[2]

1   [1993] Fam 301 at 309, [1993] 3 All ER 524 at 529–530. See also *Re P (a minor) (leave to apply: foster parents)* [1994] 2 FCR 1093, sub nom *C v Salford City Council* [1994] 2 FLR 926, per Hale J. Note also the comments in *Re A (Minors) (Residence Orders: Leave to Apply)* [1992] Fam 182, [1992] 3 All ER 872, CA, per Balcombe LJ, and *Kent County Council v C* [1993] Fam 57, [1993] 1 All ER 719, per Ewbank J.

2   Though other remedies include invoking the local authority's complaints procedure, invoking the Secretary of State's default powers, complaining to the 'local government ombudsman' or seeking a remedy at the European Court of Human Rights. See Chapter 13.

Chapter 13

CHALLENGING DECISIONS

APPEALS

1. Generally

13.1 In line with the policy of creating concurrent jurisdictions the CA 1989 provides the same right and avenue of appeal for all proceedings under the Act regardless of whether they are private or public law cases. Although with regard to the former the substantive provisions are essentially the same as under the pre-1989 Act law, the CA 1989 made fundamental changes to the public law position allowing for the first time local authorities a general right of appeal against the refusal of a care or supervision order.[1] Since the Act there has been an important procedural change in that in most cases an appeal to the Court of Appeal requires court permission.[2] The right and avenue of appeal under the CA 1989 is the same as in other proceedings concerning children.[3]

[1]   Formerly appeals were only permitted on points of law.
[2]   See CPR 52.3.
[3]   As *Clarke Hall and Morrison on Children* points out at 1[1491], although a uniform system of appeals is provided for by CPR Pt 52 so far as family proceedings are concerned that Part only governs appeals to the Court of Appeal. Appeals in family proceedings lying to the High Court are governed by the FPR 1991, r 4.22. Appeals to the House of Lords are governed by CPR Sch 1 RSC Ord 59.

13.2 With certain exceptions and subject to permission when appealing to the Court of Appeal, there is a general right of appeal against the making or refusal to make orders (including 'no orders') under the CA 1989.[1] In the private law context, any party can appeal against the making or refusal to make, for example, s 8 orders, special guardianship orders, directions under s 13, parental responsibility orders under s 4 or guardianship orders under s 5. Similarly, in the public law context anyone who had party status (including, therefore, local authorities) in the original proceedings may appeal against the making of a care or supervision order (including an interim order) or of an order varying or discharging such an order, or against the court's refusal to make such order.[2] This includes a direction made under s 38(6).[3]

13.2   Challenging decisions

1   Section 94(1). This provision also applies to orders made under the Adoption and Children Act 2002.
2   But note Johnson J's comment in *Re M (prohibited steps order: application for leave)* [1993] 1 FCR 78, [1993] 1 FLR 275 that the CA 1989, s 94(1) should not be read as limiting the class of those entitled to appeal. Hence in that case the local authority could appeal even though it was not a party to the original proceedings.
3   *Re O (minors) (medical examination)* [1992] 2 FCR 394, [1993] 1 FLR 860.

13.3 Although as a matter of principle there is no automatic embargo against appealing against a consent order, normally such an appeal will only be entertained where it is made with the leave of the court that made the order.[1] The exception is where it is alleged that the judge brought improper pressure upon a party to reach a settlement[2] or so conducted the case as to prevent the party from putting his case properly.[3] Where a consent order has been reached by the parties without involvement of the judge at all then, unless leave to appeal has been given, the proper procedure is to apply to the first instance court to vary the order.[4]

1   See *Re R (A Minor) (Consent Order: Appeal)* [1995] 1 WLR 184, [1994] 2 FCR 1251, sub nom *Re R (Contact: Consent Order)* [1995] 1 FLR 123, CA and the Supreme Court Act 1981, s 18(1).
2   See *Re R* Above, respectively at 190, 1257–1258 and 123 at 129, CA, per Stuart-Smith LJ.
3   See *Jones v National Coal Board* [1957] 2 QB 55, [1957] 2 All ER 155, CA.
4   *Re F (a minor) (appeal)* [1992] 1 FCR 167, sub nom *Re F (A Minor) (Custody: Consent Order: Procedure)* [1992] 1 FLR 561, CA.

13.4 Notwithstanding the aforesaid general right of appeal there are some limitations:

*   There is no right of appeal against the making of or refusal to make an emergency protection order.[1]
*   There is no right of appeal against a magistrates' court decision to decline jurisdiction (where it has power to do so) because it considers that the case can be more conveniently dealt with by another court.[2]

Furthermore, because it is a matter of judicial discretion, there is effectively no right of appeal. against a decision not to interview a child in private,[3] or against whether or not to ask for a welfare report.[4] It has also been said that an application to discharge a care order should be made, rather than an application for an extension to appeal out of time.[5]

1   Section 45(10) but note the criticisms in *Re P (emergency protection order)* [1996] 3 FCR 637, [1996] 1 FLR 482 and in *Essex County Council v F* [1993] 2 FCR 289, [1993] 1 FLR 847.
2   Section 94(2). Note also there is no right of appeal in relation to an interim order for periodical payments under Sch 1 to the CA 1989: CA 1989, s 94(3), see *Clarke Hall and Morrison on Children* at 4[14].
3   See *Re R (a minor) (religious sect)* [1993] 2 FCR 525, sub nom *Re R (A Minor) (Residence: Religion)* [1993] 2 FLR 163, CA.
4   *Re W (a minor) (welfare reports)* [1995] 3 FCR 793, [1995] 2 FLR 142, CA.
5   *Re S (minors) (care orders: appeal out of time)* [1996] 2 FCR 838, sub nom *Re S (Minors) (Discharge of Care Order)* [1995] 2 FLR 639, CA.

13.5 The comparatively unrestricted right of appeal, at least to the High Court from a family proceedings court, imposes a duty on advocates not to advise or encourage an appeal in cases with no hope of succeeding, however dissatisfied the party may be with the decision.[1] Legal advisers have been warned not to be carried away by the enthusiasm, frustration and hurt of their lay clients, it being observed that hopeless family appeals which have been brought without leave on public funds were all too frequent examples of public money spent to no good effect and as having an adverse effect upon the children concerned.[2]

[1] *Re D (minors) (family appeals)* [1995] 1 FCR 301, CA, per Butler-Sloss LJ. See also Handbook of Best Practice in Children Act Cases (June 1997) CAAC, para 89(a). Note also the comment in *Practice Note* [1999] 1 All ER 186, at para 7.
[2] *Re N (minors) (residence orders: sexual abuse)* [1996] 1 FCR 244, sub nom *Re N (Residence: Hopeless Appeals)* [1995] 2 FLR 230, CA, per Butler-Sloss LJ. The courts have also warned legal advisers of hopeless appeals that they might make wasted costed orders against them. See *Re G (A Minor) (Role of Appellate Court)* [1987] 1 FLR 164, CA and *Re O (a minor) (legal aid costs)* [1997] 1 FCR 159, sub nom *Re O (Costs: Liability of Legal Aid Board)* [1997] 1 FLR 465, CA. Cf *B v B (wasted costs order)* [2001] 3 FCR 724, [2001] 1 FLR 843.

13.6 In cases before the family proceedings court, advocates must not take an adversarial view of the proceedings. Accordingly, if the justices are in the process of making or appear likely to make a decision which is procedurally plainly wrong, it is the duty of the advocates, and notably those acting for the children's guardian and the local authority, to advise the justices that they are about to make a fundamental error of law.[1]

[1] *Re F (interim care order: evidence)* [1994] 1 FCR 729, sub nom *Re F (A Minor) (Care Order: Procedure)* [1994] 1 FLR 240.

2. Routes of appeal and procedure

(a) *Appeals from magistrates' courts*

13.7 The general rule, provided by, s 94(1) of the CA 1989, is that an appeal lies to the High Court against both the making and the refusal to make any order by a magistrates' court. Appeals lie to a single judge of the Family Division unless the President otherwise directs.[1] Save in the case of consent orders,[2] leave to appeal is not required.

[1] Handbook of Best Practice in Children Act Cases (June 1997) CAAC, para 87. Note: (1) applications to withdraw the appeal, have the appeal dismissed with the consent of all the parties or to amend the ground of appeal may be heard by a district judge: FPR 1991, r 4.22(7); (2) the proposal that in future appeals from magistrates' court decisions should lie to the county court, see para 13.36.
[2] See para 13.3.

13.8 Unless it is brought by way of case stated,[1] the procedure for appealing is governed by the FPR 1991, r 4.22 (which also applies to appeals against any decision of a district judge).[2] The appellant must file and serve on the parties:

• written notice of appeal setting out the grounds relied upon;
• a copy of the summons or application;
• a certified copy of the order appealed against and of any order staying its execution;

- copies of any notes of evidence; and
- copies of any reasons for the decision;
- reports and witness statements filed in the proceedings (not mentioned in the rules but regarded as important for a proper determination of the appeal).[3]

Notice of appeal must be filed and served within 14 days after the determination against which the appeal is brought or seven days where the appeal is against an interim care order or interim supervision order. Although these periods for service may be altered[4] by the High Court upon application, these time limits are strict and extensions of time will not be granted without good reason which advocates will be expected to justify.[5] Similar strict time limits[6] are laid down for respondents wishing to cross appeal or to seek a variation, or an affirmation of the decision on grounds other than those relied upon by the magistrates. No notice may be filed or served in an appeal against an order under s 38 of the CA 1989.[7]

[1] For which see CPR Sch 1 RSC Ord 55 r 1(1), (2). Note the proposal to abolish appeals by case stated, see para 13.36.
[2] Appeals from district judge to the county court circuit judge save where it is from a district judge sitting in the Principal Registry, when it lies to the High Court.
[3] *Re UT (a minor)* [1993] 2 FCR 565.
[4] Namely to a longer or shorter period: FPR 1991, r 4.22(3)(c).
[5] See Handbook of Best Practice in Children Act Cases (June 1997) CAAC, para 89(b).
[6] Namely 14 days of receipt of the notice of appeal: FPR 1991, r 4.22(5).
[7] FPR 1991, r 4.22(6).

13.9 Ideally, appeals should take place at the nearest convenient High Court centre.[1] It is vital, however, that the appeal be set down promptly and where it is unlikely that a case can be listed without delay on Circuit, arrangements will be made for the appeal to be heard in London.[2] Appellants should file a paginated bundle with a chronology together (save in the most simple cases) with a skeleton argument in advance of the hearing. Advocates must also file in advance an accurate estimate of the length of the hearing and keep the court informed of any change to that estimate.[3]

[1] *Practice Direction* [1992] 1 All ER 864 [1992] 1 WLR 261, as supplemented by the Procedural Directive [1992] 2 FLR 503, but cf *R v Oxfordshire County Council (Secure Accommodation Order)* [1992] Fam 150, sub nom *R (J) v Oxfordshire County Council* [1992] 3 All ER 660.
[2] Handbook of Best Practice in Children Act Cases (June 1997) CAAC, para 90.
[3] Handbook of Best Practice in Children Act Cases (June 1997) CAAC, para 91.

13.10 On hearing an appeal, the High Court may make such orders as may be necessary to give effect to its determination of the appeal and such incidental and consequential orders as appear just.[1] Any order made on appeal, other than that directing the application to be reheard by the magistrates, for the purposes of enforcement[2] and any power to vary, revive or discharge the order, shall be treated as if it were an order of the original magistrates' court and not the High Court.[3]

[1] Section 94(4) and (5), on which see eg *Re R (Care: Plan for Adoption: Best Interest)* [2006] 1 FLR 483 at para [18].

² Ie the Magistrates' Courts Act 1980, s 63(3), applies, see *B (BPM) v B (MM)* [1969] P 103, sub nom *B (B) v B (M)* [1969] 1 All ER 891.
³ CA 1989, s 94(9).

(b) Appeals from county courts and the High Court

13.11 Appeals generally lie to the Court of Appeal.¹ The procedure is now governed by CPR Pt 52 and the accompanying Practice Direction.

¹ County Courts Act 1984, s 77(1); Supreme Court Act 1981, s 16. But note so far as County Courts are concerned (1) there is a power in the original tribunal to review interim orders and also to order a rehearing if new evidence comes to light: County Court Rules 1991 Ord 37 r 1 (not revoked in relation to family proceedings: CPR 2.1), and (2) appeals from district judges normally lie to a circuit judge unless he is sitting in the Principal Registry when it lies to the High Court, see *Re S (a minor) (appeals from the principal registry)* [1997] 2 FCR 119, [1997] 2 FLR 856.

(I) PERMISSION TO APPEAL

13.12 Both the appellant and the respondent require permission to appeal save where the appeal is against:

- a committal order;
- a refusal to grant habeas corpus;
- a secure accommodation order made under the CA 1989, s 25; or
- as provided by the relevant practice direction.¹

Where the appeal is from a decision which itself was the determination of an appeal (ie a 'second appeal') permission to appeal is required from the Court of Appeal which will not be given unless it raises an important principle or practice or there is some other compelling reason.²

¹ CPR 52.3(1).
² CPR 52.13, CPR Pt 52 PD, para 4.9.

13.13 Save in the case of second appeals, where permission *must* be sought from the Court of Appeal,¹ permission to appeal should normally be sought from the lower court first² but if that application is refused or if no application was made at the first instance hearing, permission can then be sought from the Court of Appeal.³ If the appeal court refuses permission without a hearing the applicant has the right to ask for an oral hearing.⁴ There is, however, no appeal from a decision of the appeal court made at an oral hearing either to allow or to refuse permission to appeal to that court.⁵

¹ See para 13.12.
² CPR Pt 52 PD, para 4.6 the rationale being that because the first instance court is usually in the best position to determine whether leave to appeal should be given, where the parties are present for the delivery of the judgment it should be routine for the judge below: (a) to ask whether either party wants leave to appeal; and (b) to deal with the matter there and then. Applications should be made orally.
³ CPR 52.3(2), (3) and CPR Pt 52 PD, para 4.7.
⁴ CPR 52.3(4).
⁵ CPR Pt 52 PD, para 4.8 referring to s 54(4) of the Access to Justice Act 1999.

13.14 *Challenging decisions*

13.14 In the case of first appeals, permission to appeal will only be given where:

'(a) the court considers that the appeal would have a real prospect of success; or

(b) there is some other compelling reason why the appeal should be heard'.[1]

In the case of second appeals the test is more stringent in that the court should not give permission unless it considers that:

'(a) the appeal would raise an important point of principle or practice; or

(b) there is some other compelling reason for the Court of Appeal to hear it'.[2]

An order giving permission may limit the issues to be heard and be made subject to conditions.[3]

¹ CPR 52.3(6).
² CPR 52.13(2).
³ CPR 52.3(7).

13.15 Applications for permission to appeal should be made orally to the lower court at the hearing at which the decision to be appealed is made[1] or to the appeal court in an appeal notice.[2] Applications for permission may be considered by the appeal court without a hearing.[3] If granted the parties will be notified of that decision.[4] If refused, the parties will be informed of the reasons but this latter decision is subject to the appellant's right to have it reconsidered at an oral hearing.[5] A request for reconsideration must be filed at the appeal court within seven days after service of the notice that permission has been refused and a copy of the request must be served by the appellant on the respondent at the same time.[6]

¹ CPR Pt 52 PD, para 4.6.
² CPR 52.3(2)(b), and see para 13.16 below.
³ CPR Pt 52 PD, para 4.11. Unless the court directs otherwise such applications need not be on notice. However, such directions will usually be given if the appellant is seeking a remedy against the respondent pending the appeal: CPR Pt 52 PD, para 4.15.
⁴ CPR Pt 52 PD, para 4.12.
⁵ CPR Pt 52 PD, para 4.13.
⁶ CPR Pt 52 PD, para 4.14. If no request is made for the decision to be reconsidered, the refusal becomes binding once the time limits have expired. In children cases it is not uncommon for the Court of Appeal to adjourn the application for an oral hearing on notice with an appeal to follow if permission is granted.

13.16 Where the appellant seeks permission from the appeal court it must be requested in the appellant's notice.[1] This notice should be filed at the appeal court within such a period as may be directed by the lower court or, in the absence of any such direction, within 14 days of the date of the lower court's decision that is being appealed. If an extension of time for filing is required, the application should be made in the appellant's notice,[2] stating the reason for the delay and the steps taken before the making of the application. This appeal notice should, unless the appeal court otherwise orders, be served on each respondent as soon as practicable and in any event not later than seven days after it is filed. Similarly, where the respondent seeks permission it must be requested in the respondent's notice and filed within such period as directed by the lower court or, in the absence of any such direction, within 14 days of the date when the respondent:

(a)   is served with the appellant's notice; or
(b)   receives notification that the appeal court has given the appellant permission to appeal; or
(c)   receives notification that the application for permission to appeal and the appeal itself are to be heard together.

This notice should, unless the appeal court otherwise directs, be served on the appellant or any other respondent as soon as practicable and in any event not later than seven days after it is filed.[3] An appeal notice may not be amended without the appeal court's permission.[4]

1   CPR 52.4(1), and see Form N161.
2   See respectively CPR 52.4(2), 52.6; CPR Pt 52 PD, para 5.2 and CPR 52.4(3).
3   CPR 52.5(1), (5), (6).
4   CPR 52.8.

13.17 The granting of permission to appeal does not operate to stay the order which is the subject of appeal. Instead a specific application to stay must be made.[1] Similarly, separate applications should also be made for other remedies incidental to the appeal, eg an interim remedy or security for costs.[2]

1   CPR 52.7.
2   CPR Pt 52 PD, para 5.5.

(II) Documents to be included with the appellant's notice

13.18 Except where it relates to a refusal of permission to apply for judicial review,[1] the appellant must lodge the following documents with his notice:

'(1)   one additional copy of the appellant's notice for the appeal court;
(2)   one copy of the appellant's notice for each of the respondents;
(3)   one copy of any skeleton argument ... ;
(4)   a sealed copy of the order being appealed;
(5)   any order giving or refusing permission to appeal, together with a copy of the reasons for that decision;
(6)   any witness statements or affidavits in support of any application included in the appellant's notice; and
(7)   a bundle of documents in support of the appeal – this should include copies of the documents referred to in paragraphs (1) to (6) and any other documents which the appellant reasonably considers necessary to enable the appeal court to reach its decision on the hearing of the application or appeal. Documents which are extraneous to the issues to be considered should be excluded. The other documents will, subject to paragraph 5.7, include —
    (a)   any affidavit or witness statement filed in support of the application for permission to appeal or the appeal;
    (b)   a suitable record of the reasons for judgment of the lower court ... ;
    (c)   where permission to appeal has been given or permission is not required; any relevant transcript or note of evidence ... ;

(d)   statements of case;

(e)   any application notice (or case management documentation) relevant to the subject of the appeal;

(f)   in cases where the decision appealed was itself made on appeal, the first order, the reasons given and the appellant's notice of appeal from that order;

(g)   in cases where the appeal is from a tribunal, a copy of the tribunal's reasons for the decision, a copy of the decision reviewed by the tribunal and the reasons for the original decision;

(h)   in the case of judicial review or a statutory appeal, the original decision which was the subject of the application to the lower court;

(i)   relevant affidavits, witness statements, summaries, experts' reports and exhibits;

(j)   any skeleton arguments relied on in the lower court; and

(k)   such other documents as the court may direct.'[2]

1   CPR Pt 52 PD, para 15.3.
2   CPR Pt 52 PD, para 5.6.

(III) Skeleton Arguments

13.19 The appellant's notice must either be accompanied by a skeleton argument or such an argument may be included in the notice unless:

(*a*)   it is impracticable to do so, in which case it must be lodged and served on all respondents within 14 days of the filing of the notice; or

(*b*)   the appellant is unrepresented (though even unrepresented litigants are encouraged to do so since this is helpful to the court).[1]

1   CPR Pt 52 PD, para 5.9.

13.20 Skeleton arguments for the appeal court should contain a numbered list of points of no more than a few sentences which should both define and confine the areas of controversy. Each point should be followed by references to any documentation on which the appellant seeks to rely.[1] The appellant should also consider what other information the appeal court will need, for example, a list of persons who feature in the case or glossaries of technical terms. In most appeals a chronology of relevant events will be necessary. In relation to points of law, authorities relied upon should be cited with reference to the particular pages where the principle concerned is set out.[2]

1   CPR Pt 52 PD, para 5.10. In practice this requirement seems more honoured in the breach than in the observance.
2   CPR Pt 52 PD, para 5.11.

(IV) Procedure after permission is granted

13.21 Where the appeal court gives permission to appeal, copies of all the documents must be served on the respondent within seven days of receiving the order giving permission to appeal.[1] The Court of Appeal will send the parties notification of either the date of the hearing or the period of time (the 'listing window') during which the appeal is likely to be heard and the date by which the appeal will be heard.[2] In addition it will send the parties a questionnaire which must be completed and lodged within 14 days of the date of the letter of notification and which must include, if the appellant is legally represented, the advocate's time estimate for the hearing and details of the preparation of documents.[3]

[1] CPR Pt 52 PD, para 6.2
[2] CPR Pt 52 PD, para 6.3. In children's cases hearing dates are normally listed within 3 months of permission being granted.
[3] CPR Pt 52 PD, paras 6.4–6.6.

(c) Appeals to the House of Lords/Supreme Court

13.22 Appeals from the Court of Appeal lie to the House of Lords.[1] In exceptional cases 'leap frog' appeals may be made directly to the House of Lords from the High Court in accordance with the Administration of Justice Act 1969, ss 12 and 15.

[1] Appellate Jurisdiction Act 1876.

13.23 An appeal from the Court of Appeal to the House of Lords may only be made with leave.[1] Applications for leave must first be made in the Court of Appeal either at the hearing, or later by notice of motion. If leave is refused in the Court of Appeal, then the party must apply, by way of petition, to the House of Lords. The petition for permission to appeal must be lodged within 28 days of the order appealed against, or (if the applicant is legally aided) within 28 days of the grant or refusal of legal aid if later.[2] The petition will first be considered by the Appeal Committee of the House of Lords (which comprises three Law Lords). If that Committee is unanimous that the petition should be allowed to proceed, then the parties will be notified (and the respondent will have 14 days within which to object). If the Committee is unanimous that the petition should not succeed then permission to appeal will not be granted, and that will be the end of the process. If the Committee is divided, then the application for permission will be referred for oral hearing.[3]

[1] Administration of Justice (Appeals) Act 1934, s 1(1).
[2] Direction 25.3 of the House of Lords *Directions* as to the Procedure.
[3] See Directions 4.5 to 4.18 of the House of Lords *Directions* as to Procedure.

13.24 The appeal must be lodged within three months of the order appealed against. The form and content of the petition are set out in Direction 10.1 of the House of Lords *Directions* as to procedure. Except in certain specified cases, the appellant must lodge security for costs within one week of the presentation of the appeal, or lodge a form of consent to waiver of the security costs.[1]

[1] See Direction 11 of the House of Lords *Directions* as to Procedure.

13.25 By s 23 of the Constitutional Reform Act 2005 the Appellate Committee of the House of Lords will be replaced by the Supreme Court. At the time of writing the Supreme Court is scheduled to come into operation in October

2009 though the date is subject to planning permission being granted to refurbish Middlesex Guildhall which is where the new court will be housed. The creation of this new court will not alter the basic routes of appeal to the final court, but there may be accompanying procedural modifications.

3. The position pending appeal

13.26 Under the general powers to impose directions and conditions in private law orders under the CA 1989, s 11(7)[1] the operation of any s 8 order can be postponed pending an appeal, or other interim arrangements can be made. Stays, which should not normally be granted for more than 14 days,[2] may be granted at first instance both in the county court and High Court (cf. magistrates' powers, discussed below).[3] In these cases any stays or other interim arrangements pending an appeal imposed under s 11(7) should be made before the parties leave the court since once they have left the court and an appeal is lodged the court at first instance ceases to have jurisdiction. In cases of urgency stays can be sought and granted by the Court of Appeal over the telephone both during and outside office hours.[4] Although magistrates appear to have no power to order a stay, they are empowered under s 11(7) to make interim arrangements.[5]

[1] Discussed at paras 5.109–5.110.
[2] *Hereford and Worcester County Council v EH* [1985] FLR 975 at 977, per Wood J.
[3] Per Singer J in *Re J (a minor) (residence)* [1993] 2 FCR 636 at 642, [1994] 1 FLR 369 at 375.
[4] See *Re S (Child Proceedings: Urgent Appeals)* [2007] EWCA Civ 958, [2007] 2 FLR 1044 and the cases there cited. The business hours telephone number is 0207 947 6000, the out of hours number (the Security Offices) is 020 7947 6260.
[5] See Handbook of Best Practice in Children Act Cases (June 2007) CAAC, para 92. But see further in relation to public law cases, para 13.27 below.

13.27 In public law cases the court may, if it dismisses an application for a care order and at the time of dismissal the child is the subject of an interim care or supervision order, make either a care or supervision order, as the case may be, for a limited duration pending an appeal.[1] Similarly, upon granting a discharge, the court may order either that its decision is not to have effect or that the care or supervision order is to continue, pending the appeal.[2] In each case these orders may have effect only for the 'appeal period', that is, either between the lodging of an appeal and the determination of it, or the time during which an appeal may be made.[3]

[1] Section 40(1), (2).
[2] Section 40(3).
[3] Section 40(4) and (6).

13.28 Justices have no statutory power to grant a stay of a care order. If an appeal is being considered and a stay required, the proper course is to apply to the High Court where the judge has such power under the inherent jurisdiction.[1] It may be, however, that justices have a common law power to grant a stay of execution, which has not been affected by, s 40. In an appropriate case the court should consider the welfare of the child and the effect of a move pending appeal.[2]

4. The powers of appellate courts – the general position

13.29 An appellate court may grant or dismiss the appeal.[1] Alternatively, if it is satisfied that the original order was wrong but is unsure upon the evidence what order should be made, it can remit the case for a rehearing and in the meantime give appropriate directions. This power of remittal, at any rate in cases where the order appealed from is a final order, includes the power to remit the case to a different court level from that of first instance.[2]

1.	On hearing an appeal the High Court has a discretion to make such orders as may be necessary to give effect to its determination of the appeal and to make such incidental or consequential orders as it thinks just (CA 1989, s 94(4), (5)), see also above at para 13.10.
2.	See *Suffolk County Council v C* [1999] 1 FCR 473n, [1999] 1 FLR 259n, per Holman J explaining and distinguishing *Leicestershire County Council v G* [1995] 1 FCR 205, [1994] 2 FLR 329. See also *D v D (application for contact)* [1994] 1 FCR 694.

13.30 The appeal court has 'a wide ranging power to consider and deal with the way in which the court below came to its decision but it is not empowered to hear evidence, except in certain circumstances.'[1] It can, however, hear fresh evidence to resolve its doubts about the original decision.[2] The admission of such evidence is at the appellate court's discretion,[3] though it is normally admitted if it relates to relevant circumstances occurring between the first instance hearing and the appeal hearing. In the private law context it has been held[4] that appeals concerning children do not automatically call for an up-to-date welfare report. If fresh evidence is admitted, the appellate court will look to see if it invalidates the first instance decision, and if that decision is found wrong on the material before the court the appeal will normally be allowed.[5] Conversely, the admission of fresh evidence may justify upholding the original decision even though it would otherwise have been held to be plainly wrong.[6] Exceptionally, fresh evidence, with a view to the reopening of an appeal can be admitted to demonstrate that the earlier litigation process, whether at trial or at first appeal, had been critically undermined. This is known as a *Taylor v Lawrence* application.[7]

1.	See *Croydon London Borough v A* [1992] Fam 169, [1992] 3 All ER 788.
2.	See Lord Scarman in *B v W (wardship: appeal)* [1979] 3 All ER 83 at 95–6, HL. But note Waite LJ's comments in *Re G (A Minor) (Care: Evidence)* [1994] 2 FLR 785, 797, CA that so the so-called rule in *Ladd v Marshall* [1954] 1 WLR 1489, [1954] 3 All ER 745, CA, is applied less rigorously in children cases.
3.	*A v A (Custody Appeal: Role of Appellate Court)* [1988] 1 FLR, 193, CA; *M v M (Minor: Custody Appeal)* [1987] 1 WLR 404, CA; *Re C (A Minor) (Wardship: Proceedings)* [1984] FLR 419, CA and *Ladd v Marshall*, above
4.	*M v M (Welfare Report)* [1989] 2 FLR 354, CA.
5.	*Re G (a minor) (appeal)* [1993] 1 FCR 810, sub nom *Re C (A Minor) (Care: Child's Wishes)* [1993] 1 FLR 832; *Croydon London Borough v A* [1992] Fam 169, [1992] 3 All ER 788.
6.	*M v M (Minor: Custody Appeal)* [1987] 1 WLR 404, CA.

7   Ie after *Taylor v Lawrence* [2002] EWCA Civ 90, [2003] QB 528, [2002] 2 All ER 353. See also CPR 52.17. For an unsuccessful *Taylor v Lawrence* application made in the context of care proceedings, see *Re U (Re-Opening of Appeal)* [2005] EWCA Civ 52, [2005] 2 FLR 444 which is also authority for saying that the *Ladd v Marshall*, above, grounds used to justify a first-time appeal based on new evidence do not suffice to justify a second appeal under *Taylor v Lawrence*. In the latter case the fresh evidence must demonstrate a *powerful* probability (as opposed to a real possibility) that an erroneous result had been arrived at in earlier proceedings.

13.31 In deciding whether to allow an appeal, there are no special rules governing cases involving children. In *G v G*[1] the House of Lords held that an appellate court cannot overturn a first instance decision merely upon the basis that it disagrees with it. Rather it must be satisfied either that the judge has erred as a matter of law (ie he applied the wrong principle) or that he relied upon evidence that he should have ignored or ignored evidence that he should have taken into account, or that the decision was so 'plainly wrong' that the only legitimate conclusion was that the judge had erred in the exercise of his discretion. Applying *G v G*, Lord Nicholls has forcibly observed:[2]

> 'The Court of Appeal is not intended to be a forum in which unsuccessful litigants, where no error occurred at first instance, may have a second trial of the same issue by different judges under the guise of an appeal. The mere fact that appellate judges might have reached a different conclusion had they been carrying out the evaluation and balancing exercise does not mean that the first instance judge fall into error'.

This approach applies equally to appeals against private law or public law decisions[3] or those made in wardship[4] and regardless of whether, for example, the appeal is to the High Court from a magistrates' court decision, to a circuit judge from a district judge or to the Court of Appeal from a judge.[5] As discussed in para 13.30 above, under the *Taylor v Lawrence*[6] principle, an appeal can be allowed upon the basis that the earlier litigation process had been critically undermined.

1   [1985] 2 All ER 225, [1985] 1 WLR 647, HL.
2   *Re B (a child) (sole adoption by unmarried father)* [2001] UKHL 70, para [17], [2002] 1 FCR 150, [2002] 1 FLR 196. See also *Re C (leave to remove from jurisdiction)* [2000] 2 FCR 40, [2000] 2 FLR 457, CA.
3   See eg *Croydon London Borough Council v A* [1992] Fam 169, [1992] 3 All ER 788, *Re G (a Minor) (Care: Evidence)* [1995] 2 FCR 120, [1994] 2 FLR 785, CA and *Re S (Appeal from Principal Registry: Procedure)*[1997] 2 FCR 119, [1997] 2 FLR 856.
4   See *B v W (Wardship: Appeal)* [1979] 3 All ER 83, [1979] 1 WLR 1041, HL.
5   Per Butler-Sloss LJ in *Re W (A Child) (Illegitimate Child: Change of Surname)* [2001] Fam 1 at para [23], [1999] 3 FCR 337, [1999] 2 FLR 930, CA. See also *Re M (a minor) (contact)* [1995] 2 FCR 435,, sub nom *Re M (Section 94 Appeals)* [1995] 1 FLR 546, CA.
6   [2002] EWCA Civ 90, [2003] QB 528, [2002] 2 All ER 353.

5. The powers of the Court of Appeal

13.32 It is expressly provided by CPR 52.10 that the Court of Appeal has, in general, all the powers of the lower court and in particular can:

● affirm, set aside or vary any order or judgment made by the lower court;

● refer any claim or issue for determination by the lower court;

- order a new trial or hearing;
- make orders for the payment of interest; and
- make a costs order.

13.33 Appeals are limited to a review of the lower court's decision unless the Court of Appeal considers that in the particular case it is in the interests of justice that there be a rehearing.[1] Unless it orders otherwise the appeal court will not receive oral evidence or evidence which was not before the lower court.[2] At the appeal hearing a party may not rely on a matter that is not contained in the notice of appeal unless the appeal court gives permission.[3]

[1] CPR 52.11(1).
[2] CPR 52.11(2). But see also para 13.30.
[3] CPR 52.11(5).

13.34 The Court of Appeal will allow an appeal where the lower court's decision was:

'(a) wrong; or
(b) unjust because of a serious procedural or other irregularity in the proceedings in the lower court'.[1]

It may draw any inference of fact which it considers justified on the evidence.[2]

[1] CPR 52.11(3).
[2] CPR 52.11(4).

13.35 In all cases it is desirable that appeals should be heard as quickly as possible.[1] Failure by barristers and solicitors to exercise the greatest possible diligence in complying with time limits imposed by the courts for the preparation of appeals may be regarded as professional misconduct.[2]

[1] See Handbook of Best Practice in Children Act Cases (June 1997) CAAC, para 90.
[2] *Re M (A Minor)* (1989) Times, 29 December, CA.

6. Reform proposals

13.36 Following the response[1] to the Government's Consultation Paper, *Family Procedure Rules – A new procedural code for family proceedings*[2] it is proposed that:

- there should be a single form of appeal notice to initiate all appeals from decisions of magistrates' courts in family proceedings;
- the route of appeal from a family proceedings court be changed from the High Court to a county court to be heard by a circuit judge; and
- appeals from decisions of a family proceedings court by way of case stated be abolished.

[1] CP(R) 19/06 (22 February, 2008).
[2] CP 19/06 (30 August, 2006).

13.37 *Challenging decisions*

JUDICIAL REVIEW

1. Nature of the remedy

13.37 Judicial review is the standard administrative law remedy for correcting decisions taken by inferior courts, tribunals and other bodies. Applications are now made to the Administrative Court. As CPR 54.1(2)(a) states:

> 'a "claim for judicial review" means a claim to review the lawfulness of—
> (i)   an enactment; or
> (ii) a decision, action or failure to act in relation to the exercise of a public function'.

13.38 A claim for judicial review may only be made in respect of a decision, action or failure to act in relation to the exercise of a *public* function. It cannot be made merely to enforce private law rights against a public body.[1] Any person with a sufficient interest in the matter may bring a claim.[2]

[1]   *R v East Berkshire Health Authority, ex p Walsh* [1985] QB 152 at 162, [1984] 3 All ER 425 at 429, per Lord Donaldson MR.
[2]   Supreme Court Act 1981, s 31(3); CPR 54.1(1)(f). For further discussion see *Civil Procedure: The White Book Service 2008* at 54.1.11 ff and the *Civil Court Practice 2008* (the 'Green Book') LexisNexis at 54.1[1] ff.

13.39 No special rules apply in judicial review of children cases.[1] The function of the court, as Scott Baker J neatly expressed it, is 'to consider in each case not whether the decision itself is right or fair but whether the manner in which the decision is made is fair'.[2] Put another way, when determining a judicial review application the court is not exercising a 'best interests' or "welfare" jurisdiction nor is it the court's function in these proceedings to monitor, regulate, or police the performance by a local authority of their statutory functions on a continuing basis.[3] There are the following remedies:

- *mandatory orders*, that is, where a body is ordered to comply with statutory duty, for example, that the local authority provide some specific support service provided for in Pt III of Sch 2 to the CA 1989,[4] or to set up a complaints procedure that complies with the regulations issued under s 26;[5]
- *quashing orders*, that is, that the original order or decision be quashed as, for example, a Director of Social Services decision not to ratify a complaints panel decision that a 17 year old should be accommodated;[6]
- *prohibiting orders*, that is, restraining a body from acting unlawfully; and
- *declarations* that an action or policy is unlawful[7] and/or an *injunction* to prevent an unlawful act taking place or to prevent an unlawful policy from continuing.[8]

[1]   But this is not to say that in judging the reasonableness of a local authority's action in respect of children in their care attention should not be paid to the authority's duty to safeguard the child's interests; cf *R v Harrow London Borough Council, ex p D* [1990] Fam 133, [1990] 3 All ER 12, CA, per Butler-Sloss LJ.

² R v *Hereford and Worcester County Council, ex p D* [1992] 1 FLR 448 at 457. 'Fairness' is judged in this context against the criteria of legality, rationality and procedural propriety, see para 13.44 below.

³ Per Munby J in *R (on the application of P, W, F and G) v Essex County Council* [2004] EWHC 2027 (Admin), [2004] All ER (D) 103 (Aug) at [32]–[33] and repeated in *R (B By Her Litigation Friend MB) v London Borough of Lambeth* [2006] EWHC 639 (Admin), [2007] 1 FLR.

⁴ See *R (on the application of S) v London Borough of Wandsworth, London Borough of Hammersmith and Fulham, London Borough of Lambeth* [2001] EWHC Admin 209, [2002] 1 FLR 469, in which Lambeth and Wandsworth were ordered to make an assessment of whether the children concerned were in 'need'.

⁵ See *R v Barnet London Borough Council, ex p S* [1994] 2 FCR 781 at 788, [1994] 1 FLR 592 at 598, per Auld J. The complaints procedure is discussed at paras 13.53 ff.

⁶ See eg *Re T (accommodation by local authority)* [1995] 1 FCR 517, [1995] 1 FLR 159. If a quashing order is made the court may remit the matter to the decision-maker and direct it to reconsider the matter but if it feels there is no purpose in remitting, the court can take the decision itself: CPR 54.19.

⁷ See eg *R (on the application of Howard League for Penal Reform) v Secretary of State for the Home Department* [2002] EWHC 2497 (Admin), [2003] 1 FLR 484 and *R v Cornwall County Council, ex p LH* [2000] 1 FCR 460, [2000] 1 FLR 236.

⁸ Unlike when seeking a mandatory, prohibiting or quashing order, it is not mandatory to use the judicial review procedure laid down in CPR 54.3. Note, it is not unknown for mandatory injunctions to be sought. For an example of (unsuccessfully) seeking a declaration, see *R (on the application of M) v Hammersmith and Fulham London Borough Council* [2008] UKHL 14, [2008] 1 WLR 535, [2008] 1 FLR 1384.

13.40 It is also possible to include in a claim for judicial review a claim for damages but not to seek damages alone.¹ The court may at any time during the course of judicial review proceedings grant interim relief.² The court also has an inherent power to grant a stay.³

¹ CPR 54.3(2).
² CPR Pt 25.
³ CPR 54.10(2).

2. The requirements for judicial review

13.41 A prerequisite for a claim for judicial review is that there must be a reviewable 'decision'. In *R v Devon County Council, ex p L*,¹ for example, it was held that a social worker's letter informing the applicant's cohabitant that he was suspected of sexual abuse did not amount to a 'decision' so that the action for judicial review failed at the outset. Even if there is a reviewable 'decision' applicants must first obtain the court's permission to proceed.² Pursuant to CPR Pt 54, the claimant must first file a claim form in the Administrative Court Office. Claim forms must be filed promptly and in any event not later than three months after the grounds to make the claim first arose.³ Claims must inter alia state any remedy (including any interim remedy) being sought, and provide a detailed statement of the grounds for bringing the claim (accompanied by any written evidence in support) and a time estimate for the substantive hearing of the application for judicial review, should permission be granted.⁴

¹ [1991] 2 FLR 541. Cf *R v Chief Constable of North Wales, ex p Thorpe* [1999] QB 396, [1998] 2 FLR 571, sub nom *R v Chief Constable of North Wales Police ex p AB*, [1998] 3 All ER 310, [1998] 3 FCR 371, CA – decision of police to reveal applicant's identity (the

applicant having served sentences for rape and indecent assault) was amenable to judicial review – but the action failed on facts. See more generally, the *White Book* at 54.1.3.
2   CPR 54.4.
3   CPR 54.5. Although this time limit cannot be extended simply by agreement between the parties a court may grant an extension subject to a good reason being adduced, see, for example, *R (on the application of Raines) v Orange Grove Foster Care Agency Ltd* [2006] EWHC 1887 (Admin), [2007] 1 FLR 760. But see *Re S (Application for Judicial Review)* [1998] 1 FCR 368, [1998] 1 FLR 790, CA, where leave was refused the application being made four months after the expiration of the time limit. But note the HL left open the question whether 'promptness' is EU and human rights compliant see *R (on the application of Burkett) v Hammersmith and Fulham London Borough Council, ex p* [2002] UKHL 23, [2002] 1 WLR 1593, [2002] 3 All ER 97. See further the *White Book* at 54.5.1 and the Green Book at 54.5[2].
4   See generally CPR 8.2 and 54.2 and the accompanying Practice Direction – Judicial Review, paras 5.1, 5.6 and 5.7.

13.42   Applications for permission are generally considered on the papers alone.[1] The claimant does not have a right to have the permission determined at an oral hearing. However, there is a right to request that any decision to refuse or limit the grant of permission be reconsidered at an oral hearing.[2]

1   CPR Pt 54 PD at para 8.4.
2   CPR 54.12(3).

13.43   Leave is not a formality for, as Balcombe LJ said in *R v Lancashire County Council, ex p M*,[1] there must be a reasonable prospect of the court coming to the decision that the local authority's conclusion was so unreasonable that no reasonable local authority could ever have come to it.[2] In any event in some cases it is likely to be held that the preferable remedy is to invoke the complaints procedure.[3] It has been held,[4] for instance, that where neither fact nor law is in dispute but rather the way the local authority carried out its duty, the proper remedy is under the complaints procedure and not by judicial review. Challenges to proposed local authority care plans should generally be made in care proceedings rather than by judicial review.[5] Nevertheless the availability of an alternative remedy cannot be said as a matter of principle to mean that there cannot be a judicial review.[6]

1   [1992] 1 FLR 109 at 113, CA. See also *Re M (Care Proceedings: Judicial Review)* [2003] EWHC 850 (Admin), [2003] 2 FLR 171 in which leave was refused.
2   Given that some information is confidential (eg records compiled in relation to foster carers, see in England, the Fostering Services Regulations 2002, SI 2002/57, reg 32) having to establish even a prima facie case can be difficult.
3   Note Ward J's observation in *R v Royal Borough of Kingston-upon-Thomas, ex p T* [1994] 1 FLR 798 that it is the clear, broad legislative purpose that the complaints procedure should be invoked in preference to judicial review. See further para 13.61. But cf *Re R (recovery orders)* [1998] 3 FCR 321 at 330, [1998] 2 FLR 401 at 409 in which Wall J suggested that judicial review is the only means of challenging a local authority decision to change a 'responsible person' under a care or emergency protection order.
4   *R v Birmingham City Council, ex p A* [1997] 2 FCR 357, [1997] 2 FLR 841, per Sir Stephen Brown P (see further para 13.58) and *R v East Sussex County Council, ex p W* [1999] 1 FCR 536, [1998] 2 FLR 1082. Note also *R (on the application of M) v London Borough of Bromley* [2002] EWCA Civ 1113, [2002] 2 FLR 802 in which it was held that the appropriate remedy in respect of a decision to place a local authority employee on an index of individuals considered unsuitable to work with children, was to appeal to the Care Standards Tribunal.
5   See eg *Re M (Care Proceedings: Judicial Review)*, above, in which it was sought to challenge a local authority decision to apply for an emergency protection order in respect of a baby as soon as he was born; and *Re C (Adoption: Religious Observance)* [2002]

1 FLR 1119 where a guardian sought to challenge a local authority care plan. Cf *Re S and W (Care Proceedings)* [2007] EWCA Civ 232 [2007] 2 FLR 275 in which it was said that where the local authority decision-making is flawed (in that case by ignoring the court's views and changing the care plan without reference to the court or the guardian) and a re-hearing of care proceedings inevitable, judicial review proceedings are not only appropriate but may be necessary to protect the children from removal from the present carers without the court's approval. However, judicial review proceedings should be consolidated with the rehearing of the care proceedings and be heard at the same time by the same judge.

6   Per Cazalet J in *R v High Peak Magistrates' Court, ex p B* [1995] 3 FCR 237, [1995] 1 FLR 568. Note also *S v Knowsley Borough Council* [2004] EWHC 491 (Fam), [2004] 2 FLR 716 in which Charles J considered that it was not inappropriate to use judicial review to challenge the legality of a secure accommodation order, see [63] ff.

13.44 To substantiate a claim for judicial review, the applicant must be able to bring himself within the so-called *Wednesbury* principle[1] as interpreted by the House of Lords in *Council of Civil Service Unions v Minister for Civil Defence.*[2] According to Lord Diplock in that case,[3] there are three main heads under which court intervention may be justified:

- 'illegality' (where there was an error of law in reaching the relevant decision);
- 'procedural impropriety' (where the relevant rules have not been complied with); and
- 'irrationality' (where a decision 'is so outrageous in its defiance of logic or of accepted moral standards that no sensible person who had applied his mind to the question to be decided could have arrived at it').

1   Following *Associated Provincial Picture Houses Ltd v Wednesbury Corpn* [1948] 1 KB 223, [1947] 2 All ER 680, CA.
2   [1985] AC 374, [1984] 3 All ER 935, HL.
3   [1985] AC 374 at 410, [1984] 3 All ER 935 at 950, HL.

3. Circumstances in which judicial review has been sought

13.45 In the context of disputing local authority decisions,[1] claimants are commonly parents, foster parents, prospective adopters, the children themselves, relative and guardians.

1   Claims, concerning children, can be made against bodies other than local authorities, see eg *R (on the application of P) v Secretary of State for the Home Department*; *R (on the application of Q) v Secretary of State for the Home Department* [2001] EWCA Civ 1151, [2001] 3 FCR 416, [2001] 2 FLR 1122, CA, in which claims were brought against the Home Department (one successful and one unsuccessful) and one made against the Prison Service in respect of their policy only to allow babies up to the age of 18 months to remain in prison with their mothers. See also *R (on the application of the National Association of Guardians ad Litem and Reporting Officers) v Children and Family Court Advisory and Support Service* [2001] EWHC Admin 693, [2002] 1 FLR 255 in which the decision of the CAFCASS board not to proceed with the offer of self employment to guardians ad litem was quashed.

13.46 Although complaints have been made about a variety of local authority decisions (see the chart at para 13.50 below) by no means all were successful. One common reason for failure is a finding that the local authority was acting lawfully and reasonably.[1] In this respect it should be appreciated that it is not

13.46 *Challenging decisions*

enough to question the wisdom of a decision,[2] rather the claimant must discharge the heavy onus of showing that no reasonable authority could have reached the particular decision complained of. Another common reason for failure is that judicial review is thought to be an inappropriate remedy, as for example where challenges to a care plan should instead be made in care proceedings[3] or because it is preferable to use the complaints procedure.[4]

[1]　See eg *R (on the application of P) v London Borough of Hackney* [2007] EWHC 1365 (Admin), [2007] Fam Law 867 – local authority held to have acted reasonably in assessing a 12-year-old autistic child's needs as being best served by being with the grandmother and by attending his current day school; *R (on the application of W) v Leicestershire County Council* [2003] EWHC 704 (Admin), [2003] 2 FLR 185, removal of twins from a foster parent held to be a legitimate means of protecting the children and *R (on the application of S) v Swindon Borough Council* [2001] EWHC Admin 334, [2001] 3 FCR 702, [2001] 2 FLR 776 – only a low threshold, namely reasonable cause to suspect abuse to trigger duty under s 47 to investigate and monitor family.

[2]　See eg *Re M (Care Proceedings: Judicial Review)* [2003] EWHC 850 (Fam), [2003] 2 FLR 171.

[3]　See the cases cited at para 13.43, n 5.

[4]　See eg *R v East Sussex County Council, ex p W* [1999] 1 FCR 536, [1998] 2 FLR 1082, *R v Birmingham City Council, ex p A* [1997] 2 FCR 357, [1997] 2 FLR 841 and *R v Royal Borough of Kingston-upon-Thames, ex p T* [1994] 1 FLR 798, discussed further at para 13.58. But cf *Re R (recovery orders)* [1998] 3 FCR 321, [1998] 2 FLR 401, discussed at para 13.43, n 2.

13.47 Of those actions that were successful an important factor is the failure of the local authority either to allow the complainant to put his side of the case or otherwise to explain its reasoning. In *R v (on the application of Raines) v Orange Grove Foster Care Agency*,[1] for example, which involved the agency's termination (contrary to its adoption panel's recommendation) of the claimant's registration as an approved foster parent, judicial review succeeded inter alia because the agency's process of reasoning was unknown (there was nothing to show that it had given any weight to the panel's recommendation) nor had it given the claimant its reason for reaching the decision. The court further observed that the fact that de-registration constituted a serious stigma on the claimant prejudicing her future prospects as a foster carer was highly relevant in evaluating whether the agency's decision was procedurally unfair and/or *Wednesbury* unreasonable. Similarly in *R (v Devon County Council, ex p O (Adoption)*[2] which involved the removal of a child placed for adoption with the applicants, judicial review succeeded because the local authority failed to consult or give the applicants an opportunity to be heard. Another striking example is *R v Norfolk County Council Social Services Department, ex p M*,[3] which concerned a plumber working in a house where a teenage girl made allegations that she was sexually abused by him. She had twice previously been the victim of sexual abuse and a few days later made similar allegations against another man. After a case conference the plumber's name was entered on the Child Abuse Register as an abuser. His employers were informed and they suspended him pending a fully enquiry. The plumber first learned of these allegations through a letter informing him of the decision to place his name on the register. Waite J held that, given the serious consequences of registration for the plumber, the local authority had a duty to act fairly, which it had manifestly failed to do by not giving him an opportunity to meet the allegations.

1   [2006] EWHC 1887 (Admin), [2007] 1 FLR 760.
2   [1997] 2 FLR 388. Cf *R v Avon County Council, ex p Crabtree* [1996] 1 FLR 502, CA, where the de-registration of an approved foster parent was only made after careful consideration and consultation. Consequently the action failed.
3   [1989] QB 619, [1989] 2 All ER 359.

13.48   The *Norfolk*[1] case was exceptional and, as Butler-Sloss LJ said in *R v Harrow London Borough Council, ex p D*,[2] recourse to judicial review in respect of placing a name on the Child Protection Register ought to be rare. She further held that courts should not encourage applications to review case conference decisions or recommendations because it was important for those involved in this difficult area to 'be allowed to perform their task without having to look over their shoulder all the time for the possible intervention of the court'. She pointed out that in 'balancing adequate protection for the child and the fairness to an adult, the interest of an adult may have to take second place to the needs of the child'.[3] Notwithstanding these observations, there may still be some occasions when judicial review is appropriate, even of a decision to place a child's name on the Protection Register.[4] In *R v Cornwall County Council, ex p LH*,[5] for example, an action for judicial review succeeded against the Council in respect of their policy: (a) not to permit solicitors to attend child protection case conferences on behalf of parents, other than to read out a prepared statement; and (b) not to provide parents attending such conferences with a copy of the minutes.

1   *R v Norfolk County Council Social Services Department, ex p M* [1989] QB 619, [1989] 2 All ER 359.
2   [1990] Fam 133, [1990] 2 All ER 12, CA.
3   Above at 138 and 17 respectively. See also *R v London Borough of Wandsworth, ex p P* [1989] 1 FLR 387 at 308 in which Ewbank J said 'Foster-parents have to accept that their interests may have to be subordinated to the children they care for. Accordingly, provided the rules of fairness are complied with, the decision as to whether there is a risk or not, is one that has to be taken by the local authority. In the ordinary way, provided the rules of natural justice are complied with the foster parents have no redress'.
4   See eg *R v Hampshire County Council, ex p H* [1999] 2 FLR 359, CA.
5   [2000] 1 FCR 460, [2000] 1 FLR 236. As Scott Baker J commented (at 469 and 243 respectively) what was complained about in this case was not 'the decision of the conference but the manner in which its deliberations were conducted'.

13.49   Other examples of where judicial review has succeeded include *B v London Borough of Lewisham*[1] in which a local authority fixed, contrary to a sensible interpretation of the Special Guardianship Guidance, special guardianship allowances by reference to adoption rather than fostering allowances and *R (on the application of CD) v Isle of Anglesey County Council*[2] in which the local authority's care plan (to terminate a successful foster placement) had been fixed without giving due consideration to the child's consistently expressed views and the mother's capability to care for the child who suffered from quadriplegic cerebral palsy.

1   [2008] EWHC 738 (Admin), [2008] Fam Law 640.
2   [2004] EWHC 1635, [2005] 1 FLR 59. For other examples see the chart below.

Summary of reported judicial review cases involving children and local authorities

13.50

Case	Subject-matter	Result
R (on the application of M) v London Borough of Hammersmith and Fulham [2008] UKHL 14, [2008] 1 WLR 535, [2008] 1 FLR 1384.	The claimant, when aged 17, was told by her mother to leave home. She told the local authority she was homeless and was provided with temporary bed and breakfast accommodation under the Housing Act 1996. Following her eviction for a breach of the licence agreement she was told that no further accommodation would be provided. The claimant sought judicial review on the basis that the authority's decision to treat her as unintentionally homeless and in priority need under the 1996 Act was unlawful. She also sought a declaration that she was a 'child in need' under the CA 1989 and should have been accommodated under s 20.	Failed: It was not unlawful of the local authority to accommodate the claimant under the Housing Act 1996. While a local authority cannot side-step s 20 obligations under the CA 1989 by recording or arguing they were acting under s 17 or some other legislation. In this case there was no evidence that the children's services authority had done anything at all and it could not be said she was a 'child in need' to whom s 20 duties were owed.

Case	Subject-matter	Result
B v London Borough of Lewisham [2008] EWHC 738 (Admin), [2008] Fam Law 640.	The claimant sought judicial review of the level of financial support that the defendant local authority were offering to pay her as the special guardian of her granddaughter and of the legality of the defendant's Special Guardianship Allowance Scheme generally. That scheme allied special guardianship allowances to adoption allowances. It was argued that instead they should have been allied to fostering allowances, and that the claimant's support should have accordingly been so calculated.	*Succeeded*: Paragraph 65 of the Special Guardianship Guidance issued under s 7 of the Local Authority Social Services Act 1970 (which while not having the force of law should be followed unless there was good reason not to follow it – see *Munjaz v Ashworth Hospital* [2005] UKHL 58), was sensibly interpreted as requiring special guardianship allowances to be fixed by reference to fostering allowances. The local authority had therefore acted wrongly by *ignoring* fostering allowances when setting the special guardianship allowances.

Case	Subject-matter	Result
R (on the application of Raines) v Orange Grove Foster Care Agency [2006] EWHC 1887 (Admin), [2007] 1 FLR 760.	The claimant was approved by the defendant agency as a foster carer. She had cared for a child with severe physical disabilities but when he was returned to his usual placement staff raised concerns about his physical condition. The matter was referred to the agency's fostering panel which initially recommended de-registration. Following written representations by the claimant, however, the panel recommended instead that she undergo retraining. The agency rejected this recommendation and terminated the claimant's registration. The claimant sought judicial review of this decision.	*Succeeded*: The defendant agency's decision was procedurally unfair and unreasonable. Its process of reasoning was unknown and there was nothing to show that it had given any weight to the panel's recommendation. It was incumbent upon the Agency, having rejected the panel's recommendation, either to have provided the claimant with the minutes of the panel's proceedings or the gist of them together with the recommendation and the reasons why the recommendation had been rejected. Furthermore, the agency had wrongly refused to disclose a paediatrician's report on the child's condition which would have shed light on the details of the allegations about the claimant's care of the child. The fact that de-registration constituted a serious stigma on the claimant prejudicing her future prospects as a foster carer were 'highly relevant considerations in evaluating whether the [defendant's decision] was procedurally unfair and/or *Wednesbury* unreasonable'.

Case	Subject-matter	Result
R (B By Her Litigation Friend MB) v London Borough of Lambeth [2006] EWHC 639 (Admin), [2007] 1 FLR 2091.	A 15 year old was thrown out of the family home and became homeless. The local authority made a CA 1989 assessment which was challenged by a judicial review action. Notwithstanding a failure to particularise grounds for review, interim orders were made requiring the local authority to carry out a comprehensive assessment and to maintain the child in a specified placement meanwhile. After the completion of the core assessment the proposal was that the child live in an approved residential establishment for up to six months and to be prepared for semi independence. Disagreeing with that assessment the child continued with the judicial review proceedings finally (her solicitors had repeatedly failed to amend the grounds) alleging that the assessment failed to meet the requirements of *Framework for the Assessment of Children in Need and their Families*. In the event the case was settled, the outstanding issue being costs.	Making no order as to costs, Munby J commented on (a) the local practice in judicial review cases in challenging a public body's assessment, observing that too often inadequate thought is given to the nature of the court's role in such proceedings, namely, to review the challenged decision on public law and not welfare grounds; and (b) the lamentable failure to give proper notice of the amended grounds. Munby J warned practitioners that the courts would no longer tolerate such inappropriate challenges and that not only might some applications be summarily dismissed but lawyers might find themselves exposed to an application for a wasted costs order.

Case	Subject-matter	Result
R (on the application of M) v Sheffield Magistrates' Court [2004] EWHC 1830 (Admin), [2005] 1 FLR 81.	Local authority with child in its care applied for an ASBO against the child under the Crime and Disorder Act 1998. The judge granted the ASBO but stayed the order and gave permission for judicial review, inter alia because no-one form the social services department assisted the child in court.	*Succeeded*: A local authority would not be precluded from making an ASBO against a child in its care, but had to go through the necessary procedures properly. The allocated social worker should not participate in the decision to apply for an ASBO.
R (on the application of CD) v Isle of Anglesey County Council [2004] EWHC 1635 (Admin), [2005] 1 FLR 59.	Care plan for accommodated child with quadriplegic cerebral palsy; preparation of a new care plan for her which, contrary to the child's wishes, involved the termination of a successful foster placement and the de-registration of the foster carers as respite carers for the child.	*Succeeded*: The local authority's care plan was unlawful, in that it failed to give due consideration to the clearly and consistently expressed views of the child, and the mother's capability to deliver care within the care plan. The local authority, having encouraged the child to make a second home with the foster carers notwithstanding the unsuitability of the accommodation, could not subsequently lawfully de-register the foster carers on the basis that the accommodation did not meet the child's needs.
R (on the application of T) v A Local Authority [2003] EWHC 2515 (Admin), [2004] 1 FLR 601, [2003] All ER (D) 02 (Nov).	Accommodated child (aged 14); local authority rejected recommendation for specialist residential placement, and contended that the child's needs could be met in-house with special educational programme.	*Succeeded*: Local authority had an obligation to the child; its decision-making had been vitiated by the failure to obtain a statement of special educational needs. The court could not, however, direct the local authority to make any particular decision about the boy in the future.

Case	Subject-matter	Result
Re M (Care Proceedings: Judicial Review) [2003] EWHC 850 (Admin), [2003] 2 FLR 171.	The father (a Sch 1 offender) and mother (who had mild learning difficulties) of an unborn child sought permission to apply for judicial review to prevent the local authority commencing emergency protection or care proceedings once the child was born. It had been agreed at a pre-birth child protection conference that the parents and child would go to a residential assessment centre to be assessed, but the authority's children panel (to which meeting the parents had not been invited) subsequently decided that the proposed assessment was not appropriate and that care proceedings should be initiated.	*Failed:* It could not be said that the local authority would be acting unlawfully, unreasonably, unfairly or in breach of human rights in seeking an emergency protection or interim care order upon the child's birth. The parents' appropriate remedy if such proceedings were brought was to defend those proceedings.
R (on the application of W) v Leicestershire County Council [2003] EWHC 704 (Admin), [2003] 2 FLR 185.	Foster parent sought leave to apply for judicial review to challenge the local authority decision to remove twins placed with her and then to prevent her applying to adopt them.	*Failed:* No court could say that the twins' removal was not a legitimate way of safeguarding and promoting their welfare.
R (on the application of M) v London Borough of Bromley [2002] EWCA Civ 1113, [2002] 2 FLR 802.	A local authority employee, placed on index of individuals considered unsuitable to work with children as a result of an investigation into the centre in which he was working, sought to quash the report on the basis of alleged procedural flaws in the investigation.	*Failed:* As judicial review could only review the procedure and not the merits of the case, the appropriate remedy was to appeal to the care standards tribunal.

Case	Subject-matter	Result
Re C (Adoption: Religious Observance) [2002] 1 FLR 1119.	Guardian sought to challenge local authority's care plan to place a child of mixed heritage with a Jewish couple.	*Failed*: Challenges to care plan should be made in the care proceedings and not by judicial review.
R (on the application of W) v Lambeth London Borough [2002] EWCA Civ 613, [2002] 2 FLR 327.	Mother of two children evicted for being in arrears with rent, applied to Social Services for assistance in securing private accommodation for herself and her children which was refused.	*Failed*: Although Social Services had power under s 17 of the CA 1989 to provide accommodation for a family in need when not otherwise entitled to help from the local housing authority, the local authority was nevertheless entitled to reserve the use of that power to cope with extreme cases. The court refused to quash the local authority decision but nevertheless hoped that it might reconsider it.
R (on the application of J) v Enfield London Borough Council [2002] EWHC 432 (Admin), [2002] 2 FLR 1.	A Ghanian mother diagnosed with HIV and who had overstayed her permission to remain in the UK claimed that she should be provided with accommodation or that she and her two-year-old daughter be provided with financial assistance to enable them to secure accommodation.	*Succeeded*: Although there is no duty under s 17 of the CA 1989 to provide financial assistance to secure accommodation there was a duty to do so under s 2 of the Local Government Act 2000. A refusal to provide such assistance would amount to a breach of art 8 of the European Convention of Human Rights inasmuch as it would cause the separation of mother and child.

Case	Subject-matter	Result
R (on the application of S) v London Borough of Wandsworth, London Borough of Hammersmith and Fulham, London Borough of Lambeth [2001] EWHC Admin 709, [2002] 1 FLR 469.	After being informed that she was intentionally homeless a mother sought an assessment as to whether her children were 'in need'. She applied to Wandsworth which had temporarily housed the family; to Lambeth where the temporary accommodation was situated and to Wandsworth where the children went to school. Each authority refused to make an assessment.	*Succeeded*: Lambeth and Wandsworth were ordered to make an assessment; the children being physically present in the area which triggered their duty under s 17 of the CA 1989.
R (on the application of L) v Manchester City Council [2000] EWHC Admin 707, [2002] 1 FLR 43.	Local authority policy to pay short-term foster carers who were friends or relatives of the child a significantly lower rate in respect of child's maintenance than was paid to other foster carers.	*Succeeded*: Policy to pay lower rate to foster carers who were friends or relatives was irrational and discriminatory against both the adults and the children concerned.
R (on the application of S) v Swindon Borough Council [2001] EWHC Admin 334, [2001] 3 FCR 702, [2001] 2 FLR 776.	Complaint that notwithstanding his acquittal on sexual abuse charges two local authorities continued to treat the claimant as posing a risk to children particularly those unrelated to him. The first authority accordingly decided that there remained a need to consider and deal with the prospect of the claimant interfering with the children, while the second authority informed the ex-husband of the claimant's new partner of their risk assessment.	*Failed*: Each local authority had acted lawfully in the assessment of risk and its respective decisions were not perverse. The duty under s 47 of the CA 1989 was only triggered by a reasonable cause to suspect abuse – it did not have to be satisfied that it had taken place. The acquittal did not ipso facto mean that there was no risk.

Case	Subject-matter	Result
R (on the application of AB and SB) v Nottingham City Council [2001] EWHC Admin 235, [2001] 3 FCR 350.	Failure to carry out a proper core assessment based on the Framework for the Assessment of Children in Need and their Families document.	*Succeeded*: Failure without good cause to identify the child's needs (including housing needs); produce a care plan, and to provide identified services amounted to an impermissible departure from the Framework guidance.
R v Somerset County Council, ex p Prospects Care Services [2000] 1 FLR 636.	Decision to publish a document for promulgation to other authorities from whom enquiries were received containing information about a private fostering agency, the details of which were objected to by the agency.	*Failed*: The authority had acted intra vires in publishing the details and had acted reasonably in doing so.
R v Cornwall County Council, ex p LH [2000] 1 FLR 236, [2000] 1 FCR 460.	Local authority policy not to: (a) permit solicitors to attend child protection case conferences on behalf of parents save to read out prepared statement; and (b) give parents attending such conferences copy of the minutes.	*Succeeded*: Both policies declared to be unlawful.
R v Tameside Metropolitan Borough Council, ex p J [2000] 1 FCR 173, [2000] 1 FLR 942.	Decision to move an 'accommodated' child from residential care to foster care without parental permission.	*Succeeded*: Without parental responsibility such local authority action was ultra vires.
R v Cornwall County Council, ex p E [1999] 2 FCR 685, [1999] 1 FLR 1055, CA.	Decision to give foster parents (who had just given notice of their intention to apply for adoption) notice of removal under the Adoption Act 1976, s 30.	*Failed*: Leave refused — decision not unreasonable.

Case	Subject-matter	Result
R v Hampshire County Council, ex p H [1999] 2 FLR 359, CA.	Decision to place three siblings on Child Protection Register following allegations (later withdrawn) by one of the children that he had been physically abused by step-father.	*Succeeded in part.* Declaration granted in respect of third child since there was insufficient material to justify registration.
R v Hammersmith and Fulham London Borough Council, ex p D [1999] 1 FLR 642.	Decision not to continue to provide accommodation and a subsistence allowance for child if mother did not accept local authority offer to fund return to Sweden.	*Succeeded*: Wrong to decide or threaten to withdraw future assistance — in clear breach of statutory duty under the CA 1989, s 17.
R v East Sussex County Council, ex p W [1999] 1 FCR 536, [1998] 2 FLR 1082.	Child complaining local authority had wrongly not sought a care order.	*Failed*: Should have used complaints procedure.
R v Devon County Council, ex p A [1997] 2 FLR 388.	Prospective adopters complaining child had wrongfully been removed.	*Succeeded*: Insufficient consultation.
R v Birmingham County Council, ex p A [1997] 2 FCR 357, [1997] 2 FLR 841.	Child and mother seeking declaration that local authority had not acted with due diligence in placing child in appropriate accommodation.	*Failed*: In absence dispute of law or fact should use complaints procedure.
R v Avon County Council, ex p Crabtree [1996] 1 FLR 502, CA.	Approved foster parents complaining about their de-registration.	*Failed*: Adequate warning and consultation.
Re T (Accommodation by Local Authority) [1995] 1 FLR 159.	17-year-old child complaining about local authority decision not to accommodate her.	*Succeeded*: Director of Social Services did not accept complaints panel decision — erred in assessing, on basis of past support, child's future welfare would not be prejudiced.
R v Royal Borough of Kingston-upon-Thames, ex p T [1994] 1 FLR 798.	Complaint by mother about a refusal to accommodate child at a particular home.	*Failed*: Complaints procedure preferable — in any event decision not '*Wednesbury* unreasonable'.

Case	Subject-matter	Result
R v London Borough of Brent, ex p S [1994] 1 FLR 203, CA.	Child complaining about local authority failure to provide adequate accommodation.	*Failed*: Decision not 'Wednesbury unreasonable'.
R v Secretary of State for Health, ex p Luff [1992] 1 FLR 59.	Complaint by prospective adopters about Department of Health recommendation that applicants were unsuitable to adopt Romanian orphan.	*Failed*: Decision neither perverse nor 'Wednesbury unreasonable'.
R v Lancashire County Council, ex p M [1992] 1 FLR 109, CA.	Complaint by prospective adopters that LA (as an adoption agency) had potential adopters.	*Failed*: Decision not perverse nor 'Wednesbury unreasonable'.
R v Cornwall County Council, ex p G [1992] 1 FLR 270.	Complaint by Guardians ad Litem about Director of Social Services' decision to put limits on number of hours to be spent on any one case.	*Succeeded*: Decision unreasonable.

REVIEWS, COMPLAINTS AND OTHER REMEDIES

1. Generally

(a) Review of children's cases

13.51 Regulations made under s 26[1] require the review of the case of each child being looked after by a responsible authority (ie a local authority, voluntary organisation or a person carrying on a private children's home).[2] They provide in detail for the manner, content and frequency of reviews, the considerations to which the authority is to have regard and who is to be consulted beforehand and notified of the result afterwards. The Regulations now require the appointment of an independent reviewing officer ('IRO') in connection with the review of each case of a child who is looked after or for whom accommodation is being provided.[3]

[1] So far as England is concerned the relevant instrument is the Review of Children's Cases Regulations 1991, SI 1991/895 as amended by the Review of Children's Cases (Amendment) (England) Regulations 2004, SI 2004/1419. In Wales, the relevant instrument is the Review of Children's Cases (Wales) Regulations 2007, SI 2007/307, W 26.

[2] See in England reg 1(2) of the 1991 Regulations (as amended) and in Wales reg 1(2) of the 2007 Regulations. IROs are further discussed at at para 8.165.

(b) Complaints about after care

13.52 Every local authority must establish a procedure for considering any representations (including any complaint) made to it by a person qualifying for advice and assistance about the discharge of its functions under Pt III of the 1989 Act in relation to him.[1] This allows young people to complain if they consider that the local authority has not given them adequate preparation for leaving care, or adequate aftercare.[2]

[1] Section 24D(1), added by the Children (Leaving Care) Act 2000, s 5.
[2] Cf *R v Lambeth London Borough Council, ex p Caddell* [1998] 2 FCR 6, [1998] 1 FLR 253. See further, paras 6.70 ff.

2. Complaints procedures[1]

13.53 It is mandatory for all local authorities, voluntary authorities providing accommodation for the child and children's homes[2] to have a formal representation or complaints procedure (although the Act refers to 'representations (including any complaint)' it has always been envisaged that the procedure be used primarily for handling complaints)[3] in relation to their 'qualifying functions'.[4] To ensure that there is an independent element, s 26(4) provides that at least one person who is not a member or officer of the authority concerned must take part in any formal consideration of the complaint or representatives and in any discussions held by the authority about what action, if any, should be taken.[5] Under s 26(8) there is an obligation to publicise the complaints procedure.[6] Rules governing the scope and procedure of the complaints scheme are provided by, in England, the Children Act 1989 Representation Procedure (England) Regulations 2006 (the 2006 Regulations)[7] and, for Wales, by the Representations Procedure (Children)(Wales) Regulations 2005 (the 2005 Regulations).[8]

[1] See generally Oliver, Knight and Candappa *Advocacy for looked after children and children in need: achievements and challenges* (2006); Williams and Jordan *The Children Act 1989 (Complaints Procedure: A Study of Six Local Authority* Areas (1996) and Williams 'The practical operation of the Children Act complaints procedure' [2002] CFLQ 25.
[2] Section 26(3) as applied by reg 21 of the Representations Procedure (England) Regulations 2006, Part 5 (for Wales see the 2005 Regulations, above), issued pursuant to s 59(4), (5). Note that in England (but not Wales) the obligation to establish a representations procedure extends to those made to the authority about their discharge of specified adoption support service and special guardianship support services: CA 1989, s 26(3B) and reg 4 of the 2006 Regulations. In respect of children's homes see the Children's Homes Regulations 2001, reg 24, which requires the registered person responsible for the home to establish a written procedure for considering complaints.
[3] See the Children Act 1989 Guidance and Regulations, Vol 3, Family Placements (1991) Department of Health at para 10.3 and Vol 4, Residential Care at para 5.3
[4] Ie functions under Pts III, IV and V as specified by reg 3 of the 2006 Regulations in the case of England and by reg 7 of the 2005 Regulations in the case of Wales (note the latter are more extensive than the former inasmuch as it includes local authority's investigative functions under s 47): CA 1989, s 26(3), as amended, (3A). Failure to have a procedure or having one that fails to comply with the Regulations can be remedied by invoking the Secretary of State's default powers under s 84 (see para 13.64), per Auld J in *R v London Borough of Barnet ex p B* 1994] 2 FCR 781 at 788, [1994] 1 FLR 592 at 598. Conversely, where a complaints procedure is available judicial review is unlikely to be appropriate: see para 13.61 below.
[5] See para 13.60.
[6] Note there is also an obligation to publicise the child advocacy support services (discussed below): s 26A(5).
[7] SI 2006/1738.
[8] SI 2005/3365 (W 262).

13.54 To meet what had been identified as a priority need,[1] s 26A[2] makes provision for advocacy support for children seeking to make representations or complaints. Section 26A(1) imposes a duty on every local authority to make arrangements for the provision of assistance (including assistance by way of representation)[3] for children who make or intend to make representations under s 26 and for care-leavers complaining under s 24D. There is an obligation both to publicise these arrangements[4] and to monitor their compliance with the Regulations.[5]

[1] Ie in the response to *Listening to People* (Department of Health, 2000).
[2] Inserted into the CA 1989 by s 119 of the Adoption and Children Act 2002. Note also the Department of Health's *National Standards for the Provision of Children's Advocacy Services* (2002).
[3] Section 26A(2).
[4] Section 26A(5), including on receiving representations, to provide information about advocacy services and to offer help in finding an advocate to do so on becoming aware that a child or young person intends to make representations: Advocacy Services and Representations Procedure (Children)(Amendment) Regulations 2004, SI 2004/719, reg 4 (England) and Advocacy Services and Representations Procedure (Children)(Wales) Regulations 2004, SI 2004/1448 (W 148), reg 4 (Wales).
[5] Section 26A(4) and reg 5 of each of the above mentioned 2004 Regulations.

(a) Who may complain?

13.55 Under s 26(3) complaints may be made against the relevant body by:

- a child who is being looked after or who is not being looked after but is in need. This is intended to ensure that children are consulted on decisions taken about them.[1] It could also assist a child who believes he should be accommodated where the body is refusing to offer the service;[2]
- a parent;[3]
- any other person (other than a parent) with parental responsibility;
- any local authority foster parent;
- any person falling within CA 1989, s 24D;[4] or
- such other person as the authority consider has a sufficient interest in the child's welfare to warrant representations being considered by it about the discharge by the authority of any of their functions under Pt III in relation to the child.

[1] According to the Children Act 1989 Guidance and Regulations, Vol 3, Family Placements (1991) Department of Health, para 10.7, the responsible authority should always check with the child (subject to his understanding) that a complaint submitted on his behalf reflects his views and that he wishes the person submitting it to act on his behalf.
[2] See Ward J in *Rv Royal Borough of Kingston-upon-Thames, ex p T* [1994] 1 FLR 798 at 812.
[3] Including the unmarried father.
[4] Discussed above at para 13.52.

13.56 The procedure is available to a wide range of people. In addition to the child, parents or other persons with parental responsibility or other members of the family, who cannot achieve their objectives by applying for discharge of a care order or an application for contact with the child, are entitled to have their complaint heard. Foster parents are able to question why a child is being moved away from them or why they are being denied an enhanced fostering allowance. Other interested people can use the procedure, though this is subject to the local authority's discretion. Nevertheless while an authority may decide who it considers has a sufficient interest in the child's welfare, it would be difficult to deny that professionals in other agencies providing a service to the child would qualify.

(b) What may be complained about?

13.57 The statutory complaints procedure originally only catered for complaints about local authority support for families and their children under Pt III of the CA 1989. Although this included, as the Department of Health's Children Act 1989 Guidance and Regulations, Vol 3, Family Placements pointed out:[1]

' … complaints about day care, services to support children within their family home, accommodation of a child, after-care and decisions relating to the placement of a child or the handling of a child's case. The processes involved in decision making or the denial of a service must also be covered by the responsible authority's arrangements.'

The narrowness of the coverage proved both inconvenient and complicated[2] and accordingly the scope has been widened[3] both to include Pts IV and V of the CA 1989 as well as adoption and special guardianship support services. Complaints may be made in respect of an individual child or about matters affecting a group of children, for example, inappropriate restriction on children in foster care.[4]

[1] Children Act 1989 Guidance and Regulations, Vol 3, Family Placements (1991) Department of Health at para 10.8.
[2] Eg that a child in care under Part IV is nevertheless a 'looked after' child under Pt III. See also *R v East Sussex County Council, ex p W* [1999] 1 FCR 536, [1998] 2 FLR 1082 in which it was held that in deciding not to apply for a care order the local authority was exercising a Pt III function which was therefore amenable to a complaint under s 26.
[3] Namely by s 26(3A), (3B), inserted by the Adoption and Children Act 2002, s 117.
[4] This is an example given in *Butterworths Family Law Service* at 3A[2658].

13.58 In *R v Birmingham City Council, ex p A*[1] judicial review was sought to challenge a local authority's apparent inability speedily to place a child with special needs with an appropriate foster parent. Sir Stephen Brown P commented that, in cases such as these where neither fact nor law was in dispute but instead the ground of complaint was the way the authority was carrying out its duty, the appropriate remedy was a complaint under, s 26. Similarly it has been held[2] that the complaints procedure would in ordinary circumstances, provide a suitable alternative remedy to judicial review to question a local authority decision not to apply for a care order.

[1] [1997] 2 FLR 841.
[2] Per Scott Baker J in *R v East Sussex County Council, ex p W* [1999] 1 FCR 536, [1998] 2 FLR 1082.

(c) Procedure and outcome

13.59 As explained at para 13.53 above, the complaints procedure is now separately governed by the 2006 Regulations in the case of England and by the 2005 Regulations in the case of Wales. Although their broad thrust is similar, the two Regulations differ in detail and emphasis. One example is while both provide that representations may be made in writing or orally,[1] the Welsh Regulations expressly allow for representations to be made electronically.[2] A more significant difference is that whereas in England representations must generally be made within one year after the grounds to make representations arose,[3] no such time limit is mentioned in the Welsh Regulations. There are also crucial differences in the formal complaints process (discussed below). Both, however, make virtually identical provision for the circumstances in which a local authority will not consider or further consider representations (because effectively such consideration would prejudice other proceedings or investigation);[4] for the withdrawal of representations (ie orally or in writing at any time by the complainant or his advocate, if appointed),[5] and both provide that as soon as possible after receiving the representation the local authority must provide the complainant with information about the representations procedure, where relevant, advocacy services and offer help on following the procedure and, where appropriate, in obtaining an advocate.[6]

[1] Regulation 6 of the 2006 Regulations.
[2] Regulation 11 of the 2005 Regulations.
[3] Regulation 9(1) of the 2006 Regulations, although the local authority have a discretion to consider representations made outside the time limit, where they conclude it would not in all the circumstances be reasonable to expect the complainant to have made the representation within the year *and* it is still possible to consider the representations effectively and fairly; reg 9(2).
[4] See respectively reg 8 of each of the Regulations.
[5] See respectively reg 7 of the 2006 Regulations and reg 14 of the 2005 Regulations.
[6] See respectively reg 11 and reg 12.

13.60 The Regulations provide both an informal and formal process. In the first instance, the local authority will seek to resolve the issue by 'local resolution', which need not involve an independent person, within 10 working days (unless the representation is complex in which case the resolution can be made within 20 days).[1] Where a resolution is reached the local authority must as soon as possible provide the complainant and his advocate (if there is one) with the written terms of the resolution.[2] If a resolution has not been reached the complainant or his advocate, if there is one, can request orally or in writing a formal investigation.[3] the formal process can also be invoked if the complainant and local authority agree that the informal process is not appropriate.[4] In either event the local authority must consider the representation together with the independent person and send notice of response within 25 days.[5] If the complainant is dissatisfied with the response then, in England, he or the advocate, if there is one, can within 20 working days of receiving the response request a further investigation by a review panel comprising three independent persons.[6] That panel must meet within 20 working days of the receipt of the request and within five working days of that meeting must send its report to the local authority, the complainant, his advocate, the independent person previously appointed and any other person the panel considers has sufficient interest in the case.[7] The local authority then has 15 working days to consider the panel's recommendations and to decide how it will respond to them and what they propose to do in the light of them and to notify the complainant accordingly as well as providing information about making a complaint to a local Commissioner.[8]

[1] See reg 14 of the 2006 Regulations and reg 15(1)–(5) of the 2005 Regulations.
[2] See respectively reg 15(1) and 15(6).
[3] Regulation 15(2) of the 2006 Regulations. In Wales, under reg 15(7) of the 2005 Regulation, where no resolution is reached within 20 working days the local authority must give written notice to the complainant about his right to request a formal investigation. The complainant can request orally or in writing a formal investigation within 30 days of the representation: reg 15(8).
[4] Regulation 17(1) of the 2006 Regulations. There seems no Welsh equivalent.
[5] Regulation 17(2), (3) of the 2006 Regulation and regs 16–18 of the 2005 Regulations – which also make provision, inter alia, for medication etc.
[6] Regulations 18 and 19 of the 2006 Regulations. The position in Wales is slightly different inasmuch as the complainant can request the Welsh Assembly to appoint an independent panel: Social Services Complaints Procedure (Wales) Regulations 2005, SI 2005/3366, reg 22 issued pursuant to s 26ZB of the CA 1989.
[7] Regulation 20(2) of the 2006 Regulations.
[8] Regulation 20(3) of the 2006 Regulations, and the CA 1989, s 26(7)(b).

13.61 Although a panel decision is not binding upon the local authority,[1] as Peter Gibson LJ said in *R v London Borough of Brent, ex p S*,[2] it would be 'an unusual case when a local authority acted otherwise than in accord with the panel's recommendations and the independent person's views'. Furthermore, ignoring or failing reasonably to consider the recommendations will lay the authority open to judicial review.[3] Given that in England the Panel now comprises three independent persons instead of one previously, these comments can only be strengthened as is Ward J's observation in *R v Royal Borough of Kingston-upon-Thames, ex p T*,[4] it is the clear broad legislative purpose that the complaints procedure should be invoked in preference to judicial review in respect of matters within the remit of s 26. In any event the remedy is quicker, cheaper and more convenient.

[1] This is implicit in, s 26(7) which requires the authority, having had due regard to the findings, to 'take such steps *as are reasonably practicable*' [emphasis added].
[2] [1994] 2 FCR 996 at 1004, [1994] 1 FLR 203 at 211.
[3] Per Ward J in *Rv Royal Borough of Kingston-upon-Thames, ex p T* [1994] 1 FLR 798 at 814. Judicial review is discussed at paras 13.37 ff.
[4] Above at 815.

13.62 Local authorities are required to monitor the operation and effectiveness of their complaints procedure. To this end they are required to keep a record of each representation received, its outcome and whether there was compliance with the time limits. They must also produce an Annual Report.[1]

[1] Regulation 13 of the 2006 Regulations (England); reg 19 of the 2005 Regulations (Wales).

13.63 The effectiveness of the complaints system is an important issue, particularly as its existence was used as one of the justifications for not imposing a general duty of care in tort upon local authorities.[1] Research has suggested that in the past, at any rate, children were reluctant to complain (in part because of fear of victimisation) and did not have much confidence in the system.[2] The hope is, however, that the advocacy service will make an important difference. Time will tell though whether, given the research finding[3] that informal arrangements are generally regarded as more child-friendly, the introduction of an even more formal final procedure before a Panel of three independent persons might not be seen as the ideal solution.

1 See *X v Bedfordshire County Council* [1995] 2 AC 633, [1995] 3 All ER 353, HL, discussed further at paras 13.71 ff.
2 See Williams and Jordan 'Factors relating to publicity surrounding the complaints procedure under the Children Act' (1998) 8 CFLQ 337 and Oliver, Knight and Candappa *Advocacy for looked after children in need: achievements and challenges* (2006) at p 12.
3 Oliver et al, above at p 12.

DEFAULT POWERS OF THE SECRETARY OF STATE

13.64 Section 84, enables[1] the Secretary of State to declare a local authority in default where he is satisfied that they have without reasonable cause, failed to comply with a *duty*[2] under the Act. Such a declaration may contain such directions as are necessary to ensure compliance within a specified period and may be enforced upon the Secretary of State's application for a mandatory order.[3]

1 Ie it is only a discretionary power, the Secretary of State is not obliged to act even if a local authority is in default, see *R v London Borough of Brent, ex p S* [1994] 2 FCR 996 at 1004, [1994] 1 FLR 203 at 211, per Peter Gibson LJ.
2 Ie not simply a power, see Peter Gibson LJ in *R v London Borough of Brent, ex p S*, above. But note the power under ss 22 and 26 to grant a declaration absolving a local authority from a particular duty and thus protecting it from a s 84 order, see *Re C (Care: Consultation With Parents Not In Child's Best Interests)* [2005] EWHC 3390 (Fam), [2006] 2 FLR 787, applying the guidance set out in *Re P (Children Act 1989, ss 22 and 26: Local Authority Compliance)* [2000] 2 FLR 910.
3 Section 84(2), (3). Mandatory orders are discussed at para 13.39.

13.65 Although individuals aggrieved by a local authority decision (or lack of it) may make a complaint under s 84[1] it would be wrong to regard the provision as conferring, either expressly or by implication, on any individual a right so to appeal. As has been pointed out,[2] the Secretary of State's power exists irrespective of any complaint or representation. He can act of his own motion. Furthermore there appears to be no restriction on the material, or its sources, from which the Secretary of State may draw his conclusions. It accordingly follows that the existence of these default powers does not bar applications for judicial review.[3]

1 As was suggested in *R v Barnet London Borough Council, ex p B* [1994] 2 FCR 781, [1994] 1 FLR 592, where it was alleged that a local authority was failing to provide a day care service. During the debates on the Bill the Solicitor General commented that the general expectation was that the Secretary of State would exercise his powers, if at all, where an authority's failure to discharge its statutory duties affected a class as opposed to individual children, see HC Official Reports (6th Series) SC col 492 (13 June 1989).
2 Per Peter Gibson LJ in *R v London Borough of Brent, ex p S* [1994] 2 FCR at 1004, [1994] 1 FLR at 211. Cf. the comparable default powers under the Education Act 1996, s 497 which permits the default powers to be taken 'upon complaint by any person interested or otherwise'.
3 See *R v London Borough of Brent, ex p S*, above at 1007 and 214 respectively. Note also *R (on the application of L) v Manchester City Council* [2001] EWHC Admin 707, [2002] 1 FLR 43.

APPLYING TO THE LOCAL GOVERNMENT OMBUDSMAN

13.66 Another procedure for questioning a local authority's decisions (or the lack of them) concerning its children is to complain to the Commissioner for Local Administration ('the Local Government Ombudsman'), according to the procedure[1] set out by the Local Government Act 1974 (LGA 1974) as amended and under which investigations of written complaints of 'maladministration' may be investigated.[2]

[1] A free booklet explaining the procedure is available from the Commissioner.
[2] In Wales complaints can also be made to the Children's Commissioner for Wales, discussed at para 13.70.

13.67 Before a complaint may be made, the local authority must first be given an opportunity to address it.[1] If, however, this approach has not produced a satisfactory result, a complaint can be made. Complaints can be made directly to the Commissioner or through a councillor.[2] The Commissioner cannot normally investigate complaints concerning proceedings or events that occurred more than 12 months previously.[3]

[1] LGA 1974, s 26(5).
[2] Formerly they had to be initially referred to a local councillor, but this was changed by the LGA 1988, s 29 and Sch 3.
[3] LGA 1974, s 26(4).

13.68 To find the complaint justified the Commissioner must find there has been 'maladministration'. The Court of Appeal has ruled[1] that it is not necessary for the complainant to spell out the particular maladministration which led to the injustice complained of; it is sufficient if he specifies the action alleged to be wrong. This is generally taken to refer to the procedure by which the decision is made or put into action rather than to the merits of the particular decision itself. At the conclusion of his investigation the Commissioner issues a report and, if he has found maladministration and injustice, he may recommend an ex gratia payment.[2] Although the local authority must consider these recommendations it is not *bound* to follow them and indeed, given the passage of time, may not be able to do so if that would be inconsistent with the child's welfare.

[1] See *R v Local Comr for Administration for the North and East Area of England, ex p Bradford Metropolitan City Council* [1979] QB 287, [1979] 2 All ER 881, CA.
[2] Awards of £1,000 have been recommended where a local authority failed to follow a case conference's recommendation, and of £2,000 where children were inappropriately interviewed about allegations of sexual abuse.

13.69 As a general mechanism for scrutinising administrative action, the main drawbacks are that:

- the central concern is with procedural propriety and not the child's welfare;
- the Commissioner may have no expertise in child matters;
- the investigation is itself a long process[1] and will probably result in delaying implementation of plans for the child's long-term future (it is in any event a process concerned to judge the past and not to manage the future); and

- even if 'maladministration' is established, there is no power to interfere with the decision taken by the authority.[2]

1 Though in *Re A Subpoena (Adoption: Comr for Local Administration)* [1996] 2 FLR 629 it was held that the Commissioner was entitled to subpoena a local authority to produce adoption documents.
2 In *Z v United Kingdom* [2001] 2 FCR 246, [2001] 2 FLR 612 at para [107], EHRR, the Government accepted that in the particular circumstances of the case complaining to the Local Government Ombudsman and/or under the complaints procedure was insufficient to satisfy the requirements of art 13 of the European Convention on Human Rights – see further paras 13.84–13.85.

CHILDREN'S COMMISSIONERS

13.70 Unlike the Children's Commissioner for England,[1] the Children's Commissioner for Wales[2] has limited powers to examine cases of individual children coming within his jurisdiction. This power, however, is confined to cases where the Commissioner considers that the case raises matters of principle which have a more general application or relevance to the rights or welfare of children than those in the particular case.[3] He must also take into account whether the case has been or is being, considered by any other person.[4]

1 This post was set up by Pt I of the Children Act 2004. For a discussion of his role see *Clarke Hall and Morrison on Children*, Division 9 and Lowe and Douglas' *Bromley's Family Law* (10th edn) 509–10.
2 The post was set up pursuant to s 74 of the Care Standards Act 2000 (as amended by the Children's Commissioner for Wales Act 2001). See generally Hollingsworth and Douglas 'Creating a children's champion for Wales?' (2002) 65 MLR 58 and Rees 'The Children's Commissioner for Wales: the first five years' (2006) 222 childRIGHT 16.
3 See the Children's Commissioner for Wales Regulations 2001, SI 2001/2787 (W 237), as amended, reg 5.
4 Regulation 6.

HABEAS CORPUS

13.71 *Re S (Habeas Corpus); S v Harringey London Borough Council*[1] establishes that where care proceedings are in existence habeas corpus has no role to play; indeed recourse to such proceedings is to be deprecated. This should not be taken, however, to mean that habeas corpus is never an appropriate remedy in children cases. Indeed, it may be an appropriate remedy to challenge the validity of a secure accommodation order.[2]

1 [2003] EWHC 2734 (Admin), [2004] 1 FLR 590. Note also Munby J's clear message that where care proceedings are on foot it would only be in wholly exceptional circumstances that it would be appropriate to make a free-standing application. The proper place to ventilate relevant issues is in the care proceedings. This has been repeated and endorsed by Wall LJ in *Re V (Care Proceedings: Human Rights Claims)* [2004] EWCA Civ 54, [2004] 1 WLR 1433, [2004] 1 FCR 338, [2004] 1 FLR 944, at para [100].
2 See *LM v Essex County Council* [1999] 1 FCR 673, [1999] 1 FLR 988 but note *S v Knowsley Borough Council* [2004] EWHC 491 (Fam), [2004] 2 FLR 716 in which it was suggested that even in these cases judicial review might be the more appropriate remedy. See further para 9.10.

CLAIMS FOR DAMAGES FOR FAILURE BY LOCAL AUTHORITIES TO CARRY OUT THEIR STATUTORY DUTIES

1. Limited liability for negligence

13.72 At one time English domestic law set its face against superimposing a general common law duty of care on local authorities in relation to performance of their duties to protect children. The key case was *X (Minors) v Bedfordshire County Council*[1] which comprised five test cases, two of which concerned the way local authorities had dealt with child abuse. In one, *M v Newham London Borough*, the parents alleged that a child had been taken into care after an inadequate investigation into allegations of harm. In the other, *X v Bedfordshire County Council*, the position was reversed, the allegation being that the local authority failed properly to investigate reports suggesting that the children had been abused and therefore adequately to protect them. The five children concerned sought damages for personal injuries. In each case the action failed since the House of Lords held that a child had no cause of action for harm arising from:

- an alleged failure of a local authority to comply with its statutory duties under children's welfare legislation;
- careless performance of a statutory duty by an authority;
- negligence in respect of an alleged failure; and
- actions or decisions where a common law duty of care might arise, if they came within the ambit of a statutory discretion.

Furthermore, it held there was no right of action in private law for breach of statutory duty, although this did not necessarily exclude recourse being had to judicial review or complaint to the local government ombudsman.

[1] [1995] 2 AC 633, [1995] 3 All ER 353, [1995] 2 FLR 276, HL, on which see Cane 'Suing public authorities in tort' (1996) 112 LQR 13, Oliphant 'Tort' (1996) 49 Current Legal Problems 29 and Bailey Harris and Harris 'The Immunity of local authorities in child protection functions – Is the door now ajar?' (1998) 10 CFLQ 227.

13.73 Lord Browne-Wilkinson said that a distinction had to be drawn between those alleged negligent acts or decisions which involved policy matters, which were not justiciable in tort at all, and those which did not. Where policy matters were not involved, then it had to be shown that the local authority had exercised its jurisdiction so unreasonably that it had acted outside the discretion entrusted to it by Parliament. In this latter case the claimant would then have to bring him or herself within the tripartite test established by *Caparo Industries plc v Dickman*:[1]

- Was the damage to the claimant reasonably foreseeable?
- Was the relationship between the claimant and the defendant sufficiently proximate?
- Was it just and reasonable to impose a duty of care?

[1] [1990] 2 AC 605 at 616–17, HL.

13.74 Although *Bedfordshire* did not establish a blanket immunity for any action taken by a local authority in respect of children, it certainly seemed to limit the possibilities of action.[1] However, a number of subsequent domestic decisions have widened the scope for action in negligence. Furthermore the House of Lords decision itself has been ruled in breach of the European Convention and the Government was ordered to pay compensation to the claimants and it is now becoming apparent that ss 7 and 8 of the Human Rights Act 1998 provide an important alternative means of seeking redress. Each of these developments will now be considered.

[1] See eg *H v Norfolk County Council* [1997] 2 FCR 334, [1997] 1 FLR 384, CA in which the applicant, then aged 22, failed in his action for damages in negligence against the local authority for failing properly to monitor and supervise his foster care placement (he alleged that he had been sexually and physically abused by his foster father) and for failing to remove him from that placement. Note that this case has since been said to have been wrongly decided, see *S v Gloucestershire County Council, L v Tower Hamlets London Borough Council* [2000] 3 All ER 346, [2000] 2 FCR 345, [2000] 1 FLR 825, CA, discussed at para 13.76.

2. The retreat from Bedfordshire

13.75 In *Barrett v Enfield London Borough Council*[1] the House of Lords refused to strike out a claim for negligence against the local authority for its alleged catalogue of errors during the 17 years the claimant had been in its care, which had resulted in him leaving care with deep-seated psychological and psychiatric problems. In reaching this decision their Lordships drew a distinction between deciding to take a child into care pursuant to a statutory duty, which unless it was wholly unreasonable so as not to be a real exercise of the discretion, was not normally justiciable, and looking after a child in care, when it might be easier to establish a breach of duty. However, while their Lordships were not prepared to strike out the claim,[2] the decision by no means indicated that the claim would in fact succeed. Indeed Lord Slynn expressly said that many of the allegations would be difficult to establish and were likely to fail.

[1] [1999] 3 WLR 79, [1999] 3 All ER 193, [1999] 2 FCR 434, [1999] 2 FLR 426.
[2] Their Lordships were mindful of the obligation under art 6 of the ECHR to allow everyone to have a fair and public hearing and referred expressly to the decision in *Osman v United Kingdom* (1998) 29 EHRR 245, [1999] 1 FLR 193, ECtHR.

13.76 *Barrett* was subsequently applied in *S v Gloucester County Council, L v Tower Hamlets London Borough Council*[1] in which claims for negligence were brought against the local authorities by children who alleged that the foster fathers with whom they had been placed had abused them sexually and as a result they had suffered long-term damage. In each case the foster fathers had eventually been convicted of sexual offences with children. According to May LJ[2] the relevant law derived from *Barrett* can be summarised as follows:

'(a)   depending upon the particular facts of the case, a claim in common-law negligence may be available to a person who claims to have been damaged by failings of a local authority which was responsible under statutory powers for his care and upbringing ...

(b)   the claim will not succeed if the failings alleged comprise actions or decisions by the local authority of a kind which are not justiciable.

These may include, but will not necessarily be limited to, policy decisions and decisions about allocating public funds;

(c) the border line between what is justiciable and what is not may in a particular case be unclear. Its demarcation may require a more extensive investigation than is capable of being made from material in traditional pleadings alone;

(d) there may be circumstances in which it will not be just and reasonable to impose a duty of care of the kind contended for. It may often be necessary to conduct a detailed investigation of the facts to determine this question; and

(e) in considering whether a discretionary decision was negligent, the court will not substitute its view for that of the local authority upon which the state has placed the power to exercise discretion, unless the discretionary decision was plainly wrong. But decisions of, for example, social workers, are capable of being held to have been negligent by analogy with decisions of other professional people, Here again, it may well be necessary to conduct a detailed factual enquiry.'

Applying these principles it was held that the allegation that Gloucestershire had failed to deal with the abuse by the foster carer after being informed of it was actionable. However, in the case of Tower Hamlets there was held to be no real prospect of establishing negligence in its approval of the foster parents nor in its subsequent placement of the child with them and the action was struck out.

1 [2000] 3 All ER 346, [2000] 2 FCR 345, [2000] 1 FLR 825, CA.
2 Above at 369, 374 and 848–849 respectively.

13.77 In *W v Essex County Council*[1] a foster child, known by the social worker to be an active sexual abuser, sexually abused the birth children of the foster carers. The Court of Appeal held that while the foster parents' claim for negligence against the local authority should be struck out, the children's should not. The majority held that a social worker placing a child with foster parents had a duty of care to the foster parents' children to provide them, before and during the placement, with such information about the placed child as a reasonable social worker would provide in all the circumstances, and a local authority was vicariously liable for the conduct of its social worker relating to that. Although appeals were lodged on both counts, that relating to the children was not pursued but in relation to the action by the parents, the House of Lords held that that too should not be struck out on the basis that it could not be said that such a claim was unarguable. In a separate action against Essex County Council, adoptive parents succeeded in obtaining damages in respect of injury, loss and damage sustained during the placement (but not after the adoption) of two siblings, the local authority being liable in negligence for not disclosing the boy's serious behavioural problems, including severe violence on his sister which required constant adult supervision.[2]

1 [1999] Fam 90, [1998] 3 All ER 111, CA; revsd [2001] 2 AC 592, [2000] 2 All ER 237, [2000] 1 FCR 568, [2000] 1 FLR 657, HL. Note a local authority might be liable for negligent misstatement under common law liability, if a decision was so unreasonable, even though it could not be liable for breach of statutory duty: *T v Surrey County Council* [1994] 2 FCR 1269, a case relating to a registered childminder held to have injured a child in her care. For liability of a local education authority for not diagnosing children's special

13.77 *Challenging decisions*

education needs see *Phelps v Hillingdon London Borough Council* [2001] 2 AC 619, [2000] 2 WLR 776, [2000] 4 All ER 504, [2000] 3 FCR 102, HL.

2   See *A v Essex County Council* [2003] EWCA Civ 1848, [2004] 1 FLR 749.

3. The East Berkshire limits

13.78 Although in *D v East Berkshire Community Health NHS Trust*[1] Lord Nicholls accepted[2] that the law has moved on since the *Bedfordshire* decision (the Court of Appeal had unequivocally said that that decision did not survive the Human Rights Act 1998),[3] the House of Lords nevertheless restrained the seemingly relentless widening of the duty of care owed by professionals when dealing with a child. In that case the Lords upheld the dismissal of claims by parents that medical professionals had negligently misdiagnosed child abuse. In so ruling, the Lords upheld the Court of Appeal's ruling that a distinction had to be made between the children's position and the parents' position. While in the former there can now be said to be a duty of care towards the child in relation to the investigation of suspected child abuse and the institution and pursuit of care proceedings, the same cannot be said of the parents. All that is owed to the parent is that clinical and other investigations must be conducted in good faith.[4] The justification for the general absence of a duty of care towards parents lay (a) in the importance of allowing the investigator to act single-mindedly in the interests of the child safe in the knowledge that if the suspicions proved unfounded he or she would not be open to a claim from the distressed parent, and (b) that the general approach of the law is to oppose granting remedies to third parties for the effects of injuries to others.[5]

1   [2005] UKHL 23, [2005] 2 AC 273, [2005] 2 All ER 443, [2005] 2 FLR 284.

2   At para [82]. For a similar position of CAFCASS when investigating a case for the court see *Hinds v Liverpool County Court, Liverpool City Council* [2008] EWHC 665 (QB), [2008] 2 FLR 63.

3   [2003] EWCA Civ 1151, [2004] QB 558, [2003] 2 FLR 1166 at [83]–[85], per Lord Phillips MR.

4   See Lord Nicholls, above at para [90]. Lord Bingham dissented.

5   This summary is based on that by Douglas at [2007] Fam Law 805.

13.79 Since *East Berkshire* there have been subsequent attempts to argue that a local authority's common law duty of care should extend to parents. In *Lawrence v Pembrokeshire County Council*[1] the argument principally rested upon human rights considerations. It was submitted that 'the advent of Article 8 to our law' since the facts giving rise to the House of Lords decision called 'for an evolutionary change in our law of negligence' inter alia in recognition of the Strasbourg jurisprudence that duties of care in cases of suspected child abuse may be owed both to children and to parents suspected of abusing them. In upholding the striking out of a mother's negligence claim against the local authority in respect of its decision to place her children on the Child Protection Register, the Court of Appeal rejected the human rights argument. As it pointed out, art 8(2) requires the public body interfering with family life to justify its conduct. Were this to be put in terms of a common duty of care it would mean that a local authority would have to prove, by reference to its concern for the child's welfare, that it was not in breach. This development would amount to a plain distortion of the common law action in negligence and in any event overlooked the whole point of the *East Berkshire* solution to forestall by robust and timely intervention, if at all possible, the greater possible harm when a local authority suspected parental abuse of children in the context of family life. In the court's view, the advent of art 8 to domestic law did not undermine or weaken as a matter of public policy the primary need to protect children from abuse, or the risk of abuse from inter alia parents. In other words the cogency of the reasoning in *East Berkshire* was entirely compatible with human rights. In any event the absence of a duty of care does not preclude an action under the Human Rights Act 1998.[2]

1   [2007] EWCA Civ 446, [2007] 1 WLR 2991, [2007] 2 FLR 705.
2   Ie under s 7, discussed at paras 13.88 ff.

13.80 A subsidiary argument in *Lawrence v Pembrokeshire County Council* for not following *East Berkshire* in relation to parents was that it concerned a health authority and doctors and other healthcare professionals rather than local authorities and social workers and as such raised quite different questions. But this argument was dismissed out of hand on the basis the ratio of the majority was clearly directed to all persons engaged in child protection.

13.81 A further challenge to *East Berkshire* was rejected in *B v Reading Borough Council*,[1] namely, that the majority's reasoning in the House of Lords case was intended to be confined to cases of vicarious responsibility for breach of duty on the part of the doctor or social worker. In other words it did not apply to direct liability. In the Court of Appeal's view the House of Lords' reasoning applied both to vicarious and direct liability and there was no room to distinguish the two.

1   [2007] EWCA Civ 1313, [2008] 1 FLR 797.

13.82 One important consequence of *East Berkshire* is that parents seeking damages from local authorities in respect of action taken over their conduct over their children must either do so by bringing an action under the Human Rights Act 1998 (see paras 13.88 ff) or by complaining to the ombudsman (see paras 13.66 ff).

13.83 In cases where negligence can be established[1] the question then arises as to how to calculate the damages. In *C v A Local Authority*,[2] damages were awarded against the local authority in respect of physical, emotional and sexual abuse at the hands of members of staff at the children's home in which the claimant (now aged 36) had been placed. In upholding an award of £35,000 for pain, suffering and loss of amenities, £20,000 for his loss of past earnings, £5,000 for future loss of earnings and £10,000 for the cost of future psychotherapy, the Court of Appeal doubted whether the Judicial Studies Board Guidelines on damages for psychiatric harm applied to cases of abuse of children in care by their carers. In *KR v Bryn Alyn Community (Holdings) Ltd*,[3] however, it was considered that while the Guidelines should not be applied rigidly they did, nevertheless, provide a signpost to the general level of damages. In that case the children involved were awarded damages under various hands including general damages (ranging from £50,000 to £5,000), compensation for pain and suffering, compensation for loss of earnings and rather lower compensation for the costs of therapy. In *Pierce v Doncaster Metropolitan Borough Council*,[4] the claimant was awarded £25,000 by way of general damages.

1 For a useful guide to the practicalities of proving loss (the burden for doing so lying on the claimant) and of the difficulties of doing so, particularly in the absence of local authority records, see *Pierce v Doncaster Metropolitan Borough Council* [2007] EWHC 2968 (QB), [2008] 1 FLR 922.
2 [2001] EWCA Civ 302, [2001] 1 FCR 614, sub nom *C v Flintshire County Council* [2001] 2 FLR 33, CA.
3 [2003] EWCA Civ 85, [2003] QB 1441, [2003] 1 FLR 1203.
4 Above at n 1.

4. The Strasbourg rulings

13.84 The four children denied relief by the House of Lords[1] in the *Bedfordshire* case and both the mother and child involved in the *Newham* decision, subsequently took their claims before the European Court of Human Rights. In both cases, respectively reported as *Z v United Kingdom*[2] and *TP and KM v United Kingdom*,[3] the claim that the striking out of the negligence claims by the House of Lords amounted to a breach of art 6 of the Convention was rejected on the basis that while that Article generally safeguarded a right of access to the courts in respect of complaints of unlawful interference with civil rights, it did not guarantee a particular content of these civil rights or obligations. In other words States can properly restrict those rights provided they do so for legitimate reasons and 'there is a reasonable relationship of proportionality between the means employed and the aim sought to be achieved'. In the Court's view the UK had legitimately restricted the application of negligence. Nevertheless despite this ruling the Court found other reasons for holding the UK to be breach of the ECHR in each of the two cases.

1 [1995] 2 AC 633, [1995] 3 All ER 353, [1995] 2 FLR 276, discussed at paras 13.71–13.72.
2 [2001] 2 FCR 246, [2001] 2 FLR 612, ECtHR, on which see the excellent analysis by Bailey-Harris at [2001] Fam Law 584.
3 [2001] 2 FCR 289, [2001] 2 FLR 549, ECtHR.

13.85 In *Z v United Kingdom* the Court upheld the children's claim that there had been a breach of art 3. The local authority was found to be aware of the appalling treatment and neglect suffered over a period of years by the applicants at the hands of their parents (the UK Government did not contest the Commission's finding that the treatment suffered by the children had reached the level of severity prohibited by art 3, ie that it amounted to inhuman and degrading treatment) but had failed, despite the powers available to take it, to take effective measures to bring it to an end. Accordingly, the State too had failed in its positive obligation under art 3 to provide the applicants with adequate protection against inhuman and degrading treatment. The Court further held that notwithstanding the propriety of striking out the negligence claim, the absence of an effective remedy for the breach itself amounted to a breach of art 13 (under which everyone should have an effective remedy for a violation of a Convention right). The court awarded £32,000 compensation to each applicant.

13.86 Since art 3 was found to have been broken the Court in Z found it unnecessary to consider whether art 8 had also been breached in that case. In *TP and KM v United Kingdom*, however, the Court upheld the mother and daughter's complaint that because the child had unjustifiably been taken into care and separated from her mother, both claimants' art 8 rights had been breached. What constituted the violation in the court's view was the local authority's failure to disclose to the mother a video of the child's disclosure interview[1] which in turn deprived the mother of an effective opportunity to deal with allegations that the child could not be safely returned to her. As in Z the absence of an effective domestic remedy was found to be a breach of art 13 and each applicant was awarded £10,000 compensation.

[1]   There was some doubt as to whom the child was referring in relation to the allegations of abuse.

13.87 These two Strasbourg rulings are important not least for establishing how the Convention can be used despite the legitimate restriction of an action for negligence. However, following the implementation of the Human Rights Act 1998, such actions have now first to be brought under that Act, though if these fail it is still possible to take the case to Strasbourg.[1]

[1]   For guidance on how to bring actions in Strasbourg, see Clements, Mole and Simmonds *European human rights: taking a case under the Convention* (2nd edn, 1999).

5. Actions under ss 7 and 8 of the Human Rights Act 1998[1]

13.88 Section 7 of the Human Rights Act 1998 enables victims to bring proceedings against public authorities (which includes both local authorities and the courts)[2] in respect of acts claimed to be incompatible with a Convention right and if successful, s 8 empowers the court to grant 'such relief or remedy, or make such order, within its powers as it considers just and appropriate'. These latter powers include awarding damages. As Lord Nicholls observed in *Re S (Care Order: Implementation of Care Plan)*,[3] 'The object of these sections is to provide in English law the very remedy art 13 declares is the entitlement of everyone whose rights are violated'.

[1]   See generally the *White Book 2008*, Vol 2 3D-23–3D-41 and the Green Book 2008, Vol 2, III HUM[12] ff.
[2]   Section 6(3) of the 1998 Act, discussed at para 1.52. But when complaining about a court's action, proceedings should be brought against The Ministry of Justice: *Hinds v Liverpool County Court, Liverpool City Council* [2008] EWHC 665 (QB), [2008] 2 FLR 63. *Hinds* also illustrates an 'expert' is not a body for this purpose.
[3]   [2002] UKHL 10, [2002] 2 AC 291, [2002] 2 All ER 192, [2002] 1 FLR 815, at para [61]. As his Lordship said unlike art 13 which makes it a 'right' to have an effective remedy, ss 7 and 8 simply provide a remedy for enforcing a Convention right. Note: the UK has not incorporated art 13 into domestic law.

13.89 Actions may either be brought directly against the public authority alleged to be at fault (sometimes referred to as 'free-standing action') or can be raised in existing proceedings. Freestanding actions have to be brought in an 'appropriate court or tribunal',[1] but, as Hale LJ said, in *Re W and B (children: care plan), Re W (children) (care plan):*[2]

> 'There is no definition of the "appropriate court or tribunal" for purpose of s 7(1)(a). The amended *Practice Direction* to Pt 16 of the Civil Procedure Rules 1998 requires any party who seeks to rely on the Human Rights Act to state that and give particulars in his statement of case. A claim against a local authority under s 7(1)(a) might therefore be brought as an ordinary civil claim in the county or the High Court'.

However, her Ladyship also pointed out that a parent or child can invoke existing procedures in the CA 1989 to get the matter back before the care court and then rely upon s 7(1)(b), though it might be preferable to get the matter before higher courts rather than the family proceedings court since only they can grant an injunction and award damages.[3]

[1]   Section 7(1)(a) of the 1998 Act. Although at one time it was thought that human rights challenges to care plans and placement of children in care should be heard in the Family Division of the High Court and, if possible, by judges with experience of sitting in the administrative court, see Butler-Sloss P in *C v Bury Metropolitan Borough Council* [2002] EWHC 1438 (Fam), [2002] 2 FLR 868, it seems now to be established that such a transfer is neither necessary nor desirable: see *Re V (Care Proceedings: Human Rights)* [2004] EWCA Civ 54, [2004] 1 WLR 1433, [2004] 1 All ER 997, per Wall LJ and *Westminster City Council v RA, B and S* [2005] EWHC 970 (Fam), [2005] 2 FLR 1309, per Potter P at [50].
[2]   [2001] EWCA Civ 757 at para [74], [2001] 2 FCR 450, [2001] 2 FLR 582, not commented upon by HL on appeal.
[3]   Above at para [75].

13.90   There are important limits on the ability to invoke ss 7 and 8. First, the claimant has to show that he or she is a 'victim', that is a person who is directly affected by the act or omission.[1] It is therefore insufficient to be a secondary victim, which would have meant, for example, that the foster carers in *Re Z* would have had no action.[2] Secondly, the action must be brought within one year of the act complained of, although claims after that can be admitted at the court's discretion.[3] Thirdly, there must be no other appropriate remedy. Indeed, in *Re S (Care Order: Implementation of Care Plan)*[4] Lord Nicholls considered actions generally under s 7 to be a 'longstop remedy'. He commented 'One would not expect proceedings to be launched under s 7 until any other appropriate remedial routes have first been explored'. His Lordship did not explain why s 7 actions should be of 'last resort'.

[1]   Section 7(7) applying art 34 of the ECHR.
[2]   Cf *A and B v United Kingdom* [1998] 1 EHRLR 82 in which the father of a son who was beaten by his stepfather was not considered to be a victim.
[3]   Section 7(5). See further para 1.52.
[4]   [2002] UKHL 10, [2002] 2 AC 291, [2002] 2 All ER 192, [2002] 1 FLR 815, at para [62].

13.91   Section 8(4) directs the court in determining: (a) whether to award damages; or (b) the amount of an award to 'take into account the principles applied by the European Court of Human Rights in relation to the award of compensation under art 41 of the Convention'. According to Lord Woolf CJ in *Anufrijeva v Southwark London Borough Council*[1] the critical message is that the remedy has to be 'just and appropriate', the approach being an equitable one. This means that establishing a breach does not *entitle* the claimant to damages.[2] Where damages are appropriate then the levels of awards in respect of tests as reflected in the guidelines issued by the Judicial Studies Board and by the Parliamentary and Local Government Ombudsman provide rough guidance. Lord Woolf considered[3] the guiding principle under the 1998 Act be restitutio in integrum so that the claimant be placed as far as possible in the same position as if his rights had not been infringed. But account must first be taken of the effect of any other available remedies. Caution should be exercised when awarding damages for non-pecuniary loss: the consequences of the breach must be serious, the damage must be more than distress and frustration. The scale and the manner of the violation can also be taken into account.

[1] [2003] EWCA Civ 1406, [2004] QB 124, [2004] 1 All ER 833, [2004] 1 FLR 8.
[2] See also *Re C (Breach of Human Rights: Damages)* [2007] EWCA Civ 2, [2007] 1 FLR 1957, sub nom *P v South Gloucestershire County Council* [2007] Fam Law 393, discussed further at para 13.94.
[3] Above at paras [71] ff, summarised by the *White Book 2008*, Vol 2 at 3D-41.

13.92 In *Re M (Care: Challenging Decisions By Local Authority)*,[1] following a review of its care plan for a child in its care the local authority finally ruled out any further prospect of the child returning to live with her mother or of ever going to live with her father. In reaching this decision, however, the authority was held to have acted unfairly and therefore in breach of art 8 by not involving the parents to a degree sufficient to provide their interests with the requisite protection. Exercising his powers under s 8 of the 1998 Act upon an application by the parents under s 7, Holman J set the local authority decision aside. He also gave directions for a full hearing of the review issues and of applications for the discharge of the care orders.

[1] [2001] 2 FLR 1300.

13.93 Holman J's decision was specifically endorsed by Lord Nicholls in *Re S (Care Order: Implementation of Care Plan)*.[1] At the same time his Lordship emphasised that wide though the powers are under s 8 they are nevertheless confined to acts or proposed acts which the court finds are or would be unlawful. It does not confer a power to give relief in respect of acts by public authorities who have not and are not proposing to act in breach of a Convention right.[2]

[1] [2002] UKHL 10, [2002] 2 AC 291, [2002] 2 All ER 192, [2002] 1 FLR 815 at para [46].
[2] It was for this reason that his Lordship considered the Court of Appeal was wrong to justify the starring of care plans (discussed at paras 8.157 ff) upon the basis of ss 7 and 8.

13.94 In *Re C (Breach of Human Rights: Damages)*[1] the claimant established a breach of her art 8 rights inasmuch as although the decision taken in her absence and the subsequent removal of her baby was unlawful[2] the local authority was in breach for deciding, at the removal meeting, to abandon the care plan.[3] However, the Court of Appeal considered the breach to have been purely procedural and at the low end of the spectrum of seriousness and upheld the decision of Holman J not to award damages. There was no evidence that her exclusion from the meeting was the cause of any additional injury and in any event the local authority had mitigated the breach by going to considerable lengths to keep her lawyer informed.

1 [2007] EWCA Civ 2, [2007] 1 FLR 1957, sub nom *P v South Gloucestershire County Council* [2007] Fam Law 393.
2 The mother had made threats of serious harm to others and possibly towards herself and the baby.
3 Originally there had been a concurrent care plan giving the mother six months to demonstrate her parenting capacity but at the same time preparatory steps towards adoption were taken if removal was necessary. The plan recorded that if the baby was removed the mother would be kept fully informed.

Chapter 14
CONCLUSIONS

OVERVIEW

14.1 The aims of the CA 1989 can be broadly summarised as follows:

(a)   the creation of a unified system of modern law and procedure to provide for the welfare of children;

(b)   the integration of provisions on private and public law;

(c)   the provision of local authority support for families with children in need, and where necessary, the power to take steps to protect the child; and

(d)   unification of the court system to deal with these matters.

In this Chapter we consider again the extent to which these aims have been achieved and what might lie ahead.

14.2 A UNICEF Report[1] published in February 2007 has as its introduction:

'The true measure of a nation's standing is how well it attends to its children, their health and safety, their material security, their education and socialisation, and their sense of being loved, valued and included in the families and societies into which they were born.'

[1]   UNICEF, *Child poverty in perspective: An overview of child well-being in rich countries,* *Innocenti Report Card* 7, 2007, UNICEF Innocenti Research Centre, Florence.

14.3 The welfare checklist in s 1 of the 1989 Act is based on similar values but applies only in court proceedings. Statutory recognition has been given to the concepts more broadly in the Children Act 2004. It requires each children's services authority[1] in England to make arrangements to promote co-operation between the authority and its relevant statutory partners and such other persons or bodies as the authority considers appropriate with a view to improving the well-being of children in the authority's area so far as relating to:

(a)   physical and mental health and emotional well-being;

(b)   protection from harm and neglect;

(c)   education, training and recreation;

(d) the contribution made by them to society;
(e) social and economic well-being.

In making these arrangements the authority must have regard to the importance of parents and other persons caring for children in improving the well-being of children.

[1] Note also that cl 8 of the Children and Young Person's Bill 2008 imposes on the Secretary of State the general duty to promote the well-being of children in England and specific duties may also be imposed.

14.4 Regrettably the Report from which the UNICEF quotation is taken goes on to place the United Kingdom near the bottom of 21 of the world's well-developed countries in every dimension similar to those listed in the 2004 Act. And in June 2008 the Children's Commissioners for England, Wales, Scotland and Northern Ireland published a report[1] which led to the condemnation that the United Kingdom was a bleak place for children, where thousands are needlessly criminalised for misdemeanours and where the gap between the education and health of the rich and poor is growing. This is clearly at odds with the central tenets of both the 1989 and 2004 Acts. While the evidence for the conclusion that the well-being of children in the United Kingdom is a matter for widespread concern may be open to challenge, there is clearly a growing anxiety that a generation of troubled youth is developing. In short the aspirations of what is regarded as well-meant legislation are not matched by their implementation, a theme to which we shall return.

[1] UK Children's Commissioners' Report to the UN Committee on the Rights of the Child (June 2008).

14.5 In assessing the success of the CA 1989 legal critique has to be separated from political comment. The Act and its supplementary legislation necessarily remain extensive with its rules, regulations, orders and guidance. The Act has not created simplicity but it has been a major achievement to have a single structure, which is largely internally coherent. With the exception of legislation concerning adoption, abduction,[1] and the inspection of children's services,[2] all the law relating to the welfare of children is in one place. The Adoption and Children Act 2002 has made adoption consistent with the principles of the CA 1989. The essential principles of the Act have created a framework for good practice.

[1] The Child Abduction and Custody Act 1985, *Clarke Hall and Morrison on Children*, 2[601].
[2] The Care Standards Act 2000, *Clarke Hall and Morrison on Children*, 1A[1001].

THE FAMILY JUSTICE SYSTEM

14.6 An essential component of children's legislation is ready access to the courts, where that is in the interests of the child. It is difficult to avoid the conclusion in the light of developments since the last edition that there is a political determination to limit that access. We commented previously about the problems with the provision of court services and concern about arrangements for public funding.[1] Since then government policy has actually further reduced funding in these areas. In an attempt to meet the problems of delay local authorities are now being discouraged from taking proceedings, even though there is no evidence that applications have been made inappropriately. Matters have certainly reached a serious state when the judiciary are driven to make public statements.[2]

[1]   See 'The future of welfare law for children', White R, in 'Looking Back – Looking Forward: 150 Years of Family Law' (March 2008, in publication) Cardiff University: 'The tools with which they are now dismantling the Family Justice System are destruction of legal aid, inadequate provision of court services and as part of a wider discouragement of local authorities from taking proceedings, a massive increase in court fees.'

[2]   Lord Justice Wall in a speech to the Lancashire Family Justice Council on 10 March 2007 said: 'I am angry because I think the Family Justice System is being exploited and abused. Our dedication, our goodwill, our passionate belief that our function is to address the best interests of vulnerable children and families is not being recognised by a government which, however much it pays lip service to the welfare of children, is frankly indifferent to disadvantaged children and young people who are the subject of proceedings, and simply refuses properly to fund the Family Justice System, relying instead on the fact that we have always got by in the face of government indifference, and will continue to do so.'
Mr Justice Coleridge in a speech to the Resolution conference (April 2008) said: 'I am afraid that the time has come for family judges to speak out publicly in protest at the way in which the Family Justice System in this country has been and is being mismanaged and neglected by government.'
Mr Justice Ryder in a speech on the 25th anniversary of *Butterworths Family Law Service* (27 June 2008, see www.judicary.gov.uk) marked as one of his critical comments about the system: 'The lack of capacity in the courts to deal with an ever increasing volume of the most serious and complex cases in a timely fashion and as a consequence the downgrading of many legitimate medium risk and need cases as if we haven't got time for them'.

14.7 The Family Justice Council[1] now has a responsibility for improving outcomes for those who come into contact with the family justice system but it will be difficult for them to bring about much improvement in the current climate. Unlike criminal justice which has both the National Criminal Justice Board and a dedicated department within the Ministry of Justice, and in spite of frequent assertions about the importance of the family, family *justice* has no strong advocate within Government. We need to consider the establishment of a National Family Justice Board. There should be a statutory duty imposed on Government to take account of the views of the Board on matters relating to public policy on the family justice system, so as to ensure that individual government departments do not take inadequate or ill-considered action.

[1]   See para 1.33.

THE COURTS

14.8 The Act provided a unified jurisdiction for children's cases but not a unified court, as had been sought for many years. The system has had significant advantages in that, with a few exceptions, the High Court, the county court and the family proceedings court apply the same law and have the same powers, and each have personnel who are experienced in the application of the relevant law. Courts can interact and ensure co-ordination based on complexity and convenience rather than the nature of the case.

14.9 *Conclusions*

14.9 A central principle of the Act is that delay in deciding any question with respect to a child's upbringing is likely to prejudice the child's welfare. The continuing delay in obtaining court hearings in some areas is a most serious problem, which has led to drift rather than planned timetables operating at a pace consistent with the welfare of the child. The problem was identified in 1995 in the Booth Report.[1] When the CAAC was abolished in 1997 there was a vacuum in taking forward its functions in relation to the implementation of the Report. Its momentum was lost and has never been recovered. The *Scoping Study on Delay in Children Act Cases*[2] in 2002 showed that it was still then a problem. Statistics on care proceedings for 2005/06 demonstrate the continuing serious nature of the position.

---

1   See 'Delay in Public Law Children Act Cases: Preliminary Report' (1995), a report by
     Dame Margaret Booth on research conducted for the Lord Chancellor's Department.
2   Lord Chancellor's Department, May 2002.
3   Unpublished figures for the top five in case volume of County Court Care Centres from
     April 2005 to December 2006 showed that the average waiting times for a final hearing in
     public law care cases ranged between 48 and 53 weeks.

14.10 The lack of available judiciary, especially in the county court, was identified as a problem in the *Scoping Study* and was (and still is) a significant contribution to the problem of delay. Although delays were far more frequently brought about by the court rather than practitioners, the initial response to delay in the higher courts was to introduce strict provisions on the conduct of cases and draconian threats on costs. Practice Directions required proper arrangements for filing evidence and the use of experts, the provision of bundles of documents and a chronology, control of unnecessary examination of witnesses and preventing oral evidence, which should all be good practice in the right circumstances. Warranted as these controls on cases were, the Court Service should have made adequate provision for judges and court staff to ensure expeditious hearings and oversee the conduct of proceedings. Instead we had cuts in funding and the introduction of policies to drive down the number of cases and drive down to the lower courts the venue for those cases. Judicial continuity, which has always been important to the proper and expeditious conduct of cases, has had the support of the judiciary but has been institutionally difficult to implement, especially in London, because of the shortage of judges and management of their time.

1. Openness in courts

14.11 In 2006 the Lord Chancellor's Department published proposals intended to meet criticism of the family justice system of being secretive, biased and in some cases unjust.[1] They included allowing the media in to family courts as of right, proposals supported by media organisations and organisations like Fathers for Justice. Children, young people and organisations which protect, support and represent them strongly disagreed, and argued against the media being allowed into family courts as of right. The Ministry of Justice decided[2] that children must come first. Instead of allowing the media in to family courts as of right, they proposed to improve the openness of family courts not by the numbers or types of people going in to the courts, but by the amount and quality of information coming out of the courts. The conclusions were that the right balance is between on the one hand providing more information about proceedings at all levels to users and the public; and on the other, giving courts the discretion on who should be able to attend. The consequence has been to amend the court rules for disclosure,[3] improve consistency of access to the courts and set up pilots for increased circulation of the outcome of proceedings.[4] Whether these developments will satisfy those convinced that family proceedings should be public events remains to be seen.[5]

1   Confidence and confidentiality: Improving transparency and privacy in family courts, Lord Chancellor's Department, CP 11/06.
2   Confidence and Confidentiality: Openness in family courts – a new approach. Ministry of Justice, 20 June 2007, CP 10/07.
3   See the FPR 1991, r 10.20A and para 4.47.
4   One proposal is to make available for public viewing all judgments but this would undoubtedly lead to an even greater need for court time and discourage the delivery of expeditious judgments.
5   See for example the series of articles in *The Times* in the week beginning 7 July 2008 pressing for more open access to the courts.

2. What court?

14.12 Current policy raises questions about longer term intentions for the family justice system. Even if judicial decisions were to be less frequently required some cases will still require independent judgement. What is the likely forum? Would it be a court and if so at what level, given the current pressure for cases to be heard at a lower level? In the course of early drafting of the Public Law Outline, it was agreed that it was necessary for there to be a scoping study to assess the capacity for work in the family proceedings court but it did not take place. Yet again it is difficult to avoid the conclusion that policy is based on cost considerations without adequate analysis of the implications for outcome.

14.13 What decisions would such a body be taking? In public law cases factual matters are often not seriously in dispute. Is there a role for a binding alternative dispute resolution system, which could reach agreement on factual matters, seek to resolve less serious disputes and establish a care plan for the future, perhaps based on a less strict standard of evidence. But could such an approach attract the respect of its users and ensure that human rights are protected? And could such a system sufficiently ensure proper regard for the principles of arts 6 and 8 of the ECHR.

14.14 What are the options – a legally trained decision maker, a combination of a legally qualified chair sitting with others with relevant expertise like the Special Educational Needs and Disability Tribunal or a lay bench? For economic reasons the Government might like to delegate more powers to a local committee of people already employed to take decisions about children. This would run counter to stated intentions to ensure openness. Most importantly there would be questions about whether any such moves would be compliant with rights to a fair trial protected by art 6 of the ECHR. In the current climate of reducing judicial involvement, lawyers will have to keep a wary eye on the legitimacy of future proposals. It will remain an essential requirement that children and families have access to independent legal advice at any stage of a case, in or out of court, where their rights to family life may be prejudiced.

3. Court rules

14.15 It had been expected that new court rules to replace the Family Proceedings Rules 1991 and the Family Proceedings Courts (Children Act 1989) Rules 1991 would be in force by spring 2008. It is said that they have been held up by technical problems and are not now likely to be brought in before 2010. It is regrettable that much-needed rules are not published and that improvements in practice are delayed for reasons of poor technology.

4. Legal aid/Public funding

14.16 We noted in the third edition that one consequence of the Access to Justice Act 1999 and accompanying policy was to decrease the number of legal aid practitioners. Inevitably this has had an adverse effect, not only on access to justice, but also on the development of child jurisprudence and in due course the availability of suitable lawyers to assume judicial office. That process has continued unabated[1] and the consequences have now reached crisis point. In July 2005 the Government published 'A fairer deal for legal aid'.[2] It would be difficult to think of a more inapt title. It was nothing less than the continuation of the process of dismantling the public funding of the family justice system. This was followed by the Carter Report,[3] which focussed primarily on funding of legal aid in criminal law and had no research information about civil proceedings on which to found its proposals. This was nonetheless taken as the basis for the simultaneous publication of proposals for change in civil legal aid in 'Legal Aid: a sustainable future'.[4] This produced a public funding fee structure for children's proceedings going beyond the proposals of the Carter Report, implemented without any clear idea why legal aid spending on care proceedings had increased or what the effect of the changes would be. This has further reduced the professional base, both among solicitors and barristers.

[1]   Law Society figures show a reduction in the number of solicitors' firms having contracts with the Legal Services Commission from 4,593 in 2001 to 2,784 in 2007. As MacDonald says: 'the same Government that champions the reforms to case management signalled by the PLO risks defeating those reforms by resourcing policies which dilapidate the legal professions required to implement them', The Caustic Dichotomy – Under Resourcing in the Care System (Child and Family Law Quarterly, in publication).
[2]   Cm 6591.
[3]   Legal Aid: a market based approach to reform (July 2006, known as the Carter Report).
[4]   CP13/06 (Department for Constitutional Affairs).

5. Parental responsibility

14.17 One of the objectives of the private law provisions was to encourage those responsible for children to reach their own decisions, where appropriately jointly, without recourse to the courts. Yet the Act imposes no duty on the residential parent to consult, following the Law Commission view that such a duty was unworkable and undesirable.[1] However, the courts have created some exceptions, namely, changing the child's schooling[2] and name,[3] so that it is uncertain as to the extent which the parent with whom the child does not reside can or should be involved in the exercise of parental responsibility. In any event what is the scope of the responsibility of the non-residential parent, if there is no duty to consult?

[1]   Report on Guardianship and Custody, Law Com 1988, No 172.
[2]   *Re G (a minor)(parental responsibility: education)* [1995] 2 FCR 53, [1994] 2 FLR 964, discussed at para 3.92.
[3]   *Re C (minors)(change of surname)* [1997] 3 FCR 310, sub nom *Re PC (Change of Surname)* [1997] 2 FLR 730. See also *Re J (child's religious upbringing and circumcision)* [2000] 1 FCR 307, sub *nom Re J (Specific Issue Orders)(Muslim Upbringing and Circumcision)* [2000] 1 FLR 571, discussed at para 3.92.

14.18 We have previously discussed the role of fathers and their acquisition of parental responsibility. In practice few fathers who want parental responsibility are denied it, especially since they can acquire it by being on the birth certificate since 1 December 2003.[1] Step-parents who are married to, or in a civil partnership with, a parent can acquire it by agreement or court order.[2] There are proposals for fathers to be required to register and thus be included on the child's birth certificate.[3] It is said that this is designed to ensure that both parents are involved in a child's life, but there may also be benefits to the Treasury in helping to ensure that fathers are identified for the purposes of obtaining financial support. Birth registrars will have powers to pursue reluctant fathers who do not want to be named. Mothers will be discouraged from keeping the name of the father secret.

[1]   Adoption and Children Act 2002, s 111 which amends the CA 1989, s 4.
[2]   Adoption and Children Act 2002, s 112, which inserts s 4A into the CA 1989.
[3]   Welfare Reform Bill 2008.

14.19 Notwithstanding these prospective changes, it remains the case that, unlike Scotland, there is no general power to grant parental responsibility. Consequently, an individual other than a parent or step-parent can acquire parental responsibility only by means of a residence order, which the courts will not use purely to allocate responsibility.[1] While this was an intended effect of the Act, there does seem to be a case for extending the courts' powers to grant responsibility to others, even though they are not caring for the child.

[1]   See eg *N v B (children: order as to residence)* [1993] 1 FCR 231, sub nom *Re WB (Residence Orders)* [1995] 2 FLR 1023, where the mother's cohabitant helped bring up the child, but when a dispute arose it was discovered on the eve of the court hearing that he was not the father. Cf *Re H (shared residence: parental responsibility)* [1996] 3 FCR 321, [1995] 2 FLR 883, CA, discussed at para 5.11.

6. Private law in the courts

14.20 In 2006 total private law applications increased by 2% compared with 2005.[1] Within this, applications for parental responsibility have decreased by 6%, applications for residence have increased by 1% and applications for contact have increased by 2%. There has been a small gradual increase in the number of private law applications between 2002 and 2006. This suggests no major changes in those areas. It is applications for contact orders which have always presented particular problems. At one end of case types there are minor disputes which would be best dealt with outside the court system. At the other end the courts have to consider applications in the face of allegations of domestic violence or sexual abuse. It has become evident that the courts have had to re-think their position upon the realisation that violence perpetrated on one parent by the other can have harmful effects upon the child.[2] Then there can be difficulties in deciding whether false allegations are being made with a view to justifying the withholding of contact. Such cases need but rarely get the necessary early hearing to reach a judgment on the facts. The risk assessment now required[3] of a CAFCASS reporting officer carrying out any function under the Act if the officer is given cause to suspect that the child is at risk of harm, should assist the early identification of such problems. The impact of prospective amendments in the Children and Adoption Act 2006[4] providing for courts to make contact activity directions and conditions and contact enforcement orders will be awaited with interest.

[1] Judicial and Court Statistics 2006, Cm 7273.
[2] See the discussion at paras 5.60 ff.
[3] Children and Adoption Act 2006, s 7, adds s 16A to the CA 1989.
[4] See discussion at paras 5.180 ff.

14.21 An important amendment to the 1989 Act contained in the Adoption and Children Act 2002 is the creation of special guardianship which is designed to provide the child with a permanent family relationship without terminating the fundamental nature of the birth relationship.[1] It is being used by relatives and foster carers though to what extent is still unclear. Anecdotally it appears that increasing use is being made of the provisions to encourage the care of children within their wider family, often known as kinship care. There are benefits for children and carers in remaining within the family, while at the same time obtaining support from the local authority without the high level involvement required if the child remains in care, provided adequate assessments are made to ensure that carers can provide for the child's welfare. The extent to which they can, in cases involving family conflict, achieve a sufficient degree of protection from intrusion remains to be seen.

[1] Discussed at paras 5.161 ff. See the Judicial and Court Statistics 2006, Cm 7273 for the most recent figures.

7. The local authority context

(a) Local authority support for children and families

14.22 The provision of services for children in need and families is a central plank of the public law provisions of the Act. The duty to safeguard and promote the welfare of children in need is vital to the proper functioning of the legislation. Unfortunately it is one of those areas which has suffered most through inadequate resources, though it might reasonably be argued that there could never be sufficient.

14.23 From 2003 government policy in furtherance of the principles of the 2004 Act has focussed on the development of strategies for vulnerable children in furtherance of principles set out in the Children Act 2004.[1] There has been a series of papers under the general title 'Every Child Matters'.[2] In theory this should direct more resources to the early needs of families, but it is likely to be at the expense of children and families at the hard end of the sector.

[1]   See Every Child Matters Green Paper (2003). There are many related subsequent policy documents, including the Children's Plan (December 2007). For full details see www.everychildmatters.gov.uk/publications.

(b) Care proceedings

14.24 Concerns about how the courts would operate in the public law field, without the availability of wardship, have proved unfounded. Through flexible interpretation of the threshold criteria, the courts have acquired an ability to exercise a reasonable degree of discretion in reaching solutions in care proceedings. In spite of concerns the threshold criteria seem to have achieved a suitable balance and a recent visit by the House of Lords continues to suggest that there is no need for them to be reinterpreted.[1]

[1]   *Re B (Children) (FC)* [2008] UKHL 35, [2008] 2 FCR 339.

14.25 The Government proposals in A Fairer Deal for Legal Aid[1] hit hardest and most immediately on public law proceedings. The Government took the opportunity to announce a review of the child care proceedings system. The Review's analysis identified as significant (in relation to outcomes for families and children and to the use of resources within the child care proceedings system) forecast increases in the volume of care proceedings likely to come to court and unnecessary delay, caused by a number of problems, including poorly prepared applications to court, ineffective case management, scarcity of judicial resources, variation in quality of representation; the provision of expert evidence; the late allocation of the children's guardian, which delayed the start of their appraisal of the authority's work in preparing the application and alternative carers emerging late in proceedings.

[1]   See para 14.13.

14.26 These reasons undoubtedly contributed to problems with the framework for public law cases but rather than providing practitioners with the ability to make the much needed improvements in practice the Government determined to focus on reducing the number and length of care proceedings, as one method of reducing the costs of the family justice system. At the same time funding of the legal aid system and resources for court services were reduced. This policy was pursued although at the time of the Review the numbers of public law proceedings were actually reducing[1] and the Government had commissioned research in 2004 but not published until 2008[2] which made it clear that proceedings were not being commenced inappropriately. There are obvious repercussions for the safety and welfare of children but changes have been implemented in ways which have brought about little public debate, for example by new procedures and higher fees for local authority applications.[3]

1   In November 2007 it was noted in the report Judicial and Court Statistics 2006 (Cm 7273) that public law applications decreased by 11% compared with 2005, following an upward trend in previous years. Within this, applications for care orders decreased by 7% cent and applications for supervision orders increased by 9%.
2   Masson, Pearce and Bader 'Care Profiling Study' (2008) Ministry of Justice.
3   On 1 May 2008 fees payable by local authorities in respect of public law proceedings were increased from £150 to more than £5,000 if they went to final hearing: see SI 2008/1053 and SI 2008/1054.

14.27 The procedural mechanisms in the form of the Public Law Outline[1] set out good practice and were intended to streamline case management in order to improve outcomes for children. When set in the context of the other policies of reducing public funding, increasing court fees and failing to make provision for adequate judicial and professional (including social work) services, introduced in spite of widespread warnings to the Government, the impact of policy changes on the court care system has every potential for disaster. There has been a further massive drop in the number of care applications issued.[2] Numbers will continue to reduce and for the wrong reasons – which will be financial and an inability to prepare cases adequately. There has to be a major fear that local authorities will decline to take care proceedings where they should do so or they will delay in doing so. They are being actively encouraged to use relatives to a greater degree, where possible without proceedings as that provides a cheaper option, without necessarily carrying out the same standard of assessment of the child's need for a secure placement. Children will not be protected when they should or they will enter care when older and more damaged. This will be particularly serious in neglect and emotional abuse cases. Local authorities are likely to seek to persuade parents to agree to children being 'voluntarily' accommodated.[3] This will exacerbate the drift of children in care which we have fought so hard to deal with in the last 30 years, because planning for the child's future is frequently poorly administered.

1   See paras 8.15 ff.
2   In the Inner London and City Family Proceedings Court in the period from January 2008 to June 2008 the number of applications issued reduced to 334 by comparison with 468 in the same period in the previous year, a drop of 35%. A report to the Ministerial Group on Care Proceedings in July 2008 noted that applications across England and Wales were down between 10% and 25% and in some areas by as much as 50%.
3   Under the CA 1989, s 20.

14.28 The approach of working with parents without the framework of court proceedings as opposed to obtaining court orders to ensure structure and planning for difficult case was explored in the early years after implementation of the 1989 Act, when some argued that s 1(5) was intended to limit the use of the court, both in public and private law. As a policy it was found wanting and the number of proceedings gradually increased to ensure proper protection of children. Regrettably those deciding on policy have chosen to ignore that experience, but there is no reason to suppose that the constraints on taking proceedings will act any better in the interests of children. It is difficult to conclude other than that the current reforms to the care system are proceeding on the basis of hope and short-term economy rather than research or even expectation. They are certainly not proceeding on a foundation of evidence-based planning.[1]

[1] 'Ministers admit that they are aware of the drop in care order applications but say they hope that the reduction is because more children at risk are being cared for by family members – although they concede that they have no evidence of this.' Quote from Ministry of Justice, Times, 6 May 2008. For further analysis of the reforms see MacDonald A 'The Caustic Dichotomy – Under Resourcing in the Care System' (Child and Family Law Quarterly, in publication).

8. Privatisation of children's services

14.29 Clause 1 of the Children and Young Persons Bill 2008 makes provision to enable local authorities to delegate local authority functions in relation to looked after children to providers of social work services. Effectively this could lead to privatisation of children's services so that local authorities become merely commissioners of services rather than providers. There are of course many voluntary and private agencies which already provide fostering and adoption services, but it is relevant to ask how far this privatisation will extend. Will the next step be to privatise child protective services and what would be the consequences of that, especially given a philosophical approach which requires full recovery of costs?

9. Representation of children and their interests

14.30 The Act gave children the right to object to certain court directions and to be parties and apply for orders or seek leave to apply in some circumstances. The philosophy followed the approach of the House of Lords in *Gillick*.[1] What came to be known as 'Gillick-competent' children acquired a level of self-determination or at least an opportunity to be heard. The major difficulties which have arisen relate to how that interest should be represented in private and public law proceedings. These involve whether the child should be a party, how their position should be articulated before the court and the role of CAFCASS in promoting the interests of the child.

[1] *Gillick v West Norfolk and Wisbech Area Health Authority* [1986] AC 112, [1985] 3 All ER 402, HL.

14.31 The extent to which children should be party to and represented in private law proceedings has long been the source of contention and variable practice.[1] Section 122 of the Adoption and Children Act 2002 amended s 41 of the 1989 Act to provide that proceedings for the making, varying or discharging of a s 8 order could be specified (so as to enable more easily the appointment of the child as a party represented by a children's guardian) and for the rules of court to include provision for children to be separately represented in relevant proceedings. This provision was forced on a reluctant government in the course of parliamentary debates and they quickly reneged on the agreement. It was four more years before the debate was renewed.[2]

14.31 Conclusions

1   See eg Lowe and Murch 'Children's participation in the family justice system – translating principles into practice' [2001] CFLQ 137, a report based on research at Cardiff Law School. The current position is dealt with at paras 4.50 and at 10.30.

2   The Department for Constitutional Affairs published a Consultation Paper 'Separate Representation of Children (September 2006) to inform the content of new court rules. But there has been no further publication pursuant to that consultation and progress on separate representation seems to have stopped, with the slow progress on developing the new court rules.

14.32 There is a growing awareness of the need for child participation in proceedings. There is good evidence that children want to be treated as active participants whose thoughts about their futures are listened to and not as passive objects. Courts have always been against seeing children and this has given a wider signal which may have served to limit their involvement. Although the 1989 Act makes provision both for the child to be heard and for his or her views to be taken into account, whether sufficient provision is made for the child's active participation in legal proceedings may be questioned.[1] There is now an evolving understanding of the importance of listening to children and in some courts a willingness to provide children with the opportunity within proceedings to express directly their own wishes and feelings in all matters affecting them in addition to having their interests adequately and independently represented. Yet there remain difficulties in translating these principles into practice. Given the lack of provision for them even to be a party in private law proceedings in the family proceedings court, we have a long way to go.

1   Research has increasingly pointed to the shift of emphasis so that children are no longer seen simply as passive victims of family breakdown but increasingly as participants and actors in the family justice system. See also the comment of Munby J in *CF v Secretary of State for the Home Department* [2004] EWHC 111 (Fam), [2004] 2 FLR 517 that: 'Children are not the largely passive objects of more or less paternalistic parental or judicial … decision-making'. A Family Justice Council Sub-Committee, the Voice of the Child, is currently considering the participation of children and the extent to which they should see the judge.

14.33 We said in 1995 that the Court Welfare Service was in crisis and there were problems with the guardian ad litem service. The obvious solution, which the authors first canvassed in 1985,[1] was to construct an agency with responsibility for all aspects of welfare reporting to the court. The introduction of CAFCASS initially caused deterioration in services. We had not foreseen that, after so many years of pressure for a new service, there would be a hasty introduction of such a vital organisation and no subsequent political impetus for improvement. Recent reports by OFSTED suggest that in some areas problems remain.[2] It may be that it is hoped that the planned reductions in care proceedings will enable CAFCASS to relocate its resources effectively. Yet one consequence of the more limited intervention by local authorities under s 31 is likely to be the need for more representation of children in private law proceedings, where there has been inadequate investigation of the effect of conflict between parents on children.

1   See Lowe and White *Wards of Court* (2nd edn, 1986) Barry Rose, para 9.31.

2   See eg Report of OFSTED Inspection (15 February 2008).

14.34 In the same way that the 2003 Service Standards were notable for imposing requirements on the individual CAFCASS officer, the new National Standards are notable for moving from emphasising the personal responsibility of the individual CAFCASS officer to emphasising the corporate responsibility of CAFCASS as an organisation. The new National Standards suggest an agenda more attuned to the resources of the agency than a reflection of the needs of the child.

14.35 The challenge of providing effective representation for children outside the scope of proceedings whilst also safeguarding and promoting their welfare continues to throw up issues which present both legal and practical difficulties. There is concern that care plans approved by the court are not honoured at a time when the court's powers are limited after the making of a care order. It may be that there will be an increase in the number of children accommodated in consequence of the restrictions imposed on care proceedings, so that the court will have no say in the life of the child. The Government's proposals for managing this appear to be to strengthen the administrative oversight of practice by establishing a national body for Independent Reviewing Officers.[1] It remains to be seen whether this will be any more effective than the current, virtually unused system of permitting a local authority employed Officer to refer the matter to CAFCASS.

[1] See the Children and Young Persons Bill, cl 12 and discussion at para 8.162.

(a) Welsh devolution

14.36 Reference is made in Chapter 1 to the growing significance of Welsh devolution leading to separate subordinate legislation dealing inter alia with children's services, CAFCASS Cymru and complaints procedures.[1] More fundamental changes can be expected in the future with the acquisition of competence by the Welsh Assembly under the Government of Wales Act 2006 to pass primary legislation in any of fifteen fields including that of social welfare.

[1] See para 1.42.

(b) Children's Commissioners

14.37 The appointment of a Children's Commissioner was made in Wales in April 2001, in Northern Ireland in October 2003 and in Scotland in February 2004, so England was the last country within the United Kingdom without an independent body or individual protecting the rights of children. The Children Act 2004 came into force on 15 November 2004 and led to the Commissioner taking up post in England on 1 July 2005. In Wales he has powers to examine cases of individual children, although he is limited to cases where he considers that the case raises matters of principle which have a more general application or relevance to the rights or welfare of children than those in the particular case. It remains a concern that the Commissioner in England is barred from assisting an individual child and permitted only to 'promote awareness of the views and interests of children in England'.

11. Human rights

14.38 Since publication of the third edition the Human Rights Act 1998 has become embedded in practice. This is unsurprising since the 1989 Act was drafted with the ECHR very much in mind. Problems still remain with procedural issues such as delay, secure accommodation and the continuing failure to provide more broadly for representation of children. Given the concerns expressed at various points in this edition it would be surprising if there continued to be no successful challenges.

12. International developments

14.39 International instruments are likely to play an increasing role in shaping not just so-called international family law but domestic law as well. In particular the European Union will predictably play a much greater role. The so-called Brussels II Regulation which controls jurisdiction, recognition and enforcement of decisions in relation to parental responsibility in divorce proceedings,[1] is currently under review and is likely to be extended to parental responsibility of all children. Furthermore, though not yet binding, the European Charter of Human Rights could well lead to further attempts to harmonise domestic family law of Member States.

[1]   See further para 4.4.

14.40 The United Kingdom will bring in to force the 1996 Hague Convention on the Protection of Children in June 2010. It contains important provisions for the recognition and enforcement of measures directed both to the protection of the child's person and property and to establish the necessary co-operation between the authorities of contracting states to achieve this purpose.[1]

[1]   For a discussion of this Convention see Lowe 'The 1996 Hague Convention on the protection of children – a fresh appraisal' [2002] CFLQ 191 and the authorities there cited.

FIT FOR THE 21ST CENTURY?

14.41 The Act has been in place for nearly two decades and has withstood examination fairly well in spite of restraint on the provision of resources. If the structures and support services provided under the legislation were to be adequately resourced, there is no reason to suppose the Act will not serve well for the foreseeable future. The Act remains a good basis for the law of the 21st century. There have been diverse amendments, many of major consequence such as those under the Care Standards Act 2000, the Adoption and Children Act 2002 and the Children Act 2004, and others of significance such as enforcement of contact orders, leaving care legislation and redefinition of the meaning of accommodation of children. Given the absence of an official up to date copy of the Act with all amendments in force, there may be a need for consolidation, but it has not surprised us that in 2008 we are not writing about the need for a new framework for the Act.

14.42 It has surprised us that we are having to write about defending the structure of legislation and its implementation, so widely held in high regard, against political undermining. It is difficult to avoid the conclusion that, in spite of public proclamations to be defending the family justice system, there is a current desire to drive lawyers out and minimise the use of proceedings, without regard to the consequences for children and their families. Such far-reaching changes should not be brought about without a much more open, and open-minded on the part of the Government, debate, than has occurred so far.

Appendix 1

CHILDREN ACT 1989

CHILDREN ACT 1989

(1989 C 41)

ARRANGEMENT OF SECTIONS

PART I

INTRODUCTORY

SECTION

		PAGE
1	Welfare of the child	648
2	Parental responsibility for children	650
3	Meaning of 'parental responsibility'	651
4	Acquisition of parental responsibility by father	652
4A	Acquisition of parental responsibility by step-parent	653
5	Appointment of guardians	654
6	Guardians: revocation and disclaimer	656
7	Welfare reports	657

PART II

ORDERS WITH RESPECT TO CHILDREN IN FAMILY PROCEEDINGS

General

8	Residence, contact and other orders with respect to children	658
9	Restrictions on making section 8 orders	660
10	Power of court to make section 8 orders	661
11	General principles and supplementary provisions	664
11A	Contact activity directions	665
11B	Contact activity directions: further provision	666
11C	Contact activity conditions	667
11D	Contact activity conditions: further provision	668
11E	Contact activity directions and conditions: making	668
11F	Contact activity directions and conditions: financial assistance	669
11G	Contact activity directions and conditions: monitoring	670
11H	Monitoring contact	670
11I	Contact orders: warning notices	671
11J	Enforcement orders	671
11K	Enforcement orders: further provision	672

11L   Enforcement orders: making 673
11M   Enforcement orders: monitoring 674
11N   Enforcement orders: warning notices 674
11O   Compensation for financial loss 674
11P   Orders under section 11O(2): further provision 675
12   Residence orders and parental responsibility 676
13   Change of child's name or removal from jurisdiction 677
14   Enforcement of residence orders 677

Special Guardianship
14A   Special guardianship orders 678
14B   Special guardianship orders: making 680
14C   Special guardianship orders: effect 680
14D   Special guardianship orders: variation and discharge 681
14E   Special guardianship orders: supplementary 682
14F   Special guardianship support services 682
14G   *This section has been repealed* 684

Financial relief
15   Orders for financial relief with respect to children 684

Family assistance orders
16   Family assistance orders 685
16A   Risk assessments 686

PART III

LOCAL AUTHORITY SUPPORT FOR CHILDREN AND FAMILIES

Provision of services for children and their families
17   Provision of services for children in need, their families and others 678
17A   Direct payments 689
17B   Vouchers for persons with parental responsibility for disabled children 691
18   Day care for pre-school and other children 691
19   *This section has been repealed* 692

Provision of accommodation for children
20   Provision of accommodation for children: general 692
21   Provision for accommodation for children in police protection or detention or on remand,
       etc 694

Duties of local authorities in relation to children looked after by them
22   General duty of local authority in relation to children looked after by them 696
23   Provision of accommodation and maintenance by local authority for children whom they
       are looking after 698

Advice and assistance for certain children [and young persons]
23A   The responsible authority and relevant children 700
23B   Additional functions of the responsible authority in respect of relevant children 701
23C   Continuing functions in respect of former relevant children 702

Personal advisers and pathway plans
23D   Personal advisers 703
23E   Pathway plans 704
24   Persons qualifying for advice and assistance 704
24A   Advice and assistance 706
24B   Employment, education and training 707
24C   Information 707
24D   Representations: sections 23A to 24B 708

Secure accommodation

25   Use of accommodation for restricting liberty...709

Supplemental

26   Review of cases and inquiries into representations 710
26ZA   Representations: further consideration...714
26ZB   Representations: further consideration (Wales) 714
26A   Advocacy services...715
27   Co-operation between authorities 716
28   Consultation with local education authorities...717
29   Recoupment of cost of providing services etc 718
30   Miscellaneous...720

PART IV

CARE AND SUPERVISION

General

31   Care and supervision orders...721
31A   Care orders: care plans 724
32   Period within which application for order under this Part must be disposed of.........724

Care orders

33   Effect of care order 725
34   Parental contact etc with children in care 727

Supervision orders

35   Supervision orders...729
36   Education supervision orders 729

Powers of court

37   Powers of court in certain family proceedings 731
38   Interim orders 732
38A   Power to include exclusion requirement in interim care order....................734
38B   Undertakings relating to interim care orders...735
39   Discharge and variation etc of care orders and supervision orders.............736
40   Orders pending appeals in cases about care or supervision orders 737

Representation of child

41   Representation of child and of his interests in certain proceedings.............738
42   Right of officer of the Service to have access to local authority records.....741

PART V

PROTECTION OF CHILDREN

43   Child assessment orders 742
44   Orders for emergency protection of children 744
44A   Power to include exclusion requirement in emergency protection order.....747
44B   Undertakings relating to emergency protection orders.................................748
45   Duration of emergency protection orders and other supplemental provisions.............749
46   Removal and accommodation of children by police in cases of emergency 751
47   Local authority's duty to investigate 753
48   Powers to assist in discovery of children who may be in need of emergency protection.756
49   Abduction of children in care etc..757
50   Recovery of abducted children etc 758
51   Refuges for children at risk..760
52   Rules and regulations..761

Appendix 1 *Children Act 1989*

PART VI

COMMUNITY HOMES

53   Provision of community homes by local authorities 762
54   *This section has been repealed* 765
55   Determination of disputes relating to controlled and assisted community homes........765
56   Discontinuance by voluntary organisation of controlled or assisted community home.766
57   Closure by local authority of controlled or assisted community home.......................767
58   Financial provisions applicable on cessation of controlled or assisted community home or disposal etc of premises...768

PART VII

VOLUNTARY HOMES AND VOLUNTARY ORGANISATIONS

59   Provision of accommodation by voluntary organisations 770
60   Voluntary homes 772
61   Duties of voluntary organisations 772
62   Duties of local authorities..773

PART VIII

REGISTERED CHILDREN'S HOMES

63   Private children's homes etc 776
64   Welfare of children in children's homes 777
65   Persons disqualified from carrying on, or being employed in, children's homes 778
65A   Appeal against refusal of authority to give consent under section 65............................779

PART IX

PRIVATE ARRANGEMENTS FOR FOSTERING CHILDREN

66   Privately fostered children..779
67   Welfare of privately fostered children 781
68   Persons disqualified from being private foster parents...782
69   Power to prohibit private fostering...784
70   Offences 785

PART X

CHILD MINDING AND DAY CARE FOR YOUNG CHILDREN

71–79   *Part X has been repealed as it applies to England and Wales (but not Scotland)*..............

PART XA

CHILD MINDING AND DAY CARE FOR CHILDREN IN ENGLAND AND WALES

Introductory

79A   Child minders and day care providers 787
79B   Other definitions, etc 788

Regulations

79C   Regulations etc governing child minders and day care providers.................................790

Registration

79D   Requirement to register...792
79E   Applications for registration 793
79F   Grant or refusal of registration 794
79G   Cancellation of registration..795
79H   Suspension of registration 796

79J	Resignation of registration	797
79K	Protection of children in an emergency	798
79L	Notice of intention to take steps	799
79M	Appeals	800

Inspection: England

79N	General functions of the Chief Inspector	801
79P	*This section has been repealed*	802
79Q	Inspection of provision of child minding and day care in England	802
79R	Reports of inspections	803

Inspection: Wales

79S	General functions of the Assembly	804
79T	Inspection: Wales	804

Supplementary

79U	Rights of entry etc	805
79V	Function of local authorities	807

Checks on suitability of persons working with children over the age of seven

79W	Requirement for certificate of suitability	807

Time limit for proceedings

79X	Time limit for proceedings	808

PART XI

SECRETARY OF STATE'S SUPERVISORY FUNCTIONS AND RESPONSIBILITIES

80	Inspection of children's homes etc by persons authorised by Secretary of State	809
81	*This section has been repealed*	812
82	Financial support by Secretary of State	812
83	Research and returns of information	814
84	Local authority failure to comply with statutory duty: default power of Secretary of State	815

PART XII

MISCELLANEOUS AND GENERAL

Notification of children accommodated in certain establishments

85	Children accommodated by health authorities and local education authorities	816
86	Children accommodated in residential care, nursing or mental nursing homes [Children accommodated in care homes or independent hospitals]	817
87	*Welfare of children accommodated in independent schools* [Welfare of children in boarding schools and colleges	818
87A	Suspension of duty under section 87(3)	821
87B	Duties of inspectors under section 87A	822
87C	Boarding schools: national minimum standards	823
87D	Annual fee for boarding school inspections	824

Adoption

88	*This section has been repealed*	824

Paternity tests

89	*This section has been repealed*	825

Criminal care and supervision orders

90	Care and supervision orders in criminal proceedings	825

Effect and duration of orders etc
91   Effect and duration of orders etc 825

Jurisdiction and procedure etc
92   Jurisdiction of courts..827
93   Rules of court 829
94   Appeals 830
95   Attendance of child at hearing under Part IV or V..832
96   Evidence given by, or with respect to, children..832
97   Privacy for children involved in certain proceedings......................................833
98   Self-incrimination 835
99   *This section has been repealed* 835
100   Restrictions on use of wardship jurisdiction 835
101   Effect of orders as between England and Wales and Northern Ireland, the Channel Islands or the Isle of Man..836

Search warrants
102   Power of constable to assist in exercise of certain powers to search for children or inspect premises 838

General
103   Offences by bodies corporate..839
104   Regulations and orders 839
105   Interpretation 840
106   Financial provisions 845
107   Application to Channel Islands..845
108   Short title, commencement, extent etc 845

SCHEDULES
     Schedule A1 — Enforcement Orders 847
     Schedule 1 — Financial Provision for Children 852
     Schedule 2 — Local Authority Support for Children and Families 853
     Schedule 3 — Supervision Orders..860
     Schedule 4 — Management and Conduct of Community Homes 863
     Schedule 5 — Voluntary Homes and Voluntary Organisations 865
     Schedule 6 — Registered Children's Homes [Private Children's Homes]..............867
     Schedule 7 — Foster Parents: Limits on Number of Foster Children 868
     Schedule 8 — Privately Fostered Children..869
     Schedule 9 — Child Minding and Day Care for Young Children 871
     Schedule 9A — Child Minding and Day Care for Young Children......................872
     Schedule 10 — Amendments of Adoption Legislation..874
     Schedule 11 — Jurisdiction..875
     Schedule 12 — Minor Amendments 876
     Schedule 13 — Consequential Amendments..876
     Schedule 14 — Transitionals and Savings..876
     Schedule 15 — Repeals..876

An Act to reform the law relating to children; to provide for local authority services for children in need and others; to amend the law with respect to children's homes, community homes, voluntary homes and voluntary organisations; to make provision with respect to fostering, child minding and day care for young children and adoption; and for connected purposes

[16th November 1989]

PART I

INTRODUCTORY

1   **Welfare of the child**

(1)   When a court determines any question with respect to—

648

(a) the upbringing of a child; or

(b) the administration of a child's property or the application of any income arising from it,

the child's welfare shall be the court's paramount consideration.

(2)   In any proceedings in which any question with respect to the upbringing of a child arises, the court shall have regard to the general principle that any delay in determining the question is likely to prejudice the welfare of the child.

(3)   In the circumstances mentioned in subsection (4), a court shall have regard in particular to—

(a) the ascertainable wishes and feelings of the child concerned (considered in the light of his age and understanding);

(b) his physical, emotional and educational needs;

(c) the likely effect on him of any change in his circumstances;

(d) his age, sex, background and any characteristics of his which the court considers relevant;

(e) any harm which he has suffered or is at risk of suffering;

(f) how capable each of his parents, and any other person in relation to whom the court considers the question to be relevant, is of meeting his needs;

(g) the range of powers available to the court under this Act in the proceedings in question.

(4)   The circumstances are that—

(a) the court is considering whether to make, vary or discharge a section 8 order, and the making, variation or discharge of the order is opposed by any party to the proceedings; or

(b) the court is considering whether to make, vary or discharge [a special guardianship order or] an order under Part IV.

(5)   Where a court is considering whether or not to make one or more orders under this Act with respect to a child, it shall not make the order or any of the orders unless it considers that doing so would be better for the child than making no order at all.

Date in force

14 October 1991: SI 1991/828.

Amendment

Sub-s (4): in para (b) words 'a special guardianship order or' in square brackets inserted by the Adoption and Children Act 2002, s 115(2), (3).

Definitions

For 'court' see s 97(7); for 'child', 'upbringing' and 'special guardianship' see s 105(1); for 'harm' see s 31(9) as applied to the whole Act by s 105(1); for 'a section 8 order' see s 8(2).

References

See generally paras 2.2 ff. For jurisdiction of courts see s 92 and Sch 11; for welfare of the child, see paras 2.2 ff for 'parent' see para 3.43; for 'special guardianship see paras 5.213 ff. 'Part IV' ie ss 31–42 and Sch 3 (care and supervision). For 'family proceedings' under this Act see s 8(3), (4)(a).

Sub-s (1)

For 'paramount' see paras 2.3 ff. For the impact of the European Convention on Human Rights generally, see *Re S (children: care plan)* [2002] UKHL 10, [2002] 1 All ER 192. For where the paramountcy principle does not apply, see paras 2.13 ff. The paramountcy principle does not apply to determining whether to grant leave to apply for a s 8 order under s 10: *Re A (Minors) (Residence Orders: Leave to Apply)* [1992] Fam 182, [1992] 3 All ER 872, sub nom *Re A and W (Minors) (Residence Order: Leave to Apply)* [1992] 2 FLR 154, CA.

Sub-s (2)

For delay, prima facie, prejudicial to child's welfare, see paras 2.60 ff.

Sub-s (3)(a)

For application of the checklist, see paras 2.42 ff. Child's view does not have priority over other heads in the checklist. See *Re W (minors) (residence order)* [1992] 2 FCR 461, CA. See para 2.42.

Sub-s (5)

For the application of this principle, see para 2.64 ff. Has little or no application to applications for financial relief under Sch 1: *K v H* [1993] 1 FCR 684, [1993] 2 FLR 61. Nor to applications for secure accommodation orders: *Re M (A Minor) (Secure Accommodation Order)* [1995] Fam 108, [1995] 3 All ER 407, CA. For application to 'non-parent' applicants see *Re B (a minor) (residence order)* [1992] 2 FLR 327 and para 2.72. See also paras 2.73–2.75 of the revised Children Act 1989 Guidance and Regulations, Volume 1, Court Orders (2008) Department for Children, Schools and Families.

---

2   Parental responsibility for children

(1)   Where a child's father and mother were married to each other at the time of his birth, they shall each have parental responsibility for the child.

(2)   Where a child's father and mother were not married to each other at the time of his birth—

    (a)   the mother shall have parental responsibility for the child;

    (b)   the father [shall have parental responsibility for the child if he has acquired it (and has not ceased to have it)] in accordance with the provisions of this Act.

(3)   References in this Act to a child whose father and mother were, or (as the case may be) were not, married to each other at the time of his birth must be read with section 1 of the Family Law Reform Act 1987 (which extends their meaning).

(4)   The rule of law that a father is the natural guardian of his legitimate child is abolished.

(5)   More than one person may have parental responsibility for the same child at the same time.

(6)   A person who has parental responsibility for a child at any time shall not cease to have that responsibility solely because some other person subsequently acquires parental responsibility for the child.

(7)   Where more than one person has parental responsibility for a child, each of them may act alone and without the other (or others) in meeting that responsibility; but nothing in this Part shall be taken to affect the operation of any enactment which requires the consent of more than one person in a matter affecting the child.

(8)   The fact that a person has parental responsibility for a child shall not entitle him to act in any way which would be incompatible with any order made with respect to the child under this Act.

(9)   A person who has parental responsibility for a child may not surrender or transfer any part of that responsibility to another but may arrange for some or all of it to be met by one or more persons acting on his behalf.

(10)   The person with whom any such arrangement is made may himself be a person who already has parental responsibility for the child concerned.

(11)   The making of any such arrangement shall not affect any liability of the person making it which may arise from any failure to meet any part of his parental responsibility for the child concerned.

Date in force

14 October 1991: SI 1991/828.

Amendment

Sub-s (2): in para (b) words 'shall have parental responsibility for the child if he has acquired it (and has not ceased to have it)' in square brackets substituted by the Adoption and Children Act 2002, s 111(5).

Definitions

For 'child' see s 105(1); for 'parental responsibility' see s 3.

References

See generally paras 3.43 ff and paras 2.6 to 2.17 of the revised Children Act 1989 Guidance and Regulations, Volume 1, Court Orders (2008) Department for Children, Schools and Families. For whether a child's father and mother were married to each other at the time of his birth see sub-s (3); for father acquiring parental responsibility see s 4 and at paras 3.48 ff; for step-parent acquiring parental responsibility see s 4A and at paras 3.81 ff; for 'this part' see Part I, ss 1–7.

3   Meaning of 'parental responsibility'

(1)   In this Act 'parental responsibility' means all the rights, duties, powers, responsibilities and authority which by law a parent of a child has in relation to the child and his property.

(2)   It also includes the rights, powers and duties which a guardian of the child's estate (appointed, before the commencement of section 5, to act generally) would have had in relation to the child and his property.

(3)   The rights referred to in subsection (2) include, in particular, the right of the guardian to receive or recover in his own name, for the benefit of the child, property of whatever description and wherever situated which the child is entitled to receive or recover.

(4)   The fact that a person has, or does not have, parental responsibility for a child shall not affect—

    (a)   any obligation which he may have in relation to the child (such as a statutory duty to maintain the child); or

    (b)   any rights which, in the event of the child's death, he (or any other person) may have in relation to the child's property.

(5)   A person who—

    (a)   does not have parental responsibility for a particular child; but

    (b)   has care of the child,

may (subject to the provisions of this Act) do what is reasonable in all the circumstances of the case for the purpose of safeguarding or promoting the child's welfare.

Date in force

14 October 1991: SI 1991/828.

Definitions

For 'parental responsibility' see sub-s (1); for 'child' see s 105(1).

References

For the meaning and scope of parental responsibility, see paras 3.7 ff and paras 2.6 to2.17 of the revised Children Act 1989 Guidance and Regulations, Volume 1, Court Orders (2008) Department for Children, Schools and Families; for duration, see para 3.94 and for sharing with others, see paras 3.96 ff. For 'parent', see para 3.43; for the application of 'parental responsibility' to other enactments see s 108(5), Sch 13.

---

4   Acquisition of parental responsibility by father

(1)   Where a child's father and mother were not married to each other at the time of his birth

([, the father shall acquire parental responsibility for the child if—

(a)   he becomes registered as the child's father under any of the enactments specified in subsection (1A);

(b)   he and the child's mother make an agreement (a 'parental responsibility agreement') providing for him to have parental responsibility for the child; or

(c)   the court, on his application, orders that he shall have parental responsibility for the child.]

[(1A)   The enactments referred to in subsection (1)(a) are—

(a)   paragraphs (a), (b) and (c) of section 10(1) and of section 10A(1) of the Births and Deaths Registration Act 1953;

(b)   paragraphs (a), (b)(i) and (c) of section 18(1), and sections 18(2)(b) and 20(1)(a) of the Registration of Births, Deaths and Marriages (Scotland) Act 1965; and

(c)   sub-paragraphs (a), (b) and (c) of Article 14(3) of the Births and Deaths Registration (Northern Ireland) Order 1976.

(1B)   The [Secretary of State] may by order amend subsection (1A) so as to add further enactments to the list in that subsection.]

(2)   No parental responsibility agreement shall have effect for the purposes of this Act unless—

(a)   it is made in the form prescribed by regulations made by the Lord Chancellor; and

(b)   where regulations are made by the Lord Chancellor prescribing the manner in which such agreements must be recorded, it is recorded in the prescribed manner.

[(2A)   A person who has acquired parental responsibility under subsection (1) shall cease to have that responsibility only if the court so orders.

(3)   The court may make an order under subsection (2A) on the application—

(a)   of any person who has parental responsibility for the child; or

(b)   with the leave of the court, of the child himself,

subject, in the case of parental responsibility acquired under subsection (1)(c), to section 12(4).]

(4)   The court may only grant leave under subsection (3)(*b*) if it is satisfied that the child has sufficient understanding to make the proposed application.

Date in force

14 October 1991: SI 1991/828.

Amendment

Sub-s (1): words from ', the father shall' to 'for the child.' in square brackets substituted by the Adoption and Children Act 2002, s 111(1), (2); for further provision in relation to parental responsibility conferred on a man registered under the enactments referred to in sub-s (1A) above see sub-s (7) thereof.
Sub-ss (1A), (1B): inserted by the Adoption and Children Act 2002, s 111(1), (3).
Sub-s (1B): words 'Secretary of State' in square brackets substituted by SI 2003/3191, arts 3(a), 6, Schedule, para 1.
Sub-ss (2A), (3): substituted, for sub-s (3) as originally enacted, by the Adoption and Children Act 2002, s 111(1), (4). Date in force:

Definitions

For 'child' see s 105(1); for 'court' see s 92(7); for 'parental responsibility' see s 3; for 'parental responsibility agreement' see sub-s (1)(b); for 'prescribed' see sub-s (2).

References

See generally paras 3.48 ff. For jurisdiction of courts see s 92 and Sch 11; for appeals see s 94. For whether a child's father and mother were married to each other at the time of his birth see s 2(3), s 105(2); for duration of the order see s 12(4) (where residence order made in favour of the father) and generally s 91(7), (8); for 'family proceedings' under this Act see s 8(3), (4)(a).

Regulations

See Parental Responsibility Agreement Regulations 1991, SI 1991/1478 amended by SI 1994/3157 and SI 2005/2808.

Sub-s (1)

May ... an order. For examples where an application was refused, see para 3.69. Effect for the practical effects of an order, see para 3.73.

4A   Acquisition of parental responsibility by step-parent

[(1)   Where a child's parent ('parent A') who has parental responsibility for the child is married to[, or a civil partner of,] a person who is not the child's parent ('the step-parent')—

   (a)   parent A or, if the other parent of the child also has parental responsibility for the child, both parents may by agreement with the step-parent provide for the step-parent to have parental responsibility for the child; or
   (b)   the court may, on the application of the step-parent, order that the step-parent shall have parental responsibility for the child.

(2)   An agreement under subsection (1)(a) is also a 'parental responsibility agreement', and section 4(2) applies in relation to such agreements as it applies in relation to parental responsibility agreements under section 4.

(3)   A parental responsibility agreement under subsection (1)(a), or an order under subsection (1)(b), may only be brought to an end by an order of the court made on the application—

   (a)   of any person who has parental responsibility for the child; or

(b)   with the leave of the court, of the child himself.

(4)   The court may only grant leave under subsection (3)(b) if it is satisfied that the child has sufficient understanding to make the proposed application.]

Date in force

30 December 2005: see SI 2005/2213, art 2.

Amendment

Inserted by the Adoption and Children Act 2002, s 112.
Sub-s (1): words ', or a civil partner of,' in square brackets inserted by the Civil Partnership Act 2004, s 75(1), (2).

Definitions

For 'child' see s 105(1); for 'parent', see para 3.43; for 'court' see s 92(7); for 'parental responsibility' see s 3; for 'parental responsibility agreement' see sub-s (2).

References

See generally paras 3.81 ff. For jurisdiction of courts see s 92 and Sch 11; for appeals see s 94. For whether a child's father and mother were married to each other at the time of his birth see s 2(3), s 105(2); for duration of the order see s 12(4) (where residence order made in favour of the father) and generally s 91(7), (8); for 'family proceedings' under this Act see s 8(3), (4)(a).

---

5   Appointment of guardians

(1)   Where an application with respect to a child is made to the court by any individual, the court may by order appoint that individual to be the child's guardian if—

    (a)   the child has no parent with parental responsibility for him; or

    (b)   a residence order has been made with respect to the child in favour of a parent[, guardian or special guardian] of his who has died while the order was in force[; or

    (c)   paragraph (b) does not apply, and the child's only or last surviving special guardian dies].

(2)   The power conferred by subsection (1) may also be exercised in any family proceedings if the court considers that the order should be made even though no application has been made for it.

(3)   A parent who has parental responsibility for his child may appoint another individual to be the child's guardian in the event of his death.

(4)   A guardian of a child may appoint another individual to take his place as the child's guardian in the event of his death[; and a special guardian of a child may appoint another individual to be the child's guardian in the event of his death].

(5)   An appointment under subsection (3) or (4) shall not have effect unless it is made in writing, is dated and is signed by the person making the appointment or—

    (a)   in the case of an appointment made by a will which is not signed by the testator, is signed at the direction of the testator in accordance with the requirements of section 9 of the Wills Act 1837; or

    (b)   in any other case, is signed at the direction of the person making the appointment, in his presence and in the presence of two witnesses who each attest the signature.

(6)   A person appointed as a child's guardian under this section shall have parental responsibility for the child concerned.

(7)   Where—

    (a)   on the death of any person making an appointment under subsection (3) or (4), the child concerned has no parent with parental responsibility for him; or

    (b)   immediately before the death of any person making such an appointment, a residence order in his favour was in force with respect to the child, [or he was the child's only (or last surviving) special guardian]

the appointment shall take effect on the death of that person.

(8)   Where, on the death of any person making an appointment under subsection (3) or (4)—

    (a)   the child concerned has a parent with parental responsibility for him; and

    (b)   subsection (7)(b) does not apply,

the appointment shall take effect when the child no longer has a parent who has parental responsibility for him.

(9)   Subsections (1) and (7) do not apply if the residence order referred to in paragraph (b) of those subsections was also made in favour of a surviving parent of the child.

(10)   Nothing in this section shall be taken to prevent an appointment under subsection (3) or (4) being made by two or more persons acting jointly.

(11)   Subject to any provision made by rules of court, no court shall exercise the High Court's inherent jurisdiction to appoint a guardian of the estate of any child.

(12)   Where rules of court are made under subsection (11) they may prescribe the circumstances in which, and conditions subject to which, an appointment of such a guardian may be made.

(13)   A guardian of a child may only be appointed in accordance with the provisions of this section.

Date in force

Sub-ss (1)–(10), (13): 14 October 1991: SI 1991/828. Sub-ss (11), (12): 1 February 1992: SI 1991/828.

Amendments

Sub-s (1): in para (b) words ', guardian or special guardian' in square brackets substituted by the Adoption and Children Act 2002, s 115(2), (4)(a)(i); word '; or' immediately preceding it inserted by the Adoption and Children Act 2002, s 115(2), (4)(a)(ii).
Sub-s (4): words from '; and a special' to 'of his death' in square brackets inserted by the Adoption and Children Act 2002, s 115(2), (4)(b).
Sub-s (7): in para (b) words 'or he was the child's only (or last surviving) special guardian' in square brackets inserted by the Adoption and Children Act 2002, s 115(2), (4)(c).

Definitions

For 'child' and 'signed' see s 105(1); for 'court' see s 92(7); for 'parental responsibility' see s 3; for 'residence order' see s 8(1); for 'special guardianship see s 105(1); for a person in whose favour a residence order is in force see s 105(3).

References

See generally paras 3.104 ff. Guardianship is discussed at para 2.18–2.26 of the revised Children Act 1989 Guidance and Regulations, Volume 1, Court Orders (2008) Department for Children,

Schools and Families.For jurisdiction of courts see s 92 and Sch 11; for duration of order of appointment see s 91(7), (8); for transitional provisions see s 108(6) and Sch 14, para 12; for 'family proceedings' under this Act see s 8(3), (4)(a); for other restrictions on the use of wardship jurisdiction see s 100.

---

6   Guardians: revocation and disclaimer

(1)   An appointment under section 5(3) or (4) revokes an earlier such appointment (including one made in an unrevoked will or codicil) made by the same person in respect of the same child, unless it is clear (whether as the result of an express provision in the later appointment or by any necessary implication) that the purpose of the later appointment is to appoint an additional guardian.

(2)   An appointment under section 5(3) or (4) (including one made in an unrevoked will or codicil) is revoked if the person who made the appointment revokes it by a written and dated instrument which is signed—

(a)   by him; or
(b)   at his direction, in his presence and in the presence of two witnesses who each attest the signature.

(3)   An appointment under section 5(3) or (4) (other than one made in a will or codicil) is revoked if, with the intention of revoking the appointment, the person who made it—

(a)   destroys the instrument by which it was made; or
(b)   has some other person destroy that instrument in his presence.

[(3A)   An appointment under section 5(3) or (4) (including one made in an unrevoked will or codicil) is revoked if the person appointed is the spouse of the person who made the appointment and either—

(*a*)   *a decree of a court of civil jurisdiction in England and Wales dissolves or annuls the marriage, or*
[(a)   a court of civil jurisdiction in England and Wales by order dissolves, or by decree annuls, a marriage, or]
(b)   the marriage is dissolved or annulled and the divorce or annulment is entitled to recognition in England and Wales by virtue of Part II of the Family Law Act 1986,

unless a contrary intention appears by the appointment.]

[(3B)   An appointment under section 5(3) or (4) (including one made in an unrevoked will or codicil) is revoked if the person appointed is the civil partner of the person who made the appointment and either—

(a)   an order of a court of civil jurisdiction in England and Wales dissolves or annuls the civil partnership, or
(b)   the civil partnership is dissolved or annulled and the dissolution or annulment is entitled to recognition in England and Wales by virtue of Chapter 3 of Part 5 of the Civil Partnership Act 2004,

unless a contrary intention appears by the appointment.]

(4)   For the avoidance of doubt, an appointment under section 5(3) or (4) made in a will or codicil is revoked if the will or codicil is revoked.

(5)   A person who is appointed as a guardian under section 5(3) or (4) may disclaim his appointment by an instrument in writing signed by him and made within a reasonable time of his first knowing that the appointment has taken effect.

(6)   Where regulations are made by the Lord Chancellor prescribing the manner in which such disclaimers must be recorded, no such disclaimer shall have effect unless it is recorded in the prescribed manner.

(7)   Any appointment of a guardian under section 5 may be brought to an end at any time by order of the court—

(a)   on the application of any person who has parental responsibility for the child;

(b)   on the application of the child concerned, with leave of the court; or

(c)   in any family proceedings, if the court considers that it should be brought to an end even though no application has been made.

Date in force

14 October 1991: SI 1991/828.

Amendment

Sub-s (3A): inserted by the Law Reform (Succession) Act 1995, s 4; para (a) prospectively substituted with savings by the Family Law Act 1996, s 66(1), Sch 8, para 41(2), as from a day to be appointed, for savings see s 66(2), Sch 9, para 5 thereof.
Sub-s (3B): inserted by the Civil Partnership Act 2004, s 76.

Definitions

For 'child', and 'signed' see s 105(1); for 'court' see s 92(7); for 'parental responsibility' see s 3.

Reference

For jurisdiction of courts see s 92 and Sch 11; for 'family proceedings' under this Act see s 8(3), (4)(a).

7   Welfare reports

(1)   A court considering any question with respect to a child under this Act may—

(a)   ask [an officer of the Service] [or a Welsh family proceedings officer]; or

(b)   ask a local authority to arrange for—

(i)   an officer of the authority; or

(ii)   such other person (other than [an officer of the Service] [or a Welsh family proceedings officer]) as the authority considers appropriate,

to report to the court on such matters relating to the welfare of that child as are required to be dealt with in the report.

(2)   The Lord Chancellor may[, after consulting the Lord Chief Justice,] make regulations specifying matters which, unless the court orders otherwise, must be dealt with in any report under this section.

(3)   The report may be made in writing, or orally, as the court requires.

(4)   Regardless of any enactment or rule of law which would otherwise prevent it from doing so, the court may take account of—

(a)   any statement contained in the report; and

(b)   any evidence given in respect of the matters referred to in the report,

in so far as the statement or evidence is, in the opinion of the court, relevant to the question which it is considering.

(5)   It shall be the duty of the authority or [officer of the Service] [or a Welsh family proceedings officer] to comply with any request for a report under this section.

[(6) The Lord Chief Justice may nominate a judicial office holder (as defined in section 109(4) of the Constitutional Reform Act 2005) to exercise his functions under subsection (2).]

Date in force

14 October 1991: SI 1991/828.

Amendments

Sub-s (1): words 'an officer of the Service' in square brackets in both places they occur substituted by the Criminal Justice and Court Services Act 2000, s 74, Sch 7, Pt II, paras 87, 88(a); in paras (a), (b)(ii) words 'or a Welsh family proceedings officer' in square brackets inserted by the Children Act 2004, s 40, Sch 3, paras 5, 6.
Sub-s (2): words ', after consulting the Lord Chief Justice,' in square brackets inserted by the Constitutional Reform Act 2005, s 15(1), Sch 4, Pt 1, paras 203, 204(1), (2).
Sub-s (5): words 'officer of the Service' in square brackets substituted by the Criminal Justice and Court Services Act 2000, s 74, Sch 7, Pt II, paras 87, 88(b); words 'or a Welsh family proceedings officer' in square brackets inserted by the Children Act 2004, s 40, Sch 3, paras 5, 6.
Sub-s (6): inserted by the Constitutional Reform Act 2005, s 15(1), Sch 4, Pt 1, paras 203, 204(1), (3).

Definitions

For 'court' see s 92(7); for 'child' and 'local authority' see s 105(1).

References

See generally Chapter 10 and in particular paras 10.1 ff. For jurisdiction of courts see s 92 and Sch 11; for other evidential provisions see s 96. For the need for the court to give clear reasons for departing from the evidence of a professional witness given by way of a s 7 report, see *Re J (children) (residence: expert evidence)* [2001] 2 FCR 43 and see for where such reasons were sufficient, *Re E (children) (residence order)* [2001] EWCA Civ 567, [2001] 2 FCR 662.
To date no regulations have been issued under sub-s (2).

PART II

ORDERS WITH RESPECT TO CHILDREN IN FAMILY PROCEEDINGS

General

8   Residence, contact and other orders with respect to children

(1)   In this Act—

'a contact order' means an order requiring the person with whom a child lives, or is to live, to allow the child to visit or stay with the person named in the order, or for that person and the child otherwise to have contact with each other;

'a prohibited steps order' means an order that no step which could be taken by a parent in meeting his parental responsibility for a child, and which is of a kind specified in the order, shall be taken by any person without the consent of the court;

'a residence order' means an order settling the arrangements to be made as to the person with whom a child is to live; and

'a specific issue order' means an order giving directions for the purpose of determining a specific question which has arisen, or which may arise, in connection with any aspect of parental responsibility for a child.

(2)   In this Act 'a section 8 order' means any of the orders mentioned in subsection (1) and any order varying or discharging such an order.

(3) For the purposes of this Act 'family proceedings' means [(subject to subsection (5))] any proceedings—

(a) under the inherent jurisdiction of the High Court in relation to children; and
(b) under the enactments mentioned in subsection (4),

but does not include proceedings on an application for leave under section 100(3).

(4) The enactments are—

(a) Parts I, II and IV of this Act;
(b) the Matrimonial Causes Act 1973;
[(ba) Schedule 5 to the Civil Partnership Act 2004;]
(c) ...
[(d) the Adoption and Children Act 2002;]
(e) the Domestic Proceedings and Magistrates' Courts Act 1978;
[(ea) Schedule 6 to the Civil Partnership Act 2004;]
(f) ...
(g) Part III of the Matrimonial and Family Proceedings Act 1984.
[(h) the Family Law Act 1996.]
[(i) sections 11 and 12 of the Crime and Disorder Act 1998.]

[(5)   For the purposes of any reference in this Act to family proceedings powers which under this Act are exercisable in family proceedings shall also be exercisable in relation to a child, without any such proceedings having been commenced or any application having been made to the court under this Act, if—

(a) a statement of marital breakdown under section 5 of the Family Law Act 1996 with respect to the marriage in relation to which that child is a child of the family has been received by the court; and
(b) it may, in due course, become possible for an application for a divorce order or for a separation order to be made by reference to that statement.]

Date in force

14 October 1991: SI 1991/828.

Amendments

Sub-s (3): words 'subject to subsection (5)' in square brackets inserted with savings by the Family Law Act 1996, s 66(1), Sch 8, para 41(3); for savings see s 66(2), Sch 9, para 5 thereof. Date in force: to be appointed: see the Family Law Act 1996, s 67.
Sub-s (4): para (ba) inserted by the Civil Partnership Act 2004, s 261(1), Sch 27, para 129(1), (2); paras (c), (f) repealed by the Family Law Act 1996, s 66(1), (3), Sch 8, para 60(1), Sch 10; para (d) substituted by the Adoption and Children Act 2002, s 139(1), Sch 3, paras 54, 55; para (ea) inserted by the Civil Partnership Act 2004, s 261(1), Sch 27, para 129(1), (3); para (h) inserted by the Family Law Act 1996, s 66(1), Sch 8, para 60(1); para (i) inserted by the Crime and Disorder Act 1998, s 119, Sch 8, para 68.
Sub-s (5): inserted with savings by the Family Law Act 1996, s 66(1), Sch 8, para 41(4); for savings see s 66(2), Sch 9, paras 5, 8–10 thereof. Date in force: to be appointed: see the Family Law Act 1996, s 67(3).

Definitions

For 'contact order', 'prohibited steps order', 'residence order', 'specific issue order' see sub-s (1); for 'child' see s 105(1); for 'parental responsibility' see s 3; for 'court' see s 92(7); for 'a section 8 order' see sub-s (2); for 'family proceedings' see sub-s (3).

References

See generally Chapter 5. Section 8 orders are discussed at paras 2.27–2.54 of the revised Children Act 1989 Guidance and Regulations, Volume 1, Court Orders (2008) Department for Children,

Schools and Families. For 'parent', see para 3.43; for jurisdiction of the courts see s 92 and Sch 11. Part I of this Act: ie ss 1–7 (introductory); Pt II, ss 8–17 and Sch 1 (orders with respect to children in family and other proceedings); Pt IV, ss 31–42 and Sch 3 (care and supervision); for the effects of orders generally see s 91.

Residence order

See generally paras 5.14 ff. Can be made ex parte but only in exceptional circumstances: FPR 1991, SI 1991/1247, r 4.4(4); FPC(CA 1989)R 1991, SI 1991/1395, r 4(4); *Re B (minors) (residence orders)* [1992] Fam 162, [1992] 3 All ER 867, CA; *Re G (minors) (ex parte interim residence order)* [1993] 1 FLR 910, CA; *Re P (a minor) (ex parte interim residence order)* [1993] 1 FLR 915, CA, see paras 5.22 ff.

Contact order

See paras 5.54 ff. For contact and domestic violence, see paras 5.90 ff. For contact activity directions and conditions, see para 5.63 ff.

Prohibited steps order

See generally paras 5.94 ff. Must not be used as a disguised residence or contact order, see s 9(5) above and *Re B (minors) (residence orders)* at 165 and 869 respectively per Butler-Sloss LJ and *Nottingham County Council v P* [1993] 3 All ER 815, [1994] Fam 18 CA. There is no jurisdiction to make ouster orders: *Re D (Prohibited Steps Order)* [1996] 2 FLR 273, sub nom *D v D (Ouster Order)* [1996] 2 FCR 496, CA nor an order prohibiting parents from seeing each other as such contact is not a step which can be taken by a parent in meeting his parental responsibility towards his child: *Croydon London Borough Council v A* [1992] 3 All ER 788, [1992] 3 WLR 267, CA.. Orders can be made even though child is abroad: *Re D (a minor) (child: removal from jurisdiction)* [1992] 1 All ER 892, [1992] 1 WLR 315, CA. For prohibiting contact see *Nottingham County Council v P*, above and *Re H (prohibited steps order)* [1995] 1 FLR 638, CA, see paras 5.62.

Specific issue order

See generally paras 5.97 ff.

---

9   Restrictions on making section 8 orders

(1)   No court shall make any section 8 order, other than a residence order, with respect to a child who is in the care of a local authority.

(2)   No application may be made by a local authority for a residence order or contact order and no court shall make such an order in favour of a local authority.

(3)   A person who is, or was at any time within the last six months, a local authority foster parent of a child may not apply for leave to apply for a section 8 order with respect to the child unless—

    (a)   he has the consent of the authority;
    (b)   he is a relative of the child; or
    (c)   the child has lived with him for at least [one year] preceding the application.

(4)   ...

(5)   No court shall exercise its powers to make a specific issue order or prohibited steps order—

    (a)   with a view to achieving a result which could be achieved by making a residence or contact order; or
    (b)   in any way which is denied to the High Court (by section 100(2)) in the exercise of its inherent jurisdiction with respect to children.

(6)   [Subject to section 12(5)] no court shall make any section 8 order which is to have effect for a period which will end after the child has reached the age of sixteen unless it is satisfied that the circumstances of the case are exceptional.

(7)   No court shall make any section 8 order, other than one varying or discharging such an order, with respect to a child who has reached the age of sixteen unless it is satisfied that the circumstances of the case are exceptional.

Date in force

14 October 1991: SI 1991/828.

Amendments

Sub-s (3): in para (c) words 'one year' in square brackets substituted by the Adoption and Children Act 2002, s 113(a).
Sub-s (4): repealed by the Adoption and Children Act 2002, ss 113(b), 139(3), Sch 5.
Sub-s (6): words 'Subject to section 12(5)' in square brackets inserted by the Adoption and Children Act 2002, s 114(2).

Definitions

For 'court' see s 92(7); for 'a section 8 order' see s 8(2); for 'residence order', 'contact order', 'specific issue order' and 'prohibited steps order' see s 8(1); for 'child', 'child who is in the care of a local authority', 'local authority' and 'relative' see s 105(1); for 'local authority foster parent', see s 23(3).

References

For 'family proceedings' under this Act see s 8(3), (4)(a) and see paras 2.55 to 2.58 of the revised Children Act 1989 Guidance and Regulations, Volume 1, Court Orders (2008) Department for Children, Schools and Families; for jurisdiction of courts see s 92 and Sch 11; for power of court to make s 8 orders, person who may make an application for such orders and the need for leave to apply see s 10; for the presumption that a delay in determining any question in proceedings concerning the upbringing of a child is likely to prejudice the welfare of the child concerned see s 1(2); for timetable for s 8 proceedings and supplementary provisions see s 11; for provisions connected with residence orders see ss 12, 13 and 14; for the application of s 9(1)(2) see paras 5.105 ff and 5.125 ff and for 9(5) see para 5.102 and see *Re B (Minors) (Residence Orders)* [1992] Fam 162 at 165, [1992] 3 All ER 867 at 869, per Butler-Sloss LJ and *Nottingham County Council v P* [1994] Fam 18, [1993] 3 All ER 815, [1993] 3 WLR 637, CA. Cf *Re H (Prohibited Steps Order)* [1995] 1 FLR 638, CA. A local authority may apply for leave to apply for a specific issue order in respect of a child not in care: *Re C (a child) (HIV test)* [1999] 3 FCR 289. A parent may continue to apply for a s 8 order in respect of a child without seeking leave, notwithstanding that the child is subject to a special guardianship order: *A Local Authority v X, Y, Z* [2006] 2 FLR 41.

---

10   Power of court to make section 8 orders

(1)   In any family proceedings in which a question arises with respect to the welfare of any child, the court may make a section 8 order with respect to the child if—

    (a)   an application for the order has been made by a person who—
        (i)   is entitled to apply for a section 8 order with respect to the child; or
        (ii) has obtained the leave of the court to make the application; or
    (b)   the court considers that the order should be made even though no such application has been made.

(2)   The court may also make a section 8 order with respect to any child on the application of a person who—

    (a)   is entitled to apply for a section 8 order with respect to the child; or
    (b)   has obtained the leave of the court to make the application.

(3)   This section is subject to the restrictions imposed by section 9.

(4)   The following persons are entitled to apply to the court for any section 8 order with respect to a child—

    (a)   any parent[, guardian or special guardian] of the child;

    [(aa) any person who by virtue of section 4A has parental responsibility for the child;]

    (b)   any person in whose favour a residence order is in force with respect to the child.

(5)   The following persons are entitled to apply for a residence or contact order with respect to a child—

    (a)   any party to a marriage (whether or not subsisting) in relation to whom the child is a child of the family;

    [(aa) any civil partner in a civil partnership (whether or not subsisting) in relation to whom the child is a child of the family;]

    (b)   any person with whom the child has lived for a period of at least three years;

    (c)   any person—

        (i)   in any case where a residence order is in force with respect to the child, has the consent of each of the persons in whose favour the order was made;

        (ii)   in any case where the child is in the care of a local authority, has the consent of that authority; or

        (iii)   in any other case, has the consent of each of those (if any) who have parental responsibility for the child.

[(5A)   A local authority foster parent is entitled to apply for a residence order with respect to a child if the child has lived with him for a period of at least one year immediately preceding the application.]

(6)   A person who would not otherwise be entitled (under the previous provisions of this section) to apply for the variation or discharge of a section 8 order shall be entitled to do so if—

    (a)   the order was made on his application; or

    (b)   in the case of a contact order, he is named in the order.

(7)   Any person who falls within a category of person prescribed by rules of court is entitled to apply for any such section 8 order as may be prescribed in relation to that category of person.

[(7A)   If a special guardianship order is in force with respect to a child, an application for a residence order may only be made with respect to him, if apart from this subsection the leave of the court is not required, with such leave.]

(8)   Where the person applying for leave to make an application for a section 8 order is the child concerned, the court may only grant leave if it is satisfied that he has sufficient understanding to make the proposed application for the section 8 order.

(9)   Where the person applying for leave to make an application for a section 8 order is not the child concerned, the court shall, in deciding whether or not to grant leave, have particular regard to—

    (a)   the nature of the proposed application for the section 8 order;

    (b)   the applicant's connection with the child;

    (c)   any risk there might be of that proposed application disrupting the child's life to such an extent that he would be harmed by it; and

    (d)   where the child is being looked after by a local authority—

        (i)   the authority's plans for the child's future; and

(ii) the wishes and feelings of the child's parents.

(10) The period of three years mentioned in subsection (5)(b) need not be continuous but must not have begun more than five years before, or ended more than three months before, the making of the application.

Date in force

14 October 1991: SI 1991/828.

Amendments

Sub-s (4): in para (a) words ', guardian or special guardian' in square brackets substituted by the Adoption and Children Act 2002, s 139(1), Sch 3, paras 54, 56(a); para (aa) inserted by the Adoption and Children Act 2002, s 139(1), Sch 3, paras 54, 56(b).
Sub-s (5): para (aa) inserted by the Civil Partnership Act 2004, s 77.
Sub-s (5A): inserted by the Adoption and Children Act 2002, s 139(1), Sch 3, paras 54, 56(c).
Sub-s (7A): inserted by the Adoption and Children Act 2002, s 139(1), Sch 3, paras 54, 56(d).

Definitions

For 'family proceedings' see s 8(3); for 'child', 'guardian', 'child of the family', 'child in the care of local authority', 'local authority', 'prescribed', 'special guardian' see s 105(1); for 'court' see s 92(7); for 'a section 8 order' see s 8(2); for 'residence order', 'contact order', see s 8(1); for a 'person in whose favour a residence order is in force' see s 105(3)(b); for 'parental responsibility' see s 3; for 'harm' see s 31(9) as applied to the whole Act by s 105(1); for 'child looked after by a local authority' see s 22(1) and s 105(4).

References

See generally para 5.141 ff. For jurisdiction of courts see s 92 and Sch 11; for appeals see s 94; for persons entitled to apply for s 8 orders see sub-ss (4), (5) and (6); for 'parent' see para 3.43; for appointment of children's guardian see s 41; for duration of orders made under this section see s 11(5), (6) and ss 91(10), (11); for 'family proceedings' under this Act see s 8(3), (4)(a); for where the leave of the court may be required in order to make an application for an order under this section see s 91(14); for the making of family assistance orders under this Part, ie Pt II (ss 8–16 and Sch 1) see s 16; for the restrictions on the making of applications for a s 8 order see s 9; for the presumption that a delay in determining any question in proceedings concerning a s 8 order is likely to prejudice the welfare of the child concerned see s 1(2); for the timetable for such proceedings and supplementary provisions see s 11; for other provisions connected with residence orders see ss 12, 13 and 14. Unmarried fathers do not require leave, but parents whose child has been freed for adoption do require leave: *Re C (Minors) (Adoption: Residence Order)* [1994] Fam 1, sub nom *Re C (minors) (parent:residence order)* [1993] 3 All ER 313, [1993] 3 WLR 249, sub nom *M v C and Calderdale Metropolitan Borough Council* [1993] 1 FLR 505, CA. A child who is named in a contact order for whom he had previously obtained leave to apply does not need leave to apply for its subsequent variation, per Wilson J in *Re W (application for leave: whether necessary)* [1996] 3 FCR 337n. The grant of leave is a substantial judicial decision and generally, any application should be heard on notice to all likely to be affected, see *Re (minors)* [1992] 3 All ER 867, *Re G (minors) (ex p Residence Order)* [1992] 2 FCR 720 and *Re W (A Child)(Contact: Leave to Apply)* [2000] 1 FLR 263, FD. In deciding whether to grant adults leave the child's welfare is not the paramount consideration: *Re A (Minors) (Residence Orders: Leave to Apply)* [1992] Fam 182, [1992] 3 All ER 872, sub nom *Re A and W (Minors) (Residence Order) (Leave to Apply)* [1992] 2 FLR 154, [1992] Fam Law 439,CA. In the case of applications for leave by children, the criteria in s 10(9) do not apply but there is a conflict of opinion as to whether the child's welfare is the paramount consideration. See *Re C (A Minor) (Leave to Seek Section 8 Orders)* [1994] 1 FLR 26, where the child's welfare is the paramount consideration, per Johnson J, cf *Re SC (A Minor) (Leave to Seek Residence Order)* [1994] 1 FLR 96 and *Re C (Residence: Child's Application for Leave)* [1995] 1 FLR 927 in which Booth J and Stuart-White J respectively held that it was not. Although a local authority foster parent may not apply without the consent of the local authority, the court may make an order of its own motion in favour of the foster parent: *Gloucestershire County Council v P* [1999] 3 FCR 114, [1999] 2 FLR 61, CA.

Contact within adoption proceedings is more common but the imposition of contact on adoptions with which they are not in agreement is extremely uncommon: *Re R (a child) (adoption: contact)* [2005] EWCA Civ 1128, [2007] 1 FCR 149.

---

11 General principles and supplementary provisions

(1) In proceedings in which any question of making a section 8 order, or any other question with respect to such an order, arises, the court shall (in the light of any rules made by virtue of subsection (2))—

  (a) draw up a timetable with a view to determining the question without delay; and
  (b) give such directions as it considers appropriate for the purpose of ensuring, so far as is reasonably practicable, that that timetable is adhered to.

(2) Rules of court may—

  (a) specify periods within which specified steps must be taken in relation to proceedings in which such questions arise; and
  (b) make other provision with respect to such proceedings for the purpose of ensuring, so far as is reasonably practicable, that such questions are determined without delay.

(3) Where a court has power to make a section 8 order, it may do so at any time during the course of the proceedings in question even though it is not in a position to dispose finally of those proceedings.

(4) Where a residence order is made in favour of two or more persons who do not themselves all live together, the order may specify the periods during which the child is to live in the different households concerned.

(5) Where—

  (a) a residence order has been made with respect to a child; and
  (b) as a result of the order the child lives, or is to live, with one of two parents who each have parental responsibility for him,

the residence order shall cease to have effect if the parents live together for a continuous period of more than six months.

(6) A contact order which requires the parent with whom a child lives to allow the child to visit, or otherwise have contact with, his other parent shall cease to have effect if the parents live together for a continuous period of more than six months.

(7) A section 8 order may—

  (a) contain directions about how it is to be carried into effect;
  (b) impose conditions which must be complied with by any person—
    (i) in whose favour the order is made;
    (ii) who is a parent of the child concerned;
    (iii) who is not a parent of his but who has parental responsibility for him; or
    (iv) with whom the child is living,
  and to whom the conditions are expressed to apply;
  (c) be made to have effect for a specified period, or contain provisions which are to have effect for a specified period;
  (d) make such incidental, supplemental or consequential provision as the court thinks fit.

Date in force

14 October 1991: SI 1991/828.

Definitions

For 'a section 8 order' see s 8(2); for 'court' see s 92(7) for 'residence order' and 'contact order' see s 8(1); for 'child' see s 105(1); for a person in whose favour a residence order is made or a person with whom a child lives, or is to live, as the result of the residence order see s 105(3); for 'parental responsibility' see s 3.

References

For jurisdiction of courts see s 92 and Sch 11; for welfare of the child see Chapter 2; for the presumption that a delay in determining any question in proceedings concerning the upbringing of a child is likely to prejudice the welfare of the child concerned see s 1(2); for 'parent' see para 3.43.

Sub-s (4)

Where children were de facto spending substantial amounts of time with each of their parents, a shared residence order was an appropriate order to make and there was no need to show exceptional circumstances or a positive benefit to the children, see *Re D (children) (shared residence orders)* [2001] 1 FCR 147, [2001] 1 FLR 495 explaining *Re H (a minor) (Residence Order)* [1993] 1 FCR 671 where it had been held that it would rarely be appropriate for a shared residence order to be made other than in exceptional circumstances. See also *N v B (Children:.Orders as to Residence)* [1993] 1 FCR 231 (wrong to make a shared residence order solely to give an applicant parental responsibility).

Sub-s (7)

See generally paras 5.109 ff. The powers under sub s (7) are ancillary to the making of a s 8 order and are governed by the provisions for the making of a s 8 order. There is not power therefore to interfere with rights of occupation: per Ward LJ in *Re D (Prohibited Steps Order)* [1996] 2 FLR 273, sub nom *D v D (ouster order)* [1996] 2 FCR 496, CA and *Re D (Residence: Imposition of Conditions)* [1996] 2 FLR, CA. Conditions must not be inconsistent with any residence order granted: *Birmingham City Council v H* [1992] 2 FLR 323 and can only be imposed on persons listed (i e not local authorities): *Leeds County Council v C* [1993] 1 FLR 269. Section 11 cannot be used to interfere with the exercise by other bodies, such as local authorities or the police, of their statutory law powers: *D v D (County Court Jurisdiction: Injunctions)* [1993] 2 FLR 802, CA. It is highly exceptional to impose a condition of residence on a primary carer in circumstances other than the express restrictions on a removal of a child from the jurisdiction in s 13 of the Act: *Re S (a child) (residence order: condition)* [2001] EWCA Civ 847, [2001] 3 FCR 847 (but for an exceptional case, see *Re H (children (residence order: condition* [2001] EWCA Civ 1338, [2001] 3 FCR 182 and see also *B v B (residence: conditon limiting geographic area)* [2004] 2 FLR 979).

[11A   Contact activity directions]

[(1)   This section applies in proceedings in which the court is considering whether to make provision about contact with a child by making—

(a)   a contact order with respect to the child, or

(b)   an order varying or discharging a contact order with respect to the child.

(2)   The court may make a contact activity direction in connection with that provision about contact.

(3)   A contact activity direction is a direction requiring an individual who is a party to the proceedings to take part in an activity that promotes contact with the child concerned.

(4)   The direction is to specify the activity and the person providing the activity.

(5)   The activities that may be so required include, in particular—

(a)   programmes, classes and counselling or guidance sessions of a kind that—

(i)   may assist a person as regards establishing, maintaining or improving contact with a child;

(ii) may, by addressing a person's violent behaviour, enable or facilitate contact with a child;

(b) sessions in which information or advice is given as regards making or operating arrangements for contact with a child, including making arrangements by means of mediation.

(6)   No individual may be required by a contact activity direction—

(a) to undergo medical or psychiatric examination, assessment or treatment;

(b) to take part in mediation.

(7)   A court may not on the same occasion—

(a) make a contact activity direction, and

(b) dispose finally of the proceedings as they relate to contact with the child concerned.

(8)   Subsection (2) has effect subject to the restrictions in sections 11B and 11E.

(9)   In considering whether to make a contact activity direction, the welfare of the child concerned is to be the court's paramount consideration.]

Date in force

Inserted by the Children and Adoption Act 2006, s 1. Date in force: to be appointed: see the Children and Adoption Act 2006, s 17(2).

Definitions

For 'child', see s 105(1); for 'court' see s 92(7); for 'contact order' see s 8 (1); for 'contact activity direction' see s 11A(3)

Reference

For contact activity directions see paras 5.63 ff.

[11B   Contact activity directions: further provision]

[(1)   A court may not make a contact activity direction in any proceedings unless there is a dispute as regards the provision about contact that the court is considering whether to make in the proceedings.

(2)   A court may not make a contact activity direction requiring an individual who is a child to take part in an activity unless the individual is a parent of the child in relation to whom the court is considering provision about contact.

(3)   A court may not make a contact activity direction in connection with the making, variation or discharge of a contact order, if the contact order is, or would if made be, an excepted order.

(4)   A contact order with respect to a child is an excepted order if—

(a) it is made in proceedings that include proceedings on an application for a relevant adoption order in respect of the child; or

(b) it makes provision as regards contact between the child and a person who would be a parent or relative of the child but for the child's adoption by an order falling within subsection (5).

(5)   An order falls within this subsection if it is—

(a) a relevant adoption order;

(b) an adoption order, within the meaning of section 72(1) of the Adoption Act 1976, other than an order made by virtue of section 14 of that Act on the application of a married couple one of whom is the mother or the father of the child;

(c) a Scottish adoption order, within the meaning of the Adoption and Children Act 2002, other than an order made—

  (i) by virtue of section 14 of the Adoption (Scotland) Act 1978 on the application of a married couple one of whom is the mother or the father of the child, or

  (ii) by virtue of section 15(1)(aa) of that Act; or

(d) a Northern Irish adoption order, within the meaning of the Adoption and Children Act 2002, other than an order made by virtue of Article 14 of the Adoption (Northern Ireland) Order 1987 on the application of a married couple one of whom is the mother or the father of the child.

(6) A relevant adoption order is an adoption order, within the meaning of section 46(1) of the Adoption and Children Act 2002, other than an order made—

(a) on an application under section 50 of that Act by a couple (within the meaning of that Act) one of whom is the mother or the father of the person to be adopted, or

(b) on an application under section 51(2) of that Act.

(7) A court may not make a contact activity direction in relation to an individual unless the individual is habitually resident in England and Wales; and a direction ceases to have effect if the individual subject to the direction ceases to be habitually resident in England and Wales.]

Date in force

Inserted by the Children and Adoption Act 2006, s 1. Date in force: to be appointed: see the Children and Adoption Act 2006, s 17(2).

Definitions

For 'court' see s 92(7); for 'contact activity direction' see s 11A(3).

[**11C**   **Contact activity conditions**]

[(1) This section applies if in any family proceedings the court makes—

(a) a contact order with respect to a child, or

(b) an order varying a contact order with respect to a child.

(2) The contact order may impose, or the contact order may be varied so as to impose, a condition (a 'contact activity condition') requiring an individual falling within subsection (3) to take part in an activity that promotes contact with the child concerned.

(3) An individual falls within this subsection if he is—

(a) for the purposes of the contact order so made or varied, the person with whom the child concerned lives or is to live;

(b) the person whose contact with the child concerned is provided for in that order; or

(c) a person upon whom that order imposes a condition under section 11(7)(b).

(4) The condition is to specify the activity and the person providing the activity.

(5)   Subsections (5) and (6) of section 11A have effect as regards the activities that may be required by a contact activity condition as they have effect as regards the activities that may be required by a contact activity direction.

(6)   Subsection (2) has effect subject to the restrictions in sections 11D and 11E.]

Date in force

Inserted by the Children and Adoption Act 2006, s 1. Date in force: to be appointed: see the Children and Adoption Act 2006, s 17(2).

Definitions

For 'contact order' see s 8 (1); for 'family proceedings' see s 8 (3); for 'contact activity direction' see s 11A(3).

[11D   Contact activity conditions: further provision]

[(1)   A contact order may not impose a contact activity condition on an individual who is a child unless the individual is a parent of the child concerned.

(2)   If a contact order is an excepted order (within the meaning given by section 11B(4)), it may not impose (and it may not be varied so as to impose) a contact activity condition.

(3)   A contact order may not impose a contact activity condition on an individual unless the individual is habitually resident in England and Wales; and a condition ceases to have effect if the individual subject to the condition ceases to be habitually resident in England and Wales.]

Date in force

Inserted by the Children and Adoption Act 2006, s 1. Date in force: to be appointed: see the Children and Adoption Act 2006, s 17(2).

Definitions

For 'contact activity direction' see s 11A(3).

[11E   Contact activity directions and conditions: making]

[(1)   Before making a contact activity direction (or imposing a contact activity condition by means of a contact order), the court must satisfy itself as to the matters falling within subsections (2) to (4).

(2)   The first matter is that the activity proposed to be specified is appropriate in the circumstances of the case.

(3)   The second matter is that the person proposed to be specified as the provider of the activity is suitable to provide the activity.

(4)   The third matter is that the activity proposed to be specified is provided in a place to which the individual who would be subject to the direction (or the condition) can reasonably be expected to travel.

(5)   Before making such a direction (or such an order), the court must obtain and consider information about the individual who would be subject to the direction (or the condition) and the likely effect of the direction (or the condition) on him.

(6)   Information about the likely effect of the direction (or the condition) may, in particular, include information as to—

(a)   any conflict with the individual's religious beliefs;

(b)   any interference with the times (if any) at which he normally works or attends an educational establishment.

(7)   The court may ask an officer of the Service or a Welsh family proceedings officer to provide the court with information as to the matters in subsections (2) to (5); and it shall be the duty of the officer of the Service or Welsh family proceedings officer to comply with any such request.

(8)   In this section 'specified' means specified in a contact activity direction (or in a contact activity condition).]

Date in force

Inserted by the Children and Adoption Act 2006, s 1. Date in force: to be appointed: see the Children and Adoption Act 2006, s 17(2).

Definitions

For 'contact activity direction' see s 11A(3).

[11F   Contact activity directions and conditions: financial assistance]

[(1)   The Secretary of State may by regulations make provision authorising him to make payments to assist individuals falling within subsection (2) in paying relevant charges or fees.

(2)   An individual falls within this subsection if he is required by a contact activity direction or condition to take part in an activity that promotes contact with a child, not being a child ordinarily resident in Wales.

(3)   The National Assembly for Wales may by regulations make provision authorising it to make payments to assist individuals falling within subsection (4) in paying relevant charges or fees.

(4)   An individual falls within this subsection if he is required by a contact activity direction or condition to take part in an activity that promotes contact with a child who is ordinarily resident in Wales.

(5)   A relevant charge or fee, in relation to an activity required by a contact activity direction or condition, is a charge or fee in respect of the activity payable to the person providing the activity.

(6)   Regulations under this section may provide that no assistance is available to an individual unless—

(a)   the individual satisfies such conditions as regards his financial resources as may be set out in the regulations;

(b)   the activity in which the individual is required by a contact activity direction or condition to take part is provided to him in England or Wales;

(c)   where the activity in which the individual is required to take part is provided to him in England, it is provided by a person who is for the time being approved by the Secretary of State as a provider of activities required by a contact activity direction or condition;

(d)   where the activity in which the individual is required to take part is provided to him in Wales, it is provided by a person who is for the time being approved by the National Assembly for Wales as a provider of activities required by a contact activity direction or condition.

(7)   Regulations under this section may make provision—

(a)   as to the maximum amount of assistance that may be paid to or in respect of an individual as regards an activity in which he is required by a contact activity direction or condition to take part;

(b)   where the amount may vary according to an individual's financial resources, as to the method by which the amount is to be determined;

(c)   authorising payments by way of assistance to be made directly to persons providing activities required by a contact activity direction or condition.]

Date in force

Inserted by the Children and Adoption Act 2006, s 1. Date in force: to be appointed: see the Children and Adoption Act 2006, s 17(2).

11G   Contact activity directions and conditions: monitoring

[(1)   This section applies if in any family proceedings the court—

(a)   makes a contact activity direction in relation to an individual, or

(b)   makes a contact order that imposes, or varies a contact order so as to impose, a contact activity condition on an individual.

(2)   The court may on making the direction (or imposing the condition by means of a contact order) ask an officer of the Service or a Welsh family proceedings officer—

(a)   to monitor, or arrange for the monitoring of, the individual's compliance with the direction (or the condition);

(b)   to report to the court on any failure by the individual to comply with the direction (or the condition).

(3)   It shall be the duty of the officer of the Service or Welsh family proceedings officer to comply with any request under subsection (2).]

Date in force

Inserted by the Children and Adoption Act 2006, s 1. Date in force: to be appointed: see the Children and Adoption Act 2006, s 17(2).

Definitions

For 'family proceedings' see s 8 (3);for 'court' see s 92(7).

[11H   Monitoring contact]

[(1)   This section applies if in any family proceedings the court makes—

(a)   a contact order with respect to a child in favour of a person, or

(b)   an order varying such a contact order.

(2)   The court may ask an officer of the Service or a Welsh family proceedings officer—

(a)   to monitor whether an individual falling within subsection (3) complies with the contact order (or the contact order as varied);

(b)   to report to the court on such matters relating to the individual's compliance as the court may specify in the request.

(3)   An individual falls within this subsection if the contact order so made (or the contact order as so varied)—

(a)   requires the individual to allow contact with the child concerned;

(b)   names the individual as having contact with the child concerned; or

(c)   imposes a condition under section 11(7)(b) on the individual.

(4)   If the contact order (or the contact order as varied) includes a contact activity condition, a request under subsection (2) is to be treated as relating to the provisions of the order other than the contact activity condition.

(5)   The court may make a request under subsection (2)—

(a)   on making the contact order (or the order varying the contact order), or
(b)   at any time during the subsequent course of the proceedings as they relate to contact with the child concerned.

(6)   In making a request under subsection (2), the court is to specify the period for which the officer of the Service or Welsh family proceedings officer is to monitor compliance with the order; and the period specified may not exceed twelve months.

(7)   It shall be the duty of the officer of the Service or Welsh family proceedings officer to comply with any request under subsection (2).

(8)   The court may order any individual falling within subsection (3) to take such steps as may be specified in the order with a view to enabling the officer of the Service or Welsh family proceedings officer to comply with the court's request under subsection (2).

(9)   But the court may not make an order under subsection (8) with respect to an individual who is a child unless he is a parent of the child with respect to whom the order falling within subsection (1) was made.

(10)   A court may not make a request under subsection (2) in relation to a contact order that is an excepted order (within the meaning given by section 11B(4)).]

Date in force

Inserted by the Children and Adoption Act 2006, s 2. Date in force: to be appointed: see the Children and Adoption Act 2006, s 17(2).

Definitions

For 'family proceedings' see s 8 (3); for 'court' see s 92(7).

[11I   Contact orders: warning notices]

[Where the court makes (or varies) a contact order, it is to attach to the contact order (or the order varying the contact order) a notice warning of the consequences of failing to comply with the contact order.]

Date in force

Inserted by the Children and Adoption Act 2006, s 3; for transitional provision see s 8 thereof. Date in force: to be appointed: see the Children and Adoption Act 2006, s 17(2).

Definitions

For 'contact order' see s 8(1).

[11J   Enforcement orders]

[(1)   This section applies if a contact order with respect to a child has been made.

(2)   If the court is satisfied beyond reasonable doubt that a person has failed to comply with the contact order, it may make an order (an 'enforcement order') imposing on the person an unpaid work requirement.

(3)   But the court may not make an enforcement order if it is satisfied that the person had a reasonable excuse for failing to comply with the contact order.

(4)   The burden of proof as to the matter mentioned in subsection (3) lies on the person claiming to have had a reasonable excuse, and the standard of proof is the balance of probabilities.

(5)   The court may make an enforcement order in relation to the contact order only on the application of—

(a)   the person who is, for the purposes of the contact order, the person with whom the child concerned lives or is to live;

(b)   the person whose contact with the child concerned is provided for in the contact order;

(c)   any individual subject to a condition under section 11(7)(b) or a contact activity condition imposed by the contact order; or

(d)   the child concerned.

(6)   Where the person proposing to apply for an enforcement order in relation to a contact order is the child concerned, the child must obtain the leave of the court before making such an application.

(7)   The court may grant leave to the child concerned only if it is satisfied that he has sufficient understanding to make the proposed application.

(8)   Subsection (2) has effect subject to the restrictions in sections 11K and 11L.

(9)   The court may suspend an enforcement order for such period as it thinks fit.

(10)   Nothing in this section prevents a court from making more than one enforcement order in relation to the same person on the same occasion.

(11)   Proceedings in which any question of making an enforcement order, or any other question with respect to such an order, arises are to be regarded for the purposes of section 11(1) and (2) as proceedings in which a question arises with respect to a section 8 order.

(12)   In Schedule A1—

(a)   Part 1 makes provision as regards an unpaid work requirement;

(b)   Part 2 makes provision in relation to the revocation and amendment of enforcement orders and failure to comply with such orders.

(13)   This section is without prejudice to section 63(3) of the Magistrates' Courts Act 1980 as it applies in relation to contact orders.]

Date in force

Inserted by the Children and Adoption Act 2006, s 4(1); for transitional provision see s 8 thereof. Date in force: to be appointed: see the Children and Adoption Act 2006, s 17(2).

Definitions

For 'contact order' see s 8 (1); for 'child', see s 105(1).

[11K   Enforcement orders: further provision]

[(1)   A court may not make an enforcement order against a person in respect of a failure to comply with a contact order unless it is satisfied that before the failure occurred the person had been given (in accordance with rules of court) a copy of, or otherwise informed of the terms of—

(a)   in the case of a failure to comply with a contact order that was varied before the failure occurred, a notice under section 11I relating to the order varying the contact order or, where more than one such order has been made, the last order preceding the failure in question;

(b)   in any other case, a notice under section 11I relating to the contact order.

(2)   A court may not make an enforcement order against a person in respect of any failure to comply with a contact order occurring before the person attained the age of 18.

(3)   A court may not make an enforcement order against a person in respect of a failure to comply with a contact order that is an excepted order (within the meaning given by section 11B(4)).

(4)   A court may not make an enforcement order against a person unless the person is habitually resident in England and Wales; and an enforcement order ceases to have effect if the person subject to the order ceases to be habitually resident in England and Wales.]

Date in force

Inserted by the Children and Adoption Act 2006, s 4(1); for transitional provision see s 8 thereof. Date in force: to be appointed: see the Children and Adoption Act 2006, s 17(2).

Definitions

For 'contact order' see s 8 (1).

[11L   Enforcement orders: making]

[(1)   Before making an enforcement order as regards a person in breach of a contact order, the court must be satisfied that—

(a)   making the enforcement order proposed is necessary to secure the person's compliance with the contact order or any contact order that has effect in its place;

(b)   the likely effect on the person of the enforcement order proposed to be made is proportionate to the seriousness of the breach of the contact order.

(2)   Before making an enforcement order, the court must satisfy itself that provision for the person to work under an unpaid work requirement imposed by an enforcement order can be made in the local justice area in which the person in breach resides or will reside.

(3)   Before making an enforcement order as regards a person in breach of a contact order, the court must obtain and consider information about the person and the likely effect of the enforcement order on him.

(4)   Information about the likely effect of the enforcement order may, in particular, include information as to—

(a)   any conflict with the person's religious beliefs;

(b)   any interference with the times (if any) at which he normally works or attends an educational establishment.

(5)   A court that proposes to make an enforcement order may ask an officer of the Service or a Welsh family proceedings officer to provide the court with information as to the matters in subsections (2) and (3).

(6)   It shall be the duty of the officer of the Service or Welsh family proceedings officer to comply with any request under this section.

(7)   In making an enforcement order in relation to a contact order, a court must take into account the welfare of the child who is the subject of the contact order.]

Date in force

Inserted by the Children and Adoption Act 2006, s 4(1); for transitional provision see s 8 thereof. Date in force: to be appointed: see the Children and Adoption Act 2006, s 17(2).

[11M   Enforcement orders: monitoring]

[(1)   On making an enforcement order in relation to a person, the court is to ask an officer of the Service or a Welsh family proceedings officer—

(a)   to monitor, or arrange for the monitoring of, the person's compliance with the unpaid work requirement imposed by the order;

(b)   to report to the court if a report under paragraph 8 of Schedule A1 is made in relation to the person;

(c)   to report to the court on such other matters relating to the person's compliance as may be specified in the request;

(d)   to report to the court if the person is, or becomes, unsuitable to perform work under the requirement.

(2)   It shall be the duty of the officer of the Service or Welsh family proceedings officer to comply with any request under this section.]

Date in force

Inserted by the Children and Adoption Act 2006, s 4(1); for transitional provision see s 8 thereof. Date in force: to be appointed: see the Children and Adoption Act 2006, s 17(2).

[11N   Enforcement orders: warning notices]

[Where the court makes an enforcement order, it is to attach to the order a notice warning of the consequences of failing to comply with the order.]

Date in force

Inserted by the Children and Adoption Act 2006, s 4(1); for transitional provision see s 8 thereof. Date in force: to be appointed: see the Children and Adoption Act 2006, s 17(2).

[11O   Compensation for financial loss]

[(1)   This section applies if a contact order with respect to a child has been made.

(2)   If the court is satisfied that—

(a)   an individual has failed to comply with the contact order, and

(b)   a person falling within subsection (6) has suffered financial loss by reason of the breach,

it may make an order requiring the individual in breach to pay the person compensation in respect of his financial loss.

(3)   But the court may not make an order under subsection (2) if it is satisfied that the individual in breach had a reasonable excuse for failing to comply with the contact order.

(4)   The burden of proof as to the matter mentioned in subsection (3) lies on the individual claiming to have had a reasonable excuse.

(5) An order under subsection (2) may be made only on an application by the person who claims to have suffered financial loss.

(6) A person falls within this subsection if he is—

    (a) the person who is, for the purposes of the contact order, the person with whom the child concerned lives or is to live;

    (b) the person whose contact with the child concerned is provided for in the contact order;

    (c) an individual subject to a condition under section 11(7)(b) or a contact activity condition imposed by the contact order; or

    (d) the child concerned.

(7) Where the person proposing to apply for an order under subsection (2) is the child concerned, the child must obtain the leave of the court before making such an application.

(8) The court may grant leave to the child concerned only if it is satisfied that he has sufficient understanding to make the proposed application.

(9) The amount of compensation is to be determined by the court, but may not exceed the amount of the applicant's financial loss.

(10) In determining the amount of compensation payable by the individual in breach, the court must take into account the individual's financial circumstances.

(11) An amount ordered to be paid as compensation may be recovered by the applicant as a civil debt due to him.

(12) Subsection (2) has effect subject to the restrictions in section 11P.

(13) Proceedings in which any question of making an order under subsection (2) arises are to be regarded for the purposes of section 11(1) and (2) as proceedings in which a question arises with respect to a section 8 order.

(14) In exercising its powers under this section, a court is to take into account the welfare of the child concerned.]

Date in force

Inserted by the Children and Adoption Act 2006, s 5; for transitional provision see s 8 thereof. Date in force: to be appointed: see the Children and Adoption Act 2006, s 17(2).

Definitions

For 'contact order' see s 8 (1); for 'child', see s 105(1).

[**11P**   Orders under section 11O(2): further provision]

[(1) A court may not make an order under section 11O(2) requiring an individual to pay compensation in respect of a failure by him to comply with a contact order unless it is satisfied that before the failure occurred the individual had been given (in accordance with rules of court) a copy of, or otherwise informed of the terms of—

    (a) in the case of a failure to comply with a contact order that was varied before the failure occurred, a notice under section 11I relating to the order varying the contact order or, where more than one such order has been made, the last order preceding the failure in question;

    (b) in any other case, a notice under section 11I relating to the contact order.

(2)   A court may not make an order under section 11O(2) requiring an individual to pay compensation in respect of a failure by him to comply with a contact order where the failure occurred before the individual attained the age of 18.

(3)   A court may not make an order under section 11O(2) requiring an individual to pay compensation in respect of a failure by him to comply with a contact order that is an excepted order (within the meaning given by section 11B(4)).]

Date in force

Inserted by the Children and Adoption Act 2006, s 5; for transitional provision see s 8 thereof. Date in force: to be appointed: see the Children and Adoption Act 2006, s 17(2).

Definitions

For 'court' see s 92(7).

12   Residence orders and parental responsibility

(1)   Where the court makes a residence order in favour of the father of a child it shall, if the father would not otherwise have parental responsibility for the child, also make an order under section 4 giving him that responsibility.

(2)   Where the court makes a residence order in favour of any person who is not the parent or guardian of the child concerned that person shall have parental responsibility for the child while the residence order remains in force.

(3)   Where a person has parental responsibility for a child as a result of subsection (2), he shall not have the right—

   (a)   ...
   (b)   to agree, or refuse to agree, to the making of an adoption order, or an order under [section 84 of the Adoption and Children Act 2002], with respect to the child; or
   (c)   to appoint a guardian for the child.

(4)   Where subsection (1) requires the court to make an order under section 4 in respect of the father of a child, the court shall not bring that order to an end at any time while the residence order concerned remains in force.

[(5)   The power of a court to make a residence order in favour of any person who is not the parent or guardian of the child concerned includes power to direct, at the request of that person, that the order continue in force until the child reaches the age of eighteen (unless the order is brought to an end earlier); and any power to vary a residence order is exercisable accordingly.

(6)   Where a residence order includes such a direction, an application to vary or discharge the order may only be made, if apart from this subsection the leave of the court is not required, with such leave.]

Date in force

14 October 1991: SI 1991/828.

Amendments

Sub-s (3): para (a) repealed by the Adoption and Children Act 2002, s 139(1), (3), Sch 3, paras 54, 57(a), Sch 5; in para (b) words 'section 84 of the Adoption and Children Act 2002' in square brackets substituted by the Adoption and Children Act 2002, s 139(1), Sch 3, paras 54, 57(b).
Sub-ss (5), (6): inserted by the Adoption and Children Act 2002, s 114(1).

Definitions

For 'court' see s 92(7); for 'residence order' see s 8(1); for 'child' and 'guardian of a child' see s 105(1); for 'parental responsibility' see s 3.

References

See generally paras 3.71 and 3.87. For jurisdiction of courts see s 92, and Sch 11. For 'an order under section 4' see para 3.60; for 'parent', see para 3.43; for the duration of residence orders see s 11(5), and s 91(10), (11); for 'family proceedings' under this Act see s 8(3), (4)(a).

---

13   Change of child's name or removal from jurisdiction

(1)   Where a residence order is in force with respect to a child, no person may—

   (a)   cause the child to be known by a new surname; or
   (b)   remove him from the United Kingdom;

without either the written consent of every person who has parental responsibility for the child or the leave of the court.

(2)   Subsection (1)(*b*) does not prevent the removal of a child, for a period of less than one month, by the person in whose favour the residence order is made.

(3)   In making a residence order with respect to a child the court may grant the leave required by subsection (1)(*b*), either generally or for specified purposes.

Date in force

14 October 1991: SI 1991/828.

Definitions

For 'residence order' see s 8(1); for 'child' see s 105(1); for 'parental responsibility' see s 3; for 'court' see s 92(7); for 'the person in whose favour a residence order is in force' see s 105(3).

References

See generally paras 5.31 ff. For 'family proceedings' under this Act see s 8(3), (4)(a).

Sub-s (1)(a)

For the principles applying to change of names see *Dawson v Wearmouth* [1999] 2 AC 308, [1999] 2 All ER, [1999] 2 FCR 625, *Re W, Re A, Re B (Change of Surname)* [1999] 2 FLR 930, [1999] 3 FCR 357 and *Re R (a child)* [2001] EWCA Civ 1344, [2002] 1 FCR 170.

Sub-s (1)(b)

For the principles governing applications to remove a child from the jurisdiction see, see *Re K (applications to remove from jurisdiction)* [1999] 2 FCR 410. [1999] 2 FLR 1006 and see paras 5.39 ff. There is no presumption in favour of the applicant parent and the European Convention on Human Rights has not affected the principles of domestic law: *Payne v Payne* [2001] EWCA Civ 166, [2001] 1 FCR 425 see paras 5.44 ff. 'United Kingdom' includes Northern Ireland, see *Re H (children) (residence order: condition)* [2001] EWCA Civ 1338, [2001] 3 FCR 182 where exceptionally a prohibited steps order was made preventing the removal of children by their father to Northern Ireland see para 5.39.

---

14   Enforcement of residence orders

(1)   Where—

   (a)   a residence order is in force with respect to a child in favour of any person; and

(b)   any other person (including one in whose favour the order is also in force) is in breach of the arrangements settled by that order,

the person mentioned in paragraph (*a*) may, as soon as the requirement in subsection (2) is complied with, enforce the order under section 63(3) of the Magistrates' Courts Act 1980 as if it were an order requiring the other person to produce the child to him.

(2)   The requirement is that a copy of the residence order has been served on the other person.

(3)   Subsection (1) is without prejudice to any other remedy open to the person in whose favour the residence order is in force.

Date in force

14 October 1991: SI 1991/828.

Definitions

For 'residence order' see s 8(1); for 'child' see s 105(1); for 'the person in whose favour a residence order is in force' see s 105(3).

References

See generally para 5.160. For service of documents under the Act generally see s 105(8)–(10).

[Special guardianship]

[14A   Special guardianship orders]

[(1)   A 'special guardianship order' is an order appointing one or more individuals to be a child's 'special guardian' (or special guardians).

(2)   A special guardian—

(a)   must be aged eighteen or over; and
(b)   must not be a parent of the child in question,

and subsections (3) to (6) are to be read in that light.

(3)   The court may make a special guardianship order with respect to any child on the application of an individual who—

(a)   is entitled to make such an application with respect to the child; or
(b)   has obtained the leave of the court to make the application,

or on the joint application of more than one such individual.

(4)   Section 9(3) applies in relation to an application for leave to apply for a special guardianship order as it applies in relation to an application for leave to apply for a section 8 order.

(5)   The individuals who are entitled to apply for a special guardianship order with respect to a child are—

(a)   any guardian of the child;
(b)   any individual in whose favour a residence order is in force with respect to the child;
(c)   any individual listed in subsection (5)(b) or (c) of section 10 (as read with subsection (10) of that section);
(d)   a local authority foster parent with whom the child has lived for a period of at least one year immediately preceding the application.

(6)   The court may also make a special guardianship order with respect to a child in any family proceedings in which a question arises with respect to the welfare of the child if—

(a)   an application for the order has been made by an individual who falls within subsection (3)(a) or (b) (or more than one such individual jointly); or

(b)   the court considers that a special guardianship order should be made even though no such application has been made.

(7)   No individual may make an application under subsection (3) or (6)(a) unless, before the beginning of the period of three months ending with the date of the application, he has given written notice of his intention to make the application—

(a)   if the child in question is being looked after by a local authority, to that local authority, or

(b)   otherwise, to the local authority in whose area the individual is ordinarily resident.

(8)   On receipt of such a notice, the local authority must investigate the matter and prepare a report for the court dealing with—

(a)   the suitability of the applicant to be a special guardian;

(b)   such matters (if any) as may be prescribed by the Secretary of State; and

(c)   any other matter which the local authority consider to be relevant.

(9)   The court may itself ask a local authority to conduct such an investigation and prepare such a report, and the local authority must do so.

(10)   The local authority may make such arrangements as they see fit for any person to act on their behalf in connection with conducting an investigation or preparing a report referred to in subsection (8) or (9).

(11)   The court may not make a special guardianship order unless it has received a report dealing with the matters referred to in subsection (8).

(12)   Subsections (8) and (9) of section 10 apply in relation to special guardianship orders as they apply in relation to section 8 orders.

(13)   This section is subject to section 29(5) and (6) of the Adoption and Children Act 2002.]

Date in force

Inserted by the Adoption and Children Act 2002, s 115(1); for further effect in relation to applications for special guardianship orders see s 29(6) thereof.

Definitions

For 'special guardianship order' see sub-s (1); for 'special guardian see sub-s (2); for 'court' see s 92(7); for 'child', guardian, local authority foster parent, local authority' see s 105(1); for 'residence order' see s 8 (1); for 'family proceedings' see s 8 (3).

Reference

For 'parent' see para 3.43. For special guardianship see para 5.213 ff and paras 2.59 to 2.66 of the revised Children Act 1989 Guidance and Regulations, Volume 1, Court Orders (2008) Department for Children, Schools and Families. A party to care proceedings who has not yet obtained leave cannot give notice to the local authority, nor should a court seek to compel a local authority by a direction under sub-s (9) unless sub-s (6)(b) applies: *Birmingham City Council v R* [2006] EWCA Civ 1748, [2007] 2 WLR 1130, sub nom *Re R (a child) (special guardianship order)* [2007] 1 FCR 121. A court is entitled to make a special guardianship order in adoption proceedings subject to the appropriate local authority report being provided: *Re S (a Child) (Special guardianship order)* [2007] EWCA Civ 54, [2007] 1 FCR 271, [2007] 1 FLR 819. In a case to which s 14A(6)(b) applies, and in which the bulk of the information required for the report under s 14A(8) is already before the court in a different form, the local authority should be asked by the court to file a report, which will fulfil the terms of s 14A(8); (i) by providing the missing information; and (ii) by setting out the remaining information in the form of cross-references to the information already before the court in other reports: *Re S (a child) (adoption order or special guardianship order) (No 2)* [2007] EWCA Civ 90, [2007] 1 FCR 339, [2007] 1 FLR 855.

Regulations

See the Special Guardianship Regulations 2005, SI 2005/1109 and the Special Guardianship (Wales) Regulations 2005, SI 2005/1513.

[14B   Special guardianship orders: making]

[(1)   Before making a special guardianship order, the court must consider whether, if the order were made—

- (a)   a contact order should also be made with respect to the child, *and*
- (b)   any section 8 order in force with respect to the child should be varied or discharged,
- [(c)   where a contact order made with respect to the child is not discharged, any enforcement order relating to that contact order should be revoked, and
- (d)   where a contact activity direction has been made as regards contact with the child and is in force, that contact activity direction should be discharged].

(2)   On making a special guardianship order, the court may also—

- (a)   give leave for the child to be known by a new surname;
- (b)   grant the leave required by section 14C(3)(b), either generally or for specified purposes.]

Date in force

Inserted by the Adoption and Children Act 2002, s 115(1).
Sub-s (1): in para (a) word 'and' in italics repealed by the Children and Adoption Act 2006, s 15, Sch 2, paras 7, 8(a), Sch 3. Date in force: to be appointed: see the Children and Adoption Act 2006, s 17(2); paras (c), (d) inserted by the Children and Adoption Act 2006, s 15(1), Sch 2, paras 7, 8(b). Date in force: to be appointed: see the Children and Adoption Act 2006, s 17(2).

Definitions

For 'special guardianship order' see s 14A(1); for 'court' see s 92(7); for 'child' see s 105(1); for 'contact order' see s 8 (1); for 'section 8 order' see s 8(2).

[14C   Special guardianship orders: effect]

[(1)   The effect of a special guardianship order is that while the order remains in force—

- (a)   a special guardian appointed by the order has parental responsibility for the child in respect of whom it is made; and
- (b)   subject to any other order in force with respect to the child under this Act, a special guardian is entitled to exercise parental responsibility to the exclusion of any other person with parental responsibility for the child (apart from another special guardian).

(2)   Subsection (1) does not affect—

(a) the operation of any enactment or rule of law which requires the consent of more than one person with parental responsibility in a matter affecting the child; or

(b) any rights which a parent of the child has in relation to the child's adoption or placement for adoption.

(3) While a special guardianship order is in force with respect to a child, no person may—

(a) cause the child to be known by a new surname; or
(b) remove him from the United Kingdom,

without either the written consent of every person who has parental responsibility for the child or the leave of the court.

(4) Subsection (3)(b) does not prevent the removal of a child, for a period of less than three months, by a special guardian of his.

(5) If the child with respect to whom a special guardianship order is in force dies, his special guardian must take reasonable steps to give notice of that fact to—

(a) each parent of the child with parental responsibility; and
(b) each guardian of the child,

but if the child has more than one special guardian, and one of them has taken such steps in relation to a particular parent or guardian, any other special guardian need not do so as respects that parent or guardian.

(6) This section is subject to section 29(7) of the Adoption and Children Act 2002.]

Date in force

Inserted by the Adoption and Children Act 2002, s 115(1).

[**14D**   **Special guardianship orders: variation and discharge**]

[(1) The court may vary or discharge a special guardianship order on the application of—

(a) the special guardian (or any of them, if there are more than one);
(b) any parent or guardian of the child concerned;
(c) any individual in whose favour a residence order is in force with respect to the child;
(d) any individual not falling within any of paragraphs (a) to (c) who has, or immediately before the making of the special guardianship order had, parental responsibility for the child;
(e) the child himself; or
(f) a local authority designated in a care order with respect to the child.

(2) In any family proceedings in which a question arises with respect to the welfare of a child with respect to whom a special guardianship order is in force, the court may also vary or discharge the special guardianship order if it considers that the order should be varied or discharged, even though no application has been made under subsection (1).

(3) The following must obtain the leave of the court before making an application under subsection (1)—

(a) the child;
(b) any parent or guardian of his;
(c) any step-parent of his who has acquired, and has not lost, parental responsibility for him by virtue of section 4A;

(d)   any individual falling within subsection (1)(d) who immediately before the making of the special guardianship order had, but no longer has, parental responsibility for him.

(4)   Where the person applying for leave to make an application under subsection (1) is the child, the court may only grant leave if it is satisfied that he has sufficient understanding to make the proposed application under subsection (1).

(5)   The court may not grant leave to a person falling within subsection (3)(b)(c) or (d) unless it is satisfied that there has been a significant change in circumstances since the making of the special guardianship order.]

Date in force

Inserted by the Adoption and Children Act 2002, s 115(1).

[14E   Special guardianship orders: supplementary]

[(1)   In proceedings in which any question of making, varying or discharging a special guardianship order arises, the court shall (in the light of any rules made by virtue of subsection (3))—

(a)   draw up a timetable with a view to determining the question without delay; and

(b)   give such directions as it considers appropriate for the purpose of ensuring, so far as is reasonably practicable, that the timetable is adhered to.

(2)   Subsection (1) applies also in relation to proceedings in which any other question with respect to a special guardianship order arises.

(3)   The power to make rules in subsection (2) of section 11 applies for the purposes of this section as it applies for the purposes of that.

(4)   A special guardianship order, or an order varying one, may contain provisions which are to have effect for a specified period.

(5)   Section 11(7) (apart from paragraph (c)) applies in relation to special guardianship orders and orders varying them as it applies in relation to section 8 orders.]

Date in force

Inserted by the Adoption and Children Act 2002, s 115(1).

[14F   Special guardianship support services]

[(1)   Each local authority must make arrangements for the provision within their area of special guardianship support services, which means—

(a)   counselling, advice and information; and

(b)   such other services as are prescribed,

in relation to special guardianship.

(2)   The power to make regulations under subsection (1)(b) is to be exercised so as to secure that local authorities provide financial support.

(3)   At the request of any of the following persons—

(a)   a child with respect to whom a special guardianship order is in force;

(b)   a special guardian;

(c)   a parent;

(d)   any other person who falls within a prescribed description, a local authority may carry out an assessment of that person's needs for special guardianship support services (but, if the Secretary of State so provides in regulations, they must do so if he is a person of a prescribed description, or if his case falls within a prescribed description, or if both he and his case fall within prescribed descriptions).

(4)   A local authority may, at the request of any other person, carry out an assessment of that person's needs for special guardianship support services.

(5)   Where, as a result of an assessment, a local authority decide that a person has needs for special guardianship support services, they must then decide whether to provide any such services to that person.

(6)   If—

    (a)   a local authority decide to provide any special guardianship support services to a person, and
    (b)   the circumstances fall within a prescribed description,

the local authority must prepare a plan in accordance with which special guardianship support services are to be provided to him, and keep the plan under review.

(7)   The Secretary of State may by regulations make provision about assessments, preparing and reviewing plans, the provision of special guardianship support services in accordance with plans and reviewing the provision of special guardianship support services.

(8)   The regulations may in particular make provision—

    (a)   about the type of assessment which is to be carried out, or the way in which an assessment is to be carried out;
    (b)   about the way in which a plan is to be prepared;
    (c)   about the way in which, and the time at which, a plan or the provision of special guardianship support services is to be reviewed;
    (d)   about the considerations to which a local authority are to have regard in carrying out an assessment or review or preparing a plan;
    (e)   as to the circumstances in which a local authority may provide special guardianship support services subject to conditions (including conditions as to payment for the support or the repayment of financial support);
    (f)   as to the consequences of conditions imposed by virtue of paragraph (e) not being met (including the recovery of any financial support provided);
    (g)   as to the circumstances in which this section may apply to a local authority in respect of persons who are outside that local authority's area;
    (h)   as to the circumstances in which a local authority may recover from another local authority the expenses of providing special guardianship support services to any person.

(9)   A local authority may provide special guardianship support services (or any part of them) by securing their provision by—

    (a)   another local authority; or
    (b)   a person within a description prescribed in regulations of persons who may provide special guardianship support services,

and may also arrange with any such authority or person for that other authority or that person to carry out the local authority's functions in relation to assessments under this section.

(10)   A local authority may carry out an assessment of the needs of any person for the purposes of this section at the same time as an assessment of his needs is made under any other provision of this Act or under any other enactment.

(11)   Section 27 (co-operation between authorities) applies in relation to the exercise of functions of a local authority under this section as it applies in relation to the exercise of functions of a local authority under Part 3.]

Date in force

Inserted by the Adoption and Children Act 2002, s 115(1).

Regulations

See the Special Guardianship Regulations 2005, SI 2005/1109 and the Special Guardianship (Wales) Regulations 2005, SI 2005/1513.

[14G   ...]

[...]

Date in force

Inserted by the Adoption and Children Act 2002, s 115(1).
Repealed by the Health and Social Care (Community Health and Standards) Act 2003, ss 117(2), 196, Sch 14, Pt 2.

Financial relief

15   Orders for financial relief with respect to children

(1)   Schedule 1 (which consists primarily of the re-enactment, with consequential amendments and minor modifications, of provisions of [section 6 of the Family Law Reform Act 1969] the Guardianship of Minors Acts 1971 and 1973, the Children Act 1975 and of sections 15 and 16 of the Family Law Reform Act 1987) makes provision in relation to financial relief for children.

(2)   The powers of a magistrates' court under section 60 of the Magistrates' Courts Act 1980 to revoke, revive or vary an order for the periodical payment of money [and the power of the clerk of a magistrates' court to vary such an order] shall not apply in relation to an order made under Schedule 1.

Date in force

14 October 1991: SI 1991/828.

Amendment

Sub-s (1): words in square brackets inserted by the Courts and Legal Services Act 1990, s 116, Sch 16, para 10.
Sub-s (2): words in square brackets inserted by the Maintenance Enforcement Act 1991, s 11(1), Sch 2, para 10.

Definition

For 'child' see s 105(1).

Reference

For 'family proceedings' under this Act see s 8(3), (4)(a) and see generally paras 2.78 to 79 of the revised Children Act 1989 Guidance and Regulations, Volume 1, Court Orders (2008) Department for Children, Schools and Families.

Family assistance orders

16   Family assistance orders

(1)   Where, in any family proceedings, the court has power to make an order under this Part with respect to any child, it may (whether or not it makes such an order) make an order requiring—

(a)   [an officer of the Service] [or a Welsh family proceedings officer] to be made available; or

(b)   a local authority to make an officer of the authority available,

to advise, assist and (where appropriate) befriend any person named in the order.

(2)   The persons who may be named in an order under this section ('a family assistance order') are—

(a)   any parent[, guardian or special guardian] of the child;

(b)   any person with whom the child is living or in whose favour a contact order is in force with respect to the child;

(c)   the child himself.

(3)   No court may make a family assistance order unless—

(a)   ...

(b)   it has obtained the consent of every person to be named in the order other than the child.

(4)   A family assistance order may direct—

(a)   the person named in the order; or

(b)   such of the persons named in the order as may be specified in the order,

to take such steps as may be so specified with a view to enabling the officer concerned to be kept informed of the address of any person named in the order and to be allowed to visit any such person.

[(4A)   If the court makes a family assistance order with respect to a child and the order is to be in force at the same time as a contact order made with respect to the child, the family assistance order may direct the officer concerned to give advice and assistance as regards establishing, improving and maintaining contact to such of the persons named in the order as may be specified in the order.]

(5)   Unless it specifies a shorter period, a family assistance order shall have effect for a period of [twelve months] beginning with the day on which it is made.

[(6)   If the court makes a family assistance order with respect to a child and the order is to be in force at the same time as a section 8 order made with respect to the child, the family assistance order may direct the officer concerned to report to the court on such matters relating to the section 8 order as the court may require (including the question whether the section 8 order ought to be varied or discharged).]

(7)   A family assistance order shall not be made so as to require a local authority to make an officer of theirs available unless—

(a)   the authority agree; or

(b)   the child concerned lives or will live within their area.

(8)   ...

(9)   ...

Date in force

14 October 1991: SI 1991/828.

Amendments

Sub-s (1): in para (a) words 'an officer of the Service' in square brackets substituted by the Criminal Justice and Court Services Act 2000, s 74, Sch 7, Pt II, paras 87, 89(a); in para (a) words 'or a Welsh family proceedings officer' in square brackets inserted by the Children Act 2004, s 40, Sch 3, paras 5, 7.
Sub-s (2): in para (a) words ', guardian or special guardian' in square brackets substituted by the Adoption and Children Act 2002, s 139(1), Sch 3, paras 54, 58.
Sub-s (3): para (a) repealed by the Children and Adoption Act 2006, ss 6(1), (2), 15(2), Sch 3.
Sub-s (4A): inserted by the Children and Adoption Act 2006, s 6(1), (3).
Sub-s (5): words 'twelve months' in square brackets substituted by the Children and Adoption Act 2006, s 6(1), (4).
Sub-s (6): substituted by the Children and Adoption Act 2006, s 6(1), (5).
Sub-ss (8), (9): repealed by the Criminal Justice and Court Services Act 2000, ss 74, 75, Sch 7, Pt II, paras 87, 89(b), Sch 8.

Definitions

For 'family proceedings' see s 8(3), (4)(a); for 'court' see s 92(7); for 'child', 'local authority' and 'guardian of a child' see s 105(1); for 'special guardian' see s 14A(1); 'family assistance order' see sub-s (2); for 'contact order' see s 8(1) and 'a section 8 order' see s 8(2).

References

See generally paras 5.191 ff, paras 2.67 to 2.71 of the revised Children Act 1989 Guidance and Regulations, Volume 1, Court Orders (2008) Department for Children, Schools and Families and the *Practice Direction (Family Proceedings: Family Assistance Orders)* [2007] 1 WLR 2522, [2007] 2 FLR 626. For 'this Part' see Pt II i e ss 8–16 and Sch 1 (orders with respect to children in family and other proceedings); for 'parent' see para 3.43; for the ending of orders see sub-s (5) and for the duration of s 8 orders see s 91(10), (11); for the use of a family assistance order as a means by which a local authority can supervise contact: *Leeds County Council v C* [1993] 1 FLR 269; not by attaching a condition to the contact order under s 11(7). And see *Re DH (A Minor) (Child Abuse)* [1994] 1 FLR 679 and *Re E (family assistance order)* [1999] 3 FCR 700.

[16A   Risk assessments]

[(1) This section applies to the following functions of officers of the Service or Welsh family proceedings officers—

(a) any function in connection with family proceedings in which the court has power to make an order under this Part with respect to a child or in which a question with respect to such an order arises;

(b) any function in connection with an order made by the court in such proceedings.

(2) If, in carrying out any function to which this section applies, an officer of the Service or a Welsh family proceedings officer is given cause to suspect that the child concerned is at risk of harm, he must—

(a) make a risk assessment in relation to the child, and
(b) provide the risk assessment to the court.
(3) A risk assessment, in relation to a child who is at risk of suffering harm of a particular sort, is an assessment of the risk of that harm being suffered by the child.]

Date in force

Inserted by the Children and Adoption Act 2006, s 7.

Reference

See generally, para 2.72 of the revised Children Act 1989 Guidance and Regulations, Volume 1, Court Orders (2008) Department for Children, Schools and Families and the *Practice Direction (Children: Risk Assessments)* [2007] 1 WLR 2521, [2007] 3 FCR 784, [2007] 2 FLR 625.

PART III

LOCAL AUTHORITY SUPPORT FOR CHILDREN AND FAMILIES

Provision of services for children and their families

17   Provision of services for children in need, their families and others

(1)   It shall be the general duty of every local authority (in addition to the other duties imposed on them by this Part)—

(a)   to safeguard and promote the welfare of children within their area who are in need; and

(b)   so far as is consistent with that duty, to promote the upbringing of such children by their families,

by providing a range and level of services appropriate to those children's needs.

(2)   For the purpose principally of facilitating the discharge of their general duty under this section, every local authority shall have the specific duties and powers set out in Part I of Schedule 2.

(3)   Any service provided by an authority in the exercise of functions conferred on them by this section may be provided for the family of a particular child in need or for any member of his family, if it is provided with a view to safeguarding or promoting the child's welfare.

(4)   The Secretary of State may by order amend any provision of Part I of Schedule 2 or add any further duty or power to those for the time being mentioned there.

[(4A)   Before determining what (if any) services to provide for a particular child in need in the exercise of functions conferred on them by this section, a local authority shall, so far as is reasonably practicable and consistent with the child's welfare—

(a)   ascertain the child's wishes and feelings regarding the provision of those services; and

(b)   give due consideration (having regard to his age and understanding) to such wishes and feelings of the child as they have been able to ascertain.]

(5)   Every local authority—

(a)   shall facilitate the provision by others (including in particular voluntary organisations) of services which the authority have power to provide by virtue of this section, or section 18, 20, [23, 23B to 23D, 24A or 24B]; and

(b)   may make such arrangements as they see fit for any person to act on their behalf in the provision of any such service.

(6)   The services provided by a local authority in the exercise of functions conferred on them by this section may include [providing accommodation and] giving assistance in kind or, in exceptional circumstances, in cash.

(7)   Assistance may be unconditional or subject to conditions as to the repayment of the assistance or of its value (in whole or in part).

(8)   Before giving any assistance or imposing any conditions, a local authority shall have regard to the means of the child concerned and of each of his parents.

(9)   No person shall be liable to make any repayment of assistance or of its value at any time when he is in receipt of income support [under] [Part VII of the Social Security Contributions and Benefits Act 1992][, of any element of child tax credit other than the family element, of working tax credit] *[or of an income-based jobseeker's allowance]* [, of an income-based jobseeker's allowance or of an income-related employment and support allowance].

(10)   For the purposes of this Part a child shall be taken to be in need if—

   (a)   he is unlikely to achieve or maintain, or to have the opportunity of achieving or maintaining, a reasonable standard of health or development without the provision for him of services by a local authority under this Part;
   (b)   his health or development is likely to be significantly impaired, or further impaired, without the provision for him of such services; or
   (c)   he is disabled,

and 'family', in relation to such a child, includes any person who has parental responsibility for the child and any other person with whom he has been living.

(11)   For the purposes of this Part, a child is disabled if he is blind, deaf or dumb or suffers from mental disorder of any kind or is substantially and permanently handi-capped by illness, injury or congenital deformity or such other disability as may be prescribed; and in this Part—

   'development' means physical, intellectual, emotional, social or behavioural development; and
   'health' means physical or mental health.

[(12)   The Treasury may by regulations prescribe circumstances in which a person is to be treated for the purposes of this Part (or for such of those purposes as are prescribed) as in receipt of any element of child tax credit other than the family element or of working tax credit.]

Date in force

14 October 1991: SI 1991/828.

Amendments

Sub-s (4A): inserted by the Children Act 2004, s 53(1).
Sub-s (5): in para (a) words '23, 23B to 23D, 24A or 24B' in square brackets substituted by the Children (Leaving Care) Act 2000, s 7(1), (2).
Sub-s (6): words 'providing accommodation and' in square brackets inserted by the Adoption and Children Act 2002, s 116(1).
Sub-s (9): word 'under' in square brackets substituted by the Tax Credits Act 2002, s 47, Sch 3, paras 15, 16(1), (2)(a); words 'Part VII of the Social Security Contributions and Benefits Act 1992' in square brackets substituted by the Social Security (Consequential Provisions) Act 1992, s 4, Sch 2, para 108(a); words from ', of any element' to 'working tax credit' in square brackets inserted by the Tax Credits Act 2002, s 47, Sch 3, paras 15, 16(1), (2)(b); words 'or of an income-based jobseeker's allowance' in square brackets inserted by the Jobseekers Act 1995, s 41(4), Sch 2, para 19(2); words 'or of an income-based jobseeker's allowance' in italics repealed and subsequent words in square brackets substituted by the Welfare Reform Act 2007, s 28(1), Sch 3, para 6(1), (2).
Sub-s (12): inserted by the Tax Credits Act 2002, s 47, Sch 3, paras 15, 16(1), (3).

Definitions

For 'local authority', 'child', 'upbringing', 'service' 'functions' and 'prescribed' see s 105(1); for 'need' and 'family' see sub-s (10); for 'voluntary organisation' see s 105(1); for 'health', 'development' and 'disabled' see sub-s (11).

References

See generally Chapter 6 and the Children Act 1989 Guidance and Regulations, Volume 2, Family Support, Day Care and Educational Provision for Young Children (1991) Department of Health. For 'this Part' see Pt III i e ss 17–30 and Sch 2 (local authority support for children and families). 'Parent' i e mother and father; for the application of sub-ss (7)–(9) in relation to assistance given under s 24 see s 24(10); for the duty to publish information about the services provided under this section see Sch 2, Pt I; for co-operation between authorities see s 27; for recoupment of the cost of services see s 29; for miscellaneous supplementary provisions see s 30.

Transfer of functions

Functions of the Secretary of State, so far as exercisable in relation to Wales, transferred to the National Assembly for Wales, by the National Assembly for Wales (Transfer of Functions) Order 1999, SI 1999/672, art 2, Sch 1.

Within their area

These words have the same meaning as in other sections of the Act and physical presence is required and is sufficient to found the duty under s 17(1): *R(S) v London Borough of Wandsworth, London Borough of Hammersmith and Fulham, London Borough of Lambeth* [2001] EWHC Admin 799, [2002] 1 FLR 469.

Services

For the framework and nature of the assessment required to be undertaken by local authorities , see 'Framework for the Assessment of Children in Need (2000) (Department of Health) and also *R (on the application of AB and SB) v Nottingham City Council* [2001] EWHC Admin 235, [2001] 3 FCR 349.

Sub-s (2) Regulations

See the Children Act 1989, Section 17(12) Regulations 2003, SI 2003/2077.

Sub-s (4) Order

See the Children Act 1989 (Amendment) (Children's Services Planning) Order 1996, SI 1996/785.

Sub-s (12) Regulations

See the Children Act 1989, s 17(2) Regulations 2003, SI 2003/2077.

[17A   Direct payments]

[(1)   The Secretary of State may by regulations make provision for and in connection with requiring or authorising the responsible authority in the case of a person of a prescribed description who falls within subsection (2) to make, with that person's consent, such payments to him as they may determine in accordance with the regulations in respect of his securing the provision of the service mentioned in that subsection.

(2)   A person falls within this subsection if he is—

    (a)   a person with parental responsibility for a disabled child,
    (b)   a disabled person with parental responsibility for a child, or
    (c)   a disabled child aged 16 or 17,

and a local authority ('the responsible authority') have decided for the purposes of section 17 that the child's needs (or, if he is such a disabled child, his needs) call for the provision by them of a service in exercise of functions conferred on them under that section.

(3)   Subsections (3) to (5) and (7) of section 57 of the 2001 Act shall apply, with any necessary modifications, in relation to regulations under this section as they apply in relation to regulations under that section.

(4)   Regulations under this section shall provide that, where payments are made under the regulations to a person falling within subsection (5)—

(a)   the payments shall be made at the rate mentioned in subsection (4)(a) of section 57 of the 2001 Act (as applied by subsection (3)); and
(b)   subsection (4)(b) of that section shall not apply.

(5)   A person falls within this subsection if he is—

(a)   a person falling within subsection (2)(a) or (b) and the child in question is aged 16 or 17, or
(b)   a person who is in receipt of income support ... under Part 7 of the Social Security Contributions and Benefits Act 1992 (c 4)[, of any element of child tax credit other than the family element, of working tax credit] *or of an income-based jobseeker's allowance* [, of an income-based jobseeker's allowance or of an income-related employment and support allowance].

(6)   In this section—

'the 2001 Act' means the Health and Social Care Act 2001;
'disabled' in relation to an adult has the same meaning as that given by section 17(11) in relation to a child;
'prescribed' means specified in or determined in accordance with regulations under this section (and has the same meaning in the provisions of the 2001 Act mentioned in subsection (3) as they apply by virtue of that subsection).]

Date in force

Inserted by the Carers and Disabled Children Act 2000, s 7(1) as from 1 April 2001 (England) SI 2001/510; 1 July 2001 (Wales) SI 2001/2196.

Amendments

Substituted by the Health and Social Care Act 2001, s 58;: in para (b) words from ', of any element' to 'working tax credit' in square brackets inserted by the Tax Credits Act 2002, s 47, Sch 3, paras 15, 17; in para (b) words 'or of an income-based jobseeker's allowance' in italics repealed and subsequent words in square brackets substituted by the Welfare Reform Act 2007, s 28(1), Sch 3, para 6(1), (3).

Definitions

For 'parental responsibility' see s 3; for 'disabled child' see s 17 and for 'disabled' in relation to an adult see sub-s (6).

Regulations

See the Community Care, Services for Carers and Children's Services (Direct Payments) (England) Regulations 2003, SI 2003/762 amended by SI 2005/2114 and the Community Care, Services for Carers and Children's Services (Direct Payments) (Wales) Regulations 2004, SI 2004/1748 amended by SI 2005/3302 and SI 2006/2840.

[17B   Vouchers for persons with parental responsibility for disabled children]

[(1)   The Secretary of State may by regulations make provision for the issue by a local authority of vouchers to a person with parental responsibility for a disabled child.

(2)   'Voucher' means a document whereby, if the local authority agrees with the person with parental responsibility that it would help him care for the child if the person with parental responsibility had a break from caring, that person may secure the temporary provision of services for the child under section 17.

(3)   The regulations may, in particular, provide—

(a)   for the value of a voucher to be expressed in terms of money, or of the delivery of a service for a period of time, or both;

(b)   for the person who supplies a service against a voucher, or for the arrangement under which it is supplied, to be approved by the local authority;

(c)   for a maximum period during which a service (or a service of a prescribed description) can be provided against a voucher.]

Date in force

Inserted by the Carers and Disabled Children Act 2000, s 7(1) as from a date to be appointed.

Amendment

Inserted by the Carers and Disabled Children Act 2000, s 7(1).

Regulations

See the Carers and Disabled Children (Vouchers) (England) Regulations 2003, SI 2003/1216.

18   Day care for pre-school and other children

(1)   Every local authority shall provide such day care for children in need within their area who are—

(a)   aged five or under; and
(b)   not yet attending schools,

as is appropriate.

(2)   A local authority [in Wales] may provide day care for children within their area who satisfy the conditions mentioned in subsection (1)(a) and (b) even though they are not in need.

(3)   A local authority may provide facilities (including training, advice, guidance and counselling) for those—

(a)   caring for children in day care; or
(b)   who at any time accompany such children while they are in day care.

(4)   In this section 'day care' means any form of care or supervised activity provided for children during the day (whether or not it is provided on a regular basis).

(5)   Every local authority shall provide for children in need within their area who are attending any school such care or supervised activities as is appropriate—

(a)   outside school hours; or
(b)   during school holidays.

(6)   A local authority [in Wales] may provide such care or supervised activities for children within their area who are attending any school even though those children are not in need.

(7)   In this section 'supervised activity' means an activity supervised by a responsible person.

Date in force

14 October 1991: SI 1991/828.

Amendment

Sub-s (2): words 'in Wales' in square brackets inserted by the Childcare Act 2006, s 103(1), Sch 2, para 4(a).
Sub-s (6): words 'in Wales' in square brackets inserted by the Childcare Act 2006, s 103(1), Sch 2, para 4(b).

Definitions

For 'local authority', 'child' and 'school' see s 105(1); for 'a child in need' see s 17(19); for 'day care' see sub-s (4); for 'supervised activity' see sub-s (7).

References

See para 6.31 and the Children Act 1989 Guidance and Regulations, Volume 2, Family Support, Day Care and Educational Provision For Young Children (1991) Department of Health.

Note

Allegations of failure to make proper provision under this section should be dealt with by complaint under s 26 and, if that is not satisfactory, s 84.

19   **...**

...

Date in force

14 October 1991: SI 1991/828.

Amendments

Repealed, in relation to Scotland, by the Regulation of Care (Scotland) Act 2001, s 80, Sch 4 and, in relation to England and Wales, by virtue of the Education Act 2002, s 149(2).

Provision of accommodation for children

20   Provision of accommodation for children: general

(1)   Every local authority shall provide accommodation for any child in need within their area who appears to them to require accommodation as a result of—

    (a)   there being no person who has parental responsibility for him;
    (b)   his being lost or having been abandoned; or
    (c)   the person who has been caring for him being prevented (whether or not permanently, and for whatever reason) from providing him with suitable accommodation or care.

(2)   Where a local authority provide accommodation under subsection (1) for a child who is ordinarily resident in the area of another local authority, that other local authority may take over the provision of accommodation for the child within—

    (a)   three months of being notified in writing that the child is being provided with accommodation; or

(b)   such other longer period as may be prescribed.

(3)   Every local authority shall provide accommodation for any child in need within their area who has reached the age of sixteen and whose welfare the authority consider is likely to be seriously prejudiced if they do not provide him with accommodation.

(4)   A local authority may provide accommodation for any child within their area (even though a person who has parental responsibility for him is able to provide him with accommodation) if they consider that to do so would safeguard or promote the child's welfare.

(5)   A local authority may provide accommodation for any person who has reached the age of sixteen but is under twenty-one in any community home which takes children who have reached the age of sixteen if they consider that to do so would safeguard or promote his welfare.

(6)   Before providing accommodation under this section, a local authority shall, so far as is reasonably practicable and consistent with the child's welfare—

(a)   ascertain the child's wishes [and feelings] regarding the provision of accommodation; and
(b)   give due consideration (having regard to his age and understanding) to such wishes [and feelings] of the child as they have been able to ascertain.

(7)   A local authority may not provide accommodation under this section for any child if any person who—

(a)   has parental responsibility for him; and
(b)   is willing and able to—
   (i)   provide accommodation for him; or
   (ii)   arrange for accommodation to be provided for him,
objects.

(8)   Any person who has parental responsibility for a child may at any time remove the child from accommodation provided by or on behalf of the local authority under this section.

(9)   Subsections (7) and (8) do not apply while any person—

(a)   in whose favour a residence order is in force with respect to the child; ...
[(aa) who is a special guardian of the child; or]
(b)   who has care of the child by virtue of an order made in the exercise of the High Court's inherent jurisdiction with respect to children,

agrees to the child being looked after in accommodation provided by or on behalf of the local authority.

(10)   Where there is more than one such person as is mentioned in subsection (9), all of them must agree.

(11)   Subsections (7) and (8) do not apply where a child who has reached the age of sixteen agrees to being provided with accommodation under this section.

Date in force

14 October 1991: SI 1991/828.

Amendments

Sub-s (6): in paras (a), (b) words 'and feelings' in square brackets inserted by the Children Act 2004, s 53(2).

Sub-s (9): in para (a) word omitted repealed by the Adoption and Children Act 2002, s 139(1), (3), Sch 3, paras 54, 59, Sch 5; para (aa) inserted by the Adoption and Children Act 2002, s 139(1), Sch 3, paras 54, 59.

Definitions

For 'local authority', 'child' and 'prescribed' see s 105(1); for 'a child in need' see s 17(10) as applied to the whole Act by s 105(7); for 'parental responsibility' see s 3; for 'residence order' see s 8(1). For a person in whose favour a residence order is in force see s 105(3); for 'special guardian' see s 14A.

References

See paras 6.36 ff and the Children Act 1989 Guidance and Regulations, Volume 2, Family Support, Day Care and Educational Provision for Young Children (1991) Department of Health and the Children Act 1989 Guidance and Regulations, Volume 3, Family Placements (1991) Department of Health. For the determination of the ordinary residence of a child for the purposes of sub-s (2), 21(3) or s 29(7)–(9) see s 30(2) and s 105(6); for the general duties of local authorities in connection with the welfare of children in need see s 17; for review of case of, and representations relating to, child being looked after by local authority see s 26 and Review of Children's Cases Regulations 1991, SI 1991/895 amended by SI 1991/2033, SI 1993/3069, SI 1995/2015, SI 1997/649, SI 2002/546 (E), SI 2935 (W) and 3013 (W), SI 2004/1419 (E), 1448 (W) and 2253 (E) and SI 2005/774 (revoked in relation to Wales by SI 2007/307) and the Review of Childen's Cases (Wales) Regulations 2007, SI 2007/307; for co-operation between authorities see s 27; for recoupment for the cost of services provided see s 29; for miscellaneous supplementary provisions see s 30. If a local authority provides accommodation for a child in need, and if on the facts a duty to do so arose under s 20, the local authority must be regarded as providing that accommodation under s 20 and not under s 17: *H, Barhanu and B v London Borough of Wandsworth* [2007] EWHC 1082 (Admin), [2007] 2 FLR 822.

Sub-s (1)

These criteria reflect those formerly contained in the CCA 1980, s 2. Children in care under the section shall be treated as being provided with accommodation, provided no parental rights resolution has been passed: Sch 14, para 20. As to contact with accommodated children see the Contact with Children Regulations 1991, SI 1991/891, and Sch 2, para 15. As to arrangements for the provision of accommodation see s 23 and Arrangement for Placement of Children Regulations 1991, SI 1991/890 and note the duties of other authorities to provide help for Pt III functions by virtue of s 27.

Sub-s (7)

Objections by person with parental responsibility. The local authority does not have the power to override the wishes of a parent with parental responsibility and does not have the power to place a child with foster parents against the wishes of the parents: *R v Tameside Metropolitan Borough Council, ex p J* [2000] 1 FCR 173, [2000] 1 FLR 942, QBD.

---

21   Provision for accommodation for children in police protection or detention or on remand, etc

(1)   Every local authority shall make provision for the reception and accommodation of children who are removed or kept away from home under Part V.

(2)   Every local authority shall receive, and provide accommodation for, children—

   (a)   in police protection whom they are requested to receive under section 46(3)(f);
   (b)   whom they are requested to receive under section 38(6) of the Police and Criminal Evidence Act 1984;
   (c)   who are—
      (i)   on remand [(within the meaning of the section)] under [*paragraph 7(5) of Schedule 7 to the Powers of Criminal Courts (Sentencing) Act 2000 or section*] 23(1) of the Children and Young Persons Act 1969; *or*

[(ia) remanded to accommodation provided by or on behalf of a local authority by virtue of paragraph 4 of Schedule 1 or paragraph 6 of Schedule 8 to the Powers of Criminal Courts (Sentencing) Act 2000 (breach etc of referral orders and reparation orders);]

(ii) *the subject of a supervision order imposing a [local authority residence requirement under paragraph 5 of Schedule 6 to that Act of 2000] [or a foster parent residence requirement under paragraph 5A of that Schedule]*,

[(ii) remanded to accommodation provided by or on behalf of a local authority by virtue of paragraph 21 of Schedule 2 to the Criminal Justice and Immigration Act 2008 (breach etc of youth rehabilitation orders); or

(iii) the subject of a youth rehabilitation order imposing a local authority residence requirement or a youth rehabilitation order with fostering,]

and with respect to whom they are the designated authority.

[(2A)   In subsection (2)(c)(iii), the following terms have the same meanings as in Part 1 of the Criminal Justice and Immigration Act 2008 (see section 7 of that Act)—

'local authority residence requirement';
'youth rehabilitation order';
'youth rehabilitation order with fostering'.]

(3)   Where a child has been—

(a)   removed under Part V; or

(b)   detained under section 38 of the Police and Criminal Evidence Act 1984,

and he is not being provided with accommodation by a local authority or in a hospital vested in the Secretary of State [or a Primary Care Trust,] [or otherwise made available pursuant to arrangements made by a [Local Health Board]] [or a Primary Care Trust], any reasonable expenses of accommodating him shall be recoverable from the local authority in whose area he is ordinarily resident.

Date in force

14 October 1991: SI 1991/828.

Amendments

Sub-s (2): in para (c)(i) words '(within the meaning of the section)' in square brackets inserted by the Criminal Justice and Public Order Act 1994, s 168(1), Sch 9, para 38; in para (c)(i) words 'paragraph 7(5) of Schedule 7 to the Powers of Criminal Courts (Sentencing) Act 2000 or section' in square brackets substituted by the Powers of Criminal Courts (Sentencing) Act 2000, s 165(1), Sch 9, para 126(a); in para (c)(i) words 'paragraph 7(5) of Schedule 7 to the Powers of Criminal Courts (Sentencing) Act 2000 or' in italics repealed by the Criminal Justice and Immigration Act 2008, ss 6(2), 149, Sch 4, Pt 1, paras 33, 34(1), (2)(a), Sch 28, Pt 1; for transitional provisions and savings see s 148(2), Sch 27, Pt 1, paras 1(1), 5 thereto. Date in force: to be appointed: see the Criminal Justice and Immigration Act 2008, s 153(7); in para (c)(i) word 'or' in italics repealed by the Criminal Justice and Immigration Act 2008, ss 6(2), 149, Sch 4, Pt 1, paras 33, 34(1), (2)(a), Sch 28, Pt 1; for transitional provisions and savings see s 148(2), Sch 27, Pt 1, paras 1(1), 5 thereto. Date in force: to be appointed: see the Criminal Justice and Immigration Act 2008, s 153(7); para (c)(ia) inserted by the Criminal Justice and Immigration Act 2008, s 6(3), Sch 4, Pt 2, para 105; for transitional provisions and savings see s 148(2), Sch 27, Pt 1, paras 1(2), 5 thereto. Date in force: to be appointed: see the Criminal Justice and Immigration Act 2008, s 153(7); para (c)(ii) substituted, by subsequent para (c)(ii), (iii), by the Criminal Justice and Immigration Act 2008, s 6(2), Sch 4, Pt 1, paras 33, 34(1), (2)(b); for transitional provisions and savings see s 148(2), Sch 27, Pt 1, paras 1(1), 5 thereto. Date in force: to be appointed: see the Criminal Justice and Immigration Act 2008, s 153(7); in para (c)(ii) words 'local authority residence requirement under paragraph 5 of Schedule 6 to that Act of 2000' in square brackets substituted by the Powers of Criminal Courts (Sentencing) Act 2000, s 165(1), Sch 9, para 126(b);

in para (c)(ii) words 'or a foster parent residence requirement under paragraph 5A of that Schedule' in square brackets inserted by the Anti-social Behaviour Act 2003, s 88, Sch 2, para 5. Sub-s (2A): inserted by the Criminal Justice and Immigration Act 2008, s 6(2), Sch 4, Pt 1, paras 33, 34(1), (3); for transitional provisions and savings see s 148(2), Sch 27, Pt 1, paras 1(1), 5 thereto. Date in force: to be appointed: see the Criminal Justice and Immigration Act 2008, s 153(7).
Sub-s (3): words 'or a Primary Care Trust,' in square brackets inserted by SI 2000/90, art 3(1), Sch 1, para 24(1), (3)(a); words in square brackets beginning with the words 'or otherwise made available' inserted by the National Health Service and Community Care Act 1990, s 66(1), Sch 9, para 36(1); words 'Local Health Board' in square brackets substituted by SI 2007/961, art 3, Schedule, para 20(1), (2)(a); words 'or a Primary Care Trust' in square brackets inserted by SI 2000/90, art 3(1), Sch 1, para 24(1), (3)(b).

Definitions

For 'local authority', 'child' and 'hospital' see s 105(1); for 'in police protection' see s 46(2); for 'supervision order' see s 31(11); for 'designated authority' see s 31(8).

References

'Part V' ie ss 43–52 (protection of children). For the determination of the ordinary residence of a child see ss 30(2) and 105(6).

Sub-s (2)(c) Duty of local authority

While this provision does not impose an absolute duty to provide *secure* accommodation when this is requested by the police under s 36 of PACE, though local authorities should have in place a reasonable system for responding to such requests by the police: *R (on the application of M) v Gateshead Metropolitan Borough Council* [2006] EWCA Civ 221, [2006] QB 650, [2007] 1 All ER 1262, [2006] 3 WLR 108.

Transfer of functions

Functions of the Secretary of State, so far as exercisable in relation to Wales, transferred to the National Assembly for Wales, by the National Assembly for Wales (Transfer of Functions) Order 1999, SI 1999/672, art 2, Sch 1.

Duties of local authorities in relation to children looked after by them

22   General duty of local authority in relation to children looked after by them

(1)   In this Act, any reference to a child who is looked after by a local authority is a reference to a child who is—

(a)   in their care; or
(b)   provided with accommodation by the authority in the exercise of any functions (in particular those under this Act) which [are social services functions within the meaning of] the Local Authority Social Services Act 1970[, apart from functions under sections [17], 23B and 24B].

(2)   In subsection (1) 'accommodation' means accommodation which is provided for a continuous period of more than 24 hours.

(3)   It shall be the duty of a local authority looking after any child—

(a)   to safeguard and promote his welfare; and
(b)   to make such use of services available for children cared for by their own parents as appears to the authority reasonable in his case.

[(3A)   The duty of a local authority under subsection (3)(a) to safeguard and promote the welfare of a child looked after by them includes in particular a duty to promote the child's educational achievement.]

(4)   Before making any decision with respect to a child whom they are looking after, or proposing to look after, a local authority shall, so far as is reasonably practicable, ascertain the wishes and feelings of—

(a)   the child;

(b)   his parents;

(c)   any person who is not a parent of his but who has parental responsibility for him; and

(d)   any other person whose wishes and feelings the authority consider to be relevant,

regarding the matter to be decided.

(5)   In making any such decision a local authority shall give due consideration—

(a)   having regard to his age and understanding, to such wishes and feelings of the child as they have been able to ascertain;

(b)   to such wishes and feelings of any person mentioned in subsection (4)(*b*) to (*d*) as they have been able to ascertain; and

(c)   to the child's religious persuasion, racial origin and cultural and linguistic background.

(6)   If it appears to a local authority that it is necessary, for the purpose of protecting members of the public from serious injury, to exercise their powers with respect to a child whom they are looking after in a manner which may not be consistent with their duties under this section, they may do so.

(7)   If the Secretary of State considers it necessary, for the purpose of protecting members of the public from serious injury, to give directions to a local authority with respect to the exercise of their powers with respect to a child whom they are looking after, he may give such directions to the authority.

(8)   Where any such directions are given to an authority they shall comply with them even though doing so is inconsistent with their duties under this section.

Date in force

14 October 1991: SI 1991/828.

Amendments

Sub-s (1): Local Government Act 2000,Sch 5; Children Leaving Care Act 2000, s 2(1), (2);in para (b) words 'are social services functions within the meaning of' in square brackets substituted by the Local Government Act 2000, s 107, Sch 5, para 19; in para (b) words ', apart from functions under sections 23B and 24B' in square brackets inserted by the Children (Leaving Care) Act 2000, s 2(1), (2);: in para (b) reference to '17' in square brackets inserted by the Adoption and Children Act 2002, s 116(2).
Sub-s (3A): inserted by the Children Act 2004, s 52.

Definitions

For 'child', 'local authority' and 'child in the care of a local authority' and 'service' see s 105(1); for 'looked after by a local authority' see sub-s (1); for 'accommodation' see sub-s (2); for 'parental responsibility' see s 3.

References

See paras 6.58 ff and the Children Act 1989 Guidance and Regulations, Volume 2, Family Support, Day Care and Educational Provision for Young Children (1991) Department of Health and the Children Act 1989 Guidance and Regulations, Volume 3, Family Placements (1991) Department of Health. The Children Act 1989 Guidance and Regulations, Volume 4, Residential Care (1991) Department of Health. For inspection of premises where a child who is being looked after by a local authority is living, by a person authorised to do by the Secretary of State, see

80(1)(b); for the general duty of local authorities in connection with the welfare of children in need see s 17; for review of case of and representations relating to child being looked after by local authority see s 26 and Review of Children's Cases Regulations 1991, SI 1991/895 amended by SI 1991/2033, SI 1993/3069, SI 1995/2015, SI 1997/649, SI 2002/546 (E), SI 2935 (W) and 3013 (W), SI 2004/1419 (E), 1448 (W) and 2253 (E) and SI 2005/774 (revoked in relation to Wales by SI 2007/307) and the Review of Children's Cases (Wales) Regulations 2007, SI 2007/307 and Representations Procedure (Children) Regulations 1991, SI 1991/894 amended by SI 2002/546; for co-operation between authorities see s 27; for recoupment of the cost of services provided see s 29; for miscellaneous supplementary provisions see s 30; for transitional provisions relating to children in care under repealed enactments see s 108(6) and Sch 14, paras 15ff.

Transfer of functions

Functions of the Secretary of State, so far as exercisable in relation to Wales, transferred to the National Assembly for Wales, by the National Assembly for Wales (Transfer of Functions) Order 1999, SI 1999/672, art 2, Sch 1.

---

23   Provision of accommodation and maintenance by local authority for children whom they are looking after

(1)   It shall be the duty of any local authority looking after a child—

    (a)   when he is in their care, to provide accommodation for him; and

    (b)   to maintain him in other respects apart from providing accommodation for him.

(2)   A local authority shall provide accommodation and maintenance for any child whom they are looking after by—

    (a)   placing him (subject to subsection (5) and any regulations made by the Secretary of State) with—

        (i)   a family;

        (ii)   a relative of his; or

        (iii)   any other suitable person,

on such terms as to payment by the authority and otherwise as the authority may determine [(subject to section 49 of the Children Act 2004)];

[(aa) maintaining him in an appropriate children's home;] or

    (f)   making such other arrangements as—

        (i)   seem appropriate to them; and

        (ii)   comply with any regulations made by the Secretary of State.

[(2A)   Where under subsection (2)(aa) a local authority maintains a child in a home provided, equipped and maintained by the Secretary of State under section 82(5), it shall do so on such terms as the Secretary of State may from time to time determine.]

(3)   Any person with whom a child has been placed under subsection (2)(*a*) is referred to in this Act as a local authority foster parent unless he falls within subsection (4).

(4)   A person falls within this subsection if he is—

    (a)   a parent of the child;

    (b)   a person who is not a parent of the child but who has parental responsibility for him; or

    (c)   where the child is in care and there was a residence order in force with respect to him immediately before the care order was made, a person in whose favour the residence order was made.

(5)   Where a child is in the care of a local authority, the authority may only allow him to live with a person who falls within subsection (4) in accordance with regulations made by the Secretary of State.

[(5A)   For the purposes of subsection (5) a child shall be regarded as living with a person if he stays with that person for a continuous period of more than 24 hours].

(6)   Subject to any regulations made by the Secretary of State for the purposes of this subsection, any local authority looking after a child shall make arrangements to enable him to live with—

(a)   a person falling within subsection (4); or
(b)   a relative, friend or other person connected with him,

unless that would not be reasonably practicable or consistent with his welfare.

(7)   Where a local authority provide accommodation for a child whom they are looking after, they shall, subject to the provisions of this Part and so far as is reasonably practicable and consistent with his welfare, secure that—

(a)   the accommodation is near his home; and
(b)   where the authority are also providing accommodation for a sibling of his, they are accommodated together.

(8)   Where a local authority provide accommodation for a child whom they are looking after and who is disabled, they shall, so far as is reasonably practicable, secure that the accommodation is not unsuitable to his particular needs.

(9)   Part II of Schedule 2 shall have effect for the purposes of making further provision as to children looked after by local authorities and in particular as to the regulations that may be made under subsections (2)(*a*) and (*f*) and (5).

[(10)   In this Act—

'appropriate children's home' means a children's home in respect of which a person is registered under Part II of the Care Standards Act 2000; and
'children's home' has the same meaning as in that Act.]

Date in force

14 October 1991: SI 1991/828.

Amendments

Sub-s (2): in para (a) words '(subject to section 49 of the Children Act 2004)' in square brackets inserted by the Children Act 2004, s 49(3); para (aa) substituted, for paras (b)–(e) as originally enacted, by the Care Standards Act 2000, s 116, Sch 4, para 14(1), (3)(a).
Sub-s (2A): inserted by the Care Standards Act 2000, s 116, Sch 4, para 14(1), (3)(b).
Sub-s (5A): inserted by the Courts and Legal Services Act 1990, s 116, Sch 16, para 12.
Sub-s (10): inserted by the Care Standards Act 2000, s 116, Sch 4, para 14(3)(c).

Definitions

For 'local authority', 'child', 'relative', 'in the care of a local authority' see s 105(1); for 'looked after by a local authority' see s 22(1); for 'community home' see s 53; for 'voluntary home' see s 60; for 'registered children's home' and for 'appropriate children's home' see Sub-s (10) as applied to the whole Act by s 105(1); for 'residence order' see s 8; for 'local authority foster parent' see s 23(3); for 'parental responsibility' see s 3; for 'disabled' see s 17(11).

References

See para 6.63 ff *and* the Children Act 1989 Guidance and Regulations, Volume 3, Family Placements (1991) Department of Health and the Children Act 1989 Guidance and Regulations, Volume 4, Residential Care (1991) Department of Health. 'This Part' ie Pt III (ss 17–30 and Sch 2) (local authority support for children and families). For 'live with a person' see sub-s (5A).

Appendix 1 *Children Act 1989*

Sub-s (1) Looked after child

A child does not have to be looked after for 24 hours before either a placement under s 23(2) or an arrangement under s 23(6) can be made (*D v London Borough of Southwark* [2007] EWCA Civ 182, [2007] 1 FCR 787).

Sub-s (2) Regulations

See Sch 2, paras 12 and 13, and the Arrangements for Placement of Children (General) Regulations 1991, SI 1991/890 amended by SI 1991/2033, SI 1993/3069, SI 1995/2015, 1997/647, SI 2002/546 (E), 2469, 2935 (W) and 3013 (W) and SI 2005/774 (W) (revoked in relation to Wales by SI 2007/310); the Fostering Services Regulations 2002, SI 2002/57 amended by SI 2002/865 and SI 2006/1738; the Fostering Services (Wales) Regulations 2003, SI 2003/237 amended by SI 2003/896, SI 2005/3302 and SI 2006/3251; the Placement of Children (Wales) Regulations 2007, SI 2007/310. For disqualification as a foster parent, see *Re S* (*Foster Placement (Children) Regulations 1991*) [2000] 1 FLR 648, FD.

Sub-s (5) Regulations

See Sch 2, para 14 and the Arrangements for Placement of Children (General) Regulations 1991, SI 1991/890 amended by SI 1991/2033, SI 1993/3069, SI 1995/2015 and the Placement of Children with Parents Regulations 1991, SI 1991/893 amended by SI 1995/2015, SI 1997/649, SI 2002/546 (England), 2469, 2935 (Wales) and 3013 (Wales) and SI 2005/774 (W) (revoked in relation to Wales by SI 2007/310) and the Placement of Children (Wales) Regulations 2007, SI 2007/310.

Sub-s (10) Children's home.

For s 1 of the Care Standards Act, see note to s 53, post.

Transfer of functions

Functions of the Secretary of State, so far as exercisable in relation to Wales, transferred to the National Assembly for Wales, by the National Assembly for Wales (Transfer of Functions) Order 1999, SI 1999/672, art 2, Sch 1.

Advice and assistance for certain children [and young persons]

[23A   The responsible authority and relevant children]

[(1)   The responsible local authority shall have the functions set out in section 23B in respect of a relevant child.

(2)   In subsection (1) 'relevant child' means (subject to subsection (3)) a child who—

(a)   is not being looked after by any local authority;

(b)   was, before last ceasing to be looked after, an eligible child for the purposes of paragraph 19B of Schedule 2; and

(c)   is aged sixteen or seventeen.

(3)   The Secretary of State may prescribe—

(a)   additional categories of relevant children; and

(b)   categories of children who are not to be relevant children despite falling within subsection (2).

(4)   In subsection (1) the 'responsible local authority' is the one which last looked after the child.

(5)   If under subsection (3)(a) the Secretary of State prescribes a category of relevant children which includes children who do not fall within subsection (2)(b) (for example,

because they were being looked after by a local authority in Scotland), he may in the regulations also provide for which local authority is to be the responsible local authority for those children.]

Date in force

Inserted by the Children (Leaving Care) Act 2000, s 2(1), (4).

Definitions

For 'responsible local authority' see sub-s (4); for 'relevant child' see sub-s (2); for 'pathway plan' see s 23E(1).

Reference

See generally Chapter 6.

Sub-s (3) Regulations

See the Children Leaving Care (Wales) Regulations 2001, SI 2001/2189 amended by SI 2002/1855 and 2935 and SI 2004/1732 and the Children Leaving Care (England) Regulations 2001, SI 2001/2874 amended by SI 2002/546 and SI 2006/1738.

[23B   Additional functions of the responsible authority in respect of relevant children]

[(1)   It is the duty of each local authority to take reasonable steps to keep in touch with a relevant child for whom they are the responsible authority, whether he is within their area or not.

(2)   It is the duty of each local authority to appoint a personal adviser for each relevant child (if they have not already done so under paragraph 19C of Schedule 2).

(3)   It is the duty of each local authority, in relation to any relevant child who does not already have a pathway plan prepared for the purposes of paragraph 19B of Schedule 2—

    (a)   to carry out an assessment of his needs with a view to determining what advice, assistance and support it would be appropriate for them to provide him under this Part; and

    (b)   to prepare a pathway plan for him.

(4)   The local authority may carry out such an assessment at the same time as any assessment of his needs is made under any enactment referred to in sub-paragraphs (a) to (c) of paragraph 3 of Schedule 2, or under any other enactment.

(5)   The Secretary of State may by regulations make provision as to assessments for the purposes of subsection (3).

(6)   The regulations may in particular make provision about—

    (a)   who is to be consulted in relation to an assessment;

    (b)   the way in which an assessment is to be carried out, by whom and when;

    (c)   the recording of the results of an assessment;

    (d)   the considerations to which the local authority are to have regard in carrying out an assessment.

(7)   The authority shall keep the pathway plan under regular review.

(8)   The responsible local authority shall safeguard and promote the child's welfare and, unless they are satisfied that his welfare does not require it, support him by—

    (a)   maintaining him;

   (b)   providing him with or maintaining him in suitable accommodation; and

   (c)   providing support of such other descriptions as may be prescribed.

(9)   Support under subsection (8) may be in cash.

(10)   The Secretary of State may by regulations make provision about the meaning of 'suitable accommodation' and in particular about the suitability of landlords or other providers of accommodation.

(11)   If the local authority have lost touch with a relevant child, despite taking reasonable steps to keep in touch, they must without delay—

   (a)   consider how to re-establish contact; and

   (b)   take reasonable steps to do so,

and while the child is still a relevant child must continue to take such steps until they succeed.

(12)   Subsections (7) to (9) of section 17 apply in relation to support given under this section as they apply in relation to assistance given under that section.

(13)   Subsections (4) and (5) of section 22 apply in relation to any decision by a local authority for the purposes of this section as they apply in relation to the decisions referred to in that section.]

Date in force

Inserted by the Children (Leaving Care) Act 2000, s 2(1), (2) as from 1 October 2001.

Definitions

For 'local authority' and 'child' see s 105(1); for 'relevant child' see s 23A(2); for 'responsible local authority' see sub-s (4).

Personal adviser

An officer or employee of the local authority may be appointed as the personal adviser to a child in care but it is essential that all those involved recognise that he or she is acting as personal adviser and not in some other role: *R (on the application of J) v Caerphilly County Borough Council* [2005] EWHC 586 (Admin), [2005] 2 FLR 860.

Sub-ss (5), (6), (8), (10) Regulations

See the Children Leaving Care (Wales) Regulations 2001, SI 2001/2189 amended by SI 2002/1855 and 2935 and SI 2004/1732 and the Children Leaving Care (England) Regulations 2001, SI 2001/2874 amended by SI 2002/546 and SI 2006/1738.

[23C   Continuing functions in respect of former relevant children]

[(1)   Each local authority shall have the duties provided for in this section towards—

   (a)   a person who has been a relevant child for the purposes of section 23A (and would be one if he were under eighteen), and in relation to whom they were the last responsible authority; and

   (b)   a person who was being looked after by them when he attained the age of eighteen, and immediately before ceasing to be looked after was an eligible child,

and in this section such a person is referred to as a 'former relevant child'.

(2)   It is the duty of the local authority to take reasonable steps—

   (a)   to keep in touch with a former relevant child whether he is within their area or not; and

(b)   if they lose touch with him, to re-establish contact.

(3)   It is the duty of the local authority—

(a)   to continue the appointment of a personal adviser for a former relevant child; and

(b)   to continue to keep his pathway plan under regular review.

(4)   It is the duty of the local authority to give a former relevant child—

(a)   assistance of the kind referred to in section 24B(1), to the extent that his welfare requires it;

(b)   assistance of the kind referred to in section 24B(2), to the extent that his welfare and his educational or training needs require it;

(c)   other assistance, to the extent that his welfare requires it.

(5)   The assistance given under subsection (4)(c) may be in kind or, in exceptional circumstances, in cash.

(6)   Subject to subsection (7), the duties set out in subsections (2), (3) and (4) subsist until the former relevant child reaches the age of twenty-one.

(7)   If the former relevant child's pathway plan sets out a programme of education or training which extends beyond his twenty-first birthday—

(a)   the duty set out in subsection (4)(b) continues to subsist for so long as the former relevant child continues to pursue that programme; and

(b)   the duties set out in subsections (2) and (3) continue to subsist concurrently with that duty.

(8)   For the purposes of subsection (7)(a) there shall be disregarded any interruption in a former relevant child's pursuance of a programme of education or training if the local authority are satisfied that he will resume it as soon as is reasonably practicable.

(9)   Section 24B(5) applies in relation to a person being given assistance under subsection (4)(b) as it applies in relation to a person to whom section 24B(3) applies.

(10)   Subsections (7) to (9) of section 17 apply in relation to assistance given under this section as they apply in relation to assistance given under that section.]

Date in force

Inserted by the Children (Leaving Care) Act 2000, s 2(1), (4).

Definitions

For 'local authority' and 'child' see s 105(1); for 'relevant child' see s 23A(2); for 'former relevant child' see sub-s (1); for 'responsible local authority' see s 23A(4).

[Personal advisers and pathway plans]

[23D   Personal advisers]

[(1)   The Secretary of State may by regulations require local authorities to appoint a personal adviser for children or young persons of a prescribed description who have reached the age of sixteen but not the age of twenty-one who are not—

(a)   children who are relevant children for the purposes of section 23A;

(b)   the young persons referred to in section 23C; or

(c)   the children referred to in paragraph 19C of Schedule 2.

(2)   Personal advisers appointed under or by virtue of this Part shall (in addition to any other functions) have such functions as the Secretary of State prescribes.]

703

Date in force

Inserted by the Children (Leaving Care) Act 2000, s 3.

Sub-s (2) Prescribed

See the Children Leaving Care (Wales) Regulations 2001, SI 2001/2189 amended by SI 2002/1855 and 2935 and SI 2004/1732 and the Children Leaving Care (England) Regulations 2001, SI 2001/2874 amended by SI 2002/546 and SI 2006/1738.

[23E   Pathway plans]

[(1)   In this Part, a reference to a 'pathway plan' is to a plan setting out—

    (a)   in the case of a plan prepared under paragraph 19B of Schedule 2—

        (i)   the advice, assistance and support which the local authority intend to provide a child under this Part, both while they are looking after him and later; and

        (ii)   when they might cease to look after him; and

    (b)   in the case of a plan prepared under section 23B, the advice, assistance and support which the local authority intend to provide under this Part,

and dealing with such other matters (if any) as may be prescribed.

(2)   The Secretary of State may by regulations make provision about pathway plans and their review.]

Date in force

Inserted by the Children (Leaving Care) Act 2000, s 3.

Sub-s (1)(b) ... sub-s (2) Regulations

See the Children Leaving Care (Wales) Regulations 2001, SI 2001/2189 amended by SI 2002/546 and 1855 and the Children Leaving Care (England) Regulations 2001, SI 2001/2874 amended by SI 2002/546.

[24   Persons qualifying for advice and assistance]

[[(1)   In this Part 'a person qualifying for advice and assistance' means a person to whom subsection (1A) or (1B) applies.

(1A)   This subsection applies to a person—

    (a)   who has reached the age of sixteen but not the age of twenty-one;

    (b)   with respect to whom a special guardianship order is in force (or, if he has reached the age of eighteen, was in force when he reached that age); and

    (c)   who was, immediately before the making of that order, looked after by a local authority.

(1B)   This subsection applies to a person to whom subsection (1A) does not apply, and who—

    (a)   is under twenty-one; and

    (b)   at any time after reaching the age of sixteen but while still a child was, but is no longer, looked after, accommodated or fostered.]

(2)   In [subsection (1B)(b)], 'looked after, accommodated or fostered' means—

    (a)   looked after by a local authority;

    (b)   accommodated by or on behalf of a voluntary organisation;

(c)   accommodated in a private children's home;

(d)   accommodated for a consecutive period of at least three months—

        (i)   by any [Local Health Board], Special Health Authority, Primary Care Trust or local education authority, or

        (ii)   in any care home or independent hospital or in any accommodation provided by a National Health Service trust [or an NHS foundation trust]; or

(e)   privately fostered.

(3)   Subsection (2)(d) applies even if the period of three months mentioned there began before the child reached the age of sixteen.

(4)   In the case of a person qualifying for advice and assistance by virtue of subsection (2)(a), it is the duty of the local authority which last looked after him to take such steps as they think appropriate to contact him at such times as they think appropriate with a view to discharging their functions under sections 24A and 24B.

(5)   In each of sections 24A and 24B, the local authority under the duty or having the power mentioned there ('the relevant authority') is—

[(za) in the case of a person to whom subsection (1A) applies, a local authority determined in accordance with regulations made by the Secretary of State;]

(a)   in the case of a person qualifying for advice and assistance by virtue of subsection (2)(a), the local authority which last looked after him; or

(b)   in the case of any other person qualifying for advice and assistance, the local authority within whose area the person is (if he has asked for help of a kind which can be given under section 24A or 24B).]

Date in force

Substituted, together with ss 24A–24C, for s 24 as originally enacted, by the Children (Leaving Care) Act 2000, s 4(1).

Sub-s (1), (1A), (1B): substituted, for sub-s (1) as originally enacted, by the Adoption and Children Act 2002, s 139(1), Sch 3, paras 54, 60(a).

Sub-s (2): words 'subsection (1B)(b)' in square brackets substituted by the Adoption and Children Act 2002, s 139(1), Sch 3, paras 54, 60(b);: in para (d)(i) words 'Local Health Board' in square brackets substituted by SI 2007/961, art 3, Schedule, para 20(1), (2)(b); in para (d)(ii) words 'or an NHS foundation trust' in square brackets inserted by the Health and Social Care (Community Health and Standards) Act 2003, s 34, Sch 4, paras 75, 76.

Sub-s (5): para (za) inserted by the Adoption and Children Act 2002, s 139(1), Sch 3, paras 54, 60(c).

Definitions

For 'child', 'local authority', 'voluntary organisation', 'health authority', 'local education authority' 'special health authority', 'primary care trust', see s 105(1); for 'looked after, accommodated or fostered' see sub-s ((2); for 'a person qualifying for advice and assistance' see sub-s (1); for 'privately fostered' see s 66 as applied to the whole Act by s 105(1); for 'special guardianship order' see s 14A.

References

See paras 6.81 ff and the Children Act 1989 Guidance and Regulations, Volume 2, Family Support, Day Care and Educational Provision for Young Children (1991) Department of Health and the Children Act 1989 Guidance and Regulations, Volume 3, Family Placement (1991) Department of Health. For 'after-care' see the Children Act 1989 Guidance and Regulations, Volume 2, Family Support, Day Care and Educational Provision for Young Children (1991) Department of Health, para 2.32. 'This Part' ie Pt III (ss 17–30 and Sch 2) (local authority support for children and families).

Sub-s (5)(za) Special guardianship

See the Special Guardianship Regulations 2005, SI 2005/1109 and the Special Guardianship (Wales) Regulations 2005, SI 2005/1513.

Transfer of functions

Functions of the Secretary of State, so far as exercisable in relation to Wales, transferred to the National Assembly for Wales, by the National Assembly for Wales (Transfer of Functions) Order 1999, SI 1999/672, art 2, Sch 1

[24A   Advice and assistance]

[(1)   The relevant authority shall consider whether the conditions in subsection (2) are satisfied in relation to a person qualifying for advice and assistance.

(2)   The conditions are that—

(a)   he needs help of a kind which they can give under this section or section 24B; and

(b)   in the case of a person [to whom section 24(1A) applies, or to whom section 24(1B) applies and] who was not being looked after by any local authority, they are satisfied that the person by whom he was being looked after does not have the necessary facilities for advising or befriending him.

(3)   If the conditions are satisfied—

(a)   they shall advise and befriend him if [he is a person to whom section 24(1A) applies, or he is a person to whom section 24(1B) applies and] he was being looked after by a local authority or was accommodated by or on behalf of a voluntary organisation; and

(b)   in any other case they may do so.

(4)   Where as a result of this section a local authority are under a duty, or are empowered, to advise and befriend a person, they may also give him assistance.

(5)   The assistance may be in kind [and, in exceptional circumstances, assistance may be given—

(a)   by providing accommodation, if in the circumstances assistance may not be given in respect of the accommodation under section 24B, or

(b)   in cash].

(6)   Subsections (7) to (9) of section 17 apply in relation to assistance given under this section or section 24B as they apply in relation to assistance given under that section.]

Date in force

Substituted, together with ss 24, 24B, 24C, for s 24 as originally enacted, by the Children (Leaving Care) Act 2000, s 4(1).
Sub-s (2): in para (b) words 'to whom section 24(1A) applies, or to whom section 24(1B) applies and' in square brackets inserted by the Adoption and Children Act 2002, s 139(1), Sch 3, paras 54, 61(a).
Sub-s (3): in para (a) words from 'he is a person' to 'section 24(1B) applies and' in square brackets inserted by the Adoption and Children Act 2002, s 139(1), Sch 3, paras 54, 61(b)
Sub-s (5): words from 'and, in exceptional' to 'in cash' in square brackets substituted by the Adoption and Children Act 2002, s 116(3).

Definitions

For 'relevant authority' see s 24(5); for 'person qualifying for help and assistance' see s 24(1); for 'looked after by a local authority' see s 22(1); for 'voluntary organisation' see s 105(1).

[24B   Employment, education and training]

[(1)   The relevant local authority may give assistance to any person who qualifies for advice and assistance by virtue of [section 24(1A) or] section 24(2)(a) by contributing to expenses incurred by him in living near the place where he is, or will be, employed or seeking employment.

(2)   The relevant local authority may give assistance to a person to whom subsection (3) applies by—

(a)   contributing to expenses incurred by the person in question in living near the place where he is, or will be, receiving education or training; or

(b)   making a grant to enable him to meet expenses connected with his education or training.

(3)   This subsection applies to any person who—

(a)   is under twenty-four; and

(b)   qualifies for advice and assistance by virtue of [section 24(1A) or] section 24(2)(a), or would have done so if he were under twenty-one.

(4)   Where a local authority are assisting a person under subsection (2) they may disregard any interruption in his attendance on the course if he resumes it as soon as is reasonably practicable.

(5)   Where the local authority are satisfied that a person to whom subsection (3) applies who is in full-time further or higher education needs accommodation during a vacation because his term-time accommodation is not available to him then, they shall give him assistance by—

(a)   providing him with suitable accommodation during the vacation; or

(b)   paying him enough to enable him to secure such accommodation himself.

(6)   The Secretary of State may prescribe the meaning of 'full-time', 'further education', 'higher education' and 'vacation' for the purposes of subsection (5).]

Date in force

Substituted, together with ss 24, 24A, 24C, for s 24 as originally enacted, by the Children (Leaving Care) Act 2000, s 4(1).
Sub-s (1): words 'section 24(1A) or' in square brackets inserted by the Adoption and Children Act 2002, s 139(1), Sch 3, paras 54, 62.
Sub-s (3): in para (b) words 'section 24(1A) or' in square brackets inserted by the Adoption and Children Act 2002, s 139(1), Sch 3, paras 54, 62.

Definitions

For 'relevant local authority' see s 24(5); for 'person qualifying for help and assistance' see s 24(1).

Regulations

See the Children Leaving Care (Wales) Regulations 2001, SI 2001/2189 amended by SI 2002/1855 and 2935 and SI 2004/1732 and the Children Leaving Care (England) Regulations 2001, SI 2001/2874 amended by SI 2002/546 and SI 2006/1738.

[24C   Information]

[(1)   Where it appears to a local authority that a person—

(a)   with whom they are under a duty to keep in touch under section 23B, 23C or 24; or

(b)   whom they have been advising and befriending under section 24A; or

707

(c)   to whom they have been giving assistance under section 24B,

proposes to live, or is living, in the area of another local authority, they must inform that other authority.

(2)   Where a child who is accommodated—

(a)   by a voluntary organisation or in a private children's home;
(b)   by any [Local Health Board], Special Health Authority, Primary Care Trust or local education authority; or
(c)   in any care home or independent hospital or any accommodation provided by a National Health Service trust [or an NHS foundation trust],

ceases to be so accommodated, after reaching the age of sixteen, the organisation, authority or (as the case may be) person carrying on the home shall inform the local authority within whose area the child proposes to live.

(3)   Subsection (2) only applies, by virtue of paragraph (b) or (c), if the accommodation has been provided for a consecutive period of at least three months.]

Date in force

Substituted, together with ss 24, 24A, 24B, for s 24 as originally enacted, by the Children (Leaving Care) Act 2000, s 4(1); in para (b) words 'Local Health Board' in square brackets substituted by SI 2007/961, art 3, Schedule, para 20(1), (2)(c); in para (c) words 'or an NHS foundation trust' in square brackets inserted by the Health and Social Care (Community Health and Standards) Act 2003, s 34, Sch 4, paras 75, 77.

[24D   Representations: sections 23A to 24B]

[(1)   Every local authority shall establish a procedure for considering representations (including complaints) made to them by—

(a)   a relevant child for the purposes of section 23A or a young person falling within section 23C;
(b)   a person qualifying for advice and assistance; or
(c)   a person falling within section 24B(2),

about the discharge of their functions under this Part in relation to him.

[(1A) Regulations may be made by the Secretary of State imposing time limits on the making of representations under subsection (1).]

(2)   In considering representations under subsection (1), a local authority shall comply with regulations (if any) made by the Secretary of State for the purposes of this subsection.]

Date in force

Inserted by the Children (Leaving Care) Act 2000, s 5.
Sub-s (1A): inserted by the Adoption and Children Act 2002, s 117(1).

Reference

See para 13.53.

Sub-s (1A) Regulations

See in relation to England, the Advocacy Services and Representations Procedure (Children) (Amendment) Regulations 2004, SI 2004/719 amended by SI 2006/1738 and SI 2006/1738; Children Act 1989 Representations Procedure (England) Regulations 2006, SI 2006/1738; in relation to Wales, the Advocacy Services and Representations Procedure (Children) (Wales) Regulations 2004, SI 2004/1448, the Representations Procedure (Children) (Wales) Regulations 2005, SI 2005/3365.

Sub-s (2) Regulations

See the Children (Leaving Care) (Wales) Regulations 2001, SI 2001/2189 amended by SI 2002/1855 and 2935 and SI 2004/1732 and the Children (Leaving Care) (England) Regulations 2001, SI 2001/2874 amended by SI 2002/546.

Secure accommodation

25 Use of accommodation for restricting liberty

(1) Subject to the following provisions of this section, a child who is being looked after by a local authority may not be placed, and, if placed, may not be kept, in accommodation provided for the purpose of restricting liberty ('secure accommodation') unless it appears—

    (a)   that—
        (i)   he has a history of absconding and is likely to abscond from any other description of accommodation; and
        (ii) if he absconds, he is likely to suffer significant harm; or
    (b)   that if he is kept in any other description of accommodation he is likely to injure himself or other persons.

(2) The Secretary of State may by regulations—

    (a)   specify a maximum period—
        (i)   beyond which a child may not be kept in secure accommodation without the authority of the court; and
        (ii) for which the court may authorise a child to be kept in secure accommodation;
    (b)   empower the court from time to time to authorise a child to be kept in secure accommodation for such further period as the regulations may specify; and
    (c)   provide that applications to the court under this section shall be made only by local authorities.

(3) It shall be the duty of a court hearing an application under this section to determine whether any relevant criteria for keeping a child in secure accommodation are satisfied in his case.

(4) If a court determines that any such criteria are satisfied, it shall make an order authorising the child to be kept in secure accommodation and specifying the maximum period for which he may be so kept.

(5) On any adjournment of the hearing of an application under this section, a court may make an interim order permitting the child to be kept during the period of the adjournment in secure accommodation.

(6) No court shall exercise the powers conferred by this section in respect of a child who is not legally represented in that court unless, having been informed of his right to apply for [representation funded by the Legal Services Commission as part of the Community Legal Service or Criminal Defence Service] and having had the opportunity to do so, he refused or failed to apply.

(7) The Secretary of State may by regulations provide that—

    (a)   this section shall or shall not apply to any description of children specified in the regulations;

(b) this section shall have effect in relation to children of a description specified in the regulations subject to such modifications as may be so specified;

(c) such other provisions as may be so specified shall have effect for the purpose of determining whether a child of a description specified in the regulations may be placed or kept in secure accommodation.

(8) The giving of an authorisation under this section shall not prejudice any power of any court in England and Wales or Scotland to give directions relating to the child to whom the authorisation relates.

(9) This section is subject to section 20(8).

Date in force

14 October 1991: SI 1991/828.

Amendment

Sub-s (1) modified in relation to certain children by SI 1991/1505, regs 6, 7, see para 9.35. Sub-s (6): words 'representation funded by the Legal Services Commission as part of the Community Legal Service or Criminal Defence Service' in square brackets substituted by the Access to Justice Act 1999, s 24, Sch 4, para 45.

Definitions

For 'child' and 'local authority' see s 105(1); for 'a child who is being looked after by a local authority' see s 22(1); for 'secure accommodation' see sub-s (1); for 'harm' see s 31(9) as applied to the whole Act by s 105; as to whether harm is significant see s 31(10) as applied to the whole Act by s 105(1); for 'court' see s 92(7).

References

See generally Chapter 9,Chapter 5 of the revised Children Act 1989 Guidance and Regulations, Volume 1, Court Orders (2008) Department for Children, Schools and Families and the Children Act 1989 Guidance and Regulations, Volume 4, Residential Care (1991) Department of Health. For jurisdiction of courts see s 92 and Sch 11 and for orders made in criminal proceedings see the CJA 1991, the Crime and Disorder Act 1998 and para 9.31 ff.

Sub-s (1)

The grounds in paras (a) and (b) are disjunctive rather than conjunctive: *Re D (Secure Accommodation)* [1997] 1 FLR 197.

Sub-s (2)

'Is likely' This means a 'real possibility' that cannot sensibly be ignored: *S v Knowsley Borough Council* [2004] EWHC 491 (Fam), [2004] 2 FLR 716.

Sub-s (6) and (7) Regulations

See the Children (Secure Accommodation) Regulations 1991, SI 1991/1505 amended by 1992/2117, SI 1995/1398, SI 1996/692, SI 2000/694, SI 2001/2337, SI 2002/546 and 2935 (Wales), SI 2004/696 and SI 2006/2986 (W) and the Children (Secure Accommodation) (No 2) Regulations 1991, SI 1991/2034 amended by SI 2002/546 and 2935 and SI 2004/696.

Supplemental

26 Review of cases and inquiries into representations

(1) The Secretary of State may make regulations requiring the case of each child who is being looked after by a local authority to be reviewed in accordance with the provisions of the regulations.

(2)   The regulations may, in particular, make provision—

(a)   as to the manner in which each case is to be reviewed;

(b)   as to the considerations to which the local authority are to have regard in reviewing each case;

(c)   as to the time when each case is first to be reviewed and the frequency of subsequent reviews;

(d)   requiring the authority, before conducting any review, to seek the views of—
  (i)   the child;
  (ii)   his parents;
  (iii)   any person who is not a parent of his but who has parental responsibility for him; and
  (iv)   any other person whose views the authority consider to be relevant,
including, in particular, the views of those persons in relation to any particular matter which is to be considered in the course of the review;

(e)   requiring the authority ..., in the case of a child who is in their care—
  [(i)   to keep the section 31A plan for the child under review and, if they are of the opinion that some change is required, to revise the plan, or make a new plan, accordingly,
  (ii)   to consider], whether an application should be made to discharge the care order;

(f)   requiring the authority ..., in the case of a child in accommodation provided by the authority—
  [(i)   if there is no plan for the future care of the child, to prepare one,
  (ii)   if there is such a plan for the child, to keep it under review and, if they are of the opinion that some change is required, to revise the plan or make a new plan, accordingly,
  (iii)   to consider], whether the accommodation accords with the requirements of this Part;

(g)   requiring the authority to inform the child, so far as is reasonably practicable, of any steps he may take under this Act;

(h)   requiring the authority to make arrangements, including arrangements with such other bodies providing services as it considers appropriate, to implement any decision which they propose to make in the course, or as a result, of the review;
  (i)   requiring the authority to notify details of the result of the review and of any decision taken by them in consequence of the review to—
  (i)   the child;
  (ii)   his parents;
  (iii)   any person who is not a parent of his but who has parental responsibility for him; and
  (iv)   any other person whom they consider ought to be notified;

(j)   requiring the authority to monitor the arrangements which they have made with a view to ensuring that they comply with the regulations;

[(k)   for the authority to appoint a person in respect of each case to carry out in the prescribed manner the functions mentioned in subsection (2A) and any prescribed function].

[(2A)   The functions referred to in subsection (2)(k) are—

(a)   participating in the review of the case in question,

(b)   monitoring the performance of the authority's functions in respect of the review,

(c)   referring the case to an officer of the Children and Family Court Advisory and Support Service [or a Welsh family proceedings officer], if the person appointed under subsection (2)(k) considers it appropriate to do so.

711

(2B)   A person appointed under subsection (2)(k) must be a person of a prescribed description.

(2C)   In relation to children whose cases are referred to officers under subsection (2A)(c), the Lord Chancellor may by regulations—

  (a)   extend any functions of the officers in respect of family proceedings (within the meaning of section 12 of the Criminal Justice and Court Services Act 2000) to other proceedings,
  (b)   require any functions of the officers to be performed in the manner prescribed by the regulations.]

[(2D)   The power to make regulations in subsection (2C) is exercisable in relation to functions of Welsh family proceedings officers only with the consent of the National Assembly for Wales.]

(3)   Every local authority shall establish a procedure for considering any representations (including any complaint) made to them by—

  (a)   any child who is being looked after by them or who is not being looked after by them but is in need;
  (b)   a parent of his;
  (c)   any person who is not a parent of his but who has parental responsibility for him;
  (d)   any local authority foster parent;
  (e)   such other person as the authority consider has a sufficient interest in the child's welfare to warrant his representations being considered by them,

about the discharge by the authority of any of their [qualifying functions] in relation to the child.

[(3A)   The following are qualifying functions for the purposes of subsection (3)—

  (a)   functions under this Part,
  (b)   such functions under Part 4 or 5 as are specified by the Secretary of State in regulations.

(3B)   The duty under subsection (3) extends to representations (including complaints) made to the authority by—

  (a)   any person mentioned in section 3(1) of the Adoption and Children Act 2002 (persons for whose needs provision is made by the Adoption Service) and any other person to whom arrangements for the provision of adoption support services (within the meaning of that Act) extend,
  (b)   such other person as the authority consider has sufficient interest in a child who is or may be adopted to warrant his representations being considered by them,

about the discharge by the authority of such functions under the Adoption and Children Act 2002 as are specified by the Secretary of State in regulations.]

[(3C)   The duty under subsection (3) extends to any representations (including complaints) which are made to the authority by—

  (a)   a child with respect to whom a special guardianship order is in force,
  (b)   a special guardian or a parent of such a child,
  (c)   any other person the authority consider has a sufficient interest in the welfare of such a child to warrant his representations being considered by them, or
  (d)   any person who has applied for an assessment under section 14F(3) or (4),

about the discharge by the authority of such functions under section 14F as may be specified by the Secretary of State in regulations.]

(4)   The procedure shall ensure that at least one person who is not a member or officer of the authority takes part in—

(a)   the consideration; and
(b)   any discussions which are held by the authority about the action (if any) to be taken in relation to the child in the light of the consideration,

[but this subsection is subject to subsection (5A)].

[(4A)   Regulations may be made by the Secretary of State imposing time limits on the making of representations under this section.]

(5)   In carrying out any consideration of representations under this section a local authority shall comply with any regulations made by the Secretary of State for the purpose of regulating the procedure to be followed.

[(5A)   Regulations under subsection (5) may provide that subsection (4) does not apply in relation to any consideration or discussion which takes place as part of a procedure for which provision is made by the regulations for the purpose of resolving informally the matters raised in the representations.]

(6)   The Secretary of State may make regulations requiring local authorities to monitor the arrangements that they have made with a view to ensuring that they comply with any regulations made for the purposes of subsection (5).

(7)   Where any representation has been considered under the procedure established by a local authority under this section, the authority shall—

(a)   have due regard to the findings of those considering the representation; and
(b)   take such steps as are reasonably practicable to notify (in writing)—
     (i)   the person making the representation;
     (ii)   the child (if the authority consider that he has sufficient understanding); and
     (iii)   such other persons (if any) as appear to the authority to be likely to be affected,

of the authority's decision in the matter and their reasons for taking that decision and of any action which they have taken, or propose to take.

(8)   Every local authority shall give such publicity to their procedure for considering representations under this section as they consider appropriate.

Date in force

14 October 1991: SI 1991/828.

Amendment

Sub-s (2): in para (e) words omitted repealed by the Adoption and Children Act 2002, ss 118(1)(a), 139(3), Sch 5; in para (e) words from '(i) to keep' to '(ii) to consider' in square brackets inserted by the Adoption and Children Act 2002, s 118(1)(a); in para (f) words omitted repealed by the Adoption and Children Act 2002, ss 118(1)(b), 139(3), Sch 5; in para (f) words from '(i) if there' to '(iii) to consider' in square brackets inserted by the Adoption and Children Act 2002, s 118(1)(b); para (k) inserted by the Adoption and Children Act 2002, s 118(1)(c).
Sub-ss (2A)–(2C): inserted by the Adoption and Children Act 2002, s 118(2).
Sub-s (2A): in para (c) words 'or a Welsh family proceedings officer' in square brackets inserted by the Children Act 2004, s 40, Sch 3, paras 5, 8(1), (2).
Sub-s (2D): inserted by the Children Act 2004, s 40, Sch 3, paras 5, 8(1), (3).
Sub-s (3): words 'functions under this part' in italics repealed and subsequent words in square brackets substituted by the Adoption and Children Act 2002, s 117(2), (3).
Sub-ss (3A), (3B): inserted by the Adoption and Children Act 2002, s 117(2), (4).
Sub-s (3C): inserted by the Health and Social Care (Community Health and Standards) Act 2003, s 117(1).

Sub-s (4): words 'but this subsection is subject to subsection (5A)' in square brackets inserted by the Adoption and Children Act 2002, s 117(2), (5).
Sub-s (4A): inserted by the Adoption and Children Act 2002, s 117(2), (6).
Sub-s (5A): inserted by the Adoption and Children Act 2002, s 117(2), (7).

Definitions

For 'child' and 'local authority' see s 105(1); for 'a child who is being looked after by a local authority see s 22(1); for 'parental responsibility' see s 3; for 'care order' see s 31(11) and s 105(1); for 'local authority foster parent' see s 23(3).

References

See paras 13.55 ff and *the Children Act 1989 Guidance and Regulations, Volume 3, Family Placements* (1991) Department of Health. 'This Part' ie Pt III (ss 17–30 and Sch 2) (local authority support for children and families). For the powers and duties of local authorities under this Part to provide accommodation for children see s 20, (accommodation for certain children eg those lost or abandoned), s 23 (accommodation for and maintenance of children an authority is looking after) and s 25 (use of accommodation for restricting liberty); for reviews and representations procedure see the Children Act 1989 Guidance and Regulations, Volume 3, Family Placements (1991) Department of Health.

Sub-s (1) Regulations

See the Review of Children's Cases Regulations 1991, SI 1991/895 amended by SI 1991/2033, SI 1993/3069, SI 1995/2015, SI 1997/649, SI 2002/546 (England), 2935 (Wales) and 3013 (Wales), SI 2004/1419 (E), 1448 (W) and 2253 (E) and SI 2005/774 (W) (revoked in relation to Wales by SI 2007/307) and the Review of Children's Cases (Wales) Regulations 2007, SI 2007/307.

Sub-s (2C) Regulations

See the Children and Family Court Advisory and Support Service (Reviewed Case Referral) Regulations 2004, SI 2004/2187 amended by SI 2005/605.

Sub-s (5) (6) Regulations

See the Children Act 1989 Representations Procedure (England) Regulations 2006, SI 2006/1738.

[26ZA   ...]

[...]

Date in force

1 April 2007: see SI 2007/935, art 5(gg), (ii).

Amendment

Inserted by the Health and Social Care (Community Health and Standards) Act 2003, s 116(1). Repealed by the Education and Inspections Act 2006, ss 157, 184, Sch 14, paras 9, 10, Sch 18, Pt 5.

[26ZB   Representations: further consideration (Wales)]

[(1) The Secretary of State may by regulations make provision for the further consideration of representations which have been considered by a local authority in Wales under section 24D or section 26.

(2)   The regulations may in particular make provision—

(a)   for the further consideration of a representation by an independent panel established under the regulations;

(b) about the procedure to be followed on the further consideration of a representation;

(c) for the making of recommendations about the action to be taken as the result of a representation;

(d) about the making of reports about a representation;

(e) about the action to be taken by the local authority concerned as a result of the further consideration of a representation;

(f) for a representation to be referred back to the local authority concerned for reconsideration by the authority.

(3) The regulations may require—

(a) the making of a payment, in relation to the further consideration of a representation under this section, by any local authority in respect of whose functions the representation is made;

(b) any such payment to be—
  (i) made to such person or body as may be specified in the regulations;
  (ii) of such amount as may be specified in, or calculated or determined under, the regulations; and

(c) for an independent panel to review the amount chargeable under paragraph (a) in any particular case and, if the panel thinks fit, to substitute a lesser amount.

(4) The regulations may also—

(a) provide for different parts or aspects of a representation to be treated differently;

(b) require the production of information or documents in order to enable a representation to be properly considered;

(c) authorise the disclosure of information or documents relevant to a representation to a person or body who is further considering a representation under the regulations;

and any such disclosure may be authorised notwithstanding any rule of common law that would otherwise prohibit or restrict the disclosure.]

Date in force

1 April 2006: see SI 2005/3285, art 2(2)(b).

Amendment

Inserted by the Health and Social Care (Community Health and Standards) Act 2003, s 116(2).

Regulations

Social Services Complaints Procedure (Wales) Regulations 2005, SI 2005/3366.

[26A   Advocacy services]

[(1) Every local authority shall make arrangements for the provision of assistance to—

(a) persons who make or intend to make representations under section 24D; and

(b) children who make or intend to make representations under section 26.

(2) The assistance provided under the arrangements shall include assistance by way of representation.

[(2A)   The duty under subsection (1) includes a duty to make arrangements for the provision of assistance where representations under section 24D or 26 are further considered under section ... 26ZB.]

(3)   The arrangements—

    (a)   shall secure that a person may not provide assistance if he is a person who is prevented from doing so by regulations made by the Secretary of State; and

    (b)   shall comply with any other provision made by the regulations in relation to the arrangements.

(4)   The Secretary of State may make regulations requiring local authorities to monitor the steps that they have taken with a view to ensuring that they comply with regulations made for the purposes of subsection (3).

(5)   Every local authority shall give such publicity to their arrangements for the provision of assistance under this section as they consider appropriate.]

Date in force

1 April 2004: see SI 2003/3079

Amendment

Inserted by the Adoption and Children Act 2002, s 119.
Sub-s (2A): inserted by the Health and Social Care (Community Health and Standards) Act 2003, s 116(3); words omitted repealed by the Education and Inspections Act 2006, ss 157, 184, Sch 14, paras 9, 11, Sch 18, Pt 5.

Sub-s (3)(b) Regulations

See in relation to England: the Advocacy Services and Representations Procedure (Children) (Amendment) Regulations 2004, SI 2004/719 amended by SI 2006/1738; Children Act 1989 Representations Procedure (England) Regulations 2006, SI 2006/1738; in relation to Wales, the Advocacy Services and Representations Procedure (Children) (Wales) Regulations 2004, SI 2004/1448; Social Services Complaints Procedure (Wales) Regulations 2005, SI 2005/3365.

---

27   Co-operation between authorities

(1)   Where it appears to a local authority that any authority ... mentioned in subsection (3) could, by taking any specified action, help in the exercise of any of their functions under this Part, they may request the help of that other authority ... , specifying the action in question.

(2)   An authority whose help is so requested shall comply with the request if it is compatible with their own statutory or other duties and obligations and does not unduly prejudice the discharge of any of their functions.

(3)   The [authorities] are—

    (a)   any local authority;

    (b)   any local education authority;

    (c)   any local housing authority;

    (d)   any [[Local Health Board], Special Health Authority][, Primary Care Trust][, National Health Service trust or NHS foundation trust]; and

    (e)   any person authorised by the Secretary of State for the purposes of this section.

(4)   ...

Date in force

14 October 1991: SI 1991/828.

Amendments

Sub-s (1): words omitted repealed by the Courts and Legal Services Act 1990, ss 116, 125(7), Sch 16, para 14, Sch 20.

Sub-s (3): word 'authorities' in square brackets substituted by the Courts and Legal Services Act 1990, s 116, Sch 16, para 14; in para (d) words in square brackets ending with the words 'Special Health Authority' substituted by the Health Authorities Act 1995, s 2(1), Sch 1, para 118(5); words 'Local Health Board' in square brackets substituted by SI 2007/961, art 3, Schedule, para 20(1), (2)(d); in para (d) words ', Primary Care Trust' in square brackets inserted by SI 2000/90, art 3(1), Sch 1, para 24(1), (5); in para (d) words ', National Health Service trust or NHS foundation trust' in square brackets substituted by the Health and Social Care (Community Health and Standards) Act 2003, s 34, Sch 4, paras 75, 78.

Sub-s (4): repealed by the Education Act 1993, s 307(1), (3), Sch 19, para 147, Sch 21, Pt II.

Definitions

For 'local authority', 'functions', 'local education authority', 'local housing authority', 'health authority', 'special educational needs' see s 105(1).

References

See generally para 6.16 and the Children Act 1989 Guidance and Regulations, Volume 3, Family Placement (1991) Department of Health. 'This Part' ie Pt III (ss 17–30 and Sch 2) (local authority support for children and families). For the recovery of reasonable expenses by one local authority from another see s 29(7).

Note

This section does not give a social services authority power to require a housing authority to provide accommodation under the Housing Acts. The section does impose on a housing authority a duty to ascertain whether it could provide a solution for a homeless family with children: *R v Northavon District Council, ex p Smith* [1994] 3 WLR 403, HL.

Transfer of functions

Functions of the Secretary of State, so far as exercisable in relation to Wales, transferred to the National Assembly for Wales, by the National Assembly for Wales (Transfer of Functions) Order 1999, SI 1999/672, art 2, Sch 1.

28   Consultation with local education authorities

(1)   Where—

    (a)   a child is being looked after by a local authority; and

    (b)   the authority propose to provide accommodation for him in an establishment at which education is provided for children who are accommodated there,

they shall, so far as is reasonably practicable, consult the appropriate local education authority before doing so.

(2)   Where any such proposal is carried out, the local authority shall, as soon as is reasonably practicable, inform the appropriate local education authority of the arrangements that have been made for the child's accommodation.

(3)   Where the child ceases to be accommodated as mentioned in subsection (1)(b), the local authority shall inform the appropriate local education authority.

(4)   In this section 'the appropriate local education authority' means—

(a)   the local education authority within whose area the local authority's area falls; or,

(b)   where the child has special educational needs and a statement of his needs is maintained under [Part IV of the Education Act 1996], the local education authority who maintain the statement.

Date in force

14 October 1991: SI 1991/828.

Amendment

Sub-s (4): EA 1996, Sch 37 para 84.
Sub-s (4): words in square brackets substituted by the Education Act 1996, s 582(1), Sch 37, para 84.

Definitions

For 'child', 'local authority' and 'local education authority' see s 105(1); for 'a child who is being looked after by a local authority' see s 22(1); for 'the appropriate local education authority' see sub-s (4).

29   Recoupment of cost of providing services etc

(1)   Where a local authority provide any service under section 17 or 18, other than advice, guidance or counselling, they may recover from a person specified in subsection (4) such charge for the service as they consider reasonable.

(2)   Where the authority are satisfied that that person's means are insufficient for it to be reasonably practicable for him to pay the charge, they shall not require him to pay more than he can reasonably be expected to pay.

(3)   No person shall be liable to pay any charge under subsection (1) [for a service provided under section 17 or section 18(1) or (5)] at any time when he is in receipt of income support [under] [Part VII of the Social Security Contributions and Benefits Act 1992][, of any element of child tax credit other than the family element, of working tax credit] *[or of an income-based jobseeker's allowance]* [, of an income-based jobseeker's allowance or of an income-related employment and support allowance].

[(3A)   No person shall be liable to pay any charge under subsection (1) for a service provided under section 18(2) or (6) at any time when he is in receipt of income support under Part VII of the Social Security Contributions and Benefits Act 1992 *or of an income-based jobseeker's allowance* [, of an income-based jobseeker's allowance or of an income-related employment and support allowance].]

[(3B)   No person shall be liable to pay any charge under subsection (1) for a service provided under section 18(2) or (6) at any time when—

(a)   he is in receipt of guarantee state pension credit under section 1(3)(a) of the State Pension Credit Act 2002, or

(b)   he is a member of a [couple] (within the meaning of that Act) the other member of which is in receipt of guarantee state pension credit.]

(4)   The persons are—

(a)   where the service is provided for a child under sixteen, each of his parents;

(b)   where it is provided for a child who has reached the age of sixteen, the child himself; and

(c)   where it is provided for a member of the child's family, that member.

(5) Any charge under subsection (1) may, without prejudice to any other method of recovery, be recovered summarily as a civil debt.

(6) Part III of Schedule 2 makes provision in connection with contributions towards the maintenance of children who are being looked after by local authorities and consists of the re-enactment with modifications of provisions in Part V of the Child Care Act 1980.

(7) Where a local authority provide any accommodation under section 20(1) for a child who was (immediately before they began to look after him) ordinarily resident within the area of another local authority, they may recover from that other authority any reasonable expenses incurred by them in providing the accommodation and maintaining him.

(8) Where a local authority provide accommodation under section 21(1) or (2)(a) or (b) for a child who is ordinarily resident within the area of another local authority and they are not maintaining him in—

(a) a community home provided by them;
(b) a controlled community home; or
(c) a hospital vested in the Secretary of State [or a Primary Care Trust], [or any other hospital made available pursuant to arrangements made by [a Strategic Health Authority,] a [Local Health Board]] [or a Primary Care Trust,]

they may recover from that other authority any reasonable expenses incurred by them in providing the accommodation and maintaining him.

(9) [Except where subsection (10) applies,] where a local authority comply with any request under section 27(2) in relation to a child or other person who is not ordinarily resident within their area, they may recover from the local authority in whose area the child or person is ordinarily resident any [reasonable expenses] incurred by them in respect of that person.

[(10) Where a local authority ('authority A') comply with any request under section 27(2) from another local authority ('authority B') in relation to a child or other person—

(a) whose responsible authority is authority B for the purposes of section 23B or 23C; or
(b) whom authority B are advising or befriending or to whom they are giving assistance by virtue of section 24(5)(a),

authority A may recover from authority B any reasonable expenses incurred by them in respect of that person.]

Date in force

14 October 1991: SI 1991/828.

Amendments

Sub-s (3): words 'for a service provided under section 17 or section 18(1) or (5)' in square brackets inserted by the Local Government Act 2000, s 103(1); word 'under' in square brackets substituted by the Tax Credits Act 2002, s 47, Sch 3, paras 15, 18(a); words 'Part VII of the Social Security Contributions and Benefits Act 1992' in square brackets substituted by the Social Security (Consequential Provisions) Act 1992, s 4, Sch 2, para 108(b); words from ', of any element' to 'working tax credit' in square brackets inserted by the Tax Credits Act 2002, s 47, Sch 3, paras 15, 18(b); words 'or of an income-based jobseeker's allowance' in square brackets inserted by the Jobseekers Act 1995, s 41(4), Sch 2, para 19(3); words 'or of an income-based jobseeker's allowance' in italics repealed and subsequent words in square brackets substituted by the Welfare Reform Act 2007, s 28(1), Sch 3, para 6(1), (4).

Sub-s (3A): inserted by the Local Government Act 2000, s 103(2); words 'or of an income-based jobseeker's allowance' in italics repealed and subsequent words in square brackets substituted by the Welfare Reform Act 2007, s 28(1), Sch 3, para 6(1), (4).

Sub-s (3B): inserted by the State Pension Credit Act 2002, s 14, Sch 2, Pt 3, para 30; in para (b) word 'couple' in square brackets substituted by SI 2005/3129, art 4(4), Sch 4, para 9.

Sub-s (8): in para (c) words 'or a Primary Care Trust' in square brackets inserted by SI 2000/90, art 3(1), Sch 1, para 24(1), (6)(a); in para (c) words in square brackets beginning with the words 'or any other hospital' inserted by the National Health Service and Community Care Act 1990, s 66(1), Sch 9, para 36(3); in para (c) words 'a Strategic Health Authority,' in square brackets inserted by SI 2002/2469, reg 4, Sch 1, Pt 1, para 16(1), (2); in para (c) words 'Local Health Board' in square brackets substituted by SI 2007/961, art 3, Schedule, para 20(1), (2)(e); in para (c) words 'or a Primary Care Trust,' in square brackets inserted by SI 2000/90, art 3(1), Sch 1, para 24(1), (6)(b).

Sub-s (9): words 'Except where subsection (10) applies' in square brackets inserted by the Children (Leaving Care) Act 2000, s 7(1), (3)(a); words 'reasonable expenses' in square brackets substituted by the Courts and Legal Services Act 1990, s 116, Sch 16, para 15.

Sub-s (10): inserted by the Children (Leaving Care) Act 2000, s 7(1), (3)(b).

Definitions

For 'looked after' see s 22(1); for 'local authority', 'service', 'child' and 'hospital' see s 105(1); for 'community home' and 'controlled community home' see s 53 as applied to the whole Act by s 105(1).

References

See generally the Children Act 1989 Guidance and Regulations, Volume 2, Family Support Day Care and Educational Provision (1991) Department of Health, para 238; for the determination of the ordinary residence of a child for the purposes of sub-s (7)–(9) see s 30(2) and s 105(6). For transitional provisions for contributions for maintenance of children in care under repealed enactments see s 108(6) and Sch 14, para 24; for contributions to the maintenance of accommodated children see Sch 2, Pt III.

Transfer of functions

Functions of the Secretary of State, so far as exercisable in relation to Wales, transferred to the National Assembly for Wales, by the National Assembly for Wales (Transfer of Functions) Order 1999, SI 1999/672, art 2, Sch 1.

---

30   Miscellaneous

(1)   Nothing in this Part shall affect any duty imposed on a local authority by or under any other enactment.

(2)   Any question arising under section 20(2), 21(3) or 29(7) to (9) as to the ordinary residence of a child shall be determined by agreement between the local authorities concerned or, in default of agreement, by the Secretary of State.

(3)   Where the functions conferred on a local authority by this Part and the functions of a local education authority are concurrent, the Secretary of State may by regulations provide by which authority the functions are to be exercised.

(4)   The Secretary of State may make regulations for determining, as respects any local education authority functions specified in the regulations, whether a child who is being looked after by a local authority is to be treated, for purposes so specified, as a child of parents of sufficient resources or as a child of parents without resources.

Date in force

14 October 1991: SI 1991/828.

Definitions

For 'local authority', 'child', 'functions', 'local education authority' see s 105(1); for 'a child who is being looked after by a local authority' see s 22(1).

References

For determination of ordinary residence of a child see sub-s (2) and s 105(6). 'This Part' ie Pt III (ss 17–30 and Sch 2) (local authority support for children and families).

Transfer of functions

Functions of the Secretary of State, so far as exercisable in relation to Wales, transferred to the National Assembly for Wales, by the National Assembly for Wales (Transfer of Functions) Order 1999, SI 1999/672, art 2, Sch 1.

PART IV

CARE AND SUPERVISION

General

31   Care and supervision orders

(1)   On the application of any local authority or authorised person, the court may make an order—

(a)   placing the child with respect to whom the application is made in the care of a designated local authority; or

(b)   putting him under the supervision of a designated local authority ...

(2)   A court may only make a care order or supervision order if it is satisfied—

(a)   that the child concerned is suffering, or is likely to suffer, significant harm; and

(b)   that the harm, or likelihood of harm, is attributable to—

(i)   the care given to the child, or likely to be given to him if the order were not made, not being what it would be reasonable to expect a parent to give to him; or

(ii)   the child's being beyond parental control.

(3)   No care order or supervision order may be made with respect to a child who has reached the age of seventeen (or sixteen, in the case of a child who is married).

[(3A)   No care order may be made with respect to a child until the court has considered a section 31A plan.]

(4)   An application under this section may be made on its own or in any other family proceedings.

(5)   The court may—

(a)   on an application for a care order, make a supervision order;

(b)   on an application for a supervision order, make a care order.

(6)   Where an authorised person proposes to make an application under this section he shall—

(a)   if it is reasonably practicable to do so; and

(b)   before making the application,

consult the local authority appearing to him to be the authority in whose area the child concerned is ordinarily resident.

(7)   An application made by an authorised person shall not be entertained by the court if, at the time when it is made, the child concerned is—

   (a)   the subject of an earlier application for a care order, or supervision order, which has not been disposed of; or

   (b)   subject to—

      (i)   a care order or supervision order;

      (ii)   an order under [section 63(1) of the Powers of Criminal Courts (Sentencing) Act 2000]; or

      [(ii)   a youth rehabilitation order within the meaning of Part 1 of the Criminal Justice and Immigration Act 2008; or]

      (iii)   a supervision requirement within the meaning of [Part II of the Children (Scotland) Act 1995].

(8)   The local authority designated in a care order must be—

   (a)   the authority within whose area the child is ordinarily resident; or

   (b)   where the child does not reside in the area of a local authority, the authority within whose area any circumstances arose in consequence of which the order is being made.

(9)   In this section—

'authorised person' means—

   (a)   the National Society for the Prevention of Cruelty to Children and any of its officers; and

   (b)   any person authorised by order of the Secretary of State to bring proceedings under this section and any officer of a body which is so authorised;

'harm' means ill-treatment or the impairment of health or development [including, for example, impairment suffered from seeing or hearing the ill-treatment of another];

'development' means physical, intellectual, emotional, social or behavioural development;

'health' means physical or mental health; and

'ill-treatment' includes sexual abuse and forms of ill-treatment which are not physical.

(10)   Where the question of whether harm suffered by a child is significant turns on the child's health or development, his health or development shall be compared with that which could reasonably be expected of a similar child.

(11)   In this Act—

'a care order' means (subject to section 105(1)) an order under subsection (1)(a) and (except where express provision to the contrary is made) includes an interim care order made under section 38; and

'a supervision order' means an order under subsection (1)(b) and (except where express provision to the contrary is made) includes an interim supervision order made under section 38.

Date in force

14 October 1991: SI 1991/828.

Amendment

Sub-s (1): in para (b) words omitted repealed by the Criminal Justice and Court Services Act 2000, ss 74, 75, Sch 7, Pt II, paras 87, 90, Sch 8.
Sub-s (3A): inserted by the Adoption and Children Act 2002, s 121(1).

Sub-s (7): para (b)(ii) substituted by the Criminal Justice and Immigration Act 2008, s 6(2), Sch 4, Pt 1, paras 33, 35; for transitional provisions and savings see s 148(2), Sch 27, Pt 1, paras 1(1), 5 thereto. Date in force: to be appointed: see the Criminal Justice and Immigration Act 2008, s 153(7); in para (b)(ii) words 'section 63(1) of the Powers of Criminal Courts (Sentencing) Act 2000' in square brackets substituted by the Powers of Criminal Courts (Sentencing) Act 2000, s 165(1), Sch 9, para 127; in para (b)(iii) words 'Part II of the Children (Scotland) Act 1995' in square brackets substituted by the Children (Scotland) Act 1995, s 105(4), Sch 4, para 48(2).

Sub-s (9): in definition 'harm' words from 'including, for example,' to 'ill-treatment of another' in square brackets inserted by the Adoption and Children Act 2002, s 120.

Definitions

For 'local authority', 'child' see s 105(1); for 'court' see s 92(7); for 'designated local authority' see sub-s (8); for 'care order', 'supervision order' see sub-s (11); for 'harm' see sub-s (9) and as to whether harm is significant see sub-s (10); for 'authorised person', 'development', 'health', 'ill-treatment' see sub-s (9); for 'care plan' see s 31A.

References

See generally Chapter 8 and Chapter 3 of the revised Children Act 1989 Guidance and Regulations, Volume 1, Court Orders (2008) Department for Schools, Families and Children. See also Care Plans and Care Proceedings Under the Children Act 1989 LAC (99) 29 in *Clarke Hall and Morrison on Children* at para 1[14454] and *Handbook of Best Practice in Children Act Cases* at para 1[20001] also *Re S (children: care plan)* [2002] UKHL 10, [2002] 1 All ER 192. The principles of s 1 apply. For jurisdiction of courts see s 92 and Sch 11 and paras 4.5 ff; for appeals see s 94 and orders pending appeals s 40; for determining the 'ordinary residence' of a child see s 105(6). Care proceedings must be commenced in the magistrates' court, but may be allocated to the county court or High Court: Children (Allocation of Proceedings) Order 1991, SI 1991/1677, rr 3(i)(b) and 12, see paras 4.14 and 4.33 ff; for 'family proceedings' see s 8(3); for duty of local authority to make inquiries with respect to certain children to enable them to decide whether they should take any action to safeguard or promote the child's welfare see s 47(1); for the appointment of a children's guardian see s 41; for interim care and supervision orders see s 38; for attendance of child at hearing see s 95; for evidence given by or with respect of children see s 96; for self incrimination of witness see s 98; for powers of the court when considering whether to make a care or supervision order under this section see s 37; for variation and discharge of care and supervision orders see s 39; for duration of care orders and supervision orders see s 91(12), (13); for effect of orders see generally s 91 and for further provisions relating to care orders see s 33, 34, and for supervision orders s 35. For consent orders, see paras 8.167 ff and for the effect of a care order on other court orders, see paras 8.178 ff. The proper forum for a challenge to the care plan is in the care proceedings, rather than by way of judicial review; only in the event of a failure by a local authority to amend its proposals for the child so as to accord with the court's determination of the child's interests is it proper for the guardian to consider taking proceedings for judicial review *Re C (adoption: religious observance)* [2002] 1 FLR 1119.

Transfer of functions

Functions of the Secretary of State, so far as exercisable in relation to Wales, transferred to the National Assembly for Wales, by the National Assembly for Wales (Transfer of Functions) Order 1999, SI 1999/672, art 2, Sch 1

Sub-s (5)(b)

But does not include the making of a care order on an application under para 6(3) of Sch 3 for the extension of a supervision order *(Re A (a minor) (Supervision Order: Extension)* [1995] 3 All ER 401, [1995] 2 FCR 114.

Sub-s (8)

For the test of ordinary residence for these purposes see *Northampton County Council v Islington London Borough Council* [1999] 3 FCR 385, [1999] 2 FLR 881, *C v Plymouth City Council* [2000] 2 FCR 289, [2000] 2 FLR 875, CA and *Re BC (a minor) (care order: appropriate local authority)* [1995] 3 FCR 598. See further cases cited at para 8.170.

Appendix 1 *Children Act 1989*

Sub-s (8)(b)

Should be read as if the word 'ordinarily' preceded reside': *Gateshead Metropolitan Borough Council v B* [1996] 2 FLR 179.

[31A   Care orders: care plans]

[(1)   Where an application is made on which a care order might be made with respect to a child, the appropriate local authority must, within such time as the court may direct, prepare a plan ('a care plan') for the future care of the child.

(2)   While the application is pending, the authority must keep any care plan prepared by them under review and, if they are of the opinion some change is required, revise the plan, or make a new plan, accordingly.

(3)   A care plan must give any prescribed information and do so in the prescribed manner.

(4)   For the purposes of this section, the appropriate local authority, in relation to a child in respect of whom a care order might be made, is the local authority proposed to be designated in the order.

(5)   In section 31(3A) and this section, references to a care order do not include an interim care order.

(6)   A plan prepared, or treated as prepared, under this section is referred to in this Act as a 'section 31A plan'.]

Date in force

Inserted by the Adoption and Children Act 2002, s 121(2). Date in force: (for the purpose of making regulations) 7 December 2004; (for remaining purposes): 30 December 2005 – for provision as to care orders made before that date see the Adoption and Children Act 2002, s 121(3).

Reference

For the duty on the court to scrutinise the care plan and the right to invite the local authority to reconider the care plan if the court considers the care plan involves a course of action which the court believes is contrary to the interests of the child, see *Re S and W (children) (care proceedings: care plan)* [2007] EWCA Civ 232, [2007] 1 FCR 721, [2007] 2 FLR 275.

---

32   Period within which application for order under this Part must be disposed of

(1)   A court hearing an application for an order under this Part shall (in the light of any rules made by virtue of subsection (2))—

    (a)   draw up a timetable with a view to disposing of the application without delay; and

    (b)   give such directions as it considers appropriate for the purpose of ensuring, so far as is reasonably practicable, that that timetable is adhered to.

(2)   Rules of court may—

    (a)   specify periods within which specified steps must be taken in relation to such proceedings; and

    (b)   make other provisions with respect to such proceedings for the purpose of ensuring, so far as is reasonably practicable, that they are disposed of without delay.

Date in force

14 October 1991: SI 1991/828.

Definitions

For 'court' see s 92(7); for 'child' see s 105(1).

References

For jurisdiction of courts see s 92 and Sch 11, paras 4.3 ff. 'This Part' ie Pt IV (ss 31–42 and Sch 3) (care and supervision). For welfare of the child the paramount consideration see s 1(1). For family proceedings see s 8(3). For timetable see para 8.15.

Rules of Court

See the FPC(CA 1989)R 1991, r 15, and the FPR 1991, r 4.15, see paras 4.20 ff. For allocation of care proceedings see the Children (Allocation of Proceedings) Order 1991, see paras 4.14 and 4.33.

Care orders

33   Effect of care order

(1)   Where a care order is made with respect to a child it shall be the duty of the local authority designated by the order to receive the child into their care and to keep him in their care while the order remains in force.

(2)   Where—

  (a)   a care order has been made with respect to a child on the application of an authorised person; but

  (b)   the local authority designated by the order was not informed that that person proposed to make the application,

the child may be kept in the care of that person until received into the care of the authority.

(3)   While a care order is in force with respect to a child, the local authority designated by the order shall—

  (a)   have parental responsibility for the child; and

  (b)   have the power (subject to the following provisions of this section) to determine the extent to which[—

      (i)   a parent, guardian or special guardian of the child; or

      (ii)   a person who by virtue of section 4A has parental responsibility for the child,]

  may meet his parental responsibility for him.

(4)   The authority may not exercise the power in subsection (3)(b) unless they are satisfied that it is necessary to do so in order to safeguard or promote the child's welfare.

(5)   Nothing in subsection (3)(b) shall prevent [a person mentioned in that provision who has care of the child] from doing what is reasonable in all the circumstances of the case for the purpose of safeguarding or promoting his welfare.

(6)   While a care order is in force with respect to a child, the local authority designated by the order shall not—

  (a)   cause the child to be brought up in any religious persuasion other than that in which he would have been brought up if the order had not been made; or

(b) have the right—
    (i) ...
    (ii) to agree or refuse to agree to the making of an adoption order, or an order under [section 84 of the Adoption and Children Act 2002], with respect to the child; or
    (iii) to appoint a guardian for the child.

(7) While a care order is in force with respect to a child, no person may—

(a) cause the child to be known by a new surname; or
(b) remove him from the United Kingdom,

without either the written consent of every person who has parental responsibility for the child or the leave of the court.

(8) Subsection (7)(b) does not—

(a) prevent the removal of such a child, for a period of less than one month, by the authority in whose care he is; or
(b) apply to arrangements for such a child to live outside England and Wales (which are governed by paragraph 19 of Schedule 2).

(9) The power in subsection (3)(b) is subject (in addition to being subject to the provisions of this section) to any right, duty, power, responsibility or authority which [a person mentioned in that provision] has in relation to the child and his property by virtue of any other enactment.

Date in force

14 October 1991: SI 1991/828.

Amendment

Sub-s (3): para (b)(i), (ii) substituted by the Adoption and Children Act 2002, s 139(1), Sch 3, paras 54, 63(a).
Sub-s (5): words 'a person mentioned in that provision who has care of the child' in square brackets substituted by the Adoption and Children Act 2002, s 139(1), Sch 3, paras 54, 63(b).
Sub-s (6): para (b)(i) repealed by the Adoption and Children Act 2002, s 139(1), (3), Sch 3, paras 54, 63(c)(i), Sch 5; in para (b)(ii) words 'section 84 of the Adoption and Children Act 2002' in square brackets substituted by the Adoption and Children Act 2002, s 139(1), Sch 3, paras 54, 63(c)(ii).
Sub-s (9): words 'a person mentioned in that provision' in square brackets substituted by the Adoption and Children Act 2002, s 139(1), Sch 3, paras 54, 63(d).

Definitions

For 'care order' see s 31(11) and s 105(1); for 'child', 'local authority' and 'guardian of a child' see s 105(1); for 'designated local authority' see s 31(8); for 'authorised person' see s 31(9); for 'parental responsibility' see s 3; for 'court' see s 92(7).

References

See generally Chapter 8 and in particular para 8.122 ff and 8.178 ff and para 3.58 of the revised Children Act 1989 Guidance and Regulations, Volume 1, Court Orders (2008) Department for Schools, Families and Children. For appointment of children's guardian see s 41. For duration of care orders see s 91(12); for care and supervision orders generally see s 31; for further provisions in connection with care orders see s 34 and in connection with supervision orders see ss 35 and 36; for interim care and supervision orders see s 38; for the discharge and variation of care and supervision orders see s 39; for jurisdiction of courts see s 92 and Sch 11.

Sub-s (1)

A family proceedings court does not have power to stay a care order pending appeal to the High Court but application may be made to the High Court immediately for a stay: See *Re O (a minor)* [1992] 4 All ER 905.

Sub-s (7)

Cf s 13(1) where a residence order is in force. Application for leave must be commenced in the magistrates' court: Children (Allocation of Proceedings) Order 1991, r 2. The Secretary of State for the Home Department exercising his powers and duties under the Immigration legislation is not included in this prohibition: *Re L (Care Order: Immigration Powers to Remove)* [2007] EWHC 158(Fam) [2007] 2 FLR 789

Sub-s (8)

Cf s 13(2) where a residence order is in force.

---

34   **Parental contact etc with children in care**

(1)   Where a child is in the care of a local authority, the authority shall (subject to the provisions of this section) allow the child reasonable contact with—

   (a)   his parents;
   (b)   any guardian [or special guardian] of his;
   [(ba) any person who by virtue of section 4A has parental responsibility for him;]
   (c)   where there was a residence order in force with respect to the child immediately before the care order was made, the person in whose favour the order was made; and
   (d)   where, immediately before the care order was made a person had care of the child by virtue of an order made in the exercise of the High Court's inherent jurisdiction with respect to children, that person.

(2)   On an application made by the authority or the child, the court may make such order as it considers appropriate with respect to the contact which is to be allowed between the child and any named person.

(3)   On an application made by—

   (a)   any person mentioned in paragraphs (a) to (d) of subsection (1); or
   (b)   any person who has obtained the leave of the court to make the application,

the court may make such order as it considers appropriate with respect to the contact which is to be allowed between the child and that person.

(4)   On an application made by the authority or the child, the court may make an order authorising the authority to refuse to allow contact between the child and any person who is mentioned in paragraphs (a) to (d) of subsection (1) and named in the order.

(5)   When making a care order with respect to a child, or in any family proceedings in connection with a child who is in the care of a local authority, the court may make an order under this section, even though no application for such an order has been made with respect to the child, if it considers that the order should be made.

(6)   An authority may refuse to allow the contact that would otherwise be required by virtue of subsection (1) or an order under this section if—

   (a)   they are satisfied that it is necessary to do so in order to safeguard or promote the child's welfare; and
   (b)   the refusal—
       (i)   is decided upon as a matter of urgency; and

(ii) does not last for more than seven days.

(7) An order under this section may impose such conditions as the court considers appropriate.

(8) The Secretary of State may by regulations make provision as to—

(a) the steps to be taken by a local authority who have exercised their powers under subsection (6);

(b) the circumstances in which, and conditions subject to which, the terms of any order under this section may be departed from by agreement between the local authority and the person in relation to whom the order is made;

(c) notification by a local authority of any variation or suspension of arrangements made (otherwise than under an order under this section) with a view to affording any person contact with a child to whom this section applies.

(9) The court may vary or discharge any order made under this section on the application of the authority, the child concerned or the person named in the order.

(10) An order under this section may be made either at the same time as the care order itself or later.

(11) Before making a care order with respect to any child the court shall—

(a) consider the arrangements which the authority have made, or propose to make, for affording any person contact with a child to whom this section applies; and

(b) invite the parties to the proceedings to comment on those arrangements.

Date in force

14 October 1991: SI 1991/828.

Amendment

Sub-s (1): in para (b) words 'or special guardian' in square brackets inserted by the Adoption and Children Act 2002, s 139(1), Sch 3, paras 54, 64(a); para (ba) inserted by the Adoption and Children Act 2002, s 139(1), Sch 3, paras 54, 64(b).

Definitions

For 'child', 'local authority', 'guardian of a child' and 'child in the care of a local authority' see s 105(1). For 'special guardian' see s 14A. For 'care order' see s 31(11) and s 105(1); for 'residence order' see s 8(1); for a 'person in whose favour a residence order is in force' see s 105(3); for 'court' see s 92(7); for 'the local authority designated in a care order' see s 31(8).

References

Proceedings must be commenced in the magistrates' court: Children (Allocation of Proceedings) Order 1991, r 3, see para 4.14. See generally Chapter 8 and in particular paras 8.177 ff and paras 3.71 to 3.79 of rhe revised Children Act 1989 Guidance and Regulations, Volume 1, Court Orders (2008) Department for Schools, Families and Children, and Volume 3 Family Placements. For welfare of the child the paramount consideration see s 1(1) and Chapter 2; for appointment of a children's guardian see s 41; for care and supervision orders generally see s 31; for further provisions in connection with supervision orders see s 35 and 36; for interim care and supervision orders see s 38; for exclusion requirement in interim order, see s 38A; for the discharge and variation of care and supervisions orders see s 39; for jurisdiction of courts see s 92 and Sch 11; for refusal of contact, see para 8.214 ff.

Sub-s (3) Leave of the Court

Leave may be granted by a single justice: FPC(CA 1989)R 1991, r 2(5).

Sub-s (4)

The court may make an interim order for no contact: *West Glamorgan County Council v P* [1992] 2 FCR 378; see para 8.214.

Sub-s (8) Regulations

See the Contact with Children Regulations 1991, SI 1991/891 which provide, inter alia, for the local authority to depart from the terms of any order as to contact by agreement with the person about whom the order was made. The child must agree if of sufficient understanding and the authority must send written notification to specified persons.

Transfer of functions

Functions of the Secretary of State, so far as exercisable in relation to Wales, transferred to the National Assembly for Wales, by the National Assembly for Wales (Transfer of Functions) Order 1999, SI 1999/672, art 2, Sch 1.

Supervision orders

35   Supervision orders

(1)   While a supervision order is in force it shall be the duty of the supervisor—

(a)   to advise, assist and befriend the supervised child;
(b)   to take such steps as are reasonably necessary to give effect to the order; and
(c)   where—
   (i)   the order is not wholly complied with; or
   (ii)   the supervisor considers that the order may no longer be necessary,
to consider whether or not to apply to the court for its variation or discharge.

(2)   Parts I and II of Schedule 3 make further provision with respect to supervision orders.

Date in force

14 October 1991: SI 1991/828.

Definitions

For 'supervision order' see s 31(11); for 'supervisor', 'supervised child' see s 105(1).

References

See generally paras 8.112 ff and 8.180 ff and paras 3.80 to 3.84 of the revised Children Act 1989 Guidance and Regulations, Volume 1, Court Orders (2008) Department for Schools, Families and Children. For duration of supervision orders see s 91(13) and Sch 3, para 6(1). For care and supervision orders generally see s 31; for further provisions in connection with supervision orders see s 36 and Sch 3; for interim care and supervision orders see s 38; for the discharge and variation of care and supervision orders see s 39.

Note

Before the court can make a supervision order it must be satisfied as to the provisions of s 31. Section 35 must be read with Sch 3 in view of the detailed powers contained therein.

---

36   Education supervision orders

(1)   On the application of any local education authority, the court may make an order putting the child with respect to whom the application is made under the supervision of a designated local education authority.

(2)   In this Act 'an education supervision order' means an order under subsection (1).

(3)   A court may only make an education supervision order if it is satisfied that the child concerned is of compulsory school age and is not being properly educated.

(4)   For the purposes of this section, a child is being properly educated only if he is receiving efficient full-time education suitable to his age, ability and aptitude and any special educational needs he may have.

(5)   Where a child is—

    (a)   the subject of a school attendance order which is in force under [section 437 of the Education Act 1996] and which has not been complied with; or

    [(b)   is not attending regularly within the meaning of section 444 of that Act—
        (i)   a school at which he is a registered pupil,
        (ii)   any place at which education is provided for him in the circumstances mentioned in subsection (1) of section 444ZA of that Act, or
        (iii)   any place which he is required to attend in the circumstances mentioned in subsection (2) of that section],

then, unless it is proved that he is being properly educated, it shall be assumed that he is not.

(6)   An education supervision order may not be made with respect to a child who is in the care of a local authority.

(7)   The local education authority designated in an education supervision order must be—

    (a)   the authority within whose area the child concerned is living or will live; or
    (b)   where—
        (i)   the child is a registered pupil at a school; and
        (ii)   the authority mentioned in paragraph (a) and the authority within whose area the school is situated agree,

the latter authority.

(8)   Where a local education authority propose to make an application for an education supervision order they shall, before making the application, consult the ... appropriate local authority.

(9)   The appropriate local authority is—

    (a)   in the case of a child who is being provided with accommodation by, or on behalf of, a local authority, that authority; and
    (b)   in any other case, the local authority within whose area the child concerned lives, or will live.

(10)   Part III of Schedule 3 makes further provision with respect to education supervision orders.

Date in force

14 October 1991: SI 1991/828.

Amendment

Sub-s (5): in para (a) words 'section 437 of the Education Act 1996' in square brackets substituted by the Education Act 1996, s 582(1), Sch 37, para 85; para (b) substituted by the Education Act 2005, s 117, Sch 18, para 1.
Sub-s (8): words omitted repealed by the Education Act 1993, s 307(1), (3), Sch 19, para 149, Sch 21, Part II.

Definitions

For 'local education authority', 'child', 'child who is in the care of a local authority', 'local authority' see s 105(1); for 'court' see s 92(7); for 'designated local authority' see sub-s (7); for 'education supervision order' see sub-s (2); for 'being properly educated' see sub-s (4), (5); for 'registered pupil' see s 105(1) and the EA 1996 s 434(5); for 'special educational needs' see s 105(1) and the EA 1996 s 312(1); for 'appropriate local authority' see sub-s (9); for 'accommodation provided by or on behalf of a local authority' see s 105(5).

References

See generally paras 8.191 ff. For jurisdiction of courts see s 92 and Sch 11, paras 4.5 ff; proceedings under this section must be commenced in the magistrates' court: Children (Allocation of Proceedings) Order 1991; for attendance of child at hearing see s 95; for evidence given by or with respect to children see s 96; for self incrimination of witness see s 98.

Powers of court

37   Powers of court in certain family proceedings

(1)   Where, in any family proceedings in which a question arises with respect to the welfare of any child, it appears to the court that it may be appropriate for a care or supervision order to be made with respect to him, the court may direct the appropriate authority to undertake an investigation of the child's circumstances.

(2)   Where the court gives a direction under this section the local authority concerned shall, when undertaking the investigation, consider whether they should—

(a)   apply for a care order or for a supervision order with respect to the child;
(b)   provide services or assistance for the child or his family; or
(c)   take any other action with respect to the child.

(3)   Where a local authority undertake an investigation under this section, and decide not to apply for a care order or supervision order with respect to the child concerned, they shall inform the court of—

(a)   their reasons for so deciding;
(b)   any service or assistance which they have provided, or intend to provide, for the child and his family; and
(c)   any other action which they have taken, or propose to take, with respect to the child.

(4)   The information shall be given to the court before the end of the period of eight weeks beginning with the date of the direction, unless the court otherwise directs.

(5)   The local authority named in a direction under subsection (1) must be—

(a)   the authority in whose area the child is ordinarily resident; or
(b)   where the child [is not ordinarily resident] in the area of a local authority, the authority within whose area any circumstances arose in consequence of which the direction is being given.

(6)   If, on the conclusion of any investigation or review under this section, the authority decide not to apply for a care order or supervision order with respect to the child—

(a)   they shall consider whether it would be appropriate to review the case at a later date; and
(b)   if they decide that it would be, they shall determine the date on which that review is to begin.

Date in force

14 October 1991: SI 1991/828.68

Amendment

Sub-s (5): words in square brackets substituted by the Courts and Legal Services Act 1990, s 116, Sch 16, para 16.

Definitions

For 'family proceedings' see s 8(3), (4)(a); for 'child', 'local authority' see s 105(1); for 'court' see s 92(7) (a single justice may make the direction: FPC(CA 1989)R 1991, r 2(5); for 'care order' see s 31(11) and s 105(1); for 'supervision order' see s 31(11); for 'appropriate authority' see sub-s (5); for 'ordinary residence' see s 105(6).

References

See generally paras 5.206 and 7.25 ff, the FPR 1991, r 4.26 and FPC(CA 1989)R 1991, r 27. For welfare of the child as paramount consideration see s 1(1); for jurisdiction of courts see s 92 and Sch 11; for the bringing to an end of an interim order made under s 38 as a result of a direction by the court under sub-s (1) see s 38(4); for the appointment of a children's guardian see s 41 and para 10.21; for the provision of services and assistance by local authorities see Pt III ie ss 17–30 and Sch 2 (local authority support for children and families); for interim orders see s 38; for exclusion requirement in interim order see s 38A. For 'family proceedings' under this Act see s 8(3), (4)(a). See also s 47 for investigations by the local authority.

Investigation

A court should only order an investigation where it appears that it may be appropriate to make a public law order: *Re CE (section 37 direction)* [1995] 1 FLR 26; *Re L (a minor) (section 37 direction)* [1999] 3 FCR 642, [1999] 1 FLR 984, CA.

---

38   Interim orders

(1)   Where—

   (a)   in any proceedings on an application for a care order or supervision order, the proceedings are adjourned; or

   (b)   the court gives a direction under section 37(1),

the court may make an interim care order or an interim supervision order with respect to the child concerned.

(2)   A court shall not make an interim care order or interim supervision order under this section unless it is satisfied that there are reasonable grounds for believing that the circumstances with respect to the child are as mentioned in section 31(2).

(3)   Where, in any proceedings on an application for a care order or supervision order, a court makes a residence order with respect to the child concerned, it shall also make an interim supervision order with respect to him unless satisfied that his welfare will be satisfactorily safeguarded without an interim order being made.

(4)   An interim order made under or by virtue of this section shall have effect for such period as may be specified in the order, but shall in any event cease to have effect on whichever of the following events first occurs—

   (a)   the expiry of the period of eight weeks beginning with the date on which the order is made;

   (b)   if the order is the second or subsequent such order made with respect to the same child in the same proceedings, the expiry of the relevant period;

   (c)   in a case which falls within subsection (1)(a), the disposal of the application;

(d) in a case which falls within subsection (1)(b), the disposal of an application for a care order or supervision order made by the authority with respect to the child;

(e) in a case which falls within subsection (1)(b) and in which—

  (i) the court has given a direction under section 37(4), but

  (ii) no application for a care order or supervision order has been made with respect to the child,

the expiry of the period fixed by that direction.

(5) In subsection (4)(b) 'the relevant period' means—

(a) the period of four weeks beginning with the date on which the order in question is made; or

(b) the period of eight weeks beginning with the date on which the first order was made if that period ends later than the period mentioned in paragraph (a).

(6) Where the court makes an interim care order, or interim supervision order, it may give such directions (if any) as it considers appropriate with regard to the medical or psychiatric examination or other assessment of the child; but if the child is of sufficient understanding to make an informed decision he may refuse to submit to the examination or other assessment.

(7) A direction under subsection (6) may be to the effect that there is to be—

(a) no such examination or assessment; or

(b) no such examination or assessment unless the court directs otherwise.

(8) A direction under subsection (6) may be—

(a) given when the interim order is made or at any time while it is in force; and

(b) varied at any time on the application of any person falling within any class of person prescribed by rules of court for the purposes of this subsection.

(9) Paragraphs 4 and 5 of Schedule 3 shall not apply in relation to an interim supervision order.

(10) Where a court makes an order under or by virtue of this section it shall, in determining the period for which the order is to be in force, consider whether any party who was, or might have been, opposed to the making of the order was in a position to argue his case against the order in full.

Date in force

14 October 1991: SI 1991/828.

Definitions

For 'care order' see s 31(11) and s 105(1); for 'supervision order' see s 31(11); for 'court' see s 92(7); for 'child' see s 105(1); for 'residence order' see s 8(1); for 'the relevant period' see sub-s (5); for 'the authority' see s 37(1), (5).

References

See generally paras 8.112 ff and paras 3.44 to 3.57 of the revised Children Act 1989 Guidance and Regulations, Volume 1, Court Orders (2008) Department for Schools, Families and Children. For application for care order or supervision order see s 31; for jurisdiction of courts see s 92 and Sch 11, paras 4.5 ff; for attendance of child at hearing see s 95 and the FPR 1991, r 4.16 and the FPC(CA 1989)R 1991, r 16; for evidence given by or with respect to children see s 96 and the Children (Admissibility of Hearsay Evidence) Order 1993, SI 1993/621; for self-incrimination of witness see s 98. For making of interim care orders after a full hearing, see paras 8.149 ff and *Re S (Minors) (Care Order; Implementation of Care Plan); Re W (Minors) (Care Orders: Adequacy of Care Plan)* [2002] UKHL 10, [2002] 2 WLR 720, [2002] 1 FLR 815.

Appendix 1 *Children Act 1989*

Sub-s (1) Court

An interim order may be made by a single justice or justices' clerk in certain circumstances: FPC(CA 1989)R 1991, r 28.

Sub-s (3)

This creates a presumption that the court shall make an interim supervision order in the circumstances described, but it must also be satisfied as to sub-s (2). Even where the criteria for an interim order are satisfied, such an order may only be made where it is in the interests of the child to do so: *Re A (children) (interim care order)* [2001] 3 FCR 402. For the use of interim orders in relation to care plans, see *Re S (children: care plan)* [2002] UKHL 10, [2002] 1 All ER 192.

Sub-ss (4) and (5)

The effect of these provisions is that the court can make interim orders initially for up to eight weeks or any part thereof including any unspent period of eight weeks from the date of the first order, and thereafter for one or more periods of up to four weeks. Note s 1 on the avoidance of delay and s 32 on the requirement to establish a timetable.

Sub-s (6)

See generally para 8.113 ff. In addition to directions under this sub-s, the court can impose requirements under Sch 3, paras 1–3, on orders under s 8, in addition to a supervision order. The directions may be varied: sub-s (8) on the application of specified persons: FPR 1991, r 4.2 and FPC(CA 1989)R 1991, r 2 and subject to appeal: *Re O (minors) (medical examination)* [1992] 2 FCR 394. The court may direct a local authority to carry out an assessment even though the authority is unwilling to do so: *Re C (A Minor) (Interim Care Order: Residential Assessment)* [1997] 1 FLR 1, HL. For the steps to be taken before ordering a residential assessment, see *Sheffield City Council v V (Legal Services Commission Intervening)* [2006] EWHC 1861 (Fam), [2007] 1 FCR 279 and, for the circumstances where an assessment would not be useful, see *Re L and another (children) (care order: residential assessment)* [2007] EWCA Civ 213, [2007] 3 FCR 258, [2007] 1 FLR 1370.

[38A   Power to include exclusion requirement in interim care order]

[(1) Where—

- (a) on being satisfied that there are reasonable grounds for believing that the circumstances with respect to a child are as mentioned in section 31(2)(a) and (b)(i), the court makes an interim care order with respect to a child, and
- (b) the conditions mentioned in subsection (2) are satisfied,

the court may include an exclusion requirement in the interim care order.

(2) The conditions are—

- (a) that there is reasonable cause to believe that, if a person ('the relevant person') is excluded from a dwelling-house in which the child lives, the child will cease to suffer, or cease to be likely to suffer, significant harm, and
- (b) that another person living in the dwelling-house (whether a parent of the child or some other person)—
  - (i) is able and willing to give to the child the care which it would be reasonable to expect a parent to give him, and
  - (ii) consents to the inclusion of the exclusion requirement.

(3) For the purposes of this section an exclusion requirement is any one or more of the following—

- (a) a provision requiring the relevant person to leave a dwelling-house in which he is living with the child,
- (b) a provision prohibiting the relevant person from entering a dwelling-house in which the child lives, and

734

    (c)   a provision excluding the relevant person from a defined area in which a dwelling-house in which the child lives is situated.

(4)   The court may provide that the exclusion requirement is to have effect for a shorter period than the other provisions of the interim care order.

(5)   Where the court makes an interim care order containing an exclusion requirement, the court may attach a power of arrest to the exclusion requirement.

(6)   Where the court attaches a power of arrest to an exclusion requirement of an interim care order, it may provide that the power of arrest is to have effect for a shorter period than the exclusion requirement.

(7)   Any period specified for the purposes of subsection (4) or (6) may be extended by the court (on one or more occasions) on an application to vary or discharge the interim care order.

(8)   Where a power of arrest is attached to an exclusion requirement of an interim care order by virtue of subsection (5), a constable may arrest without warrant any person whom he has reasonable cause to believe to be in breach of the requirement.

(9)   Sections 47(7), (11) and (12) and 48 of, and Schedule 5 to, the Family Law Act 1996 shall have effect in relation to a person arrested under subsection (8) of this section as they have effect in relation to a person arrested under section 47(6) of that Act.

(10)   If, while an interim care order containing an exclusion requirement is in force, the local authority have removed the child from the dwelling-house from which the relevant person is excluded to other accommodation for a continuous period of more than 24 hours, the interim care order shall cease to have effect in so far as it imposes the exclusion requirement.]

Date in force

Inserted by the Family Law Act 1996, Sch 6, para 1 as from 1 October 1997.

Definitions

For 'child', 'local authority' see s 105(1); for 'court' see s 92(7); for 'relevant person' see sub-s (2); for 'exclusion requirement' see sub-s (3).

Reference

For interim care orders see s 38 and see paras 4.53 to 4.56 of the revised Children Act 1989 Guidance and Regulations, Volume 1, Court Orders (2008) Department for Schools, Families and Children.

[38B   Undertakings relating to interim care orders]

[(1)   In any case where the court has power to include an exclusion requirement in an interim care order, the court may accept an undertaking from the relevant person.

(2)   No power of arrest may be attached to any undertaking given under subsection (1).

(3)   An undertaking given to a court under subsection (1)—

    (a)   shall be enforceable as if it were an order of the court, and
    (b)   shall cease to have effect if, while it is in force, the local authority have removed the child from the dwelling house from which the relevant person is excluded to other accommodation for a continuous period of more than 24 hours.

(4)   This section has effect without prejudice to the powers of the High Court and county court apart from this section.

(5)   In this section 'exclusion requirement' and 'relevant person' have the same meaning as in section 38A.]

Date in force

Inserted by the Family Law Act 1996, Sch 6, para 1 as from 1 October 1997.

Reference

For 'court' see s 92(7); for 'relevant person' and 'exclusion requirement' see sub-s (5) and s 38A(2)(3).

---

39   Discharge and variation etc of care orders and supervision orders

(1)   A care order may be discharged by the court on the application of—

(a)   any person who has parental responsibility for the child;
(b)   the child himself; or
(c)   the local authority designated by the order.

(2)   A supervision order may be varied or discharged by the court on the application of—

(a)   any person who has parental responsibility for the child;
(b)   the child himself; or
(c)   the supervisor.

(3)   On the application of a person who is not entitled to apply for the order to be discharged, but who is a person with whom the child is living, a supervision order may be varied by the court in so far as it imposes a requirement which affects that person.

[(3A)   On the application of a person who is not entitled to apply for the order to be discharged, but who is a person to whom an exclusion requirement contained in the order applies, an interim care order may be varied or discharged by the court in so far as it imposes the exclusion requirement.

(3B)   Where a power of arrest has been attached to an exclusion requirement of an interim care order, the court may, on the application of any person entitled to apply for the discharge of the order so far as it imposes the exclusion requirement, vary or discharge the order in so far as it confers a power of arrest (whether or not any application has been made to vary or discharge any other provision of the order).]

(4)   Where a care order is in force with respect to a child the court may, on the application of any person entitled to apply for the order to be discharged, substitute a supervision order for the care order.

(5)   When a court is considering whether to substitute one order for another under subsection (4) any provision of this Act which would otherwise require section 31(2) to be satisfied at the time when the proposed order is substituted or made shall be disregarded.

Date in force

14 October 1991: SI 1991/828.

Amendment

Sub-ss (3A), (3B): inserted by the Family Law Act 1996, s 52, Sch 6, para 2.

Definitions

For 'care order' see s 31(11) and s 105(1); for 'court' see s 92(7); for parental responsibility see s 3; for 'child', 'local authority', 'supervision' see s 105(1). For 'supervision order' see s 31(11); for 'exclusion requirement' see s 38A(3).

References

See generally paras 8.178 and 8.220 ff and paras 3.65 to 3.69 of the revised Children Act 1989 Guidance and Regulations, Volume 1, Court Orders (2008) Department for Schools, Families and Children. For jurisdiction of courts see s 92 and Sch 11, paras 4.3 ff; for attendance of child at hearing see s 95; for evidence given by or with respect to children see s 96; for self incrimination of witness see s 98; for 'family proceedings' under this Act see s 8(3), (4)(a); for limitation on repeated applications see s 91(14)(15).

Note

This section is silent on the test to be applied, but obviously the principles of s 1 must apply. While sub-ss (4) and (5) empower the court to substitute a supervision order for a care order solely on the application of those principles, substitution of a care order for a supervision order requires the conditions in s 31(2) to be satisfied again. The making of a residence order discharges a care order: s 91(1).

Sub-s (1)(b)

There is no need for the child first to apply for leave before making an application: *Re A (Care: Discharge Application by Child)* [1995] 2 FCR 686, [1995] 1 FLR 599.

---

40   Orders pending appeals in cases about care or supervision orders

(1)   Where—

    (a)   a court dismisses an application for a care order; and

    (b)   at the time when the court dismisses the application, the child concerned is the subject of an interim care order,

the court may make a care order with respect to the child to have effect subject to such directions (if any) as the court may see fit to include in the order.

(2)   Where—

    (a)   a court dismisses an application for a care order, or an application for a supervision order; and

    (b)   at the time when the court dismisses the application, the child concerned is the subject of an interim supervision order,

the court may make a supervision order with respect to the child to have effect subject to such directions (if any) as the court may see fit to include in the order.

(3)   Where a court grants an application to discharge a care order or supervision order, it may order that—

    (a)   its decision is not to have effect; or

    (b)   the care order, or supervision order, is to continue to have effect but subject to such directions as the court sees fit to include in the order.

(4)   An order made under this section shall only have effect for such period, not exceeding the appeal period, as may be specified in the order.

(5)   Where—

    (a)   an appeal is made against any decision of a court under this section; or

    (b)   any application is made to the appellate court in connection with a proposed appeal against that decision.

the appellate court may extend the period for which the order in question is to have effect, but not so as to extend it beyond the end of the appeal period.

(6)   In this section 'the appeal period' means—

    (a)   where an appeal is made against the decision in question, the period between the making of that decision and the determination of the appeal; and

    (b)   otherwise, the period during which an appeal may be made against the decision.

Date in force

14 October 1991: SI 1991/828.

Definitions

For 'court' see s 92(7); for 'care order' see s 31(11) and s 105(1); for 'child' see s 105(1); for 'supervision order' see s 31(11); for 'appeal period' see sub-s (6).

References

See para 8.225. For interim care and supervision orders see s 38; for discharge of care or supervision orders see s 39; for appeals see s 94 and the FPR 1991. Note the court may also make an order under s 8 with directions or conditions under s 11(7), pending the outcome of an appeal. The High Court has no power to make a care order pending the determination of the appeal. But can make a care order under s 38 of the Act: *Croydon London Borough Council v A (No 2)* [1992] 1WLR 984, [1992] 2 FCR 858.

[Representation of child]

41   **Representation of child and of his interests in certain proceedings**

(1)   For the purpose of any specified proceedings, the court shall appoint [an officer of the Service] [or a Welsh family proceedings officer] for the child concerned unless satisfied that it is not necessary to do so in order to safeguard his interests.

(2)   The [officer of the Service] [or Welsh family proceedings officer] shall—

    (a)   be appointed in accordance with the rules of court; and

    (b)   be under a duty to safeguard the interests of the child in the manner prescribed by such rules.

(3)   Where—

    (a)   the child concerned is not represented by a solicitor; and

    (b)   any of the conditions mentioned in subsection (4) is satisfied,

the court may appoint a solicitor to represent him.

(4)   The conditions are that—

    (a)   no [officer of the Service] [or Welsh family proceedings officer] has been appointed for the child;

    (b)   the child has sufficient understanding to instruct a solicitor and wishes to do so;

    (c)   it appears to the court that it would be in the child's best interests for him to be represented by a solicitor.

(5)   Any solicitor appointed under or by virtue of this section shall be appointed, and shall represent the child, in accordance with rules of court.

(6)   In this section 'specified proceedings' means any proceedings—

    (a)   on an application for a care order or supervision order;

(b) in which the court has given a direction under section 37(1) and has made, or is considering whether to make, an interim care order;

(c) on an application for the discharge of a care order or the variation or discharge of a supervision order;

(d) on an application under section 39(4);

(e) in which the court is considering whether to make a residence order with respect to a child who is the subject of a care order;

(f) with respect to contact between a child who is the subject of a care order and any other person;

(g) under Part V;

(h) on an appeal against—

    (i) the making of, or refusal to make, a care order, supervision order or any order under section 34;

    (ii) the making of, or refusal to make, a residence order with respect to a child who is the subject of a care order; or

    (iii) the variation or discharge, or refusal of an application to vary or discharge, an order of a kind mentioned in sub-paragraph (i) or (ii);

    (iv) the refusal of an application under section 39(4); or

    (v) the making of, or refusal to make, an order under Part V; or

[(hh) on an application for the making or revocation of a placement order (within the meaning of section 21 of the Adoption and Children Act 2002);]

(i) which are specified for the time being, for the purposes of this section, by rules of court.

[(6A) The proceedings which may be specified under subsection (6)(i) include (for example) proceedings for the making, varying or discharging of a section 8 order.]

(7) ...

(8) ...

(9) ...

(10) Rules of court may make provision as to—

(a) the assistance which any [officer of the Service] [or Welsh family proceedings officer] may be required by the court to give to it;

(b) the consideration to be given by any [officer of the Service] [or Welsh family proceedings officer], where an order of a specified kind has been made in the proceedings in question, as to whether to apply for the variation or discharge of the order;

(c) the participation of [officers of the Service] [or Welsh family proceedings officers] in reviews, of a kind specified in the rules, which are conducted by the court.

(11) Regardless of any enactment or rule of law which would otherwise prevent it from doing so, the court may take account of—

(a) any statement contained in a report made by [an officer of the Service] [or a Welsh family proceedings officer] who is appointed under this section for the purpose of the proceedings in question; and

(b) any evidence given in respect of the matters referred to in the report,

in so far as the statement or evidence is, in the opinion of the court, relevant to the question which the court is considering.

[(12) ...]

Date in force

14 October 1991: SI 1991/828.

Appendix 1 *Children Act 1989*

Amendment

Sub-s (1): words 'an officer of the Service' in square brackets substituted by the Criminal Justice and Court Services Act 2000, s 74, Sch 7, Pt II, paras 87, 91(a); words 'or a Welsh family proceedings officer' in square brackets inserted by the Children Act 2004, s 40, Sch 3, paras 5, 9(1), (2).
Sub-s (2): words 'officer of the Service' in square brackets substituted by the Criminal Justice and Court Services Act 2000, s 74, Sch 7, Pt II, paras 87, 91(b); words 'or Welsh family proceedings officer' in square brackets inserted by the Children Act 2004, s 40, Sch 3, paras 5, 9(1), (3).
Sub-s (4): in para (a) words 'officer of the Service' in square brackets substituted by the Criminal Justice and Court Services Act 2000, s 74, Sch 7, Pt II, paras 87, 91(b); in para (a) words 'or Welsh family proceedings officer' in square brackets inserted by the Children Act 2004, s 40, Sch 3, paras 5, 9(1), (3).
Sub-s (6): para (hh) inserted by the Adoption and Children Act 2002, s 122(1)(a).
Sub-s (6A): inserted by the Adoption and Children Act 2002, s 122(1)(b).
Sub-ss (7)–(9): repealed by the Criminal Justice and Court Services Act 2000, ss 74, 75, Sch 7, Pt II, paras 87, 91(d), Sch 8.
Sub-s (10): words 'officer of the Service' in square brackets in both places they occur substituted by the Criminal Justice and Court Services Act 2000, s 74, Sch 7, Pt II, paras 87, 91(b); in paras (a), (b) words 'or Welsh family proceedings officer' in square brackets inserted by the Children Act 2004, s 40, Sch 3, paras 5, 9(1), (4)(a); in para (c) words 'officers of the Service' in square brackets substituted by the Criminal Justice and Court Services Act 2000, s 74, Sch 7, Pt II, paras 87, 91(c); in para (c) words 'or Welsh family proceedings officers' in square brackets inserted by the Children Act 2004, s 40, Sch 3, paras 5, 9(1), (4)(b).
Sub-s (11): in para (a) words 'an officer of the Service' in square brackets substituted by the Criminal Justice and Court Services Act 2000, s 74, Sch 7, Pt II, paras 87, 91(a); in para (a) words 'or a Welsh family proceedings officer' in square brackets inserted by the Children Act 2004, s 40, Sch 3, paras 5, 9(1), (5).
Sub-s (12): inserted by the Courts and Legal Services Act 1990, s 116, Sch 16, para 17; repealed by the Criminal Justice and Court Services Act 2000, ss 74, 75, Sch 7, Pt II, paras 87, 91(d), Sch 8.

Definitions

For specified proceedings' and 'placement order' see sub-s (6); for 'court' see s 92(7); for 'child', prescribed', 'officer of the Service', 'Welsh family proceedings officer' see s 105(1); for 'care order' see s 31(11) and s 105(1); for 'supervision order' see s 31(11); for 'residence order' see s 8(1).

References

See generally Chapter 10 and in particular paras 10.35 ff. For the power to make interim care orders see s 38(1). Part V ie ss 43–52 (protection of children).

Sub-ss (2) and (10)

See the FPR 1991, r 4.10, and the FPC(CA 1989)R 1991, r 10. A children's guardian may be appointed by a single justice: FPC(CA 1989)R 1991, r 2(5).

Sub-s (5)

See para 10.41 for duties of the solicitor and *Re H (a minor) (care proceedings)* [1992] 2 FCR 330, [1993] 1 FLR 440, *Re M (Minors) (Care Proceedings)* [1994] 1 FCR 866, [1994] 1 FLR 749; and for duties re appeal, see R v Plymouth Juvenile Court, ex p F [1987] 1 FLR 169.

Sub-s (6)(i) and 10

An application under s 8 of the Act for a prohibited steps order is not a 'specified proceeding': *Re M (Prohibited Steps Order: Application for Leave)* [1993] 1 FCR 78, [1993] 1 FLR 275.For specified proceedings see also the FPR 1991, r 4.2 and the FPC(CA 1989)R 1991, r 2. As to the duties of the children's guardian see the FPR 1991, r 4.11 and 4.11A and the FPC(CA 1989)R 1991, r 11 and 11A.

Transfer of Functions

Functions of the Secretary of State, so far as exercisable in relation to Wales, transferred to the National Assembly for Wales, by the National Assembly for Wales (Transfer of Functions) Order 1999, SI 1999/672, art 2, Sch 1.

---

42   [Right of officer of the Service to have access to local authority records]

(1)   Where [an officer of the Service] [or Welsh family proceedings officer] has been appointed [under section 41] he shall have the right at all reasonable times to examine and take copies of—

(a)   any records of, or held by, a local authority [or an authorised person] which were compiled in connection with the making, or proposed making, by any person of any application under this Act with respect to the child concerned;
...

(b)   any ... records of, or held by, a local authority which were compiled in connection with any functions which [are social services functions within the meaning of] the Local Authority Social Services Act 1970, so far as those records relate to that child [; or

(c)   any records of, or held by, an authorised person which were compiled in connection with the activities of that person, so far as those records relate to that child].

(2)   Where [an officer of the Service] [or Welsh family proceedings officer] takes a copy of any record which he is entitled to examine under this section, that copy or any part of it shall be admissible as evidence of any matter referred to in any—

(a)   report which he makes to the court in the proceedings in question; or
(b)   evidence which he gives in those proceedings.

(3)   Subsection (2) has effect regardless of any enactment or rule of law which would otherwise prevent the record in question being admissible in evidence.

[(4)   In this section 'authorised person' has the same meaning as in section 31.]

Date in force

14 October 1991: SI 1991/828.

Amendments

Section heading: substituted by the Criminal Justice and Court Services Act 2000, s 74, Sch 7, Pt II, paras 87, 92(c); words 'an officer of the Service' in square brackets substituted by the Criminal Justice and Court Services Act 2000, s 74, Sch 7, Pt II, paras 87, 92(a)(i);words 'or Welsh family proceedings officer' in square brackets inserted by the Children Act 2004, s 40, Sch 3, paras 5, 10; words 'under section 41' in square brackets substituted by the Criminal Justice and Court Services Act 2000, s 74, Sch 7, Pt II, paras 87, 92(a)(ii); in para (a) words 'or an authorised person' in square brackets inserted by the Courts and Legal Services Act 1990, s 116, Sch 16, para 18(2); in para (a) words omitted repealed by the Courts and Legal Services Act 1990, s 125(7), Sch 20; in para (b) words omitted repealed by the Courts and Legal Services Act 1990, s 125(7), Sch 20; in para (b) words 'are social services functions within the meaning of' in square brackets substituted by the Local Government Act 2000, s 107, Sch 5, para 20; para (c) and word '; or' immediately preceding it inserted by the Courts and Legal Services Act 1990, s 116, Sch 16, para 18(3).
Sub-s (2): words 'an officer of the Service' in square brackets substituted by the Criminal Justice and Court Services Act 2000, s 74, Sch 7, Pt II, paras 87, 92(b); words 'or Welsh family proceedings officer' in square brackets inserted by the Children Act 2004, s 40, Sch 3, paras 5, 10.
Sub-s (4): inserted by the Courts and Legal Services Act 1990, s 116, Sch 16, para 18(4).

Appendix 1 *Children Act 1989*

Definitions

For 'officer of the Service', 'Welsh family proceedings officer', 'local authority' and 'child' see s 105(1). For 'authorised person' see sub-s (4).

References

For other evidential provisions see s 96; for the right of the children's guardian to examine records, see paras 10.47 and 11.65.

Records

Include the case record relating to prospective adopters: *Re T (a minor) (Guardian ad litem: case records)* [1994] 2 All ER 526, [1994] 1 FLR 632; and a document prepared by an Area Child Protection Committee for a 'Part 8 Review' (part 8 of the *Working Together under the Children Act 1989*) : *Re R (Care proceedings: Disclosure)* [2000] 3 FCR 721, [2000] 2 FLR 751, CA. If the document falls within CA 1989 s 42, public interest immunity does not arise so far as the guardian's inspection is concerned: *Re J (care proceedings: disclosure)* [2003] EWHC 976 (Fam), [2003] 2 FLR 522.

PART V

PROTECTION OF CHILDREN

43 Child assessment orders

(1) On the application of a local authority or authorised person for an order to be made under this section with respect to a child, the court may make the order if, but only if, it is satisfied that—

  (a) the applicant has reasonable cause to suspect that the child is suffering, or is likely to suffer, significant harm;
  (b) an assessment of the state of the child's health or development, or of the way in which he has been treated, is required to enable the applicant to determine whether or not the child is suffering, or is likely to suffer, significant harm; and
  (c) it is unlikely that such an assessment will be made, or be satisfactory, in the absence of an order under this section.

(2) In this Act 'a child assessment order' means an order under this section.

(3) A court may treat an application under this section as an application for an emergency protection order.

(4) No court shall make a child assessment order if it is satisfied—

  (a) that there are grounds for making an emergency protection order with respect to the child; and
  (b) that it ought to make such an order rather than a child assessment order.

(5) A child assessment order shall—

  (a) specify the date by which the assessment is to begin; and
  (b) have effect for such period, not exceeding 7 days beginning with that date, as may be specified in the order.

(6) Where a child assessment order is in force with respect to a child it shall be the duty of any person who is in a position to produce the child—

  (a) to produce him to such person as may be named in the order; and
  (b) to comply with such directions relating to the assessment of the child as the court thinks fit to specify in the order.

(7)   A child assessment order authorises any person carrying out the assessment, or any part of the assessment, to do so in accordance with the terms of the order.

(8)   Regardless of subsection (7), if the child is of sufficient understanding to make an informed decision he may refuse to submit to a medical or psychiatric examination or other assessment.

(9)   The child may only be kept away from home—

   (a)   in accordance with directions specified in the order;
   (b)   if it is necessary for the purposes of the assessment; and
   (c)   for such period or periods as may be specified in the order.

(10)   Where the child is to be kept away from home, the order shall contain such directions as the court thinks fit with regard to the contact that he must be allowed to have with other persons while away from home.

(11)   Any person making an application for a child assessment order shall take such steps as are reasonably practicable to ensure that notice of the application is given to—

   (a)   the child's parents;
   (b)   any person who is not a parent of his but who has parental responsibility for him;
   (c)   any other person caring for the child;
   (d)   any person in whose favour a contact order is in force with respect to the child;
   (e)   any person who is allowed to have contact with the child by virtue of an order under section 34; and
   (f)   the child,

before the hearing of the application.

(12)   Rules of court may make provision as to the circumstances in which—

   (a)   any of the persons mentioned in subsection (11); or
   (b)   such other person as may be specified in the rules,

may apply to the court for a child assessment order to be varied or discharged.

(13)   In this section 'authorised person' means a person who is an authorised person for the purposes of section 31.

Date in force

14 October 1991: SI 1991/828.

Definitions

For 'local authority' and 'child' see s 105(1); for 'authorised person' see sub-s (13); for 'court' see s 92(7); for 'harm' see s 31(9) as applied to the whole Act by s 105(1) and as to whether harm is significant see s 31(10) as applied to the whole Act by s 105(1); for 'a child assessment order' see sub-s (2); for 'emergency protection order' see s 44(4) as applied to the whole Act by s 105(1); for 'parental responsibility' see s 3; for 'contact order' see s 8(1).

References

See generally Chapter 7, paras 7.53 ff and paras 4.10 to 4.24 of the revised Children Act 1989 Guidance and Regulations, Volume 1, Court Orders (2008) Department for Schools, Families and Children. Proceedings must be commenced in the magistrates' court: Children (Allocation of Proceedings) Order 1991, r 3, see para 4.15. For jurisdiction of courts see s 92 and Sch 11, para 4.5; for attendance of child at hearing see s 95 and the Children (Admissibility of Hearsay Evidence) Order 1991; for evidence given by or with respect to children see s 96; for self-incrimination of witness see s 98.

Appendix 1   *Children Act 1989*

Rules of court

See FPC(CA 1989)R 1991, r 2(3).

---

44   Orders for emergency protection of children

(1)   Where any person ('the applicant') applies to the court for an order to be made under this section with respect to a child, the court may make the order if, but only if, it is satisfied that—

(a)   there is reasonable cause to believe that the child is likely to suffer significant harm if—
  (i)   he is not removed to accommodation provided by or on behalf of the applicant; or
  (ii)   he does not remain in the place in which he is then being accommodated;
(b)   in the case of an application made by a local authority—
  (i)   enquiries are being made with respect to the child under section 47(1)(b); and
  (ii)   those enquiries are being frustrated by access to the child being unreasonably refused to a person authorised to seek access and that the applicant has reasonable cause to believe that access to the child is required as a matter of urgency; or
(c)   in the case of an application made by an authorised person—
  (i)   the applicant has reasonable cause to suspect that a child is suffering, or is likely to suffer, significant harm;
  (ii)   the applicant is making enquiries with respect to the child's welfare; and
  (iii)   those enquiries are being frustrated by access to the child being unreasonably refused to a person authorised to seek access and the applicant has reasonable cause to believe that access to the child is required as a matter of urgency.

(2)   In this section—

(a)   'authorised person' means a person who is an authorised person for the purposes of section 31; and
(b)   'a person authorised to seek access' means—
  (i)   in the case of an application by a local authority, an officer of the local authority or a person authorised by the authority to act on their behalf in connection with the enquiries; or
  (ii)   in the case of an application by an authorised person, that person.

(3)   Any person—

(a)   seeking access to a child in connection with enquiries of a kind mentioned in subsection (1); and
(b)   purporting to be a person authorised to do so,

shall, on being asked to do so, produce some duly authenticated document as evidence that he is such a person.

(4)   While an order under this section ('an emergency protection order') is in force it—

(a)   operates as a direction to any person who is in a position to do so to comply with any request to produce the child to the applicant;
(b)   authorises—
  (i)   the removal of the child at any time to accommodation provided by or on behalf of the applicant and his being kept there; or
  (ii)   the prevention of the child's removal from any hospital, or other place, in which he was being accommodated immediately before the making of the order; and

(c)   gives the applicant parental responsibility for the child.

(5)   Where an emergency protection order is in force with respect to a child, the applicant—

   (a)   shall only exercise the power given by virtue of subsection (4)(b) in order to safeguard the welfare of the child;
   (b)   shall take, and shall only take, such action in meeting his parental responsibility for the child as is reasonably required to safeguard or promote the welfare of the child (having regard in particular to the duration of the order); and
   (c)   shall comply with the requirements of any regulations made by the Secretary of State for the purposes of this subsection.

(6)   Where the court makes an emergency protection order, it may give such directions (if any) as it considers appropriate with respect to—

   (a)   the contact which is, or is not, to be allowed between the child and any named person;
   (b)   the medical or psychiatric examination or other assessment of the child.

(7)   Where any direction is given under subsection (6)(b), the child may, if he is of sufficient understanding to make an informed decision, refuse to submit to the examination or other assessment.

(8)   A direction under subsection (6)(a) may impose conditions and one under subsection (6)(b) may be to the effect that there is to be—

   (a)   no such examination or assessment; or
   (b)   no such examination or assessment unless the court directs otherwise.

(9)   A direction under subsection (6) may be—

   (a)   given when the emergency protection order is made or at any time while it is in force; and
   (b)   varied at any time on the application of any person falling within any class of person prescribed by rules of court for the purposes of this subsection.

(10)   Where an emergency protection order is in force with respect to a child and—

   (a)   the applicant has exercised the power given by subsection (4)(b)(i) but it appears to him that it is safe for the child to be returned; or
   (b)   the applicant has exercised the power given by subsection (4)(b)(ii) but it appears to him that it is safe for the child to be allowed to be removed from the place in question,

he shall return the child or (as the case may be) allow him to be removed.

(11)   Where he is required by subsection (10) to return the child the applicant shall—

   (a)   return him to the care of the person from whose care he was removed; or
   (b)   if that is not reasonably practicable, return him to the care of—
      (i)   a parent of his;
      (ii)   any person who is not a parent of his but who has parental responsibility for him; or
      (iii)   such other person as the applicant (with the agreement of the court) considers appropriate.

(12)   Where the applicant has been required by subsection (10) to return the child, or to allow him to be removed, he may again exercise his powers with respect to the child (at any time while the emergency protection order remains in force) if it appears to him that a change in the circumstances of the case makes it necessary for him to do so.

745

(13)   Where an emergency protection order has been made with respect to a child, the applicant shall, subject to any direction given under subsection (6), allow the child reasonable contact with—

   (a)   his parents;

   (b)   any person who is not a parent of his but who has parental responsibility for him;

   (c)   any person with whom he was living immediately before the making of the order;

   (d)   any person in whose favour a contact order is in force with respect to him;

   (e)   any person who is allowed to have contact with the child by virtue of an order under section 34; and

   (f)   any person acting on behalf of any of those persons.

(14)   Wherever it is reasonably practicable to do so, an emergency protection order shall name the child; and where it does not name him it shall describe him as clearly as possible.

(15)   A person shall be guilty of an offence if he intentionally obstructs any person exercising the power under subsection (4)(b) to remove, or prevent the removal of, a child.

(16)   A person guilty of an offence under subsection (15) shall be liable on summary conviction to a fine not exceeding level 3 on the standard scale.

Date in force

14 October 1991: SI 1991/828.

Definitions

For 'court' see s 92(7); for 'child', 'local authority', 'hospital' see s 105(1); for 'harm' see s 31(9) as applied to the whole Act by s 105(1) and as to whether harm is significant see s 31(10) as applied to the whole Act by s 105(1); for 'applicant' see sub-s (1); for 'a person authorised to seek access' see sub-s (2)(b); for 'authorised person' see sub-s (2)(a); for 'emergency protection order' see sub-s (4); for 'parental responsibility' see s 3; for 'contact order' see s 8(1).

References

See generally Chapter 7 and in particular paras 7.63 ff and the FPC(CA 1989)R 1991. For welfare of the child as paramount consideration see s 1(1). For jurisdiction of courts see s 92 and Sch 11, paras 4.5 ff; for attendance of child at hearing see s 95, FPR 1991, r 4.16 and FPC(CA 1989)R 1991, r 16; for evidence given by or with respect to children see s 45(7), s 96, and and paras 4.25 to 4.63 of the revised Children Act 1989 Guidance and Regulations, Volume 1, Court Orders (2008) Department for Schools, Families and Children, and the Children (Admissibility of Hearsay Evidence) Order 1993; for self-incrimination of witness see s 98; for application by the police when child is in police protection see s 46(7), (8); for power to include exclusion requirement in emergency protection order see s 44A; for undertakings relating to emergency protection orders see s 44B; for duration of an emergency protection order see s 45; for duty of local authority to make inquiries with respect to certain children to enable them to decide whether they should take any action to safeguard or promote the child's welfare see s 47(1); for powers to assist in discovery of children who may be in need of emergency protection see s 48; for local authority responsibility in relation to accommodation see s 21; for 'the standard scale' see the CJA 1982, s 37(2), (3) as amended; for 'likely to suffer significant harm', see paras 7.66 ff and 8.19 ff and *Newham London Borough v AG* [1992] 2 FCR 119, CA.

Transfer of functions

Functions of the Secretary of State, so far as exercisable in relation to Wales, transferred to the National Assembly for Wales, by the National Assembly for Wales (Transfer of Functions) Order 1999, SI 1999/672, art 2, Sch 1.

Sub-s (1)

This application may be made ex parte to a single justice with the leave of the justices' clerk: FPC(CA 1989)R 1991, rr 2 and 4. Where the applicant is not the authority in whose area the child is ordinarily resident, that authority may have responsibility transferred to it: Emergency Protection Order (Transfer of Responsibilities) Regulations 1991, SI 1991/1414.

Sub-s (9) Rules

See the FPC(CA 1989)R 1991, r 2(4).

Sub-s (11) Agreement of the court

Agreement may be given by a single justice: FPC(CA 1989)R 1991, r 2(5).

[44A   Power to include exclusion requirement in emergency protection order]

[(1)   Where—

(a)   on being satisfied as mentioned in section 44(1)(a), (b) or (c), the court makes an emergency protection order with respect to a child, and
(b)   the conditions mentioned in subsection (2) are satisfied,

the court may include an exclusion requirement in the emergency protection order.

(2)   The conditions are—

(a)   that there is reasonable cause to believe that, if a person ('the relevant person') is excluded from a dwelling-house in which the child lives, then—
  (i)   in the case of an order made on the ground mentioned in section 44(1)(a), the child will not be likely to suffer significant harm, even though the child is not removed as mentioned in section 44(1)(a)(i) or does not remain as mentioned in section 44(1)(a)(ii), or
  (ii)   in the case of an order made on the ground mentioned in paragraph (b) or (c) of section 44(1), the enquiries referred to in that paragraph will cease to be frustrated, and
(b)   that another person living in the dwelling-house (whether a parent of the child or some other person)—
  (i)   is able and willing to give to the child the care which it would be reasonable to expect a parent to give him, and
  (ii)   consents to the inclusion of the exclusion requirement.

(3)   For the purposes of this section an exclusion requirement is any one or more of the following—

(a)   a provision requiring the relevant person to leave a dwelling-house in which he is living with the child,
(b)   a provision prohibiting the relevant person from entering a dwelling-house in which the child lives, and
(c)   a provision excluding the relevant person from a defined area in which a dwelling-house in which the child lives is situated.

(4)   The court may provide that the exclusion requirement is to have effect for a shorter period than the other provisions of the order.

(5)   Where the court makes an emergency protection order containing an exclusion requirement, the court may attach a power of arrest to the exclusion requirement.

(6)   Where the court attaches a power of arrest to an exclusion requirement of an emergency protection order, it may provide that the power of arrest is to have effect for a shorter period than the exclusion requirement.

(7) Any period specified for the purposes of subsection (4) or (6) may be extended by the court (on one or more occasions) on an application to vary or discharge the emergency protection order.

(8) Where a power of arrest is attached to an exclusion requirement of an emergency protection order by virtue of subsection (5), a constable may arrest without warrant any person whom he has reasonable cause to believe to be in breach of the requirement.

(9) Sections 47(7), (11) and (12) and 48 of, and Schedule 5 to, the Family Law Act 1996 shall have effect in relation to a person arrested under subsection (8) of this section as they have effect in relation to a person arrested under section 47(6) of that Act.

(10) If, while an emergency protection order containing an exclusion requirement is in force, the applicant has removed the child from the dwelling-house from which the relevant person is excluded to other accommodation for a continuous period of more than 24 hours, the order shall cease to have effect in so far as it imposes the exclusion requirement.]

Amendment

Inserted by the Family Law Act 1996, Sch 6, para 3.

Definitions

For 'court' see s 92(7); for 'child' see s 105(1); for 'exclusion requirement' see sub-s (3); for 'relevant person' see sub-s (2); for 'harm' see s 31(9) as applied to the whole Act by s 105(1); and as to whether harm is significant see s 31(10) as applied to the whole Act by s 105(1).

Reference

See para 7.93.

[44B   Undertakings relating to emergency protection orders]

[(1) In any case where the court has power to include an exclusion requirement in an emergency protection order, the court may accept an undertaking from the relevant person.

(2) No power of arrest may be attached to any undertaking given under subsection (1).

(3) An undertaking given to a court under subsection (1)—

  (a) shall be enforceable as if it were an order of the court, and
  (b) shall cease to have effect if, while it is in force, the applicant has removed the child from the dwelling-house from which the relevant person is excluded to other accommodation for a continuous period of more than 24 hours.

(4) This section has effect without prejudice to the powers of the High Court and county court apart from this section.

(5) In this section 'exclusion requirement' and 'relevant person' have the same meaning as in section 44A.]

Date in force

Inserted by the Family Law Act 1996, Sch 6, para 3 as from.

Definitions

For 'court' see s 92(7); for 'child' see s 105(1); for 'exclusion requirement' see sub-s (5); for 'relevant person' see sub-s (5).

---

45   Duration of emergency protection orders and other supplemental provisions

(1)   An emergency protection order shall have effect for such period, not exceeding eight days, as may be specified in the order.

(2)   Where—

    (a)   the court making an emergency protection order would, but for this subsection, specify a period of eight days as the period for which the order is to have effect; but

    (b)   the last of those eight days is a public holiday (that is to say, Christmas Day, Good Friday, a bank holiday or a Sunday),

the court may specify a period which ends at noon on the first later day which is not such a holiday.

(3)   Where an emergency protection order is made on an application under section 46(7), the period of eight days mentioned in subsection (1) shall begin with the first day on which the child was taken into police protection under section 46.

(4)   Any person who—

    (a)   has parental responsibility for a child as the result of an emergency protection order; and

    (b)   is entitled to apply for a care order with respect to the child,

may apply to the court for the period during which the emergency protection order is to have effect to be extended.

(5)   On an application under subsection (4) the court may extend the period during which the order is to have effect by such period, not exceeding seven days, as it thinks fit, but may do so only if it has reasonable cause to believe that the child concerned is likely to suffer significant harm if the order is not extended.

(6)   An emergency protection order may only be extended once.

(7)   Regardless of any enactment or rule of law which would otherwise prevent it from doing so, a court hearing an application for, or with respect to, an emergency protection order may take account of—

    (a)   any statement contained in any report made to the court in the course of, or in connection with, the hearing; or

    (b)   any evidence given during the hearing,

which is, in the opinion of the court, relevant to the application.

(8)   Any of the following may apply to the court for an emergency protection order to be discharged—

    (a)   the child;

    (b)   a parent of his;

    (c)   any person who is not a parent of his but who has parental responsibility for him; or

    (d)   any person with whom he was living immediately before the making of the order.

[(8A)   On the application of a person who is not entitled to apply for the order to be discharged, but who is a person to whom an exclusion requirement contained in the

749

order applies, an emergency protection order may be varied or discharged by the court in so far as it imposes the exclusion requirement.

(8B)   Where a power of arrest has been attached to an exclusion requirement of an emergency protection order, the court may, on the application of any person entitled to apply for the discharge of the order so far as it imposes the exclusion requirement, vary or discharge the order in so far as it confers a power of arrest (whether or not any application has been made to vary or discharge any other provision of the order).]

(9)   No application for the discharge of an emergency protection order shall be heard by the court before the expiry of the period of 72 hours beginning with the making of the order.

[(10)   No appeal may be made against—

(a)   the making of, or refusal to make, an emergency protection order;
(b)   the extension of, or refusal to extend, the period during which such an order is to have effect;
(c)   the discharge of, or refusal to discharge, such an order; or
(d)   the giving of, or refusal to give, any direction in connection with such an order.]

(11)   Subsection (8) does not apply—

(a)   where the person who would otherwise be entitled to apply for the emergency protection order to be discharged—
(i)   was given notice (in accordance with rules of court) of the hearing at which the order was made; and
(ii)   was present at that hearing; or
(b)   to any emergency protection order the effective period of which has been extended under subsection (5).

(12)   A court making an emergency protection order may direct that the applicant may in exercising any powers which he has by virtue of the order, be accompanied by a registered medical practitioner, registered nurse or [registered midwife], if he so chooses.

[(13)   The reference in subsection (12) to a registered midwife is to such a midwife who is also registered in the Specialist Community Public Health Nurses' Part of the register maintained under article 5 of the Nursing and Midwifery Order 2001.]

Date in force

14 October 1991: SI 1991/828.

Amendment

Sub-ss (8A), (8B): inserted by the Family Law Act 1996, s 52, Sch 6, para 4.
Sub-s (10): substituted by the Courts and Legal Services Act 1990, s 116, Sch 16, para 19.
Sub-s (12): words 'registered midwife' in square brackets substituted by SI 2002/253, art 54(3), Sch 5, para 10(a).
Sub-s (13): inserted by SI 2004/1771, art 3, Schedule, Pt 1, para 4(a).

Definitions

For 'emergency protection order' see s 44(4); for 'court' see s 92(7); for 'bank holiday', 'child' see s 105(1); for 'parental responsibility' see s 3; for 'care order' see s 31(11); for 'harm' see s 31(9) as applied to the whole Act by s 105(1); and as to whether harm is significant see s 31(10) as applied to the whole Act by s 105(1); for 'applicant' see s 44(1); for 'exclusion requirement' see s 44A(3).

References

See generally paras 7.95 ff and and paras 4.57 and 4.58 of the revised Children Act 1989 Guidance and Regulations, Volume 1, Court Orders (2008) Department for Schools, Families and Children. For persons entitled to apply for care order see s 31(1)(9); for 'parent' see para 3.43; for further provisions see note to s 44; for jurisdiction of courts see s 92(7) and Sch 11, paras 4.5 ff.

Sub-s (4)

Any person other than the local authority or the NSPCC who has obtained an emergency protection order under s 44, cannot obtain an extension of the order, since they are not entitled to apply for a care order: see s 31(1) and (9).

Sub-s (10)

There is no appeal procedure under this section; refusal includes any decision not to make an order: *Essex County Council v F* [1993] 1 FLR 847, see para 7.97.

---

46   Removal and accommodation of children by police in cases of emergency

(1)   Where a constable has reasonable cause to believe that a child would otherwise be likely to suffer significant harm, he may—

(a)   remove the child to suitable accommodation and keep him there; or

(b)   take such steps as are reasonable to ensure that the child's removal from any hospital, or other place, in which he is then being accommodated is prevented.

(2)   For the purposes of this Act, a child with respect to whom a constable has exercised his powers under this section is referred to as having been taken into police protection.

(3)   As soon as is reasonably practicable after taking a child into police protection, the constable concerned shall—

(a)   inform the local authority within whose area the child was found of the steps that have been, and are proposed to be, taken with respect to the child under this section and the reasons for taking them;

(b)   give details to the authority within whose area the child is ordinarily resident ('the appropriate authority') of the place at which the child is being accommodated;

(c)   inform the child (if he appears capable of understanding)—
(i)   of the steps that have been taken with respect to him under this section and of the reasons for taking them; and
(ii)   of the further steps that may be taken with respect to him under this section;

(d)   take such steps as are reasonably practicable to discover the wishes and feelings of the child;

(e)   secure that the case is inquired into by an officer designated for the purposes of this section by the chief officer of the police area concerned; and

(f)   where the child was taken into police protection by being removed to accommodation which is not provided—
(i)   by or on behalf of a local authority; or
(ii)   as a refuge, in compliance with the requirements of section 51,
secure that he is moved to accommodation which is so provided.

(4)   As soon as is reasonably practicable after taking a child into police protection, the constable concerned shall take such steps as are reasonably practicable to inform—

(a)   the child's parents;

(b)   every person who is not a parent of his but who has parental responsibility for him; and

751

> (c)   any other person with whom the child was living immediately before being taken into police protection,

of the steps that he has taken under this section with respect to the child, the reasons for taking them and the further steps that may be taken with respect to him under this section.

(5)   On completing any inquiry under subsection (3)(e), the officer conducting it shall release the child from police protection unless he considers that there is still reasonable cause for believing that the child would be likely to suffer significant harm if released.

(6)   No child may be kept in police protection for more than 72 hours.

(7)   While a child is being kept in police protection, the designated officer may apply on behalf of the appropriate authority for an emergency protection order to be made under section 44 with respect to the child.

(8)   An application may be made under subsection (7) whether or not the authority know of it or agree to its being made.

(9)   While a child is being kept in police protection—

> (a)   neither the constable concerned nor the designated officer shall have parental responsibility for him; but
> (b)   the designated officer shall do what is reasonable in all the circumstances of the case for the purpose of safeguarding or promoting the child's welfare (having regard in particular to the length of the period during which the child will be so protected).

(10)   Where a child has been taken into police protection, the designated officer shall allow—

> (a)   the child's parents;
> (b)   any person who is not a parent of the child but who has parental responsibility for him;
> (c)   any person with whom the child was living immediately before he was taken into police protection;
> (d)   any person in whose favour a contact order is in force with respect to the child;
> (e)   any person who is allowed to have contact with the child by virtue of an order under section 34; and
> (f)   any person acting on behalf of any of those persons,

to have such contact (if any) with the child as, in the opinion of the designated officer, is both reasonable and in the child's best interests.

(11)   Where a child who has been taken into police protection is in accommodation provided by, or on behalf of, the appropriate authority, subsection (10) shall have effect as if it referred to the authority rather than to the designated officer.

Date in force

14 October 1991: SI 1991/828.

Definitions

For 'child', 'hospital' and 'local authority' see s 105(1); for 'harm' see s 31(9) as applied to the whole Act by s 105(1) and as to whether harm is significant see s 31(10) as applied to the whole Act by s 105(1); for 'police protection' see sub-s (2); for 'ordinary residence' see s 105(6); for 'appropriate authority' see sub-s (3)(b); for 'emergency protection order' see s 44(4); for 'designated officer' see sub-s (3)(e). For 'parental responsibility' see s 3; for 'contact order' see s 8(1).

References

See generally paras 7.88 ff and and paras 4.64 to 4.72 of the revised Children Act 1989 Guidance and Regulations, Volume 1, Court Orders (2008) Department for Schools, Families and Children. For 'parent' see para 3.43; for the maximum duration of an emergency protection order taken under sub-s (7) see s 45(3); for the welfare of the child the paramount consideration see s 1(1); for duty of local authority to make inquiries with respect to certain children to enable them to decide whether they should take any action to safeguard or promote the child's welfare see s 47(1); for powers to assist in discovery of children who may be in need of emergency protection see s 48; for local authority responsibility in relation to accommodation see s 21; for refuges for children at risk see s 51. A constable is not precluded from using this power where the statutory criteria are satisfied because an emergency protection order is in force *Langley v Liverpool City Council* [2005] EWCA Civ 1173, [2006] 2 All ER 202, [2006] 1 WLR 375, [2005] 3 FCR 303.

Sub-s (6)

'72 hours' in this section, the period is not extended by public holidays. Cf s 45(2).

Sub-s (7)

The maximum period of eight days for such an order begins with the first day on which the child is taken into police protection: s 45(3).

---

47   Local authority's duty to investigate

(1)   Where a local authority—

(a)   are informed that a child who lives, or is found, in their area—
    (i)   is the subject of an emergency protection order; or
    (ii)   is in police protection; or
    [(iii)   has contravened a ban imposed by a curfew notice within the meaning of Chapter I of Part I of the Crime and Disorder Act 1998; or]
(b)   have reasonable cause to suspect that a child who lives, or is found, in their area is suffering, or is likely to suffer, significant harm,

the authority shall make, or cause to be made, such enquiries as they consider necessary to enable them to decide whether they should take any action to safeguard or promote the child's welfare.

[In the case of a child falling within paragraph (a)(iii) above, the enquiries shall be commenced as soon as practicable and, in any event, within 48 hours of the authority receiving the information.]

(2)   Where a local authority have obtained an emergency protection order with respect to a child, they shall make, or cause to be made, such enquiries as they consider necessary to enable them to decide what action they should take to safeguard or promote the child's welfare.

(3)   The enquiries shall, in particular, be directed towards establishing—

(a)   whether the authority should make any application to the court, or exercise any of their other powers under this Act [or section 11 of the Crime and Disorder Act 1998 (child safety orders)], with respect to the child;
(b)   whether, in the case of a child—
    (i)   with respect to whom an emergency protection order has been made; and
    (ii)   who is not in accommodation provided by or on behalf of the authority,
it would be in the child's best interests (while an emergency protection order remains in force) for him to be in such accommodation; and
(c)   whether, in the case of a child who has been taken into police protection, it would be in the child's best interests for the authority to ask for an application to be made under section 46(7).

(4)   Where enquiries are being made under subsection (1) with respect to a child, the local authority concerned shall (with a view to enabling them to determine what action, if any, to take with respect to him) take such steps as are reasonably practicable—

    (a) to obtain access to him; or

    (b) to ensure that access to him is obtained, on their behalf, by a person authorised by them for the purpose,

unless they are satisfied that they already have sufficient information with respect to him.

(5)   Where, as a result of any such enquiries, it appears to the authority that there are matters connected with the child's education which should be investigated, they shall consult the relevant local education authority.

[(5A)   For the purposes of making a determination under this section as to the action to be taken with respect to a child, a local authority shall, so far as is reasonably practicable and consistent with the child's welfare—

    (a) ascertain the child's wishes and feelings regarding the action to be taken with respect to him; and

    (b) give due consideration (having regard to his age and understanding) to such wishes and feelings of the child as they have been able to ascertain.]

(6)   Where, in the course of enquiries made under this section—

    (a) any officer of the local authority concerned; or

    (b) any person authorised by the authority to act on their behalf in connection with those enquiries—

        (i) is refused access to the child concerned; or

        (ii) is denied information as to his whereabouts,

the authority shall apply for an emergency protection order, a child assessment order, a care order or a supervision order with respect to the child unless they are satisfied that his welfare can be satisfactorily safeguarded without their doing so.

(7)   If, on the conclusion of any enquiries or review made under this section, the authority decide not to apply for an emergency protection order, a child assessment order, a care order or a supervision order they shall—

    (a) consider whether it would be appropriate to review the case at a later date; and

    (b) if they decide that it would be, determine the date on which that review is to begin.

(8)   Where, as a result of complying with this section, a local authority conclude that they should take action to safeguard or promote the child's welfare they shall take that action (so far as it is both within their power and reasonably practicable for them to do so).

(9)   Where a local authority are conducting enquiries under this section, it shall be the duty of any person mentioned in subsection (11) to assist them with those enquiries (in particular by providing relevant information and advice) if called upon by the authority to do so.

(10)   Subsection (9) does not oblige any person to assist a local authority where doing so would be unreasonable in all the circumstances of the case.

(11)   The persons are—

    (a) any local authority;

    (b) any local education authority;

(c)   any local housing authority;

(d)   any [[Local Health Board], Special Health Authority][, Primary Care Trust][, National Health Service trust or NHS foundation trust]; and

(e)   any person authorised by the Secretary of State for the purposes of this section.

(12)   Where a local authority are making enquiries under this section with respect to a child who appears to them to be ordinarily resident within the area of another authority, they shall consult that other authority, who may undertake the necessary enquiries in their place.

Date in force

14 October 1991: SI 1991/828.

Amendment

Sub-s (1): para (a)(iii) inserted by the Crime and Disorder Act 1998, s 15(4)(a); words from 'In the case' to 'the information.' in square brackets inserted by the Crime and Disorder Act 1998, s 15(4)(b).

Sub-s (3): words from 'or section 11' to '(child safety orders)' in square brackets inserted by the Crime and Disorder Act 1998, s 119, Sch 8, para 69.

Sub-s (5A): inserted by the Children Act 2004, s 53(3).

Sub-s (11): in para (d) words in square brackets ending with the words 'Special Health Authority' substituted by the Health Authorities Act 1995, s 2(1), Sch 1, para 118(7); in para (d) words 'Local Health Board' in square brackets substituted by SI 2007/961, art 3, Schedule, para 20(1), (2)(f); in para (d) words ', Primary Care Trust' in square brackets inserted by SI 2000/90, art 3(1), Sch 1, para 24(1), (7); in para (d) words ', National Health Service trust or NHS foundation trust' in square brackets substituted by the Health and Social Care (Community Health and Standards) Act 2003, s 34, Sch 4, paras 75, 79.

Definitions

For 'local authority', 'child', 'local education authority', 'local housing authority', 'health authority', ' Special Health Authority', 'Primary Care Trust', 'National Health Service Trust' see s 105(1); for 'emergency protection order' see s 44(4); for 'police protection' see s 46(2); for 'harm' see s 31(9) as applied to the whole Act by s 105(1); as to whether harm is significant see s 31(10) as applied to the whole Act by s 105(1); for 'court' see s 92(7); for 'accommodation provided by or on behalf of a local authority' see s 105(5); for 'care order', 'supervision order' see s 31(11); for 'ordinary residence' see s 105(6). For 'child assessment order' see s 43(2).

References

See generally paras 7.7 ff and and paras 4.73 to 4.82 of the revised Children Act 1989 Guidance and Regulations, Volume 1, Court Orders (2008) Department for Schools, Families and Children and *Handbook of Best Practice in Children Act Cases* in *Clarke Hall and Morrison on Children* at para 1[20001]. For welfare of the child the paramount consideration see s 1(1); for emergency protection orders see s 44 and for child assessment orders see s 43.

Transfer of functions

Functions of the Secretary of State, so far as exercisable in relation to Wales, transferred to the National Assembly for Wales, by the National Assembly for Wales (Transfer of Functions) Order 1999, SI 1999/672, art 2, Sch 1.

Sub-s (1) Reasonable cause to suspect

Ie a local authority is not required to make a finding on the balance of probabilities as to past conduct before assessing risk and taking any necessary steps: *Re S (sexual abuse allegations: local authority response)* [2001] EWHC Admin 334, [2001] 3 FCR 702, [2001] 2 FLR 776.

Appendix 1   *Children Act 1989*

48   **Powers to assist in discovery of children who may be in need of emergency protection**

(1)   Where it appears to a court making an emergency protection order that adequate information as to the child's whereabouts—

    (a)   is not available to the applicant for the order; but
    (b)   is available to another person,

it may include in the order a provision requiring that other person to disclose, if asked to do so by the applicant, any information that he may have as to the child's whereabouts.

(2)   No person shall be excused from complying with such a requirement on the ground that complying might incriminate him or his spouse [or civil partner] of an offence; but a statement or admission made in complying shall not be admissible in evidence against either of them in proceedings for any offence other than perjury.

(3)   An emergency protection order may authorise the applicant to enter premises specified by the order and search for the child with respect to whom the order is made.

(4)   Where the court is satisfied that there is reasonable cause to believe that there may be another child on those premises with respect to whom an emergency protection order ought to be made, it may make an order authorising the applicant to search for that other child on those premises.

(5)   Where—

    (a)   an order has been made under subsection (4);
    (b)   the child concerned has been found on the premises; and
    (c)   the applicant is satisfied that the grounds for making an emergency protection order exist with respect to him,

the order shall have effect as if it were an emergency protection order.

(6)   Where an order has been made under subsection (4), the applicant shall notify the court of its effect.

(7)   A person shall be guilty of an offence if he intentionally obstructs any person exercising the power of entry and search under subsection (3) or (4).

(8)   A person guilty of an offence under subsection (7) shall be liable on summary conviction to a fine not exceeding level 3 on the standard scale.

(9)   Where, on an application made by any person for a warrant under this section, it appears to the court—

    (a)   that a person attempting to exercise powers under an emergency protection order has been prevented from doing so by being refused entry to the premises concerned or access to the child concerned; or
    (b)   that any such person is likely to be so prevented from exercising any such powers,

it may issue a warrant authorising any constable to assist the person mentioned in paragraph (*a*) or (*b*) in the exercise of those powers, using reasonable force if necessary.

(10)   Every warrant issued under this section shall be addressed to, and executed by, a constable who shall be accompanied by the person applying for the warrant if—

    (a)   that person so desires; and
    (b)   the court by whom the warrant is issued does not direct otherwise.

(11)   A court granting an application for a warrant under this section may direct that the constable concerned may, in executing the warrant, be accompanied by a registered medical practitioner, registered nurse or [registered midwife] if he so chooses.

[(11A)   The reference in subsection (11) to a registered midwife is to such a midwife who is also registered in the Specialist Community Public Health Nurses' Part of the register maintained under article 5 of the Nursing and Midwifery Order 2001.]

(12)   An application for a warrant under this section shall be made in the manner and form prescribed by rules of court.

(13)   Wherever it is reasonably practicable to do so, an order under subsection (4), an application for a warrant under this section and any such warrant shall name the child; and where it does not name him it shall describe him as clearly as possible.

Date in force

14 October 1991: SI 1991/828.

Amendment

Sub-s (2): words 'or civil partner' in square brackets inserted by the Civil Partnership Act 2004, s 261(1), Sch 27, para 130.
Sub-s (11): words 'registered midwife' in square brackets substituted by SI 2002/253, art 54(3), Sch 5, para 10(b).
Sub-s (11A): inserted by SI 2004/1771, art 3, Schedule, Pt 1, para 4(b).

Definitions

For 'court' see s 92(7); for 'emergency protection order' see s 44(4); for 'child' see s 105(1); for 'applicant' see s 44(1).

References

See generally paras 7.88 ff and and paras 4.43 to 4.48 of the revised Children Act 1989 Guidance and Regulations, Volume 1, Court Orders (2008) Department for Children, Schools and Families. For grounds for making an emergency protection order see s 44(1); for 'the standard scale' see the CJA 1982, s 37(2)(3) as amended.

Sub-s (3)

Note this provision is permissive. It needs to be used with sub-s (9) if the help of the police and reasonable force to gain entry is required. See also the powers in s 50.

Sub-s (4) Court

A single justice may make this order: FPC(CA 1989)R 1991.

Sub-s (9) Court

A single justice may make this order ex parte with leave of the justices' clerk: FPC(CA 1989)R 1991, rr 2(5) and 4(4).

---

49   Abduction of children in care etc

(1)   A person shall be guilty of an offence if, knowingly and without lawful authority or reasonable excuse, he—

(a)   takes a child to whom this section applies away from the responsible person;
(b)   keeps such a child away from the responsible person; or
(c)   induces, assists or incites such a child to run away or stay away from the responsible person.

(2)   This section applies in relation to a child who is—

- (a)   in care;
- (b)   the subject of an emergency protection order; or
- (c)   in police protection,

and in this section 'the responsible person' means any person who for the time being has care of him by virtue of the care order, the emergency protection order, or section 46, as the case may be.

(3)   A person guilty of an offence under this section shall be liable on summary conviction to imprisonment for a term not exceeding six months, or to a fine not exceeding level 5 on the standard scale, or to both.

Date in force

14 October 1991: SI 1991/828.91.

Definitions

For 'child' and 'child who is in care' see s 105(1); for 'the responsible person' see sub-s (2); for 'emergency protection order' see s 44(4); for 'in police protection' see s 46(2).

References

See paras 7.3 and 7.104, and paras 4.83 and 4.84 of the revised Children Act 1989 Guidance and Regulations, Volume 1, Court Orders (2008) Department for Children, Schools and Families. For 'the standard scale' see the CJA 1982, s 37(2) (3) as amended.

Sub-s (2)

The local authority may designate who the responsible person should be at any given time: *Re R (Recovery Orders)* [1998] 3 FCR 321, [1998] 2 FLR 401.

---

50   Recovery of abducted children etc

(1)   Where it appears to the court that there is reason to believe that a child to whom this section applies—

- (a)   has been unlawfully taken away or is being unlawfully kept away from the responsible person;
- (b)   has run away or is staying away from the responsible person; or
- (c)   is missing,

the court may make an order under this section ('a recovery order').

(2)   This section applies to the same children to whom section 49 applies and in this section 'the responsible person' has the same meaning as in section 49.

(3)   A recovery order—

- (a)   operates as a direction to any person who is in a position to do so to produce the child on request to any authorised person;
- (b)   authorises the removal of the child by any authorised person;
- (c)   requires any person who has information as to the child's whereabouts to disclose that information, if asked to do so, to a constable or an officer of the court;
- (d)   authorises a constable to enter any premises specified in the order and search for the child, using reasonable force if necessary.

(4)   The court may make a recovery order only on the application of—

(a) any person who has parental responsibility for the child by virtue of a care order or emergency protection order; or

(b) where the child is in police protection, the designated officer.

(5) A recovery order shall name the child and—

(a) any person who has parental responsibility for the child by virtue of a care order or emergency protection order; or

(b) where the child is in police protection, the designated officer.

(6) Premises may only be specified under subsection (3)(d) if it appears to the court that there are reasonable grounds for believing the child to be on them.

(7) In this section—

'an authorised person' means—
    (a) any person specified by the court;
    (b) any constable;
    (c) any person who is authorised—
        (i) after the recovery order is made; and
        (ii) by a person who has parental responsibility for the child by virtue of a care order or an emergency protection order,
    to exercise any power under a recovery order; and

'the designated officer' means the officer designated for the purposes of section 46.

(8) Where a person is authorised as mentioned in subsection (7)(c)—

(a) the authorisation shall identify the recovery order; and

(b) any person claiming to be so authorised shall, if asked to do so, produce some duly authenticated document showing that he is so authorised.

(9) A person shall be guilty of an offence if he intentionally obstructs an authorised person exercising the power under subsection (3)(b) to remove a child.

(10) A person guilty of an offence under this section shall be liable on summary conviction to a fine not exceeding level 3 on the standard scale.

(11) No person shall be excused from complying with any request made under subsection (3)(c) on the ground that complying with it might incriminate him or his spouse [or civil partner] of an offence; but a statement or admission made in complying shall not be admissible in evidence against either of them in proceedings for an offence other than perjury.

(12) Where a child is made the subject of a recovery order whilst being looked after by a local authority, any reasonable expenses incurred by an authorised person in giving effect to the order shall be recoverable from the authority.

(13) A recovery order shall have effect in Scotland as if it had been made by the Court of Session and as if that court had had jurisdiction to make it.

(14) In this section 'the court', in relation to Northern Ireland, means a magistrates' court within the meaning of the Magistrates' Courts (Northern Ireland) Order 1981.

Date in force

14 October 1991: SI 1991/828.

Amendment

Sub-s (11): words 'or civil partner' in square brackets inserted by the Civil Partnership Act 2004, s 261(1), Sch 27, para 131.

Appendix 1 *Children Act 1989*

Definitions

For 'court' see s 92(7) and sub-ss (13) (Scotland) and (14) (Northern Ireland); for 'child' and 'local authority' see s 105(1); for 'the responsible person' see sub-s (2) and s 49(2); for 'a recovery order' see sub-s (1); for 'authorised person' and 'designated officer' see sub-s (7); for 'parental responsibility' see s 3; for 'care order' sees 31(11) and s 105(1); for 'emergency protection order' see s 44(4); for 'in police protection' see s 46(2); for 'child looked after by a local authority' see s 22(1).

References

See generally paras 7.3 and 7.104, and and paras 4.85 to 4.89 of the revised Children Act 1989 Guidance and Regulations, Volume 1, Court Orders (2008) Department for Children, Schools and Families. Application may be made ex parte with the leave of the justices' clerk: FPC(CA 1989)R 1991, rr 2(5) and 4(4). For 'the standard scale' see the CJA 1982, s 37(2) (3) as amended.

51 Refuges for children at risk

(1) Where it is proposed to use a voluntary home or [private] children's home to provide a refuge for children who appear to be at risk of harm, the Secretary of State may issue a certificate under this section with respect to that home.

(2) Where a local authority or voluntary organisation arrange for a foster parent to provide such a refuge, the Secretary of State may issue a certificate under this section with respect to that foster parent.

(3) In subsection (2) 'foster parent' means a person who is, or who from time to time is, a local authority foster parent or a foster parent with whom children are placed by a voluntary organisation.

(4) The Secretary of State may by regulations—

    (a) make provision as to the manner in which certificates may be issued;
    (b) impose requirements which must be complied with while any certificate is in force; and
    (c) provide for the withdrawal of certificates in prescribed circumstances.

(5) Where a certificate is in force with respect to a home, none of the provisions mentioned in subsection (7) shall apply in relation to any person providing a refuge for any child in that home.

(6) Where a certificate is in force with respect to a foster parent, none of those provisions shall apply in relation to the provision by him of a refuge for any child in accordance with arrangements made by the local authority or voluntary organisation.

(7) The provisions are—

    (a) section 49;
    [(b) sections 82 (recovery of certain fugitive children) and 83 (harbouring) of the Children (Scotland) Act 1995, so far as they apply in relation to anything done in England and Wales;]
    (c) section 32(3) of the Children and Young Persons Act 1969 (compelling, persuading, inciting or assisting any person to be absent from detention, etc), so far as it applies in relation to anything done in England and Wales;
    (d) section 2 of the Child Abduction Act 1984.

Date in force

14 October 1991: SI 1991/828.

Amendment

In section 51(7) (enactments which do not apply where a child is granted refuge), for paragraph (b) substitute '(b) sections 82 (recovery of certain fugitive children) and 83 (harbouring) of the Children (Scotland) Act 1995, so far as they apply in relation to anything done in England and Wales;' (Children (Scotland) Act 1995, Sch 4, para 48).'

Sub-s (1): word 'private' in square brackets substituted by the Care Standards Act 2000, s 116, Sch 4, para 14(1), (7).

Sub-s (7): para (b) substituted by the Children (Scotland) Act 1995, s 105(4), Sch 4, para 48(3).

Definitions

For 'voluntary home' see s 60(2); for 'child', 'local authority', 'private children's home' and 'voluntary organisation' see s 105(1); for 'harm' see s 31(9) as applied to the whole Act by s 105(1); for 'foster parent' see sub-s (3); for 'local authority foster parent' see s 23(3).

References

See generally para 6.43 ff.

Transfer of functions

Functions of the Secretary of State, so far as exercisable in relation to Wales, transferred to the National Assembly for Wales, by the National Assembly for Wales (Transfer of Functions) Order 1999, SI 1999/672, art 2, Sch 1.

References

For 'children's home' see s 23(10) as applied to the whole Act by s 105(1) and see note to s 53, post.

Sub-s (4) Regulations

See the Refuges (Children's Homes and Foster Placements) Regulations 1991, SI 1991/1507 amended by SI 2002/546 (E) and 2935 (W).

52　Rules and regulations

(1)　Without prejudice to section 93 or any other power to make such rules, rules of court may be made with respect to the procedure to be followed in connection with proceedings under this Part.

(2)　The rules may, in particular make provision—

    (a)　as to the form in which any application is to be made or direction is to be given;

    (b)　prescribing the persons who are to be notified of—

        (i)　the making, or extension, of an emergency protection order; or

        (ii)　the making of an application under section 45(4) or (8) or 46(7); and

    (c)　as to the content of any such notification and the manner in which, and person by whom, it is to be given.

(3)　The Secretary of State may by regulations provide that, where—

    (a)　an emergency protection order has been made with respect to a child;

    (b)　the applicant for the order was not the local authority within whose area the child is ordinarily resident; and

    (c)　that local authority are of the opinion that it would be in the child's best interests for the applicant's responsibilities under the order to be transferred to them, that authority shall (subject to their having complied with any requirements imposed by the regulations) be treated, for the purposes of this Act, as though they and not the original applicant had applied for, and been granted, the order.

(4)   Regulations made under subsection (3) may, in particular, make provision as to—

(a)   the considerations to which the local authority shall have regard in forming an opinion as mentioned in subsection (3)(c); and

(b)   the time at which responsibility under any emergency protection order is to be treated as having been transferred to a local authority.

Date in force

14 October 1991: SI 1991/828.

Definitions

For 'emergency protection order' see s 44(4); for 'child' and 'local authority' see s 105(1); for 'ordinary residence' see s 105(6).

References

See generally the FPC(CA 1989)R 1991, and the FPR 1991. 'This Part' ie Pt V (ss 43–52) (protection of children).

Transfer of functions

Functions of the Secretary of State, so far as exercisable in relation to Wales, transferred to the National Assembly for Wales, by the National Assembly for Wales (Transfer of Functions) Order 1999, SI 1999/672, art 2, Sch 1.

Regulations

See the Emergency Protection Order (Transfer of Responsibility) Regulation 1991, SI 1991/1414.

PART VI

COMMUNITY HOMES

53   Provision of community homes by local authorities

(1)   Every local authority shall make such arrangements as they consider appropriate for securing that homes ('community homes') are available—

(a)   for the care and accommodation of children looked after by them; and

(b)   for purposes connected with the welfare of children (whether or not looked after by them),

and may do so jointly with one or more other local authorities.

(2)   In making such arrangements, a local authority shall have regard to the need for ensuring the availability of accommodation—

(a)   of different descriptions; and

(b)   which is suitable for different purposes and the requirements of different descriptions of children.

(3)   A community home may be a home—

(a)   provided, [equipped, maintained and (subject to subsection (3A)) managed] by a local authority; or

(b)   provided by a voluntary organisation but in respect of which a local authority and the organisation—

>   (i) propose that, in accordance with an instrument of management, the
>   [equipment, maintenance and (subject to subsection (3B)) management]
>   of the home shall be the responsibility of the local authority; or
>   (ii) so propose that the management, equipment and maintenance of the
>   home shall be the responsibility of the voluntary organisation.

[(3A)   A local authority may make arrangements for the management by another person of accommodation provided by the local authority for the purpose of restricting the liberty of children.

(3B)   Where a local authority are to be responsible for the management of a community home provided by a voluntary organisation, the local authority may, with the consent of the body of managers constituted by the instrument of management for the home, make arrangements for the management by another person of accommodation provided for the purpose of restricting the liberty of children.]

(4)   Where a local authority are to be responsible for the management of a community home provided by a voluntary organisation, the authority shall designate the home as a controlled community home.

(5)   Where a voluntary organisation are to be responsible for the management of a community home provided by the organisation, the local authority shall designate the home as an assisted community home.

(6)   Schedule 4 shall have effect for the purpose of supplementing the provisions of this Part.

Date in force

14 October 1991: SI 1991/828.

Amendment

Sub-s (3): words in square brackets substituted by the Criminal Justice and Public Order Act 1994, s 22(2)(a).
Sub-ss (3A), (3B): inserted by the Criminal Justice and Public Order Act 1994, s 22(2)(b).

Definitions

For 'local authority', 'child', 'voluntary organisation' see s 105(1); for 'child who is looked after by a local authority' see s 22(1); for 'controlled community home' see sub-s (4) and 'assisted community home' see sub-s (5).

Reference

'This Part' i e Pt VI (ss 53–58 and Sch 4) (community homes).

Note

Part VI of the CA 1989 gives a local authority wide discretion to make such arrangements as they consider appropriate to provide community homes for children whether looked after by them or not. They may operate jointly with one or more other local authorities. There are three types of home: a home provided, managed, equipped and maintained by the local authority; a controlled community home provided by a voluntary organisation but managed by the local authority; and an assisted community home provided and managed by the voluntary organisation. See Sch 4 for organisation and management of controlled and assisted homes. See s 82(4) for the power of the Secretary of State to pay grants to voluntary organisations for the establishment, maintenance and improvement of assisted community homes. For contracting out of management of community homes, see the Contracting Out (Management functions in relations to certain Community Homes) Order 1996, SI 1996/586.

Appendix 1   *Children Act 1989*

Conduct, registration and inspection of children's homes

The Care Standards Act 2000 Act makes provision for the conduct, registration and inspection of children's homes.

Section 1 of the 2000 Act defines a 'children's home' as follows:

'Children's homes.

(1)   Subsections (2) to (6) have effect for the purposes of this Act.

(2)   An establishment is a children's home (subject to the following provisions of this section) if it provides care and accommodation wholly or mainly for children.

(3)   An establishment is not a children's home merely because a child is cared for and accommodated there by a parent or relative of his or by a foster parent.

(4)   An establishment is not a children's home if it is—
    (a)   a health service hospital;
    (b)   an independent hospital or an independent clinic; or
    (c)   a residential family centre,
or if it is of a description excepted by regulations.

(5)   Subject to subsection (6), an establishment is not a children's home if it is a school.

(6)   A school is a children's home at any time if at that time accommodation is provided for children at the school and either—
    (a)   in each year that fell within the period of two years ending at that time, accommodation was provided for children, either at the school or under arrangements made by the proprietor of the school, for more than 295 days; or
    (b)   it is intended to provide accommodation for children, either at the school or under arrangements made by the proprietor of the school, for more than 295 days in any year;
and in this subsection 'year' means a period of twelve months.

But accommodation shall not for the purposes of paragraph (a) be regarded as provided to children for a number of days unless there is at least one child to whom it is provided for that number of days; and paragraph (b) shall be construed accordingly.

(7)   For the purposes of this section a person is a foster parent in relation to a child if—
    (a)   he is a local authority foster parent in relation to the child;
    (b)   he is a foster parent with whom a child has been placed by a voluntary organisation under section 59(1)(a) of the 1989 Act; or
    (c)   he fosters the child privately.'

This definition encompasses (subject to the exemptions in the section) community homes, voluntary homes and private (formerly registered) children's homes as defined in the Children Act 1989.

Any person who carries on or manages an establishment or agency of any description within the meaning of Part I of the CSA 2000 is required to be registered under Part II of the Act with the National Care Standards Commission or, in Wales, with the National Assembly. Failure to register in accordance with the CSA 2000 incurs criminal sanctions.

The conduct of children's homes is regulated by the Children's Homes Regulations 2001, SI 2001/3967 amended by SI 2002/865 and 2469, SI 2005/1541, SI 2006/1738; and the Children's Homes (Wales) Regulations 2002, SI 2002/327 amended by SI 2002/2622 and 3295, SI 2003/947, 1004 and 1703, SI 2004/1314, 1756 and 2414, SI 2005/1541, 2929 and 3302, SI 2006/3251 made under s 22 of the Care Standards Act 2000. In addition, the Secretary of State has published *Children's Homes – National Minimum Standards* (Dept of Health 2002) in accordance with s 23(1) of the 2000 Act. These standards must be taken into account in respect of Part II of the 2000 Act by the registration authority in the making of any decision, in proceedings for an emergency cancellation of registration, any appeal against cancellation of registration and any proceedings for an offence under that Part.

Sub-s (2) Shall have regard

Consider but not place any particular weight on the needs and requirements of different children.

54   ...

...

Repealed by the CSA 2000, s 117, Sch 6.

55   Determination of disputes relating to controlled and assisted community homes

(1)   Where any dispute relating to a controlled community home arises between the local authority specified in the home's instrument of management and—

    (a)   the voluntary organisation by which the home is provided; or

    (b)   any other local authority who have placed, or desire or are required to place, in the home a child who is looked after by them,

the dispute may be referred by either party to the Secretary of State for his determination.

(2)   Where any dispute relating to an assisted community home arises between the voluntary organisation by which the home is provided and any local authority who have placed, or desire to place, in the home a child who is looked after by them, the dispute may be referred by either party to the Secretary of State for his determination.

(3)   Where a dispute is referred to the Secretary of State under this section he may, in order to give effect to his determination of the dispute, give such directions as he thinks fit to the local authority or voluntary organisation concerned.

(4)   This section applies even though the matter in dispute may be one which, under or by virtue of Part II of Schedule 4, is reserved for the decision, or is the responsibility, of—

    (a)   the local authority specified in the home's instrument of management; or

    (b)   (as the case may be) the voluntary organisation by which the home is provided.

(5)   Where any trust deed relating to a controlled or assisted community home contains provision whereby a bishop or any other ecclesiastical or denominational authority has power to decide questions relating to religious instruction given in the home, no dispute which is capable of being dealt with in accordance with that provision shall be referred to the Secretary of State under this section.

(6)   In this Part 'trust deed', in relation to a voluntary home, means any instrument (other than an instrument of management) regulating—

    (a)   the maintenance, management or conduct of the home; or

    (b)   the constitution of a body of managers or trustees of the home.

Date in force

14 October 1991: SI 1991/828.

Definitions

For 'controlled community home' see s 53(4). For 'local authority', 'voluntary organisation', 'child' see s 105(1); for 'child who is looked after by a local authority' see s 22(1); for 'assisted community home' see s 53(5); for 'trust deed' see sub-s (6).

References

For instruments of management see Sch 4, Pt I. This Part' ie Pt VI (ss 53–58 and Sch 4) (community homes).

Appendix 1 *Children Act 1989*

Transfer of functions

Functions of the Secretary of State, so far as exercisable in relation to Wales, transferred to the National Assembly for Wales, by the National Assembly for Wales (Transfer of Functions) Order 1999, SI 1999/672, art 2, Sch 1.

Note

The Secretary of State is enabled to settle disputes between a local authority and a voluntary organisation about a controlled or assisted home. If the trust deed of the home gives power to an ecclesiastical authority to decide questions on religious instruction, the dispute shall not be referred to the Secretary of State.

---

56 Discontinuance by voluntary organisation of controlled or assisted community home

(1) The voluntary organisation by which a controlled or assisted community home is provided shall not cease to provide the home except after giving to the Secretary of State and the local authority specified in the home's instrument of management not less than two years' notice in writing of their intention to do so.

(2) A notice under subsection (1) shall specify the date from which the voluntary organisation intend to cease to provide the home as a community home.

(3) Where such a notice is given and is not withdrawn before the date specified in it, the home's instrument of management shall cease to have effect on that date and the home shall then cease to be a controlled or assisted community home.

(4) Where a notice is given under subsection (1) and the home's managers give notice in writing to the Secretary of State that they are unable or unwilling to continue as its managers until the date specified in the subsection (1) notice, the Secretary of State may by order—

(a) revoke the home's instrument of management; and
(b) require the local authority who were specified in that instrument to conduct the home until—
    (i) the date specified in the subsection (1) notice; or
    (ii) such earlier date (if any) as may be specified for the purposes of this paragraph in the order,
as if it were a community home provided by the local authority.

(5) Where the Secretary of State imposes a requirement under subsection (4)(b)—

(a) nothing in the trust deed for the home shall affect the conduct of the home by the local authority;
(b) the Secretary of State may by order direct that for the purposes of any provision specified in the direction and made by or under any enactment relating to community homes (other than this section) the home shall, until the date or earlier date specified as mentioned in subsection (4)(b), be treated as a controlled or assisted community home;
(c) except in so far as the Secretary of State so directs, the home shall until that date be treated for the purposes of any such enactment as a community home provided by the local authority; and
(d) on the date or earlier date specified as mentioned in subsection (4)(b) the home shall cease to be a community home.

Date in force

14 October 1991: SI 1991/828.

Definitions

For 'voluntary organisation', 'local authority' see s 105(1); for 'controlled community home' see s 53(4); for 'assisted community home' see s 53(5); for 'trust deed' see s 55(6).

References

For instruments of management see Sch 4, Pt I; for service of notices under the Act generally see s 105(8)–(10); for the financial provisions which apply on the cessation of a community home see s 58.

Transfer of functions

Functions of the Secretary of State, so far as exercisable in relation to Wales, transferred to the National Assembly for Wales, by the National Assembly for Wales (Transfer of Functions) Order 1999, SI 1999/672, art 2, Sch 1.

---

57   Closure by local authority of controlled or assisted community home

(1)   The local authority specified in the instrument of management for a controlled or assisted community home may give—

(a)   the Secretary of State; and
(b)   the voluntary organisation by which the home is provided,

not less than two years' notice in writing of their intention to withdraw their designation of the home as a controlled or assisted community home.

(2)   A notice under subsection (1) shall specify the date ('the specified date') on which the designation is to be withdrawn.

(3)   Where—

(a)   a notice is given under subsection (1) in respect of a controlled or assisted community home;
(b)   the home's managers give notice in writing to the Secretary of State that they are unable or unwilling to continue as managers until the specified date; and
(c)   the managers' notice is not withdrawn,

the Secretary of State may by order revoke the home's instrument of management from such date earlier than the specified date as may be specified in the order.

(4)   Before making an order under subsection (3), the Secretary of State shall consult the local authority and the voluntary organisation.

(5)   Where a notice has been given under subsection (1) and is not withdrawn, the home's instrument of management shall cease to have effect on—

(a)   the specified date; or
(b)   where an earlier date has been specified under subsection (3), that earlier date,

and the home shall then cease to be a community home.

Date in force

14 October 1991: SI 1991/828.

Definitions

For 'local authority', 'voluntary organisation' see s 105(1); for 'community home' see s 53; for 'controlled community home' see s 53(4); for 'assisted community home' see s 53(5); for 'the specified date' see sub-s (2).

Appendix 1 *Children Act 1989*

References

For instruments of management see Sch 4, Pt I. For service of notices under the Act generally see s 105(8)–(10). For the financial provisions which apply on the cessation of a community home see s 58.

Transfer of functions

Functions of the Secretary of State, so far as exercisable in relation to Wales, transferred to the National Assembly for Wales, by the National Assembly for Wales (Transfer of Functions) Order 1999, SI 1999/672, art 2, Sch 1.

---

58   Financial provisions applicable on cessation of controlled or assisted community home or disposal etc of premises

(1)   Where—

  (a) the instrument of management for a controlled or assisted community home is revoked or otherwise ceases to have effect under section ..., 56(3) or (4)(a) or 57(3) or (5); or

  (b) any premises used for the purposes of such a home are (at any time after 13th January 1987) disposed of, or put to use otherwise than for those purposes,

the proprietor shall become liable to pay compensation ('the appropriate compensation') in accordance with this section.

(2)   Where the instrument of management in force at the relevant time relates—

  (a) to a controlled community home; or

  (b) to an assisted community home which, at any time before the instrument came into force, was a controlled community home,

the appropriate compensation is a sum equal to that part of the value of any premises which is attributable to expenditure incurred in relation to the premises, while the home was a controlled community home, by the authority who were then the responsible authority.

(3)   Where the instrument of management in force at the relevant time relates—

  (a) to an assisted community home; or

  (b) to a controlled community home which, at any time before the instrument came into force, was an assisted community home,

the appropriate compensation is a sum equal to that part of the value of the premises which is attributable to the expenditure of money provided by way of grant under section 82, section 65 of the Children and Young Persons Act 1969 or section 82 of the Child Care Act 1980.

(4)   Where the home is, at the relevant time, conducted in premises which formerly were used as an approved school or were an approved probation hostel or home, the appropriate compensation is a sum equal to that part of the value of the premises which is attributable to the expenditure—

  (a) of sums paid towards the expenses of the managers of an approved school under section 104 of the Children and Young Persons Act 1933; ...

  (b) of sums paid under section 51(3)(c) of the Powers of Criminal Courts Act 1973 [or section 20(1)(c) of the Probation Service Act 1993] in relation to expenditure on approved probation hostels or homes[; or

  (c) of sums paid under section 3, 5 or 9 of the Criminal Justice and Court Services Act 2000 in relation to expenditure on approved premises (within the meaning of Part I of that Act)].

(5)   The appropriate compensation shall be paid—

768

(a)   in the case of compensation payable under subsection (2), to the authority who were the responsible authority at the relevant time; and

(b)   in any other case, to the Secretary of State.

(6)   In this section—

'disposal' includes the grant of a tenancy and any other conveyance, assignment, transfer, grant, variation or extinguishment of an interest in or right over land, whether made by instrument or otherwise;

'premises' means any premises or part of premises (including land) used for the purposes of the home and belonging to the proprietor;

'the proprietor' means—

(a)   the voluntary organisation by which the home is, at the relevant time, provided; or

(b)   if the premises are not, at the relevant time, vested in that organisation, the persons in whom they are vested;

'the relevant time' means the time immediately before the liability to pay arises under subsection (1); and

'the responsible authority' means the local authority specified in the instrument of management in question.

(7)   For the purposes of this section an event of a kind mentioned in subsection (1)(b) shall be taken to have occurred—

(a)   in the case of a disposal, on the date on which the disposal was completed or, in the case of a disposal which is effected by a series of transactions, the date on which the last of those transactions was completed;

(b)   in the case of premises which are put to different use, on the date on which they first begin to be put to their new use.

(8)   The amount of any sum payable under this section shall be determined in accordance with such arrangements—

(a)   as may be agreed between the voluntary organisation by which the home is, at the relevant time, provided and the responsible authority or (as the case may be) the Secretary of State; or

(b)   in default of agreement, as may be determined by the Secretary of State.

(9)   With the agreement of the responsible authority or (as the case may be) the Secretary of State, the liability to pay any sum under this section may be discharged, in whole or in part, by the transfer of any premises.

(10)   This section has effect regardless of—

(a)   anything in any trust deed for a controlled or assisted community home;

(b)   the provisions of any enactment or instrument governing the disposition of the property of a voluntary organisation.

Date in force

14 October 1991: SI 1991/828. But note s 58(1)(b) for disputes after 13 January 1987.

Amendment

Sub-s (1): in para (a) reference omitted repealed by the Care Standards Act 2000, s 117(2), Sch 6.
Sub-s (4): in para (a) word omitted repealed by the Criminal Justice and Court Services Act 2000, ss 74, 75, Sch 7, Pt II, paras 87, 93(a), Sch 8; in para (b) words 'or section 20(1)(c) of the Probation Service Act 1993' in square brackets inserted by the Probation Service Act 1993, s 32, Sch 3, para 9(2); para (c) and word '; or' immediately preceding it inserted by the Criminal Justice and Court Services Act 2000, s 74, Sch 7, Pt II, paras 87, 93(b).

Appendix 1 *Children Act 1989*

Definitions

For 'controlled community home' see s 53(4); for 'assisted community home' see s 53(5); for 'appropriate compensation', see sub-s (1); for 'the relevant time', 'disposal', 'premises', 'the proprietor', 'relevant premises', 'the responsible authority', see sub-s (6); for 'trust deed' see s 55(6).

References

For instruments of management see Sch 4, Pt I; for disposal or change of use of premises see sub-s (7); for the amount of any sum payable under this section see sub-s (8) and for the payment of such funds into the consolidated fund see s 106(2).

Transfer of functions

Functions of the Secretary of State, so far as exercisable in relation to Wales, transferred to the National Assembly for Wales, by the National Assembly for Wales (Transfer of Functions) Order 1999, SI 1999/672, art 2, Sch 1.

PART VII

VOLUNTARY HOMES AND VOLUNTARY ORGANISATIONS

59 Provision of accommodation by voluntary organisations

(1) Where a voluntary organisation provide accommodation for a child, they shall do so by—

(a) placing him (subject to subsection (2)) with—
  (i) a family;
  (ii) a relative of his; or
  (iii) any other suitable person,
on such terms as to payment by the organisation and otherwise as the organisation may determine [(subject to section 49 of the Children Act 2004)];
[(aa) maintaining him in an appropriate children's home;] or
(f) making such other arrangements (subject to subsection (3)) as seem appropriate to them.

[(1A) Where under subsection (1)(aa) a local authority maintains a child in a home provided, equipped and maintained by the Secretary of State under section 82(5), it shall do so on such terms as the Secretary of State may from time to time determine.]

(2) The Secretary of State may make regulations as to the placing of children with foster parents by voluntary organisations and the regulations may, in particular, make provision which (with any necessary modifications) is similar to the provision that may be made under section 23(2)(a).

(3) The Secretary of State may make regulations as to the arrangements which may be made under subsection (1)(f) and the regulations may, in particular, make provision which (with any necessary modifications) is similar to the provision that may be made under section 23(2)(f).

(4) The Secretary of State may make regulations requiring any voluntary organisation who are providing accommodation for a child—

(a) to review his case; and
(b) to consider any representations (including any complaint) made to them by any person falling within a prescribed class of person,

in accordance with the provisions of the regulations.

(5)   Regulations under subsection (4) may in particular make provision which (with any necessary modifications) is similar to the provision that may be made under section 26.

(6)   Regulations under subsections (2) to (4) may provide that any person who, without reasonable excuse, contravenes or fails to comply with a regulation shall be guilty of an offence and liable on summary conviction to a fine not exceeding level 4 on the standard scale.

Date in force

14 October 1991: SI 1991/828.109.

Amendments

Sub-s (1): in para (a) words '(subject to section 49 of the Children Act 2004)' in square brackets inserted by the Children Act 2004, s 49(4); para (aa) substituted, for paras (b)–(e) as originally enacted, by the Care Standards Act 2000, s 116, Sch 4, para 14(1), (8)(a).
Sub-s (1A): inserted by the Care Standards Act 2000, s 116, Sch 4, para 14(1), (8)(b).

Definitions

For 'voluntary organisation', 'child' and 'relative' see s 105(1); for 'appropriate children's home' see s 23; for 'the standard scale' see the CJA 1982, s 37(2) (3) as amended.

Note

This section places voluntary organisations in the same position as local authorities with respect to the provision of accommodation cf s 23(2). Voluntary homes are provided by not-for-profit organisations (voluntary organisations) and must be registered with the Secretary of State (for procedure, see note to s 53, above). For placement of a child by a voluntary organisation see s 60. For the duty on a voluntary organisation to safeguard and promote the welfare of any child it arranges or provides accommodation for see s 61. For duties on local authorities regarding any voluntary organisation within its area or any voluntary organisation outside its area providing accommodation for a child on behalf of the authority see s 62.

Registration and inspection of children's homes

See the note to s 53, above.

Sub-s (2) Foster parents

The placing of a child with foster parents by a voluntary organisation is not private fostering and is not subject to the provisions of Part IX (ss 66–70 and Sch 8) (see Sch 8, para 2(1)(c)) although the 'usual fostering limit' will apply so that where more than three children who are not siblings with respect to each other are placed by a voluntary organisation, that placement will be treated as a placement in a children's home unless it is exempted by the local authority (Sch 7).

Regulations

See the Arrangements for Placement of Children (General) Regulations 1991, SI 1991/890 amended by SI 1991/2033, SI 1993/3069, SI 1995/2015, SI 1997/649, SI 2002/546, 2469, 2935 (Wales) and 3013 (W) and SI 2005/774 (W) (revoked in relation to Wales by SI 2007/310); the Fostering Services Regulations 2002, SI 2002/57 amended by SI 2002/865 and 2469, SI 2005/1541 and SI 2006/1738; the Fostering Services (Wales) Regulations 2003, SI 2003/237 amended by SI 2003/896, SI 2005/3302 and SI 2006/3251.

Sub-s (3) Regulations

See the Arrangements for Placement of Children (General) Regulations 1991, SI 1991/890 as amended and the Placement of Children (Wales) Regulations 2007, SI 2007/310.

Sub-s (4), (5) Regulations

See the Review of Children's Cases Regulations 1991, SI 1991/895 amended by SI 1991/2033, SI 1993/3069, SI 1995/2015, SI 1997/649, SI 2002/546 (England), 2935 (Wales), 3013 (Wales), SI 2004/1419 (E) and 1448 (W) and 2253 (E) and SI 2005/774 (W) (revoked in relation to Wales by SI 2007/310); the Review of Children's Cases (Wales) Regulations 2007, SI 2007/307; the Adoption Agencies (Wales) Regulations 2005, SI 2005/1313 amended by SI 2006/362; Representations Procedure (England) Regulations 2006, SI 2006/1738.

---

60   [Voluntary homes]

(1)   ...

(2)   ...

[(3)   In this Act 'voluntary home' means a children's home which is carried on by a voluntary organisation but does not include a community home.]

(4)   Schedule 5 shall have effect for the purpose of supplementing the provisions of this Part.

Date in force

14 October 1991: SI 1991/828.

Amendment

Section heading: words 'Voluntary homes' in square brackets substituted by the Care Standards Act 2000, s 116, Sch 4, para 14(1), (9)(a).
Sub-ss (1), (2): repealed by the Care Standards Act 2000, s 117(2), Sch 6.
Sub-s (3): substituted by the Care Standards Act 2000, s 116, Sch 4, para 14(1), (9)(b).

Definitions

For for 'community home' see s 53.

References

' This Part' ie Pt VII (ss 59–62 and Sch 5) (voluntary homes and voluntary organisations). For the circumstances in which the Secretary of State may make a grant to a voluntary organisation in connection with a voluntary home see s 82(4); for the power to inspect a voluntary home and to hold inquiries into any matter connected with a voluntary home see ss 80 and 81.

Note

'Voluntary home' is defined so as to exclude establishments which are regulated by other statutory provisions. Regulations as to the conduct of voluntary homes may be made by the Secretary of State under the Care Standards Act 2000. Regulations may also provide for the disqualification of persons in relation to voluntary homes.

Transfer of functions

Functions of the Secretary of State, so far as exercisable in relation to Wales, transferred to the National Assembly for Wales, by the National Assembly for Wales (Transfer of Functions) Order 1999, SI 1999/672, art 2, Sch 1.

---

61   Duties of voluntary organisations

(1)   Where a child is accommodated by or on behalf of a voluntary organisation, it shall be the duty of the organisation—

(a)   to safeguard and promote his welfare;

(b)   to make such use of the services and facilities available for children cared for by their own parents as appears to the organisation reasonable in his case; and

(c)   to advise, assist and befriend him with a view to promoting his welfare when he ceases to be so accommodated.

(2)   Before making any decision with respect to any such child the organisation shall, so far as is reasonably practicable, ascertain the wishes and feelings of—

(a)   the child;

(b)   his parents;

(c)   any person who is not a parent of his but who has parental responsibility for him; and

(d)   any other person whose wishes and feelings the organisation consider to be relevant,

regarding the matter to be decided.

(3)   In making any such decision the organisation shall give due consideration—

(a)   having regard to the child's age and understanding, to such wishes and feelings of his as they have been able to ascertain;

(b)   to such other wishes and feelings mentioned in subsection (2) as they have been able to ascertain; and

(c)   to the child's religious persuasion, racial origin and cultural and linguistic background.

Date in force

14 October 1991: SI 1991/828.

Definitions

For 'child' and 'voluntary organisation' see s 105(1); for 'parental responsibility' see s 3.

Note

Compare the similar duties imposed on local authorities in respect of children they are looking after: s 22(2). A local authority has a duty to provide aftercare for children formerly looked after by a voluntary organisation (s 24).

Applications for orders under section 8

The embargo under s 9(2) against local authorities applying for residence or contact orders does not apply to voluntary organisations, but the circumstances in which the court will give leave to apply for such orders must be limited. By applying for such an order the applicant would be circumventing the general principle applicable to local authorities, that the 'threshold criteria' in s 31(2) must be satisfied before the authority can intervene compulsorily in family life. Although an application by a voluntary organisation may not necessarily be equated with intervention by the State, such an organisation perhaps may not be seen to be in a similar position to an individual.

---

62   Duties of local authorities

(1)   Every local authority shall satisfy themselves that any voluntary organisation providing accommodation—

(a)   within the authority's area for any child; or

(b)   outside that area for any child on behalf of the authority,

are satisfactorily safeguarding and promoting the welfare of the children so provided with accommodation.

773

(2)   Every local authority shall arrange for children who are accommodated within their area by or on behalf of voluntary organisations to be visited, from time to time, in the interests of their welfare.

(3)   The Secretary of State may make regulations—

    (a)   requiring every child who is accommodated within a local authority's area, by or on behalf of a voluntary organisation, to be visited by an officer of the authority—

        (i)   in prescribed circumstances; and

        (ii)   on specified occasions or within specified periods; and

    (b)   imposing requirements which must be met by any local authority, or officer of a local authority, carrying out functions under this section.

(4)   Subsection (2) does not apply in relation to community homes.

(5)   Where a local authority are not satisfied that the welfare of any child who is accommodated by or on behalf of a voluntary organisation is being satisfactorily safeguarded or promoted they shall—

    (a)   unless they consider that it would not be in the best interests of the child, take such steps as are reasonably practicable to secure that the care and accommodation of the child is undertaken by—

        (i)   a parent of his;

        (ii)   any person who is not a parent of his but who has parental responsibility for him; or

        (iii)   a relative of his; and

    (b)   consider the extent to which (if at all) they should exercise any of their functions with respect to the child.

(6)   Any person authorised by a local authority may, for the purpose of enabling the authority to discharge their duties under this section—

    (a)   enter, at any reasonable time, and inspect any premises in which children are being accommodated as mentioned in subsection (1) or (2);

    (b)   inspect any children there;

    (c)   require any person to furnish him with such records of a kind required to be kept by regulations made under [section 22 of the Care Standards Act 2000] (in whatever form they are held), or allow him to inspect such records, as he may at any time direct.

(7)   Any person exercising the power conferred by subsection (6) shall, if asked to do so, produce some duly authenticated document showing his authority to do so.

(8)   Any person authorised to exercise the power to inspect records conferred by subsection (6)—

    (a)   shall be entitled at any reasonable time to have access to, and inspect and check the operation of, any computer and any associated apparatus or material which is or has been in use in connection with the records in question; and

    (b)   may require—

        (i)   the person by whom or on whose behalf the computer is or has been so used; or

        (ii)   any person having charge of, or otherwise concerned with the operation of, the computer, apparatus or material,

to afford him such assistance as he may reasonably require.

(9)   Any person who intentionally obstructs another in the exercise of any power conferred by subsection (6) or (8) shall be guilty of an offence and liable on summary conviction to a fine not exceeding level 3 on the standard scale.

[(10) This section does not apply in relation to any voluntary organisation which is an institution within the further education sector, as defined in section 91 of the Further and Higher Education Act 1992, or a school.]

Date in force

14 October 1991: SI 1991/828.115.

Amendment

Sub-s (6): in para (c) words 'section 22 of the Care Standards Act 2000' in square brackets substituted by the Care Standards Act 2000, s 116, Sch 4, para 14(1), (10)(a).
Sub-s (10): inserted by the Care Standards Act 2000, s 105(5).

Definitions

For 'local authority', 'voluntary organisation', 'child', 'functions' and 'relative' see s 105(1); for 'community home' see s 53; for 'parental responsibility' see s 3.

References

For power to issue warrant to authorise a constable to assist in exercising the power under sub-ss (6) or (8) see s 102; for 'the standard scale' see the CJA 1982, s 37(2) (3) as amended.

Transfer of functions

Functions of the Secretary of State, so far as exercisable in relation to Wales, transferred to the National Assembly for Wales, by the National Assembly for Wales (Transfer of Functions) Order 1999, SI 1999/672, art 2, Sch 1

Sub-s (2) From time to time

This section is based on provisions formerly contained in the CCA 1980, s 68. The regulation making powers of the 1980 Act were not used and accordingly the frequency and nature of the visiting was left to the discretion of the local authority. At the time of writing no regulations have yet been made under s 62(3) of the 1989 Act. However, the frequency of visits by a local authority is prescribed by the Foster Placement (Children) Regulations 1991 and now the Fostering Services Regulations 2002.

Sub-s (3) Regulations

See the Foster Placement (Children) Regulations 1991, SI 1991/910 amended by SI 1995/2015, SI 1997/2308 and SI 1999/2768 and SI 2001/2992 (E) and 3443 (W) (revoked in so far as they apply to England and substituted by the Fostering Services Regulations 2002, SI 2002/57 amended by SI 2002/865.

Sub-s (6) May enter

If they so choose, but they cannot force entry. Their remedy is to seek a warrant under s 102(1) where entry has been prevented or refused or they are likely to be prevented from using these powers. The warrant of entry will be executed by a constable who may be accompanied by the person applying for the warrant.

Sub-s (8)

For where access is refused see s 102(1) for warrant of entry.

Sub-s (9) Intentionally obstructs

The former legislation merely required an obstruction (CCA 1980, s 68(5)). 'Obstructs' need not involve physical violence: *Hinchliffe v Sheldon* [1955] 3 All ER 406, [1955] 1 WLR 1207. Doing anything which makes it more difficult for a person to carry out his duty may amount to obstruction: *Rice v Connolly* [1966] 2 QB 414, [1966] 2 All ER 649, but standing by and doing nothing, in the absence of a legal duty to act, is not obstruction: *Swallow v LCC* [1916] 1 KB 224.

For cases on 'wilful obstruction': *Hills v Ellis* [1983] QB 680, [1983] 1 All ER 667; *Moore v Green* [1983] 1 All ER 663; *Willmott v Atack* [1977] QB 498, [1976] 3 All ER 794, 141 JP 35.

PART VIII

PRIVATE CHILDREN'S HOMES

63   [Private children's homes etc]

(1)   ...

(2)   ...

(3)   ...

(4)   ...

(5)   ...

(6)   ...

(7)   ...

(8)   ...

(9)   ...

(10)   ...

(11)   Schedule 6 shall have effect with respect to [private] children's homes.

(12)   Schedule 7 shall have effect for the purpose of setting out the circumstances in which a person may foster more than three children without being treated[, for the purposes of this Act and the Care Standards Act 2000,] as carrying on a children's home.

Date in force

14 October 1991: SI 1991/828.

Amendment

Section heading: words 'Private children's homes etc' in square brackets substituted by the Care Standards Act 2000, s 116, Sch 4, para 14(1), (11)(a).
Sub-ss (1)–(10): repealed by the Care Standards Act 2000, s 177(2), Sch 6.
Sub-s (11): word 'private' in square brackets inserted by the Care Standards Act 2000, s 116, Sch 4, para 14(1), (11)(b).
Sub-s (12): words ', for the purposes of this Act and the Care Standards Act 2000,' in square brackets inserted by the Care Standards Act 2000, s 116, Sch 4, para 14(1), (11)(c).

Definitions

For 'private children's home see s 105(1).

References

For 'the standard scale' see the CJA 1982, s 37(2)(3) as amended; for the inspection of private children's homes see s 80(1)(a); for the power to hold inquiries into any matter connected with a private children's home see s 81; for transitional provisions see s 108(6) and Sch 14, para 32.

Registration and inspection of children's homes

See the note to s 53 above. For the welfare of children in private children's homes, and the duty on the person carrying on the home to safeguard and protect the children's welfare see s 64.

64   Welfare of children in children's homes

(1)   Where a child is accommodated in a [private] children's home, it shall be the duty of the person carrying on the home to—

- (a)   safeguard and promote the child's welfare;
- (b)   make such use of the services and facilities available for children cared for by their own parents as appears to that person reasonable in the case of the child; and
- (c)   advise, assist and befriend him with a view to promoting his welfare when he ceases to be so accommodated.

(2)   Before making any decision with respect to any such child the person carrying on the home shall, so far as is reasonably practicable, ascertain the wishes and feelings of—

- (a)   the child;
- (b)   his parents;
- (c)   any other person who is not a parent of his but who has parental responsibility for him; and
- (d)   any person whose wishes and feelings the person carrying on the home considers to be relevant,

regarding the matter to be decided.

(3)   In making any such decision the person concerned shall give due consideration—

- (a)   having regard to the child's age and understanding, to such wishes and feelings of his as he has been able to ascertain;
- (b)   to such other wishes and feelings mentioned in subsection (2) as he has been able to ascertain; and
- (c)   to the child's religious persuasion, racial origin and cultural and linguistic background.

(4)   Section 62, except subsection (4), shall apply in relation to any person who is carrying on a [private] children's home as it applies in relation to any voluntary organisation.

Date in force

14 October 1991: SI 1991/828.

Amendments

Sub-s (1): word 'private' in square brackets inserted by the Care Standards Act 2000, s 116, Sch 4, para 14(1), (12).
Sub-s (4): word 'private' in square brackets inserted by the Care Standards Act 2000, s 116, Sch 4, para 14(1), (12).

Definitions

For 'child', 'voluntary organisation' and 'private children's home' see s 105(1); for 'children's home' see s 63(3) and s 23(10) as applied to the whole Act by s 105(1) and see note to s 53, above; for 'parental responsibility' see s 3.

Reference

For power to issue a warrant to authorise a constable to assist in exercising the power under sub-s (4) see s 102.

Appendix 1   *Children Act 1989*

Note

Sections 64 and 65 apply whether or not a private children's home is currently registered- for example, during the period when an application for registration is being considered or where a home should be registered but is not and the welfare of the children in the home is in issue. Cf a local authority's duties under ss 22 and 24(1).

Sub-s (4)

The duties of local authorities to ensure that the welfare of the children are being satisfactorily safeguarded and promoted.

---

65   Persons disqualified from carrying on, or being employed in, children's homes

(1)   A person who is disqualified (under section 68) from fostering a child privately shall not carry on, or be otherwise concerned in the management of, or have any financial interest in, a children's home unless he has—

    (a)   disclosed to [the appropriate authority] the fact that he is so disqualified; and
    (b)   obtained [its] written consent.

(2)   No person shall employ a person who is so disqualified in a children's home unless he has—

    (a)   disclosed to [the appropriate authority] the fact that that person is so disqualified; and
    (b)   obtained [its] written consent.

(3)   Where [the appropriate authority refuses to give its consent under this section, it] shall inform the applicant by a written notice which states—

    (a)   the reason for the refusal;
    [(b)   the applicant's right to appeal under section 65A against the refusal to the Tribunal established under section 9 of the Protection of Children Act 1999]; and
    (c)   the time within which he may do so.

(4)   Any person who contravenes subsection (1) or (2) shall be guilty of an offence and liable on summary conviction to imprisonment for a term not exceeding six months or to a fine not exceeding level 5 on the standard scale or to both.

(5)   Where a person contravenes subsection (2) he shall not be guilty of an offence if he proves that he did not know, and had no reasonable grounds for believing, that the person whom he was employing was disqualified under section 68.

[(6)   In this section and section 65A 'appropriate authority' means—

    (a)   in relation to England, [Her Majesty's Chief Inspector of Education, Children's Services and Skills]; and
    (b)   in relation to Wales, the National Assembly for Wales.]

Date in force

14 October 1991: SI 1991/828.

Amendments

Sub-s (1): words 'the appropriate authority' and 'its' in square brackets substituted by the Care Standards Act 2000, s 116, Sch 4, para 14(1), (13)(a).
Sub-s (2): words 'the appropriate authority' and 'its' in square brackets substituted by the Care Standards Act 2000, s 116, Sch 4, para 14(1), (13)(a).

Sub-s (3): words 'the appropriate authority refuses to give its consent under this section, it' in square brackets substituted by the Care Standards Act 2000, s 116, Sch 4, para 14(1), (13)(b); para (b) substituted by the Care Standards Act 2000, s 116, Sch 4, para 14(1), (13)(c).

Sub-s (6): inserted by the Care Standards Act 2000, s 116, Sch 4, para 14(1), (13)(d); in para (a) words 'Her Majesty's Chief Inspector of Education, Children's Services and Skills' in square brackets substituted by the Education and Inspections Act 2006, s 157, Sch 14, paras 9, 12.

Definitions

For 'fostering a child privately' see s 66(1)(b) as applied to the whole Act by s 105(1); for 'children's home' see s 63(3) see sub-s (6); for 'the responsible authority' see Sch 6, Pt I para 3(1); for 'the appropriate authority'.

References

For service of notices under the Act generally see s 105(8)–(10); for 'the standard scale' see the CJA 1982, s 37(2) (3) as amended.

Person disqualified

Persons disqualified from fostering privately are disqualified under s 65. The Secretary of State has power under s 68(2) to make regulations prescribing those persons who are disqualified from being private foster parents: see the Disqualification for Caring for Children (England) Regulations 2002, SI 2002/635 and the Disqualification for Caring for Children (Wales) Regulations 2004, SI 2004/2695.

Sub-s (5) If he proves

On the balance of probabilities: *R v Carr-Briant* [1943] KB 607, [1943] 2 All ER 156, 107 JP 167, CCA. Under the former CHA 1982, s 10(4) the prosecution had to prove beyond reasonable doubt that the defendant knowingly employed a disqualified person. Now once the prosecution have proved that such a person was employed by the defendant, he must prove not only that he did not know of the disqualification but also a further requirement that he had no reasonable cause to know of the disqualification.

[65A   Appeal against refusal of authority to give consent under section 65]

[(1)   An appeal against a decision of an appropriate authority under section 65 shall lie to the Tribunal established under section 9 of the Protection of Children Act 1999.

(2)   On an appeal the Tribunal may confirm the authority's decision or direct it to give the consent in question.]

Date in force

England: 1 April 2002: SI 2002/1493, art 3(2)(b); date in force (in relation to Wales): 1 April 2002: SI 2002/920, art 3(3)(d).

Amendment

Inserted by the Care Standards Act 2000, s 116, Sch 4 para 14(1), (14).

PART IX

PRIVATE ARRANGEMENTS FOR FOSTERING CHILDREN

66   Privately fostered children

1)   In this Part—

(a) 'a privately fostered child' means a child who is under the age of sixteen and who is cared for, and provided with accommodation [in their own home] by, someone other than—

    (i) a parent of his;

    (ii) a person who is not a parent of his but who has parental responsibility for him; or

    (iii) a relative of his; and

(b) 'to foster a child privately' means to look after the child in circumstances in which he is a privately fostered child as defined by this section.

(2)   A child is not a privately fostered child if the person caring for and accommodating him—

(a) has done so for a period of less than 28 days; and

(b) does not intend to do so for any longer period.

(3)   Subsection (1) is subject to—

(a) the provisions of section 63; and

(b) the exceptions made by a paragraphs 1 to 5 of Schedule 8.

(4)   In the case of a child who is disabled, subsection (1)(a) shall have effect as if for 'sixteen' there were substituted 'eighteen'.

[(4A)   The Secretary of State may by regulations make provision as to the circumstances in which a person who provides accommodation to a child is, or is not, to be treated as providing him with accommodation in the person's own home.]

(5)   Schedule 8 shall have effect for the purposes of supplementing the provision made by this Part.

Date in force

14 October 1991: SI 1991/828.

Amendments

Sub-s (1): in para (a) words 'in their own home' in square brackets inserted by the Care Standards Act 2000, s 116, Sch 4, para 14(1), (15)(a).
Sub-s (4A): inserted by the Care Standards Act 2000, s 116, Sch 4, para 14(1), (15)(b).

Definitions

For 'a privately fostered child' see sub-s (1)(a); for 'parental responsibility' see s 3; for 'relative' see s 105(1); for 'to foster a child privately' see sub-s (1)(b); for 'disabled' see s 17(11) as applied to the whole Act by s 105(1).

References

'This Part' ie Part IX, ss 66–70 and Sch 8 (private arrangements for fostering children). For transitional provisions see s 108(6) and Sch 14, para 32.

Sub-s (1) Relative

This is defined as a 'grandparent, brother, sister, uncle or aunt (whether of the full blood or half blood or by affinity) or step-parent.

Note

A person may be a foster parent notwithstanding he receives no reward or financial assistance for caring for the child. A privately fostered child is defined by a series of negative definitions which exclude the application of the provisions if the child is in the care of an agency, in certain premises or (sub-s (2)) for limited periods.

Sub-s (2) Period of less than 28 days

In *Surrey County Council v Battersby* [1965] 2 QB 194, [1965] 1 All ER 273, 129 JP 116, a case under the CA 1958 where the relevant period was described as 'for a period of more than 27 days' it was held that the provisions were aimed at the intention of the person taking in the child, and that intention could be inferred from the facts. In that case the parents agreed with the foster parent that the child would remain with the foster parent for an indefinite period, returning to the parents for periodical weekends. It was held that the weekends did not interrupt the overall period.

---

67   Welfare of privately fostered children

(1)   It shall be the duty of every local authority to satisfy themselves that the welfare of children who are [or are proposed to be] privately fostered within their area is being [or will be] satisfactorily safeguarded and promoted and to secure that such advice is given to those [concerned with] them as appears to the authority to be needed.

(2)   The Secretary of State may make regulations—

- (a)   requiring every child who is privately fostered within a local authority's area to be visited by an officer of the authority—
  - (i)   in prescribed circumstances; and
  - (ii)   on specified occasions or within specified periods; and
- (b)   imposing requirements which are to be met by any local authority, or officer of a local authority, in carrying out functions under this section.

[(2A)   Regulations under subsection (2)(b) may impose requirements as to the action to be taken by a local authority for the purposes of discharging their duty under subsection (1) where they have received notification of a proposal that a child be privately fostered.]

(3)   Where any person who is authorised by a local authority [for the purpose] has reasonable cause to believe that—

- (a)   any privately fostered child is being accommodated in premises within the authority's area; or
- (b)   it is proposed to accommodate any such child in any such premises,

he may at any reasonable time inspect those premises and any children there.

(4)   Any person exercising the power under subsection (3) shall, if so required, produce some duly authenticated document showing his authority to do so.

(5)   Where a local authority are not satisfied that the welfare of any child who is [or is proposed to be] privately fostered within their area is being [or will be] satisfactorily safeguarded or promoted they shall—

- (a)   unless they consider that it would not be in the best interests of the child, take such steps as are reasonably practicable to secure that the care and accommodation of the child is undertaken by—
  - (i)   a parent of his;
  - (ii)   any person who is not a parent of his but who has parental responsibility for him; or
  - (iii)   a relative of his; and
- (b)   consider the extent to which (if at all) they should exercise any of their functions under this Act with respect to the child.

[(6)   The Secretary of State may make regulations requiring a local authority to monitor the way in which the authority discharge their functions under this Part (and the regulations may in particular require the authority to appoint an officer for that purpose).]

Date in force

14 October 1991: SI 1991/828.

Amendments

Sub-s (1): words 'or are proposed to be' in square brackets inserted by the Children Act 2004, s 44(1), (2)(a); words 'or will be' in square brackets inserted by the Children Act 2004, s 44(1), (2)(b); words 'concerned with' in square brackets substituted by the Children Act 2004, s 44(1), (2)(c).
Sub-s (2A): inserted by the Children Act 2004, s 44(1), (3).
Sub-s (3): words 'for the purpose' in square brackets substituted by the Children Act 2004, s 44(1), (4).
Sub-s (5): words 'or is proposed to be' in square brackets inserted by the Children Act 2004, s 44(1), (5)(a); words 'or will be' in square brackets inserted by the Children Act 2004, s 44(1), (5)(b).
Sub-s (6): inserted by the Children Act 2004, s 44(1), (6).

Definitions

For 'local authority', 'child', 'relative', 'functions' see s 105(1); for 'a privately fostered child' see s 66(1)(a); for 'parental responsibility' see s 3.

References

For the offence of intentionally obstructing a person exercising the power under sub-s (3) see s 70(1)(c) in particular and s 70(4) concerning the punishment for such offence. For the inspection of premises where a foster child is living see s 80(1)(g). For power to issue a warrant to authorise a constable to assist in exercising the power under sub-s (3) see s 102.

Transfer of functions

Functions of the Secretary of State, so far as exercisable in relation to Wales, transferred to the National Assembly for Wales, by the National Assembly for Wales (Transfer of Functions) Order 1999, SI 1999/672, art 2, Sch 1

Sub-s (2) Regulations

See the Children (Private Arrangements for Fostering) Regulations 2005, SI 2005/1533 and the Children (Private Arrangements for Fostering) (Wales) Regulations 2006, SI 2006/940.

Premises

This will mean the whole of the premises in which the child is being accommodated not just that part in which the child has a room. The FCA 1980, s 8 referred to premises in the whole or any part of which the child was kept. This provision does not appear to have affected the position.

Sub-s (5) Local authority functions

eg under Pt III or make application for an emergency protection order s 44, child assessment order s 43 or commence care proceedings s 31

---

68   Persons disqualified from being private foster parents

(1)   Unless he has disclosed the fact to the appropriate local authority and obtained their written consent, a person shall not foster a child privately if he is disqualified from doing so by regulations made by the Secretary of State for the purposes of this section.

(2)   The regulations may, in particular, provide for a person to be so disqualified where—

(a) an order of a kind specified in the regulations has been made at any time with respect to him;

(b) an order of a kind so specified has been made at any time with respect to any child who has been in his care;

(c) a requirement of a kind so specified has been imposed at any time with respect to any such child, under or by virtue of any enactment;

(d) he has been convicted of an offence of a kind specified, or ... discharged absolutely or conditionally for any such offence;

(e) a prohibition has been imposed on him at any time under section 69 or under any other specified enactment;

(f) his rights and powers with respect to a child have at any time been vested in a specified authority under a specified enactment.

[(2A) A conviction in respect of which a probation order was made before 1st October 1992 (which would not otherwise be treated as a conviction) is to be treated as a conviction for the purposes of subsection (2)(d).]

(3) Unless he has disclosed the fact to the appropriate local authority and obtained their written consent, a person shall not foster a child privately if—

(a) he lives in the same household as a person who is himself prevented from fostering a child by subsection (1); or

(b) he lives in a household at which any such person is employed.

[(3A) A person shall not foster a child privately if—

(a) he is barred from regulated activity relating to children (within the meaning of section 3(2) of the Safeguarding Vulnerable Groups Act 2006); or

(b) he lives in the same household as a person who is barred from such activity.]

(4) Where an authority refuse to give their consent under this section, they shall inform the applicant by a written notice which states—

(a) the reason for the refusal;

(b) the applicant's right under paragraph 8 of Schedule 8 to appeal against the refusal; and

(c) the time within which he may do so.

(5) In this section—

'the appropriate authority' means the local authority within whose area it is proposed to foster the child in question; and

'enactment' means any enactment having effect, at any time, in any part of the United Kingdom.

Date in force

4 October 1991: SI 1991/828.

Definitions

For 'the appropriate local authority' and 'enactment' see sub-s (5); for 'to foster a child privately' see s 66(1)(b); for 'child', 'local authority' see s 105(1).

Amendments

Sub-s (2): in para (d) words omitted repealed by the Criminal Justice Act 2003, ss 304, 332, Sch 32, Pt 1, paras 59, 60(1), (2), Sch 37, Pt 7.
Sub-s (2A): inserted by the Criminal Justice Act 2003, s 304, Sch 32, Pt 1, paras 59, 60(1), (3).
Sub-s (3A): inserted by the Safeguarding Vulnerable Groups Act 2006, s 63(1), Sch 9, Pt 2, para 12.

Appendix 1 *Children Act 1989*

References

For appeal to the court by a person aggrieved by a refusal of consent under this section see Sch 8, para 8; for offences see s 70.

Regulations

See the Disqualification for Caring for Children (England) Regulations 2002, SI 2002/635 and the Disqualification for Caring for Children (Wales) Regulations 2004, SI 2004/2695.

Transfer of functions

Functions of the Secretary of State, so far as exercisable in relation to Wales, transferred to the National Assembly for Wales, by the National Assembly for Wales (Transfer of Functions) Order 1999, SI 1999/672, art 2, Sch 1.

Sub-s (2)

A conviction followed by an absolute or conditional discharge is not normally a conviction for the purposes of any proceedings other than those in which the order is made (PCC(S)A 2000, s 1C) and the inclusion of these words is necessary to give a local authority opportunity to consider the case.

Sub-s (3)

Same household The former provisions in the FCA 1980, s 7(2) referred to persons in the 'same premises'. The new restriction seems therefore to be drawn more closely. But note the defence to a prosecution in s 70(2).

---

69 Power to prohibit private fostering

(1) This section applies where a person—

    (a) proposes to foster a child privately; or
    (b) is fostering a child privately.

(2) Where the local authority for the area within which the child is proposed to be, or is being, fostered are of the opinion that—

    (a) he is not a suitable person to foster a child;
    (b) the premises in which the child will be, or is being, accommodated are not suitable; or
    (c) it would be prejudicial to the welfare of the child for him to be, or continue to be, accommodated by that person in those premises,

the authority may impose a prohibition on him under subsection (3).

(3) A prohibition imposed on any person under this subsection may prohibit him from fostering privately—

    (a) any child in any premises within the area of the local authority; or
    (b) any child in premises specified in the prohibition;
    (c) a child identified in the prohibition, in premises specified in the prohibition.

(4) A local authority who have imposed a prohibition on any person under subsection (3) may, if they think fit, cancel the prohibition—

    (a) of their own motion; or
    (b) on an application made by that person,

if they are satisfied that the prohibition is no longer justified.

(5) Where a local authority impose a requirement on any person under paragraph 6 of Schedule 8, they may also impose a prohibition on him under subsection (3).

(6)   Any prohibition imposed by virtue of subsection (5) shall not have effect unless—

(a)   the time specified for compliance with the requirement has expired; and
(b)   the requirement has not been complied with.

(7)   A prohibition imposed under this section shall be imposed by notice in writing addressed to the person on whom it is imposed and informing him of—

(a)   the reason for imposing the prohibition;
(b)   his right under paragraph 8 of Schedule 8 to appeal against the prohibition; and
(c)   the time within which he may do so.

Date in force

14 October 1991: SI 1991/828.

Definitions

For 'child', 'local authority' see s 105(1); for 'to foster a child privately' see s 66(1)(b).

References

For 'required notice' see Sch 8, para 7; for service of notices under this Act generally see s 105(8)–(10); for appeal to the court by a person aggrieved by a prohibition imposed under this section see Sch 8, para 8; for offences see s 70; for inspection of premises where a child is privately fostered see s 67(3).

Sub-s (1) Is fostering

Formerly the power of prohibition existed only where the foster parent had failed to give the authority notice of his proposal to foster. Now the power exists even where the placement had at first been deemed suitable but where circumstances may have changed and the local authority may need to act to safeguard the child.

Sub-s (2) Impose a prohibition

The prohibition appears to be effective pending appeal under Sch 8, para (1). Cf effect of an appeal on a requirement under para 6 (requirements).

Sub-s (7) Notice in writing

May be given by post, s 105(8).

---

70   Offences

(1)   A person shall be guilty of an offence if—

(a)   being required, under any provision made by or under this Part, to give any notice or information—
  (i)   he fails without reasonable excuse to give the notice within the time specified in that provision; or
  (ii)   he fails without reasonable excuse to give the information within a reasonable time; or
  (iii)   he makes, or causes or procures another person to make, any statement in the notice or information which he knows to be false or misleading in a material particular;
(b)   he refuses to allow a privately fostered child to be visited by a duly authorised officer of a local authority;
(c)   he intentionally obstructs another in the exercise of the power conferred by section 67(3);
(d)   he contravenes section 68;

(e)   he fails without reasonable excuse to comply with any requirement imposed by a local authority under this Part;

(f)   he accommodates a privately fostered child in any premises in contravention of a prohibition imposed by a local authority under this Part;

(g)   he knowingly causes to be published, or publishes, an advertisement which he knows contravenes paragraph 10 of Schedule 8.

(2)   Where a person contravenes section 68(3), he shall not be guilty of an offence under this section if he proves that he did not know, and had no reasonable ground for believing, that any person to whom section 68(1) applies was living or employed in the premises in question.

(3)   A person guilty of an offence under subsection (1)(a) shall be liable on summary conviction to a fine not exceeding level 5 on the standard scale.

(4)   A person guilty of an offence under subsection (1)(b), (c) or (g) shall be liable on summary conviction to a fine not exceeding level 3 on the standard scale.

(5)   A person guilty of an offence under subsection (1)(d) or (f) shall be liable on summary conviction to imprisonment for a term not exceeding six months, or to a fine not exceeding level 5 on the standard scale, or to both.

(6)   A person guilty of an offence under subsection (1)(e) shall be liable on summary conviction to a fine not exceeding level 5 on the standard scale.

(7)   If any person who is required, under any provision of this Part, to give a notice fails to give the notice within the time specified in that provision, proceedings for the offence may be brought at any time within six months from the date when evidence of the offence came to the knowledge of the local authority.

(8)   Subsection (7) is not affected by anything in section 127(1) of the Magistrates' Courts Act 1980 (time limit for proceedings).

Date in force

14 October 1991: SI 1991/828.

Definitions

For 'a privately fostered child' see s 66(1)(a); for 'local authority' see s 105(1).

References

'This Part' ie Pt IX, s 66–70 and Sch 8 (private arrangements for fostering children). For 'the standard scale' see the CJA 1982, s 37(2)(3) as amended.

Sub-s (1)

Note that these provisions require the failure in s 70(1)(a)(i) (ii) and (e) to be without reasonable excuse and that statement in sub-s (iii) to be false in a material particular.

Intentionally obstructs

The former provision referred to 'wilfully obstructs' but the law probably remains the same.

Sub-s (2)

He proves that he did not know Ie the burden of proof is on the defendant but on the balance of probabilities: *R v Carr-Briant* [1943] KB 607, [1943] 2 All ER 156, 107 JP 167, CCA.

Sub-s (8)

The normal time limit for criminal proceedings in respect of summary offences is six months: Magistrates' Courts Act 1980, s 127(1).

PART X

CHILD MINDING AND DAY CARE FOR YOUNG CHILDREN

Part X is repealed as it applies to England and Wales (but not Scotland) by s 79 of the Care Standards Act. For the provisions of Part X, see the second edition of this work.

PART XA

CHILD MINDING AND DAY CARE FOR CHILDREN IN ENGLAND AND WALES

Introductory

[79A   Child minders and day care providers]

[(1)   This section and section 79B apply for the purposes of this Part.

(2)   'Act as a child minder' means (subject to the following subsections) look after one or more children under the age of eight on domestic premises for reward; and 'child minding' shall be interpreted accordingly.

(3)   A person who—

   (a)   is the parent, or a relative, of a child;
   (b)   has parental responsibility for a child;
   (c)   is a local authority foster parent in relation to a child;
   (d)   is a foster parent with whom a child has been placed by a voluntary organisation; or
   (e)   fosters a child privately,

does not act as a child minder when looking after that child.

(4)   Where a person—

   (a)   looks after a child for the parents ('P1'), or
   (b)   in addition to that work, looks after another child for different parents ('P2'),

and the work consists (in a case within paragraph (a)) of looking after the child wholly or mainly in P1's home or (in a case within paragraph (b)) of looking after the children wholly or mainly in P1's home or P2's home or both, the work is not to be treated as child minding.

(5)   In subsection (4), 'parent', in relation to a child, includes—

   (a)   a person who is not a parent of the child but who has parental responsibility for the child;
   (b)   a person who is a relative of the child.

(6)   'Day care' means care provided at any time for children under the age of eight on premises other than domestic premises.

(7)   This Part does not apply in relation to a person who acts as a child minder, or provides day care on any premises, unless the period, or the total of the periods, in any day which he spends looking after children or (as the case may be) during which the children are looked after on the premises exceeds two hours.

(8)   In determining whether a person is required to register under this Part for child minding, any day on which he does not act as a child minder at any time between 2am and 6pm is to be disregarded.]

Date in force

England: 2 July 2001: see SI 2001/1210, art 2.

Amendment

Inserted by s 79 of the Care Standards Act 2000.

Definitions

For 'act as a child minder' see sub-s (2) as applied to the whole Act by s 105(5A); for 'relative', 'child', 'voluntary organization' see 105(1); for 'domestic premises' see s 79B(6); for 'parent' see sub-s (5); for 'parental responsibility' see s 3; for 'local authority foster parent' see s 23(3); for 'fosters a child privately' see 66(1)(b); for 'day care' see sub-s (6).

Reference

'This Part' ie Part XA ss 79A–79X and Sch 9A (child minding and day care for young children).

Note

Part XA provides new definitions of child minding and day care which, particularly as regards child minding, clarifies some of the concepts which were doubtful in the former legislation (Part X of the 1989 Act) eg nannies, unless they work for more than two families are exempt from the definition of day care; 'day care' includes care given at any time of the day or night; and babysitters, provided they work for no more than 2 hours a day or between 6pm and 2 am are not 'child minders'. (See generally, the *Explanatory Notes to the Care Standards Act 2000* The Stationery Office Limited ISBN 0105614009).

In addition, provision is made for checks on the suitability of persons working with older children.

In England the responsibility for child minding and day care regulation is transferred from local authorities to Her Majesty's Chief Inspector of Schools for England (HMCIS) and in Wales to the National Assembly and the Chief Inspector of Education and Training in Wales (the 'registration authorities').

Criteria are established for applicants to be registered and for suspension or cancellation of registration. Whilst it is an offence to act as an unregistered day care provider an unregistered child minder only commits an offence if he or she acts as such without reasonable excuse whilst an enforcement notice is in effect. The register of child minders and providers of day care must be publicly available. Registration may be voluntarily given up which may assist in ensuring that information provided for parents seeking child care provision relates only to those who are currently providing these services.

A magistrates' court may make, on application by the registration authority, an emergency order in respect of a registered childminder or day care provider where the registration authority believes that a child in their care is suffering, or is likely to suffer, significant harm.

[79B   Other definitions, etc]

[(1)   *The registration authority in relation to England is [Her Majesty's Chief Inspector of Education, Children's Services and Skills] (referred to in this Part as the Chief Inspector) and references to the Chief Inspector's area are references to England.*

(2)   *The registration authority in relation to Wales is the National Assembly for Wales (referred to in this Act as 'the Assembly').*

[(2)   In this Act 'the Assembly' means the National Assembly for Wales.]

(3)   A person is qualified for registration for child minding if—

    (a)   he, and every other person looking after children on any premises on which he is or is likely to be child minding, is suitable to look after children under the age of eight;

(b) every person living or employed on the premises in question is suitable to be in regular contact with children under the age of eight;

(c) the premises in question are suitable to be used for looking after children under the age of eight, having regard to their condition and the condition and appropriateness of any equipment on the premises and to any other factor connected with the situation, construction or size of the premises; and

(d) he is complying with regulations under section 79C and with any conditions imposed [under this Part].

(4) A person is qualified for registration for providing day care on particular premises if—

[(a) he has made adequate arrangements to ensure that—
   (i) every person (other than himself and the responsible individual) looking after children on the premises is suitable to look after children under the age of eight; and
   (ii) every person (other than himself and the responsible individual) living or working on the premises is suitable to be in regular contact with children under the age of eight;

(b) the responsible individual—
   (i) is suitable to look after children under the age of eight, or
   (ii) if he is not looking after such children, is suitable to be in regular contact with them;]

(c) the premises are suitable to be used for looking after children under the age of eight, having regard to their condition and the condition and appropriateness of any equipment on the premises and to any other factor connected with the situation, construction or size of the premises; and

(d) he is complying with regulations under section 79C and with any conditions imposed [under this Part].

(5) For the purposes of subsection [(4)(a)] a person is not treated as working on the premises in question if—

(a) none of his work is done in the part of the premises in which children are looked after; or

(b) he does not work on the premises at times when children are looked after there.

[(5ZA) For the purposes of subsection (4), 'the responsible individual' means—

(a) in a case of one individual working on the premises in the provision of day care, that person;

(b) in a case of two or more individuals so working, the individual so working who is in charge.]

[(5A) Where, for the purposes of determining a person's qualification for registration under this Part—

(a) *the registration authority* [the Assembly] requests any person ('A') to consent to the disclosure to the authority by another person ('B') of any information relating to A which is held by B and is of a prescribed description, and

(b) A does not give his consent (or withdraws it after having given it),

the registration authority [the Assembly] may, if regulations so provide and it thinks it appropriate to do so, regard A as not suitable to look after children under the age of eight, or not suitable to be in regular contact with such children.]

(6) 'Domestic premises' means any premises which are wholly or mainly used as a private dwelling and 'premises' includes any area and any vehicle.

(7) *'Regulations' means*—

(a) *in relation to England, regulations made by the Secretary of State;*
(b) *in relation to Wales, regulations made by the Assembly.*

[(7) 'Regulations' means regulations made by the Assembly.]

(8) 'Tribunal' means the Tribunal established by section 9 of the Protection of Children Act 1999.

(9) Schedule 9A (which supplements the provisions of this Part) shall have effect.]

Date in force

1 July 2001: see SI 2001/2190; SI 2001/2041.

Amendment

Inserted by the Care Standards Act 2000, s 79(1).
Sub-s (1): repealed by the Childcare Act 2006, s 103, Sch 2, para 7(a), Sch 3, Pt 2; words 'Her Majesty's Chief Inspector of Education, Children's Services and Skills' in square brackets substituted by the Education and Inspections Act 2006, s 157, Sch 14, paras 9, 13.
Sub-s (2): substituted by the Childcare Act 2006, s 103(1), Sch 2, para 7(b). Date in force: to be appointed: see the Childcare Act 2006, ss 109(2), 110(1), (5)(c).
Sub-s (3): in para (d) words 'under this Part' in square brackets substituted by the Children Act 2004, s 48, Sch 4, paras 1, 2(1).
Sub-s (4): paras (a), (b) substituted by the Children Act 2004, s 48, Sch 4, paras 1, 6(a) in para (d) words 'under this Part' in square brackets substituted by the Children Act 2004, s 48, Sch 4, paras 1, 2(1).
Sub-s (5): reference to '(4)(a)' in square brackets substituted by the Children Act 2004, s 48, Sch 4, paras 1, 6(b).
Sub-s (5ZA): inserted by the Children Act 2004, s 48, Sch 4, paras 1, 6(c).
Sub-s (5A): inserted by the Education Act 2002, s 152, Sch 13, para 1; words 'the registration authority' in italics in both places they occur repealed and subsequent words in square brackets substituted by the Childcare Act 2006, s 103(1), Sch 2, para 6. Date in force: to be appointed: see the Childcare Act 2006, ss 109(2), 110(1), (5)(c).
Sub-s (7): substituted by the Childcare Act 2006, s 103(1), Sch 2, para 7(c). Date in force: to be appointed: see the Childcare Act 2006, ss 109(2), 110(1), (5)(c).

Definitions

For 'the registration authority' and 'Chief Inspector' see sub-s (1)(2); for 'the Assembly' see sub-s (2); for 'child minding' see s 79A(1) as applied to the whole Act by s 105(5A); for 'premises' see sub-s (6); for 'day care' see s 79A(6).

Reference

'This Part' ie Part XA, ss 79A–79X and Sch 9A (child minding and day care for young children).

Sub-s (5A) Regulations

See the Day Care and Child Minding (Suitability) (England) Regulations 2005, SI 2005/229.

[**79C   Regulations etc governing child minders and day care providers**]

[(1) *The Secretary of State may, after consulting the Chief Inspector and any other person he considers appropriate, make regulations governing the activities of registered persons who act as child minders, or provide day care, on premises in England.*

(2) The Assembly may make regulations governing the activities of registered persons who act as child minders, or provide day care, on premises in Wales.

(3) The regulations under this section may deal with the following matters (among others)—

(a)   the welfare and development of the children concerned;
(b)   suitability to look after, or be in regular contact with, children under the age of eight;
(c)   qualifications and training;
(d)   the maximum number of children who may be looked after and the number of persons required to assist in looking after them;
(e)   the maintenance, safety and suitability of premises and equipment;
(f)   the keeping of records;
(g)   the provision of information.

(4)   *In relation to activities on premises in England, the power to make regulations under this section may be exercised so as to confer powers or impose duties on the Chief Inspector in the exercise of his functions under this Part.*

(5)   *In particular they may be exercised so as to require or authorise the Chief Inspector, in exercising those functions, to have regard to or meet factors, standards and other matters prescribed by or referred to in the regulations.*

(6)   If the regulations require any person (other than *the registration authority* [the Assembly]) to have regard to or meet factors, standards and other matters prescribed by or referred to in the regulations, they may also provide for any allegation that the person has failed to do so to be taken into account—

(a)   by *the registration authority* [the Assembly] in the exercise of its functions under this Part, or
(b)   in any proceedings under this Part.

(7)   Regulations may provide—

(a)   that a registered person who without reasonable excuse contravenes, or otherwise fails to comply with, any requirement of the regulations shall be guilty of an offence; and
(b)   that a person guilty of the offence shall be liable on summary conviction to a fine not exceeding level 5 on the standard scale.]

Date in force

England: 16 March 2001 / 2 July 2001: see SI 2001/1210; SI 2001/2041.

Amendment

Inserted by the Care Standards Act 2000, s 79(1).
Sub-s (1): repealed by the Childcare Act 2006, s 103, Sch 2, para 8, Sch 3, Pt 2. Date in force: to be appointed: see the Childcare Act 2006, ss 109(2), 110(1), (5)(c), (6)(b).
Sub-ss (4), (5): repealed by the Childcare Act 2006, s 103, Sch 2, para 8, Sch 3, Pt 2. Date in force: to be appointed: see the Childcare Act 2006, ss 109(2), 110(1), (5)(c), (6)(b).
Sub-s (6): words 'the registration authority' in italics in both places they occur repealed and subsequent words in square brackets substituted by the Childcare Act 2006, s 103(1), Sch 2, para 6. Date in force: to be appointed: see the Childcare Act 2006, ss 109(2), 110(1), (5)(c).

Definitions

For 'the Chief Inspector' see s 79B(1); for 'act as a child minder' see s 79A(2) as applied to the whole Act by s 105(5A); for 'day care' see s 79A(6); for 'premises' see s 79B(6); for 'the Assembly' see s 79B(2); for 'the registration authority' see s 79B(1)(2).

Reference

For 'the standard scale' see the CJA 1982 s 37(2) (3) as amended.

Appendix 1 *Children Act 1989*

Without reasonable excuse

The defendant will have the evidential burden of raising the defence of reasonable excuse but the final burden of proving his guilt beyond reasonable doubt will remain with the prosecution throughout. What amounts to a reasonable excuse in the circumstances of a particular case will be for the court to decide.

Regulations

See the Child Minding and Day Care (Wales) Regulations 2002, SI 2002/812 amended by SI 2002/2171 and 2622, SI 2003/2708, SI 2004/2414, SI 2005/2929 and SI 2006/3251, the Day Care and Child Minding (National Standards) (England) Regulations 2003, SI 2003/1996 amended by SI 2005/2303, the Disqualification from Caring for Children (Wales) Regulations 2004, SI 2004/2695 and the Day Care and Child Minding (Disqualification) (England) Regulations 2005, SI 2005/2296 amended by SI 2007/197 and 603.

Registration

[79D   Requirement to register]

[*(1) No person shall*—

    (*a*)   *act as a child minder in England unless he is registered under this Part for child minding by the Chief Inspector; or*

    (*b*)   *act as a child minder in Wales unless he is registered under this Part for child minding by the Assembly.*

[(1) No person shall act as a child minder in Wales unless he is registered under this Part for child minding by the Assembly.]

(2) Where it appears to *the registration authority* [the Assembly] that a person has contravened subsection (1), the authority may serve a notice ('an enforcement notice') on him.

(3) An enforcement notice shall have effect for a period of one year beginning with the date on which it is served.

(4) If a person in respect of whom an enforcement notice has effect contravenes subsection (1) without reasonable excuse (*whether the contravention occurs in England or Wales*), he shall be guilty of an offence.

(5) No person shall provide day care on any premises [in Wales] unless he is registered under this Part for providing day care on those premises by *the registration authority* [the Assembly].

(6) If any person contravenes subsection (5) without reasonable excuse, he shall be guilty of an offence.

(7) A person guilty of an offence under this section shall be liable on summary conviction to a fine not exceeding level 5 on the standard scale.]

Date in force

England: 2 July 2001: see SI 2001/2041.

Amendment

Inserted by the Care Standards Act 2000, s 79(1).
Sub-s (1): substituted by the Childcare Act 2006, s 103(1), Sch 2, para 9(a). Date in force: to be appointed: see the Childcare Act 2006, ss 109(2), 110(1), (5)(c).
Sub-s (2): words 'the registration authority' in italics repealed and subsequent words in square brackets substituted by the Childcare Act 2006, s 103(1), Sch 2, para 6. Date in force: to be appointed: see the Childcare Act 2006, ss 109(2), 110(1), (5)(c).

Sub-s (4): words '(whether the contravention occurs in England or Wales)' in italics repealed by the Childcare Act 2006, s 103, Sch 2, para 9(b), Sch 3, Pt 2. Date in force: to be appointed: see the Childcare Act 2006, ss 109(2), 110(1), (5)(c), (6)(b).
Sub-s (5): words 'in Wales' in square brackets inserted by the Childcare Act 2006, s 103(1), Sch 2, para 9(c). Date in force: to be appointed: see the Childcare Act 2006, ss 109(2), 110(1), (5)(c); words 'the registration authority' in italics repealed and subsequent words in square brackets substituted by the Childcare Act 2006, s 103(1), Sch 2, para 6. Date in force: to be appointed: see the Childcare Act 2006, ss 109(2), 110(1), (5)(c).

Definitions

For 'act as a child minder' see s 79A(2) as applied to the whole Act by s 105(5A); for 'the Chief Inspector' see s 79B(1); for 'the registration authority' see s 79B(1)(2); for 'the Assembly' see s 79B(2); for 'an enforcement notice' see sub-s (2); for 'premises' see s 79B(6); for 'day care' see s 79A(6).

References

'This Part' i e Part XA ss 79A–79X and Sch 9A (child minding and day care for young children). For 'the standard scale' see the CJA 1982 s 37(2) (3) as amended.

Without reasonable excuse

The defendant will have the evidential burden of raising the defence of reasonable excuse but the final burden of proving his guilt beyond reasonable doubt will remain with the prosecution throughout. What amounts to a reasonable excuse in the circumstances of a particular case will be for the court to decide.

[79E   Applications for registration]

[(1)   A person who wishes to be registered under this Part shall make an application to *the registration authority* [the Assembly].

(2)   The application shall—

    (a)   give prescribed information about prescribed matters;
    (b)   give any other information which *the registration authority* [the Assembly] reasonably requires the applicant to give;
    [(c)   be accompanied by the prescribed fee].

(3)   Where a person provides, or proposes to provide, day care on different premises, he shall make a separate application in respect of each of them.

(4)   Where *the registration authority* [the Assembly] has sent the applicant notice under section 79L(1) of its intention to refuse an application under this section, the application may not be withdrawn without the consent of the authority.

(5)   A person who, in an application under this section, knowingly makes a statement which is false or misleading in a material particular shall be guilty of an offence and liable, on summary conviction, to a fine not exceeding level 5 on the standard scale.]

Date in force

England: 16 March 2001 / 2 July 2001: see SI 2001/1210; SI 2001/2041.

Amendment

Inserted by the Care Standards Act 2000, s 79(1).
Sub-s (1): words 'the registration authority' in italics repealed and subsequent words in square brackets substituted by the Childcare Act 2006, s 103(1), Sch 2, para 6. Date in force: to be appointed: see the Childcare Act 2006, ss 109(2), 110(1), (5)(c).

Sub-s (2): in para (b) words 'the registration authority' in italics repealed and subsequent words in square brackets substituted by the Childcare Act 2006, s 103(1), Sch 2, para 6. Date in force: to be appointed: see the Childcare Act 2006, ss 109(2), 110(1), (5)(c); para (c) inserted by the Children Act 2004, s 48, Sch 4, paras 1, 3(1).

Sub-s (4): words 'the registration authority' in italics repealed and subsequent words in square brackets substituted by the Childcare Act 2006, s 103(1), Sch 2, para 6. Date in force: to be appointed: see the Childcare Act 2006, ss 109(2), 110(1), (5)(c).

Definitions

For 'the registration authority' see s 79B(1)(2); for 'day care' see s 79A(6); for 'premises' see s 79B(6); for 'act as a child minder' see s 79A(2) as applied to the whole Act by s 105(5A).

References

'This Part' ie Part XA ss 79A–79X and Sch 9A (child minding and day care for young children). For 'the standard scale' see the CJA 1982 s 37(2) (3) as amended.

Sub-s (2) Prescribed information

See the Child Minding and Day Care (Applications for Registration (England) Regulations 2001, SI 2001/1829 amended by SI 2003/1995 and SI 2005/2448, the Registration of Social Care and Independent Health Care (Wales) Regulations 2002, SI 2002/919 amended by SI 2002/2622 and 2935, SI 2003/710,2527 and 2709, SI 2004/219, 1756 and SI 2006/3251 and 3302 and SI 2006/3251 and the Day Care and Child Minding (Registration Fees) (England) Regulations 2005, SI 2005/2301 amended by SI 2006/2081 and SI 2007/1769.

[79F   Grant or refusal of registration]

[(1)   If, on an application [under section 79E] by a person for registration for child minding—

(a)   *the registration authority* [the Assembly] is of the opinion that the applicant is, and will continue to be, qualified for registration for child minding (so far as the conditions of section 79B(3) are applicable); ...

(b)   ...

the authority [the Assembly] shall grant the application; otherwise, it shall refuse it.

(2)   If, on an application [under section 79E] by any person for registration for providing day care on any premises—

(a)   *the registration authority* [the Assembly] is of the opinion that the applicant is, and will continue to be, qualified for registration for providing day care on those premises (so far as the conditions of section 79B(4) are applicable); ...

(b)   ...

the authority [the Assembly] shall grant the application; otherwise, it shall refuse it.

(3)   An application may, as well as being granted subject to any conditions *the authority* [the Assembly] thinks necessary or expedient for the purpose of giving effect to regulations under section 79C, be granted subject to any other conditions *the authority* [the Assembly] thinks fit to impose.

(4)   *The registration authority* [The Assembly] may as it thinks fit vary or remove any condition to which the registration is subject or impose a new condition.

(5)   Any register kept by *a registration authority* [the Assembly] of persons who act as child minders or provide day care shall be open to inspection by any person at all reasonable times.

(6) A registered person who without reasonable excuse contravenes, or otherwise fails to comply with, any condition imposed on his registration shall be guilty of an offence.

(7) A person guilty of an offence under subsection (6) shall be liable on summary conviction to a fine not exceeding level 5 on the standard scale.]

Date in force

England: 16 March 2001 / 2 July 2001: see SI 2001/1210; SI 2001/2041.

Amendment

Inserted by the Care Standards Act 2000, s 79(1).
Sub-s (1): words 'under section 79E' in square brackets inserted by the Children Act 2004, s 48, Sch 4, paras 1, 3(2)(a); in para (a) words 'the registration authority' in italics repealed and subsequent words in square brackets substituted by the Childcare Act 2006, s 103(1), Sch 2, para 6. Date in force: to be appointed: see the Childcare Act 2006, ss 109(2), 110(1), (5)(c); para (b) and word omitted immediately preceding it repealed by the Children Act 2004, ss 48, 64, Sch 4, paras 1, 3(2)(b), Sch 5, Pt 2; words 'the authority' in italics repealed and subsequent words in square brackets substituted by the Childcare Act 2006, s 103(1), Sch 2, para 6. Date in force: to be appointed: see the Childcare Act 2006, ss 109(2), 110(1), (5)(c).
Sub-s (2): words 'under section 79E' in square brackets inserted by the Children Act 2004, s 48, Sch 4, paras 1, 3(2)(a); in para (a) words 'the registration authority' in italics repealed and subsequent words in square brackets substituted by the Childcare Act 2006, s 103(1), Sch 2, para 6. Date in force: to be appointed: see the Childcare Act 2006, ss 109(2), 110(1), (5)(c); para (b) and word omitted immediately preceding it repealed by the Children Act 2004, ss 48, 64, Sch 4, paras 1, 3(2)(b), Sch 5, Pt 2; words 'the authority' in italics repealed and subsequent words in square brackets substituted by the Childcare Act 2006, s 103(1), Sch 2, para 6. Date in force: to be appointed: see the Childcare Act 2006, ss 109(2), 110(1), (5)(c).
Sub-s (3): words 'the authority' in italics in both places they occur repealed and subsequent words in square brackets substituted by the Childcare Act 2006, s 103(1), Sch 2, para 6. Date in force: to be appointed: see the Childcare Act 2006, ss 109(2), 110(1), (5)(c).
Sub-s (4): words 'The registration authority' in italics repealed and subsequent words in square brackets substituted by the Childcare Act 2006, s 103(1), Sch 2, para 6. Date in force: to be appointed: see the Childcare Act 2006, ss 109(2), 110(1), (5)(c).
Sub-s (5): words 'a registration authority' in italics repealed and subsequent words in square brackets substituted by the Childcare Act 2006, s 103(1), Sch 2, para 6. Date in force: to be appointed: see the Childcare Act 2006, ss 109(2), 110(1), (5)(c).

Definitions

For 'child minding' see s 79A (2) as applied to the whole Act by s 105(5A); for 'the registration authority' see s 79B(1)(2); for 'day care' see s 79A(6); for 'premises' see s 79B(6).

Reference

For 'the standard scale' see the CJA 1982 s 37(2) (3) as amended.

Without reasonable excuse

The defendant will have the evidential burden of raising the defence of reasonable excuse but the final burden of proving his guilt beyond reasonable doubt will remain with the prosecution throughout. What amounts to a reasonable excuse in the circumstances of a particular case will be for the court to decide.

[79G   Cancellation of registration]

[(1) *The registration authority* [The Assembly] may cancel the registration of any person if—

(a)   in the case of a person registered for child minding, *the authority* [the Assembly] is of the opinion that the person has ceased or will cease to be qualified for registration for child minding;

(b)   in the case of a person registered for providing day care on any premises, *the authority* [the Assembly] is of the opinion that the person has ceased or will cease to be qualified for registration for providing day care on those premises,

or if [a fee] which is due from the person has not been paid.

(2)   Where a requirement to make any changes or additions to any services, equipment or premises has been imposed on a registered person ..., his registration shall not be cancelled on the ground of any defect or insufficiency in the services, equipment or premises if—

(a)   the time set for complying with the requirements has not expired; and

(b)   it is shown that the defect or insufficiency is due to the changes or additions not having been made.

(3)   Any cancellation under this section must be in writing.]

Date in force

England: 2 July 2001: see SI 2001/2041.

Amendment

Inserted by the Care Standards Act 2000, s 79(1).
Sub-s (1): words 'The registration authority' in italics repealed and subsequent words in square brackets substituted by the Childcare Act 2006, s 103(1), Sch 2, para 6. Date in force: to be appointed: see the Childcare Act 2006, ss 109(2), 110(1), (5)(c); words 'the authority' in italics in both places they occur repealed and subsequent words in square brackets substituted by the Childcare Act 2006, s 103(1), Sch 2, para 6. Date in force: to be appointed: see the Childcare Act 2006, ss 109(2), 110(1), (5)(c); words 'a fee' in square brackets substituted by the Children Act 2004, s 48, Sch 4, paras 1, 4(1).
Sub-s (2): words omitted repealed by the Children Act 2004, ss 48, 64, Sch 4, paras 1, 2(2), Sch 5, Pt 2.

Definitions

For 'the registration authority' see s 79B(1)(2); for 'child minding' see s 79A(2) as applied to the whole Act by s 105(5A); for 'day care' see s 79A(6); for 'premises' see s 79B(6).

[79H   Suspension of registration]

[(1)   Regulations may provide for the registration of any person for acting as a child minder or providing day care to be suspended for a prescribed period by *the registration authority* [the Assembly] in prescribed circumstances.

(2)   Any regulations made under this section shall include provision conferring on the person concerned a right of appeal to the Tribunal against suspension.

[(3)   *A person registered under this Part for child minding by the Chief Inspector shall not act as a child minder in England at a time when that registration is suspended in accordance with regulations under this section.*

(4)   A person registered under this Part for child minding by the Assembly shall not act as a child minder in Wales at a time when that registration is so suspended.

(5)   A person registered under this Part for providing day care on any premises shall not provide day care on those premises at any time when that registration is so suspended.

(6) If any person contravenes subsection (3), (4) or (5) without reasonable excuse, he shall be guilty of an offence and liable on summary conviction to a fine not exceeding level 5 on the standard scale.]]

Date in force

England: 16 March 2001 / 2 July 2001: see SI 2001/1210; SI 2001/2041.

Amendment

Inserted by the Care Standards Act 2000, s 79(1).
Sub-s (1): words 'the registration authority' in italics repealed and subsequent words in square brackets substituted by the Childcare Act 2006, s 103(1), Sch 2, para 6. Date in force: to be appointed: see the Childcare Act 2006, ss 109(2), 110(1), (5)(c).
Sub-ss (3)–(6): inserted by the Education Act 2002, s 152, Sch 13, para 2.
Sub-s (3): repealed by the Childcare Act 2006, s 103, Sch 2, para 10, Sch 3, Pt 2. Date in force: to be appointed: see the Childcare Act 2006, ss 109(2), 110(1), (5)(c), (6)(b).

Definitions

For 'act as a child minder' see s 79A(2) as applied to the whole Act by s 105(5A); for 'day care' see s 79A(6); for 'the registration authority' see s 79B(1)(2); for 'the Tribunal' see s 79B(8).

Sub-s (1) Regulations

See the Child Minding and Day Care (Suspension of Registration) (England) Regulations 2003, SI 2003/332 amended by SI 2007/197 and 603 and the Suspension of Day Care Providers and Child Minders (Wales) Regulations 2004, SI 2004/3282.

[79J   Resignation of registration]

[(1)   A person who is registered for acting as a child minder or providing day care may by notice in writing to *the registration authority* [the Assembly] resign his registration.

(2)   But a person may not give a notice under subsection (1)—

    (a)   if *the registration authority* [the Assembly] has sent him a notice under section 79L(1) of its intention to cancel the registration, unless the authority has decided not to take that step; or

    (b)   if *the registration authority* [the Assembly] has sent him a notice under section 79L(5) of its decision to cancel the registration and the time within which an appeal may be brought has not expired or, if an appeal has been brought, it has not been determined.]

Date in force

England: 2 July 2001: see SI 2001/2041.

Amendment

Inserted by the Care Standards Act 2000, s 79(1).
Sub-ss (1), (2): words 'the registration authority' in italics in each place they occur repealed and subsequent words in square brackets substituted by the Childcare Act 2006, s 103(1), Sch 2, para 6. Date in force: to be appointed: see the Childcare Act 2006, ss 109(2), 110(1), (5)(c).

Definitions

For 'act as a child minder' see s 79A(2) as applied to the whole Act by s 105(5A); for 'day care' see s 79A(6); for 'the registration authority' see s 79B(1)(2); for 'the Tribunal' see s 79B(8).

Appendix 1 *Children Act 1989*

For service of documents see s 105(8)–(10).

[79K   Protection of children in an emergency]

[(1)   If, in the case of any person registered [under this Part] for acting as a child minder or providing day care—

  (a)   *the registration authority* [the Assembly] applies to a justice of the peace for an order—
      (i)   cancelling the registration;
      (ii)   varying or removing any condition to which the registration is subject; or
      (iii)   imposing a new condition; and
  (b)   it appears to the justice that a child who is being, or may be, looked after by that person, or (as the case may be) in accordance with the provision for day care made by that person, is suffering, or is likely to suffer, significant harm,

the justice may make the order.

(2)   The cancellation, variation, removal or imposition shall have effect from the time when the order is made.

(3)   An application under subsection (1) may be made without notice.

(4)   An order under subsection (1) shall be made in writing.

(5)   Where an order is made under this section, *the registration authority* [the Assembly] shall serve on the registered person, as soon as is reasonably practicable after the making of the order—

  (a)   a copy of the order;
  (b)   a copy of any written statement of *the authority's* [the Assembly's] reasons for making the application for the order which supported that application; and
  (c)   notice of any right of appeal conferred by section 79M.

(6)   Where an order has been so made, *the registration authority* [the Assembly] shall, as soon as is reasonably practicable after the making of the order, notify the local authority in whose area the person concerned acts or acted as a child minder, or provides or provided day care, of the making of the order.]

Date in force

England: 2 July 2001: see SI 2001/2041.

Amendment

Inserted by the Care Standards Act 2000, s 79(1).
Sub-s (1): words 'under this Part' in square brackets inserted by the Childcare Act 2006, s 103(1), Sch 2, para 11. Date in force: to be appointed: see the Childcare Act 2006, ss 109(2), 110(1), (5)(c); in para (a) words 'the registration authority' in italics repealed and subsequent words in square brackets substituted by the Childcare Act 2006, s 103(1), Sch 2, para 6. Date in force: to be appointed: see the Childcare Act 2006, ss 109(2), 110(1), (5)(c).
Sub-ss (5), (6): words 'the registration authority' in italics repealed and subsequent words in square brackets substituted by the Childcare Act 2006, s 103(1), Sch 2, para 6. Date in force: to be appointed: see the Childcare Act 2006, ss 109(2), 110(1), (5)(c).
Sub-s (5): in para (b) words 'the authority's' in italics repealed and subsequent words in square brackets substituted by virtue of the Childcare Act 2006, s 103(1), Sch 2, para 6. Date in force: to be appointed: see the Childcare Act 2006, ss 109(2), 110(1), (5)(c).

Definitions

For 'act as a child minder' see s 79A(2) as applied to the whole Act by s 105(5A); for 'day care' see s 79A(6); for 'the registration authority' see s 79B(1)(2); for 'harm' see s 31(9) and as to whether harm is significant see s 31(10) as applied to the whole Act by s 105(1); for 'local authority' see s 105(1).

References

For 'likely to suffer significant harm' see s 31 and see generally Chapter 8.

Service of documents

See s 105(8)–(10).

[79L   Notice of intention to take steps]

[(1)   Not less than 14 days before—

(a)   refusing an application for registration;

(b)   cancelling a registration;

(c)   removing or varying any condition to which a registration is subject or imposing a new condition; or

(d)   refusing to grant an application for the removal or variation of any condition to which a registration is subject,

the registration authority [the Assembly] shall send to the applicant, or (as the case may be) registered person, notice in writing of its intention to take the step in question.

(2)   Every such notice shall—

(a)   give *the authority's* [the Assembly's] reasons for proposing to take the step; and

(b)   inform the person concerned of his rights under this section.

(3)   Where the recipient of such a notice informs *the authority* [the Assembly] in writing of his desire to object to the step being taken, *the authority* [the Assembly] shall afford him an opportunity to do so.

(4)   Any objection made under subsection (3) may be made orally or in writing, by the recipient of the notice or a representative.

(5)   If *the authority* [the Assembly], after giving the person concerned an opportunity to object to the step being taken, decides nevertheless to take it, it shall send him written notice of its decision.

(6)   A step of a kind mentioned in subsection (1)(b) or (c) shall not take effect until the expiry of the time within which an appeal may be brought under section 79M or, where such an appeal is brought, before its determination.

(7)   Subsection (6) does not prevent a step from taking effect before the expiry of the time within which an appeal may be brought under section 79M if the person concerned notifies *the registration authority* [the Assembly] in writing that he does not intend to appeal.]

Date in force

England: 2 July 2001: see SI 2001/2041.

Amendment

Inserted by the Care Standards Act 2000, s 79(1).

Sub-s (1): words 'the registration authority' in italics repealed and subsequent words in square brackets substituted by the Childcare Act 2006, s 103(1), Sch 2, para 6. Date in force: to be appointed: see the Childcare Act 2006, ss 109(2), 110(1), (5)(c).

Sub-s (2): in para (a) words 'the authority's' in italics repealed and subsequent words in square brackets substituted by virtue of the Childcare Act 2006, s 103(1), Sch 2, para 6. Date in force: to be appointed: see the Childcare Act 2006, ss 109(2), 110(1), (5)(c).

Sub-s (3): words 'the authority' in italics in both places they occur repealed and subsequent words in square brackets substituted by the Childcare Act 2006, s 103(1), Sch 2, para 6. Date in force: to be appointed: see the Childcare Act 2006, ss 109(2), 110(1), (5)(c).

Sub-s (5): words 'the authority' in italics repealed and subsequent words in square brackets substituted by the Childcare Act 2006, s 103(1), Sch 2, para 6. Date in force: to be appointed: see the Childcare Act 2006, ss 109(2), 110(1), (5)(c).

Sub-s (7): words 'the registration authority' in italics repealed and subsequent words in square brackets substituted by the Childcare Act 2006, s 103(1), Sch 2, para 6. Date in force: to be appointed: see the Childcare Act 2006, ss 109(2), 110(1), (5)(c).

Definitions

For 'the registration authority' see s 79B(1)(2).

Service of documents

See s 105(8)–(10).

Representative

No professional qualifications are required for a representative who may, therefore, be any person nominated for the purpose.

[79M   Appeals]

[(1)   An appeal against—

   (a)   the taking of any step mentioned in section 79L(1); ...
   (b)   an order under section 79K, [or
   (c)   a determination made by *the registration authority* [the Assembly] under this Part (other than one falling within paragraph (a) or (b)) which is of a prescribed description,]

shall lie to the Tribunal.

(2)   On an appeal, the Tribunal may—

   (a)   confirm the taking of the step or the making of the order [or determination] or direct that it shall not have, or shall cease to have, effect; and
   (b)   impose, vary or cancel any condition.]

Date in force

Appointment (in relation to England, for certain purposes): 16 March 2001: see SI 2001/1210, art 2.

Amendment

Inserted by the Care Standards Act 2000, s 79(1).
Sub-s (1): in para (a) word omitted repealed by the Education Act 2002, s 215(2), Sch 22, Pt 3; para (c) and word 'or' immediately preceding it inserted by the Education Act 2002, s 148, Sch 13, para 3(1), (2); in para (c) words 'the registration authority' in italics repealed and subsequent words in square brackets substituted by the Childcare Act 2006, s 103(1), Sch 2, para 6. Date in force: to be appointed: see the Childcare Act 2006, ss 109(2), 110(1), (5)(c).
Sub-s (2): in para (a) words 'or determination' in square brackets inserted by the Education Act 2002, s 148, Sch 13, para 3(1), (3).

Definition

For 'the Tribunal' see s 79B(8).

Sub-s (1)(c) Prescribed descripton

See the Disqualification from Caring for Children (Wales) Regulations 2004, SI 2004/2695 and the Day Care and Child Minding (Disqualification) (England) Regulations 2005, SI 2005/2296 amended by SI 2007/197 and 603.

Inspection: England

[79N   General functions of the Chief Inspector]

[[(1)   ...

(1A)   ...]

(2)   ...

(3)   ...

(4)   *The Chief Inspector may secure the provision of training for persons who provide or assist in providing child minding or day care, or intend to do so.*

(5)   *Regulations may confer further functions on the Chief Inspector relating to child minding and day care provided in England.*

(6)   ...]

Date in force

England: 16 March 2001 / 2 July 2001: see SI 2001/1210; SI 2001/2041.

Amendment

Inserted by the Care Standards Act 2000, s 79(1).
Repealed by the Childcare Act 2006, s 103, Sch 2, para 12, Sch 3, Pt 2. Date in force: to be appointed: see the Childcare Act 2006, ss 109(2), 110(1), (5)(c), (6)(b).
Sub-ss (1), (1A): substituted, for sub-s (1) as originally enacted, by the Education Act 2005, s 53, Sch 7, Pt 1, para 1(1), (2).
Sub-ss (1)–(3): repealed by the Education and Inspections Act 2006, ss 157, 184, Sch 14, paras 9, 14, Sch 18, Pt 5.
Sub-s (6): repealed by the Education and Inspections Act 2006, ss 157, 184, Sch 14, paras 9, 14, Sch 18, Pt 5.

Definitions

For 'child minding' see s 79A(2) as applied to the whole Act by s 105(5A); for 'day care' see s 79A(6); for 'premises' see s 79B(6).

Sub-s (5) Regulations

The Child Minding and Day Care (Disclosure Functions) (England) Regulations 2004, SI 2004/3136 prescribe the circumstances for the disclosure by the Chief Inspector of certain information gathered while regulating childcare to parents, the police and various organisations concerned with the provision of care for, or with protecting, children and the Childcare Act 2006 (Provision of Information to Parents) (England) Regulations 2007, SI 2007/3490 prescribe information which must be provided by English local authorities to parents and prospective parents as a result of the duty imposed by section 12 of the Childcare Act 2006.

Appendix 1   *Children Act 1989*

[79P   ...]

[...]

Date in force

2 July 2001.

Amendment

Inserted by the Care Standards Act 2000, s 79(1).
Repealed by the Education Act 2005, ss 53, 123, Sch 7, Pt 1, para 2, Sch 19, Pt 1.

[79Q   *Inspection of provision of child minding and day care in England*]

[(1)   *The Chief Inspector may at any time require any registered person to provide him with any information connected with the person's activities as a child minder, or [provider] of day care, which the Chief Inspector considers it necessary to have for the purposes of his functions under this Part.*

(2)   *The Chief Inspector shall [at prescribed intervals inspect, ..., any child minding provided in England by a registered person].*

(3)   *The Chief Inspector shall [at prescribed intervals inspect, ..., any day care provided by a registered person on any premises in England].*

(4)   ...

(5)   *In prescribing the intervals mentioned in subsection (2) or (3) the Secretary of State may make provision as to the period within which the first inspection of child minding or day care provided by any person or at any premises is to take place.*

[(5A)   *Regulations may make provision requiring a registered person, except in prescribed cases, to notify prescribed persons of the fact that any child minding or day care provided by the registered person is to be inspected under this section.*]

[(6)   *When conducting an inspection under this section the Chief Inspector shall report in writing on—*

   (a)   *the quality and standards of the child minding or day care provided,*
   (b)   *how far the child minding or day care meets the needs of the range of children for whom it is provided,*
   (c)   *the contribution made by the child minding or day care to the well-being of the children for whom it is provided, and*
   (d)   *in the case of day care, the quality of leadership and management in connection with its provision.*

(6A)   *In subsection (6)(c), the reference to well-being is a reference to well-being having regard to the matters mentioned in section 10(2) of the Children Act 2004.*]

(7)   ...]

Date in force

16 March 2001 / 2 July 2001 / 2 September 2002: see SI 2001/1210; SI 2001/2041.

Amendment

Inserted by the Care Standards Act 2000, s 79(1).
Repealed by the Childcare Act 2006, s 103, Sch 2, para 12, Sch 3, Pt 2.
Sub-s (1): word 'provider' in square brackets substituted by the Education Act 2005, s 53, Sch 7, Pt 1, para 3(1), (2).

Sub-s (2): words from 'at prescribed intervals' to 'a registered person' in square brackets substituted by the Education Act 2002, s 148, Sch 13, para 4(1), (2); words omitted repealed by the Education Act 2005, ss 53, 123, Sch 7, Pt 1, para 3(1), (3), Sch 19, Pt 1.
Sub-s (3): words from 'at prescribed intervals' to 'premises in England' in square brackets substituted by the Education Act 2002, s 152, Sch 13, para 4(1), (3); words omitted repealed by the Education Act 2005, ss 53, 123, Sch 7, Pt 1, para 3(1), (4), Sch 19, Pt 1.
Sub-s (4): repealed by the Education Act 2005, ss 53, 123, Sch 7, Pt 1, para 3(1), (5), Sch 19, Pt 1.
Sub-s (5A): inserted by the Education Act 2005, s 53, Sch 7, Pt 1, para 3(1), (6).
Sub-ss (6), (6A): substituted, for sub-s (6) as originally enacted, by the Education Act 2005, s 53, Sch 7, Pt 1, para 3(1), (7).
Sub-s (7): repealed by the Education Act 2005, ss 53, 123, Sch 7, Pt 1, para 3(1), (8), Sch 19, Pt 1.

Definitions

For 'act as a child minder' see s 79A(2) as applied to the whole Act by s 105(5A); for 'day care' see s 79A(6); for 'premises' see s 79B(6); for 'registered inspector' see s 79P(5).

Regulations

See the Day Care and Child Minding (Inspections) (Prescribed Matters) (England) Regulations 2005, SI 2005/2300.

[**79R** *Reports of inspections*]

[*(1)* ...

(2) ...

[(3) Where the Chief Inspector reports on an inspection under section 79Q he—

- (a) may send a copy of the report to the Secretary of State, and shall do so without delay if the Secretary of State requests a copy;
- (b) shall ensure that a copy of the report is sent to the registered person providing the child minding or day care that was inspected;
- (c) shall ensure that copies of the report, or such parts of it as he considers appropriate, are sent to such other authorities or persons as may be prescribed; and
- (d) may arrange for the report (or parts of it) to be further published in any manner he considers appropriate.]

[(3A) Regulations may make provision—

- (a) requiring a registered person to make a copy of any report sent to him under subsection (3)(b) available for inspection by prescribed persons,
- (b) requiring a registered person, except in prescribed cases, to provide a copy of the report to prescribed persons, and
- (c) authorising a registered person in prescribed cases to charge a fee for providing a copy of the report.]

[(4) Subsections (2) to (4) of section 11 of the Education Act 2005 (publication of inspection reports) shall apply in relation to the publication of a report under subsection (3) as they apply in relation to the publication of a report under any of the provisions mentioned in subsection (2) of section 11.]]

Date in force

16 March 2001 / 2 July 2001: see SI 2001/1210; SI 2001/2041.

Amendment

Inserted by the Care Standards Act 2000, s 79(1).

Appendix 1 *Children Act 1989*

Repealed by the Childcare Act 2006, s 103, Sch 2, para 12, Sch 3, Pt 2. Date in force: to be appointed: see the Childcare Act 2006, ss 109(2), 110(1), (5)(c), (6)(b).
Sub-ss (1), (2): repealed by the Education Act 2005, ss 53, 123, Sch 7, Pt 1, para 4(1), (2), Sch 19, Pt 1.
Sub-s (3): substituted by the Education Act 2005, s 53, Sch 7, Pt 1, para 4(1), (3).
Sub-s (3A): inserted by the Education Act 2005, s 53, Sch 7, Pt 1, para 4(1), (4).
Sub-s (4): substituted by the Education Act 2005, s 53, Sch 7, Pt 1, para 4(1), (5).

Regulations

See the Day Care and Child Minding (Inspections) (Prescribed Matters) (England) Regulations 2005, SI 2005/2300.

[Inspection: Wales]

[79S   General functions of the Assembly]

[(1)   The Assembly may secure the provision of training for persons who provide or assist in providing child minding or day care, or intend to do so.

(2)   In relation to child minding and day care provided in Wales, the Assembly shall have any additional function specified in regulations made by the Assembly; *but the regulations may only specify a function corresponding to a function which, by virtue of section 79N(5), is exercisable by the Chief Inspector in relation to child minding and day care provided in England.*]

Date in force

Appointment (in relation to England, for certain purposes): 16 March 2001: see SI 2001/1210, art 2.

Amendment

Inserted by the Care Standards Act 2000, s 79(1).
Sub-s (2): words from 'but the regulations' to the end repealed by the Childcare Act 2006, s 103, Sch 2, para 13, Sch 3, Pt 2. Date in force: to be appointed: see the Childcare Act 2006, ss 109(2), 110(1), (5)(c), (6)(b).

Definitions

For 'the Assembly' see 79B(2); for 'child minding' see s 79A(2) as applied to the whole Act by s 105(5A); for 'day care' see s 79A(6).

[79T   Inspection: Wales]

[(1)   The Assembly may at any time require any registered person to provide it with any information connected with the person's activities as a child minder or provision of day care which the Assembly considers it necessary to have for the purposes of its functions under this Part.

(2)   The Assembly may by regulations make provision—

    (a)   for the inspection of ... child minding provided in Wales by registered persons and of day care provided by registered persons on premises in Wales;

    (b)   for the publication of reports of the inspections in such manner as the Assembly considers appropriate.

(3)   The regulations may provide for the inspections to be organised by—

    (a)   the Assembly; or

(b) Her Majesty's Chief Inspector of Education and Training in Wales, or any other person, under arrangements made with the Assembly.

(4) The regulations may provide for subsections (2) to (4) of [section 29 of the Education Act 2005] to apply with modifications in relation to the publication of reports under the regulations.]

Date in force

Appointment (in relation to England, for certain purposes): 16 March 2001: see SI 2001/1210, art 2.

Amendment

Inserted by the Care Standards Act 2000, s 79(1).
Sub-s (2): in para (a) words omitted repealed by the Education Act 2005, ss 53, 123, Sch 7, Pt 1, para 5(1), (2), Sch 19, Pt 1.
Sub-s (4): words 'section 29 of the Education Act 2005' in square brackets substituted by the Education Act 2005, s 53, Sch 7, Pt 1, para 5(1), (3).

Definitions

For 'the Assembly' see 79B(2); for 'act as a child minder' see s 79A(2) as applied to the whole Act by s 105(5A); for 'day care' see s 79A(6).

[Supplementary]

[79U   Rights of entry etc]

[(1) [Any person authorised for the purposes of this subsection by *the registration authority* [the Assembly]] may at any reasonable time enter any premises in *England or* Wales on which child minding or day care is at any time provided.

(2) Where [a person who is authorised for the purposes of this subsection by *the registration authority* [the Assembly]] has reasonable cause to believe that a child is being looked after on any premises in contravention of this Part, he may enter those premises at any reasonable time.

[(2A) Authorisation under subsection (1) or (2)—

(a) may be given for a particular occasion or period;
(b) may be given subject to conditions.]

(3) [A person entering premises under this section may (subject to any conditions imposed under subsection (2A)(b))—]

(a) inspect the premises;
(b) inspect, and take copies of—
   (i) any records kept by the person providing the child minding or day care; and
   (ii) any other documents containing information relating to its provision;
(c) seize and remove any document or other material or thing found there which he has reasonable grounds to believe may be evidence of a failure to comply with any condition or requirement imposed by or under this Part;
(d) require any person to afford him such facilities and assistance with respect to matters within the person's control as are necessary to enable him to exercise his powers under this section;
(e) take measurements and photographs or make recordings;
(f) inspect any children being looked after there, and the arrangements made for their welfare;
(g) interview in private the person providing the child minding or day care; and

   (h)   interview in private any person looking after children, or living or working, there who consents to be interviewed.

(4) [Section 58 of the Education Act 2005] (inspection of computer records for purposes of Part I of that Act) shall apply for the purposes of subsection (3) as it applies for the purposes of Part I of that Act.

(5) ...

(6) A person exercising any power conferred by this section shall, if so required, produce some duly authenticated document showing his authority to do so.

(7) It shall be an offence wilfully to obstruct a person exercising any such power.

(8) Any person guilty of an offence under subsection (7) shall be liable on summary conviction to a fine not exceeding level 4 on the standard scale.

(9) In this section—

   ...

   'documents' and 'records' each include information recorded in any form.]

Date in force

England: 2 July 2001: see SI 2001/2041.

Amendment

Inserted by the Care Standards Act 2000, s 79(1).
Sub-s (1): words 'Any person authorised for the purposes of this subsection by the registration authority' in square brackets substituted by the Education Act 2002, s 152, Sch 13, para 5(1), (2).
Sub-s (1): words 'the registration authority' in italics repealed and subsequent words in square brackets substituted by the Childcare Act 2006, s 103(1), Sch 2, para 6. Date in force: to be appointed: see the Childcare Act 2006, ss 109(2), 110(1), (5)(c); words 'England or' in italics repealed by the Childcare Act 2006, s 103, Sch 2, para 14, Sch 3, Pt 2. Date in force: to be appointed: see the Childcare Act 2006, ss 109(2), 110(1), (5)(c), (6)(b).
Sub-s (2): words 'a person who is authorised for the purposes of this subsection by the registration authority' in square brackets substituted by the Education Act 2002, s 152, Sch 13, para 5(1), (3); words 'the registration authority' in italics repealed and subsequent words in square brackets substituted by the Childcare Act 2006, s 103(1), Sch 2, para 6. Date in force: to be appointed: see the Childcare Act 2006, ss 109(2), 110(1), (5)(c).
Sub-s (2A): inserted by the Education Act 2002, s 152, Sch 13, para 5(1), (4).
Sub-s (3): words 'A person entering premises under this section may (subject to any conditions imposed under subsection (2A)(b))—' in square brackets substituted by the Education Act 2002, s 152, Sch 13, para 5(1), (5).
Sub-s (4): words 'Section 58 of the Education Act 2005' in square brackets substituted by the Education Act 2005, s 53, Sch 7, Pt 1, para 6.
Sub-s (5): repealed by the Education Act 2002, ss 152, 215(2), Sch 13, para 5(1), (6), Sch 22, Pt 3.
Sub-s (9): definition 'authorised inspector' (omitted) repealed by the Education Act 2002, ss 152, 215(2), Sch 13, para 5(1), (7), Sch 22, Pt 3.

Definitions

For 'authorised inspector', 'documents', 'records' see sub-s (9); for 'premises' see s 79B(6); for 'child minding' see s 79A(2) as applied to the whole Act by s 105(5A); for 'day care' see s 79A(6); for 'the registration authority' see s 79B(1)(2).

References

'This Part' ie Part XA ss 79A–79X and Sch 9A (child minding and day care for young children). For 'the standard scale' see the CJA 1982 s 37(2) (3) as amended.

Wilfully obstructs

'Obstructs' need not involve physical violence: *Hinchliffe v Sheldon* [1955] 3 All ER 406, [1955] 1 WLR 1207. Doing anything which makes it more difficult for a person to carry out his duty may amount to obstruction: *Rice v Connolly* [1966] 2 QB 414, [1966] 2 All ER 649, but standing by and doing nothing, in the absence of a legal duty to act, is not obstruction: *Swallow v LCC* [1916] 1 KB 224. For cases on 'wilful obstruction': *Hills v Ellis* [1983] QB 680, [1983] 1 All ER 667; *Moore v Green* [1983] 1 All ER 663; *Willmott v Atack* [1977] QB 498, [1976] 3 All ER 794, 141 JP 35.

[79V   Function of local authorities]

[Each local authority [in Wales] shall, in accordance with regulations, secure the provision—

  (a)   of information and advice about child minding and day care; and
  (b)   of training for persons who provide or assist in providing child minding or day care.]

Date in force

England: 16 March 2001 / 2 July 2001: see SI 2001/1210; SI 2001/2041.

Amendment

Words 'in Wales' in square brackets inserted by the Childcare Act 2006, s 103(1), Sch 2, para 15. Date in force: to be appointed: see the Childcare Act 2006, ss 109(2), 110(1), (5)(c).

Definition

For 'local authority' see s 105(1).

Regulations

See the Day Care and Child Minding (Functions of Local Authorities: Information, Advice and Training) (England) Regulations 2001, SI 2001/2746 amended by SI 2005/2302.

Checks on suitability of persons working with children over the age of seven

[79W   Requirement for certificate of suitability]

[(1)   This section applies to any person not required to register under this Part who looks after, or provides care for, children [in Wales] and meets the following conditions.
    References in this section to children are to those under the age of 15 or (in the case of disabled children) 17.

(2)   The first condition is that the period, or the total of the periods, in any week which he spends looking after children or (as the case may be) during which the children are looked after exceeds five hours.

(3)   The second condition is that he would be required to register under this Part (or, as the case may be, this Part if it were subject to prescribed modifications) if the children were under the age of eight.

(4)   Regulations may require a person to whom this section applies to hold a certificate issued by *the registration authority* [the Assembly] as to his suitability, and the suitability of each prescribed person, to look after children.

(5)   The regulations may make provision about—

  (a)   applications for certificates;

807

(b) the matters to be taken into account by *the registration authority* [the Assembly] in determining whether to issue certificates;

(c) the information to be contained in certificates;

(d) the period of their validity.

(6) The regulations may provide that a person to whom this section applies shall be guilty of an offence—

(a) if he does not hold a certificate as required by the regulations; or

(b) if, being a person who holds such a certificate, he fails to produce it when reasonably required to do so by a prescribed person.

(7) The regulations may provide that a person who, for the purpose of obtaining such a certificate, knowingly makes a statement which is false or misleading in a material particular shall be guilty of an offence.

(8) The regulations may provide that a person guilty of an offence under the regulations shall be liable on summary conviction to a fine not exceeding level 5 on the standard scale.]

Date in force

England: 16 March 2001 / 2 July 2001: see SI 2001/1210; SI 2001/2041.

Amendment

Inserted by the Care Standards Act 2000, s 79(1).
Sub-s (1): words 'in Wales' in square brackets inserted by the Childcare Act 2006, s 103(1), Sch 2, para 16. Date in force: to be appointed: see the Childcare Act 2006, ss 109(2), 110(1), (5)(c).
Sub-s (4): words 'the registration authority' in italics repealed and subsequent words in square brackets substituted by the Childcare Act 2006, s 103(1), Sch 2, para 6. Date in force: to be appointed: see the Childcare Act 2006, ss 109(2), 110(1), (5)(c).
Sub-s (5): in para (b) words 'the registration authority' in italics repealed and subsequent words in square brackets substituted by the Childcare Act 2006, s 103(1), Sch 2, para 6. Date in force: to be appointed: see the Childcare Act 2006, ss 109(2), 110(1), (5)(c).

Definitions

For 'child' see sub-s (1).

References

'This Part' ie Part XA ss 79A–79X and Sch 9A (child minding and day care for young children). For 'the standard scale' see the CJA 1982 s 37(2) (3) as amended.

[Time limit for proceedings]

[**79X   Time limit for proceedings**]

[Proceedings for an offence under this Part or regulations made under it may be brought within a period of six months from the date on which evidence sufficient in the opinion of the prosecutor to warrant the proceedings came to his knowledge; but no such proceedings shall be brought by virtue of this section more than three years after the commission of the offence.]

Date in force

England: 2 July 2001: see SI 2001/2041.

Amendment

Inserted by the Care Standards Act 2000, s 79(1).

Time limit for proceedings

The normal time limit for criminal proceedings in respect of summary offences is six months: Magistrates' Courts Act 1980, s 127(1).

PART XI

SECRETARY OF STATE'S SUPERVISORY FUNCTIONS AND RESPONSIBILITIES

80   Inspection of children's homes etc by persons authorised by Secretary of State

(1)   *The Secretary of State may cause to be inspected from time to time any—*

    (a)   *[private] children's home;*

    (b)   *premises in which a child who is being looked after by a local authority is living;*

    (c)   *premises in which a child who is being accommodated by or on behalf of a local education authority or voluntary organisation is living;*

    (d)   *premises in which a child who is being accommodated by or on behalf of a [[Local Health Board], Special Health Authority] [, Primary Care Trust][, National Health Service trust or NHS foundation trust] is living;*

    (e)   *...*

    (f)   *...*

    (g)   *premises in which a privately fostered child, or child who is treated as a foster child by virtue of paragraph 9 of Schedule 8, is living or in which it is proposed that he will live;*

    (h)   *premises on which any person is acting as a child minder;*

    (i)   *premises with respect to which a person is registered under section 71(1)(b) [or with respect to which a person is registered for providing day care under Part XA];*

    [(j)   *care home or independent hospital used to accommodate children;]*

    (k)   *premises which are provided by a local authority and in which any service is provided by that authority under Part III;*

    (l)   *independent school [school or college] providing accommodation for any child.*

(2)   *An inspection under this section shall be conducted by a person authorised to do so by the Secretary of State.*

(3)   *An officer of a local authority shall not be so authorised except with the consent of that authority.*

(4)   *The Secretary of State may require any person of a kind mentioned in subsection (5) to furnish him with such information, or allow him to inspect such records (in whatever form they are held), relating to—*

    (a)   *any premises to which subsection (1) or, in relation to Scotland, subsection (1)(h) or (i) applies;*

    (b)   *any child who is living in any such premises;*

    (c)   *the discharge by the Secretary of State of any of his functions under this Act;*
    ...

    (d)   *the discharge by any local authority of any of their functions under this Act,*

as the Secretary of State may at any time direct.

(5)   *The persons are any—*

    (a)   *local authority;*

    (b)   *voluntary organisation;*

    (c)   *person carrying on a [private] children's home;*

(d)   proprietor of an independent school [or governing body of any other school];

[(da) governing body of an institution designated under section 28 of the Further and Higher Education Act 1992;

(db) further education corporation;]

(e)   person fostering any privately fostered child or providing accommodation for a child on behalf of a local authority, local education authority, [[Local Health Board], Special Health Authority,] [Primary Care Trust,] [National Health Service trust] [, NHS foundation trust] or voluntary organisation;

(f)   local education authority providing accommodation for any child;

(g)   person employed in a teaching or administrative capacity at any educational establishment (whether or not maintained by a local education authority) at which a child is accommodated on behalf of a local authority or local education authority;

(h)   person who is the occupier of any premises in which any person acts as a child minder (within the meaning of Part X) or provides day care for young children (within the meaning of that Part);

[(hh) person who is the occupier of any premises—

   (i)   in which any person required to be registered for child minding under Part XA acts as a child minder (within the meaning of that Part); or

   (ii)   with respect to which a person is required to be registered under that Part for providing day care;]

(i)   person carrying on any home of a kind mentioned in subsection (1)(j)

[(j)   person carrying on a fostering agency].

(6)   Any person inspecting any home or other premises under this section may—

(a)   inspect the children there; and

(b)   make such examination into the state and management of the home or premises and the treatment of the children there as he thinks fit.

(7)   Any person authorised by the Secretary of State to exercise the power to inspect records conferred by subsection (4)—

(a)   shall be entitled at any reasonable time to have access to, and inspect and check the operation of, any computer and any associated apparatus or material which is or has been in use in connection with the records in question; and

(b)   may require—

   (i)   the person by whom or on whose behalf the computer is or has been so used; or

   (ii)   any person having charge of, or otherwise concerned with the operation of, the computer, apparatus or material,

to afford him such reasonable assistance as he may require.

(8)   A person authorised to inspect any premises under this section shall have a right to enter the premises for that purpose, and for any purpose specified in subsection (4), at any reasonable time.

(9)   Any person exercising that power shall, if so required, produce some duly authenticated document showing his authority to do so.

(10)   Any person who intentionally obstructs another in the exercise of that power shall be guilty of an offence and liable on summary conviction to a fine not exceeding level 3 on the standard scale.

(11)   The Secretary of State may by order provide for subsections (1), (4) and (6) not to apply in relation to such homes, or other premises, as may be specified in the order.

(12)   Without prejudice to section 104, any such order may make different provisions with respect to each of those subsections.

[(13)   *In this section*—

'*college*' *means an institution within the further education sector as defined in section 91 of the Further and Higher Education Act 1992;*
'*fostering agency*' *has the same meaning as in the Care Standards Act 2000;*
'*further education corporation*' *has the same meaning as in the Further and Higher Education Act 1992.*]

Date in force

14 October 1991: SI 1991/828.

Amendments

Repealed, in relation to Scotland, by the Regulation of Care (Scotland) Act 2001, s 80(1), Sch 4. Sub-s (1): in para (a) word 'private' in square brackets inserted by the Care Standards Act 2000, s 116, Sch 4, para 14(1), (16)(a); in para (d) words in square brackets ending with the words 'Special Health Authority' substituted by the Health Authorities Act 1995, s 2(1), Sch 1, para 118(8); in para (d) words 'Local Health Board' in square brackets substituted by SI 2007/961, art 3, Schedule, para 20(1), (2)(g); in para (d) words ', Primary Care Trust' in square brackets inserted by SI 2000/90, art 3(1), Sch 1, para 24(1), (8)(a); in para (d) words ', National Health Service trust or NHS foundation trust' in square brackets substituted by the Health and Social Care (Community Health and Standards) Act 2003, s 34, Sch 4, paras 75, 80(a); paras (e), (f) repealed by the Adoption and Children Act 2002, s 139(1), (3), Sch 3, paras 54, 65, Sch 5; in para (i) words from 'or with respect' to 'under Part XA' in square brackets inserted by the Care Standards Act 2000, s 116, Sch 4, para 14(1), (16)(b); para (j) substituted by the Care Standards Act 2000, s 116, Sch 4, para 14(1), (16)(c); in para (l) words 'independent school' repealed and subsequent words in square brackets substituted by the Care Standards Act 2000, s 109(1), (2). Sub-s (4): in para (c) word omitted repealed by the Care Standards Act 2000, s 117(2), Sch 6. Sub-s (5): in para (c) word 'private' in square brackets inserted by the Care Standards Act 2000, s 116, Sch 4, para 14(1), (16)(a); in para (d) words 'or governing body of any other school' in square brackets inserted by the Care Standards Act 2000, s 109(1), (3)(a); paras (da), (db) inserted by the Care Standards Act 2000, s 109(1), (3)(b); in para (e) words in square brackets ending with the words 'Special Health Authority,' substituted by the Health Authorities Act 1995, s 2(1), Sch 1, para 118(8); in para (e) words 'Local Health Board' in square brackets substituted by SI 2007/961, art 3, Schedule, para 20(1), (2)(g); in para (e) words 'Primary Care Trust,' in square brackets inserted by SI 2000/90, art 3(1), Sch 1, para 24(1), (8)(b); in para (e) words 'National Health Service trust' in square brackets inserted by the National Health Service and Community Care Act 1990, s 66(1), Sch 9, para 36(4)(b); in para (e) words ', NHS foundation trust' in square brackets inserted by the Health and Social Care (Community Health and Standards) Act 2003, s 34, Sch 4, paras 75, 80(b); para (hh) inserted by the Care Standards Act 2000, s 116, Sch 4, para 14(1), (16)(d); para (j) inserted by the Care Standards Act 2000, s 109(1), (3)(c). Sub-s (13): inserted by the Care Standards Act 2000, s 109(1), (4).

Definitions

For 'children home' see s 63(3) and s 23(10) as applied to the whole Act by s 105(1) and see note to s 53, above; for 'child', 'local authority', 'local education authority', 'voluntary organisation', 'health authority', 'adoption agency', 'protected child', 'residential care home', 'nursing home', 'mental nursing home', 'independent school', 'school' and 'service' see s 105(1); for 'college', 'fostering agency' and 'further education corporation' see sub-s (13); for 'child who is looked after by a local authority' see s 22(1); for 'accommodation provided by or on behalf of a local authority' see s 105(5); for 'privately fostered child' see s 66(1) as applied to the whole Act by s 105(1); for 'child minder' see s 71(2)(a) as applied to the whole Act by s 105(1) and s 79A as applied to the whole Act by s 105(5A).

References

'Part III' ie ss 17–30 and Sch 2 (local authority support for children and families). For proprietor of an independent school see the EA 1996, s 579(1); for power to issue warrant to authorise a constable to assist in exercising the power under this section see s 102; for 'the standard scale' see the CJA 1982, s 37(2) (3) as amended.

811

Appendix 1 *Children Act 1989*

Transfer of functions

Functions of the Secretary of State, so far as exercisable in relation to Wales, transferred to the National Assembly for Wales, by the National Assembly for Wales (Transfer of Functions) Order 1999, SI 1999/672, art 2, Sch 1.

Note

Part XI contains the Secretary of State's supervisory functions and responsibilities. Although it largely reproduces the pre-existing law, the CA 1989 also implemented proposals made in The Law on Child Care and Family Services (1987, Cm 62). The Government was of the view that the opportunity should be taken to bring together in child care legislation the provisions relating to general matters such as research and training and the giving of grants to voluntary organisations. Also a general power should be included for the Secretary of State through the Social Services Inspectorate to inspect the work that local authority social services departments carry out for families with children and that this would include the inspection of records. (Cm 62, para 84). The powers of the Secretary of State to inspect premises where a child has been placed away from his home are rationalised and extended by s 80. Matters to note are the new provisions in sub-s 1(*h*) and (*i*) in relation to child minding and day care where formerly only the local authority had a power of inspection. Other powers of inspection now given to the Secretary of State in addition to the local authority include sub-s (1)(*a*) (children's homes) and (1)(*g*) (private foster children). Sub-s 1(*j*) reflects the desire to include within the welfare provisions of the ChA 1989, placements for children under general health and welfare legislation such as the National Health Service Act 1977. Sub-s 1(*l*) is a new power for the Secretary of State for Social Services to inspect the schools specified therein.

---

81   ...

...

Date in force

14 October 1991: SI 1991/828.

Amendment

Repealed by the Inquiries Act 2005, ss 48(1), 49(2), Sch 2, Pt 1, para 12, Sch 3.

Definitions

For 'functions' see sub-s (5); for 'local authority', 'child', 'adoption agency', 'voluntary organisa-tion', 'residential care home', 'nursing home', 'mental nursing home', see s 105(1); for 'voluntary home' see s 60(3).

Children

The plural includes the singular and therefore an inquiry may be held in respect of an individual child: IA 1978, s 6(c).

---

82   Financial support by Secretary of State

(1) The Secretary of State may (with the consent of the Treasury) defray or contribute towards—

    (a)   any fees or expenses incurred by any person undergoing approved child care training;

    (b)   any fees charged, or expenses incurred, by any person providing approved child care training or preparing material for use in connection with such training; or

    (c)   the cost of maintaining any person undergoing such training.

(2) The Secretary of State may make grants to local authorities in respect of expenditure incurred by them in providing secure accommodation in community homes other than assisted community homes.

(3) Where—

(a) a grant has been made under subsection (2) with respect to any secure accommodation; but

(b) the grant is not used for the purpose for which it was made or the accommodation is not used as, or ceases to be used as, secure accommodation,

the Secretary of State may (with the consent of the Treasury) require the authority concerned to repay the grant, in whole or in part.

(4) The Secretary of State may make grants to voluntary organisations towards—

(a) expenditure incurred by them in connection with the establishment, maintenance or improvement of voluntary homes which, at the time when the expenditure was incurred—
(i) were assisted community homes; or
(ii) were designated as such; or

(b) expenses incurred in respect of the borrowing of money to defray any such expenditure.

(5) The Secretary of State may arrange for the provision, equipment and maintenance of homes for the accommodation of children who are in need of particular facilities and services which—

(a) are or will be provided in those homes; and

(b) in the opinion of the Secretary of State, are unlikely to be readily available in community homes.

(6) In this Part—

'child care training' means training undergone by any person with a view to, or in the course of—
(a) his employment for the purposes of any of the functions mentioned in section 83(9) or in connection with the adoption of children or with the accommodation of children in a [care home or independent hospital]; or
(b) his employment by a voluntary organisation for similar purposes;
'approved child care training' means child care training which is approved by the Secretary of State; and
'secure accommodation' means accommodation provided for the purpose of restricting the liberty of children.

(7) Any grant made under this section shall be of such amount, and shall be subject to such conditions, as the Secretary of State may (with the consent of the Treasury) determine.

Date in force

14 October 1991: SI 1991/828.

Amendments

Sub-s (6): in definition 'child care training' words 'care home or independent hospital' in square brackets substituted by the Care Standards Act 2000, s 116, Sch 4, para 14(1), (18).

Definitions

For 'child care training', 'approved child care training', 'secure accommodation' see sub-s (6); for 'local authority', 'voluntary organisation' see s 105(1); for 'community home' and 'assisted community home' see s 53 as applied to the whole Act by s 105(1); for 'voluntary home' see s 60(3).

Reference

'This Part' ie Pt XI ss 80–84 (Secretary of State's supervisory functions and responsibilities).

Transfer of functions

Functions of the Secretary of State, so far as exercisable in relation to Wales, transferred to the National Assembly for Wales, by the National Assembly for Wales (Transfer of Functions) Order 1999, SI 1999/672, art 2, Sch 1

Sub-s (5)

A home under this provision (known as 'Youth Treatment Centre') is currently maintained at Glenthorne, Birmingham.

---

83   Research and returns of information

(1)   The Secretary of State may conduct, or assist other persons in conducting, research into any matter connected with—

   (a)   his functions, or the functions of local authorities, under the enactments mentioned in subsection (9);

   (b)   the adoption of children; or

   (c)   the accommodation of children in a [care home or independent hospital].

(2)   Any local authority may conduct, or assist other persons in conducting, research into any matter connected with—

   (a)   their functions under the enactments mentioned in subsection (9);

   (b)   the adoption of children; or

   (c)   the accommodation of children in a [care home or independent hospital].

(3)   Every local authority shall, at such times and in such form as the Secretary of State may direct, transmit to him such particulars as he may require with respect to—

   (a)   the performance by the local authority of all or any of their functions—

      (i)   under the enactments mentioned in subsection (9); or

      (ii)   in connection with the accommodation of children in a [care home or independent hospital]; and

   (b)   the children in relation to whom the authority have exercised those functions.

(4)   Every voluntary organisation shall, at such times and in such form as the Secretary of State may direct, transmit to him such particulars as he may require with respect to children accommodated by them or on their behalf.

[(4A)   Particulars required to be transmitted under subsection (3) or (4) may include particulars relating to and identifying individual children.]

(5)   The Secretary of State may direct the [designated officer for] each magistrates' court to which the direction is expressed to relate to transmit—

   (a)   to such person as may be specified in the direction; and

   (b)   at such times and in such form as he may direct;

such particulars as he may require with respect to proceedings of the court which relate to children.

(6)   The Secretary of State shall in each year lay before Parliament a consolidated and classified abstract of the information transmitted to him under subsections (3) to (5).

(7)   The Secretary of State may institute research designed to provide information on which requests for information under this section may be based.

(8)   The Secretary of State shall keep under review the adequacy of the provision of child care training and for that purpose shall receive and consider any information from or representations made by—

   (a)   the Central Council for Education and Training in Social Work;
   (b)   such representatives of local authorities as appear to him to be appropriate; or
   (c)   such other persons or organisations as appear to him to be appropriate,

concerning the provision of such training.

(9)   The enactments are—

   (a)   this Act;
   (b)   the Children and Young Persons Acts 1933 to 1969;
   (c)   section 116 of the Mental Health Act 1983 (so far as it relates to children looked after by local authorities);
   (d)   ...

Date in force

14 October 1991: SI 1991/828.

Amendment

Sub-s (1): in para (c) words 'care home or independent hospital' in square brackets substituted by the Care Standards Act 2000, s 116, Sch 4, para 14(1), (19).
Sub-s (2): in para (c) words 'care home or independent hospital' in square brackets substituted by the Care Standards Act 2000, s 116, Sch 4, para 14(1), (19).
Sub-s (3): in para (a)(ii) words 'care home or independent hospital' in square brackets substituted by the Care Standards Act 2000, s 116, Sch 4, para 14(1), (19).
Sub-s (4A): inserted by the Children Act 2004, s 54.
Sub-s (5): words 'designated officer for' in square brackets substituted by the Courts Act 2003, s 109(1), Sch 8, para 336.
Sub-s (9): para (d) repealed by SI 2005/2078, art 16(1), Sch 3.

Definitions

For 'functions', 'local authority', 'child', 'residential care home', 'nursing home', 'mental nursing home', 'voluntary organisation' and 'independent hospital' see s 105(1); for 'care home' see s 23(10) as applied to the whole Act by s 105(1) and see note to s 53, above; for 'child care training' see s 82(6).

Transfer of functions

Functions of the Secretary of State, so far as exercisable in relation to Wales, transferred to the National Assembly for Wales, by the National Assembly for Wales (Transfer of Functions) Order 1999, SI 1999/672, art 2, Sch 1.

84   Local authority failure to comply with statutory duty: default power of Secretary of State

(1)   If the Secretary of State is satisfied that any local authority has failed, without reasonable excuse, to comply with any of the duties imposed on them by or under this Act he may make an order declaring that authority to be in default with respect to that duty.

(2)   An order under subsection (1) shall give the Secretary of State's reasons for making it.

(3)   An order under subsection (1) may contain such directions for the purpose of ensuring that the duty is complied with, within such period as may be specified in the order, as appears to the Secretary of State to be necessary.

(4)   Any such direction shall, on the application of the Secretary of State, be enforceable by mandamus.

Date in force

14 October 1991: SI 1991/828.

Definition

For 'local authority', see s 105(1).

Reference

See paras 13.64 ff.

Transfer of functions

Functions of the Secretary of State, so far as exercisable in relation to Wales, transferred to the National Assembly for Wales, by the National Assembly for Wales (Transfer of Functions) Order 1999, SI 1999/672, art 2, Sch 1.

PART XII

MISCELLANEOUS AND GENERAL

Notification of children accommodated in certain establishments

85   Children accommodated by health authorities and local education authorities

(1)   Where a child is provided with accommodation by any [[Local Health Board], Special Health Authority,] [Primary Care Trust,] [National Health Service trust][, NHS foundation trust] or local education authority ('the accommodating authority')—

(a)   for a consecutive period of at least three months; or
(b)   with the intention, on the part of that authority, of accommodating him for such a period,

the accommodating authority shall notify the responsible authority.

(2)   Where subsection (1) applies with respect to a child, the accommodating authority shall also notify the responsible authority when they cease to accommodate the child.

(3)   In this section 'the responsible authority' means—

(a)   the local authority appearing to the accommodating authority to be the authority within whose area the child was ordinarily resident immediately before being accommodated; or
(b)   where it appears to the accommodating authority that a child was not ordinarily resident within the area of any local authority, the local authority within whose area the accommodation is situated.

(4)   Where a local authority have been notified under this section, they shall—

   (a) take such steps as are reasonably practicable to enable them to determine whether the child's welfare is adequately safeguarded and promoted while he is accommodated by the accommodating authority; and

   (b) consider the extent to which (if at all) they should exercise any of their functions under this Act with respect to the child.

Date in force

14 October 1991: SI 1991/828.

Amendment

Sub-s (1): words in square brackets ending with the words 'Special Health Authority,' substituted by the Health Authorities Act 1995, s 2(1), Sch 1, para 118(9); words 'Local Health Board' in square brackets substituted by SI 2007/961, art 3, Schedule, para 20(1), (2)(h); words 'Primary Care Trust,' in square brackets inserted by SI 2000/90, art 3(1), Sch 1, para 24(1), (9); words 'National Health Service trust' in square brackets inserted by the National Health Service and Community Care Act 1990, s 66(1), Sch 9, para 36(5); words ', NHS foundation trust' in square brackets inserted by the Health and Social Care (Community Health and Standards) Act 2003, s 34, Sch 4, paras 75, 81.

Definitions

For 'child', 'Health Authority', 'Special Health Authority', 'Primary Care Trust', 'National Health Service Trust', 'local education authority', 'local authority' see 105(1); for 'the accommodating authority' see sub-s (1); for 'the responsible authority' see sub-s (3); for 'ordinarily resident' see s 105(6).

86   [Children accommodated in care homes or independent hospitals]

(1)   Where a child is provided with accommodation in any [care home or independent hospital]—

   (a) for a consecutive period of at least three months; or

   (b) with the intention, on the part of the person taking the decision to accommodate him, of accommodating him for such period,

the person carrying on the home shall notify the local authority within whose area the home is carried on.

(2)   Where subsection (1) applies with respect to a child, the person carrying on the home shall also notify that authority when he ceases to accommodate the child in the home.

(3)   Where a local authority have been notified under this section, they shall—

   (a) take such steps as are reasonably practicable to enable them to determine whether the child's welfare is adequately safeguarded and promoted while he is accommodated in the home; and

   (b) consider the extent to which (if at all) they should exercise any of their functions under this Act with respect to the child.

(4)   If the person carrying on any home fails, without reasonable excuse, to comply with this section he shall be guilty of an offence.

(5)   A person authorised by a local authority may enter any [care home or independent hospital] within the authority's area for the purpose of establishing whether the requirements of this section have been complied with.

(6)   Any person who intentionally obstructs another in the exercise of the power of entry shall be guilty of an offence.

(7)   Any person exercising the power of entry shall, if so required, produce some duly authenticated document showing his authority to do so.

(8)   Any person committing an offence under this section shall be liable on summary conviction to a fine not exceeding level 3 on the standard scale.

Date in force

14 October 1991: SI 1991/828.

Amendment

Section heading: words 'Children accommodated in care homes or independent hospitals' in square brackets substituted by the Care Standards Act 2000, s 116, Sch 4, para 14(1), (20)(a).
Sub-s (1): words 'care home or independent hospital' in square brackets substituted by the Care Standards Act 2000, s 116, Sch 4, para 14(1), (20)(b).
Sub-s (5): words 'care home or independent hospital' in square brackets substituted by the Care Standards Act 2000, s 116, Sch 4, para 14(1), (20)(b).

Definitions

For 'child', 'residential care home', 'nursing home', 'mental nursing home', 'local authority', 'care home', 'independent hospital' see s 105(1).

References

For power to issue warrant to authorise a constable to assist in exercising the power under this section see s 102. For 'the standard scale' see the CJA 1982, s 37(2) (3) as amended; 'level 3' ie £1000.

Note

A number of children may be cared for away from home for fairly long periods and in circumstances where social services departments had, under the former legislation, no clear responsibilities for them. The powers and duties of local authorities to support families with children come from two main streams of law: health and welfare legislation and child care legislation. Health and Welfare legislation enables the provision of services to children as part of the local authority's responsibilities to particular groups of all ages, such as those who are mentally handicapped or physically disabled (see for example the National Health Service Act 1977, the National Assistance Act 1948 and the Chronically Sick and Disabled Persons Act 1970). Some children might have to stay in health establishments for considerable periods especially where they are handicapped or chronically ill. Others are placed in residential schools. Accordingly the Act provides that where a child has been in an NHS establishment a duty rests on the health authority to notify the appropriate social services department. This is to obviate concern that for a number of children contact with their families may diminish and the child's welfare suffer. Similar duties apply to care homes and independent hospitals. See s 85 for children accommodated by health authorities and local education authorities and s 87 for children accommodated in independent schools. See also ss 27 (co-operation between authorities) and 28 (consultation with local education authorities).

---

87   *Welfare of children accommodated in independent schools* [Welfare of children in boarding schools and colleges]

[(1)   Where a school or college provides accommodation for any child, it shall be the duty of the relevant person to safeguard and promote the child's welfare.

(2)   Subsection (1) does not apply in relation to a school or college which is a children's home or care home.

(3)   Where accommodation is provided for a child by any school or college the appropriate authority shall take such steps as are reasonably practicable to enable them

to determine whether the child's welfare is adequately safeguarded and promoted while he is accommodated by the school or college.

(4) Where [the Chief Inspector for England is] of the opinion that there has been a failure to comply with subsection (1) in relation to a child provided with accommodation by a school or [college in England, he shall]—

(a) in the case of a school other than an independent school or a special school, notify the local education authority for the area in which the school is situated;

(b) in the case of a special school which is maintained by a local education authority, notify that authority;

(c) in any other case, notify the Secretary of State.

(4A) Where the National Assembly for Wales are of the opinion that there has been a failure to comply with subsection (1) in relation to a child provided with accommodation by a school or college [in Wales], they shall—

(a) in the case of a school other than an independent school or a special school, notify the local education authority for the area in which the school is situated;

(b) in the case of a special school which is maintained by a local education authority, notify that authority.

(5) Where accommodation is, or is to be, provided for a child by any school or college, a person authorised by the appropriate authority may, for the purpose of enabling that authority to discharge its duty under this section, enter at any time premises which are, or are to be, premises of the school or college.]

(6) Any person [exercising] the power conferred by subsection (5) may carry out such inspection of premises, children and records as is prescribed by regulations made by the Secretary of State for the purposes of this section.

(7) Any person exercising that power shall, if asked to do so, produce some duly authenticated document showing his authority to do so.

(8) Any person authorised by the regulations to inspect records—

(a) shall be entitled at any reasonable time to have access to, and inspect and check the operation of, any computer and any associated apparatus or material which is or has been in use in connection with the records in question; and

(b) may require—

(i) the person by whom or on whose behalf the computer is or has been so used; or

(ii) any person having charge of, or otherwise concerned with the operation of, the computer, apparatus or material,

to afford him such assistance as he may reasonably require.

(9) Any person who intentionally obstructs another in the exercise of any power conferred by this section or the regulations shall be guilty of an offence and liable on summary conviction to a fine not exceeding level 3 on the standard scale.

[(9A) Where [the Chief Inspector for England] or the National Assembly for Wales exercises the power conferred by subsection (5) in relation to a child, [that authority must] publish a report on whether the child's welfare is adequately safeguarded and promoted while he is accommodated by the school or college.

(9B) Where [the Chief Inspector for England] or the National Assembly for Wales publishes a report under this section, [that authority must]—

(a) send a copy of the report to the school or college concerned; and

(b)   make copies of the report available for inspection at its offices by any person at any reasonable time.

(9C)   Any person who requests a copy of a report published under this section is entitled to have one on payment of such reasonable fee (if any) as [the Chief Inspector for England] or the National Assembly for Wales (as the case may be) considers appropriate.]

[(10)   In this section and sections 87A to 87D—

'the 1992 Act' means the Further and Higher Education Act 1992;
'appropriate authority' means—
    (a)   in relation to England, [the Chief Inspector for England];
    (b)   in relation to Wales, the National Assembly for Wales;
['the Chief Inspector for England' means Her Majesty's Chief Inspector of Education, Children's Services and Skills;]
'college' means an institution within the further education sector as defined in section 91 of the 1992 Act;
   ...
'further education corporation' has the same meaning as in the 1992 Act;
'local education authority' and 'proprietor' have the same meanings as in the Education Act 1996'.

(11)   In this section and sections 87A and 87D 'relevant person' means—

(a)   in relation to an independent school, the proprietor of the school;
(b)   in relation to any other school, or an institution designated under section 28 of the 1992 Act, the governing body of the school or institution;
(c)   in relation to an institution conducted by a further education corporation, the corporation.

(12)   Where a person other than the proprietor of an independent school is responsible for conducting the school, references in this section to the relevant person include references to the person so responsible.]

Date in force

14 October 1991: SI 1991/828.

Amendment

Section heading: substituted by the Care Standards Act 2000, s 116, Sch 4, para 14(1), (21).
Sub-ss (1)–(5): substituted by the Care Standards Act 2000, s 105(1), (2).
Sub-s (4): words 'the Chief Inspector for England is' in square brackets substituted by the Education and Inspections Act 2006, s 157, Sch 14, paras 9, 16(1), (2)(a); words 'college in England, he shall' in square brackets substituted by the Education and Inspections Act 2006, s 157, Sch 14, paras 9, 16(1), (2)(b).
Sub-s (4A): words 'in Wales' in square brackets inserted by the Education and Inspections Act 2006, s 157, Sch 14, paras 9, 16(1), (3).
Sub-s (6): word 'exercising' in square brackets substituted by the Care Standards Act 2000, s 105(1), (3).
Sub-ss (9A)–(9C): inserted by the Health and Social Care (Community Health and Standards) Act 2003, s 111.
Sub-s (9A): words 'the Chief Inspector for England' in square brackets substituted by the Education and Inspections Act 2006, s 157, Sch 14, paras 9, 16(1), (4)(a); words 'that authority must' in square brackets substituted by the Education and Inspections Act 2006, s 157, Sch 14, paras 9, 16(1), (4)(b).
Sub-s (9B): words 'the Chief Inspector for England' in square brackets substituted by the Education and Inspections Act 2006, s 157, Sch 14, paras 9, 16(1), (4)(a); words 'that authority must' in square brackets substituted by the Education and Inspections Act 2006, s 157, Sch 14, paras 9, 16(1), (4)(b).

Sub-s (9C): words 'the Chief Inspector for England' in square brackets substituted by the Education and Inspections Act 2006, s 157, Sch 14, paras 9, 16(1), (4)(a).
Sub-ss (10)–(12): substituted, for sub-s (10) as originally enacted, by the Care Standards Act 2000, s 105(1), (4).
Sub-s (10): in definition 'appropriate authority' in para (a) words 'the Chief Inspector for England' in square brackets substituted by the Education and Inspections Act 2006, s 157, Sch 14, paras 16(1), (5)(a); definition 'the Chief Inspector for England' inserted by the Education and Inspections Act 2006, s 157, Sch 14, paras 9, 16(1), (5)(b); definition 'the Commission' (omitted) repealed by the Education and Inspections Act 2006, ss 157, 184, Sch 14, paras 9, 16(1), (5)(c), Sch 18, Pt 5.

Definitions

For 'proprietor' see sub-s (10); for 'child', 'independent school', 'school', 'local authority', 'care home', 'residential care home' see s 105(1); for 'the appropriate authority', 'the Commission', 'college', 'further education corporation' see sub-s (10); for 'relevant person' see sub-s (11); for 'local education authority' see sub-s (10) as applied to the whole Act by s 105(1).

Sub-s (6) Regulations

See the National Care Standards Commission (Inspection of Schools and Colleges) Regulations 2002, SI 2002/552 and the Inspection of Boarding Schools and Colleges (Powers and Fees) (Wales) Regulations 2002, SI 2002/316.

[87A   Suspension of duty under section 87(3)]

[(1)   The Secretary of State may appoint a person to be an inspector for the purposes of this section if—

(a)   that person already acts as an inspector for other purposes in relation to schools or colleges to which section 87(1) applies, and

(b)   the Secretary of State is satisfied that the person is an appropriate person to determine whether the welfare of children provided with accommodation by such schools or colleges is adequately safeguarded and promoted while they are accommodated by them.

(2)   Where—

(a)   the relevant person enters into an agreement in writing with a person appointed under subsection (1),

(b)   the agreement provides for the person so appointed to have in relation to the school or college the function of determining whether section 87(1) is being complied with, and

(c)   the appropriate authority receive from the person mentioned in paragraph (b) ('the inspector') notice in writing that the agreement has come into effect,

the appropriate authority's duty under section 87(3) in relation to the school or college shall be suspended.

(3)   Where the appropriate authority's duty under section 87(3) in relation to any school or college is suspended under this section, it shall cease to be so suspended if the appropriate authority receive—

(a)   a notice under subsection (4) relating to the inspector, or

(b)   a notice under subsection (5) relating to the relevant agreement.

(4)   The Secretary of State shall terminate a person's appointment under subsection (1) if—

(a)   that person so requests, or

(b)   the Secretary of State ceases, in relation to that person, to be satisfied that he is such a person as is mentioned in paragraph (b) of that subsection, and shall give notice of the termination of that person's appointment to the appropriate authority.

(5) Where—

    (a)   the appropriate authority's duty under section 87(3) in relation to any school or college is suspended under this section, and

    (b)   the relevant agreement ceases to have effect,

the inspector shall give to the appropriate authority notice in writing of the fact that it has ceased to have effect.

(6)   In this section references to the relevant agreement, in relation to the suspension of the appropriate authority's duty under section 87(3) as regards any school or college, are to the agreement by virtue of which the appropriate authority's duty under that provision as regards that school or college is suspended.]

Date in force

1 January 1996.

Amendment

Inserted by the Deregulation and Contracting Out Act 1994, s 38.
Substituted by the Care Standards Act 2000, s 106(1).

Definitions

For 'relevant agreement' see sub-s (6).

Transfer of functions

Functions of the Secretary of State, so far as exercisable in relation to Wales, transferred to the National Assembly for Wales, by the National Assembly for Wales (Transfer of Functions) Order 1999, SI 1999/672, art 2, Sch 1.

[87B   Duties of inspectors under section 87A]

[(1)   The Secretary of State may impose on a person appointed under section 87A(1) ('an authorised inspector') such requirements relating to, or in connection with, the carrying out under substitution agreements of the function mentioned in section 87A(2)(b) as the Secretary of State thinks fit.

(2)   Where, in the course of carrying out under a substitution agreement the function mentioned in section 87A(2)(b), it appears to an authorised inspector that there has been a failure to comply with section 87(1) in the case of a child provided with accommodation by the school [or college] to which the agreement relates, the inspector shall give notice of that fact

    [(a)   in the case of a school other than an independent school or a special school, to the local education authority for the area in which the school is situated;

    (b)   in the case of a special school which is maintained by a local education authority, to that authority;

    (c)   in any other case, to the Secretary of State].

(3)   Where, in the course of carrying out under a substitution agreement the function mentioned in section 87A(2)(b), it appears to an authorised inspector that a child provided with accommodation by the school [or college] to which the agreement relates is suffering, or is likely to suffer, significant harm, the inspector shall—

    (a)   give notice of that fact to the local authority in whose area the school [or college] is situated, and

(b) where the inspector is required to make inspection reports to the Secretary of State, supply that local authority with a copy of the latest inspection report to have been made by the inspector to the Secretary of State in relation to the school [or college].

[(4) In this section 'substitution agreement' means an agreement by virtue of which the duty of the appropriate authority under section 87(3) in relation to a school or college is suspended.]]

Date in force

1 January 1996.

Amendment

Inserted by the Deregulation and Contracting Out Act 1994, s 38.
Sub-s (2): words 'or college' in square brackets inserted by the Care Standards Act 2000, s 106(2)(a); paras (a)–(c) substituted by the Care Standards Act 2000, s 106(2)(b).
Sub-s (3): words 'or college' in square brackets in each place they occur inserted by the Care Standards Act 2000, s 106(2)(a).
Sub-s (4): substituted by the Care Standards Act 2000, s 106(2)(c).

Definitions

For 'an authorised inspector' see sub-s (1); for 'child', 'school', 'local authority' see s 105(1); for 'substitution agreement' see sub-s (3).

Transfer of functions

Functions of the Secretary of State, so far as exercisable in relation to Wales, transferred to the National Assembly for Wales, by the National Assembly for Wales (Transfer of Functions) Order 1999, SI 1999/672, art 2, Sch 1.

[87C   Boarding schools: national minimum standards]

[(1) The Secretary of State may prepare and publish statements of national minimum standards for safeguarding and promoting the welfare of children for whom accommodation is provided in a school or college.

(2) The Secretary of State shall keep the standards set out in the statements under review and may publish amended statements whenever he considers it appropriate to do so.

(3) Before issuing a statement, or an amended statement which in the opinion of the Secretary of State effects a substantial change in the standards, the Secretary of State shall consult any persons he considers appropriate.

(4) The standards shall be taken into account—

(a) in the making by the appropriate authority of any determination under section 87(4) or (4A);
(b) in the making by a person appointed under section 87A(1) of any determination under section 87B(2); and
(c) in any proceedings under any other enactment in which it is alleged that the person has failed to comply with section 87(1).]

Date in force

England: 1 April 2002: see SI 2001/3852. Wales: 1 July 2001: see SI 2001/2190.

Appendix 1 *Children Act 1989*

Amendment

Inserted by the Care Standards Act 2000, s107.

Definitions

For 'child', 'school' see s 105(1); for 'college', 'appropriate authority' see s 87A(10).

Transfer of functions

Functions of the Secretary of State, so far as exercisable in relation to Wales, transferred to the National Assembly for Wales, by the National Assembly for Wales (Transfer of Functions) Order 1999, SI 1999/672, art 2, Sch 1.

[87D   Annual fee for boarding school inspections]

[(1)   Regulations under subsection (2) may be made in relation to any school or college in respect of which the appropriate authority is required to take steps under section 87(3).

(2)   The Secretary of State may by regulations require the relevant person to pay the appropriate authority an annual fee of such amount, and within such time, as the regulations may specify.

(3)   A fee payable by virtue of this section may, without prejudice to any other method of recovery, be recovered summarily as a civil debt.]

Date in force

England: 1 April 2002: see SI 2001/3852. Wales: 1 July 2001: see SI 2001/2190.

Amendment

Inserted by the Care Standards Act 2000, s108.

Definitions

For 'school' see s 105(1); for 'college' see s 87A(10).

Sub-s (2) Regulations

Her Majesty's Chief Inspector of Education, Children's Services and Skills (Fees and Frequency of Inspections) (Children's Homes etc.) Regulations 2007, SI 2007/694 in addition to making provision for fees, provide for the frequency of inspection in relation to each of the establishments, agencies and local authority adoption and fostering functions. In Wales the prescribed fee is nil: Care Standards Act 2000 and Children Act 1989 (Abolition of Fees) (Wales) Regulations 2006, SI 2006/878. Inspection of Boarding Schools and Colleges (Powers and Fees) (Wales) Regulations 2002, Commission for Social Care Inspection (Fees and Frequency of Inspections) Regulations 2007, SI 2007/556.

Transfer of functions

Functions of the Secretary of State, so far as exercisable in relation to Wales, transferred to the National Assembly for Wales, by the National Assembly for Wales (Transfer of Functions) Order 1999, SI 1999/672, art 2, Sch 1.

Adoption

88   Amendments of adoption legislation

(1)   ...

(2) *The Adoption (Scotland) Act 1978 shall have effect subject to the amendments made by Part II of Schedule 10.*

Paternity tests

89

Repealed by the Child Support, Pensions and Social Security Act 2000, s 85, Sch 9, Pt IX.

Criminal care and supervision orders

90   Care and supervision orders in criminal proceedings

(1)   The power of a court to make an order under subsection (2) of section 1 of the Children and Young Persons Act 1969 (care proceedings in [youth courts]) where it is of the opinion that the condition mentioned in paragraph (f) of that subsection ('the offence condition') is satisfied is hereby abolished.

(2)   The powers of the court to make care orders—

> (a)   under section 7(7)(a) of the Children and Young Persons Act 1969 (alteration in treatment of young offenders etc); and
> (b)   under section 15(1) of that Act, on discharging a supervision order made under section 7(7)(b) of that Act,

are hereby abolished.

(3)   The powers given by that Act to include requirements in supervision orders shall have effect subject to amendments made by Schedule 12.

Date in force

14 October 1991: SI 1991/828.

Amendment

Sub-s (1): words in square brackets substituted by the Criminal Justice Act 1991, s 100, Sch 11, para 40.

Effect and duration of orders etc

91   Effect and duration of orders etc

(1)   The making of a residence order with respect to a child who is the subject of a care order discharges the care order.

(2)   The making of a care order with respect to a child who is the subject of any section 8 order discharges that order.

[(2A)   Where a contact activity direction has been made as regards contact with a child, the making of a care order with respect to the child discharges the direction.]

(3)   The making of a care order with respect to a child who is the subject of a supervision order discharges that other order.

(4)   The making of a care order with respect to a child who is a ward of court brings that wardship to an end.

(5)   The making of a care order with respect to a child who is the subject of a school attendance order made under [section 437 of the Education Act 1996] discharges the school attendance order.

[(5A)   The making of a special guardianship order with respect to a child who is the subject of—

(a)   a care order; or
(b)   an order under section 34,

discharges that order.]

(6)   Where an emergency protection order is made with respect to a child who is in care, the care order shall have effect subject to the emergency protection order.

(7)   Any order made under section 4(1), [4A(1)] or 5(1) shall continue in force until the child reaches the age of eighteen, unless it is brought to an end earlier.

(8)   Any—

(a)   agreement under section 4 [or 4A]; or
(b)   appointment under section 5(3) or (4),

shall continue in force until the child reaches the age of eighteen, unless it is brought to an end earlier.

(9)   An order under Schedule 1 has effect as specified in that Schedule.

(10)   A section 8 order shall, if it would otherwise still be in force, cease to have effect when the child reaches the age of sixteen, unless it is to have effect beyond that age by virtue of section 9(6) [or 12(5)].

(11)   Where a section 8 order has effect with respect to a child who has reached the age of sixteen, it shall, if it would otherwise still be in force, cease to have effect when he reaches the age of eighteen.

(12)   Any care order, other than an interim care order, shall continue in force until the child reaches the age of eighteen, unless it is brought to an end earlier.

(13)   Any order made under any other provision of this Act in relation to a child shall, if it would otherwise still be in force, cease to have effect when he reaches the age of eighteen.

(14)   On disposing of any application for an order under this Act, the court may (whether or not it makes any other order in response to the application) order that no application for an order under this Act of any specified kind may be made with respect to the child concerned by any person named in the order without leave of the court.

(15)   Where an application ('the previous application') has been made for—

(a)   the discharge of a care order;
(b)   the discharge of a supervision order;
(c)   the discharge of an education supervision order;
(d)   the substitution of a supervision order for a care order; or
(e)   a child assessment order,

no further application of a kind mentioned in paragraphs (a) to (e) may be made with respect to the child concerned, without leave of the court, unless the period between the disposal of the previous application and the making of the further application exceeds six months.

(16)   Subsection (15) does not apply to applications made in relation to interim orders.

(17)   Where—

(a) a person has made an application for an order under section 34;
(b) the application has been refused; and
(c) a period of less than six months has elapsed since the refusal,

that person may not make a further application for such an order with respect to the same child, unless he has obtained the leave of the court.

Date in force

14 October 1991: SI 1991/828.

Amendment

Sub-s (2A): inserted by the Children and Adoption Act 2006, s 15(1), Sch 2, paras 7, 9. Date in force: to be appointed: see the Children and Adoption Act 2006, s 17(2).
Sub-s (5): words in square brackets substituted by the Education Act 1996, s 582(1), Sch 37, para 90.
Sub-s (5A): inserted by the Adoption and Children Act 2002, s 139(a), Sch 3, paras 54, 68(a).
Sub-s (7): reference to '4A(1)' in square brackets inserted by the Adoption and Children Act 2002, s 139(1), Sch 3, paras 54, 68(b).
Sub-s (8): in para (a) words 'or 4A' in square brackets inserted by the Adoption and Children Act 2002, s 139(1), Sch 3, paras 54, 68(c).
Sub-s (10): words 'or 12(5)' in square brackets inserted by the Adoption and Children Act 2002, s 114(3).

Definitions

For 'residence order' see s 8(1); for 'child' see s 105(1); for care order' see s 31(11) and s 105(1); for 'a section 8 order' see s 8(2); for 'supervision order' see s 31(11); for 'emergency protection order' see s 44 as applied to the whole Act by s 105(1); for 'court' see s 92(7); for 'education supervision order' see s 36; for 'child assessment order' see s 43(2).

References

For the duration of supervision orders see also Sch 3, Pt II, para 6; for the discharge and variation of care and supervision orders see s 39; for interim orders see s 38.

Sub-s (2)

Where the court made a care order and made no order in respect of a pending application for a residence order, the application for a residence order was deemed to have been dismissed: *Hounslow London Borough Council v A* [1993] 1 FLR 702.

Sub-s (14)

For the application of this provision, see generally paras 5.202 ff.

Jurisdiction and procedure etc

92 Jurisdiction of courts

(1) The name 'domestic proceedings', given to certain proceedings in magistrates' courts, is hereby changed to 'family proceedings' and the names 'domestic court' and 'domestic court panel' are hereby changed to 'family proceedings court' and 'family panel', respectively.

(2) Proceedings under this Act shall be treated as family proceedings in relation to magistrates' courts.

(3) Subsection (2) is subject to the provisions of section 65(1) and (2) of the Magistrates' Courts Act 1980 (proceedings which may be treated as not being family proceedings), as amended by this Act.

(4)   A magistrates' court shall not be competent to entertain any application, or make any order, involving the administration or application of—

    (a)   any property belonging to or held in trust for a child; or
    (b)   the income of any such property.

(5)   The powers of a magistrates' court under section 63(2) of the Act of 1980 to suspend or rescind orders shall not apply in relation to any order made under this Act.

(6)   Part I of Schedule 11 makes provision, including provision for the Lord Chancellor to make orders, with respect to the jurisdiction of courts and justices of the peace in relation to—

    (a)   proceedings under this Act; and
    (b)   proceedings under certain other enactments.

(7)   For the purposes of this Act 'the court' means the High Court, a county court or a magistrates' court.

(8)   Subsection (7) is subject to the provision made by or under Part I of Schedule 11 and to any express provision as to the jurisdiction of any court made by any other provision of this Act.

(9)   The Lord Chancellor may[, after consulting the Lord Chief Justice,] by order make provision for the principal registry of the Family Division of the High Court to be treated as if it were a county court for such purposes of this Act, or of any provision made under this Act, as may be specified in the order.

(10)   Any order under subsection (9) may make such provision as the Lord Chancellor thinks expedient[, after consulting the Lord Chief Justice,] for the purpose of applying (with or without modifications) provisions which apply in relation to the procedure in county courts to the principal registry when it acts as if it were a county court.

[(10A)   The Lord Chief Justice may nominate a judicial office holder (as defined in section 109(4) of the Constitutional Reform Act 2005) to exercise his functions under subsection (9) or (10).]

(11)   Part II of Schedule 11 makes amendments consequential on this section.

Date in force

14 October 1991: SI 1991/828.

Amendment

Sub-s (9): words ', after consulting the Lord Chief Justice,' in square brackets inserted by the Constitutional Reform Act 2005, s 15(1), Sch 4, Pt 1, paras 203, 205(1), (2).
Sub-s (10): words ', after consulting the Lord Chief Justice,' in square brackets inserted by the Constitutional Reform Act 2005, s 15(1), Sch 4, Pt 1, paras 203, 205(1), (3).
Sub-s (10A): inserted by the Constitutional Reform Act 2005, s 15(1), Sch 4, Pt 1, paras 203, 205(1), (4).

Regulations

See the Children (Allocation of Proceedings) Order 1991, SI 1991/1677 amended by SI 1997/1897, SI 2001/775, SI 2005/520 and SI 2005/2797.

Reference

For the application of sub-s (2): *R v Oxfordshire County Council* [1992] Fam 150, [1992] 3 All ER 660.

---

93   Rules of court

(1) An authority having power to make rules of court may make such provision for giving effect to—

  (a)   this Act;
  (b)   the provisions of any statutory instrument made under this Act; or
  (c)   any amendment made by this Act in any other enactment,

as appears to that authority to be necessary or expedient.

(2)   The rules may, in particular, make provision—

  (a)   with respect to the procedure to be followed in any relevant proceedings (including the manner in which any application is to be made or other proceedings commenced);
  (b)   as to the persons entitled to participate in any relevant proceedings, whether as parties to the proceedings or by being given the opportunity to make representations to the court;
  [(bb) for children to be separately represented in relevant proceedings,]
  (c)   with respect to the documents and information to be furnished, and notices to be given, in connection with any relevant proceedings;
  (d)   applying (with or without modification) enactments which govern the procedure to be followed with respect to proceedings brought on a complaint made to a magistrates' court to relevant proceedings in such a court brought otherwise than on a complaint;
  (e)   with respect to preliminary hearings;
  (f)   for the service outside [England and Wales], in such circumstances and in such manner as may be prescribed, of any notice of proceedings in a magistrates' court;
  (g)   for the exercise by magistrates' courts, in such circumstances as may be prescribed, of such powers as may be prescribed (even though a party to the proceedings in question is [or resides] outside England and Wales);
  (h)   enabling the court, in such circumstances as may be prescribed, to proceed on any application even though the respondent has not been given notice of the proceedings;
  (i)   authorising a single justice to discharge the functions of a magistrates' court with respect to such relevant proceedings as may be prescribed;
  (j)   authorising a magistrates' court to order any of the parties to such relevant proceedings as may be prescribed, in such circumstances as may be prescribed, to pay the whole or part of the costs of all or any of the other parties.

(3)   In subsection (2)—

  'notice of proceedings' means a summons or such other notice of proceedings as is required; and 'given', in relation to a summons, means 'served';
  'prescribed' means prescribed by the rules; and
  'relevant proceedings' means any application made, or proceedings brought, under any of the provisions mentioned in paragraphs (*a*) to (*c*) of subsection (1) and any part of such proceedings.

(4)   This section and any other power in this Act to make rules of court are not to be taken as in any way limiting any other power of the authority in question to make rules of court.

(5)   When making any rules under this section an authority shall be subject to the same requirements as to consultation (if any) as apply when the authority makes rules under its general rule making power.

Date in force

14 October 1991: SI 1991/828.

Amendment

Sub-s (2): para (bb) inserted by the Adoption and Children Act 2002, s 122(2); in para (f) words 'England and Wales' in square brackets substituted by the Courts and Legal Services Act 1990, s 116, Sch 16, para 22; in para (g) words 'or resides' in square brackets inserted by the Courts and Legal Services Act 1990, s 116, Sch 16, para 22.

Definitions

For 'notice of proceedings', 'prescribed' and 'relevant proceedings' see sub-s (3).

Rules of court

See also the Courts Act 2003 for provision for 'Family Procedure Rules' governing practice and procedure in family proceedings in the High Court, county courts and magistrates' courts (s75) to be made by the Family Procedure Rules Committee (s 77) in accordance with statutory procedures (s 79).

94   Appeals

(1)   [Subject to any express provisions to the contrary made by or under this Act, an] appeal shall lie to the High Court against—

    (a)   the making by a magistrates' court of any order under this Act [or the Adoption and Children Act 2002]; or

    (b)   any refusal by a magistrates' court to make such an order.

(2)   Where a magistrates' court has power, in relation to any proceedings under this Act [or the Adoption and Children Act 2002], to decline jurisdiction because it considers that the case can more conveniently be dealt with by another court, no appeal shall lie against any exercise by that magistrates' court of that power.

(3)   Subsection (1) does not apply in relation to an interim order for periodical payments made under Schedule 1.

(4)   On an appeal under this section, the High Court may make such orders as may be necessary to give effect to its determination of the appeal.

(5)   Where an order is made under subsection (4) the High Court may also make such incidental or consequential orders as appear to it to be just.

(6)   Where an appeal from a magistrates' court relates to an order for the making of periodical payments, the High Court may order that its determination of the appeal shall have effect from such date as it thinks fit to specify in the order.

(7)   The date so specified must not be earlier than the earliest date allowed in accordance with rules of court made for the purposes of this section.

(8)   Where, on an appeal under this section in respect of an order requiring a person to make periodical payments, the High Court reduces the amount of those payments or discharges the order—

    (a)   it may order the person entitled to the payments to pay to the person making them such sum in respect of payments already made as the High Court thinks fit; and

    (b)   if any arrears are due under the order for periodical payments, it may remit payment of the whole, or part, of those arrears.

(9)   Any order of the High Court made on an appeal under this section (other than one directing that an application be re-heard by a magistrates' court) shall, for the purposes—

(a)   of the enforcement of the order; and
(b)   of any power to vary, revive or discharge orders,

be treated as if it were an order of the magistrates' court from which the appeal was brought and not an order of the High Court.

(10)   The Lord Chancellor may[, after consulting the Lord Chief Justice,] by order make provision as to the circumstances in which appeals may be made against decisions taken by courts on questions arising in connection with the transfer, or proposed transfer, of proceedings by virtue of any order under paragraph 2 of Schedule 11.

(11)   Except to the extent provided for in any order made under subsection (10), no appeal may be made against any decision of a kind mentioned in that subsection.

[(12)   The Lord Chief Justice may nominate a judicial office holder (as defined in section 109(4) of the Constitutional Reform Act 2005) to exercise his functions under subsection (10).]

Date in force

14 October 1991: SI 1991/828.

Amendment

Sub-s (1): words from 'Subject to any' to 'this Act, an' in square brackets substituted by the Courts and Legal Services Act 1990, s 116, Sch 16, para 23; in para (a) words 'or the Adoption and Children Act 2002' in square brackets inserted by the Adoption and Children Act 2002, s 100.
Sub-s (2): words 'or the Adoption and Children Act 2002' in square brackets inserted by the Adoption and Children Act 2002, s 100.
Sub-s (10): words ', after consulting the Lord Chief Justice,' in square brackets inserted by the Constitutional Reform Act 2005, s 15(1), Sch 4, Pt 1, paras 203, 206(1), (2).
Sub-s (12): inserted by the Constitutional Reform Act 2005, s 15(1), Sch 4, Pt 1, paras 203, 206(1), (3).

References

See generally Chapter 13; *Handbook of Best Practice in Children Act Cases* (June 1997) CAAC in *Clarke, Hall and Morrison on Children* at para [?????????????].

Practice Directions

See *Practice Direction* [1992] 1 All ER 864 and in relation to magistrates' courts *Practice Direction (Children Act 1989 – Appeals)* [1992] 2 FLR 503.
There is no power for a magistrates' court to stay an order pending appeal but an application for a stay may be made to the High Court *Re O (a minor)* [1992] 4 All ER 905 and *Re J (a minor) (Residence)* [1993] 2 FCR 636, [1994] 1 FLR 369 but see para 13.24. On an appeal from a family proceedings court, the High Court may remit the matter for rehearing before any county court which is a care centre: *Suffolk County Council v C* [1999] 1 FCR 473n, [1999] 1 FLR 259n.

Regulations

See the Children (Allocation of Proceedings) (Appeals) Order 1991, SI 1991/1801.

---

95 Attendance of child at hearing under Part IV or V

(1) In any proceedings in which a court is hearing an application for an order under Part IV or V, or is considering whether to make any such order, the court may order the child concerned to attend such stage or stages of the proceedings as may be specified in the order.

(2) The power conferred by subsection (1) shall be exercised in accordance with rules of court.

(3) Subsections (4) to (6) apply where—

(a) an order under subsection (1) has not been complied with; or
(b) the court has reasonable cause to believe that it will not be complied with.

(4) The court may make an order authorising a constable, or such person as may be specified in the order—

(a) to take charge of the child and to bring him to the court; and
(b) to enter and search any premises specified in the order if he has reasonable cause to believe that the child may be found on the premises.

(5) The court may order any person who is in a position to do so to bring the child to the court.

(6) Where the court has reason to believe that a person has information about the whereabouts of the child it may order him to disclose it to the court.

Date in force

14 October 1991: SI 1991/828.

Definitions

For 'court' see s 92(7); for 'child' see s 105(1).

References

See generally Chapter 8. Part IV ie ss 31–42 and Sch 3 (care and supervision); Part V ie ss 43–52 (protection of children).

---

96 Evidence given by, or with respect to, children

(1) Subsection (2) applies where a child who is called as a witness in any civil proceedings does not, in the opinion of the court, understand the nature of an oath.

(2) The child's evidence may be heard by the court if, in its opinion—

(a) he understands that it is his duty to speak the truth; and
(b) he has sufficient understanding to justify his evidence being heard.

(3) The Lord Chancellor may[, with the concurrence of the Lord Chief Justice,] by order make provision for the admissibility of evidence which would otherwise be inadmissible under any rule of law relating to hearsay.

(4) An order under subsection (3) may only be made with respect to—

(a) civil proceedings in general or such civil proceedings, or class of civil proceedings, as may be prescribed; and
(b) evidence in connection with the upbringing, maintenance or welfare of a child.

(5) An order under subsection (3)—

(a) may, in particular, provide for the admissibility of statements which are made orally or in a prescribed form or which are recorded by any prescribed method of recording;

(b) may make different provision for different purposes and in relation to different descriptions of court; and

(c) may make such amendments and repeals in any enactment relating to evidence (other than in this Act) as the Lord Chancellor considers necessary or expedient in consequence of the provision made by the order.

(6) Subsection (5)(b) is without prejudice to section 104(4).

(7) In this section—

['civil proceedings' means civil proceedings, before any tribunal, in relation to which the strict rules of evidence apply, whether as a matter of law or by agreement of the parties, and references to 'the court' shall be construed accordingly;]
'prescribed' means prescribed by an order under subsection (3).

Date in force

Sub-ss (1), (2): 14 October 1991: SI 1991/828. Sub-ss (3)–(7): 16 November 1989.

Amendment

Sub-s (3): words ', with the concurrence of the Lord Chief Justice,' in square brackets inserted by the Constitutional Reform Act 2005, s 15(1), Sch 4, Pt 1, paras 203, 207.
Sub-s (7): definition 'civil proceedings' substituted, for definitions 'civil proceedings and 'court' as originally enacted, by the Civil Evidence Act 1995, s 15(1), Sch 1, para 16.

Definitions

For 'child' see s 105(1); for 'court', 'civil proceedings' and 'prescribed' see sub-s (7).

Sub-s (3)

See the Children (Admissibility of Hearing Evidence) Order 1993, SI 1993/621 and para 11.20.

97   Privacy for children involved in certain proceedings

(1) *Rules made under section 144 of the Magistrates' Courts Act 1980* [Family Procedure Rules] may make provision for a magistrates' court to sit in private in proceedings in which any powers under this Act [or the Adoption and Children Act 2002] may be exercised by the court with respect to any child.

(2) No person shall publish [to the public at large or any section of the public] any material which is intended, or likely, to identify—

(a) any child as being involved in any proceedings before [the High Court, a county court or] a magistrates' court in which any power under this Act [or the Adoption and Children Act 2002] may be exercised by the court with respect to that or any other child; or

(b) an address or school as being that of a child involved in any such proceedings.

(3) In any proceedings for an offence under this section it shall be a defence for the accused to prove that he did not know, and had no reason to suspect, that the published material was intended, or likely, to identify the child.

(4) The court or the [Lord Chancellor] may, if satisfied that the welfare of the child requires it [and, in the case of the Lord Chancellor, if the Lord Chief Justice agrees], by order dispense with the requirements of subsection (2) to such extent as may be specified in the order.

(5) For the purposes of this section—

'publish' includes—
[(a) include a programme service (within the meaning of the Broadcasting Act 1990);] or
(b) cause to be published; and
'material' includes any picture or representation.

(6) Any person who contravenes this section shall be guilty of an offence and liable, on summary conviction, to a fine not exceeding level 4 on the standard scale.

(7) Subsection (1) is without prejudice to—

(a) *the generality of the rule making power in section 144 of the Act of 1980; or*
(b) any other power of a magistrates' court to sit in private.

(8) [Sections 69 (sittings of magistrates' courts for family proceedings) and 71 (newspaper reports of certain proceedings) of the Act of 1980] shall apply in relation to any proceedings [(before a magistrates' court)] to which this section applies subject to the provisions of this section.

[(9) The Lord Chief Justice may nominate a judicial office holder (as defined in section 109(4) of the Constitutional Reform Act 2005) to exercise his functions under subsection (4).]

Date in force

14 October 1991: SI 1991/828.

Amendments

Sub-s (1): words 'Rules made under section 144 of the Magistrates' Courts Act 1980' in italics repealed and subsequent words in square brackets substituted by the Courts Act 2003, s 109(1), Sch 8, para 337(1), (2). Date in force: to be appointed: see the Courts Act 2003, s 110(1); words 'or the Adoption and Children Act 2002' in square brackets inserted by the Adoption and Children Act 2002, s 101(3).
Sub-s (2): words 'to the public at large or any section of the public' in square brackets inserted by the Children Act 2004, s 62(1); in para (a) words 'the High Court, a county court or' in square brackets inserted by the Access to Justice Act 1999, s 72(a); in para (a) words 'or the Adoption and Children Act 2002' in square brackets inserted by the Adoption and Children Act 2002, s 101(3).
Sub-s (4): words 'Lord Chancellor' in square brackets substituted by SI 1992/709, art 3(2), Sch 2; words 'and, in the case of the Lord Chancellor, if the Lord Chief Justice agrees' in square brackets inserted by the Constitutional Reform Act 2005, s 15(1), Sch 4, Pt 1, paras 203, 208(1), (2).
Sub-s (5): in definition 'publish' words in square brackets substituted by the Broadcasting Act 1990, s 203(1), Sch 20, para 53.
Sub-s (7): para (a) repealed by the Courts Act 2003, s 109(1), (3), Sch 8, para 337(1), (3), Sch 10. Date in force: to be appointed: see the Courts Act 2003, s 110(1); words from 'Sections 69' to 'Act of 1980' in square brackets substituted by the Courts and Legal Services Act 1990, s 116, Sch 16, para 24.
Sub-s (8): words '(before a magistrates' court)' in square brackets inserted by the Access to Justice Act 1999, s 72(b).
Sub-s (9): inserted by the Constitutional Reform Act 2005, s 15(1), Sch 4, Pt 1, paras 203, 208(1), (3).

Definitions

For 'child' and 'school' see 105(1); for 'publish' and 'material' see sub-s (5).

References

See generally paras 4.47 ff. For 'the standard scale' see the CJA 1982 s 37(2)(3) as amended.

98   Self-incrimination

(1)   In any proceedings in which a court is hearing an application for an order under Part IV or V, no person shall be excused from—

(a)   giving evidence on any matter; or
(b)   answering any question put to him in the course of his giving evidence,

on the ground that doing so might incriminate him or his spouse [or civil partner] of an offence.

(2)   A statement or admission made in such proceedings shall not be admissible in evidence against the person making it or his spouse [or civil partner] in proceedings for an offence other than perjury.

Date in force

14 October 1991: SI 1991/828.

Amendment

Sub-s (1): words 'or civil partner' in square brackets inserted by the Civil Partnership Act 2004, s 261(1), Sch 27, para 132.
Sub-s (2): words 'or civil partner' in square brackets inserted by the Civil Partnership Act 2004, s 261(1), Sch 27, para 132.

Definition

For 'court' see s 92(7).

References

'Part IV' ie ss 31–42 and Sch 3 (care and supervision); 'Part V' ie ss 43–52 (protection of children) for discussion on immunity from self-incrimination, see para 11.64 ff and see *Re M (disclosure: police investigation)* [2002] 1 FCR 655 where the court declined to order disclosure of a mother's admission of assault in care proceedings made subsequent to the closing of an inconclusive police investigation.

99   ...

(1)–(4)   ...

(5)   ...

Amendment

Repealed by the Access to Justice Act 1999, s 106, Sch 15, Pt I.

Legal Aid

Now replaced by the Community Legal Service under the provisions of the Access to Justice Act 1999.

100   Restrictions on use of wardship jurisdiction

(1)   ...

(2)   No court shall exercise the High Court's inherent jurisdiction with respect to children—

  (a)   so as to require a child to be placed in the care, or put under the supervision, of a local authority;

  (b)   so as to require a child to be accommodated by or on behalf of a local authority;

  (c)   so as to make a child who is the subject of a care order a ward of court; or

  (d)   for the purpose of conferring on any local authority power to determine any question which has arisen, or which may arise, in connection with any aspect of parental responsibility for a child.

(3)   No application for any exercise of the court's inherent jurisdiction with respect to children may be made by a local authority unless the authority have obtained the leave of the court.

(4)   The court may only grant leave if it is satisfied that—

  (a)   the result which the authority wish to achieve could not be achieved through the making of any order of a kind to which subsection (5) applies; and

  (b)   there is reasonable cause to believe that if the court's inherent jurisdiction is not exercised with respect to the child he is likely to suffer significant harm.

(5)   This subsection applies to any order—

  (a)   made otherwise than in the exercise of the court's inherent jurisdiction; and

  (b)   which the local authority is entitled to apply for (assuming, in the case of any application which may only be made with leave, that leave is granted).

Date in force

14 October 1991: SI 1991/828.

Amendment

Sub-s (1): repeals the Family Law Reform Act 1969, s 7.

Definitions

For 'local authority', 'child' see s 105(1); for 'care order' see s 31(11) and s 105(1); for 'parental responsibility' see s 3; for 'harm' see s 31(9) as applied to the whole Act by s 105(1) and as to whether harm is significant see s 31(10) as applied to the whole Act by s 105(1).

References

See generally paras 12.4 ff, wardship and 12.25 ff, inherent jurisdiction. For exclusion of applications under s 100(3) from the definition of 'family proceedings' under this Act see s 8(3).

---

101   Effect of orders as between England and Wales and Northern Ireland, the Channel Islands or the Isle of Man

(1)   The Secretary of State may make regulations providing—

  (a)   for prescribed orders which—

    (i)   are made by a court in Northern Ireland; and

    (ii)   appear to the Secretary of State to correspond in their effect to orders which may be made under any provision of this Act,

to have effect in prescribed circumstances, for prescribed purposes of this Act, as if they were orders of a prescribed kind made under this Act;

  (b)   for prescribed orders which—

    (i)   are made by a court in England and Wales; and

(ii) appear to the Secretary of State to correspond in their effect to orders which may be made under any provision in force in Northern Ireland,

to have effect in prescribed circumstances, for prescribed purposes of the law of Northern Ireland, as if they were orders of a prescribed kind made in Northern Ireland.

(2)   Regulations under subsection (1) may provide for the order concerned to cease to have effect for the purposes of the law of Northern Ireland, or (as the case may be) the law of England and Wales, if prescribed conditions are satisfied.

(3)   The Secretary of State may make regulations providing for prescribed orders which—

(a)   are made by a court in the Isle of Man or in any of the Channel Islands; and
(b)   appear to the Secretary of State to correspond in their effect to orders which may be made under this Act,

to have effect in prescribed circumstances for prescribed purposes of this Act, as if they were orders of a prescribed kind made under this Act.

(4)   Where a child who is in the care of a local authority is lawfully taken to live in Northern Ireland, the Isle of Man or any of the Channel Islands, the care order in question shall cease to have effect if the conditions prescribed in regulations made by the Secretary of State are satisfied.

(5)   Any regulations made under this section may—

(a)   make such consequential amendments (including repeals) in—
(i)   section 25 of the Children and Young Persons Act 1969 (transfers between England and Wales and Northern Ireland); or
(ii)   section 26 (transfers between England and Wales and Channel Islands or Isle of Man) of that Act,
as the Secretary of State considers necessary or expedient; and
(b)   modify any provision of this Act, in its application (by virtue of the regulations) in relation to an order made otherwise than in England and Wales.

Date in force

14 October 1991: SI 1991/828.

Definitions

For 'court' see s 92(7); for 'prescribed' see s 105(1); for 'care order' see s 31(11) and s 105(1).

Transfer of functions

Functions of the Secretary of State, so far as exercisable in relation to Wales, transferred to the National Assembly for Wales, by the National Assembly for Wales (Transfer of Functions) Order 1999, SI 1999/672, art 2, Sch 1.

Regulations

See the Children (Prescribed Orders – Northern Ireland, Guernsey and Isle of Man) Regulations 1991, SI 1991/2032 amended by SI 2006/837.

Search warrants

102   Power of constable to assist in exercise of certain powers to search for children or inspect premises

(1)   Where, on an application made by any person for a warrant under this section, it appears to the court—

   (a)   that a person attempting to exercise powers under any enactment mentioned in subsection (6) has been prevented from doing so by being refused entry to the premises concerned or refused access to the child concerned; or

   (b)   that any such person is likely to be so prevented from exercising any such powers,

it may issue a warrant authorising any constable to assist that person in the exercise of those powers, using reasonable force if necessary.

(2)   Every warrant issued under this section shall be addressed to, and executed by, a constable who shall be accompanied by the person applying for the warrant if—

   (a)   that person so desires; and

   (b)   the court by whom the warrant is issued does not direct otherwise.

(3)   A court granting an application for a warrant under this section may direct that the constable concerned may, in executing the warrant, be accompanied by a registered medical practitioner, registered nurse or [registered midwife] if he so chooses.

[(3A)   The reference in subsection (3) to a registered midwife is to such a midwife who is also registered in the Specialist Community Public Health Nurses' Part of the register maintained under article 5 of the Nursing and Midwifery Order 2001.]

(4)   An application for a warrant under this section shall be made in the manner and form prescribed by rules of court.

(5)   Where—

   (a)   an application for a warrant under this section relates to a particular child; and

   (b)   it is reasonably practicable to do so,

the application and any warrant granted on the application shall name the child; and where it does not name him it shall describe him as clearly as possible.

(6)   The enactments are—

   (a)   sections 62, 64, 67, 76, [79U,] 80, 86 and 87;

   (b)   paragraph 8(1)(b) and (2)(b) of Schedule 3;

   (c)   ...

Date in force

14 October 1991: SI 1991/828.

Amendment

Sub-s (3): words 'registered midwife' in square brackets substituted by SI 2002/253, art 54(3), Sch 5, para 10(c).
Sub-s (3A): inserted by SI 2004/1771, art 3, Schedule, Pt 1, para 4(c).
Sub-s (6): in para (a) reference to '76,' in italics repealed, in relation to Scotland, by the Regulation of Care (Scotland) Act 2001, s 80(1), Sch 4; in para (a) reference to '79U,' in square brackets inserted by the Care Standards Act 2000, s 116, Sch 4, para 14(1), (22); para (c) repealed by the Adoption and Children Act 2002, s 139(1), (3), Sch 3, paras 54, 69, Sch 5.

Definitions

For 'court' see s 92(7); for 'child', 'prescribed' see s 105(1).

Reference

For 'premises' see the note to s 72.

Procedure

Application may only be made to a magistrates' court: SI 1991/1395, arts 2(1)(m) and 6(2). With the leave of the justices' clerk, application may be made ex parte in which case the applicant must file an application for each child in Forms C1 and C19 prescribed in SI 1991/1395, Sch 1 either at the time the application is made or as directed by the justices' clerk: SI 1991/1395, r 4(4)(ii). An ex parte application may be heard before a single justice: s 93(2)(i) and SI 1991/1395, r 2(5)(a). Where the court or a single justice refuses to make an order or an ex parte application it may direct that the application be made inter partes: r 4(5).

Inter partes applications

The applicant must file with the justices' clerk the application and sufficient copies for one to be served on each respondent. The clerk will consider whether there should be a directions appointment to consider the matters specified in SI 1991/1395, r 14 (and see r 16 (attendance at directions appointment)). The clerk will then fix the date, time and place for a hearing or directions appointment (allowing sufficient time for the applicant to give the required notice to the respondent). The clerk will endorse the date so fixed on the copy applications which are returned to the applicant who thereupon serves a copy application on the person referred to in s 102(1) and any person preventing or likely to prevent such a person from exercising powers under enactments mentioned in sub-s (6) of that section at least one day before the day fixed for the hearing or directions appointment. The rules of service are provided for in SI 1991/1395, r 8, and service may be effected by first class post. The parties to the proceedings must file with the court and serve on the other parties written statements of the substance of the oral evidence which they intend to adduce at the directions appointment or hearing as provided for by SI 1991/1395, r 17.

General

103 Offences by bodies corporate

(1) This section applies where any offence under this Act is committed by a body corporate.

(2) If the offence is proved to have been committed with the consent or connivance of or to be attributable to any neglect on the part of any director, manager, secretary or other similar officer of the body corporate, or any person who was purporting to act in any such capacity he (as well as the body corporate) shall be guilty of the offence and shall be liable to be proceeded against and punished accordingly.

Date in force

14 October 1991: SI 1991/828.

---

104 Regulations and orders

(1) Any power of the Lord Chancellor[, the Treasury] *or the Secretary of State* [, the Secretary of State or the National Assembly for Wales] under this Act to make an order, regulations, or rules, except an order under section ..., 56(4)(*a*), 57(3), 84 or 97(4) or paragraph 1(1) of Schedule 4, shall be exercisable by statutory instrument.

(2)   Any such statutory instrument, except one made under section [4(1B),] 17(4), 107 or 108(2), shall be subject to annulment in pursuance of a resolution of either House of Parliament.

[(2A)   Subsection (2) does not apply to a statutory instrument made solely by the National Assembly for Wales.]

(3)   An order under section [4(1B) or] 17(4) shall not be made unless a draft of it has been laid before, and approved by a resolution of, each House of Parliament.

(4)   Any statutory instrument made under this Act may—

    (a)   make different provision for different cases;
    (b)   provide for exemptions from any of its provisions; and
    (c)   contain such incidental, supplemental and transitional provisions as the person making it considers expedient.

Date in force

14 October 1991:SI 1991/828.

Amendment

Sub-s (1): words ', the Treasury' in square brackets inserted by the Tax Credits Act 2002, s 47, Sch 3, paras 15, 19;words 'or the Secretary of State' in italics repealed and subsequent words in square brackets substituted by the Children and Adoption Act 2006, s15(1), Sch 2, paras 7, 10(a). Date in force: to be appointed: see the Children and Adoption Act 2006, s 17(2); reference omitted repealed by the Care Standards Act 2000, s 117(2), Sch 6.
Sub-s (2): reference to '4(1B),' in square brackets inserted by the Adoption and Children Act 2002, s 111(6)(a).
Sub-s (2A): inserted by the Children and Adoption Act 2006, s 15(1), Sch 2, paras 7, 10(b). Date in force: to be appointed: see the Children and Adoption Act 2006, s 17(2).
Sub-s (3): words '4(1)(B) or' in square brackets inserted by the Adoption and Children Act 2002, s 111(6)(b).

Transfer of functions

Functions of the Secretary of State, so far as exercisable in relation to Wales, transferred to the National Assembly for Wales, by the National Assembly for Wales (Transfer of Functions) Order 1999, SI 1999/672, art 2, Sch 1.

---

105   Interpretation

(1)   In this Act—

    'adoption agency' means a body which may be referred to as an adoption agency by virtue of [section 2 of the Adoption and Children Act 2002];
    ['appropriate children's home' has the meaning given by section 23;]
    'bank holiday' means a day which is a bank holiday under the Banking and Financial Dealings Act 1971;
    ['care home' has the same meaning as in the Care Standards Act 2000;]
    'care order' has the meaning given by section 31(11) and also includes any order which by or under any enactment has the effect of, or is deemed to be, a care order for the purposes of this Act; and any reference to a child who is in the care of an authority is a reference to a child who is in their care by virtue of a care order;
    'child' means, subject to paragraph 16 of Schedule 1, a person under the age of eighteen;
    'child assessment order' has the meaning given by section 43(2);
    'child minder' has the meaning given by section 71;

['child of the family', in relation to parties to a marriage, or to two people who are
civil partners of each other, means—
- (a) a child of both of them, and
- (b) any other child, other than a child placed with them as foster parents by
a local authority or voluntary organisation, who has been treated by
both of them as a child of their family;]

['children's home' has the meaning given by section 23;]

'community home' has the meaning given by section 53;

['contact activity condition' has the meaning given by section 11C;]

['contact activity direction' has the meaning given by section 11A;]

'contact order' has the meaning given by section 8(1);

'day care' [(except in Part XA)] has the same meaning as in section 18;

'disabled', in relation to a child, has the same meaning as in section 17(11);

...

'domestic premises' has the meaning given by section 71(12);

[dwelling-house' includes—
- (a) any building or part of a building which is occupied as a dwelling;
- (b) any caravan, house-boat or structure which is occupied as a dwelling;

and any yard, garden, garage or outhouse belonging to it and occupied with it;]

'education supervision order' has the meaning given in section 36;

'emergency protection order' means an order under section 44;

['enforcement order' has the meaning given by section 11J;]

'family assistance order' has the meaning given in section 16(2);

'family proceedings' has the meaning given by section 8(3);

'functions' includes powers and duties;

'guardian of a child' means a guardian (other than a guardian of the estate of a
child) appointed in accordance with the provisions of section 5;

'harm' has the same meaning as in section 31(9) and the question of whether harm
is significant shall be determined in accordance with section 31(10);

...

'health service hospital' [means a health service hospital within the meaning given
by the National Health Service Act 2006 or the National Health Service (Wales)
Act 2006];

'hospital' [(except in Schedule 9A)] has the same meaning as in the Mental Health
Act 1983, except that it does not include a *special hospital within the meaning
of that Act* [hospital at which high security psychiatric services within the
meaning of that Act are provided];

'ill-treatment' has the same meaning as in section 31(9);

['income-based jobseeker's allowance' has the same meaning as in the Jobseekers
Act 1995;]

['income-related employment and support allowance' means an income-related
allowance under Part 1 of the Welfare Reform Act 2007 (employment and
support allowance);]

['independent hospital' has the same meaning as in the Care Standards Act 2000;]

'independent school' has the same meaning as in [the Education Act 1996];

'local authority' means, in relation to England ... , the council of a county, a
metropolitan district, a London Borough or the Common Council of the City of
London[, in relation to Wales, the council of a county or a county borough] and,
in relation to Scotland, a local authority within the meaning of section 1(2) of
the Social Work (Scotland) Act 1968;

'local authority foster parent' has the same meaning as in section 23(3);

'local education authority' has the same meaning as in [the Education Act 1996];

['Local Health Board' means a Local Health Board established under section 11 of
the National Health Service (Wales) Act 2006;]

'local housing authority' has the same meaning as in the Housing Act 1985;

...

...

['officer of the Service' has the same meaning as in the Criminal Justice and Court Services Act 2000;]

'parental responsibility' has the meaning given in section 3;

'parental responsibility agreement' has the meaning given in [sections 4(1) and 4A(2)];

'prescribed' means prescribed by regulations made under this Act;

['private children's home' means a children's home in respect of which a person is registered under Part II of the Care Standards Act 2000 which is not a community home or a voluntary home;]

['Primary Care Trust' means a Primary Care Trust established under [section 18 of the National Health Service Act 2006];]

'privately fostered child' and 'to foster a child privately' have the same meaning as in section 66;

'prohibited steps order' has the meaning given by section 8(1);

...

...

'registered pupil' has the same meaning as in [the Education Act 1996];

'relative', in relation to a child, means a grandparent, brother, sister, uncle or aunt (whether of the full blood or half blood or [by marriage or civil partnership)] or step-parent;

'residence order' has the meaning given by section 8(1);

...

'responsible person', in relation to a child who is the subject of a supervision order, has the meaning given in paragraph 1 of Schedule 3;

'school' has the same meaning as in [the Education Act 1996] or, in relation to Scotland, in the Education (Scotland) Act 1980;

['section 31A plan' has the meaning given by section 31A(6);]

'service', in relation to any provision made under Part III, includes any facility;

'signed', in relation to any person, includes the making by that person of his mark;

'special educational needs' has the same meaning as in [the Education Act 1996];

['special guardian' and 'special guardianship order' have the meaning given by section 14A;]

['Special Health Authority' means a Special Health Authority established under [section 28 of the National Health Service Act 2006 or section 22 of the National Health Service (Wales) Act 2006,];]

'specific issue order' has the meaning given by section 8(1);

['Strategic Health Authority' means a Strategic Health Authority established under [section 13 of the National Health Service Act 2006];]

'supervision order' has the meaning given by section 31(11);

'supervised child' and 'supervisor', in relation to a supervision order or an education supervision order, mean respectively the child who is (or is to be) under supervision and the person under whose supervision he is (or is to be) by virtue of the order;

'upbringing', in relation to any child, includes the care of the child but not his maintenance;

'voluntary home' has the meaning given by section 60;

'voluntary organisation' means a body (other than a public or local authority) whose activities are not carried on for profit;

['Welsh family proceedings officer' has the meaning given by section 35 of the Children Act 2004].

(2) References in this Act to a child whose father and mother were, or (as the case may be) were not, married to each other at the time of his birth must be read with section 1 of the Family Law Reform Act 1987 (which extends the meaning of such references).

(3)   References in this Act to—

(a)   a person with whom a child lives, or is to live, as the result of a residence order; or

(b)   a person in whose favour a residence order is in force,

shall be construed as references to the person named in the order as the person with whom the child is to live.

(4)   References in this Act to a child who is looked after by a local authority have the same meaning as they have (by virtue of section 22) in Part III.

(5)   References in this Act to accommodation provided by or on behalf of a local authority are references to accommodation so provided in the exercise of functions [of that or any other local authority which are social services functions within the meaning of] the Local Authority Social Services Act 1970.

[(5A)   References in this Act to a child minder shall be construed—

(a)   …;

(b)   in relation to *England and* Wales, in accordance with section 79A.]

[(5B)   References in this Act to acting as a child minder and to a child minder shall be construed, in relation to Scotland, in accordance with section 2(17) of the Regulation of Care (Scotland) Act 2001 (asp 8).]

(6)   In determining the 'ordinary residence' of a child for any purpose of this Act, there shall be disregarded any period in which he lives in any place—

(a)   which is a school or other institution;

(b)   in accordance with the requirements of a supervision order under this Act *or an order under [section 63(1) of the Powers of Criminal Courts (Sentencing) Act 2000]; or*

[(ba) in accordance with the requirements of a youth rehabilitation order under Part 1 of the Criminal Justice and Immigration Act 2008; or]

(c)   while he is being provided with accommodation by or on behalf of a local authority.

(7)   References in this Act to children who are in need shall be construed in accordance with section 17.

(8)   Any notice or other document required under this Act to be served on any person may be served on him by being delivered personally to him, or being sent by post to him in a registered letter or by the recorded delivery service at his proper address.

(9)   Any such notice or other document required to be served on a body corporate or a firm shall be duly served if it is served on the secretary or clerk of that body or a partner of that firm.

(10)   For the purposes of this section, and of section 7 of the Interpretation Act 1978 in its application to this section, the proper address of a person—

(a)   in the case of a secretary or clerk of a body corporate, shall be that of the registered or principal office of that body;

(b)   in the case of a partner of a firm, shall be that of the principal office of the firm; and

(c)   in any other case, shall be the last known address of the person to be served.

Date in force

14 October 1991: SI 1991/828.

Appendix 1   *Children Act 1989*

Amendment

Sub-s (1): in defintion 'adoption agency' words 'section 2 of the Adoption and Children Act 2002' in square brackets substituted by the Adoption and Children Act 2002, s 139(1), Sch 3, paras 54, 70(a); definition 'appropriate children's home' inserted by the Care Standards Act 2000, s 116, Sch 4, para 14(1), (23)(a)(i); definition 'care home' inserted by the Care Standards Act 2000, s 116, Sch 4, para 14(1), (23)(a)(ii); definition 'child minder' repealed by the Care Standards Act 2000, s 117(2), Sch 6; definition 'child of the family' substituted by the Civil Partnership Act 2004, s 75(1), (3); definition 'children's home' substituted by the Care Standards Act 2000, s 116, Sch 4, para 14(1), (23)(a)(iii); definition 'contact activity condition' inserted by the Children and Adoption Act 2006, s 15(1), Sch 2, paras 7, 11. Date in force: to be appointed: see the Children and Adoption Act 2006, s 17(2); definition 'contact activity direction' inserted by the Children and Adoption Act 2006, s 15(1), Sch 2, paras 7, 11. Date in force: to be appointed: see the Children and Adoption Act 2006, s 17(2); in definition 'day care' words '(except in Part XA)' in square brackets inserted by the Care Standards Act 2000, s 116, Sch 4, para 14(1), (23)(a)(iv); definition 'district health authority' (omitted) repealed by the Health Authorities Act 1995, ss 2(1), 5(1), Sch 1, para 118(10)(a), Sch 3; definition 'dwelling house' inserted by the Family Law Act 1996, s 52, Sch 6, para 5; definition 'enforcement order' inserted by the Children and Adoption Act 2006, s 15(1), Sch 2, paras 7, 11. Date in force: to be appointed: see the Children and Adoption Act 2006, s 17(2); definition 'Health Authority' (omitted) repealed by the National Health Service (Consequential Provisions) Act 2006, s 2, Sch 1, paras 124, 125(a); in definition 'health service hospital' words from 'means a health' to 'National Health Service (Wales) Act 2006' in square brackets substituted by the National Health Service (Consequential Provisions) Act 2006, s 2, Sch 1, paras 124, 125(b); in definition 'hospital' words '(except in Schedule 9A)' in square brackets inserted by the Care Standards Act 2000, s 116, Sch 4, para 14(1), (23)(a)(v); in definition 'hospital' words 'special hospital within the meaning of that Act' in italics repealed and subsequent words in square brackets substituted, in relation to England and Wales only, by SI 2000/90, arts 2(1), 3(2), Sch 2, para 5; definition 'income-based jobseeker's allowance' inserted by the Jobseekers Act 1995, s 41(4), Sch 2, para 19(4); definition 'income-related employment and support allowance' inserted, in relation to England and Wales, by the Welfare Reform Act 2007, s 28(1), Sch 3, para 6(1), (5); definition 'independent hospital' inserted by the Care Standards Act 2000, s 116, Sch 4, para 14(1), (23)(a)(vi); in definitions 'independent school', 'local education authority', 'registered pupil', 'school' and 'special educational needs' words 'the Education Act 1996' in square brackets substituted by the Education Act 1996, s 582(1), Sch 37, para 91; in definition 'local authority' words omitted repealed by the Local Government (Wales) Act 1994, ss 22(4), 66(8), Sch 10, para 13, Sch 18;in definition 'local authority' words ', in relation to Wales, the council of a county or a county borough' in square brackets inserted by the Local Government (Wales) Act 1994, ss 22(4), 66(8), Sch 10, para 13; definition 'Local Health Board' inserted by SI 2007/961, art 3, Schedule, para 20(1), (3); definition 'mental nursing home' (omitted) repealed by the Care Standards Act 2000, s 117(2), Sch 6; definition 'nursing home' (omitted) repealed by the Care Standards Act 2000, s 117(2), Sch 6; definition 'officer of the Service' inserted by the Criminal Justice and Court Services Act 2000, s 74, Sch 7, Pt II, paras 87, 95; in definition 'parental responsibility agreement' words 'sections 4(1) and 4A(2)' in square brackets substituted by the Adoption and Children Act 2002, s 139(1), Sch 3, paras 54, 70(c); definition 'private children's home' inserted by the Care Standards Act 2000, s 116, Sch 4, para 14(1), (23)(a)(vii); definition 'Primary Care Trust' inserted, in relation to England and Wales only, by SI 2000/90, arts 2(1), 3(1), Sch 1, para 24(1), (10); in definition 'Primary Care Trust' words 'section 18 of the National Health Service Act 2006' in square brackets substituted by the National Health Service (Consequential Provisions) Act 2006, s 2, Sch 1, paras 124, 125(c); definition 'protected child' (omitted) repealed by the Adoption and Children Act 2002, s 139(1), (3), Sch 3, paras 54, 70(d), Sch 5; definition 'registered children's home' (omitted) repealed by the Care Standards Act 2000, s 117(2), Sch 6; in definition 'relative' words 'by marriage or civil partnership)' in square brackets substituted by the Civil Partnership Act 2004, s 75(1), (4); definition 'residential care home' (omitted) repealed by the Care Standards Act 2000, s 117(2), Sch 6; definition 'section 31A plan' inserted by the Adoption and Children Act 2002, s 139(1), Sch 3, paras 54, 70(b); definition 'special guardian' and 'special guardianship order' inserted by the Adoption and Children Act 2002, s 139(1), Sch 3, paras 54, 70(e); definition 'Special Health Authority' substituted by the Health Authorities Act 1995, ss 2(1), 5(1), Sch 1, para 118(10)(c); in definition 'Special Health Authority' words from 'section 28 of' to 'National Health Service (Wales) Act 2006,' in square brackets substituted by the National Health Service (Consequential Provisions) Act 2006, s 2, Sch 1, paras 124, 125(d); definition 'Strategic Health Authority' inserted by SI 2002/2469, reg 4, Sch 1, Pt 1, para 16(1), (3); in definition 'Strategic Health Authority' words 'section 13 of the National Health Service Act 2006' in square brackets substituted by the National Health Service (Consequential Provisions) Act 2006, s 2, Sch 1, paras 124, 125(e).

Sub-s (1): definition 'Welsh family proceedings officer' inserted by the Children Act 2004, s 40, Sch 3, paras 5, 11.

Sub-s (5): words from 'of that or any other' to 'within the meaning of' in square brackets substituted by the Local Government Act 2000, s 107, Sch 5, para 22.

Sub-s (5A): inserted by the Care Standards Act 2000, s 116, Sch 4, para 14(1), (23)(b); para (a) repealed, in relation to Scotland, by the Regulation of Care (Scotland) Act 2001, s 79, Sch 3, paras 15(1), (2)(a); in para (b) words 'England and' in italics repealed by the Childcare Act 2006, s 103, Sch 2, para 17, Sch 3, Pt 2.

Sub-s (5B): inserted, in relation to Scotland, by the Regulation of Care (Scotland) Act 2001, s 79, Sch 3, paras 15(1), (2)(b).

Sub-s (6): in para (b) words from 'or an order' to the end repealed by the Criminal Justice and Immigration Act 2008, ss 6(2), 149, Sch 4, Pt 1, paras 33, 36(a), Sch 28, Pt 1; for transitional provisions and savings see s 148(2), Sch 27, Pt 1, paras 1(1), 5 thereto. Date in force: to be appointed: see the Criminal Justice and Immigration Act 2008, s 153(7); in para (b) words 'section 63(1) of the Powers of Criminal Courts (Sentencing) Act 2000' in square brackets substituted by the Powers of Criminal Courts (Sentencing) Act 2000, s 165(1), Sch 9, para 129; para (ba) inserted by the Criminal Justice and Immigration Act 2008, s 6(2), Sch 4, Pt 1, paras 33, 36(b); for transitional provisions and savings see s 148(2), Sch 27, Pt 1, paras 1(1), 5 thereto. Date in force: to be appointed: see the Criminal Justice and Immigration Act 2008, s 153(7).

---

106   Financial provisions

(1)   Any—

    (a)   grants made by the Secretary of State under this Act; and

    (b)   any other expenses incurred by the Secretary of State under this Act,

shall be payable out of money provided by Parliament.

(2)   Any sums received by the Secretary of State under section 58, or by way of the repayment of any grant made under section 82(2) or (4) shall be paid into the Consolidated Fund.

Date in force

14 October 1991: SI 1991/828.

Transfer of functions

Functions of the Secretary of State, so far as exercisable in relation to Wales, transferred to the National Assembly for Wales, by the National Assembly for Wales (Transfer of Functions) Order 1999, SI 1999/672, art 2, Sch 1.

---

107   Application to Channel Islands

Her Majesty may by Order in Council direct that any of the provisions of this Act shall extend to any of the Channel Islands with such exceptions and modifications as may be specified in the Order.

Date in force

14 October 1991: SI 1991/828.

---

108   Short title, commencement, extent etc

(1)   This Act may be cited as the Children Act 1989.

(2)   Sections 89 and 96(3) to (7), and paragraph 35 of Schedule 12, shall come into force on the passing of this Act and paragraph 36 of Schedule 12 shall come into force at the end of the period of two months beginning with the day on which this Act is passed but otherwise this Act shall come into force on such date as may be appointed by order made by the Lord Chancellor or the Secretary of State, or by both acting jointly.

(3)   Different dates may be appointed for different provisions of this Act and in relation to different cases.

(4)   The minor amendments set out in Schedule 12 shall have effect.

(5)   The consequential amendments set out in Schedule 13 shall have effect.

(6)   The transitional provisions and savings set out in Schedule 14 shall have effect.

(7)   The repeals set out in Schedule 15 shall have effect.

(8)   An order under subsection (2) may make such transitional provisions or savings as appear to the person making the order to be necessary or expedient in connection with the provisions brought into force by the order, including—

    (a)   provisions adding to or modifying the provisions of Schedule 14; and
    (b)   such adaptations—
        (i)   of the provisions brought into force by the order; and
        (ii)   of any provisions of this Act then in force,
as appear to him necessary or expedient in consequence of the partial operation of this Act.

(9)   The Lord Chancellor may by order make such amendments or repeals, in such enactments as may be specified in the order, as appear to him to be necessary or expedient in consequence of any provision of this Act.

(10)   This Act shall, in its application to the Isles of Scilly, have effect subject to such exceptions, adaptations and modifications as the Secretary of State may by order prescribe.

(11)   The following provisions of this Act extend to Scotland—

...
section 25(8);
section 50(13);
...

...
section 88;
section 104 (so far as necessary);
section 105 (so far as necessary);
subsections (1) to (3), (8) and (9) and this subsection;
in Schedule 2, paragraph 24;
in Schedule 12, paragraphs 1, 7 to 10, 18, 27, 30(a) and 41 to 44;
in Schedule 13, paragraphs 18 to 23, 32, 46, 47, 50, 57, 62, 63, 68(a) and (b) and 71;
in Schedule 14, paragraphs 1, 33 and 34;
in Schedule 15, the entries relating to—
    (a)   the Custody of Children Act 1891;
    (b)   the Nurseries and Child Minders Regulation Act 1948;
    (c)   section 53(3) of the Children and Young Persons Act 1963;
    (d)   section 60 of the Health Services and Public Health Act 1968;
    (e)   the Social Work (Scotland) Act 1968;
    (f)   the Adoption (Scotland) Act 1978;
    (g)   the Child Care Act 1980;

(h)   the Foster Children (Scotland) Act 1984;
(i)   the Child Abduction and Custody Act 1985; and
(j)   the Family Law Act 1986.

(12)   The following provisions of this Act extend to Northern Ireland—

section 50;
section 101(1)(b), (2) and (5)(a)(i);
subsections (1) to (3), (8) and (9) and this subsection;
in Schedule 2, paragraph 24;
in Schedule 12, paragraphs 7 to 10, 18 and 27;
in Schedule 13, paragraphs 21, 22, 46, 47, 57, 62, 63, 68(c) to (e) and 69 to 71;
in Schedule 14, paragraphs ... , 28 to 30 and 38(a); and
in Schedule 15, the entries relating to the Guardianship of Minors Act 1971, the
   Children Act 1975, the Child Care Act 1980, and the Family Law Act 1986.

Dates in force

Sub-ss (1), (3), (5)–(12), sub-ss (2), (4), certain purposes: 14 October 1991: SI 1991/828.
Sub-s (4), certain purposes: 16 January 1990: s 108(2). Sub-ss (2), (4), remaining purposes:
16 November 1989, s 108(2).

Amendment

Sub-s (11): first words omitted repealed by the Regulation of Care (Scotland) Act 2001, s 80(1),
Sch 4; second words omitted repealed by the Regulation of Care (Scotland) Act 2001, s 80(1),
Sch 4; final words omitted repealed by the Regulation of Care (Scotland) Act 2001, s 80(1), Sch 4.
Sub-s (12): figure omitted repealed by the Courts and Legal Services Act 1990, ss 116, 125(7),
Sch 16, para 25, Sch 20.

Regulations

See the Children Act 1989 (Commencement and Transitional Provisions) Order 1991,
SI 1991/828, the Children Act 1989 (Consequential Amendment of Enactments) Order 1991,
SI 1991/1881 and the Children Act 1989 (Commencement No 2—Amendment and Transitional
Provisions) Order 1991, SI 1991/1990.

[SCHEDULE A1

Enforcement Orders]

[Part 1

Unpaid Work Requirement]

[*General*

1   Subject to the modifications in paragraphs 2 and 3, Chapter 4 of Part 12 of the
Criminal Justice Act 2003 has effect in relation to an enforcement order as it has effect
in relation to a community order (within the meaning of Part 12 of that Act).

References to an offender

2   Subject to paragraph 3, references in Chapter 4 of Part 12 of the Criminal Justice
Act 2003 to an offender are to be treated as including references to a person subject to
an enforcement order.

Specific modifications

3 (1)   The power of the Secretary of State by order under section 197(3) to amend the definition of 'responsible officer' and to make consequential amendments includes power to make any amendments of this Part (including further modifications of Chapter 4 of Part 12 of the Criminal Justice Act 2003) that appear to the Secretary of State to be necessary or expedient in consequence of any amendment made by virtue of section 197(3)(a) or (b).

(2)   In section 198 (duties of responsible officer)—

(a)   in subsection (1)—
(i)   at the end of paragraph (a) insert 'and', and
(ii)   omit paragraph (c) and the word 'and' immediately preceding it, and
(b)   after subsection (1) insert—

'(1A)   Subsection (1B) applies where—

(a)   an enforcement order is in force, and
(b)   an officer of the Children and Family Court Advisory and Support Service or a Welsh family proceedings officer (as defined in section 35 of the Children Act 2004) is required under section 11M of the Children Act 1989 to report on matters relating to the order.

(1B)   The officer of the Service or the Welsh family proceedings officer may request the responsible officer to report to him on such matters relating to the order as he may require for the purpose of making a report under section 11M(1)(c) or (d); and it shall be the duty of the responsible officer to comply with such a request.'

(3)   In section 199 (unpaid work requirement)—

(a)   in subsection (2) (minimum and maximum hours of unpaid work) for paragraph (b) substitute—
'(b)   not more than 200.',
(b)   omit subsections (3) and (4), and
(c)   in subsection (5) for the words from the beginning to 'of them' substitute 'Where on the same occasion and in relation to the same person the court makes more than one enforcement order imposing an unpaid work requirement'.

(4)   In section 200 (obligations of person subject to unpaid work requirement), for subsection (2) substitute—

'(2)   Subject to paragraphs 7 and 9 of Schedule A1 to the Children Act 1989, the work required to be performed under an unpaid work requirement imposed by an enforcement order must be performed during a period of twelve months.

(2A)   But the period of twelve months is not to run while the enforcement order is suspended under section 11J(9) of the Children Act 1989.'

(5)   Section 217 (requirement to avoid conflict with religious beliefs, etc) is omitted.

(6)   In section 218 (availability of arrangements in local area), subsection (1) (condition for imposition of unpaid work requirement) is omitted.

(7)   Section 219 (provision of copies of relevant order) is omitted.

(8)   The power of the Secretary of State to make rules under section 222 in relation to persons subject to relevant orders may also be exercised in relation to persons subject to enforcement orders.

(9)   The power of the Secretary of State by order under section 223(1) to amend the provision mentioned in section 223(1)(a) includes power to amend this Part so as to

make such modifications of Chapter 4 of Part 12 of the Criminal Justice Act 2003 as appear to the Secretary of State to be necessary or expedient in consequence of any amendment of the provision mentioned in section 223(1)(a).]

Date in force

To be appointed: see the Children and Adoption Act 2006, s 17(2).

Amendment

Inserted by the Children and Adoption Act 2006, s 4(2), Sch 1; for transitional provision see s 8 thereof. Date in force: to be appointed: see the Children and Adoption Act 2006, s 17(2).

[PART 2

REVOCATION, AMENDMENT OR BREACH OF ENFORCEMENT ORDER]

[Power to revoke

4 (1) This paragraph applies where a court has made an enforcement order in respect of a person's failure to comply with a contact order and the enforcement order is in force.

(2) The court may revoke the enforcement order if it appears to the court that—

    (a) in all the circumstances no enforcement order should have been made,

    (b) having regard to circumstances which have arisen since the enforcement order was made, it would be appropriate for the enforcement order to be revoked, or

    (c) having regard to the person's satisfactory compliance with the contact order or any contact order that has effect in its place, it would be appropriate for the enforcement order to be revoked.

(3) The enforcement order may be revoked by the court under sub-paragraph (2) of its own motion or on an application by the person subject to the enforcement order.

(4) In deciding whether to revoke the enforcement order under sub-paragraph (2)(b), the court is to take into account—

    (a) the extent to which the person subject to the enforcement order has complied with it, and

    (b) the likelihood that the person will comply with the contact order or any contact order that has effect in its place in the absence of an enforcement order.

(5) In deciding whether to revoke the enforcement order under sub-paragraph (2)(c), the court is to take into account the likelihood that the person will comply with the contact order or any contact order that has effect in its place in the absence of an enforcement order.

Amendment by reason of change of residence

5 (1) This paragraph applies where a court has made an enforcement order in respect of a person's failure to comply with a contact order and the enforcement order is in force.

(2) If the court is satisfied that the person has changed, or proposes to change, his residence from the local justice area specified in the order to another local justice area, the court may amend the order by substituting the other area for the area specified.

(3) The enforcement order may be amended by the court under sub-paragraph (2) of its own motion or on an application by the person subject to the enforcement order.

Amendment of hours specified under unpaid work requirement

6 (1) This paragraph applies where a court has made an enforcement order in respect of a person's failure to comply with a contact order and the enforcement order is in force.

(2) If it appears to the court that, having regard to circumstances that have arisen since the enforcement order was made, it would be appropriate to do so, the court may reduce the number of hours specified in the order (but not below the minimum specified in section 199(2)(a) of the Criminal Justice Act 2003).

(3) In amending the enforcement order under sub-paragraph (2), the court must be satisfied that the effect on the person of the enforcement order as proposed to be amended is no more than is required to secure his compliance with the contact order or any contact order that has effect in its place.

(4) The enforcement order may be amended by the court under sub-paragraph (2) of its own motion or on an application by the person subject to the enforcement order.

Amendment to extend unpaid work requirement

7 (1) This paragraph applies where a court has made an enforcement order in respect of a person's failure to comply with a contact order and the enforcement order is in force.

(2) If it appears to the court that, having regard to circumstances that have arisen since the enforcement order was made, it would be appropriate to do so, the court may, in relation to the order, extend the period of twelve months specified in section 200(2) of the Criminal Justice Act 2003 (as substituted by paragraph 3).

(3) The period may be extended by the court under sub-paragraph (2) of its own motion or on an application by the person subject to the enforcement order.

Warning and report following breach

8 (1) This paragraph applies where a court has made an enforcement order in respect of a person's failure to comply with a contact order.

(2) If the responsible officer is of the opinion that the person has failed without reasonable excuse to comply with the unpaid work requirement imposed by the enforcement order, the officer must give the person a warning under this paragraph unless—

(a) the person has within the previous twelve months been given a warning under this paragraph in relation to a failure to comply with the unpaid work requirement, or

(b) the responsible officer reports the failure to the appropriate person.

(3) A warning under this paragraph must—

(a) describe the circumstances of the failure,
(b) state that the failure is unacceptable, and
(c) inform the person that, if within the next twelve months he again fails to comply with the unpaid work requirement, the warning and the subsequent failure will be reported to the appropriate person.

(4) The responsible officer must, as soon as practicable after the warning has been given, record that fact.

(5) If—

(a) the responsible officer has given a warning under this paragraph to a person subject to an enforcement order, and

(b) at any time within the twelve months beginning with the date on which the warning was given, the responsible officer is of the opinion that the person has since that date failed without reasonable excuse to comply with the unpaid work requirement imposed by the enforcement order,

the officer must report the failure to the appropriate person.

(6) A report under sub-paragraph (5) must include a report of the warning given to the person subject to the enforcement order.

(7) The appropriate person, in relation to an enforcement order, is the officer of the Service or the Welsh family proceedings officer who is required under section 11M to report on matters relating to the enforcement order.

(8) 'Responsible officer', in relation to a person subject to an enforcement order, has the same meaning as in section 197 of the Criminal Justice Act 2003 (as modified by paragraph 2).

Breach of an enforcement order

9 (1) This paragraph applies where a court has made an enforcement order ('the first order') in respect of a person's failure to comply with a contact order.

(2) If the court is satisfied beyond reasonable doubt that the person has failed to comply with the unpaid work requirement imposed by the first order, the court may—

(a) amend the first order so as to make the requirement more onerous, or

(b) make an enforcement order ('the second order') in relation to the person and (if the first order is still in force) provide for the second order to have effect either in addition to or in substitution for the first order.

(3) But the court may not exercise its powers under sub-paragraph (2) if it is satisfied that the person had a reasonable excuse for failing to comply with the unpaid work requirement imposed by the first order.

(4) The burden of proof as to the matter mentioned in sub-paragraph (3) lies on the person claiming to have had a reasonable excuse, and the standard of proof is the balance of probabilities.

(5) The court may exercise its powers under sub-paragraph (2) in relation to the first order only on the application of a person who would be able to apply under section 11J for an enforcement order if the failure to comply with the first order were a failure to comply with the contact order to which the first order relates.

(6) Where the person proposing to apply to the court is the child with respect to whom the contact order was made, subsections (6) and (7) of section 11J have effect in relation to the application as they have effect in relation to an application for an enforcement order.

(7) An application to the court to exercise its powers under sub-paragraph (2) may only be made while the first order is in force.

(8) The court may not exercise its powers under sub-paragraph (2) in respect of a failure by the person to comply with the unpaid work requirement imposed by the first order unless it is satisfied that before the failure occurred the person had been given (in accordance with rules of court) a copy of, or otherwise informed of the terms of, a notice under section 11N relating to the first order.

(9) In dealing with the person under sub-paragraph (2)(a), the court may—

(a) increase the number of hours specified in the first order (but not above the maximum specified in section 199(2)(b) of the Criminal Justice Act 2003, as substituted by paragraph 3);

(b) in relation to the order, extend the period of twelve months specified in section 200(2) of the Criminal Justice Act 2003 (as substituted by paragraph 3).

(10) In exercising its powers under sub-paragraph (2), the court must be satisfied that, taking into account the extent to which the person has complied with the unpaid work requirement imposed by the first order, the effect on the person of the proposed exercise of those powers—

(a) is no more than is required to secure his compliance with the contact order or any contact order that has effect in its place, and

(b) is no more than is proportionate to the seriousness of his failures to comply with the contact order and the first order.

(11) Where the court exercises its powers under sub-paragraph (2) by making an enforcement order in relation to a person who has failed to comply with another enforcement order—

(a) sections 11K(4), 11L(2) to (7), 11M and 11N have effect as regards the making of the order in relation to the person as they have effect as regards the making of an enforcement order in relation to a person who has failed to comply with a contact order;

(b) this Part of this Schedule has effect in relation to the order so made as if it were an enforcement order made in respect of the failure for which the other order was made.

(12) Sub-paragraph (2) is without prejudice to section 63(3) of the Magistrates' Courts Act 1980 as it applies in relation to enforcement orders.

Provision relating to amendment of enforcement orders

10 Sections 11L(2) to (7) and 11M have effect in relation to the making of an order under paragraph 6(2), 7(2) or 9(2)(a) amending an enforcement order as they have effect in relation to the making of an enforcement order; and references in sections 11L(2) to (7) and 11M to an enforcement order are to be read accordingly.]

Date in force

To be appointed: see the Children and Adoption Act 2006, s 17(2).

Amendment

Inserted by the Children and Adoption Act 2006, s 4(2), Sch 1; for transitional provision see s 8 thereof. Date in force: to be appointed: see the Children and Adoption Act 2006, s 17(2).

SCHEDULE 1

FINANCIAL PROVISION FOR CHILDREN

Section 15(1)

[Not reproduced]

SCHEDULE 2

LOCAL AUTHORITY SUPPORT FOR CHILDREN AND FAMILIES

Sections 17, 23, 29

PART I

PROVISION OF SERVICES FOR FAMILIES

Identification of children in need and provision of information

1

[Children's services plans

1A

Maintenance of a register of disabled children

2

Note

The Children Act 1989 Guidance and Regulations, Volume 2, Family Support, Day Care and Educational Provision for Young Children (Dept of Health, 1991) at para 2.19 recommends that local authorities, local education authorities and health authorities should draw up a common register.

Appendix 1 *Children Act 1989*

Assessment of children's needs

3

Prevention of neglect and abuse

4

Provision of accommodation in order to protect child

5

Provision for disabled children

6

Provision to reduce need for care proceedings etc

7

Provision for children living with their families

8

Family centres

9

Maintenance of the family home

10

Duty to consider racial groups to which children in need belong

11

Date in force

14 October 1991: SI 1991/828.

Amendment

Para 1: in sub-para (2)(a)(i) words '20, 23B to 23D, 24A and 24B' in square brackets substituted by the Children (Leaving Care) Act 2000, s 7(1), (4).
Para 1A: inserted by SI 1996/785, art 2; repealed by the Children Act 2004, s 64, Sch 5, Pt 1.
Para 3: in sub-para (b) words 'Part IV of the Education Act 1996' in square brackets substituted by the Education Act 1996, s 582(1), Sch 37, para 92.

Definitions

For 'local authority', 'child', 'voluntary organisation', 'service' see s 105(1); for 'child in need' and 'family' see s 17(10); for 'disabled' see s 17(11); for 'ill-treatment', 'harm', see s 31(9) as applied to the whole Act by s 105(1); for 'care order', 'supervision order' see s 31(11); for 'family proceedings' see s 8(3)(4)(a); for 'secure accommodation' see s 25(1); for 'family centre' see para (9); for 'parental responsibility' see s 3.

Reference

'Part III of this Act' ie ss 17–30 and Sch 2 (local authority support for children and families).

Transfer of functions

Functions of the Secretary of State, so far as exercisable in relation to Wales, transferred to the National Assembly for Wales, by the National Assembly for Wales (Transfer of Functions) Order 1999, SI 1999/672, art 2, Sch 1.

PART II

CHILDREN LOOKED AFTER BY LOCAL AUTHORITIES

Regulations as to placing of children with local authority foster parents

12

Note

See the Arrangements for Placement of Children (General) Regulations 1991, SI 1991/890 amended by SI 1991/2033, SI 1993/3069 and SI 1995/2015, SI 1997/649, SI 2002/546 (England), 2469 and 2935 (Wales) and 3013 (W) and SI 2005/774 (W) (revoked in relation to Wales by SI 2007/310); the Fostering Services Regulations 2002, SI 2002/57 amended by SI 2002/865 and 2469, SI 2005/1541 and SI 2006/1738; the Fostering Services (Wales) Regulations 2003, SI 2003/237 amended by SI 2003/896, SI 2005/3302 and SI 2006/3251; the Placement of Children (Wales) Regulations 2007, SI 2007/310. For disqualification as a foster parent, see *Re S (Foster Placement (Children) Regulations 1991)* [2000] 1 FLR 648, FD.

Regulations as to arrangements under section 23(2)(f)

13

Note

See the Arrangements for Placement of Children (General) Regulations 1991, SI 1991/890 amended by SI 1991/2033, SI 1993/3069 and SI 1995/2015, SI 1997/649, SI 2002/546 (England), 2469 and 2935 (Wales) and 3013 (W) and SI 2005/774 (W) (revoked in relation to Wales by SI 2007/310); the Placement of Children (Wales) Regulations 2007, SI 2007/310.

Regulations as to conditions under which child in care is allowed to live with parent, etc

14

Note

See the Arrangements for Placement of Children (General) Regulations 1991, SI 1991/890 amended by SI 1991/2033, SI 1993/3069, SI 1995/2015, 1997/647, SI 2002/546 (E), 2469, 2935 (W) and 3013 (W) and SI 2005/774 (W) (revoked in relation to Wales by SI 2007/310); the Fostering Services Regulations 2002, SI 2002/57 amended by SI 2002/865; the Fostering Services (Wales) Regulations 2003, SI 2003/237 amended by SI 2003/896 and SI 2005/3302; the Placement of Children (Wales) Regulations 2007, SI 2007/310.

Promotion and maintenance of contact between child and family

15

Visits to or by children: expenses

16

Appointment of visitor for child who is not being visited

17

Note

See the Definition of Independent Visitors (Children) Regulations 1991, SI 1991/892 amended by SI 2001/2237 (England).

Power to guarantee apprenticeship deeds etc

18

Arrangements to assist children to live abroad

19

Note

For the application of this provision, see *Re G* (*child in care: arrangements to live abroad*) [1994] 2 FCR 359, CA and for whether or not parental consent is being withheld unreasonably, see *Re W* (*an infant*) [1971] AC 682, (*Re G* (*child in care: arrangements to live abroad*) [1994] 2 FCR 359, CA). A local authority can place for adoption abroad a child in their care only if they obtain the approval of the court even if all those with parental responsibility for the child agreed, see *Re A* (*Adoption: Placement outside Jurisdiction* [2004] EWCA 515, [2005] Fam 105, [2004] 3 WLR 1207 sub nom *Re B* (*children*) (*adoption: removal from jurisdiction*) [2004] FCR 129.

[Preparation for ceasing to be looked after

19A

19B

(1)   A local authority shall have the following additional functions in relation to an eligible child whom they are looking after.

(2)   In sub-paragraph (1) 'eligible child' means, subject to sub-paragraph (3), a child who—

   (a)   is aged sixteen or seventeen; and
   (b)   has been looked after by a local authority for a prescribed period, or periods amounting in all to a prescribed period, which began after he reached a prescribed age and ended after he reached the age of sixteen.

(3)   The Secretary of State may prescribe—

   (a)   additional categories of eligible children; and

(b)   categories of children who are not to be eligible children despite falling within sub-paragraph (2).

(4)   For each eligible child, the local authority shall carry out an assessment of his needs with a view to determining what advice, assistance and support it would be appropriate for them to provide him under this Act—

(a)   while they are still looking after him; and
(b)   after they cease to look after him,

and shall then prepare a pathway plan for him.

(5)   The local authority shall keep the pathway plan under regular review.

(6)   Any such review may be carried out at the same time as a review of the child's case carried out by virtue of section 26.

(7)   The Secretary of State may by regulations make provision as to assessments for the purposes of sub-paragraph (4).

(8)   The regulations may in particular provide for the matters set out in section 23B(6).

Regulations

See the Children Leaving Care (Wales) Regulations 2001, SI 2001/2189 amended by SI 2002/1855 and the Children Leaving Care (England) Regulations 2001, SI 2001/2874 amended by SI 2002/546 and SI 2006/1738.

Personal advisers

19C

A local authority shall arrange for each child whom they are looking after who is an eligible child for the purposes of paragraph 19B to have a personal adviser.]

Duty of the local authority

A local authority may not substitute an alternative process whatever its merits, *R (on the application of P) v London Borough of Newham* [2004] EWHC 2210 (Admin), [2005] 1 FCR 170.

Death of children being looked after by local authorities

20

(1)   If a child who is being looked after by a local authority dies, the authority—

(a)   shall notify the Secretary of State [and (in the case of a local authority in England) Her Majesty's Chief Inspector of Education, Children's Services and Skills];
(b)   shall, so far as is reasonably practicable, notify the child's parents and every person who is not a parent of his but who has parental responsibility for him;
(c)   may, with the consent (so far as it is reasonably practicable to obtain it) of every person who has parental responsibility for the child, arrange for the child's body to be buried or cremated; and
(d)   may, if the conditions mentioned in sub-paragraph (2) are satisfied, make payments to any person who has parental responsibility for the child, or any

relative, friend or other person connected with the child, in respect of travelling, subsistence or other expenses incurred by that person in attending the child's funeral.

(2)   The conditions are that—

(a)   it appears to the authority that the person concerned could not otherwise attend the child's funeral without undue financial hardship; and

(b)   that the circumstances warrant the making of the payments.

(3)   Sub-paragraph (1) does not authorise cremation where it does not accord with the practice of the child's religious persuasion.

(4)   Where a local authority have exercised their power under sub-paragraph (1)(c) with respect to a child who was under sixteen when he died, they may recover from any parent of the child any expenses incurred by them.

(5)   Any sums so recoverable shall, without prejudice to any other method of recovery, be recoverable summarily as a civil debt.

(6)   Nothing in this paragraph affects any enactment regulating or authorising the burial, cremation or anatomical examination of the body of a deceased person.

Date in force

14 October 1991: SI 1991/828.

Amendment

Para 14: sub-para (d) inserted by the Courts and Legal Services Act 1990, s 116, Sch 16, para 26. Para 19: in sub-para (4) words 'special guardian,' in square brackets inserted by the Adoption and Children Act 2002, s 139(1), Sch 3, paras 54, 72(a); in sub-para (6) words from 'Section 85 of' to 'the United Kingdom)' in square brackets substituted by the Adoption and Children Act 2002, s 139(1), Sch 3, paras 54, 72(b); sub-para (9) inserted by the Adoption and Children Act 2002, s 139(1), Sch 3, paras 54, 72(c).
Paras 19A–19C: inserted by the Children (Leaving Care) Act 2000, s 1.
Para 20: in sub-para (1)(a) words 'and (in the case of a local authority in England) Her Majesty's Chief Inspector of Education, Children's Services and Skills' in square brackets substituted by the Education and Inspections Act 2006, s 157, Sch 14, paras 9, 17.

Definitions

For 'a child who is looked after by a local authority' see s 22(1); for 'child', 'local authority', 'relative', 'child who is in the care of a local authority' see s 105(1); for 'local authority foster parent' see s 23(3); for 'parental responsibility' see s 3; for 'the receiving authority', 'the transferring authority' see para 15(3); for 'court' see s 92(7); for 'appeal period' see para 19(8).

References

For 'welfare of the child' see paras 2.2 ff. For 'the standard scale' see the CJA 1982, s 37(2), (3) as amended.

Para 20(1)(c)

If the child dies any order in respect of him terminates. The local authority or other person who had parental responsibility under an order is not entitled to arrange for burial or cremation; the authority is given power to do so with the consent of the person having parental responsibility or in default. This would appear to be the effect of *R v Gwynedd County Council, ex p B* [1992] 3 All ER 317, [1991] 2 FLR 365, CA, a case under the CCA 1980, s 25.

PART III

CONTRIBUTIONS TOWARDS MAINTENANCE OF CHILDREN LOOKED AFTER BY
LOCAL AUTHORITIES

Liability to contribute

21

Note

It should be noted that, unlike the provisions in Sch 1, para 4, above, there is no reference in Sch 2
to the requirement for the court to have regard to the child's needs nor even of the the local
authority's expenditure on behalf of the child, *see Re C (a minor) (Contribution Notice)* [1994]
1 FLR 111.

Agreed contributions

22

Note

Paragraph 22(4) is permissive only and not mandatory: *Re C (A minor) (Contribution Notice)*
[1994] 1 FLR 111.

Contribution orders

23

Court

FPC(CA 1989)R 1991, r 30.

Para 23(3)(b)

Due regard to means the liability is not prior to other items of reasonable expenditure: *Re C (a
minor: contribution notice)* [1994] 1 FLR 111.

Enforcement of contribution orders etc

24

Date in force

14 October 1991: SI 1991/828.

Amendments

Para 21: in sub-para (4) word 'under' in square brackets substituted by the Tax Credits Act 2002,
s 47, Sch 3, paras 15, 20(a). Date in force: 6 April 2003: see SI 2003/962, art 2(1), (3)(b), (d)(iii);
for savings and transitional provisions see arts 3–5 thereof; in sub-para (4) words 'Part VII of the
Social Security Contributions and Benefits Act 1992' in square brackets substituted by the Social
Security (Consequential Provisions) Act 1992, s 4, Sch 2, para 108(c); in sub-para (4) words from
', of any element' to 'working tax credit' in square brackets inserted by the Tax Credits Act 2002,
s 47, Sch 3, paras 15, 20(b). Date in force: 6 April 2003: see SI 2003/962, art 2(1), (3)(b), (d)(iii);
for savings and transitional provisions see arts 3–5 thereof; in sub-para (4) words 'or of an
income-based jobseeker's allowance' in square brackets inserted by the Jobseekers Act 1995,

s 41(4), Sch 2, para 19(5); in sub-para (4) words 'or of an income-based jobseeker's allowance' in italics repealed and subsequent words in square brackets substituted by the Welfare Reform Act 2007, s 28(1), Sch 3, para 6(1), (6); in sub-para (7)(c) words 'section 92 of the Powers of Criminal Courts (Sentencing) Act 2000' in square brackets substituted by the Powers of Criminal Courts (Sentencing) Act 2000, s 165(1), Sch 9, para 130.

Para 24: in sub-para (6)(b) words 'designated officer for' in square brackets substituted by the Courts Act 2003, s 109(1), Sch 8, para 340.

References

For 'charging for services' see Department of Health Guidance Volume 2, para 2.38. 'This Part of this Schedule' ie Pt III, paras 21–25 made under s 29(6). For interim care orders see s 38; for service of notices generally under the Act see s 105(8)–(10).

Transfer of functions

Functions of the Secretary of State, so far as exercisable in relation to Wales, transferred to the National Assembly for Wales, by the National Assembly for Wales (Transfer of Functions) Order 1999, SI 1999/672, art 2, Sch 1.

SCHEDULE 3

SUPERVISION ORDERS

Sections 35, 36

PART I

GENERAL

Meaning of 'responsible person'

1

Power of supervisor to give directions to supervised child

2

Imposition of obligations on responsible person

3

Psychiatric and medical examinations

4

Psychiatric and medical treatment

5

Date in force

14 October 1991: SI 1991/828.

Definitions

For 'the responsible person' see para 1; for 'supervised child', 'child', 'supervisor' 'health service hospital', 'hospital', 'mental nursing home' see s 105(1); for 'parental responsibility' see s 3; for 'court' see s 92(7).

Note

Paragraphs 4 and 5 do not apply in relation to an interim supervision order s 38(9). For discussion of the imposition of requirements in a supervision order, see paras 8. 183 ff.

PART II

MISCELLANEOUS

Life of supervision order

6

Note

A supervision order may be made for a period of less than twelve months: *M v Warwickshire County Council* [1994] 2 FCR 121, [1994] 2 FLR 593. The threshold conditions of s 31(2) need not be satisfied on an application to extend a supervision order during the period of its currency; there is no jurisdiction to make an interim care order under s 31(5)(b) to replace the supervision order: *Re A (a minor) (Supervision Order: Extension)* [1995] 3 All ER 401, [1995] 2 FCR 114.

7

... (Repealed by the CLSA 1990, Sch 16, para 27, Sch 20.)

Information to be given to supervisor etc

8

Selection of supervisor

9

Effect of supervision order on earlier orders

10

Local authority functions and expenditure

11

Date in force

14 October 1991: SI 1991/828.

Amendment

Para 7: repealed by the Courts and Legal Services Act 1990, ss 116, 125(7), Sch 16, para 27, Sch 20.
Para 9: sub-paras (2)–(5) repealed by the Criminal Justice and Court Services Act 2000, ss 74, 75, Sch 7, Pt II, paras 87, 96, Sch 8.

Definitions

For 'supervision order' see s 31(11); for 'supervisor', 'supervised child', 'local authority', 'functions' see s 105(1); for 'court' see s 92(7); for 'the responsible person' see para 1; for 'the appropriate authority' see para 9(3); for power to issue a warrant to authorise a constable to assist in exercising the power under para 8(1)(b), (2)(b) see s 102. For power to issue a warrant to authorise a constable to assist in exercising the power under para 8(1)(*b*), (2)(*b*) see s 102.

PART III

EDUCATION SUPERVISION ORDERS

Effect of orders

12

13

Effect where child also subject to supervision order

14

Duration of orders

15

Information to be given to supervisor etc

16

Discharge of orders

17

Offences

18

Persistent failure of child to comply with directions

19

Miscellaneous

20

Interpretation

21

Date in force

14 October 1991: SI 1991/828.

Amendments

Para 13: in sub-para (1) words 'sections 7 and 444 of the Education Act 1996 (duties to secure education of children and' in square brackets substituted by the Education Act 1996, s 582(1), Sch 37, para 93(1), (2)(a); in sub-para (2)(a)(i) words 'section 437 of the Education Act 1996' in square brackets substituted by the Education Act 1996, s 582(1), Sch 37, para 93(1), (2)(b)(i); in sub-para (2)(b)(i) words 'section 437' in square brackets substituted by the Education Act 1996, s 582(1), Sch 37, para 93(1), (2)(b)(ii); in sub-para (2)(b)(ii) words 'section 9 of that Act' in square brackets substituted by the Education Act 1996, s 582(1), Sch 37, para 93(1), (2)(b)(iii); in sub-para (2)(b)(iii) words 'sections 411 and 423 of that Act' in square brackets substituted by the Education Act 1996, s 582(1), Sch 37, para 93(1), (2)(b)(iv); sub-para (2)(c) substituted by the Criminal Justice and Immigration Act 2008, s 6(2), Sch 4, Pt 1, paras 33, 37(1), (2); for transitional provisions and savings see s 148(2), Sch 27, Pt 1, paras 1(1), 5 thereto. Date in force: to be appointed: see the Criminal Justice and Immigration Act 2008, s 153(7);in sub-para (2)(c) words 'paragraph 7 of Schedule 6 to the Powers of Criminal Courts (Sentencing) Act 2000' in square brackets substituted by the Powers of Criminal Courts (Sentencing) Act 2000, s 165(1), Sch 9, para 131(1), (2).

Para 14: in sub-para (1) words 'order under section 63(1) of the Powers of Criminal Courts (Sentencing) Act 2000' in italics repealed and subsequent words in square brackets substituted by the Criminal Justice and Immigration Act 2008, s 6(2), Sch 4, Pt 1, paras 33, 37(1), (3)(a); for transitional provisions and savings see s 148(2), Sch 27, Pt 1, paras 1(1), 5 thereto. Date in force: to be appointed: see the Criminal Justice and Immigration Act 2008, s 153(7); in sub-para (1) words 'section 63(1) of the Powers of Criminal Courts (Sentencing) Act 2000' in square brackets substituted by the Powers of Criminal Courts (Sentencing) Act 2000, s 165(1), Sch 9, para 131(1), (3); in sub-para (2) words 'or instruction' in square brackets inserted by the Criminal Justice and Immigration Act 2008, s 6(2), Sch 4, Pt 1, paras 33, 37(1), (3)(b); for transitional provisions and savings see s 148(2), Sch 27, Pt 1, paras 1(1), 5 thereto. Date in force: to be appointed: see the Criminal Justice and Immigration Act 2008, s 153(7).

Para 21: words 'the Education Act 1996' in square brackets substituted by the Education Act 1996, s 582(1), Sch 37, para 93(1), (3).

SCHEDULE 4

MANAGEMENT AND CONDUCT OF COMMUNITY HOMES

Section 53(6)

PART I

INSTRUMENTS OF MANAGEMENT

Instruments of management for controlled and assisted community homes

1

2

Date in force

14 October 1991: SI 1991/828.

Amendment

Para 1: in sub-paras (1), (2), (4), (5), (6), (8), (9) words omitted repealed by the Courts and Legal Services Act 1990, ss 116, 125(7), Sch 16, para 28, Sch 20.

Definitions

For 'voluntary home' see s 60(3); for 'designated' and 'foundation managers' see para 1(9); for 'controlled community home' see s 53(4); for 'assisted community home' see s 53(5); for 'voluntary organisation', 'local authority', 'child' see s 105(1); for 'trust deed' see s 55(6).

Para 2(1) Instrument of management

Cannot alter the basic purposes for which premises comprising a voluntary home are held. When an organisation holds premises on trust for purposes inconsistent with use as a community home, it is for that organisation to secure appropriate modification of the trust deed. This cannot by virtue of para 2(2) be done by the instrument of management, and para (4) which deals with inconsistencies between the instrument of management and a trust deed is expressly made subject to para 2(2).

Para 2(4) Trust deed

The definition in s 55(6) is wide and is not confined to trust deeds properly so described. Para 2(5) Section 36(5) of the CCA 1980 formerly provided that the Secretary of State might vary or revoke any provisions of the instrument of management by a further instrument of management. Now any variation etc will be by order.

Transfer of functions

Functions of the Secretary of State, so far as exercisable in relation to Wales, transferred to the National Assembly for Wales, by the National Assembly for Wales (Transfer of Functions) Order 1999, SI 1999/672, art 2, Sch 1.

PART II

MANAGEMENT OF CONTROLLED AND ASSISTED COMMUNITY HOMES

3

Date in force

14 October 1991: SI 1991/828.

Amendments

Para 3: in sub-paras (4), (5) words in square brackets inserted by the Criminal Justice and Public Order Act 1994, s 22(3).

Definitions

For 'controlled community home' see s 53(4); for 'local authority', 'voluntary organisation', 'functions' see s 105(1); for 'assisted community home' see s 53(5); for 'home', 'the managers', 'the responsible body' see para 3(3).

References

For service of notices under the Act generally see s 105(8)–(10).

Para 3(a): Employment

These arrangements would enable (if the instrument of management so provides) the employees of the voluntary organisation or, for example, members of religious orders, to undertake the care of children in a controlled community home.

PART III

REGULATIONS

4

Date in force

14 October 1991: SI 1991/828.

Definitions

For 'child', 'local authority', 'voluntary organisation', see s 105(1). For "community home' see s 53. For 'assisted community home' see s 53(5). For 'a child who is looked after by a local authority' see s 22(1). For 'controlled community home' see s 53(4).

Regulations

See the Arrangements for Placement of Children (General) Regulations 1991, SI 1991/890, amended by SI 1991/2033, SI 1993/3069, SI 1995/2015, SI 1997/649, SI 2002/546 (England), 2469 and 2935 (Wales) and 3013 (W) and SI 2005/774 (W) (revoked in relation to Wales by SI 2007/310); the Secure Accommodation Regulations 1991, SI 1991/1505 amended by 1992/2117, SI 1995/1398, SI 1996/692, SI 2000/694, SI 2001/2337, SI 2002/546 and 2395 (Wales), SI 2004/696 and SI 2006/2986 (W); the Review of Children's Cases (Wales) Regulations 2007, SI 2007/307 and the Placement of Children (Wales) Regulations 2007, SI 2007/310.

SCHEDULE 5

VOLUNTARY HOMES AND VOLUNTARY ORGANISATIONS

Section 60(4)

PART I

REGISTRATION OF VOLUNTARY HOMES

General

1

Procedure

2

Right to make representations

3

Decision of Secretary of State

4

Appeals

5

Notification of particulars with respect to voluntary homes

6

Date in force

14 October 1991: SI 1991/828.

Amendment

This Part repealed by the Care Standards Act 2000, s 117(2), Sch 6.

PART II

REGULATIONS AS TO VOLUNTARY HOMES

Regulations as to conduct of voluntary homes

7   (1) The Secretary of State may make regulations—

(a)   as to the placing of children in voluntary homes;

(b)   ...

(c)   ...

(2) ...

(3) ...

(4) ...

Date in force

14 October 1991: SI 1991/828.

Amendments

Para 7: sub-paras (1)(b), (c), (2)–(4) repealed by the Care Standards Act 2000, s 117(2), Sch 6.
Para 8: repealed by the Care Standards Act 2000, s 117(2), Sch 6.

Definitions

For 'voluntary home' see s 60(3) see s 105(1).

Transfer of functions

Functions of the Secretary of State, so far as exercisable in relation to Wales, transferred to the National Assembly for Wales, by the National Assembly for Wales (Transfer of Functions) Order 1999, SI 1999/672, art 2, Sch 1.

Note

See the Arrangements for Placement of Children (General) Regulations 1991, SI 1991/890, amended by SI 1991/2033, SI 1993/3069, SI 1995/2015, SI 1997/649, SI 2002/546 (England), 2469 and 2935 (Wales) and 3013 (W) and SI 2005/774 (W) (revoked in relation to Wales by SI 2007/310); the Secure Accommodation Regulations 1991, SI 1991/1505 amended by 1992/2117, SI 1995/1398, SI 1996/692, SI 2000/694, SI 2001/2337, SI 2002/546 and 2395 (Wales), SI 2004/696 and SI 2006/2986 (W); the Review of Children's Cases (Wales) Regulations 2007, SI 2007/307 and the Placement of Children (Wales) Regulations 2007, SI 2007/310.

...

8

...

Note

Para 8: repealed by the Care Standards Act 2000, s 117(2), Sch 6.

SCHEDULE 6

PRIVATE CHILDREN'S HOMES

Section 63(11)

PART I

REGISTRATION

This Part repealed by the Care Standards Act 2000, s 117(2), Sch 6.

PART II

REGULATIONS

10

Date in force

14 October 1991: SI 1991/828.

Definitions

For child' and 'registered children's home' now private children's home' see s 105(1); .

Amendment

Para 10: in sub-para (1)(a) word 'private' in square brackets substituted by the Care Standards Act 2000, s 116, Sch 4, para 14(1), (25)(b); sub-paras (1)(b), (c), (2)(a)–(k), (3), (4) repealed by the Care Standards Act 2000, s 117(2), Sch 6; sub-para (2)(jj) inserted by the Criminal Justice and Public Order Act 1994, ss 19(2)(b), 168(3), Sch 11.

Reference

For 'the standard scale', see the CJA 1982, s 37(2), (3) as amended.

Regulations

See the Arrangements for Placement of Children (General) Regulations 1991, SI 1991/890, amended by SI 1991/2033, SI 1993/3069, SI 1995/2015, SI 1997/649, SI 2002/546 (England), 2469 and 2935 (Wales) and 3013 (W) and SI 2005/774 (W) (revoked in relation to Wales by SI 2007/310); the Secure Accommodation Regulations 1991, SI 1991/1505 amended by 1992/2117, SI 1995/1398, SI 1996/692, SI 2000/694, SI 2001/2337, SI 2002/546 and 2395 (Wales), SI 2004/696 and SI 2006/2986 (W); the Review of Children's Cases (Wales) Regulations 2007, SI 2007/307 and the Placement of Children (Wales) Regulations 2007, SI 2007/310.

SCHEDULE 7

FOSTER PARENTS: LIMITS ON NUMBER OF FOSTER CHILDREN

Section 63(12)

Interpretation

1

The usual fostering limit

2

Siblings

3

Exemption by local authority

4

Effect of exceeding fostering limit

5

Complaints etc

6

Date in force

14 October 1991: SI 1991/828.

Definitions

For 'local authority foster parent' see s 23(3); for 'child', 'local authority', and 'voluntary organisation' see s 105(1); for 'to foster a child privately' see s 66(1)(b); for 'the usual fostering limit' see para 2.

References

For service of notices under the Act generally see s 105(8)–(10); for duty to register a children's home see s 63.

Para 4(5) Regulations

See the Foster Placement (Children) Regulations 1991, SI 1991/910 amended by SI 1995/2015, SI 1997/2308 and SI 1999/2768 and SI 2001/2992 (E) and 3443 (W) reg 11 revoked in so far as they apply to England and substituted by the Fostering Services Regulations 2002, SI 2002/57 amended by SI 2002/865 reg 38.

Para 6

A private foster parent may appeal to the court against a refusal to make an exemption, or to vary or cancel such an exemption, or against a condition imposed in such an exemption (Sch 8, para 1(e)–(g). The right of appeal does not extend to those who would otherwise be a local authority foster parent or with whom a child would be placed by a voluntary organisation (Sch 8, para (8)).

Para 6(2) Regulations

See the Representations Procedure (England) Regulations 2006, SI 2006/1738; Representations Procedure (Children) (Wales) Regulations 2005, SI 2005/3365.

Representations Procedure (Children) (Wales) Regulations 2005, SI 2005/3365 (made under para 6).

Transfer of functions

Functions of the Secretary of State, so far as exercisable in relation to Wales, transferred to the National Assembly for Wales, by the National Assembly for Wales (Transfer of Functions) Order 1999, SI 1999/672, art 2, Sch 1.

SCHEDULE 8

PRIVATELY FOSTERED CHILDREN

Section 66(5)

Exemptions

1

2

3

4

5

Power of local authority to impose requirements

6

Regulations requiring notification of fostering etc

7

Appeals

8

Extension of Part IX to certain school children during holidays

9

Prohibition of advertisements relating to fostering

10

Avoidance of insurances on lives of privately fostered children

11

Date in force

14 October 1991: SI 1991/828.

Appendix 1 *Children Act 1989*

Amendment

Para 3: sub-para (a) substituted by the Criminal Justice and Immigration Act 2008, s 6(2), Sch 4, Pt 1, paras 33, 38; for transitional provisions and savings see s 148(2), Sch 27, Pt 1, paras 1(1), 5 thereto; in sub-para (a) words 'section 63(1) of the Powers of Criminal Courts (Sentencing) Act 2000' in square brackets substituted by the Powers of Criminal Courts (Sentencing) Act 2000, s 165(1), Sch 9, para 132; in sub-para (b) words 'Part II of the Children (Scotland) Act 1995' in square brackets substituted by the Children (Scotland) Act 1995, s 105(4), Sch 4, para 48(5).
Para 5: words from 'he is placed' to 'Adoption (Northern Ireland) Order 1987' in square brackets substituted by the Adoption and Children Act 2002, s 139(1), Sch 3, paras 54, 73; words from 'or while he' to 'of Intercountry Adoption).' in square brackets inserted by the Children and Adoption Act 2006, s 14(3).
Para 7A: inserted by the Children Act 2004, s 44(7).
Para 9: in sub-para (1) words omitted repealed by the Care Standards Act 2000, ss 110, 117(2), Sch 6; in sub-para (1)(b) reference to '2(1)(c) and (d)' in square brackets substituted by the Care Standards Act 2000, s 116, Sch 4, para 14(1), (27)(b); in sub-para (1) words from 'But this sub-paragraph' to 'appropriate children's home' in square brackets inserted by the Care Standards Act 2000, s 116, Sch 4, para 14(1), (27)(b).

Definitions

For 'child', 'local authority', 'relative', 'voluntary organisation', 'health service hospital', 'residential care home', 'nursing home', 'mental nursing home', 'protected child', 'local education authority', 'school' see s 105(1); for 'children's home' see s 63(3) as applied to the whole Act by s 105(1); for 'child who is looked after by a local authority' see s 22(1); for 'privately fostered child' see s 66(1)(a); for 'parental responsibility' see s 3; for 'court' see s 92(7); for 'requirement' see para 6(6)(b); for 'the appropriate authority' see para 6(6)(a); for 'pupil', 'maintained' see EA 1944, s 114; for 'ordinarily resident' see s 105(6).

References

For 'premises' see the note to s 72; for service of notices generally under the Act see s 105(8)–(10).

Premises

Common sense suggests this should be interpreted as household.

Para 6 May impose on him requirements

Responsibilities under this Act stand referred to the Social Services Committee. By the Local Government Act 1972, s 10(1), any functions of the authority can be delegated to a committee, sub-committee or officer. It is therefore a matter for the discretion of the committee whether it delegates powers under this section to officers. Arrangements to be made with respect to their health and safety will include medical arrangements to be made for protecting the health of the children and fire precautions.

Right of appeal

See Sch 8, para 8 for right of appeal. If there is an appeal a requirement shall not have effect pending appeal: Sch 8, para 8(3).

Notice in writing

May be given by post: s 105(8).

Para 7 Regulations

See the Children (Private Arrangements for Fostering) Regulations 2005, SI 2005/1533 and the Children (Private Arrangements for Fostering) (Wales) Regulations 2006, SI 2006/940. An obligation is placed on a parent or a person with parental responsibility to give notice where he knows it is proposed that the child be fostered privately. In addition persons involved, or who propose to be involved, directly or indirectly in arranging for a child to be fostered privately can be required to notify the appropriate local authority, but no regulations have been made.

Para 8 Person aggrieved

A person who has suffered a legal grievance or against whom a decision has been pronounced which has wrongfully deprived him of something, or wrongfully refused him something or wrongfully affected his title to something: *Re Baron, ex p The Debtor v Official Receiver* [1943] Ch 177 at 179; *R v London Quarter Sessions, ex p Westminster Corpn* [1951] 2 KB 508, [1951] 1 All ER 1032, 115 JP 350.

Within 14 days

Not including the day on which the notice is received.

Para 9

This continues similar provisions formerly contained in the Foster Children Act 1980, s 17 and is designed to apply, for example, provisions as to disqualification of individuals and inspection of premises to schools not maintained by a local education authority, which accommodate children during the school holidays.

Transfer of functions

Functions of the Secretary of State, so far as exercisable in relation to Wales, transferred to the National Assembly for Wales, by the National Assembly for Wales (Transfer of Functions) Order 1999, SI 1999/672, art 2, Sch 1.

SCHEDULE 9

CHILD MINDING AND DAY CARE FOR YOUNG CHILDREN

Section 71(16)

[Repealed by the Care Standards Act 2000, s 79(5)]

Appendix 1 *Children Act 1989*

SCHEDULE 9A

CHILD MINDING AND DAY CARE FOR YOUNG CHILDREN

[Section 79B(9)]

[Exemption of certain schools

1

Exemption for other establishments

2

Exemption for occasional facilities

3

Disqualification for registration

4

5

Certificates of registration

6

Annual fees

7

Cooperation between authorities

8

Date in force

England: 16 March 2001/2 July 2001: see SI 2001/1210; SI 2001/2041.
Wales (for the purposes of enabling subordinate legislation to be made): 1 July 2001: see SI 2001/2190.

Amendment

Inserted by the Care Standards Act 2000, s 79, Sch 3. Date in force (in relation to England for remaining purposes): 2 July 2001: see SI 2001/2041, art 2(1)(b); for transitional, transitory and savings provisions see art 3, Schedule thereto. Date in force (in relation to Wales for remaining purposes): 1 April 2002: see SI 2002/920, art 3(3)(b); for transitional provisions see arts 2, 3(2), Sch 2 thereto.
Para 1: in sub-para (1)(c) words 'the Secretary of State or' in italics repealed by the Childcare Act 2006, s 103, Sch 2, para 18(1), (3), Sch 3, Pt 2. Date in force: to be appointed: see the Childcare Act 2006, ss 109(2), 110(1), (5)(c), (6)(b).
Para 2A: inserted by the Children Act 2004, s 48, Sch 4, paras 1, 7.
Para 3: in sub-para (1) words 'the registration authority' in italics repealed and subsequent words in square brackets substituted by the Childcare Act 2006, s 103(1), Sch 2, para 6. Date in force: to be appointed: see the Childcare Act 2006, ss 109(2), 110(1), (5)(c).
Para 4: in sub-para (1) words 'in Wales' in square brackets inserted by the Childcare Act 2006, s 103(1), Sch 2, para 18(1), (4)(a). Date in force: to be appointed: see the Childcare Act 2006, ss 109(2), 110(1), (5)(c); sub-para (2)(a), (b) repealed by the Safeguarding Vulnerable Groups

Act 2006, s 63(2), Sch 10. Date in force: to be appointed: see the Safeguarding Vulnerable Groups Act 2006, s 65; sub-para (2)(b) substituted by the Education Act 2002, s 215(1), Sch 21, para 9; in sub-para (2)(b) words 'or on grounds relating to his health' in square brackets inserted by the Childcare Act 2006, s 102(1), (2)(a); sub-para (2)(ba) inserted by the Safeguarding Vulnerable Groups Act 2006, s 63(1), Sch 9, Pt 1, para 1. Date in force: to be appointed: see the Safeguarding Vulnerable Groups Act 2006, s 65; in sub-para (2)(f) words ', or Part 3 of the Childcare Act 2006,' in square brackets inserted by the Childcare Act 2006, s 103(1), Sch 2, para 18(1), (4)(b). Date in force: to be appointed: see the Childcare Act 2006, ss 109(2), 110(1), (5)(c); in sub-para (2)(g) words omitted repealed by the Criminal Justice Act 2003, ss 304, 332, Sch 32, Pt 1, paras 59, 61(1), (2), Sch 37, Pt 7. Date in force: 4 April 2005: see SI 2005/950, art 2(1), Sch 1, para 42(1), (24); for savings in relation to offences committed before that date see Sch 2, para 5 thereof; sub-para (2)(ga) inserted by the Childcare Act 2006, s 102(1), (2)(b); in sub-para (3) words 'in Wales' in square brackets in both places they occur inserted by the Childcare Act 2006, s 103(1), Sch 2, para 18(1), (4)(c). Date in force: to be appointed: see the Childcare Act 2006, ss 109(2), 110(1), (5)(c); sub-para (3A) inserted by the Education Act 2002, s 152, Sch 13, para 6; in sub-para (3A) words from '(and may in' to 'sub-paragraphs (4) and (5))' in square brackets inserted by the Children Act 2004, s 48, Sch 4, paras 1, 5(a); in sub-para (3A) words 'the registration authority' in italics in both places they occur repealed and subsequent words in square brackets substituted by the Childcare Act 2006, s 103(1), Sch 2, para 6. Date in force: to be appointed: see the Childcare Act 2006, ss 109(2), 110(1), (5)(c); in sub-para (3A)(b) words omitted repealed by the Children Act 2004, ss 48, 64, Sch 4, paras 1, 5(b), Sch 5, Pt 2; in sub-para (4) words 'in Wales' in square brackets in each place they occur inserted by the Childcare Act 2006, s 103(1), Sch 2, para 18(1), (4)(d). Date in force: to be appointed: see the Childcare Act 2006, ss 109(2), 110(1), (5)(c); in sub-para (4) word 'directly' in square brackets inserted by the Children Act 2004, s 48, Sch 4, paras 1, 8(a); in sub-para (4) words omitted repealed by the Children Act 2004, ss 48, 64, Sch 4, paras 1, 8(b), Sch 5, Pt 2; in sub-para (5) words 'in Wales' in square brackets in both places they occur inserted by the Childcare Act 2006, s 103(1), Sch 2, para 18(1), (4)(e). Date in force: to be appointed: see the Childcare Act 2006, ss 109(2), 110(1), (5)(c); sub-para (6) substituted by the Childcare Act 2006, s 102(1), (3); sub-para (7) inserted by the Criminal Justice Act 2003, s 304, Sch 32, Pt 1, paras 59, 61(1), (3). Date in force: 4 April 2005: see SI 2005/950, art 2(1), Sch 1, para 42(1), (24); for savings in relation to offences committed before that date see Sch 2, para 5 thereof.

Para 5: in sub-para (1)(a) words 'in Wales' in square brackets in both places they occur inserted by the Childcare Act 2006, s 103(1), Sch 2, para 18(1), (5)(a). Date in force: to be appointed: see the Childcare Act 2006, ss 109(2), 110(1), (5)(c); in sub-para (1)(b) words 'any of sub-paragraphs (3) to (5)' in italics repealed and subsequent words in square brackets substituted by the Childcare Act 2006, s 103(1), Sch 2, para 18(1), (5)(b). Date in force: to be appointed: see the Childcare Act 2006, ss 109(2), 110(1), (5)(a);sub-para (2) substituted by the Childcare Act 2006, s 103(1), Sch 2, para 18(1), (5)(c). Date in force: to be appointed: see the Childcare Act 2006, ss 109(2), 110(1), (5)(a).

Para 5A: inserted by the Children Act 2004, s 48, Sch 4, paras 1, 9.

Para 6: in sub-paras (1), (3), (4) words 'the registration authority' and 'the authority' in italics repealed and subsequent words in square brackets substituted by the Childcare Act 2006, s 103(1), Sch 2, para 6. Date in force: to be appointed: see the Childcare Act 2006, ss 109(2), 110(1), (5)(c); in sub-para (5)(a) words '(in England or in Wales)' in italics repealed and subsequent words in square brackets substituted by the Childcare Act 2006, s 103(1), Sch 2, para 18(1), (6)(a). Date in force: to be appointed: see the Childcare Act 2006, ss 109(2), 110(1), (5)(c); in sub-para (5)(b) words 'in Wales' in square brackets inserted by the Childcare Act 2006, s 103(1), Sch 2, para 18(1), (6)(b). Date in force: to be appointed: see the Childcare Act 2006, ss 109(2), 110(1), (5)(c).

Para 7 heading: word omitted repealed by the Children Act 2004, ss 48, 64, Sch 4, paras 1, 4(2)(a), Sch 5, Pt 2; words 'the registration authority' in italics in both places they occur repealed and subsequent words in square brackets substituted by the Childcare Act 2006, s 103(1), Sch 2, para 6. Date in force: to be appointed: see the Childcare Act 2006, ss 109(2), 110(1), (5)(c); words from ', at or by' to 'under Part XA' in square brackets substituted by the Children Act 2004, s 48, Sch 4, paras 1, 4(2)(b).

Para 8: sub-para (1) repealed by the Childcare Act 2006, s 103, Sch 2, para 18(1), (7), Sch 3, Pt 2. Date in force: to be appointed: see the Childcare Act 2006, ss 109(2), 110(1), (5)(c), (6)(b).

Appendix 1 *Children Act 1989*

Definitions

For 'day care' see s 79A(6); for 'assisted', 'maintained school' see para 1(3); for 'appropriate children's home', 'care home' see s 23 as applied to the whole Act by s 105(1); for 'hospital' see para 2(1)(c); for 'premises' see s 79B(6); for 'year' see para 3(2).

Para 1 Regulations

See the Day Care (Application to Schools) Regulations 2003, SI 2003/1992 and the Day Care (Application to Schools) (Wales) Regulations 2005, SI 2005/118.

Para 4 Regulations

See the Disqualification for Caring for Children (England) Regulations 2002, SI 2002/635, the Disqualification for Caring for Children (Wales) Regulations 2004, 2004/2695 and the Day Care and Child Minding (Disqualification) (England) Regulations 2005, SI 2005/2296 amended by SI 2007/197 and 603.

Para 4(2)(g) Convicted of an offence

A conviction of an offence for which a person was discharged conditionally or absolutely is deemed not to be a conviction for any purpose other than the purposes of the proceedings in which the order is made and in any event must be disregarded for the purposes of any enactment or instrument which imposes any disqualification or disability upon convicted persons or authorises or requires the imposition of any such disqualification or disability: Powers of Criminal Courts (Sentencing) Act 2000, s 14.

Para 6 Regulations

See the Child Minding and Day Care (Certificates of Registration) (England) Regulations 2001, SI 2001/1830, the Registration of Social Care and Independent Health Care (Wales) Regulations 2002, SI SI 2002/919 amended by SI 2002/2622, 2709 and 2935, SI 2003/710 and 2527, SI 2004/219, 1756 and 3302 and SI 2006/878 and 3251 and the Day Care and Child Minding (Registration Fees) (England) Regulations 2005, SI 2005/2301 amended by SI 2006/2081 and SI 2007/1769.

SCHEDULE 10

AMENDMENTS OF ADOPTION LEGISLATION

Section 88

PART I

AMENDMENTS OF ADOPTION ACT 1976

Repealed by the Adoption and Children Act 2002, s 139(1), (3), Sch 3, paras 54, 74, Sch 5.

PART II

AMENDMENTS OF ADOPTION (SCOTLAND) ACT 1978

Repealed by the Adoption and Children (Scotland) Act 2007, s 120(2), Sch 3. Date in force: to be appointed: see the Adoption and Children (Scotland) Act 2007, s 121(2).

SCHEDULE 11

JURISDICTION

Section 92

PART I

GENERAL

Commencement of proceedings

1

Transfer of proceedings

2

Hearings by single justice

3

General

4

Date in force

14 October 1991: SI 1991/828.

Amendments

Para 1: in sub-paras (1), (2), (3) words ', after consulting the Lord Chief Justice,' in square brackets inserted by the Constitutional Reform Act 2005, s 15(1), Sch 4, Pt 1, paras 203, 210(1), (2); words 'the Adoption and Children Act 2002' in square brackets in each place they occur substituted by the Adoption and Children Act 2002, s 139(1), Sch 3, paras 54, 75; sub-para (2A) inserted by the Child Support Act 1991, s 45(3), (4); sub-para (2A)(a) substituted by the Child Support, Pensions and Social Security Act 2000, s 83(5), Sch 8, para 10(1), (2)(a); in sub-para (2A)(b) words 'of the Child Support Act 1991' in square brackets substituted by the Child Support, Pensions and Social Security Act 2000, s 83(5), Sch 8, paras 10(1), (2)(b); sub-para (3)(bb) inserted by the Child Support Act 1991, s 45(3), (5); in sub-para (3)(bb) words omitted repealed by the Child Support, Pensions and Social Security Act 2000, s 85, Sch 9, Pt IX.
Para 2: in sub-para (1) words ', after consulting the Lord Chief Justice,' in square brackets inserted by the Constitutional Reform Act 2005, s 15(1), Sch 4, Pt 1, paras 203, 210(1), (3)(a); words 'the Adoption and Children Act 2002' in square brackets in each place they occur substituted by the Adoption and Children Act 2002, s 139(1), Sch 3, paras 54, 75; sub-para (3)(ba) inserted by the Child Support, Pensions and Social Security Act 2000, s 83(5), Sch 8, para 10(1), (3)(a); sub-para (3)(bb) inserted by the Child Support Act 1991, s 45(3), (5); in sub-para (3)(bb) words 'any proceedings under' in square brackets inserted by the Child Support, Pensions and Social Security Act 2000, s 83(5), Sch 8, para 10(1), (3)(b); in sub-para (3)(bb) words omitted repealed by the Child Support, Pensions and Social Security Act 2000, s 85, Sch 9, Pt IX; in sub-para (5) words ', after consulting the Lord Chief Justice,' in square brackets inserted by the Constitutional Reform Act 2005, s 15(1), Sch 4, Pt 1, paras 203, 210(1), (3)(b).
Para 3: in sub-para (1) words ', after consulting the Lord Chief Justice,' in square brackets inserted by the Constitutional Reform Act 2005, s 15(1), Sch 4, Pt 1, paras 203, 210(1), (4).
Para 4: in sub-para (5)(a) words 'after consulting the Lord Chief Justice,' in square brackets inserted by the Constitutional Reform Act 2005, s 15(1), Sch 4, Pt 1, paras 203, 210(1), (5)(a); sub-para (6) inserted by the Constitutional Reform Act 2005, s 15(1), Sch 4, Pt 1, paras 203, 210(1), (5)(b).

Appendix 1 *Children Act 1989*

References

See generally the Children (Allocation of Proceedings) Order 1991 and Chapter 4 at paras 4.15 ff.

PART II

CONSEQUENTIAL AMENDMENTS

[Not reproduced]

SCHEDULE 12

MINOR AMENDMENTS

Section 108(4)

[Not reproduced]

SCHEDULE 13

CONSEQUENTIAL AMENDMENTS

Section 108(5)

[Not reproduced]

SCHEDULE 14

TRANSITIONAL AND SAVINGS

Section 108(6)

[Not reproduced]

SCHEDULE 15

REPEALS

Section 108(7)

[Not reproduced]

Appendix 2

SECONDARY LEGISLATION

FAMILY PROCEEDINGS RULES 1991

(SI 1991/1247)

PART I
PRELIMINARY

1.1   Citation and commencement

These rules may be cited as the Family Proceedings Rules 1991 and shall come into force on 14th October 1991.

1.2

(1)   In these rules, unless the context otherwise requires—

"the Act of 1973" means the Matrimonial Causes Act 1973;
"the Act of 1984" means the Matrimonial and Family Proceedings Act 1984;
"the Act of 1986" means the Family Law Act 1986;
"the Act of 1989" means the Children Act 1989;
["the Act of 1991" means the Child Support Act 1991;]
...
"business day" has the meaning assigned to it by rule 1.5(6);
["cause" means—
    (a)   a matrimonial cause or a civil partnership cause, or
    (b)   proceedings under section 19 of the Act of 1973 (presumption of death and dissolution of marriage), or
    (c)   proceedings under section 55 of the Act of 2004 (presumption of death);]
["child", except in Part IV, in relation to one or both of the parties to a marriage or civil partnership, includes an illegitimate child of that party or, as the case may be, of both parties;
"child of the family" has, except in Part IV, the meaning assigned to it by section 105(1) of the Act of 1989;
"civil partnership cause" has the meaning assigned to it by section 32 of the Act of 1984;
"civil partnership order" means one of the orders mentioned in section 37 of the Act of 2004;
"civil partnership proceedings county court" means a county court so designated by the Lord Chancellor under section 36A of the Act of 1984;]
["consent order" means—
    (a)   in matrimonial proceedings, an order under section 33A of the Act of 1973, and
    (b)   in civil partnership proceedings, an order under paragraph 66 of Schedule 5 to the Act of 2004;]
["Contracting State" means—
    [(a) one of the parties to the Council Regulation, that is to say, Belgium, Cyprus, Czech Republic, Germany, Greece, Spain, Estonia, France,

Hungary, Ireland, Italy, Latvia, Lithuania, Luxembourg, Malta, Netherlands, Austria, Poland, Portugal, Slovakia, Slovenia, Finland, Sweden
and the United Kingdom,] and
  (b)   a party which has subsequently adopted the Council Regulation;]
["the Council Regulation" means Council Regulation (EC) No [2201/2003 of 27th
November 2003 concerning] jurisdiction and the recognition and enforcement
of judgments in matrimonial matters and [the] matters of parental responsibility
…;]
"court" means a judge or the district judge;
…
"district judge", in relation to proceedings in the principal registry, a district
registry or a county court, means the district judge or one of the district judges
of that registry or county court, as the case may be;
["district registry", except in rule 4.22(2A), means—
  (a)   in matrimonial proceedings, any district registry having a divorce county
        court within its district;
  (b)   in civil partnership proceedings, any district registry having a civil
        partnership proceedings county court within its district; and
  (c)   in any other case, any district registry having a designated county court
        within its district;]
"divorce county court" means a county court so designated by the Lord Chancellor
pursuant to section 33(1) of the Act of 1984;
"divorce town", in relation to any matrimonial proceedings, means a place at
which sittings of the High Court are authorised to be held outside the Royal
Courts of Justice for the hearing of such proceedings or proceedings of the class
to which they belong;
"document exchange" means any document exchange for the time being approved
by the Lord Chancellor;
"family proceedings" has the meaning assigned to it by section 32 of the Act of
1984;
…
"judge" does not include a district judge;
["matrimonial cause" has the meaning assigned to it by section 32 of the Act of
1984;]
"notice of intention to defend" has the meaning assigned to it by rule 10.8;
["officer of the service" has the same meaning as in the Criminal Justice and Court
Services Act 2000;]
…
"the President" means the President of the Family Division or, in the case of his
absence or incapacity through illness or otherwise or of a vacancy in the office
of President, the senior puisne judge of that Division;
["the President of Gender Recognition Panels" means the office in paragraph 2(1)
of Schedule 1 to the Gender Recognition Act 2004;]
"principal registry" means the Principal Registry of the Family Division;
"proper officer" means—
  (a)   in relation to the principal registry, the [family proceedings department
        manager], and
  (b)   in relation to any other court or registry, the [court manager],
or other officer of the court or registry acting on his behalf in accordance with
directions given by the Lord Chancellor;
…
"Royal Courts of Justice", in relation to matrimonial proceedings pending in a
divorce county court [or civil partnership proceedings pending in a civil
partnership proceedings county court], means such place, being the Royal
Courts of Justice or elsewhere, as may be specified in directions given by the
Lord Chancellor pursuant to section 42(2)(a) of the Act of 1984;

"senior district judge" means the senior district judge of the Family Division or, in his absence from the principal registry, the senior of the district judges in attendance at the registry;

...

(2)   Unless the context otherwise requires, a cause begun by petition shall be treated as pending for the purposes of these rules notwithstanding that a final decree [or civil partnership order has been made on the petition, or it has been otherwise finally disposed of].

(3)   Unless the context otherwise requires, a rule or Part referred to by number means the rule or Part so numbered in these rules.

(4)   In these rules a form referred to by number means the form so numbered in Appendix 1 [or 1A] to these rules with such variation as the circumstances of the particular case may require.

(5)   In these rules any reference to an Order and rule is—

(a)   if prefixed by the letters "CCR", a reference to that Order and rule in the County Court Rules 1981, and

(b)   if prefixed by the letters "RSC", a reference to that Order and rule in the Rules of the Supreme Court 1965.

[(5A)   In these rules a reference to a Part or rule, if prefixed by the letters "CPR", is a reference to that Part or rule in the Civil Procedure Rules 1998.]

[(6)   References in these rules to a county court shall—

(a)   in matrimonial proceedings, be construed as references to a divorce county court, and

(b)   in civil partnership proceedings, be construed as references to a civil partnership proceedings county court.]

(7)   In this rule and in rule 1.4, "matrimonial proceedings" means proceedings of a kind with respect to which divorce county courts have jurisdiction by or under section 33, 34 or 35 of the Act of 1984.

[(8)   In this rule and in rule 1.4, "civil partnership proceedings" means proceedings of a kind with respect to which civil partnership proceedings county courts have jurisdiction by or under section 36A, 36B or 36C of the Act of 1984.

(9)   In these Rules—

(a)   a reference to a conditional order is a reference to an order made under Chapter 2 of Part 2 of the Act of 2004 of a kind mentioned in section 37(1)(a), (b) or (c) of that Act which has not been made final; and

(b)   except in rule 8.1 and 8.1A, a reference to a final order is a reference to such an order which has been made final.]

Date in force

14 October 1991: see r 1.1.

Amendment

Para (1): definition "the Act of 1991" inserted by SI 1993/295, r 3; definition "the Act of 2004" inserted by SI 2005/2922, r 3(a)(i); definitions of "child" substituted, for definition "'child' and 'child of the family'" as originally enacted, by SI 2005/2922, r 3(a)(v); definition "Contracting State" inserted by SI 2001/821, r 8(a); in definition "Contracting State" para (a) substituted by SI 2005/264, r 4(a);definition "the Council Regulation" inserted by SI 2001/821, r 8(a); in definition "the Council Regulation" words "2201/2003 of 27th November 2003 concerning" in square brackets substituted by SI 2005/264, r 4(b)(i); in definition "the Council Regulation" word "the" in square brackets substituted by SI 2005/264, r 4(b)(ii); in definition "the Council Regulation" words omitted revoked by SI 2005/264, r 4(b)(iii); definition "district registry" substituted by SI 2005/2922, r 3(a)(ix); in definition "proper officer" in para (a) words "family proceedings department manager" in square brackets substituted by SI 1997/1056, r 6; in definition "proper office" in para (b) words "court manager" in square brackets substituted by SI 1997/1056, r 6; in definition "Royal Courts of Justice" words "or civil partnership proceedings pending in a civil partnership proceedings county court" in square brackets inserted by SI 2005/2922, r 3(a)(xvi).

Para (2): words "or civil partnership order has been made on the petition, or it has been otherwise finally disposed of" in square brackets substituted by SI 2005/2922, r 3(b)

Para (4): words "or 1A" in square brackets inserted by SI 1999/3491, rr 2, 4(1).

Para (5A): inserted by SI 1999/3491, rr 2, 4(2).

Para (6): substituted by SI 2005/2922, r 3(c).

Paras (8), (9): inserted by SI 2005/2922, r 3(d).

Note

Only those definitions relevant to this work are printed here.

1.3   Application of other rules

(1)   Subject to the provisions of these rules and of any enactment the County Court Rules 1981 and the Rules of the Supreme Court 1965 shall [continue to] apply, with the necessary modifications, to family proceedings in a county court and the High Court respectively.

(2)   For the purposes of paragraph (1) any provision of these rules authorising or requiring anything to be done in family proceedings shall be treated as if it were, in the case of proceedings pending in a county court, a provision of the County Court Rules 1981 and, in the case of proceedings pending in the High Court, a provision of the Rules of the Supreme Court 1965.

Date in force

14 October 1991: see r 1.1.

Amendment

Para (1): words "continue to" in square brackets inserted by SI 1999/1012, rr 2, 3(2).

1.4   County court proceedings in principal registry

[(1)   Subject to the provisions of these rules—

    (a)   matrimonial proceedings pending at any time in the principal registry which, if they had been begun in a divorce county court, would be pending at that time in such a court, shall be treated, for the purposes of these rules and of any provision of the County Court Rules 1981 and the County Courts Act 1984, as pending in a divorce county court and not in the High Court, and

    (b)   civil partnership proceedings pending at any time in the principal registry which, if they had been begun in a civil partnership proceedings county court, would be pending at that time in such a court, shall be treated, for the purposes of these rules and of any provision of the County Court Rules 1981 and the County Courts Act 1984, as pending in a civil partnership proceedings county court and not in the High Court.]

(2)   Unless the context otherwise requires, any reference to a divorce county court [or a civil partnership proceedings county court or a designated county court] in any

provision of these rules which relates to the commencement or prosecution of proceedings in ..., or the transfer of proceedings to or from[,] such a court, includes a reference to the principal registry.

Date in force

14 October 1991: see r 1.1.

Amendment

Para (1): substituted by SI 2005/2922, r 4(a).
Para (2): words "or a civil partnership proceedings county court or a designated county court" in square brackets inserted by SI 2005/2922, r 4(b)(i); words omitted revoked by SI 2005/2922, r 4(b)(ii); reference to "," in square brackets inserted by SI 2005/2922, r 4(b)(iii).

1.5   Computation of time

(1)   Any period of time fixed by these rules, or by any rules applied by these rules, or by any decree, judgment, order or direction for doing any act shall be reckoned in accordance with the following provisions of this rule.

(2)   Where the act is required to be done not less than a specified period before a specified date, the period starts immediately after the date on which the act is done and ends immediately before the specified date.

(3)   Where the act is required to be done within a specified period after or from a specified date, the period starts immediately after that date.

(4)   Where, apart from this paragraph, the period in question, being a period of seven days or less, would include a day which is not a business day, that day shall be excluded.

(5)   Where the time so fixed for doing an act in the court office expires on a day on which the office is closed, and for that reason the act cannot be done on that day, the act shall be in time if done on the next day on which the office is open.

(6)   In these rules "business day" means any day other than—

    (a)   a Saturday, Sunday, Christmas Day or Good Friday; or
    (b)   a bank holiday under the Banking and Financial Dealings Act 1971, in England and Wales.

Date in force

14 October 1991: see r 1.1.

[PART II
MATRIMONIAL AND CIVIL PARTNERSHIP CAUSES]

PART III
OTHER MATRIMONIAL ETC PROCEEDINGS

PART IV
PROCEEDINGS UNDER THE CHILDREN ACT 1989

4.1   Interpretation and application

(1)   In this Part of these rules, unless a contrary intention appears—

a section or schedule referred to means the section or schedule so numbered in the Act of 1989;

"a section 8 order" has the meaning assigned to it by section 8(2);

"application" means an application made under or by virtue of the Act of 1989 or under these rules, and "applicant" shall be construed accordingly;

"child", in relation to proceedings to which this Part applies—

    (a)   means, subject to sub-paragraph (b), a person under the age of 18 with respect to whom the proceedings are brought, and

    (b)   where the proceedings are under Schedule 1, also includes a person who has reached the age of 18;

["children and family reporter" means an officer of the service [or a Welsh family proceedings officer] who has been asked to prepare a welfare report under section 7(1)(a);]

["children's guardian"—

    (a)   means an officer of the service [or a Welsh family proceedings officer] appointed under section 41 for the child with respect to whom the proceedings are brought; but

    (b)   does not include such an officer appointed in relation to proceedings specified by Part IVA;]

"directions appointment" means a hearing for directions under rule 4.14(2);

"emergency protection order" means an order under section 44;

["family assistance order report" means a report to the court pursuant to a direction in a family assistance order under section 16(6);]

...

"leave" includes permission and approval;

"note" includes a record made by mechanical means;

"parental responsibility" has the meaning assigned to it by section 3;

"recovery order" means an order under section 50;

["risk assessment" has the meaning assigned to it by section 16A(3);]

["special guardianship order" has the meaning assigned to it by section 14A;]

"specified proceedings" has the meaning assigned to it by section 41(6) and rule 4.2(2); and

"welfare officer" means a person who has been asked to prepare a welfare report under [section 7(1)(b)].

(2)   Except where the contrary intention appears, the provisions of this Part apply to proceedings in the High Court and the county courts

    (a)   on an application for a section 8 order;

    (b)   on an application for a care order or a supervision order;

    (c)   on an application under section [4(1)(c)], 4(3), [4A(1)(b), 4A(3),] 5(1), 6(7), 13(1), [14A, 14C(3), 14D,] ... 33(7), 34(2), 34(3), 34(4), 34(9), 36(1), 38(8)(b), 39(1), 39(2), 39(3), 39(4), 43(1), 43(12), 44, 45, 46(7), 48(9)[, 50(1) or 102(1)]];

    (d)   under Schedule 1, except where financial relief is also sought by or on behalf of an adult,

    (e)   on an application under paragraph 19(1) of Schedule 2;

    (f)   on an application under paragraph 6(3), 15(2) or 17(1) of Schedule 3;

    (g)   on an application under paragraph 11(3) or 16(5) of Schedule 14; or

    (h)   under section 25.

Date in force

14 October 1991: see r 1.1.

Amendment

Para (1): definition "children and family reporter" inserted by SI 2001/821, r 15(a); in definition "children and family reporter" words "or a Welsh family proceedings officer" in square brackets inserted by SI 2005/559, r 16; definition "children's guardian" inserted by SI 2001/821, r 15(a); in definition "children's guardian" in para (a) words "or a Welsh family proceedings officer" in square brackets inserted by SI 2005/559, r 16; definition "family assistance order report" inserted by SI 2007/2187, rr 2, 7(a)(i); definition "guardian ad litem" (omitted) revoked by SI 2001/821, r 15(b); definition "risk assessment" inserted by SI 2007/2187, rr 2, 7(a)(ii); definition "special guardianship order" inserted by SI 2005/2922, r 75(a); in definition "welfare officer" words "section 7(1)(b)" in square brackets substituted by SI 2001/821, r 15(c)

Para (2): in sub-para (c) reference to "4(1)(c)" in square brackets substituted by SI 2003/2839, r 4; in sub-para (c) reference to "4A(1)(b), 4A(3)," in square brackets inserted by SI 2005/2922, r 75(b)(i); in sub-para (c) reference to "14A, 14C(3), 14D," in square brackets inserted by SI 2005/2922, r 75(b)(ii); in sub-para (c) reference omitted revoked by SI 2007/2187, rr 2, 7(b); in sub-para (c) words ", 50(1) or 102(1)" in square brackets substituted by SI 1991/2113, r 5.

4.2   Matters prescribed for the purposes of the Act of 1989

(1)   The parties to proceedings in which directions are given under section 38(6), and any person named in such a direction, form the prescribed class for the purposes of section 38(8) (application to vary directions made with interim care or interim supervision order).

(2)   The following proceedings are specified for the purposes of section 41 in accordance with subsection (6)(i) thereof—

    (a)   proceedings under section 25;
    (b)   applications under section 33(7);
    (c)   proceedings under paragraph 19(1) of Schedule 2;
    (d)   applications under paragraph 6(3) of Schedule 3.
    [(e)   appeals against the determination of proceedings of a kind set out in sub-paragraphs (a) to (d)].

(3)   The applicant for an order that has been made under section 43(1) and the persons referred to in section 43(11) may, in any circumstances, apply under section 43(12) for a child assessment order to be varied or discharged.

(4)   The following persons form the prescribed class for the purposes of section 44(9) (application to vary directions)—

    (a)   the parties to the application for the order in respect of which it is sought to vary the directions;
    (b)   the [children's guardian];
    (c)   the local authority in whose area the child concerned is ordinarily resident;
    (d)   any person who is named in the directions.

Date in force

14 October 1991: see r 1.1.

Amendment

Para (2): sub-para (e) inserted by SI 1991/2113, r 8.
Para (4): in sub-para (b) words "children's guardian" in square brackets substituted by SI 2001/821, r 16(a).

4.3   Application for leave to commence proceedings

(1)   Where the leave of the court is required to bring any proceedings to which this Part applies, the person seeking leave shall file—

    (a)   a written request for leave [in Form C2] setting out the reasons for the application; and [(b) a draft of the application (being the documents referred to in rule 4.4(1A)) for the making of which leave is sought together with sufficient copies for one to be served on each respondent].

(2) On considering a request for leave filed under paragraph (1), the court shall—

(a) grant the request, whereupon the proper officer shall inform the person making the request [and any local authority that is preparing, or has prepared, a report under section 14A(8) or (9)] of the decision, or

(b) direct that a date be fixed for the hearing of the request, whereupon the proper officer shall fix such a date and give such notice as the court directs to the person making the request [and any local authority that is preparing, or has prepared, a report under section 14A(8) or (9)] and to such other persons as the court requires to be notified, of the date so fixed.

(3) Where leave is granted to bring proceedings to which this Part applies the application shall proceed in accordance with rule 4.4; but paragraph (1)(a) of that rule shall not apply.

(4) In the case of a request for leave to bring proceedings under Schedule 1, the draft application under paragraph (1) shall be accompanied by a statement setting out the financial details which the person seeking leave believes to be relevant to the request and containing a declaration that it is true to the maker's best knowledge and belief, together with sufficient copies for one to be served on each respondent.

Date in force

14 October 1991: see r 1.1.

Amendment

Para (1): in sub-para (a) words "in Form C2" inserted, and sub-para (b) substituted, by SI 1994/3155, r 4.
Para (2): in sub-paras (a), (b) words from "and any local authority" to "section 14A(8) or (9)" in square brackets inserted by SI 2005/2922, r 76.

4.4   Application

(1) Subject to paragraph (4), an applicant shall—

[(a) file the documents referred to in paragraph (1A) below (which documents shall together be called the "application") together with sufficient copies for one to be served on each respondent, and]

(b) serve a copy of the application [together with Form C6 and such (if any) of Forms [C1A,] C7 and C10A as are given to him by the proper officer under paragraph (2)(b)] on each respondent such number of days prior to the date fixed under paragraph (2)(a) as is specified for that application in column (ii) of Appendix 3 to these rules.

[(1A) The documents to be filed under paragraph (1)(a) above are—

(a)
(i) whichever is appropriate of Forms [C1, C2, C3, C4] or C51, and
(ii) such of the supplemental Forms C10 or C11 to C20 as may be appropriate, [and
(iii) in the case of an application for a section 8 order or an order under section 4(1)(c) where question 7 on Form C1, or question 4 on Form C2, is answered in the affirmative, supplemental Form C1A], or

    (b)   where there is no appropriate form a statement in writing of the order sought, and where the application is made in respect of more than one child, all the children shall be included in one application.]

(2) On receipt of the documents filed under paragraph (1)(a) the proper officer shall—

    (a)   fix the date for a hearing or a directions appointment, allowing sufficient time for the applicant to comply with paragraph (1)(b),

    (b)   endorse the date so fixed upon [Form C6 and, where appropriate, Form C6A], and

    [(c)   return forthwith to the applicant the copies of the application and Form C10A if filed with it, together with Form C6 and such of Forms C6A and C7 as are appropriat[, and, in the case of an application for a section 8 order or an order under section 4(1)(c), Form C1A]e].

[(3) The applicant shall, at the same time as complying with paragraph (1)(b), serve Form C6A on the persons set out for the relevant class of proceedings in column (iv) of Appendix 3 to these rules.]

(4) An application for—

    (a)   a [section 8 order],
    (b)   an emergency protection order,
    (c)   a warrant under section 48(9), ...
    (d)   a recovery order, [or
    (e)   a warrant under section 102(1),]

may be made ex parte in which case the applicant shall—

    (i)   file the application ... in the appropriate form in Appendix 1 to these rules—
        (a)   where the application is made by telephone, within 24 hours after the making of the application, or
        (b)   in any other case, at the time when the application is made, and
    (ii) in the case of an application for a [section 8 order] or an emergency protection order, serve a copy of the application on each respondent within 48 hours after the making of the order.

(5) Where the court refuses to make an order on an ex parte application it may direct that the application be made inter partes.

(6) In the case of proceedings under Schedule 1, the application under paragraph (1) shall be accompanied by a statement [in Form C10A] setting out the financial details which the applicant believes to be relevant to the application ... , together with sufficient copies for one to be served on each respondent.

Date in force

14 October 1991: see r 1.1.

Amendment

Para (1): sub-para (a) substituted by SI 1994/3155, r 5(a); in sub-para (b) words from "together with" to "paragraph (2)(b)" in square brackets substituted by SI 1994/3155, r 5(b); in sub-para (b) reference to "C1A," in square brackets inserted by SI 2004/3375, r 3
Para (1A): inserted by SI 1994/3155, r 6; in sub-para (a)(i) references to "C1, C2, C3, C4" in square brackets substituted by SI 2004/3375, r 4(a); sub-para (a)(iii) and word "and" immediately preceding it inserted by SI 2004/3375, r 4(b).
Para (2): in sub-para (b) words "Form C6 and, where appropriate, Form C6A" in square brackets substituted by SI 1994/3155, r 7(a); sub-para (c) substituted by SI 1994/3155, r 7(b); in sub-para (c) words from ", and, in the" to "section 4(1)(c), Form C1A" in square brackets inserted by SI 2004/3375, r 5

Para (3): substituted by SI 1994/3155, r 8.
Para (4): words "section 8 order" in both places where they occur substituted by SI 1992/2067, r 9; in sub-para (c) word omitted revoked and sub-para (e) and the word "or" immediately preceding it inserted, by SI 1991/2113, r 9; in sub-para (i) words omitted revoked by SI 1994/3155, r 9.
Para (6): words "in Form C10A" inserted and words omitted revoked, by SI 1994/3155, r 10.

4.5   Withdrawal of application

(1)   An application may be withdrawn only with leave of the court.

(2)   Subject to paragraph (3), a person seeking leave to withdraw an application shall file and serve on the parties a written request for leave setting out the reasons for the request.

(3)   The request under paragraph (2) may be made orally to the court if the parties and either the [children's guardian][,] the [welfare officer[,] children and family reporter][, or the officer of the service or the Welsh family proceedings officer who is preparing or has prepared a family assistance order report or a risk assessment] are present.

(4)   Upon receipt of a written request under paragraph (2) the court shall—

    (a)   if—
        (i)   the parties consent in writing,
        (ii)   the [children's guardian] has had an opportunity to make representations, and
        (iii)   the court thinks fit,
grant the request, in which case the proper officer shall notify the parties, [any local authority that is preparing, or has prepared, a report under section 14A(8) or (9),] the [children's guardian] and the [welfare officer or children and family reporter] of the granting of the request, or

    (b)   direct that a date be fixed for the hearing of the request in which case the proper officer shall give at least 7 days' notice to the parties, [any local authority that is preparing, or has prepared, a report under section 14A(8) or (9),] the [children's guardian][,] the [welfare officer[,] children and family reporter][[a]nd the officer of the service or the Welsh family proceedings officer who is preparing or has prepared a family assistance order report or a risk assessment] , of the date fixed.

Date in force

14 October 1991: see r 1.1.

Amendment

Para (3): words "children's guardian" in square brackets substituted by SI 2001/821, r 16(a); comma in square brackets in both places it occurs substituted by SI 2007/2187, rr 2, 8(a)(i), (ii); words "welfare officer or children and family reporter" in square brackets substituted by SI 2001/821, r 16(b); words from ", or the officer" to "a risk assessment" in square brackets inserted by SI 2007/2187, rr 2, 8(a)(iii).
Para (4): in sub-para (a)(ii) words "children's guardian" in square brackets substituted by SI 2001/821, r 16(a); in sub-paras (a), (b) words from "any local authority" to "section 14A(8) or (9)," in square brackets inserted by SI 2005/2922, r 77; in sub-para (a) words "children's guardian" in square brackets substituted by SI 2001/821, r 16(a); in sub-para (a) words "welfare officer or children and family reporter" in square brackets substituted by SI 2001/821, r 16(b); in sub-para (b) words "children's guardian" in square brackets substituted by SI 2001/821, r 16(a); comma in square brackets in both places it occurs substituted by SI 2007/2187, rr 2, 8(b)(ii)(aa), (bb); in sub-para (b) words "welfare officer or children and family reporter" in square brackets

substituted by SI 2001/821, r 16(b); in sub-para (b) words from "and the officer" to "a risk assessment" in square brackets inserted by SI 2007/2187, rr 2, 8(b)(ii)(cc).

4.6   Transfer ...

(1)   Where an application is made, in accordance with the provisions of [the Allocation Order], to a county court for an order transferring proceedings from a magistrates' court following the refusal of the magistrates' court to order such a transfer, the applicant shall—

(a)   file the application in Form [C2], together with a copy of the certificate issued by the magistrates' court, and

(b)   serve a copy of the documents mentioned in sub-paragraph (a) personally on all parties to the proceedings which it is sought to have transferred,

within 2 days after receipt by the applicant of the certificate.

(2)   Within 2 days after receipt of the documents served under paragraph (1)(b), any party other than the applicant may file written representations.

(3)   The court shall, not before the fourth day after the filing of the application under paragraph (1), unless the parties consent to earlier consideration, consider the application and either—

(a)   grant the application, whereupon the proper officer shall inform the parties [and any local authority that is preparing, or has prepared, a report under section 14A(8) or (9)] of that decision, or

(b)   direct that a date be fixed for the hearing of the application, whereupon the proper officer shall fix such a date and give not less than 1 day's notice to the parties [and any local authority that is preparing, or has prepared, a report under section 14A(8) or (9)] of the date so fixed.

(4)   Where proceedings are transferred from a magistrates' court to a county court in accordance with the provisions of [the Allocation Order], the county court shall consider whether to transfer those proceedings to the High Court in accordance with that Order and either—

(a)   determine that such an order need not be made,

(b)   make such an order,

(c)   order that a date be fixed for the hearing of the question whether such an order should be made, whereupon the proper officer shall give such notice to the parties [and any local authority that is preparing, or has prepared, a report under section 14A(8) or (9)] as the court directs of the date so fixed, or

(d)   invite the parties to make written representations, within a specified period, as to whether such an order should be made; and upon receipt of the representations the court shall act in accordance with sub-paragraph (a), (b) or (c).

(5)   The proper officer shall notify the parties [and any local authority that is preparing, or has prepared, a report under section 14A(8) or (9)] of an order transferring the proceedings from a county court or from the High Court made in accordance with the provisions of [the Allocation Order].

[(6)   Before ordering the transfer of proceedings from a county court to a magistrates' court in accordance with the Allocation Order, the county court shall notify the magistrates' court of its intention to make such an order and invite the views of the clerk to the justices on whether such an order should be made.

(7)   An order transferring proceedings from a county court to a magistrates' court in accordance with the Allocation Order shall—

(a)   be in form [C49], and

(b) be served by the court on the parties.

(8) In this rule "the Allocation Order" means the Children (Allocation of Proceedings) Order 1991 or any Order replacing that Order.]

Date in force

14 October 1991: see r 1.1.

Amendment

Provision heading: words omitted revoked by SI 1991/2113, r 11.
Para (1): words "the Allocation Order" substituted by SI 1991/2113, r 10; in sub-para (a) figure "C2" substituted by SI 1994/3155, r 11.
Para (3): in sub-paras (a), (b) words from "and any local authority" to "section 14A(8) or (9)" in square brackets inserted by SI 2005/2922, r 78.
Para (4): words "the Allocation Order" in square brackets substituted by SI 1991/2113, r 10; in sub-para (c) words from "and any local authority" to "section 14A(8) or (9)" in square brackets inserted by SI 2005/2922, r 78.
Para (5): words from "and any local authority" to "section 14A(8) or (9)" in square brackets inserted by SI 2005/2922, r 78; words "the Allocation Order" in square brackets substituted by SI 1991/2113, r 10.
Paras (6)–(8): inserted by SI 1991/2113, r 12.
Para (7): in sub-para (a) reference to "C49" in square brackets substituted by SI 1994/3155, r 12.

4.7 Parties

(1) The respondents to proceedings to which this Part applies shall be those persons set out in the relevant entry in [column (iii)] of Appendix 3 to these rules.

(2) In proceedings to which this Part applies, a person may file a request [in Form C2] that he or another person—

(a) be joined as a party, or
(b) cease to be a party.

(3) On considering a request under paragraph (2) the court shall, subject to paragraph (4)—

(a) grant it without a hearing or representations, save that this shall be done only in the case of a request under paragraph (2)(a), whereupon the proper officer shall inform the parties [and any local authority that is preparing, or has prepared, a report under section 14A(8) or (9)] and the person making the request of that decision, or
(b) order that a date be fixed for the consideration of the request, whereupon the proper officer shall give notice of the date so fixed, together with a copy of the request—
  (i) in the case of a request under paragraph (2)(a), to the applicant [and any local authority that is preparing, or has prepared, a report under section 14A(8) or (9)], and
  (ii) in the case of a request under paragraph (2)(b), to the parties [and any local authority that is preparing, or has prepared, a report under section 14A(8) or (9)], or
(c) invite the parties or any of them to make written representations, within a specified period, as to whether the request should be granted; and upon the expiry of the period the court shall act in accordance with sub-paragraph (a) or (b).

(4) Where a person with parental responsibility requests that he be joined under paragraph (2)(a), the court shall grant his request.

(5)   In proceedings to which this Part applies the court may direct—

(a)   that a person who would not otherwise be a respondent under these rules be joined as a party to the proceedings, or
(b)   that a party to the proceedings cease to be a party.

Date in force

14 October 1991: see r 1.1.

Amendment

Para (1): words "column (iii)" in square brackets substituted by SI 1992/2067, r 7.;Para (2): words "in Form C2" in square brackets substituted by SI 1994/3155, r 13.
Para (3): in sub-paras (a), (b) words from "and any local authority" to "section 14A(8) or (9)" in square brackets in each place they occur inserted by SI 2005/2922, r 79.

4.8   Service

(1)   Subject to the requirement in rule 4.6(1)(b) of personal service, where service of a document is required under this Part (and not by a provision to which section 105(8) (Service of notice or other document under the Act) applies) it may be effected—

(a)   if the person to be served is not known by the person serving to be acting by solicitor—
   (i)   by delivering it to him personally, or
   (ii)   by delivering it at, or by sending it by first-class post to, his residence or his last known residence, or
(b)   if the person to be served is known by the person serving to be acting by solicitor—
   (i)   by delivering the document at, or sending it by first-class post to, the solicitor's address for service,
   (ii)   where the solicitor's address for service includes a numbered box at a document exchange, by leaving the document at that document exchange or at a document exchange which transmits documents on every business day to that document exchange, or
   (iii)   by sending a legible copy of the document by facsimile transmission to the solicitor's office.

(2)   In this rule "first-class post" means first-class post which has been pre-paid or in respect of which pre-payment is not required.

(3)   Where a child who is a party to proceedings to which this Part applies [is not prosecuting or defending them without a next friend or guardian ad litem under rule 9.2A and] is required by these rules or other rules of court to serve a document, service shall be effected by—

(a)   the solicitor acting for the child, or
(b)   where there is no such solicitor, [the children's guardian or] the guardian ad litem, or
(c)   where there is neither such a solicitor [nor a children's guardian] nor a guardian ad litem, the court.

(4)   Service of any document on a child [who is not prosecuting or defending the proceedings concerned without a next friend or guardian ad litem under rule 9.2A] shall, subject to any direction of the court, be effected by service on—

(a)   the solicitor acting for the child, or
(b)   where there is no such solicitor, [the children's guardian or] the guardian ad litem, or

(c)   where there is neither such a solicitor [nor a children's guardian] nor a guardian ad litem, with leave of the court, the child.

(5)   Where the court refuses leave under paragraph (4)(c) it shall give a direction under paragraph (8).

(6)   A document shall, unless the contrary is proved, be deemed to have been served—

(a)   in the case of service by first-class post, on the second business day after posting, and

(b)   in the case of service in accordance with paragraph (1)(b)(ii), on the second business day after the day on which it is left at the document exchange.

(7)   At or before the first directions appointment in, or hearing of, proceedings to which this Part applies the applicant shall file a statement [in Form C9] that service of—

(a)   a copy of the application [and other documents referred to in rule 4.4(1)(b)] has been effected on each respondent, and

(b)   notice of the proceedings has been effected under rule 4.4(3);

and the statement shall indicate—

(i)   the manner, date, time and place of service, or

(ii)   where service was effected by post, the date, time and place of posting.

[(8)   In proceedings to which this Part applies, where these rules or other rules of court require a document to be served, the court may, without prejudice to any power under rule 4.14, direct that—

(a)   the requirement shall not apply;

(b)   the time specified by the rules for complying with the requirement shall be abridged to such extent as may be specified in the direction;

(c)   service shall be effected in such manner as may be specified in the direction.]

Date in force

14 October 1991: see r 1.1.

Amendment

Para (3): words from "is not prosecuting" to "rule 9.2A and" in square brackets inserted by SI 1992/456, r 3; in sub-para (b) words "the children's guardian or" in square brackets inserted by SI 2001/821, r 17(a)(i); in sub-para (c) words "nor a children's guardian" in square brackets inserted by SI 2001/821, r 17(a)(ii).

Para (4): words from "who is not prosecuting" to "rule 9.2A" in square brackets inserted by SI 1992/456, r 4;in sub-para (b) words "the children's guardian or" in square brackets substituted by SI 2001/821, r 17(b)(i); in sub-para (c) words "nor a children's guardian" in square brackets inserted by SI 2001/821, r 17(b)(ii).

Para (7): words "in Form C9" and "and other documents referred to in rule 4.4(1)(b)", inserted by SI 1994/3155, r 14.

Para (8): substituted by SI 1992/2067, r 19.

4.9   Answer to application

(1)   Within 14 days of service of [an application for an order under section 4(1)(c),] an application for a section 8 order[, a special guardianship order] [or an application under Schedule 1], each respondent shall file, and serve on the parties, an [acknowledgment of] the application in Form [C7] [and, if both parts of question 6 or question 7 (or both) on Form C7 are answered in the affirmative, Form C1A].

(2)   ...

(3) Following service of an application to which this Part applies, other than an application under rule 4.3[, for an order under section 4(1)(c)] or for a section 8 order [or special guardianship order], a respondent may, subject to paragraph (4), file a written answer, which shall be served on the other parties.

(4) An answer under paragraph (3) shall, except in the case of an application under section 25, 31, 34, 38, 43, 44, 45, 46, 48 or 50, be filed, and served, not less than 2 days before the date fixed for the hearing of the application.

Date in force

14 October 1991: see r 1.1.

Amendment

Para (1): words "an application for an order under section 4(1)(c)," in square brackets inserted by SI 2004/3375, r 6(a); words ", a special guardianship order" in square brackets inserted by SI 2005/2922, r 80(a). ; words "or an application under Schedule 1" in square brackets inserted by SI 1994/3155, r 15(a); words "acknowledgment of" in square brackets and reference to "C7" in square brackets substituted by SI 1994/3155, r 15(a); words from "and, if both" to "affrmative, Form C1A" in square brackets inserted by SI 2004/3375, r 6(b).
Para (2): revoked by SI 1994/3155, r 15(b).
Para (3): words ", for an order under section 4(1)(c)" in square brackets inserted by SI 2004/3375, r 7;words "or special guardianship order" in square brackets inserted by SI 2005/2922, r 80(b).

4.10   Appointment of [children's guardian]

(1) As soon as practicable after the commencement of specified proceedings, or the transfer of such proceedings to the court, the court shall appoint a [children's guardian], unless—

   (a)   such an appointment has already been made by the court which made the transfer and is subsisting, or

   (b)   the court considers that such an appointment is not necessary to safeguard the interests of the child.

(2) At any stage in specified proceedings a party may apply, without notice to the other parties unless the court directs otherwise, for the appointment of a [children's guardian].

(3) The court shall grant an application under paragraph (2) unless it considers such an appointment not to be necessary to safeguard the interests of the child, in which case it shall give its reasons; and a note of such reasons shall be taken by the proper officer.

(4) At any stage in specified proceedings the court may, of its own motion, appoint a [children's guardian].

[(4A) The court may, in specified proceedings, appoint more than one children's guardian in respect of the same child.]

(5) The proper officer shall, as soon as practicable, notify the parties and any [welfare officer or children and family reporter] of an appointment under this rule or, as the case may be, of a decision not to make such an appointment.

(6) Upon the appointment of a [children's guardian] the proper officer shall, as soon as practicable, notify him of the appointment and serve on him copies of the application and of documents filed under rule 4.17(1).

[(7) A children's guardian appointed by the court under this rule shall not—

(a) be a member, officer or servant of a local authority which, or an authorised person (within the meaning of section 31(9)) who, is a party to the proceedings;

(b) be, or have been, a member, officer or servant of a local authority or voluntary organisation (within the meaning of section 105(1)) who has been directly concerned in that capacity in arrangements relating to the care, accommodation or welfare of the child during the five years prior to the commencement of the proceedings; or

(c) be a serving probation officer who has, in that capacity, been previously concerned with the child or his family.]

(8) When appointing a [children's guardian] the court shall consider the appointment of anyone who has previously acted as [children's guardian] of the same child.

(9) The appointment of a [children's guardian] under this rule shall continue for such time as is specified in the appointment or until terminated by the court.

(10) When terminating an appointment in accordance with paragraph (9), the court shall give its reasons in writing for so doing.

(11) Where the court appoints a [children's guardian] in accordance with this rule or refuses to make such an appointment, the court or the proper officer shall record the appointment or refusal in Form [C47].

Date in force

14 October 1991: see r 1.1.

Amendment

Provision heading: words "children's guardian" in square brackets substituted by SI 2001/821, r 16(a).
Para (1): words "children's guardian" in square brackets substituted by SI 2001/821, r 16(a)
Para (2): words "children's guardian" in square brackets substituted by SI 2001/821, r 16(a).
Para (4): words "children's guardian" in square brackets substituted by SI 2001/821, r 16(a).
Para (4A): inserted by SI 2001/821, r 18(a).
Para (5): words "welfare officer or children and family reporter" in square brackets substituted by SI 2001/821, r 16(b).
Para (6): words "children's guardian" in square brackets substituted by SI 2001/821, r 16(a).
Para (7): substituted by SI 2001/821, r 18(b).
Para (8): words "children's guardian" in square brackets in both places they occur substituted by SI 2001/821, r 16(a).
Para (9): words "children's guardian" in square brackets substituted by SI 2001/821, r 16(a).
Para (11): words "children's guardian" in square brackets substituted by SI 2001/821, r 16(a); reference to "C47" substituted by SI 1994/3155, r 16.

[4.11   Powers and duties of officers of the service [and Welsh family proceedings officers]]

[(1) In carrying out his duty under section 7(1)(a)[, section 16(6), section 16A] section 41(2), the officer of the service [or the Welsh family proceedings officer] shall have regard to the principle set out in section 1(2) and the matters set out in section 1(3)(a) to (f) as if for the word "court" in that section there were substituted the words ["officer of the Service or Welsh family proceedings officer"].

(2) The officer of the service [or the Welsh family proceedings officer] shall make such investigations as may be necessary for him to carry out his duties and shall, in particular—

(a) contact or seek to interview such persons as he thinks appropriate or as the court directs;

(b) obtain such professional assistance as is available to him which he thinks appropriate or which the court directs him to obtain.

(3)   In addition to his duties, under other paragraphs of this rule, or rules 4.11A[, 4.11AA] and 4.11B, the officer of the service [or the Welsh family proceedings officer] shall provide to the court such other assistance as it may require.

(4)   A party may question the officer of the service [or the Welsh family proceedings officer] about oral or written advice tendered by him to the court.]

Amendment

Substituted by SI 2001/821, r 19. Date in force: 1 April 2001: see SI 2001/821, r 1(b).
Provision heading: words "and Welsh family proceedings officers" in square brackets inserted by SI 2005/559, r 17(a).
Para (1): words ", section 16(6), section 16A" in square brackets substituted by SI 2007/2187, rr 2, 9(a).
Paras (1)–(4): words "or the Welsh family proceedings officer" in square brackets inserted by SI 2005/559, r 17(b).
Para (1): words ""officer of the Service or Welsh family proceedings officer"" in square brackets substituted by SI 2005/559, r 17(c).
Para (3): reference ", 4.11AA" in square brackets inserted by SI 2007/2187, rr 2, 9(b).

[4.11A   Additional powers and duties of children's guardian]

[(1)   The children's guardian shall—

(a) appoint a solicitor to represent the child unless such a solicitor has already been appointed; and
(b) give such advice to the child as is appropriate having regard to his understanding and, subject to rule 4.12(1)(a), instruct the solicitor representing the child on all matters relevant to the interests of the child including possibilities for appeal, arising in the course of proceedings.

(2)   Where the children's guardian is an officer of the service authorised by the Service in the terms mentioned by and in accordance with section 15(1) of the Criminal Justice and Court Services Act 2000, paragraph (1)(a) shall not require him to appoint a solicitor for the child if he intends to have conduct of the proceedings on behalf of the child unless—

(a) the child wishes to instruct a solicitor direct; and
(b) the children's guardian or the court considers that he is of sufficient understanding to do so.

[(2A)   Where the children's guardian is a Welsh family proceedings officer authorised by the National Assembly for Wales in the terms mentioned by and in accordance with section 37(1) of the Children Act 2004, paragraph (1)(a) shall not require him to appoint a solicitor for the child if he intends to have conduct of the proceedings on behalf of the child unless—

(a) the child wishes to instruct a solicitor direct; and
(b) the children's guardian or the court considers that he is of sufficient understanding to do so.]

(3)   Where it appears to the children's guardian that the child—

(a) is instructing his solicitor direct; or
(b) intends to conduct and is capable of conducting the proceedings on his own behalf,

he shall inform the court and from then he—

    (i)   shall perform all of his duties set out in rule 4.11 and this rule, other than those duties under paragraph (1)(a) of this rule, and such other duties as the court may direct;

   (ii)   shall take such part in the proceedings as the court may direct; and

  (iii)   may, with the leave of the court, have legal representation in the conduct of those duties.

(4)   Unless excused by the court, the children's guardian shall attend all directions appointments in and hearings of the proceedings and shall advise the court on the following matters—

  (a)   whether the child is of sufficient understanding for any purpose including the child's refusal to submit to a medical or psychiatric examination or other assessment that the court has the power to require, direct or order.

  (b)   the wishes of the child in respect of any matter relevant to the proceedings including his attendance at court;

  (c)   the appropriate forum for the proceedings;

  (d)   the appropriate timing of the proceedings or any part of them;

  (e)   the options available to it in respect of the child and the suitability of each such option including what order should be made in determining the application; and

  (f)   any other matter concerning which the court seeks his advice or concerning which he considers that the court should be informed.

(5)   The advice given under paragraph (4) may, subject to any order of the court, by given orally or in writing; and if the advice be given orally, a note of it shall be taken by the court or the proper officer.

(6)   The children's guardian shall, where practicable, notify any person whose joinder as a party to those proceedings would be likely, in the opinion of the children's guardian, to safeguard the interests of the child of that person's right to apply to be joined under rule 4.7(2) and shall inform the court—

  (a)   of any such notification given;

  (b)   of anyone whom he attempted to notify under this paragraph but was unable to contact; and

  (c)   of anyone whom he believes may wish to be joined to the proceedings.

(7)   The children's guardian shall, unless the court otherwise directs, not less than 14 days before the date fixed for the final hearing of the proceedings—

  (a)   file a written report advising on the interests of the child; and

  (b)   serve a copy of the filed report on the other parties [and any local authority that is preparing, or has prepared, a report under section 14A(8) or (9)].

(8)   The children's guardian shall serve and accept service of documents on behalf of the child in accordance with rule 4.8(3)(b) and (4)(b) and, where the child has not himself been served, and has sufficient understanding, advise the child of the contents of any document so served.

(9)   If the children's guardian inspects records of the kinds referred to in section 42, he shall bring to the attention of—

  (a)   the court; and

  (b)   unless the court otherwise directs, the other parties to the proceedings,

all records and documents which may, in his opinion, assist in the proper determination of the proceedings.

(10)   The children's guardian shall ensure that, in relation to a decision made by the court in the proceedings—

(a)   if he considers it appropriate to the age and understanding of the child, the child is notified of that decision; and

(b)   if the child is notified of the decision, it is explained to the child in a manner appropriate to his age and understanding.]

Amendment

Inserted by SI 2001/821, r 20. Date in force: 1 April 2001: see SI 2001/821, r 1(b).
Para (2A): inserted by SI 2005/559, r 18.
Para (7): in sub-para (b) words from "and any local authority" to "section 14A(8) or (9)" in square brackets inserted by SI 2005/2922, r 81.

[4.11AA   Additional powers and duties of officers of the service and Welsh family proceedings officers: family assistance order reports and risk assessments]

[(1)   This rule applies where an officer of the service or a Welsh family proceedings officer is preparing or has prepared—

(a)   a family assistance order report; or

(b)   a risk assessment.

(2)   When an officer of the service or a Welsh family proceedings officer is preparing a family assistance order report or a risk assessment he must consider whether—

(a)   to notify the child of such of the contents of the report or assessment as he considers appropriate to the age and understanding of the child;

(b)   to recommend in the report or assessment that the court lists a hearing for the purposes of considering the report or assessment;

(c)   it is in the best interests of the child for the child to be made a party to the proceedings.

(3)   If the officer of the service or the Welsh family proceedings officer decides to notify the child of any of the contents of the report or assessment, he must explain those contents to the child in a manner appropriate to the child's age and understanding.

(4)   If the officer of the service or the Welsh family proceedings officer considers that the child should be made a party to the proceedings he must notify the court of his opinion together with the reasons for that opinion.

(5)   If the officer of the service or the Welsh family proceedings officer considers that the court should exercise its discretion under rule 4.17AA(2) in relation to service of a risk assessment, he must state in the risk assessment—

(a)   the way in which he considers the court should exercise its discretion (including his view on the length of any suggested delay in service); and

(b)   his reasons for reaching his view.

(6)   The officer of the service or the Welsh family proceedings officer must file the report or assessment with the court—

(a)   at or by the time directed by the court;

(b)   in the absence of any such direction, at least 14 days before a relevant hearing; or

(c)   where there has been no direction from the court and no relevant hearing is listed, as soon as possible following completion of the report or assessment.

(7)   In paragraph (6), a hearing is a relevant hearing if the proper officer has given the officer of the service or the Welsh family proceedings officer notice that the report or assessment is to be considered at it.

(8)   When an officer of the service or a Welsh family proceedings officer prepares a family assistance order report, he shall, as soon as practicable, serve copies of that report on—

(a)   each party; and
(b)   any local authority that is preparing or has prepared a report under section 14A(8) or (9).

(9)   At any hearing where a family assistance order report or a risk assessment is considered, any party may question the officer of the service or the Welsh family proceedings officer about the report or assessment.]

Amendment

Inserted by SI 2007/2187, rr 2, 3(a), 10.

[**4.11B**   **Additional powers and duties of a children and family reporter**]

[(1)   The children and family reporter shall—

(a)   notify the child of such contents of his report (if any) as he considers appropriate to the age and understanding of the child, including any reference to the child's own views on the application and the recommendation of the children and family reporter; and
(b)   if he does notify the child of any contents of his report, explain them to the child in a manner appropriate to his age and understanding.

(2)   Where the court has—

(a)   directed that a written report be made by a children and family reporter;

and

(b)   notified the children and family reporter that his report is to be considered at a hearing,
the children and family reporter shall—
    (i)   file the report; and
    (ii)   serve a copy on the other parties[, any local authority that is preparing, or has prepared, a report under section 14A(8) or (9)] and on the children's guardian (if any),
by such time as the court may direct, and if no direction is given, not less than 14 days before that hearing.

(3)   The court may direct that the children and family reporter attend any hearing at which his report is to be considered.

(4)   The children and family reporter shall advise the court if he considers that the joinder of a person as a party to the proceedings would be likely to safeguard the interests of the child.

(5)   The children and family reporter shall consider whether it is in the best interests of the child for the child to be made a party to the proceedings.

(6)   If the children and family reporter considers the child should be made a party to the proceedings he shall notify the court of his opinion together with the reasons for that opinion.]

Amendment

Inserted by SI 2001/821, r 20. Date in force: 1 April 2001: see SI 2001/821, r 1(b).
Para (2): in sub-para (b)(ii) words from ", any local authority" to "section 14A(8) or (9)" in square brackets inserted by SI 2005/2922, r 82.

4.12   Solicitor for child

(1)   A solicitor appointed under section 41(3) or in accordance with [rule 4.11A (1)(a)] shall represent the child—

(a)   in accordance with instructions received from the [children's guardian] (unless the solicitor considers, having taken into account the views of the [children's guardian] and any direction of the court under [rule 4.11A(3)], that the child wishes to give instructions which conflict with those of the [children's guardian] and that he is able, having regard to his understanding, to give such instructions on his own behalf in which case he shall conduct the proceedings in accordance with instructions received from the child), or

(b)   where no [children's guardian] has been appointed for the child and the condition in section 41(4)(b) is satisfied, in accordance with instructions received from the child, or

(c)   in default of instructions under (a) or (b), in furtherance of the best interests of the child.

(2)   A solicitor appointed under section 41(3) or in accordance with [rule 4.11A (1)(a)] shall serve and accept service of documents on behalf of the child in accordance with rule 4.8(3)(a) and (4)(a) and, where the child has not himself been served and has sufficient understanding, advise the child of the contents of any document so served.

(3)   Where the child wishes an appointment of a solicitor under section 41(3) or in accordance with [rule 4.11A (1)(a)] to be terminated, he may apply to the court for an order terminating the appointment; and the solicitor and the [children's guardian] shall be given an opportunity to make representations.

(4)   Where the [children's guardian] wishes an appointment of a solicitor under section 41(3) to be terminated, he may apply to the court for an order terminating the appointment; and the solicitor and, if he is of sufficient understanding, the child, shall be given an opportunity to make representations.

(5)   When terminating an appointment in accordance with paragraph (3) or (4), the court shall give its reasons for so doing, a note of which shall be taken by the court or the proper officer.

(6)   Where the court appoints a solicitor under section 41(3) or refuses to make such an appointment, the court or the proper officer shall record the appointment or refusal in Form [C48].

Date in force

14 October 1991: see r 1.1.

Amendment

Para (1): words "rule 4.11A (1)(a)" in square brackets substituted by SI 2001/821, r 21(a); in sub-para (a) words "children's guardian" in square brackets in each place they occur substituted by SI 2001/821, r 16(a); in sub-para (a) words "rule 4.11A(3)" in square brackets substituted by SI 2001/821, r 21(b); in sub-para (b) words "children's guardian" in square brackets substituted by SI 2001/821, r 16(a).
Para (2): words "rule 4.11A (1)(a)" in square brackets substituted by SI 2001/821, r 21(a).
Para (3): words "rule 4.11A (1)(a)" in square brackets substituted by SI 2001/821, r 21(a); words "children's guardian" in square brackets substituted by SI 2001/821, r 16(a).
Para (4): words "children's guardian" in square brackets substituted by SI 2001/821, r 16(a).
Para (6): figure "C48" substituted by SI 1994/3155, r 17.

[4.13   Welfare officer]

[(1)   Where the court has directed that a written report be made by a welfare officer [in accordance with section 7(1)(b)], the report shall be filed at or by such time as the court directs or, in the absence of such a direction, at least 14 days before a relevant hearing; and the proper officer shall, as soon as practicable, serve a copy of the report on the parties[, any local authority that is preparing, or has prepared, a report under section 14A(8) or (9)] and any [children's guardian].

(2)   In paragraph (1), a hearing is relevant if the proper officer has given the welfare officer notice that his report is to be considered at it.

(3)   After the filing of a report by a welfare officer, the court may direct that the welfare officer attend any hearing at which the report is to be considered; and

(a)   except where such a direction is given at a hearing attended by the welfare officer, the proper officer shall inform the welfare officer of the direction; and

(b)   at the hearing at which the report is considered any party may question the welfare officer about his report.

[(3A)   The welfare officer shall consider whether it is in the best interests of the child for the child to be made a party to the proceedings.

(3B)   If the welfare officer considers the child should be made a party to the proceedings he shall notify the court of his opinion together with the reasons for that opinion.]

(4)   This rule is without prejudice to any power to give directions under rule 4.14.]

Amendment

Substituted by SI 1992/2067, r 12.
Para (1): words "in accordance with section 7(1)(b)" in square brackets inserted by SI 2001/821, r 22(a); words from ", any local authority" to "section 14A(8) or (9)" in square brackets inserted by SI 2005/2922, r 82; words "children's guardian" in square brackets substituted by SI 2001/821, r 16(a).
Paras (3A), (3B): inserted by SI 2001/821, r 22(b).

[4.13A   Local authority officers preparing family assistance order reports]

[Where a family assistance order directs a local authority officer to prepare a family assistance order report, rules 4.5, 4.13, 4.14(1)(a)(i) and (2), 4.15(2) and 4.17(1) shall apply to, or in respect of, the local authority officer preparing a family assistance order report as they would apply to, or in respect of, a welfare officer preparing a report in accordance with section 7(1)(b).]

Date in force

14 October 1991: see r 1.1.

Amendment

Inserted by SI 2007/2187, rr 2, 3(b), 11.

4.14   Directions

[(1)   In this rule, "party" includes the children's guardian and, where a request or direction is or are concerned with—

(a)   a report under—
(i)   section 7, the welfare officer or children and family reporter;

(ii) section 14A(8) or (9), the local authority preparing that report;
(b) a family assistance order report, the officer of the service or the Welsh family proceedings officer who is preparing the report;
(c) a risk assessment, the officer of the service or the Welsh family proceedings officer who is preparing the assessment.]

(2) In proceedings to which this Part applies the court may, subject to paragraph (3), give, vary or revoke directions for the conduct of the proceedings, including—

(a) the timetable for the proceedings;
(b) varying the time within which or by which an act is required, by these rules or by other rules or court, to be done;
(c) the attendance of the child;
[(d) the appointment of a children's guardian, a guardian ad litem, or of a solicitor under section 41(3);]
(e) the service of documents;
(f) the submission of evidence including experts' reports;
(g) the preparation of welfare reports under section 7;
(h) the transfer of the proceedings to another court;
[(i) consolidation with other proceedings;
(j) the preparation of reports under section 14A(8) or (9);
(k) the attendance of the person who prepared the report under section 14A(8) or (9) at any hearing at which the report is to be considered][;
(l) the preparation of family assistance order reports;
(m) listing a hearing for the purposes of considering the contents of a risk assessment].

(3) Directions under paragraph (2) may be given, varied or revoked either—

(a) of the court's own motion having given the parties notice of its intention to do so, and an opportunity to attend and be heard or to make written representations,
(b) on the written request [in Form C2] of a party specifying the direction which is sought, filed and served on the other parties, or
(c) on the written request [in Form C2] of a party specifying the direction which is sought, to which the other parties consent and which they or their representatives have signed.

(4) In an urgent case the request under paragraph (3)(b) may, with the leave of the court, be made—

(a) orally, or
(b) without notice to the parties, or
(c) both as in sub-paragraph (a) and as in sub-paragraph (b).

(5) On receipt of a written request under paragraph (3)(b) the proper officer shall fix a date for the hearing of the request and give not less than 2 days' notice [in Form C6] to the parties of the date so fixed.

(6) On considering a request under paragraph (3)(c) the court shall either—

(a) grant the request, whereupon the proper officer shall inform the parties of the decision, or
(b) direct that a date be fixed for the hearing of the request, whereupon the proper officer shall fix such a date and give not less than 2 days' notice to the parties of the date so fixed.

(7) A party may apply for an order to be made under section 11(3) or, if he is entitled to apply for such an order, under section 38(1) in accordance with paragraph (3)(b) or (c).

(8)   Where a court is considering making, of its own motion, a section 8 order, or an order under section [14A, 14D,] 31, 34 or 38, the power to give directions under paragraph (2) shall apply.

(9)   Directions of a court which are still in force immediately prior to the transfer of proceedings to which this Part applies to another court shall continue to apply following the transfer, subject to any changes of terminology which are required to apply those directions to the court to which the proceedings are transferred, unless varied or discharged by directions under paragraph (2).

[(9A)   After the filing of a family assistance order report or a risk assessment, the court may direct that the officer of the service or the Welsh family proceedings officer attend any hearing at which the report or assessment is to be considered.]

(10)   The court or the proper officer shall take a note of the giving, variation or revocation of a direction under this rule and serve, as soon as practicable, a copy of the note on any party who was not present at the giving, variation or revocation.

Date in force

14 October 1991: see r 1.1.

Amendment

Para (1): substituted by SI 2007/2187, rr 2, 12(a).
Para (2): sub-para (d) substituted by SI 2001/821, r 23; sub-paras (i)–(k) substituted, for sub-para (i) as originally enacted, by SI 2005/2922, r 83(b); sub-paras (l), (m) and semi-colon immediately preceding it inserted by SI 2007/2187, rr 2,12(b).
Para (3): words "in Form C2" inserted by SI 1994/3155, r 18.
Para (5): words "in Form C6" inserted by SI 1994/3155, r 19.
Para (8): reference to "14A, 14D," in square brackets inserted by SI 2005/2922, r 83(c). Date in force: 30 December 2005: see SI 2005/2922, r 1(2); for transitional provisions see r 123 thereof.
Para (9A): inserted by SI 2007/2187, rr 2, 12(c).

4.15   Timing of proceedings

(1)   Where these rules or other rules of court provide a period of time within which or by which a certain act is to be performed in the course of proceedings to which this Part applies, that period may not be extended otherwise than by direction of the court under rule 4.14.

(2)   At the—

(a)   transfer to a court of proceedings to which this Part applies,
(b)   postponement or adjournment of any hearing or directions appointment in the course of proceedings to which this Part applies, or
(c)   conclusion of any such hearing or directions appointment other than one at which the proceedings are determined, or so soon thereafter as is practicable,

the court or the proper officer shall—

(i)   fix a date upon which the proceedings shall come before the court again for such purposes as the court directs, which date shall, where paragraph (a) applies, be as soon as possible after the transfer, and
(ii)   give notice to the parties, [any local authority that is preparing, or has prepared, a report under section 14A(8) or (9),] the [children's guardian][,] the [welfare officer[, the] children and family reporter][or the officer of the service or the Welsh family proceedings officer who is preparing or has prepared a family assistance order report or a risk assessment] of the date so fixed.

Date in force

14 October 1991: see r 1.1.

Amendment

Para (2): in sub-para (ii) words from "any local authority" to "section 14A(8) or (9)," in square brackets inserted by SI 2005/2922, r 84; in sub-para (ii) words "children's guardian" in square brackets substituted by SI 2001/821, r 16(a); in sub-para (ii) comma in square brackets substituted by SI 2007/2187, rr 2, 13(a). Date in force: 1 October 2007: see SI 2007/2187, r 1; in sub-para (ii) words "welfare officer or children and family reporter" in square brackets substituted by SI 2001/821, r 16(b). Date in force: 1 April 2001: see SI 2001/821, r 1(b); in sub-para (ii) word ", the" in square brackets substituted by SI 2007/2187, rr 2, 13(b); in sub-para (ii) words from "or the officer" to "a risk assessment" in square brackets inserted by SI 2007/2187, rr 2, 13(c).

4.16   Attendance at directions appointment and hearing

(1)   Subject to paragraph (2), a party shall attend a directions appointment of which he has been given notice in accordance with rule 4.14(5) unless the court otherwise directs.

(2)   Proceedings or any part of them shall take place in the absence of any party, including the child, if—

(a)   the court considers it in the interests of the child, having regard to the matters to be discussed or the evidence likely to be given, and

(b)   the party is represented by a [children's guardian] or solicitor;

and when considering the interests of the child under sub-paragraph (a) the court shall give the [children's guardian], the solicitor for the child and, if he is of sufficient understanding, the child an opportunity to make representations.

(3)   Subject to paragraph (4), where at the time and place appointed for a hearing or directions appointment the applicant appears but one or more of the respondents do not, the court may proceed with the hearing or appointment.

(4)   The court shall not begin to hear an application in the absence of a respondent unless—

(a)   it is proved to the satisfaction of the court that he received reasonable notice of the date of the hearing; or

(b)   the court is satisfied that the circumstances of the case justify proceeding with the hearing.

(5)   Where, at the time and place appointed for a hearing or directions appointment one or more of the respondents appear but the applicant does not, the court may refuse the application or, if sufficient evidence has previously been received, proceed in the absence of the applicant.

(6)   Where at the time and place appointed for a hearing or directions appointment neither the applicant nor any respondent appears, the court may refuse the application.

(7)   Unless the court otherwise directs, a hearing of, or directions appointment in, proceedings to which this Part applies shall be in chambers.

Date in force

14 October 1991: see r 1.1.

Appendix 2   *Family Proceedings Rules 1991*

Amendment

Para (2): words "children's guardian" in square brackets in both places they occur substituted by SI 2001/821, r 16(a).

4.17   Documentary evidence

(1)   Subject to paragraphs (4) and (5), in proceedings to which this Part applies a party shall file and serve on the parties, [any local authority that is preparing, or has prepared, a report under section 14A(8) or (9),] any [welfare officer[, any] children and family reporter][, any officer of the service or any Welsh family proceedings officer who is preparing or has prepared a family assistance order report or a risk assessment] and any [children's guardian] of whose appointment he has been given notice under rule 4.10(5)—

    (a)   written statements of the substance of the oral evidence which the party intends to adduce at a hearing of, or a directions appointment in, those proceedings, which shall—
       (i)   be dated,
      (ii)   be signed by the person making the statement, ...
     (iii)   contain a declaration that the maker of the statement believes it to be true and understands that it may be placed before the court; and
    [(iv)   show in the top right hand corner of the first page—
         (a)   the initials and surname of the person making the statement,
         (b)   the number of the statement in relation to the maker,
         (c)   the date on which the statement was made, and
         (d)   the party on whose behalf it is filed; and]
    (b)   copies of any documents, including experts' reports, upon which the party intends to rely at a hearing of, or a directions appointment in, those proceedings,

at or by such time as the court directs or, in the absence of a direction, before the hearing or appointment.

(2)   A party may, subject to any direction of the court about the timing of statements under this rule, file and serve on the parties a statement which is supplementary to a statement served under paragraph (1).

(3)   At a hearing or a directions appointment a party may not, without the leave of the court—

    (a)   adduce evidence, or
    (b)   seek to rely on a document,

in respect of which he has failed to comply with the requirements of paragraph (1).

(4)   In proceedings for a section 8 order [or a special guardianship order] a party shall—

    (a)   neither file nor serve any document other than as required or authorised by these rules, and
    (b)   in completing a form prescribed by these rules, neither give information, nor make a statement, which is not required or authorised by that form,

without the leave of the court.

(5)   In proceedings for a section 8 order [or a special guardianship order] no statement or copy may be filed under paragraph (1) until such time as the court directs.

Date in force

14 October 1991: see r 1.1.

Amendment

Para (1): words from "any local authority" to "section 14A(8) or (9)," in square brackets inserted by SI 2005/2922, r 85(a); words "welfare officer or children and family reporter" in square brackets substituted by SI 2001/821, r 16(b); word ", any" in square brackets substituted by SI 2007/2187, rr 2, 14(a); words from ", any officer of" to "a risk assessment" in square brackets inserted by SI 2007/2187, rr 2, 14(b); words "children's guardian" in square brackets substituted by SI 2001/821, r 16(a); in sub-para (a)(ii) word omitted revoked by SI 1992/2067, r 20; sub-para (a)(iv) inserted by SI 1992/2067, r 20.

Para (4): words "or a special guardianship order" in square brackets inserted by SI 2005/2922, r 85(b)

Para (5): words "or a special guardianship order" in square brackets inserted by SI 2005/2922, r 85(b).

[4.17A   Disclosure of report under section 14A(8) or (9)]

[(1)   In proceedings for a special guardianship order, the local authority shall file the report under section 14A(8) or (9) within the timetable fixed by the court.

(2)   The court shall consider whether to give a direction that the report under section 14A(8) or (9) be disclosed to each party to the proceedings.

(3)   Before giving such a direction the court shall consider whether any information should be deleted including information which reveals the party's address in a case where he has declined to reveal it in accordance with rule 10.21 (disclosure of addresses).

(4)   The court may direct that the report will not be disclosed to a party.

(5)   The proper officer shall serve a copy of the report filed under paragraph (1)—

      (i)   in accordance with any direction given under paragraph (2); and

      (ii)   on any children's guardian, welfare officer or children and family reporter.]

Amendment

Inserted by SI 2005/2922, r 86.

[4.17AA   Service of risk assessments]

[(1)   Where an officer of the service or a Welsh family proceedings officer has filed a risk assessment with the court, subject to paragraph (2), the proper officer shall as soon as practicable serve copies of the risk assessment on—

    (a)   each party; and

    (b)   any local authority that is preparing or has prepared a report under section 14A(8) or (9).

(2)   Before serving the risk assessment, the court must consider whether, in order to prevent a risk of harm to the child, it is necessary for—

    (a)   information to be deleted from a copy of the risk assessment before that copy is served on a party; or

    (b)   service of a copy of the risk assessment (whether with information deleted from it or not) on a party to be delayed for a specified period,

and may direct accordingly.]

Amendment

Inserted by SI 2007/2187, rr 2, 3(c), 15.

4.18   Expert evidence—examination of child

(1)   No person may, without the leave of the court, cause the child to be medically or psychiatrically examined, or otherwise assessed, for the purpose of the preparation of expert evidence for use in the proceedings.

(2)   An application for leave under paragraph (1) shall, unless the court otherwise directs, be served on all parties to the proceedings and on the [children's guardian].

(3)   Where the leave of the court has not been given under paragraph (1), no evidence arising out of an examination or assessment to which that paragraph applies may be adduced without the leave of the court.

Date in force

14 October 1991: see r 1.1.

Amendment

Para (2): words "children's guardian" in square brackets substituted by SI 2001/821, r 16(a). .

4.19   Amendment

(1)   Subject to rule 4.17(2), a document which has been filed or served in proceedings to which this Part applies, may not be amended without the leave of the court which shall, unless the court otherwise directs, be requested in writing.

(2)   On considering a request for leave to amend a document the court shall either—

   (a)   grant the request, whereupon the proper officer shall inform the person making the request of that decision, or
   (b)   invite the parties or any of them to make representations, within a specified period, as to whether such an order should be made.

(3)   A person amending a document shall file it and serve it on those persons on whom it was served prior to amendment; and the amendments shall be identified.

Date in force

14 October 1991: see r 1.1.

4.20   Oral evidence

The court or the proper officer shall keep a note of the substance of the oral evidence given at a hearing of, or directions appointment in, proceedings to which this Part applies.

Date in force

14 October 1991: see r 1.1.

4.21   Hearing

(1)   The court may give directions as to the order of speeches and evidence at a hearing, or directions appointment, in the course of proceedings to which this Part applies.

(2)   Subject to directions under paragraph (1), at a hearing of, or directions appointment in, proceedings to which this Part applies, the parties and the [children's guardian] shall adduce their evidence in the following order—

(a)   the applicant,
(b)   any party with parental responsibility for the child,
(c)   other respondents,
(d)   the [children's guardian],
(e)   the child, if he is a party to the proceedings and there is no [children's guardian].

[(2A)   At the hearing at which the report under section 14A(8) or (9) is considered a party to whom the report, or part of it, has been disclosed may question the person who prepared the report about it.]

(3)   After the final hearing of proceedings to which this Part applies, the court shall deliver its judgment as soon as is practicable.

[(4)   When making an order or when refusing an application, the court shall—

(a)   where it makes a finding of fact state such finding and complete Form C22; and
(b)   state the reason's for the court's decision].

(5)   An order made in proceedings to which this Part applies shall be recorded, by the court or the proper officer, either in the appropriate form in Appendix 1 to these rules or, where there is no such form, in writing.

(6)   Subject to paragraph (7), a copy of an order made in accordance with paragraph (5) shall, as soon as practicable after it has been made, be served by the proper officer on the parties to the proceedings in which it was made [and] on any person with whom the child is living[, and where applicable, on the local authority that prepared the report under section 14A(8) or (9)].

(7)   Within 48 hours after the making ex parte of—

(a)   a [section 8 order], or
(b)   an order under section 44, 48(4), 48(9) or 50,

the applicant shall serve a copy of the order in the appropriate form in Appendix 1 to these Rules on—

(i)   each party,
(ii)   any person who has actual care of the child or who had such care immediately prior to the making of the order, and
(iii)   in the case of an order referred to in sub-paragraph (b), the local authority in whose area the child lives or is found.

(8)   At a hearing of or directions appointment in, an application which takes place outside the hours during which the court office is normally open, the court or the proper officer shall take a note of the substance of the proceedings.

Date in force

14 October 1991: see r 1.1.

Amendment

Para (2): words "children's guardian" in square brackets substituted by SI 2001/821, r 16(a). ; in sub-para (d) words "children's guardian" in square brackets substituted by SI 2001/821, r 16(a); in sub-para (e) words "children's guardian" in square brackets substituted by SI 2001/821, r 16(a)
Para (2A): inserted by SI 2005/2922, r 87(a).
Para (4): substituted by SI 1994/3155, r 20.
Para (6): word "and" in square brackets inserted by SI 1992/456, r 14; words from ", and where applicable," to "section 14A(8) or (9)" in square brackets inserted by SI 2005/2922, r 87(b)
Para (7): in sub-para (a) words "section 8 order" in square brackets substituted by SI 1992/2067, r 10.

[4.21A   Attachment of penal notice]

[CCR Order 29, rule 1 (committal for breach of order or undertaking) shall apply to section 8 orders and orders under section 14A, 14B(2)(b), 14C(3)(b), or 14D as if for paragraph (3) of that rule there were substituted the following—

"(3)   In the case of a section 8 order (within the meaning of section 8(2) of the Children Act 1989) or an order under section 14A, 14B(2)(b), 14C(3)(b), or 14D of the Children Act 1989 enforceable by committal order under paragraph (1), the judge or the district judge may, on the application of the person entitled to enforce the order, direct that the proper officer issue a copy of the order, endorsed with or incorporating a notice as to the consequences of disobedience, for service in accordance with paragraph (2); and no copy of the order shall be issued with any such notice endorsed or incorporated save in accordance with such a direction.]

Amendment

Inserted by SI 1992/2067, r 13.
Substituted by SI 2005/2922, r 88.

4.22   Appeals

(1)   Where an appeal lies—

   (a)   to the High Court under section 94, or
   (b)   from any decision of a district judge to the judge of the court in which the decision was made,

it shall be made in accordance with the following provisions; and references to "the court below" are references to the court from which, or person from whom, the appeal lies.

(2)   The appellant shall file and serve on the parties to the proceedings in the court below, and on any [children's guardian] [and where applicable, on the local authority that prepared a report under section 14A(8) or (9)],

   (a)   notice of the appeal in writing, setting out the grounds upon which he relies;
   (b)   a certified copy of the summons or application and of the order appealed against, and of any order staying its execution;
   (c)   a copy of any notes of the evidence;
   (d)   a copy of any reasons given for the decision.

[(2A)   In relation to an appeal to the High Court under section 94, the documents required to be filed by paragraph (2) shall,—

   (a)   where the care centre listed in column (ii) of Schedule 2 to the Children (Allocation of Proceedings) Order 1991 against the entry in column (i) relating to the [local justice area] in which the court below is situated—
     (i)   is the principal registry, or
     (ii)   has a district registry in the same place,
   be filed in that registry, and
   (b)   in any other case, be filed in the district registry, being in the same place as a care centre within the meaning of article 2(c) of the said Order, which is nearest to the court below.]

(3)   The notice of appeal shall be filed and served in accordance with paragraph (2)(a)—

   (a)   within 14 days after the determination against which the appeal is brought, or

(b)   in the case of an appeal against an order under section 38(1), within 7 days after the making of the order, or

(c)   with the leave of the court to which, or judge to whom, the appeal is to be brought, within such other time as that court or judge may direct.

(4)   The documents mentioned in paragraph (2)(b) to (d) shall, subject to any direction of the court to which, or judge to whom, the appeal is to be brought, be filed and served as soon as practicable after the filing and service of the notice of appeal under paragraph (2)(a).

(5)   Subject to paragraph (6), a respondent who wishes—

(a)   to contend on the appeal that the decision of the court below should be varied, either in any event or in the event of the appeal being allowed in whole or in part, or

(b)   to contend that the decision of the court below should be affirmed on grounds other than those relied upon by that court, or

(c)   to contend by way of cross-appeal that the decision of the court below was wrong in whole or in part,

shall, within 14 days of receipt of notice of the appeal, file and serve on all other parties to the appeal a notice in writing, setting out the grounds upon which he relies.

(6)   No notice under paragraph (5) may be filed or served in an appeal against an order under section 38.

(7)   In the case of an appeal mentioned in paragraph (1)(a), an application to—

(a)   withdraw the appeal,
(b)   have the appeal dismissed with the consent of all the parties, or
(c)   amend the grounds of appeal,

may be heard by a district judge.

(8)   An appeal of the kind mentioned in paragraph (1)(a) shall, unless the President otherwise directs, be heard and determined by a single judge.

Date in force

14 October 1991: see r 1.1.

Amendment

Para (2): words "children's guardian" in square brackets substituted by SI 2001/821, r 16(a); words from "and where applicable," to "section 14A(8) or (9)" in square brackets inserted by SI 2005/2922, r 89.
Para (2A): inserted by SI 1992/2067, r 4; in sub-para (a) words "local justice area" in square brackets substituted by SI 2005/617, art 2, Schedule, para 127.

4.23   ...

...

Amendment

Revoked by SI 2005/1976, rr 2, 4.

4.24   Notification of consent

[(1)]   Consent for the purposes of—

(a)   section 16(3), [or]

[(b)   section 38A(2)(b)(ii) or 44A(2)(b)(ii), or]

(c)   paragraph 19(3)(c) or (d) of Schedule 2,

shall be given either—

(i)   orally in court, or

(ii)   in writing to the court signed by the person giving his consent.

[(2)   Any written consent given for the purposes of subsection (2) of section 38A or section 44A, shall include a statement that the person giving consent—

(a)   is able and willing to give to the child the care which it would be reasonable to expect a parent to give him; and

(b)   understands that the giving of consent could lead to the exclusion of the relevant person from the dwelling-house in which the child lives.]

Date in force

14 October 1991: see r 1.1.

Amendment

Para (1): numbered as such by SI 1997/1893, rr 3(1), 9; in sub-para (a) word "or" inserted by SI 1992/456, r 15.; original sub-para (b) revoked by SI 1992/456, r 15; new sub-para (b) inserted by SI 1997/1893, rr 3(2), 9.

Para (2): inserted by SI 1997/1893, rr 3(2), 9.

[4.24A   Exclusion requirements: interim care orders and emergency protection orders]

[(1)   This rule applies where the court includes an exclusion requirement in an interim care order or an emergency protection order.

(2)   The applicant for an interim care order or emergency protection order shall—

(a)   prepare a separate statement of the evidence in support of the application for an exclusion requirement;

(b)   serve the statement personally on the relevant person with a copy of the order containing the exclusion requirement (and of any power of arrest which is attached to it);

(c)   inform the relevant person of his right to apply to vary or discharge the exclusion requirement.

(3)   Where a power of arrest is attached to an exclusion requirement in an interim care order or an emergency protection order, a copy of the order shall be delivered to the officer for the time being in charge of the police station for the area in which the dwelling-house in which the child lives is situated (or of such other station as the court may specify) together with a statement showing that the relevant person has been served with the order or informed of its terms (whether by being present when the order was made or by telephone or otherwise).

(4)   Rules 3.9(5), 3.9A (except paragraphs (1) and (3)) and 3.10 shall apply, with the necessary modifications, for the service, variation, discharge and enforcement of any exclusion requirement to which a power of arrest is attached as they apply to an order made on an application under Part IV of the Family Law Act 1996.

(5)   The relevant person shall serve the parties to the proceedings with any application which he makes for the variation or discharge of the exclusion requirement.

(6)   Where an exclusion requirement ceases to have effect whether—

(a)   as a result of the removal of a child under section 38A(10) or 44A(10),

(b) because of the discharge of the interim care order or emergency protection order, or

(c) otherwise,

the applicant shall inform—

(i) the relevant person,

(ii) the parties to the proceedings,

(iii) any officer to whom a copy of the order was delivered under paragraph (3), and

(iv) (where necessary) the court.

(7) Where the court includes an exclusion requirement in an interim care order or an emergency protection order of its own motion, paragraph (2) shall apply with the omission of any reference to the statement of the evidence.]

Amendment

Inserted by SI 1997/1893, rr 4, 9.

4.25 Secure accommodation—evidence

In proceedings under section 25, the court shall, if practicable, arrange for copies of all written reports before it to be made available before the hearing to—

(a) the applicant;

(b) the parent or guardian of the child;

(c) any legal representative of the child;

(d) the [children's guardian]; and

(e) the child, unless the court otherwise directs;

and copies of such reports may, if the court considers it desirable, be shown to any person who is entitled to notice of the proceedings in accordance with these rules.

Date in force

14 October 1991: see r 1.1.

Amendment

In para (d) words "children's guardian" in square brackets substituted by SI 2001/821, r 16(a).

4.26 Investigation under section 37

(1) This rule applies where a direction is given to an appropriate authority by the High Court or a county court under section 37(1).

(2) On giving a direction the court shall adjourn the proceedings and the court or the proper officer shall record the direction [in Form C40].

(3) A copy of the direction recorded under paragraph (2) shall, as soon as practicable after the direction is given, be served by the proper officer on the parties to the proceedings in which the direction is given and, where the appropriate authority is not a party, on that authority.

(4) When serving the copy of the direction on the appropriate authority the proper officer shall also serve copies of such of the documentary evidence which has been, or is to be, adduced in the proceedings as the court may direct.

(5) Where a local authority informs the court of any of the matters set out in section 37(3)(a) to (c) it shall do so in writing.

Date in force

14 October 1991: see r 1.1.

Amendment

Para (2): words "in Form C40" substituted by SI 1994/3155, r 21.

4.27 Direction to local education authority to apply for education supervision order

(1) For the purposes of section 40(3) and (4) of the Education Act 1944 a direction by the High Court or a county court to a local education authority to apply for an education supervision order shall be given [in writing].

(2) Where, following such a direction, a local education authority informs the court that they have decided not to apply for an education supervision order, they shall do so in writing.

Date in force

14 October 1991: see r 1.1.

Amendment

Para (1): words "in writing" in square brackets substituted by SI 1997/1893, r 15.

[4.27A Stay under the Council Regulation]

[(1) An application for an order under Article 19 of the Council Regulation shall be made to a district judge, who may determine the application or refer the application, or any question arising thereon, to a judge for his decision.

(2) Where at any time after an application under rule 4.4 is made, it appears to the court that, under Articles 16 to 19 of the Council Regulation, the court does not have jurisdiction to hear the application and is required or may be required to stay the proceedings, the court will stay the proceedings and fix a date for a hearing to determine the questions of jurisdiction and whether there should be a stay or other order and shall serve notice of the hearing on the parties to the proceedings.

(3) The court must give reasons for its decision under Articles 16 to 19 of the Council Regulation and, where it makes a finding of fact state such a finding of fact.

(4) A declaration under Article 17 of the Council Regulation that the court has no jurisdiction over the proceedings shall be recorded by the court or proper officer in writing.

(5) The court may, if all parties agree, deal with any question about the jurisdiction of the court without a hearing.]

Amendment

Inserted by SI 2005/264, r 6.

4.28 Transitional provision

Nothing in any provision of this Part of these rules shall affect any proceedings which are pending (within the meaning of paragraph 1 of Schedule 14 to the Act of 1989) immediately before these rules come into force.

Date in force

14 October 1991: see r 1.1.

[PART IVA
PROCEEDINGS UNDER SECTION 30 OF THE HUMAN FERTILISATION AND EMBRYOLOGY
ACT 1990]

[Not reproduced]

PART V
WARDSHIP

[Not reproduced]

PART VI
CHILD ABDUCTION AND CUSTODY ...

[Not reproduced]

PART VII
ENFORCEMENT OF ORDERS

[Not reproduced]

PART VIII
APPEALS

[Not reproduced]

PART IX
DISABILITY

9.1   Interpretation and application of Part IX

(1)   In this Part—

["the 2005 Act" means the Mental Capacity Act 2005;]
["child" means a person under 18;]
["deputy" has the meaning given in section 16(2)(b) of the 2005 Act;]
["enduring power of attorney" has the meaning given in Schedule 4 to the 2005
    Act;]
["lasting power of attorney" has the meaning given in section 9 of the 2005 Act;]
...
...
...

["protected party" means a party, or an intended party, who lacks capacity (within
    the meaning of the 2005 Act) to conduct the proceedings;]

(2)   So far as they relate to [children] [who are the subject of applications], the
provisions of this Part of these rules shall not apply to proceedings which are specified
proceedings within the meaning of section 41(6) of the Children Act 1989 and, with
respect to proceedings which are dealt with together with specified proceedings, this
Part shall have effect subject to the said section 41 and Part IV of these rules.

[(3)   Rule 9.2A shall apply only to proceedings under the Act of 1989 or the inherent
jurisdiction of the High Court with respect to [children].]

Date in force

14 October 1991: see r 1.1.

Amendment

Para (1): definition "the 2005 Act" inserted by SI 2007/2187, rr 2, 16(b); definition "child" inserted by SI 2007/2187, rr 2, 16(b); definition "deputy" inserted by SI 2007/2187, rr 2, 16(b); definition "enduring power of attorney" inserted by SI 2007/2187, rr 2, 16(b); definition "lasting power of attorney" inserted by SI 2007/2187, rr 2, 16(b); definition "patient" (omitted) revoked by SI 2007/2187, rr 2, 16(1)(a)(i); definition "person under disability" (omitted) revoked by SI 2007/2187, rr 2, 16(1)(a)(ii); definition "Part VII" (omitted) revoked by SI 2007/2187, rr 2, 16(1)(a)(iii); definition "protected party" inserted by SI 2007/2187, rr 2, 16(b)
Para (2): word "children" in square brackets substituted by SI 2007/2187, rr 2, 16(2); words "who are the subject of applications" inserted by SI 1991/2113, r 16.
Para (3): inserted by SI 1992/456, r 6; word "children" in square brackets substituted by SI 2007/2187, rr 2, 16(3).

9.2 **[Child or protected party] must sue by next friend etc**

(1) [Except where rule 9.2A or any other rule otherwise provides, a [child or protected party] may begin and prosecute any family proceedings only by his next friend and may defend any such proceedings only] by his guardian ad litem and, except as otherwise provided by this rule, it shall not be necessary for a guardian ad litem to be appointed by the court.

(2) No person's name shall be used in any proceedings as next friend of a [child or protected party] unless he is the Official Solicitor or the documents mentioned in paragraph (7) have been filed.

(3) Where a person [has authority as a deputy] to conduct legal proceedings in the name of a [protected party] or on his behalf, that person shall, subject to [paragraph (2)], be entitled to be next friend or guardian ad litem of the [protected party] in any family proceedings to which his [power] extends.

(4) Where a person entitled to defend any family proceedings is a [protected party] and there is no person [with authority as a deputy] to defend the proceedings in his name or on his behalf, then—

  (a) the Official Solicitor shall, if he consents, be the [protected party's] guardian ad litem, but at any stage of the proceedings an application may be made on not less than four days' notice to the Official Solicitor, for the appointment of some other person as guardian;
  (b) in any other case, an application may be made on behalf of the [protected party] for the appointment of a guardian ad litem;

and there shall be filed in support of any application under this paragraph the documents mentioned in paragraph (7).

(5) Where a petition, answer, originating application or originating summons has been served on a person whom there is reasonable ground for believing to be a [child or protected party] and no notice of intention to defend has been given, or answer or affidavit in answer filed, on his behalf, the party at whose instance the document was served shall, before taking any further steps in the proceedings, apply to a district judge for directions as to whether a guardian ad litem should be appointed to act for that person in the cause, and on any such application the district judge may, if he considers it necessary in order to protect the interests of the person served, order that some proper person be appointed his guardian ad litem.

(6) [Except where a [child] is prosecuting or defending proceedings under rule 9.2A, no] notice of intention to defend shall be given, or answer or affidavit in answer filed, by or on behalf of a person under disability unless the person giving the notice or filing the answer or affidavit—

(a) is the Official Solicitor or, in a case to which paragraph (4) applies, is the Official Solicitor or has been appointed by the court to be guardian ad litem; or

(b) in any other case, has filed the documents mentioned in paragraph (7).

(7) The documents referred to in paragraphs (2), (4) and (6) are—

(a) a written consent to act by the proposed next friend or guardian ad litem;

(b) where the person ... is a [protected party] and the proposed next friend or guardian ad litem is [has authority as a deputy] to conduct the proceedings in his name or on his behalf, an office copy, sealed with the seal of the Court of Protection, of [the document conferring his authority to act]; and

(c) except where the proposed next friend or guardian ad litem is authorised as mentioned in sub-paragraph (b), a certificate by the solicitor acting for the person under disability—

(i) that he knows or believes that the person to whom the certificate relates is a [child] or [protected party], stating (in the case of a [protected party]) the grounds of his knowledge or belief and, where the person ... is a [protected party], that there is no person [with authority as a deputy to conduct the proceedings in the name of a protected party or on his behalf], and

(ii) that the person named in the certificate as next friend or guardian ad litem has no interest in the cause or matter in question adverse to that of the [child or protected party] and that he is a proper person to be next friend or guardian.

Date in force

14 October 1991: see r 1.1.

Amendment

Provision heading: words "Child or protected party" in square brackets substituted by SI 2007/2187, rr 2, 17(1).
Para (1): words from "Except where rule" to "such proceedings only" substituted by SI 1992/456, r 7; words "child or protected party" in square brackets substituted by SI 2007/2187, rr 2, 17(2)(a)
Para (2): words "child or protected party" in square brackets substituted by SI 2007/2187, rr 2, 17(2)(a).
Para (3): words "has authority as a deputy" in square brackets substituted by SI 2007/2187, rr 2, 17(2)(d); words "protected party" in square brackets in both places they occur substituted by SI 2007/2187, rr 2, 17(2)(b);: words "paragraph (2)" substituted by SI 1991/2113, r 17; word "power" in square brackets substituted by SI 2007/2187, rr 2, 17(3).
Para (4): words "protected party" in square brackets in both places they occur substituted by SI 2007/2187, rr 2, 17(2)(b); words "with authority as a deputy" in square brackets substituted by SI 2007/2187, rr 2, 17(4); in sub-para (a) words "protected party's" in square brackets substituted by virtue of SI 2007/2187, rr 2, 17(2)(b).
Para (5): words "child or protected party" in square brackets substituted by SI 2007/2187, rr 2, 17(2)(a).
Para (6): words "Except where a minor is prosecuting or defending proceedings under rule 9.2A, no" substituted by SI 1992/456, r 8. Para (6): word "child" in square brackets substituted by SI 2007/2187, rr 2, 17(2)(c).
Para (7): in sub-para (b) words omitted revoked by SI 2007/2187, rr 2, 17(5)(a)(i); in sub-para (b) words "protected party" in square brackets substituted by SI 2007/2187, rr (2), 17(2)(b); in sub-para (b) words "has authority as a deputy" in square brackets substituted by SI 2007/2187,

rr 2, 17(2)(d); in sub-para (b) words "the document conferring his authority to act" in square brackets substituted by SI 2007/2187, rr 2, 17(5)(a)(ii); in sub-para (c)(i) word "child" in square brackets substituted by SI 2007/2187, rr 2, 17(2)(c); in sub-para (c)(i) words "protected party" in square brackets in each place they occur substituted by SI 2007/2187, rr 2, 17(2)(b);: in sub-para (b) words omitted revoked by SI 2007/2187, rr 2, 17(5)(b)(i); in sub-para (c)(i) words from "with authority as" to "on his behalf" in square brackets substituted by SI 2007/2187, rr 2, 17(5)(b)(ii); in sub-para (c)(ii) words "child or protected party" in square brackets substituted by SI 2007/2187, rr 2, 17(2)(a).

[9.2A   Certain [children] may sue without next friend etc]

[(1)   Where a person entitled to begin, prosecute or defend any proceedings to which this rule applies, is a [child] to whom this Part applies, he may, subject to paragraph (4), begin, prosecute or defend, as the case may be, such proceedings without a next friend or guardian ad litem—

- (a)   where he has obtained the leave of the court for that purpose; or
- (b)   where a solicitor—
  - (i)   considers that the [child] is able, having regard to his understanding, to give instructions in relation to the proceedings; and
  - (ii)   has accepted instructions from the [child] to act for him in the proceedings and, where the proceedings have begun, is so acting.

(2)   A [child] shall be entitled to apply for the leave of the court under paragraph (1)(a) without a next friend or guardian ad litem either—

- (a)   by filing a written request for leave setting out the reasons for the application, or
- (b)   by making an oral request for leave at any hearing in the proceedings.

(3)   On considering a request for leave filed under paragraph (2)(a), the court shall either—

- (a)   grant the request, whereupon the proper officer shall communicate the decision to the [child] and, where the leave relates to the prosecution or defence of existing proceedings, to the other parties to those proceedings, or
- (b)   direct that the request be heard *ex parte*, whereupon the proper officer shall fix a date for such a hearing and give to the [child] making the request such notice of the date so fixed as the court may direct.

(4)   Where a [child] has a next friend or guardian ad litem in proceedings and the [child] wishes to prosecute or defend the remaining stages of the proceedings without a next friend or guardian ad litem, the [child] may apply to the court for leave for that purpose and for the removal of the next friend or guardian ad litem; and paragraph (2) shall apply to the application as if it were an application under paragraph (1)(a).

(5)   On considering a request filed under paragraph (2) by virtue of paragraph (4), the court shall either—

- (a)   grant the request, whereupon the proper officer shall communicate the decision to the [child] and next friend or guardian ad litem concerned and to all other parties to the proceedings, or
- (b)   direct that the request be heard, whereupon the proper officer shall fix a date for such a hearing and give to the [child] and next friend or guardian ad litem concerned such notice of the date so fixed as the court may direct;

provided that the court may act under sub-paragraph (a) only if it is satisfied that the next friend or guardian ad litem does not oppose the request.

(6)   Where the court is considering whether to

- (a)   grant leave under paragraph (1)(a), or

(b)   grant leave under paragraph (4) and remove a next friend or guardian ad litem,

it shall grant the leave sought and, as the case may be, remove the next friend or guardian ad litem if it considers that the [child] concerned has sufficient understanding to participate as a party in the proceedings concerned or proposed without a next friend or guardian ad litem.

[(6A)   In exercising its powers under paragraph (6) the court may order the next friend or guardian ad litem to take such part in the proceedings as the court may direct.]

(7)   Where a request for leave is granted at a hearing fixed under paragraph (3)(b) (in relation to the prosecution or defence of proceedings already begun) or (5)(b), the proper officer shall forthwith communicate the decision to the other parties to the proceedings.

(8)   The court may revoke any leave granted under paragraph (1)(a) where it considers that the child does not have sufficient understanding to participate as a party in the proceedings concerned without a next friend or guardian ad litem.

(9)   Without prejudice to any requirement of CCR Order 50, rule 5 or RSC Order 67, where a solicitor is acting for a [child] in proceedings which the [child] is prosecuting or defending without a next friend or guardian ad litem by virtue of paragraph (1)(b) and either of the conditions specified in paragraph (1)(b)(i) and (ii) cease to be fulfilled, he shall forthwith so inform the court.

(10)   Where—

(a)   the court revokes any leave under paragraph (8), or
(b)   either of the conditions specified in paragraph (1)(b)(i) and (ii) is no longer fulfilled,

the court may, if it considers it necessary in order to protect the interests of the [child] concerned, order that some proper person be appointed his next friend or guardian ad litem.

(11)   Where a [child] is of sufficient understanding to begin, prosecute or defend proceedings without a next friend or guardian ad litem—

(a)   he may nevertheless begin, prosecute or defend them by his next friend or guardian ad litem; and
(b)   where he is prosecuting or defending proceedings by his next friend or guardian ad litem, the respective powers and duties of the [child] and next friend or guardian ad litem, except those conferred or imposed by this rule, shall not be affected by the minor's ability to dispense with a next friend or guardian ad litem under the provisions of this rule.]

Amendment

Inserted by SI 1992/456, r 9.
Provision heading: word "children" in square brackets substituted by SI 2007/2187, rr 2, 18(1).
Paras (1)–(6): word "child" in square brackets in each place they occur substituted by SI 2007/2187, rr 2, 18(2).
Paras (9)–(11): word "child" in square brackets in each place they occur substituted by SI 2007/2187, rr 2, 18(2).

9.3   Service on [child or protected party]

(1)   Where a document to which rule 2.9 applies is required to be served on a [child or protected party] ... , it shall be served—

(a)   in the case of a [child] who is not also a [protected party], on his father or guardian or, if he has no father or guardian, on the person with whom he resides or in whose care he is;

(b)   in the case of a [protected party]—

[(i)   on the person (if any) who is the attorney of a registered enduring power of attorney, donee of a lasting power of attorney or deputy of the protected party, or]

(ii)   if there is no [attorney of a registered enduring power of attorney, donee of a lasting power of attorney or deputy of the protected party], on the Official Solicitor if he has consented under rule 9.2(4) to be the guardian ad litem of the [protected party], or

(iii)   in any other case, on the person with whom the [protected party] resides or in whose care he is:

Provided that the court may order that a document which has been, or is to be, served on the [child or protected party] or on a person other than one mentioned in sub-paragraph (a) or (b) shall be deemed to be duly served on the [child or protected party].

(2)   Where a document is served in accordance with paragraph (1) it shall be indorsed with a notice in Form M24; and after service has been effected the person at whose instance the document was served shall, unless the Official Solicitor is the guardian ad litem of the [child or protected party] or the court otherwise directs, file an affidavit by the person on whom the document was served stating whether the contents of the document were, or its purport was, communicated to the [child or protected party] and, if not, the reasons for not doing so.

Date in force

14 October 1991: see r 1.1.

Amendment

Provision heading: words "child or protected party" in square brackets substituted by SI 2007/2187, rr 2, 19(1).

Para (1): words "child or protected party in square brackets substituted by SI 2007/2187, rr 2, 19(2)(a); words omitted revoked by SI 1992/2067, r 21; in sub-para (a) word "child" in square brackets substituted by SI 2007/2187, rr 2, 19(3); in sub-para (a) words "protected party" in square brackets substituted by SI 2007/2187, rr 2, 19(2)(b); in sub-para (b) words "protected party" in square brackets substituted by SI 2007/2187, rr 2, 19(2)(b); sub-para (b)(i) substituted by SI 2007/2187, rr 2, 19(4); in sub-para (b)(ii) words from "attorney of a" to "the protected party" in square brackets substituted by SI 2007/2187, rr 2,19(5); in sub-para (b)(ii) words "protected party" in square brackets substituted by SI 2007/2187, rr 2, 19(2)(b); in sub-para (b)(iii) words "protected party" in square brackets substituted by SI 2007/2187, rr 2, 19(2)(b); in sub-para (b) words "child or protected party" in square brackets substituted by SI 2007/2187, rr 2, 19(2)(a).

Para (2): words "child or protected party" in square brackets in both places they occur substituted by SI 2007/2187, rr 2, 19(2)(a).

9.4

...

9.5   Separate representation of children

[(1)Without prejudice to rules 2.57 and 9.2A [and to paragraph 2 of Appendix 4], if in any family proceedings it appears to the court that it is in the best interest of any child to be made a party to the proceedings, the court may appoint—

(a)   an officer of the service [or a Welsh family proceedings officer];

(b) (if he consents) the Official Solicitor; or

(c) (if he consents) some other proper person,

to be the guardian ad litem of the child with authority to take part in the proceedings on the child's behalf.]

(2)   An order under paragraph (1) may be made by the court of its own motion or on the application of a party to the proceedings or of the proposed guardian ad litem.

(3)   The court may at any time direct that an application be made by a party for an order under paragraph (1) and may stay the proceedings until the application has been made.

(4)   ...

(5)   Unless otherwise directed, a person appointed under this rule or rule 2.57 [or under paragraph 2 of Appendix 4] to be the guardian ad litem of a child in any family proceedings shall be treated as a party for the purpose of any provision of these rules requiring a document to be served on or notice to be given to a party to the proceedings.

[(6)   Where the guardian ad litem appointed under this rule is an officer of the service [or a Welsh family proceedings officer], rules 4.11 and 4.11A shall apply to him as they apply to a children's guardian appointed under section 41 of the Children Act 1989.]

Date in force

14 October 1991: see r 1.1.

Amendment

Para (1): substituted by SI 2001/821, r 31(a); words "and to paragraph 2 of Appendix 4" in square brackets inserted by SI 2005/2922, r 102(a); in sub-para (a) words "or a Welsh family proceedings officer" in square brackets inserted by SI 2005/559, r 16.
Para (4): revoked by SI 2001/821, r 31(b).
Para (5): words "or under paragraph 2 of Appendix 4" in square brackets inserted by SI 2005/2922, r 102(b).
Para (6): inserted by SI 2001/821, r 31(c); words "or a Welsh family proceedings officer" in square brackets inserted by SI 2005/559, r 16.

PART X
PROCEDURE (GENERAL)

PART X
PROCEDURE (GENERAL)

...

[**10.20A**   **Communication of information relating to proceedings**]

[(1)   This rule applies to proceedings held in private to which these Rules apply where the proceedings—

(a) relate to the exercise of the inherent jurisdiction of the High Court with respect to minors;

(b) are brought under the Act of 1989; or

(c) otherwise relate wholly or mainly to the maintenance or upbringing of a minor.

(2)   For the purposes of the law relating to contempt of court, information relating to the proceedings (whether or not contained in a document filed with the court) may be communicated—

(a)   where the court gives permission;

(b)   subject to any direction of the court, in accordance with paragraphs (3) or (4) of this rule; or

(c)   where the communication is to—
   (i) a party,
   (ii) the legal representative of a party,
   (iii) a professional legal adviser,
   (iv) an officer of the service or a Welsh family proceedings officer,
   (v) the welfare officer,
   (vi) the Legal Services Commission,
   (vii) an expert whose instruction by a party has been authorised by the court, or
   (viii) a professional acting in furtherance of the protection of children.

(3)   A person specified in the first column of the following table may communicate to a person listed in the second column such information as is specified in the third column for the purpose or purposes specified in the fourth column.

Communication of information without permission of the court

Communicated by	To	Information	Purpose
A party	A lay adviser or a McKenzie Friend	Any information relating to the proceedings	To enable the party to obtain advice or assistance in relation to the proceedings.
A party	The party's spouse, [civil partner,] cohabitant or close family member		For the purpose of confidential discussions enabling the party to receive support from his spouse, [civil partner,] cohabitant or close family member.
A party	A health care professional or a person or body providing counselling services for children or families		To enable the party or any child of the party to obtain health care or counselling.

Communicated by	To	Information	Purpose
[A party	The Secretary of State, a McKenzie Friend, a lay adviser or an appeal tribunal dealing with an appeal made under section 20 of the Child Support Act 1991		For the purposes of making or responding to an appeal under section 20 of the Child Support Act 1991 or the determination of such an appeal.
A party	An adoption panel		For the purposes of making or responding to an appeal under section 20 of the Child Support Act 1991 or the determination of such an appeal.]
A party or any person lawfully in receipt of information	The Children's Commissioner or the Children's Commissioner for Wales		To refer an issue affecting the interests of children to the Children's Commissioner or the Children's Commissioner for Wales.
A party or a legal representative	A mediator		For the purpose of mediation in relation to the proceedings.
A party, any person lawfully in receipt of information or a proper officer	A person or body conducting an approved research project		For the purpose of an approved research project.
A party, a legal representative or a professional legal adviser	A person or body responsible for investigating or determining complaints in relation to legal representatives or professional legal advisers		For the purposes of making a complaint or the investigation or determination of a complaint in relation to a legal representative or a professional legal adviser.

Communicated by	To	Information	Purpose
A legal representative or a professional legal adviser	A person or body assessing quality assurance systems		To enable the legal representative or professional legal adviser to obtain a quality assurance assessment.
A legal representative or a professional legal adviser	An accreditation body	Any information relating to the proceedings providing that it does not, or is not likely to, identify any person involved in the proceedings	To enable the legal representative or professional legal adviser to obtain accreditation.
A party	An elected representative or peer	The text or summary of the whole or part of a judgment given in the proceedings	To enable the elected representative or peer to give advice, investigate any complaint or raise any question of policy or procedure.
A party	The General Medical Council		For the purpose of making a complaint to the General Medical Council.
A party	A police officer		For the purpose of a criminal investigation.
A party or any person lawfully in receipt of information	A member of the Crown Prosecution Service		To enable the Crown Prosecution Service to discharge its functions under any enactment.

(4) A person in the second column of the table in paragraph (3) may only communicate information relating to the proceedings received from a person in the first column for the purpose or purposes—

    (a) for which he received that information, or

    (b) of professional development or training, providing that any communication does not, or is not likely to, identify any person involved in the proceedings without that person's consent.

(5)   In this rule—

"accreditation body" means—
  (a)   The Law Society,
  (b)   Resolution, or
  (c)   The Legal Services Commission;
["adoption panel" means a panel established in accordance with regulation 3 of the Adoption Agencies Regulations 2005 or regulation 3 of the Adoption Agencies (Wales) Regulations 2005;]
"approved research project" means a project of research—
  (a)   approved in writing by a Secretary of State after consultation with the President of the Family Division,
  (b)   approved in writing by the President of the Family Division, or
  (c)   conducted under section 83 of the Act of 1989 or section 13 of the Criminal Justice and Court Services Act 2000;
"body assessing quality assurance systems" includes—
  (a)   The Law Society,
  (b)   The Legal Services Commission, or
  (c)   The General Council of the Bar;
"body or person responsible for investigating or determining complaints in relation to legal representatives or professional legal advisers" means—
  (a)   The Law Society,
  (b)   The General Council of the Bar,
  (c)   The Institute of Legal Executives, or
  (d)   The Legal Services Ombudsman;
["cohabitant" means one of two persons who are neither married to each other nor civil partners of each other but are living together as husband and wife or as if they were civil partners;]
"criminal investigation" means an investigation conducted by police officers with a view to it being ascertained—
  (a)   whether a person should be charged with an offence, or
  (b)   whether a person charged with an offence is guilty of it;
"elected representative" means—
  (a)   a member of the House of Commons,
  (b)   a member of the National Assembly for Wales, or
  (c)   a member of the European Parliament elected in England and Wales;
"health care professional" means—
  (a)   a registered medical practitioner,
  (b)   a registered nurse or midwife,
  (c)   a clinical psychologist, or
  (d)   a child psychotherapist;
"lay adviser" means a non-professional person who gives lay advice on behalf of an organisation in the lay advice sector;
"legal representative" means a barrister or a solicitor, solicitor's employee or other authorised litigator (as defined in the Courts and Legal Services Act 1990) who has been instructed to act for a party in relation to the proceedings;
"McKenzie Friend" means any person permitted by the court to sit beside an unrepresented litigant in court to assist that litigant by prompting, taking notes and giving him advice;
"mediator" means a family mediator who is—
  (a)   undertaking, or has successfully completed, a family mediation training course approved by the United Kingdom College of Family Mediators, or
  (b)   a member of the Law Society's Family Mediation Panel;
"peer" means a member of the House of Lords as defined by the House of Lords Act 1999;
"professional acting in furtherance of the protection of children" includes—

(a)   an officer of a local authority exercising child protection functions,

(b)   a police officer who is—
  (i)   exercising powers under section 46 of the Act of 1989, or
  (ii)   serving in a child protection unit or a paedophile unit of a police force;

(c)   any professional person attending a child protection conference or review in relation to a child who is the subject of the proceedings to which the information relates, or

(d)   an officer of the National Society for the Prevention of Cruelty to Children;

"professional legal adviser" means a barrister or a solicitor, solicitor's employee or other authorised litigator (as defined in the Courts and Legal Services Act 1990) who is providing advice to a party but is not instructed to represent that party in the proceedings;

"welfare officer" means a person who has been asked to prepare a report under section 7(1)(b) of the Act of 1989.]

Amendment

Inserted by SI 2005/1976, rr 2, 6. Date in force: 31 October 2005: see SI 2005/1976, r 1.
Para (3): Table: in second entry words 'civil partner,' in square brackets in both places they occur inserted by SI 2005/2922, r 114(a). Date in force: 5 December 2005: see SI 2005/2922, r 1(2); for transitional provisions see r 123 thereof.
Para (3): Table: fourth and fifth entries inserted by SI 2007/2187, rr 2, 20. Date in force: 1 October 2007: see SI 2007/2187, r 1.
Para (5): definition 'adoption panel' inserted by SI 2007/2187, rr 2, 20(1), (3). Date in force: 1 October 2007: see SI 2007/2187, r 1.
Para (5): definition 'cohabitant' substituted by SI 2005/2922, r 114(b). Date in force: 5 December 2005: see SI 2005/2922, r 1(2); for transitional provisions see r 123 thereof.

...

APPENDIX 1
FORMS

See Schedule 1 to the Family Proceedings Courts (Children Act 1989) Rules 1991

APPENDIX [1A]

[Not reproduced]

APPENDIX 2
CONTENTS OF PETITION (UNLESS OTHERWISE DIRECTED UNDER RULE 2.3)

[Not reproduced]

APPENDIX 3
NOTICES AND RESPONDENTS (RR, 4.4, 4.7)

[(i)   (ii)   (iii)   (iv)

Provision under which proceedings brought	Minimum number of days prior to hearing or directions appointment for service under rule 4.4(1)(b)	Respondents	Persons to whom notice is to be given
All applications	See separate entries below	Subject to separate entries below:—	Subject to separate entries below:—
		every person whom the applicant believes to have parental responsibility for the child;	local authority providing accommodation for the child;
		where the child is the subject of a care order, every person whom the applicant believes to have had parental responsibility immediately prior to the making of the care order;	persons who are caring for the child at the time when the proceedings are commenced;
		in the case of an application to extend, vary or discharge an order, the parties to the proceedings leading to the order which it is sought to have extended, varied or discharged;	in the case of proceedings brought in respect of a child who is alleged to be staying in a refuge which is certificated under section 51(1) or (2), the person who is providing the refuge.
		in the case of specified proceedings, the child.	
Section [4(1)(c)], 4(3), [4A(1)(b), 4A(3),] 5(1), 6(7), 8, 13(1), [14A, 14C(3), 14D,] ... , 33(7), Schedule 1, paragraph 19(1) of Schedule 2, or paragraph 11(3) or 16(5) of Schedule 14.	14 days	As for all applications above, and:	As for "all applications" above, and:

in the case of proceedings under Schedule 1, those persons whom the applicant believes to be interested in or affected by the proceedings;

in the case of an application under paragraph 11(3)(b) or 16(5) of Schedule 14, any person, other than the child, named in the order or directions which it is sought to discharge or vary;

[in the case of an application under section 14A, if a care order is in force with respect to the child, the child.]

in the case of an application for a section 8 order [or an application under section 14A or 14D], every person whom the applicant believes—

(i) to be named in a court order with respect to the same child, which has not ceased to have effect,

(ii) to be a party to pending proceedings in respect of the same child, or

(iii) to be a person with whom the child has lived for at least 3 years prior to the application, unless, in a case to which (i) or (ii) applies, the applicant believes that the court order or pending proceedings are not relevant to the application;

in the case of an application under paragraph 19(1) of Schedule 2, the parties to the proceedings leading to the care order;

in the case of an application under section 5(1), the father of the child if he does not have parental responsibility;

[in the case of an application under section 14A, if the child is not being accommodated by the local authority, the local authority in whose area the applicant is ordinarily resident;

in the case of an application under section 14D—

(a) as for applications under section 14A above, and

(b) the local authority that prepared the report under section 14A(8) or (9) in the proceedings leading to the order which it is sought to have varied or discharged, if different from any local authority that will otherwise be notified.]

Section 36(1), 39(1), 39(2), 39(3), 39(4), 43(1), or paragraph 6(3), 15(2) or 17(1) of Schedule 3.	7 days	As for "all applications" above and:	As for "all applications" above, and:
		in the case of an application under section 39(2) or (3), the supervisor;	in the case of an application for an order under section 43(1)—
		in the case of proceedings under paragraph 17(1) of Schedule 3, the local education authority concerned;	(i) every person whom the applicant believes to be a parent of the child,
		in the case of proceedings under section 36 or paragraph 15(2) or 17(1) of Schedule 3, the child.	(ii) every person whom the applicant believes to be caring for the child,

925

			(iii) every person in whose favour a contact order is in force with respect to the child, and
			(iv) every person who is allowed to have contact with the child by virtue of an order under section 34.
Section 31, 34(2), 34(3), 34(4), 34(9) or 38(8)(b).	3 days	As for "all applications" above, and:	As for "all applications" above, and:
		in the case of an application under section 34, the person whose contact with the child is the subject of the application.	in the case of an application under section 31—
			(i) every person whom the applicant believes to be a party to pending relevant proceedings in respect of the same child, and
			(ii) every person whom the applicant believes to be a parent without parental responsibility for the child.
Section 43(12)	2 days	As for "all applications" above.	Those of the persons referred to in section 43(11)(a) to (e) who were not party to the application for the order which it is sought to have varied or discharged.
Section 25, 44(1), 44(9)(b), 45(4), 45(8), 46(7), 48(9), 50(1) or 102(1)	1 day	As for "all applications" above, and:	Except for applications under section 102(1), as for "all applications" above, and:

		in the case of an application under section 44(9)(b)—	in the case of an application under section 44(1), every person whom the applicant believes to be a parent of the child;
		(i) the parties to the application for the order in respect of which it is sought to vary the directions;	in the case of an application under section 44(9)(b)—
		(ii) any person who was caring for the child prior to the making of the order, and	(i) the local authority in whose area the child is living, and
		(iii) any person whose contact with the child is affected by the direction which it is sought to have varied;	(ii) any person whom the applicant believes to be affected by the direction which it is sought to have varied;
		in the case of an application under section 50, the person whom the applicant alleges to have effected or to have been or to be responsible for the taking or keeping of the child.	in the case of an application under section 102(1), the person referred to in section 102(1) and any person preventing or likely to prevent such a person from exercising powers under enactments mentioned in subsection (6) of that section.
[section 30 of the Human Fertilisation and Embryology Act 1990]	[14 days]	[the birth parents (except where the applicants seek to dispense with their agreement under section 30(6) of the Human Fertilisation and Embryology Act 1990) and any other persons or body with parental responsibility for the child at the date of the application]	[any local authority or voluntary organisation that has at any time provided accommodation for the child]]

927

Amendment

Substituted by SI 1992/2067, r 8, Sch 1.
In entry beginning "Section 4(1)(c)" in column (i) reference to "4(1)(c)" in square brackets substituted by SI 2003/2839, r 8.
In entry beginning "Section 4(1)(c)" in column (i) reference to "4A(1)(b), 4A(3)," in square brackets inserted by SI 2005/2922, r 120(a)(i).
In entry beginning "Section 4(1)(c)" in column (i) reference to "14A, 14C(3), 14D," in square brackets inserted by SI 2005/2922, r 120(a)(ii).
In entry beginning "Section 4(1)(c)" in column (i) reference omitted revoked by SI 2007/2187, rr 2, 24.
In entry beginning "Section 4(1)(c)" in column (iii) words from "in the case" to "child, the child." in square brackets inserted by SI 2005/2922, r 120(b).
In entry beginning "Section 4(1)(c)" in column (iv) words "or an application under section 14A or 14D" in square brackets inserted by SI 2005/2922, r 120(c)(i).
In entry beginning "Section 4(1)(c)" in column (iv) words from "in the case" to "otherwise be notified." in square brackets inserted by SI 2005/2922, r 120(c)(ii).
Final entries in columns (i)–(iv) inserted by SI 1994/2165, r 6.

[APPENDIX 4]

Amendment

Inserted by SI 2005/2922, r 121, Sch 2.

[rules 3.1(10), 3.5(1), 3.6(10), 3.8(13), 3.18(3) and (6), 3.19(5)]

Amendment

Inserted by SI 2005/2922, r 121, Sch 2.

[1   In this Appendix a reference to a paragraph by number alone is a reference to a paragraph of this Appendix.

Representation of children on applications under Act of 1984 and under Schedule 7 to the Act 2004

2   (1)   Sub-paragraph (2) applies where, on an application for financial relief under Part III of the Act of 1984 or under Schedule 7 to the Act of 2004, an application is made for an order for a variation of settlement.

(2)   The court must, unless it is satisfied that the proposed variation does not adversely affect the rights or interests of any children concerned, direct that the children be separately represented on the application, either by a solicitor or by a solicitor and counsel, and may appoint the Official Solicitor or other fit person to be guardian ad litem of the children for the purpose of the application.

(3)   On any other application for financial relief under Part III of the Act of 1984 or under Schedule 7 to the Act of 2004 the court may give such a direction or make such appointment as it is empowered to give or make by sub-paragraph (2).

(4)   Before a person other than the Official Solicitor is appointed guardian ad litem under this rule the solicitor acting for the children must file a certificate that the person proposed as guardian has no interest in the matter adverse to that of the children and that he is a proper person to be such guardian.

Evidence on application for financial relief or avoidance of transaction order under
Act of 1984 or under Schedule 7 to Act of 2004

3 (1) Where an application is made for financial relief or an avoidance of transaction order under Part III of the Act of 1984 or under Schedule 7 to the Act of 2004, the affidavit in support must contain, so far as known to the applicant, full particulars—

    (a)   in the case of an application for a transfer or settlement of property—

        (i) of the property in respect of which the application is made, and

        (ii) of the property to which the party against whom the application is made is entitled either in possession or reversion;

    (b)   in the case of an application for an order for a variation of settlement—

        (i) of all relevant settlements, made on the spouses or civil partners, as the case may be, and

        (ii) of the funds brought into settlement by each spouse or civil partner;

    (c)   in the case of an application for an avoidance of transaction order—

        (i) of the property to which the disposition relates, and

        (ii) of the person in whose favour the disposition is alleged to have been made,

and in the case of a disposition alleged to have been made by way of settlement, of the trustees and the beneficiaries of the settlement.

(2) Where an application for a property adjustment order or an avoidance of transaction order relates to land, the affidavit in support must identify the land and—

    (a)   state whether the title to the land is registered or unregistered and, if registered, the Land Registry title number; and

    (b)   give particulars, so far as known to the applicant, of any mortgage of the land or other interest in it.

(3) A copy of Form M26 or M27 as the case may be, together with a copy of the supporting affidavit, must, as well as being served on the respondent, be served—

    (a)   in the case of an application for an order for a variation of settlement, on the trustees of the settlement and the settlor if living;

    (b)   in the case of an application for an avoidance of transaction order, on the person in whose favour the disposition is alleged to have been made; and

    (c)   in the case of an application to which sub-paragraph (2) refers, on any mortgagee of whom particulars are given pursuant to that paragraph, and on such other persons, if any, as the district judge may direct.

(4) Any person who is served with an application pursuant to sub-paragraph (3) may within 14 days after service file an affidavit in answer.

(5) In this rule a relevant settlement—

    (a)   in relation to a marriage, is an ante-nuptial or post-nuptial settlement; and

    (b)   in relation to a civil partnership, is a settlement made during its subsistence or in anticipation of its formation, on the civil partners including one made by will or codicil, but not including one in the form of a pension arrangement (within the meaning of Part 4 of Schedule 5 to the Act of 2004).

Service of affidavit on application for alteration of maintenance agreement

4 (1) This paragraph applies to an affidavit filed in support of an application under section 35 or 36 of the Act of 1973 or paragraphs 69 or 73 of Schedule 5 to the Act of 2004.

(2)   This paragraph, apart from sub-paragraph (3), also applies to an affidavit filed in support of an application under section 27 of the Act of 1973 or Part 9 of Schedule 5 to the Act of 2004 which contains an allegation of adultery or of an improper association with a person named.

(3)   Where a person files an affidavit to which this sub-paragraph applies he must at the same time serve a copy on the opposite party.

(4)   Where an affidavit to which this paragraph applies contains an allegation of adultery or of an improper association with a named person ("the named person") the court may direct that the party who filed the affidavit serve a copy of all or part of it on the named person together with Form F (the references to ancillary relief in that form being substituted by references to the provision under which the application is made).

(5)   Where the court makes a direction under sub-paragraph (4) the named person may file an affidavit in answer to the allegations.

(6)   The named person may intervene in the proceedings by applying for directions under paragraph 7(4) within seven days of service of the affidavit on him.

(7)   Rule 2.37(3) applies to a person served with an affidavit under sub-paragraph (4) as it applies to a co-respondent.

Information on application for consent orders on application for failure to provide reasonable maintenance or for financial provision under Act of 1984 or Schedule 7 to Act of 2004

5   (1)   This paragraph applies to an application for a consent order—

(a)   under section 27 of the Act of 1973 or Part 9 of Schedule 5 to the Act of 2004; and

(b)   under Part III of the Act of 1984 or Schedule 7 to the Act of 2004.

(2)   Subject to sub-paragraphs (3) and (4), there must be lodged with every application to which this paragraph applies two copies of a draft of the order in the terms sought, one of which must be indorsed with a statement signed by the respondent to the application signifying his agreement, and a statement of information (which may be made in more than one document) which must include—

(a)   the duration of the marriage or civil partnership, as the case may be, the age of each party and of any minor or dependent child of the family;

(b)   an estimate in summary form of the approximate amount or value of the capital resources and net income of each party and of any minor child of the family;

(c)   what arrangements are intended for the accommodation of each of the parties and any minor child of the family;

(d)   whether either party has subsequently married or formed a civil partnership or has any present intention to do so or to cohabit with another person;

(e)   where the order includes provision to be made—

(i)   under section 17(1)(a) of the Act of 1984 of a kind which could be made by an order under section 25B or 25C of the Act of 1973;

(ii)   under section 17(1)(b) of the Act of 1984; or

(iii)   under paragraph 9(2) of Schedule 7 to the Act of 2004 of a kind which could be made by an order under paragraphs 15, 25 or 26 of Schedule 5 to that Act,

a statement confirming that the person responsible for the pension arrangement in question has been served with the documents required by rule 2.70(11) and that no objection to such an order has been made by that person within 21 days from such service;

(f)   where the terms of the order provide for a transfer of property, a statement confirming that any mortgagee of that property has been served with notice of the application and that no objection to such a transfer has been made by the mortgagee within 14 days from such service; and

(g)   any other especially significant matters.

(3)   Where an application is made—

(a)   for a consent order for interim periodical payments pending the determination of the application; or

(b)   for an order varying an order for periodical payments,

the statement of information required by sub-paragraph (2) need include only the information in respect of net income mentioned in sub-paragraph (2)(b).

(4)   Where all or any of the parties attend the hearing of an application for financial relief the court may dispense with the lodging of a statement of information in accordance with sub-paragraph (2) and give directions for the information which would otherwise be required to be given in such a statement to be given in such a manner as it sees fit.

Investigation by district judge of application under section 27 of Act of 1973 or under Part 9 of Schedule 5 to Act of 2004

6   (1)   On or after the filing of a notice in Form M19 an appointment must be fixed for the hearing of the application by the district judge.

(2)   An application for an avoidance of disposition order must, if practicable, be heard at the same time as any related application.

(3)   Notice of the appointment must be given in Form M20 by the proper officer to every party to the application.

(4)   Any party may apply to the court for an order that any person do attend an appointment (an "inspection appointment") before the court and produce any documents to be specified or described in the order, the inspection of which appears to the court to be necessary for disposing fairly of the application to which it relates or for saving costs.

(5)   No person shall be required by an order under sub-paragraph (4) to produce any document at an inspection appointment which he could not be required to produce at the final hearing of the application.

(6)   The court must permit any person attending an inspection appointment pursuant to an order under sub-paragraph (4) to be represented at the appointment.

Further provision about certain applications

7   (1)   This paragraph applies to—

(a)   an application under section 27 of the Act of 1973 or under Part 9 of Schedule 5 to the Act of 2004;

(b)   an application under section 35 and 36 of the Act of 1973 or under paragraphs 69 and 73 of Schedule 5 to the Act of 2004;

(c)   an application under section 17 of the Married Women's Property Act 1882 or under section 66 of the Act of 2004;

(d)   an application under section 33, 35 and 36 of the Family Law Act 1996 and applications for transfer of tenancy under that Act; and

(2)   This paragraph, apart from sub-paragraph (3) also applies to an application for financial relief under Part III of the Act of 1984 or under Schedule 7 to the Act of 2004.

(3)   At the hearing of an application to which this paragraph applies the district judge must, subject to paragraphs 8 and 9(5) and rule 10.10 investigate the allegations made in support of and in answer to the application, and may take evidence orally and may at any stage of the proceedings, whether before or during the hearing, order the attendance of any person for the purpose of being examined or cross-examined and order the disclosure and inspection of any document or require further affidavits.

(4)   The district judge may at any stage of the proceedings give directions as to the filing and service of pleadings and as to the further conduct of the proceedings.

(5)   Where any party to such an application intends on the day appointed for the hearing to apply for directions, he must file and serve on every other party a notice to that effect.

(6)   Subject to any directions given by the court, any party to an application to which this sub-paragraph applies may by letter require any other party to give further information concerning any matter contained in any affidavit filed by or on behalf of that other party or any other relevant matter, or to provide a list of relevant documents or to allow inspection of any such document, and may, in default of compliance by such other party, apply to the district judge for directions.

Order on certain applications

8   (1)   This paragraph applies to—

(a)   an application under section 27 of the Act of 1973 or under Part 9 of Schedule 5 to the Act of 2004;

(b)   an application under section 35 and 36 of the Act of 1973 or under paragraphs 69 and 73 of Schedule 5 to the Act of 2004;

(c)   an application under section 17 of the Married Women's Property Act 1882 or under section 66 of the Act of 2004;

(2)   Subject to paragraph 9(5) the district judge must, after completing his investigation under paragraph 7, make such order as he thinks just.

(3)   Pending the final determination of the application, the district judge may make an interim order upon such terms as he thinks just.

(4)   RSC Order 31, rule 1 (power to order sale of land) shall apply to applications to which this rule applies as though that application were a cause or matter in the Chancery Division.

Arrangements for hearing applications etc by judge

9   (1)   This paragraph applies to

(a)   an application under section 27 of the Act of 1973 or under Part 9 of Schedule 5 to the Act of 2004;

(b)   an application under section 35 of the Act of 1973 or under paragraphs 69 of Schedule 5 to the Act of 2004;

(c)   an application under section 17 of the Married Women's Property Act 1882 or under section 66 of the Act of 2004.

(2)   This paragraph, apart from sub-paragraphs (5), (8), (9) and (10), applies to an application under section 24 of the Act of 1984 or under paragraph 17 of Schedule 7 to the Act of 2004 for an order preventing transactions.

(3)   Sub-paragraphs (5) to (7) of this paragraph apply to an application under section 36 of the Act of 1973 or under paragraph 73 of Schedule 5 to the Act of 2004;

(4)   Sub-paragraphs (6) and (7) of this paragraph apply to an application for financial relief under the Act of 1984 or under Schedule 7 to the Act of 2004.

(5)   The district judge may at any time refer an application of a kind referred to in sub-paragraph (1), or any question arising thereon, to a judge for his decision.

(6)   Where an application of a kind mentioned in sub-paragraph (1), (2) or (3) is referred or adjourned to a judge, the proper officer must fix a date, time and place for the hearing of the application or the consideration of the question and give notice of that date to all parties.

(7)   The hearing or consideration must, unless the court otherwise directs, take place in chambers.

(8)   In an application under the Married Women's Property Act 1882 or under section 27 or 35 of the Act of 1973, where the application is proceeding in a divorce county court which is not a court of trial or is pending in the High Court and proceeding in a district registry which is not in a divorce town, the hearing or consideration shall take place at such court of trial or divorce town as in the opinion of the district judge is the nearest or most convenient.

(9)   In an application under section 66 of the Act of 2004 or under Part 9 or paragraph 69 of Schedule 5 to the Act of 2004, where the application is proceeding in a civil partnership proceedings county court which is not a court of trial or is pending in the High Court and proceeding in a district registry which is not in a dissolution town, the hearing or consideration shall take place at such court of trial or dissolution town as in the opinion of the district judge is the nearest or most convenient.

(10)   For the purposes of sub-paragraph (8) and (9) the Royal Courts of Justice shall be treated as a divorce town or a dissolution town, as the case may be.

(11)   In respect of any application referred to him under this rule, a judge shall have the same powers as a district judge has under paragraph 7(4).]

Amendment

Inserted by SI 2005/2922, r 121, Sch 2.

FAMILY PROCEEDINGS COURTS (CHILDREN ACT 1989) RULES 1991

(SI 1991/1395)

PART I
INTRODUCTORY

1   Citation, commencement and interpretation

(1)   These Rules may be cited as the Family Proceedings Courts (Children Act 1989) Rules 1991 and shall come into force on 14th October 1991.

(2)   Unless a contrary intention appears—

a section or schedule referred to means the section or schedule in the Act of 1989,
   "application" means an application made under or by virtue of the Act of 1989 or under these Rules, and "applicant" shall be construed accordingly,
"business day" means any day other than—
   (a)   a Saturday, Sunday, Christmas Day or Good Friday; or

  (b) a bank holiday, that is to say, a day which is, or is to be observed as, a bank holiday, or a holiday, under the Banking and Financial Dealings Act 1971, in England and Wales,

"child"

  (a) means, in relation to any relevant proceedings, subject to sub-paragraph (b), a person under the age of 18 with respect to whom the proceedings are brought, and

  (b) where paragraph 16(1) of Schedule 1 applies, also includes a person who has reached the age of 18;

["children and family reporter" means an officer of the service [or a Welsh family proceedings officer] who has been asked to prepare a welfare report under section 7(1)(a)][,]

["children's guardian"—

  (a) means an officer of the service [or a Welsh family proceedings officer] appointed under section 41 for the child with respect to whom the proceedings are brought; but

  (b) does not include such an officer appointed in relation to proceedings specified by rule 21A][,]

"contribution order" has the meaning assigned to it by paragraph 23(2) of Schedule 2,

["the Council Regulation" means Council Regulation (EC) 2201/2003 of 27 November 2003 concerning jurisdiction and the recognition and enforcement of judgments in matrimonial matters and the matters of parental responsibility,]

"court" means a family proceedings court constituted in accordance with sections 66 and 67 of the Magistrates' Courts Act 1980 or, in respect of those proceedings prescribed in rule 2(5), a single justice who is a member of a family panel,

"directions appointment" means a hearing for directions under rule 14(2),

"emergency protection order" means an order under section 44,

["family assistance order report" means a report to the court pursuant to a direction in a family assistance order under section 16(6);]

"file" means deposit with the [designated officer for a magistrates' court],

"form" means a form in Schedule 1 to these Rules with such variation as the circumstances of the particular case may require,

...

[...]

"justices' clerk" has the meaning assigned to it by section 70 of the Justices of the Peace Act 1979 and includes any person who performs a justices' clerk's functions by virtue of rule 32,

"leave" includes approval,

"note" includes a record made by mechanical means,

["officer of the service" has the same meaning as in the Criminal Justice and Court Services Act 2000,]

["Member State" means—

  (a) those parties contracting to the Council Regulation, that is to say, Belgium, Cyprus, Czech Republic, Germany, Greece, Spain, Estonia, France, Hungary, Ireland, Italy, Latvia, Lithuania, Luxembourg, Malta, Netherlands, Austria, Poland, Portugal, Slovakia, Slovenia, Finland, Sweden and the United Kingdom.

  (b) a party which has subsequently adopted the Council Regulation,]

"parental responsibility" has the meaning assigned to it by section 3,

"parties" in relation to any relevant proceedings means the respondents specified for those proceedings in the third column of Schedule 2 to these Rules, and the applicant,

"recovery order" means an order under section 50,

"relevant proceedings" has the meaning assigned to it by section 93(3),

["risk assessment" has the meaning assigned to it by section 16A(3);]
"section 8 order" has the meaning assigned to it by section 8(2),
["special guardianship order" has the meaning assigned to it by section 14A,]
"specified proceedings" has the meaning assigned to it by section 41(6) and
    rule 2(2),
"the 1981 rules" means the Magistrates' Courts Rules 1981,
"the Act of 1989" means the Children Act 1989,
"welfare officer" means a person who has been asked to prepare a welfare report
    under [section 7(1)(b)],
["Welsh family proceedings officer" has the same meaning as in the Children
    Act 2004].

Date in force

14 October 1991: see para (1) above.

Amendment

Para (2): definition "children and family reporter" inserted by SI 2001/818, rr 2, 3(a)(i). Date in force: 1 April 2001: see SI 2001/818, r 1.

Para (2): in definition "children and family reporter" words "or a Welsh family proceedings officer" in square brackets inserted by SI 2005/585, rr 2, 3(a). Date in force: 1 April 2005: see SI 2005/585, r 1(1); for transitional provisions see rr 8, 9 thereof.

Para (2): definition "children's guardian" inserted by SI 2001/818, rr 2, 3(a)(ii). Date in force: 1 April 2001: see SI 2001/818, r 1.

Para (2): in definition "children's guardian" in para (a) words "or a Welsh family proceedings officer" in square brackets inserted by SI 2005/585, rr 2, 3(b). Date in force: 1 April 2005: see SI 2005/585, r 1(1); for transitional provisions see rr 8, 9 thereof.

Para (2): definition "the Council Regulation" inserted by SI 2005/229, r 4(a). Date in force: 1 March 2005: see SI 2005/229, r 1.

Para (2): definition "family assistance order report" inserted by SI 2007/2188, rr 2, 4(a). Date in force: 1 October 2007: see SI 2007/2188, r 1.

Para (2): in definition "file" words "designated officer for a magistrates' court" in square brackets substituted by SI 2005/617, art 2, Schedule, para 129(a). Date in force: 1 April 2005: see SI 2005/617, art 1.

Para (2): definition "guardian ad litem" (omitted) revoked by SI 2001/818, rr 2, 3(b). Date in force: 1 April 2001: see SI 2001/818, r 1.

Para (2): definition "justices' chief executive" (omitted) inserted by SI 2001/615, r 2(xx), Schedule, para 94. Date in force: 1 April 2001: see SI 2001/615, r 1.

Para (2): definition "justices' chief executive" (omitted) revoked by SI 2005/617, art 2, Schedule, para 129(b). Date in force: 1 April 2005: see SI 2005/617, art 1.

Para (2): definition "officer of the service" inserted by SI 2001/818, rr 2, 3(a)(iii). Date in force: 1 April 2001: see SI 2001/818, r 1.

Para (2): definition "Member State" inserted by SI 2005/229, r 4(b). Date in force: 1 March 2005: see SI 2005/229, r 1.

Para (2): definition "risk assessment" inserted by SI 2007/2188, rr 2, 4(b). Date in force: 1 October 2007: see SI 2007/2188, r 1.

Para (2): definition "special guardianship order" inserted by SI 2005/2930, r 2(e), Sch 1, para 34. Date in force: 30 December 2005: see SI 2005/2930, r 1(2).

Para (2): in definition "welfare officer" words "section 7(1)(b)" in square brackets substituted by SI 2001/818, rr 2, 3(c). Date in force: 1 April 2001: see SI 2001/818, r 1.

Para (2): definition "Welsh family proceedings officer" inserted by SI 2005/585, rr 2, 3(c). Date in force: 1 April 2005: see SI 2005/585, r 1(1); for transitional provisions see rr 8, 9 thereof.

---

2   Matters prescribed for the purposes of the Act of 1989

(1) The parties to proceedings in which directions are given under section 38(6), and any person named in such a direction, form the prescribed class for the purposes of section 38(8)(b) (application to vary directions made with interim care or interim supervision order).

(2) The following proceedings [(in a family proceedings court)] are specified for the purposes of section 41 in accordance with subsection (6)(i) thereof—

    (a) proceedings under section 25;
    (b) applications under section 33(7);
    (c) proceedings under paragraph 19(1) of Schedule 2;
    (d) applications under paragraph 6(3) of Schedule 3.

(3) The applicant for an order that has been made under section 43(1) and the persons referred to in section 43(11) may, in any circumstances, apply under section 43(12) for a child assessment order to be varied or discharged.

(4) The following persons form the prescribed class for the purposes of section 44(9)(b) (application to vary directions)—

    (a) the parties to the application for the order in respect of which it is sought to vary the directions;
    (b) the [children's guardian];
    (c) the local authority in whose area the child concerned is ordinarily resident;
    (d) any person who is named in the directions.

(5) The following proceedings are prescribed for the purposes of section 93(2)(i) as being proceedings with respect to which a single justice may discharge the functions of a family proceedings court, that is to say, proceedings—

    (a) where an ex parte application is made, under sections 10, 44(1), 48(9), 50(1), 75(1) or 102(1),
    (b) subject to rule 28, under sections 11(3) or 38(1),
    (c) under sections 4(3)(b), [4A(3)(b),] 7, 14, 34(3)(b), 37, 41, 44(9)(b) and (11)(b)(iii), 48(4), 91(15) or (17), or paragraph 11(4) of Schedule 14,
    (d) in accordance with any Order made by the Lord Chancellor under Part I of Schedule 11, and
    (e) in accordance with rules 3 to 8, 10 to 19, 21, 22, or 27.

Date in force

14 October 1991: see r 1(1).

Amendment

Para (2): words "(in a family proceedings court)" in square brackets inserted by SI 1991/1991, r 26, Sch 2, para 8(1).
Para (4): in sub-para (b) words "children's guardian" in square brackets substituted by SI 2001/818, rr 2, 4(a). Date in force: 1 April 2001: see SI 2001/818, r 1.
Para (5): in sub-para (c) reference to "4A(3)(b)," in square brackets inserted by SI 2005/2930, r 2(e), Sch 1, para 35. Date in force: 30 December 2005: see SI 2005/2930, r 1(2).

PART II
GENERAL

3 Application for leave to commence proceedings

(1) Where the leave of the court is required to bring any relevant proceedings, the person seeking leave shall file—

    (a) a written request for leave [in Form C2] setting out the reasons for the application; and
    [(b) a draft of the application (being the documents referred to in rule 4(1A)) for the making of which leave is sought together with sufficient copies for one to be served on each respondent.]

(2)   On considering a request for leave filed under paragraph (1), the court shall—

  (a)   grant the request, whereupon the [designated officer for the court] shall inform the person making the request [and any local authority that is preparing, or has prepared, a report under section 14A(8) or (9)] of the decision, or

  (b)   direct that a date be fixed for a hearing of the request, whereupon the justices' clerk shall fix such a date and [the [designated officer for the court] shall] give such notice as the court directs to the person making the request [and any local authority that is preparing, or has prepared, a report under section 14A(8) or (9)] and to such other persons as the court requires to be notified, of the date so fixed.

(3)   Where leave is granted to bring any relevant proceedings, the application shall proceed in accordance with rule 4; but paragraph (1)(a) of that rule shall not apply.

Date in force

14 October 1991: see r 1(1).

Amendment

Para (1): in sub-para (a) words in square brackets inserted, and sub-para (b) substituted, by SI 1994/3156, r 4.
Para (2): in sub-paras (a), (b) words "designated officer for the court" in square brackets substituted by SI 2005/617, art 2, Schedule, para 128. Date in force: 1 April 2005: see SI 2005/617, art 1.
Para (2): in sub-paras (a), (b) words "and any local authority that is preparing, or has prepared, a report under section 14A(8) or (9)" in square brackets inserted by SI 2005/2930, r 2(e), Sch 1, para 36. Date in force: 30 December 2005: see SI 2005/2930, r 1(2).
Para (2): in sub-para (b) words from "the" to "shall" in square brackets inserted by SI 2001/615, r 2(xx), Schedule, para 97. Date in force: 1 April 2001: see SI 2001/615, r 1.

---

4   Application

(1)   Subject to paragraph (4), an applicant shall—

  [(a)   file the documents referred to in paragraph (1A) below (which documents shall together be called the "application") together with sufficient copies for one to be served on each respondent, and]

  (b)   serve a copy of the application [together with Form C6 and such (if any) of Forms [C1A,] C7 and C10A as are given to him by the [designated officer for the court] under paragraph 2(b)] on each respondent such minimum number of days prior to the date fixed under paragraph (2)(a) as is specified in relation to that application in column (ii) of Schedule 2 to these Rules.

[(1A)   The documents to be filed under paragraph (1)(a) above are—

  (a)
    (i)   whichever is appropriate of Forms [C1, C2, C3, C4, C5] or C51, and
    (ii)   such of the supplemental Forms C10 or C11 to C20 as may be appropriate, [and
    (iii)   in the case of an application for a section 8 order or an order under section 4(1)(c) where question 7 on Form C1, or question 4 on Form C2, is answered in the affirmative, supplemental Form C1A,] or

  (b)   where there is no appropriate form a statement in writing of the order sought,

and where the application is made in respect of more than one child, all the children shall be included in one application.]

[(2)   On receipt by the [designated officer for the court] of the documents filed under paragraph (1)(a)—

(a)   the justices' clerk shall fix the date, time and place for a hearing or a directions appointment, allowing sufficient time for the applicant to comply with paragraph (1)(b), and

(b)   the [designated officer for the court] shall—
   (i)   endorse the date, time and place so fixed upon Form C6, and where appropriate, Form C6A, and
   (ii)   return forthwith to the applicant the copies of the application and Form C10A if filed with it, together with Form C6, and such of Forms C6A and C7 as are appropriat[, and, in the case of an application for a section 8 order or an order under section 4(1)(c), Form C1A]e.]

[(3)   The applicant shall, at the same time as complying with paragraph (1)(b), serve Form C6A on the persons set out in relation to the relevant class of proceedings in column (iv) of Schedule 2 to these Rules.]

(4)   An application for—

(a)   [section 8 order],
(b)   an emergency protection order,
(c)   a warrant under section 48(9),
(d)   a recovery order, or
(e)   a warrant under section 102(1),

may, with leave of the justices' clerk, be made ex parte in which case the applicant shall—

   (i)   file with the [designated officer for the court] or the court the application < ... > in the appropriate form in Schedule 1 to these Rules at the time when the application is made or as directed by the justices' clerk, and
   (ii)   in the case of an application for a [section 8 order] or an emergency protection order, and also in the case of an application for an order under section 75(1) where the application is ex parte, serve a copy of the application on each respondent within 48 hours after the making of the order.

(5)   Where the court refuses to make an order on an ex parte application it may direct that the application be made inter partes.

(6)   In the case of proceedings under Schedule 1, the application under paragraph (1) shall be accompanied by a statement [in Form C10A] setting out the financial details which the applicant believes to be relevant to the application ... , together with sufficient copies for one to be served on each respondent.

Date in force

14 October 1991: see r 1(1).

Amendment

Para (1): sub-para (a) substituted by SI 1994/3156, r 5(a).
Para (1): in sub-para (b) words from "together with Form C6" to "under paragraph 2(b)" in square brackets substituted by SI 1994/3156, r 5(b).
Para (1): in sub-para (b) reference to "C1A," in square brackets inserted by SI 2004/3376, r 3. Date in force: 31 January 2005 (except in relation to proceedings commenced before that date): see SI 2004/3376, rr 1(1), 2.
Para (1): in sub-para (b) words "designated officer for the court" in square brackets substituted by SI 2005/617, art 2, Schedule, para 128. Date in force: 1 April 2005: see SI 2005/617, art 1.
Para (1A): inserted by SI 1994/3156, r 6.

Para (1A): in sub-para (a)(i) references to "C1, C2, C3, C4, C5" in square brackets substituted by SI 2004/3376, r 4(a). Date in force: 31 January 2005 (except in relation to proceedings commenced before that date): see SI 2004/3376, rr 1(1), 2.

Para (1A): sub-para (a)(iii) and word "and" immediately preceding it inserted by SI 2004/3376, r 4(b). Date in force: 31 January 2005 (except in relation to proceedings commenced before that date): see SI 2004/3376, rr 1(1), 2.

Para (2): substituted by SI 2001/615, r 2(xx), Schedule, para 100. Date in force: 1 April 2001: see SI 2001/615, r 1.

Para (2): words "designated officer for the court" in square brackets in both places they occur substituted by SI 2005/617, art 2, Schedule, para 128. Date in force: 1 April 2005: see SI 2005/617, art 1.

Para (2): in sub-para (b)(ii) words from ", and, in the" to "section 4(1)(c), Form C1A" in square brackets inserted by SI 2004/3376, r 5. Date in force: 31 January 2005 (except in relation to proceedings commenced before that date): see SI 2004/3376, rr 1(1), 2.

Para (3): substituted by SI 1994/3156, r 8.

Para (4): words "section 8 order" in square brackets in both places they occur substituted by SI 1992/2068, r 2, Schedule, para 1.

Para (4): in sub-para (i) words "designated officer for the court" in square brackets substituted by SI 2005/617, art 2, Schedule, para 128. Date in force: 1 April 2005: see SI 2005/617, art 1.

Para (4): in sub-para (i) words omitted revoked by SI 1994/3156, r 9.

Para (6): words in square brackets inserted, and words omitted revoked, by SI 1994/3156, r 10.

---

5 Withdrawal of application

(1) An application may be withdrawn only with leave of the court.

(2) Subject to paragraph (3), a person seeking leave to withdraw an application shall file and serve on the parties a written request for leave setting out the reasons for the request.

(3) The request under paragraph (2) may be made orally to the court if the parties and, if appointed, the [children's guardian] or the [welfare officer or children and family reporter] are present.

(4) Upon receipt of a written request under paragraph (2), the court shall—

    (a) if—
        (i) the parties consent in writing,
        (ii) any [children's guardian] has had an opportunity to make representations, and
        (iii) the court thinks fit,
grant the request; in which case the [designated officer for the court] shall notify the parties, [any local authority that is preparing, or has prepared, a report under section 14A(8) or (9),] the [children's guardian][,] the [welfare officer[, the] children and family reporter] [and the officer of the service or the Welsh family proceedings officer who is preparing or has prepared a family assistance order report or a risk assessment] of the granting of the request; or

    (b) the justices' clerk shall fix a date for the hearing of the request and [the [designated officer for the court] shall] give at least 7 days' notice to the parties, [any local authority that is preparing, or has prepared, a report under section 14A(8) or (9),] the [children's guardian][,] the [welfare officer[, the] children and family reporter] [and the officer of the service or Welsh family proceedings officer who is preparing or has prepared a family assistance order report or a risk assessment] of the date fixed.

Date in force

14 October 1991: see r 1(1).

Appendix 2   *Family Proceedings Courts (CA 1989) Rules 1991*

Amendment

Para (3): words "children's guardian" in square brackets substituted by SI 2001/818, rr 2, 4(a). Date in force: 1 April 2001: see SI 2001/818, r 1.

Para (3): words "welfare officer or children and family reporter" in square brackets substituted by SI 2001/818, rr 2, 4(b). Date in force: 1 April 2001: see SI 2001/818, r 1.

Para (4): words "children's guardian" in square brackets in each place they occur substituted by SI 2001/818, rr 2, 4(a). Date in force: 1 April 2001: see SI 2001/818, r 1.

Para (4): in sub-paras (a), (b) words "designated officer for the court" in square brackets substituted by SI 2005/617, art 2, Schedule, para 128. Date in force: 1 April 2005: see SI 2005/617, art 1.

Para (4): in sub-paras (a), (b) words "any local authority that is preparing, or has prepared, a report under section 14A(8) or (9)," in square brackets inserted by SI 2005/2930, r 2(e), Sch 1, para 37. Date in force: 30 December 2005: see SI 2005/2930, r 1(2).

Para (4): in sub-para (a) comma in square brackets substituted by SI 2007/2188, rr 2, 5(a)(i). Date in force: 1 October 2007: see SI 2007/2188, r 1.

Para (4): words "welfare officer or children and family reporter" in square brackets in both places they occur substituted by SI 2001/818, rr 2, 4(b). Date in force: 1 April 2001: see SI 2001/818, r 1.

Para (4): in sub-para (a) word ", the" in square brackets substituted by SI 2007/2188, rr 2, 5(a)(ii). Date in force: 1 October 2007: see SI 2007/2188, r 1.

Para (4): in sub-para (a) words from "and the officer" to "a risk assessment" in square brackets inserted by SI 2007/2188, rr 2, 5(a)(iii). Date in force: 1 October 2007: see SI 2007/2188, r 1.

Para (4): in sub-para (b) words from "the" to "shall" in square brackets inserted by SI 2001/615, r 2(xx), Schedule, para 97. Date in force: 1 April 2001: see SI 2001/615, r 1.

Para (4): in sub-para (b) comma in square brackets substituted by SI 2007/2188, rr 2, 5(b)(i). Date in force: 1 October 2007: see SI 2007/2188, r 1.

Para (4): in sub-para (b) word ", the" in square brackets substituted by SI 2007/2188, rr 2, 5(b)(ii). Date in force: 1 October 2007: see SI 2007/2188, r 1.

Para (4): in sub-para (b) words from "and the officer" to "a risk assessment" in square brackets inserted by SI 2007/2188, rr 2, 5(b)(iii). Date in force: 1 October 2007: see SI 2007/2188, r 1.

---

6   Transfer of proceedings

(1)   Where, in any relevant proceedings, the [designated officer for the court] or the court receives a request in writing from a party that the proceedings be transferred to another family proceedings court or to a county court, the [designated officer for the court] or court shall issue [an order or certificate] in the appropriate form in Schedule 1 to these Rules, granting or refusing the request in accordance with any Order made by the Lord Chancellor under Part I of Schedule 11.

(2)   Where a request is granted under paragraph (1), the [designated officer for the court] shall send a copy of the [order]—

(a)   to the parties,

[(aa) to any local authority that is preparing, or has prepared, a report under section 14A(8) or (9),]

(b)   to any [children's guardian], and

(c)   to the family proceedings court or to the county court to which the proceedings are to be transferred.

(3)   Any consent given or refused by a justices' clerk in accordance with any Order made by the Lord Chancellor under Part I of Schedule 11 shall be recorded in writing by the justices' clerk at the time it is given or refused or as soon as practicable thereafter.

(4)   Where a request to transfer proceedings to a county court is refused under paragraph (1), the person who made the request may apply in accordance with rule 4.6 of the Family Proceedings Rules 1991 for an order under any Order made by the Lord Chancellor under Part I of Schedule 11.

Date in force

14 October 1991: see r 1(1).

Amendment

Para (1): words "designated officer for the court" in square brackets in both places they occur substituted by SI 2005/617, art 2, Schedule, para 128. Date in force: 1 April 2005: see SI 2005/617, art 1.
Para (1): words "an order or certificate" in square brackets substituted by SI 1994/3156, r 11.
Para (2): words "designated officer for the court" in square brackets substituted by SI 2005/617, art 2, Schedule, para 128. Date in force: 1 April 2005: see SI 2005/617, art 1.
Para (2): word "order" in square brackets substituted by SI 1994/3156, r 11.
Para (2): sub-para (aa) inserted by SI 2005/2930, r 2(e), Sch 1, para 38. Date in force: 30 December 2005: see SI 2005/2930, r 1(2).
Para (2): in sub-para (b) words "children's guardian" in square brackets substituted by SI 2001/818, rr 2, 4(a). Date in force: 1 April 2001: see SI 2001/818, r 1.

---

7   Parties

(1)   The respondents to relevant proceedings shall be those persons set out in the relevant entry in column (iii) of Schedule 2 to these Rules.

(2)   In any relevant proceedings a person may file a request [in Form C2] that he or another person—

   (a)   be joined as a party, or
   (b)   cease to be a party.

(3)   On considering a request under paragraph (2) the court shall, subject to paragraph (4)—

   (a)   grant it without a hearing or representations, save that this shall be done only in the case of a request under paragraph (2)(a), whereupon the [designated officer for the court] shall inform the parties [and any local authority that is preparing, or has prepared, a report under section 14A(8) or (9)] and the person making the request of that decision, or
   (b)   order that a date be fixed for the consideration of the request, whereupon the [designated officer for the court] shall give notice of the date so fixed, together with a copy of the request—
      (i)   in the case of a request under paragraph (2)(a), to the applicant [and any local authority that is preparing, or has prepared, a report under section 14A(8) or (9)], and
      (ii)   in the case of a request under paragraph (2)(b), to the parties [and any local authority that is preparing, or has prepared, a report under section 14A(8) or (9)], or
   (c)   invite the parties or any of them to make written representations, within a specified period, as to whether the request should be granted; and upon the expiry of the period the court shall act in accordance with sub-paragraph (a) or (b).

(4)   Where a person with parental responsibility requests that he be joined under paragraph (2)(a), the court shall grant his request.

(5)   In any relevant proceedings the court may direct—

   (a)   that a person who would not otherwise be a respondent under these Rules be joined as a party to the proceedings, or
   (b)   that a party to the proceedings cease to be a party.

Date in force

14 October 1991: see r 1(1).

Amendment

Para (2): words in square brackets substituted by SI 1994/3156, r 12.
Para (3): in sub-paras (a), (b) words "designated officer for the court" in square brackets substituted by SI 2005/617, art 2, Schedule, para 128. Date in force: 1 April 2005: see SI 2005/617, art 1.
Para (3): in sub-paras (a), (b) words "and any local authority that is preparing, or has prepared, a report under section 14A(8) or (9)" in square brackets in each place they occur inserted by SI 2005/2930, r 2(e), Sch 1, para 39. Date in force: 5 December 2005: see SI 2005/2930, r 1(2).

8   Service

(1)   Where service of a document is required by these Rules (and not by a provision to which section 105(8) (service of notice or other document under the Act) applies) it may be effected—

   (a)   if the person to be served is not known by the person serving to be acting by solicitor—
      (i)   by delivering it to him personally, or
      (ii)   by delivering it at, or by sending it by first-class post to, his residence or his last known residence, or

   (b)   if the person to be served is known by the person serving to be acting by solicitor—
      (i)   by delivering the document at, or sending it by first-class post to, the solicitor's address for service,
      (ii)   where the solicitor's address for service includes a numbered box at a document exchange, by leaving the document at that document exchange or at a document exchange which transmits documents on every business day to that document exchange, or
      (iii)   by sending a legible copy of the document by facsimile transmission to the solicitor's office.

(2)   In this rule, "first-class post" means first-class post which has been pre-paid or in respect of which pre-payment is not required.

(3)   Where a child who is a party to any relevant proceedings is required by these Rules to serve a document, service shall be effected by—

   (a)   the solicitor acting for the child,
   (b)   where there is no such solicitor, the [children's guardian], or
   (c)   where there is neither such a solicitor nor a [children's guardian], the [designated officer for the court].

(4)   Service of any document on a child shall, subject to any direction of the justices' clerk or the court, be effected by service on—

   (a)   the solicitor acting for the child,
   (b)   where there is no such solicitor, the [children's guardian], or
   (c)   where there is neither such a solicitor nor a [children's guardian], with leave of the justices' clerk or the court, the child.

(5)   Where the justices' clerk or the court refuses leave under paragraph (4)(c), a direction shall be given under paragraph (8).

(6)   A document shall, unless the contrary is proved, be deemed to have been served—

(a) in the case of service by first-class post, on the second business day after posting, and

(b) in the case of service in accordance with paragraph (1)(b)(ii), on the second business day after the day on which it is left at the document exchange.

(7) At or before the first directions appointment in, or hearing of, relevant proceedings, whichever occurs first, the applicant shall file a statement [in Form C9] that service of—

(a) a copy of the application [and other documents referred to in rule 4(1)(b)] has been effected on each respondent, and

(b) notice of the proceedings has been effected under rule 4(3);

and the statement shall indicate—

(i) the manner, date, time and place of service, or

(ii) where service was effected by post, the date, time and place of posting.

[(8) In any relevant proceedings, where these rules require a document to be served, the court or the justices' clerk may, without prejudice to any power under rule 14, direct that—

(a) the requirement shall not apply;

(b) the time specified by the rules for complying with the requirement shall be abridged to such extent as may be specified in the direction;

(c) service shall be effected in such manner as may be specified in the direction.]

Date in force

14 October 1991: see r 1(1).

Amendment

Para (3): words "children's guardian" in square brackets in both places they occur substituted by SI 2001/818, rr 2, 4(a). Date in force: 1 April 2001: see SI 2001/818, r 1.
Para (3): in sub-para (c) words "designated officer for the court" in square brackets substituted by SI 2005/617, art 2, Schedule, para 128. Date in force: 1 April 2005: see SI 2005/617, art 1.
Para (4): words "children's guardian" in square brackets in both places they occur substituted by SI 2001/818, rr 2, 4(a). Date in force: 1 April 2001: see SI 2001/818, r 1.
Para (7): words "in Form C9" in square brackets inserted by SI 1994/3156, r 13.
Para (7): in sub-para (a) words "and other documents referred to in rule 4(1)(b)" in square brackets inserted by SI 1994/3156, r 13.
Para (8): substituted by SI 1992/2068, r 2, Schedule, para 2.

[9 **Acknowledgement of application**]

[Within 14 days of service of [an application for an order under section 4(1)(c),] an application for a section 8 order[, a special guardianship order] or an application under Schedule 1, each respondent shall file and serve on the parties an acknowledgement of the application in Form C7 [and, if both parts of question 6 or question 7 (or both) on Form C7 are answered in the affirmative, Form C1A].]

Amendment

Substituted by SI 1994/3156, r 14.
Words "an application for an order under section 4(1)(c)," in square brackets inserted by SI 2004/3376, r 6(a). Date in force: 31 January 2005 (except in relation to proceedings commenced before that date): see SI 2004/3376, rr 1(1), 2.
Words ", a special guardianship order" in square brackets inserted by SI 2005/2930, r 2(e), Sch 1, para 40. Date in force: 30 December 2005: see SI 2005/2930, r 1(2).
Words from "and, if both" to "affirmative, Form C1A" in square brackets inserted by

SI 2004/3376, r 6(b). Date in force: 31 January 2005 (except in relation to proceedings commenced before that date): see SI 2004/3376, rr 1(1), 2.

10 Appointment of [children's guardian]

(1) As soon as practicable after the commencement of specified proceedings or the transfer of such proceedings to the court, the justices' clerk or the court shall appoint a [children's guardian] unless—

    (a) such an appointment has already been made by the court which made the transfer and is subsisting, or

    (b) the justices' clerk or the court considers that such an appointment is not necessary to safeguard the interests of the child.

(2) At any stage in specified proceedings a party may apply, without notice to the other parties unless the justices' clerk or the court otherwise directs, for the appointment of a [children's guardian].

(3) The justices' clerk or the court shall grant an application under paragraph (2) unless it is considered that such an appointment is not necessary to safeguard the interests of the child, in which case reasons shall be given; and a note of such reasons shall be taken by the justices' clerk.

(4) At any stage in specified proceedings the justices' clerk or the court may appoint a [children's guardian] even though no application is made for such an appointment.

[(4A) The [designated officer for the court] or the court may, in specified proceedings, appoint more than one children's guardian in respect of the same child.]

(5) The [designated officer for the court] shall, as soon as practicable, notify the parties and any [welfare officer or children and family reporter] of an appointment under this rule or, as the case may be, of a decision not to make such an appointment.

(6) Upon the appointment of a [children's guardian] the [designated officer for the court] shall, as soon as practicable, notify him of the appointment and serve on him copies of the application and of documents filed under rule 17(1).

[(7) A children's guardian appointed by the [designated officer for the court] or by the court under this rule shall not—

    (a) be a member, officer or servant of a local authority which, or an authorised person (within the meaning of section 31(9)) who, is a party to the proceedings;

    (b) be, or have been, a member, officer or servant of a local authority or voluntary organisation (within the meaning of section 105(1)) who has been directly concerned in that capacity in arrangements relating to the care, accommodation or welfare of the child during the five years prior to the commencement of the proceedings; or

    (c) be a serving probation officer who has, in that capacity, been previously concerned with the child or his family.]

(8) When appointing a [children's guardian], the justices' clerk or the court shall consider the appointment of anyone who has previously acted as [children's guardian] of the same child.

(9) The appointment of a [children's guardian] under this rule shall continue for such time as is specified in the appointment or until terminated by the court.

(10) When terminating an appointment in accordance with paragraph (9), the court shall give reasons in writing for so doing, a note of which shall be taken by the justices' clerk.

(11) Where the justices' clerk or the court appoints a [children's guardian] in accordance with this rule or refuses to make such an appointment, the justices' clerk shall record the appointment or refusal in the appropriate form in Schedule 1 to these Rules.

Date in force

14 October 1991: see r 1(1).

Amendment

Provision heading: words "children's guardian" in square brackets substituted by SI 2001/818, rr 2, 4(a). Date in force: 1 April 2001: see SI 2001/818, r 1.
Para (1): words "children's guardian" in square brackets substituted by SI 2001/818, rr 2, 4(a). Date in force: 1 April 2001: see SI 2001/818, r 1.
Para (2): words "children's guardian" in square brackets substituted by SI 2001/818, rr 2, 4(a). Date in force: 1 April 2001: see SI 2001/818, r 1.
Para (4): words "children's guardian" in square brackets substituted by SI 2001/818, rr 2, 4(a). Date in force: 1 April 2001: see SI 2001/818, r 1.
Para (4A): inserted by SI 2001/818, rr 2, 5(a). Date in force: 1 April 2001: see SI 2001/818, r 1.
Para (4A): words "designated officer for the court" in square brackets substituted by SI 2005/617, art 2, Schedule, para 128. Date in force: 1 April 2005: see SI 2005/617, art 1.
Para (5): words "designated officer for the court" in square brackets substituted by SI 2005/617, art 2, Schedule, para 128. Date in force: 1 April 2005: see SI 2005/617, art 1.
Para (5): words "welfare officer or children and family reporter" in square brackets substituted by SI 2001/818, rr 2, 4(b). Date in force: 1 April 2001: see SI 2001/818, r 1.
Para (6): words "children's guardian" in square brackets substituted by SI 2001/818, rr 2, 4(a). Date in force: 1 April 2001: see SI 2001/818, r 1.
Para (6): words "designated officer for the court" in square brackets substituted by SI 2005/617, art 2, Schedule, para 128. Date in force: 1 April 2005: see SI 2005/617, art 1.
Para (7): substituted by SI 2001/818, rr 2, 5(b). Date in force: 1 April 2001: see SI 2001/818, r 1.
Para (7): words "designated officer for the court" in square brackets substituted by SI 2005/617, art 2, Schedule, para 128. Date in force: 1 April 2005: see SI 2005/617, art 1.
Para (8): words "children's guardian" in square brackets in both places they occur substituted by SI 2001/818, rr 2, 4(a). Date in force: 1 April 2001: see SI 2001/818, r 1.
Para (9): words "children's guardian" in square brackets substituted by SI 2001/818, rr 2, 4(a). Date in force: 1 April 2001: see SI 2001/818, r 1.
Para (11): words "children's guardian" in square brackets substituted by SI 2001/818, rr 2, 4(a). Date in force: 1 April 2001: see SI 2001/818, r 1.

[11   Powers and duties of officers of the service [and Welsh family proceedings officers]]

[(1) In carrying out his duty under section 7(1)(a)[, section 16(6), section 16A] or section 41(2), the officer of the service [or the Welsh family proceedings officer] shall have regard to the principle set out in section 1(2) and the matters set out in section 1(3)(a) to (f) as if for the word "court" in that section there were substituted the words ["officer of the service or Welsh family proceedings officer"].

(2) The officer of the service [or the Welsh family proceedings officer] shall make such investigations as may be necessary for him to carry out his duties and shall, in particular—

(a) contact or seek to interview such persons as he thinks appropriate or as the court directs;
(b) obtain such professional assistance as is available to him which he thinks appropriate or which the justices' clerk or the court directs him to obtain.

(3)   In addition to his duties, under other paragraphs of this rule, or rules [11A, 11AA or 11B], the officer of the service [or the Welsh family proceedings officer] shall provide to the [designated officer for the court], the justices' clerk and the court such other assistance as he or it may require.

(4)   A party may question the officer of the service [or the Welsh family proceedings officer] about oral or written advice tendered by him to the [designated officer for the court], the justices' clerk or the court.]

Amendment

Substituted by SI 2001/818, rr 2, 6. Date in force: 1 April 2001: see SI 2001/818, r 1.
Provision heading: words "and Welsh family proceedings officers" in square brackets inserted by SI 2005/585, rr 2, 4(a). Date in force: 1 April 2005: see SI 2005/585, r 1(1); for transitional provisions see rr 8, 9 thereof.
Para (1): words ", section 16(6), section 16A" in square brackets inserted by SI 2007/2188, rr 2, 6(a). Date in force: 1 October 2007: see SI 2007/2188, r 1.
Para (1): words "or the Welsh family proceedings officer" in square brackets inserted by SI 2005/585, rr 2, 4(b). Date in force: 1 April 2005: see SI 2005/585, r 1(1); for transitional provisions see rr 8, 9 thereof.
Para (1): words ""officer of the service or Welsh family proceedings officer"" in square brackets substituted by SI 2005/585, rr 2, 4(c). Date in force: 1 April 2005: see SI 2005/585, r 1(1); for transitional provisions see rr 8, 9 thereof.
Para (2): words "or the Welsh family proceedings officer" in square brackets inserted by SI 2005/585, rr 2, 4(b). Date in force: 1 April 2005: see SI 2005/585, r 1(1); for transitional provisions see rr 8, 9 thereof.
Para (3): words "11A, 11AA or 11B" in square brackets substituted by SI 2007/2188, rr 2, 6(b). Date in force: 1 October 2007: see SI 2007/2188, r 1.
Para (3): words "or the Welsh family proceedings officer" in square brackets inserted by SI 2005/585, rr 2, 4(b). Date in force: 1 April 2005: see SI 2005/585, r 1(1); for transitional provisions see rr 8, 9 thereof.
Para (3): words "designated officer for the court" in square brackets substituted by SI 2005/617, art 2, Schedule, para 128. Date in force: 1 April 2005: see SI 2005/617, art 1.
Para (4): words "or the Welsh family proceedings officer" in square brackets inserted by SI 2005/585, rr 2, 4(b). Date in force: 1 April 2005: see SI 2005/585, r 1(1); for transitional provisions see rr 8, 9 thereof.
Para (4): words "designated officer for the court" in square brackets substituted by SI 2005/617, art 2, Schedule, para 128. Date in force: 1 April 2005: see SI 2005/617, art 1.

[11A   Additional powers and duties of children's guardian]

[(1)   The children's guardian shall—

(a)   appoint a solicitor to represent the child unless such a solicitor has already been appointed; and

(b)   give such advice to the child as is appropriate having regard to his understanding and, subject to rule 12(1)(a), instruct the solicitor representing the child on all matters relevant to the interests of the child including possibilities for appeal, arising in the course of proceedings.

(2)   Where it appears to the children's guardian that the child—

(a)   is instructing his solicitor direct; or

(b)   intends to conduct and is capable of conducting the proceedings on his own behalf,

he shall inform the court through the [designated officer for the court] and from then he—

(i)   shall perform all of his duties set out in rule 11 and this rule, other than those duties under paragraph (1)(a) of this rule, and such other duties as the justices' clerk or the court may direct;

     (ii) shall take such part in the proceedings as the justices' clerk or the court may direct; and

    (iii) may, with the leave of the justices' clerk or the court, have legal representation in the conduct of those duties.

(3)   Unless excused by the justices' clerk or the court, the children's guardian shall attend all directions appointments in and hearings of the proceedings and shall advise the court on the following matters—

(a)   whether the child is of sufficient understanding for any purpose including the child's refusal to submit to a medical or psychiatric examination or other assessment that the court has the power to require, direct or order;

(b)   the wishes of the child in respect of any matter relevant to the proceedings including his attendance at court;

(c)   the appropriate forum for the proceedings;

(d)   the appropriate timing of the proceedings or any part of them;

(e)   the options available to it in respect of the child and the suitability of each such option including what order should be made in determining the application; and

(f)   any other matter concerning which the [designated officer for the court], the justices' clerk or the court seeks his advice or concerning which he considers that the [designated officer for the court], the justices' clerk or the court should be informed.

(4)   The advice given under paragraph (3) may, subject to any order of the court, be given orally or in writing; and if the advice be given orally, a note of it shall be taken by the justices' clerk or the court.

(5)   The children's guardian shall, where practicable, notify any person whose joinder as a party to those proceedings would be likely, in the opinion of the officer of the service [or the Welsh family proceedings officer], to safeguard the interests of the child of that person's right to apply to be joined under rule 7(2) and shall inform the [designated officer for the court] or the court—

(a)   of any such notification given;

(b)   of anyone whom he attempted to notify under this paragraph but was unable to contact; and

(c)   of anyone whom he believes may wish to be joined to the proceedings.

(6)   The children's guardian shall, unless the justices' clerk or the court otherwise directs, not less than 14 days before the date fixed for the final hearing of the proceedings—

(a)   file a written report advising on the interests of the child;

(b)   serve a copy of the filed report on the other parties [and any local authority that is preparing, or has prepared, a report under section 14A(8) or (9)].

(7)   The children's guardian shall serve and accept service of documents on behalf of the child in accordance with rule 8(3)(b) and (4)(b) and, where the child has not himself been served, and has sufficient understanding, advise the child of the contents of any document so served.

(8)   If the children's guardian inspects records of the kinds referred to in section 42, he shall bring to the attention of—

(a)   the court, through the [designated officer for the court]; and

(b)   unless the court or the justices' clerk otherwise directs, the other parties to the proceedings,

all records and documents which may, in his opinion, assist in the proper determination of the proceedings.

(9) The children's guardian shall ensure that, in relation to a decision made by the justices' clerk or the court in the proceedings—

(a) if he considers it appropriate to the age and understanding of the child, the child is notified of that decision; and

(b) if the child is notified of the decision, it is explained to the child in a manner appropriate to his age and understanding.]

Amendment

Inserted by SI 2001/818, rr 2, 7. Date in force: 1 April 2001: see SI 2001/818, r 1.
Para (2): words "designated officer for the court" in square brackets substituted by SI 2005/617, art 2, Schedule, para 128. Date in force: 1 April 2005: see SI 2005/617, art 1.
Para (3): in sub-para (f) words "designated officer for the court" in square brackets in both places they occur substituted by SI 2005/617, art 2, Schedule, para 128. Date in force: 1 April 2005: see SI 2005/617, art 1.
Para (5): words "or the Welsh family proceedings officer" in square brackets inserted by SI 2005/585, rr 2, 5. Date in force: 1 April 2005: see SI 2005/585, r 1(1); for transitional provisions see rr 8, 9 thereof.
Para (5): words "designated officer for the court" in square brackets substituted by SI 2005/617, art 2, Schedule, para 128. Date in force: 1 April 2005: see SI 2005/617, art 1.
Para (6): in sub-para (b) words "and any local authority that is preparing, or has prepared, a report under section 14A(8) or (9)" in square brackets inserted by SI 2005/2930, r 2(e), Sch 1, para 41. Date in force: 30 December 2005: see SI 2005/2930, r 1(2).
Para (8): in sub-para (a) words "designated officer for the court" in square brackets substituted by SI 2005/617, art 2, Schedule, para 128. Date in force: 1 April 2005: see SI 2005/617, art 1.

[11AA Additional powers and duties of officers of the service and Welsh family proceedings officers: family assistance order reports and risk assessments]

[(1) This rule applies where an officer of the service or a Welsh family proceedings officer is preparing or has prepared—

(a) a family assistance order report; or

(b) a risk assessment.

(2) Where an officer of the service or a Welsh family proceedings officer is preparing a family assistance order report or a risk assessment, he must consider whether—

(a) to notify the child of such of the contents of the report or assessment as he considers appropriate to the age and understanding of the child;

(b) to recommend in the report or assessment that the court lists a hearing for the purposes of considering the report or assessment;

(c) it is in the best interests of the child for the child to be made a party to the proceedings.

(3) If the officer of the service or the Welsh family proceedings officer decides to notify the child of any of the contents of the report or assessment, he must explain those contents to the child in a manner appropriate to the child's age and understanding.

(4) If the officer of the service or the Welsh family proceedings officer considers that the child should be made a party to the proceedings, he must notify the court of his opinion together with the reasons for that opinion.

(5) If the officer of the service or the Welsh family proceedings officer considers that the court should exercise the discretion under rule 17AA(2) in relation to service of a risk assessment, he must state in the risk assessment—

(a) the way in which he considers the discretion should be exercised (including his view on the length of any suggested delay in service); and

(b)   his reasons for reaching his view.

(6)   The officer of the service or the Welsh family proceedings officer must file the report or assessment with the court—

(a)   at or by the time directed by the court;
(b)   in the absence of any such direction, at least 14 days before a relevant hearing; or
(c)   where there has been no direction from the court and no relevant hearing is listed, as soon as possible following completion of the report or assessment.

(7)   In paragraph (6), a hearing is a relevant hearing if the justices' clerk has given the officer of the service or the Welsh family proceedings officer notice that the report or assessment is to be considered at it.

(8)   When an officer of the service or a Welsh family proceedings officer prepares a family assistance order report, he shall as soon as practicable serve copies of the report on—

(a)   each party; and
(b)   any local authority that is preparing or has prepared a report under section 14A(8) or (9).

(9)   At any hearing where a family assistance order report or risk assessment is considered any party may question the officer of the service or the Welsh family proceedings officer about the report or the assessment.]

Amendment

Inserted by SI 2007/2188, rr 2, 3(a), 7. Date in force: 1 October 2007: see SI 2007/2188, r 1.

[11B   Additional powers and duties of a children and family reporter]

[(1)   In addition to his duties under rule 11, the children and family reporter shall—

(a)   notify the child of such contents of his report (if any) as he considers appropriate to the age and understanding of the child, including any reference to the child's own views on the application and the recommendation of the children and family reporter; and
(b)   if he does notify the child of any contents of his report, explain them to the child in a manner appropriate to his age and understanding.

(2)   Where the court has—

(a)   directed that a written report be made by a children and family reporter; and
(b)   notified the children and family reporter that his report is to be considered at a hearing,

the children and family reporter shall—
(i)   file his report; and
(ii)   serve a copy on the other parties[, any local authority that is preparing, or has prepared, a report under section 14A(8) or (9)] and on the children's guardian (if any),

by such time as the court may direct and if no direction is given, not less than 14 days before that hearing.

(3)   The court may direct that the children and family reporter attend any hearing at which his report is to be considered.

(4)   The children and family reporter shall advise the court if he considers that the joinder of a person as a party to the proceedings would be likely to safeguard the interests of the child.

(5)   The children and family reporter shall consider whether it is in the best interests of the child for the child to be made a party to the proceedings.

(6)   If the children and family reporter considers the child should be made a party to the proceedings he shall notify the court of his opinion together with the reasons for that opinion.]

Amendment

Inserted by SI 2001/818, rr 2, 7. Date in force: 1 April 2001: see SI 2001/818, r 1.
Para (2): and in sub-para (b)(ii) words ", any local authority that is preparing, or has prepared, a report under section 14A(8) or (9)" in square brackets inserted by SI 2005/2930, r 2(e), Sch 1, para 42. Date in force: 30 December 2005: see SI 2005/2930, r 1(2).

---

12   Solicitor for child

(1)   A solicitor appointed under section 41(3) or in accordance with [rule 11A(1)(a)] shall represent the child—

(a)   in accordance with instructions received from the [children's guardian] (unless the solicitor considers, having taken into account the views of the [children's guardian] and any direction of the court under [rule 11A(2)], that the child wishes to give instructions which conflict with those of the [children's guardian] and that he is able, having regard to his understanding, to give such instructions on his own behalf in which case he shall conduct the proceedings in accordance with instructions received from the child), or

(b)   where no [children's guardian] has been appointed for the child and the condition in section 41(4)(b) is satisfied, in accordance with instructions received from the child, or

(c)   in default of instructions under (a) or (b), in furtherance of the best interests of the child.

(2)   A solicitor appointed under section 41(3) or in accordance with [rule 11A(1)(a)] shall serve and accept service of documents on behalf of the child in accordance with rule 8(3)(a) and (4)(a) and, where the child has not himself been served and has sufficient understanding, advise the child of the contents of any document so served.

(3)   Where the child wishes an appointment of a solicitor under section 41(3) or in accordance with [rule 11A(1)(a)] to be terminated, he may apply to the court for an order terminating the appointment; and the solicitor and the [children's guardian] shall be given an opportunity to make representations.

(4)   Where the [children's guardian] wishes an appointment of a solicitor under section 41(3) to be terminated, he may apply to the court for an order terminating the appointment; and the solicitor and, if he is of sufficient understanding, the child, shall be given an opportunity to make representations.

(5)   When terminating an appointment in accordance with paragraph (3) or (4), the court shall give reasons for so doing, a note of which shall be taken by the justices' clerk.

(6)   Where the justices' clerk or the court appoints a solicitor under section 41(3) or refuses to make such an appointment, the justices' clerk shall record the appointment or refusal in the appropriate form in Schedule 1 to these Rules and [the [designated officer for the court] shall] serve a copy on the parties and, where he is appointed, on the solicitor.

Date in force

14 October 1991: see r 1(1).

Amendment

Para (1): words "rule 11A(1)(a)" in square brackets substituted by SI 2001/818, rr 2, 8(a). Date in force: 1 April 2001: see SI 2001/818, r 1.
Para (1): words "children's guardian" in square brackets in each place they occur substituted by SI 2001/818, rr 2, 4(a). Date in force: 1 April 2001: see SI 2001/818, r 1.
Para (1): in sub-para (a) words "rule 11A(2)" in square brackets substituted by SI 2001/818, rr 2, 8(b). Date in force: 1 April 2001: see SI 2001/818, r 1.
Para (2): words "rule 11A(1)(a)" in square brackets substituted by SI 2001/818, rr 2, 8(a). Date in force: 1 April 2001: see SI 2001/818, r 1.
Para (3): words "rule 11A(1)(a)" in square brackets substituted by SI 2001/818, rr 2, 8(a). Date in force: 1 April 2001: see SI 2001/818, r 1.
Para (3): words "children's guardian" in square brackets substituted by SI 2001/818, rr 2, 4(a). Date in force: 1 April 2001: see SI 2001/818, r 1.
Para (4): words "children's guardian" in square brackets substituted by SI 2001/818, rr 2, 4(a). Date in force: 1 April 2001: see SI 2001/818, r 1.
Para (6): words from "the" to "shall" in square brackets inserted by SI 2001/615, r 2(xx), Schedule, para 97. Date in force: 1 April 2001: see SI 2001/615, r 1.
Para (6): words "designated officer for the court" in square brackets substituted by SI 2005/617, art 2, Schedule, para 128. Date in force: 1 April 2005: see SI 2005/617, art 1.

[13   Welfare officer]

[(1)   Where the court or a justices' clerk has directed that a written report be made by a welfare officer [in accordance with section 7(1)(b)], the report shall be filed at or by such time as the court or justices' clerk directs or, in the absence of such a direction, at least 14 days before a relevant hearing; and the [designated officer for the court] shall, as soon as practicable, serve a copy of the report on the parties[, any local authority that is preparing, or has prepared, a report under section 14A(8) or (9)] and any [children's guardian].

(2)   In paragraph (1), a hearing is relevant if the [designated officer for the court] has given the welfare officer notice that his report is to be considered at it.

(3)   After the filing of a written report by a welfare officer, the court or the justices' clerk may direct that the welfare officer attend any hearing at which the report is to be considered; and

    (a)   except where such a direction is given at a hearing attended by the welfare officer, the [designated officer for the court] shall inform the welfare officer of the direction; and

    (b)   at the hearing at which the report is considered any party may question the welfare officer about his report.

[(3A)   The welfare officer shall consider whether it is in the best interests of the child for the child to be made a party to the proceedings.

(3B)   If the welfare officer considers the child should be made a party to the proceedings he shall notify the court of his opinion together with the reasons for that opinion.]

(4)   This rule is without prejudice to the court's power to give directions under rule 14.]

Amendment

Substituted by SI 1992/2068, r 2, Schedule, para 3.
Para (1): words "in accordance with section 7(1)(b)" in square brackets inserted by SI 2001/818, rr 2, 9(a). Date in force: 1 April 2001: see SI 2001/818, r 1.
Para (1): words "designated officer for the court" in square brackets substituted by SI 2005/617, art 2, Schedule, para 128. Date in force: 1 April 2005: see SI 2005/617, art 1.
Para (1): words ", any local authority that is preparing, or has prepared, a report under section 14A(8) or (9)" in square brackets inserted by SI 2005/2930, r 2(e), Sch 1, para 42. Date in force: 30 December 2005: see SI 2005/2930, r 1(2).
Para (1): words "children's guardian" in square brackets substituted by SI 2001/818, rr 2, 4(a). Date in force: 1 April 2001: see SI 2001/818, r 1.
Para (2): words "designated officer for the court" in square brackets substituted by SI 2005/617, art 2, Schedule, para 128. Date in force: 1 April 2005: see SI 2005/617, art 1.
Para (3): in sub-para (a) words "designated officer for the court" in square brackets substituted by SI 2005/617, art 2, Schedule, para 128. Date in force: 1 April 2005: see SI 2005/617, art 1.
Paras (3A), (3B): inserted by SI 2001/818, rr 2, 9(b). Date in force: 1 April 2001: see SI 2001/818, r 1.

[13A   Local authority officer preparing a family assistance order report]

[Where a family assistance order directs a local authority officer to prepare a family assistance order report, rules 5(4)(a) and (b), 13, 14(1)(a)(i) and (2), 15(5) and 17(1) shall apply to, or in respect of, the local authority officer as they would apply to, or in respect of, a welfare officer preparing a report in accordance with section 7(1)(b).]

Amendment

Inserted by SI 2007/2188, rr 2, 3(b), 8. Date in force: 1 October 2007: see SI 2007/2188, r 1.

14   Directions

[(1)   In this rule, "party" includes the children's guardian and, where a request or directions is or are concerned with—

(a)   a report under—
   (i)   section 7, the welfare officer or children and family reporter;
   (ii)   section 14A(8) or (9), the local authority preparing that report;
(b)   a family assistance order report, the officer of the service or the Welsh family proceedings officer who is preparing the report;
(c)   a risk assessment, the officer of the service or the Welsh family proceedings officer who is preparing the assessment.]

(2)   In any relevant proceedings the justices' clerk or the court may, subject to paragraph (5), give, vary or revoke directions for the conduct of the proceedings, including—

(a)   the timetable for the proceedings;
(b)   varying the time within which or by which an act is required, by these Rules, to be done;
(c)   the attendance of the child;
(d)   the appointment of a [children's guardian] ..., or of a solicitor under section 41(3);
(e)   the service of documents;
(f)   the submission of evidence including experts' reports;
(g)   the preparation of welfare reports under section 7;
(h)   the transfer of the proceedings to another court in accordance with any Order made by the Lord Chancellor under Part I of Schedule 11;

(i) consolidation with other proceedings;

[(j) the preparation of reports under section 14A(8) or (9);

(k) the attendance of the person who prepared the report under section 14A(8) or (9) at any hearing at which the report is to be considered;]

[(l) the preparation of family assistance order reports;

(m) listing a hearing for the purposes of considering the contents of a risk assessment.]

and the justices' clerk shall, on receipt of an application [by the] [designated officer for the court], or where proceedings have been transferred to his court, consider whether such directions need to be given.

(3) Where the justices' clerk or a single justice who is holding a directions appointment considers, for whatever reason, that it is inappropriate to give a direction on a particular matter, he shall refer the matter to the court which may give any appropriate direction.

(4) Where a direction is given under paragraph (2)(h), [an order] shall be issued in the appropriate form in Schedule 1 to these Rules and the [designated officer for the court] shall follow the procedure set out in rule 6(2).

(5) Directions under paragraph (2) may be given, varied or revoked either—

(a) of the justices' clerk or the court's own motion [the [d]esignated officer for the court] having given the parties notice of the intention to do so and an opportunity to attend and be heard or to make written representations,

(b) on the written request [in Form C2] of a party specifying the direction which is sought, filed and served on the other parties, or

(c) on the written request [in Form C2] of a party specifying the direction which is sought, to which the other parties consent and which they or their representatives have signed.

(6) In an urgent case, the request under paragraph (5)(b) may, with the leave of the justices' clerk or the court, be made—

(a) orally,

(b) without notice to the parties, or

(c) both as in sub-paragraph (a) and as in sub-paragraph (b).

(7) On receipt of a request [by the [d]esignated officer for the court] under paragraph (5)(b) the justices' clerk shall fix a date for the hearing of the request and [the [designated officer for the court] shall] give not less than 2 days' notice [in Form C6] to the parties of the date so fixed.

(8) On considering a request under paragraph (5)(c) the justices' clerk or the court shall either—

(a) grant the request, whereupon the [designated officer for the court] shall inform the parties of the decision, or

(b) direct that a date be fixed for the hearing of the request, whereupon the justices clerk shall fix such a date and [the [designated officer for the court] shall] give not less than 2 days' notice to the parties of the date so fixed.

(9) Subject to rule 28, a party may request, in accordance with paragraph 5(b) or (c), that an order be made under section 11(3) or, if he is entitled to apply for such an order, under section 38(1), and paragraphs (6), (7) and (8) shall apply accordingly.

(10) Where, in any relevant proceedings, the court has power to make an order of its own motion, the power to give directions under paragraph (2) shall apply.

(11) Directions of the justices' clerk or a court which are still in force immediately prior to the transfer of relevant proceedings to another court shall continue to apply

following the transfer, subject to any changes of terminology which are required to apply those directions to the court to which the proceedings are transferred, unless varied or discharged by directions under paragraph (2).

[(11A) After the filing of a family assistance order report or a risk assessment, the court may direct that the officer of the service or the Welsh family proceedings officer attend any hearing at which the report or assessment is to be considered.]

(12) The justices' clerk or the court shall [record] the giving, variation or revocation of a direction under this rule [in the appropriate form in Schedule 1 to these Rules] and [the [designated officer for the court] shall] serve, as soon as practicable, a copy of [the form] on any party who was not present at the giving, variation or revocation.

Date in force

14 October 1991: see r 1(1).

Amendment

Para (1): substituted by SI 2007/2188, rr 2, 9(a). Date in force: 1 October 2007: see SI 2007/2188, r 1.
Para (2): in sub-para (d) words "children's guardian" in square brackets substituted by SI 2001/818, rr 2, 4(a). Date in force: 1 April 2001: see SI 2001/818, r 1.
Para (2): in sub-para (d) words omitted revoked by SI 2001/818, rr 2, 10. Date in force: 1 April 2001: see SI 2001/818, r 1.
Para (2): sub-paras (j), (k) inserted by SI 2005/2930, r 2(e), Sch 1, para 43(b). Date in force: 30 December 2005: see SI 2005/2930, r 1(2).
Para (2): sub-paras (l), (m) inserted by SI 2007/2188, rr 2, 9(b). Date in force: 1 October 2007: see SI 2007/2188, r 1.
Para (2): words in square brackets beginning with the words "by the" inserted by SI 2001/615, r 2(xx), Schedule, para 99. Date in force: 1 April 2001: see SI 2001/615, r 1.
Para (2): words "designated officer for the court" in square brackets substituted by SI 2005/617, art 2, Schedule, para 128. Date in force: 1 April 2005: see SI 2005/617, art 1.
Para (4): words "an order" in square brackets substituted by SI 1994/3156, r 15.
Para (4): words "designated officer for the court" in square brackets substituted by SI 2005/617, art 2, Schedule, para 128. Date in force: 1 April 2005: see SI 2005/617, art 1.
Para (5): in sub-para (a) words in square brackets beginning with the word "the" inserted by SI 2001/615, r 2(xx), Schedule, para 98. Date in force: 1 April 2001: see SI 2001/615, r 1.
Para (5): in sub-para (a) words "designated officer for the court" in square brackets substituted by SI 2005/617, art 2, Schedule, para 128. Date in force: 1 April 2005: see SI 2005/617, art 1.
Para (5): words "in Form C2" in square brackets in both places they occur inserted by SI 1994/3156, rr 16, 17.
Para (7): words in square brackets beginning with the words "by the" inserted by SI 2001/615, r 2(xx), Schedule, para 99. Date in force: 1 April 2001: see SI 2001/615, r 1.
Para (7): words "designated officer for the court" in square brackets in both places they occur substituted by SI 2005/617, art 2, Schedule, para 128. Date in force: 1 April 2005: see SI 2005/617, art 1.
Para (7): words from "the" to "shall" in square brackets inserted by SI 2001/615, r 2(xx), Schedule, para 97. Date in force: 1 April 2001: see SI 2001/615, r 1.
Para (7): words "in Form C6" in square brackets inserted by SI 1994/3156, rr 16, 17.
Para (8): in sub-paras (a), (b) words "designated officer for the court" in square brackets substituted by SI 2005/617, art 2, Schedule, para 128. Date in force: 1 April 2005: see SI 2005/617, art 1.
Para (8): in sub-para (b) words from "the" to "shall" in square brackets inserted by SI 2001/615, r 2(xx), Schedule, para 97. Date in force: 1 April 2001: see SI 2001/615, r 1.
Para (11A): inserted by SI 2007/2188, rr 2, 9(c). Date in force: 1 October 2007: see SI 2007/2188, r 1.
Para (12): word "record" in square brackets substituted by SI 1991/1991, r 26, Sch 2, para 8(2).
Para (12): words "in the appropriate form in Schedule 1 to these Rules" in square brackets inserted by SI 1991/1991, r 26, Sch 2, para 8(2).
Para (12): words from "the" to "shall" in square brackets inserted by SI 2001/615, r 2(xx), Schedule, para 97. Date in force: 1 April 2001: see SI 2001/615, r 1.

Para (12): words "designated officer for the court" in square brackets substituted by SI 2005/617, art 2, Schedule, para 128. Date in force: 1 April 2005: see SI 2005/617, art 1.
Para (12): words "the form" in square brackets substituted by SI 1991/1991, r 26, Sch 2, para 8(2).

---

15   Timing of proceedings

(1)   Any period of time fixed by these Rules, or by any order or direction, for doing any act shall be reckoned in accordance with this rule.

(2)   Where the period, being a period of 7 days or less, would include a day which is not a business day, that day shall be excluded.

(3)   Where the time fixed for filing a document with the [designated officer for the court] expires on a day on which the [office of the [designated officer for the court]] is closed, and for that reason the document cannot be filed on that day, the document shall be filed in time if it is filed on the next day on which the [office of the [designated officer for the court]] is open.

(4)   Where these Rules provide a period of time within which or by which a certain act is to be performed in the course of relevant proceedings, that period may not be extended otherwise than by a direction of the justices' clerk or the court under rule 14.

(5)   At the—

    (a)   transfer to a court of relevant proceedings,
    (b)   postponement or adjournment of any hearing or directions appointment in the course of relevant proceedings, or
    (c)   conclusion of any such hearing or directions appointment other than one at which the proceedings are determined, or so soon thereafter as is practicable,
[(i)   the justices' clerk shall fix a date upon which the proceedings shall come before him or the court again for such purposes as he or the court directs, which date shall, where paragraph (a) applies, be as soon as possible after the transfer, and
   (ii)   the [designated officer for the court] shall give notice to the parties[, any local authority that is preparing, or has prepared, a report under section 14A(8) or (9)] and to the [children's guardian][,] the [welfare officer[, the] children and family reporter] [or the officer of the service or the Welsh family proceedings officer who is preparing or has prepared a family assistance order report or a risk assessment] of the date so fixed].

Date in force

14 October 1991: see r 1(1).

Amendment

Para (3): words "designated officer for the court" in square brackets in each place they occur substituted by SI 2005/617, art 2, Schedule, para 128. Date in force: 1 April 2005: see SI 2005/617, art 1.
Para (3): words in square brackets beginning with the words "office of the" in both places they occur substituted by SI 2001/615, r 2(xx), Schedule, para 95. Date in force: 1 April 2001: see SI 2001/615, r 1.
Para (5): sub-paras (i), (ii) substituted by SI 2001/615, r 2(xx), Schedule, para 96. Date in force: 1 April 2001: see SI 2001/615, r 1.
Para (5): in sub-para (ii) words "designated officer for the court" in square brackets substituted by SI 2005/617, art 2, Schedule, para 128. Date in force: 1 April 2005: see SI 2005/617, art 1.
Para (5): in sub-para (ii) words ", any local authority that is preparing, or has prepared, a report under section 14A(8) or (9)" in square brackets inserted by SI 2005/2930, r 2(e), Sch 1, para 44. Date in force: 30 December 2005: see SI 2005/2930, r 1(2).

Para (5): in sub-para (ii) words "children's guardian" in square brackets substituted by SI 2001/818, rr 2, 4(a). Date in force: 1 April 2001: see SI 2001/818, r 1.
Para (5): in sub-para (c)(ii) comma and word ", the" in square brackets substituted by SI 2007/2188, rr 2, 10(a), (b). Date in force: 1 October 2007: see SI 2007/2188, r 1.
Para (5): in sub-para (ii) words "welfare officer or children and family reporter" in square brackets substituted by SI 2001/818, rr 2, 4(b). Date in force: 1 April 2001: see SI 2001/818, r 1.
Para (5): in sub-para (c)(ii) words from "or the officer" to "a risk assessment" inserted by SI 2007/2188, rr 2, 10(c). Date in force: 1 October 2007: see SI 2007/2188, r 1.

---

16   Attendance at directions appointment and hearing

(1)   Subject to paragraph (2), a party shall attend a directions appointment of which he has been given notice in accordance with rule 14(5) unless the justices' clerk or the court otherwise directs.

(2)   Relevant proceedings shall take place in the absence of any party including the child if—

  (a)   the court considers it in the interests of the child, having regard to the matters to be discussed or the evidence likely to be given, and
  (b)   the party is represented by a [children's guardian] or solicitor;

and when considering the interests of the child under sub-paragraph (a) the court shall give the [children's guardian], solicitor for the child and, if he is of sufficient understanding, the child, an opportunity to make representations.

(3)   Subject to paragraph (4) below, where at the time and place appointed for a hearing or directions appointment the applicant appears but one or more of the respondents do not, the justices' clerk or the court may proceed with the hearing or appointment.

(4)   The court shall not begin to hear an application in the absence of a respondent unless—

  (a)   it is proved to the satisfaction of the court that he received reasonable notice of the date of the hearing; or
  (b)   the court is satisfied that the circumstances of the case justify proceeding with the hearing.

(5)   Where, at the time and place appointed for a hearing or directions appointment, one or more respondents appear but the applicant does not, the court may refuse the application or, if sufficient evidence has previously been received, proceed in the absence of the applicant.

(6)   Where at the time and place appointed for a hearing or directions appointment neither the applicant nor any respondent appears, the court may refuse the application.

(7)   If the court considers it expedient in the interests of the child, it shall hear any relevant proceedings in private when only the officers of the court, the parties, their legal representatives and such other persons as specified by the court may attend.

Date in force

14 October 1991: see r 1(1).

Amendment

Para (2): words "children's guardian" in square brackets in both places they occur substituted by SI 2001/818, rr 2, 4(a). Date in force: 1 April 2001: see SI 2001/818, r 1.

---

17   Documentary Evidence

(1)   Subject to paragraphs (4) and (5), in any relevant proceedings a party shall file and serve on the parties, [any local authority that is preparing, or has prepared, a report under section 14A(8) or (9),] any [welfare officer[, any] children and family reporter] [, any officer of the service or any Welsh family proceedings officer who is preparing or has prepared a family assistance order report or a risk assessment] and any [children's guardian] of whose appointment he has been given notice under rule 10(5)—

(a)   written statements of the substance of the oral evidence which the party intends to adduce at a hearing of, or a directions appointment in, those proceedings, which shall—
   (i)   be dated,
   (ii)   be signed by the person making the statement, …
   (iii)   contain a declaration that the maker of the statement believes it to be true and understands that it may be placed before the court, and
   [(iv)   show in the top right hand corner of the first page—
       (a)   the initials and surname of the person making the statement,
       (b)   the number of the statement in relation to the maker,
       (c)   the date on which the statement was made, and
       (d)   the party on whose behalf it is filed; and]
(b)   copies of any documents, including, subject to rule 18(3), experts' reports, upon which the party intends to rely, at a hearing of, or a directions appointment in, those proceedings,

at or by such time as the justices' clerk or the court directs or, in the absence of a direction, before the hearing or appointment.

(2)   A party may, subject to any direction of the justices' clerk or the court about the timing of statements under this rule, file and serve on the parties a statement which is supplementary to a statement served under paragraph (1).

(3)   At a hearing or directions appointment a party may not, without the leave of the justices' clerk, in the case of a directions appointment, or the court—

(a)   adduce evidence, or
(b)   seek to rely on a document,

in respect of which he has failed to comply with the requirements of paragraph (1).

(4)   In proceedings for a section 8 order [or a special guardianship order] a party shall—

(a)   neither file nor serve any document other than as required or authorised by these Rules, and
(b)   in completing a form prescribed by these Rules, neither give information, nor make a statement, which is not required or authorised by that form,

without the leave of the justices' clerk or the court.

(5)   In proceedings for a section 8 order [or a special guardianship order], no statement or copy may be filed under paragraph (1) until such time as the justices' clerk or the court directs.

Date in force

14 October 1991: see r 1(1).

Amendment

Para (1): words "any local authority that is preparing, or has prepared, a report under section 14A(8) or (9)," in square brackets inserted by SI 2005/2930, r 2(e), Sch 1, para 45(a).

Date in force: 30 December 2005: see SI 2005/2930, r 1(2).
Para (1): words "welfare officer or children and family reporter" in square brackets substituted by SI 2001/818, rr 2, 4(b). Date in force: 1 April 2001: see SI 2001/818, r 1.
Para (1): word ", any" in square brackets substituted by SI 2007/2188, rr 2, 11(a). Date in force: 1 October 2007: see SI 2007/2188, r 1.
Para (1): words from ", any officer of" to "a risk assessment" in square brackets inserted by SI 2007/2188, rr 2, 11(b). Date in force: 1 October 2007: see SI 2007/2188, r 1.
Para (1): words "children's guardian" in square brackets substituted by SI 2001/818, rr 2, 4(a). Date in force: 1 April 2001: see SI 2001/818, r 1.
Para (1): in sub-para (a)(ii) word omitted revoked by SI 1992/2068, r 2, Schedule, para 4.
Para (1): sub-para (a)(iv) inserted by SI 1992/2068, r 2, Schedule, para 4.
Para (4): words "or a special guardianship order" in square brackets inserted by SI 2005/2930, r 2(e), Sch 1, para 45(b). Date in force: 30 December 2005: see SI 2005/2930, r 1(2).
Para (5): words "or a special guardianship order" in square brackets inserted by SI 2005/2930, r 2(e), Sch 1, para 45(b). Date in force: 30 December 2005: see SI 2005/2930, r 1(2).

[17A   Disclosure of report under section 14A(8) or (9)]

[(1)   In proceedings for a special guardianship order, the local authority shall file the report under section 14A(8) or (9) within the timetable fixed by the court.

(2)   The justices' clerk or the court shall consider whether to give a direction that the report under section 14A(8) or (9) be disclosed to each party to the proceedings.

(3)   Before giving such a direction the justices' clerk or the court shall consider whether any information should be deleted including information which reveals the party's address in a case where he has declined to reveal it in accordance with rule 33A (disclosure of addresses).

(4)   The justices' clerk or the court may direct that the report will not be disclosed to a party.

(5)   The designated officer shall serve a copy of the report filed under paragraph (1)—

    (a)   in accordance with any direction given under paragraph (2); and
    (b)   on any children's guardian, welfare officer or children and family reporter.]

Amendment

Inserted by SI 2005/2930, r 2(e), Sch 1, para 46. Date in force: 30 December 2005: see SI 2005/2930, r 1(2).

[17AA   Service of risk assessment]

[(1)   Where an officer of the service or Welsh family proceedings officer has filed a risk assessment with the court, subject to paragraph (2), the justices' clerk shall as soon as practicable serve copies of the risk assessment on—

    (a)   each party; and
    (b)   any local authority that is preparing or has prepared a report under section 14A(8) or (9).

(2)   Before serving the risk assessment, the court must consider whether, in order to prevent a risk of harm to the child, it is necessary for—

    (a)   information to be deleted from a copy of the risk assessment before that copy is served on a party; or
    (b)   service of a copy of the risk assessment (whether with information deleted from it or not) on a party to be delayed for a specified period,

and may direct accordingly.]

Amendment

Inserted by SI 2007/2188, rr 2, 12. Date in force: 1 October 2007: see SI 2007/2188, r 1.

18   Expert evidence – examination of child

(1)   No person may, without the leave of the justices' clerk or the court, cause the child to be medically or psychiatrically examined, or otherwise assessed, for the purpose of the preparation of expert evidence for use in the proceedings.

(2)   An application for leave under paragraph (1) shall, unless the justices' clerk or the court otherwise directs, be served on all the parties to the proceedings and on the [children's guardian].

(3)   Where the leave of the justices' clerk or the court has not been given under paragraph (1), no evidence arising out of an examination or assessment to which that paragraph applies may be adduced without the leave of the court.

Date in force

14 October 1991: see r 1(1).

Amendment

Para (2): words "children's guardian" in square brackets substituted by SI 2001/818, rr 2, 4(a). Date in force: 1 April 2001: see SI 2001/818, r 1.

19   Amendment

(1)   Subject to rule 17(2), a document which has been filed or served in any relevant proceedings may not be amended without the leave of the justices' clerk or the court which shall, unless the justices' clerk or the court otherwise directs, be requested in writing.

(2)   On considering a request for leave to amend a document the justices' clerk or the court shall either—

    (a)   grant the request, whereupon the [designated officer for the court] shall inform the person making the request of that decision, or

    (b)   invite the parties or any of them to make representations, within a specified period, as to whether such an order should be made.

(3)   A person amending a document shall file it with the [designated officer for the court] and serve it on those persons on whom it was served prior to amendment; and the amendments shall be identified.

Date in force

14 October 1991: see r 1(1).

Amendment

Para (2): in sub-para (a) words "designated officer for the court" in square brackets substituted by SI 2005/617, art 2, Schedule, para 128. Date in force: 1 April 2005: see SI 2005/617, art 1.
Para (3): words "designated officer for the court" in square brackets substituted by SI 2005/617, art 2, Schedule, para 128. Date in force: 1 April 2005: see SI 2005/617, art 1.

20 Oral Evidence

The justices' clerk or the court shall keep a note of the substance of the oral evidence given at a hearing of, or directions appointment in, relevant proceedings.

Date in force

14 October 1991: see r 1(1).

---

21 Hearing

(1) Before the hearing, the justice or justices who will be dealing with the case shall read any documents which have been filed under rule 17 in respect of the hearing.

(2) The justices' clerk at a directions appointment, or the court at a hearing or directions appointment, may give directions as to the order of speeches and evidence.

(3) Subject to directions under paragraph (2), at a hearing of, or directions appointment in, relevant proceedings, the parties and the [children's guardian] shall adduce their evidence in the following order—

    (a) the applicant,
    (b) any party with parental responsibility for the child,
    (c) other respondents,
    (d) the [children's guardian],
    (e) the child if he is a party to the proceedings and there is no [children's guardian].

[(3A) At the hearing at which the report under section 14A(8) or (9) is considered a party to whom the report, or part of it, has been disclosed may question the person who prepared the report about it.]

(4) After the final hearing of relevant proceedings, the court shall make its decision as soon as is practicable.

(5) Before the court makes an order or refuses an application or request, the justices' clerk shall record in writing—

    (a) the names of the justice or justices constituting the court by which the decision is made, and
    (b) in consultation with the justice or justices, the reasons for the court's decision and any findings of fact.

[(6) When making an order or when refusing an application, the court, or one of the justices constituting the court by which the decision is made shall

    (a) where it makes a finding of fact state such finding and complete Form C22; and
    (b) state the reasons for the court's decision.]

[(7) As soon as practicable after the court announces its decision—

    (a) the justices' clerk shall make a record of any order made in the appropriate form in Schedule 1 to these Rules or, where there is no such form, in writing; and
    (b) subject to paragraph (8), the [designated officer for the court] shall serve a copy of any order made on the parties to the proceedings and on any person with whom the child is living[, and where applicable, on the local authority that prepared the report under section 14A(8) or (9)].]

(8) Within 48 hours after the making of an order under section 48(4) or the making, ex parte, of—

(a) [section 8 order], or

(b) an order under section 44, 48(9), 50, [or] 75(1) ... ,

the applicant shall serve a copy of the order in the appropriate form in Schedule 1 to these Rules on—

(i) each party,

(ii) any person who has actual care of the child, or who had such care immediately prior to the making of the order, and

(iii) in the case of an order referred to in sub-paragraph (b), the local authority in whose area the child lives or is found.

Date in force

14 October 1991: see r 1(1).

Amendment

Para (3): words "children's guardian" in square brackets in each place they occur substituted by SI 2001/818, rr 2, 4(a). Date in force: 1 April 2001: see SI 2001/818, r 1.

Para (3A): inserted by SI 2005/2930, r 2(e), Sch 1, para 47(a). Date in force: 30 December 2005: see SI 2005/2930, r 1(2).

Para (6): substituted by SI 1994/3156, r 18.

Para (7): substituted by SI 2001/615, r 2(xx), Schedule, para 101. Date in force: 1 April 2001: see SI 2001/615, r 1.

Para (7): in sub-para (b) words "designated officer for the court" in square brackets substituted by SI 2005/617, art 2, Schedule, para 128. Date in force: 1 April 2005: see SI 2005/617, art 1.

Para (7): in sub-para (b) words ", and where applicable, on the local authority that prepared the report under section 14A(8) or (9)" in square brackets inserted by SI 2005/2930, r 2(e), Sch 1, para 47(b). Date in force: 30 December 2005: see SI 2005/2930, r 1(2).

Para (8): in sub-para (a) words "section 8 order" in square brackets substituted by SI 1992/2068, r 2, Schedule, paras 1, 5.

Para (8): in sub-para (b) word "or" in square brackets inserted by SI 1992/2068, r 2, Schedule, paras 1, 5.

Para (8): in sub-para (b) words omitted revoked by SI 1992/2068, r 2, Schedule, paras 1, 5.

[Part IIA
Proceedings under Section 30 of the Human Fertilisation and Embryology
Act 1990]

Amendment

Inserted by SI 1994 No 2166, r 4.

[21A   Interpretation]

[(1)   In this Part of these Rules—

"the 1990 Act" means the Human Fertilisation and Embryology Act 1990;

"the birth father" means the father of the child, including a person who is treated as being the father of the child by section 28 of the 1990 Act where he is not the husband within the meaning of section 30 of the 1990 Act;

"the birth mother" means the woman who carried the child;

"the birth parents" means the birth mother and the birth father;

...

"the husband and wife" means the persons who may apply for a parental order where the conditions set out in section 30(1) of the 1990 Act are met;

"parental order" means an order under section 30 of the 1990 Act (parental orders in favour of gamete donors) providing for a child to be treated in law as a child of the parties to a marriage;

["parental order reporter" means an officer of the service [or a Welsh family proceedings officer] appointed under section 41 of the Children Act 1989 in relation to proceedings specified by paragraph (2)].

(2) Applications under section 30 of the 1990 Act are specified proceedings for the purposes of section 41 of the Children Act 1989 in accordance with section 41(6)(i) of that Act.]

Amendment

Inserted by SI 1994/2166, r 4.
Para (1): definition "the guardian ad litem" (omitted) revoked by SI 2001/818, rr 2, 11(a). Date in force: 1 April 2001: see SI 2001/818, r 1.
Para (1): definition "parental order reporter" inserted by SI 2001/818, rr 2, 11(b). Date in force: 1 April 2001: see SI 2001/818, r 1.
Para (1): in definition "parental order reporter" words "or a Welsh family proceedings officer" in square brackets inserted by SI 2005/585, rr 2, 6. Date in force: 1 April 2005: see SI 2005/585, r 1(1); for transitional provisions see rr 8, 9 thereof.

[21B   Application of the remaining provisions of these Rules]

[Subject to the provisions of this Part, the remaining provisions of these Rules shall apply as appropriate with any necessary modifications to proceedings under this Part except that rules 7(1), 9, 10(1)(b), 10(11), [11A(1)], [11A(2)] and 12 shall not apply.]

Amendment

Inserted by SI 1994/2166, r 4.
Reference to "11A(1)" in square brackets substituted by SI 2001/818, rr 2, 12(a). Date in force: 1 April 2001: see SI 2001/818, r 1.
Reference to "11A(2)" in square brackets substituted by SI 2001/818, rr 2, 12(b). Date in force: 1 April 2001: see SI 2001/818, r 1.

[21C   Parties]

[The applicants shall be the husband and wife and the respondents shall be the persons set out in the relevant entry in column (iii) of Schedule 2.]

Amendment

Inserted by SI 1994/2166, r 4.

[21D   [Acknowledgement]]

[Within 14 days of the service of an application for a parental order, each respondent shall file and serve on all the other parties an [acknowledgement in Form C52].]

Amendment

Inserted by SI 1994/2166, r 4.
Rule heading: substituted by SI 1994/3156, r 19(a).
Words in square brackets substituted by SI 1994/3156, r 19(b).

[21E   Appointment and duties of the [parental order reporter]]

[(1)   As soon as practicable after the application has been filed, the justices' clerk shall consider the appointment of a [parental order reporter] in accordance with section 41(1) of the Children Act 1989.

(2)   ...

(3)   In addition to such of the matters set out in [rules 11 and 11A] as are appropriate, the [parental order reporter] shall—

(i)   investigate the matters set out in section 30(1) to (7) of the 1990 Act;

(ii)   so far as he considers necessary, investigate any matter contained in the application form or other matter which appears relevant to the making of a parental order;

(iii)   advise the court on whether there is any reason under section 6 of the Adoption Act 1976, as applied with modifications by the Parental Orders (Human Fertilisation and Embryology) Regulations 1994, to refuse the parental order.]

Amendment

Inserted by SI 1994/2166, r 4.
Provision heading: words "parental order reporter" in square brackets substituted by SI 2001/818, rr 2, 13(a). Date in force: 1 April 2001: see SI 2001/818, r 1.
Para (1): words "parental order reporter" in square brackets substituted by SI 2001/818, rr 2, 13(a). Date in force: 1 April 2001: see SI 2001/818, r 1.
Para (2): revoked by SI 2001/818, rr 2, 13(b). Date in force: 1 April 2001: see SI 2001/818, r 1.
Para (3): words "rules 11 and 11A" in square brackets substituted by SI 2001/818, rr 2, 13(c). Date in force: 1 April 2001: see SI 2001/818, r 1.
Para (3): words "parental order reporter" in square brackets substituted by SI 2001/818, rr 2, 13(a). Date in force: 1 April 2001: see SI 2001/818, r 1.

[21F   Personal attendance of applicants]

[The court shall not make a parental order except upon the personal attendance before it of the applicants.]

Amendment

Inserted by SI 1994/2166, r 4.

[21G   Copies of orders]

[(1)   Where a parental order is made by a court sitting in Wales in respect of a child who was born in Wales and the applicants so request before the order is drawn up, the [designated officer for the court] shall obtain a translation into Welsh of the particulars set out in the order.

(2)   Within 7 days after the making of a parental order, the [designated officer for the court] shall send a copy of the order to the Registrar General.

(3)   A copy of any parental order may be supplied to the Registrar General at his request.]

Amendment

Inserted by SI 1994/2166, r 4.
Para (1): words "designated officer for the court" in square brackets substituted by SI 2005/617, art 2, Schedule, para 128. Date in force: 1 April 2005: see SI 2005/617, art 1.

Para (2): words "designated officer for the court" in square brackets substituted by SI 2005/617, art 2, Schedule, para 128. Date in force: 1 April 2005: see SI 2005/617, art 1.

[21H   Amendment and revocation of orders]

[(1)   Any application made under paragraph 4 of Schedule 1 to the Adoption Act 1976 as modified by the Parental Orders (Human Fertilisation and Embryology) Regulations 1994 for the amendment of a parental order or for the revocation of a direction to the Registrar General shall be made to a family proceedings court for the same [local justice area] as the family proceedings court which made the parental order, by delivering it to or sending it by post to the [designated officer for the court].

(2)   Notice of the application shall be given by the [designated officer for the court] to such persons (if any) as the court thinks fit.

(3)   Where the application is granted, the [designated officer for the court] shall send to the Registrar General a notice specifying the amendments or informing him of the revocation and shall give sufficient particulars of the order to enable the Registrar General to identify the case.]

Amendment

Inserted by SI 1994/2166, r 4.
Para (1): words "local justice area" in square brackets substituted by SI 2005/617, art 2, Schedule, para 130. Date in force: 1 April 2005: see SI 2005/617, art 1.
Para (1): words "designated officer for the court" in square brackets substituted by SI 2005/617, art 2, Schedule, para 128. Date in force: 1 April 2005: see SI 2005/617, art 1.
Para (2): words "designated officer for the court" in square brackets substituted by SI 2005/617, art 2, Schedule, para 128. Date in force: 1 April 2005: see SI 2005/617, art 1.
Para (3): words "designated officer for the court" in square brackets substituted by SI 2005/617, art 2, Schedule, para 128. Date in force: 1 April 2005: see SI 2005/617, art 1.

[21I   Keeping of registers, custody, inspection and disclosure of documents and information]

[(1)   Such part of the register kept in pursuance of rules made under the Magistrates' Courts Act 1980 as relates to proceedings for parental orders shall be kept in a separate book and the book shall not contain particulars of any other proceedings.

(2)   The book kept in pursuance of paragraph (1) and all other documents relating to the proceedings for a parental order shall, while they are in the custody of the court, be kept in a place of special security.

(3)   Any person who obtains information in the course of, or relating to proceedings for a parental order, shall treat that information as confidential and shall only disclose it if—

    (a)   the disclosure is necessary for the proper exercise of his duties, or
    (b)   the information is requested—
        (i)   by a court or public authority (whether in Great Britain or not) having the power to determine proceedings for a parental order and related matters, for the purpose of the discharge of its duties in that behalf, or
        (ii)   by a person who is authorised in writing by the Secretary of State to obtain the information for the purposes of research.]

Amendment

Inserted by SI 1994/2166, r 4.

[21J   Application for removal, return etc of child]

[(1)   An application under sections 27(1), 29(1) or 29(2) of the Adoption Act 1976 as applied with modifications by the Parental Orders (Human Fertilisation and Embryology) Regulations 1994 shall be made by complaint to the family proceedings court in which the application under section 30 of the 1990 Act is pending.

(2)   The respondents shall be all the parties to the proceedings under section 30 and such other person or body, not being the child, as the court thinks fit.

(3)   The [designated officer for the court] shall serve notice of the time fixed for the hearing, together with a copy of the complaint on the guardian ad litem who may attend on the hearing of the application and be heard on the question of whether the application should be granted.

(4)   The court may at any time give directions as to the conduct of the application under this rule.

(5)   Where an application under this rule is determined, the [designated officer for the court] shall serve notice of the determination on all the parties.

(6)   A search warrant issued by a justice of the peace under section 29(4) of the Adoption Act 1976 (applied as above) (which relates to premises specified in an information to which an order made under the said section 29(1) relates, authorising a constable to search the said premises and if he finds the child to return the child to the person on whose application the said order was made) shall be in a warrant form as if issued under section 102 of the Children Act 1989 (warrant to search for or remove a child) or a form to the like effect.]

Amendment

Inserted by SI 1994/2166, r 4.
Para (3): words "designated officer for the court" in square brackets substituted by SI 2005/617, art 2, Schedule, para 128. Date in force: 1 April 2005: see SI 2005/617, art 1.
Para (5): words "designated officer for the court" in square brackets substituted by SI 2005/617, art 2, Schedule, para 128. Date in force: 1 April 2005: see SI 2005/617, art 1.

[PART IIB
PROCEEDINGS IN RESPECT OF THE COUNCIL REGULATION]

Amendment

Inserted by SI 2005/229, r 5. Date in force: 1 March 2005: see SI 2005/229, r 1.

[21K   Application by a party for transfer of proceedings to a court of another Member State]

[(1)   A party may make an application that proceedings, or a specific part of those proceedings, be heard in another Member State pursuant to Article 15 of the Council Regulation.

(2)   An application under paragraph (1) shall be made—

    (a)   to the court in which the relevant parental responsibility proceedings (within the meaning of the Council Regulation) are pending; and
    (b)   on notice in form C1; and
    (c)   such notice shall be filed and served on the respondents not less than 5 business days before the hearing of the application.

(3)   An application made under paragraph (1) must be supported by an affidavit, which should contain evidence of the child's particular connection to the other Member State in accordance with Article 15(3) of the Council Regulation. In this paragraph the child referred to is the child subject of the parental responsibility proceedings.

(4)   The respondents referred to in paragraph (2)(c) mean any other parties, the child and the Central Authority of the relevant Member State.]

Amendment

Inserted by SI 2005/229, r 5. Date in force: 1 March 2005: see SI 2005/229, r 1.

[21L   Application by a court of another Member State for transfer of proceedings]

[(1)   A court of another Member State may make an application that proceedings, or a specific part of those proceedings, be heard in that Member State pursuant to Article 15 of the Council Regulation.

(2)   An application under paragraph (1) should be made in the first instance to the Central Authority of England and Wales.

(3)   The Central Authority will forward an application made under paragraph (1) to the court in which the parental responsibility proceedings are pending, or where there are no pending proceedings to the principal registry.

(4)   When a court receives the application the court shall serve all other parties in England and Wales not less than 5 business days before the hearing of the application.

(5)   A decision to accept or refuse jurisdiction under Article 15 of the Council Regulation is to be served on all parties, the Central Authority of the relevant Member State and the Central Authority of England and Wales. Service on a Central Authority or court of another Member State shall be made by the Central Authority of England and Wales.]

Amendment

Inserted by SI 2005/229, r 5. Date in force: 1 March 2005: see SI 2005/229, r 1.

[21M   A certified copy of a judgment for enforcement in other Member States]

[(1)   An application for a certified copy of a judgment or certificate referred to in Article 37(1), 39 or 45(1) of the Council Regulation must be made to the court which made the order by witness statement or affidavit without notice being served on any other party.

(2)   A witness statement or affidavit by which an application for a certified copy of a judgment is made must—

    (a)   give particulars of the proceedings in which the judgment was obtained;
    (b)   have annexed to it—
        (i)   a copy of the petition or application by which the proceedings were begun;
        (ii)   evidence of service on the respondent;
        (iii)   copies of the pleadings and particulars, if any; and
        (iv)   a statement of the grounds on which the judgment was based together, where appropriate, with any document showing that the applicant is entitled to legal aid or assistance by way of representation for the purposes of the proceedings;

(c) state whether the respondent did or did not object to the jurisdiction, and if so, on what grounds;

(d) show that the judgment has been served in accordance with rule 8 and is not subject to any order for the stay of proceedings;

(e) state that the time for appealing has expired, or, as the case may be, the date on which it will expire and in either case whether notice of appeal against the judgment has been given; and

(f) state—
  (i) whether the judgment provides for the payment of a sum of money;
  (ii) whether interest is recoverable on the judgment or part thereof and if so, the rate of interest, the date from which interest is recoverable, and the date on which interest ceases to accrue.

(3) A witness statement or affidavit by which an application for a certificate is made must give—

(a) particulars of the proceedings in which the judgment was obtained;

(b) the full name, country and place of birth and date of birth of the parties;

(c) details of the type of certificate applied for and the reasons for making the application; and

(d) where the application is for a certificate under Annex II to the Council Regulation—
  (i) the full name and, if known, the address and the date and place of birth of any other persons with parental responsibility;
  (ii) information as to whether or not the judgment entails the return of a child wrongfully removed or retained in another Member State and, if so, the full name and address of the person to whom the child should be returned.

(4) The certified copy of the judgment shall be an office copy sealed with the seal of the court and signed by the justices' clerk and there shall be issued with the copy of the judgment a certified copy of any order which has varied any of the terms of the original order.]

Amendment

Inserted by SI 2005/229, r 5. Date in force: 1 March 2005: see SI 2005/229, r 1.

[21N Application for a certificate in accordance with Article 41]

[(1) An application for a certificate in accordance with Article 41 can be made, after judgment, by any party.

(2) An application under paragraph (1) should be made to the court in which the relevant judgment was made and must be supported by an affidavit, which should contain evidence of the cross-border character of the case.]

Amendment

Inserted by SI 2005/229, r 5. Date in force: 1 March 2005: see SI 2005/229, r 1.

[21P Rectification of certificates issued under Article 41]

[(1) The court may rectify an error in a certificate issued under Article 41.

(2) The court may rectify the certificate of its own motion or pursuant to an application made by any party to the proceedings, or the court or Central Authority of another Member State.]

Amendment

Inserted by SI 2005/229, r 5. Date in force: 1 March 2005: see SI 2005/229, r 1.

PART III
MISCELLANEOUS

22   Costs

(1)   In any relevant proceedings, the court may, at any time during the proceedings in that court, make an order that a party pay the whole or any part of the costs of any other party.

(2)   A party against whom the court is considering making a costs order shall have an opportunity to make representations as to why the order should not be made.

Date in force

14 October 1991: see r 1(1).

[22A   Power of court to limit cross-examination]

[The court may limit the issues on which an officer of the service [or a Welsh family proceedings officer] may be cross-examined.]

Amendment

Inserted by SI 2001/818, rr 2, 14. Date in force: 1 April 2001: see SI 2001/818, r 1.
Words "or a Welsh family proceedings officer" in square brackets inserted by SI 2005/585, rr 2, 6.
Date in force: 1 April 2005: see SI 2005/585, r 1(1); for transitional provisions see rr 8, 9 thereof.

23   Confidentiality of documents

(1)   [Subject to rule 23A] no document, other than a record of an order, held by the court and relating to relevant proceedings shall be disclosed, other than to—

    (a)   a party,
    (b)   the legal representative of a party,
    (c)   the [children's guardian],
    (d)   the [Legal Services Commission], or
    (e)   a [welfare officer or children and family reporter], [or
    (f)   an expert whose instruction by a party has been authorised by the court,]

without leave of the justices' clerk or the court.

(2)   Nothing in this rule shall prevent the notification by the Court or the [designated officer for the court] of a direction under section 37(1) to the authority concerned.

[(3)   Nothing in this rule shall prevent the disclosure of a document prepared by an officer of the service or a Welsh family proceedings officer for the purpose of—

    (a)   enabling a person to perform functions required under section 62(3A) of the Justices of the Peace Act 1997;
    (b)   enabling a person to perform functions required under section 38(1) of the Children Act 2004; or
    (c)   assisting an officer of the service or a Welsh family proceedings officer who is appointed by the court under any enactment to perform his functions.]

[(4) Nothing in this rule shall prevent the disclosure of any document relating to proceedings by [an officer of the service or a Welsh family proceedings officer to any other officer of the service or Welsh family proceedings officer] unless that other officer is involved in the same proceedings but on behalf of a different party.]

Date in force

14 October 1991: see r 1(1).

Amendment

Para (1): words "Subject to rule 23A" in square brackets inserted by SI 2005/1977, rr 2, 4. Date in force: 31 October 2005: see SI 2005/1977, r 1.
Para (1): in sub-para (c) words "children's guardian" in square brackets substituted by SI 2001/818, rr 2, 4(a). Date in force: 1 April 2001: see SI 2001/818, r 1.
Para (1): in sub-para (d) words "Legal Services Commission" in square brackets substituted by virtue of the Access to Justice Act 1999, s 105, Sch 14, Pt II, para 3(3). Date in force: 1 April 2000 (subject to transitional provisions and savings): see SI 2000/774, arts 2, 5.
Para (1): in sub-para (e) words "welfare officer or children and family reporter" in square brackets substituted by SI 2001/818, rr 2, 4(b). Date in force: 1 April 2001: see SI 2001/818, r 1.
Para (1): sub-para (f) and word "or" immediately preceeding it inserted by SI 2001/818, rr 2, 15(a). Date in force: 1 April 2001: see SI 2001/818, r 1.
Para (2): words "designated officer for the court" in square brackets substituted by SI 2005/617, art 2, Schedule, para 128. Date in force: 1 April 2005: see SI 2005/617, art 1.
Para (3): inserted by SI 1997/1895, r 2.
Para (3): substituted by SI 2005/585, rr 2, 7(a). Date in force: 1 April 2005: see SI 2005/585, r 1(1); for transitional provisions see rr 8, 9 thereof.
Para (4): inserted by SI 2001/818, rr 2, 15(c). Date in force: 1 April 2001: see SI 2001/818, r 1.
Para (4): words from "an officer of the service" to "Welsh family proceedings officer" in square brackets substituted by SI 2005/585, rr 2, 7(b). Date in force: 1 April 2005: see SI 2005/585, r 1(1); for transitional provisions see rr 8, 9 thereof.

[23A   Communication of information relating to proceedings]

[(1)   For the purposes of the law relating to contempt of court, information relating to relevant proceedings held in private (whether or not contained in a document filed with the court) may be communicated—

    (a) where the justices' clerk or the court gives permission;
    (b) subject to any direction of the justices' clerk or the court, in accordance with paragraphs (2) or (3) of this rule; or
    (c) where the communication is to—
        (i) a party,
        (ii) the legal representative of a party,
        (iii) a professional legal adviser,
        (iv) an officer of the service or a Welsh family proceedings officer,
        (v) the welfare officer,
        (vi) the Legal Services Commission,
        (vii) an expert whose instruction by a party has been authorised by the court, or
        (viii) a professional acting in furtherance of the protection of children.

(2)   A person specified in the first column of the following table may communicate to a person listed in the second column such information as is specified in the third column for the purpose or purposes specified in the fourth column.

Communication of information without permission of the court

Communicated by	To	Information	Purpose
A party	A lay adviser or a McKenzie Friend	Any information relating to the proceedings	To enable the party to obtain advice or assistance in relation to the proceedings.
A party	The party's spouse, [civil partner,] cohabitant or close family member		For the purpose of confidential discussions enabling the party to receive support from his spouse, [civil partner,] cohabitant or close family member.
A party	A health care professional or a person or body providing counselling services for children or families		To enable the party or any child of the party to obtain health care or counselling.
[A party	The Secretary of State, a McKenzie Friend, a lay adviser or an appeal tribunal dealing with an appeal made under section 20 of the Child Support Act 1991		For the purposes of making or responding to an appeal under section 20 of the Child Support Act 1991 or the determination of such an appeal.
A party	An adoption panel		To enable the adoption panel to discharge its functions as appropriate.]

Communicated by	To	Information	Purpose
A party or any person lawfully in receipt of information	The Children's Commissioner or the Children's Commissioner for Wales		To refer an issue affecting the interests of children to the Children's Commissioner or the Children's Commissioner for Wales.
A party or a legal representative	A mediator		For the purpose of mediation in relation to the proceedings.
A party, any person lawfully in receipt of information or a designated officer	A person or body conducting an approved research project		For the purpose of an approved research project.
A party, a legal representative or a professional legal adviser	A person or body responsible for investigating or determining complaints in relation to legal representatives or professional legal advisers		For the purposes of making a complaint or the investigation or determination of a complaint in relation to a legal representative or a professional legal adviser.
A legal representative or a professional legal adviser1	A person or body assessing quality assurance systems		To enable the legal representative or professional legal adviser to obtain a quality assurance assessment.
A legal representative or a professional legal adviser	An accreditation body	Any information relating to the proceedings providing that it does not, or is not likely to, identify any person involved in the proceedings	To enable the legal representative or professional legal adviser to obtain accreditation.

Communicated by	To	Information	Purpose
A party	An elected representative or peer	The text or summary of the whole or part of a judgment given in the proceedings	To enable the elected representative or peer to give advice, investigate any complaint or raise any question of policy or procedure.
A party	The General Medical Council		For the purpose of making a complaint to the General Medical Council.
A party	A police officer		For the purpose of a criminal investigation.
A party or any person lawfully in receipt of information	A member of the Crown Prosecution Service		To enable the Crown Prosecution Service to discharge its functions under any enactment.

(3) A person in the second column of the table in paragraph (3) may only communicate information relating to the proceedings received from a person in the first column for the purpose or purposes—

(a) for which he received that information, or

(b) of professional development or training, providing that any communication does not, or is not likely to, identify any person involved in the proceedings without that person's consent.

(4) In this rule—

"accreditation body" means—
(a) The Law Society,
(b) Resolution, or
(c) The Legal Services Commission;

["adoption panel" means a panel established in accordance with regulation 3 of the Adoption Agencies Regulations 2005 or regulation 3 of the Adoption Agencies (Wales) Regulations 2005;]

"approved research project" means a project of research—
(a) approved in writing by a Secretary of State after consultation with the President of the Family Division,
(b) approved in writing by the President of the Family Division,
(c) conducted under section 83, or
(d) conducted under section 13 of the Criminal Justice and Court Services Act 2000;

"body assessing quality assurance systems" includes—

    (a)   The Law Society,
    (b)   The Legal Services Commission, or
    (c)   The General Council of the Bar;
"body or person responsible for investigating or determining complaints in relation to legal representatives or professional legal advisers" means—
    (a)   The Law Society,
    (b)   The General Council of the Bar,
    (c)   The Institute of Legal Executives, or
    (d)   The Legal Services Ombudsman;
["cohabitant" means one of two persons who are neither married to each other nor civil partners of each other but are living together as husband and wife or as if they were civil partners;]
"criminal investigation" means an investigation conducted by police officers with a view to it being ascertained—
    (a)   whether a person should be charged with an offence, or
    (b)   whether a person charged with an offence is guilty of it;
"elected representative" means—
    (a)   a member of the House of Commons,
    (b)   a member of the National Assembly for Wales, or
    (c)   a member of the European Parliament elected in England and Wales;
"health care professional" means—
    (a)   a registered medical practitioner,
    (b)   a registered nurse or midwife,
    (c)   a clinical psychologist, or
    (d)   a child psychotherapist;
"lay adviser" means a non-professional person who gives lay advice on behalf of an organisation in the lay advice sector;
"legal representative" means a barrister or a solicitor, solicitor's employee or other authorised litigator (as defined in the Courts and Legal Services Act 1990) who has been instructed to act for a party in relation to the proceedings;
"McKenzie Friend" means any person permitted by the court to sit beside an unrepresented litigant in court to assist that litigant by prompting, taking notes and giving him advice;
"mediator" means a family mediator who is—
    (a)   undertaking, or has successfully completed, a family mediation training course approved by the United Kingdom College of Family Mediators, or
    (b)   member of the Law Society's Family Mediation Panel;
"peer" means a member of the House of Lords as defined by the House of Lords Act 1999;
"professional acting in furtherance of the protection of children" includes—
    (a)   an officer of a local authority exercising child protection functions,
    (b)   a police officer who is—
        (i)   exercising powers under section 46, or
        (ii)   serving in a child protection unit or a paedophile unit of a police force;
    (c)   any professional person attending a child protection conference or review in relation to a child who is the subject of the proceedings to which the information relates, or
    (d)   an officer of the National Society for the Prevention of Cruelty to Children;
"professional legal adviser" means a barrister or a solicitor, solicitor's employee or other authorised litigator (as defined in the Courts and Legal Services Act 1990) who is providing advice to a party but is not instructed to represent that party in the proceedings.]

Amendment

Inserted by SI 2005/1977, rr 2, 5. Date in force: 31 October 2005: see SI 2005/1977, r 1.
Para (2): in the second entry words "civil partner," in square brackets in both places they occur inserted by SI 2005/2930, r 2(e), Sch 1, para 48(a). Date in force: 5 December 2005: see SI 2005/2930, r 1(2).
Para (2): fourth and fifth entries inserted by SI 2007/2188, rr 2, 13(1), (2). Date in force: 1 October 2007: see SI 2007/2188, r 1.
Para (4): definition "adoption panel" inserted by SI 2007/2188, rr 2, 13(1), (3). Date in force: 1 October 2007: see SI 2007/2188, r 1.
Para (4): definition "cohabitant" substituted by SI 2005/2930, r 2(e), Sch 1, para 48(b). Date in force: 5 December 2005: see SI 2005/2930, r 1(2).

24   Enforcement of residence order [or special guardianship order]

Where a person in whose favour a residence order [or special guardianship order] is in force wishes to enforce it he shall file a written statement describing the alleged breach of the arrangements settled by the order, whereupon the justices' clerk shall fix a date, time and place for a hearing of the proceedings and [the [designated officer for the court] shall] give notice, as soon as practicable, to the person wishing to enforce the residence order [or special guardianship order] and to any person whom it is alleged is in breach of the arrangements settled by that order, of the date fixed.

Date in force

14 October 1991: see r 1(1).

Amendment

Provision heading: words "or special guardianship order" in square brackets inserted by SI 2005/2930, r 2(e), Sch 1, para 49. Date in force: 30 December 2005: see SI 2005/2930, r 1(2).
Words "or special guardianship order" in square brackets in both places they occur inserted by SI 2005/2930, r 2(e), Sch 1, para 49. Date in force: 30 December 2005: see SI 2005/2930, r 1(2).
Words from "the" to "shall" in square brackets inserted by SI 2001/615, r 2(xx), Schedule, para 97. Date in force: 1 April 2001: see SI 2001/615, r 1.
Words "designated officer for the court" in square brackets substituted by SI 2005/617, art 2, Schedule, para 128. Date in force: 1 April 2005: see SI 2005/617, art 1.

25   Notification of consent

[(1)]   Consent for the purposes of—

    (a)   section 16(3), [or]
    [(b)   section 38A(2)(b)(ii) or 44A(2)(b)(ii), or]
    (c)   paragraph 19(1) of Schedule 2,

shall be given either—

    (i)   orally in court, or
    (ii)   in writing to the [designated officer for the court] or the court and signed by the person giving his consent.

[(2)   Any written consent given for the purposes of subsection (2) of section 38A or section 44A, shall include a statement that the person giving consent—

    (a)   is able and willing to give to the child the care which it would be reasonable to expect a parent to give him; and
    (b)   understands that the giving of consent could lead to the exclusion of the relevant person from the dwelling-house in which the child lives.]

Date in force

14 October 1991: see r 1(1).

Amendment

Para (1): numbered as such, in relation to proceedings issued on or after 1 October 1997, by SI 1997/1895, rr 3(1), 8.
Para (1): in sub-para (a) word "or" in square brackets inserted by SI 1992/2068, r 2, Schedule, para 6.
Para (1): original sub-para (b) revoked by SI 1992/2068, r 2.
Para (1): new sub-para (b) inserted, in relation to proceedings issued after 1 October 1997, by SI 1997/1895, rr 3(1), 8.
Para (1): in sub-para (ii) words "designated officer for the court" in square brackets substituted by SI 2005/617, art 2, Schedule, para 128. Date in force: 1 April 2005: see SI 2005/617, art 1.
Para (2): inserted, in relation to proceedings issued on or after 1 October 1997, by SI 1997/1895, rr 3(2), 8.

[25A   Exclusion requirements: interim care orders and emergency protection orders]

[(1)   This rule applies where the court includes an exclusion requirement in an interim care order or an emergency protection order.

(2)   The applicant for an interim care order or emergency protection order shall

    (a)   prepare a separate statement of the evidence in support of the application for an exclusion requirement;

    (b)   serve the statement personally on the relevant person with a copy of the order containing the exclusion requirement (and of any power of arrest which is attached to it);

    (c)   inform the relevant person of his right to apply to vary or discharge the exclusion requirement.

(3)   Where a power of arrest is attached to an exclusion requirement in an interim care order or an emergency protection order, a copy of the order shall be delivered to the officer for the time being in charge of the police station for the area in which the dwelling-house in which the child lives is situated (or of such other station as the court may specify) together with a statement that the relevant person has been served with the order or informed of its terms (whether by being present when the order was made or by telephone or otherwise).

(4)   Rules 12A(3), 20 (except paragraphs (1) and (3)) and 21 of the Family Proceedings Courts (Matrimonial Proceedings etc) Rules 1991 shall apply, with the necessary modifications, for the service, variation, discharge and enforcement of any exclusion requirement to which a power of arrest is attached as they apply to an order made on an application under Part IV of the Family Law Act 1996.

(5)   The relevant person shall serve the parties to the proceedings with any application which he makes for the Variation or discharge of the exclusion requirement.

(6)   Where an exclusion requirement ceases to have effect whether—

    (a)   as a result of the removal of a child under section 38A(10) or 44A(10),

    (b)   because of the discharge of the interim care order or emergency protection order, or

    (c)   otherwise, the applicant shall inform—

        (i)   the relevant person,

        (ii) the parties to the proceedings,

> (iii)   any officer to whom a copy of the order was delivered under para-
> graph (3), and
> (iv)   (where necessary) the court.

(7)   Where the court includes an exclusion requirement in an interim care order or an emergency protection order of its own motion, paragraph (2) shall apply with the omission of any reference to the statement of the evidence.]

Amendment

Inserted, in relation to proceedings issued on or after 1 October 1997, by SI 1997/1895, rr 4, 8.

---

26   Secure accommodation

In proceedings under section 25, the [designated officer for the court] shall, if practicable, arrange for copies of all written reports before the court to be made available before the hearing to—

(a)   the applicant,
(b)   the parent or guardian of the child,
(c)   any legal representative of the child,
(d)   the [children's guardian], and
(e)   the child, unless the [designated officer for the court] or the court otherwise directs;

and copies of such reports may, if the court considers it desirable, be shown to any person who is entitled to notice of the proceedings in accordance with these Rules.

Date in force

14 October 1991: see r 1(1).

Amendment

Words "designated officer for the court" in square brackets in both places they occur substituted by SI 2005/617, art 2, Schedule, para 128. Date in force: 1 April 2005: see SI 2005/617, art 1.
In para (d) words "children's guardian" in square brackets substituted by SI 2001/818, rr 2, 4(a). Date in force: 1 April 2001: see SI 2001/818, r 1.

---

27   Investigation under section 37

(1)   This rule applies where a direction is given to an appropriate authority by a family proceedings court under section 37(1).

(2)   On giving a direction the court shall adjourn the proceedings and the justices' clerk or the court shall record the direction [in Form C40].

(3)   A copy of the direction recorded under paragraph (2) shall, as soon as practicable after the direction is given, be served by the [designated officer for the court] on the parties to the proceedings in which the direction is given and, where the appropriate authority is not a party, on that authority.

(4)   When serving the copy of the direction on the appropriate authority the [designated officer for the court] shall also serve copies of such of the documentary evidence which has been, or is to be, adduced in the proceedings as the court may direct.

(5)   Where a local authority informs the court of any of the matters set out in section 37(3)(a) to (c) it shall do so in writing.

Date in force

14 October 1991: see r 1(1).

Amendment

Para (2): words in square brackets substituted by SI 1994/3156, r 20.
Para (3): words "designated officer for the court" in square brackets substituted by SI 2005/617, art 2, Schedule, para 128. Date in force: 1 April 2005: see SI 2005/617, art 1.
Para (4): words "designated officer for the court" in square brackets substituted by SI 2005/617, art 2, Schedule, para 128. Date in force: 1 April 2005: see SI 2005/617, art 1.

28   Limits on the power of a justices' clerk or a single justice to make an order under section 11(3) or section 38(1)

A justices' clerk or single justice shall not make an order under section 11(3) or section 38(l) unless—

    (a)   a written request for such an order has been made to which the other parties and any [children's guardian] consent and which they or their representatives have signed,

    (b)   a previous such order has been made in the same proceedings, and

    (c)   the terms of the order sought are the same as those of the last such order made.

Date in force

14 October 1991: see r 1(1).

Amendment

In para (a) words "children's guardian" in square brackets substituted by SI 2001/818, rr 2, 4(a). Date in force: 1 April 2001: see SI 2001/818, r 1.

29   Appeals to a family proceedings court under section 77(6) and paragraph 8(1) of Schedule 8

(1)   An appeal under section 77(6) or paragraph 8(1) of Schedule 8 shall be by application in accordance with rule 4.

(2)   An appeal under section 77(6) shall be brought within 21 days from the date of the step to which the appeal relates.

Date in force

14 October 1991: see r 1(1).

30   Contribution orders

(1)   An application for a contribution order under paragraph 23(1) of Schedule 2 shall be accompanied by a copy of the contribution notice served in accordance with paragraph 22(1) of that Schedule and a copy of any notice served by the contributor under paragraph 22(8) of that Schedule.

(2)   Where a local authority notifies the court of an agreement reached under paragraph 23(6) of Schedule 2, it shall do so in writing through the [designated officer for the court].

(3) An application for the variation or revocation of a contribution order under paragraph 23(8) of Schedule 2 shall be accompanied by a copy of the contribution order which it is sought to vary or revoke.

Date in force

14 October 1991: see r 1(1).

Amendment

Para (2): words "designated officer for the court" in square brackets substituted by SI 2005/617, art 2, Schedule, para 128. Date in force: 1 April 2005: see SI 2005/617, art 1.

---

31 Direction to local education authority to apply for education supervision order

(1) For the purposes of section 40(3) and (4) of the Education Act 1944, a direction by a magistrates' court to a local education authority to apply for an education supervision order shall be given [in writing].

(2) Where, following such a direction, a local education authority informs the court that they have decided not to apply for an education supervision order, they shall do so in writing.

Date in force

14 October 1991: see r 1(1).

Amendment

Para (1): words "in writing" in square brackets substituted by SI 1997/1895, r 5.

[31A Applications and orders under sections 33 and 34 of the Family Law Act 1986]

[(1) In this rule "the 1986 Act" means the Family Law Act 1986.

(2) An application under section 33 of the 1986 Act shall be in Form C4 and an order made under that section shall be in Form C30.

(3) An application under section 34 of the 1986 Act shall be in Form C3 and an order made under that section shall be in Form C31.

(4) An application under section 33 or section 34 of the 1986 Act may be made ex parte in which case the applicant shall file the application—

    (a) where the application is made by telephone, within 24 hours after the making of the application, or

    (b) in any other case at the time when the application is made,

and shall serve a copy of the application on each respondent 48 hours after the making of the order.

(5) Where the court refuses to make an order on an ex parte application it may direct that the application be made inter partes.]

Amendment

Inserted by SI 1994/3156, r 22.

---

32   Delegation by justices' clerk

(1)   In this rule, "employed as a clerk in court" has the same meaning as in rule 2(1) of the Justices' Clerks (Qualifications of Assistants) Rules 1979.

(2)   Anything authorised to be done by, to or before a justices' clerk under these Rules, or under paragraphs 13 to 15C of the Schedule to the Justices' Clerks Rules 1970 as amended by Schedule 3 to these Rules, may be done instead by, to or before a person employed as a clerk in court where that person is appointed by the [Lord Chancellor] to assist him and where that person has been specifically authorised by the justices' clerk for that purpose.

(3)   Any authorisation by the justices' clerk under paragraph (2) shall be recorded in writing at the time the authority is given or as soon as practicable thereafter.

Date in force

14 October 1991: see r 1(1).

Amendment

Para (2): words "Lord Chancellor" in square brackets substituted by SI 2005/617, art 2, Schedule, para 131. Date in force: 1 April 2005: see SI 2005/617, art 1.

33   Application of section 97 of the Magistrates' Courts Act 1980

Section 97 of the Magistrates' Courts Act 1980 shall apply to relevant proceedings in a family proceedings court as it applies to a hearing of a complaint under that section.

Date in force

14 October 1991: see r 1(1).

[33A   Disclosure of addresses]

[(1)   Nothing in these rules shall be construed as requiring any party to reveal the address of their private residence (or that of any child) except by order of the court.

(2)   Where a party declines to reveal an address in reliance upon paragraph (1) he shall give notice of that address to the court in Form C8 and that address shall not be revealed to any person except by order of the court.]

Amendment

Inserted by SI 1994/3156, r 23.

[33B   Setting aside on failure of service]

[Where an application has been sent to a respondent in accordance with rule 8(1) and, after an order has been made on the application, it appears to the court that the application did not come to the knowledge of the respondent in due time, the court may of its own motion set aside the order and may give such directions as it thinks fit for the rehearing of the application.]

Amendment

Inserted by SI 1997/1895, r 6.

34 Consequential and minor amendments, savings and transitionals

(1) Subject to paragraph (3) the consequential and minor amendments in Schedule 3 to these Rules shall have effect.

(2) Subject to paragraph (3), the provisions of the 1981 rules shall have effect subject to these Rules.

(3) Nothing in these Rules shall affect any proceedings which are pending (within the meaning of paragraph 1 of Schedule 14 to the Act of 1989) immediately before these Rules come into force.

Date in force

14 October 1991: see r 1(1).

[SCHEDULE 1
FORMS]

Rule 3

[[C1	Application	for an order]
[C1A		Supplemental Information Form]
C2	Application	for an order or directions in existing family proceedings
	Application	to be joined as, or cease to be, a party in existing family proceedings
	Application	for leave to commence proceedings
C3	Application	for an order authorising search for, taking charge of, and delivery of a child
C4	Application	for an order for disclosure of a child's whereabouts
C5	Application	concerning the registration of a child-minder or a provider of day care
C6	Notice	of proceedings (Hearing) (Directions Appointment) (*Notice to parties*)
C6A	Notice	of proceedings (Hearing) (Directions Appointment) (*Notice to non-parties*)
C7		Acknowledgement
C8		Confidential Address
[C9	Statement	of Service]
C10	Supplement	for an application for financial provision for a child or for variation of financial provision for a child
C10A	Statement	of Means
[C11	Supplement	for an application for an Emergency Protection Order]
C12	Supplement	for an application for a Warrant to assist a person authorised by an Emergency Protection Order
C13	Supplement	for an application for a Care or Supervision Order
[C13A	Supplement	for an application for a Special Guardianship Order]
C14	Supplement	for an application for authority to refuse contact with a child in care
C15	Supplement	for an application for contact with a child in care
C16	Supplement	for an application for a Child Assessment Order
C17	Supplement	for an application for an Education Supervision Order
C17A	Supplement	for an application for an extension of an Education Supervision Order
C18	Supplement	for an application for a Recovery Order

C19	Supplement	for a Warrant of Assistance
C20	Supplement	for an application for an order to hold a child in Secure Accommodation
C21	Order or direction	Blank
C22	Record	of hearing
[C23	Order	Emergency Protection Order]
C24	Order	Variation of an Emergency Protection Order
		Extension of an Emergency Protection Order
		Discharge of an Emergency Protection Order
C25	Warrant	To assist a person authorised by an Emergency Protection Order
C26	Order	Authority to keep a child in Secure Accommodation
C27	Order	Authority to search for another child
C28	Warrant	To assist a person to gain access to a child or entry to premises
C29	Order	Recovery of a child
C30	Order	To disclose information about the whereabouts of a missing child
C31	Order	Authorising search for, taking charge of, and delivery of a child
C32	Order	Care Order
		Discharge of a Care Order
[C33	Order	Interim Care Order]
C34	Order	Contact with a child in care
		Authority to refuse contact with a child in care
C35	Order	Supervision Order
		Interim Supervision Order
C36	Order	Substitution of a Supervision Order for a Care Order
		Discharge of a Supervision Order
		Variation of a Supervision Order
		Extension of a Supervision Order
C37	Order	Education Supervision Order
C38	Order	Discharge of an Education Supervision Order
		Extension of an Education Supervision Order
C39	Order	Child Assessment Order
C40	Direction	To undertake an investigation
C41	Order	Cancellation of the registration of a child-minder or a provider of day care
		Removal, Variation or Imposition of a requirement on a child-minder or a provider of day care
C42	Order	Family Assistance Order
C43	Order	Residence Order
		Contact Order
		Specific Issue Order
		Prohibited Steps Order
[C43A	Order	Special Guardianship Order]
C44	Order	Leave to change the surname by which a child is known
		Leave to remove a child from the United Kingdom
C45	Order	Parental Responsibility Order
		Termination of a Parental Responsibility Order
C46	Order	Appointment of a guardian
		Termination of the appointment of a guardian

C47	Order	Making or refusing the appointment of a [children's guardian] Termination of the appointment of a [children's guardian]
C48	Order	Appointment of a solicitor for a child Refusal of the appointment of a solicitor for a child Termination of the appointment of a solicitor for a child
C49	Order	Transfer of Proceedings to (the High Court) (a county court) (a family proceedings court)
C50	Certificate	Refusal to transfer proceedings
C51	Application	for a Parental Order
C52		Acknowledgment of an application for a Parental Order
C53	Order	Parental Order
C54	Notice	of Refusal of a Parental Order]

Amendment

Entry for Form C1: substituted by SI 2001/818, rr 2, 16(a), Schedule. Date in force: 1 April 2001: see SI 2001/818, r 1.
Entry for Form C1A: inserted by SI 2004/3376, r 7(b). Date in force: 31 January 2005 (except in relation to proceedings commenced before that date): see SI 2004/3376, rr 1(1), 2.
Entry for Form C9: substituted by SI 2001/818, rr 2, 16(a), Schedule. Date in force: 1 April 2001: see SI 2001/818, r 1.
Entry for Form C11: substituted, in relation to proceedings issued on or after 1 October 1997, by SI 1997/1895, rr 7, 8, Schedule.
Entry for Form C13A: inserted by SI 2005/2930, r 2(e), Sch 1, para 50(a)(i). Date in force: 30 December 2005: see SI 2005/2930, r 1(2).
Entry for Form C23: substituted, in relation to proceedings issued on or after 1 October 1997, by SI 1997/1895, rr 7, 8, Schedule.
Entry for Form C33: substituted, in relation to proceedings issued on or after 1 October 1997, by SI 1997/1895, rr 7, 8, Schedule.
Entry for Form C43A: inserted by SI 2005/2930, r 2(e), Sch 1, para 50(a)(ii). Date in force: 30 December 2005: see SI 2005/2930, r 1(2).
Form C47: words "children's guardian" in square brackets in both places they occur substituted by SI 2001/818, rr 2, 4(a); Form C47 further amended by r 16(d) thereof. Date in force: 1 April 2001: see SI 2001/818, r 1.

SCHEDULE 2
RESPONDENTS AND NOTICE

Rules 4, 7

(i) *Provision under which proceedings brought*	(ii) *Minimum number of days prior to hearing or directions appointment for service under rule 4(1)(b)*	(iii) *Respondents*	(iv) *Persons to whom notice is to be given*
All applications.	See separate entries below.	Subject to separate entries below,	Subject to separate entries below,

| | | every person whom the applicant believes to have parental responsibility for the child; | the local authority providing accommodation for the child; |

| | | where the child is the subject of a care order, every person whom the applicant believes to have had parental responsibility immediately prior to the making of the care order; | persons who are caring for the child at the time when the proceedings are commenced; |

| | | in the case of an application to extend, vary or discharge an order, the parties to the proceedings leading to the order which it is sought to have extended, varied or discharged; | in the case of proceedings brought in respect of a child who is alleged to be staying in a refuge which is certificated under section 51(1) or (2), the person who is providing the refuge. |

| | | in the case of specified proceedings, the child. | |

| ... | ... | ... | ... |

| Section [4(1)(c)], 4(3), [4A(1)(b), 4A(3),] 5(1), 6(7), [8], 13(1), [14A, 14C(3), 14D,] ... , 33(7), 77(6), [Schedule 1], paragraph 19(1), 23(1) or 23(8) of Schedule 2, paragraph 8(1) of Schedule 8, or paragraph 11(3) or 16(5) of Schedule 14. | 14 days | Except for proceedings under section 77(6), Schedule 2, or paragraph 8(1) of Schedule 8, as for "all applications" above, and: | As for "all applications" above, and: |

[in the case of proceedings under Schedule 1, those persons whom the applicant believes to be interested in or affected by the proceedings;]

in the case of an application under paragraph 19(1) of Schedule 2, the parties to the proceedings leading to the care order;

in the case of an application under paragraph 11(3)(b) or 16(5) of Schedule 14, any person, other than the child, named in the order or directions which it is sought to discharge or vary;

in the case of an application under section 5(1), the father of the child if he does not have parental responsibility.

[in the case of proceedings] under section 77(6), the local authority against whose decision the appeal is made;

in the case of an application under paragraph 23(1) of Schedule 2, the contributor;

in the case of an application under paragraph 23(8) of Schedule 2—

(i) if the applicant is the local authority, the contributor, and

(ii) if the applicant is the contributor, the local authority.

In the case of an application under paragraph 8(1) of Schedule 8, the local authority against whose decision the appeal is made.

[in the case of an
application for a
section 8 order,
every person
whom the
applicant
believes—

(i)to be named in a
court order with
respect to the same
child, which has
not ceased to have
effect,

(ii)to be a party to
pending
proceedings in
respect of the same
child, or

(iii)to be a person
with whom the
child has lived for
at least three years
prior to the
application,

unless, in a case to
which (i) or (ii)
applies, the
applicant believes
that the court
order or pending
proceedings are
not relevant to the
application.]

[in the case of an application under section 14A, if a care order is in force with respect to the child, the child]

[in the case of an application under section 14A—
(a)if the child is not being accommodated by the local authority, the local authority in whose area the applicant is ordinarily resident, and
(b)every other person whom the applicant believes—
(i)to be named in a court order with respect to that child which remains in force,
(ii)to be a party to pending proceedings in respect of the same child,
(iii)to be a person with whom the child has lived for at least 3 years prior to the application,
unless, in a case to which (i) or (ii) applies, the applicant believes that the court order or pending proceedings are not relevant to the application;
in the case of an application under section 14D—
(a)as for applications under section 14A above, and
(b)the local authority that prepared the report under section 14A(8) or (9) in the proceedings leading to the order which it is sought to have varied or discharged, if different from any local authority that will be otherwise be notified]

Section 36(1), 39(1), 39(2), 39(3), 39(4), 43(1), or paragraph 6(3), 15(2) or 17(1) of Schedule 3.	7 days	As for "all applications" above, and:	As for "all applications" above, and:
		in the case of an application under section 39(2) or (3), the supervisor;	in the case of an application for an order under section 43(1)—
		in the case of proceedings under paragraph 17(1) of Schedule 3, the local education authority concerned;	(i)every person whom the applicant believes to be a parent of the child,
		in the case of proceedings under section 36 or paragraph 15(2) or 17(1) of Schedule 3, the child.	(ii)every person whom the applicant believes to be caring for the child,
			(iii)every person in whose favour a contact order is in force with respect to the child, and
			(iv)every person who is allowed to have contact with the child by virtue of an order under section 34.
Section 31,34(2), 34(3), 34(4), 34(9) or 38(8)(b).	3 days	As for "all applications" above, and:	As for "all applications" above, and:
		in the case of an application under section 34, the person whose contact with the child is the subject of the application.	in the case of an application under section 31—
			(i)every person whom the applicant believes to be a party to pending relevant proceedings in respect of the same child, and

987

			(ii)every person whom the applicant believes to be a parent without parental responsibility for the child.
Section 43(12).	2 days	As for "all applications" above.	Those of the persons referred to in section 43(11)(a) to (e) who were not party to the application for the order which it is sought to have varied or discharged.
Section 25,44(1), 44(9)(b), 45(4), 45(8), 46(7), 48(9), 50(1), 75(1) or 102(1).	1 day	Except for applications under section 75(1) or 102(1), as for "all applications" above, and:	As for "all applications" above, and:
		in the case of an application under section 44(9)(b)	in the case of an application under section 44(1), every person whom the applicant believes to be a parent of the child;
		(i)the parties to the application for the order in respect of which it is sought to vary the directions;	in the case of an application under section 44(9)(b)—
		(ii)any person who was caring for the child prior to the making of the order; and	(i)the local authority in whose area the child is living, and
		(iii)any person whose contact with the child is affected by the direction which it is sought to have varied;	(ii)any person whom the applicant believes to be affected by the direction which it is sought to have varied.

		in the case of an application under section 50, the person whom the applicant alleges to have effected or to have been or to be responsible for the taking or keeping of the child; in the case of an application under section 75(1), the registered person; in the case of an application under section 102(1), the person referred to in section 102(1) and any person preventing or likely to prevent such a person from exercising powers under enactments mentioned in subsection (6) of that section.	
[section 30 of the Human Fertilisation and Embryology Act 1990]	14 days	the birth parents (except where the applicants seek to dispense with their agreement under section 30(6) of the Human Fertilisation and Embryology Act 1990) and any other persons or body with parental responsibility for the child at the date of the application	any local authority or voluntary organisation that has at any time provided accommodation for the child]

Date in force

14 October 1991: see r 1(1).

Amendment

Entry relating to Section 8 and Sch 1 (omitted) revoked by SI 1992/2068, r 2, Schedule, para 8. In entry beginning "Section 4(1)(c), 4(3)" in column (i) reference to "4(1)(c)" in square brackets substituted by SI 2003/2840, r 3. Date in force: this amendment came into force on 1 December 2003 (being the date on which the Adoption and Children Act 2002, s 111 came into force): see SI 2003/3079, art 2 and SI 2003/2840, r 1.

In entry beginning "Section 4(1)(c), 4(3)" in column (i) references to "4A(1)(b), 4A(3)" inserted by SI 2005/2930, r 2(e), Sch 1, para 51(a)(i). Date in force: 30 December 2005: see SI 2005/2930, r 1(2).

In entry beginning "Section 4(1)(c), 4(3)" in column (i) reference to "8" in square brackets inserted by SI 1992/2068, r 2, Schedule, para 9(a).

In entry beginning "Section 4(1)(c), 4(3)" in column (i) references to "14A, 14C(3), 14D," in square brackets inserted by SI 2005/2930, r 2(e), Sch 1, para 51(a)(ii). Date in force: 30 December 2005: see SI 2005/2930, r 1(2).

In entry beginning "Section 4(1)(c)" in column (i) reference omitted revoked by SI 2007/2188, rr 2, 15. Date in force: 1 October 2007: see SI 2007/2188, r 1.

In entry beginning "Section 4(1)(c), 4(3)" in column (i) words "Schedule 1" in square brackets inserted by SI 1992/2068, r 2, Schedule, para 9(b).

In entry beginning "Section 4(1)(c), 4(3)" in column (iii) words from "in the case" to "by the proceedings;" in square brackets inserted by SI 1992/2068, r 2, Schedule, para 9(d).

In entry beginning "Section 4(1)(c), 4(3)" in column (iii) words "in the case of proceedings" in square brackets substituted by SI 1992/2068, r 2, Schedule, para 9(c).

In entry beginning "Section 4(1)(c), 4(3)" in column (iii) words from "in the case" to "to the application." in square brackets inserted by SI 1992/2068, r 2, Schedule, para 9(e).

In entry beginning "Section 4(1)(c), 4(3)" in column (iii) words from "in the case" to "child, the child" in square brackets inserted by SI 2005/2930, r 2(e), Sch 1, para 51(b). Date in force: 30 December 2005: see SI 2005/2930, r 1(2).

In entry beginning "section 4(1)(c), 4(3)" in column (iv) words from "in the case" to "otherwise be notified" in square brackets inserted by SI 2005/2930, r 2(e), Sch 1, para 51(c). Date in force: 30 December 2005: see SI 2005/2930, r 1(2).

Entry relating to "section 30 of the Human Fertilisation and Embryology Act 1990" inserted by SI 1994/2166, r 6.

SCHEDULE 3
CONSEQUENTIAL AND MINOR AMENDMENTS

Rule 34(1)

[Not reproduced]

CHILDREN (ALLOCATION OF PROCEEDINGS) ORDER 1991

(SI 1991/1677)

Citation, commencement and interpretation

1

(1)   This Order may be cited as the Children (Allocation of Proceedings) Order 1991 and shall come into force on 14th October 1991.

(2)   In this Order, unless the context otherwise requires—

"child"—
    (a)   means, subject to sub-paragraph (b), a person under the age of 18 with respect to whom proceedings are brought, and
    (b)   where the proceedings are under Schedule 1, [or are for adoption under the Adoption and Children Act 2002,] also includes a person who has reached the age of 18;

["Convention adoption order" means an adoption order which, by virtue of regulations under section 1 of the Adoption (Intercountry Aspects) Act 1999 (regulations giving effect to the Convention), is made as a Convention adoption order;]

...

["local justice area" has the same meaning as in the Courts Act 2003; and]
"the Act" means the Children Act 1989, and a section, Part or Schedule referred to by number alone means the section, Part or Schedule so numbered in that Act.

Date in force

14 October 1991: see para (1) above.

Amendment

Para (2): in definition "child" in para (b) words "or are for adoption under the Adoption and Children Act 2002," in square brackets inserted by SI 2005/2797, arts 3, 4(a);definition "Convention adoption order" inserted by SI 2005/2797, arts 3, 4(b); definition "London commission area" (omitted) revoked by SI 2005/520, art 2(a); definition "local justice area" substituted, for definition "petty sessions area" as originally enacted, by SI 2005/520, art 2(b).

Classes of county court

2

For the purposes of this Order there shall be the following classes of county court:

[(a) designated county courts, being those courts designated for the time being—
   (i) as divorce county courts by an order under section 33 of the Matrimonial and Family Proceedings Act 1984;
   (ii) as civil partnership proceedings county courts by an order under section 36A of the Matrimonial and Family Proceedings Act 1984; or
   (iii) as both divorce county courts and civil partnership proceedings county courts by such orders;]
(b) family hearing centres, being those courts set out in Schedule 1 to this Order;
(c) care centres, being those courts set out in column (ii) of Schedule 2 to this Order[;
(d) adoption centres, being those courts set out in Schedule 3 to this Order;
(e) intercountry adoption centres, being those courts set out in Schedule 4 to this Order].

Date in force

14 October 1991: see art 1(1).

Amendment

Para (a) substituted by SI 2005/2797, arts 3, 5(a). Date in force: 5 December 2005: see SI 2005/2797, art 1(a).
Paras (d), (e) inserted by SI 2005/2797, arts 3, 5(b). Date in force: 30 December 2005: see SI 2005/2797, art 1(b); for savings and transitional provisions see art 2 thereof.

Commencement of Proceedings

Proceedings to be commenced in magistrates' court

3

(1) Subject to paragraphs (2) and (3) and to article 4, proceedings under any of the following provisions shall be commenced in a magistrates' court:

(a)   section 25 (use of accommodation for restricting liberty);
(b)   section 31 (care and supervision orders);
(c)   section 33(7) (leave to change name of or remove from United Kingdom child in care);
(d)   section 34 (parental contact);
(e)   section 36 (education supervision orders);
(f)   section 43 (child assessment orders);
(g)   section 44 (emergency protection orders);
(h)   section 45 (duration of emergency protection orders etc);
(i)   section 46(7) (application for emergency protection order by police officer);
(j)   section 48 (powers to assist discovery of children etc);
(k)   section 50 (recovery orders);
(l)   section 75 (protection of children in an emergency);
(m)   section 77(6) (appeal against steps taken under section 77(1));
(n)   section 102 (powers of constable to assist etc);
(o)   paragraph 19 of Schedule 2 (approval of arrangements to assist child to live abroad);
(p)   paragraph 23 of Schedule 2 (contribution orders);
(q)   paragraph 8 of Schedule 8 (certain appeals);
[(r)   section 23 of the Adoption and Children Act 2002 (varying placement orders);]
[(s)   ...
(t)   section 20 of the Child Support Act 1991 (appeals) where the proceedings are to be dealt with in accordance with the Child Support Appeals (Jurisdiction of Courts) Order 1993;]
[(u)   section 30 of the Human Fertilisation and Embryology Act 1990 (parental orders in favour of gamete donors).]

(2)   Notwithstanding paragraph (1) and subject to paragraph (3), proceedings of a kind set out in sub-paragraph (b), (e), (f), (g), (i) or (j) of paragraph (1), and which arise out of an investigation directed, by the High Court or a county court, under section 37(1), shall be commenced—

(a)   in the court which directs the investigation, where that court is the High Court or a care centre, or
(b)   in such care centre as the court which directs the investigation may order.

(3)   Notwithstanding paragraphs (1) and (2), proceedings of a kind set out in sub-paragraph (a) to (k), (n) or (o) of paragraph (1) shall be [commenced in] a court in which are pending other proceedings, in respect of the same child, which are also of a kind set out in those sub-paragraphs.

Date in force

14 October 1991: see art 1(1).

Amendment

Para (1): sub-para (r) substituted by SI 2005/2797, arts 3, 6; sub-para (s) inserted by SI 1993/624, art 3; sub-para (s) revoked by SI 2001/775, arts 3, 4; sub-para (t) inserted by SI 1993/624, art 3; sub-para (u) inserted by SI 1994/2164, art 3; words "commenced in" in square brackets substituted by SI 1993/624, art 5.

[Proceedings to be commenced in the High Court or a county court]

Amendment

Inserted by SI 2005/2797, arts 3, 7.

[3A]

[Proceedings for a Convention adoption order or an adoption order where section 83 of the Adoption and Children Act 2002 (restriction on bringing children in) applies shall be commenced in the High Court or in a county court.]

Amendment

Inserted by SI 2005/2797, arts 3, 7.

[Application where proceedings pending]

Amendment

Inserted by SI 2005/2797, arts 3, 7.

[3B]

[(1)   Where an application has been made for an adoption order and has not been disposed of, an application for—

 (a) leave to apply for a residence order under section 29(4)(b) of the Adoption and Children Act 2002;

 (b) leave to apply for a special guardianship order under section 29(5)(b) of the Adoption and Children Act 2002;

 (c) a residence order under section 8 where section 28(1)(a) or 29(4)(b) of the Adoption and Children Act 2002 applies (leave obtained to make application for a residence order);

 (d) an order under section 14A where section 28(1)(b) or 29(5)(b) of the Adoption and Children Act 2002 applies (leave obtained to make application for a special guardianship order);

 (e) leave to remove the child under section 37(a) of the Adoption and Children Act 2002; or

 (f) leave to oppose the making of an adoption order under section 47(3) or (5) of the Adoption and Children Act 2002

shall be commenced in the court in which the adoption proceedings are pending.

(2)   Where an application has been made for a placement order and has not been disposed of, an application for leave to remove a child from accommodation provided by the local authority under section 30(2)(b) of the Adoption and Children Act 2002 shall be commenced in the court in which the proceedings for the placement order are pending.

(3)   Where an application has been made for leave under section 42(6) of the Adoption and Children Act 2002 and has not been disposed of, an application for leave to remove a child under section 38(3)(a) or 40(2)(a) of that Act shall be commenced in the court in which the proceedings under section 42(6) of that Act are pending.]

Amendment

Inserted by SI 2005/2797, arts 3, 7.

[Application where order already in force]

Amendment

Inserted by SI 2005/2797, arts 3, 7.

[3C]

[(1) Where a special guardianship order is in force in respect of a child, an application for leave to change child's name or remove child from United Kingdom under section 14C(3) shall be commenced in the court which made the special guardianship order.

(2) Where a placement order is in force in respect of a child, an application for—

(a) leave to apply to revoke the placement order under section 24(2)(a) of the Adoption and Children Act 2002;

(b) leave to place child for adoption under section 24(5) of that Act;

(c) leave to apply for a contact order under section 26(3)(f) of that Act;

(d) leave to apply to change child's name or remove child from United Kingdom under section 28(2)(b) of that Act; or

(e) a contact order under section 26 of that Act

shall be commenced in the court which made the placement order.]

Amendment

Inserted by SI 2005/2797, arts 3, 7.

Application to extend, vary or discharge order

4

(1) Subject to paragraphs (2) and (3), proceedings under the Act ...—

(a) to extend, vary or discharge an order, or

(b) the determination of which may have the effect of varying or discharging an order,

shall be [commenced in] the court which made the order.

[(1A) Proceedings under the Adoption and Children Act 2002, save for proceedings under section 23 of that Act, to vary or revoke an order shall be commenced in the court which made the order.]

(2) Notwithstanding paragraph (1), an application for an order under section 8[, 14A or 14D] which would have the effect of varying or discharging an order made, by a county court, in accordance with section 10(1)(b)[, 14A(6)(b) or 14D(2) respectively] shall be made to a [designated] county court.

(3) Notwithstanding paragraph (1), an application to extend, vary or discharge an order made, by a county court, under section 38, or for an order which would have the effect of extending, varying or discharging such an order, shall be made to a care centre.

(4) A court may transfer proceedings [commenced] in accordance with paragraph (1) [or (1A)] to any other court in accordance with the provisions of articles 5 to 13.

Date in force

14 October 1991: see art 1(1).

Amendment

Para (1): words omitted revoked by SI 2005/2797, arts 3, 8(a); words "commenced in" in square brackets substituted by SI 1993/624, arts 2, 5.
Para (1A): inserted by SI 2005/2797, arts 3, 8(b).

Para (2): words ", 14A or 14D" in square brackets inserted by SI 2005/2797, arts 3, 8(c)(i); words ", 14A(6)(b) or 14D(2) respectively" in square brackets inserted by SI 2005/2797, arts 3, 8(c)(ii); word "designated" in square brackets substituted by SI 2005/2797, arts 3, 8(c)(iii).
Para (4): word "commenced" in square brackets substituted by SI 1993/624, arts 2, 6; words "or (1A)" in square brackets inserted by SI 2005/2797, arts 3, 8(d).

Transfer of Proceedings

Disapplication of enactments about transfer

5

Sections 38 and 39 of the Matrimonial and Family Proceedings Act 1984 shall not apply to proceedings under the Act or under the [Adoption and Children Act 2002].

Date in force

14 October 1991: see art 1(1).

Amendment

Words "Adoption and Children Act 2002" in square brackets substituted by SI 2005/2797, arts 3, 9.

Transfer from one magistrates' court to another

6

[(1)] A magistrates' court (the "transferring court") shall transfer proceedings [to which this article applies] to another magistrates' court (the "receiving court") where—

  (a) having regard to the principle set out in section 1(2) [and, where applicable, section 1(3) of the Adoption and Children Act 2002], the transferring court considers that the transfer is in the interests of the child—
    (i) because it is likely significantly to accelerate the determination of the proceedings,
    (ii) because it would be appropriate for those proceedings to be heard together with other family proceedings which are pending in the receiving court, or
    (iii) for some other reason, and
  (b) the receiving court, by its justices' clerk (as defined by rule 1(2) of the Family Proceedings Courts (Children Act 1989) Rules 1991), consents to the transfer.

[(2) This article applies to proceedings—

  (a) under the Act;
  (b) under the [Adoption and Children Act 2002];
  (c) of the kind mentioned in sub-paragraph [... (t) or (u)] of article 3(1) [and under section 55A of the Family Law Act 1986][;
  (d) under section 11 of the Crime and Disorder Act 1998 (child safety orders)].]

Date in force

14 October 1991: see art 1(1).

Amendment

Para (1): numbered as such by SI 1993/624, arts 2, 4(a).

Para (1): words "to which this article applies" in square brackets substituted by SI 1993/624, arts 2, 4(b). Para (1): in sub-para (a) words "and, where applicable, section 1(3) of the Adoption and Children Act 2002" in square brackets inserted by SI 2005/2797, arts 3, 10.
Para (2): inserted by SI 1993/624, arts 2, 4(c); in sub-para (b) words "Adoption and Children Act 2002" in square brackets substituted by SI 2005/2797, arts 3, 9; in sub-para (c) words in square brackets ending with the words "(t) or (u)" substituted by SI 1994/2164, art 4; in sub-para (c) reference omitted revoked by SI 2001/775, arts 3, 5(a); in sub-para (c) words "and under section 55A of the Family Law Act 1986" in square brackets inserted by SI 2001/775, arts 3, 5(b; sub-para (d) inserted by SI 1998/2166, art 2. Date in force: 30 September 1998: see SI 1998/2166, art 1.

Transfer from magistrates' court to county court by magistrates' court

7

(1) Subject to paragraphs (2), (3) and (4) and to articles 15 to 18, a magistrates' court may, upon application by a party or of its own motion, transfer to a county court proceedings of any of the kinds mentioned in article 3(1) [or proceedings under section 55A of the Family Law Act 1986] where it considers it in the interests of the child to do so having regard, first, to the principle set out in section 1(2) [and, where applicable, section 1(3) of the Adoption and Children Act 2002] and, secondly, to the following questions:

(a) whether the proceedings are exceptionally grave, important or complex, in particular—
  (i) because of complicated or conflicting evidence about the risks involved to the child's physical or moral well-being or about other matters relating to the welfare of the child;
  (ii) because of the number of parties;
  (iii) because of a conflict with the law of another jurisdiction;
  (iv) because of some novel and difficult point of law; or
  (v) because of some question of general public interest;
(b) whether it would be appropriate for those proceedings to be heard together with other family proceedings which are pending in another court; and
(c) whether transfer is likely significantly to accelerate the determination of the proceedings, where—
  (i) no other method of doing so, including transfer to another magistrates' court, is appropriate, and
  (ii) delay would seriously prejudice the interests of the child who is the subject of the proceedings.

(2) Notwithstanding paragraph (1), proceedings of the kind mentioned in sub-paragraph (g) to (j), (l), (m), (p) or (q) of article 3(1) shall not be transferred from a magistrates' court.

(3) Notwithstanding paragraph (1), proceedings of the kind mentioned in sub-paragraph (a) or (n) of article 3(1) shall only be transferred from a magistrates' court to a county court in order to be heard together with other family proceedings which arise out of the same circumstances as gave rise to the proceedings to be transferred and which are pending in another court.

(4) Notwithstanding paragraphs (1) and (3), proceedings of the kind mentioned in article 3(1)(a) shall not be transferred from a magistrates' court which is not a family proceedings court within the meaning of section 92(1).

Date in force

14 October 1991: see art 1(1).

Amendment

Para (1): words "or proceedings under section 55A of the Family Law Act 1986" in square brackets inserted by SI 2001/775, arts 3, 6; words "and, where applicable, section 1(3) of the Adoption and Children Act 2002" in square brackets inserted by SI 2005/2797, arts 3, 10.

8

Subject to articles 15 to 18, a magistrates' court may transfer to a county court proceedings under the Act or under the [Adoption and Children Act 2002], being proceedings to which article 7 does not apply, where, having regard to the principle set out in section 1(2) [and, where applicable, section 1(3) of the Adoption and Children Act 2002], it considers that in the interests of the child the proceedings can be dealt with more appropriately in that county court.

Date in force

14 October 1991: see art 1(1).

Amendment

Words "Adoption and Children Act 2002" in square brackets substituted by SI 2005/2797, arts 3, 9.
Words "and, where applicable, section 1(3) of the Adoption and Children Act 2002" in square brackets inserted by SI 2005/2797, arts 3, 10.

Transfer from magistrates' court following refusal of magistrates' court to transfer

9

(1)   Where a magistrates' court refuses to transfer proceedings under article 7, a party to those proceedings may apply to the care centre listed in column (ii) of Schedule 2 to this Order against the entry in column (i) for the [local justice area] in which the magistrates' court is situated for an order under paragraph (2).

(2)   Upon hearing an application under paragraph (1) the court may transfer the proceedings to itself where, having regard to the principle set out in section 1(2) [and, where applicable, section 1(3) of the Adoption and Children Act 2002] and the questions set out in article 7(1)(a) to (c), it considers it in the interests of the child to do so.

(3)   Upon hearing an application under paragraph (1) the court may transfer the proceedings to the High Court where, having regard to the principle set out in section 1(2) [and, where applicable, section 1(3) of the Adoption and Children Act 2002], it considers—

   (a)   that the proceedings are appropriate for determination in the High Court, and
   (b)   that such determination would be in the interests of the child.

[(4)   This article shall apply (with the necessary modifications) to proceedings brought under Parts I and II as it applies where a magistrates' court refuses to transfer proceedings under article 7.]

Date in force

14 October 1991: see art 1(1).

Amendment

Para (1): words "local justice area" in square brackets substituted by SI 2005/520, art 3.

Para (2): words "and, where applicable, section 1(3) of the Adoption and Children Act 2002" in square brackets inserted by SI 2005/2797, arts 3, 10.
Para (3): words "and, where applicable, section 1(3) of the Adoption and Children Act 2002" in square brackets inserted by SI 2005/2797, arts 3, 10.
Para (4): inserted by SI 1997/1897, art 2.

Transfer from one county court to another

10

[(1)]   Subject to articles 15 [and 16], a county court (the "transferring court") shall transfer proceedings [to which this article applies] to another county court (the "receiving court") where—

(a)   the transferring court, having regard to the principle set out in section 1(2) [and, where applicable, section 1(3) of the Adoption and Children Act 2002], considers the transfer to be in the interests of the child, and

(b)   the receiving court is—

   (i)   of the same class or classes, within the meaning of article 2, as the transferring court, or

   (ii) to be presided over by a judge or district judge who is specified by directions under section 9 of the Courts and Legal Services Act 1990 for the same purposes as the judge or district judge presiding over the transferring court.

[(2)   This article applies to proceedings—

(a)   under the Act;

(b)   under the [Adoption and Children Act 2002];

(c)   of the kind mentioned in sub-paragraph [... (t) or (u)] of article 3(1) [and under section 55A of the Family Law Act 1986].]

Date in force

14 October 1991: see art 1(1).

Amendment

Para (1): numbered as such by SI 1993/624, arts 2, 4(a); words "and 16" in square brackets substituted by SI 2005/2797, arts 3, 11(a); words "to which this article applies" in square brackets substituted by SI 1993/624, arts 2, 4(b); in sub-para (a) words "and, where applicable, section 1(3) of the Adoption and Children Act 2002" in square brackets inserted by SI 2005/2797, arts 3, 10. Date in force: 30 December 2005: see SI 2005/2797, art 1(b); for savings and transitional provisions see art 2 thereof.
Para (2): inserted by SI 1993/624, arts 2, 4(c); in sub-para (b) words "Adoption and Children Act 2002" in square brackets substituted by SI 2005/2797, arts 3, 11(b); in sub-para (c) words in square brackets ending with the words "(t) or (u)" substituted by SI 1994/2164, art 4; in sub-para (c) reference omitted revoked by SI 2001/775, arts 3, 5(a); in sub-para (c) words "and under section 55A of the Family Law Act 1986" in square brackets inserted by SI 2001/775, arts 3, 5(b).

Transfer from county court to magistrates' court by county court

11

[(1)]   A county court may transfer to a magistrates' court before trial proceedings which were transferred under article 7(1) where the county court, having regard to the principle set out in section 1(2) [and, where applicable, section 1(3) of the Adoption and Children Act 2002] and the interests of the child, considers that the criterion cited by the magistrates' court as the reason for transfer—

(a)   in the case of the criterion in article 7(1)(a), does not apply,

(b)   in the case of the criterion in article 7(1)(b), no longer applies, because the proceedings with which the transferred proceedings were to be heard have been determined,

(c)   in the case of the criterion in article 7(1)(c), no longer applies.

[(2)   Paragraph (1) shall apply (with the necessary modifications) to proceedings under Parts I and II brought in, or transferred to, a county court as it applies to proceedings transferred to a county court under article 7(1).]

Date in force

14 October 1991: see art 1(1).

Amendment

Para (1): renumbered as such by SI 1997/1897, art 3. Date in force: 1 October 1997: see SI 1997/1897, art 1; words "and, where applicable, section 1(3) of the Adoption and Children Act 2002" in square brackets inserted by SI 2005/2797, arts 3, 10.
Para (2): inserted by SI 1997/1897, art 3.

Transfer from county court to High Court by county court

12

[(1)]   A county court may transfer proceedings [to which this article applies] to the High Court where, having regard to the principle set out in section 1(2) [and, where applicable, section 1(3) of the Adoption and Children Act 2002], it considers—

(a)   that the proceedings are appropriate for determination in the High Court, and

(b)   that such determination would be in the interests of the child.

[(2)   This article applies to proceedings—

(a)   under the Act;

(b)   under the [Adoption and Children Act 2002];

(c)   of the kind mentioned in sub-paragraph [... (t) or (u)] of article 3(1) [and under section 55A of the Family Law Act 1986].]

Date in force

14 October 1991: see art 1(1).

Amendment

Para (1): numbered as such by SI 1993/624, arts 2, 4(a); words "to which this article applies" in square brackets substituted by SI 1993/624, arts 2, 4(b);words "and, where applicable, section 1(3) of the Adoption and Children Act 2002" in square brackets inserted by SI 2005/2797, arts 3, 10.
Para (2): inserted by SI 1993/624, arts 2, 4(c); in sub-para (b) words "Adoption and Children Act 2002" in square brackets substituted by SI 2005/2797, arts 3, 9; in sub-para (c) words in square brackets ending with the words "(t) or (u)" substituted by SI 1994/2164, art 4; in sub-para (c) reference omitted revoked by SI 2001/775, arts 3, 5(a): in sub-para (c) words "and under section 55A of the Family Law Act 1986" in square brackets inserted by SI 2001/775, arts 3, 5(b).

Transfer from High Court to county court

13

[(1)]   Subject to articles 15 [to] 18, the High Court may transfer to a county court proceedings [to which this article applies] where, having regard to the principle set out in section 1(2) [and, where applicable, section 1(3) of the Adoption and Children Act 2002], it considers that the proceedings are appropriate for determination in such a court and that such determination would be in the interests of the child.

[(2)   This article applies to proceedings—

    (a)   under the Act;

    (b)   under the [Adoption and Children Act 2002];

    (c)   of the kind mentioned in sub-paragraph [... (t) or (u)] of article 3(1) [and under section 55A of the Family Law Act 1986].]

Date in force

14 October 1991: see art 1(1).

Amendment

Para (1): numbered as such by SI 1993/624, arts 2, 4(a); word "to" in square brackets substituted by SI 2005/2797, arts 3, 12(a); words "to which this article applies" in square brackets substituted by SI 1993/624, arts 2, 4(b); words "and, where applicable, section 1(3) of the Adoption and Children Act 2002" in square brackets inserted by SI 2005/2797, arts 3, 10.
Para (2): inserted by SI 1993/624, arts 2, 4(c); in sub-para (b) words "Adoption and Children Act 2002" in square brackets substituted by SI 2005/2797, arts 3, 12(b); in sub-para (c) words in square brackets ending with the words "(t) or (u)" substituted by SI 1994/2164, art 4; in sub-para (c) reference omitted revoked by SI 2001/775, arts 3, 5(a); in sub-para (c) words "and under section 55A of the Family Law Act 1986" in square brackets inserted by SI 2001/775, arts 3, 5(b).

Allocation of Proceedings to Particular County Courts

Commencement

14

[(1)]   Subject to [articles 3B(c) and (d), 18 and 19] and to rule 2.40 of the Family Proceedings Rules 1991 (Application under Part I or II of the Children Act 1989 where ... cause is pending), an application under the Act ... which is to be [made to] a county court shall be [made to] a [designated] county court.

[(2)   Subject to paragraph (3), an application under the Adoption and Children Act 2002 which is to be made to a county court shall be commenced in an adoption centre.

(3)   An application for a Convention adoption order or an adoption order where section 83 of the Adoption and Children Act 2002 applies which is to be made to a county court shall be commenced in an intercountry adoption centre.]

Date in force

14 October 1991: see art 1(1).

Amendment

Para (1): numbered as such by SI 2005/2797, arts 3, 13; words "articles 3B(c) and (d), 18 and 19" in square brackets substituted by SI 2005/2797, arts 3, 13(a); first word omitted revoked by SI 2005/2797, arts 3, 13(b)(i); final words omitted revoked by SI 2005/2797, arts 3, 13(b)(ii); words "made to" in square brackets in both places they occur substituted by SI 1993/624, arts 2, 7; word "designated" in square brackets substituted by SI 2005/2797, arts 3, 13(c).
Paras (2), (3): inserted by SI 2005/2797, arts 3, 13(d).

Proceedings under Part I or II or Schedule 1

15

(1)   Subject to paragraph (3), where an application under Part I or II or Schedule 1 is to be transferred from a magistrates' court to a county court, it shall be transferred to a [designated] county court.

(2)   Subject to paragraph (3), where an application under Part I or II or Schedule 1, other than an application for an order under section 8 [or 14A], is to be transferred from the High Court to a county court, it shall be transferred to a [designated] county court.

(3)   Where an application under Part I or II or Schedule 1, other than an application for an order under section 8 [or 14A], is to be transferred to a county court for the purpose of consolidation with other proceedings, it shall be transferred to the court in which those other proceedings are pending.

Date in force

14 October 1991: see art 1(1).

Amendment

Para (1): word "designated" in square brackets substituted by SI 2005/2797, arts 3, 14(a).
Para (2): words "or 14A" in square brackets inserted by SI 2005/2797, arts 3, 14(b); word "designated" in square brackets substituted by SI 2005/2797, arts 3, 14(a).
Para (3): words "or 14A" in square brackets inserted by SI 2005/2797, arts 3, 14(b).

Orders under section 8 of the Children Act 1989

16

(1)   An application for an order under section 8 [or 14A] in a [designated] county court, which is not also a family hearing centre, shall, if the court is notified that the application will be opposed, be transferred for trial to a family hearing centre.

(2)   Subject to paragraph (3), where an application for an order under section 8 [or 14A] is to be transferred from the High Court to a county court it shall be transferred to a family hearing centre.

(3)   Where an application for an order under section 8 [or 14A] is to be transferred to a county court for the purpose of consolidation with other proceedings, it may be transferred to the court in which those other proceedings are pending whether or not it is a family hearing centre; but paragraph (1) shall apply to the application following the transfer.

Date in force

14 October 1991: see art 1(1).

Amendment

Para (1): words "or 14A" in square brackets inserted by SI 2005/2797, arts 3, 14(b); word "designated" in square brackets substituted by SI 2005/2797, arts 3, 14(a). Date in force: 5 December 2005: see SI 2005/2797, art 1(a).
Para (2): words "or 14A" in square brackets inserted by SI 2005/2797, arts 3, 14(b).
Para (3): words "or 14A" in square brackets inserted by SI 2005/2797, arts 3, 14(b).

[Application under the Adoption and Children Act 2002]

Amendment

Substituted by SI 2005/2797, arts 3, 15. Date in force: 30 December 2005: see SI 2005/2797, art 1(b); for savings and transitional provisions see art 2 thereof.

---

[17]

[(1)   Subject to paragraph (2), where proceedings under the Adoption and Children Act 2002, save for proceedings under section 23 of that Act, are to be transferred from the High Court or a magistrates' court to a county court, they shall be transferred to an adoption centre.

(2)   Where proceedings for a Convention adoption order or an adoption order where section 83 of the Adoption and Children Act 2002 applies are to be transferred from the High Court to a county court, they shall be transferred to an intercountry adoption centre.]

Amendment

Substituted by SI 2005/2797, arts 3, 15.

Applications under Part III, IV or V

18

(1)   An application under Part III, IV or V, if it is to be [made to] a county court, shall be [made to] a care centre.

(2)   An application under Part III, IV or V which is to be transferred from the High Court to a county court shall be transferred to a care centre.

(3)   An application under Part III, IV or V which is to be transferred from a magistrates' court to a county court shall be transferred to the care centre listed against the entry in column (i) of Schedule 2 to this Order for the [local justice area] in which the relevant magistrates' court is situated.

Date in force

14 October 1991: see art 1(1).

Amendment

Para (1): words "made to" in square brackets in both places they occur substituted by SI 1993/624, arts 2, 7.
Para (3): words "local justice area" in square brackets substituted by SI 2005/520, art 3.

Principal Registry of the Family Division

19

The principal registry of the Family Division of the High Court shall be treated, for the purposes of this Order, as if it were a [designated] county court, a family hearing centre and a care centre listed against every entry in column (i) of Schedule 2 to this Order (in addition to the entries against which it is actually listed) [and an adoption centre and intercountry adoption centre].

Date in force

14 October 1991: see art 1(1).

Amendment

Word "designated" in square brackets substituted by SI 2005/2797, arts 3, 16(a).
Words "and an adoption centre and intercountry adoption centre" in square brackets inserted by SI 2005/2797, arts 3, 16(b).

...

Amendment

Revoked by SI 2005/2797, arts 3, 17. Date in force: 30 December 2005: see SI 2005/2797, art 1(b); for savings and transitional provisions see art 2 thereof.

20 ...

...

Amendment

Revoked by SI 2005/2797, arts 3, 17.

Miscellaneous

Contravention of provision of this Order

21

Where proceedings are commenced or transferred in contravention of a provision of this Order, the contravention shall not have the effect of making the proceedings invalid; and no appeal shall lie against the determination of proceedings on the basis of such contravention alone.

Date in force

14 October 1991: see art 1(1).

...

Amendment

Revoked by SI 2005/2797, arts 3, 17.

22

...

Amendment

Revoked by SI 2005/2797, arts 3, 17.

Appendix 2 *Children (Allocation of Proceedings) Order 1991*

SCHEDULE 1
FAMILY HEARING CENTRES

Article 2

[London Region

Barnet County Court
Bow County Court
Brentford County Court
Bromley County Court
[Clerkenwell & Shoreditch County Court]
Croydon County Court
Edmonton County Court
Ilford County Court
Kingston-upon-Thames County Court
Romford County Court
Wandsworth County Court
Willesden County Court]

[Midlands Region]

Birmingham County Court
Coventry County Court
Derby County Court
[Dudley County Court]
[...]
Leicester County Court
Lincoln County Court
Mansfield County Court
Northampton County Court
Nottingham County Court
...
...
Stafford County Court
Stoke-on-Trent County Court
Telford County Court
Walsall County Court
Wolverhampton County Court
Worcester County Court

[North West Region]

Blackburn County Court
Bolton County Court
Carlisle County Court
Lancaster County Court
Liverpool County Court
Manchester County Court
[Oldham County Court]
Stockport County Court

[North East Region]

Barnsley County Court
Bradford County Court
Darlington County Court
Dewsbury County Court
Doncaster County Court
Durham County Court

[Grimsby County Court]
Halifax County Court
Harrogate County Court
Huddersfield County Court
Keighley County Court
Kingston-upon-Hull County Court
Leeds County Court
Newcastle-upon-Tyne County Court
Pontefract County Court
Rotherham County Court
Scarborough County Court
Sheffield County Court
Skipton County Court
Sunderland County Court
Teesside County Court
Wakefield County Court
York County Court

[South East Region]

[...]
[Bedford County Court]
Brighton County Court
...
...

...
Cambridge County Court
Canterbury County Court
Chelmsford County Court
Chichester County Court
Colchester and Clacton County Court

...
[Dartford County Court]
...
Guildford County Court
Hitchin County Court

...
Ipswich County Court
[King's Lynn County Court]
...
Luton County Court
Maidstone County Court
Medway County Court
Milton Keynes County Court
Norwich County Court
[Oxford County Court
Peterborough County Court]
Reading County Court

...
Slough County Court
Southend County Court

...
Watford County Court
...

[Wales and Cheshire Region]

Aberystwyth County Court
Caernarfon County Court

Cardiff County Court
Carmarthen County Court
Chester County Court
Crewe County Court
Haverfordwest County Court
Llangefni County Court
Macclesfield County Court
Merthyr Tydfil County Court
Newport (Gwent) County Court
[Pontypridd County Court]
Rhyl County Court
Swansea County Court
Warrington County Court
Welshpool and Newtown County Court

[South West Region]

[Barnstaple County Court]
Wrexham County Court
Basingstoke County Court
[Bath County Court]
Bournemouth County Court
Bristol County Court
Exeter County Court
Gloucester County Court
Plymouth County Court
Portsmouth County Court
[Salisbury County Court]
Southampton County Court
Swindon County Court
Taunton County Court
Truro County Court
[Weymouth County Court]
[Yeovil County Court]

Date in force

14 October 1991: see art 1(1).

Amendment

London Region: inserted by SI 2005/520, art 4(a).
London Region: entry "Clerkenwell & Shoreditch County Court" inserted by SI 2006/1541, arts 2, 3.
Midlands Region: words "Midlands Region" in square brackets substituted by SI 2005/520, art 4(b).
Midlands Region: entry "Dudley County Court" inserted by SI 1994/3138, art 3.
Midlands Region: entry "Grimsby County Court" (omitted) inserted by SI 1994/3138, art 3.
Midlands Region: entry "Grimsby County Court" (omitted) revoked by SI 2001/775, arts 3, 7(1), (2)(b).
Midlands Region: entry "Oxford County Court" (omitted) revoked by SI 2001/775, arts 3, 7(1), (2)(b).
Midlands Region: entry "Peterborough County Court" (omitted) revoked by SI 2001/775, arts 3, 7(1), (2)(b).
North West Region: words "North West Region" in square brackets substituted by SI 2005/520, art 4(c).
North West Region: entry "Oldham County Court" inserted by SI 1999/524, art 2(a).
North East Region: words "North East Region" in square brackets substituted by SI 2005/520, art 4(d).

North East Region: entry "Grimsby County Court" inserted by SI 2001/775, arts 3, 7(1), (3).
South East Region: words "South East Region" in square brackets substituted by SI 2005/520, art 4(e). D
South East Region: entry "Barnet County Court" (omitted) inserted by SI 2000/2670, art 2.
South East Region: entry "Barnet County Court" (omitted) revoked by SI 2005/520, art 4(f)(i).
South East Region: entries "Bedford County Court", "Dartford County Court" and "King's Lynn County Court" inserted by SI 1994/3138, art 3.
South East Region: entry "Bow County Court" (omitted) revoked by SI 2005/520, art 4(f)(ii).
South East Region: entry "Brentford County Court" (omitted) revoked by SI 2005/520, art 4(f)(iii).
South East Region: entry "Bromley County Court" (omitted) revoked by SI 2005/520, art 4(f)(iv).
South East Region: entry "Croydon County Court" (omitted) revoked by SI 2005/520, art 4(f)(v).
South East Region: entry "Edmonton County Court" (omitted) revoked by SI 2005/520, art 4(f)(vi).
South East Region: entry "Ilford County Court" (omitted) revoked by SI 2005/520, art 4(f)(vii).
South East Region: entry "Kingston-upon-Thames County Court" (omitted) revoked by SI 2005/520, art 4(f)(viii).
South East Region: entries "Oxford County Court" and "Peterborough County Court" inserted by SI 2001/775, arts 3, 7(1), (4).
South East Region: entry "Romford County Court" (omitted) revoked by SI 2005/520, art 4(f)(ix).
South East Region: entry "Wandsworth County Court" (omitted) revoked by SI 2005/520, art 4(f)(x).
South East Region: entry "Willesden County Court" (omitted) revoked by SI 2005/520, art 4(f)(xi).
Wales and Cheshire Region: words "Wales and Cheshire Region" in square brackets substituted by SI 2005/520, art 4(g).
Wales and Cheshire Region: entry "Pontypridd County Court" inserted by SI 1995/1649, art 2.
South West Region: words "South West Region" in square brackets substituted by SI 2005/520, art 4(h).
South West Region: entry "Barnstaple County Court" inserted by SI 1999/524, art 2(b). D
South West Region: entries "Bath County Court" and "Weymouth County Court" inserted by SI 1994/3138, art 3.
South West Region: entry "Salisbury County Court" inserted by SI 1997/1897, art 5.
South West Region: entry "Yeovil County Court" inserted by SI 2001/1656, art 2. D
#AnnotationE

[SCHEDULE 2
CARE CENTRES]

Amendment

Substituted by SI 2005/520, art 5.

[Article 2]

[London Region

(*i*) *Local Justice Area*	(*ii*) *Care Centre*
Barking and Dagenham	Principal Registry of the Family Division
Barnet	Principal Registry of the Family Division
Bexley	Principal Registry of the Family Division
Brent	Principal Registry of the Family Division
Bromley	Principal Registry of the Family Division
Camden and Islington	Principal Registry of the Family Division
City of London	Principal Registry of the Family Division

Appendix 2 *Children (Allocation of Proceedings) Order 1991*

[London Region

(i) *Local Justice Area*	(ii) *Care Centre*
City of Westminster	Principal Registry of the Family Division
Croydon	Principal Registry of the Family Division
Ealing	Principal Registry of the Family Division
Enfield	Principal Registry of the Family Division
Greenwich and Lewisham	Principal Registry of the Family Division
Hackney and Tower Hamlets	Principal Registry of the Family Division
Hammersmith and Fulham and Kensington and Chelsea	Principal Registry of the Family Division
Haringey	Principal Registry of the Family Division
Harrow Gore	Principal Registry of the Family Division
Havering	Principal Registry of the Family Division
Hillingdon	Principal Registry of the Family Division
Hounslow	Principal Registry of the Family Division
Kingston-upon-Thames	Principal Registry of the Family Division
Lambeth and Southwark	Principal Registry of the Family Division
Merton	Principal Registry of the Family Division
Newham	Principal Registry of the Family Division
Redbridge	Principal Registry of the Family Division
Richmond-upon-Thames	Principal Registry of the Family Division
Sutton	Principal Registry of the Family Division
Waltham Forest	Principal Registry of the Family Division
Wandsworth	Principal Registry of the Family Division

Midlands Region

(i) *Local Justice Area*	(ii) *Care Centre*
Ashby-De-La-Zouch	Leicester County Court
Birmingham	Birmingham County Court
Boston	Lincoln County Court
Bourne and Stamford	Lincoln County Court
Bromsgrove and Redditch	Worcester County Court
Central and South West Staffordshire	Stoke-on-Trent County Court
Corby	Northampton County Court
Coventry District	Coventry County Court
Daventry	Northampton County Court
Drayton	Telford County Court
Dudley	Wolverhampton County Court
Elloes	Lincoln County Court
Gainsborough	Lincoln County Court
Grantham	Lincoln County Court
Herefordshire	Worcester County Court
High Peak	Derby County Court
Kettering	Northampton County Court
Kidderminster	Worcester County Court
Leicester	Leicester County Court
Lincoln District	Lincoln County Court

Loughborough	Leicester County Court
Mansfield	Nottingham County Court
Market Bosworth	Leicester County Court
Market Harborough and Lutterworth	Leicester County Court
Melton, Belvoir and Rutland	Leicester County Court
Newark and Southwell	Nottingham County Court
Northampton	Northampton County Court
North East Derbyshire and Dales	Derby County Court
North Staffordshire	Stoke-on-Trent County Court
Nottingham	Nottingham County Court
Oswestry	Telford County Court
Shrewsbury	Telford County Court
Skegness	Lincoln County Court
Sleaford	Lincoln County Court
Solihull	Birmingham County Court
South Shropshire	Telford County Court
South East Staffordshire	Stoke-on-Trent County Court or Derby County Court
Southern Derbyshire	Derby County Court
South Worcestershire	Worcester County Court
Stourbridge and Halesowen	Wolverhampton County Court
Sutton Coldfield	Birmingham County Court
Telford and Bridgnorth	Telford County Court
Towcester	Northampton County Court
Warley	Wolverhampton County Court
Walsall and Aldridge	Wolverhampton County Court
Warwickshire	Coventry County Court
Wellingborough	Northampton County Court
West Bromwich	Wolverhampton County Court
Wolds	Lincoln County Court
Wolverhampton	Wolverhampton County Court
Worksop and Retford	Nottingham County Court

North East Region

(i) *Local Justice Area*	(ii) *Care Centre*
Alnwick	Newcastle-upon-Tyne County Court
Barnsley District	Sheffield County Court
Batley and Dewsbury	Leeds County Court
Berwick-upon-Tweed	Newcastle-upon-Tyne County Court
Beverley and the Wolds	Kingston-upon-Hull County Court
Bradford	Leeds County Court
Bridglington	Kingston-upon-Hull County Court
Calderdale	Leeds County Court
Doncaster	Sheffield County Court
Gateshead District	Newcastle-upon-Tyne County Court
Grimsby and Cleethorpes	Kingston-upon-Hull County Court
Goole and Howdenshire	Kingston-upon-Hull County Court
Harrogate	York County Court or Leeds County Court
Hartlepool	Middlesbrough County Court
Houghton-le-Spring	Sunderland County Court
Huddersfield	Leeds County Court
Hull and Holderness	Kingston-upon-Hull County Court

Keighley	Leeds County Court
Langbaurgh East	Middlesbrough County Court
Leeds District	Leeds County Court
Newcastle-upon-Tyne District	Newcastle-upon-Tyne County Court
Northallerton and Richmond	Middlesbrough County Court
North Durham	Newcastle-upon-Tyne County Court or Sunderland County Court
North Lincolnshire	Kingston-upon-Hull County Court
North Tyneside District	Newcastle-upon-Tyne County Court
Pontefract	Leeds County Court
Rotherham	Sheffield County Court
Scarborough	York County Court
Selby	York County Court
Sheffield	Sheffield County Court
Skipton	Leeds County Court
South Durham	Newcastle-upon-Tyne County Court or Middlesbrough County Court
South East Northumberland	Newcastle-upon-Tyne County Court
South Tyneside District	Sunderland County Court
Sunderland	Sunderland County Court
Teesside	Middlesbrough County Court
Tynedale	Newcastle-upon-Tyne County Court
Wakefield	Leeds County Court
York	York County Court

North West Region

(i) *Local Justice Area*	(ii) *Care Centre*
Blackburn, Darwen and Ribble Valley	Blackburn County Court
Bolton	Manchester County Court
Burnley, Pendle and Rossendale	Blackburn County Court
Bury	Manchester County Court
Carlisle and District	Carlisle County Court
[Chester, Ellesmere Port and Neston	Chester County Court]
Chorley	Blackburn County Court
City of Salford	Manchester County Court
Eden	Carlisle County Court
Furness and District	Lancaster County Court
Fylde Coast	Lancaster County Court
[Halton	Warrington County Court]
Hyndburn	Blackburn County Court
Knowsley	Liverpool County Court
Lancaster	Lancaster County Court
Liverpool	Liverpool County Court
[Macclesfield	Warrington County Court]
Manchester City	Manchester County Court
North Sefton District	Liverpool County Court
Oldham	Manchester County Court
Ormskirk	Liverpool County Court
Preston	Blackburn County Court
Rochdale, Middleton and Heywood	Manchester County Court
St Helens	Liverpool County Court
[South Cheshire	Stoke-on-Trent County Court]
South Lakeland	Lancaster County Court

South Ribble	Blackburn County Court
South Sefton District	Liverpool County Court
Stockport	Manchester County Court
Tameside	Manchester County Court
Trafford	Manchester County Court
[Vale Royal	Chester County Court
Warrington	Warrington County Court]
West Allerdale and Keswick	Carlisle County Court
Whitehaven	Carlisle County Court
Wigan and Leigh	Liverpool County Court or Manchester County Court
Wirral	Liverpool County Court

South East Region

(i) *Local Justice Area*	(ii) *Care Centre*
Bedford and Mid-Bedfordshire	Luton County Court
Cambridge	Cambridge County Court
Central Buckinghamshire	Milton Keynes County Court
Central Kent	Medway County Court
Central Hertfordshire	Watford County Court
Central Norfolk	Norwich County Court
East Berkshire	Reading County Court
East Cambridgeshire	Cambridge County Court
East Hertfordshire	Watford County Court
East Kent	Canterbury County Court
Fenland	Peterborough County Court
Great Yarmouth	Norwich County Court
Huntingdonshire	Peterborough County Court
Luton and South Bedfordshire	Luton County Court
Mid-North Essex	Chelmsford County Court
Mid-South Essex	Chelmsford County Court
Milton Keynes	Milton Keynes County Court
North-East Essex	Chelmsford County Court
North East Suffolk	Ipswich County Court
North Hertfordshire	Watford County Court
North Kent	Medway County Court
North Norfolk	Norwich County Court
Northern Oxfordshire	Oxford County Court
North Surrey	Guildford County Court
North-West Essex	Chelmsford County Court
North West Surrey	Guildford County Court
Norwich	Norwich County Court
Oxford	Oxford County Court
Peterborough	Peterborough County Court
Reading	Reading County Court
South-East Essex	Chelmsford County Court
South East Suffolk	Ipswich County Court
South East Surrey	Guildford County Court
South West Surrey	Guildford County Court
South Norfolk	Norwich County Court
Southern Oxfordshire	Oxford County Court
South-West Essex	Chelmsford County Court
Sussex (Central)	Brighton County Court

Sussex (Eastern)	Brighton County Court
Sussex (Northern)	Brighton County Court
Sussex (Western)	Brighton County Court
West Berkshire	Reading County Court
West Hertfordshire	Watford County Court
West Norfolk	Norwich County Court
West Suffolk	Ipswich County Court
Wycombe and Beaconsfield	Milton Keynes County Court

South West Region

(i) Local Justice Area	(ii) Care Centre
Bath and Wansdyke	Bristol County Court
Bristol	Bristol County Court
Central Devon	Exeter County Court
East Cornwall	Truro County Court
East Dorset	Bournemouth County Court
Gloucestershire	Bristol County Court
Isle of Wight	Portsmouth County Court
Mendip	Taunton County Court
New Forest	Portsmouth County Court
North Avon	Bristol County Court
North Devon	Exeter County Court
North East Hampshire	Portsmouth County Court
North Somerset	Bristol County Court
North West Hampshire	Portsmouth County Court
North West Wiltshire	Swindon County Court
Plymouth District	Plymouth County Court
Sedgemoor	Taunton County Court
Southampton	Portsmouth County Court
South Devon	Exeter County Court
South East Hampshire	Portsmouth County Court
South East Wiltshire	Swindon County Court
South Hampshire	Portsmouth County Court
South Somerset	Taunton County Court
Swindon	Swindon County Court
Taunton Deane and West Somerset	Taunton County Court
West Cornwall	Truro County Court
West Dorset	Bournemouth County Court

Wales ...

(i) Local Justice Area	(ii) Care Centre
Cardiff	Cardiff County Court
Carmarthen	Swansea County Court
Ceredigion	Swansea County Court
< ... >	...
Conwy	Caernarfon County Court or Rhyl County Court
Cynon Valley	Pontypridd County Court
De Brycheiniog	Pontypridd County Court
< ... >	...
Denbighshire	Rhyl County Court
Dinefwr	Swansea County Court

1012

Flintshire	Rhyl County Court
Gwynedd	Caernarfon County Court
< ... >	...
Llanelli	Swansea County Court
...	...
Merthyr Tydfil	Pontypridd County Court
Miskin	Pontypridd County Court
[Montgomeryshire	[Wrexham County Court]]
Neath Port Talbot	Swansea County Court
Newcastle and Ogmore	Cardiff County Court
...	...
North West Gwent	Cardiff County Court or Newport (Gwent) County Court or Pontypridd County Court
[Pembrokeshire	Swansea County Court]
Radnorshire and North Brecknock	Pontypridd County Court
< ... >	...
South East Gwent	Cardiff County Court or Newport (Gwent) County Court or Pontypridd County Court
...	...
Swansea County	Swansea County Court
Vale of Glamorgan	Cardiff County Court
...	...
< ... >	...
...	...
[Wrexham	Wrexham County Court]
Wrexham Maelor	[Wrexham County Court]
Ynys Mòn/Anglesey	Caernarfon County Court]

Amendment

Substituted by SI 2005/520, art 5.
North West Region: entry relating to "Chester, Ellesmore Port and Neston" inserted by SI 2007/1099, arts 3, 4(1)(a).
North West Region: entry relating to "Halton" inserted by SI 2007/1099, arts 3, 4(1)(b).
North West Region: entry relating to "Macclesfield" inserted by SI 2007/1099, arts 3, 4(1)(c).
North West Region: entry relating to "South Cheshire" inserted by SI 2007/1099, arts 3, 4(1)(d).
North West Region: entries relating to "Vale Royal" and "Warrington" inserted by SI 2007/1099, arts 3, 4(1)(e).
Wales heading: words omitted revoked by SI 2007/1099, arts 3, 4(2)(a). .
Wales: entry relating to "Chester, Ellesmere Port and Neston" (omitted) revoked by SI 2007/1099, arts 3, 4(2)(b).
Wales: entry relating to "De Maldwyn" (omitted) revoked by SI 2006/1541, arts 2, 4(a).
Wales: entry relating to "Halton" (omitted) revoked by SI 2007/1099, arts 3, 4(2)(b).
Wales: entry relating to "Macclesfield" (omitted) revoked by SI 2007/1099, arts 3, 4(2)(b).
Wales: entry relating to "Montgomeryshire" inserted by SI 2006/1541, arts 2, 4(b).
Wales: in entry relating to "Montgomeryshire" words "Wrexham County Court" in square brackets substituted by SI 2007/1099, arts 3, 4(2)(c).
Wales: entry relating to "North Pembrokeshire" (omitted) revoked by SI 2006/1541, arts 2, 4(a).
Wales: entry relating to "Pembrokeshire" inserted by SI 2006/1541, arts 2, 4(c).
Wales: entry relating to "South Cheshire" (omitted) revoked by SI 2007/1099, arts 3, 4(2)(b).
Wales: entry relating to "South Pembrokeshire" (omitted) revoked by SI 2006/1541, arts 2, 4(a).
Wales: entries relating to "Vale Royal" and "Warrington" (omitted) revoked by SI 2007/1099, arts 3, 4(2)(b).
Wales: entry relating to "Welshpool" (omitted) revoked by SI 2006/1541, arts 2, 4(a).

Wales: in entry relating to "Wrexham Maelor" words "Wrexham County Court" in square brackets substituted by SI 2007/1099, arts 3, 4(2)(d).

[SCHEDULE 3
ADOPTION CENTRES]

Amendment

Inserted by SI 2005/2797, arts 3, 18, Schedule. Date in force: 30 December 2005: see SI 2005/2797, art 1(b); for savings and transitional provisions see art 2 thereof.

[Article 2]

Amendment

Inserted by SI 2005/2797, arts 3, 18, Schedule. Date in force: 30 December 2005: see SI 2005/2797, art 1(b); for savings and transitional provisions see art 2 thereof.

[Aberystwyth County Court

Birmingham County Court

Blackburn County Court

Bolton County Court

Bournemouth County Court

Bow County Court

Bradford County Court

Brentford County Court

Brighton County Court

Bristol County Court

Bromley County Court

Cambridge County Court

Canterbury County Court

Cardiff County Court

Carlisle County Court

Chelmsford County Court

Chester County Court

Coventry County Court

Croydon County Court

Derby County Court

Exeter County Court

Guildford County Court

Ipswich County Court

Kingston Upon Hull County Court

Lancaster County Court

Leeds County Court

Leicester County Court

Lincoln County Court

Liverpool County Court

Llangefni County Court

Luton County Court

Macclesfield County Court

Manchester County Court

Medway County Court

Middlesbrough County Court at Teesside Combined Court

Milton Keynes County Court

Newcastle upon Tyne County Court

Newport (Gwent) County Court

Northampton County Court

Norwich County Court

Nottingham County Court

Oxford County Court

Peterborough County Court

Plymouth County Court

Pontypridd County Court

Portsmouth County Court

Reading County Court

Rhyl County Court

Romford County Court

Sheffield County Court

Southampton County Court

Stockport County Court

Stoke On Trent County Court

Sunderland County Court

Swansea County Court

Swindon County Court

Taunton County Court

Teesside County Court

Telford County Court

Truro County Court

Warrington County Court

Watford County Court

Wolverhampton County Court

Worcester County Court

[Wrexham County Court]

York County Court]

Amendment

Inserted by SI 2005/2797, arts 3, 18, Schedule. Date in force: 30 December 2005: see SI 2005/2797, art 1(b); for savings and transitional provisions see art 2 thereof.
Entry "Wrexham County Court" inserted by SI 2007/1099, arts 3, 5. Date in force: 2 April 2007: see SI 2007/1099, art 1.

[SCHEDULE 4
INTERCOUNTRY ADOPTION CENTRES]

Amendment

Inserted by SI 2005/2797, arts 3, 18, Schedule.

[Article 2]

Amendment

Inserted by SI 2005/2797, arts 3, 18, Schedule.

[Birmingham County Court

Bournemouth County Court

Bristol County Court

Cardiff County Court

Chester County Court

Exeter County Court

Leeds County Court

Liverpool County Court

Manchester County Court

Newcastle upon Tyne County Court

Nottingham County Court

Portsmouth County Court]

[Wrexham County Court]

Amendment

Inserted by SI 2005/2797, arts 3, 18, Schedule.
Entry "Wrexham County Court" inserted by SI 2007/1099, arts 3, 6.

Appendix 3

THE PUBLIC LAW OUTLINE

GUIDE TO CASE MANAGEMENT IN PUBLIC LAW PROCEEDINGS

Foreword

April 2008

The Protocol for Judicial Case Management in Public Law Children Act Cases came into operation in November 2003, distilling good practice and focusing on a new approach to case management. While the Protocol has become well-established as the framework for case management and has encouraged parties and the courts to tackle the causes of delay in resolving cases for children, both the Thematic Review published by the Judicial Review Team (JRT) in December 2005 and the Government Child Care Proceedings Review of May 2006 identified areas where it has not achieved its objective and in which practice needs improvement.

Analysis of the causes of delay has revealed a number of exacerbating features. For example, many cases have proved unwieldy through having been brought to court before local authority pre-proceedings work is complete. In others, lack of robust judicial case management has led to widespread failure to identify early, and concentrate upon resolving, the determinative issues in the case. It is also clear that children can suffer because parents and families are insufficiently engaged in the process both pre-proceedings and during the progress of the case. Acting on those findings, the JRT, in consultation with their colleagues and the other key agencies in the Family Justice System have formulated the streamlined and simplified case management procedures which are set out in the Public Law Outline (PLO), and supported by a detailed Practice Direction.

At the same time, the Department for Children, Schools and Families and Welsh Assembly Government have revised their statutory guidance for local authorities (The Children Act 1989 Guidance and Regulations) in liaison with the JRT so as to ensure that the PLO and the Guidance complement each other and the best use is made of resources. In all cases where it is safe and practicable to do so, courts will expect local authorities to have completed procedures and involved families in accordance with the pre-proceedings stage of the PLO.

The PLO has been tested in various centres across England and Wales, and the family magistrates and judiciary trying care cases have been trained to identify and remain focussed on the key issues in the case with the aim of making the best decisions within the timetable for the child.

I have been much encouraged throughout the process, in particular at the seminars and other training events organised or overseen by the trainers of the Judicial Studies Board, to see the enthusiasm with which judges and magistrates have applied themselves to mastering the details of the PLO, accepting the need for careful and decisive case management within its structure, identifying the essential issues, setting the timetable for their disposal, and eliminating unnecessary evidence or hearings in respect of non-determinative matters.

Particular thanks are due to those who have drafted the provisions of the PLO and its supporting documentation and to those who have devised and delivered the necessary training. Please may I urge all of you to put it into practice with your customary dedication.

Sir Mark Potter

President of the Family Division

April 2008

Appendix 3   *The Public Law Outline*

The Public Law Outline
The Practice Direction below is made by the President of the Family Division under the powers delegated to him by the Lord Chief Justice under Schedule 2, Part 1, paragraph 2(2) of the Constitutional Reform Act 2005, and is approved by the Lord Chancellor.

Scope

1.1 This Practice Direction applies to care and supervision proceedings. In so far as practicable, it is to be applied to all other Public Law Proceedings.
1.2 This Practice Direction will come into effect on 1st April 2008. It does not apply to applications issued before 1st April 2008 but the court may direct in any individual case that the Case Management Tools and Case Management Documentation referred to in the Direction will apply either wholly or partly to those applications. This is subject to the overriding objective below and to the proviso that such a direction will neither cause further delay nor involve repetition of steps already taken or decisions already made in the case.
1.3 This Practice Direction is to be read with the Rules and is subject to them.
1.4 A Glossary of terms is at paragraph 25.

The overriding objective

2.1 This Practice Direction has the overriding objective of enabling the court to deal with cases justly, having regard to the welfare issues involved.

Dealing with a case justly includes, so far as is practicable—
(1)   ensuring that it is dealt with expeditiously and fairly;
(2)   dealing with the case in ways which are proportionate to the nature, importance and complexity of the issues;
(3)   ensuring that the parties are on an equal footing;
(4)   saving expense; and
(5)   allotting to it an appropriate share of the court's resources, while taking into account the need to allot resources to other cases.The Public Law Outline

Application by the court of the overriding objective

2.2 The court must seek to give effect to the overriding objective when it—
(1)   exercises the case management powers referred to in this Practice Direction; or
(2)   interprets any provision of this Practice Direction.

Duty of the parties

2.3 The parties are required to help the court further the overriding objective.

Court case management

THE MAIN PRINCIPLES

3.1 The main principles underlying court case management in Public Law Proceedings are—
(1)   judicial continuity: each case will be allocated to one or not more than two case management judges (in the case of magistrates' courts, case managers), who will be responsible for every case management stage in the proceedings through to the Final Hearing and, in relation to the High Court or county court, one of whom may be – and where possible should be – the judge who will conduct the Final Hearing;
(2)   main case management tools: each case will be managed by the court by using the appropriate main case management tools;

(3)   active case management: each case will be actively case managed by the court with a view at all times to furthering the overriding objective;

(4)   consistency: each case will, so far as compatible with the overriding objective, be managed in a consistent way and using the standardised steps provided for in this Direction.

THE MAIN CASE MANAGEMENT TOOLS

THE TIMETABLE FOR THE CHILD

3.2 The court will set an appropriate Timetable for the Child who is the subject of the proceedings.

3.3 The Timetable for the Child will be set by the court to take account of all significant steps in the child's life that are likely to take place during the proceedings. Those steps include not only legal steps but also social, care, health and education steps.

3.4 Examples of the dates the court will record and take into account when setting the Timetable for the Child are the dates of—

(1)   any formal review by the Local Authority of the case of a looked after child (within the meaning of section 22(1) of the 1989 Act);

(2)   the child taking up a place at a new school;

(3)   any review by the Local Authority of any statement of the child's special educational needs;

(4)   an assessment by a paediatrician or other specialist; The Public Law Outline

(5)   the outcome of any review of Local Authority plans for the child, for example, any plans for permanence through adoption, Special Guardianship or placement with parents or relatives;

(6)   a change or proposed change of the child's placement.

CASE MANAGEMENT DOCUMENTATION

3.5 The case management documents include the—

(1)   Application form;
(2)   Supplementary Form PLO1;
(3)   Schedule of Proposed Findings;
(4)   Allocation Record and the Timetable for the Child;
(5)   Case Analysis and Recommendations provided by Cafcass or Cafcass Cymru;
(6)   Local Authority Case Summary;
(7)   Other Parties' Case Summaries;
(8)   Draft Case Management Orders.

3.6 The court will encourage the use of those case management documents which are not prescribed by the Rules.

THE CASE MANAGEMENT RECORD

3.7 The court's filing system for the case will be known as the Case Management Record and will include the following main documents—

(1)   the Supplementary Form PLO1 which will be the index of documents on the Record;

(2)   in care and supervision proceedings, any Letter Before Proceedings and any related subsequent correspondence confirming the Local Authority's position to parents and others with parental responsibility for the child;

(3)   the Case Management Documentation;

(4)   Standard Directions on Issue and on First Appointment;

(5)   the Draft Case Management Orders approved by the court.

3.8 Parties or their legal representatives will be expected to retain their own record containing copies of the documents on the court's Case Management Record.

Appendix 3 *The Public Law Outline*

THE FIRST APPOINTMENT

3.9 The purpose of the First Appointment is to confirm allocation of the case and give initial case management directions.

THE DRAFT CASE MANAGEMENT ORDER

3.10 The draft form of a Case Management Order is a special form of order containing terms of general application to be used as appropriate for each case. The form of order is not only to be used for drawing up orders in the form prescribed by the Rules at the end of a hearing. The form is also to be used as a case management checklist. The form contains standard provisions designed to help parties, their legal representatives and the court – The Public Law Outline
(1)   identify the relevant issues and the procedural directions which may be required;
(2)   monitor changes to the relevant issues and compliance with the court's directions;
(3)   focus on what the proceedings are intended to achieve.

ADVOCATES DISCUSSION/MEETING

3.11 The court will consider directing advocates to have discussions before the Case Management Conference and the Issues Resolution Hearing. Advocates may well find that the best way to have these discussions is to meet. Such discussion is intended to facilitate agreement and to narrow the issues for the court to consider. Advocates and litigants in person may take part in the Advocates' meeting or discussions.

THE CASE MANAGEMENT CONFERENCE

3.12 In each case there will be a Case Management Conference to enable the case management judge or case manager, with the co-operation of the parties, actively to manage the case and, at the earliest practicable opportunity to—
(1)   identify the relevant and key issues; and
(2)   give full case management directions including confirming the Timetable for the Child.

THE ISSUES RESOLUTION HEARING

3.13 In each case there will be an Issues Resolution Hearing before the Final Hearing to—
(1)   identify any remaining key issues; and
(2)   as far as possible, resolve or narrow those issues.

ACTIVE CASE MANAGEMENT

3.14 The court must further the overriding objective by actively managing cases.
3.15 Active case management includes—
(1)   identifying the Timetable for the Child;
(2)   identifying the appropriate court to conduct the proceedings and transferring the proceedings as early as possible to that court;
(3)   encouraging the parties to co-operate with each other in the conduct of the proceedings;
(4)   retaining the Case Management Record;
(5)   identifying all facts and matters that are in issue at the earliest stage in the proceedings and at each hearing;
(6)   deciding promptly which issues need full investigation and hearing and which do not;
(7)   deciding the order in which issues are to be resolved;
(8)   identifying at an early stage who should be a party to the proceedings;
(9)   considering whether the likely benefits of taking a particular step justify any delay which will result and the cost of taking it;
(10)   directing discussion between advocates and litigants in person before the Case Management Conference and Issues Resolution Hearing;The Public Law Outline

(11)   requiring the use of the Draft Case Management Order and directing advocates and litigants in person to prepare or adjust the draft order where appropriate;

(12)   standardising, simplifying and regulating—
   (a)   the use of Case Management Documentation and forms;
   (b)   the court's orders and directions;

(13)   controlling—
   (a)   the use and cost of experts;
   (b)   the nature and extent of the documents which are to be disclosed to the parties and presented to the court;
   (c)   whether and, if so, in what manner the documents disclosed are to be presented to the court;
   (d)   the progress of the case;

(14)   where it is demonstrated to be in the interests of the child, encouraging the parties to use an alternative dispute resolution procedure if the court considers such a procedure to be appropriate and facilitating the use of such procedure;

(15)   helping the parties to reach agreement in relation to the whole or part of the case;

(16)   fixing the dates for all appointments and hearings;

(17)   dealing with as many aspects of the case as it can on the same occasion;

(18)   where possible dealing with additional issues which may arise from time to time in the case without requiring the parties to attend at court;

(19)   making use of technology; and

(20)   giving directions to ensure that the case proceeds quickly and efficiently.

The Expectations

4.1 The expectations are that proceedings should be—

(1)   conducted using the Case Management Tools and Case Management Documentation referred to in this Practice Direction in accordance with the Table contained in paragraph 9 below and known as the Public Law Outline;

(2)   finally determined within the timetable fixed by the court in accordance with the Timetable for the Child – the target times in the Public Law Outline being adhered to and being taken as the maximum permissible time for the taking of the step referred to in the Outline.

4.2 However, there may be cases where the court considers that the child's welfare requires a different approach from the one contained in the Public Law Outline. In those cases, the court will—

(1)   determine the appropriate case management directions and timetable; and

(2)   record on the face of the order the reasons for departing from the approach in the Public Law Outline. The Public Law Outline

How the parties should help court case management

MAIN METHODS OF HELPING

GOOD CASE PREPARATION

5.1 The applicant should prepare the case before proceedings are issued. In care and supervision proceedings the Local Authority should use the Pre-proceedings Checklist.

THE ALLOCATION RECORD AND THE TIMETABLE FOR THE CHILD

5.2 The applicant must prepare and file the Allocation Record and the Timetable for the Child. The Allocation Record must contain the applicant's allocation proposal and a record of the court's allocation decision and reasons. The Timetable for the Child will be part of the Allocation Record. The applicant should provide information to update the Timetable regularly. The applicant is to be responsible for updating the Allocation Record including the Timetable after each hearing.

Appendix 3 *The Public Law Outline*

CASE MANAGEMENT DOCUMENTATION

5.3 The parties must use the Case Management Documentation.

CO-OPERATION

5.4 The parties and their representatives should co-operate with the court in case management, including the fixing of timetables to avoid unacceptable delay, and in the crystallisation and resolution of the issues on which the case turns.

DIRECTIONS

5.5 The parties or their legal representatives will—
(1)   monitor compliance with the court's directions; and
(2)   tell the court or court officer about any failure to comply with a direction of the court or any other delay in the proceedings.

THE CASE MANAGEMENT RECORD

5.6 The parties or their legal representatives are expected to retain a record containing copies of the documents on the court's Case Management Record.

THE DRAFT CASE MANAGEMENT ORDER

5.7 Parties should start to consider the content of the Draft Case Management Order at the earliest opportunity either before or in the course of completing applications to the court or the response to the application. They should in any event consider the Draft Case Management Order after the First Appointment.
5.8 There should be ongoing consideration of the Draft Case Management Orders throughout the proceedings. The Draft Case Management Orders should serve as an aide memoire to everyone involved in the proceedings of—
(1)   the Timetable for the Child;
(2)   the case management decisions;
(3)   the identified issues. The Public Law Outline

5.9 Only one Draft Case Management Order should be filed with the court for each of the Case Management Conference and the Issues Resolution Hearing. It is the responsibility of the advocate for the applicant, which in care and supervision proceedings will ordinarily be the Local Authority, to prepare those drafts and be responsible for obtaining comments from the advocates and the parties.
5.10 In paragraphs 5.3, 5.7 and 5.9 "parties" includes parties' legal representatives.

Ethnicity, Language, Religion and Culture

6 At each case management stage of the proceedings, particularly at the First Appointment and Case Management Conference, the court will consider giving directions regarding the obtaining of evidence about the ethnicity, language, religion and culture of the child and other significant persons involved in the proceedings. The court will subsequently consider the implications of this evidence for the child in the context of the issues in the case.

Adults who may be protected parties

7.1 The court will investigate as soon as possible any issue as to whether an adult party or intended party to the proceedings lacks capacity (within the meaning of the Mental Capacity Act 2005) to conduct the proceedings. An adult who lacks capacity to conduct the proceedings is a protected party and must have a representative (a litigation friend, next friend or guardian ad litem) to conduct the proceedings on his or her behalf.

7.2 Any issue as to the capacity of an adult to conduct the proceedings must be determined before the court gives any directions relevant to that adult's role within the proceedings.

7.3 Where the adult is a protected party, his or her representative should be involved in any instruction of an expert, including the instruction of an expert to assess whether the adult, although a protected party, is competent to give evidence. The instruction of an expert is a significant step in the proceedings. The representative will wish to consider (and ask the expert to consider), if the protected party is competent to give evidence, their best interests in this regard. The representative may wish to seek advice about 'special measures'. The representative may put forward an argument on behalf of the protected party that the protected party should not give evidence.

7.4 If at any time during the proceedings, there is reason to believe that a party may lack capacity to conduct the proceedings, then the court must be notified and directions sought to ensure that this issue is investigated without delay.

Child likely to lack capacity to conduct the proceedings when he reaches 18

8 Where it appears that a child is—
(1)   a party to the proceedings and not the subject of them;
(2)   nearing his or her 18th birthday; and
(3)   considered likely to lack capacity to conduct the proceedings when he reaches 18,

the court will consider giving directions relating to the investigation of a child's capacity in this respect. The Public Law Outline

Outline of the process and how to use the main Case Management Tools

9.1 The Public Law Outline set out in the Table below contains an outline of—
(1)   the order of the different stages of the process;
(2)   the purposes of the main case management hearings and matters to be considered at them;
(3)   the latest timescales within which the main stages of the process should take place.

9.2 In the Public Law Outline—
(1)   "CMC" means the Case Management Conference;
(2)   "FA" means the First Appointment;
(3)   "IRH" means the Issues Resolution Hearing;
(4)   "OS" means the Official Solicitor.

Public Law Outline

PRE-PROCEEDINGS
PRE-PROCEEDINGS CHECKLIST
The Checklist Documents:

Documents to be disclosed from the LA's files:	• Pre-existing care plans (e.g. child in need plan, looked after child plan & child protection plan)
• Previous court orders & judgments/reasons • Any relevant Assessment Materials – Initial and core assessments – Section 7 & 37 reports – Relatives & friends materials (e.g. a genogram) • Other relevant Reports & Records – Single, joint or inter-agency materials (e.g. health & education/Home Office & Immigration documents) – records of discussions with the family – Key LA minutes & records for the child (including Strategy Discussion Record)	• Social Work Chronology • Letters Before Proceedings **Documents to be prepared for the proceedings:** • Schedule of Proposed Findings • Initial Social Work Statement • Care Plan • Allocation Record & Timetable for the Child

STAGE 1 – ISSUE AND THE FIRST APPOINTMENT	
ISSUE	FIRST APPOINTMENT
On DAY 1 and by DAY 3	**By DAY 6**
Objectives: To ensure compliance with pre-proceedings checklist; to allocate proceedings; to obtain the information necessary for initial case management at the FA	**Objectives:** To confirm allocation; to give initial case management directions
On Day 1:	• Parties notify LA & court of need for a contested hearing
• The LA files: – Application Form — Supplementary Form PLO1 – Checklist documents • Court officer issues application • Court nominates case manager(s) • Court gives standard directions on issue including: – Pre-proceedings checklist compliance – Allocate and/or transfer – Appoint children's guardian – Appoint solicitor for the child – Case Analysis for FA – Invite OS to act for protected persons (non subject children & incapacitated adults) – List FA by Day 6 – Make arrangements for contested hearing (if necessary) **By Day 3** • Allocation of a children's guardian expected • LA serves the Application Form, Supplementary Form PLO1 and the Checklist Documents on parties	• Court makes arrangements for a contested hearing • Initial case management by Court including: – Confirm Timetable for the Child – Confirm allocation or transfer – Identify additional parties & representation (including allocation of children's guardian) – Identify "Early Final Hearing" cases – Scrutinise Care Plan • Court gives standard directions on FA including: – Case Analysis and Recommendations for Stages 2 & 3 – LA Case Summary – Other Parties' Case Summaries – Parties' initial witness statements – For the Advocates' Meeting – List CMC or (if appropriate) an Early Final Hearing – Upon transfer

STAGE 2 – CASE MANAGEMENT CONFERENCE	
ADVOCATES' MEETING	CMC
No later than 2 days before CMC	No later than day 45
Objectives: To prepare the Draft Case Management Order; to identify experts and draft questions for them	**Objectives:** To identify issue(s); to give full case management directions
<ul><li>Consider all other parties' Case Summaries and Case Analysis and Recommendations</li><li>Identify proposed experts and draft questions in accordance with Experts Practice Direction</li><li>Draft Case Management Order</li><li>Notify court of need for a contested hearing</li><li>File Draft Case Management Order with the case manager/case management judge by 11am one working day before the CMC</li></ul>	<ul><li>Detailed case management by the court</li></ul> – Scrutinise compliance with directions – Confirm Timetable for the Child – Identify key issue(s) – Confirm allocation or transfer – Consider case management directions in the Draft Case Management Order – Scrutinise Care Plan – Check compliance with Experts Practice Direction <ul><li>Court issues Case Management Order</li><li>Court lists IRH and, where necessary, a warned period for Final Hearing</li></ul>

STAGE 3 – ISSUES RESOLUTION HEARING	
ADVOCATES' MEETING	IRH
Between 2 and 7 days before the IRH	**Between 16 & 25 weeks**
Objective: To prepare or update the Draft Case Management Order	**Objectives:** To resolve and narrow issue(s); to identify any remaining key issues

• Consider all other parties' Case Summaries and Case Analysis and Recommendations
• Draft Case Management Order
• Notify court of need for a contested hearing/time for oral evidence to be given
• File Draft Case Management Order with the case manager/case management judge by 11am one working day before the IRH
	• Identification by the court of the key issue(s) (if any) to be determined
	
	• Final case management by the court:
	  – Scrutinise compliance with directions
	
	  – Consider case management directions in the Draft Case Management Order
	
	  – Scrutinise Care Plan
	  – Give directions for Hearing documents:
	    – Threshold agreement or facts/issues remaining to be determined
	    – Final Evidence & Care Plan
	    – Case Analysis and Recommendations
	    – Witness templates
	    – Skeleton arguments
	    – Judicial reading list/reading time/judgment writing time
	    – Time estimate
	    – Bundles Practice Direction compliance
	    – List or confirm Hearing
	• Court issues Case Management Order

STAGE 4
HEARING

In accordance with the Timetable for the Child

Objective: To determine remaining issues

• All file & serve updated case management documents & bundle	• Judgment/Reasons
• Draft final order(s) in approved form	• Disclose documents as required after hearing

Starting the Proceedings

10.1 The applicant, which in care and supervision proceedings will ordinarily be the Local Authority, must file the Supplementary Form PLO1 with the application form. The applicant must also file an Allocation Record and Timetable for the Child which includes the applicant's allocation proposal.

Pre-proceedings Checklist

10.2 The documents which the court will expect to see attached to the application form for a care or supervision order are set out in the Pre-proceedings Checklist in the Public Law Outline. The Pre-proceedings Checklist should be used at the earliest opportunity as a guide to what documents the court will expect to see at the start of the proceedings and should be filed with the application form. The Pre-proceedings Checklist will promote good case preparation.

Compliance with Pre-proceedings Checklist

10.3 It is recognised that in some cases the circumstances are such that the safety and welfare of the child may be jeopardised if the start of proceedings is delayed until all of the documents appropriate to the case and referred to in the Pre-proceedings Checklist are available. The court recognises that the preparation may need to be varied to suit the circumstances of the case. The court is likely to make directions relating to the preparation of any missing documentation at the start of the proceedings and at the First Appointment. The court also recognises that some documents on the Pre-proceedings Checklist may not exist and may never exist, for example, the Section 37 report, and that in urgent proceedings no Letter Before Proceedings may have been sent.

What the Court will do at the Issue of Proceedings

Objectives

11.1 The objectives at this stage are for the court—
(1)   in care and supervision proceedings, to ensure compliance with the Pre-proceedings Checklist;
(2)   to allocate proceedings;
(3)   to obtain the information necessary to enable initial case management at the First Appointment.

11.2 The steps which the court will take once proceedings have been issued include those set out in paragraphs 11.3 to 11.5 below.

Allocation

11.3 The court will consider allocation of the case and transfer those cases to the county court which are obviously suitable for immediate transfer. An example of a case of this kind is where there is evidence that a parent may be a protected party and require representation which currently cannot be obtained in the magistrates' court.The Public Law Outline 13

Other Steps to be taken by the Court

Directions

11.4 The court will—
(1)   consider giving directions—
    (a)   appropriate to the case including Standard Directions On Issue;
    (b)   in care and supervision proceedings, relating to the preparation and filing of documents on the Pre-proceedings Checklist which are not yet available;
    (c)   relating to representation of any protected party and where appropriate invite the Official Solicitor to act for a protected party or any child who is a party to, but is not the subject of, the proceedings and where appropriate invite the Official Solicitor to act as his or her guardian ad litem;
(2)   appoint a children's guardian in specified proceedings (in relation to care and supervision proceedings the court will expect that Cafcass or Cafcass Cymru will have received notice from the Local Authority that proceedings were going to be started);
(3)   appoint a solicitor for the child under section 41(3) of the 1989 Act where appropriate;
(4)   request the children's guardian or if appropriate another officer of the service or Welsh family proceedings officer to prepare a Case Analysis and Recommendations for the First Appointment;
(5)   make arrangements for a contested hearing, if necessary.

Setting a date for the First Appointment

11.5 The court will set a date for the First Appointment normally no later than 6 days from the date of issue of the proceedings and in any event in line with the draft Timetable for the Child.

Case Managers in the Magistrates' Courts

11.6 In the magistrates' courts, the justices' clerk may nominate one but not more than two case managers.

The First Appointment

Objectives

12.1 The First Appointment is the first hearing in the proceedings. The main objectives of the First Appointment are to—
(1)   confirm allocation; and
(2)   give initial case management directions having regard to the Public Law Outline.

12.2 The steps which the court will take at the First Appointment include those set out in paragraphs 12.3 to 12.6 below.The Public Law Outline 14

Steps to be taken by the Court

12.3 The court will—
(1)   confirm the Timetable for the Child;

(2)   make arrangements for any contested interim hearing such as an application for an interim care order;

(3)   confirm the allocation of the case or, if appropriate, transfer the case;

(4)   request the children's guardian or if appropriate another officer of the service or Welsh family proceedings officer to prepare a Case Analysis and Recommendations for the Case Management Conference or Issues Resolution Hearing;

(5)   scrutinise the Care Plan;

(6)   consider giving directions relating to –

    (a)   those matters in the Public Law Outline which remain to be considered;

    (b)   the joining of a person who would not otherwise be a respondent under the Rules as a party to the proceedings;

    (c)   where any person to be joined as a party may be a protected party, an investigation of that person's capacity to conduct the proceedings and the representation of that person and if appropriate invite the Official Solicitor to act for that person;

    (d)   the identification of family and friends as proposed carers and any overseas, immigration, jurisdiction and paternity issues;

    (e)   in Public Law Proceedings other than care and supervision proceedings, the documents to be filed with the court;

    (f)   evidence to be obtained as to whether a parent who is a protected party is competent to make his or her own statement.

Early Final Hearing Cases

12.4 Cases which are suitable for an Early Final Hearing are likely to be those cases where the child has no parents, guardians, relatives who want to care for the child, or other carers. Examples are those cases where the child is an abandoned baby or where a child has been brought into this country and abandoned. The court will—

(1)   identify at the First Appointment whether the case is one which is suitable for an Early Final Hearing; and

(2)   set a date for that Final Hearing.

Setting a date for the Case Management Conference

12.5 The court will set a date for the Case Management Conference normally no later than 45 days from the date of issue of the proceedings and in any event in line with the Timetable for the Child.

Advocates' Meeting/discussion and the Draft Case Management Order

12.6 The court will consider directing a discussion between the parties' advocates and any litigant in person and the preparation of a Draft Case Management Order as outlined below.The Public Law Outline 15

Experts

12.7 A party who wishes to instruct an expert should comply with the Experts Practice Direction. Where the parties are agreed on any matter relating to experts or expert evidence, the draft agreement must be submitted for the court's approval as early as possible in the proceedings.

Advocates' Meeting/discussion and the Draft Case Management Order

13.1 The main objective of the Advocates' Meeting or discussion is to prepare the Draft Case Management Order.

13.2 Where there is a litigant in person the court will consider the most effective way in which that person can be involved in the advocates' discussions and give directions as appropriate including directions relating to the part to be played by any McKenzie Friend.

13.3 Timing of the discussions is of the utmost importance. The need for discussions outside the "court room door" of matters, which could have been discussed at an earlier time, is to be avoided. Discussions are to take place no later than 2 days before the Case Management Conference or the Issues Resolution Hearing whichever is appropriate. The discussions may take place earlier than 2 days before those hearings, for example, up to 7 days before them.

13.4 Following discussion the advocates should prepare or adjust the Draft Case Management Order. In practice the intention is that the advocate for the applicant, which in care and supervision proceedings will ordinarily be the Local Authority, should take the lead in preparing and adjusting the Draft Case Management Order following discussion with the other advocates.

13.5 Where it is not possible for the advocates to agree the terms of the Draft Case Management Order, the advocates should specify on the Draft Case Management Order, or on a separate document if more practicable—

(1)   those provisions on which they agree; and

(2)   those provisions on which they disagree.

13.6 Unless the court directs otherwise, the Draft Case Management Order must be filed with the court no later than 11am on the day before the Case Management Conference or the Issues Resolution Hearing whichever may be appropriate.

13.7 At the Advocates' Meeting or discussion before the Case Management Conference, the advocates should also try to agree the questions to be put to any proposed expert (whether jointly instructed or not) if not previously agreed. Under the Experts Practice Direction the questions on which the proposed expert is to give an opinion are a crucial component of the expert directions which the court is required to consider at the Case Management Conference.

Case Management Conference

Objectives

14.1 The Case Management Conference is the main hearing at which the court manages the case. The main objectives of the Conference are to—

(1)   identify key issues; and

(2)   give full case management directions.The Public Law Outline 16

14.2 The steps which the court will take at the Case Management Conference include those steps set out in paragraphs 14.3 to 14.5 below.

Steps to be taken by the Court

14.3 The court will—

(1)   review and confirm the Timetable for the Child;

(2)   confirm the allocation or the transfer of the case;

(3)   scrutinise the Care Plan;

(4)   identify the key issues;

(5)   identify the remaining case management issues;

(6)   resolve remaining case management issues by reference to the Draft Case Management Order;

(7)   identify any special measures such as the need for access for the disabled or provision for vulnerable witnesses;

(8)   scrutinise the Case Management Record to check whether directions have been complied with and if not, consider making further directions as appropriate;

(9)   where expert evidence is required, check whether the parties have complied with the Experts Practice Direction, in particular section 4 (Preparation for the relevant hearing) and consider giving directions as appropriate.

Appendix 3   *The Public Law Outline*

Case Management Order

14.4 The court will issue the approved Case Management Order. Parties or their legal representatives will be expected to submit in electronic form the final approved Draft Case Management Order on the conclusion of, and the same day as, the Case Management Conference.

Setting a date for the Issues Resolution Hearing/Final Hearing

14.5 The court will set—
(1)   a date for the Issues Resolution Hearing normally at any time between 16 and 25 weeks from the date of issue of the proceedings and in any event in line with the Timetable for the Child; and
(2)   if necessary, specify a period within which the Final Hearing of the application is to take place unless a date has already been set.

The Issues Resolution Hearing

Objectives

15.1 The objectives of this hearing are to—
(1)   resolve and narrow issues; and
(2)   identify key remaining issues requiring resolution.

15.2 The Issues Resolution Hearing is likely to be the hearing before the Final Hearing. Final case management directions and other preparations for the Final Hearing will be made at this hearing.The Public Law Outline 17

Steps to be taken by the Court

15.3 The court will—
(1)   identify the key issues (if any) to be determined;
(2)   review and confirm the Timetable for the Child;
(3)   consider giving case management directions relating to—
        (a)   any outstanding matter contained in the Draft Case Management Order;
        (b)   the preparation and filing of final evidence including the filing of witness templates;
        (c)   skeleton arguments;
        (d)   preparation and filing of bundles in accordance with the Bundles Practice Direction;
        (e)   any agreement relating to the satisfaction of the threshold criteria under section 31 of the 1989 Act or facts and issues remaining to be determined in relation to it or to any welfare question which arises;
        (f)   time estimates;
        (g)   the judicial reading list and likely reading time and judgment writing time;
(4)   issue the Case Management Order.

15.4 For the avoidance of doubt the purpose of an Issues Resolution Hearing is to—
(1)   identify key issues which are not agreed;
(2)   examine if those key issues can be agreed; and
(3)   where those issues cannot be agreed, examine the most proportionate method of resolving those issues.

15.5 The expectation is that the method of resolving the key issues which cannot be agreed will be at a hearing (ordinarily the Final Hearing) where there is an opportunity for the relevant oral evidence to be heard and challenged.

Attendance at the Case Management Conference and the Issues Resolution Hearing

16 An advocate who has conduct of the Final Hearing should ordinarily attend the Case Management Conference and the Issues Resolution Hearing. Where the attendance of this advocate is not possible, then an advocate who is familiar with the issues in the proceedings should attend.

Flexible Powers of the Court

17.1 Attention is drawn to the flexible powers of the court either following the issue of the application in that court, the transfer of the case to that court or at any other stage in the proceedings.The Public Law Outline 18

17.2 The court may give directions without a hearing including setting a date for the Final Hearing or a period within which the Final Hearing will take place. The steps, which the court will ordinarily take at the various stages of the proceedings provided for in the Public Law Outline, may be taken by the court at another stage in the proceedings if the circumstances of the case merit this approach.

17.3 The flexible powers of the court include the ability for the court to cancel or repeat a particular hearing. For example, if the issue on which the case turns can with reasonable practicability be crystallised and resolved by having an Early Final Hearing, then in the fulfilment of the overriding objective, such a flexible approach must be taken to secure compliance with section 1(2) of the 1989 Act.

Alternative Dispute Resolution

18.1 The court will encourage the parties to use an alternative dispute resolution procedure and facilitate the use of such a procedure where it is—
(1)   readily available;
(2)   demonstrated to be in the interests of the child; and
(3)   reasonably practicable and safe.

18.2 At any stage in the proceedings, the parties can ask the court for advice about alternative dispute resolution.

18.3 At any stage in the proceedings the court itself will consider whether alternative dispute resolution is appropriate. If so, the court may direct that a hearing or proceedings be adjourned for such specified period as it considers appropriate—
(1)   to enable the parties to obtain information and advice about alternative dispute resolution; and
(2)   where the parties agree, to enable alternative dispute resolution to take place.

18.4 It is expressly recognised that no party can or should be obliged to enter into any form of alternative dispute resolution if they are unwilling to do so.

Co-operation

19.1 Throughout the proceedings the parties and their representatives should co-operate wherever reasonably practicable to help towards securing the welfare of the child as the paramount consideration.

19.2 At each court appearance the court will ask the parties and their legal representatives—
(1)   what steps they have taken to achieve co-operation and the extent to which they have been successful;
(2)   if appropriate the reason why co-operation could not be achieved; and
(3)   the steps needed to resolve any issues necessary to achieve co-operation.The Public Law Outline 19

Appendix 3 *The Public Law Outline*

Agreed Directions

20.1 The parties, their advisers and the children's guardian, are encouraged to try to agree directions for the management of the proceedings.

20.2 To obtain the court's approval the agreed directions must—

(1)   set out a Timetable for the Child by reference to calendar dates for the taking of steps for the preparation of the case;

(2)   include a date when it is proposed that the next hearing will take place.

Variation of case management timetable

21 It is emphasised that a party or the children's guardian must apply to the court at the earliest opportunity if they wish to vary by extending the dates set by the court for—

(1)   a directions appointment;

(2)   a First Appointment;

(3)   a Case Management Conference;

(4)   an Issues Resolution Hearing;

(5)   the Final Hearing;

(6)   the period within which the Final Hearing of the application is to take place; or

(7)   any discussion between advocates or for the filing of the Draft Case Management Orders.

Who performs the functions of the Court

22.1 Where this Practice Direction provides for the Court to perform case management functions, then except where any Rule, Practice Direction, any other enactment or the Family Proceedings (Allocation to Judiciary) Directions ((1999) 2 FLR 799) provides otherwise, the functions may be performed—

(1)   in relation to proceedings in the High Court or in a district registry, by any judge or district judge of that Court including a district judge of the principal registry;

(2)   in relation to proceedings in the county court, by any judge or district judge including a district judge of the principal registry when the principal registry is treated as if it were a county court; and

(3)   in relation to proceedings in a magistrates' court by—

    (a)   any family proceedings court constituted in accordance with sections 66 and 67 of the 1980 Act;

    (b)   a single justice; or

    (c)   a justices' clerk.

22.2 The case management functions to be exercised by a justices' clerk may be exercised by an assistant justices' clerk provided that person has been specifically authorised by a justices' clerk to exercise case management functions. Any reference in this Practice Direction to a justices' clerk is to be taken to include an assistant justices' clerk so authorised. The justices' clerk may in particular appoint one but not more than two assistant justices' clerks as case managers for each case.

22.3 In proceedings in a magistrates' court, where a party considers that there are likely to be issues arising at a hearing (including the First Appointment, Case Management Conference and Issues Resolution Hearing) which need to be decided by a family proceedings court, rather than a justices' clerk, then that party should give the court written notice of that need at least 2 days before the hearing.

22.4 Family proceedings courts may consider making arrangements to ensure a court constituted in accordance with s 66 of the 1980 Act is available at the same time as Issues Resolution Hearings are being heard by a justices' clerk. Any delay as a result of the justices' clerk considering for whatever reason that it is inappropriate for a justices' clerk to perform a case management function on a particular matter and the justices' clerk's referring of that matter to the court should then be minimal.

Technology

23 Where the facilities are available to the court and the parties, the court will consider making full use of technology including electronic information exchange and video or telephone conferencing.

Other Practice Directions

24.1 This Practice Direction must be read with the Bundles Practice Direction.

24.2 The Bundles Practice Direction is applied to Public Law Proceedings in the High Court and county court with the following adjustments—

(1)   add "except the First Appointment, Case Management Conference, and Issues Resolution Hearing referred to in the Practice Direction: Guide to Case Management in Public Law Proceedings where there are no contested applications being heard at those hearings" to paragraph 2.2 ;

(2)   the reference to—

    (a)   the "Protocol for Judicial Case Management in Public law Children Act Cases (2003) 2 FLR 719" in paragraph 6.1;

    (b)   the "Practice Direction: Care Cases: Judicial Continuity and Judicial Case Management" in paragraph 15; and

    (c)   "the Public Law Protocol" in paragraph 15

shall be read as if it were a reference to this Practice Direction.

24.3 This Practice Direction replaces Practice Direction: Care Cases: Judicial Continuity and Judicial Case Management appended to the Protocol for Judicial Case Management in Public Law Children Act Cases (2003) 2 FLR 719.

Glossary

25 In this Practice Direction—

(1)   "the 1989 Act" means the Children Act 1989;

(2)   "the 1980 Act" means the Magistrates' Courts Act 1980;

(3)   "advocate" means a person exercising a right of audience as a representative of, or on behalf of, a party;

(4)   "Allocation Record and the Timetable for the Child" means a document containing—

    (a)   the Local Authority's proposal for allocation;

    (b)   the Local Authority's proposed Timetable for the Child;

    (c)   the court's allocation decisions and reasons; and

    (d)   the court's approved Timetable for the Child;

(5)   "alternative dispute resolution" means the methods of resolving a dispute other than through the normal court process;

(6)   "assistant justices' clerk" has the meaning assigned to it by section 27(5) of the Courts Act 2003;

(7)   "the Bundles Practice Direction" means the Practice Direction Family Proceedings: Court Bundles (Universal Practice to be Applied in all Courts other than Family Proceedings Court) of 27 July 2006;

(8)   "Case Analysis and Recommendations" means a written or oral outline of the case from the child's perspective prepared by the children's guardian or other officer of the service or Welsh family proceedings officer at different stages of the proceedings requested by the court, to provide—

    (a)   an analysis of the issues that need to be resolved in the case including-

        (i)   any harm or risk of harm;

        (ii)   the child's own views;

        (iii)   the family context including advice relating to ethnicity, language, religion and culture of the child and other significant persons;

        (iv)   the Local Authority work and proposed care plan;

        (v)   advice about the court process including the Timetable for the Child; and

        (vi)   identification of work that remains to be done for the child in the short and longer term; and

(b)   recommendations for outcomes, in order to safeguard and promote the best interests of the child in the proceedings;

(9)   "Case Management Documentation" includes the documents referred to in paragraph 3.5;

(10)   "Case Management Record" means the court's filing system for the case which includes the documents referred to at paragraph 3.7;

(11)   "case manager" means the justices' clerk or assistant justices' clerk who manages the case in the magistrates' courts;

(12)   "Care Plan" means a "section 31A plan" referred to in section 31A of the 1989 Act;The Public Law Outline 22

(13)   "Core Assessment" means the assessment undertaken by the Local Authority in accordance with The Framework for the Assessment of Children in Need and their Families (Department of Health, 2000);

(14)   "court" means the High Court, county court or the magistrates' court;

(15)   "court officer" means—

(a)   in the High Court or a county court, a member of court staff; and

(b)   in a magistrates' court, the designated officer;

(16)   "Draft Case Management Order" means the draft case management document in the form of an order set out at Annex C to this Practice Direction;

(17)   "Experts Practice Direction" means the Practice Direction on Experts in Family Proceedings relating to Children which is to come into force on the same date as this Practice Direction;

(18)   "genogram" means a family tree, setting out in diagrammatic form the family's background;

(19)   "hearing" includes a directions appointment;

(20)   "Initial Assessment" means the assessment undertaken by the Local Authority in accordance with The Framework for the Assessment of Children in Need and their Families (Department of Health, 2000);

(21)   "Initial Social Work Statement" means a statement prepared by the Local Authority strictly limited to the following evidence—

(a)   the precipitating incident(s) and background circumstances relevant to the grounds and reasons for making the application including a brief description of any referral and assessment processes that have already occurred;

(b)   any facts and matters that are within the social worker's personal knowledge limited to the findings sought by the Local Authority;

(c)   any emergency steps and previous court orders that are relevant to the application;

(d)   any decisions made by the Local Authority that are relevant to the application;

(e)   information relevant to the ethnicity, language, religion, culture, gender and vulnerability of the child and other significant persons in the form of a 'family profile' together with a narrative description and details of the social care and other services that are relevant to the same;

(f)   where the Local Authority is applying for an interim order: the Local Authority's initial proposals for the child (which are also to be set out in the Care Plan) including placement, contact with parents and other significant persons and the social care services that are proposed;

(g)   the Local Authority's initial proposals for the further assessment of the parties during the proceedings including twin track /concurrent planning (where more than one permanence option for the child is being explored by the Local Authority);

(22)   "legal representative" means a barrister or solicitor, solicitor's employee or other authorised litigator (as defined in the Courts and Legal Services Act 1990) who has been instructed to act for a party in relation to the proceedings;

(23)   "Letter Before Proceedings" means any letter from the Local Authority containing written notification to the parents and others with parental responsibility for the child of the Local Authority's plan to apply to court for a care or supervision order;The Public Law Outline 23

(24)   "Local Authority Case Summary" means a summary for each case management hearing in the form set out at Annex B to this Practice Direction which must include the following information—

(a)   the applications which have been issued in the current proceedings;

(b)   any previous proceedings in relation to the child[ren] and any orders made in previous proceedings or in the current proceedings to which the child[ren] is/are subject;

(c)   the present living arrangements for the child[ren] and arrangements for contact between the child[ren] and parent(s) or other relevant adult or child;

(d)   a very brief summary of the incident(s) or circumstances giving rise to the application and of the background to the proceedings;

(e)   a summary of any concerns the Local Authority may have about the mental capacity of an adult to care for the child or the capacity of the adult to prepare for the proceedings;

(f)   the Key Issues in the case;

(g)   any agreements that there are as to the Key Issues or the findings of fact sought by the Local Authority;

(h)   whether an application for placement for adoption is among the range of options that will have to be considered;

(i)   any current or proposed proceedings (e.g. criminal proceedings, other family proceedings, disciplinary, immigration or mental capacity/health determinations) which are relevant to the determination of the application(s);

(j)   the issues and directions which the court will need to consider at the Case Management Conference/Issues Resolution Hearing, including any interim orders sought;

(k)   any steps which have not been taken or directions not complied with, an explanation of the reasons and the effect, if any, on the Timetable for the Child;

(l)   a recommended reading list and suggested reading time;

(m)   any additional information relevant to the Timetable for the Child or for the conduct of the hearing or the proceedings;

(n)   the contact details of all advocates, their solicitors (where appropriate) and other significant persons e.g. the Local Authority key worker or team manager and the children's guardian;

(25)   "justices' clerk" has the meaning assigned to it by section 27(1) of the Courts Act 2003;

(26)   "McKenzie Friend" means any person permitted by the court to sit beside an unrepresented litigant in court to assist the litigant by prompting, taking notes and giving advice to the litigant;

(27)   "Other Parties' Case Summaries" means summaries by parties other than the Local Authority containing—

(a)   the party's proposals for the long term future of the child (to include placement and contact);

(b)   the party's reply to the Local Authority's Schedule of Proposed Findings;

(c)   any proposal for assessment / expert evidence; and

(d)   the names, addresses and contact details of any family or friends who it is suggested be approached in relation to long term care/contact or respite;

(28)   "Pre-proceedings Checklist" means the checklist of documents set out in the Public Law Outline; The Public Law Outline 24

(29)   "Public Law Proceedings" means proceedings for—

(a)   a residence order under section 8 of the 1989 Act with respect to a child who is the subject of a care order;

(b)   a secure accommodation order under section 25 of the 1989 Act;

(c)   a care order under section 31(1)(a) of the 1989 Act or the discharge of such an order under section 39(1) of the 1989 Act;

(d)   an order giving permission to change a child's surname or remove a child from the United Kingdom under section 33(7) of the 1989 Act;

(e)   a supervision order under section 31(1)(b) of the 1989 Act, the discharge or variation of such an order under section 39(2) of that Act, or the extension or further extension of such an order under paragraph 6(3) of Schedule 3 to that Act;

(f)   an order making provision for contact under section 34(2) to (4) of the 1989 Act or an order varying or discharging such an order under section 34(9) of that Act;

(g)   an education supervision order, the extension of an education supervision order under paragraph 15(2) of Schedule 3 to the 1989 Act, or the discharge of such an order under paragraph 17(1) of Schedule 3 to that Act;

(h)   an order varying directions made with an interim care order or interim supervision order under section 38(8)(b) of the 1989 Act;

(i) an order under section 39(3) of the 1989 Act varying a supervision order in so far as it affects a person with whom the child is living but who is not entitled to apply for the order to be discharged;

(j) an order under section 39(3A) of the 1989 Act varying or discharging an interim care order in so far as it imposes an exclusion requirement on a person who is not entitled to apply for the order to be discharged;

(k) an order under section 39(3B) of the 1989 Act varying or discharging an interim care order in so far as it confers a power of arrest attached to an exclusion requirement;

(l) the substitution of a supervision order for a care order under section 39(4) of the 1989 Act;

(m) a child assessment order or the variation or discharge of such an order under section 43(12) of the 1989 Act;

(n) an order permitting the Local Authority to arrange for any child in its care to live outside England and Wales under paragraph 19(1) of Schedule 2 to the 1989 Act;

(o) a contribution order, or the variation or revocation of such an order under paragraph 23(8), of Schedule 2 to the 1989 Act;

(30) "Rules" means rules of court governing the practice and procedure to be followed in Public Law Proceedings;

(31) "Schedule of Proposed Findings" means the schedule of findings of fact prepared by the Local Authority sufficient to satisfy the threshold criteria under section 31(2) of the 1989 Act and to inform the Care Plan;

(32) "Section 7 report" means any report under section 7 of the 1989 Act;

(33) "Section 37 report" means any report by the Local Authority to the court as a result of a direction under section 37 of the 1989 Act;The Public Law Outline 25

(34) "Social Work Chronology" means a schedule containing—

 (a) a succinct summary of the significant dates and events in the child's life in chronological order – a running record to be updated during the proceedings;

 (b) information under the following headings—

  (i) serial number;

  (ii) date;

  (iii) event-detail;

  (iv) witness or document reference (where applicable);

(35) "specified proceedings" has the meaning assigned to it by section 41(6) of the 1989 Act;

(36) "Standard Directions on Issue and on First Appointment" includes the directions set out in the Public Law Outline, Stage 1;

(37) "Strategy Discussion Record" means a note of the strategy discussion within the meaning of "Working Together to Safeguard Children" (2006);

(38) "Supplementary Form PLO1" means the form set out at Annex A to this Practice Direction which is to be filed with the application form and then used as the Index to the Court's Case Management Record;

(39) "Timetable for the Child " means the timetable set by the court which is appropriate for the child who is the subject of the proceedings and forms part of the Allocation Record.

ANNEX A

SUPPLEMENTARY FORM PLO 1

Application for a care order or supervision order: Supplementary Form

PART 1 - Pre-proceedings checklist

This checklist must be completed and filed by the local authority with any application for a care order or supervision order to specify the pre-proceedings documents filed with the application [Column (a)] and to identify those which are not applicable [N/A]. If any relevant document is not filed with the application, the reason and any expected date of filing must be stated [Column (d)]. Columns (b) and (c) are for use by the court to record any pre-proceedings documents filed subsequently.

All documents filed with the application must be clearly marked with their description and numbered consecutively in the following sequence

	Category	Document	N/A	(a) Filed on issue	(b) Filed by FA	(c) Filed by CMC	(d) Reason not filed/ expected date of filing
	Documents prepared for the proceedings						
1	Schedule of Proposed Findings						
2	Initial Social Work Statement						
3	Care Plan						
4	Allocation Record and Timetable for the Child						
	Documents held by the local authority						
5	Previous proceedings	Orders					
		Judgment/reasons						
6	Any relevant assessment materials	Initial/core assessment					
		Section 7 & 37 reports						
		Relatives and friends materials (e.g. a genogram)						
7	Other relevant reports and records	Single, joint or inter-agency materials					
		Records of discussions with the family						
		Key LA minutes and records for the child, (inc. Strategy Discussion Record)						
8	Pre-existing care plans (e.g. child in need plan, looked after child plan & child protection plan)						
9	Social Work Chronology						
10	Letters Before Proceedings						
11	Other relevant pre-proceedings documents (specify)						

PART 2 - Record of case management documents filed

This Part is for use by the court to record case management documents filed with the court for Stages 1, 2 and 3

		Filed for FA	Filed for CMC	Filed for IRH	Notes
1	Local Authority Case Summary				
2	Other Parties' Case Summaries				M
					F
					Other
3	Parties' initial witness statements				M
					F
					Other
4	CAFCASS/ CAFCASS CYMRU Case Analysis and Recommendations				
5	Draft Case Management order for CMC/IRH				
6	Other case management documents (specify)				

ANNEX B

The Local Authority's Case Summary

Applications and previous proceedings

1. The applications that have been issued in these proceedings are:

Applicant	Order Sought	Date	Bundle ref.

2. The child[ren] is/are subject to the following orders previously made in these/other proceedings:

Order	in favour of	Court	Date of order	Case no.	Bundle ref.

Arrangements for the child[ren]

3. The present arrangements for the child[ren] is/are

   (a) Living arrangements:

Child	Living with:

   (b) contact arrangements:

Child	Having contact with:	Frequency

Appendix 3 *The Public Law Outline*

Summary of precipitating events and background

4. The following is a brief summary of the incident(s) or circumstances giving rise to the application and of the background to the proceedings:

Mental Capacity

5. The local authority has no/ the following concerns about the mental capacity of the mother/ father/ *[other adult]* to care for the child or to prepare for the proceedings:

Key issues and findings

1. The Key Issues in the case are:

a)	
b)	
c)	
d)	

2. With reference to the above Key Issues the following are agreed:

a)	
b)	
c)	
d)	

3. In addition, the following findings of fact sought by the local authority are agreed on the following basis:

Finding sought	Basis of agreement

1042

Related applications/proceedings

4. This is / is not a case where an application for placement for adoption is among the range of options that will have to be considered.

5. The following current or proposed proceedings (eg criminal proceedings, other family proceedings, disciplinary, immigration or mental capacity/health determinations) are relevant to the determination of the application(s):

Proceedings	Parties	Court/Body	Stage reached	Comments.

Issues and directions for CMC/IRH

6. At the Case Management Conference/Issues Resolution Hearing the following issues, directions and interim orders will need to be considered by the court:

a)
b)
c)
d)
e)
f)

Compliance

7. The following steps have not been taken for the reasons explained and the effect on the timetable is as follows:

Key Date	Step to be taken	Reason for non-compliance	Expected date of compliance/ Effect on timetable

Appendix 3 *The Public Law Outline*

Recommended reading list and reading time

8. The following are the key documents to be read in preparation for the hearing:

Document	Author	Status/role	Date	Bundle page

9. The suggested reading time required for the hearing is:

Additional information

10. The following additional information is relevant to the timetable for the child(ren) or for the conduct of the hearing or of the proceedings

Contact details: advocates, solicitors and key professionals

Party	Status	Name	Tel:	Email:
Applicant Local Authority	Advocate Solicitor Key worker/team manager			
Respondents: (1) Mother	(1) Advocate Solicitor			
(2) Father	(2) Advocate Solicitor			
(3) Other party	(3) Advocate Solicitor			
Child(ren)	Advocate Solicitor Guardian:			

ANNEX C

Draft Case Management Order   Case No

                                                        Child(ren) No

[   ] Family Proceedings / County Court

The High Court sitting at [   ]

The Principal Registry of the Family Division

PART 1 – Preliminary

The child[ren] is / are:

Name	Boy/Girl	Date of Birth
(1)		
(2)		
(3)		

Date of this Order:

Ordered by:

Sitting in private/public

at the Case Management Conference / Issues Resolution Hearing

or at the [contested] hearing of an application [made without notice] by

for

or [other]

The court heard the advocates for the following parties:

Party	Status	Counsel/solicitor/Advocate
Applicant	Local Authority	
Respondents:		
(1) **X**	Mother	
(2) **Y**	Father	
(3) **Z**	Other	
Child(ren)	Guardian:	

And the following parties in person:

Party	Status

The court has heard and read the evidence set out on the Record of Hearing [Form C22]

This order is made on the basis of the information recorded in Part 3 about the timetable for the child(ren), the key issues and any agreements and decisions made

---

PART 2 - Order

The Court Orders that:

Orders relating to the child

1   *Record of Prescribed Forms of Order which are to be issued separately [C23 to C49]*
    e.g. Interim care order / interim supervision order / interim residence order / contact order

Joinder of parties/parentage issues

2   Party status

3   Paternity / Maternity and tracing / involvement of absent parent / previous carers

Appointment of Children's Guardian / Children's Solicitor / Official Solicitor

4.   Appointment of children's guardian / solicitor for the child

5.   Appointment of Official Solicitor as guardian ad litem / litigation friend for a non-subject child or protected party

Transfer / Allocation to Case Manager / Case Management Judge

6.   Transfer

7.   Allocation

Evidence to be filed

8.   Evidence
     a.   local authority
     b.   parents
     c.   [other]
     d.   children's guardian

9.   Assessments
     a.   Core and initial
     b.   Parenting (inc residential)
     c.   Friends and Family
     d.   [other, inc specialist]

10. Care planning

Other documents

11. LA's Schedule of Proposed Findings

12. LA Case Summary, Other Parties' Case Summaries and the Case Analysis and Recommendations

13. Disclosure of documents (whether to be filed and/or served)
    a. Key LA minutes and records not disclosed as pre-proceedings documents
    b. Health records (inc GP, HV, clinic and hospital)
    c. Education records (inc SEN)
    d. Police records (inc DV logs)
    e. Contact notes

Expert evidence

14. Identification of expert

15. Identification of Key Issue(s) to be addressed

16. Permission to instruct
    a. Responsibility for instruction (joint/sole)
    b. Letter of instruction
    c. Timetable
    d. Filing and service of report (paper/electronic)
    e. Questions to expert
    f. Permission to examine/observe child
    g. Funding
    h. Arrangements for expert to give oral evidence (in person or by video/audio-link)

17. Experts' meeting
    a. Responsibility to arrange and chair
    b. Questions
    c. Schedule of agreements and disagreements

Advocates' Meeting

18. Meeting

19. Draft Case Management Order and experts proposals

Further Hearings

20. The next hearing is at [   ][a.m.][p.m.] on [   ]

    at [   ] and is:

    [The Issues Resolution Hearing]

    [An Early Final Hearing]

    [A Fact Finding Hearing at which the findings set out in the local authority's schedule of findings are to be determined]

    [The Final Hearing at which   ]

    [Other (specify the AIM of the hearing)   ]

21. Special Measures and Security

22. Attendance at court

23. Use of Technology and Special requirements
    a. videolink
    b. conference telephone link
    c. hearing assistance
    d. DDA requirements
    e. translation directions

Other applications

24. Directions in other concurrent applications (e.g. for Residence/Contact)

25. Directions in Placement for Adoption Applications

Bundles for hearings

26. Bundles Practice Direction requirements
    a. Agreed or revised Threshold / Schedule of Findings
    b. Witness Template
    c. Skeleton arguments
    d. Judicial Reading List
    e. Time estimate to specify reading time and judgment writing time
    f. Other (eg [The parties must comply with the President's Practice Direction (Family Proceedings: Court Bundles), 27 July 2006, [2006] 2 FLR 199. The Direction applies to all hearings in this case regardless of the estimated length of the hearing.]

Other orders

27. No document other than a document specified in these directions or filed in accordance with the Rules or any Practice Direction shall be filed by any party without the court's permission.

28. Any application to vary these directions or for any other order is to be made to the allocated judge on notice to [   ] all parties.

Compliance with directions

29. All parties must immediately inform the Court/Court Officer on
[contact telephone / e-mail] if any party fails to adhere to any date specified for a direction or the filing of any document.

Dated   **(signed)**

                                   HCJ/HHJ/DJ/DJ(MC)/JP/[Assistant] JC
Court address:

PART 3 - Recitals

The timetable for the child(ren)

And key issues, agreements and decisions

It is recorded that:

1. The key dates and events in the Timetable for the Child(ren) are:

a)	
b)	
c)	
d)	

2. There is no [the following] delay in the timetable for the proceedings fixed by the court ir accordance with the Timetable for the Child *(specify any delay and reasons)*

3. The Key Issue(s) in the case are:

a)	
b)	
c)	
d)	

4. The parties have agreed the following Key Issues and/or findings of fact:

a)	
b)	
c)	
d)	

5. The court makes the following findings or decisions as the basis for this order:

a)	
b)	
c)	
d)	

Flowchart: Pre-proceedings - Public Law Outline

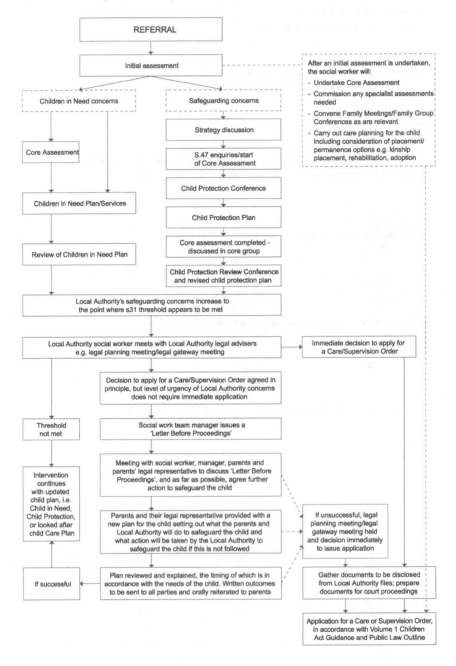

Flowchart: Court Proceedings - Public Law Outline

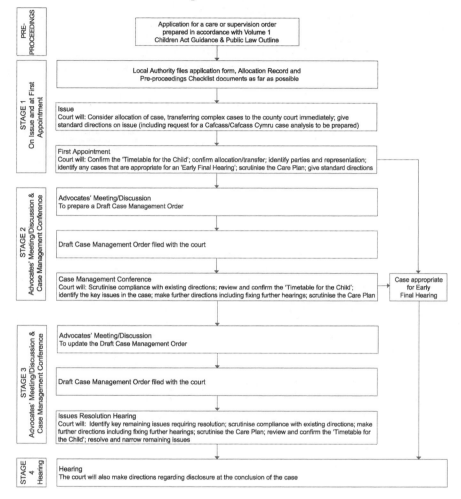

PRACTICE DIRECTION

PRACTICE DIRECTION – EXPERTS IN FAMILY PROCEEDINGS RELATING TO CHILDREN

The Practice Direction below is made by the President of the Family Division under the powers delegated to him by the Lord Chief Justice under Schedule 2, Part 1, paragraph 2(2) of the Constitutional Reform Act 2005, and is approved by the Lord Chancellor

1. INTRODUCTION

1.1 This Practice Direction deals with the use of expert evidence and the instruction of experts in family proceedings relating to children, and comes into force on 1st April 2008. The guidance supersedes, for such proceedings, that contained in Appendix C (the *Code of Guidance for Expert Witnesses in Family Proceedings*) to the Protocol of June 2003 (*Judicial Case Management in Public Law Children Act Cases*) and in the Practice Direction to Part 17 (*Experts*) of the Family Procedure (Adoption) Rules 2005[1] ("FP(AR) 2005") with effect on and from 1st April 2008.

Where the guidance refers to "an expert" or "the expert", this includes a reference to an expert team.

1.2 For the purposes of this guidance, the phrase "family proceedings relating to children" is a convenient description. It is not a legal term of art and has no statutory force. In this guidance it means[2]-

– placement and adoption proceedings, or
– family proceedings held in private which
– relate to the exercise of the inherent jurisdiction of the High Court with respect to children,
– are brought under the Children Act 1989 in any family court, or
– are brought in the High Court and county courts and "otherwise relate wholly or mainly to the maintenance or upbringing of a minor".

---

[1]   SI 2005/2795.
[2]   Following rule 10.20A(1) of the Family Proceedings Rules 1991, SI 1991/1247 ("FPR 1991") which defines the application of rule 10.20A (*Communication of information relating to proceedings*). Compare the definition of "relevant proceedings" in section 93(3) of the Children Act 1989 (*Rules of court*), applied in the equivalent rule 23A (*Confidentiality of documents*) of the Family Proceedings Courts (Children Act 1989) Rules 1991, SI 1991/1395 ("FPC(ChA)R 1991").

Aims of the guidance

1.3 The guidance aims to provide the court in family proceedings relating to children with early information to determine whether an expert or expert evidence will assist the court to:

– identify, narrow and where possible agree the issues between the parties;
–– provide an opinion about a question that is not within the skill and experience of the court;

– encourage the early identification of questions that need to be answered by an expert; and

– encourage disclosure of full and frank information between the parties, the court and any expert instructed.

1.4 The guidance does not aim to cover all possible eventualities. Thus it should be complied with so far as consistent in all the circumstances with the just disposal of the matter in accordance with the rules and guidance applying to the procedure in question.

Permission to instruct an expert or to use expert evidence

1.5 In family proceedings relating to children, the court's permission is required to instruct an expert. Such proceedings are confidential and, in the absence of the court's permission, disclosure of information and documents relating to such proceedings risks contravening the law of contempt of court or the various statutory provisions protecting this confidentiality. Thus, for the purposes of the law of contempt of court, information relating to such proceedings (whether or not contained in a document filed with the court or recorded in any form) may be communicated only to an expert whose instruction by a party has been permitted by the court.[3] Additionally, in proceedings under the Children Act 1989, the court's permission is required to cause the child to be medically or psychiatrically examined or otherwise assessed for the purpose of the preparation of expert evidence for use in the proceedings; and, where the court's permission has not been given, no evidence arising out of such an examination or assessment may be adduced without the court's permission.[4]

1.6 In practice, the need to have the court's permission to disclose information or documents to an expert – and, in Children Act 1989 proceedings, to have the child examined or assessed – means that in proceedings relating to children the court strictly controls the number, fields of expertise and identity of the experts who may be first instructed and then called.

1.7 Before permission is obtained from the court to instruct an expert in family proceedings relating to children, it will be necessary for the party wishing to instruct an expert to make enquiries designed so as to provide the court with information about that expert which will enable the court to decide whether or not to give permission. In practice, enquiries may need to be made of more than one expert for this purpose. This will in turn require each expert to be given sufficient information about the case to enable that expert to decide whether or not he or she is in a position to accept instructions. Such preliminary enquiries, and the disclosure of anonymised information about the case which is a necessary part of such enquiries, will not require the court's permission and will not amount to a contempt of court: see sections 4.1 and 4.2 (*Preliminary Enquiries of the Expert* and *Expert's Response to Preliminary Enquiries*).

1.8 Section 4 (*Preparation for the relevant hearing*) gives guidance on applying for the court's permission to instruct an expert, and on instructing the expert, in family proceedings relating to children. The court, when granting permission to instruct an expert, will also give directions for the expert to be called to give evidence, or for the expert's report to be put in evidence: see section 4.4 (*Draft Order for the relevant hearing*).

When should the court be asked for permission?

1.9 The key event is "the relevant hearing", which is any hearing at which the court's permission is sought to instruct an expert or to use expert evidence. Both expert issues should be raised with the court – and, where appropriate, with the other parties – as early as possible. This means:-

– in public law proceedings under the Children Act 1989, by or at the Case Management Conference: see the *Practice Direction: Guide to Case Management in Public Law Proceedings*, paragraphs 13.7, 14.3 and 25(29) which contains the definition of public law proceedings for the purposes of that practice direction;
– in private law proceedings under the Children Act 1989, by or at the First Hearing Dispute Resolution Appointment: see the *Private Law Programme* (9th November 2004), section 4 (*Process*);
– in placement and adoption proceedings, by or at the First Directions Hearing: see FP(A)R 2005 rule 26 and the *President's Guidance: Adoption: the New Law and Procedure* (March 2006), paragraph 23.

³   FPR 1991 rule 10.20A(2)(vii); FPC(ChA)R 1991 rule 23A(1)(c)(vii); FP(A)R 2005 rule 78(1)(c)(vii).

⁴   FPR 1991 rule 4.18(1) and (3); FPC(ChA)R 1991 rule 18(1) and (3).

2. GENERAL MATTERS

Scope of the Guidance

2.1 This guidance does not apply to cases issued before 1st April 2008, but in such a case the court may direct that this guidance will apply either wholly or partly. This is subject to the overriding objective for the type of proceedings, and to the proviso that such a direction will neither cause further delay nor involve repetition of steps already taken or of decisions already made in the case.

2.2 This guidance applies to all experts who are or have been instructed to give or prepare evidence for the purpose of family proceedings relating to children in a court in England and Wales.

Pre-application instruction of experts

2.3 When experts' reports are commissioned before the commencement of proceedings, it should be made clear to the expert that he or she may in due course be reporting to the court and should therefore consider himself or herself bound by this guidance. A prospective party to family proceedings relating to children (for example, a local authority) should always write a letter of instruction when asking a potential witness for a report or an opinion, whether that request is within proceedings or pre-proceedings (for example, when commissioning specialist assessment materials, reports from a treating expert or other evidential materials); and the letter of instruction should conform to the principles set out in this guidance.

Emergency and urgent cases

2.4 In emergency or urgent cases – for example, where, before formal issue of proceedings, a without-notice application is made to the court during or out of business hours; or where, after proceedings have been issued, a previously unforeseen need for (further) expert evidence arises at short notice – a party may wish to call expert evidence without having complied with all or any part of this guidance. In such circumstances, the party wishing to call the expert evidence must apply forthwith to the court – where possible or appropriate, on notice to the other parties – for directions as to the future steps to be taken in respect of the expert evidence in question.

Orders

2.5 Where an order or direction requires an act to be done by an expert, or otherwise affects an expert, the party instructing that expert – or, in the case of a jointly instructed expert, the lead solicitor – must serve a copy of the order or direction on the expert forthwith upon receiving it.

Adults who may be protected parties

2.6 The court will investigate as soon as possible any issue as to whether an adult party or intended party to family proceedings relating to children lacks capacity (within the meaning of the Mental Capacity Act 2005) to conduct the proceedings. An adult who lacks capacity to act as a party to the proceedings is a protected party and must have a representative (a litigation friend, next friend or guardian ad litem) to conduct the proceedings on his or her behalf.

2.7 Any issue as to the capacity of an adult to conduct the proceedings must be determined before the court gives any directions relevant to that adult's role in the proceedings.

2.8 Where the adult is a protected party, his or her representative should be involved in any instruction of an expert, including the instruction of an expert to assess whether the adult, although a protected party, is competent to give evidence. The instruction of an expert is a significant step in the proceedings. The representative will wish to consider (and ask the expert to consider), if the protected party is competent to give evidence, their best interests in this regard. The representative may wish to seek advice about "special measures". The representative may put forward an argument on behalf of the protected party that the protected party should not give evidence.

2.9 If at any time during the proceedings there is reason to believe that a party may lack capacity to conduct the proceedings, then the court must be notified and directions sought to ensure that this issue is investigated without delay.

Child likely to lack capacity to conduct the proceedings on when he or she reaches 18

2.10 Where it appears that a child is—

– a party to the proceedings and not the subject of them;
– nearing his or her 18th birthday, and
– considered likely to lack capacity to conduct the proceedings when he or she attains the age of 18,

the court will consider giving directions for the child's capacity in this respect to be investigated.

3. THE DUTIES OF EXPERTS

Overriding Duty

3.1 An expert in family proceedings relating to children has an overriding duty to the court that takes precedence over any obligation to the person from whom the expert has received instructions or by whom the expert is paid.

Particular Duties

3.2 Among any other duties an expert may have, an expert shall have regard to the following duties:

1) to assist the court in accordance with the overriding duty;
2) to provide advice to the court that conforms to the best practice of the expert's profession;
3) to provide an opinion that is independent of the party or parties instructing the expert;
4) to confine the opinion to matters material to the issues between the parties and in relation only to questions that are within the expert's expertise (skill and experience);
5) where a question has been put which falls outside the expert's expertise, to state this at the earliest opportunity and to volunteer an opinion as to whether another expert is required to bring expertise not possessed by those already involved or, in the rare case, as to whether a second opinion is required on a key issue and, if possible, what questions should be asked of the second expert;
6) in expressing an opinion, to take into consideration all of the material facts including any relevant factors arising from ethnic, cultural, religious or linguistic contexts at the time the opinion is expressed;
7) to inform those instructing the expert without delay of any change in the opinion and of the reason for the change.

Content of the Expert's Report

3.3 The expert's report shall be addressed to the court and prepared and filed **in accordance with the court's timetable** and shall:

1) give details of the expert's qualifications and experience;
2) contain a statement setting out the substance of all material instructions (whether written or oral) summarising the facts stated and instructions given to the expert which are material to the conclusions and opinions expressed in the report;
3) identify materials that have not been produced either as original medical or other professional records or in response to an instruction from a party, as such materials may contain an assumption as to the standard of proof, the admissibility or otherwise of hearsay evidence, and other important procedural and substantive questions relating to the different purposes of other enquiries (for example, criminal or disciplinary proceedings);
4) identify all requests to third parties for disclosure and their responses in order to avoid partial disclosure which tends only to prove a case rather than give full and frank information;
5) make clear which of the facts stated in the report are within the expert's own knowledge;
6) state who carried out any test, examination or interview which the expert has used for the report and whether or not the test, examination or interview has been carried out under the expert's supervision;
7) give details of the qualifications of any person who carried out the test, examination or interview;
8) in expressing an opinion to the court:
   (a) take into consideration all of the material facts including any relevant factors arising from ethnic, cultural, religious or linguistic contexts at the time the opinion is expressed, identifying the facts, literature and any other material including research material that the expert has relied upon in forming an opinion;

  (b) describe their own professional risk assessment process and process of differential diagnosis, highlighting factual assumptions, deductions from the factual assumptions, and any unusual, contradictory or inconsistent features of the case;

  (c) highlight whether a proposition is an hypothesis (in particular a controversial hypothesis), or an opinion deduced in accordance with peer-reviewed and -tested technique, research and experience accepted as a consensus in the scientific community;

  (d) indicate whether the opinion is provisional (or qualified, as the case may be), stating the qualification and the reason for it, and identifying what further information is required to give an opinion without qualification;

9) where there is a range of opinion on any question to be answered by the expert:

  (a) summarise the range of opinion;

  (b) highlight and analyse within the range of opinion an "unknown cause", whether on the facts of the case (for example, there is too little information to form a scientific opinion) or because of limited experience, lack of research, peer review or support in the field of expertise which the expert professes;

  (c) give reasons for any opinion expressed: the use of a balance sheet approach to the factors that support or undermine an opinion can be of great assistance to the court;

10) contain a summary of the expert's conclusions and opinions;

11) contain a statement that the expert understands his or her duty to the court and has complied and will continue to comply with that duty;

12) contain a statement that the expert:

  (a) has no conflict of interest of any kind, other than any conflict disclosed in his or her report;

  (b) does not consider that any interest disclosed affects his or her suitability as an expert witness on any issue on which he or she has given evidence;

  (c) will advise the instructing party if, between the date of the expert's report and the final hearing, there is any change in circumstances which affects the expert's answers to (a) or (b) above;

13) be verified by a statement of truth in the following form:

'I confirm that insofar as the facts stated in my report are within my own knowledge I have made clear which they are and I believe them to be true, and that the opinions I have expressed represent my true and complete professional opinion.'

4. PREPARATION FOR THE RELEVANT HEARING

Preliminary Enquiries of the Expert

4.1 In good time for the information requested to be available for the relevant hearing or for the advocates' meeting or discussion where one takes place before the relevant hearing, the solicitor for the party proposing to instruct the expert (or lead solicitor or solicitor for the child if the instruction proposed is joint) shall approach the expert with the following information:

1) the nature of the proceedings and the issues likely to require determination by the court;

2) the questions about which the expert is to be asked to give an opinion (including any ethnic, cultural, religious or linguistic contexts);
3) the date when the court is to be asked to give permission for the instruction (or if – unusually – permission has already been given, the date and details of that permission);
4) whether permission is to be asked of the court for the instruction of another expert in the same or any related field (that is, to give an opinion on the same or related questions);
5) the volume of reading which the expert will need to undertake;
6) whether or not permission has been applied for or given for the expert to examine the child;
7) whether or not it will be necessary for the expert to conduct interviews – and, if so, with whom;
8) the likely timetable of legal and social work steps;
9) when the expert's report is likely to be required;
10) whether and, if so, what date has been fixed by the court for any hearing at which the expert may be required to give evidence (in particular the Final Hearing).

It is essential that there should be proper co-ordination between the court and the expert when drawing up the case management timetable: the needs of the court should be balanced with the needs of the expert whose forensic work is undertaken as an adjunct to his or her main professional duties, whether in the National Health Service or elsewhere.

The expert should be informed at this stage of the possibility of making, through his or her instructing solicitor, representations to the court about being named or otherwise identified in any public judgment given by the court.

Expert's Response to Preliminary Enquiries

4.2 In good time for the relevant hearing or for the advocates' meeting or discussion where one takes place before the relevant hearing, the solicitors intending to instruct the expert shall obtain confirmation from the expert:

1) that acceptance of the proposed instructions will not involve the expert in any conflict of interest;
2) that the work required is within the expert's expertise;
3) that the expert is available to do the relevant work within the suggested time scale;
4) when the expert is available to give evidence, of the dates and times to avoid and, where a hearing date has not been fixed, of the amount of notice the expert will require to make arrangements to come to court (or to give evidence by video link) without undue disruption to his or her normal professional routines;
5) of the cost, including hourly or other charging rates, and likely hours to be spent, attending experts' meetings, attending court and writing the report (to include any examinations and interviews);
6) of any representations which the expert wishes to make to the court about being named or otherwise identified in any public judgment given by the court.

Where parties have not agreed on the appointment of a single joint expert before the relevant hearing, they should obtain the above confirmations in respect of all experts whom they intend to put to the court as candidates for the appointment.

Appendix 4 *Practice Direction*

The proposal to instruct an expert

4.3 Any party who proposes to ask the court for permission to instruct an expert shall, **by 11 a.m. on the business day before the relevant hearing**, file and serve a written proposal to instruct the expert in the following detail:

1) the name, discipline, qualifications and expertise of the expert (by way of C.V. where possible);
2) the expert's availability to undertake the work;
3) the relevance of the expert evidence sought to be adduced to the issues in the proceedings and the specific questions upon which it is proposed that the expert should give an opinion (including the relevance of any ethnic, cultural, religious or linguistic contexts);
4) the timetable for the report;
5) the responsibility for instruction;
6) whether or not the expert evidence can properly be obtained by the joint instruction of the expert by two or more of the parties;
7) whether the expert evidence can properly be obtained by only one party (for example, on behalf of the child);
8) why the expert evidence proposed cannot be given by social services undertaking a core assessment or by the Children's Guardian in accordance with their respective statutory duties;
9) the likely cost of the report on an hourly or other charging basis: where possible, the expert's terms of instruction should be made available to the court;
10) the proposed apportionment (at least in the first instance) of any jointly instructed expert's fee; when it is to be paid; and, if applicable, whether public funding has been approved.

Draft Order for the relevant hearing

4.4 Any party proposing to instruct an expert shall, **by 11 a.m. on the business day before the relevant hearing**, submit to the court a draft order for directions dealing in particular with:

1) the party who is to be responsible for drafting the letter of instruction and providing the documents to the expert;
2) the issues identified by the court and the questions about which the expert is to give an opinion;
3) the timetable within which the report is to be prepared, filed and served;
4) the disclosure of the report to the parties and to any other expert;
5) the organisation of, preparation for and conduct of an experts' discussion;
6) the preparation of a statement of agreement and disagreement by the experts following an experts' discussion;
7) making available to the court at an early opportunity the expert reports in electronic form;
8) the attendance of the expert at court to give oral evidence (alternatively, the expert giving his or her evidence in writing or remotely by video link), whether at or for the Final Hearing or another hearing; unless agreement about the opinions given by the expert is reached at or before the Issues Resolution Hearing ("IRH") or, if no IRH is to be held, by a specified date prior to the hearing at which the expert is to give oral evidence ("the specified date").

5. LETTER OF INSTRUCTION

5.1 The solicitor instructing the expert shall, **within 5 business days after the relevant hearing,** prepare (in agreement with the other parties where appropriate), file and serve a letter of instruction to the expert which shall:

1) set out the context in which the expert's opinion is sought (including any ethnic, cultural, religious or linguistic contexts);
2) set out the specific questions which the expert is required to answer, ensuring that they:
   (a) are within the ambit of the expert's area of expertise;
   (b) do not contain unnecessary or irrelevant detail;
   (c) are kept to a manageable number and are clear, focused and direct; and
   (d) reflect what the expert has been requested to do by the court.

The Annex to this guidance sets out suggested questions in letters of instruction to (1) child mental health professionals or paediatricians, and (2) adult psychiatrists and applied psychologists, in Children Act 1989 proceedings;

3) list the documentation provided, or provide for the expert an indexed and paginated bundle which shall include:
   (a) a copy of the order (or those parts of the order) which gives permission for the instruction of the expert, immediately the order becomes available;
   (b) an agreed list of essential reading; and
   (c) a copy of this guidance;
4) identify materials that have not been produced either as original medical (or other professional) records or in response to an instruction from a party, as such materials may contain an assumption as to the standard of proof, the admissibility or otherwise of hearsay evidence, and other important procedural and substantive questions relating to the different purposes of other enquiries (for example, criminal or disciplinary proceedings);
5) identify all requests to third parties for disclosure and their responses, to avoid partial disclosure, which tends only to prove a case rather than give full and frank information;
6) identify the relevant people concerned with the proceedings (for example, the treating clinicians) and inform the expert of his or her right to talk to them provided that an accurate record is made of the discussions;
7) identify any other expert instructed in the proceedings and advise the expert of his or her right to talk to the other experts provided that an accurate record is made of the discussions;
8) subject to any public funding requirement for prior authority, define the contractual basis upon which the expert is retained and in particular the funding mechanism including how much the expert will be paid (an hourly rate and overall estimate should already have been obtained), when the expert will be paid, and what limitation there might be on the amount the expert can charge for the work which he or she will have to do. In cases where the parties are publicly funded, there should also be a brief explanation of the costs and expenses excluded from public funding by Funding Code criterion 1.3 and the detailed assessment process.

Asking the court to settle the letter of instruction to a joint expert

5.2 Where the court has directed that the instructions to the expert are to be contained in a jointly agreed letter and the terms of the letter cannot be agreed, any instructing party may submit to the court a written request, which must be copied to the other instructing parties, that the court settle the letter of instruction. Where possible, the written request should be set out in an e-mail to the court, preferably sent directly to the judge dealing with the proceedings (or, in the Family Proceedings Court, to the legal adviser who will forward it to the appropriate judge or justices), and be copied by e-mail to the other instructing parties. The court will settle the letter of instruction, usually without a hearing to avoid delay; and will send (where practicable, by e-mail) the settled letter to the lead solicitor for transmission forthwith to the expert, and copy it to the other instructing *parties for information.*

Keeping the expert up to date with new documents

5.3 As often as may be necessary, the expert should be provided promptly with a copy of any new document filed at court, together with an updated document list or bundle index.

6. THE COURT'S CONTROL OF EXPERT EVIDENCE: CONSEQUENTIAL ISSUES

Written Questions

6.1 Any party wishing to put written questions to an expert for the purpose of clarifying the expert's report must put the questions to the expert **not later than 10 business days after receipt of the report.**

The court will specify the timetable according to which the expert is to answer the written questions.

Experts' Discussion or Meeting: Purpose

6.2 By the specified date, the court may – if it has not already given such a direction – direct that the experts are to meet or communicate:

1) to identify and narrow the issues in the case;
2) where possible, to reach agreement on the expert issues;
3) to identify the reasons for disagreement on any expert question and what, if any, action needs to be taken to resolve any outstanding disagreement or question;
4) to explain or add to the evidence in order to assist the court to determine the issues;
5) to limit, wherever possible, the need for the experts to attend court to give oral evidence.

Experts' Discussion or Meeting: Arrangements

6.3 In accordance with the directions given by the court, the solicitor or other professional who is given the responsibility by the court ("the nominated professional") shall – **within 15 business days after the experts' reports have been filed and copied to the other parties** – make arrangements for the experts to meet or communicate. Where applicable, the following matters should be considered:

1) where permission has been given for the instruction of experts from different disciplines, a global discussion may be held relating to those questions that concern all or most of them;

2) separate discussions may have to be held among experts from the same or related disciplines, but care should be taken to ensure that the discussions complement each other so that related questions are discussed by all relevant experts;

3) **5 business days prior to a discussion or meeting**, the nominated professional should formulate an agenda including a list of questions for consideration. The agenda should contain only those questions which are intended to clarify areas of agreement or disagreement. Questions which repeat questions asked in the letter of instruction or which seek to rehearse cross-examination in advance of the hearing should be rejected as likely to defeat the purpose of the meeting.

The agenda may usefully take the form of a list of questions to be circulated among the other parties in advance. The agenda should comprise all questions that each party wishes the experts to consider. The agenda and list of questions should be sent to each of the experts **not later than 2 clear business days before the discussion;**

4) the nominated professional may exercise his or her discretion to accept further questions after the agenda with list of questions has been circulated to the parties. **Only in exceptional circumstances should questions be added to the agenda within the 2-day period before the meeting. Under no circumstances should any question received on the day of or during the meeting be accepted.** Strictness in this regard is vital, for adequate notice of the questions enables the parties to identify and isolate the issues in the case before the meeting so that the experts' discussion at the meeting can concentrate on those issues;

5) the discussion should be chaired by the nominated professional. A minute must be taken of the questions answered by the experts, and a Statement of Agreement and Disagreement must be prepared which should be agreed and signed by each of the experts who participated in the discussion. The statement should be served and filed **not later than 5 business days after the discussion has taken place;**

6) in each case, whether some or all of the experts participate by telephone conference or video link to ensure that minimum disruption is caused to professional schedules and that costs are minimised.

Meetings or conferences attended by a jointly instructed expert

6.4 Jointly instructed experts should not attend any meeting or conference which is not a joint one, unless all the parties have agreed in writing or the court has directed that such a meeting may be held, and it is agreed or directed who is to pay the expert's fees for the meeting or conference. Any meeting or conference attended by a jointly instructed expert should be proportionate to the case.

Court-directed meetings involving experts in public law Children Act cases

6.5 In public law Children Act proceedings, where the court gives a direction that a meeting shall take place between the local authority and any relevant named experts for the purpose of providing assistance to the local authority in the formulation of plans and proposals for the child, the meeting shall be arranged, chaired and minuted in accordance with the directions given by the court.

7. POSITIONS OF THE PARTIES

7. Where a party refuses to be bound by an agreement that has been reached at an experts' discussion or meeting, that party must inform the court and the other parties in writing, **within 10 business days after the discussion or meeting or, where an IRH is to be held, not less than 5 business days before the IRH,** of his reasons for refusing to accept the agreement.

8. ARRANGEMENTS FOR EXPERTS TO GIVE EVIDENCE

Preparation

8.1 Where the court has directed the attendance of an expert witness, the party who is responsible for the instruction of the expert shall, **by the specified date or, where an IRH is to be held, by the IRH,** ensure that:

1) a date and time (if possible, convenient to the expert) are fixed for the court to hear the expert's evidence, substantially in advance of the hearing at which the expert is to give oral evidence and no later than a specified date prior to that hearing or, where an IRH is to be held, than the IRH;

2) if the expert's oral evidence is not required, the expert is notified as soon as possible;

3) the witness template accurately indicates how long the expert is likely to be giving evidence, in order to avoid the inconvenience of the expert being delayed at court;

4) consideration is given in each case to whether some or all of the experts participate by telephone conference or video link, or submit their evidence in writing, to ensure that minimum disruption is caused to professional schedules and that costs are minimised.

Experts attending Court

8.2 Where expert witnesses are to be called, all parties shall, **by the specified date or, where an IRH is to be held, by the IRH,** ensure that:

1) the parties' advocates have identified (whether at an advocates' meeting or by other means) the issues which the experts are to address;

2) wherever possible, a logical sequence to the evidence is arranged, with experts of the same discipline giving evidence on the same day;

3) the court is informed of any circumstance where all experts agree but a party nevertheless does not accept the agreed opinion, so that directions can be given for the proper consideration of the experts' evidence and of the party's reasons for not accepting the agreed opinion;

4) in the exceptional case the court is informed of the need for a witness summons.

9. ACTION AFTER THE FINAL HEARING

9.1 Within 10 business days after the Final Hearing, the solicitor instructing the expert shall inform the expert in writing of the outcome of the case, and of the use made by the court of the expert's opinion.

9.2 Where the court directs preparation of a transcript, it may also direct that the solicitor instructing the expert shall send a copy to the **expert within 10 business days after receiving the transcript.**

9.3 After a Final Hearing in the Family Proceedings Court, the (lead) solicitor instructing the expert shall send the expert a copy of the court's written reasons for its decision **within 10 business days after receiving the written reasons.**

ANNEX[5]

Questions in letters of instruction to child mental health professional or paediatrician in Children Act 1989 proceedings

A. The Child(ren) – TO B

1. Please describe the child(ren)'s current health, development and functioning (according to your area of expertise), and identify the nature of any significant changes which have occurred

- Behavioural
- Emotional
- Attachment organisation
- Social/peer/sibling relationships
- Cognitive/educational
- Physical
  - Growth, eating, sleep
  - Non-organic physical problems (including wetting and soiling)
  - Injuries
  - Paediatric conditions

2. Please comment on the likely explanation for/aetiology of the child(ren)'s problems/difficulties/injuries

- History/experiences (including intrauterine influences, and abuse and neglect)
- Genetic/innate/developmental difficulties
- Paediatric/psychiatric disorders

3. Please provide a prognosis and risk if difficulties not addressed above.

4. Please describe the child(ren)'s needs in the light of the above

- Nature of care-giving
- Education
- Treatment

in the short and long term (subject, where appropriate, to further assessment later).

B. The parents/primary care-givers – TO B

5. Please describe the factors and mechanisms which would explain the parents' (or primary care-givers') harmful or neglectful interactions with the child(ren) (if relevant)

1065

6. What interventions have been tried and what has been the result?

7. Please assess the ability of the parents or primary care-givers to fulfil the child(ren)'s identified needs now.

8. What other assessments of the parents or primary care-givers are indicated

- Adult mental health assessment
- Forensic risk assessment
- Physical assessment
- Cognitive assessment

9. What, if anything, is needed to assist the parents or primary care-givers now, within the child(ren)'s time scales and what is the prognosis for change

- Parenting work
- Support
- Treatment/therapy

C. Alternatives – TO B

10. Please consider the alternative possibilities for the fulfilment of the child(ren)'s needs.

- What sort of placement
- Contact arrangements

Please consider the advantages, disadvantages and implications of each for the child(ren).

Questions in letters of instruction to adult psychiatrists and applied psychologists in Children Act 1989 proceedings

1. Does the parent/adult have – whether in his/her history or presentation – a mental illness/disorder (including substance abuse) or other psychological/emotional difficulty and, if so, what is the diagnosis?

2. How do any/all of the above (and their current treatment if applicable) affect his/her functioning, including interpersonal relationships?

3. If the answer to Q1 is yes, are there any features of either the mental illness or psychological/emotional difficulty or personality disorder which could be associated with risk to others, based on the available evidence base (whether published studies or evidence from clinical experience)?

1.[4.] What are the experiences/antecedents/aetiology which would explain his/her difficulties, if any, (taking into account any available evidence base or other clinical experience)?

5. What treatment is indicated, what is its nature and the likely duration?

6. What is his/her capacity to engage in/partake of the treatment/therapy?

7. Are you able to indicate the prognosis for, time scales for achieving, and likely durability of, change?

8. What other factors might indicate positive change?

(It is assumed that this opinion will be based on collateral information as well as interviewing the adult).

_____The Right Honourable Date:

Sir Mark Potter

The President of the Family Division

_____

The Lord Chancellor Date:

5   Drafted by the Family Justice Council.

TIMELINE

Timeline for developments towards a unified family court		
Date	*Development*	*Comments*
1969 1989 1991 1996	The Finer Report The Children Act 1989 was passed The 1989 Act implemented The Booth Report	The start of the concept? First report on the problems of delay.
2002	*Scoping study on Delay in Children Act cases* LCD	Led to Lord Chancellor's Advisory Committee on judicial case management in Public cases and the creation of the Protocol for Judicial Case Management.
2002 September	Lord Chancellor's Working Party on Delay in FPCs under the Children Act 1989	Chairman HHJ Cryan.
2003 1 November	*Judicial Protocol*	Protocol for Judicial Case Management in public law Children Act cases came into effect on 1 November 2003.
2004 May	*Delays in Public Law Children Act Cases* E Finch	Ineffective case management was one of the main factors to have an adverse impact on case progression. Case Progression Officers a way for court to be more proactive and provide support for the judiciary for case management.
2004 9 November	*Private Law Programme*	Reduce delays in private law cases such as contact: conciliation at first appointment, effective court control including judicial continuity and close cooperation with CAFCASS.

Appendix 5 *Timeline*

Timeline for developments towards a unified family court		
Date	*Development*	*Comments*
2005 3 February	**A Single Civil Court?** *The scope for unifying the civil jurisdictions of the High Court, the county courts and the Family Proceedings Courts* **Consultation Paper CP 06/05** **Published 3 February 2005**	This consultation paper was the first phase in a scoping study that assessed the case for unifying the jurisdictions of the High Court, the county courts and the family proceedings courts. The paper considered the potential for creating a single civil court of first instance in England and Wales by amalgamating the High Court and the county courts. The jurisdiction of the family proceedings courts was also considered.
2005 17 February	HMCS Management Proposals to Develop a Unified Family Service	
2005 1 March	Report of the Constitutional Affairs Select Committee	HC 116–1.
2005 July	*Judicial Resources Review* commenced	Arose partly from LC announcement that there will be no increase in the overall numbers of High Court Judges, requiring cascading down of work.
2005 July	*A Fairer Deal for Legal Aid*	Cm 6591. *Legal Aid Review* led to *Review of the Child Care Proceedings System in England and Wales* (May 2006) and the *Carter Review*.
2005 September	The Child Care Proceedings Review: Key Issues Summary	DCA Working Party.
2005 September – 2006 August	*Family case progression officers*	Piloted in six courts in September 2005 for 12 months. Revised guidance from April 2007.

Timeline for developments towards a unified family court		
Date	*Development*	*Comments*
2005 October	*Focusing Judicial Resources Appropriately*	Judicial Resources Review Report – joint work of the Judiciary and the DCA.
2005 7 November	Moving Towards a Single Family Court	DCA News Release.
2005 14 December	*Thematic Review of the Protocol for Judicial Case Management in Public Law Children Act Cases* (JRT)	Consultation exercise on effectiveness of the Protocol.
2006 May	*Review of the Child Care Proceedings System in England and Wales*	DCA.
2006 13 July	*Review of Legal Aid Procurement – Lord Carter of Coles* *Legal Aid: A Sustainable Future – Consultation Paper* *Legal Aid – A Market Based Approach to Reform*	Carter Review. DCA/LSC Consultation Paper. DCA/LSC Consultation Paper.
2006 30 August	*Family Procedure Rules – a new procedural code for family proceedings*	DCA Consultation Paper.
2006/2007	Unified family court service	*HMCS working to establish a Unified Family Service to bring together FPCs and family business in county courts.* (See HMCS *Working Together* Annual Report).
2006 November	November 2006 President accepted JRT recommendations. '*Framework for Family Courts – blueprint for integrated Family Court*'	
2007 Early	*Draft Public Law Outline (PLO) prepared*	Meeting of JRT and Designated Family Judges and following this meeting draft PLO prepared.
2007 June – September	Consultation on PLO June – September 2007 and introduced in 7 further areas.	Arising from the Judicial Review Team *Thematic Review of the protocol for Judicial Case Management in Public Law Children Act Cases.*

Appendix 5 *Timeline*

Timeline for developments towards a unified family court		
Date	*Development*	*Comments*
2008 22 February	Ministry of Justice announced proposals for new rules which would align the differing procedures for different levels of courts and follow the example set by the Civil Procedure Rules	News Release 020–08.
2008 1 April	Public Law Outline implemented	
2009/10	New Family Proceedings Rules?	

Index

[all references are to paragraph number]

Abduction
ambit of the Act, and, 1.14
wardship, and, 12.20–12.23
welfare principle, and, 2.7
Abuse prevention
local authority support services, and,
6.25
Accommodation of children
And see Local authority support
services
arrangement planning, 6.48
ascertaining child's wishes, 6.47
children who may be
accommodated, 6.39
children who must be
accommodated, 6.36–6.38
consent of parents, 6.56
general duty, 6.36–6.46
homeless adolescents, 6.42
homeless families, 6.40–6.41
limits, 6.50–6.53
miscellaneous duties, 6.48–6.49
parental agreement, 6.48
partnership with parents, 6.55–6.56
placement arrangements, 6.48
records, 6.49
refuges for children at risk,
6.43–6.46
representations, 6.49
restriction on removal, 6.54
Administration of child's property
welfare principle, and, 2.7
Adoption
ambit of the Act, and, 1.14
parental responsibility, and, 3.13
special guardianship orders, and,
5.233–5.234
Advice and assistance
local authority support services, and,
6.81–6.82
Advisory Board on Family Law
liaison network, and, 1.32

Advocates' meeting
advocates' meeting, 8.126–8.128
issues resolution hearing, 8.135
"After-care"
And see 'Looked after' children
duties to 'eligible child', 6.75–6.76
duties to 'former relevant children',
6.80
duties to 'relevant child', 6.77–6.79
education support, 6.86
employment support, 6.86
financial support, 6.85
generally, 6.70–6.71
local authorities' duties, 6.72–6.74
Pathway Plans, 6.83
Personal Adviser, 6.84
persons qualifying for advice and
assistance, 6.81–6.82
training support, 6.86
Age of child
welfare principle, and, 2.48
Allocation of proceedings
care proceedings, and, 8.96–8.97
commencement, on, 4.15–4.16
introduction, 4.14
review
complexity, 4.338
Draft President's guidance, 4.41
introduction, 4.32
private law, 4.39–4.40
public law, 4.33–4.36
transfer, on, 4.17–4.18
Alternative dispute resolution
care proceedings, and, 8.86
Ambit of the Act
generally, 1.12–1.14
Appeals
appellant's notice
generally, 13.16
supporting documentation, 13.18
care orders, and, 8.225–8.226

Index

Appeals—*contd*
county courts, from
introduction, 13.11
permission to appeal,
13.12–13.17
post-permission procedure, 13.21
skeleton arguments, 13.19–13.20
supporting documentation, 13.18
court's powers
Court of Appeal, in, 13.32–13.35
generally, 13.29–13.31
generally, 13.1–13.6
High Court, from
introduction, 13.11
permission to appeal,
13.12–13.17
post-permission procedure, 13.21
skeleton arguments, 13.19–13.20
supporting documentation, 13.18
House of Lords, to, 13.22–13.25
"leapfrog" appeals, 13.22
limitations, 13.4
permission to appeal, 13.12–13.17
position pending appeal,
13.26–13.28
post-permission procedure, 13.21
reform proposals, 13.36
routes
county courts, from, 13.11–13.21
High Court, from, 13.11–13.21
House of Lords, to, 13.22–13.25
magistrates' court, from,
13.7–13.10
secure accommodation orders, and
civil proceedings, 9.29
criminal proceedings, 9.40
skeleton arguments, 13.19–13.20
supervision orders, and, 8.96–8.97
Supreme Court, to, 13.22–13.25
Applications
care proceedings, and
applicants, 8.89
checklist, 8.90–8.91
consideration, 8.62–8.64
generally, 8.87–8.8
pre-proceedings stage, 8.65–8.74
filing, 4.22
forms, 4.21
secure accommodation orders, and
civil proceedings, 9.17
criminal proceedings, 9.32
service, 4.24
Applications for section 8 orders
in favour of third person, 5.159
introduction, 5.143
with leave
criteria for leave, 5.148–5.157
introduction, 5.146–5.147
procedure for leave, 5.158
without leave, 5.144–5.145

Appointment of guardian
parental responsibility, and
introduction, 3.13
non-parents, 3.88
unmarried fathers, 3.53
Ascertainable wishes and feelings of child
welfare principle, and, 2.42–2.43
Assessment of needs
local authority support services, and,
6.12–6.15
Attendance of child
oral evidence, 4.51–4.54
private law proceedings, 4.50
specified proceedings, 4.49

Background of child
welfare principle, and, 2.49–2.54
'Beyond parental control'
care orders, and, 8.52
Blind children
local authority support services, and,
6.21–6.22
Burden of proof
evidence, and, 11.5
Burial of deceased child
parental responsibility, and, 3.13
Butler-Sloss Report (1987)
child abuse, and, 1.5–1.6

CAFCASS
attendance of officers at court,
10.29
background, 10.13–10.14
Domestic Violence Toolkit, 10.19
functions, 10.14
National Practice Standards,
10.17–10.18
officers, 10.15–10.16
Safeguarding Framework, 10.19
welfare reports, 10.20–10.28
Capability of parents to meet child's needs
welfare principle, and, 2.58
Care centres
county court jurisdiction, and, 4.8
Care contact orders
court powers, 8.208–8.211
discharge, 8.212–8.213
generally, 8.202–8.207
variation, 8.212–8.213
Care orders
advocates' meeting
advocates' meeting, 8.126–8.128
issues resolution hearing, 8.135
allocation, 8.96–8.97
alternative dispute resolution, 8.86
appeals, 8.225–8.226
applications
applicants, 8.89
checklist, 8.90–8.91

Care orders—*contd*
  applications—*contd*
    consideration, 8.62–8.64
    generally, 8.87–8.8
    pre-proceedings stage, 8.65–8.74
  'attributable', 8.46–8.49
  'beyond parental control', 8.52
  burden of proof, 8.21–8.27
  care given to the child, 8.50–8.51
  care plans, 8.58–8.60
  case management, 8.79–8.82
  case management conference
    advocates' meeting, 8.126–8.128
    case management order,
      8.129–8.132
    generally, 8.133–8.134
    introduction, 8.125
  case management order
    generally, 8.129–8.132
    issues resolution hearing, 8.136
  change of name, and, 8.175
  'child concerned', 8.28–8.29
  concurrent criminal proceedings,
    8.106
  consent orders, 8.167–8.168
  contact arrangements, 8.61
  contact with child, and
    care contact order, 8.202–8.207
    court's powers, 8.208–8.211
    discharge, 8.212–8.213
    duty to child in care, 8.201
    duty to promote contact,
      8.199–8.200
    introduction, 8.197–8.198
    procedure, 8.145–8.152
    refusal, 8.214–8.218
    variation, 8.212–8.213
  'designated authority', 8.170
  discharge, 8.220–8.224
  early final hearing, 8.104
  effect
    change of name, 8.175
    other orders, on, 8.178–8.179
    parental responsibility,
      8.171–8.174
    permanent removal from
      jurisdiction, 8.177
    temporary removal from
      jurisdiction, 8.176
  experts, 8.105
  final hearing
    consent orders, 8.167–8.168
    decision as to type of order,
      8.164–8.166
    form of order, 8.146–8.148
    interim care order, and,
      8.149–8.154
    introduction, 8.141–8.142
    split hearings, 8.143–8.145
    supervising care plans,
      8.155–8.163
  first appointment, 8.93

Care orders—*contd*
  grounds
    contact arrangements, 8.61
    generally, 8.18
    threshold criteria, 8.19–8.53
    welfare of child, 8.54–8.60
  'harm', 8.40–8.41
  interim orders
    conditions, 8.108
    directions for assessment,
      8.113–8.119
    duration, 8.122–8.123
    effect, 8.112
    exclusion requirement, and,
      8.120–8.121
    final hearing, and, 8.149–8.154
    grounds, 8.109–8.110
    guidance on applications, 8.111
    introduction, 8.107
    renewal, 8.124
  'is likely to suffer', 8.36–8.39
  'is suffering', 8.30–8.35
  issue, 8.92
  issues resolution hearing
    advocates' meeting, 8.135
    case management order, 8.136
    generally, 8.137–8.140
  kinship care
    pre-proceedings stage, 8.68
    welfare of child, 8.57
  local authorities' powers, 8.17
  meaning, 8.16
  need, 8.16–8.17
  overriding objective, 8.76–8.77
  parental responsibility, and,
    8.171–8.174
  parties, 8.98–8.103
  placement orders, and, 8.169
  pre-proceedings stage
    assessment, 8.67
    Children Act 1989 Guidance
      Volume 1, 8.65
    communications with parents and
      child, 8.70
    inter-agency cooperation, 8.69
    key principles, 8.66
    kinship care, 8.68
    letter before proceedings, 8.71
    meeting with parents, 8.72–8.74
  procedure
    allocation, 8.96–8.97
    alternative dispute resolution,
      8.86
    applications, 8.87–8.91
    case management, 8.79–8.82
    case management conference,
      8.125–8.134
    concurrent care and criminal
      proceedings, 8.106
    consistency, 8.83
    early final hearing, 8.104
    expectations, 8.84–8.85

Care orders—*contd*
  procedure—*contd*
    experts, 8.105
    final hearing, 8.141–8.168
    first appointment, 8.93
    interim orders, 8.107–8.124
    issue, 8.92
    issues resolution hearing,
        8.135–8.140
    judicial continuity, 8.78
    key principles, 8.75
    overriding objective, 8.76–8.77
    parties, 8.98–8.103
    placement order applications,
        8.169
    timetable for proceedings,
        8.94–8.95
    transfer, 8.96–8.97
  proportionality, 8.56
  removal from jurisdiction, and
    permanent, 8.177
    temporary, 8.176
  'significant harm', 8.42–8.44
  split hearings, 8.143–8.145
  supervising care plans, 8.155–8.163
  standard of proof, 8.21–8.27
  threshold criteria
    agreed threshold, 8.53
    'attributable', 8.46–8.49
    'beyond parental control', 8.52
    burden of proof, 8.21–8.27
    care given to the child, 8.50–8.51
    'child concerned', 8.28–8.29
    generally, 8.19–8.20
    'harm', 8.40–8.41
    'is likely to suffer', 8.36–8.39
    'is suffering', 8.30–8.35
    'significant harm', 8.42–8.44
    similar child comparison, 8.45
    standard of proof, 8.21–8.27
  timetable for proceedings, 8.94–8.95
  transfer of proceedings, 8.96–8.97
  variation, 8.219
  welfare of child
    care plans, 8.58–8.60
    introduction, 8.54
    kinship care, 8.57
    paramountcy, 8.55
    proportionality, 8.56
    statutory checklist, 8.55
  withdrawal, 8.227
Care plans
  generally, 8.58–8.60
Care proceedings
  care contact orders
    court powers, 8.208–8.211
    discharge, 8.212–8.213
    generally, 8.202–8.207
    variation, 8.212–8.213
  care orders
    applications, 8.62–8.169
    contact arrangements, 8.61

Care proceedings—*contd*
  care orders—*contd*
    discharge, 8.220–8.224
    effect, 8.170–8.179
    grounds, 8.18–8.61
    need, 8.16–8.17
    threshold criteria, 8.19–8.53
    variation, 8.219
    welfare issue, 8.54–8.60
  Care Proceedings Review (2005),
      8.12–8.13
  Case Management Protocol (2003),
      8.8–8.11
  Children Act 1989 Guidance Volume
      1, 8.14
  conclusions, 8.228–8.239,
      14.24–14.28
  contact with children in care
    care contact orders, 8.202–8.213
    local authorities' duties,
        8.199–8.201
    refusal of contact, 8.214–8.218
    summary, 8.197–8.198
  introduction, 8.1–8.6
  Public Law Outline
    background, 8.7–8.14
    generally, 8.15
  supervision orders
    appeals, 8.225–8.226
    applications, 8.62–8.169
    contact arrangements, 8.61
    discharge, 8.220–8.224
    effect, 8.180–8.1196
    grounds, 8.18–8.61
    need, 8.16–8.17
    threshold criteria, 8.19–8.53
    variation, 8.219
    welfare issue, 8.54–8.60
  withdrawal, 8.227
Carers
  parental responsibility, and, 3.103
Case management
  care proceedings, and
    conference, 8.125–8.134
    generally, 8.79–8.82
    order, 8.129–8.132
  issues resolution hearing, 8.136
  generally, 4.31
Certificate of conviction
  evidence, and, 11.18
Challenging decisions
  appeals
    appellant's notice, 13.16
    court's powers, 13.29–13.35
    generally, 13.1–13.6
    permission to appeal,
        13.12–13.17
    position pending appeal,
        13.26–13.28
    post-permission procedure, 13.21
    reform proposals, 13.36
    routes, 13.7–13.11

Challenging decisions—*contd*
  appeals—*contd*
    skeleton arguments, 13.19–13.20
    supporting documentation, 13.18
  Children's Commissioners, and,
    13.70
  complaints about after-care
    complainants, 13.55–13.56
    generally, 13.53—13.54
    introduction, 13.52
    outcome, 13.59–13.63
    relevant matters, 13.57–13.58
  default powers of SoS, 13.64–13.65
  habeas corpus, 13.71
  judicial review
    introduction, 13.37–13.40
    requirements, 13.41–13.44
    summary of cases, 13.50
    types of claims, 13.45–13.49
  Local Government Ombudsman,
    and, 13.66–13.69
  negligence claims
    generally, 13.72–13.74
    HRA 1998, under, 13.88–13.94
    Strasbourg rulings, 13.84–13.87
    widening liability, 13.75–13.83
  reviews, 13.51
Change in circumstances
  welfare principle, and, 2.45–2.47
Change of child's surname
  care orders, and, 8.175
  residence orders, and, 5.31–5.38
Charges
  local authority support services, and,
    6.3
Child abduction
  ambit of the Act, and, 1.14
  wardship, and, 12.20–12.23
  welfare principle, and, 2.7
Child aged 16 or over
  section 8 orders, and, 5.122–5.123
Child and family reporter
  representation of children, and,
    10.15
Child assessment orders
  criteria, 7.53–7.57
  effect, 7.61–7.62
  procedure, 7.58–7.60
Child-parent and baby
  welfare principle, and, 2.30–2.32
Children Act 1989
  and see under individual headings
  ambit, 1.12–1.14
  background, 1.3–1.9
  conclusions, 14.1–14.5
  development, 1.10–1.11
  general principles, 2.1–2.78
  introduction, 1.1–1.2
  key changes, 1.15–1.38
  parental responsibility, 3.1–3.129
  subsequent changes, 1.39–1.54

Children Act Advisory Committee
  liaison network, and, 1.30–1.31
Children in need
  And see Local authority support
    services
  assessment, 6.12–6.15
  children with disabilities, 6.21–6.22
  co-operation between authorities,
    6.16
  definitions
    'development', 6.10
    'family', 6.11–6.11
    'health', 6.10
    'in need', 6.9
  identification of, 6.24
  local authorities' duties, 6.17–6.20
  specific powers and duties,
    6.23–6.34
Children with conflicting interests
  welfare principle, and
    child-parent and baby, 2.30–2.32
    introduction, 2.29
    siblings, 2.33–2.35
Children with disabilities
  and see Local authority support
    services
  generally, 6.21–6.22
Children's Commissioners
  conclusions, 14.37
  generally, 13.70
Children's guardian
  appointment, 10.39–10.41
  duties, 10.42–10.46
  inspection of records, 10.47–10.48
  introduction, 10.15
  'specified proceedings', 10.35–10.38
Children's homes
  placement of children, and, 6.68
Child's wishes and feelings
  accommodation of children, and,
    6.47
  welfare principle, and, 2.42–2.43
Circuit judges
  generally, 4.11
Civil Procedure Rules 1998
  post-Act changes, and, 1.43
Cleveland Report (1987)
  child abuse, and, 1.5–1.6
Commencement of proceedings
  generally, 4.15–4.16
Committal for breach of section 8
    orders
  considerations, 5.175
  county court, in, 5.164–5.170
  High Court, in, 5.164–5.170
  introduction, 5.163
  limitations of powers, 5.176–5.177
  magistrates' court, in, 5.171–5.174
Compensation for financial loss orders
  contact, and, 5.185–5.189
Complaints about after-care
  complainants, 13.55–13.56

Complaints about after-care—*contd*
  generally, 13.53—13.54
  introduction, 13.52
  outcome, 13.59–13.63
  relevant matters, 13.57–13.58
Conflicting interests
  child-parent and baby, 2.30–2.32
  introduction, 2.29
  siblings, 2.33–2.35
Consent of parents
  accommodation of children, and,
    6.56
Consent orders
  care proceedings, and, 8.167–8.168
Considering racial groups
  local authority support services, and,
    6.30
Contact
  children in care, and
    care contact orders, 8.202–8.213
    local authorities' duties,
      8.199–8.201
    refusal of contact, 8.214–8.218
    summary, 8.197–8.198
  looked after children, and, 6.62
  parental responsibility, and,
    3.23–3.25
Contact orders
  alienation of parent, and, 5.82
  applicants, 5.143
  applications
    in favour of third person, 5.159
    introduction, 5.143
    with leave, 5.146–5.159
    without leave, 5.144–5.145
  applications with leave
    criteria for leave, 5.148–5.157
    introduction, 5.146–5.147
    procedure for leave, 5.158
  care contact orders
    court powers, 8.208–8.211
    discharge, 8.212–8.213
    generally, 8.202–8.207
    variation, 8.212–8.213
  committal for contempt
    considerations, 5.175
    county court, in, 5.164–5.170
    High Court, in, 5.164–5.170
    introduction, 5.163
    limitations of powers,
      5.176–5.177
    magistrates' court, in,
      5.171–5.174
  conditions
    generally, 5.111–5.121
    introduction, 5.108
  contact activity conditions
    financial support, 5.70–5.71
    generally, 5.67–5.69
    introduction, 5.63
  contact activity directions
    financial support, 5.70–5.71

Contact orders—*contd*
  contact activity directions—*contd*
    generally, 5.64–5.66
    introduction, 5.63
  considerations
    general, 5.56–5.72
    human rights, 5.75–5.77
    legal, 5.55
    practical, 5.78–5.93
    procedural, 5.73–5.74
  contact enforcement orders,
    5.179–5.184
  denying contact with a parent,
    5.86–5.88
  directions
    interim orders, 5.109–5.110
    introduction, 5.108
    limited duration orders,
      5.109–5.110
  domestic violence, and, 5.90–5.93
  duration, 5.55
  enforcement
    committal for contempt,
      5.163–5.177
    considerations, 5.175
    contact enforcement orders,
      5.179–5.184
    county court, in, 5.164–5.170
    financial compensation orders,
      5.185–5.189
    fines, 5.164, 5.171
    FLA 1986, under, 5.161–5.162
    High Court, in, 5.164–5.170
    introduction, 5.160
    magistrates' court, in,
      5.171–5.174
    search and recover order,
      5.161–5.162
    sequestration, 5.164
    warning notices, 5.178
  financial compensation orders,
    5.185–5.189
  fines
    considerations, 5.175
    county court, in, 5.164
    High Court, in, 5.164
    magistrates' court, in, 5.171
  general considerations
    contact activity directions and
      conditions, 5.63–5.71
    interim contract orders, 5.61
    introduction, 5.56–5.60
    monitoring contact, 5.72
    prohibiting contact, 5.62
  generally, 5.54
  human rights considerations,
    5.75–5.77
  indirect contact, 5.55
  interim contract orders, 5.61
  lapse, 5.60
  legal considerations, 5.55
  monitoring contact, 5.72

Contact orders—*contd*
  parental alienation, and, 5.82
  practical considerations
    denying contact with a parent,
      5.86–5.88
    domestic violence, 5.90–5.93
    general difficulties, 5.78–5.82
    predisposition to maintain
      contact, 5.83–5.89
  predisposition to maintain contact
    denying contact with a parent,
      5.86–5.88
    generally, 5.83–5.85
    statutory form, 5.89
  procedural considerations, 5.73–5.74
  prohibited steps orders, and,
    5.102–5.103
  prohibition of contact, 5.62
  'reasonable contact', 5.58
  relevant proceedings
    'any child', 5.140
    application of BIIR, 5.128
    application of FLA 1986,
      5.129–5.133
    'family proceedings', 5.134–5.139
    introduction, 5.127
    'upon application', 5.141–5.142
  restrictions
    child aged 16 or over,
      5.122–5.123
    child in local authority care,
      5.124
    local authorities, on, 5.125
    other, 5.126
  right to respect for private and
    family life, and, 5.76–5.77
  sexual abuse allegations, and, 5.74
  specific issue orders, and,
    5.102–5.103
  texting, 5.55
  unwilling parents, and, 5.56
  warning notices, 5.178
Contact enforcement orders
  generally, 5.179–5.184
Convictions
  evidence, and, 11.18
Costs
  generally, 4.58
  legal representative, against, 4.59
  wasted costs order, 4.59
County court
  jurisdiction, 4.8
Court jurisdiction
  county court, 4.8
  High Court, 4.7
  introduction, 4.5–4.6
  magistrates' courts
    generally, 4.9
    justices' clerk, 4.10
Court powers
  special guardianship orders, and
    basic principles, 5.221

Court powers—*contd*
  special guardianship orders, and—*contd*
    considerations, 5.222–5.224
    discharge, 5.228
    effect of orders, 5.225–5.227
    generally, 5.214–5.217
    jurisdiction, 5.218
    local authority involvement,
      5.219–5.220
    variation, 5.228
  termination of guardianship, and,
    3.129
  welfare principle, and, 2.59
Court procedure
  allocation of proceedings
    commencement, on, 4.15–4.16
    introduction, 4.14
    review, 4.32–4.41
    transfer, on, 4.17–4.18
  applications
    fees, 4.23
    filing, 4.22
    form, 4.21
    service, 4.24
  attendance of child
    oral evidence, 4.51–4.54
    private law proceedings, 4.50
    specified proceedings, 4.49
  case management, 4.31
  commencement of proceedings,
    4.15–4.16
  costs
    generally, 4.58
    legal representative, against, 4.59
    wasted costs order, 4.59
  county court jurisdiction, 4.8
  decision
    generally, 4.55
    justices' reasons, 4.56–4.57
  delay, and, 4.1
  directions, 4.28–4.30
  evidence, 4.48
  fees, 4.23
  filing, 4.22
  First Hearing, 4.27
  forms, 4.21
  hearings
    attendance of child, 4.49–4.54
    evidence, 4.48
    order of speeches, 4.48
    privacy, 4.47
    reporting restrictions, 4.47
  High Court jurisdiction, 4.7
  introduction, 4.1
  judiciary, 4.11
  jurisdiction of the courts
    county court jurisdiction, 4.8
    High Court jurisdiction, 4.7
    introduction, 4.5–4.6
    magistrates' courts, 4.9–4.10
  legal profession, 4.12

Court procedure—*contd*
  magistrates' courts jurisdiction
    generally, 4.9
    justices' clerk, 4.10
  McKenzie friends, 4.13
  order of speeches, 4.48
  overriding objective, 4.2
  parties, 4.25–4.26
  privacy, 4.47
  Private Law Programme, 4.19
  Public Law Outline, 4.19
  reading time, 4.46
  relevant venue, 4.2
  reporting restrictions, 4.47
  review of allocation
    complexity, 4.338
    Draft President's guidance, 4.41
    introduction, 4.32
    private law, 4.39–4.40
    public law, 4.33–4.36
  Rules, 4.20
  service
    applications, 4.24
    statements, 4.44
  timetable, 4.43
  transfer of proceedings, 4.17–4.18
  unrepresented friends, 4.13
  venue for proceedings, 4.3–4.4
  welfare reports, order for, 4.42
Court User Committees
  liaison network, and, 1.37
Covert video surveillance
  evidence, and, 11.28
Credibility of witnesses
  expert evidence, and, 11.56—11.58
Cremation of deceased child
  parental responsibility, and, 3.13
Criminal proceedings
  care orders, and, 8.106
Criminal remands
  secure accommodation orders, and,
    9.31
Cultural background
  welfare principle, and, 2.53–2.54

Day care
  local authority support services, and,
    6.31–6.32
Deaf children
  local authority support services, and,
    6.21–6.22
Death of child
  guardianship, and, 3.127
Death of guardian
  guardianship, and, 3.128
Decision
  generally, 4.55
  justices' reasons, 4.56–4.57
Default powers of SoS
  challenging decisions, and,
    13.64–13.65

Delay
  court procedure, and, 4.1
  principles, and, 2.60–2.63
Delegation
  parental responsibility, and, 3.102
Dental treatment
  children, and, 3.31–3.34
  court's powers, 3.35–3.37
  introduction, 3.26
  person with parental responsibility,
    and, 3.27–3.30
Department of Health guidance and
    advice
  local authority support services, and,
    6.7
Deprivation of liberty
  generally, 9.2–9.3
  parental responsibility, 9.4–9.6
Designated authority
  care orders, and, 8.170
Designated care judges
  county court jurisdiction, and, 4.8
Directions
  generally, 4.28–4.30
  interim care proceedings, and,
    8.113–8.119
  section 8 orders, and
    interim orders, 5.109–5.110
    introduction, 5.108
    limited duration orders,
      5.109–5.110
  secure accommodation orders, and,
    9.21
Directions appointments
  generally, 4.29
Disabled children
  and see Local authority support
    services
  generally, 6.21–6.22
Discharge of orders
  care contact orders, and,
    8.212–8.213
  care orders, and, 8.220–8.224
  emergency protection orders, and,
    7.98
  special guardianship orders, and,
    5.228
Discipline
  parental responsibility, and, 3.20
Disclosure
  conclusions, 11.100–11.103
  court order, by, 11.79–11.92
  general duty, 11.59–11.61
  no proceedings, where, 11.93–11.96
  reasons for withholding information
    parents, by, 11.72–11.78
    public immunity interest,
      11.62–11.70
    real harm, 11.71
  solicitors, by, 11.97–11.99

Discovery of children
emergency protection orders, and,
7.89
District judges
generally, 4.11
Domestic violence
contact orders, and, 5.90–5.93
representation of children, and,
10.19
Dumb, deaf and blind children
local authority support services, and,
6.21–6.22

Education of child
parental responsibility, and,
3.38–3.40
Education supervision orders
generally, 8.191–8.196
Educational needs
welfare principle, and, 2.44
Educational support
'looked after' children, and, 6.86
Emergency protection orders
appeals, and, 7.97
applications, 7.75–7.77
applications without notice,
7.79–7.80
automatic directions, 7.84–7.85
contact, and, 7.92
denial of access to the child,
7.68–7.69
discharge, 7.98
discovery of other children, 7.89
discretionary directions
contact, 7.92
discovery of other children, 7.89
exclusion requirement, 7.93–7.94
introduction, 7.87
medical examination, 7.91
search for child, 7.88
tracing of child, 7.88
warrants, 7.90
duration, 7.95–7.96
effect
automatic directions, 7.84–7.85
discretionary directions,
7.87–7.94
parental responsibility, 7.86
exclusion requirement, 7.93–7.94
grounds, 7.66–7.74
hearings, 7.81–7.83
introduction, 7.63–7.65
judicial guidance, 7.71–7.74
likely to suffer harm, 7.67
medical examination, 7.91
parental responsibility, and, 3.91,
7.86
police protection, 7.99–7.103
relevant proceedings, 7.78
search for child, 7.88
statutory guidance, 7.70
tracing of child, 7.88

Emergency protection orders—*contd*
venue of proceedings, 7.78
warrants, 7.90
Emotional needs
welfare principle, and, 2.44
Employment support
'looked after' children, and, 6.86
Enforcement
Children and Adoption Act 2006
contact enforcement orders,
5.179–5.184
financial compensation orders,
5.185–5.189
overview, 5.190
warning notices, 5.178
committal for contempt
considerations, 5.175
county court, in, 5.164–5.170
High Court, in, 5.164–5.170
introduction, 5.163
limitations of powers,
5.176–5.177
magistrates' court, in,
5.171–5.174
considerations, 5.175
contact enforcement orders,
5.179–5.184
county court, in, 5.164–5.170
financial compensation orders,
5.185–5.189
fines
considerations, 5.175
county court, in, 5.164
High Court, in, 5.164
FLA 1986, under, 5.161–5.162
High Court, in, 5.164–5.170
introduction, 5.160
magistrates' court, in, 5.171–5.174
section 8 orders
committal for contempt,
5.163–5.177
considerations, 5.175
county court, in, 5.164–5.170
fines, 5.164
FLA 1986, under, 5.161–5.162
High Court, in, 5.164–5.170
introduction, 5.160
magistrates' court, in,
5.171–5.174
search and recover order,
5.161–5.162
sequestration, 5.164
search and recover order,
5.161–5.162
sequestration, 5.164
supervision orders, 8.189
warning notices, 5.178
Enhanced residence orders
generally, 5.209–5.212
Estoppel
evidence, and, 11.24–11.27

European Convention on the Exercise of Children's Rights
representation of children, and, 10.6
European Convention on Human Rights
background to the Act, and, 1.7
representation of children, and, 10.5
Evidence
attendance of child, and, 4.51–4.54
burden of proof, 11.5
certificate of conviction, 11.18
child, from
generally, 11.48–11.54
recorded interviews, 11.55
convictions, of, 11.18
covert video surveillance, 11.28
credibility, 11.56—11.58
disclosure
conclusions, 11.100–11.103
court order, by, 11.79–11.92
general duty, 11.59–11.61
no proceedings, where,
11.93–11.96
reasons for withholding
information, 11.62–11.78
solicitors, by, 11.97–11.99
estoppel, and, 11.24–11.27
expert witness, from
credibility, 11.56—11.58
duties, 11.46–11.47
generally, 11.29–11.32
instructions, 11.40–11.45
leave, 11.33–11.39
generally, 11.12–11.16
harm, of, 11.17
hearsay, 11.19–11.23
introduction, 11.1–11.4
order of giving, 4.48
procedural changes, and, 1.26–1.27
proving the case
burden of proof, 11.5
certificate of conviction, 11.18
covert video surveillance, 11.28
estoppel, 11.24–11.27
harm, 11.17
standard of proof, 11.6–11.11
reasons for withholding information
parents, by, 11.72–11.78
public immunity interest,
11.62–11.70
real harm, 11.71
section 8 orders, and, 11.11
secure accommodation orders, and
civil proceedings, 9.24
criminal proceedings, 9.36
standard of proof
commentary, 11.10–11.11
generally, 11.6–11.9
***Ex parte* orders**
residence orders, and, 5.26–5.29
Exclusion from home
prohibited steps orders, and, 5.101

Exclusion from home—*contd*
specific issue orders, and, 5.101
wardship, and, 12.33–12.34
Exclusion orders
emergency protection orders, and,
7.93–7.94
Expert witness
credibility, 11.56—11.58
duties, 11.46–11.47
generally, 11.29–11.32
instructions, 11.40–11.45
leave, 11.33–11.39
External relocation
care orders, and
permanent, 8.177
temporary, 8.176
residence orders, and
applications, 5.44–5.50
for less than one month,
5.40–5.41
for more than one month,
5.42–5.43
generally, 5.39
holidays, 5.40

Family assistance orders
duration, 5.199
effect, 5.197–5.198
introduction, 5.191–5.192
practice, 5.200–5.201
relevant proceedings, 5.193–5.196
Family centres
local authority support services, and,
6.35
Family Court Business Committees
liaison network, and, 1.34
Family Court Forums
liaison network, and, 1.35–1.36
Family Division Liaison Judge
liaison network, and, 1.29
Family hearing centres
county court jurisdiction, and, 4.8
Family Justice Council
Chairperson, 4.8
conclusions, 14.7
generally, 1.33
Family Proceedings Rules
generally, 14.15
Feelings and wishes
accommodation of children, and,
6.47
welfare principle, and, 2.42–2.43
Financial support
'looked after' children, and, 6.85
Fines for breach of section 8 orders
considerations, 5.175
county court, in, 5.164
High Court, in, 5.164
First Hearing
introduction, 4.27

Forms
generally, 4.21

Gender change
parental responsibility, and, 3.45
General principles
and see under individual headings
delay is prejudicial, 2.60–2.63
introduction, 2.1
non-intervention
application, 2.65–2.74
background, 2.64
form of order, 2.75
inter-relationship with human
rights, 2.78
inter-relationship with welfare
principle, 2.76–2.77
introduction, 2.64
practical application, 2.73
substantive law, 2.69–2.72
welfare of child
application, 2.7–2.28
checklist, 2.38–2.59
children with conflicting interests,
2.29–2.35
comparison with UN Convention,
2.5
introduction, 2.2
paramountcy, 2.33
welfare, 2.36–2.37
Gillick **capacity**
background to the Act, and, 1.9
Guardian, appointment of
court, by
applicants, 3.110
considerations, 3.112–3.114
generally, 3.107–3.109
relevant children, 3.111
effect, 3.125–3.126
Official Solicitor, and, 3.115
parental responsibility, and
introduction, 3.13
non-parents, 3.88
unmarried fathers, 3.53
parents, by
disclaimer, 3.123–3.124
effective date, 3.120–3.122
generally, 3.116–3.118
revocation, 3.119
Guardians ad litem
representation of children, and,
10.31
Guardianship
appointment
and see above
generally, 3.107–3.126
introduction, 3.104–3.106
special guardianship orders
And see Special guardianship
orders
adoption orders, and,
5.233–5.234

Guardianship—*contd*
special guardianship orders—*contd*
discharge, 5.228
duration, 5.229
introduction, 5.213–5.214
power of court, 5.215–5.228
residence orders, and,
5.235–5.236
support services, 5.230–5.232
use, 5.233–5.234
variation, 5.228
termination
court order, by, 3.129
death of child, by, 3.127
death of guardian, by, 3.128
majority of child, on, 3.128
marriage of child, on, 3.128

Habeas corpus
generally, 13.71
Harm
evidence, and, 11.17
welfare principle, and, 2.55
Head of Family Justice
generally, 4.11
Hearings
attendance of child, 4.49–4.54
care proceedings, and
consent orders, 8.167–8.168
decision as to type of order,
8.164–8.166
form of order, 8.146–8.148
interim care order, and,
8.149–8.154
introduction, 8.141–8.142
issues resolution, 8.135–8.140
split hearings, 8.143–8.145
supervising care plans,
8.155–8.163
evidence, 4.48
order of speeches, 4.48
privacy, 4.47
reporting restrictions, 4.47
secure accommodation orders, and
evidence, 9.24
introduction, 9.22
presence of child, 9.23
Hearsay evidence
generally, 11.19–11.23
High Court
jurisdiction, 4.7
Holidays
care orders, and, 8.176
residence orders, and, 5.39–5.51
Housing for homeless
adolescents, 6.42
families, 6.40–6.41
Housing the child
parental responsibility, and, 3.19
Human rights
care proceedings, and, 8.2–8.6
conclusions, 14.38

Human rights—*contd*
  non-intervention principle, and, 2.78
  local authority support services, and,
    6.1
  paramountcy principle, and, 2.4
  post-Act changes, and, 1.44–1.54
  representation of children, and,
    10.5–10.6
  secure accommodation, and
    generally, 9.2–9.3
    parental responsibility, 9.4–9.6
  welfare principle, and, 2.4

Identification of children in need
  local authority support services, and,
    6.24
Independent action
  parental responsibility, and, 3.96
Indirect contact
  contact orders, and, 5.55
Inherent jurisdiction of court
  local authority use, and
    circumstances in which leave
      criteria satisfied,
      12.38–12.41
    criteria for grant of leave,
      12.36–12.37
    inherent jurisdiction, under,
      12.35–12.41
    leave to apply, 12.35
    pre-Act position, 12.4–12.9
  prohibited steps orders, and, 5.104
  specific issue orders, and, 5.104
  wardship, and
    court's powers, 12.28
    exclusion from home,
      12.33–12.34
    individual's use, 12.42–12.43
    jurisdiction, 12.27
    local authority use, 12.35–12.41
    procedure, 12.25–12.26
    restrictions on exercise of powers,
      12.29–12.32
  welfare principle, and, 2.7
Injunctions
  child protection, and, 7.105–7.107
Interim orders
  care proceedings, and
    conditions, 8.108
    directions for assessment,
      8.113–8.119
    duration, 8.122–8.123
    effect, 8.112
    exclusion requirement, and,
      8.120–8.121
    final hearing, and, 8.149–8.154
    grounds, 8.109–8.110
    guidance on applications, 8.111
    introduction, 8.107
    renewal, 8.124
  section 8 orders
    contact orders, and, 5.61

Interim orders—*contd*
  section 8 orders—*contd*
    generally, 5.109–5.110
    residence orders, and, 5.24–5.25
  secure accommodation orders, and,
    9.25
Investigation
  assessment principles
    child centred approach, 7.34
    child development, 7.35
    concurrent action, 7.44
    continuing process, 7.43
    ecological approach, 7.36
    equality of opportunity, 7.37
    evidence-based knowledge,
      7.45–7.46
    inter-agency approach, 7.42
    introduction, 7.33
    strengths and weaknesses, 7.41
    working with child and family,
      7.38–7.39
  assessment process
    cardinal principles, 7.33–7.46
    framework, 7.31–7.32
    interviewing children, 7.48–7.52
    judicial guidance, 7.47
  court-directed enquiry, 7.25–7.30
  interviewing children, 7.48–7.52
  judicial guidance, 7.47
  local authority enquiry
    section 17 duty, 7.6
    section 47 duty, 7.7–7.24
  section 17 enquiry, 7.6
  section 37 enquiry
    criteria, 7.25–7.26
    local authority duty, 7.30
    procedure upon grant, 7.27–7.29
  section 47 enquiry
    aims, 7.13–7.14
    general duty, 7.7
    process, 7.15–7.23
    strategy discussion, 7.24
    threshold, 7.8–7.12
Investigation of child's circumstances
  generally, 5.206
Issues resolution hearing
  advocates' meeting, 8.135
  case management order, 8.136
  generally, 8.137–8.140

Joint orders
  residence orders, and, 5.17–5.23
Judicial review
  introduction, 13.37–13.40
  requirements, 13.41–13.44
  summary of cases, 13.50
  types of claims, 13.45–13.49
Judiciary
  generally, 4.11
Jurisdiction of the courts
  county court, 4.8
  High Court, 4.7

Jurisdiction of the courts—*contd*
introduction, 4.5–4.6
magistrates' courts
generally, 4.9
justices' clerk, 4.10

Key changes subsequent to the Act
Civil Procedure Rules 1998, 1.43
Human Rights Act 1998, 1.44–1.54
introduction, 1.39–1.41
Welsh devolution, 1.42
Key changes under the Act
general principles, 1.23–1.24
new concepts, 1.15–1.18
procedural changes, 1.25–1.38
public law, 1.19–1.22
Kinship care
pre-proceedings stage, 8.68
welfare of child, 8.57

Law Commission reports
parental responsibility, and, 1.4, 3.1
Law on Child Care and Family Services (**White Paper, 1987**)
generally, 1.3
Legal aid
generally, 14.16
Legal representation for children
attendance of child at court, and,
10.60–10.65
CAFCASS Legal
generally, 10.57–10.58
introduction, 10.56
non-specified proceedings,
10.53–10.55
Official Solicitor, by, 10.59
secure accommodation orders, and,
9.20
solicitors, by
non-specified proceedings, in,
10.53–10.55
specified proceedings, in,
10.49–10.52
specified proceedings
duties of solicitor, 10.50
generally, 10.49
instructions from child, 10.51
termination of instructions, 10.52
Liaison network
Advisory Board on Family Law, 1.32
Children Act Advisory Committee,
1.30–1.31
Court User Committees, 1.37
Family Court Business Committees,
1.34
Family Court Forums, 1.35–1.36
Family Division Liaison Judge, 1.29
Family Justice Council, 1.33
introduction, 1.28
Limited duration orders
and see Interim orders

Limited duration orders—*contd*
generally, 5.109–5.110
Linguistic background
welfare principle, and, 2.53
Local authorities
parental responsibility, and, 3.92
section 8 orders, and, 5.125
wardship, and
circumstances in which leave
criteria satisfied,
12.38–12.41
criteria for grant of leave,
12.36–12.37
inherent jurisdiction, under,
12.35–12.41
leave to apply, 12.35
pre-Act position, 12.4–12.9
Local authority support services
accommodation of children
arrangement planning, 6.48
ascertaining child's wishes, 6.47
children who may be
accommodated, 6.39
children who must be
accommodated, 6.36–6.38
consent of parents, 6.56
general duty, 6.36–6.46
homeless adolescents, 6.42
homeless families, 6.40–6.41
limits, 6.50–6.53
miscellaneous duties, 6.48–6.49
parental agreement, 6.48
partnership with parents,
6.55–6.56
placement arrangements, 6.48
records, 6.49
refuges for children at risk,
6.43–6.46
representations, 6.49
restriction on removal, 6.54
assessment of needs, 6.12–6.15
blind children, 6.21–6.22
changes under the Act, and,
1.19–1.21
charges, and, 6.3
'child', 6.8
children in need
assessment, 6.12–6.15
children with disabilities,
6.21–6.22
co-operation between authorities,
6.16
definitions, 6.8–6.11
identification of, 6.24
local authorities' duties,
6.17–6.20
specific powers and duties,
6.23–6.34
children under five years old, 6.33
children with disabilities, 6.21–6.22
conclusions, 14.22–14.23
consider racial groups, 6.30

Local authority support services—*contd*
  co-operation between authorities,
    6.16
  day care, 6.31–6.32
  deaf children, 6.21–6.22
  definitions
    child, 6.8
    development, 6.10
    family, 6.11
    health, 6.10
    in need, 6.9
  Department of Health guidance and
    advice, 6.7
  'development', 6.10
  disabled children, 6.21–6.22
  dumb children, 6.21–6.22
  duties
    delegation, 6.3
    general scheme, 6.2
    guiding principle, 6.4
  'family', 6.11
  family centres, and, 6.35
  'health', 6.10
  human rights, and, 6.1
  implementation of, 6.87–6.92
  identification of children in need,
    6.24
  'in need', 6.9
  introduction, 6.1–6.7
  involvement of families, and, 6.4
  leaving 'looked after' provision
    duties to 'eligible child',
      6.75–6.76
    duties to 'former relevant
      children', 6.80
    duties to 'relevant child',
      6.77–6.79
    education support, 6.86
    employment support, 6.86
    financial support, 6.85
    generally, 6.70–6.71
    local authorities' duties,
      6.72–6.74
    Pathway Plans, 6.83
    Personal Adviser, 6.84
    persons qualifying for advice and
      assistance, 6.81–6.82
    training support, 6.86
  'looked after' children
    introduction, 6.57
    leaving provision, and, 6.70–6.
    local authorities' duties,
      6.58–6.62
    placement, 6.63–6.69
    promotion of contact, 6.62
    rehabilitation, 6.59–6.61
  maintenance of family home, 6.29
  mentally disabled children,
    6.21–6.22
  placement of 'looked after' children
    children's homes, in, 6.68
    foster parents, with, 6.66–6.67

Local authority support services—*contd*
  placement of 'looked after' children—*contd*
    friends, with, 6.65
    introduction, 6.63
    outside the jurisdiction, 6.69
    parents, with, 6.64
    relatives, with, 6.65
  prevention of abuse, 6.25
  promotion of upbringing, 6.28
  provision of accommodation,
    6.26–6.27
  right to respect fir private and
    family life, and, 6.1
  scheme duties, 6.2
  special guardianship orders, and,
    5.230–5.232
  'working in partnership', and,
    6.4–6.5
Local Government Ombudsman
  generally, 13.66–13.69
Local Safeguarding Children's Boards
  generally, 1.21
'Looked after' children
  And see Local authority support
    services
  education support, 6.86
  employment support, 6.86
  'eligible child', 6.75–6.76
  financial support, 6.85
  'former relevant children', 6.80
  introduction, 6.57
  leaving 'looked after' provision
    duties to 'eligible child',
      6.75–6.76
    duties to 'former relevant
      children', 6.80
    duties to 'relevant child',
      6.77–6.79
    education support, 6.86
    employment support, 6.86
    financial support, 6.85
    generally, 6.70–6.71
    local authorities' duties,
      6.72–6.74
    Pathway Plans, 6.83
    Personal Adviser, 6.84
    persons qualifying for advice and
      assistance, 6.81–6.82
    training support, 6.86
  local authorities' duties
    generally, 6.58–6.62
    leaving 'looked after' provision,
      6.72–6.74
  local authorities' duties (leaving
    provision)
    'eligible child', to, 6.75–6.76
    'former relevant children', to,
      6.80
    generally, 6.72–6.74
    'relevant child', to, 6.77–6.79
  Pathway Plans, 6.83
  Personal Adviser, 6.84

'Looked after' children—*contd*
  persons qualifying for advice and
    assistance, 6.81–6.82
  placement
    children's homes, in, 6.68
    foster parents, with, 6.66–6.67
    friends, with, 6.65
    introduction, 6.63
    outside the jurisdiction, 6.69
    parents, with, 6.64
    relatives, with, 6.65
  promotion of contact, 6.62
  rehabilitation, 6.59–6.61
  'relevant child', 6.77–6.79
  training support, 6.86
Looking after the child
  parental responsibility, and, 3.19
Lord Chief Justice
  generally, 4.11

Magistrates' court
  jurisdiction, 4.9
  justices' clerk, 4.10
Majority of child
  guardianship, and, 3.128
Marriage of child
  guardianship, and, 3.128
Married child
  parental responsibility, and, 3.93
Married parents
  parental responsibility, and, 3.43
McKenzie friends
  generally, 4.13
Medical examination or assessment
  emergency protection orders, and,
    7.91
  supervision orders, and,
    8.187–8.188
Medical treatment
  children, position of, 3.31–3.34
  court's powers, 3.35–3.37
  introduction, 3.26
  person with parental responsibility,
    position of, 3.27–3.30
Mentally disabled children
  local authority support services, and,
    6.21–6.22

National Practice Standards
  generally, 10.17–10.19
  minimum standards, 10.10
  principles, 10.18
Neglect prevention
  local authority support services, and,
    6.25
Negligence claims
  East Berkshire limits, 13.78–13.83
  generally, 13.72–13.74
  HRA 1998, under, 13.88–13.94
  Strasbourg rulings, 13.84–13.87
  widening liability, 13.75–13.83

Nominated care judges
  county court jurisdiction, and, 4.8
Nominated district judges
  county court jurisdiction, and, 4.8
'No-order' principle
  application, 2.65–2.74
  background, 2.64
  form of order, 2.75
  inter-relationship with human rights,
    2.78
  inter-relationship with welfare
    principle, 2.76–2.77
  introduction, 2.64
  practical application, 2.73
  substantive law, 2.69–2.72
Non-parents
  parental responsibility after birth,
    and
    emergency protection orders,
      under, 3.91
    guardians, 3.88
    introduction, 3.87
    local authorities, 3.92
    residence orders, under, 3.90
    special guardians, 3.89
  parental responsibility at birth, and,
    3.46
'Non-intervention' principle
  application, 2.65–2.74
  background, 2.64
  form of order, 2.75
  inter-relationship with human rights,
    2.78
  inter-relationship with welfare
    principle, 2.76–2.77
  introduction, 2.64
  practical application, 2.73
  substantive law, 2.69–2.72

Occupation orders
  prohibited steps orders, and, 5.101
  specific issue orders, and, 5.101
Official Solicitor
  guardianship, and, 3.115
  representation of children, and,
    10.59
Openness
  court system, and, 14.11
Order of speeches
  court procedure, and, 4.48
Ouster orders
  prohibited steps orders, and, 5.101
  specific issue orders, and, 5.101
  wardship, and, 12.33–12.34
Overriding objective
  care proceedings, and, 8.76–8.77

'Paramountcy' principle
  administration of child's property,
    and, 2.7

'Paramountcy' principle—*contd*
application
  exclusions, 2.13–2.28
  generally, 2.7–2.12
checklist of considerations
  age, 2.48
  ascertainable wishes and feelings,
    2.42–2.43
  background, 2.49–2.54
  capability of parents to meet
    child's needs, 2.58
  court's powers, 2.59
  cultural background, 2.53–2.54
  educational needs, 2.44
  effect of change in circumstances,
    2.45–2.47
  emotional needs, 2.44
  harm suffered, 2.55
  introduction, 2.38–2.39
  linguistic background, 2.53
  physical needs, 2.44
  racial origin, 2.53–2.54
  relevant proceedings, 2.40–2.41
  religious upbringing, 2.49–2.52
  risk of suffering, 2.56–2.57
  sex, 2.48
child-parent and baby, and,
  2.30–2.32
children with conflicting interests,
  and
  child-parent and baby, 2.30–2.32
  introduction, 2.29
  siblings, 2.33–2.35
comparison with UN Convention,
  2.5
exclusion by statutory provision,
  and, 2.26–2.28
human rights, and, 2.4
introduction, 2.2–2.3
non-intervention principle, and,
  2.76–2.77
outside of litigation, and, 2.14–2.15
siblings, and, 2.33–2.35
upbringing of child, and
  generally, 2.16–2.19
  introduction, 2.7
  other areas of uncertainty,
    2.24–2.25
  procedural issues, 2.22–2.23
  publicity issues, 2.20–2.21
"welfare", 2.36–2.37
Parental agreement
accommodation of children, and,
  6.55–6.56
Parental guardianship
abolition, 3.2
Parental order reporter
representation of children, and,
  10.15
Parental responsibility
ambit of the Act, and, 1.16

Parental responsibility—*contd*
appointment as guardian, and
  non-parents, 3.88
  unmarried fathers, 3.53
background to the Act, and, 1.4
birth of child, after
  introduction, 3.47
  local authorities, by, 3.92
  non-parents, by, 3.87–3.91
  step-parents, by, 3.81–3.86
  unmarried fathers, by, 3.48–3.80
birth of child, at
  gender change, and, 3.45
  local authorities, 3.92
  married parents, 3.43
  non-parents, 3.46
  other individuals, 3.87–3.91
  step-parents, 3.81–3.86
  unmarried fathers, 3.47–3.80
  unmarried parents, 3.44
carers, and, 3.103
conclusions, 14.17–14.19
contact with the child, 3.23–3.25
delegation of, 3.102
discipline, 3.20
duration of, 3.94–3.95
education of child, 3.38–3.40
emergency protection orders, under,
  3.91
gender change, and, 3.45
guardians, and
  non-parents, 3.88
  unmarried fathers, 3.53
housing the child, 3.19
independent action, and, 3.96
introduction, 3.1–3.2
local authorities, of, 3.92
looking after the child, 3.19
married child, and, 3.93
married parents, of, 3.43
meaning
  generally, 3.9–3.12
  preliminary observations,
    3.13–3.17
  purpose, 3.7–3.8
  Scotland, in, 3.11
medical treatment
  children, position of, 3.31–3.34
  court's powers, 3.35–3.37
  introduction, 3.26
  person with parental
    responsibility, position of,
    3.27–3.30
non-parents after birth, by
  emergency protection orders,
    under, 3.91
  guardians, 3.88
  introduction, 3.87
  local authorities, 3.92
  residence orders, under, 3.90
  special guardians, 3.89
non-parents at birth, by, 3.46

Parental responsibility—*contd*
  parental responsibility agreement,
      under
    effect, 3.73–3.75
    generally, 3.54–3.59
    termination, 3.79–3.80
  parental responsibility order, under
    considerations, 3.63–3.70
    effect, 3.73–3.75
    generally, 3.60–3.62
    termination, 3.79–3.80
  practical effect, 3.6
  prohibited steps orders, and,
      5.99–5.100
  protection of the child, 3.21–3.22
  registration on birth certificate, by,
      3.50–3.52
  relevant children, 3.93
  relevant contexts, 3.3–3.5
  religious upbringing, 3.41–3.42
  residence orders, under
    generally, 5.30
    non-parents, 3.90
    unmarried fathers, 3.71–3.72
  scope, 3.18
  secure accommodation, and, 9.4–9.6
  sharing of
    introduction, 3.96
    married parents, by, 3.97–3.99
    non-parent, with, 3.100–3.101
  special guardians, and, 3.89
  specific issue orders, and,
      5.99–5.100
  step-parents, of, 3.81–3.86
  subsequent marriage, and, 3.49
  unmarried fathers, of
    appointment as guardian, by, 3.53
    checklist of responsibilities,
        3.76–3.78
    introduction, 3.48
    parental responsibility agreement,
        under, 3.54–3.59
    parental responsibility order,
        under, 3.60–3.70
    registration on birth certificate,
        by, 3.50–3.52
    residence orders, under, 3.71–3.72
    subsequent marriage, by, 3.49
  unmarried parents, of, 3.44
Parental responsibility agreement
  effect, 3.73–3.75
  generally, 3.54–3.59
  termination, 3.79–3.80
Parental responsibility order
  considerations, 3.63–3.70
  effect, 3.73–3.75
  generally, 3.60–3.62
  termination, 3.79–3.80
Parental rights and duties
  and see Parental responsibility
  generally, 3.1

Parties
  care proceedings, and, 8.98–8.103
  generally, 4.25–4.26
Pathway plans
  'looked after' children, and, 6.83
Pending appeal, orders
  care orders, and, 8.130
Permission to appeal
  appeals, and, 13.12–13.17
Personal advisers
  'looked after' children, and, 6.84
Physical needs
  welfare principle, and, 2.44
Placement of children
  care proceedings, and, 8.169
  children's homes, in, 6.68
  foster parents, with, 6.66–6.67
  friends, with, 6.65
  introduction, 6.63
  outside the jurisdiction, 6.69
  parents, with, 6.64
  relatives, with, 6.65
Police protection
  generally, 7.99–7.103
Prevention of abuse
  local authority support services, and,
      6.25
Principal Registry of the Family
    Division
  county court jurisdiction, and, 4.8
  generally, 4.11
Privacy
  court procedure, and, 4.47
Private family proceedings
  representation of children, and,
      10.30–10.34
Private law orders
  and see under individual headings
  background, 5.1–5.3
  conclusions, 14.20–14.21
  contact orders
    applicants, 5.143–5.159
    conditions, 5.108–5.121
    considerations, 5.55–5.93
    directions, 5.108–5.121
    enforcement, 5.160–5.177
    generally, 5.54
    relevant proceedings, 5.127–5.142
    restrictions, 5.122–5.126
  court's powers, 5.5–5.6
  enforcement under Children and
      Adoption Act 2006
    financial compensation orders,
        5.185–5.189
    contact enforcement orders,
        5.179–5.184
    overview, 5.190
    warning notices, 5.178
  family assistance orders
    duration, 5.199
    effect, 5.197–5.198
    introduction, 5.191–5.192

Private law orders—*contd*
 family assistance orders—*contd*
  practice, 5.200–5.201
  relevant proceedings, 5.193–5.196
 general strategy, 5.4
 introduction, 5.1–5.3
 investigation of child's
   circumstances, 5.206
 prohibited steps orders
  applicants, 5.143–5.159
  conditions, 5.108–5.121
  directions, 5.108–5.121
  enforcement, 5.160–5.177
  generally, 5.94–5.96
  limits on court's powers,
   5.99–5.107
  relevant proceedings, 5.127–5.142
  restrictions, 5.122–5.126
 public law proceedings, and,
   5.207–5.208
 residence orders
  applicants, 5.143–5.159
  conditions, 5.108–5.121
  directions, 5.108–5.121
  enforcement, 5.160–5.177
  generally, 5.14–5.53
  relevant proceedings, 5.127–5.142
  restrictions, 5.122–5.126
 restricting further applications,
   order, 5.202–5.205
 risk assessments, 5.11–5.12
 section 8 orders
  applicants, 5.143–5.159
  conditions, 5.108–5.121
  contact orders, 5.54–5.93
  court's powers, 5.5–5.6
  directions, 5.108–5.121
  enforcement, 5.160–5.177
  introduction, 5.13
  prohibited steps order, 5.94–5.96
  relevant proceedings, 5.127–5.142
  residence orders, 5.14–5.53
  restrictions, 5.122–5.126
  specific issue order, 5.97–5.98
 specific issue orders
  applicants, 5.143–5.159
  conditions, 5.108–5.121
  directions, 5.108–5.121
  enforcement, 5.160–5.177
  generally, 5.97–5.98
  limits on court's powers,
   5.99–5.107
  relevant proceedings, 5.127–5.142
  restrictions, 5.122–5.126
 statistics, 5.7–5.10
Private Law Programme
 generally, 4.19
Procedural changes
 evidence, 1.26–1.27
 introduction, 1.25

Procedural changes—*contd*
 liaison network
  Advisory Board on Family Law,
   1.32
  Children Act Advisory
   Committee, 1.30–1.31
  Court User Committees, 1.37
  Family Court Business
   Committees, 1.34
  Family Court Forums, 1.35–1.36
  Family Division Liaison Judge,
   1.29
  Family Justice Council, 1.33
  introduction, 1.28
 role of the courts, 1.38
Prohibited steps orders
 applicants, 5.143–5.159
 applications
  in favour of third person, 5.159
  introduction, 5.143
  with leave, 5.146–5.159
  without leave, 5.144–5.145
 applications with leave
  criteria for leave, 5.148–5.157
  introduction, 5.146–5.147
  procedure for leave, 5.158
 committal for contempt
  considerations, 5.175
  county court, in, 5.164–5.170
  High Court, in, 5.164–5.170
  introduction, 5.163
  limitations of powers,
   5.176–5.177
  magistrates' court, in,
   5.171–5.174
 conditions
  generally, 5.111–5.121
  introduction, 5.108
 directions
  interim orders, 5.109–5.110
  introduction, 5.108
  limited duration orders,
   5.109–5.110
 enforcement
  committal for contempt,
   5.163–5.177
  considerations, 5.175
  county court, in, 5.164–5.170
  fines, 5.164, 5.171
  FLA 1986, under, 5.161–5.162
  High Court, in, 5.164–5.170
  introduction, 5.160
  limitations of powers,
   5.176–5.177
  magistrates' court, in,
   5.171–5.174
  search and recover order,
   5.161–5.162
  sequestration, 5.164
 fines
  considerations, 5.175
  county court, in, 5.164

Prohibited steps orders—*contd*
fines—*contd*
  High Court, in, 5.164
  magistrates' court, in, 5.171
generally, 5.94–5.96
limits
  disguised contact or residence
    orders, 5.102–5.103
  inherent jurisdiction, 5.104
  Nottingham decision,
    5.105–5.107
  occupation orders, 5.101
  ouster orders, 5.101
  parental responsibility,
    5.99–5.100
relevant proceedings
  'any child', 5.140
  application of BIIR, 5.128
  application of FLA 1986,
    5.129–5.133
  'family proceedings', 5.134–5.139
  introduction, 5.127
  'upon application', 5.141–5.142
restrictions
  child aged 16 or over,
    5.122–5.123
  child in local authority care,
    5.124
  local authorities, on, 5.125
  other, 5.126
Promotion of upbringing
And see Upbringing of child
local authority support services, and,
  6.28
Proportionality
care proceedings, and, 8.56
Protection of children
ancillary protection under care
  order, 7.105–7.107
assessment principles
  child centred approach, 7.34
  child development, 7.35
  concurrent action, 7.44
  continuing process, 7.43
  ecological approach, 7.36
  equality of opportunity, 7.37
  evidence-based knowledge,
    7.45–7.46
  inter-agency approach, 7.42
  introduction, 7.33
  strengths and weaknesses, 7.41
  working with child and family,
    7.38–7.39
assessment process
  cardinal principles, 7.33–7.46
  framework, 7.31–7.32
  interviewing children, 7.48–7.52
  judicial guidance, 7.47
child assessment orders
  criteria, 7.53–7.57
  effect, 7.61–7.62
  procedure, 7.58–7.60

Protection of children—*contd*
emergency measures, and, 7.3
emergency protection orders
  appeals, and, 7.97
  applications, 7.75–7.77
  applications without notice,
    7.79–7.80
  automatic directions, 7.84–7.85
  contact, and, 7.92
  denial of access to the child,
    7.68–7.69
  discharge, 7.98
  discovery of other children, 7.89
  discretionary directions,
    7.87–7.94
  duration, 7.95–7.96
  effect, 7.84–7.94
  exclusion requirement, 7.93–7.94
  grounds, 7.66–7.74
  hearings, 7.81–7.83
  introduction, 7.63–7.65
  judicial guidance, 7.71–7.74
  likely to suffer harm, 7.67
  medical examination, 7.91
  parental responsibility, 7.86
  police protection, 7.99–7.103
  relevant proceedings, 7.78
  search for child, 7.88
  statutory guidance, 7.70
  tracing of child, 7.88
  venue of proceedings, 7.78
  warrants, 7.90
enquiry
  assessment process, 7.31–7.
  section 17 duty, 7.6
  section 37, under, 7.25–7.30
  section 47 duty, 7.7–7.24
exclusion orders, 7.93–7.94
human rights, and, 7.4
injunctions, 7.105–7.107
interviewing children, 7.48–7.52
introduction, 7.1–7.5
investigation
  assessment process, 7.31–7.46
  court-directed, 7.25–7.30
  local authority, by, 7.6–7.24
judicial guidance, 7.47
local authority enquiry
  section 17 duty, 7.6
  section 47 duty, 7.7–7.24
parental responsibility, and,
  3.21–3.22
receivers, 7.105–7.107
recovery orders, 7.104
section 17 investigation, 7.6
section 37 investigation
  criteria, 7.25–7.26
  local authority duty, 7.30
  procedure upon grant, 7.27–7.29
section 47 investigation
  aims, 7.13–7.14
  enquiry process, 7.15–7.23

Protection of children—*contd*
　section 47 investigation—*contd*
　　general duty, 7.7
　　strategy discussion, 7.24
　　threshold for enquiry, 7.8–7.12
Proving the case
　burden of proof, 11.5
　certificate of conviction, 11.18
　covert video surveillance, 11.28
　estoppel, 11.24–11.27
　harm, 11.17
　standard of proof, 11.6–11.11
Psychiatric examination or assessment
　emergency protection orders, and,
　　7.91
　supervision orders, and,
　　8.187–8.188
Public funding
　generally, 14.16
Public interest immunity
　evidence, and, 11.62–11.70
Public Law Outline
　care proceedings, and
　　background, 8.7–8.14
　　generally, 8.15
　generally, 4.19
Public law proceedings
　private law orders, and,
　　5.207–5.208
　welfare principle, and, 2.11

Racial origin
　welfare principle, and, 2.53–2.54
Reading time
　court procedure, and, 4.46
Real harm
　evidence, and, 11.71
Recorded interviews
　evidence, and, 11.55
Recorders
　generally, 4.11
Recovery orders
　protection of children, and, 7.104
Refuges for children at risk
　accommodation of children, and,
　　6.43–6.46
**Registration of name on birth
　certificate**
　parental responsibility, and,
　　3.67–3.68
Rehabilitation
　'looked after' children, and,
　　6.59–6.61
Religious upbringing
　parental responsibility, and
　　3.41–3.42
　welfare principle, and, 2.49–2.52
Removal of child from UK
　care orders, and
　　permanent, 8.177
　　temporary, 8.176

Removal of child from UK—*contd*
　external relocation
　　applications, 5.44–5.50
　　for less than one month,
　　　5.40–5.41
　　for more than one month,
　　　5.42–5.43
　　generally, 5.39
　　holidays, 5.40
　internal relocation, 5.51
　residence orders, and
　　external relocation, 5.40–5.50
　　internal relocation, 5.51
　　introduction, 5.39
Reporting officer
　representation of children, and,
　　10.15
Reporting restrictions
　court procedure, and, 4.47
Representation of children
　CAFCASS, and
　　attendance of officers at court,
　　　10.29
　　background, 10.13–10.14
　　Domestic Violence Toolkit, 10.19
　　functions, 10.14
　　National Practice Standards,
　　　10.17–10.18
　　officers, 10.15–10.16
　　Safeguarding Framework, 10.19
　　welfare reports, 10.20–10.28
　child and family reporter, 10.15
　children's guardian, and
　　appointment, 10.39–10.41
　　duties, 10.42–10.46
　　inspection of records,
　　　10.47–10.48
　　introduction, 10.15
　　'specified proceedings',
　　　10.35–10.38
　conclusions, 14.30–14.34
　context
　　developmental issues, 10.11
　　introduction, 10.2
　　rights verses welfare, 10.12
　　'voice of the child', 10.3–10.10
　court procedure, and, 4.42
　developmental issues, 10.11
　Domestic Violence Toolkit, 10.19
　European Convention on the
　　Exercise of Children's Rights,
　　and, 10.6
　European Court of Human Rights,
　　and, 10.5
　guardians ad litem, 10a.31
　hearsay evidence, and, 10.20
　introduction, 10.1
　legal representation
　　And see Legal representation of
　　　children
　　attendance of child at court, and,
　　　10.60–10.65

Representation of children—*contd*
legal representation—*contd*
CAFCASS Legal, 10.56–10.58
non-specified proceedings,
10.53–10.55
Official Solicitor, by, 10.59
solicitors, by, 10.49–10.55
specified proceedings,
10.49–10.52
National Practice Standards
generally, 10.17–10.19
minimum standards, 10.10
principles, 10.18
parental order reporter, 10.15
private family proceedings, in,
10.30–10.34
reporting officer, 10.15
rights verses welfare, 10.12
Safeguarding Framework, 10.19
UN Convention on the Rights of the
Child, and, 10.4
welfare of the child, and, 10.1
welfare officer, 10.15
'voice of the child', 10.3–10.10

Residence orders
applicants, 5.143–5.159
applications
in favour of third person, 5.159
introduction, 5.143
with leave, 5.146–5.159
without leave, 5.144–5.145
applications with leave
criteria for leave, 5.148–5.157
introduction, 5.146–5.147
procedure for leave, 5.158
change of child's surname,
5.31–5.38
committal for contempt
considerations, 5.175
county court, in, 5.164–5.170
High Court, in, 5.164–5.170
introduction, 5.163
limitations of powers,
5.176–5.177
magistrates' court, in,
5.171–5.174
conditions
generally, 5.111–5.121
introduction, 5.108
directions
interim orders, 5.109–5.110
introduction, 5.108
limited duration orders,
5.109–5.110
effects
change of child's surname,
5.31–5.38
parental responsibility, 5.30
removal of child from UK,
5.39–5.51
shared residence, 5.52–5.53

Residence orders—*contd*
enforcement
committal for contempt,
5.163–5.177
considerations, 5.175
county court, in, 5.164–5.170
fines, 5.164, 5.171
FLA 1986, under, 5.161–5.162
High Court, in, 5.164–5.170
introduction, 5.160
magistrates' court, in,
5.171–5.174
search and recover order,
5.161–5.162
sequestration, 5.164
enhanced residence orders,
5.209–5.212
ex parte orders, 5.26–5.29
external relocation of child
applications, 5.44–5.50
for less than one month,
5.40–5.41
for more than one month,
5.42–5.43
generally, 5.39
holidays, 5.40
fines
considerations, 5.175
county court, in, 5.164
High Court, in, 5.164
magistrates' court, in, 5.171
generally, 5.14–5.16
interim orders, 5.24–5.25
internal relocation, 5.51
joint orders, 5.17–5.23
parental responsibility, and
generally, 5.30
non-parents, 3.90
unmarried fathers, 3.71–3.72
shared residence, 5.52–5.53
prohibited steps orders, and,
5.102–5.103
relevant proceedings
'any child', 5.140
application of BIIR, 5.128
application of FLA 1986,
5.129–5.133
'family proceedings', 5.134–5.139
introduction, 5.127
'upon application', 5.141–5.142
removal of child from UK
external relocation, 5.40–5.50
internal relocation, 5.51
introduction, 5.39
restrictions
child aged 16 or over,
5.122–5.123
child in local authority care,
5.124
local authorities, on, 5.125
other, 5.126

Residence orders—*contd*
shared residence orders
effects, 5.52–5.53
generally, 5.17–5.23
specific issue orders, and,
5.102–5.103
**Restrict further applications, orders
which**
generally, 5.202–5.205
welfare principle, and, 2.12
Review of Child Care Law (DHSS,
1984)
generally, 1.3
Reviews
challenging decisions, and, 13.51
**Right to respect for private and family
life**
care proceedings, and, 8.4
contact orders, and, 5.76–5.77
local authority support services, and,
6.1
Risk assessments
section 8 orders, and, 5.11–5.12
Risk of suffering
welfare principle, and, 2.56–2.57
Role of the courts
procedural changes, and, 1.38
Routes of appeal
county courts, from, 13.11
High Court, from, 13.11
magistrates' court, from, 13.7–13.10
Rules
court procedure, and, 4.20

Safeguarding Framework
representation of children, and,
10.19
Search and recover orders
enforcement of section 8 orders,
and, 5.161–5.162
section 8 orders
and see under individual headings
ambit of the Act, and, 1.17–1.18
applicants, 5.143–5.159
applications
in favour of third person, 5.159
introduction, 5.143
with leave, 5.146–5.159
without leave, 5.144–5.145
applications with leave
criteria for leave, 5.148–5.157
introduction, 5.146–5.147
procedure for leave, 5.158
conditions
generally, 5.111–5.121
introduction, 5.108
background, 5.1–5.3
committal for contempt
considerations, 5.175
county court, in, 5.164–5.170
High Court, in, 5.164–5.170
introduction, 5.163

section 8 orders—*contd*
committal for contempt—*contd*
limitations of powers,
5.176–5.177
magistrates' court, in,
5.171–5.174
contact orders
applicants, 5.143–5.159
conditions, 5.108–5.121
directions, 5.108–5.121
enforcement, 5.160–5.177
generally, 5.54–5.93
relevant proceedings, 5.127–5.142
restrictions, 5.122–5.126
court's powers, 5.5–5.6
directions
interim orders, 5.109–5.110
introduction, 5.108
limited duration orders,
5.109–5.110
enforcement
committal for contempt,
5.163–5.177
considerations, 5.175
county court, in, 5.164–5.170
fines, 5.164, 5.171
FLA 1986, under, 5.161–5.162
High Court, in, 5.164–5.170
introduction, 5.160
magistrates' court, in,
5.171–5.174
search and recover order,
5.161–5.162
sequestration, 5.164
evidence, and, 11.11
fines
considerations, 5.175
county court, in, 5.164
High Court, in, 5.164
magistrates' court, in, 5.171
general strategy, 5.4
introduction, 5.13
prohibited steps orders
applicants, 5.143–5.159
conditions, 5.108–5.121
directions, 5.108–5.121
enforcement, 5.160–5.177
generally, 5.94–5.96
limits on court's powers,
5.99–5.107
relevant proceedings, 5.127–5.142
restrictions, 5.122–5.126
relevant proceedings
'any child', 5.140
application of BIIR, 5.128
application of FLA 1986,
5.129–5.133
'family proceedings', 5.134–5.139
introduction, 5.127
'upon application', 5.141–5.142
residence orders
applicants, 5.143–5.159

section 8 orders—*contd*
  residence orders—*contd*
    conditions, 5.108–5.121
    directions, 5.108–5.121
    enforcement, 5.160–5.177
    generally, 5.14–5.53
    relevant proceedings, 5.127–5.142
    restrictions, 5.122–5.126
    restrictions
      child aged 16 or over,
        5.122–5.123
      child in local authority care,
        5.124
      local authorities, on, 5.125
      other, 5.126
    risk assessments, 5.11–5.12
    shared residence orders
      effects, 5.52–5.53
      generally, 5.17–5.23
  specific issue orders
    applicants, 5.143–5.159
    conditions, 5.108–5.121
    directions, 5.108–5.121
    enforcement, 5.160–5.177
    generally, 5.97–5.98
    limits on court's powers,
      5.99–5.107
    relevant proceedings, 5.127–5.142
    restrictions, 5.122–5.126
  statistics, 5.7–5.10
  welfare principle, and
    checklist, 2.40
    generally, 2.10
section 17 investigations
  generally, 7.6
section 37 investigations
  criteria, 7.25–7.26
  generally, 5.206
  local authority duty, 7.30
  procedure upon grant, 7.27–7.29
section 47 investigations
  aims, 7.13–7.14
  enquiry process, 7.15–7.23
  general duty, 7.7
  strategy discussion, 7.24
  threshold for enquiry, 7.8–7.12
Secure accommodation
  approved accommodation,
    9.12–9.13
  authorised use, 9.12–9.13
  criteria for use, 9.10–9.11
  definition, 9.8–9.9
  deprivation of liberty, and, 9.2–9.6
  general rule, 9.7
  introduction, 9.1
  orders for use
    and see Secure accommodation
      orders
    civil proceedings, in, 9.16–9.29
    criminal proceedings, in,
      9.30–9.40
  parental responsibility, and, 9.4–9.6

Secure accommodation—*contd*
  relevant person, 9.8–9.9
  restriction on use, 9.7
  unauthorised use, 9.14–9.15
Secure accommodation orders (civil
    proceedings)
  appeals, 9.29
  applicant, 9.17
  appointment of guardian, 9.19
  directions, 9.21
  duration, 9.26
  effect, 9.27
  hearing
    evidence, 9.24
    introduction, 9.22
    presence of child, 9.23
  interim orders, 9.25
  introduction, 9.16
  legal representation, 9.20
  renewal, 9.28
  transfer of proceedings, 9.18
Secure accommodation orders (criminal
    proceedings)
  appeals, 9.40
  application, 9.32
  criminal remands, and, 9.30
  criteria, 9.34
  Crown Court, in, 9.39
  duration, 9.37
  evidence, 9.36
  introduction, 9.30
  procedure, 9.35
  relevant court, 9.33
  renewal, 9.38
  security requirement, 9.31
Security requirement
  secure accommodation orders, and,
    9.31
Sequestration
  enforcement of section 8 orders,
    and, 5.164
Service
  applications, 4.24
  statements, 4.44
Services by local authorities
  accommodation of children
    arrangement planning, 6.48
    ascertaining child's wishes, 6.47
    children who may be
      accommodated, 6.39
    children who must be
      accommodated, 6.36–6.38
    consent of parents, 6.56
    general duty, 6.36–6.46
    homeless adolescents, 6.42
    homeless families, 6.40–6.41
    limits, 6.50–6.53
    miscellaneous duties, 6.48–6.49
    parental agreement, 6.48
    partnership with parents,
      6.55–6.56
    placement arrangements, 6.48

Services by local authorities—*contd*
　accommodation of children—*contd*
　　records, 6.49
　　refuges for children at risk,
　　　6.43–6.46
　　representations, 6.49
　　restriction on removal, 6.54
　assessment of needs, 6.12–6.15
　blind children, 6.21–6.22
　changes under the Act, and,
　　1.19–1.21
　charges, and, 6.3
　'child', 6.8
　children in need
　　assessment, 6.12–6.15
　　children with disabilities,
　　　6.21–6.22
　　co-operation between authorities,
　　　6.16
　　definitions, 6.8–6.11
　　identification of, 6.24
　　local authorities' duties,
　　　6.17–6.20
　　specific powers and duties,
　　　6.23–6.34
　children under five years old, 6.33
　children with disabilities, 6.21–6.22
　consider racial groups, 6.30
　co-operation between authorities,
　　6.16
　day care, 6.31–6.32
　deaf children, 6.21–6.22
　definitions
　　child, 6.8
　　development, 6.10
　　family, 6.11
　　health, 6.10
　　in need, 6.9
　Department of Health guidance and
　　advice, 6.7
　'development', 6.10
　disabled children, 6.21–6.22
　dumb children, 6.21–6.22
　duties
　　delegation, 6.3
　　general scheme, 6.2
　　guiding principle, 6.4
　'family', 6.11
　family centres, and, 6.35
　'health', 6.10
　human rights, and, 6.1
　implementation of, 6.87–6.92
　identification of children in need,
　　6.24
　'in need', 6.9
　introduction, 6.1–6.7
　involvement of families, and, 6.4
　leaving 'looked after' provision
　　duties to 'eligible child',
　　　6.75–6.76
　　duties to 'former relevant
　　　children', 6.80

Services by local authorities—*contd*
　leaving 'looked after' provision—*contd*
　　duties to 'relevant child',
　　　6.77–6.79
　　education support, 6.86
　　employment support, 6.86
　　financial support, 6.85
　　generally, 6.70–6.71
　　local authorities' duties,
　　　6.72–6.74
　　Pathway Plans, 6.83
　　Personal Adviser, 6.84
　　persons qualifying for advice and
　　　assistance, 6.81–6.82
　　training support, 6.86
　'looked after' children
　　introduction, 6.57
　　leaving provision, and, 6.70–6.
　　local authorities' duties,
　　　6.58–6.62
　　placement, 6.63–6.69
　　promotion of contact, 6.62
　　rehabilitation, 6.59–6.61
　maintenance of family home, 6.29
　mentally disabled children,
　　6.21–6.22
　placement of 'looked after' children
　　children's homes, in, 6.68
　　foster parents, with, 6.66–6.67
　　friends, with, 6.65
　　introduction, 6.63
　　outside the jurisdiction, 6.69
　　parents, with, 6.64
　　relatives, with, 6.65
　prevention of abuse, 6.25
　promotion of upbringing, 6.28
　provision of accommodation,
　　6.26–6.27
　right to respect fir private and
　　family life, and, 6.1
　scheme duties, 6.2
　special guardianship orders, and,
　　5.230–5.232
　'working in partnership', and,
　　6.4–6.5
Sex of child
　welfare principle, and, 2.48
Shared residence orders
　effects, 5.52–5.53
　generally, 5.17–5.23
Sharing of parental responsibility
　introduction, 3.96
　married parents, by, 3.97–3.99
　non-parent, with, 3.100–3.101
Siblings
　welfare principle, and, 2.33–2.35
Significant harm
　care proceedings, and, 8.42–8.44
Skeleton arguments
　appeals, and, 13.19–13.20

Solicitor representation
children in non-specified
proceedings, 10.53–10.55
children in specified proceedings
duties of solicitor, 10.50
generally, 10.49
instructions from child, 10.51
termination of instructions, 10.52
Special guardianship orders
adoption orders, and, 5.233–5.234
applicants, 5.216
appointees, 5.215
basic principles, 5.221
considerations, 5.222–5.224
discharge, 5.228
duration, 5.229
effect, 5.225–5.227
introduction, 5.213–5.214
jurisdiction, 5.218
local authorities, and
applicants, and, 5.215
involvement in applications,
5.219–5.220
parental responsibility, and, 3.89
powers of court
basic principles, 5.221
considerations, 5.222–5.224
discharge, 5.228
effect of orders, 5.225–5.227
generally, 5.214–5.217
jurisdiction, 5.218
local authority involvement,
5.219–5.220
variation, 5.228
residence orders, and, 5.235–5.236
support services, 5.230–5.232
use, 5.233–5.234
variation, 5.228
Specific issue orders
applicants, 5.143–5.159
applications
in favour of third person, 5.159
introduction, 5.143
with leave, 5.146–5.159
without leave, 5.144–5.145
applications with leave
criteria for leave, 5.148–5.157
introduction, 5.146–5.147
procedure for leave, 5.158
committal for contempt
considerations, 5.175
county court, in, 5.164–5.170
High Court, in, 5.164–5.170
introduction, 5.163
limitations of powers,
5.176–5.177
magistrates' court, in,
5.171–5.174
conditions
generally, 5.111–5.121
introduction, 5.108

Specific issue orders—*contd*
directions
interim orders, 5.109–5.110
introduction, 5.108
limited duration orders,
5.109–5.110
enforcement
committal for contempt,
5.163–5.177
considerations, 5.175
county court, in, 5.164–5.170
fines, 5.164, 5.171
FLA 1986, under, 5.161–5.162
High Court, in, 5.164–5.170
introduction, 5.160
magistrates' court, in,
5.171–5.174
search and recover order,
5.161–5.162
sequestration, 5.164
fines
considerations, 5.175
county court, in, 5.164
High Court, in, 5.164
magistrates' court, in, 5.171
generally, 5.97–5.98
limits
disguised contact or residence
orders, 5.102–5.103
inherent jurisdiction, 5.104
Nottingham decision,
5.105–5.107
occupation orders, 5.101
ouster orders, 5.101
parental responsibility,
5.99–5.100
relevant proceedings
'any child', 5.140
application of BIIR, 5.128
application of FLA 1986,
5.129–5.133
'family proceedings', 5.134–5.139
introduction, 5.127
'upon application', 5.141–5.142
restrictions
child aged 16 or over,
5.122–5.123
child in local authority care,
5.124
local authorities, on, 5.125
other, 5.126
Specified proceedings
children's guardian, representation
by
appointment, 10.39–10.41
duties, 10.42–10.46
inspection of records,
10.47–10.48
introduction, 10.15
'specified proceedings',
10.35–10.38

Specified proceedings—*contd*
legal representation for children, and
duties of solicitor, 10.50
generally, 10.49
instructions from child, 10.51
termination of instructions, 10.52
Split hearings
care proceedings, and, 8.143–8.145
Standard of proof
commentary, 11.10–11.11
generally, 11.6–11.9
Step-parents
parental responsibility, and,
3.81–3.86
Subsequent marriage
parental responsibility, and, 3.49
Suffering or likely to suffer
'is likely to suffer', 8.36–8.39
'is suffering', 8.30–8.35
Supervision orders
advocates' meeting
advocates' meeting, 8.126–8.128
issues resolution hearing, 8.135
allocation, 8.96–8.97
alternative dispute resolution, 8.86
appeals, 8.225–8.226
applications
applicants, 8.89
checklist, 8.90–8.91
consideration, 8.62–8.64
generally, 8.87–8.8
pre-proceedings stage, 8.65–8.74
'attributable', 8.46–8.49
'beyond parental control', 8.52
burden of proof, 8.21–8.27
care given to the child, 8.50–8.51
care plans, 8.58–8.60
case management, 8.79–8.82
case management conference
advocates' meeting, 8.126–8.128
case management order,
8.129–8.132
generally, 8.133–8.134
introduction, 8.125
case management order
generally, 8.129–8.132
issues resolution hearing, 8.136
'child concerned', 8.28–8.29
concurrent criminal proceedings,
8.106
consent orders, 8.167–8.168
contact arrangements, 8.61
'designated authority', 8.170
discharge, 8.220–8.224
duration, 8.182
early final hearing, 8.104
education supervision orders,
8.191–8.196
effect, 8.180–8.181
enforcement, 8.189
experts, 8.105

Supervision orders—*contd*
final hearing
consent orders, 8.167–8.168
decision as to type of order,
8.164–8.166
form of order, 8.146–8.148
interim care order, and,
8.149–8.154
introduction, 8.141–8.142
split hearings, 8.143–8.145
supervising care plans,
8.155–8.163
first appointment, 8.93
grounds
contact arrangements, 8.61
generally, 8.18
threshold criteria, 8.19–8.53
welfare of child, 8.54–8.60
'harm', 8.40–8.41
interim orders
conditions, 8.108
directions for assessment,
8.113–8.119
duration, 8.122–8.123
effect, 8.112
exclusion requirement, and,
8.120–8.121
final hearing, and, 8.149–8.154
grounds, 8.109–8.110
guidance on applications, 8.111
introduction, 8.107
renewal, 8.124
'is likely to suffer', 8.36–8.39
'is suffering', 8.30–8.35
issue, 8.92
issues resolution hearing
advocates' meeting, 8.135
case management order, 8.136
generally, 8.137–8.140
kinship care
pre-proceedings stage, 8.68
welfare of child, 8.57
local authorities' powers, 8.17
meaning, 8.16
medical examination or treatment,
8.187–8.188
need, 8.16–8.17
overriding objective, 8.76–8.77
parties, 8.98–8.103
placement orders, and, 8.169
pre-proceedings stage
assessment, 8.67
Children Act 1989 Guidance
Volume 1, 8.65
communications with parents and
child, 8.70
inter-agency cooperation, 8.69
key principles, 8.66
kinship care, 8.68
letter before proceedings, 8.71
meeting with parents, 8.72–8.74

Supervision orders—*contd*
procedure
  allocation, 8.96–8.97
  alternative dispute resolution,
    8.86
  applications, 8.87–8.91
  case management, 8.79–8.82
  case management conference,
    8.125–8.134
  concurrent care and criminal
    proceedings, 8.106
  consistency, 8.83
  early final hearing, 8.104
  expectations, 8.84–8.85
  experts, 8.105
  final hearing, 8.141–8.168
  first appointment, 8.93
  interim orders, 8.107–8.124
  issue, 8.92
  issues resolution hearing,
    8.135–8.140
  judicial continuity, 8.78
  key principles, 8.75
  overriding objective, 8.76–8.77
  parties, 8.98–8.103
  placement order applications,
    8.169
  timetable for proceedings,
    8.94–8.95
  transfer, 8.96–8.97
proportionality, 8.56
psychiatric examination or
  treatment, 8.187–8.188
requirements
  medical examination or treatment,
    8.187–8.188
  psychiatric examination or
    treatment, 8.187–8.188
  responsible person, 8.184–8.186
  supervised child, 8.183
responsible person, 8.184–8.186
'significant harm', 8.42–8.44
split hearings, 8.143–8.145
supervised child, 8.183
supervising care plans, 8.155–8.163
standard of proof, 8.21–8.27
threshold criteria
  agreed threshold, 8.53
  'attributable', 8.46–8.49
  'beyond parental control', 8.52
  burden of proof, 8.21–8.27
  care given to the child, 8.50–8.51
  'child concerned', 8.28–8.29
  generally, 8.19–8.20
  'harm', 8.40–8.41
  'is likely to suffer', 8.36–8.39
  'is suffering', 8.30–8.35
  'significant harm', 8.42–8.44
  similar child comparison, 8.45
  standard of proof, 8.21–8.27
timetable for proceedings, 8.94–8.95
transfer of proceedings, 8.96–8.97

Supervision orders—*contd*
use, 8.190
variation, 8.219
welfare of child
  care plans, 8.58–8.60
  introduction, 8.54
  kinship care, 8.57
  paramountcy, 8.55
  proportionality, 8.56
  statutory checklist, 8.55
withdrawal, 8.227
Support services
accommodation of children
  arrangement planning, 6.48
  ascertaining child's wishes, 6.47
  children who may be
    accommodated, 6.39
  children who must be
    accommodated, 6.36–6.38
  consent of parents, 6.56
  general duty, 6.36–6.46
  homeless adolescents, 6.42
  homeless families, 6.40–6.41
  limits, 6.50–6.53
  miscellaneous duties, 6.48–6.49
  parental agreement, 6.48
  partnership with parents,
    6.55–6.56
  placement arrangements, 6.48
  records, 6.49
  refuges for children at risk,
    6.43–6.46
  representations, 6.49
  restriction on removal, 6.54
assessment of needs, 6.12–6.15
blind children, 6.21–6.22
changes under the Act, and,
  1.19–1.21
charges, and, 6.3
'child', 6.8
children in need
  assessment, 6.12–6.15
  children with disabilities,
    6.21–6.22
  co-operation between authorities,
    6.16
  definitions, 6.8–6.11
  identification of, 6.24
  local authorities' duties,
    6.17–6.20
  specific powers and duties,
    6.23–6.34
children under five years old, 6.33
children with disabilities, 6.21–6.22
conclusions, 14.22–14.23
consider racial groups, 6.30
co-operation between authorities,
  6.16
day care, 6.31–6.32
deaf children, 6.21–6.22
definitions
  child, 6.8

Index

Support services—*contd*
  definitions—*contd*
    development, 6.10
    family, 6.11
    health, 6.10
    in need, 6.9
  Department of Health guidance and
      advice, 6.7
  'development', 6.10
  disabled children, 6.21–6.22
  dumb children, 6.21–6.22
  duties
    delegation, 6.3
    general scheme, 6.2
    guiding principle, 6.4
  'family', 6.11
  family centres, and, 6.35
  'health', 6.10
  human rights, and, 6.1
  implementation of, 6.87–6.92
  identification of children in need,
      6.24
  'in need', 6.9
  introduction, 6.1–6.7
  involvement of families, and, 6.4
  leaving 'looked after' provision
    duties to 'eligible child',
        6.75–6.76
    duties to 'former relevant
        children', 6.80
    duties to 'relevant child',
        6.77–6.79
    education support, 6.86
    employment support, 6.86
    financial support, 6.85
    generally, 6.70–6.71
    local authorities' duties,
        6.72–6.74
    Pathway Plans, 6.83
    Personal Adviser, 6.84
    persons qualifying for advice and
        assistance, 6.81–6.82
    training support, 6.86
  'looked after' children
    introduction, 6.57
    leaving provision, and, 6.70–6.
    local authorities' duties,
        6.58–6.62
    placement, 6.63–6.69
    promotion of contact, 6.62
    rehabilitation, 6.59–6.61
  maintenance of family home, 6.29
  mentally disabled children,
      6.21–6.22
  placement of 'looked after' children
    children's homes, in, 6.68
    foster parents, with, 6.66–6.67
    friends, with, 6.65
    introduction, 6.63
    outside the jurisdiction, 6.69
    parents, with, 6.64
    relatives, with, 6.65

Support services—*contd*
  prevention of abuse, 6.25
  promotion of upbringing, 6.28
  provision of accommodation,
      6.26–6.27
  right to respect fir private and
      family life, and, 6.1
  scheme duties, 6.2
  special guardianship orders, and,
      5.230–5.232
  'working in partnership', and,
      6.4–6.5
Surgical treatment
  children, position of, 3.31–3.34
  court's powers, 3.35–3.37
  introduction, 3.26
  person with parental responsibility,
      position of, 3.27–3.30

Temporary removal from UK
  care orders, and, 8.176
  residence orders, and, 5.39–5.51
Termination of guardianship
  court order, by, 3.129
  death of child, by, 3.127
  death of guardian, by, 3.128
  majority of child, on, 3.128
  marriage of child, on, 3.128
Threshold for care and supervision
  changes under the Act, and, 1.22
Timetable for proceedings
  care orders, and, 8.94–8.95
  generally, 4.43
Training support
  'looked after' children, and, 6.86
Transfer of proceedings
  care orders, and, 8.96–8.97
  generally, 4.17–4.18

UN Convention on the Rights of the
    Child (1989)
  background to the Act, and, 1.7
  representation of children, and, 10.4
  welfare principle, and, 2.5
UNICEF Report (2007)
  generally, 14.2
Unmarried fathers
  parental responsibility, and
    appointment as guardian, by, 3.53
    checklist of responsibilities,
        3.76–3.78
    introduction, 3.48
    parental responsibility agreement,
        under, 3.54–3.59
    parental responsibility order,
        under, 3.60–3.70
    registration on birth certificate,
        by, 3.50–3.52
    residence orders, under, 3.71–3.72
    subsequent marriage, by, 3.49

Unmarried fathers—*contd*
registration on birth certificate, and,
3.50–3.52
Unmarried parents
parental responsibility, and, 3.44
Unrepresented parties
generally, 4.13
Upbringing of child
generally, 2.16–2.19
introduction, 2.7
local authority support services, and,
6.28
other areas of uncertainty, 2.24–2.25
procedural issues, 2.22–2.23
publicity issues, 2.20–2.21

Variation of orders
care contact orders, and,
8.212–8.213
care orders, and, 8.219
special guardianship orders, and,
5.228
supervision orders, and, 8.219
Venue for proceedings
emergency protection orders, and,
7.78
generally, 4.3–4.4
'Voice of the child'
representation of children, and,
10.3–10.10

Wales, devolution in
post-Act changes, and, 1.42
Wardship
abduction, and, 12.20–12.23
court's inherent powers
general extent, 12.28
originating summons procedure,
and, 12.13–12.19
restrictions on exercise,
12.29–12.32
exclusion from home, 12.33–12.34
impact of the Act
private law, 12.10–12.24
public law, 12.4–12.9
individual's use of jurisdiction,
12.42–12.43
inherent jurisdiction, and
court's powers, 12.28
exclusion from home,
12.33–12.34
individual's use, 12.42–12.43
jurisdiction, 12.27
local authority use, 12.35–12.41
procedure, 12.25–12.26
restrictions on exercise of powers,
12.29–12.32
international element, 12.24
introduction, 12.1–12.3

Wardship—*contd*
local authorities' use of jurisdiction
circumstances in which leave
criteria satisfied,
12.38–12.41
criteria for grant of leave,
12.36–12.37
inherent jurisdiction, under,
12.35–12.41
leave to apply, 12.35
pre-Act position, 12.4–12.9
originating summons procedure,
and, 12.13–12.19
private law
abduction, and, 12.20–12.23
introduction, 12.10
remaining uses of wardship
proceedings, 12.13–12.19
status, 12.11–12.12
procedure, 12.25–12.26
public law
incompatibility of wardship with
care, 12.6–12.7
lack of power to commit ward
into care, 12.4–12.5
use by local authority of
proceedings, 12.8–12.9
restrictions on exercise of powers
express, 12.29
other, 12.30–12.32
welfare principle, and, 2.7
Warning notices
contact, and, 5.178
Warrant to enter and search
police protection, and, 7.104
Wasted costs order
generally, 4.59
Welfare of child
changes under the Act, and, 1.23
meaning, 2.36–2.37
representation of children, and, 10.1
Welfare officer
representation of children, and,
10.15
'Welfare' principle
administration of child's property,
and, 2.7
application
exclusions, 2.13–2.28
generally, 2.7–2.12
ascertainable wishes and feelings,
2.42–2.43
capability of parents to meet child's
needs, 2.58
care orders, and
care plans, 8.58–8.60
introduction, 8.54
kinship care, 8.57
paramountcy, 8.55
proportionality, 8.56
statutory checklist, 8.55
withdrawal, 8.227

'Welfare' principle—*contd*
  checklist of considerations
    age, 2.48
    ascertainable wishes and feelings,
      2.42–2.43
    background, 2.49–2.54
    capability of parents to meet
      child's needs, 2.58
    conclusions, 14.3
    court's powers, 2.59
    cultural background, 2.53–2.54
    educational needs, 2.44
    effect of change in circumstances,
      2.45–2.47
    emotional needs, 2.44
    harm suffered, 2.55
    introduction, 2.38–2.39
    linguistic background, 2.53
    physical needs, 2.44
    racial origin, 2.53–2.54
    relevant proceedings, 2.40–2.41
    religious upbringing, 2.49–2.52
    risk of suffering, 2.56–2.57
    sex, 2.48
    wishes and feelings, 2.42–2.43
  child-parent and baby, and,
    2.30–2.32
  children with conflicting interests,
    and
    child-parent and baby, 2.30–2.32
    introduction, 2.29
    siblings, 2.33–2.35
  comparison with UN Convention,
    2.5
  conclusions, 14.3
  cultural background, 2.53–2.54
  educational needs, 2.44
  effect of change in circumstances,
    2.45–2.47
  emotional needs, 2.44
  exclusion by statutory provision,
    and, 2.26–2.28
  harm suffered, 2.55
  introduction, 2.2
  linguistic background, 2.53
  non-intervention principle, and,
    2.76–2.77
  outside of litigation, and, 2.14–2.15
  paramountcy
    generally, 2.3
    human rights compliance, 2.4
  physical needs, 2.44
  racial origin, 2.53–2.54
  relevant proceedings, 2.40–2.41
  religious upbringing, 2.49–2.52
  risk of suffering, 2.56–2.57
  sex, 2.48
  siblings, and, 2.33–2.35
  supervision orders, and
    care plans, 8.58–8.60
    introduction, 8.54
    kinship care, 8.57

'Welfare' principle—*contd*
  supervision orders, and—*contd*
    paramountcy, 8.55
    proportionality, 8.56
    statutory checklist, 8.55
    withdrawal, 8.227
  welfare of child
    care plans, 8.58–8.60
    introduction, 8.54
    kinship care, 8.57
    paramountcy, 8.55
    proportionality, 8.56
    statutory checklist, 8.55
    withdrawal, 8.227
  upbringing of child, and
    generally, 2.16–2.19
    introduction, 2.7
    other areas of uncertainty,
      2.24–2.25
    procedural issues, 2.22–2.23
    publicity issues, 2.20–2.21
    "welfare", 2.36–2.37
  wishes and feelings, 2.42–2.43
Welfare reporting
  CAFCASS, and
    attendance of officers at court,
      10.29
    background, 10.13–10.14
    Domestic Violence Toolkit, 10.19
    functions, 10.14
    National Practice Standards,
      10.17–10.18
    officers, 10.15–10.16
    Safeguarding Framework, 10.19
    welfare reports, 10.20–10.28
  child and family reporter, 10.15
  children's guardian, and
    appointment, 10.39–10.41
    duties, 10.42–10.46
    inspection of records,
      10.47–10.48
    introduction, 10.15
    'specified proceedings',
      10.35–10.38
  context
    developmental issues, 10.11
    introduction, 10.2
    rights verses welfare, 10.12
    'voice of the child', 10.3–10.10
  court procedure, and, 4.42
  developmental issues, 10.11
  Domestic Violence Toolkit, 10.19
  European Convention on the
    Exercise of Children's Rights,
    and, 10.6
  European Court of Human Rights,
    and, 10.5
  guardians ad litem, 10a.31
  hearsay evidence, and, 10.20
  introduction, 10.1

Welfare reporting—*contd*
legal representation
And see Legal representation of
children
attendance of child at court, and,
10.60–10.65
CAFCASS Legal, 10.56–10.58
non-specified proceedings,
10.53–10.55
Official Solicitor, by, 10.59
solicitors, by, 10.49–10.55
specified proceedings,
10.49–10.52
National Practice Standards
generally, 10.17–10.19
minimum standards, 10.10
principles, 10.18
parental order reporter, 10.15

Welfare reporting—*contd*
private family proceedings, in,
10.30–10.34
reporting officer, 10.15
rights verses welfare, 10.12
Safeguarding Framework, 10.19
UN Convention on the Rights of the
Child, and, 10.4
welfare of the child, and, 10.1
welfare officer, 10.15
'voice of the child', 10.3–10.10
Welsh devolution
generally, 14.36
Wishes and feelings
accommodation of children, and,
6.47
welfare principle, and, 2.42–2.43
Withdrawal of applications
care orders, and, 8.36